A History of the English Language

A History of the English Language

Joseph P. McGowan

WILEY

This edition first published 2027

Registered Offices
John Wiley & Sons, Inc., 111 River Street, Hoboken, NJ 07030, USA
John Wiley & Sons Ltd, New Era House, 8 Oldlands Way, Bognor Regis, West Sussex, PO22 9NQ, UK

For details of our global editorial offices, customer services, and more information about Wiley products visit us at www.wiley.com.

The manufacturer's authorized representative according to the EU General Product Safety Regulation is Wiley-VCH GmbH, Boschstr. 12, 69469 Weinheim, Germany, e-mail: Product_Safety@wiley.com.

Wiley also publishes its books in a variety of electronic formats and by print-on-demand. Some content that appears in standard print versions of this book may not be available in other formats.

Library of Congress Cataloging-in-Publication Data
Names: McGowan, Joseph P. author
Title: A history of the English language / Joseph P. McGowan.
Description: Hoboken, NJ : Wiley, 2027. | Includes bibliographical references and index.
Identifiers: LCCN 2025045114 (print) | LCCN 2025045115 (ebook) | ISBN 9781405192330 paperback | ISBN 9781118326695 adobe pdf | ISBN 9781118326688 epub
Subjects: LCSH: English language–History
Classification: LCC PE1075 .M586 2026 (print) | LCC PE1075 (ebook)
LC record available at https://lccn.loc.gov/2025045114
LC ebook record available at https://lccn.loc.gov/2025045115

Cover Design: Wiley
Cover Image: Courtesy of the John Carter Brown Library

Set in 10.5/13pt STIXTwoText by Straive, Pondicherry, India
Printed and bound by CPI Group (UK) Ltd, Croydon, CR0 4YY
C9781405192330_190826

Contents

List of Plates/Figures/Maps

Preface and Acknowledgements

Any new volume on the subject of the history of English will naturally be expected to offer some rationale, or at least excuse, for its appearance, especially a single-author work of such length. There are a number of very fine books on the subject, many, if not most of them, by multiple authors (or teams of them). The most enduring is Albert Croll Baugh's *A History of the English Language*, originally published in 1935 and now, with revisions and additions by Thomas Cable, in its 6th edition (2013). Excellent among the multivolume sets is *The Cambridge History of the English Language* (6 vols., 1992–2001; these and other texts may be found in the Abbreviations section and References to Chapter 1); it is now under revision under general editor Raymond Hickey and expected to appear in 2026. Perhaps the most significant new development in the earlier history of English is the two volumes in the Oxford *A Linguistic History of English* series by noted historical linguist and Indo-Europeanist Don Ringe. These two volumes, *From Proto-Indo-European to Proto-Germanic* (2nd ed. 2017) and *The Development of Old English* (Ringe and Taylor 2014; see References to Chapter 4), in their 1000 pages, bring to bear the latest work in historical linguistics on linguistic reconstruction to a field that began in the philological tradition with Baugh (a professor in the Department of English at the University of Pennsylvania, which is also Ringe's home institution, in the Department of Linguistics). The densely argued sections on every sound change from Proto-Indo-European (ca. 3500 BC) through to late Old English (ca. 1050–1100) are filled with asterisked proto-forms. It will take some time for the many new or fuller explanations of early English phonological and morphological developments to work their way from these volumes into the broader literature of the subject. And that is one of the reasons, or excuses, for the present volume. A division in focus and labor between Departments of English and Linguistics has broadened into an expansive gulf, one that the 'language persons' in the Departments of English (those few left who still teach Old English or History of the English Language classes) may despair of bridging. This volume is written with Departments of English and their students in mind, who, as intriguing as they may find the subject, may find the reconstructed proto-forms and phonetic transcriptions and 'sound laws' and grammatical paradigms daunting. The guiding principle has been to tell the history of English as also a 'history,' or, as Herodotus first meant it, an 'inquiry' into the subject, a story still worth telling in terms of not just phonemes, morphemes, IPA symbols – without which it cannot be told – but also of the people who spoke and shaped the language. One addition to this story, a useful one it is hoped, is the chapter (Chapter 3) on the Celtic *Sprachraum* ('speech-area') into which Germanic tribes entered in the waves of Angles, Saxons, Jutes, and Frisians familiar from the usual version of the story of English. A subject often quickly dispensed with in many accounts of the history of the language, here it is given greater play, introducing those peoples of Britain who had been there for many centuries before the 'coming of the Saxons' (*adventus Saxonum*), who had been Romanized to an extent (perhaps not as great as had the Celtic peoples of Gaul), introduced to Christianity and the Latin language and Roman script, and gave names in their Celtic languages to rivers and hills and springs. The examination of Celtic and Roman Britain is meant to set a template for those other eras of the history of the language, from the Anglo-Saxon to Anglo-Norman to the heady Early Modern Elizabethans, proud of a tongue that produced a golden age of drama and poised to bring that tongue to its new colonies. And that moment, as recorded in the early narratives of exploration of a Raleigh or Hariot, is what set English on its path to its present global status. English began its history expanding into a land of Celtic languages, and then into Cornwall, Wales, Scotland, and abroad for the first time in Ireland, a pattern to take flight with the encounters in North America with speakers of Algonquian and other Native American languages. The story is as extraordinary as it was in some ways unlikely.

Many debts have been incurred in writing this volume, particularly as it took so long to bring to a close. Long overdue thanks are due to teachers and colleagues who have since passed: Rev. Ladislaus Magyar, Sch.P., Rev. Stephen Mustos, Sch.P., John M. Hunt, Effie Natsis Coughanowr, Rev. John Hagen, O.S.A., Edward B. Irving, Jr., James L. Rosier, Paul Fussell, Ludo Rocher, Phillip Pulsiano, Rev. John Rotelle, O.S.A., Sr. Elizabeth Walsh, RSCJ. Thanks are due also to many other teachers, colleagues, and friends: Siegfried Wenzel, Fred Miller Robinson, Edward Jaworowski, Vincent P. McCarren, Rosane Rocher, M.A. and C.A.H. Rollo, Sr. Mary Hotz, RSCJ, Gardner Campbell, Dougal MacGregor, Katie McGowan, M.A. Monroe, and Russell Ceccola. At Wiley-Blackwell, who suffered too many long delays, Emma Bennett and Ben Thatcher in the early days (when still Blackwell), Nicole Allen, and in the final stages the kindly helpful Pascal Raj François and Shakila Suresh and team at Puducherry. Being at a teaching university has drawn out the process considerably, but at the University of San Diego many thanks are due to Alex Moran of the Interlibrary Loan department at the Helen K. and James S. Copley Library who handled quite literally many hundreds of requests. *Optimis parentibus*: the late Joseph Peter McGowan and Joan Patricia (Moore) McGowan, speakers of non-rhotic varieties of English (Providence, RI; Flatbush, Brooklyn).

CHAPTER 1

The Approach to English

1.1 INTRODUCTION

In the past, the subject of the history or story of English has customarily been approached from a 'year zero,' normally AD 449 or thereabouts – the standard *adventus Saxonum*, the coming of the Angles, Saxons, and Jutes of Bede and the textbooks – and brought to a Present-Day English (PDE) of within a half-decade or decade of time of publication. To be certain, a number of modern texts have included material relating to the linguistic background and prehistory of the English language incorporating the great advances made in the past century and a half in Indo-European studies and historical linguistics. The narrative has normally, too, been paced chronologically forward: Strang (1970) the interesting exception in her backward look at the history of English. Chronology of course has its place in anything claiming to be or at least appropriating the title 'history' in a modern sense, and the normative forward pacing will be employed here. The approach to the subject in narrative form is a challenge to conflicting loyalties: to the flow of the history of a living, natural human language through time; to the disciplines of philology and linguistics, with their traditional deconstructing of human language into phonology, morphology, syntax, semantics/lexis, and, more recently, pragmatics. The Cambridge multivolume chronological history of English (6 vols.; Hogg et al. 1992–2001) strikes an admirable balance, though fidelity to the linguistic compartmentalization means a reader often finds oneself starting over again with each chronological period with the phonology, morphology, syntax, and so forth of Old English, early Middle English, late Middle English, Early Modern English, and so on. The advantage of the multivolume approach is the sheer mass of detail on offer, the thoroughness of investigation permitted the authors before moving on to the next topical subsection (late West Saxon, Middle English syntax, etc.).

The recent Oxford Linguistic History of English (Ringe and Taylor 2014; Ringe 2017) represents another signal development in the study of the history of the English language: the increasing specialization in a subject that has grown so vast that it encompasses literally scores of scholarly journals, with representative professional societies for the proliferating subspecializations: an established, major organization such as the American Dialect Society, with its organ of publication *American Speech*, has a membership comprising dialectologists, sociolinguists, folklorists, literary critics, anthropologists, historians, and journalists. The Cambridge History can be said to have bridged a widening disciplinary divide – that between philologists, 'language' specialists who may not adhere to the label 'scientific,' literary specialists and those often housed in departments of English and literature in English-speaking academic institutions, and historical linguists, sociolinguists, and other linguistic researchers who view their discipline as the 'scientific' investigation of human language (or language as a human cognitive faculty). The Oxford Linguistic History, of which two volumes have appeared to date (Ringe 2017; Ringe and Taylor 2014), is a major departure in the writing of the history of English in that it is the work rather of a historical linguist (an Indo-Europeanist) primarily concerned with the linguistic structure of English from its prehistory to its attested history. As such, it begins with a first volume consisting entirely of the reconstructed forms of historical linguistics; jarring to readers of traditional narrative histories of (primarily recorded) English may be Ringe's statement in his General Introduction "Since this entire volume deals with the undocumented past…" (Ringe 2017, 2). Nonetheless, this is a window onto the past that historical linguistics has opened for anyone investigating the complete story of English: we are not only able to understand that English is part of a broader grouping of human languages (the West Germanic subbranch within the Germanic branch of Indo-European), but to have for comparison reconstructed proto-forms, serving as a shorthand of the linguistic changes between forms in the proto-language and reflexes in the daughter languages, generated by the patient work of generations of scholars following a general notion of the regularity of sound change in human languages (the uniformitarian principle). These reconstructions change, of course, with advances in scholarship, representing at time of use the best knowledge available on the basis of the comparative method. So too with any 'history' of English, the methodological tools and presumptions have shifted or been utterly altered over the decades.

The great advances in historical linguistics since the 1960s (the working out of the 'laryngeal theory' among them) have been matched by those in other areas of linguistic investigation: the impact of sociolinguistics, particularly the work of William Labov, of the generative framework of Noam Chomsky (especially valuable in its investigation of syntax, an area that for historical linguists poses great difficulties in reconstruction), pidgin and Creole studies (conjoined now too with the approaches of postcolonial theory in literary and cultural studies). Add to this revisionist trends and simple revisiting of standard narratives in history and other disciplines relevant to the story of English – the revising of the canons of English, American, and Anglophone literatures, for example. A veritable embarrassment of riches confronts the investigator of the history of English today, as does the divide between humanities-based researchers and more scientifically based linguists in approaching the language. There are many fine books on the subject, including such standard textbooks as Baugh and Cable (now in its 6th edition; Baugh and Cable 2013), Pyles and Algeo (in its 7th edition under John Algeo and Carmen Acevedo Butcher; Algeo and Butcher 2013), and Millward (2nd ed. 1996), the Cambridge multivolume history (Hogg et al. 1992–2001; *The New Cambridge*

History of the English Language, under the general editorship of Raymond Hickey, likewise in 6 volumes, is due to appear in 2026); increasingly, volumes such as the *Oxford History of English* (Mugglestone 2006) employ multiple authors, the chapters parceled out by subspecialty (to the historical linguist, syntactician, post-Chomskyan generativist, etc.). For departments of English language and literature, texts such as Baugh and Cable have remained a staple for their inclusion of extralinguistic history and data: the literature, folkways, culture high and popular, the political developments (which can and do have genuine, observable linguistic consequences), social movements, trends, and fads. As the English language has passed through a number of linguistically and culturally significant turning points, so too the writing of its history – and it may sit at a crossroads at the present moment. The path taken by the Oxford Linguistic History of English represents that of the relatively young discipline of linguistics (modern linguistics can be said to date from the 1960s): despite persistent squabbles over the generative approach (Chomskyan and post-Chomskyan models), the relatively more stable methodology and practice of historical linguistics seems to indicate that there is no going back. Across the disciplinary divide the findings of modern linguistics have made their way into more humanities-based histories of the language; the rise of schools of postmodern theory from departments of philosophy and literature has had its impact (if less precisely observable than the reconstructions of historical linguistics). If something has had to give, it has perhaps been the historical and literary-cultural component of the history of the language, which has declined since the days of Albert Croll Baugh's first edition of his *A History of the English Language*, in which, in 1957, he had sensed the need to "present the historical development of English in such a way as to preserve a proper balance between what may be called internal history – sounds and inflections – and external history – the political, social, and intellectual forces that have determined the course of that development at different periods. The writer is convinced that the soundest basis for an understanding of PDE and for an enlightened attitude toward questions affecting the language today is a knowledge of the path which it has pursued in becoming what it is" (Baugh 1957, v).

Given advances in both the internal and external histories of English, the methodological advances and realignments, and the global spread of English as an L2 and postcolonial medium of communication, there seems room enough for one more synthetic history of the language. The study of the language is of course a study of its users, their linguistic activities acrolectal (literature, speeches, and other formal uses) and popular, to an extent their very being insofar as it is given linguistic expression. To return to the matter of presenting the story of English in its traditional chronology, AD 449 to present: English is a relatively young language, though we are able now, through linguistic reconstruction, archaeology, comparative mythology, and other disciplines, to say something of its prehistory, to place it within broader groupings of peoples (on the basis of genetics and material culture, for example) and speech communities (the Indo-European super-family of languages). As such, that is, considering English as a West Germanic language (whose higher-order genetic affiliations are Germanic and Indo-European), we may think of English as part of a continuum; and as long as there are speakers of English it shall have a future. One of the most fascinating aspects of North American and World Englishes is the growth of the language beyond ethnic equivalency – namely, that while the Japanese language is overwhelmingly spoken by ethnically Japanese speakers, English in America, the Caribbean, Africa, South Asia, and elsewhere is used as an L1 or L2 by peoples from literally hundreds of ethnicities. It is always difficult to conclude any investigation of the history of English with consideration of 'future trends': who in AD 650 could have imagined the status and global use of English in the 21st century? Nonetheless, this investigation of English is also a consideration of human language in general: Don Ringe recently closed the introduction to his linguistic study of the prehistory of English by noting that "human language is a single phenomenon, and an understanding of one instantiation is automatically a partial understanding of every other" (Ringe 2017, 4).

The chapters following this pursue the history of the English language in the traditional chronological fashion, though the subdivisions to chapters are as often as not arranged not simply according to a linguistic domain – phonology, morphology, syntax – but around a thematic, historical, or cultural heading. The language is, of course, treated in its parts in each era, though the intention is to broaden the linguistic analysis to the cultural and historical context in which English developed; as a younger Indo-European language, English provides the researcher the good fortune of an essentially continuous written record for most of its 1,400 years. As one of the best attested human languages in terms of the written record, particular attention will be given to its literatures. Areas of signal advances in the past half-century – taking Albert Croll Baugh's 1935 *A History of the English Language* (2nd ed., 1957) as a benchmark in the academic study of the language (or at least as a starting point for History of the English Language as a subdiscipline) – are given prominence (and, quite often, their own subsection): the debate over the West Saxon *Schriftsprache* associated with Winchester in the later Anglo-Saxon period; the legacy of the Vikings, whose raids and settlements and dynastic disputes in England span AD 793–1066 and beyond (recent work has concentrated on the Norse influence on medieval English lexis); the major advances in Middle English dialectology and the role of Geoffrey Chaucer in promoting, indeed likely shaping, the English language in a 14th-century environment that had seen Latin and French as the dominant prestige languages of England; the broad reassessment of the Reformation and Counter Reformation and the great impact of translation of Scripture into English – though the high watermark is the King James Bible of 1611, there had always been a tradition of making vernacular versions of Scripture in English; the development of pidgin and Creole studies as a discipline and the tremendous impact this has had upon the understanding of the 'birth' of languages, the nature of contact varieties, the linguistic consequences of colonization and imperialism, and the nature of language acquisition and language learning; the understanding of the linguistic and cultural power associated with the prestige and status of a language or language variety: the implications extend to modern analyses of social class and social organization (the purview of sociology and, since the 1960s, of sociolinguistics) as they can be encoded in speech and writing, and to heritage and minority languages in a century of decolonization and postcolonial language debates: from the status of Irish as the official language of Éire, the return of Welsh as an L1 in Wales, attempts at reviving Manx and Cornish, heated language debates in India post-1948, French-English language debates in officially bilingual Canada, to the status of English-based pidgins and Creoles in a number of postcolonial nations (Tok Pisin of Papua New Guinea a salient example); and the matter of English as a global language (at least as a global L2) in the 'digital age': while the dominance of English in 'cyberspace' has fallen short of predictions for the Internet Age, undoubtedly the English language is being shaped once again – to what extent is a matter of great uncertainty – by technological innovation, as it had been in 1476 with the introduction of the printing press to England by William Caxton.

Throughout maximal use has been made of example, extended examples quite often, of text or recorded speech to illustrate not only the linguistic phenomena critical to the development of English but the cultural, political, and technological influences that provide the crucible of change. The risk of over-explanation has been taken; it has been the object to incur the reader's fatigue at a perceived or actual surfeit of explanation and example rather than his or her or their frustration with under-explanation. The Scots say *Mony a mickle maks a muckle*; disregarding that warning, every effort has been made here to include as much pertinent, up-to-date information as is possible in a single-volume treatment of the subject.

1.2 THE APPROACH TO ENGLISH

Any approach to the history of the English language is essentially retrospective insofar as historians of this living language – in distinction to formal and historical linguists, literary theorists, and historians proper – must generally await the production of observable data: namely, the spoken or written use of the language by L1 (native or first-language) and L2 (non-native or second-language) users – whether this constitutes, at the present moment, actual in-person conversation, television/cable/Internet broadcasts and programming, text-messaging, e-mail, printed matter, literature, and likely a dozen other types of communication. To be sure, studies of the development of English often end with consideration of 'future trends,' 'the future of English,' or the like; reasonable predictions can be made about the spread of English as a 'global language,' or the continued growth of its lexicon and diversification of sources of loanwords into English. But there is much that one could be wrong about in anticipating the future of English, as with all prognostications, however conservative.

Historical linguists, on the other hand, work 'backward' from recorded data comparatively (with the data of other known related languages) to plausible protoforms; that is, 'primitive' or 'original' forms ancestral to the recorded forms. The reliability of the **comparative method** has been borne out by the discovery of earlier texts and the decipherment of early scripts hitherto uninterpretable. For example, the **laryngeal theory** (Chapter 2) was bolstered by the identification of cuneiform documents from the Hittite empire that recorded not a Semitic language – as expected – but an Anatolian Indo-European language (Hittite) that did have reflexes of PIE laryngeal consonants (a discovery made by Polish linguist Jerzy Kuryłowicz). A caveat to linguistic reconstruction has to do with time-depth: those reconstructed forms closer in time to the extant recorded forms of the 'daughter' languages can be, in general but not absolutely, more secure than those of the more distant past – for example, reconstructed Proto-West Germanic or Proto-Germanic (ca. 500 BC) forms involve rather less a speculative leap than for Proto-Indo-European (ca. 3500 BC or earlier), even though the overall span of evidence is greater across the rest of the IE family. There have been many great advances by historical linguists in understanding language history, the genetic typology of human languages (how languages may be grouped by families and branches), and the nature of language change (and that it is, especially with sound change, largely regular, except when 'spontaneous'). A look over the past century of reconstruction of proto-forms for PIE or PGmc will show significant changes – with individual sounds, or clusters (or whether PIE had diphthongs), and certainly with morphological paradigms (the verb 'to be' has always been a contested matter). The proposed reconstructed forms can vary by 'school' of thought (German and other 'Continental' vs. British vs. American, etc.) or even by individual scholar. But historical linguistics in the past half-century has come to an increasingly secure level of precision (if not universal agreement). This is a long-winded explanation in anticipation of questions regarding how linguists can claim to know (or at least propose to reconstruct) how English was pronounced before the invention of recording devices (besides writing, that is).

If there is one thing consideration of the history of English shows, it is the sheer implausibility of what did indeed happen. Unlike other former Roman provinces, Britain did not develop a Romance language in the wake of the Empire's collapse. For one, Germanic invaders and settlers arrived before and throughout the 'collapse' of Roman Britain (Chapter 3); Latin, it seems, did not fully disappear and was soon restored to an important position as one of the island's languages – in Kent, at first, but in both instances it was the language also of Christianity. Extended Scandinavian invasions and settlement in England, AD 793–1066, significantly altered the language's lexis but English remained a West Germanic language (while the modern Scandinavian languages belong to the North Germanic branch). The Norman Conquest of 1066 replaced West Saxon Old English with Norman French as the prestige language of the country for over the next three centuries; remarkably, the language of the masses won out, and French ceased to be a living tongue in England (though it survived in personal and place-names, and continues as the major source of loan-words to English). A relatively small island nation at the western edge of Europe would in the wake of its four historically recorded invasions (Roman, Germanic, Viking/Scandinavian, Norman) become a major imperial power – a feat often attributed to its fleets, though empire began with the conquest of the remaining Celtic lands in Britain and, starting in the 12th century, the invasion and occupation of Ireland. The linguistic impact of this expansion has been staggering: counts of numbers of speakers (L1 and L2) of English approach or reach over 3 billion, more than one-third of the world's population. There are no signs of any retraction; if American English is now the most influential set of varieties of the language, having surpassed British English in the postcolonial age, the observation has been made that English may have grown past its traditional British and American moorings to encompass a 'circle' or 'circles' of World Englishes: from a historically original (or older) core of Great Britain, the United States, Canada, Australia, and New Zealand (and Pacific Island varieties and pidgins and Creoles), to Caribbean, African (West, East, and Southern), and Asian (South and East) varieties (McArthur 1987; Kachru 1988; Mesthrie 2008).

A subject so vast – now literally global in scale – seemingly defies adequate treatment; indeed, History of the English Language (HEL) is a university subject of long-standing, a professional academic discipline of its own, an industry even (ESL and EFL programs generate revenue for universities and private concerns on the basis of the 'access' a knowledge of English is said to provide). Nonetheless, considering human language as a single phenomenon, the dialects and varieties of a language by their mutual intelligibility enable speech communities to form and function, and by association develop other bonds. The discipline of sociolinguistics has pursued this latter concern: the ties that form in sharing a language, across the many forms of distinction by which human beings have historically separated themselves. Speakers of English participate in Anglophone speech communities: to what extent this participation leads to other forms of identification (cultural, political, and so forth) varies widely. As one example, a salient point of postmodern 24-hour media coverage is the widespread use of the English language by political protesters the world over: the appeal is not just to English-speakers for their sheer number, but to some political mindset or framework many of these speakers presumably share as well as to the governmental and nongovernmental organizations that may more immediately be reached or appealed to by the use of English. As with the study of globalization itself, one needs to specify the identification of English, despite its increasingly global use, with 'Western' culture; this access it allows to 'the West' may be precisely one of its appeals.

Worth repeating here is the simple fact of the relatively young age of the English language: at 1,300–1,400 years old, English is, even within the Indo-European family of languages, a relative newcomer. Of great importance is that English has been recorded in writing for most of its 13 or 14 centuries, as this allows the historian of the language to deal in specifics. And in order to do so, relevant terminology and theoretical approaches must be turned to in at least a preliminary fashion.

1.3 LINGUISTIC METHOD

If the rise of post-Structuralist modern linguistics can be dated to the publication of Noam Chomsky's *Syntactic Structures* in 1957, developments within and discoveries in historical linguistics have since the mid-20th century – notably the Laryngeal theory (see Chapter 2) – greatly refined our ability to describe language change and the environment for changes in the sounds, inflections, syntax, and vocabulary (both lexis, the total set of words that comprise the vocabulary, and semantics, the meanings of those words) of a language. The development of sociolinguistics has re-focused attention on the broader environment of language development: the nature of speech communities and social networks, the role of class, ethnicity, gender, even religion in linguistic social stratification. The rise of pidgin and Creole studies, that is, the study of language contact varieties such as the English-based varieties of the Caribbean and Pacific Islands, has given valuable insight into the language contact situations that produce change (such as loan formations or inflectional changes) or give birth to wholly new varieties that can serve as the L1 of a speech community (Creoles), besides the insight gleaned with regard to child language development and language acquisition. And the refinement of linguistic taxonomy – one of the signal advances in linguistic knowledge of the Enlightenment – allows us to begin to ground the analysis of English in specifics.

1.4 GENETIC CLASSIFICATION

The English language is an Indo-European language, and while this is a subject reserved for more detail in the following chapter, it needs to be said at the outset that this 'taxonomic' classification has significant entailments. While the 'genetic classification' of human languages involves some metaphorical abstraction, nonetheless, one can think of human languages as having 'heritable' features and of more closely 'related' languages sharing in common more core features (in sounds, grammar, syntax, and vocabulary) than those less closely related. Thus historical linguists speak of 'parent' and 'daughter' languages. For English, the genetic classification is Indo-European, Germanic, West Germanic, in terms of its super- or macro-family, branch, and subbranch relationships (the particular terms for groupings of related languages as used in family-tree diagrams can vary slightly). West Germanic comprises German, Yiddish, Dutch, Afrikaans, Frisian, and English; Yiddish (from German *Jüdisch*, i.e., 'Jewish' German contact variety of German and Hebrew) and Afrikaans (from Dutch *Afrikaansch* 'African,' also called 'the Taal' or Cape Dutch contact variety of Dutch, English, Zulu, Xhosa, and other African languages) are Creoles often given in a listing of West Germanic languages – somewhat unusually for contact language varieties, they have historically been written down, Yiddish in particular with a rich literature of its own. Germanic is comprised of two living branches and one extinct branch: West Germanic, North Germanic (Greenlandic, Icelandic, Faroese, Norn [now extinct, formerly spoken on Shetland and the Orkneys and parts of Northern Scotland], Norwegian, Swedish, and Danish), and East Germanic (an extinct branch including Gothic, of which we have the translation of Greek Scripture by Ulfilas, and likely Vandalic [Hartmann 2020], a line of which may be preserved in the *Latin Anthology* in addition to some personal names in classical sources, Burgundian, and Crimean Gothic). The relative relatedness of Germanic to other branches in the Indo-European macro-family of languages is a matter of continued debate, but there seems to be a good case for some degree of closer affiliation to Baltic (see Chapter 2). At the super- or macro-family level, English is part of a family of languages spanning, in the pre-colonial period, Western Europe to South Asia; perhaps half the world's population speaks an Indo-European tongue as a first or second language, in large part due to the numbers of speakers of such IE languages as English, Hindi, Spanish, Russian, and French.

The entire notion of 'relatedness' among languages relies upon a good number of theoretical underpinnings; for the moment, one presumption involves the ultimate unitary phenomenon that is human language: that all human languages, living and recorded, derive from an original Ur-language, that they all share linguistic universals in common, or that human language evolved just once (none of these points going uncontested in the scholarly literature). For our purposes, this means that the English language has antecedents or ancestors more closely or distantly related. English in this sense is 'inherited' from Proto-Germanic and Proto-Indo-European – to leave it at levels that can be reconstructed by historical linguists – its core phonology, morphology, syntax, and semantics; it is enormously difficult to ascertain non-Indo-European influences at the level of proto-English: perhaps only non-Celtic 'pre-English' hydronyms and place-names and place-name elements can be suggested with any security at present (see Chapter 3). That English developed as it has is no doubt due to a number of external, historical forces, but the raw material, the DNA so to speak, of English, is an inheritance. It is found in other recorded Germanic and Indo-European languages or can be reconstructed on the basis of regular sound changes and inflectional changes found in the IE daughter languages.

Despite the great number of speakers of Indo-European languages, the family comprises approximately only 445 languages – to the Austronesian family, by comparison, belong over 1,200 languages. General estimates of the world's living languages usually fall between 6,000 and 7,000. Perhaps the most detailed count is that given by the Ethnologue project of the SIL (Summer Institute of Linguistics): 7,159 living languages (2025 estimate). The latest version of the Ethnologue data notes "an increase of 103 previously unidentified languages. Most of these are not newly discovered languages, but are ones that had been previously considered dialects of another language" (17 new languages added since 2024; Ethnologue 2025). Their data suggest 1,554 languages in the Niger-Congo family of languages (spoken throughout western and southwestern Africa, with some 600 million speakers), 1,257 languages in the Austronesian family (with approximately 330–380 million speakers), member languages spoken throughout the Pacific, with the greatest linguistic diversity being in Papua New Guinea: not included in this total are the 482 languages grouped as 'Trans-New Guinea,' spoken primarily both sides of the Papua New Guinea-Indonesia border; 445 languages in Indo-European (this includes extinct languages and a number of varieties considered dialects by other linguists or national governments; their estimate of the number of speakers is 3.4 billion; L2 speakers of English and French likely make this figure much higher), 462 languages in Sino-Tibetan (with an estimate of 1.4 billion speakers, mainly of varieties of Chinese, for this the second most widely spoken family of languages in the world), and 391 languages in Afro-Asiatic (with approximately 500 million speakers). The SIL and its Ethnologue project were founded in Arkansas in 1934 not as a linguistic organization but to foster evangelical Christian missionary work abroad; a concern with learning local languages for this work led to training in the tongues and the translation of Scripture into minority languages (in association with Wycliffe Bible Translators); this in turn led to concern with the preservation of minority languages and an attempt to classify the world's languages by accepted linguistic principles. The activity has not been without controversy, particularly in Latin America (Gow 2001). The Endangered Language Fund, based at Yale University, by comparison, also attempts to support minority, endangered languages – that is, those classified as 'moribund,' with few native speakers left, a common predicament with the languages of indigenous groups in the Americas and Asia – though without the evangelical program; nonetheless, both the SIL and ELF are involved in what is termed 'language planning.'

Thus, in terms of genetic classification, English is a member of the Indo-European family of languages – the largest in terms of numbers of speakers, with a number of member languages continuing to function as colonial and postcolonial prestige varieties (English, French, Spanish, Portuguese, Dutch, and German).

1.5 THE SPEAKERS OF ENGLISH

Estimates of the number of speakers of English vary significantly and often seem tinged either by hand-wringing or triumphalism: as with everything involving the history of the language, controversy can flare up over what the facts indeed are and their interpretation. As English derived its status as a 'global language' from imperialism – and it might be remembered that this began in the British Isles centuries before 1492 – it owes its numbers and influence to linguistic displacement, however much this may be motivated in the 21st century by 'opportunity.' An attempt will be made nonetheless at a dispassionate estimate of the numbers of speakers. The plural form 'numbers' is used as one must first distinguish between native or first-language speakers (L1) and second-language users (L2). As to the first group of speakers, those who have English as their native, heritage, or primary language (that is, in terms that language acquisition researchers use, as their acquired language system, acquired through a largely subconscious process) a figure of over half a billion seems likely (500–750 million, with 320 million alone in the United States). While the number of predominantly Anglophone nations is relatively small (the United Kingdom, the United States, Australia, New Zealand, and Canada), the number of countries in which English is an L1 and postcolonial L2 (often with status as an 'official language') adds greatly to the figure and spans the globe (calling to mind the imperial boast that 'the sun never sets on the British Empire'): from South Asia (Pakistan, India, Nepal, and Bangladesh), to West Africa (Nigeria, Ghana, the Gambia, and the American English example, Liberia), East Africa (Kenya and Tanzania), Southern Africa (South Africa, Namibia, Zimbabwe, and Zambia), Latin America and the Caribbean (Panama, Belize, Patagonia in Chile and Argentina, Bahamas, Caymans, Bermuda, and Jamaica), East Asia and the Pacific (Hong Kong, Singapore, Philippines, Papua New Guinea, and Solomon Islands). The spread of English beyond the British and American Empires (the United States developed its empire relatively late, in earnest following the Spanish-American War of April–August 1898) is a singular development of the 20th and 21st centuries: Spanish has become a hemispheric language, restricted now largely to former American colonies (Central and South America and the Caribbean) with retraction in Asia and Africa, while French, despite growth in West Africa and the Maghreb, has also been restricted largely to former colonies (with retraction in Southeast Asia, former Indochine). British and American business interests and military presence, including the worldwide spread of American military bases and relatively frequent military interventions, have led the way for an Anglo-American postcolonial expansion of use in the language and brought American-accented English to 'spheres of influence' that once belonged to 'old Europe.' English is frequently the *lingua franca* of peace-keeping operations and occupations under the banner of NATO or the UN: Bosnia-Hercegovina, Kosovo, East Timor, Afghanistan, and Iraq – Rwanda, formerly under Belgian administration and since independence seen as part of 'la Francophonie,' being a notable exception. Precise figures for L2 usage are impossible, but estimates can be drawn up on the basis of government figures, book sales, online material, media broadcasting in English, numbers of students enrolling in English-language lessons and courses, and the like, and have ranged from 1 to 2 billion (see, e.g., Crystal 2018). While Mandarin Chinese may still have more L1 speakers than English, nearly 900 million by Ethnologue's estimate (the figure for Mandarin is difficult to estimate given its status as the 'official language' of China, even in areas with other native languages), it has, in an inversion of the pattern for English (which very likely has more L2 users than L1 speakers), far fewer L2 users (Ethnologue nonetheless estimates these at 178 million). One can say at least that, L1 and L2 speakers combined, English is the most widely spoken language in the world; whether the expansion in speakers will continue steadily or exponentially is the subject of some speculation. Suffice it to say that the development of English from ca. AD 600 when it was the language of Germanic tribes then inhabiting only half the island of Britain to the present-day global language used by perhaps 2–3 billion speakers is in itself a remarkable story.

1.6 PHONOLOGY

Simply put, phonology is the study of sounds, with phonemes being the discrete units of sound-meaning correspondence, that is, the smallest sound segments by which meaningful (semantic) distinctions can be drawn. It is normal practice to transcribe phonemes in rightward slanting brackets, for example, /p/ /t/ /k/ (the voiceless stops in English), and to illustrate the phonemic inventory of the language with minimal pairs: with *pit* [pɪt] and *bit* [bɪt] and *tin* [tɪn] and *din* [dɪn] the contrastive sound segments, that is, the *phonemes*, are /p/ and /b/, /t/ and /d/. In these basic examples, only the initial consonant has been varied between the pairs, but the simple fact that to speaker-hearers of English the sound segments are distinct enough so as to produce two different words in each case constitutes *phonemic* contrast. The phoneme /p/, for instance, is in some ways a linguistic abstraction (Fox 1995, 38f.), it is the 'p'-sound considered in isolation; such metalinguistic abstraction is not a modern phenomenon; we know the Sanskrit grammarians made like observations (see Chapter 2); in a syllable or word, that is, in real-world use of sounds, abstract phonemes can behave differently (i.e., suprasegmentally, in linguistic parlance) – the importance being that the variation is not so great as to be considered another sound (languages tend to resist overlap and redundancy in their sound systems). Short of this phonemic distinction, as between /p/ and /b/ and /t/ and /d/ in the examples above, one can observe allophonic variation. *Allophones* are variants of phonemes; for example, /p/ in *pot* is realized phonetically as [p^{h}], the aspirated allophone of /p/, while in *spot* we have simply [p] (unaspirated *p*, call it 'pure' *p*). Likewise, the /t/ in *top* [tɒp] (BrE) [t^{h}ɑ:p] (AmE) vs. that in *stop* [stɒp], [stɑ:p]. The phonetic transcription in square brackets is an attempt to record with as much fidelity as possible actual speech; it will be used throughout this study to indicate how an utterance was actually pronounced as opposed to how it was graphically realized (e.g., the recordings of dialects in Mark Twain's *Adventures of Huckleberry Finn* employ 'phonetic' spellings in the popular sense rather than that of modern linguistics).

Two other brief notes might be made with regard to our minimal pairs above: /p/ and /b/ are both bilabial stops (they are similar in their place and manner of articulation); the distinguishing feature, that is, what makes them two different sounds (phonemes), is *voicing*, the vibration of the vocal cords (the folds of membrane across the larynx, located approximately behind the Adam's apple): the vocal cords in the articulation of /p/ are relaxed, producing a *voiceless* sound, while in the articulation of /b/ the vocal cords close over and vibrate with the exhalation of air. With /d/ and /t/, we again have two consonants similar in their articulation, in the place and manner of articulation, but differing by one feature in that /t/ is the voiceless alveolar stop, /d/ the voiced alveolar stop. This last example might be expanded briefly to consider an enormously common type of sound change: the interdental fricatives /θ/, voiceless as in *think*, and /ð/, voiced as in *though*, are relatively rare sounds in the phonemic inventories of the world's languages. One hears quite often in L2 (non-native or foreign) production of L1 English norms *substitution* for these interdental fricatives: native Italian and Spanish speakers, among others, may substitute alveolar stops: the 'dis, dat, dese, dose, dem' of, for example, South Philadelphia Italian American speech for the pronouns and determinatives 'this, that, these, those, them'; native French speakers may substitute alveolar fricatives (thus 'sis' [si:s] and 'zose' [zo:s] or something similar for 'these' and 'those'). Substitution and other forms of sound change can be noted for both their frequency and regularity: they can be productive of temporary, allophonic variation, or more lasting dialectal variety, or persist to an extent that one can say the language has undergone a sound change by which the previous realization of the sound has been altered for good. Linguists can speak of *phonemicization*, or *phonologization,* by which what may have been allophonic variation, such as that marking varieties within a dialect or marking off dialects within a language, becomes realized in the language as separate phonemes (the "reanalysis as two distinct phonemes"; Janda in Joseph and Janda 2003, 410); historically, for English, one sees this in allophonic /v/ (the voiced labiodental fricative) for Old English /f/, as in *fœt* 'vessel, cup,' which underwent *phonemic split* in the Middle English period (1100–1500). Such observations are vital to any description of the sound changes that mark the stages of English; before proceeding further, it is necessary to introduce the sounds of PDE as a touchstone for discussions of the earlier stages of the language.

The prefatory tables of IPA (International Phonetic Association) symbols for sounds and charts of the sounds of English will here be pared down to present-day examples. If one of the most vital distinctions to be drawn in describing the phonemic inventory of the language is between consonants and vowels, it is one nearly as difficult in its precise description as it is obvious and simple in observation. Traditionally, the distinction holds that the consonants are sounds involving occlusion or obstruction of the air flow in their articulation, and the vowels being those sounds produced without such occlusion or obstruction. One will also find such terms as *resonants* and *sonorants*, which, in their broadest sense, can include vowels and voiced consonants excluding stops and affricates: namely, *m* [m], *ng* /ŋ/, *n* /n/, *l* /l/, *r* /r/, *y* /j/, and *w* /w/. Consonants can be grouped according to three distinctive features: (1) place of articulation (what articulator has the primary role in the formation of the sound); (2) manner of articulation (by and large, the manner of occlusion or obstruction of airflow); (3) voicing (voiced, voiceless: the operation or non-operation of the vocal cords during articulation). Thus an inventory of the consonants according to these three distinctive features:

/p/ voiceless bilabial stop (**p**etrol, **p**um**p**kin)
/b/ voiced bilabial stop (**b**and, **b**a**bb**le)
/t/ voiceless alveolar stop (**t**est, **t**o**t**al)
/d/ voiced alveolar stop (**d**raw, **d**oo**d**le)

/k/ voiceless velar stop (**c**all, **c**a**ck**le)
/g/ voiced velar stop (**g**rin, **g**i**g**)

/f/ voiceless labiodental fricative (**f**ive, **F**i**f**e)
/v/ voiced labiodental fricative (**v**at, **v**al**v**e)
/θ/ voiceless interdental fricative (**th**ink, wi**th**, though the latter form can often be realized as [wɪð])
/ð/ voiced interdental fricative (**th**ough, wi**th**out, though it can also be realized as unvoiced [θ] in medial position by many speakers)
/s/ voiceless alveolar fricative (**s**imple, **s**a**ss**)
/z/ voiced alveolar fricative (**z**oo, ha**z**e)
/ʃ/ or /š/ voiceless alveolopalatal fricative (**sh**oc, spla**sh**)
/ʒ/ or/ž/ voiced alveolopalatal fricative(mea**s**ure, gara**g**e)
/h/ voiceless glottal fricative

/tʃ/ or /č/ voiceless alveolopalatal affricate (**ch**ur**ch**)
/dʒ/ or /ǰ / or voiced alveolopalatal affricate (**j**u**dg**e)

/m/ voiced bilabial nasal (**M**o**m**)
/n/ voiced alveolar nasal (**n**o**n**e)
/ŋ/ voiced velar nasal (si**ng**)

/r/ voiced alveolar (retroflex) liquid (**r**ight)
/l/ voiced alveolar (lateral) liquid (**l**ike)

/j/ voiced palatal (semi-vowel) glide (**y**oke)
/w/ voiced labiovelar (semi-vowel) glide (**w**ell)

As will be noticed, there is an overall consistent pattern of voiceless/voiced pairs of consonants, with one exception: there is no voiced complement to the glottal fricative /h/; it is entirely possible to produce one in English, it is just not found in English speech as semantically distinctive, as phonemic, that is, in formal speech: one does hear the voiced glottal fricative /ɦ/ produced in informal interjections such as *uh-huh* or *unh-unh* (indicating doubt, suspicion, or disbelief). It is indeed possible to produce a great many other consonantal sounds; one could, for example, produce *f*- and *v*-like sounds not with the top teeth pressed to the bottom lip, the normal pattern of articulation, but the other way around. It may sound curious, but it is possible; it is just not employed in the English language. Conversely, absent from this list above is the common sound [ʔ], the voiceless glottal stop, as found medially in the interjection *uh-oh*, in child language (commonly substituted for medial stops), and in Cockney (*bottle* realized as [bɔ:ʔl]). As it primarily occurs as an allophone or nonstandard dialectal variant and is thus not recorded in standard orthography, it is absent above but will be found elsewhere in transcriptions of actual use. It is also clear that the line between consonant and vowel is blurred by the label 'semi-vowel' (or glide or approximant). This may refer either to a sound having vowel-like quality but employed as a consonant (/w/, /j/), or having consonant-like quality but employed like a vowel (as can be the nasals and liquids). Even so, imprecisions abound in any attempt at employing these symbols, as the fields of auditory and articulatory phonetics have become increasingly complex (Ladefoged 1996, 2005). Clearly, the *l*-sounds in *like* and *milk* are not the same: the initial [l] in *like* [laɪk] is clearly alveolar, while the noninitial pre-consonantal [l] in *milk* [mɪɫk], sometimes called 'dark'-*l*, is velarized (one can feel and hear resonance at the velum or soft palate in articulation): all the more so in the dialectal pronunciation *melk* [mɛɫk].

It is often remarked that vowels carry the most frequent variation in English and that one will find the greatest variation in the varieties of English in their articulation of vowels. Most noticeable to even casual observers are the vowel changes between *rhotic* and *non-rhotic* varieties of English, that is, those retaining or losing, partially to fully, /r/ in medial and final positions. It is one of the conventional dividing lines between BrE and AmE varieties, though it is not at all universal: while RP is standardly non-rhotic (as are standard varieties deriving from BrE in former colonies), one finds rhotic varieties in Western England and in areas where Celtic languages were or still are spoken (Irish-English varieties are rhotic); while non-rhotic varieties of English were more predominant in colonial America (there were notable exceptions, such as Philadelphia and the Appalachians), rhotic AmE varieties now predominate and non-rhotic varieties (New England east of the Connecticut River, the New York City region, and Charleston, South Carolina, for instance) are in the minority geographically and numerically. The retention or loss of medial and final [r] affects the preceding vowels, and is one of the reasons why chapters on the more recent history of English will require separate transcriptions for AmE and BrE varieties.

If consonants may be classified by three markings or distinctive features (voicing, place of articulation, and manner of articulation), vowels are somewhat more complexly described by five distinctive features: length (long/tense, short/lax); simple or diphthong (a two-part vowel sound, even more simply if not exactly described as 'two vowel sounds in one syllable'); rounding (referring to the rounding or pursing of the lips, vowels can be placed on a scale from unrounded, such as /ɪ/ or /ɛ / or /æ/, to rounded, such as /ɔ /, /o/, /u/); front/central/back: with regard to where the position of the tongue directs the airflow in articulation, as by its elevation; high/mid/low: specifying the elevation of the tongue in the process of articulation – with a high vowel the tongue is elevated, while with the production of a low vowel the tongue is more depressed (thus a doctor asks a patient to produce a low vowel, normally /ɑ/ 'ah,' to have a look at the patient's tonsils). All vowels are voiced; they are often described as 'continuous' sounds, if only in contradistinction to the general observation that consonants normally involve some form of obstruction or occlusion of airflow in articulation. Based on the distinctive features of vowels outlined above, a preliminary catalogue of the major vowels of PDE may be given (IPA descriptions follow, where they may differ in terminology):

simple vowels (monophthongs)
/i/ high front unrounded (IPA: close for 'high')
/y/ high near front rounded (close)
/ɪ/ high-mid front unrounded (near close, near front)
/e/ mid-high front unrounded (close mid)
/ɛ/ mid-low front unrounded (open mid)
/æ/ low-mid front unrounded (near open)
/a/ low front unrounded (open)
/ɘ/ mid-high central unrounded (close mid; this symbol is seen particularly in BrE examples)
/ə/ mid central unrounded (the 'schwa' vowel)

/ɜ/ mid-low central unrounded (open mid)
/ʊ/ back high-mid rounded (near close, near back)
/ʌ/ back mid-low unrounded (open mid)
/ɒ/ low back rounded (open)
/ɑ/ low back unrounded (open)
/u/ high back rounded (close)
/o/ mid-high back rounded (close mid)
/ɔ/ mid-low back rounded (open mid; the 'aw' sound, as in New York City pronunciation of *call* [kɔ:l])

diphthongs
/aɪ/ (l**i**ne)
/ɑʊ/ (h**ou**se, n**ow**)
/ei/ (pl**ay**)
/oʊ/ (b**oa**t)
/ɔɪ/ (t**oy**)
/ɛə/ (RP b**ea**r)
/ɪə/ (RP b**ee**r)
/ʊə/ (RP p**oo**r)
/ɛu/ (Southern California t**o**tally [tɛu:təli:])
/iæ/ (Southern California Sp**a**nish [spiæ:nɪš])

Not all of the symbols from the IPA chart appear here for the vowels of English, and it is with the vowels that the most significant phonological variation occurs among the varieties of English. The vowel catalogue above at least represents the cardinal vowels for standard BrE (RP) and AmE; there are various estimates as to the number of sounds in English – of course depending upon the variety of BrE or AmE one speaks – but it may be fair enough to give a figure of approximately 37–47 sounds (Greenbaum 1996). The number of diphthongs varies widely among speakers of English; RP speakers may employ eight or so diphthongs, and AmE speakers five or so (for RP see Trudgill et al. 2012, 46–47). One primary factor for the difference is the non-rhotic nature of RP, which accounts for the diphthongs /ɛə/, /ɪə/, /ʊə/ – a sound change conditioned here by loss of final /r/. Variation in AmE can involve a number of shifts in the monophthongs and diphthongs; the change is bidirectional. Breaking/diphthongization involves the 'split' of a simple vowel into a two-part vowel or diphthong, conditioned, historically and synchronically (in dialects of PDE), by a number of factors; one hears, for instance, in Southern California and Philadelphia (in the city in particular, but spreading to the tri-state, PA-NJ-DE, greater metropolitan area) a number of vowel shifts involving breaking: the aforementioned SoCal 'teutally' ([o] > [ɛu]) and 'Speeanish' ([æ] > [iæ], heard also in *can't* [ki:ænt]), Philadelphia 'sheuw' ([o]~[ɛʊ] in *show*), among a number of others. Conversely, monophthongization/smoothing involves the reduction or coalescence of a two-part vowel (diphthong) into a simple vowel (monophthong): thus in Philadelphia working- to lower-middle-class English, the two-syllable days of the week have the *-day* [dei] reduced to 'dee' [di:], hence *Mondee, Teuzdee* [tɛuzdi:], *Wenzdee* [wɛnzdi:], *Thursdee* [θərzdi:], and *Fridee* [fraidi:], but the shift in stress is altered in the three-syllable sequence, *Saturday* [sætərdei]. Whether English genuinely has triphthongs (a monosyllabic vowel sound of three vocalic components) is a matter of contention: is the RP pronunciation of *hour* [aʊə] really monosyllabic? Southern American Mountain speech may exhibit triphthongs (as in the Appalachian pronunciation of *mountain*) or the working-class Philadelphia pronunciation of *now* [ni:æʊ]. Reference will be made throughout the volume to the 'KIT standard lexical set' deployed by J.C. Wells in the three volumes to his *Accents of English* (Wells 1982; cf. Wells 1982, 1, xviii–xix, 127–167); this sets out 'test words' for the phonetic representation of the vowels of RP (British English 'Received Pronunciation') and General American English (GenAmE):

	RP	**GenAm**
1. KIT	ɪ	ɪ
2. DRESS	e	ɛ
3. TRAP	æ	æ
4. LOT	ɒ	ɑ
5. STRUT	ʌ	ʌ
6. FOOT	ʊ	ʊ
7. BATH	ɑ:	æ
8. CLOTH	ɒ	ɔ
9. NURSE	3:	3r
10. FLEECE	i:	I
11. FACE	eɪ	eɪ
12. PALM	ɑ:	ɑ
13. THOUGHT	ɔ:	ɔ
14. GOAT	əʊ	o
15. GOOSE	u:	u
16. PRICE	aɪ	aɪ
17. CHOICE	ɔɪ	ɔɪ
18. MOUTH	aʊ	aʊ
19. NEAR	ɪə	ɪ(r
20. SQUARE	ɛə	ɛ(r[1]

[1] One of the great difficulties in any attempt to represent English pronunciation – as English is one of those languages now generally *not* spelled as pronounced – is the variability in systems of phonetic transcription, theories of phonology (which should not affect phonetic representation, but do), and differences of opinion not so much about production as perception of a sound. The OED currently lists for *square* an RP value [skwɛ:], that is, no longer diphthongized after historical loss of /r/: this may be true for 'Estuary English,' but is it so for RP? Both are, arguably, affected accents. AHD5 for AmE gives, in their own idiosyncratic system [skwâr], for which the IPA equivalent would be [skwɛər] or [skweər] (one of the disadvantages of the AHD5 and ANAE is that they have not employed IPA in their transcriptions). The latter seems the more common one among younger generations of speakers; *pace* the 'KIT set,' Americans generally do diphthongize the vowel in *square*, with quite a bit of regional variability: in non-rhotic varieties one can hear [skwɛ:] unbroken or with breaking (Boston, Providence); in some Southern Mountain varieties (e.g., Eastern Kentucky) one can hear [skwɑ:r], that is rhyming with *are*.

21. START	ɑ:	ɑ(r
22. NORTH	ɔ:	ɔ(r
23. FORCE	ɔ:	o(r
24. CURE	ʊə	ʊ(r
25. happY	i	ɪ
26. lettER	ə	ə(r
27. commA	ə	ə

For the four-volume *Varieties of English* survey of World Englishes, editor Edgar W. Schneider provided a greatly expanded version of the 'KIT set' to try to account for international varieties (e.g., nearly a dozen realizations of the vowel – usually, but not always, a diphthong – in PRICE – e.g., Australian English /ɑe/, /ɔe/; Horvath in Burridge and Kortmann 2008, 92).

The use of IPA symbols allows for an *approximate* phonetic representation of the spoken language; the IPA alphabet is enormously useful to linguists, who seek to record the sounds of human speech precisely, and to educators, for whom the IPA transcriptions can serve *in loco magistri* ('in place of a teacher'), as a guide in their absence as to how students should sound out a word in the language they are learning (the IPA is in common use in ESL dictionaries and handbooks).

Nonetheless, the reader will notice soon enough that IPA transcriptions often miss the nuances any perceptive hearer observes in dialectal speech. The subtleties of Southern American Mountain speech (such as Appalachian speech of Eastern Kentucky), or of Scouse, and so forth, will elude exact graphic representation. But the conventions of phonetic transcription are essential to metalinguistic analysis: to talking and writing about linguistic, here phonological, variation. One can at least, with the basic catalogue of sounds above, begin to describe the sound changes of early English, for which we have only written evidence; what little acoustic evidence there can be said to exist derives from 'vestigial' pronunciation in dialects that escaped some of the sound changes in the major varieties. For PDE, the description of sounds is much more elaborate and complex as we have had since the 19th century the technological means to record the sound of the human voice. A look at the ANAE (Labov et al. 2006) will bear out this general observation; while the oppositional classification of the vowels of English and other Germanic languages as tense/long and lax/short, indicating the expenditure of energy in their production (the tenser the articulation the greater the effort of production) and often given the notation [±tense], is standard, observations of recorded dialects of PDE have produced a much more complex phonological picture – if only because the recorded data are richer.

Recent work with vowel chain-shifts has suggested the importance of 'phonetic space,' of peripheral 'tracks' in which these shifts occur; this descriptive phenomenon will be seen in more detail in the discussion of the Northern Cities Vowel Shift in AmE, but in the "Germanic and Baltic language families, and those Romance languages influenced by Germanic, peripherality is the principal feature determining the direction of movement within the tense and lax subsystems"

(Labov 1994, 231; see also Labov et al. 2006, 16–18). The concept of the 'phonetic space' of vowels is important at this point in that one can visualize such from the trapezoidal representations of the vowels of English: when a vowel moves, it can intrude on the space of an adjacent vowel, triggering dissimilative change by the affected vowel so as to avoid overlap in pronunciation (see, for instance, Wolfram and Schilling-Estes 2006, 75–76). This can, in turn, produce a change in another vowel adjacent to the second vowel (that affected by the first shift), and so on, until a chain of shifts occurs; one has here the basic concept by which a phenomenon like the Great Vowel Shift, by which the vowels of Middle English developed into those of Early Modern English, can be understood. This is, of course, a process of change not limited to vowels, but one which, in the modern period, is more robustly attested among the vowels of PDE dialects.

The category of sounds, or phonemic inventory, of English above and the types of sound change detailed in later chapters, while interesting in and of themselves to linguists, of the utmost practical value when they explain what actually occurs in the use of the language. Emphasis has been placed upon the regularity of sound change, and without agreement on this regularity, historical linguists would be unable to make their reconstructions. The observable output of speakers of PDE provides ample evidence for the patterns of the types of change. More than one change may be involved in the variation. Thus, the very common loss of glide /j/ in BrE and AmE can involve the loss of one sound or an entire syllable: RP *figure* [fɪgjʊə(r)] varies with [fɪgə(r)], in AmE [fɪgjər] with [fɪgər] or [fɪgɛr]. The BrE examples will vary not just by the feature [±rhotic] but by the presence or absence of the glide (the loss of glide also produces smoothing of the RP diphthong /ʊə/). In AmE the rhotic pronunciation is more common, and that with the glide /j/ is more standard: the pronunciation [fɪgɛr], with loss of glide and fronting of the central vowel [ə], can be found in a number of regions, especially in Southern American English, and can be class-marked (tending more toward working class), while New York City [fɪgɑ] is generally working class and associated less with Manhattan than Brooklyn and the Bronx. What can happen with *accurate* is more complicated: RP [ækjʊərət] with loss of glide can involve syncopation of either just the glide [j] or the sequence [jʊ], with a loss of syllable to produce disyllabic [ækrət] or [ækrɪt], the latter form highly common in AmE with fronting and raising of central /ə/ to /ɪ/. The particular contours of the sound patterning of a word, the syllable-patterning and number of syllables, and the environment in which a given sound occurs in a word (intervocalic, postvocalic, interconsonantal, in final position, etc.), matter in explanations of sound variation and change. Geoffrey Chaucer wrote *in forme of speche is chaunge* (*Troilus and Criseyde* II.22), and this is perhaps nowhere more so true than with the sounds of speech.

1.7 MORPHOLOGY

Morphology is in the simplest definition the study of forms; in the linguistic context, this study of a language's forms involves their composition, and inflectional and derivational processes. L1 students of English often count it as a blessed relief that English underwent 'inflectional decay' in its history, leaving it, by comparison with a kindred West Germanic language such as German – and certainly by comparison with the Romance languages, and all the more so classical languages such as Greek and Latin – a relatively lightly inflected language and thus 'easier' to learn: no conjugations to memorize (as with Latin, Spanish, French, and so forth), none of the maddening concord in nominal inflections of case, number, and gender as in German, and nothing approaching the inflectional complexity of Greek or Sanskrit. Except that this is, as are nearly all oversimplifications in matters of language, not necessarily true. In what is a kind of law of conservation of forms, what one does not affix to achieve grammatical meaning, to make distinctions in terms of case, number, or gender with nominal forms (nouns, pronouns, and other substantives), or in time, voice, mood, aspect, and so forth with verbal systems, one often winds up expressing in periphrastic forms, that is, roundabout, multi-word, or phrasal form. Broadly speaking, we are dealing with *morphological typology*, a subject to be treated in more detail in the next chapter, but one that is useful for the moment in comparing *synthetic* and *analytic* languages among the Germanic and Indo-European relatives of English. Compare, for example, the inflectional means by which grammatical information is encoded in more synthetic IE languages:

Sanskrit (Indo-European, Indo-Iranian, Indic)
अस्ति गौतमारण्ये प्रस्तुतयज्ञः कश्चिद् ब्रह्मणः । स च यज्ञार्थं ग्रामान्तराच्छागमुपक्रीय स्कन्धे कृत्वा गच्छन् धूर्तत्रयेन अवलोकितः

asti: 3rd sing. pres. act. indic. *as* 'to be' = 'he/she is' (here either 'There is,' or with sense of historical present 'there was')
gautamāraṇye: a *karmadhāraya* compound (see Chapter 4.3): *Gautama,* a patronymic of a proper name *Gotama* + *araṇya*, n. 'forest; wilderness' = 'in the Gautama forest'
prastutayajñaḥ: a *tatpuruṣa* compound, here an adj. meaning 'having one's sacrifice begun'; case here is nom. sing. (*-nas* before **sandhi** [rules for euphonic combination]) < *pra-stu* 'praise, begin, introduce' + *yajña, m.* 'worship, sacrifice'
kaścid brāhmaṇaḥ: *cid* an enclitic particle with *kaś-cid* = 'a certain'; *brāhmaṇa*, m. 'the one who prays/praises; brahmin'
sa: 3rd sing. masc. pronoun/definite article: here as pron. 'he'
ca: conj. 'and'
yajñārthaṃ: an *avyayībhāva* adverbial compound; *yajña* + *artham* (the latter is acc. sing. neuter in form producing an adv.); *artha*, m. 'aim, purpose, object'
grāmāntarāc|chāgamupakrīya skandhe kṛtvā: sandi assimilates final *-t* of *grāmāntarāt*: *grāma*, m. + *antara*., n., 'interior' in ablative case produces 'from another village'; *chāgam*, acc. sing. of *chāga*, m., 'goat'
upakrīya means 'having bought or purchased' (from a literal sense of 'bring something to someone'): a gerund of *upa-kṛ*
skandhe: loc. sing of *skandha*, m. 'shoulder'
kṛtvā: gerund of *kṛ*; literally 'doing, making, performing'
gacchan: present participle of *gam* 'to go'
dhūrtatrayena, instr. sing. of this *dhūrta* + *traya* ('triad of rogues')
avalokitaḥ: nom. sing. masc. (going with preceding *brāhmaṇaḥ*) of the past passive participle of *ava-lok* – thus the sense of 'was seen,' 'was beheld'

This story of "The brahmin, the goat, and the three rogues" from the classical Sanskrit *Hitopadeśa* ('upcountry wisdom') presents folk-tale wisdom and caste satire in a grammatically purified acrolectal standard. A literal rendering in English gives a sense of how much information a reader of the Sanskrit 'unpacked' from the inflections and how different is the syntax from any English rendering:

There is [=was, historic present] in the Gautama forest [expressed here with one compound formation, a *karmadhāraya* descriptive, appositional compound] having begun his sacrifice [all expressed by a *tatpuruṣa* determinative compound] a certain brahmin, he and [the copula is postpositioned quite often in Sanskrit] for the purpose of a sacrifice [all packed into an adverbial *avyayībhāva* compound] from another village having purchased a goat [ablative adverbial compound + noun in accusative singular + gerund] on his shoulder [noun in locative singular case] put it [translating somewhat loosely another gerund] in going was by a rogue-triad beheld [present participle + *karmadhāraya* compound in instrumental singular case + past ptc.].

Somewhat less literally, the sense is that our brahmin, having purchased a goat for a sacrifice in another village, is upon his going back beheld by a trio of rogues; they scheme to part brahmin and goat, playing upon an ironic, proverbial Brahmanical naïveté found in ancient Indian folklore as well as the brahmin's abhorrence of ritual impurity. Each rogue stations himself behind a tree a 'calling distance' (*krośa*) away from the other two to emerge and tell the brahmin that he has upon his shoulder not a goat but an unclean dog. By the second time this happens, the brahmin is described as 'having a wavering mind' (by means of the *karmadhāraya* compound *dolāyamāna-matis*); by the third time, he decides to play it safe, laying aside the goat (the gerund *tyakṛtvā* < *tyaj* 'to lay aside') and going home to bathe (the gerund *snātvā* < *snā* 'to bathe'). Needless to say, the three rogues snatch up the goat and carrying it off (the gerund *nītvā* < *nī* 'to carry off') consumed it (the past ptc. *bhakṣita* < *bhakṣ* 'to eat, consume').

Two morphological tendencies in Sanskrit stand out in a literal parsing and English rendering of the original – the very frequent use in Sanskrit of compound formations and their seemingly at-will creation, and of verbal participles and gerunds. Sanskrit, though an Indo-European language, seems morphologically distant from English: the literal English rendering shows how much wordier a PDE rendering must be without the many inflections of Sanskrit. The simple distinction that Sanskrit is much more a *synthetic* language in its morphological typology and English rather more *analytic* holds up to a certain extent; of interest is that Modern German still preserves a highly productive system of nominal compound formations (though not nearly as complex as Sanskrit), as did Old English, especially Old English poetry with its kennings (allusive, often circumlocutive compound formations). English once was a much more synthetic language, though always part of its story is what can be called 'inflectional decay': the loss of word endings and the communication of the grammatical information they encoded by other means, as by periphrastic constructions; the simplest example being the loss of the genitive (possessive case) singular ending in *-es* replaced, for instance, by a prepositional 'of X' phrase denoting possession (Old English *stanes*, MdE *of stone* or *stone's*).

Runic Germanic (Indo-European, Germanic, North Germanic) [see also Chapter 4.6]

Möjbro stone. Uppland, Sweden. 300 CE.
anahahaislaginaz frawaradaz = *ana hahai slaginaz frawaradaz*
on + steed + slain + Frawaradaz
PREP + N (dat. sing.) + p.p. + N (proper; nom. sing.)
'Slain on his steed, Frawaradaz' (the inscription appears on the stone in retrograde order)

Gallehus gold horn. South Jutland, Denmark. 400 CE.
ek hlewagastiz holtijaz horna tawido
I + Hlewagastiz + (son of) Holtijaz + (drinking) horn + made
PRON (1st person nom. sing.) + N (proper; nom. sing.) + N (patronymic) + N (acc. sing.) + V (3rd sing. pret.)
'I, Hlewagastiz, son of Holtagastiz, made the horn'

Epigraphic conventions tend toward brevity in expression if not overall brevity (Roman inscriptions could be famously prolix), though the compression found here is also the result of inflections; the SOV syntactic order of the Gallehus inscription is of significance (MdE is normally SVO, and Md German employs SVO and SOV). But one can see nonetheless close similarities, in morphology, syntax, and lexis, with English, and Old English all the more so (which was also recorded graphically in Runic).

Runic Old English (Indo-European, Germanic, West Germanic)

fisc.flodu ahof	**on fergenberig.**
warþ gasric grorn	**þær he on greut giswom.**
hronæsban.	

This is the famous Runic poetic passage from the Franks casket of approximately the 7th century; the whalebone box on its front panel has this riddlic verse that ends with an identification of the source of the material from which it was made: whalebone. The alliterative OE verse tersely explains: 'Fish the flood [wave] heaved up on the mountain cliff [steep shore]. Became the terror-/storm-/ocean-king sad when he onto gravel-shore swam.'[2] As will be discussed in more detail in Chapter 4, OE poetry is marked by highly productive patterns of nominal composition, some of which remind one of the *karmadhāraya* descriptive/appositional compounds in Sanskrit; here, though the meaning of Runic OE **GĀ:SRĪC** is uncertain, something like 'ocean-king' or 'storm-king' for 'whale' makes good descriptive sense; the steep gravelly shore upon which the whale beaches is both *grēot*, a simplex, and *fergenberig* (a compound *fyrgen-beorg* 'mountain-rock' or '-cliff'). Besides the difficulties presented to the modern reader by such allusive compound forms, some of the

[2] The translation follows suggestions recorded in the *DOE*, s.vv. *fyrgen-beorg*, *gā:srīc*, *grēot*.

inflections may give initial pause: *ahof* ('hove, heaved up') is the 3rd singular preterite form of the verb *ahebban*, *giswom* the preterite of *swimman* with the *ġe-* preverbal familiar as it survives in Modern German. This carved whale-ivory box begins its series of narrations with, on the front panel, an explanation, charming in its allusive simplicity, of its own material origin: the solution to the 'riddle' is *hronæsban*, *hronæs* = *hrones* genitive singular of OE *hron* + *ban*: 'whale's-bone.'

One last example looks to the evidence of English diachronically (through time):

Old English version	**Vulgate Latin text**	**Middle English metrical version**
Ēadiġ bið se wer þe ne gæð on ġeþeaht unrihtwīsra, ne on þām weġe ne stent synfulra, ne on heora wōlbærendum setle ne sitt;	Beatus vir qui non abiit in consilio impiorum et in via peccatorum non stetit et in cathedra pestilentiae non sedit;	Seli bern, þat noght is gan In þe rede of wicked man; And in strete of sinfulle noght he stode, Ne sat in setel of storme un-gode.

Psalm 1:1 is given here in three versions of great significance in the history of the language and English liturgy: the Vulgate Latin version of St. Jerome (ca. 340–420), in the middle column, was until the Reformation *the* text of the Bible in England. Despite Reformation-era propaganda, translations of Scripture into English abounded – a fact for which we are fortunate as translations of biblical texts (such as the Book of Psalms) and liturgical books present us an orthographical and dialectal corpus afforded by texts in multiple copies. Thus the earliest translations of the Psalms into English, from the Old English period (ca. 500–1100), survive in about 40 copies, 11 of which are continuous interlinear glossings (Pulsiano 2001: vii, xix–xxx). The King James Version (KJV) of 1611 of Ps 1:1 can serve as a basis of comparison for these earlier English versions ca. 700–1500: "Blessed *is* the man that walketh not in the counsel of the ungodly, nor standeth in the way of sinners, nor sitteth in the seat of the scornful."

Beatus ('happy, fortunate'): eadig bið (OE) / seli (ME) / blessed be (eMdE)
vir ('man'): se wer / bern / the man
qui ('who'): þe / þat / that
non abiit ('not goes away/off to'): ne gæð / noght is gan /walketh not
in consilio impiorum ('in the counsel of the impious'): on geþeaht unrihtwisra / in þe rede of wicked man / in the counsel of the ungodly

The Latin past participle *beatus*, from the first conjugation verb *bēāre* 'to make happy, gladden; to bless, enrich (with)' (OLD, s.v.), with a form of the verb 'to be' understood, is rendered more expansively literally in the OE version *eadig bið*, 'blessed be,' setting a translation standard through to 1611; interestingly, the ME version follows the Latin in having the form of 'to be' in ellipsis (i.e., "Blessed [be] the one…"). Latin did not have the definite article but demonstratives, which came to fulfill that function in the Romance languages: Latin *ille, illa, illud* 'that, that one' one can see in

Spanish *el* (masc.) and *la* (fem.), French *il* (m.), *la* (f.); the OE and eMdE spell this out (*se wer, the man*). The first element of the tricolon of types of company the righteous do not keep is rendered in OE with a fairly literal compound equivalent: *on geþeaht unrihtwisra* ('in the counsel of the un-right-wise [not right-thinking]'), while the KJV gives a semantically satisfactory equivalent to Latin *impius* with 'ungodly.'[3] The ME rendering *rede*, 'counsel, advice,' to which the OED gives the usage labels 'archaic, poetic, dialectal,' from the verb *rede(n)* (ME), *rædan* (OE), appears as a variant, *ðere rede <ve>l þæhte* ('of their advice or counsel') in the OE gloss to the Eadwine Psalter (Cambridge, Trinity College, R.17.1, of ca. 1155–1160).[4]

The syntax of the second element in the OE rendering is of interest: *ne on þām weġe ne stent synfulra*, very literally, 'not in the way not stand of the sinful.' OE employed the 'double negative' (as do modern Romance languages: compare French *ne...pas* constructions) and the split of the noun phrase *on þām weġe synfulra* ('in the way of the sinful') and insertion of the second *ne* emphasize the negation by doubling it: the righteous 'not in the way,' 'not do they stand, of the sinful.' It is odd syntax to a user of PDE, though one must always ascribe to OE translations of Latin texts some degree of artificiality or influence of source language on target language (and much of surviving OE prose involves translations made from Latin);[5] nonetheless the third element, *ne on heora wōlbærendum setle ne sitt*, 'nor on of them the pestilential/destructive seat not sit,' is likewise odd to modern ears (a user of PDE would rearrange the OE to *ne sitt on heora wōlbærendum setle*, which, of course, is not good Old English). What is interesting, morphologically speaking, is the persistence of some of the inflections of English through to 1611 and beyond; the register of religious use is often conservative, with prayers and liturgical formulas preserving archaic forms well after their loss in contemporary speech: many Catholics still pray the *Ave Maria* as 'Hail Mary full of grace, the Lord is with thee. Blest are thou. ...' The fuller verbal inflections of the English verb – OE, already subject to 'inflectional decay' preserved four verb forms in the present stem (1st, 2nd, 3rd singular, and a general plural form) – still appear in the KJV and persisted well into the 20th century until new standard translations came into widespread liturgical use (e.g., the RSV and NRSV). Thus the OE verb for *ne gæð* ('not goeth') is rendered in the KJV by a different lexical choice

[3] Latin *impius*, the Vulgate rendering, has originally to do with a Roman cultural complex: "Showing no regard for the divinely imposed moral duties governing men's relationships with the gods and between themselves" (OLD, s.v.).

[4] The Cambridge Psalter, of the 12th century, is a 'triple psalter,' with a Latin gloss to the Gallicanum version of the psalter, Anglo-Norman gloss to the Hebraicum, and OE gloss to the Romanum (Pulsiano 2001, xxii). The Romanum is Jerome's first version of Psalms from the *Vetus Latinus*, 'Old Latin,' and was used in the Roman Missal; the Gallicanum is his second version made from the Greek of the Hexapla (Origen's edition of six versions of the Hebrew Bible) and incorporated into the *Biblia vulgata* or Vulgate version of the Bible; the Hebraicum was the third translation Jerome made of the Psalms, this time from pre-Masoretic Hebrew texts of the *Tehillim* (the Hebrew title rendered *Psalmi* in Latin).

[5] Susan Irvine noted of West Saxon texts of the Alfredian period (the second half of the 9th century) that some of the "convoluted syntax...may be attributed to the attempt...to apply Latin syntactic constructions to a linguistic structure not entirely suited to them" (Irvine 2006, 47).

(*walk*) but one that preserves the 3rd singular present active indicative termination -*eth* (*walketh*), which appears in the other two verbs of the verse (*standeth, sitteth*). But there has been loss in the nominal inflections: the OE genitive plural forms *unrihtwisra, synfulra, heora* are rendered by *of*-possessive phrases in both the ME (*of wicked man, of sinfulle, of storme ungode*) and eMdE versions (*of the ungodly, of sinners, of the scornful*). One way or the other – by the inflections suffixed or by periphrastic constructions, such as prepositional phrases – the language encodes the vital grammatical information to achieve meaning. As with the study of sounds, the study of forms allows us to plot out the language's development, this time by means of such grammatical distinctions as concord between subject and verb, number, tense and other markings of verbs, and the indicators of agency, possession, object status, and so forth with substantives that were once called *case* in English (Modern German still preserves case distinctions for nouns, pronouns, adjectives, and articles and determiners – Nominativ, Akkusativ, Genitiv, Dativ).

In the chapters that follow the morphology of English will be traced historically; it may be useful to set out some basic terminology at the outset. Broadly speaking, morphology – as the study of (linguistic) forms – is divided between **inflectional** and **derivational** morphology. Inflectional morphology concerns affixes that carry the grammatical distinctions of the language that, in English, are added to the **stem**. The last term is often a point of confusion in that English inflectional morphology is generally schematized as **root > stem > affix**. A **root** is the 'base' or essentially the irreducible form that carries meaning, and though this term can be used variably by linguists, examples from Sanskrit or Latin of 'verbal roots' make the concept clearer: what are called *dhātus* in Sanskrit are the basic meaning-bearing essential forms that are neither finite nor infinitive forms of the verb. For example, Sanskrit *dā* 'give' is the verbal root rather than the infinitive form proper (which is *dātum* and may indeed be glossed as 'to give'); Sanskrit verbs, like those in Greek and Latin, are often cited by their 'principal parts,' which vary according to the particular language. Thus the first conjugation Latin verb for 'to love' is often cited as *amō* (first person singular present indicative active), *amāre* (the present active infinitive, the unconjugated form, that is, not marked for person, number, tense, voice, mood, or aspect), *amāvi* (first person singular perfect indicative active), and *amatum* (the perfect passive participle, in the neuter singular form; as it can function as an adjective, in addition to the composition of compound tenses, the fuller form would be *amatus* [masc.], *amata* [fem.], *amatum* [neut.]). Linguists often classify these various base forms (here the Latin first conjugation verb *amō*) as belonging to the **lexeme** AMO (see Bauer 1983, 11–13); in a sense this is what one finds in the dictionary: derivative forms cross-referenced with the 'base' form, for example, the deverbal forms *take away (food)* and trendy *take aw ay* [impression, result] belong to the phrasal verb **to take away**; interestingly, AmE uses *takeaway* in the latter sense even though a food order to go is much more commonly called *takeout* or *(food)* (a *to go order*). One could speak, for instance, of a similar verbal root in English of **-struct-*, which is, contrary to some theoretical linguistic formulations, not without meaning as it derives from Latin third conjugation verb *struo, struere* (*struxi, structus*), which has the sense of 'pile up, build.' By means of **derivational morphology**, one has the Latinate English verbs *instruct* and *construct* (as well as *destruct*). A quick distinction between inflectional and derivational morphology might be made with the **-struct-* examples:

Inflectional	**Derivational**
construct (infinitive & present tense)	**con**struct > **con**structi**on** (deverbal noun)
construct**ed** (past and past ptc)	**de**structi**on**, **decon**structi**on**
construct**ing** (present ptc)	**in**structi**on**

Verbal inflections that mark tense include *instructs, instructed, constructing*; derivational morphemes, that is, those by which we derive new forms or words (and not just mark grammatical distinctions), include *de-con-struct-io-n* (PREFIX + PREFIX + STEM + NOMINAL SUFFIX) and *structure* (STEM + NOMINAL SUFFIX). Here we have two affixes, suffixes, by which noun forms may be derived from verbs that are highly productive in English: *-tion* and *-(t)ure*. The distinction between inflectional and derivational morphology is simple but vital. Inflectional morphology indicates morphological change that is grammatical, often by affixation, though there are 'zero-formations' such as the conjugation of MdE *hit*: *hit / hit / hit*. Of course, this is only true for the modern reflex of this late Old English (*hyttan*) borrowing from Old Norse (*hitta*), which has historical forms such as past tense *hytte* (OE), *hutte* (ME), and past participle *y-hyt* (ME), *hittin* and *hot* (late ME – eMdE, Northern and Scots).

Derivational morphology denotes those processes by which we derive new words in English, often by **conversion**, from one part of speech to another, often, but not always, by affixation of derivational morphemes. These include, in Modern English, the common suffix *-ise* (BrE) / *-ize* (AmE) for the derivation of verbs from nouns (*televise/televize* < *television*) or adjectives (*digitise/digitze* < *digital*). Derivational processes can be quite active and even in a way have a kind of circularity: for example, *digit* > *digital* > *digitise/digitize* > *digitilisation/digitilization*. Though the last example would seem, intuitively, to involve a pattern of building from *digit* (here in its computer '0/1' sense) outward to *digitise/digitize* then *digitalisation/digitalization*, technology-wise the process seems rather N > ADJ (+ – *al*) > V (+ *-ise/-ize* on the original stem *digit*) > N (+ *-isation/ization* added to the adjectival stem). If one were to refer to a *digital* copy of an old motion picture, the adjective *digital* was derived from an existing noun by affixation (the adjectival suffix *-al*); we could refer to the old film as having undergone *digitisation/digitization* or *digitalisation/digitalization*: the latter form is now preferred for the process of moving material in existing media to digital form, the former referring to information converted from analog to digital, bypassing questions of whether the forms in popular usage have collapsed due to confusion or whether the former might have involved a contraction of the latter in the spoken form. At any rate, the addition of *-al* to form an adjective or *-isation/-ization* to form a noun are derivational processes. Having the digital copies of old films, one might refer to *digitalisations/digitalizations*, the *-s* plural marker being an inflection, pluralization being one of a number of grammatical distinctions that belong to inflectional morphology.

Derivational morphology in the history of English has been productive and robust; the study of word-formation in English may be said to be an entire subdiscipline. The processes of compounding, such as of two-word or two-morpheme formations, or of phrases, are complex, as is their surface expression in writing – printed distinctly as separate forms, then hyphenated, then as one form is a common pattern historical and ongoing: for example, *high technology* > *high-tech gadget* (with clipping) > *hightech*. Affixation can involve prefixation and suffixation, as well as zero-morpheme formation (e.g., *kiss a kiss* [V, then N], *under the bridge* [N], *to bridge a gap* [V]); this is the approach to analysis of compound formations in Hans Marchand's classic treatment. *The Categories and Types of Present-Day English Word-Formation* (Marchand 1969) followed fairly closely Laurie Bauer's two highly useful studies in categorization *English Word-Formation* (Bauer 1983) and *An Introduction to English Lexicology* (Bauer 2022). Bauer's 'taxonomic' approach to English compounds (Bauer 1983, 201–240) lists some 28 basic forms of compounding in English, from NOUN + NOUN (in German what is called *Nomenkompositum*) through N + V, N + Adj, to Particle + N (or, PREP + N: *off-Broadway*), and through various other permutations involving N, V, Adj, and Particle (mainly PREP; V + Prep is highly productive: *dropout, dropoff, cutoff*, etc. – though the first two examples are nouns, the third can be a N or Adj). What the Sanskrit grammarians classed as *tatpuruṣa* (literally, 'that man') and *bahuvrīhi* (literally 'having much rice,' but allusively describing something 'rich' or 'fertile') compound formations modern linguists call **endocentric** (where the first element is **attributive**, the second **substantive**: *nightlight*, i.e., a type of light) and **exocentric** (where the formation does not seem to have a 'head,' rather the formation is descriptive of an implied head: *blueblood* can refer to members of the upper class, and *blue ribbon* to something of superior quality). Marchand's study is highly programmatic, often classified by types based on examples: for example, endocentric compounds of the type such as MdE *housekeeping*, *handwriting*, and *bookkeeping*, or Old English *gōdspellbodung*, literally 'good-spell-announcing,' that is, 'preaching of the gospel [good-spell]' (which is in turn a recursive or double compound, *gōd* + *spell* [Adj + N] + *bodung* [deverbal N, a feminine abstract noun]). It may be said that the 'Germanic' nature of English (its 'belonging' to the Germanic branch of Indo-European) is readily apparent in its ready formation of compounds; while not quite so productive as the at-will forming of compounds in German (*zusammengesetztes Substantiv*, literally 'together-set noun,' or *Nominalkompositum*), English seems to set only one limit on its productivity in such formations: that it make a kind of sense, directly or allusively, to the speaker. A recent approach from the vantage of a historical linguist is Ringe 2021, which is particularly valuable for its concentrated focus on Middle English morphology – a period of rapid expansion of the vocabulary of English, especially of Latin- and French-derived words.

1.8 SYNTAX

Greek σύνταξις (*súntaxis*) has literally to do with 'arranging together,' and 'word order' is the simplest explanation available in English. Of course the 'word order' of a language involves the normally occurring (a descriptive approach) and normative (prescriptive approach) patterns of words – those as they occur in ordinary speech and those considered desirable in prescriptive education and use – and all subsidiary rules, conventions, and customs of what governs what and which possible pattern is more desirable than another. Despite prescriptive advice otherwise, there has never been any particular bar, for example, to ending a sentence with a preposition nor beginning one with a conjunction. Nonetheless, every user of English has felt at some time or other the guiding influence of prescriptive norms, especially with written standards. In the same way that spoken English is stratified by levels of acceptability and desirability, so too the written use of the language, here especially in observation of grammatical and syntactic norms. Popular usage often employs *grammar* as a cover term, as including morphology and syntax. For the analysis of the language, the two concerns are usually separated to allow for easier description of the linguistic phenomena involved. Thus one encounters studies of Old English nominal composition (the formation of nouns and other substantives, as by affixation or compounding), or Middle English syntax. All of the parts of language work together in achieving meaning (or at least expression, however abstract); but parts are discernible. Thus, for the moment, word-level considerations of grammatical form, inflections, affixes, word-formation (of compound formations, clipped forms, acronyms, neologies, etc.), markings for case and tense, number and gender, and so forth, will be considered the province of morphology. The composition of phrases and clauses, rules involved with one part of speech governing another, transformations realized in word order (from indicative to interrogative sentences types, or active to passive constructions), will be considered the province of syntax. The term *morphosyntax* was coined to cover the obvious interrelations between grammar (word-level morphological considerations) and syntax; for example, English verbs in the complex tenses (e.g., a form such as the present progressive or past passive progressive) are phrasal (*will go*, *should have gone*), pronouns normally have antecedents (they can be in ellipsis, but without a clear antecedent ambiguity arises), conjunctions by their morphological description link other elements (words, phrases, clauses, whole sentences) – these can be considered morphosyntactic matters, and they are to be found in every stage of the history of English.[6]

Three great historical studies of English syntax, Mustanoja 1960 (on Middle English), Visser 1963–1973 (covering the whole history of the language), and Mitchell 1985 (on Old English), followed essentially a philological/Neogrammarian approach, much to the benefit of later researchers who, whatever their methodology (generative or other frameworks), had a diachronic sketch in place based on actual samples from literary and subliterary texts analyzed by the researcher – corpus linguistics has expanded the quantity of texts the researcher can study, but the judgement of the researcher is still of paramount importance in developing any picture of historical syntax. With an approach as such, the parsing – ostensibly from Latin *pars* 'part,' as in *pars orationis*, 'part of speech' – of phrases, clauses, and sentences is fundamental. The age-old tradition of labeling by parts of speech, an inheritance of the classical

[6] For a practical application of the approach, see Payne 1997; a specific application, to the verb in Homeric Greek, is to be found in Leinieks 1964.

grammarians (from Varro to Priscian, to name but two), is to be paired with their preoccupation with regularity in form: *analogia* (vs. irregularity in grammatical forms: *anomalia*) This regularity in form and derivation (OLD: 'Similarity in the inflections and derivatives of words; the use of this in forming inflections and derivatives'; s.v. *analogia*) was an essential part of one's training under the *grammaticus*, the classical young person's tutor in language, and *rhetor*, the instructor in forms of argumentation, reasoning, speech-writing and -making, and so forth. Indeed, though now lost to us, Julius Caesar wrote a treatise entitled *De analogia*. The great survey of classical grammar was the 6th-century *Institutiones grammaticae* by Priscian, who, at the dawn of the postclassical period, in 18 books, sought to preserve the learning of his predecessors and put the reader through all the morphological paces of Latin: every nominal declension is pursued through the cases (nominative [subject/agent], genitive [possessive], dative [indirect object], accusative [direct object], ablative [the 'from' case, generally expressing motion away from], vocative [direct address]) and genders (masculine, feminine, neuter, as in Old English), the five conjugations of Latin verbs parsed with multiple examples. In a method imitated by authors of comprehensive grammars of languages to this day, Priscian illustrates his grammatical and syntactic points with illustrative quotations from a range of Roman authors (some of whose work survives only by such quotation). Following his order *de partibus* ('on the parts of speech'), we are introduced to nouns and adjectives, pronouns, verbs, adverbs, participles, conjunctions, prepositions, and interjections (with mention of articles, which he explains do not occur in Latin as they do in Greek). This is essentially the parsing regimen familiar to learners to this day (we would fold participles into verbs for consideration).

The advent of transformational-generative and other frameworks in postmodern linguistics has relied to a great extent on a syntactic reduction of the parts of speech to their function in head-driven phrase structures: for example, a noun as the head of a noun phrase (NP $\rightarrow$ N) and a preposition as the head of a prepositional phrase (PP $\rightarrow$ P). The five resultant types of syntactic structures, NP, VP, PP, AdjP, and AdvP (the last two of which usually appear recursively inside NPs and VPs, respectively), were accompanied by cover terms such as determiner (DET), which modifies a noun referentially, that is, less in terms of attributes (which are semantically driven and have semantic content) than in terms of specificity or quantity (what are traditionally termed articles and demonstrative, relative, indefinite pronouns and adjectives, and the like). The meaning of the word *sentence* encapsulates both the essential matters of syntax and the difficulties in delimiting its range of analysis; it derives from Latin *sententia*, and etymologically has to do with 'sense knowledge,' 'thought,' and had a range of meanings, from 'a way of thinking, opinion, sentiment,' to the legalistic, procedural 'opinion expressed in the senate in response to an *interrogatio*' (which is not unlike the use of 'question' in present parliamentary procedure), to 'an authoritative decision, decree; (esp. a judicial pronouncement, sentence, judgement),' and, the last sense (sense 8) given in the OLD, 'a self-contained group of words, a sentence, clause' (s.v. *sententia*). This brings us to how the term will be used here, and the purview of syntax as it will be termed for the purposes of this study. The use of Greek and Latin terms for parts of speech, syntax and syntactical constructions (parataxis, hypotaxis), and rhetorical figures (hyperbaton, anacoluthon, litotes) is inescapable and shows clearly how English bears the imprint of both the legacy of the classical tradition and the study of the classics by speakers of English throughout its history. The labels may not always fit the particulars of this Germanic language, but they have shaped how students of English have used, thought about, and tried to describe the language. The text of Priscian would be excerpted by an English writer, working sometime in the 10th century, whose *excerptiones de Prisciano* would be used by Ælfric of Eynsham in the writing of his landmark *Grammar*, an introduction to the Latin language in English for novitiates; while the text, written sometime 992 × 1002, is meant to teach Latin, the interplay of the two languages, Latin and Old English, and the accompanying bilingual *Glossary* tell us much also about English in this important era (Porter 2002, 1–2, 23–30).

English in its history has been said to have had a 'freer' syntax in its earlier phases when the language was, morphologically, richer in inflections (on Old English, see Irvine 2006). This balance, of sorts, between what is encoded in inflectional affixes and what is expressed by the order of words and particles in a language has been aptly – if in somewhat oversimplified fashion – rendered in a comparison of an expression in Latin (IE, Italic) and English (IE, Germanic). Latin *canis hominem momordit* is the normal order for expressing 'dog bit man' in the language. Subject and object are designated by case: *canis* is nominative singular and the subject, and *hominem* is the accusative singular of *homo* and thus the direct object (the verb *momordit* is the 3rd singular reduplicated perfect form of the second conjugation verb *mordēre* 'to bite'); the inflections bear the bulk of the grammatical information in this sentence, thus the potential order is freer: *canis momordit hominem*, *hominem canis momordit*, *momordit canis hominem*, etc., still mean 'dog bit man.' The order in MdE is not so free, as a simple comparison of 'dog bit man' and 'man bit dog' will attest (to say the latter in Latin, one would have *homo canem momordit*). In addition to the morphological distinction, an essential distinction of *syntactic typology* can also be made here: Latin is normally an SOV language (following the order subject–object–verb in indicative statements), Modern English SVO (subject–verb–object). By comparison, Modern German is SVO in main clauses, and can follow SOV in dependent clauses; the Celtic languages are normatively VSO. There are other variations among the world's languages, though SVO is a common type (Spanish and French are SVO languages). Even if the changes in English syntax seem less dramatic by comparison with those to its sound system, grammar, and lexis, attempts have always been made to describe how to construe its written form. Among the earliest written attestations of English are glosses, which are normally lexical, giving semantic equivalents within a language or between languages; for instance, rendering Latin *ecclesia* as *ċiriċe* ('church') and *(ge)laþung* ('assembly') indicates the OE glossator's knowledge of the meanings of the original; while most glossing activity is word-for-word or phrase-for-phrase, we do find English readers attempting to understand Latin syntax by 'construe' marks, alphabetic or other forms of notation indicating what goes with what syntactically, as well as *merographs*, partial glosses that carry not semantic explanation but grammatical and syntactic information – for example, the OE gloss *-ce*, with the rest of the word in ellipsis, indicates an adverb or adverbial.[7] Such means of construing are a long way from the tree-and-branch diagrams of post-1957 Chomskyan generative grammar and the 'sentence diagramming' once quite popular in American primary education, but all of them indicate a sense that the syntax of the written language can be appreciated visually. Speech is linear, while the graphic representation of speech on the page or screen allows for easier analysis of what was produced. Postmodern generative linguistics has focused, perhaps to a fault, much more upon syntax than semantics – indeed, attempts at accounting for semantics led the new discipline nearly to the point of schism, as will be seen shortly.

1.9 SEMANTICS

Semantics as a branch of linguistics has to do with meaning, namely the relationship between linguistic signs or symbols and meaning (OED, s.v.); the OED lists as its two earliest attestations of *semantic* studies appearing in the *American Journal of Philology* by Edwin W. Fay on 'Agglutination and Adaptation' (1894, a study cautioning against arguing for the 'inviolability' of phonetic law) and Maurice Bloomfield "On Assimilation and Adaptation in Congeneric Classes of Words" (1895); Bloomfield opens with the query: "What is the influence of the lexical value – as distinguished from morphological structure – of words and expressions upon one another, and what constructive power has this influence in shaping the broader categories of words and expressions?"; 409). Fay's reference is to interchange of *r* and *l* in historical development of forms; his examples from Old Indic, Greek, and Latin, pertaining to demonstratives and indefinites (that is, particles, pronouns, and adjectives), were in support of an apparent PIE r_2 that "became *l* in the European languages and remained *r* in the Asiatic" (432 n. 1): for example, an earlier Latin demonstrative *olle* (for *ille*) is compared with Latin *ultra* and Umbrian *uru* ~ *ulo*, or Greek ἄλλος (*állos*) and Latin *alius* ('other') < *ar_2 + *yo*. Fay had concluded this subsection of his study by noting that: "Thus freedom of interchange of *r* and *l* is limited by semantic considerations" (432–433 n. 1). Fay's argument and reconstructions would be seriously modified by modern historical linguists, but his notion, and first recorded mention, of 'semantic conditioning' of changes still obtains. Bloomfield's use of 'semantic' is worth noting, as his more general observation concerning 'congeneric' forms touches upon semantic considerations still under study: "Reduplication in early glottogonic periods of language cannot have represented anything more than an attempt to make an idea tarry. It is a rudimentary rhetorical device. In historical periods of I.E. speech, the habit ceases in general to be productive, just as the semantic value of the older reduplications is entirely lost. German *beben* and even Sk. [Sanskrit] *bibheti* contain no longer any trace of the early semasy [meaning, signification] of the reduplication; the reduplication is a fossil. The productivity of languages becomes 'analytic' rather than 'synthetic,' and a set of analytic devices takes

[7]The example is from the Brussels manuscript of Aldhelm's prose *De virginitate* (Brussels, Bibliothèque royale 1650) with OE glosses copied into it about the middle of the 11th century; on theses glosses and merographs, see the close study in Gretsch 1999, 105, 135–136, *et passim*.

the place of the old synthetic reduplications. English *hurly-burly, fiffle-faddle, tittle-tattle, zig zag, rogey-pogey*, Germ. *tick-tack, piff paff puff*, and the like are the closest modern approaches to reduplication" (412–413). Some of Bloomfield's terminology is dated, *glottogonic* (having to do with the origin of language), and *semasy* (meaning, the sense of the meaning), but the morphological-semantic point is of continuing interest: English did indeed in its history shift from a more synthetic morphological typology to a more analytic one, and the change from reduplicated forms (such as reduplicated preterite forms found in older IE languages) to more analytic constructions (phrasal verbs) is well documented. And this calls to mind the phenomena called *grammaticalization* and *semantic bleaching* by modern linguists: the shift from a form having semantic value to one being primarily grammatical: for example, when the English verbs *keep* and *go* developed uses as auxiliaries, as in *She kept reading* or *He's going to tell them soon*. The 'semantic bleaching' is the (partial) loss of the original non-grammaticalized sense of the word; while the original semantic content has been 'reduced,' the form has gained an aspectual use in such verb phrases as those above (Fox 1995, 203; Givón 2001).

This brings up the distinction sometimes marked between *semantics*, the study of meaning, and *semasiology*, which also covers changes in meaning, historical and synchronic developments in sense, and the logical-philosophical matters of 'what does X mean?' (*onomasiology* approaches from the other direction, studying how something, a meaning or thing or concept, gains expression: what terms are used in its expression). For the purposes of the chapters that follow, our main concern is with *semantic change*, diachronic change (through time) and synchronic variation (at a moment in time; e.g., in varieties of PDE), and *lexicology*, the linguistic study of words, word meanings, semantic groupings, and semantic range. Semantics as a field has generated much controversy in the subdisciplines of linguistics, the search for 'meaning' seemingly put off by some linguists – especially those after the nature of language or the origin of the language faculty in human beings. Others begin with semantics: the theory of *semantic primes*, as promulgated by Anna Wierzbicka and colleagues (cf. Wierzbicka 1996 especially), that argues for an underlying universal set of concepts that become expressed as words in the many extant human natural languages; a similar, and even more controversial, theory concerns a language of concepts shared by all human beings, sometimes called *mentalese*, that finds surface expression in the speaker's particular language. There are a number of factors underlying such semantic theories: the Chomskyan notion of 'speed of acquisition': that human beings could not learn so complex a system as a natural language in so short a period were there not some elements – the human ability to grasp and work with the patterns of language, for instance – innately 'hard-wired' in the human brain or even human DNA. Or the notion that cross-cultural communication would not be possible without an underlying commonality of concepts. At any rate, the interest here is more with words, their meaning, shades of and shifts in meaning.

In looking to the vocabulary of English, one can at least begin to outline the types of semantic change recorded by etymology (word origins) and diachronic and synchronic semantic change. Any observer of the language notes that words can have multiple meanings – words with a semantic polyvalence, or *polysemy* – and shifts in meaning over time or among present-day users. Shifts in style, along scalar continua from informal to formal, nonstandard to standard, and so forth, are productive of semantic variation and change. Most noticeable, especially in PDE, is the variation produced by slang usage; *slang* – the word itself, intriguingly, is of unknown origin[8] – is, generally speaking, informal, in-group usage (Macaulay 2006). Highly important is the distinction, the label, *informal* – it belongs to particular registers, uses among peer groups, often age- and gender-specific, and to certain styles of speech: from jocular to invective. It is usually said not to belong to formal discourse or writing, excepting its use in dialogue in fiction, to produce a naturalistic, 'authentic' style. It is, despite much hand-wringing, essentially universal; its use is perhaps no more prevalent than it ever was, except that modern media broadcast it more frequently and widely than ever before (that Southern California is where so many television programs are made is why so many American teenagers, no matter where the shopping mall is located, use 'SoCal' slang: not least of which is 'like,' as in phrasal verb forms *And I'm like..*). Probably not given enough attention or credence by many linguists is the role of affectation, the 'putting on' of a non-native or non-natural speech style, especially its slang or jargon, to affect a state or allegiance or fashion one would not otherwise connect to. This will be treated in much more detail in later chapters: suffice it to say, popular satire has caught wind of the phenomenon of middle- to upper-class whites affecting 'hip-hop' style and using AAVE forms in an effort to co-opt a 'street cred' they do not otherwise have (call it, in Britain, the 'Ali G effect,' its more widespread American counterpart has been variously termed).

Nonetheless, it is not just in fluid, highly productive informal strata of the vocabulary that one observes semantic change and innovation. Technological progress, or at least innovation, in medicine, computer sciences, and dozens of other fields, calls always for terminology with which to describe their phenomena, and to write and communicate about it professionally. It may be useful at this point to introduce some of the types of semantic change and innovation that will be encountered throughout the history of English.

1.9.1 Neology

Simply put, in its etymological Greek sense, neologies are 'new words,' or coinages. These can be words given new meanings, or older forms 'recycled'; the examples are many and often obvious, though the matter is more complex than the simple designation 'new word' may imply. Relatively rare, though not uncommon, is the genuinely abstract or *de novo* ('from the new') creation, that is, the 'made-up' word. A seemingly silly example can illustrate the difficulty in delineating a 'made-up' word: the popular children's cartoon series and collectible miniatures involving the *Smurfs* were created in 1958 by Belgian comics writer Pierre Culliford (who goes by the name Peyo); in the Belgian original, the Smurfs were called *Les Schtroumpfs*, after *schtroumpf*, a stopgap nonsense word Peyo had used in conversation with a friend. As the series evolved, the word for the miniature blue creatures became part of the language they spoke and

[8] The OED only ventures the observation that it is "A word of cant origin, the ultimate source of which is not apparent" (s.v. *slang*).

underwent *conversion*: the process by which a form changes word class while preserving its basic semantic sense (e.g., *to kiss* [V] → *a kiss* [N]); it seems, in Smurf usage (that is familiar to English-speaking audiences), to have then undergone broadening: *smurf* → *smurfing*, etc., become polyvalent and productive of derivative forms (*smurfy* and so forth). The silliness, of course, mirrors the simplicity of child language, but also its production of new forms from a limited lexis (such as 'baby-talk'; child language forms are called *Lallwörter* 'babble words' in German. In the Belgian series, 'Smurfdom' was divided along north-south lines, and apparently along a linguistic (or at least dialectal) line: evidently poking fun at the French (Walloon)-Flemish (Vlaams) linguistic divide in Belgium. And so here a stopgap word, one used in place of a word one has forgotten – or to mark a syntactic pause as one thinks of what to say next – engenders a whole sub-vocabulary. Trademarked names are often new coinages, sometimes chosen for their phonological quality (alliteration, assonance, or onomatopoeic forms) or their resemblance to known forms. These can be pseudo-loans, such as the tendency for producers of economy cars to give their luxury market entries pseudo-Latinate or classical-sounding names in the United States: Acura (produced by Honda of Japan), Lexus (by Toyota of Japan), and Infiniti (Nissan, Japan). The new coinages are technically semantically empty, but by sound resemblance and allusion to classical languages – in a phenomenon belonging partly to semantics and partly to psycholinguistics – they *connote* reliable manufacture (*Acura ~ accurate*), luxury (*Lexus*), durability, freedom of movement, and perhaps even some sort of 'classiness' (*Infiniti*, with its jarring, grating *-i* termination for *– y*). Prescription drug makers have done the same thing with brand drug names; indeed, faux-Latin and -Greek are a staple of 'up-market' advertising culture. Words go in and out of fashion, and those that go out of fashion, but do not disappear entirely (to be given usage labels such as *archaic* or *obsolete* in the dictionaries), can be 'recycled,' sometimes with an altered sense or application: the jocular AmE revival of 1960s and 1970s *groovy* is one example (and began well before the Austin Powers series of films).

1.10 PRAGMATICS AND DISCOURSE

'Pragmatic' concerns of language involve areas of overlap between linguistics and philosophy; indeed, it is an area in which the signal advances were as often as not made by 'philosophers of language.' John Langshaw Austin's *How to Do Things with Words* (1962) was a landmark study in the philosophy of language and introduced the term *illocutionary act*: while philosophers had tended to classify utterances as descriptive or *constative*, being either true or false, Austin had drawn attention to those that did not fit these categories. He has used the term *performatives* for statements that do not necessarily state or describe anything but perform *speech acts*, such as *I promise to drop it off tomorrow*, or *I do hereby resolve...*, and perhaps also imperatives (*Go!* for instance performs a command, of the type of explicit performative utterances). Philosopher John R. Searle examined speech acts and the *illocutionary force* of utterances: whether they make a statement, or question, or command, or express a desire or possibility – what traditional grammatical accounts explained in morphological terms as verbal mood and aspect and sentence types (indicative, imperative, subjunctive; Searle 1969).

Areas of active pragmatic research include *deixis*, or context-dependency, *implicature* (what an utterance implies or suggests; Grice 1989), and the role of presuppositions. Deictic expressions are commonly temporal or locative: a letter indicating *Please respond within two weeks* is useless if undated; likewise, directions stating, *Take a left when you get to downtown* won't necessarily get you anywhere without a starting point or direction.

1.11 PRESCRIPTIVE AND DESCRIPTIVE APPROACHES

The Roman writer Varro, who lived ca. 116–127 BC, summed up the case rather well in Book IX of his *De lingua latina* ('On the Latin language'):

> Quare qui ad consuetudinem nos vocant, si ad rectam, sequemur: in eo quoque enim est analogia; si ad eam invitant quae est depravata, nihilo magis sequemur, nisi eum erit necesse, quam in ceteris rebus mala exempla: nam ea quoque, cum aliqua vis urget, inviti sequemur. Neque enim Lysippus artificum priorum potius <secutus> est vitiosa quam artem; sic populus facere debet, etiam singuli, sine offensione quod fiat populi (IX.xii–xiii.18; Kent 1951, 452).
>
> Wherefore, those who call on us to follow according to custom, insofar as it is correct, we will follow; for in this also there is analogy [regularity]; if they induce us to that which is distorted, we should no more follow them, unless it should become necessary, than we would bad examples in other matters: for we follow them too when urged, as by some other force. Nor did Lysippus follow the faults of prior artists, rather more their art; thus ought people do [in their speech], even individuals, without that which would cause the people offense.

His appeal to the great sculptor Lysippus, favored by Alexander the Great and, artistically, positioned at the transition from classical Greek to Hellenistic art, is telling. There is no simple appeal to the old, to unvaried tradition, but to what was the best. In this classical view, there is room for innovation in speech as in art, for adhering to established norms, all within moderation. Few things about language capture the public imagination so much than its perceived decline: the increase in grammatical solecisms (the 'death of the apostrophe,' for instance), the influx of slang and jargon into standard usage, and the deleterious effects of e-mail and texting upon writing skills. Self-appointed 'language mavens' rail against the abuses, holding them up to ridicule, and correct users of standard varieties nod in agreement and remain firm in their grammatical orthodoxy, sometimes self-righteously so. Linguists, especially those writing for popular audiences, in turn deplore the carping of the mavens and their fetishization of an unchanging standard variety – impossible for a living language, which is always subject to change. Both views are exaggerations of course. Everyone makes judgements about usage, correcting their use upward to conform to standard varieties when necessary (in formal letter-writing, speeches to large, mixed audiences – i.e., not consisting entirely of one's peers – for work, etc.), and downward to connote familiarity, jocularity, or some affectation (a streetwise toughness perhaps unearned). The audience, and our expectations of their expectations, shape the varieties we use. Most users of English can readily understand varieties of English along a continuum of standardness; they may not like what they hear (and this often affects, in biased fashion, pronouncements of intelligibility), but they understand it. And most users have been instructed to modify their speech and writing according to established norms – for English, with no governing language academy, this is from schooling, dictionaries, media, or prestige users. The divide between what is and what ought to be has even been cast in moral terms: well-known is the stigmatization of American Black speech, and not only in the South; the speech of poor whites in the American South, that is, of 'Tobacco Road,' or 'white trash,' can also be seen as a moral failing by élites. This has led to perhaps some over-reaction from the professors in their battle against prescriptivism.

While the *prescriptive* approach to language, that is, of guiding language use according to established norms, can be taken to extremes and produce nonsensical 'rules' that have never obtained in the history of English, it can be a matter of communicative effectiveness, not to mention courtesy and manners, to write or speak in as communicable and widely understood a variety as possible in matters of importance (the proverbial illegibility of doctors' prescriptions comes to mind). The *descriptive* approach, which looks to describe language as it is actually used, whether in accordance with standard usage or not, is of the utmost value to any account of the history of the language. Recent sociolinguistic work has suggested that innovation and variation in language is not a top-down process, but has to do with influential users in social networks within speech communities (Labov 2001 in Labov 1994-2010). The history of stigmatization of nonstandard varieties of English is a long one, and is inextricably connected to discrimination against the users of such varieties. Slang, that great innovative segment of the lexis of English, by nature informal, in-group usage, is a change from below of sorts. That change can come from below is demonstrable in the earlier history of the language, in the Anglo-Norman era, when French was the prestige language of the English court and judiciary, and English the language of the commons. For the story of English, both approaches are necessary: no history of the language can even approximate completeness without examining actual, everyday use of the language (which is predominantly informal usage), and it is difficult to overestimate the shaping power of prescriptive education and the cultural power of a literary standard.

1.12 DIACHRONIC AND SYNCHRONIC APPROACHES

Since the mid-19th century the focus of the energies of linguistic researchers has shifted from older stages of IE languages – familiar from Neogrammarian handbooks, grammars, and glossaries with modifiers such as *altindische*, *altenglische*, *althochdeutsche* ('Old Indic,' i.e., Sanskrit and Vedic, 'Old English,' 'Old High German') in the titles – to variation in contemporary languages (the great dialect atlases of the first half of the 20th century) to a modern split in effort: works such as Bruce Mitchell's *Old English Syntax*, as full a description of the syntax of English in one of its phases as exists (Mitchell 1985) or *A Linguistic Atlas of Late Medieval English* (McIntosh et al. 1986) draw from both the Neogrammarian tradition and refinements made to historical linguistic methodology in the 1950s and 1960s, while the *Dictionary of American Regional English* (Cassidy 1985–2012) and *ANAE* of Labov et al. (2006) have set new standards for the study of contemporary variation. And here is a simple, fundamental distinction in approach: between studies looking at linguistic variation through time (the *diachronic* approach) and at a given moment in time, or nonhistorically (the *synchronic* approach). Both approaches are of use in a history of the English language, and the student of such is fortunate in having a written corpus for most of the language's history and in the development of methodologies for analyzing synchronic variation by Anglo-American academics – English has very frequently been the proving ground for their methods, making it, arguably, the best-studied language in its contemporary expression.

1.13 FROM PHILOLOGICAL TO GENERATIVE APPROACHES – PHILOLOGICAL/NEOGRAMMARIAN APPROACH – THE COMPARATIVE METHOD

The *Junggrammatiker* ('Neogrammarians') of the University of Leipzig in the 1870s included in their number Otto Behaghel (who edited the Old Saxon *Heliand* and *Genesis* poems), Wilhelm Braune (an Old High German specialist, whose grammar of the language is still in print in its 15th edition; Braune 2004), Karl Brugmann (author of a Greek grammar and a fundamental handbook of IE studies), Berthold Delbrück (an Indologist who co-authored an IE handbook with Brugmann), Adolf Noreen (Old Icelandic, Scandinavian languages), Hermann Paul (prolific scholar of Germanic languages), Eduard Sievers (specialist in Old English and Old High German, writing a grammar of the former and, with Elias Steinmeyer, editing in five volumes the corpus of Old High German glosses [Steinmeyer and Sievers 1879–1922]; he wrote a fundamental text on Germanic meter), and Karl Verner (of Verner's Law; cf. Jankowsky 1972; Fox 1995, 31ff.). The 'Young Grammarians' or Neogrammarians are best known for their notion of the regularity of sound change (with Verner's Law as an example: 'law' here is a linguistic use, as sound changes can admit of exceptions in the face of an overall regularity of occurrence) and their formulation of historical grammars of the 'elder' tongues still in use for students of Germanic and IE languages. Generations of students have been educated in their method, especially (and to this day) in Germany; their work on the earlier stages of English was invaluable to the writing of its history. If modern linguists have departed from their primarily historical focus and emphasis on sound laws, their standards of philological exactness are still remarkable, as is the breadth of their interests and publishing efforts.

While this will be covered in more detail in the next chapter, the approaches of *internal reconstruction*, by which one derives proto-forms from within the system of a single language, and the *comparative method* might be usefully distinguished. The former have their origin in what later came to be called *structuralism*, which traces its beginnings to the signal work of Swiss linguist Ferdinand de Saussure, who drew the distinction between actual use of language (which he called the *parole* – literally 'word') and the system behind this use (*langue*, 'language') – this will call to mind the generative conceptualization of deep structure and surface structure, and not without reason (Chomsky had intellectual forebears in Saussure and the Port-Royal grammarians, authors of the *Logique de Port-Royal* of 1662). Saussure was interested in linguistic signs (the field of semiotics would develop around the study of signs), in the relationship between the *signified* (the semantic component, what is meant by the signs) and the *signifier* (the sound pattern of the signified; de Saussure 1993, 2006). Saussure is credited with a break from strict historicist approaches to language, and in emphasizing the independence of a language's internal system, such as its sound patterning and the regularity of sound changes, allowed for reconstruction of its earlier (unrecorded) stages, or for that of its proto-family (cf. de Saussure 2006; Fox 1995, 145–146). The *comparative method* that Saussure helped shape looks to comparisons of linguistic features, in terms of their similarity or dissimilarity, such as the sounds or phonemes of languages, to determine relationships between languages (internal reconstruction studies one language, for example, its particular stages of development). The ability to group languages into families (genetic classification) is a product of the comparative method; while previous attempts at classifying languages in families had focused upon morphology and lexis, the comparative method placed emphasis upon phonology and the sound changes that can be mapped from records of the languages and, on that basis, securely reconstructed for earlier, unrecorded stages of the languages. It has become the dominant method of historical linguistics, an exception being the mass comparison method of the late Joseph Greenberg, famous for his proposed genetic classifications of the indigenous languages of the Americas and the languages of Africa (Greenberg 1970, 1987). As a theory of linguistic reconstruction, its principles, though practiced in the 19th century, awaited more explicit formulation by linguists of the American Structuralist school (Hoenigswald 1960). It begins with linguistic correspondences that are not simply genetically related but equivalent; thus when one compares daughter languages of IE in the Germanic branch, for instance, one looks to similarities among the languages – in the vocabulary, or lexis, and especially in the sound system: "The most important procedural principle that we must invoke in establishing equivalences, however, derives from the *regularity of the correspondence*. According to this principle, changes are not isolated and erratic but *regular*, in the sense that the same phoneme will develop identically under the same conditions in a particular language" (Fox 1995, 65); one moves then to reconstruction of the proto-phonemes (as considered abstract units of sound in the proto-language) for comparison between the sets of two or more languages, and then to assigning phonetic value to the proto-phonemes (i.e., how they actually sound, as allophones of proto-phonemes; Fox 1995, 69–87). In establishing the relationships between 'member' languages of a family, one accounts for processes of historical change; thus PIE *p is realized as /p/ in Greek, Latin, and Sanskrit, /f/ in English and the other Germanic languages: thus for 'father,' Greek πατήρ (*patēr*), Latin *pater*, Gothic *fadar*, Old English *fæder*. In the next chapter, the specific data to the prehistory of English will be seen in much more detail.

1.14 THE CHOMSKYAN REVOLUTION

Perhaps the most fundamental underpinning to transformational grammar is the notion of *deep structure*, which determines the semantic interpretation of a given sentence, and *surface structure*, "which determines its phonetic interpretation" (Chomsky 1965, 16). Transformations allow for the 'mapping' of the deep structure – or its core semantic components, or the logical form (LF): all of which is a contentious matter – onto the surface structure. Sometimes called transformational-generative grammar (TGG), the Chomskyan systems, in their permutations, have sought rather to understand human language as a phenomenon rather than the grammar of any particular natural language. It is likely in this former sphere of study that the Chomskyan program has made its most lasting contributions.

Major theories associated with the Chomskyan program may be briefly mentioned insofar as they have altered the writing of the history of English or the general context in which an understanding of language is attempted.

1.14.1 Innateness Hypothesis

Essentially, this is the notion that our capacity to learn and use human language must be, to some extent, hard-wired in our brain, a biological phenomenon (again, to *some* extent), part of our genetic makeup. Components of the hypothesis are the *poverty of stimulus* argument – that one is not exposed in early development to enough data to allow for a *tabula rasa* behaviorist experiential learning of one's native language (L1) – and speed of acquisition argument: that one could not possibly learn so complex a system – capable of generating sentences never before uttered (a point contested by Roman Jakobson; Mehta 1971) – in so short a time-frame in childhood. In doing battle with American behaviorists (B.F. Skinner, a foremost opponent), Chomsky undoubtedly carried the day among theoretical linguists: for students of early language acquisition and second-language learning, the Chomskyan approach has become standard.

1.14.2 Speaker-hearers

The human language faculty is seen as consisting of two distinct skills or abilities: to decode the particular language data received; to grasp the 'deep structure,' or deconstruct the surface representation into 'mentalese,' the underlying concepts: there is not a little disagreement over what ultimately underlies an instance of human speech activity, as a 'hearer' of human language; and to 'encode' human thought in the surface representations of a human language through speech acts as a 'speaker' of the language. A fluent user of a human language is therefore a 'speaker-hearer'; some support for this concept is provided by the differing levels of ability in second-language learners: it is not unusual for one's ability to listen to and comprehend utterances in a language one is learning to be better, for a time, than one's ability to produce cogent, fluent responses in that language. It is a common phenomenon with 'heritage languages': immigrants who have come to an English-speaking region and have not found a native-language speech community often find, with the passage of time, that their ability to speak the heritage language has declined even though they may feel that they still 'understand' the language (e.g., listening to or watching radio or television broadcasts in that language, etc.). Second-generation immigrants, the children born to parents who emigrated from the home country, may find that their ability to understand the heritage language of their parents and grandparents is not matched by their ability to speak in that language.

The concept of Universal Grammar (UG) envisions *linguistic universals* that are common to all human (natural) languages; a common example is the declaration that all natural languages have nouns and verbs. Like all declarations by postmodern theoretical linguists, workers with the natural languages (those conducting field studies of indigenous languages, linguistic taxonomists, and so forth) do not always concur with the sweeping generalizations of the theorists. But for the theory of universal grammar, such linguistic universals need to be postulated to allow for the grammar's utility in saying something useful about the human language faculty, language and mind, and the biological bases of human cognition.

This is where the paths of theoretical and historical linguists often part. While the theories of the former have been influential across all of the subdisciplines of linguistics, and historical linguists in studying the recorded forms, and generating reconstructed (and unrecorded) proto-forms, participate also in the study of a single linguistic phenomenon (human language – according to the uniformitarian principle), their results are guided by disciplinary and data-driven constraints: a theoretical linguist may have recourse to actual examples from English use insofar as they are useful to the elaboration of theory having predictive power for the nature of grammar and the human language faculty, or insofar as rules in English are seen to have been predicted by their overall theory of grammar. For the historical linguist, the data of the particular language under study is nearly everything; the language or language family is traced back as far as the data and principles generated by them permit, the extent and time-depth of reconstruction limited by the recorded histories of the languages and the certitude of the sound laws posited for them. And this is where a natural choice in the study of the history of the English language can be made: to follow the particular data of its recorded history and, insofar as the certitude of Proto-Germanic and Proto-Indo-European reconstructions permits, to trace its plausible prehistory.

1.15 'JOHN IS EASY TO PLEASE' – RECEPTION OF THE CHOMSKYAN APPROACH

The 'revolution' in linguistic thinking ushered in by the Chomskyan program generated no small amount of controversy. Some of this was over ideas: the behaviorist model of language learning had its adherents and resisted displacement by the revived 'mentalist' position Chomsky advocated. As Chomskyan linguistics has adopted the rubric, prose style, and attitudes of the 'hard sciences,' criticism has come too from those of Popperian (after the philosopher of science, Karl Popper) or other stances; the scientific certainty often advanced with transformational-generative claims has led to questions over what empirical results have actually been produced by a system that in the end has to deal with the often messy data of actual human speech acts.

Of course, much theoretical linguistic work deals with formal languages, those, such as of symbolic logic or constructed with logical and mathematical symbols, or constructed without semantic content to allow for abstraction about syntactic patterns (and thus able to say something about the 'innate' human language faculty).

The most intense controversy involved Chomsky and factions of his former students, many of whom went on to develop major programs in theoretical linguistics at other universities. What was involved came to be called 'generative semantics,' which developed out of transformational-generative grammar's seeming inability or reluctance to account for semantics; the latter indeed occurred, with semantics sometimes put off until a number of questions, concerning syntactic patterns or the relation of language and mind, could be answered first. As an enterprise, modern linguistics seeks to solve linguistic problems (Labov 1994); naturally, there was some impatience in 'getting to' semantics – a sort of 'Holy Grail' of linguistic analysis. Chomsky's own emphasis upon grammaticality and acceptability played a role; in his *Syntactic Structures* (Chomsky 1957), he had used the example of *Colorless green ideas sleep furiously* to falsify the claim that grammatical, well-formed sentences always make sense. Descriptive linguistic work observed also levels of acceptability: from nonstandard utterances that exist and work (they achieve meaning for their users) but are stigmatized by users of a standard variety to scalar varieties of standard to what might be called a hyperstandard variety that is grammatically 'pure' but sounds affected, stuffy, or pretentious to the average hearer – unlike the traditional class-marking of BrE RP, AmE standard varieties are more usually located in the college-educated middle classes. The desire by 'generative semanticists,' such as Chomsky's former students George Lakoff, Paul Postal, and James McCawley, to account for meaning led to some theories that equated, or approximately equated, deep structure and semantics: that the meaning drove the representations, as realized by transformations in the surface structure. The generative semantics program lost the battle with 'orthodox' Chomskyan theoretical linguists in a fight that became highly partisan, perhaps not entirely for intellectual reasons (a history of the controversy and the personalities involved is to be found in Harris 1993).

The irony pointed up in Ved Mehta's brief journey in modern linguistics (Mehta 1971; see also Wolfe 2016) comes starkly into relief in the interview of Noam Chomsky by comedian Sacha Baron Cohen's Staines 'gangsta' Ali G ("Me woz born in da heart off da Staines ghetto") in his *Da Ali G Show*. Cohen's 'Jafaican' wannabe-gangsta – a satire on linguistic and social affectation at a number of levels – asks the professor in his Massachusetts Institute of Technology (MIT) office a series of increasingly ridiculous questions – 'How many words does you know?' about the least offensive – and Chomsky remains oblivious to Ali G's patent satire. While Chomsky was admittedly adhering to a scientific register and attempting to explain plainly general observations about language, it seems nonetheless odd that the satire should be missed with the glaring visual cues (Cohen's get-up as Ali G is vaudevillian) and, more importantly for a linguist, obvious verbal cues. This may point out one of the great theoretical divides between linguistic and philological approaches. As linguistics has increasingly laid claim to the rubric of 'science,' and at least mimicked its norms, spoken its language, and – understandably – sought its much richer pool of government and foundation funding, it seems to have lost touch with a literary sense to the study of language (the 'love' of language etymologically pronounced in *philology*). Cohen's humor played also upon popular confusion over what a linguist studies: nominally this would seem to involve the study of languages, though it has increasingly been used to refer to the study of the human language faculty. This has been exacerbated by the complaint that the Chomskyan approach has been too reliant on the monolingual, deriving too much of its data from English.

The advances of transformational-generative grammar have, perhaps surprisingly, had a relatively minor impact on the writing of the history of the English language overall, if viewed in comparison with, say, the comparative method of historical linguistics, without which the modern discipline could not exist. Nonetheless, the influence of Chomsky's theories about language and the human language faculty pervade essentially all the literature of linguistics.

1.16 COGNITIVE APPROACHES

While Chomskyan linguistics had emphasized the role and independence of a human language faculty – indeed of a language acquisition device (LAD) that enables one to work with the patterns of a human language and acquire the system with the aid of the particular data of a natural language – cognitive linguists reject any independent language facility and consider language ability part of general human cognition. The famous example of the Sapir-Whorf hypothesis is taken as an answer to the age-old chicken-or-egg question of whether thought influences language or the particular language shapes the expression of thought: both, language shapes cognition and is shaped by it. American linguists Edward Sapir, noted for his work with Native American languages, and his student Benjamin Lee Whorf, relying on data from a number of languages (commonly studied IE languages and indigenous languages of the Americas), suggested that the nature of particular languages (their morphological typology, for instance, or their lexis) affects not only the expression of reality by the mind but its cognition too. All of this was highly controversial (particularly Whorf's observations concerning the concept of 'time' in the Hopi language), if not entirely new (Wilhelm von Humboldt has proposed similar ideas in the 19th century). It did run counter to the work of a number of psychologists and of linguist Noam Chomsky, who viewed particular language data from natural languages as instantiations of a universal human language faculty. This theory of *linguistic relativity* was put to the test, such as by famous experiments with primary color terms: having speakers of different languages sort variously colored pieces of paper into piles by 'color.' A universal conceptual system would have at least generally an equal number of piles of paper as sorted by color; a linguistic relativistic conceptual system would find variation in the number of color categories on the basis of the language spoken. A critic of linguistic relativity was Eric Lenneberg, who taught both linguistics and neuroscience and adhered to a more innatist position; Lenneberg developed the 'critical age' or 'period' hypothesis of language acquisition: the notion that though a human language faculty is innate, there is a critical period in early development in which comprehensible linguistic input must occur for the proper acquisition of the linguistic system (Lenneberg 1967). Studies were cases of deprivation of input, such as that of the 'Wild Boy of Aveyron,' a feral child found in a forest in Southern France in 1797 who was unable to speak comprehensibly; considered at first an 'idiot,' Victor (as he came to be called) was taken under the care of Dr. Jean Marc Gaspard Itard (played by director François Truffaut in his 1970 film *L'enfant sauvage,* based on Victor's life), who sought to teach him language and 'socialize' him. Itard was more successful with the boy's emotional than linguistic education, but the case of Victor, and a number of other 'feral' children, led to the notion of a 'critical period' for language acquisition.

The cognitive approach to language produced an alternative to the prevailing Chomskyan model. Ronald Langacker, of the University of California-San Diego, developed over the course of several decades a system of *cognitive grammar*, which, in contradistinction to the transformational-generative approach, envisions language activity as part of overall cognitive activity and pairs the semantic component of language with its phonological expression or labeling by means of 'symbolic structures' (the two volumes of Langacker 1987–1991 are the fullest exposition of the system; see also Taylor 2003).

1.17 THE SOCIOLINGUISTIC APPROACH

Even some disagreement has occurred over what *sociolinguistics* itself means to linguists, and William Labov sought to clarify whether his own work fell under the rubric as it has developed since his famous New York City study first came out: "If this term refers to the use of data from the speech community to solve problems of linguistic theory, then I would agree that it applies to the research described here. But *sociolinguistics* is more frequently used to suggest a new interdisciplinary field – the comprehensive description of the relations of language and society. This seems to me an unfortunate notion, foreshadowing a long series of purely descriptive studies with little bearing on the central theoretical problems of linguistics or of sociology. My own intention was to solve linguistic problems, bearing in mind that these are ultimately problems in the analysis of social behavior: the description of continuous variation, of overlapping and multilayered phonemic systems; the subjective correlates of linguistic variation; the causes of linguistic differentiation and the mechanism of linguistic change" (Labov 2006, viii). So vast a field of study as 'language in society' and the sociocultural and sociohistorical forces that shape, for one, dialects of English, can perhaps best be distilled by specific example. Labov's study of the social stratification of NYC English (Labov 2006) brought into sharp relief a sensitive subject to 'the Academy': while since the 1960s sexism, racism, ethnic identity (what is sometimes called, or derided, as 'identity politics'), sexual orientation, and other matters of sociological study (to limit it to one discipline for this example) have been investigated and have seen subdisciplines and academic departments grow around such investigation (departments of Women's Studies, LGBTQ Studies, Black/Africana Studies, Chicano/a Studies, and so forth), somewhat less trumpeted has been the study of class. It has gone on nonetheless, somewhat more quietly; it is perhaps this relative silence that bespeaks its real significance and, in the view of left-leaning critics, gives indication of the real work of institutions of higher learning – which are indeed in the business of turning out future members of at least the middle classes, or replicating for the children the success of the parents in having obtained that status. The proud display, in America, of college and university names on car window decals is but one minor indicator of this class anxiety (and was skewered in Paul Fussell's *Class*; Fussell 1983). But it is known to any speaker of English that one is judged immediately upon opening one's mouth; the judgements can be variable, depending upon the hearer, with one found to be uneducated, low-class, a peer or 'Mensch,' or a pretentious snob. It becomes a shorthand as to whether one belongs: in a certain class, group, speech community, or quite simply, geographically (in that neighborhood or part of town or even street). Particular concern has been expressed over the role of social stratification in educational and employment access, and discrimination faced by speakers of nonstandard varieties. Noteworthy is the pressure to conform, to change one's way of speaking – which can again be variable, from modifying one's speech patterns upward for acceptance or greater communicability across the class system, or downward, to connote genuineness, 'folksiness,' or toughness (urban 'street cred'). And the role of class, important and pervasive as it is, is but one social factor at work in shaping the varieties and dialects of English. Other factors can include (following here the useful elaboration in Wolfram and Schilling-Estes 2006, 29–43):

1.17.1 Settlement Patterns

The culture of origin of settlers can be as important as the heritage language (if not English); settlers from the British Isles brought with them either a Celtic language or regional varieties of British English. Despite the mobility of modern America, early settlement patterns have had linguistic consequences that persist to this day (just as the 5th-century settlements of Germanic-speaking tribes had in Britain). Delineation of the broad dialectal bands of AmE (Kurath et al. 1939–1943; Kurath 1949, Carver 1987) bears out the 16th–18th-century patterns of settlement; these will be seen in detail later but the general, larger patterns of Puritan and Dissenter New England – whose religious sentiments soon produced new dissenters (e.g., Roger Williams of Rhode Island) – Dutch-English New York, William Penn's 'Quaker State' of Pennsylvania, Catholic-tolerating Maryland, 'Cavalier' Virginia, and so on, while vast oversimplifications, were distinct in their groups of settlers from the British Isles and the varieties of BrE they spoke or came to speak.

1.17.2 Migration Routes and Patterns

American English follows, of course, the path of westward expansion of its peoples. Original settlement of speakers of varieties of BrE tended (with exceptions, of course) to expand according to established routes, geographical barriers, and contacts in new areas (often people from their own communities). Scots-Irish from Virginia and the Carolinas passed through the Cumberland gap to Kentucky and Tennessee (some later heading to the Texas territory); some settlers from Upstate New York headed across the upper Midwest. Generally observable is an 'east-west fanning pattern'; an exception is the movement in the 19th century, greatly accelerated during post-Civil War Reconstruction through to the 1930s and later, of American Blacks from south to north: a coastal-oriented movement from the Carolinas to Washington, DC, Baltimore, MD, Wilmington, DE, Philadelphia, PA; a movement from the Mississippi Delta and 'Deep South' northward to St. Louis, MO, Chicago, IL, Detroit, MI, and Milwaukee, WI.

1.17.3 Language Contact

Pidgins and Creoles are recorded from the colonial Americas: there were regionally specific varieties and more broadly used contact varieties, as among the *coureurs des bois* of lower Canada and the Upper Midwest; so too was general language contact with Native American languages, African-European contact varieties, and other colonial languages (Dutch in New York; French in Canada, New England, along the Missouri-Mississippi riverine system, the Ozarks, Louisiana, and Texas; Spanish in Florida to the Southwest).

1.17.4 Communication Networks

These exist within and between neighborhoods and are generally set on a scale from 'high-density' (in frequent contact, interaction) to 'low-density' (less frequent contact and interaction); involved here is the type of neighborhood (or town or village in more rural settings), and speech community or communities within it, density of population, types of housing, frequency of contact, position within the network (who is the local 'go-to' person for information, gossip, advice, etc.).

1.17.5 Group Reference

One's voluntary/involuntary group association(s) can affect the speech variety; bearing in mind affectation and other factors, it is possible that people "may project their group membership via a complex array of grammatical, phonological, and lexical structures" (Wolfram and Schilling-Estes 2006, 41). Involuntary association may involve racial and ethnic groups, involuntary in the sense that such identity may be applied to one by others (if not inescapably: the multiracial complexities of America witnessed the phenomenon of 'passing,' that is, of light-skinned Black Americans, whose racial status was often quantified by law in the United States, being classified as whites). Voluntary association can involve groups one wishes to be considered as belonging to – a linguistic consequence of such desire is the willingness to affect the relevant speech style for acceptance.

1.17.6 Personal Identity

Perhaps the most salient contemporary example of how this factor can affect all of the other social factors is succinctly given by Wolfram and Schilling-Estes (2006): "speakers of varieties associated with lower classes or with certain minority ethnic groups are often considered to be tough and street-smart at the same time as they are held to be poor and uneducated. Because of the association of dialect features with character traits, speakers may use language to project personal qualities in addition to group membership status. For example, a European American teenager who wants to be 'cool' may adopt features of African American English..." (42). The pattern of course is well-established in AmE (and BrE), if the players filling the roles have shifted. American gangster films (not to be underestimated in the reach of their cultural influence) have in their history reflected the machismo and tragic rise-and-fall narrative pattern of crime fiction and reporting: from the Bowery Boys onward, the ethnic and racial makeup of the 'criminal underclass' has shifted (from lower-class English and Irish gang-members in Herbert Asbury's 1928 *The Gangs of New York*, to Jewish and Italian mobsters, to Black and Latino gangsters) while maintaining a normally urban setting. The glamorization of the 'criminal element' in popular culture is standard, and very profitable, especially its latest incarnation alluded to above. The contradictory impulses mentioned by the authors are worth highlighting: a simultaneous stigmatization of an urban underclass with poverty and educational failure, disease and crime – such as the Irish of New York City's Lower East Side in the second half of the 19th century until the neighborhoods were razed – and covert prestige engendered by 'counter-cultural,' anti-authoritarian cachet. As pervasive as this phenomenon may be (the character of Ali G mentioned above simply takes it to an absurd extreme), the motivation for such changes to speech styles may also arise from discomfort with one's identity. Comfort with an identity, as with a group association, may also lead to its exaggeration. So too the alteration of one's own variety may occur as a strategy of conversation.

1.17.7 Economic Ecology

The role of socioeconomic forces in settlement and residential patterns must be considered – to a certain degree these forces produce involuntary movements: zoning laws blamed for *ghettoization*, or *gentrification*, earlier *slum-clearances*, that replace lower-income, high-density housing with more upscale, lower-density 'luxury' properties; the availability of either land (for farming) or work (shipping, trade, mining, timber, city services, heavy industry). Other patterns to some degree involve volition: there are many examples in American immigration history of settlements concentrated by ethnic or national origin: heavy Slavic presence in 19th-century industrial cities from Pittsburgh (steel) to Chicago (steel-works and meat-packing); Irish, Italian, and Mexican miners in Colorado; German grocers and farmers throughout the Midland and Midwestern regions; Italian shopkeepers, cobblers, tailors, and stone-masons in big cities of the Northeast; Mexican agricultural workers in the Southwest.

1.18 LINGUISTIC VARIATION: LANGUAGES AND DIALECTS, PIDGINS, AND CREOLES

1.18.1 Mutual Intelligibility

This is perhaps the only *linguistic* test that passes muster of whether a particular variety is to be classified as the dialect (subset of variants) of a language or as a separate language. Popular usage can apply *dialect* to nonstandard usage, in a general, not systematic, sense, and sometimes derogatorily ('they speak in that dialect,' 'they have their own dialect'). A common observation is that a language is a dialect with an army and navy,[9] and this brings up the matter of governmental language policies. Thus one can hear, on the one hand, charges of linguistic, cultural, or political separatism leveled in the face of declarations of 'language' status for what governments officially classify as 'dialects'; Catalan (Català) and Galician (Gallego) in Spain, Occitan (Lenga d'òc/ Langue d'oc; Provençal referring to a dialect of Occitan or as the term for the variety more generally) in France, Ligurian in Italy, and a number of other examples obtain just among the Romance Indo-European languages of Western Europe. Governments have been wary of the connection between linguistic self-assertion and separatism, and linguistic separatism and political autonomy and separatist movements and, more often than not, have sought to assert the primacy of a supra-dialectal national standard (normatively based on a prestige dialect; e.g., Île-de-France French). This can lead to a gulf between official government language proclamations and linguistic reality; but for linguists, the matter is one of mutual intelligibility: if speakers in an area genuinely have difficulty understanding one another we may speak of 'varieties,' perhaps even languages (a further specification can be drawn once language contact varieties, pidgins and Creoles, have been introduced). There is of course a distinction between linguistic fact – that languages do differ in phonology, morphology, syntax, and lexis to the point that mutual intelligibility is significantly hampered (as between Spanish and Portuguese) or simply impossible (as between Russian, a Slavic language of Indo-European, and Arabic, a Semitic language of the Afroasiatic family) – and the perceptions of speakers, who may be more likely to ascribe unintelligibility to varieties used by groups of speakers they may not like (the stigmatization of American Black speech, for example). And so if, indeed, the variants hampering mutually intelligible communication obtain in the phonology, morphology, etc., we are probably talking about two different languages, not simply two dialects. The matter is made more complex by the uses to which *dialect* has been put: historical linguists often speak of *dialects* of Indo-European (namely, the reconstructed Proto-Indo-European), by which they mean 'daughter languages'; *dialect* can refer to an overall variety of a speech community involving significant *substratum* influence (here we may be talking about contact varieties or pidginized varieties of immigrant communities); and dialect is often popularly used to stand in for 'language' if the name of that language is not known or when the speaker means some unintelligible variety (in their estimate) which may or may not be 'officially' considered a separate language. Governments naturally have a tendency to consider regional languages genetically related to the official tongue as 'dialects'; linguists normally consider Catalan and Gallego Ibero-Romance *languages*, Occitan a Western Romance language, Ligurian North Italic, Frisian, and the Creoles Afrikaans and Yiddish West Germanic (all within the Indo-European super-family of languages). Conversely, the term language can be used for varieties or dialects given political status; for example, the vexed matter of Norwegian (Norsk: the official, standard forms *Bokmål* and *Nynorsk*) and Swedish (Svenska, *Nysvenska*),

[9]This is traditionally traced to the remark of Yiddish language scholar Max Weinreich: "A shprakh iz a dialekt mit an armey un flot"; Weinreich 1945.

both descended from Old Norse, given political-linguistic distinction by the separate national entities and histories.

We can at least say, in broad terms, that for the purposes of studying the development of English, the traditional use of *dialects* as referring to subsets of variants arising from regional and social conditioning factors will be accepted; this entails the popular (if linguistically imprecise) use of referring to 'speakers' of dialects, for example, that one speaks 'Pittsburghese' (of the Western Pennsylvania city and its environs, the 'Three Rivers' region) or Scouse (Liverpudlian, Merseyside). If it is more precise to say that one speaks 'Liverpool English' the tag Scouse is still useful as a register of perceptions of dialects of English. One of the great contemporary questions linguists and dialectologists have been examining is the matter of *convergence* or *divergence* of dialects and varieties of English, that is, are the dialects of English growing closer (linguistically more homogenous, ever more mutually intelligible) or are they drifting apart, becoming less mutually intelligible? This is always a matter to be considered with regard to living languages, and it is more complex than the bidirectional scheme implied by the pair of terms; the history of English itself gives evidence of patterns of both convergence and divergence of varieties/dialects. One factor would be the shift in the standard, prestige variety; in the history of English, it had not always had its locus in the city of London. The answers linguists have been coming up with may seem contradictory (Labov et al. 2006), but they have been made weighing the many and varied factors that condition dialect 'drift' and convergence.

The status of pidgins and Creoles shifted in the 20th century with the many other changes wrought by the historical forces that shaped the colonial world into the postcolonial. Newly independent nations enacted language planning policies of their own, with varying results; inevitably, the colonial languages persisted in some form: as prestige varieties spoken by postcolonial élites, in governments, universities, and chambers of commerce; or in pidgin and Creole language contact systems. Linguistic ties proved among the more durable. Many reasons obtain for the phenomenon observed; for instance, in essentially all the former British territories (whether they joined the Commonwealth or not), ties of language were productive of a sense of affiliation (even in the face of political contention), immigration strengthened the link with a 'mother country' (as between Britain and Jamaica or South Asia) and fostered continued communication and travel between Britain and the territories, and economic development schemes that emphasized trade and tourism. This will be the subject of more detailed discussion in Chapters 10 and 11, but one remarkable development may be observed at this early juncture: English-based contact varieties have been granted official or co-official status with English and indigenous languages in a number of former colonies and territories. The matter is enormously complex, and often linked inextricably with 'Creole' racial status – the useful parallel example is to the concept of *mestizaje* in Spanish America, Mexico in particular: the many, sometimes obvious, other times more subtle layers to a racially and linguistically stratified (post)colonial society. The categories can be fluid, but there is usually in the modern postcolonial era some recognized if not precisely quantifiable border or 'cut-off' point between strata, such as, for example, between *mestizo/mestiza* and *indio/india* in Mexico and among Chicanos in the United States. This social and racial stratification inevitably, if not always fully overlappingly, manifests itself linguistically: the levels of English-based Jamaican

Creole or French-based Haitian patois are scalar, and very often intersect with the type of contact variety spoken (and knowledge of the base language). A university-educated government minister, in the Caribbean for this example, will likely know the base language (RP English or Parisian French) and a local standard variety, and an acrolectal variety of the Creole and often be, in the Caribbean racial hierarchy, considered 'Creole.' Those speaking mesolectal or basilectal varieties may be identified more closely as Caribbean Blacks, and more likely living in rural or inland towns and villages. The famous Anansi folk stories, deriving from West Africa, are associated with 'deeper' Jamaican Creole varieties – that is, with a culture more African in heritage and identification (than Anglo-Caribbean) and tending toward the mesolectal and basilectal in the contact variety scale (Lalla and D'Costa 1990; Patrick 1992, 1999). This is by no means universal, and is undergoing steady change, though it is finding new expression and reinforcement in emigré communities in Britain (London especially), the United States (Philadelphia, New York, Boston), and Canada (Toronto). English-based contact varieties, derided historically as 'broken English,' have in the postmodern era 'arrived.' Tok Pisin is an official variety in linguistically diverse Papua New Guinea and one of the media languages of the Australian Broadcasting Corporation. Bislama, the English-based Creole of Vanuatu with a significant number of loans from French, serves as a *lingua franca* among the islands of Vanuatu and fulfills official functions, as on its currency: the 500-vatu note is trilingual, issued by the Reserve Bank of Vanuatu/Banque de reserve de Vanuatu/Reserve Bank Blong Vanuatu, with the seal in Bislama: *Long God yumi stanap*, 'Let us stand firm in God' (literally, 'With God you-me [= 'we'] stand up').

REFERENCES AND BIBLIOGRAPHY

Algeo, John and Carmen Acevedo Butcher, *The Origins and Development of the English Language*. 7th ed. Boston, MA: Cengage Learning, 2013

Asbury, Herbert. *The Gangs of New York: An Informal History of the Underworld*. New York: Knopf, 1928

Austin, John Langshaw. *How to Do Things with Words*. Cambridge, MA: Harvard University Press, 1962

Bauer, Laurie. *English Word-Formation*. Cambridge: Cambridge University Press, 1983

Bauer, Laurie. *An Introduction to English Lexicology*. Edinburgh: Edinburgh University Press, 2022

Baugh, Albert C. *A History of the English Language*. 2nd New York: Appleton-Century-Crofts, 1957

Baugh, Albert C. and Thomas Cable, *A History of the English Language*. London: Routledge, 2013

Bloomfield, Maurice, "On assimilation and adaptation in congeneric classes of words," *American Journal of Philology* 16.4 (1895), 409–434

Braune, Wilhelm. *Althochdeutsche Grammatik*. 15th ed. Ed. Ingo Reiffenstein. Tübingen: Niemeyer, 2004

Burridge, Kate and Bernd Kortmann, eds. *Varieties of English 3: The Pacific and Australia*. Berlin: Mouton de Gruyter, 2008

Carr, Charles Telford. *Nominal Compounds in Germanic.* London: Published for St. Andrews University by H. Milford, 1939

Carver, Craig. *American Regional Dialects: A Word Geography.* Ann Arbor, MI: University of Michigan Press, 1987

Chambers, J.K. and Peter Trudgill. *Dialectology.* 2nd ed. Cambridge: Cambridge University Press, 1998

Chambers, J.K., Peter Trudgill, Natalie Schilling-Estes, *The Handbook of Language Variation and Change.* Malden, MA: Blackwell, 2002

Chomsky, Noam. *Syntactic Structures.* 's-Gravenhage: Mouton, 1957

Chomsky, Noam. *Current Issues in Linguistic Theory.* The Hague: Mouton, 1964

Chomsky, Noam. *Aspects of the Theory of Syntax.* Cambridge, MA: MIT Press, 1965

Chomsky, Noam. *Language and Mind.* Enlarged ed. New York: Harcourt, Brace, Jovanovich, 1972a

Chomsky, Noam. *Studies on Semantics in Generative Gramar.* The Hague: Mouton, 1972b

Chomsky, Noam. *The Logical Structure of Linguistic Theory.* New York: Plenum Press, 1975

Chomsky, Noam. *Rules and Representations.* New York, Columbia University Press, 1980

Chomsky, Noam. *Barriers.* Cambridge, MA: MIT Press, 1986

Chomsky, Noam. *Lectures on Government and Binding: The Pisa Lectures.* 7th ed. Berlin: Mouton de Gruyter, 1993

Chomsky, Noam. *Cartesian Linguistics: A Chapter in the History of Rationalist Thought.* 3rd ed. Ed. James McGilvray. Cambridge: Cambridge University Press, 2009

Chomsky, Noam and Morris Halle. *The Sound Pattern of English.* New York: Harper & Row, 1968/rpt. Cambridge, MA: MIT Press, 1991

Comrie, Bernard. *Aspect: An Introduction to the Study of Verbal Aspect and Related Problems.* Cambridge: Cambridge University Press, 1976

Comrie, Bernard. *Language Universals and Linguistic Typology: Syntax and Morphology.* Oxford: Blackwell, 1981

Comrie, Bernard. *Tense.* Cambridge: Cambridge University Press, 1985

Comrie, Bernard, ed. *The World's Major Languages.* New York: Oxford University Press, 1987

Comrie, Bernard, Stephen Matthews, Maria Polinsky, eds. *The Atlas of Languages: The Origin and Development of Languages Throughout the World.* Revised ed. New York: Facts on File, 2003

Crystal, David. *The Cambridge Encyclopedia of the English Language.* 3rd ed. Cambridge: Cambridge University Press, 2018

Daniels, Peter T. And William Bright, *The World's Writing Systems.* New York: Oxford University Press, 1996

DARE = Dictionary of American Regional English. 6 vols. Ed. Frederic G. Cassidy and Joan Houston Hall. Cambridge, MA: The Belknap Press of Harvard University Press, 1985–2013

The Endangered Language Fund (New Haven, CT), (1997). http://www.endangeredlanguagefund.org/

Ethnologue: Languages of the World. SIL Global (Summer Institute of Linguistics). 27th ed. 2024. http://www.ethnologue.com

Fay, Edwin W., "I. – agglutination and adaptation," *American Journal of Philology* 15.4 (1894), 409–442

Fox, Anthony. *Linguistic Reconstruction: An Introduction to Theory and Method.* Oxford: Oxford University Press, 1995

Frawley, William J., ed. *International Encyclopedia of Linguistics*, 4 vols. 2nd ed. Oxford: Oxford University Press, 2003

Fussell, Paul. *Class: A Guide Through the American Status System.* New York: Summit Books, 1983/illustrated ed. New York: Simon & Schuster, 1992

Givón, Talmy. *Syntax: An Introduction.* 2. Rev Amsterdam: John Benjamins, 2001

Gow, Peter. *An Amazonian Myth and Its History.* Oxford: Oxford University Press, 2001

Greenbaum, Sidney. *Oxford English Grammar.* Oxford: Oxford University Press, 1996

Greenberg, Joseph. *The Languages of Africa.* 3rd Bloomington, IN: Indiana University Press, 1970

Greenberg, Joseph. *Language in the Americas.* Stanford, CA: Stanford University Press, 1987

Gretsch, Mechthild. *The Intellectual Foundations of the English Benedictine Reform.* Cambridge Studies in Anglo-Saxon England 25. Cambridge: Cambridge University Press, 1999

Grice, H. Paul. *Studies in the Way of Words.* Cambridge, MA: Harvard University Press, 1989

Harris, Randy Allen. *The Linguistics Wars.* New York: Oxford University Press, 1993

Harris, Zellig. *Methods in Structural Linguistics.* Chicago: University of Chicago Press, 1951/rpt. *Structural Linguistics.* Chicago: University of Chicago Press, 1986

Harris, Zellig. *A Grammar of English on Mathematical Principles.* New York: Wiley, 1982

Hartmann, Frederik. *The Vandalic Language – Origins and Relationships.* Indogermanische Bibliothek. Dritte Reihe: Untersuchungen. Heidelberg: Universitätsverlag Winter, 2020

Hoenigswald, Henry M. *Language Change and Linguistic Reconstruction.* Chicago: University of Chicago Press, 1960

Hogg, Richard and David Denison, *A History of the English Language.* Cambridge: Cambridge University Press, 2006

Holm, John A. *Pidgins and Creoles.* 2 vols. Cambridge: Cambridge University Press, 1988–1989

Holm, John A. *An Introduction to Pidgins and Creoles.* Cambridge: Cambridge University Press, 2000

Holm, John A. and Susanne Michaelis, eds. *Contact Languages: Critical Concepts in Language Studies.* 5. Abingdon: Routledge, 2009

Horvath, Barbara M., "Australian English: Phonology," in *Varieties of English,* volume 3: *The Pacific and Australasia*, Burridge, Kate and Bernd Kortmann. Berlin: Mouton de Gruyter, 2008, pp. 88–110

Huck, Geoffrey J. and John A. Goldsmith, "Gaps in the paradigm," *Contemporary Linguistics* 1 (1994), 1–55

Huck, Geoffrey J. and John A. Goldsmith. *Ideology and Linguistic Theory: Noam Chomsky and the Deep Structure Debates.* London: Routledge, 1995

Huddleston, Rodney and Geoffrey K. Pullum. *The Cambridge Grammar of the English Language.* Cambridge: Cambridge University Press, 2002

Irvine, Susan, "Beginnings and Transitions: Old English," in *Varieties of English*, volume 3: *The Pacific and Australasia*, Mugglestone, Lynda, Oxford: Oxford University Press, 2006, pp. 32–60

Jankowsky, Kurt R. *The Neogrammarians: A Re-evaluation of their Place in the Development of Linguistic Science*. The Hague: Mouton, 1972

Joseph, Brian D. and Richard Janda. *The Handbook of Historical Linguistics*. Oxford: Blackwell, 2003

Kachru, Braj, "The sacred cows of English," *English Today* 4 (1988), 3–8

Kent, Roland G., ed. and tr. *Varro. On the Latin Language*. 2 vols. Loeb Classical Library vols. 333–334. Cambridge, MA: Harvard University Press, 1951/rpt. 1999

Kortmann, Bernd and Clive Upton, eds. *Varieties of English 1: The British Isles*. Berlin: Mouton de Gruyter, 2008

Kretzschmar, William A., Jr. *The Linguistics of Speech*. Cambridge: Cambridge University Press, 2009

Kretzschmar, William A., Jr., Virginia G. McDavid, Theodore K. Lerud, Ellen Johnson. *Handbook of the Linguistic Atlas of the Middle and South Atlantic States*. Chicago: University of Chicago Press, 1993

Kurath, Hans. *A Word Geography of the Eastern United States*. Ann Arbor, MI: University of Michigan Press, 1949

Kurath, Hans et al., eds. *Linguistic Atlas of New England*. 3 vols. Providence: Brown University, 1939–1943

Labov, William. *Language in the Inner City: Studies in the Black English Vernacular*. Philadelphia: University of Pennsylvania Press, 1972

Labov, William. *Principles of Linguistic Change, vol. 1: Internal factors* (1994), *vol. 2: Social factors* (2001), vol.3: *Cognitive and Cultural Factors (2010)*. Oxford: Blackwell, 1994–2010

Labov, William. *The Social Stratification of English in New York City*. 2nd ed. Cambridge: Cambridge University Press, 2006

Labov, William, Sharon Ash, Charles Boberg. *The Atlas of North American English*. Berlin: Mouton de Gruyter, 2006 [= ANAE]

Ladefoged, Peter. *Elements of Acoustic Phonetics*. Chicago: University of Chicago Press, 1996

Ladefoged, Peter. *Vowels and Consonants: An Introduction to the Sounds of Languages*. Oxford: Blackwell, 2005

Lakoff, George. *Women, Fire, and Dangerous Things: What Categories Reveal about the Mind*. Chicago: University of Chicago Press, 1987

Lakoff, George and Mark Johnson. *Metaphors We Live By*. Chicago: University of Chicago Press, 2003

Lakoff, Robin Tolmach. *The Language War*. Berkeley, CA: University of California Press, 2000

Lalla, Barbara and Jean D'Costa. *Language in Exile: Three Hundred Years of Jamaican Creole*. Tuscaloosa, AL: University of Alabama Press, 1990

LALME McIntosh, Angus, M.L. Samuels, and Michael Benskin. *A Linguistic Atlas of Late Middle English*. 4 vols. Aberdeen: Aberdeen University Press, 1986

Langacker, Ronald W. *Foundations of Cognitive Grammar,* vol. 1: *Theoretical Prerequisites;* vol. 2: *Descriptive Application.* Stanford, CA: Stanford University Press, 1987–1991

Langacker, Ronald W. *Concept, Image, and Symbol: The Cognitive Basis of Grammar.* Berlin: Mouton de Gruyter, 1990

Langacker, Ronald W. *Grammar and Conceptualization.* Berlin: Mouton de Gruyter, 1999

Langacker, Ronald W. *Cognitive Grammar: A Basic Introduction.* Oxford: Oxford University Press, 2008

Lanman, Charles Rockwell. *A Sanskrit Reader: Text and Vocabulary and Notes.* Cambridge, MA: Harvard University Press, 1920/rpt. 1984

Lass, Roger. *Phonology: An Introduction to Basic Concepts.* Cambridge: Cambridge University Press, 1984

Lass, Roger. *Historical Linguistics and Language Change.* Cambridge: Cambridge University Press, 1997

Leech, Geoffrey and Jan Svartvik. *A Communicative Grammar of English.* 3rd ed. London: Longman, 2002

Leinieks, Valdis. *Morphosyntax of the Homeric Greek Verb.* The Hague: Mouton, 1964

Lenneberg, Eric. *Biological Foundations of Language.* With appendices by Noam Chomsky and Otto Marx. New York: Wiley, 1967

Liberman, Anatoly. *An Analytic Dictionary of English Etymology: An Introduction.* Minneapolis, MN: University of Minnesota Press, 2008

McArthur, Tom, "The English language?" *English Today* 3 (1987), 9–13

Macaulay, Ronald K.S. *The Social Art: Language and Its Uses.* 2nd ed. Oxford: Oxford University Press, 2006

McCawley, James D. *Thirty Million Theories of Grammar.* London: Croom Helm, 1982

McCawley, James D. *The Syntactic Phenomena of English.* 2 vols. Chicago: University of Chicago Press, 1988

McGilvray, James A. *Chomsky: Language, Mind, and Politics.* Malden, MA: Blackwell, 1999

McGilvray, James, ed. *The Cambridge Companion to Chomsky.* Cambridge: Cambridge University Press, 2005

Marchand, Hans. *The Categories and Types of Present-Day English Word-Formation.* Munich: C.H. Beck'sche Verlagsbuchhandlung, 1969

Mehta, Ved. *John is Easy to Please: Encounters with the Written and the Spoken Word.* New York: Farrar, Straus & Giroux, 1971

Mesthrie, Rajend, "English circling the globe," *English Today* 24 (2008), 28–32

Mitchell, Bruce. *Old English Syntax.* 2 vols. Oxford: Clarendon Press, 1985

Momma, Haruko and Michael Matto, *A Companion to the History of the English Language.* Oxford: Blackwell, 2008

Mufwene, Salikoko S. *The Ecology of Language Evolution.* Cambridge: Cambridge University Press, 2001

Mufwene, Salikoko S. *Language Evolution: Contact, Competition and Change.* New York: Continuum, 2008

Mugglestone, Lynda, ed. *The Oxford History of English.* Oxford: Oxford University Press, 2006

Mustanoja, Tauno F. *A Middle English Syntax, Part 1: The Parts of Speech.* Helsinki: Société néophilologique, 1960

Patrick, Peter L. *Linguistic Variation in Urban Jamaican Creole.* Diss., University of Pennsylvania, 1992

Patrick, Peter L. *Urban Jamaican Creole: Variation in the Mesolect.* Amsterdam: John Benjamins, 1999

Payne, Thomas E. *Describing Morphosyntax: A Guide for Field Linguists.* Cambridge: Cambridge University Press, 1997

Porter, David W., ed. *Excerptiones de Prisciano: The Sources for Ælfric's Latin-Old English Grammar.* Anglo-Saxon Texts 4. Cambridge: D.S. Brewer, 2002

Postal, Paul M. *On Raising: One Rule of English Grammar and its Theoretical Implications.* Cambridge, MA: MIT Press, 1974

Postal, Paul M. *Three Investigations of Extraction.* Cambridge, MA: MIT Press, 1998

Postal, Paul M. *Skeptical Linguistic Essays.* Oxford: Oxford University Press, 2004

Pulsiano, Phillip. *Old English Glossed Psalters: Psalms 1-50.* Toronto Old English Series 11. Toronto: University of Toronto Press, 2001

Quirk, Randolph, Sidney Greenbaum, Geoffrey Leech, Jan Svartvik. *A Comprehensive Grammar of the English Language.* London: Longman, 1985

Ringe, Don. *From Proto-Indo-European to Proto-Germanic.* A Linguistic History of English, Volume I. Oxford: Oxford University Press, 2017

Ringe, Don. *A Historical Morphology of English.* Edinburgh Textbooks on the English Language. Advanced. Edinburgh: Edinburgh University Press, 2021

Ringe, Don and Ann Taylor. *The Development of Old English.* A Linguistic History of English, Volume II. Oxford Linguistics. Oxford: Oxford University Press, 2014

Romaine, Suzanne. *Socio-Historical Linguistics: Its Status and Methodology.* Cambridge: Cambridge University Press, 1982

Romaine, Suzanne. *Pidgin and Creole Languages.* London: Longman, 1988

Romaine, Suzanne. *Bilingualism.* 2nd ed. Oxford: Blackwell, 1995

Romaine, Suzanne. *Language in Society: An Introduction to Sociolinguistics.* 2nd ed. Oxford: Oxford University Press, 2000

Ruhlen, Merritt. *A Guide to the World's Languages.* Vol. 1 *Classification* Stanford, CA: Stanford University Press, 1987

Saussure, Ferdinand de. *Troisième cours de linguistique générale (1910-11)/ Saussure's Third Course of Lectures on General Linguistics: from the notebooks of Émile Constantin.* Tr. Roy Harris. Oxford: Pergamon Press, 1993

Saussure, Ferdinand de. *Writings in General Linguistics (Écrits de linguistique générale).* London: Oxford University Press, 2006

Searle, John R. *Speech Acts: An Essay in the Philosophy of Language.* London: Cambridge University Press, 1969

Sievers, Eduard and Karl Brunner. *Abriss der altenglischen (angelsächsischen) Grammatik.* 16th ed. Tübingen: Max Niemeyer, 1963

Steinmeyer, Elias and Eduard Sievers, eds. *Die althochdeutschen Glossen.* 5 vols. Berlin: Weidmann, 1879–1922

Strang, Barbara M.H. *A History of English*. London: Methuen & Co., 1970

Svartvik, Jan and Geoffrey Leech. *English: One Tongue, Many Voices*. Basingstoke: Palgrave Macmillan, 2006

Tagliamonte, Sali. *Analysing Sociolinguistic Variation*. Cambridge: Cambridge University Press, 2006

Taylor, John R. *Cognitive Grammar*. Oxford: Oxford University Press, 2003

Thomason, Sarah. *Language Contact: An Introduction*. Washington, DC: Georgetown University Press, 2001

Todd, Loreto. *Pidgins and Creoles*. 2nd ed. London: Routledge, 1990

Trudgill, Peter. *The Dialects of England*. 2nd ed. Oxford: Blackwell, 1999

Trudgill, Peter. *New-Dialect Formation: The Inevitability of Colonial Englishes*. Edinburgh: Edinburgh University Press, 2006

Trudgill, Peter and Jean Hannah. *International English: A Guide to Varieties of Standard English*. 5th ed. London: Hodder, 2008

Trudgill, Peter, Arthur Hughes, Dominic Watt. *English Accents and Dialects: An Introduction to Social and Regional Varieties of English in the British Isles*. 5th ed. London: Hodder Arnold, 2012

Vigouroux, Cécile B. and Salikoko S. Mufwene, edd. *Globalization and Language Vitality: Perspectives from Africa*. New York: Continuum, 2008

Visser, Fredericus Theodorus. *An Historical Syntax of the English Language*, 3 vols. in 4 pts. Leiden: E.J. Brill, 1963–1973

Watts, Richard and Peter Trudgill, *Alternative Histories of English*. London: Routledge, 2002

Weinreich, Max, "Der YIVO [Yidisher Visnshaftlekher Institut] un di problemen fun undzer tsayt/The YIVO and the Problems of our Age," *YIVO Bleter* 25.1 (1945), 3–18

Wells, J.C. *Accents of English*. 3 vols. *1: An Introduction. 2: The British Isles. 3: Beyond the British Isles*. Cambridge: Cambridge University Press, 1982

Wierzbicka, Anna. *The Semantics of Grammar*. Philadelphia: John Benjamins, 1988

Wierzbicka, Anna. *Semantics: Primes and Universals*. Oxford: Oxford University Press, 1996

Wolfe, Tom. *The Kingdom of Speech*. Boston: Little, Brown and Company, 2016

Wolfram, Walt and Natalie Schilling-Estes. *American English: Dialects and Variation*. 2nd ed. Oxford: Blackwell, 2006

CHAPTER 2

Before English: Indo-European and Proto-Germanic

2.1 SIR WILLIAM JONES AND THE 'DISCOVERY' OF SANSKRIT

Though not the first scholar to posit an 'Indo-European' family of languages, the British jurist Sir William Jones was appointed to the Supreme Court of Bengal in 1783 and the following year founded in Calcutta the Asiatic Society. In his Third Discourse (annual address) to the Society in February 1786, Welshman Jones (1746–1794) would offer a cogent formulation of what comparative historical philology could achieve as a discipline with its principles systematically applied; his own intensive study of Sanskrit had been the impetus to his 'discovery':

> The Sanscrit language, whatever be its antiquity, is of a wonderful structure; more perfect than the Greek, more copious than the Latin, and more exquisitely refined than either, yet bearing to both of them a stronger affinity, both in the roots of verbs and the forms of grammar, than could possibly have been produced by accident; so strong indeed, that no philologer could examine them all three, without believing them to have sprung from some common source, which, perhaps, no longer exists; there is a similar reason, though not quite so forcible, for supposing that both the Gothick and the Celtick, though blended with a very different idiom, had the same origin with the Sanscrit; and the old Persian might be added to the same family ... (Cannon 1990, 245).

Jones was celebrated in his day as an 'orientalist,' translating for the first time Kālidāsa's *Ābhijnānaśākuntalam* ('Revealing Śākuntalā'), the masterpiece of India's greatest classical dramatist, setting off a literary rage for the playwright (no less than Goethe was moved by the play's 'perfection'). He is known better now as a 'father' of Indo-European studies (in the German academy, *Indogermanisch* is the term: a distinction that has figured in scholarly debates over an Indo-European homeland or *Urheimat*). Refinements would come, new member languages be discovered – Hittite and other Anatolian languages, Tocharian A and B, the decipherment of Linear B and its identification as a form of early Greek by Michael Ventris in 1952 – but the comparative method had been put on a good footing by Jones, Bopp, the Grimms,[1] and others of an early generation of historical linguists.

While one naturally encounters treatments of Modern English in a global context (common are locutions such as 'English as a world language' or 'Global Englishes'), the discoveries of the early historical linguists of the 18th and 19th centuries, the philologists, were such as to place English, as an Indo-European language, in what would have seemed a global context to pre-Modern peoples. From the Greenland and Iceland (and then, by somewhat before AD 1000, Atlantic Canada) of the Norse settlements to the Indian subcontinent, the geographic spread of Indo-European is rivaled by the numbers of speakers and prestige of some of the more widely spoken of its 455 or so related languages. The conventional figure is not an exaggeration: approximately half the world's population speaks an Indo-European language as their L1 or an L2, particularly in postcolonial nations. English is still spoken in many nations that broke away from or were granted independence of the British Empire or subsequent Commonwealth; French and French-based Creoles are widely used in West Africa, the Caribbean, and in some Pacific territories and island nations; Spanish and Portuguese predominate from Mexico to the Southern Cone. (Many other examples will be considered in chs. 10 and 11 with consideration of 'Postcolonial Englishes.') If exploration, conquest, and imperialism were paramount in the Early Modern spread of Indo-European languages such as English, French, Spanish, Portuguese, and Dutch, the causes to the original spread of the early Indo-European dialects are rather more a matter of contention.

Two major schools of thought in British Indo-European studies are in competition to explain the breakup of Proto-Indo-European – a hypothetical Ur- or proto-language or group of dialects existing entirely now in the reconstructions of historical linguists – somewhere around 6000 years before present into dialects or groups of dialects seen as proto-forms of the 'branches' of the superfamily. This process did not, of course, happen all at once, and historical linguists generally date the emergence of splits of branches on the basis of recorded changes (especially those phonological) or the perceived conservatism of the morphology of a member language. Speakers of these proto-varieties (Proto-Indo-Iranian, Proto-Celtic, Proto-Baltic, Proto-Germanic, and so forth) spread eastward and westward, either by conquest or by diffusion. The latter school of thinking has as its chief exponent British archaeologist Colin Renfrew, who has looked to the diffusion of agricultural techniques from Anatolia (Modern

[1]Franz Bopp (1791–1867) carried out considerable work on a number of the branches of Indo-European (especially Indo-Iranian), clarifying their inter-relations; his monumental *Comparative Grammar* of Indo-European languages appeared in 6 vols. (Bopp 1833–1837).

Turkey) as the vector for the spread of the Indo-European languages (Renfrew 1987). A rival explanation, often associated with another British archaeologist, J.P. Mallory, attributes the spread of the Indo-European languages to conquest, particularly by horse-borne warriors known also for their use of the chariot (Mallory 1989).[2] This view has much internal, cultural evidence to commend it: earlier Indo-European cultures, in the widely cited Dumézilian scheme, that is, of linguist and comparative mythographer Georges Dumézil, classified by a tripartite division of society into priestly/warrior/cultivator castes, produced literatures that have their 'heroic' phases or ages (see, for instance, Dumézil 1970 and Bonnefoy 1991). Indeed, epic poetry characterizes most of the Indo-European cultures for which we have early written records (Watkins 1995). From Hittite epics to the Homeric, the great Sanskrit *Mahābhārata* to the medieval Irish *Táin bó Cúailnge* ('Cattle Raid on Cooley'), Indo-European epic verse often celebrated chariot-borne warriors and their conquests, among other epic conventions. The connections and parallels run deep among the cultures and offer corroborating evidence of relatedness among Indo-European societies and cultures as does the internal linguistic evidence for the genetic relationship among the languages viewed as constituents of the Indo-European family.

The placement of English within Indo-European thus yields linguistic and cultural information if one approaches the subject comparatively. Genetically speaking, that is, in terms of relatedness between languages determined by shared features of phonology, morphology, syntax, and semantics, English is an Indo-European language, in the Germanic branch, and West Germanic subbranch. Its nearest 'sister' languages in West Germanic are German, Dutch, Frisian, Afrikaans, and Yiddish. If a family analogy is pursued further, however figuratively, a 'first-cousin' relationship can be said to exist between the languages of the West Germanic subbranch and those of the North Germanic (Greenlandic, Icelandic, Faroese, Norn, Shelta/Hjalta, Norwegian, Swedish, and Danish) and extinct East Germanic (Gothic, perhaps also Vandalic and Burgundian) subbranches. At the branch-level, at what might be the level of 'second-cousin' relatedness or a few more degrees removed, the Romance languages, descended from Vulgar Latin in the transitional period following the breakup of the Western Roman Empire traditionally dated to AD 476, are divided among the Western Romance (Italian, French, Provençal, Spanish, Portuguese, perhaps also Catalan) and Eastern Romance (Romantsch, one of four official languages of Switzerland, Romanian, Aromanian/Vlach, and Istro-Romanian) subbranches. Historical and comparative linguists base the grouping of languages into families upon perceived 'consanguinity,' that

[2] The latter proposal is the 'Renfrew' hypothesis, after the archaeologist Colin Renfrew who has written extensively on the suggestion that the Indo-European dispersal began out of Anatolia and was based on the diffusion of farming techniques rather than the efforts of waves of horse-borne warriors: "It seems likely then that the first Indo-European languages came to Europe from Anatolia around 6000 BC, together with the first domesticated plants and animals, and that they were in fact spoken by the first farmers in Europe" (Renfrew 1987, 288). A choice has been made here to follow rather the view espoused in Mallory (1989) and others, of an Indo-European expansion from around the Pontic-Caspian region that was largely hostile (or portrayed so in the epic literature of early Indo-European cultures).

is, upon observed shared features in the sound systems, grammar, syntax, and lexis. Historical phonology, the classification of the inventory of a language's sounds and discernment of the operation of regular processes of sound change, and comparative morphology, the classification of inflectional properties among languages more synthetic in their morphological typology – as English was in its early history before processes of 'inflectional decay,' as it may loosely be termed, worked changes that make Modern English a more analytic language – are particularly valuable to the task of genetic classification and predominate in the handbooks and grammars of early forms of the languages. What Sir William Jones advanced in his lectures in Calcutta would help found an entire field – Indo-European studies – that spans a number of disciplines: linguistics, archaeology, history, comparative religion and mythology, anthropology, and comparative literary study (not to mention the specialized data relating to the homeland question yielded by dendrochronology or ethnobotany). At that moment in 1786, the British colonization of India – in the service of which were Oxford men like Jones – would bring English, linguistically, full circle. Here was an older relative of English, descended from the same ancestor, a fact discernible by shared similarities more numerous "than could possibly have been produced by accident." The terminology to the discipline of historical linguistics would come in the next century, but Jones seemed cognizant of many of the major concerns of the discipline that persist to this day, such as the uses of binary comparisons of languages (two languages at a time), or the caveat about the factor of chance in apparent similarities. Though the philological method of the 19th century owes much to the German university system, it was nonetheless Jones's acuity that would enable us to extend the history of English back beyond the Angles, Saxons, and Jutes of the Venerable Bede.

2.2 *INDOGERMANISCH*: THE COMPARATIVE METHOD AND INTERNAL RECONSTRUCTION

A central if muted irony of English historiography is that, for English-speaking students of history, much of what we know, or believe we know, about the early Germans, and our attitude toward the Germanic-speaking tribes of antiquity, is an adoptive classical mindset. Speakers of a 'barbarian' tongue – Anglo-Saxon, or *Englisc* – have adopted the attitudes of Greek and especially Roman historians toward those dwelling in the dark forests beyond the Roman *limites* and threatening Roman garrisons along the Rhine frontier. The *locus classicus* in this regard is Edward Gibbon's *The History of the Decline and Fall of the Roman Empire* (1776–1788), a masterwork of English classical scholarship and English prose style, whose author seems of a decidedly Tacitean cast of mind. And it would be Caesar (100–44 BC) and Tacitus (AD 56–117), the *Commentaries* of the former and *Germania* and *Agricola* of the latter, that generations of English students read in their Latin lessons. The classical curriculum exerted a double influence: students developed a historiographical perspective that identified with the Romans over the Germans (all the more so as the English *imperium* developed), and they understood the workings of language through the prism of the classical languages. Case forms in the declensions, verbal conjugations, figures of speech, and rhetorical devices – all this came to be identified in a wholly borrowed classical lexicon: nominative, genitive, active, and passive. In German education, a similar pattern took hold, though it was infused throughout the 19th century with pulsing tides of German nationalism – *Germania* had a much more concrete sense in German schools. Nowhere else in Europe was philology pursued so methodically – so much so that many of the 'laws' (Grimm's Law, Verner's Law, Grassmann's Law) of sound change and morphology bear names of their German progenitors; through to Eduard Prokosch's *A Comparative Germanic Grammar* (Prokosch 1939[3]), the philological method taught in universities in Great Britain and North America was in many respects a German method. Prokosch's seminal comparative grammar marked the late stage of the Neogrammarian period, as American Structuralism would come to dominate until the 1960s (when the Chomskyan 'revolution' would alter dramatically departments of linguistics in North America, if somewhat less so in Europe). That philological study is of course not entirely immune to extralinguistic considerations is apparent enough in locutions historical linguists employ: Indo-European, Indo-européen, and so forth in the major non-German scholarly journals, but *Indogermanisch* (Indo-Germanic) in the German-speaking academies.

The German stamp on Proto-Indo-European, Proto-Germanic, and history of the English language scholarship is pronounced (in the earlier stages of English, it can even be dominant, especially in historical phonology and morphology). One reason of course is the premier German role in developing the methodology employed in historical linguistics; another, a desire for the light cast by English evidence on the other West Germanic languages. The study of Old and Middle English in particular was cultivated in German universities, reaching a peak in doctoral dissertations published around the turn of the 20th century (let the examples of Middendorff 1902, Köhler 1906, and Schlemilch 1914 suffice).

Some basic principles and methodologies might be outlined here; their application in historical linguistics to the reconstruction of Proto-Indo-European bears directly and indirectly upon the history of English, such as its higher-order genetic relationship with Germanic and Indo-European, or the role of reconstructed protoforms in explaining the relation of English reflexes with PGmc and PIE roots. Two major methods of linguistic reconstruction are employed by historical linguists. The comparative method, of binary (two languages or branches at a time) or, more controversially, multilateral comparison (a number of languages or branches, or in Nostraticist[4] work, entire language families, at a time; cf. Ringe 1999; Manaster Ramer and Hitchcock 1996), in seeking agreement between languages on a feature (a word,

[3]Prokosch was a native of Bohemia, trained in Austria, who taught Germanic philology at American universities, latterly at Yale.

[4]The 'Nostratic Theory' posits a Eurasian linguistic superfamily encompassing Indo-European, Uralic (including the Finno-Ugric family of languages – languages of Europe such as Finnish, Saami, Estonian, and Hungarian that are non-Indo-European), Kartvelian, and, depending upon the school or particular theorist involved, often also Altaic, Afroasiatic, and Dravidian and Proto-Dravidian languages (see, for instance, Bomhard and Kerns 1994); as Nostraticists work at a level of linguistic reconstruction that goes much further back than with Indo-European, and as many Indo-Europeanists have remained skeptical about Nostraticist claims, Nostratic is only touched upon very briefly here (Clackson 2007, 20–23).

or sound, or sound change, morphological feature, etc.). On the basis of a significant number of shared features not arising from chance, the historical linguist proceeds to classify the nature of a language family in terms of overall structure of the 'family tree' (as of Indo-European, Afroasiatic, Uralic, Sino-Tibetan, and others) and the inter-relationship of the branches and subbranches of the family. The method of internal reconstruction relies upon the data of just one language to answer questions about underlying forms, especially the earlier stages or prehistory of a language in an effort, as Herbert Penzl remarked about the reconstruction of Proto-Germanic, "to fill gaps within the historical period" and to aid in the "recovery of the immediate prehistory of each Gmc. dialect" (Penzel in Van Coetsem and Kufner 1972, 8). There is generally observed a distinction in the results of the comparative method, whose reconstructions are called proto-forms (proto-phonemes, proto-languages, etc.), and those of the method of internal reconstruction, which are called pre-forms (pre-phonemes, pre-morphemes, etc.; Fox 1995, 150). A classic example of the latter method in operation is the positing of laryngeals in Indo-European by Swiss linguist Ferdinand de Saussure. Saussure had been looking at ablaut – vowel gradation, as when indicating change in grammatical function; compare MdE *sing sang sung*, the grammatical information conveyed by the root vowel change – in Sanskrit and noticed patterns of gradation in forms of verbs such as *yuj* 'yoke, harness' (class 7) and *pū* 'cleanse, purify' (class 9) such that in the morphological pattern 3rd sing. pres./3rd sing. fut./infinitive one has the vowel gradation series[5] *u ~ o ~ o* (*yunakti / yokṣyati /yoktum*) and *u ~ a ~ a* (*punāti / paviṣyati/pavitum*). To Saussure the second series seemed problematic: the *-ā-* of *punāti* and *-i-* before the future and infinitive endings; Saussure suspected that some element lost in *pū* had made it conjugate less like verbs such as *yuj*, and this reduced grade of the vowel appears as *i* in Sanskrit class 9 verbs (example taken from Fortson 2010, 81–83). Similar suspected discrepancies were noticed in Greek; and so at first two, then three, laryngeal consonants were posited by historical linguists for PIE but largely lost in the daughter languages (reflexes of the laryngeals were identified in Hittite). It is conventional now to represent the laryngeals with the symbols h_1 h_2 h_3; though it is uncertain precisely how these consonants were sounded, they have been thought to be laryngeal (or pharyngeal) fricatives, with the first a neutral laryngeal, the second 'a-colored,' the third 'o-colored' (with reference to the effect of the preceding laryngeal on following PIE **e*; Mallory and Adams 2006, 48–49).

Thus PIE **$h_2$ówis* 'sheep' lies behind Sanskrit *ávi-* (and ultimately MdE *ewe*), **h_2ŕtk'os* 'bear' behind Greek ἄρκτος (*árktos*). What happened to the laryngeals is an enormously complicated matter: loss between vowels led to vowel coalescence, loss in a cluster -VH (word ending in a vowel plus a laryngeal) or VHC (vowel-laryngeal-consonant) produced compensatory lengthening. This we will see in Germanic when consonant loss produces compensatory lengthening of the preceding vowel – OE *riht*

[5]Sanskrit had three vowel 'grades,' simple/positive, *guṇa* ('quality'), *vṛddhi* ('growth, increment'), for example, *i / e / ai*, with the change resulting from a 'prefixed' *a-* vowel (*a-* + *i* > *e*, *a-* + *e* > *ai*); the vowel change is observed in tense-formation (a root such as *dviṣ* 'hate' forms the 3rd sing. pres. in the guṇa grade, *dveṣṭi*, *duh* 'milk' in the 3rd sing. pres. is *dogdhi*), or derivational morphology: for example, the formation of denominative adjectives by *vṛddhi*-increment, thus *daivya* 'of the gods, divine' < *deva* 'god.'

[rixt] > [ri:t], the root vowel of which breaks during the Great Vowel Shift to produce [raɪt] – English orthography fossilized during the tail-end of the GVS, and our spelling *right* preserves the lost consonant. Initial laryngeals could also be vocalized (change into a vowel): PIE *h_2*nér* 'man' > Greek ἀνήρ (*anér*). Despite controversies over the number (here three have been listed, following Ringe 2017, Fortson 2010); four are employed in Mallory and Adams 2006) of laryngeals and their quality, linguists are increasingly confident in what was once called the 'laryngeal theory,' in the face of phonological (the 'trace' left behind by a disappeared laryngeal) and morphological evidence in favor of the laryngeals and the explicative power of their inclusion in reconstructions (Puhvel 1953; Fox 1995, 173–181; Lindeman 1997; Fortson 2010, 62–64). It was the decipherment of Hittite that gave linguists more confidence not only in the 'laryngeal theory' but in their methods of reconstruction also, as Hittite preserves the second and perhaps also third laryngeal as the sound transcribed *ḫ* (Hittite *paḫḫur* < PIE **péh*$_2$*ur* 'fire',[6] Greek πῦρ [*pûr*], OE *fȳr*), in a number of the positions that Saussure had anticipated (an identification made in Kuryłowicz 1927; see also Polomé 1952), and so the comparative method provided corroboration to a product of the method of internal reconstruction (Fox 1995, 146).

2.3 ENGLISH AS A 'GERMANIC' LANGUAGE

English is an Indo-European language, in the super- or macro-family's Germanic branch, within that branch in the West Germanic subbranch or -grouping. The simple formulation that the genetic classification is Indo-European/Germanic/West Germanic belies the historical linguistic enterprise behind linguistic taxonomy and leaves abbreviated the broader implications of grouping the world's languages into families on the basis of linguistic relatedness. In the first instance, the classification gives a sense of chronology. The West Germanic languages – German, English, Dutch, Frisian, Afrikaans, and Yiddish the main representatives – are a relatively young grouping in Indo-European. Though we have, comparatively, an excellent written record for the elder phases of the West Germanic dialects (here 'dialect' is used in the manner of earlier historical linguists: as a reflex of a parent tongue), we are dealing with relatively modern linguistic phenomena – with languages whose origins (or 'birth') are by and large within recorded history. This is certainly the case with English.

One can set *terminus post quem* for English to AD 449 – allowing additionally for the generation or two following the coming of the Germanic tribes for dissimilative distance to form between the Continental dialects of the invaders and those developing in the early Anglo-Saxon kingdoms. Apart from colonial-era pidgins and Creoles, it is relatively rare to witness much less date the 'crucible of change' that leads to language birth. But one can discern traces of English in its 'infancy' of sorts, in manuscripts recording 'early Old English'; a parallel obtains for Old High German, ancestor of modern standard German varieties (Hochdeutsch, Standarddeutsch): we first see

[6]Ringe reconstructs the PIE form as **páh*$_2$*wr̥*, oblique **ph*$_2$*uén-*; the Germanic forms underwent an initial consonant shift by Grimm's Law (ON *fýrr*, Old English *fȳr*; Ringe 2017, 309).

Old High German recorded in the *Vocabularius Sancti Galli* (the 'St. Gall Vocabulary'), St. Gallen, Stiftsbibliothek MS 913 (pp. 181–206 – a manuscript that has been paginated rather than foliated), a small-format glossary manuscript dating to ca. 800 produced in a Swiss abbey founded on the site of an early-7th-century hermitage established by the Irish monk Gallus; St. Gallen would become one of the premier manuscript centers of the early medieval period, its school one in which Irish and English masters instructed German students. Here one finds, in Latin-Old High German pairings, the beginning of the written record of High German in the 'St. Gallen Vocabulary':

domus: huus [Haus, house]
ignis: fuir [Feuer, fire]
cineres: asga [Asche, ashes]
ciuitas: purc [i.e., *burg*; Burg, -burg(h)]
triticus: corn [Korn, corn]
ualles: tal [Tal, -thal, dale]
alto: hoho [Hoch, high]
arena: sant [Sand, sand]
rex: cuninc [König, king]
regina: cuningin [Köningin, queen]
uilla: dorf [Dorf, village (-thorp[e])][7]

The relationship between the Old High German (ca. 6th through 11th centuries) and Modern German, and between earlier and modern forms of German and MdE is clear to see; they are even clearer when we add in Old English correspondences: *huus* (OHG): *hus* (OE), *fuir*: *fȳr*, *asga*: *æsce*, *purc* [*burg*]: *burh*, *corn*: *corn*, *tal*: *dæl*, *hoho* [*hôh*]: *hēah*, *sant*: *sand*, *cuninc*: *cyning*, *dorf*: *þorp* (*cuningin* '[female] king, queen' presents the one anomaly here with the feminine termination *-in*; OE *cwēn* 'queen' presents an interesting development in English; < PGmc **kʷēniz*, compare Old Saxon *quān*, though Old Frisian and Old High German lack cognates; cf. Ringe in Ringe and Taylor 2014, 146). The spelling *purc*, with voiced stops devoiced, may give evidence of the High (or second) German consonant shift; we see early evidence of it in Lombard legal documents in Latin (e.g., *berg* as *perg* in the *Edictum Rotharii* of 643). What is of moment at this juncture is the composition of the West Germanic subbranch of Indo-European (Figure 2.1): the set of Germanic languages most closely related to English. The matter has, over the history of the scholarship since the early 19th century, become rather complex in terms of the constitution of branches of Germanic languages and chronology, but it can be useful to begin with the traditional groupings.

The branches of Germanic above include both languages whose descendants are living tongues and others that have gone extinct – indeed, the East Germanic branch as a whole is considered extinct, though Crimean Gothic may have survived as late

[7]The entries appear in St. Gallen MS 913 at the following pages (letters refer to the columns of glossary text): 181cd (*huus*); 183cd (*fuir, asga*); 184cd (*corn*); 185ab (*tal*); 185cd (*hoho, sant*); 186cd (*cuninc, cuningin*); an online facsimile of the manuscript is available at *e-codices, St. Gallen, Stiftsbibliothek*: http://www.e-codices.unifr.ch/en/description/csg/0913.

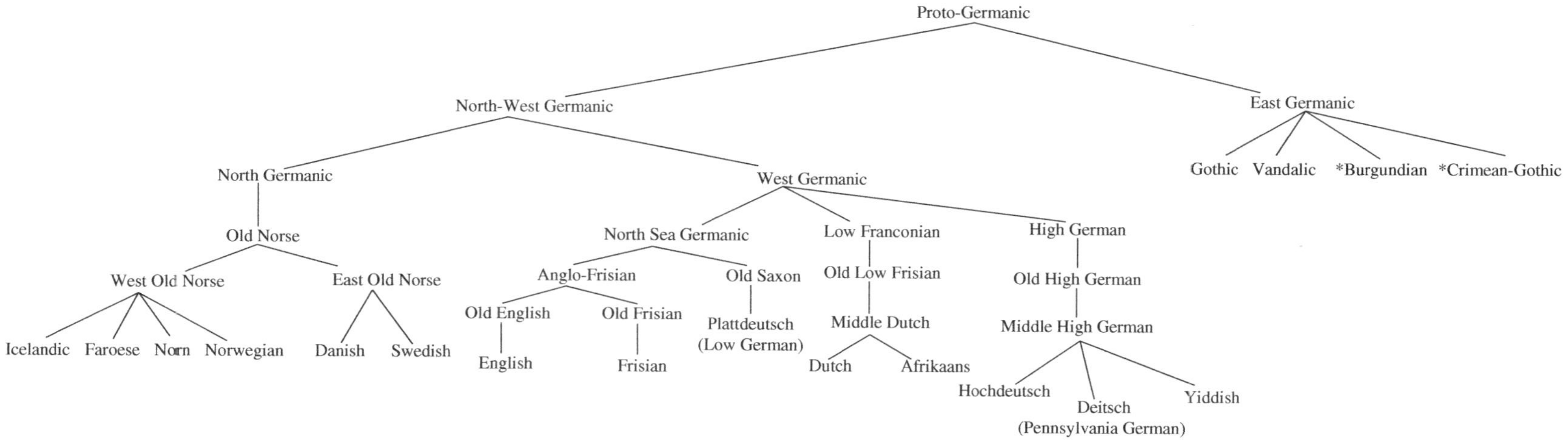

FIGURE 2.1 The Germanic family tree (collated with Harbert 2007, Ringe and Taylor 2014; the notation * indicates extinct languages).

West Germanic	**North Germanic**	**East Germanic**
Old English	Early Runic	Gothic
Old Frisian	Old Norse	*Vandalic
Old Saxon	West Old Norse	*Burgundian
Old Low Franconian	East Old Norse	*Crimean Gothic
Old High German		

as the 18th century. The division of West Germanic into three geographic branches reflects Tacitus's placement of the Ingaevones, Istvaeones, and Hermiones into, respectively, the North Sea coast, Rhine-Weser, and Elbe regions. While Tacitus's scheme was not accurate in terms of tribal names, the linguistic adoption, for a time, of these terms allowed for a more specific subbranching of West Germanic languages: English and Frisian (Frysk) derive from the 'Anglo-Frisian' of this classification, and Low German (Plattdeutsch/Plattdüütsch) from Old Saxon; in the Istvaeonic branch, Low Franconian or 'Old Dutch' lies behind Dutch, while High Franconian was a dialect of OHG; the Irminonic branch included varieties of 'Upper German' OHG (Alemannic, Bairisch). It is to the designations Ingvaeonic and 'Anglo-Frisian' that we shall return in Chapter 4, as here one finds the cradle of English – and to some extent, the early English may have been conscious of a cultural link: Ingvaeonic is the Latinized form for 'people of Yngvi,' Yngvi likely associated with ON *Ingr*, a god-name often thought to be a byname for Freyr, god of fertility; the *ing*-rune (for /ŋ/) appears in the elder futhark as ◇.

While Old English, Old High German, and Old Norse are richly attested in the manuscripts, other languages survive only in fragmentary form, or only in personal or place-names; what little there is of Vandalic may include this late Roman view from North Africa of Germanic table manners:

> Inter 'eils' Goticum 'scapia matzia ia drincan'
> non audet quisquam dignos edicere versus (Shackleton Bailey 1982, no. 279)
>
> Midst Gothic 'Heils' and 'Bring fọod, bring drink,'
> no one dares utter lines any more worthy.

A Roman North African epigrammatist of the end of the empire looks askance at the barbarians at the *convivium*; the formal dinner with its courses and entertainments in the banqueting room with *triclinia* (low couches); the *Goticum* here may be Vandalic, the Vandals having overrun the late Roman North Africa that was the milieu of a number of the poems in the Latin Anthology. If the Roman eye observes caustically the barbarian German manners at the once-formal dinner custom, the ear for early Germanic seems fairly accurate – accurate enough that we can instantly recognize *eils* as the greeting *Heils* (Heil, hail) and *drincan* 'to drink' as the infinitive form (OE *drincan*), accurate enough, in fact, that with the help of Gothic, we can recognize it as East Germanic. One imagines that our bemused Roman North African must have had more than a passing familiarity with the language of the now ascendant barbarian Germanic tribes:

scapia: compare Gothic *ga-skapjan* ('make' – perhaps here in sense of 'furnish, provide')
matzia: Gothic *matjan* ('to eat')
ia: Gothic *jah* ('and')
drincan: Gothic *drigkan* ('to drink')

The *drincan* ('to drink') example from the Latin Anthology verse allows for a comparison across the branches of Germanic languages: the possibly Vandalic *drincan*,

Gothic *drigkan* in East Germanic, OE *drincan* and OHG *trinkan* in West Germanic, and Old Norse *drekka* (with assimilation of *-nk-* to *-kk-*) in North Germanic, evidence not only how closely related the daughter languages are but also the phonological changes that map out the geographical labels – that is, why there are such branches. The evidence of *cognates* – literally, forms sharing their birth together, deriving from the same source form, having the same etymology – is invaluable to linguistic reconstruction of earlier forms in the 'parent' languages. Here, the 'parent' language is a reconstructed Proto-Germanic, conventionally placed ca. 500 BC, with some ancestor to Proto-Germanic and Italo-Celtic being spoken for perhaps some two millennia earlier than the Proto-Germanic period. That is, Proto-Germanic as a reconstructible ancestor to English did not break off from Proto-Indo-European directly: the time-depth has deepened and the family tree of Indo-European languages has been realigned and modified with advances in historical linguistics in the past 40 years especially. What may be said about the prehistory of English can span centuries prior to its 'birth' in the AD 5th century; the evidence of cognates, the regularity of sound changes, and the tools of the comparative method to offer reconstructions that reach back from the attested early stages of languages allow for linguistic 'prehistory.'

Reconstruction can also fill in gaps in recorded histories of languages too. The OHG *cuninc* ('king') form from the St. Gallen glossary above has cognates in OE (*cyning*) and ON (*konungr*); its etymology is debated, a common hypothesis being that the Germanic word for 'king' has to do with 'kin' (OE *cyning* and *cynn*). As Gothic was preserved largely in the 4th-century biblical translation by St. Ulfilas, made from the Greek, we find there Gothic *kaisar* for Greek καῖσαρ (*kaîsar*) 'Caesar' and *þiudans* for βασιλεύς (*basileūs*) 'king' (compare OE *þeoden* 'chief of a tribe, ruler, prince'); but we see also *kuni* 'family, tribe' and can conceivably imagine a Gothic cognate was possible (but not recorded). Working backwards, in a sense, one moves from the narrowest of genetic groupings for English, West Germanic, to a broader (and older) branch grouping, Germanic. The St. Gallen manuscript gives a sense of how closely related the West Germanic languages OE and OHG were despite the variation the Second Germanic Consonant Shift produced; the Gothic examples, from East Germanic, in conjunction with cognates from West and North Germanic languages, give in brief form a sense of the relatedness among Germanic languages across the three subbranches (East, West, and North).

What then does it mean to say that English is a Germanic language? The similarities between earlier stages of West Germanic languages do not prevent some confusion about the nature of contemporary English; as will be seen, English has in its development borrowed extensively from other languages (over 300, by the count of the OED), especially from Greek, and Latin, and the Romance languages. French remains a principal source of loanwords into English, and in the post-Conquest (1066 and later) period, it has also exerted phonological influence. The simplest explanation is that English, borrowings and influence from Latin and Romance languages notwithstanding, is genetically and historically a Germanic tongue. This means, quite simply, that English developed from a parent Germanic tongue, normatively reconstructed as Proto-Germanic, and so has as its inheritance core phonological, morphological, syntactic, and lexical features that are Germanic and shared by the daughter languages. In the case of English, its 'Germanic-ness' is easier to see the earlier the records of its history one examines: Old English the modern learner generally approaches as one would a foreign tongue, with a grammar and glossary at the ready; Middle English is still grammatically and orthographically distant from contemporary usage but more familiar in its pronoun system and vocabulary; by the Early Modern period, with inflectional decay (deflexion) and increasing orthographical stability (a product of both the printing press and educational standards), what is unfamiliar to the modern eye becomes rather the exception. In a loose sense, English becomes superficially an outlier in the Germanic family of languages, its particular history of the utmost value in determining the causes to such seeming dramatic change in the course of the language's evolution. But to the comparatist's eye, English is Germanic.[8]

In the classic treatment of the earlier Germanic languages and the basis for reconstructing proto-Germanic Eduard Prokosch provided 'specimen texts' to illustrate core features and divergences (largely phonological, occasionally grammatical and syntactic); given the source of the introduction of writing to the early Germanic tribes, the texts that recur across the branches of Germanic were all Biblical, and range from the 4th century (Gothic) through the 8th and 9th centuries (Old Saxon, Old High German), reflecting either the time of conversion and introduction of Roman or Greek-derived script (the Gothic script developed by Ulfilas), or the organization of scriptoria with native scribes (such as those Old High German-speaking scribes at St. Gallen trained by Irish and English missionaries). Though a much-used example, the translations of the 'Paternoster' (*Pater noster*, 'Our Father') have enormous illustrative value. Though translating from Greek rather than the Latin Vulgate, Ulfilas's Gothic version is the earliest into a Germanic language[9]:

Οὕτος οὖν προσεύχεσθε ὑμεῖς·	Swa nu bidjaiþ jus:
Πάτηρ ἡμῶν ὁ ἐν τοῖς οὐρανοῖς·	atta unsar þu in himinam,
ἁγιασθήτω τὸ ὄνομά σου·	weihnai namo þein.
ἐλθέτω ἡ βασιλεία σου·	qimai þiudinassus þeins.
γενηθήτω τὸ θέλημά σου,	Wairþai wilja þeins,
ὡς ἐν ουρανῷ καὶ ἐπὶ γῆς·	swe in himina jah ana airþai.
τὸν ἄρτον ἡμῶν τὸν ἐπιούσιον δὸς ἡμῖν σήμερον·	hlaif unsarana þana sinteinan gif uns himma daga.
καὶ ἄφες ἡμῖν τὰ ὀφειλήματα ἡμῶν,	jah aflet uns þatei skulans sijaima,
ὡς καὶ ἡμεῖς ἀφήκαμεν τοῖς ὀφειλέταις ἡμῶν·	swaswe jah weis afletam þaim skulam unsaraim.
καὶ μὴ εἰσενέγκῃς ἡμᾶς εἰς πειρασμόν,	jah ni briggais uns in fraistubnjai,
ἀλλὰ ῥῦσαι ἡμᾶς ἀπὸ τοῦ πονηροῦ (Mt 6: 9–13).	ak lausei uns af þamma ubilin;
	unte þeina ist þiudangardi jah mahts jah

[8]Harbert (2007) had noted that "English is in many respects a typological outlier in the GMC [Gmc] family" (13); this will indeed be seen in terms of such matters as the pronoun system, the lack of an indefinite *man*-type pronoun in English, its loss of grammatical gender, and other features – all, however, in the face of a conventional acceptance of English as Germanic in its genetic typology.

[9]Greek taken from Streitberg and Scardigli (2000), collated with Aland et al. (1998); Gothic from Streitberg and Scardigli (2000).

[Hoútos oun proseúchesthe humeis / Páter hēmōn ho en tois ouranois, / Hagiasthēto to ónomá sou, / Elthéto hē basileía sou, / Genēthéto to thélēmá sou, / Hōs en ouranō kai epi gēs, / ton árton hēmōn ton epioúsion dos hēmin sēmeron, / kai áphes hēmin ta ophei-lémata hēmōn, / Hōs kai mē hēmeis aphḗkamen tois opheilétais hēmōn, / kai mē eisenegkēs hēmas eis peirasmón, / alla rhusai hēmas apo tou ponērou.]

wulþus in aiwins amen.

Following the Gothic version, very literally, we have: "So now pray ye: father our thou in heavens, may be holy name thine, come kingdom thine. Come to be will thine, as in heaven so on earth. Loaf our the daily give us this-day. And release us that debtors we be, just as we release them debtors ours. But loose us from the evil one. For thine is kingdom and might and glory in eternity. Amen." When the Gothic and Old English translations are compared, the correspondences are many, if some are obscured by the developments across the branches of Germanic:

Gothic	**Old English**
atta unsar þu in himinam	fæder ūre þū þe eart on heofenum
weihnai namo þein	sī þīn nama ġehālgod
qimai þiudinassus þeins	tōbecume þīn rīce

Gothic *atta* preserves an old form of respectful address for older males (PIE **átta*), 'dad, father,' with which may be compared Hittite *attas* 'father,' Greek *ἄττα* (*átta* 'father,' as a term of address from younger to older males), and Latin *atta* ('father,' 'term of respect used when addressing old men'; OLD, s.v.); OE *fæder* like Latin *pater* descends from PIE *ph_2tér* (cf. Ringe 2017, 89). Dative plural forms *himinam* (Gothic) and *heofenum* (OE) evidence developments in WGmc departing from PGmc **himinaz* (whence Gothic *himins* 'heaven'): OE *heofun* descends from northern WGmc **hebun* whereas the Old High German and Old Saxon *himil* (and Modern German *Himmel*) descend from PWGmc **himil*, though the change is not yet understood (Ringe in Ringe and Taylor 2014, 272 and n. 29). Gothic *weihnai* and OE *ġe-hālgod*, derive, respectively, from the weak verbs (see Chapter 4.3) *weihnan* (class IV) and *ġe-hālgian* (class II), 'to make holy,' the translators choosing 3rd singular present subjunctive (***weihnai*** *namo þein* 'may be holy name thine') and the periphrastic past subjunctive (***sī*** *þīn nama* ***ġehālgod*** 'may be thine name hallowed': *sī(e)* 3rd sing. pres. subjunctive of *wesan* 'to be, exist' + past ptc. *ġehālgod*; emphasis added). Gothic *qimai* and OE *tōbecume* do not at first seem to correspond, but they do quite closely. Both are 3rd sing. pres. subjunctive forms, of class 4 strong verbs *qiman* and *cuman*, the OE verb a prepositional form: *tō-* + *be-* + *cuman*, with an intensified sense of 'become, come about.' Both verbs derive from PIE **gwem-* 'step, go' (compare Sanskrit *gam*, *gacchati* 'go'), with /g/ > /k/ by Grimm's Law; PGmc *k^wemaną* 'to go, come' > PWGmc **kweman*, with the apparent shift *wi > *u in West Germanic. As East Germanic Gothic [q] represented /kʷ/ *qiman* is closer to the PGmc form while in West Germanic **kweman* > **kwiman* > **kuman*. The 'kingdom' in 'Thy kingdom come,' Gothic *þiudinassus* and OE *rīċe* (< PGmc **rīkją* 'kingdom, rule; power') involve lexical choice, and OE did have as well cognate forms of Gothic *þiudinassus* (< *þiudan* 'ruler, leader, king' + suffix *-assus* < **-assu*, in Gothic the deverbal abstract noun suffix *-inassu-* = 'kingdom'; Lehmann 1986, 361–362; Ringe 2017, 325; Ringe in Ringe and Taylor 2014, 131–132): OE *þēodnes* 'association, assembly' < *þēoden* 'chieftain, prince' + *-nes*. Here the OE translator of the West Saxon version of the 'Our Father' chose *rīċe* over the much lower-frequency *þēodnes*.

The corpus of Gothic that remains to us is very limited: what remains of Ulfilas's translation of the Bible – parts of the Gospels of Matthew and John, most of Luke and Mark, a fairly good part of the Pauline epistles, and just Nehemiah from the Old Testament; the *Skeireins* – 'explanation, interpretation,' the word itself appears in Ulfilas's translation at 1 Cor 12:10; compare the verb *ga-skeirjan* 'to explain, interpret, clarify,' and adjective *skeirs* 'clear' – preserved in a palimpsest in the Vatican Library (Biblioteca Apostolica Vaticana, Vat. lat. 5750); a fragmentary 'Gothic calendar' in Codex Ambrosianus A; various brief documents, including a deed preserved on a Naples papyrus dating to 551 and recent discoveries in the 1970s of further biblical fragments (see Scardigli in Streitberg and Scardigli 2000, 499–515). What is of interest is that the early remains of Old English, Old Saxon, and Old High German consist of most of the same types of materials. To return to Prokosch's 'specimen texts,' we might compare the opening of the 'Paternoster' in West Germanic languages, which were translated from the Vulgate Latin version (*Pater noster, qui es in celis*, "Our Father, who art in heaven"):

Old English (West Saxon Gospels)

Fæder ūre þū þe eart on heofonum, si þīn nama gehālgōd.

Old Saxon (Heliand, 'The Savior,'[10])

Fadar ûsa, thu bist an them himila rīkea. Geuuīhid sī thīn namo.

Old High German

Fater unsēr, dū pist in himilum, kauuīhit sī namo dīn. [the 'Freisinger Paternoster,' 9th-century 'bairisch'/Bavarian OHG dialect]

Fater unseer, thū pist in himile, uuīhi namun dīnan [the 'Sankt Galler Paternoster,' from the *Abrogans* glossary manuscript, St. Gallen, Stiftsbibliothek 911[11]]

Fater unser, thū thār bist in himile, sī giheilagōt thīn namo [from the OHG version of Tatian's gospel harmony the *Diatessaron*, in early 9th-century East Franconian dialect]

Fater unsēr, thu in himilon bist, giuuīhit sī namo thīn [from the 'Weissenburger catechism,' of the late 8th century, in the South Rhine Franconian dialect][12]

[10]Based on what survives of OE, OS, and OHG poetry, poems of an epic cast based on Biblical paraphrase (and recasting) were fairly popular: for example, some 600 lines of the OS *Genesis* appear in OE as *Genesis B* in the Junius manuscript (Bodleian Library, MS Junius 11).

[11]The St. Gallen Alemannic OHG Paternoster is to be found at pp. 320–322 of MS 911; a digital facsimile is available at: http://www.e-codices.unifr.ch/en/description/csg/0911.

[12]Cf. Prokosch (1939), 32–34, 294–295; Ebbinghaus and Braune (1994).

One notices in these early Germanic versions of the Lord's Prayer, from Gothic in the 4th century (preserved in an early-6th-century manuscript) to Old High German versions of the 8th and 9th centuries, broad similarities in the 'Germanicization' of the Greek and Latin originals; by and large, for instance, the dative plural form in the opening line, ἐν τοῖς οὐρανοῖς / *in celis* ('in the heavens') is rendered by dative plural forms in the Gmc (Gothic *in himinam*; OE *on heofonum*; OHG *in himilum*). The OHG Tatian renders the dat. pl. original as dat. sing. *in himile*, and one finds, in North Germanic, ON versions in both numbers (*í hifne* [dat. sing.], *í himnum* [dat. pl.]). Vocabulary for 'to hallow' (in 'hallowed be Thy Name') is split between two forms: those cognate with modern English 'hallow' (OE *ġe-hālgian* and OHG *[gi-]heilagon*, OS *helagon* < PGmc. **hailags-* 'holy'), and those cognate with *Weih-* as in MdG *Weihnachten* ('in the Holy Nights; Christmas'; **weihs-*, 'holy,' perhaps < PIE **weyk-*; it has been suggested that *weihs*-forms belong to southern Gmc dialects, with **hailags* the northern form[13]). Interestingly, Old English preserves reflexes of both PGmc forms: *hāliġ* ('holy'), *hālgian* ('to hallow, sanctify, consecrate') and related forms seem to have been fully Christianized and became part of an Anglo-Saxon liturgical lexis, while *weih-* forms, appearing in OE as *wēoh-* or much more commonly *wiġ-* (not to be confused with *wīgan* 'to fight' and *wīg-* 'battle, fight' compounds, which derive from a separate etymological complex: PGmc **wiganą* 'to fight'; Ringe in Ringe and Taylor 2014, 36) often have to do with 'heathen' or 'pagan' customs: *wiġle* 'divination,' *wiġlere* 'soothsayer, wizard,' *wiġlian* 'to take auspices, divine,' *wiġlung* 'soothsaying, augury, witchcraft.'[14] Orthography aside – we see the preverbal variously as *ge-* (OS, and OE), *ka-* ('Bavarian' OHG), *gi-* (East Franconian OHG) – the affinities of WGmc dialects are readily apparent. And Gothic, separated by time and geographical space, seems nonetheless not all that distant in its relation.

With regard to the history of English, the chronology and geography of the early Germanic-speaking tribes are of interest to placing English in its Germanic context. The Proto-Germanic period puts us largely beyond the historical in at least two ways: prior to the recorded observations of Greek and Roman historians on the Germanic 'barbarians' (Herodotus and Pytheas of Massalia among the first to mention them; see Chapter 3 for more on the classical historians) and prior to the earliest inscriptions recording an early Germanic tongue. Nearly every matter regarding 'Germanic' is subject to controversy, historical or linguistic. But the comparative wealth of writing that survives in early Germanic languages allows nonetheless for quite some precision, enough that we can speak with some assurance of the place of English within West Germanic, of West Germanic within Germanic, and of Germanic within Indo-European.

---

[13]Cf. Scardigli (1973); Lehmann (1986), s.v. *weihs* (1) at 398–399; the type of verb involved here *weihan*, a factitive 'to make X' (X being the adjective from which the verb has been derived; thus 'to make holy, hallow'), may derive from PIE; cf. Ringe 2017, 204).

[14]Mallory and Adams (2006) also mention possible association with PIE **weik-* 'appear,' in the sense that *wēoh* = 'image, idol' (325–326).

Much more complex is the move from branch to superfamily, Indo-European. But it is important in terms of the Indo-European and Germanic 'inheritance' of English, of how English is Indo-European and Germanic, and of what significance such designations may be.

2.4 THE INDO-EUROPEAN LANGUAGES

The Indo-European family of languages is, linguistically speaking, the most intensively studied of the world's language families – to a certain extent, the discipline of historical linguistics with its comparative method developed in tandem with the 'discovery' and the classification of the branches of Indo-European, from the days of Sir William Jones (1746–1794) to the decipherment of Hittite (the oldest recorded IE language) in the early decades of the 20th century and of Linear B by Michael Ventris and John Chadwick in 1951–1953 (Ventris announced the decipherment in a BBC radio broadcast 1 July 1952; cf. Chadwick 1990). If Indo-European has lost its central place in linguistics,[15] a product of the increasing distance between 'philology' and the modern 'science' of linguistics and the increasingly theoretical orientation of many Anglo-American departments of linguistics, its study has nonetheless produced a number of exciting developments since the 1960s. There are somewhat more than 455 languages, living and extinct in the family (Ethnologue 2025 count), of which 70–100 can be considered 'major' in terms of numbers of speakers. Roughly half the world's population speaks an Indo-European tongue as a first or second language; the space on the world map in which an Indo-European language is not either primary or official (in government language policy) can be closed over when considering either colonial legacies (as with Egypt or Kenya, or Singapore or the Philippines) or factors of globalization, spurring especially the learning of English as an educational, scientific, or financial *lingua franca* (as with China, Saudi Arabia, Kuwait, and the Gulf States; see Chapter 12). Advances in linguistic cladistics are such that the early *Stammbaumtheorie* (family-tree-theory) of German linguist August Schleicher (1821–1868) has been supplanted by more mathematical and phylogenetic approaches. As the notion of languages being genetically related in terms of descent from parent languages involved a biological metaphor to begin with, the recent developments are not surprising. Two competing tree-models or phylogenies, the 2002 New Zealand model (Bouckaert et al. 2012) and the 2002 Pennsylvania tree (Ringe et al. 2002), will be examined briefly in terms of the placement of Germanic and English within the Indo-European family of languages. How English 'behaves' as a language, the nature of its phonemic inventory, the cumulative change wrought by sound laws, the conditioning of morphological processes, and syntactic tendencies (as with subject–verb order, dependent clauses, etc.) are in good part an Indo-European inheritance. And English, Old English especially, because of its long recorded history (in the face of its relative youth as a

---

[15]See, for instance, Clackson (2007), 1.

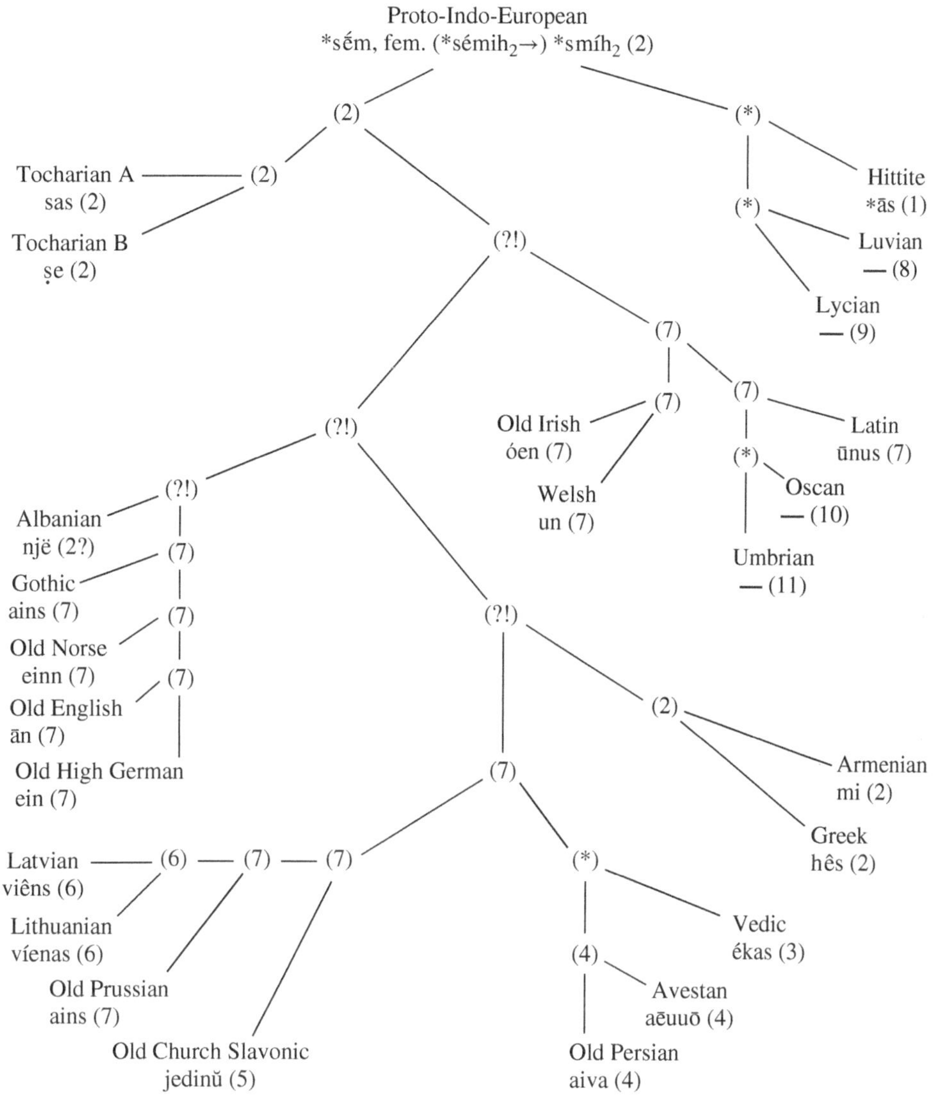

FIGURE 2.2 Pennsylvania tree, IE forms for 'one'. *Source:* Modified from Ringe et al. (2002).

spoken tongue), in turn supplies evidence for the reconstruction of proto-forms in Proto-Germanic and Proto-Indo-European (Figure 2.2).

It is important to note methodological differences between the teams of researchers: the New Zealand team relied primarily upon the lexis, vocabulary tokens, of modern IE languages in drawing up their tree diagram, while the Pennsylvania team also considered morphological and especially phonological tokens from the earliest recorded IE languages (cf. Clackson 2007, 10–15). Member languages in either phylogeny range in age from Hittite, whose earliest records (in Old Hittite) date to the early kingdom period ca. 1800 BC, to the Nuristani languages of Eastern Afghanistan:

their study is ongoing – Ethnologue lists six member languages (Ashkun, Kateviri, Komviri, Prasuni, Tregami, and Waigali; Ethnologue 2025) – and classifies them as Indo-European/Indo-Iranian/Nuristani. The Nuristani languages present something of a puzzle to linguists, as they clearly share phonological developments with Iranian languages, but "preserve some features of reconstructed Proto-Indo-Iranian that are not found elsewhere in the branch" (Fortson 2010, 203). The decipherment of Hittite and Linear B (identified as a Mycenaean form of Greek) pushed back the datable evidence (Linear B to approximately 1400 BC); our other early evidence comes from Mitanni, and this case, largely lexical evidence of Hurrian in what is otherwise a non-Indo-European language, raises a number of difficulties and methodological points. Archaeology plays a significant role here in initial identification of once-lost cultures by means of the material culture: pottery types, village or city planning, temple-building and other monumental architecture, and the iconography of the corpus of sculpture – evidence that can be all the more vital if no written records are found or if those discovered remain indecipherable. 'New' Indo-European languages can be discovered either through further linguistic fieldwork, refinements to language cladistics (as in the case of the more recently identified Nuristani languages), or by the decipherment of previously unreadable texts. Hittite was recorded in both hieroglyphic and, more commonly, cuneiform writing systems. Documents appearing in copies in multilingual archives opened the door to decipherment: such as at Amarna in Egypt, the 14th-century BC archive of pharaoh Akhenaten, where a cache of some 300 cuneiform tablets recording diplomatic correspondence attested to relations among the major powers of the Eastern Mediterranean (Egyptians, Syrians, Akkadians, Hittites, and others), or at Boğazköy in North-Central Turkey, the site of the Hittite capital Hattušas and its sacred city Yazılıkaya and the royal archives (Macqueen 1986, 26–32). Indeed, monuments in Hieroglyphic Hittite in Northern Syria and across much of Anatolia (Asia Minor) first led archaeologists to associate the unknown culture behind them with the Hittites, a people previously known mainly from contemporaneous records of other peoples – including the Hebrew Bible: when Sarah dies aged 127 at Kiriatharba (Hebron) in the land of Canaan, Abraham arranges to purchase Machpelah (known thereafter as the cave of the patriarchs) from Ephron the Hittite, for at that time the 'people of the land' were the *filii Heth* (Vulgate) or 'sons of Heth' (KJV): the Hittites.

It may seem a long way between cuneiform tablets of ca. 1800 BC adapting the Semitic Akkadian syllabary to Indo-European Hittite usage to the 'sons of Heth' in the English Bible of 1611, but the methods employed in the decipherment of Hittite, drawing on what was known of other Indo-European languages once it was determined that Hittite was indeed Indo-European, are those essential to any historical linguistic reconstruction. To return to the Mitanni, several difficult matters present themselves: the Indo-Aryan material discovered in Mitanni appears to form part of a **superstrate** (or *superstratum*): that is, a language in a contact situation that has more prestige or power (as through conquest).[16] In this case, it may be that the Indo-Aryan

[16]The matter of substrate (*substratum*) influence will be discussed in the following chapters in regard to the conquest of Celtic-speaking Britain by Germanic-speaking tribes and the contentious matter of what sorts of substrate influence Celtic languages in Britain exerted upon early English.

element was introduced to a Hurrian-speaking population in what is now Southeastern Turkey, Northern Syria, and Northwestern Iraq by military elites who formed the Mitanni empire from the Hurrian kingdom. A mid-14th-century BC treaty between King Suppululiuma(s) I of the Hittites and Shattiwaza of the Mitanni has the Mitanni king, after acknowledging the overlordship of his Hittite father-in-law, swear an oath by a constellation of gods, the majority of them familiar Near Eastern deities (Anu, Enlil, and the ever-present Storm God in Hittite texts [unnamed here, usually Pirwa is meant]) but toward the end of the series come *Mi-it-ra* (compare Indic Mitra), *Aru-na* (Indic Varuṇa), *In-da-ra* (Indic Indra), and *Na-ša-at-iyas* (the Nasatyas, or Aśvins; compare Avestan *Nåŋhaiθya*; West 2007, 187). These are familiar names from the *Ṛgveda*, the early Vedic pairing Mitra-Varuṇa – appearing in Vedic in the dual form *Mitravaruṇau*; the dual number in declensional morphology we shall see Old English preserved in its personal pronoun system – and Indra (compare Avestan *Indar*), the king of the gods, a god of war and thunder with his thunderbolt (Thor a Germanic counterpart). Hittite texts also preserve Indo-Aryan forms, including the famous horse-training manual of Kikkuli (ca. 1350 BC; Kammenhuber 1961); the trainer himself is called *assussani*, an Indo-Aryan form cognate with Sanskrit *aśva-sani*, and terms for laps on the race-course also have clear Sanskrit cognates: *a-i-ka-wa-ar-ta-an-na* ('consisting of a lap'), *pa-an-za-wa-ar-ta-an-na* ('consisting of five laps'); the second half of the compounds may be compared with Sanskrit *vartana* ('turning,' from *vṛt* 'turn'), and the numerals in the compounds may be compared with Vedic (and later Sanskrit) *eka* 'one' and *pañca* 'five' (Mallory 1989, 36–42; Fortson 2010, 206–207).

The parallels are more than linguistic, but point to the equine culture of the Indo-Europeans, expansion by horse-borne warriors, a martial culture noted for horse-drawn chariots, and even a sacral role for and veneration of horses. The Vedic *aśva-medha*, or 'horse-sacrifice,' in kingly consecrations was an elaborate ritual, mentioned in the *Ṛgveda* Book I and detailed more fully in the *Yajurveda*; the ritual is performed under Yudhiṣṭhira in Book XIV of the *Mahābhārata* (the *aśva-medhika-parvan*). The culture of the pahlavāns (horse-borne warriors; 'heroes, champions') pervades the heroic age books of the Persian *Shāh-nāma*, the hero Rustam accompanied by his steed Raksh ('luminous one'). There are parallels across the branches of Indo-European and a number, somewhat less close, or more attenuated, in Celtic and Germanic (Mallory and Adams 2006, 154, 437; West 2007, 187–192, 417–419, 496–498). In short, we find here a cultural complex accompanying the linguistic cognates. The parallels in god names between Mitanni and Vedic point to the controversial but rapidly developing notions about Indo-European religion; Old Persian preserves cognate forms as well, and we see here evidence of similarity in the naming and cultivation of divinities (often associated with hierarchical roles and natural forces) across a wide swath of the Eastern reach of the Indo-European family: from Anatolia through Persia to India. The early date to the Indo-Aryan loans in Mitanni "attests the existence of a very archaic form of the Indic language as early as 1600 BC. This indicates that a separate Indo-Aryan language had already diverged from Iranian by this time and that the putative period of proto-Indo-Iranian 'unity' must predate this, perhaps by as much as a half millennium or more" (Mallory 1989, 38).

So far, the oldest branches in the Indo-European family of languages have been touched upon. Anatolian includes Hittite, the oldest and best attested language in this branch, as well as Lycian, Lydian, and the relatively poorly attested Palaic, Carian, Pisidian, and Sidetic (Fortson 2010, 170–198, for descriptions and text samples). Luwian (or Luvian) is found also in two dialects, Hieroglyphic Luwian and Cuneiform Luwian (Payne 2004; Woudhuizen 2018); Lycian, of Southwestern Anatolia (the region around classical Xanthos), is less well-attested in inscriptions dated later (5th century BC), including the famous Xanthos stele preserving on its four sides a trilingual inscription in Lycian, Greek, and Aramaic; the surviving stele was built as part of a cult of Leto and bears witness to the process of Hellenization in Lycia, and a recent study suggests that the Lycian dynast behind the monument was Gergis (the Greek form of Lycian *xeriga*; Domingo Gygax and Tietz 2005). On the sides of the stele itself, Lycian appears in two forms: the Lycian A known from other inscriptions and, on two of the sides, what is called Lycian B or Milyan; Lycian employed a Greek-derived script. Lydian survives in inscriptions dating to the 8th through 4th centuries BC in alphabetic scripts deriving from Greek or Old Phrygian (Fortson 2010, 195–196); again, an inscription involving more than one language helps in reading the lesser known or as-yet-undeciphered language from a known language, in this case the ca. 400 BC bilingual Lydian-Aramaic inscription from Sardis, the Lydian capital (Gusmani 1964). Phrygian was an Indo-European language spoken in Anatolia but its filiation within the family is not known, and so it appears outside the tree diagrams (as often do Thracian, Illyrian, Macedonian [once spoken in the area from Bulgaria to Northern Greece], Venetic and Messapic, from Italy's northeast and southeast, and Lusitanian [Portugal]). Phrygian achieved fame in Herodotus's story (*The History*, Book II) of Pharaoh Psammetichus I (Psamtik I), who inquired into what the world's original language might be; infants were removed from their parents, their first words awaited. One day, one of the infants uttered the word *bekos*, Phrygian for 'bread,' and so the pharaoh had his answer (cf. also Fortson 2010, 460–463). It might be added, coincidental to this look at Anatolia as an Indo-European language area, that Herodotus was born in Caria in Western Anatolia, a native of Halicarnassus, his father a Greek-speaker, his mother's language Carian.

Our next oldest branch in Indo-European is Indo-Iranian; as mentioned previously, scholars have debated the date of the breakup of this large grouping of IE languages; the Indo-Aryan forms in Mitanni alluded to earlier would necessitate a date certainly before the middle of the 2nd millennium BC. At any rate, Indo-Iranian is attested as the second oldest branch of IE, and one with, in the Indic subbranch, a large number of extant daughter languages descended from the Prakrits in regular spoken use (Sanskrit reserved for sacral uses): from such Prakrits derive many of the modern languages of India: Hindi, Punjabi, Sindhi, Bengali, Gujarati, Marathi, Sinhalese, and Romany (the language of the Roma, or 'Gypsies'). The Iranian languages are attested earliest in the language of the Zoroastrian scriptures (the Gathas, or *Gāθās*), Avestan, and in Old Persian, the language of the early inscriptions, such as the bilingual Behistun inscription ca. 500 BC of Darius the Great; modern daughter languages include Farsi (Persian), Kurdish, Balochi, Pashto and Dari of Afghanistan, Luri, and Tajik – some 83 languages by Ethnologue's count (Ethnologue 2025). How closely related Old Persian and Old Indic are can be seen in the formulaic royal title repeated in the inscriptions of Darius I: *xšāyaθiya xšāyaθiyānām*, 'king of kings' (Kent 1989, 134); a grammatical and lexical parallel may be found in Sanskrit *kṣatriya kṣatriyānām*, which is not a title for ancient Indian kings but reflects the cultural tradition of the *kṣatriya* caste as one of warrior-rulers – a pattern with cultural cognates across Indo-European finding expression in the Indic branch in Vedic literature and Sanskrit heroic epics such as the *Mahābhārata*.

Here, we might turn for a moment to examples of sound laws, instrumental in determining linguistic filiation within families and branches of families. The Proto-Indo-European root *b^hewd^h-* (Ringe 2017, 22) 'observe, be aware' has a reflex in Sanskrit *budh-* (< **bhudh-*) 'awaken'; the addition of the past participle marker *-tá-* produced **bhudh-tó* > *buddha-* 'awakened, [therefore] enlightened.' A phonological change has spread through clusters of obstruents (clusters in which a voiced aspirate was followed by a voiceless aspirate), a rightward movement of the aspiration through the cluster with voicing of the second voiceless consonant. The phenomenon is called Bartholomae's Law, named, according to convention, after the scholar who described the pattern's operation (the German Indo-Europeanist Christian Bartholomae). The phenomenon was observed primarily in Indo-Iranian, and only the Indic branch of IE still preserves the voiced aspirates (*bh, dh, gh*; Ringe 2017, 22; Fortson 2010, 203–204; Bennett 1966). The Proto-Indic form in the *buddha* example above involves the operation of another sound law, by which the first aspirate was lost: Grassmann's Law. Here a sequence in which aspirated stops follow one another in separate syllables loses the aspiration in the first member: thus **bh-* in the sequence **bhudh-tó* loses its aspiration by Grassmann's Law – a phonological phenomenon observed also in Greek, and named after the German mathematician and philologist Hermann Grassmann (1809–1877). One more sound law operant in Indo-Iranian may be noted; PIE **dóru-* 'tree, wood' (we will see later that in Celtic it could mean specifically 'oak,' as in Irish *doire*) appears in Indo-Iranian as Vedic and Sanskrit *dāru*, Avestan *dāuru*, and Old Persian *dāru*. Here, original **o* appears in Indo-Iranian as *ā* in open syllables; though not a 'law' without exceptions, one can contrast Greek *póda* and Sanskrit *pādam* 'foot' – and this is Brugmann's Law, named after the eminent German Indo-Europeanist Karl Brugmann (1849–1919), author of the *Grundriss der vergleichenden Grammatik der indogermanischen Sprachen* ("Outline of the Comparative Grammar of the Indo-European Languages"; Brugmann 1886–1900; Clackson 1994, 23, 61; Fortson 2010, 205, 210–211). Our seeming digression into Indo-Iranian sound laws (Bartholomae's Law, Grassmann's Law, Brugmann's Law) has actually much to do with the history of English in that sound changes near and far within a language family have their legacy over time – some more observable than others, and not all changes affecting all (or even most) branches. Methodologically, an understanding of the concept of 'sound laws' is fundamental; much closer to home for English and the Germanic languages will be Grimm's Law and Verner's Law, discussed in chapters that follow.

The eastern geographical outlier in Indo-European is the Tocharian group; deciphered only in the last century (the Mahāyāna Buddhist texts appear in some cases in bilingual versions, generally in the North Indian Brahmī script), Tocharian A and Tocharian B are known from records dating to the AD 6th through 8th centuries (archaeology and linguistic reconstruction point to a much earlier occupation of the area by Indo-European speakers). The people known as Τοχάριοι (*Tókharioi*) to the Greeks seem to represent the furthest eastward expansion of Indo-Europeans, to the Tarim Basin in what is now the Xinjiang region of China (populated by the Turkic Uighurs).

The archaeological and literary findings associated with the Tocharians have sparked much interest and controversy: the Tarim Basin mummies and Chinese accounts of the Yuezhi – if these may be linked – point to a population some of whose members were tall, fair-haired, blue-eyed, and who produced characteristic plaid fabrics (Mallory and Mair 2000). What does seem startling about the Tocharian languages is how close some forms are to those reconstructed for PIE – a reconstruction undertaken before the rediscovery of Tocharian:

Tocharian B *tkācer*, Tocharian A *ckācar* < PIE *d^hugh_2tēr* 'daughter' (compare Sanskrit *duhitṛ*)
Tocharian B *yakwe*, Tocharian A *yuk* < PIE **éḱwos* 'horse' (compare Latin *equus*)
Tocharian B *kante*, Tocharian A *känt* < PIE **ḱm̥tóm* (compare Latin *centum*, OE *hundred /hundrað*)

The last example brings up the matter of the *centum-satəm* division in the Indo-European family between those languages which the initial palatal **ḱ* merged with **k* (as in Latin *centum*, or Proto-Germanic **hundą* [English *hundred*, German *Hundert*]) and those in which * *ḱ* > *s* (as in Avestan *satəm* or Sanskrit *śata*). Tocharian threw a wrench into the works in drawing a West-East distinction between *centum-satəm* languages; one solution was that Tocharian broke off from the rest of PIE very early on (which would help explain the relatively extreme geographical position of the languages). A number of puzzles remain about Tocharian; for the moment it is kept separate from other branches in family trees, and, along with Anatolian, marked off as one of the earliest branchings from PIE (see Adams 1988; Fortson 2010, 400–413); Ringe 1988–1990 investigates a number of problems in locating Tocharian in IE, including the tantalizing problem of the root **tēk-* 'touch' in both Germanic and Tocharian, of whether this co-occurrence is the result of chance or some unknown contact between pre-Tocharian and pre-Germanic, the direction of borrowing unknown.[17]

Greek is generally treated as a branching in IE by itself, though one does see the term 'Hellenic' used. In both the Pennsylvania and New Zealand trees we see Greek and Armenian branching off early from a parent that included the other branches of IE excluding Anatolian and Tocharian (New Zealand), or from a node that produced

[17]The matter is interesting in throwing light on methodological problems in drawing up the family tree of IE: "Very little of the evidence adduced for the original position of Tocharian in the IE family has any probative value. The shape of the noun 'tear' [PIE **dák′ru*, in western IE languages with an initial consonant, Old Irish *dér*, Gothic *tagr*, in the eastern IE languages the initial consonant presumably lost, as in Sanskrit *aśru*, Tocharian A *ākär*, Tocharian B plural *akrūna*] shows that pre-Tocharian was an eastern dialect of PIE…a (relatively) northeastern dialect of PIE, adjacent to Balto-Slavic and perhaps also to Germanic.… Even later contact between Tocharian and other branches of IE remains problematic, except for the intimate and prolonged association of Tocharian and Iranian" (Ringe 1988–1990, 115). Elided here was an extended discussion by Ringe of Tocharian verbal morphology ("Morphological Changes: Stative Presents and ā-Preterites," 83–96); important are the difficulties in plotting out linguistic relationships in geographical space in the face of the Indo-European homeland question.

Greek and Armenian and a branching that gave rise to Balto-Slavic and Indo-Iranian (Pennsylvania, which removes Germanic in one consideration for a 'best fit' *Stammbaum*, and includes a number of other complexities). In essence, there is general agreement that, in approximately this order, Anatolian, Tocharian, Greek, Armenian, Indo-Iranian broke off earlier from PIE, as evidenced by more conservative morphological features for instance (i.e., reflecting more closely those morphological features reconstructed for Proto-Indo-European). The position and age of Greek are better understood now with the decipherment of Linear B and the identification of the language it recorded as Mycenaean, an early form of Greek (cf. Chadwick 1990; Fortson 2010, 248–263). Balto-Slavic is generally seen now as a high-order grouping, comprising two branches. Baltic includes the modern languages Lithuanian and Latvian in the East Baltic subgrouping, which are attested in writing only in the Early Modern period; Old Prussian, attested in the later medieval period, went extinct in the Early Modern period and is the sole known West Baltic language. The Baltic languages are *satəm* languages (referring to the initial consonant in the word for '100') and morphologically conservative, and links between Balto-Slavic and Indo-Iranian have been posited on the basis of sound changes as well (the 'ruki' rule, a change of **s* when following **r*, **u*, **k*, or **i*; Fortson 2010, 414–416; Clackson 2007, 32). Baltic also shares some morphological similarities with Germanic, a geographically proximate branch in the Baltic Sea area, as well as cultural similarities. The Slavic languages are grouped into three geographical branches: East (Russian, Belarussian, and Ukrainian), South (Serbo-Croatian, Slovenian, Macedonian, Bulgarian, and the liturgical Old Church Slavonic), and West (Polish, Sorb, Czech, and Slovak). The Slavs migrated into the Balkans and other territories of the Byzantine Empire in the early medieval period, and entered the written record with their conversion to Christianity; a line of division in Europe that essentially remains to this day in terms of script reflects the conversion of the Slavs to either the Western (Roman) or Eastern (Byzantine) Catholic churches (or, after the 11th century, Orthodox). Poles and other West Slavs were converted to the Roman Church and use the Roman alphabet; Eastern Slavs were converted by Byzantine missionaries and use the Greek-derived Cyrillic alphabet attributed to the 9th-century missionary brothers from Thessaloniki, the 'apostles to the Slavs,' Cyril and Methodius.

If there has been some controversy over the grouping Balto-Slavic, all the more so is true with Italo-Celtic (if one follows, as here, the Pennsylvania tree); that there are morphological similarities between Italic and Celtic is certain, but whether these rise to the level of an 'Italo-Celtic' branch has been disputed. Even if treated separately (as in Fortson 2010, 274–337, and see 276–277 on the question), we move now to branches in IE closer to Germanic geographically and historically; a salient example that touches upon these three branches – Italic, Celtic, and Germanic – is the debate over the origin of Runic. A near-consensus view points to North Italic scripts (such as Greek-derived Etruscan), which seemed to enjoy a fairly wide currency in the last few centuries BC; we find Celtic inscriptions in Spain employing what look to be Runic characters, such as Celtiberian inscriptions on coins from Bolskan, Castulo, Saguntum, and Sekaisa during the Greek and Roman colonial periods. The Italic languages include of course Latin – which in turn gave rise to the Romance languages descending from late Vulgar Latin – and other IE languages of the Italian peninsula in the Latino-Faliscan (Latin,

Faliscan) and Sabellic or Osco-Umbrian branches (Oscan, Sabellian, South Picenian, Umbrian, and, surviving in relatively few inscriptions, Aequian, Marrucinian, Marsian, Paeliginian, Sabine, Vestinian, and Volscian). The names of the Italic languages beside Latin will seem familiar to any student of Roman history: they are also a list of peoples eventually subordinated to Rome, despite the resistance a number of them offered (especially the Sabines, Volscians, and Marsians). The aforementioned Etruscan script was used by a number of older Italic languages; it is important to note here that Etruscan is a language isolate, it is not Indo-European and has to date no known linguistic filiation. Nonetheless, scripts, which serve to record speech graphically, can pass between cultures whose languages may or may not be related – a point important to the development of English, which has employed in its history two scripts, Runic and Roman.

The Celtic languages too are morphologically conservative and have been important in reconstructions of PIE; they are divided into Continental and Insular branches, though Celtic was once spread across the European continent from Spain to Bohemia (the earliest identifiable Celtic cultures, Hallstatt and La Tène, are named after findsites in Austria and Switzerland). The Continental Celtic languages include Gaulish (the best attested), Lepontic, Celtiberian, and possibly Lusitanian and Tartessian (Lejeune 1971). The Galatians, to whom St. Paul addressed one of his epistles, were part of the eastward Celtic expansion that descended upon Greece, the Balkans, and then Anatolia. Though it seems to have survived as a spoken language into the medieval period, little survives from Galatian besides proper names. And there likely may have been other Continental Celtic languages in the eastern range of the 'Celtic empire' – a designation more useful in describing the range of Celtic expansion in the second half of the 1st millennium BC than denoting any entity. The Insular Celtic languages are further subdivided into the Brythonic (Welsh, Cornish, Breton; historical British and Cumbric) and Goidelic (Irish, Scots Gaelic, Manx) subbranches. The Celtic languages shall be turned to again and again as the ancestral Sprachraum ('speech area') of English involves the meeting of Celtic- and Germanic-speaking tribes, first on the continent, then in Britain in the AD 4th and 5th centuries.

In addition to Greek, two other languages are treated as separate branchings from the PIE stock: the previously mentioned Armenian and Albanian. Armenian exhibits a number of conservative morphological features, that is, elements of its morphology that seem, by comparison, to be archaic (lost or nonexistent in younger IE daughter languages), and therefore closer to the presumed PIE system. For example, Armenian has seven case forms (nominative, accusative, genitive-dative [the case distinct only with pronouns], locative, ablative, and instrumental), while PIE is believed to have had at least eight, including the vocative, and perhaps a ninth, the allative, a locative case indicating 'place something is brought to'; there is some evidence of the marking of allative in the Baltic languages, while it is found in Finnish and Hungarian, non-Indo-European languages often grouped into a Finno-Ugric family, which includes also Estonian (a geographically Baltic language, but non-Indo-European), which language has often been classified as part of the Uralic family. Sanskrit, a highly conservative IE language morphologically, employs eight cases in its declensional morphology (the seven found in Armenian plus the vocative) and three numbers (singular, dual, and plural – the dual survived in Old English in the pronoun system). Loanwords from

Hittite, an IE language of the Anatolian branch, and non-Indo-European languages such as Hurrian and Urartian (neighboring languages such as Akkadian and Canaanite were Semitic languages in the Afroasiatic family) indicate the early date of the arrival of the Armenians in Anatolia (arriving presumably from the Balkans), somewhere in the later 2nd millennium BC (cf. Fortson 2010, 382–399; Adjarian 1909; Adjarian 1926–1935). With Armenian we have another case of a language coming into the written record with Christianization; the originator of another Greek-derived alphabet this time was St. Mesrop Mashtots, at the start of the 5th century AD. Attempts at linking Armenian to other branches of IE have been controversial: perhaps it is to be linked with Greek and Albanian (Clackson 1994), or even more broadly with Anatolian and Indo-Iranian.

In its own branch in IE, the classification of Albanian has been hindered by the late date it comes into writing (generally postmedieval). There have been attempts to link Albanian to Illyrian, an idea that has cultural and political parallels in claims of descent from the Illyrians native to the Southern Balkans in the classical period. The major dialectal division in Albanian is between the Northern Gheg and Southern Tosk, which in their spoken varieties (as opposed to literary standard varieties) are not always fully mutually intelligible. Albania has been throughout its history a crossroads: Greek colonies were founded in Illyria in the later 8th to 7th centuries BC; it was split between the Roman provinces of Illyricum and Macedonia, remained under the Byzantines for centuries, and then from the 15th century until 1912 was part of the Ottoman Empire. Until the conquest by Ottoman Turks, Albanians had been Roman Catholics: the Albanian national hero Skanderbeg reconverted to Catholicism – he had been converted to Islam as a janissary – during his rebellion against the Ottomans 1443–1468; the language is written in the Roman script. Romance loanwords have had a profound influence upon the lexis of Albanian (e.g., *librin* 'book'); it has also felt the influence of neighboring Slavic languages (Fortson 2010, 446–458).

And so the major branches of the Indo-European family of languages – Anatolian, Tocharian, Indo-Iranian, Greek, Italic, Celtic, Germanic, Armenian, Balto-Slavic, Romance,[18] and Albanian (given approximately in terms of age of written records attesting to the languages) – help situate English in the broader context of its macro- or superfamily genetic classification. The efforts of the comparative method – analysis of the phonemic inventories of each member language, discernment of regular sound correspondences and changes (and, where warranted, the formulation of sound 'laws'), description of morphological systems, and so forth – help delineate the path of descent from reconstructed parent language to daughter languages and the nature of the inheritance – what is Indo-European, for instance, about English. As with genetics, one can say, somewhat loosely, that the Indo-European inheritance of English is to a certain extent determinative – while decay and innovation in lexis can on occasion, over centuries, be pronounced, the phonology, morphology, and syntax of English, by their descent through Germanic

[18] As Romance languages developed from Latin in the Italic branch at a relatively late date, the AD 5th through 7th centuries, they do not figure primarily in IE cladistics drawing upon the earliest attested languages.

and Indo-European, were bound to exhibit similarities with other Germanic and Indo-European languages. But the similarities are not limited to just the linguistic.

2.5 URHEIMAT: PROTO-INDO-EUROPEAN LANGUAGE AND CULTURE

Inevitable perhaps was that proponents of two of the major theories of the Indo-European 'homeland question' should happen to be archaeologists; there is a danger, at times, in the midst of asterisked proto-forms and tree diagrams to lose sight of the Indo-Europeans – the people themselves who brought their culture out of the original homeland: the Southern Russian steppes and forest-steppes of the Pontic-Caspian region (Mallory 1989), or Anatolia (Renfrew 1987), ca. 6,000 years ago and dispersed eastward, ultimately to India, and westward, to Spain and the British Isles. As indispensable as the linguistic evidence is – and here we depend especially upon lexis – inevitably that data must be mapped against material culture in known find-sites productive of a match. While historically the homeland or *Urheimat* question has been subject to a variety of biases, some scholarly, some even nationalistic (Mallory 1989, 144, 152–153), the linguistic constraints allow for a fairly wide geographic range in which to place the homeland. These constraints involve isoglosses and shared lexical items; if a preponderance of early IE languages evidence a particular lexical token, a type of plant- or tree-name for instance, the PIE reconstructed form may be diagnostic. With enough significant tokens, the linguistic evidence could be determinative – depending upon how the archaeologists weigh in. But as one gathers bundles of isoglosses to begin to draw a dialectal map (as of British or North American dialects of English), so one attempts to reconstruct the vocabulary of not just an Indo-European homeland, but of a Proto-Indo-European culture.

Terms for flora and fauna, topographical features, meteorological phenomena are among the lexical tokens employed in IE homeland debates; where the terms are reconstructible, their occurrence in multiple branches might be of probative value. But there is a history in the last half-century of 'false positives' and methodological disagreements that have made relatively little certain even in the terms of the debate. The 'beech-line' and salmon arguments are of interest. Reflexes of PIE **bheh$_2$ǵos* 'beech' are found in five of the branches of IE, Greek φηγός (*phēgós* the Attic form; Doric φαγός, *phāgós*), Latin *fagus*, Gaulish *bāgos*, OE *bōc, bēce*, Albanian *bung*, Russian *buz*. While the western IE terms refer to the European common beech proper (*Fagus sylvatica*), the eastern terms refer now to other types of trees, the durmast oak (*Quercus petraea*) in the case of Albanian, the elder in Russian; the notion is that east of the 'beech line,' running north-to-south from Kaliningrad (Königsberg) to Odessa, where the European common beech is not found, the original PIE term for 'beech' was transferred to other trees (though there is an eastern beech, *Fagus orientalis*, found across Northern Anatolia to the Southern Pontic-Caspian area). Thus the 'beech'-argument is not now seen as probative (Mallory 1989, 115–116, 160; Fortson 2010, 45; Lane 1967; Mallory and Adams 2006, 153). There was a similar outcome to the 'salmon'-argument: PIE **laks-* (the Atlantic *Salmo salar*; there are other proposed reconstructed forms) was thought for a time to limit the PIE homeland to a northerly 'salmon-line' running across Northern Europe (thus proposals to locate the *Urheimat* in the Baltic region). But more recent work suggested that the PIE form referred to salmonids, such as the salmon trout, *Salmo trutta*, which has a much wider and more easterly range.

Nonetheless, linguists have been able to reconstruct a good many PIE forms that help give a sense of the homeland's environment. PIE flora include terms for *alder* (*$*h_2$élis-*), *apple* (*$*h_2$ébVl-* [V for an indeterminate vowel or *$*h_2$ébōl-*], and *$*meh_2$lom*, whence Latin *mālum*), *birch* (*$*bherh_x$ǵos*, the laryngeal to be reconstructed not determined), *willow* (ultimately from a PIE root **wel-* 'turn, twist')), *yew* (*$*h_1$eiwos*/ *$*$yéw$h_1$os*). A difficulty with terms for flora, the plant- and tree-names of PIE, is that they tend to be better attested in the western IE languages; thus, it has been difficult to say how many would be of probative value with regard to the homeland question (Mallory and Adams 2006, 156–161; Friedrich 1970). Mallory and Adams 2006 place the PIE vocabulary reconstructed to date in thesaurus-like groupings: for example, from ' physical world,' fauna, flora, anatomy, family and kinship, hearth and home, clothing and textiles, material culture, and food and drink (Mallory and Adams 2006, 120–265). A number of these reconstructed PIE and PGmc forms will be encountered in the following two chapters, on the Celtic *Sprachraum* in which English developed (Chapter 3) and on Old English (Chapter 4), with a view also to where one finds innovation in Gmc. We know, for instance, of a special kinship bond felt for the 'mother's brother' (OE *ēam*, 'maternal uncle,' Gm *Oheim*) in Germanic (< PGmc **auhaim*; Ringe in Ringe and Taylor 2014, 126), with some parallels more broadly in other branches of IE (see, e.g., Bajema 1994; Bremmer 1997), though the PIE form has not been securely reconstructed (Mallory and Adams 2006, 209–218 at 214; see also Rau 2011). This may serve as a caveat on the limits of reconstruction or of how closely vocabulary serves as a register of culture.

Among the fauna, the general term **péḱu* 'livestock' (compare Latin *pecus*, Old English *feoh*, MdE *fee*) underwent a semantic extension in a number of the branches, from a term for 'cattle, livestock' to one denoting 'money, wealth'; *$*b^heb^hrus$* 'beaver' (Sanskrit *babhrús*, Latin *fiber*) one can trace through the history of English: OE *beofor*, ME *bever*, MdE *beaver*; PIE **udrós-* > PGmc **utraz* 'otter,' though the root simply indicates an aquatic animal (compare *hydro-*; Ringe in Ringe and Taylor 2014, 27); *$*w\c{l}k^wos$* 'wolf' (Greek λύκος [*lúkos*], whence the *lyco-* prefix in Greek loans to English; Latin *lupus*), of which the OE reflex is *wulf* 'wolf,' but with *$*h_2$ŕ̥tḱos* 'bear' (Ringe in Ringe and Taylor 2014, 511; Sanskrit *ṛkṣa*, Greek ἄρκτος [*árktos*], Latin *ursus*) the Germanic forms are terms meaning 'brown (one)': OHG *bero* (MdG *Bär*) and OE *bera*. Reconstructed too are terms for *mouse*, *otter*, *elk*, *sheep*, *piglet*; **pórḱos*, Latin *porcus*, returns by a circuitous route through Romance as ME *porc*; the OE reflex of the PIE form is *fearh* 'little pig, hog,' which survives with semantic shift in MdE *farrow* 'litter of pigs.' And *horse*: *$*h_1$éḱwos*, Sanskrit *aśva*, Greek ἵππος (*híppos*), Latin *equus*, the OE reflex of which was *eoh*; MdE *horse*, and related Germanic forms (OE and OFris. *hors*, OS and OHG *hros*, ON *hross*) is of uncertain etymology, but may have to do with 'running' and so derive from PIE **ḱers-* (whence Latin *currō*, MdE *course*, *current*); PGmc. **hanhistaz* gave rise to terms for '(male) horse, stallion,' including ON *hestr*, OE *hengest* (MdG *Hengst*), and the name of one of the two brothers leading the (semi-)legendary Germanic invasion of Britain in AD 449: Hengest/Hengist and Horsa – likely an incarnation of an inherited PIE 'horse' and an example of the 'twinning' theme.[19] Many of the cultural elements reconstructed for PIE society on the basis of archaeology, comparative religion and mythology, and anthropology will be visited in the next two chapters, especially insofar as the early Germanic society of Anglo-Saxon England exhibited Indo-European and Germanic features (the mythic patterning of Hengest and Horsa is but one small example).

A recent study of East Germanic and broader Germanic genetic/phylogenetic classification seems to bear out, in general outline, the traditional picture of a Germanic clade (branch) divided into West, North, and East Germanic sub-clades/subbranches. The East Germanic subbranch has proved the most controversial in Gmc cladistics: there does not seem to be a direct line of descent from Wulfilan (Biblical) Gothic to Crimean Gothic, which was likely extinct by the end of the 18th century (it was perhaps in decline in everyday use by the time of the word-list recorded in the letters of Flemish diplomat Ogier Ghiselin de Busbecq [1522–1592]). If not a direct line of descent, there may be rather a 'continuum' in East Germanic as there are shared phonological and morphological features between Biblical and Crimean Gothic (nom. & acc. sing. in neuter pronoun forms in *-ata* the shared morphological feature; Kim 2024, 38). The raising of long mid vowels is found among languages traditionally classed as 'East Germanic' (though it may "be considered an example of diffusion or parallel innovation"; Kim 2024, 38); so too the smoothing/monophthongization of PGmc **ai* and **au* (Kim 2024, 38; Hartmann 2020, 82–83). This leaves a somewhat less determinative East branching of Proto-Germanic > East Germanic 'continuum' (Biblical Gothic, *Ostrogothic, Crimean Gothic, Vandalic, Burgundian, and perhaps a few other lightly attested East Germanic languages; Kim 2024, 39–40). Intact are the West branching Proto-Germanic > Proto-Northwest Germanic > Proto-West Germanic and the Proto-North Germanic branch.

2.6 FROM WEST GERMANIC TO EARLY OLD ENGLISH

Earlier in this Chapter (2.3), we saw examples from a Latin-OHG glossary (the *Vocabularius Sancti Galli*) and early Germanic translations of the *Pater noster* that gave some indications of the close relatedness of languages in the Germanic branch, and, in turn, in the West Germanic branch that comprises the modern languages German, English, Dutch, Frisian, Afrikaans, and Yiddish. Though much of what has been covered in this chapter concerns language history well before the invasion of Britain by Germanic-speakers (which had begun before the conventional date of AD 449, and continued for some time thereafter), we are drawing closer to the ancestral *Sprachraum* of pre-English and the earliest Old English (ca. 500–650). The *Völkerwanderung* ('wanderings of the peoples') of the early centuries AD would bring Germanic-speakers further west, impinging

[19]While repeating a warning of "the danger of seeing Dioskouroi in every pair of brothers occurring in saga," M.L. West takes the case of Hengest (Hengist) and Horsa as fitting in with an IE mythic pattern: "They were descended from Woden. Their names mean Stallion and Horse, and it seems significant that the same names, Hengist and Hors, were given to pairs of horses' heads that used to adorn farmhouse gables in Lower Saxony and Schleswig-Holstein, perhaps a relic of pagan cult" (West 2007, 190, with reference to de Vries 1956).

on the Roman frontier and its Celtic client-chiefdoms in Gaul, and then Britain. As Visigoths attacked Rome in AD 410, Roman legions departed Britain. The 3rd and 2nd millennia BC are largely beyond the reach of linguists, outside of the evidence of the Anatolian languages, except in their reconstructions; the Indo-Europeans were expanding then, as archaeologists and historians trace them (Mallory 1989, 107–109, 222–265), and would continue to do so into the 1st millennium BC. And here we move from whatever intermediary nodes in the family tree come between PIE and Proto-Indo-Iranian, Proto-Celtic, and so forth, to the proto-forms of branches of IE still in existence. The movement of presumable speakers of Proto-Germanic southward and westward continually pressed upon Celtic tribes who had occupied much of Western and Central Europe (a range spanning Galicia in Spain to Galatia in Anatolia). In some sense, the 'wandering of the peoples' meets its culmination in the push of Celtic-speakers to their present Western margins: the British Isles, Northwestern France, a movement back across the Channel by Britons, now 'Bretons,' under pressure from the Germanic invaders in Britain; in another, the Indo-European migration has never really ended, but accelerated in the Age of Imperialism into that of globalization: "Over a period of 6,000 years we have witnessed the emergence and expansion of a language family until it embraces nearly half the population of this planet" (Mallory 1989, 265). But first a matter of smaller compass: into what sort of land, society, and speech area did the Angles, Saxons, and Jutes expand?

REFERENCES AND BIBLIOGRAPHY

Adams, Douglas Q. *Tocharian Historical Phonology and Morphology*. American Oriental Series Volume 71. New Haven, CT: American Oriental Society, 1988

Adjarian, Hrachia. *Classification des dialectes arméniens*. Paris: Librairie Honoré Champion, 1909

Adjarian, Hrachia. *Hayeren Armatakan Bararan (Armenian Etymological Dictionary)*. 4. Yerevan: Erevani Petakan Hamalsaran/Yerevan State University, 1926–1935

Aland, Kurt, Matthew Black, Carlo M. Martini, Bruce M. Metzger, Allen Wikgren, eds. *The Greek New Testament*. 4th rev. ed. Stuttgart: Deutsche Bibelgesellschaft, 1998

Antonsen, Elmer H. *A Concise Grammar of the Older Runic Inscriptions*. Sprachstrukturen. Reihe A: Historische Sprachstrukturen. Tübingen: Max Niemeyer Verlag, 1975

Antonsen, Elmer H. *Runes and Germanic Linguistics*. Berlin: Mouton de Gruyter, 2002

Atkinson, Q.D., G. Nicholls, D. Welch, R.D. Gray. "From words to dates: Water into wine, mathemagic or phylogenetic inference?" *Transactions of the Philological Society* 103 (2005), 193–219

Bailey, D.R. Shackleton ed. *Anthologia Latina*. Vol. 1. Stuttgart: B.G. Teubner, 1982

Bajema, Ingeborg M. "The mother's brother: An investigation into the meaning of old English *eam*," *Neophilologus* 78 (1994), 633–644

Beckman, Gary. *Hittite Diplomatic Texts*. Atlanta, GA: Society of Biblical Literature, 1999

Bennett, William. "The Germanic evidence for Bartholomae's law," *Language* 42.4 (1966), 733–737

Bomhard, Allan R. and John C. Kerns. *The Nostratic Macrofamily: A Study in Distant Language Relationship*. Trends in Linguistics. Berlin: Walter de Gruyter, 1994

Bonnefoy, Yves, compiler. *Mythologies*. 2 vols. Chicago: University of Chicago Press, 1991

Bopp, Franz. *Vergleichende Grammatik des Sanskrit, Send, Armenischen, Griechischen, Lateinischen, Litauischen, Altslavischen, Gothischen und Deutschen*, 6 vols. Berlin: Ferdinand Dümmler's Verlag, 1833–1837

Bouckaert, Remco, Philippe Lemey, Michael Dunn et al., "Mapping the origins and expansion of the Indo-European language family," *Science* 337 (2012), 957–960

Bremmer, Rolf. "The Germanic context of 'Cynewulf and Cyneheard' revisited," *Neophilologus* 81 (1997), 445–465

Brugmann, Karl and Berthold Delbrück.. *Grundriss der vergleichenden Grammatik der indogermanischen Sprachen*, 5 vols. Strassburg: Karl J. Trübner, 1886–1900

Buck, Carl Darling. *A Dictionary of Selected Synonyms in the Principal Indo-European Languages: A Contribution to the History of Ideas*. Chicago: University of Chicago Press, 1949

Cannon, Garland. *The Life and Mind of Oriental Jones: Sir William Jones, the Father of Modern Linguistics*. Cambridge: Cambridge University Press, 1990

Cavalli-Sforza, Luca Luigi, Paolo Menozzi, Alberto Piazza. *The History and Geography of Human Genes*. Princeton, NJ: Princeton University Press, 1994

Chadwick, John. *The Decipherment of Linear B*. 2nd Cambridge: Cambridge University Press, 1990. 1968/rpt

Clackson, James. *The Linguistic Relationship between Armenian and Greek*. Publications of the Philological Society 30. Oxford: Blackwell, 1994

Clackson, James. *Indo-European Linguistics: An Introduction*. Cambridge: Cambridge University Press, 2007

de Vries, Jan. *Altgermanische Religionsgeschichte*, 2. 2nd Berlin: Walter de Gruyter, 1956

Domingo Gygax, Marc and Werner Tietz "'He who of all mankind set up the most numerous trophies to Zeus': The Inscribed Pillar of Xanthos reconsidered," *Anatolian Studies* 55 (2005), 89–98

Dumézil, Georges. *Archaic Roman Religion*, 2 vols. Tr. Philip Krapp. Chicago: University of Chicago Press, 1970

Ebbinghaus, Ernst A. and Wilhelm Braune. *Althochdeutsches Lesebuch*. 17th ed. Tübingen: Max Niemeyer, 1994

Fortson, Benjamin W. IV. *Indo-European Language and Culture: An Introduction*. 2nd Oxford: Wiley-Blackwell, 2010

Fox, Anthony. *Linguistic Reconstruction: An Introduction to Theory and Method*. Oxford: Oxford University Press, 1995

Friedrich, Paul. *Proto-Indo-European Trees: The Arboreal System of a Prehistoric People*. Chicago: University of Chicago Press, 1970

Gamkrelidze, Thomas V. and Vyacheslav V. Ivanov. "Sprachtypologie und die Rekonstruktion der gemeinindogermanischen Verschlüsse," *Phonetica* 27 (1973), 150–156

Gamkrelidze, Thomas V. and Vyacheslav V. Ivanov. *Indoevropejskij jazyk I indoevropejcy. Tblisi: Izdatel'stvo Tblisskogo Universiteta, 1984*. Tr. Johanna Nichols, *Indo-European and the Indo-Europeans*. Berlin: Mouton de Gruyter, 1995

Garrett, Andrew. "Convergence in the Formation of Indo-European Subgroups: Phylogeny and Chronology," in *Phylogenetic Methods and the Prehistory of Languages* Ed. Peter Forster and Colin Renfrew. Cambridge: McDonald Institute for Archaeological Research, 2006. Pp. 139–151

Gusmani, Roberto. *Lydisches Wörterbuch, mit grammatischer Skizze und Inschriftensammlung.* Indogermanische Bibliothek. 2. Reihe: Worterbucher. Heidelberg: Carl Winter, 1964

Harbert, Wayne. *The Germanic Languages.* Cambridge: Cambridge University Press, 2007

Hartmann, Frederik. *The Vandalic Language – Origins and Relationships.* Indogermanische Bibliothek, 3. Reihe: Untersuchungen. Heidelberg: Universitätsverlag Winter, 2020

Heizmann, Wilhelm and Astrid van Nahl, eds. *Runica, Germanica, Mediaevalia.* Erganzungsbande zum Reallexikon der Germanischen Altertumskunde 37. Berlin: Walter de Gruyter, 2003

Hock, Hans Heinrich. *Principles of Historical Linguistics.* Berlin: Walter de Gruyter, 1986

Hoenigswald, Henry. *Language Change and Linguistic Reconstruction.* Chicago: University of Chicago Press, 1960

Jasanoff, J.H. *Hittite and the Indo-European Verb*, Oxford: Oxford University Press, 2003

Kammenhuber, Annelies. *Hippologia hethitica.* Wiesbaden: Otto Harrassowitz, 1961

Kent, Roland G. *Old Persian: Grammar, Texts, Lexicon.* 2nd New Haven, CT, American Oriental Society1989. 1953/rpt

Kim, Ronald I., "On the Phylogenetic Status of East Germanic," in *The Method Works: Studies on Language Change in Honor of Don Ringe*, ed. Joseph F. Eska, Olav Hackstein, Ronald I. Kim, and Jean-François Mondon. Cham: Palgrave Macmillan, 2024. Pp. 21–43

Kiparsky, Paul. "Indo-European Origins of Germanic Syntax," in *Clause Structure and Language Change*, ed. Adrian Battye and Ian Roberts.. Oxford Studies in Comparative Syntax. Oxford: Oxford University Press, 1995. Pp. 140–169

Klingenberg, Heinz. *Runenschrift, Schriftdenken, Runeninschriften.* Heidelberg: Carl Winter, 1973

Köhler, Johann Jakob. *Die altenglischen Fischnamen. Anglistische Forschungen 21.* Heidelberg: Carl Winter, 1906

Krause, Wolfgang. *Runeninschriften im älteren Futhark.* Halle: Vandenhoeck & Ruprecht, 1937

Krause, Wolfgang. *Die Sprache der urnordischen Runeninschriften.* Germanische Bibliothek. 3 vols. Reihe: Untersuchungen und Einzeldarstellungen. Heidelberg: Carl Winter, 1971

Kuryłowicz, Jerzy. "ə indo-européen et ḫ hittite," in *Symbolae Grammaticae in Honorem Ioannis Rozwadowski*, ed. W. Taszycki and W. Doroszewski. Krakow: Gebethner & Wolff, 1927. Pp. 95–104

Lane, G.S. "The beech argument," *Zeitschrift für vergleichende Sprachforschung* 81 (1967), 197–202

Lehmann, Winfred P. *A Gothic Etymological Dictionary.* Leiden: E.J. Brill, 1986

Lejeune, Michel. *Lepontica.* Paris: Société d'édition "Les Belles Lettres," 1971

Lindeman, Fredrik O. *Introduction to the Laryngeal Theory. 3rd ed.* Innsbrucker Beitrage zur Sprachwissenschaft. Innsbruck: Institut für Sprachwissenschaft der Universität Innsbruck, 1997

Lloyd, Albert L. "Indo-European unstressed short *e* in Germanic," *Modern Language Notes* 76 (1961) 847–851

Macqueen, J.G. *The Hittites: and their contemporaries in Asia Minor*. London: Thames & Hudson, 1986

Mallory, J.P. *In Search of the Indo-Europeans: Language, Archaeology, and Myth*. London: Thames & Hudson, 1989

Mallory, J.P. and Douglas Q. Adams. *The Oxford Introduction to Proto-Indo-European and the Proto-Indo-European World*. Oxford Linguistics. Oxford: Oxford University Press, 2006

Mallory, J.P. and Victor H. Mair. *The Tarim Mummies: Ancient China and the Mystery of the Earliest Peoples from the West*. London: Thames & Hudson, 2000

Ramert, A.M. and C.R. Hitchcock "Glass houses: Greenberg, Ringe, and the mathematics of comparative linguistics," *Anthropological Linguistics* 38 (1996), 601–620

Middendorff, Heinrich. *Altenglisches Flurnamenbuch*. Halle: Max Niemeyer, 1902

Must, Gustav. "The problem of the inscription on helmet B of Negau," *Harvard Studies in Classical Philology* 62 (1957), 51–59

Nedoma, Robert. *Die Inschrift auf dem Helm B von Negau. Möglichkeiten und Grenzen der Deutung norditalischer epigraphischer Denkmäler*. Philologica Germanica 17. Vienna: Verlag Fassbaender, 1995

Page, R.I. *Runes and Runic Inscriptions: Collected Essays on Anglo-Saxon and Viking Runes*. Rochester, NY: Boydell Press, 1995

Page, R.I. *An Introduction to English Runes*. 2nd ed. Woodbridge: Boydell and Brewer, 1999

Payne, Annick. *Hieroglyphic Luwian. Elementa Linguarum Orientis 3*. Wiesbaden: Harrassowitz Verlag, 2004

Penzl, Herbert, "Methods of Comparative Germanic Linguistics," in *Toward a Grammar of Proto-Germanic*, Coetsem, Frans Van and Herbert L. Kufner. Tübingen: Max Niemeyer, 1972, pp. 1–42

Pokorny, Julius. *Indogermanisches etymologisches Wörterbuch*. 2. Bern: Francke, 1959

Polomé, Edgar G.C. "On the source of Hittite ḫ," *Language* 28.4 (1952), 444–456

Prokosch, Eduard. *A Comparative Germanic Grammar*. Baltimore: Linguistic Society of America, 1939

Puhvel, Jaan. "Laryngeals and the Indo-European desiderative," *Language* 29.4 (1953), 454–456

Rau, Jeremy, "Indo-European kinship terminology: *ph$_2$tr-ou̯/ph$_2$tr̥u̯– and its derivatives," *Historische Sprachforschung* 124 (2011), 1–25

Renfrew, Colin. *Archaeology and Language: The Puzzle of Indo-European Origins*. Cambridge: Cambridge University Press, 1987

Ringe, Donald A. "Evidence for the position of Tocharian in the Indo-European family?" *Die Sprache* 34 (1988–1990), 59–123

Ringe, Don, "How hard is it to match CVC-roots?" *Transactions of the Philological Society* 97 (1999), 213–244

Ringe, Donald A. *From Proto-Indo-European to Proto-Germanic*.. A Linguistic History of English, Volume I. Oxford: Oxford University Press, 2017. 2006/rev. ed

Ringe, Donald A. and Ann Taylor. *The Development of Old English.* A Linguistic History of English, Volume II. Oxford: Oxford University Press, 2014

Ringe, Don, Tandy Warnow, and Ann Taylor, "Indo-European and computational cladistics," *Transactions of the Philological Society* 100 (2002), 59–129

Scardigli, Piergiuseppe. *Die Goten. Sprache und Kultur.* Munich: C.H. Beck, 1973

Schlemilch, Willy. *Beiträge zur Sprache und Orthographie spätaltengl. Sprachdenkmäler der Übergangszeit (1000–1150).* Halle: Max Niemeyer, 1914

Streitberg, Wilhelm and Piergiuseppe Scardigli. *Die Gotische Bibel.* 2 ed. 7th Heidelberg: Carl Winter, 2000

Coetsem, Frans Van and Herbert L. Kufner. *Toward a Grammar of Proto-Germanic.* Tübingen: Max Niemeyer, 1972

Watkins, Calvert. *How to Kill a Dragon: Aspects of Indo-European Poetics.* New York: Oxford University Press, 1995

West, Martin L. *The East Face of Helicon: West Asiatic Elements in Greek Poetry and Myth.* Oxford: Clarendon Press, 1997

West, Martin L. *Indo-European Poetry and Myth.* Oxford: Oxford University Press, 2007

Woudhuizen, Fred. *The Luwians of Western Anatolia: Their Neighbours and Predecessors.* Bicester: Archaeopress, 2018

CHAPTER 3

Britannia

DAE COVEN
VINOMATH
VS V L S M

D(e)ae Coven(tinae) | Vinomath | us v(otum) s(olvit) l(ibens) m(erito)

[To the goddess Coventina, Vinomathus fulfills his vow, willingly, deservedly.]

[Carrawburgh fort (Roman Brocolitia) shrine to Coventina, the nymphs, and the 'spirit of the place' (*genius loci*), at Hadrian's Wall; RIB 1528]

Some fourteen inscriptions in dedication to British water-goddess Coventina are extant from Carrawburgh, Northumberland, known in Roman times as Brocolitia (or Procolitia), a Latinized native place-name apparently meaning 'infested with badgers'; the first element cognate with Welsh *broc* < Proto-Celtic **brokko-* (Matasović 2009, 80; Sims-Williams 2003, 150). The man who made the dedication may have been a German or Celt; if the former, he was perhaps a soldier serving in the Batavian or Frisiavonian cohorts stationed there at the Wall (*cohors I Batavorum, cohors I Frisiavonum*).[1] An *optio*, a junior officer serving under a centurion or decurion, of the Frisiavonian cohort named Maus (or Mausaeus or Musaeus) offered his own dedication to Coventina at the same shrine:

DE CONVETI
VOT RETV
LIT MAVS
OPTIO CHO
P FRIXIAV

[1] Holder, *Alt-celtischer Sprachschatz,* Band II (1904, 459), lists the second element *-mathus* as Celtic, while Werle 1910 saw it as Germanic.

Dea(ae) Conveti(nae) | vot(um) ret(t)|u(l)lit Maus(aeus) | optio c(o)ho(rtis) | p(rimae) Frixiav(onum)

[To the goddess Coventina, Mausaeus, optio of the First Cohort of Frisiavones, has carried out his vow.]
[RIB 1523]

Other Germans made dedications at Carrawburgh to Coventina: *Crotus Germanus* ('Crotus, a German'; RIB 1525), and Maduhus (RIB 1526), their respective units not mentioned in their inscriptions. Cohorts of Tungrians, Batavians, and Frisiavones are well attested along the Wall from dedicatory and funerary inscriptions from the AD 1st century onward. The Frisiavones and Frisii seem to have been two distinct Germanic peoples, with the Frisiavones living along the Waal near modern Nijmegen in the Netherlands, while the Frisii (Frisians, though Saxon settlers to Frisia later came under this ethnic name also) living further to the northeast in what is now Friesland. We are among some of the peoples whose descendants will invade and settle Britain some four centuries later; but we have, already, a Germanic presence in Britain, and inscriptions bearing the names of Germanic-speaking peoples and Germanic gods.

The survey of the last chapter of Proto-Indo-European and Proto-Germanic was a largely linguistic affair; now we meet the 'gods and men' of the Migration and Heroic Ages (*goða ok manna*, the phrase of epic cast in Snorri Sturluson's *Edda*; here in the gen. pl. form, 'of gods and men'). In an effort to describe the *Sprachraum* (literally 'speech-room,' or speech area) in which English would develop, it is necessary to look at Celtic Britain in the centuries of Roman rule. The inscriptions, letters (on wooden tablets), and other documents of Roman Britain provide the first glimpses of literacy in the British Isles (along with the earliest ogam inscriptions and the Caistor-by-Norwich deer bone Runic inscription). The linguistic interactions and contact situation in Roman and sub-Roman Britain are vital not just in providing a template for examining those following the Saxon conquest AD 449 and later, but to tracing the earliest loanwords to enter English. And recent work on the Brittonic languages and British Latin may suggest that the influence of these languages, once thought limited to vocabulary, may have been more extensive (Schrijver 2002, and the important overview and synthesis in Parsons 2011). The pre-410 *Sprachraum* or speech area of Celtic Britain involves a largely to nearly totally Celtic-speaking island, with Celtic-speaking neighbors to the west (Man, Ireland), south (Gaul to those Celtiberian regions of Spain), and Germanic-speakers to the southeast (the Low Countries). The 'problem of Pictish' remains, namely, its status as IE or non-IE (with recent assessments split; Forsyth 1997; Sims-Williams 2012). If the traditional view is that there are relatively few Brittonic/Celtic loans in Old English apart from place-names (a view that has been challenged and is slowly changing), there are even fewer *alteuropäisch*/Old European or non-IE pre-English loans, and a number of these have since been satisfactorily explained as Celtic – Welsh *broc* cited above remains unexplained: "This word has no known cognates in other IE languages, and it has all but replaced the inherited word for badger *tasko-. It may have been borrowed from some non-IE language into Proto-Celtic" (Matasović 2009, 80). But why would the native word have been displaced? The matter of loanwords, their absorption into the borrowing language, instances of lexical displacement, and what loan chronology can tell us about the history of English in its *Sprachraum* merits a digression on badgers.

Proto-Celtic **tasko-* had reflexes in a number of Gaulish personal names, *Tascos*, *Tasco-uanus* ('badger-slayer'; Matasović 2009, 80), *Tasco*, *Tasgius*, *Tasgia* (and the diminutive forms *Tasgillus*, *Tascilla*), *Taxi-magulus* ('badger-prince,' with metathesis of /-sk/ > /-ks-/); **brokko-* also generated a number of Celtic personal names in Gaulish (*Broco-maglus*, also 'badger-prince'), Welsh *Brochmael* (cognate with Gaulish *Broco-maglus*), and Old Irish (*Broccán*; Delamarre 2003, 90, 291–292). It is believed to appear in at least two place-names in Roman Britain, the *Brocolitia* of the Coventina inscriptions above, and the Roman fort *Brocavum*, perhaps most likely < **Broccāwon* 'place of badgers' < British **brocco-* 'badger'(= Brougham, Westmorland; *Brougham* < Old English *burg-hām*, the homestead by the burg; Rivet and Smith 1979, 283–284; Ekwall 1960, 69). The **brokko-/*tasko* 'badger' etymological complex seems conjoined with what might be termed a mythological complex as well: the preponderance of forms in Gaulish seems connected to ideas of a taboo or shame in killing badgers, and of warrior-royal association with a totemic badger; the slaying of badgers appears to indicate a feat of no great significance, and this may derive from a vestigial prohibition (at least by certain persons) of killing badgers.[2] But a more serious ritual or mythic complex may lay behind the later pejorized version: the name of the British king Tasciouanus (father of Cunobelinus, Shakespeare's Cymbeline) literally means 'badger-killer' (< **task(j)o-g^{w}onos*). Tasciovanus (Tasciouanos) ruled the Catuvellauni from ca. 20s BC to about AD 9/10 from their major settlement at Verlamion (Verulamium in the Roman period). The Catuvellauni formed a major pre-Roman Celtic late Iron Age kingdom in parts of the East Midlands and Southeast: Verlamion in Hertfordshire, Bedfordshire, Buckinghamshire, parts of Oxfordshire and Berkshire, and, to the east, parts of Cambridgeshire, Essex, and the northern environs of London. Tasciovanus is known to us primarily from his coin legends, having begun minting coins soon after assuming rule, including some particularly fine gold staters. Besides the abbreviated TASCIO legend (set in a small tablet with rotae [Celtic wheel design] above and below), we find the legend RICO/RICONI (< **rigonos*, 'great king,' in nominative and genitive singular forms). Tasciovanus would also mint coins for a time at Colchester, known in pre-Roman and Romano-British times as Camulodunum (< British **Camulodunon*; Rivet and Smith 1979, 294–295). The place-name *Camulo-dunum* is itself a theonym with a productive second element: *-dunum* < Proto-Celtic **dūno-* 'hill, fort, rampart' (Matasović 2009, 108; Rivet and Smith 1979, 274–275). Camulos (Camulus) was a Celtic

[2] Delamarre traced the Gaulish > French colloquial idea of 'killers-of-badgers' as pejorizing toward ironic praise: "Le mot [Gaulish *broccos/taxos*, French *blaireau* 'badger'], employé comme soubriquet, a souvent une connotation négative dans les langues modernes...et il est probable que cette situation prévalait aussi autrefois, d'où l'emploi dans l'anthroponymie gauloise qui présente des 'tueurs-de-blaireaux' (dénotant un fait de gloire en soi limité, au sens littéral, sauf utilisé ironiquement"; Delamarre 2003, 291: "The word, employed as a nickname, often has a negative connotation in the modern languages...and it is likely that this situation prevailed as well in the past, thus its use in the Gaulish system of personal names that have to do with 'killers of badgers' (denoting a heroic act in its own right, in the literal sense, except when used ironically)." Other Celtic evidence suggests a ritual taboo at work.

war-god known throughout Celtic-speaking regions (from Iberia to Galatia), and of particular prominence in Gaul (Whatmough 1970, 796, 1101–1102). An altar dedicated to Mars Camulus (DEO MARTI CAMULO; RIB 2166) was found in Scotland at Bar Hill Fort (East Dunbartonshire, the fort dating to ca. AD 142) on the Antonine Wall, while the Ravenna Cosmography (more on which below) mentions a *Presidium Camulosessa*, a Roman garrison not located yet but thought to be in Southern Scotland; *Camulo-sessa* is < **Camulo-sed-ta*, 'Camulo's seat' (Rivet and Smith 1979, 296).

(a) Gold stater and (b) quarter staters of Tasciovanus, 1st century BC.
Sources: (a) Cleveland Museum of Art / CCO 1.0 / https://www.clevelandart.org/art/1969.150 / last accessed by Sep 29, 2025; (b) The Norweb Collection 1969.151/ Cleveland Museum of Art / Public Domain.

The Celtic place-name element **dūno-*, appearing in Gaulish and Gallo-Roman place-names as *-dunum* (< **dūnom*; and so also in Romano-British *Camulodunum*) leads to consideration of the complexities in determining the origin of place-names. The highly productive Old English place-name element *dūn* ('hill') is behind many of the English place-names with *-dun*, but not all: *Bredon* (Worcestershire) is a Celtic-OE hybrid, and tautological (literally 'hill-hill,' < OE *Breodun*, W *bre* 'hill, hillside' < Primitive Welsh **breʒ* < early British **brigā*), with Anglo-Saxon settlers taking the

Welsh common form as a proper name and adding OE *dūn* 'hill' – this is not without parallel, of course, as with Welsh *afon* 'river' (< British **abonā*; compare Irish *abhainn* 'river,' pronounced [ɑːwɪn], [ɑu'wɪn]). *Hambledon* (Hampshire, and Surrey) seems to literally mean 'mutilated hill,' likely referring to a hill bare of trees (or with trees cut down; but Rivet and Smith have 'crooked or flat-topped hill'), the first element from an OE **hamel-* (compare the attested verb form *hamelian*, 'to hamstring, mutilate'; CHM, s.v.). *Snowdon* (Gwynedd) < OE *snāw-dūn*; the Welsh name is *Yr Wyddfa*, 'the mound,' and *Swindon* (Gloucestershire, Staffordshire, and Wiltshire) < OE *swīn-dūn*) are fairly transparent, as 'snow hill' and 'swine hill' respectively, but *Dun-* presents a number of challenges: *Dundon* (Somerset) is simply 'hill valley' (< OE *dūn-denu*; on *dūn* 'hill' and *denu* 'valley' as place-name elements, see CDEPN, xliii), while *Dunchideock* (Devon) is perhaps a hybrid, the first element Welsh or Cornish *dun* ('fort') possibly under the influence of OE *dūn*, while the second element is Celtic (Welsh *coediog* 'wooded' < British **caito* 'wood' + the adjectival suffix *-āco*; Ekwall ODEPN and CDEPN, s.v.). In general, but by no means absolutely, place-names in the historical or present border zones between England proper (the regions of historical Anglo-Saxon settlement) and former or current indigenous Celtic-speaking areas of Britain will reflect the Celtic background and often the historical interaction (as by hybrid place-names). Thus the *Dun-* in *Dunbar* (East Lothian; < Scots Gaelic *dùn barr*, 'fort of the summit'), *Dunblane* (Stirling; < Scots Gaelic *dùn Blaan*, 'St. Blane's Hill'), *Dunkeld* (Perth and Ross; < *Duncalden*, 'fort of the Caldeonians') are all Celtic, as are most of the *Dun-* names from Ireland: the port of Dublin, 'Leary's fort,' *Dún Laoghaire* is named for the 5th-century *ard rí* (High King) Lóegaire mac Néill, son of Níall Noígíollach (Níall of the Nine Hostages), a place-name firmly within heroic tradition, while the more down-to-earth but poetic *Duneane* (Co. Antrim) is from *Dún dá Éan* ('fort of two birds,' but also the sort of toponymy Flann O'Brien [pen-name of Brian O'Nolan] poked fun at in his 1939 novel *At Swim-Two-Birds*). Yet *Duncote* (Northamptonshire), *Dunham* (Nottinghamshire), *Dunsford* (Devon), *Dunstable* (Bedfordshire), *Dunster* (Somerset), *Dunthrop* (Oxfordshire) are all English, the first element being an Anglo-Saxon personal name *Dunn(a)*. The digression within a digression on *dūn* points not just to a difficulty with the evidence – is it Celtic or OE, which direction was the loan made, and so forth – indeed, OE *dūn* may have been a 'pre-Insular' loan to Germanic, that is, a loan from Gaulish, likely, into Continental Germanic that was then brought to England by Germanic-speakers who once again interacted with Celtic-speakers and grappled with their place-names. But we see a line of linguistic history made (relatively) plain in these place-names and place-name elements, and that linguistic history encodes what people said and thought not just about but *in* a landscape, a landscape that in Celtic Britain (and to some extent too in pagan Anglo-Saxon England) could be viewed as sacred, even living ('living waters,' holy mountains), and lest that seem too 'New Agey' there is abundant evidence from the literature (and etymological echoes) of the elder mythology of Britain.

To return to the badger-slaying king of Britain, Tasciovanus, Celticist John Koch had suggested that the first and third branches of the medieval Welsh *Mabinogion* might allude to early chieftains or kings of British tribes such as Tasciovanus and his son Cunobelinus of the Catuvellauni (who had succeeded Cassivellaunus in the chieftaincy), or Mandubracius, son of Imanuentius (Imannuetios) of the Trinovantes. These historical figures appear in Caesar's account (the *De Bello Gallico*, 'On the Gallic War') and, in briefest compass, involve the resistance of Cassivellaunus to Caesar's second invasion of Britain (54 BC), the encroachment of the Catuvellauni on Trinovantian territory and exile of their chieftain Mandubracius to Gaul (under Roman protection), and the 'betrayal' of the resistance by Mandubracius's strategic alliance with Caesar to regain his throne. The move of the Trinovantes to the Roman side was said to lead five other British tribes to do likewise: the Cenimagni (possibly the Iceni, of later fame with Boudicca's revolt AD 60/61), Segontiaci, Ancalites, Bibroci, and Cassi (Salway 2003, 33–39).

Of additional significance to the history of English (besides the inherited Celtic place-names and vocabulary) is the role played by some of these figures in the 'Matter of Britain': Cassivellaunus appears as Casswallawn, son of Beli Mawr (Beli the Great), in Welsh tradition, in the triads (*Trioedd Ynys Prydein*, the 'Triads of the Isle of Britain') and *Mabinogion*, and as Cassibelanus in Geoffrey of Monmouth's *Historia regum Britanniae* ('History of the Kings of Britain'). Koch had advanced the idea that the cryptic nature of the names of father and son Pwyll and Pryderi in the *Mabinogion* (meaning, respectively, 'care' and 'anxiety') might be explicable in that the onomastic puns mask historico-legendary figures from the earliest layer of the 'Matter of Britain': that Pwyll is Tasciovanus, Pryderi Cunobelinus, and Mandubracius is Manawydan son of Llŷr (the same Lir of Irish myth, and the Lear of Shakespeare; Koch 1986, 1992). The most intriguing element of Koch's analysis is the mysterious episode of the 'badger in the bag' ruse by which Pwyll wins back Rhiannon from his rival Gwawl in the first branch of the *Mabinogion*. When Pwyll, having foolishly promised a mysterious stranger (Gwawl) whatever he should want at what was to be the wedding feast of Rhiannon and Pwyll, and that suppliant's request being the hand of Rhiannon, Pwyll must follow Rhiannon's advice to reverse his outwitting. An etiological myth ensues in which we get the first playing of *broch yg got* 'badger in the bag' (*Ac yna gyntaf y guarywyt broch yg got*, "and that was the first [time] was played badger in the bag"; Williams 1978, 17, 136–137); Pwyll, in a role reversal so common in the *Mabinogion*, plays now the suppliant who asks Gwawl for as much food as his bag can carry, having Gwawl step into the bag to tamp it down and promptly trapping him in it, and then the rest of his men. As each of Pwyll's men enters the hall, they strike the bags a blow and ask what is inside, to which the reply is *broch* ('badger'). The origin story of 'badger in the bag' seems less odd, in Koch's view, if "the hero had once been known by the traditional name or epithet 'badger-slayer, -smiter' *Tasciovanus*" (Koch 1992, 112).

Adding to what is likely a Celtic mythological complex would be the semi-legendary Irish warrior Tadc (Tadg) mac Céin, whose name may very well ultimately mean 'badger' and whose *geis* (Old Irish for 'personal taboo or prohibition') involves the eating of badgers. Firmly rooted in both Irish legendary history and Otherworld adventures, son of Cian and grandson of Ailill Aulomm (Ailill 'bare-ear') and great grandson of Conn Cétchathach (Conn of the 'Hundred Battles'), and perhaps to be fitted into the AD 3rd century, Tadg assists Cormac mac Airt in the Battle of Crinna (the *Cath Crinna* from the Middle Irish Cycle of Kings) but is cheated of his reward of land by Cormac; the *Eachtra Thaidhg mhic Céin* ('Adventure of Tadg mac Céin') relates his Otherworldly adventures. Old Irish *tadc/tadg* is usually interpreted as 'poet' (as in the gloss *tadg i<d est> fili*, 'tadg, that is *poet*'; DIL, s.v. *tadg*) though Mac an Bhaird (1980) has traced it to **tazgo* 'badger.' The animal was associated with Tadg mac Céin in a totemic fashion (Koch 1992, 102; there is also a dissenting view in Toorians 2015), and we read in *Cormac's Glossary* (*Sanas Cormaic*) of the prohibition Tadg was under regarding the consumption of badgers (Meyer 1912, 56, 77). On the mythical notion that one is prohibited from eating one's namesake (as Setanta/Cú Chulainn's taboo involved dogs), Tadg's name in the Old Irish period apparently still meant 'badger.' Conn Cétchathach's sometime rival was Mug Nuadat (or Eógan Mór), whose name means 'servant of Nuada'; Nuada was the mythical king of the Tuatha Dé Danann who led them into Ireland, and lost an arm to the Fir Bolg warrior Sreng at the first battle of Moytura (Magh Tuireadh). As the king's body is to be without blemish in an old sovereignty myth, the first stratagem devised by Dian Cécht (physician god of the Tuatha, and a sort of proto-druid) to restore Nuada is the creation of a silver arm, hence the addition of his epithet *Airgeadlámh* ('Silver-Arm'). That we are dealing here not just with an Irish myth can be seen in the cognate forms and myths found in Brittonic: the Welsh mythic hero Nudd from the Triads bore the epithet *Llaw Ereint* ('silver hand'),[3] and Nuada and Nudd likely descend from the British god Nodons/Nodens (< **Nowdont-*; Matasović 2009, 350) whose famous sanctuary was found at the Romano-British temple and baths complex at Lydney Park (Gloucestershire; the Roman site was built upon an earlier Iron Age Celtic *oppidum* or hill-fort). Curse tablets in bronze and lead include the famous curse levied on Senicianus by Silvianus for the alleged theft of a ring; Silvianus offers the god Nodens (DEVO NODENTI, 'to the god Nodens') half the value of the ring for its successful retrieval (RIB 306). Examples of such Celtic mythic complexes could be multiplied, but an important point for the story of English is the old religion and mythos of Celtic Britain embedded in place-names inherited by English and broader parallels of the Proto-Indo-European inheritance in Celtic and Germanic.

Turning back to the specific matter of Celtic loan-words in English, the OED lists its first attestation for *brock* 'badger' as from the late OE *Leechdoms* (ca. 1000), likely an early loan from Celtic (Welsh and Cornish *broch* < British **broccos* < **brokko-*). English *brock* is now seen as chiefly dialectal (in British English), having been displaced by *badger* in the 16th century (a form of uncertain etymology, though probably via a Romance language). Later that century, in his *The Noble Arte of Venerie or Hunting* (1575, a translation of Jacques de Fouilloux's *La venerie* [1561]), George Gascoigne observes: "If you finde a Badgerde abroad, it shall not be from hir burrow lightly." In a treatise on hunting, where one might expect the older English form, the new word holds sway. Here we can see loan formations at two ends of a chronological

[3] To this complex might perhaps be added the AD 3rd-century Caledonian Argentocoxus ('Silver Leg'), a remark of whose wife to Julia Domna, empress and consort of Septimius Severus, is recorded by Dio Cassius (LXXVII.16); cf. Birley 1980, 28, 166; LHEB 536 n. 2, 537 n. 1.

scale: a loan from Celtic into earliest English (*brock*), and the supplanting of that loan by another form (*badger*) in Early Modern English.

The overview of the last chapter of Proto-Indo-European and Proto-Germanic attempted to fill out the 'prehistory' of the English language, the features it inherited by being a branching off of Northwest Germanic, in turn a branching off from Common Germanic, traceable through Proto-Germanic back to Proto-Indo-European. Limiting the time-scale to the formative period of English's development (the 5th to 6th centuries), that is a span of at least 4,500 years. The prehistory to the *Sprachraum* of English in Celtic Britain spans the four centuries of Roman Britain before the invasion of Hengist and Horsa traditionally dated to AD 449, and at least four centuries before those that saw Insular Celtic (which would branch off into Q-Celtic Goidelic and P-Celtic Brittonic) develop from Common Celtic (and this is the conservative estimate; Celtic may have been spoken in the British Isles even earlier than 350 BC). Most histories of the language nod to PIE and PGmc, but begin in Britain with the invasions and settlements of the Angles, Saxons, Jutes, and Frisians (as does the excellent CHEL; Hogg 1992, 1–25). In a sense, this is the beginning of the story of English *in medias res*; as the example of OE *dūn* (ultimately a loan from Celtic) shows, Celtic-Germanic interaction began on the Continent (the Rhine delta is one such zone of interaction). And the 'dark' centuries of the development of English, the 5th to 6th centuries, were not just an expansion of Germanic-speakers northward and westward from the beachhead in the east and southeast, but a complex process of encounter with native speakers of other languages – some of whom formed communities within the early Anglo-Saxon kingdoms. British was spoken north of the Thames, and in more heavily wooded areas; Saxons may have taken the valleys, leaving Celts to their hilltop *oppida* (forts). The kingdoms of Elmet, Bernicia, and Deira resisted for a time absorption into Northumbria. King Offa of Mercia constructed a massive earthwork to deal with the 'Welsh problem'; Cumbric, the Brittonic of the 'North Welsh,' seems to have survived the Anglo-Saxons in the Old North (*Yr Hen Ogledd*) and fades only with the end of Alt Clut in the 11th and early 12th centuries, the Kingdom of Strathclyde being absorbed into the Kingdom of Scotland (the expansion for centuries of Goidelic brought by Irish settlers to Western Scotland had been reshaping the toponymy of Scotland as well). Cornish survived to the 18th century, perhaps a little later, while Welsh remained in active use and grew again with language revival efforts in the 20th century. The story of English is one of its 'triumph,' or at least advance, first within the British Isles, then globally. But English has never been alone in its linguistic homeland, and it is a necessary step in tracing its development to take account of the linguistic environment that obtained in Britain 'before English.'

3.1 BEFORE 'ENGLAND'

In the previous chapter, an overview was made of the earliest roots of English that historians of the language can possibly trace. Though mention was made of longer-range reconstructions than Proto-Indo-European (which takes us back to ca. 4000 BC in the conventional estimate), this chapter will focus on the language situation in Britain from the late Bronze (traditionally to ca. 800 BC) and Iron Ages (ca. 800 BC–AD 43, the latter date that of the Claudian invasion of England) to the four centuries of Roman rule in Britain (from Caesar's first invasion in 55 BC to the withdrawal of the legions ca. AD 410–417). Place-name evidence, particularly of hydronyms, may provide what little tentative evidence there is of the pre- and non-Celtic languages of Britain (Ouse, Soar, Solent, Tweed, Tyne, possibly Thames); but even here it may be more a matter of etymologies not fully worked out: the CDEPN lists the *Ouse* (Yorks.) as 'Unexplained,' and though attempts have been made to reconstruct a Primitive Welsh **Ūs* from British **Usso-* ultimately deriving from the zero-grade of PIE **wed-* 'water,' "The name is probably pre-Celtic, possibly pre-IE" (Jackson in LHEB had rejected the proposed PrW **Ūs* on phonological grounds as an impossible development of late British **Ussī*; 342). The Solent is likewise listed as 'Unexplained': no known PIE root has been adequately produced for it (a presumable **sol-*), nor has any convincing attempt been made to link it to a non-IE root ("Speculative attempts to associate **sol-* with a non-IE language such as Phoenician can neither be accepted nor rejected in the present state of knowledge"; CDEPN, s.v.).

To stay for a moment with river-names, which, along with terms for other natural features, seem particularly durable, we see among them one of the richest sources of Celtic loans to English. The endurance of indigenous or native terms for rivers, springs, mountains, headlands, and so forth is certainly not unique to Britain, and will be seen again when English in the Americas is turned to. Native American names for rivers and other bodies of water proliferate on the East coast and in the Midwest, with a somewhat greater rate of replacement by English or other colonial names (e.g., Rio Grande, the Brazos River – originally Río de los Brazos de Dios, 'River of the Arms of God') as one moves further west. In the Eastern United States, names from Algonquian and other Native languages families are predominant for the major rivers: Aroostook, Connecticut, Housatonic, Kennebec, Merrimack, Mystic (Missi-tuk), Neponset, Niantic, Penobscot, Quinnipiac, Saugatuck, Taconic, Willimantic in just New England, while other major rivers of the Mid-Atlantic to Upper Southern seaboard include the Monongahela, Susquehanna, Potomac, Rappahannock, and Roanoke. One of the Native names of the famed Hudson River was the Mahicantuck, from the Mohican language, though there were also Iroquois and Delaware names for the river – this river and its various renamings serve as a signal example of colonial linguistic interactions in New Amsterdam-New York. The example of Native American river-names quite interestingly offers another parallel for the British-English centuries under consideration (AD 1st–6th centuries): major rivers often, though certainly not always, maintained their original or native name in early contact areas; in the British example one thinks of the Tweed, Tyne, Tees, Eden, Ribble, Ure, Derwent, Ouse, Trent, Nene, Severn, Wye, Avon, Stour, Tamar, Taw, Exe, Thames, and Medway, which are nearly all certainly Celtic (or pre-Celtic British in a few debated instances).

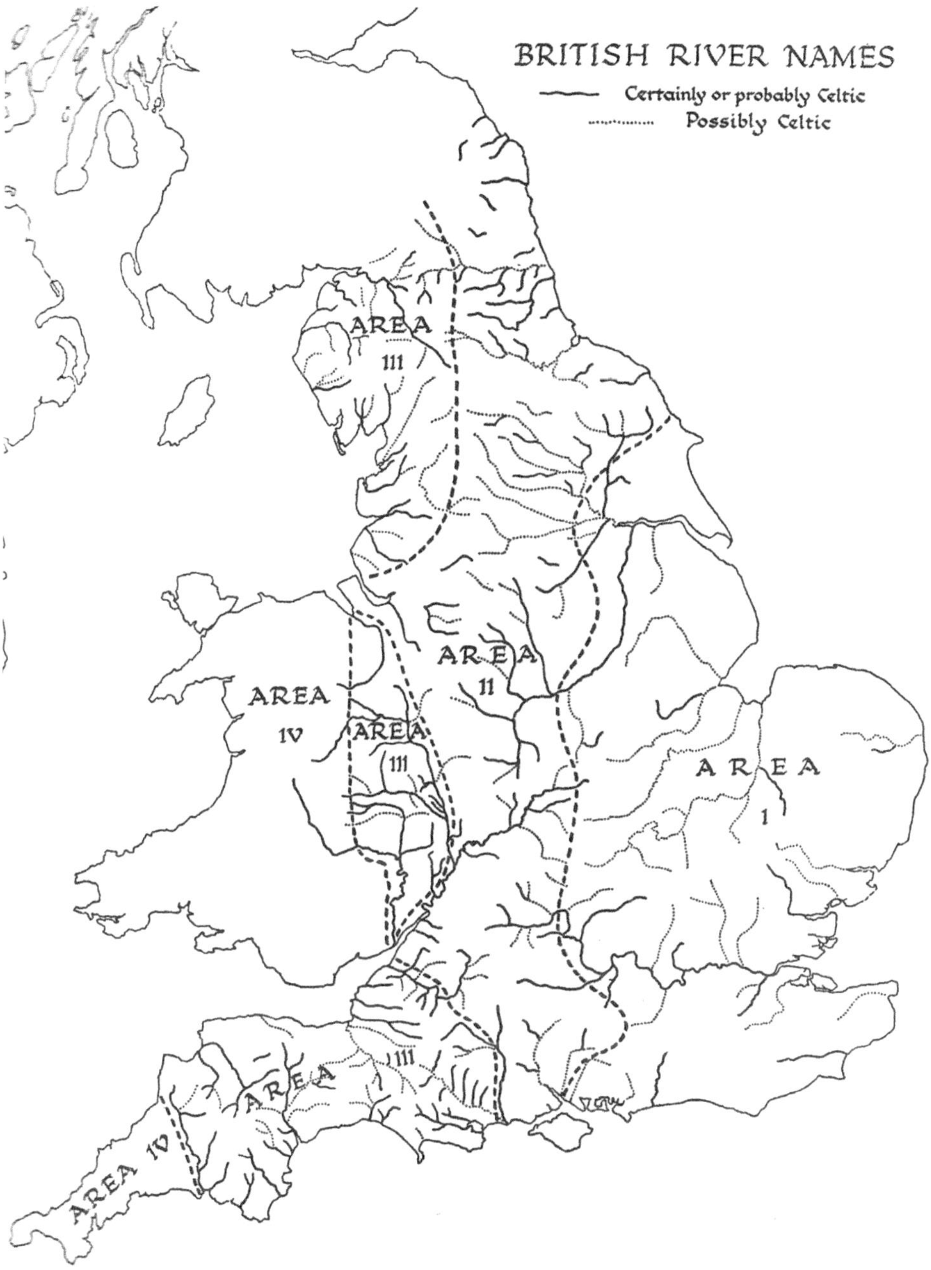

British River-Names; LHEB 220.
Source: Reprinted with permission from Jackson, Language and History in Britain (1953) / Four Courts Press.

British river-names Max Förster's *Der Flussname Themse und seine Sippe* ("The River-Name Thames and its Kindred (Terms)"; Förster 1941) is the most extensive study of English hydronymy (system of names for bodies of water). Förster had tabulated some 444 river-names in Britain deriving from Celtic (Förster 1941, 101–102) – this can be pared down with variant forms for the same river, and for different rivers bearing the same name, if in different spellings or derivative or variant form: the Derwent-Darent-Dart or Thames-Tamar-Tame-Team-Teme-Thame complexes of hyrdronyms. There continues to be great debate if not controversy over the 'Celticity' of the hydronyms, and much depends on matters of linguistic reconstruction, archaeology, and even genetics that span the Indo-European spectrum (especially, but not limited to, Western Indo-European). Very few river-names are now thought to be non-Indo-European, and what few there may be are all to be found in north and western Scotland (Kitson 1996, 106). Though the debate over Pictish leans toward its identification as Brittonic (a recent dissenting view is Sims-Williams 2012, 431), recent revisionist work has suggested 'proto-English' forms for some river-names, envisioning groups of Germanic-speakers in Britain much earlier than traditionally thought (a popular revisionist treatment is Oppenheimer 2007). There is little at present to recommend a Germanic settlement of Britain picture as other than traditionally drawn, that is, the 5th-century invasions and migrations as recorded by Bede: these would be the determinative movements of Germanic-speakers – determinative for the history of England and the English language, though it has been mentioned in this chapter that Germans were present in Britain throughout the Roman occupation. 'Celtoskepticism' seems to have induced particularly fine hair-splitting when it comes to river-names, for which the Celtic legacy is, even by a conservative estimate, immense. English river-names from the Anglo-Saxon period, when not just Anglicizations of Celtic (*Taff* for *Taf*) or hybrid formations, are of course *re-namings*. The Britons had their own terms for all the rivers of Britain. The notion of 'Old European' (*alteuropäisch*) explanations for river-names such as the Thames as indicating non-Indo-European origin seems to have fallen out of favor (Kitson 1996, 113), and attributing difficult-to-explain hydronyms to non-Celtic Indo-European can involve arguing *ignotum per ignotius* (explaining the unknown by the even more unknown). Allowing for a generous interpretation of 'Celtic' river-names in Britain – including those definitely to likely Celtic, and those perhaps at least Celticized or which passed through Celtic to English, such as those labeled 'Old European' (i.e., Indo-European, but perhaps not exclusively Celtic) but which are preserved and (often) transmitted through British, Welsh, Cumbric, and Cornish (these have been marked with an asterisk) – an impressive list presents itself. Among these hydronyms are:

Alan and Camel (the main and upper courses of this river in Cornwall; as would be expected, Celtic forms predominate in the southwest, Wales and adjacent English counties, and north)
Cale (Somerset; perhaps meaning 'creel river'; CDEPN, s.v.)
Cam and *Granta (Cambridgeshire)
Dacre (Cumberland; < PrW **Dagr* < **dakru-* 'tear,' Modern Welsh *deigryn*; the sense is 'trickling stream

Lugg (Hereford and Worcester; this, like Luke Brook, Marstow, Herefordshire, means 'bright' [British **leuc-*; LHEB 557]
Lune (Lancashire-Westmorland; this hydronym is thought to be possibly cognate with Irish river-name Slaney (< *Sláine*) with sense 'health-giving' river)
Dart, Darent, Derwent (one of a number of complexes of river-names from British)
Dee (Cheshire)
Irthing (Cumbria-Northumberland)
Loddon (Berkshire-Hampshire; perhaps meaning 'muddy river')
Lympne (Kent; of interest in that this comes from Förster's Area I, the east and southeast, which shows the lowest number of Celtic forms)
Ock (Oxfordshire; this tributary of the Thames means 'salmon' river, from Proto-Brittonic **esāko-*, compare Old Cornish *ehoc*; Matasović 2009, s.v. **esok-*)
*Ouse (North Yorkshire)
*Solent (Hampshire; the name for the strait that separates the Isle of Wight, which bears a Celtic name, from the mainland has resisted satisfactory explanation)
*Stour (name of rivers in Kent, and Cambridgeshire-Essex-Suffolk)
Tern (Shropshire)
*Thames (and Tame, Tavy, Taw, Team, Teme, Thame, all part of the same river-name complex)
Trent (Derbyshire, like the Tarrant in Dorset, from British *Trisantonā*)
*Tweed (Northumberland)
*Tyne (Northumberland)
Ure (North Yorkshire, from British **Isurā*, which gave its name, evidently also that of a river-goddess, to the Roman site *Isurium Brigantum* at Aldborough)
Usk (like the *Esk* and *Exe*, from British *Isca*, simply meaning 'water' – cf. Irish *uisce*, Scots Gaelic *uisge*, Manx *ushtey*; the modern Brittonic languages have reflexes of Proto-Celtic **dubro-* 'dark [water],' Welsh *dŵr*, Cornish *dhowr*, Breton *dour*; this latter Celtic root produced the names for the rivers Dore, Hereford and Worcester, and Dove, Derbyshire and North Yorkshire, the 'dark river,' as well as the Dawlish [Devon], Dowlish [Somerset], and Divelish [Dorset]; LHEB 274–278)
Wellow (Avon; Hampshire; likely cognate is the *Welloe* in Cornwall, both with the sense of 'winding, turning' river)
Wharfe (North Yorkshire; from Romano-British *Verbeia*, apparently the name of an eponymous river-goddess to whom an altar was dedicated at Ilkley, West Yorkshire, which fort likely bore the name of the river and goddess; Clodius Fronto, prefect of the second cohort of Lingones, soldiers from the Gaulish tribe of that name, set up the altar as 'sacred to Verbeia': VERBEIAE | SACRVM | CLODIVS | FRONTO | PRAEF COH | II LINGON; RIB 635; Latin *v-* / British *u-* > Old English *w(h)-* and *-b-* > *-v-* > *-f-*, lenition of British *b* then devoicing [LHEB 558] – the change is observed with the Severn, British *Sabrina* > Old English *Sæfern*, with metathesis of *r*)

(*continued*)

(*continued*)

*Wye (Derbyshire; Ekwall is likely right that this and the identical Wey in Dorset are old British hydronyms; the Garren in Herefordshire is a tributary of the Wye, and Luke Brook feeds into the Garren; these both are Celtic; Förster 1941, 191 and n. 2)
*Yare (Norfolk; it appeared in Ptolemy's *Geography*, ca. AD 150, as Γαριέννος/*Gariénnos*)
Yeo (Dorset; in this case, likely from British **gabliā*, **gablio-* 'fork' (cf. Welsh *gafl* < **gefl* 'fork,' referring to the forking in the river); *Yeo* in Somerset and vicinity occurs also as a dialectal form of Old English *ēa* 'water,' a generic for a stream or river, used to replace a native Celtic term; related forms are Yeovil, Ivel)

Border counties in the north, west, south-southwest have the highest number of Celtic hydronyms, a not unexpected result: Cumberland (39 river-names), Devon (36), Somerset (28), Gloucestershire (25), Lancashire (25), Worcestershire (23), Dorset (23), and Northumberland (22) top the list assembled (with some repeated names) in Förster's nearly thousand-page study of British hydronyms (Förster 1941, 101; and for further examples of Celtic hydronyms adopted into Old and Middle English, see 117–125).

Kenneth Jackson's *Language and History in Early Britain* (Jackson 1953 [= LHEB]) remains the major work on the subject, and it has stood the test of time and scrutiny by other linguists (see in particular Sims-Williams 2003, who examined every proposed sound change from LHEB). Based on his own work and that earlier from Ekwall (*English River-Names* [Ekwall 1928]) and Max Förster (his *Der Flussname Themse und seine Sippe* [*The River-Name Thames and Its Kindred*; Förster, 1941] is the most detailed study of Brittonic hydronyms), Jackson noted areas of clustering of surviving Brittonic river-names: Area I (which would form the core Anglo-Saxon settlement zone) preserved the lowest number of Brittonic names, mainly mid- to larger-size rivers such as the Trent, Thames, Thame, and Darent (LHEB 221); Areas II–IV saw higher concentrations of Brittonic names the more west and north ones goes, with, as would be expected, particularly high concentrations in Cumbria, Wales, and Cornwall, and, interestingly, the upland region between the Tyne and Tees, not fully settled until late in the Anglian settlement of Northumbria. Toponyms, hydronyms in particular here, can allow at times for a plotting of linguistic contact, sound change, and loan formation in the history of early English – or, in the broader perspective in this chapter, the linguistic history of Britain in a multilingual perspective. The Trent appears three times in Bede's *Ecclesiastical History* [HE]: at HE II.16 (*in fluvio Treenta* [with the variant *Trenta*]), III.24 (*fluvio Treanta*), and IV.21 (*iuxta fluvium Treabta* 'beside the River Trent'). The loan seems (following Jackson and Ekwall) to be from Primitive Welsh **Trihanton* to Old English *Treānte*; ancestral to the PrW form is British **Trisantonā*. A number of sound changes are evident in the course from the native British name to the OE: the reduction of /ɪ/ to /ə/ (Ekwall had envisaged an intermediary **Trəhanton*) for which OE substituted /e/, and the shift /s-/ > /h-/: the /s/ here is /s-/ as the head of the second element of a compound British name **Tri-Santonā* < British **tri-* 'across' + **santon-*, perhaps cognate with the Gaulish tribal name *Santones*, as recorded by Caesar, and preserved in the city name Saintes (Roman *Mediolanum Santonum*) and its historical province Saintonge in the modern département Charente-Maritime (see Dauzat and Rostaing 1989, 638). Rivet and Smith (*The Place-Names of Roman Britain*) present other derivations (Rivet and Smith 1979, 476–477), but return to Ekwall's explanation, though they tender the possibility that the river-name may be related to the tribal name Setantii and the theonym Sentona (a 'goddess of the way'), though this presents phonological difficulties – there is however the example Gaulish **sentu-* 'path, road,' with Gallo-Roman place-name *Sentiniacus* > *Sainteny* (département Manche; Delamarre 2003, 270; Whatmough 1970, 1144–1145; Dauzat and Rostaing 1989, 638, s.v. *Sainteny* [*Sentiniacus* < personal name **Sentennus*]). The Gaulish Santones figure in a passage from the *Mosella* of AD 4th-century Gallo-Roman poet Ausonius's tribute to the Moselle:

> non tibi se Liger anteferet, non Axona praeceps,
> Matrona non, Gallis Belgisque intersita finis,
> Santonico refluus non ipse Carantonus aestu (*Mosella* ll. 461–463).

Not the Liger [Loire] prefers himself before you, nor plunging Axona [Aisne],
not Matrona [Marne], interposed as limit between Gauls and Belgae,
not even Carantonus [Charente] himself turned back by the Santonian tide.

The Moselle and other rivers of Gaul are personified and honored by Ausonius as living, life-giving and -bearing entities – gods even, as river deities were a religious and mythological commonplace in the classical world; the Belgae of Gaul and Britain (as this tribe was found on both sides of the channel) and other Celtic tribes inhabited a landscape of sacred waters (not to speak of groves, hills, valleys and peaks), and it was in such a landscape that English would develop – and it had its roots in lands of sacrificial bogs and springs (there is a vast literature on the subject: a recent overview is Aldhouse-Green 2018, 77–117; see also Cunliffe 2018, 272–309). For our purposes, the immediate interest is in that earliest layer of Celtic loanwords in Old English, river-names in particular.

Here a number of broader matters present themselves: for one, attempts at explaining the origin of the name for the Trent (< *Trisantonā*) have looked to an etymological sense of 'wandering, winding,' or 'liable to flood,' and possibly to a theonym (feminine) behind the second half of the compound form (in those proposals that take it as such). That the waters of this river might be connected to, or personified as, a 'goddess of the waters' would be well within keeping of what is known of early Celtic religious beliefs (with their sacrality of springs, wells, rivers, lakes, and other watery places such as bogs and moors). Aquae Sulis (Bath) and Coventina's Well (Carrawburgh, on Hadrian's Wall) come to mind, the latter with a history of worship throughout the Romano-British period (by the evidence of votive inscriptions and continued offerings of coins at the wellspring). At the phonological level, changes in this Brittonic loan to OE allow it to be dated reasonably securely: the shift /Σ-/ to /h-/ (or /s-/ > /h-/)[4] Jackson

[4]The symbol /Σ/ Jackson used in LHEB to indicate a "softer" /s/ distinct from that in Latin, which would give rise to the change /s/ > /h/: "The process is certainly one of loosening or slackening of articulation, a kind of weak lisping" such that "for the Britons it was phonemically quite distinct from the sharply hissed Latin *s*" (LHEB 516–517); Sims-Williams states more definitively: "The symbol /Σ/ denotes a sibilant deriving from IE and Celtic **s*, which remained distinct from Latin *s*, was borrowed as /s/ in loans into Old English, and, unlike Latin *s*, developed into /h/ or zero in Brittonic" (Sims-Williams 2003, 106).

dated to the AD 6th century, and Sims-Williams places it among those sound changes dating to the "first half or middle of sixth century" (Sims-Williams 2003, 394). And we know that the loan is from Brittonic rather than Latin as the latter would have preserved the /s-/. These two matters are fairly neatly encompassed in another British river-name, that of the Severn: deriving from British *Sabrina*, borrowed into OE as *Sæfern*, but appearing in Welsh as *Hafren* (after undergoing the /s-/ > /h-/ shift in the later 6th century). The river figures in British myth in Geoffrey of Monmouth's 12th-century recounting of the legend of Habren (Hafren), the daughter of Locrinus, King of the Britons, by his Germanic mistress Princess Estrildis. Locrinus's spurned wife Gwendolen, daughter of Corineus, King of Cornwall, raised in her native Cornwall an army against Locrinus, whom she defeats, then drowning Estrildis and Habren in the river that now bears the latter's name.

Geoffrey's legendary account of the drowning of Hafren, and her eponymous association with the river known in English as the Severn, in Welsh the Hafren, occurs in Book II of his *Historia regum Britanniae* ('History of the Kings of Britain'), completed around 1136–1138, a work most notable in literary history as a wellspring of Arthurian myth. His *Prophetiae Merlini* ('prophecies of Merlin') was composed a few years earlier and circulated independently and as part of the *Historia*. With particular relevance to the language contact situation at hand with British river-names borrowed by Old English, Geoffrey seems to be of Brittonic origin himself – not Welsh as previously thought, but perhaps a Breton descended from those Bretons William of Normandy had brought with him in the Conquest of 1066 and placed in charge of Wales. His own appellation, Galfridus Arturus, may indicate that his father's name was Arthur, and the contemporary Norman-Breton lord of Monmouthshire was Guihenoc de la Boussac (or Withenoc, Wihenoc), whose father Caradoc held estates in Brittany at Dol (Caradog a name that figures in Arthurian legend as one of the Knights of the Round Table and derives the AD 1st-century chieftain of the Catuvellauni Caratacus). Williams' canny imperial policy was to control one group of Brittonic speakers in Wales with the assistance of another from Brittany. Though it is a vexed matter to determine which Britons had made the migration to Armorica in late Roman and sub-Roman Britain to found Brittany, some were certainly from Southeast and Southern Britain and Cornwall, while others may have been from Wales. Breton, as its name suggests, is descended from Brittonic, and was likely in the 11th and 12th centuries more mutually intelligible with Welsh than at present. Geoffrey wrote in Latin, the language of his ecclesiastical career (he was appointed bishop of St. Asaph's in Wales in 1152), and likely spoke Norman French as well as Breton (Faletra 2008, 10–11). He adopted in his writings an affinity for Welsh and British myth and legend, and engaged in myth-making of his own.

Book II opens with the birth of Brutus's three sons by his Queen Innogin (the spelling Ignogen occurs in Layamon's *Brut* from later in the century, late 12th to very early 13th), and Geoffrey engages in some legendary etymologizing: after the passing of Brutus, Locrinus the eldest son comes to rule Logres – essentially that part of Britain that will become Anglo-Saxon England, from the Humber south to Kent west to the Severn. The *Loegria* in Geoffrey's Latin text is Welsh Lloegyr, which can now refer to all of England and appears in medieval Welsh literature from the *Armes Prydein* ('The Prophecy of Britain') of the Book of Taliesin to the *Mabinogion*. It is of uncertain etymology, with some scholars attempting to connect it to the Romano-British name for Leicester – OE *Ligora/Ligera ceaster* looks to be a formation indicating a tribal name with the first element in gen. pl. (if **Legra* is taken as an earlier name for the Soar on which Leicester is sited; the old Roman name was *Legorensis civitas*) – while in the Brill *Etymological Dictionary of Proto-Celtic* Ranko Matasović supplied a hypothesized root **lāyko-* 'warrior' which may have generated Lloegyr from a collective form **lāykor* (a tentative solution as the only attestation for such a root would be Old Irish *láech*, usually seen as a loan of Latin *lāicus* 'lay, of the people'; Matasović 2009, 234–235). At any rate, Locrinus assumes dominion over Logres, and his brothers Albanactus and Kamber over Alban (Scotland) and Wales (Cambria, Cymry) respectively. As these events are projected back onto the 8th century BC, we have a mythologized national myth of Celtic Britain – and in typical Celtic tripartite fashion with three brothers holding three kingdoms – which narrative turns then to eponymous river forms. After a long period of peaceful rule, Humber the Hun, in Geoffrey's telling, invades Alba (Scotland) and dispatches Albanactus; Locrinus joins forces with his youngest brother Kamber and engages Humber to the south of the Humber estuary, putting the Hunnish king to flight, who then drowns in the waters of the river that now bears his name (*associauit sibi Kambrum fratrem suum et collegit totam iuuentutem patriae et iuit obuiam regi Hunorum citra fluuium qui nunc uocatur Humber. Inito ergo congressu, compulit Humbrum in fugam; qui usque ad fluuium diffugiens submersus est infra fluctus et nomen suum flumini reliquit*; Reeve and Wright 2007, II.24). Among the plunder Locrinus seizes from the late Hun are three girls of wondrous beauty (*tres puellae mirae pulchritudinis*), one, Estrildis, the daughter of a Germanic chieftain, and the events relayed just above proceed such that Gwendolen's rage sees Estrildis and her daughter Habren (and Gwendolen's stepdaughter) drowned on Gwendolen's order in the river that now bears Habren's name:

> Iubet enim Estrildidem et filiam eius Habren praecipitari in fluuium qui nunc Sabrina dicitur fecitque editum per totam Britanniam ut flumen nomine puellae uocaretur; uolebat etenim honorem aeternitatis illi impendere quia maritus suus eam generauerat (Reeve and Wright 2007, II.25).

> She (Gwendolen) ordered Estrildis and her daughter Habren to be hurled into the river which is now called the Sabrina (Severn), and made the decree through all of Britain that the river should be called by her name; for she wished that she (Habren) should be granted the honor of eternity as her husband had fathered her.

In Gwendolen's onslaught Locrinus has let slip the 'joys of this life' pierced with an arrow by the banks of another British river, the Stour (*...iuxta fluuium Sturam, ubi Locrinus ictu sagittae percussus gaudia uitae amisit*; II.25). A similar formula of eponymy obtains (Humber > Humber, Habren > Hafren), and Geoffrey adds a linguistic note to explain the Welsh Hafren and English Severn: *Vnde contigit quod usque in hunc diem appellatum est flumen Britannica lingua Habren, quod per corruptionem nominis alia lingua Sabrina uocatur* ("Thus has it come to pass that to this day the river is called Habren in the British tongue, but through corruption is it called Sabrina [Severn] in the other tongue"; II.25). The Humber, the Stour, the Severn, the 'other tongue' – Geoffrey's imaginative pseudo-history of ancient Britain has its notes of linguistic rightness (*Sæfern* < *Sabrina*, the role of eponyms in British to OE loans – even if fanciful in these instances), and the consciousness of that 'other' or alien tongue evinces not just Geoffrey's pro-Welsh sentiments (from someone who could be said to have been employed in Wales's conquest) but a way of looking at the expansion of English in a Celtic Britain that in his day saw British multilingualism broaden to encompass Norman French, late Old English - early Middle English, and Breton.

3.2 PRETANNIA: BEFORE 449

Πρετάννια (*Pretannia*): our earliest mentions of Britain and its inhabitants are to be found in the Greek geographical writers, for whom geography could be a philosophical concern as well as one of more practical application; their philosophical concerns could encompass such matters as the influence of climate and terrain on culture, the nature of child-rearing, the organization of society, customs, diet, religion – subjects that belong now to the modern anthropologist, ethnographer, sociologist, and all of which were within the purview of the 5th-century BC 'father of History' Herodotus of Halicarnassus, whose 'Inquiries' (ἱστορίαι, *historíai*) makes early mention of the Celts. An early writer such as Hecataeus of Miletus, born in the mid-6th century BC, writes of Massalia – the Greek form, the Latin for which was Massilia, modern Marseilles – founded as a Greek colony by Phocaeans ca. 600 BC in Ligurian territory (see also Thucydides I.13), but, he says, lay in close proximity to Celts; he mentions too a Celtic city – perhaps a fortified town or hill-fort (*oppidum*) as Celts of the time were not known for city-building – called Nyrax (possibly Noreia in what is now Austria; Rankin 2002). Herodotus says that the Danube rises in Celtic territory near Pyrene (II.33); Pytheas of Massalia, of the 4th century BC, in his *Periplous*, may have described an early circumnavigation of the British Isles (Mette 1952). This last title, *periplous* (a 'sailing or going around,' pl. *periploi*) was the term for a genre of Greek geographical writing, recording voyages by sea, such as those of Hecataeus of Miletus or the later (perhaps AD 1st century) *Periplous of the Erythraean Sea*, which encompasses sea and trades routes of not just the Erythraean (i.e., Red) Sea but, as in the Greek notion of that region, the Arabian Gulf and Indian Ocean. One of the earliest of these texts was a Greek translation of a Carthaginian travel report, and this account of the Carthaginian commander or admiral Hanno, to indulge in a brief digression, leads us by a circuitous route back to the story of English.

Hanno (Punic Annôn) departed Carthage sometime late in the 6th century BC at the head of 60 ships and, tasked with establishing Carthaginian colonies in Northwestern Africa, passed through the Pillars of Herakles (the Strait of Gibraltar). He seems to have traveled some way further, quite possibly to modern Sierra Leone or vicinity in West Africa. It is from his account – which he is said to have put onto a tablet and then nailed it up in the temple of Baal-Ammon in Carthage, and was subsequently translated into Greek – by which it came to be known to Arrian, historian of the campaigns and travels of Alexander the Great, and to Pliny the Elder (the prolific polymath whose *Historia naturalis* ['Natural History'] makes important early references to Britain), that we have the first mention of the hirsute creatures he encountered along the African coast: the Greek form in the text is accusative plural γορίλλας (*gorillas*), which appears in a 1799 English translation as *Gorillae* (it is the first attestation given in OED: 'Another island full of savage people...whose bodies were hairy, and whom our interpreters called Gorillae'; s.v. *gorilla*). The American missionary Rev. Dr. Thomas S. Savage, writing from Cape Palmas, Liberia, named one of his naturalistic discoveries *Troglodytes gorilla* (Liberia had its own curious role in the history of American English as it was the chief town of the Liberian 'state of Maryland' – briefly, 1854–1857, the Republic of Maryland – that the American-based Maryland State Colonization Society encouraged American Blacks, free-born and freedmen, to settle starting in 1834). Savage adopted Hanno's term in his 1847 report published in the *Journal of the Boston Natural History Society*. The preferred classification became *Gorilla gorilla*, but the line extending from Hanno in the late 6th or early 5th century BC to the 19th-century American settlement of Liberia traces an etymological course: γορίλλας > *Gorillae* > *gorillas*.

It was another Carthaginian explorer, Himilco 'the Navigator' of the 5th century BC, who reputedly made it as far as the British Isles. Pliny (II.169ff.) and Rufius Festus Avienus refer to Himilco's lost account, of his trading for tin in Brittany (among the Oestrumnides), apparently following the route employed by Tartessians, who were one of the vanished peoples of ancient Iberia, and a linguistic puzzle as their surviving inscriptions seem to have been syllabo-alphabetic, likely based on the Phoenician system, and genetic classification of the language, beyond links to Lusitanian and other ancient pre-Indo-European languages of Iberia, is highly uncertain (see Untermann 1998; of interest are similarities in character form and epigraphic style between Tartessian and other Iberian and Runic monuments; Guerra 2002, 222–224, figures 2–5; Koch 2011, 2013). Greek curiosity with Carthaginian naval exploits, and no doubt some sense of competition, spurred their interest in *periploi* accounts, which they were soon to write themselves. Early writers such as Skylax (or Pseudo-Skylax) of the 6th century BC and Pytheas of Massalia of the late 4th century BC help trace the earliest outlines of the Celts in Western Europe; if Skylax's account, which survives only in citations by later classical writers, is accurate, the Celts had in his day not yet arrived in Spain (though they had pushed the Ligurians there ahead of them); by the time of Pytheas, who had claimed a circumnavigation of the British Isles, the Celts had spread further westward.

The time of Celtic settlement of the British Isles is a highly contentious matter, likewise that of how many migrations there were. The traditional conservative estimate is that Ireland had been settled by the 3rd century BC (or perhaps not earlier than 500 BC), Britain somewhat earlier; linguistic evidence, such as the chronology of P-Celtic and Q-Celtic languages, likely suggests an earlier dating (this alludes to an initial consonant shift in Proto-Celtic evidenced in the surviving daughter languages: e.g., '5' in Welsh is *pump*, in Irish *cúig*, British Latin *Patricius* > Old Irish *Cothriche* [St. Patrick]). We can say that by the 5th (or 4th in some more skeptical accounts) century BC the spread of Celts westward (to Spain and the British Isles) and eastward – through Eastern Europe, Thrace, and with three tribes eventually settling in central Asia Minor, modern Turkey, in what would be called Galatia – thrust them into history. While reference has sometimes been made to a 'Celtic Empire,' a misnomer on a number of counts – not the least of which was the lack of any central government across the Celtic regions: a point noted by Greek writers and seized upon by Roman generals – one can see broad similarities across the culture groups, with strong indicators such as the persistence of La Tène artistic types from what is now the Czech Republic to Spain, and, of course, the evidence of linguistic filiation in the reconstructed hypothetical early Italo-Celtic branch of Indo-European and the surviving testimony of Continental and Insular Celtic languages. This period 'before English,' of a Celtic world (or at least a Celtic-speaking one), spans at least the 4th century BC to the AD 5th century. It is not simply the background against which English would emerge, but the cultural, historical, geographical, and even genetic (with the caveats of Sims-Williams 2012) context for contact between speakers of languages from two branches of the Indo-European family of languages, Celtic and Germanic, to describe the groups of peoples least controversially in ethnolinguistic terms. This last point has great significance to how the story of English has been written. The story of anything 'Celtic' has been subjected to withering skepticism, particularly in English academic writing; it is a matter that will be returned to again, but for this early period one can see some scholarship veer between poles of 'Celtomania' and 'Celtoskepticism,' or what the Swiss medievalist Johannes Duft termed *Iromanie* and *Irophobie* (roughly 'Irish-' or 'Hiberno-mania' and '-phobia,' from *Die Iren*, 'the Irish'). As mentioned in the previous chapter, the Celtic languages broke away from the Indo-European stock fairly early, perhaps in an Italo-Celtic branching, as attested by conservatism in daughter languages (notably Old Irish), while the Germanic dialects diverged some time around 500 BC. The geographic homelands of the Celtic and Germanic branches of IE do not appear to have been immediately contiguous (Germanic to the north, around what is now Southern Denmark and the Baltic coast; Celtic to the east, though the spread westward to Northern Italy must have been fairly early), nor synchronous – the changes in Celtic are older. In the classical period too we hear of the Celts first; by the later classical period, contact is sustained, with Germanic tribes exerting pressure on settled Celtic tribes, some of whom had been either Hellenized (such as those of Galatia) or Romanized (the Gaulish tribes), nearly all of whom had engaged in hostilities with Greeks, Macedonians, Romans, and others.

The Celts of Gaul under two war leaders named Brennus threatened Greece and Rome in the 4th to 3rd centuries BC. The earlier Brennus led his Gaulish bands (he himself was leader of the Senones, whom Caesar would fight 53 BC onward), south across the Alps, pushed out the Umbrians (speakers of an Italic Indo-European language), settled his people into the region of the March of Ancona and came into conflict with Rome. In a shock that would reverberate down the centuries, the Romans were defeated at the Battle of the Allia (a small tributary of the Tiber) ca. 390–387 BC, and Rome itself was sacked but for the Capitoline Hill; the Romans sued for peace and, in Livy's famous account (V.34–49), Brennus's men produced scales and balances with which to weigh the promised thousand pounds of gold. When the Romans complained that the balances were rigged, Brennus is said to have thrown his sword into the scales and cried out *Vae victis!* ('Woe to the vanquished!'). The Romans would not solve their Senones problem until 283 BC, when Publius Cornelius Dolabella defeated the Gauls under

Britomaris (who had defeated a Roman army the previous year); Britomaris would be executed during Dolabella's triumph. The later Brennus led Gauls against Macedon, then Greece, during the Celtic-Greek wars of the 3rd century BC; the historian Dio Cassius records an anecdote of Brennus at the Athenian sanctuary-treasury at Delphi in his History (XXII.97), and Pausanias records the Celtic-Greek battle at Thermopylae (Greek historians had a tendency to model the Celtic-Greek wars of the 3rd century on the Greco-Persian wars of the 5th; Rankin 2002). An interesting sidenote is the conflation of the two Brennoi or Brenni as Brennius, conqueror of Rome, in 12th-century Geoffrey of Monmouth's *History of the Kings of Britain*; history and pseudo-history of the Celtic forebears of the Britons was well established as a preoccupation of British and English writers in the medieval period.

And there was plenty of heroic material to choose from: Bolgius (or Bolgios, Belgius) led his Gauls against Illyria, Macedon, then Greece; in 279 BC he made his mark as the first Celtic war-leader to kill in battle a Greek king: Ptolemy Keraunos, of the Ptolemies of Egypt, a descendant of one of the Diadochoi ('Successors') of Alexander the Great, had made his way to Thrace then Macedon in a series of Greek dynastic intrigues, all of which he survived only to fall to the Celts. The 3rd century BC sees still more battles, but for our purposes, most significant is the westward extent of the Celtic settlement; they are by this time well established in France, Spain, and the British Isles. The Hellenistic Greek historian Polybius (born ca. 203 BC) records that Celts (Gauls) were along with Hannibal as allies in 218 BC during the Punic Wars (Xenophon, in his *Hellenica*, had recorded that Celtic mercenaries had been dispatched to Sparta to assist them against Thebes; VII.1.20); here and there he records information of some ethnographic interest: the great value they placed upon friendship (II.17–18), their love of mead and the bond of the *gaisatai* ('warrior bands'; a comparison is inevitable with the Germanic *comitatus*; II.27), and that, being naturally inclined to warlike behavior, Celts fell into duels that served as an entertainment of sorts for Hannibal's army on the march (III.62). We come, then, within reach chronologically of *Britannia*, the land of the Britons as it begins to emerge in Roman accounts of the 1st century BC. A late writer, but one who claimed to have drawn upon very early sources (as far back as the 6th century BC), brings us to the British Isles proper; Rufius Festus Avienus in his *Ora maritima* ('The Shore of the Sea') mentions Albion ('an old name for Britain,' OLD, s.v., mentioned also by Pliny, HN IV.102, and in Apuleius's *De mundo* VII), Hibernia (the Latin name for Ireland relatively infrequent in occurrence – it appears in Caesar, Pliny, Tacitus, and Apuleius – no doubt owing in part to the Roman failure to colonize that other British isle), and the Oestrymnides, which are described as islands but may in fact refer to Cornwall, that is, the 'Tin Islands,' or the tribe traded with for tin, likely actually in Brittany. The scope now narrows to what could be called a 'proto-English' period or phase: the Germanic 'dialects' (those daughter languages of Proto-Germanic since its emergence from Indo-European ca. 500 BC) had been undergoing the regular sound changes one must take note of for the prehistory of the English language – Grimm's Law, Verner's Law of the previous chapter – even if their relative chronology is not entirely certain (the chronology in Ringe 2017, which refines the consensus, is essentially followed here). In the linguistic Proto-Germanic period, the actual Germanic tribes would expand westward from the Baltic shores and the great river deltas of what is now Germany and Poland, and press increasingly upon Celtic territory. The story of

English is a continuation of this nearly millennium-long phenomenon: the Germanic invasions of Britain in the AD 5th century are part of a recurrent pattern, and one that had not reached its end with AD 449; indeed the movement of the Franks and Lombards, across France, and into Italy, and of the Visigoths and Vandals, into Spain and North Africa, are part of this era that would last into early Middle Ages. The Germanic tribes did not expand into uninhabited wastes and, while population pressures (and movement of still other tribes from further eastward) played a role in the *Völkerwanderung*, we are not certain of the precise factors behind the 'wandering of the peoples' (neither do we fully understand the factors behind the Viking Age emigration of Scandinavians 793–ca. 1100). One can say at least that by the 1st century BC both Britannia and Germania emerge more fully into the written record, again through classical eyes.

3.3 FURTHEST BRITAIN

Britannia, as it occurs in extant Latin writers, is a relatively rare form; it must not have been at the time. While not as fully within the orbit of *Romanitas* as was Gaul, Britain, in the relevant periods of the Roman settlement, was, to the walls of Hadrian and Antoninus Pius in the north, and to Southwestern Wales, thoroughly Romanized. To be sure, British (Celtic) ways obtained and survived within both the Roman town and townlands – Londinium itself, which form appears in Tacitus (Rivet and Smith 1979, 48), Eboracum (York), Rutupiae (Richborough; the major port of entry for Roman Britain), Camulodunum (Colchester), and so forth – and in the areas under client-kings; they predominated in the more rural districts even well into the medieval period. *Britannia*, the feminine Latin national term, occurs in a letter from Cicero to his brother Quintus (*o iucundas mihi tuas de Britannia litteras!* – "What a joy to me your letters from Britain!"; II.15.14), and in the poems of Catullus and Propertius, in the epigrams of Spanish Celtic writer Martial, Pliny, and Caesar of course. In Book IV of the *Gallic War*, he moves his troops into the territory of the Morini, Belgic Celts (the name means 'sea people'), whence the crossing to Britain was shortest (IV.21; Hammond 2008, 80); in Book V Caesar has Indutiomarus of the Treveri, a Gallic tribe on the Rhine frontier (the Roman town Augusta Treverorum now Trier, Trèves), produce 200 hostages as Caesar had not wanted to fight the Treveri as he prepared for his *Britannicum bellum* ('British war,' V.4; Hammond 2008, 91). Pliny describes the sea between the Rhine and Seine as *Britannicus*: *inter Rhenum et Sequanum Britannicus (oceanus)*, HN IV.109; the *Sequana* is both the river Seine and its tutelary goddess: compare the inscription DEAE SEQVANA<E> RVFVS DONAVIT, CIL 13.2865; "Rufus has given (this) to the goddess Sequana"). Cicero refers to this 'British sea' as rough or stormy (*aestus maritimi Britannici*; *De natura deorum* III.24); east of Boulogne to Utrecht the name *mare Germanicum* could be applied (Roman forms for this Rhine 'ford' or 'crossing-place' such as *Ad Traiectum* or *Ultraiectum* would produce the modern place-name (Utrecht); compare *Traiectum ad Mosam*, Maastricht). The ancestors of the English would cross this in the AD 5th century. The corpus of Roman inscriptions preserves evidence of units serving in Britain (COHORT <ALARV>M BRITANICINIARVM, CIL 3.1919, and [ALA] I FLAVIA BRITANICIANA, CIL 16.47), of a British merchant (NEGOTIATOR

BRITANICIANVS, CIL 13.8164a), and of the island itself personified (deified?) in a dedicatory inscription (BRITANNIAE SANCTAE, CIL 7.232; the form *Britanicianus*, 'of Britain,' was replaced by *Britannicus*, or *Brittanicus*; see Kennedy 1977, 250–251). The root vowel /i/ could vary with /e/ (BRET[ANNIA], CIL 3.249), a spelling that occurred in Old English, especially in the Anglo-Saxon Chronicle: the *Brettas* of the British Library Tiberius B.iv manuscript and survive also in the archaic appellative *Brett* with lowered vowel (applied formerly to Strathclyde Britons into the early Middle English period; OED, s.v. *Brett*). The term has its literary genealogy: Layamon in his *Brut*, a text vital to English re-imaginings of Britons and Britain, writes, in his version of the conjoining of the Troy story to that of his own nation (echoing Virgil with his *Aeneid*), that *þa Troinisce men þa temden hine to hærre, æfter Brutone Brutons heom cleopede* (line 1958; "the Trojan men swore allegiance to him as lord, so after Brutus did they call themselves Britons"), while Geoffrey Chaucer, in Book III of *The House of Fame*, his dream-vision poetical meditation on fame dating to approximately 1379–1380, invokes a congeries of famous harpers:

Ther herde I pleyen on an harpe,
That sowned both wel and sharpe,
Orpheus ful craftely,
And on his syde, faste by,
Sat the harper Orion,
And Eacides Chiron,
And other harpers many oon,
And the Bret Glascurion (Benson 1987, ll. 1201–1208).

Orpheus, Chiron the centaur, and 'the Bret Glascurion': here 'Bret' means Welshman, as Chaucer's British harper/bard is usually identified with Glasgerion (of Child's Ballads, 3:136, no. 67), who is perhaps the 'Blue Bard Keraint' ('y Bardd Glas Keraint'), by legend, a 10th-century bard and scholar (compiler of a first grammar of Welsh), brother to King Morgan Hên of Glamorgan, who went to London with other Welsh bards to enter the service of King Alfred the Great. F.N. Robinson, in his Riverside edition of the works of Chaucer, had ventured that "Nothing is known of the Blue Bard to account for Chaucer's mention of him here, and the source of Chaucer's information is undiscovered" – but, in a plausible solution that reminds one that cultural contact was continuous: "Possibly he got it from some of his Welsh friends" (Benson 1987, 986). Subsequent use of the ethnic form in English literature seems quite often linked to Roman Britain, or at least how late Roman Britain, and its fall, could figure in a moral scheme that normatively gave the advantage to Saxon over Briton: William Tyndale, in his prologue to Jonah (ca. 1531), intones that "Gyldas preached repentaunce vn to the olde Britaynes that inhabited englond: they repented not," and William Fulke, in a 1579 anti-Catholic tract rather fulsomely titled *D. Heskins, D. Sanders, and M. Rastel, accounted three pillers of the popish synagogue, and ouerthrowne (Heskins parleament repealed; A confutation of Sanders treatise; A refutation of Rastels confutation)* could make the appeal "As Ninnius a Britaine doeth testifie" (OED, s.v. *Britain*, n. 1). Striking are the Reformation-era citations of Gildas, author of the *De excidio Britanniae* ('On the Fall of Britain'), and

Nennius (or pseudo-Nennius; hence 'Nennius' is used to indicate the uncertainty surrounding the figure), reputed author of a *Historia Brittonum* ('History of the Britons'). Gildas was a 6th-century British priest perhaps from Strathclyde; the two medieval lives of Gildas, one by an anonymous writer at the Breton monastic foundation at Rhuys, the other by the Welsh cleric Caradoc of Llancarfan, differ in many significant details, while 'Nennius' was of perhaps the 8th century, though the text attributed to him may be by an unknown 9th-century writer (Dumville 1972–1973, 1975–1976, 1990). This notion of a beleaguered native population, deprived of God's providence by their moral failings, is a remarkably malleable and resonant theme, whether deployed by Gerald of Wales or Geoffrey of Monmouth in the Middle Ages, or by even more dour polemicists of the Reformation.

The period of roughly 400–450 BC was the setting of a pre-Roman Celtic background in Britain; Britain appears hazily, from hearsay or from offshore in the accounts of circumnavigations real or imagined, in the *periploi*. But *Britannia* comes more clearly into focus by the intervention of one man in particular: Caesar.

3.4 ROMANITAS

The campaigns of Gaius Julius Caesar 55–54 BC in Britain, described in *De Bello Gallico* Books IV-V, had been preceded by his campaigns against the Celtic Helvetii and the Germans under Ariovistus (Bk. I), against the Continental Belgae, the Veneti, Aquitani, and other Northwestern Gallic tribes (Bk. III). Caesar's seven commentaries on the Gallic campaigns, in their 'plain style,' give what is seen, variably, as a partisan account of his wars in Gaul, Britain, and the German frontier (an eighth is by one of Caesar's legates, Aulus Hirtius, who would figure, with former tribune Gaius Vibius Pansa Caetronianus, in the post-assassination politics of the late Republic, serving as consul with Pansa in 43 BC and commanding senatorial legions with him also in the civil war). The movements of Caesar's legions were through much of what would become the extended *Sprachraum* ('language area') of English: the tribes of Northern and Northwestern Gaul, the area of the Belgic tribes (later Belgica), and frontier Germanic territory (later Germania Inferior). From the tribes of northwest Gaul (later called Brittany after Britons began moving cross-channel ca. AD 300), the Veneti, Osismi, and Coriosolites (or Curiosolites; their coinage, among those issued from Armorica, show strong iconographic similarities to British issues of the 1st century BC), to those of the central North (Parisii, Bellovaci, Atrebates) and those in the territory of the Belgic confederacy and German frontier; Caesar's battles, negotiations, hostage exchanges, legations, and treaties – which are the real subject of his commentaries – help fill out the cultural genealogy to the cradle of English. The Claudian invasion in AD 43 under Aulus Plautius would bring Britain into the Roman world for approximately the next four centuries.

The complexity of this period, the nature of town-planning and road-building, of imperial and military administration, of trade and exploration, its remains (villas, temples, forts, inscriptions, votive tablets, and so forth) have become much better known with the past century of scholarship and a flourishing of Romano-British Studies, especially in the past few decades (the journal *Britannia*, devoted to the study of Roman Britain, was launched in 1970). The Romano-British world, even after the withdrawal of the legions in AD 410, and despite whatever degree of Celtic British reassertion there may have been in the next few decades, is as much the cultural and geographic crucible of English as are Germania Inferior and Magna Germania (or Germania Transrhenana); just east beyond the Menapii, Tungri, and Batavi – all of whom served in the Roman army in Britain – were the Frisii, the Frisians. The shifting fault line between Celtic and Germanic can be placed along the *Rhenus*, the Rhine, and while Germans would serve in Roman legions in great numbers, this fault line is also one between degrees of Romanization: Germania would never be as Romanized as Gallia, even Britannia. One immediate consequence for the history of thc language concerns literacy and literary culture. While Germans would have recourse to writing (the earliest Runic inscriptions appear to date to the AD 1st century), the matter of 'literary culture,' as opposed to essential literacy, is of great consequence (a theme given stress by Gildas). Britain before the Germanic invasions mid- AD 5th century was already within the orbit of Mediterranean learning, of a literary culture that not only produced a wide-ranging corpus of writing (lyric and epic poetry, legal, medical and other scientific writing, political treatises and orations – and survivals such as the Vindolanda tablets from Roman Britain attest to the epistolary output), but a culture that celebrated writing and writers, that demanded records be kept, laws written down, history committed to the page. The contrast between the Roman world and its *litteras* ('writing, letters') and the barbarians of the forests, with their 'songs,' is noted by authors Roman (Caesar, Tacitus) and Greek (Poseidonios, Polybius, Strabo).

Though Caesar's account hews closely to tactics, personages (commanders and legionnaires and, somewhat begrudgingly, native leaders), and, despite the use, as in Xenophon's *Anabasis*, of third-person narration (which can serve as a sort of veracity device), in Book VI.11–28 he gives an ethnographic account of Celts (Gauls) and Germans. For the story of English Caesar offers two types of ethnographic evidence of interest: the picture of larger Celtic society (alliances among Gallic and other Celtic tribes, across regions and cross-Channel), and of early British society. Prior to Book VI's more extended account, here and there one gets glimpses of the information Romans were known to collect about their adversaries; in Book I, we are introduced to Diviciacus, brother of the Aedui chief Dumnorix, and a 'chief magistrate' (I.3; I.16); with mention of Diviciacus and Liscus, the Gallic term for this chief magistracy *vergobret* is introduced. As Dumnorix's intransigence sets in, Caesar comes to negotiate more and more with Diviciacus (I.16–20), playing the brothers against each other, or, by separating the two magistrates, Diviciacus and Liscus, obtaining information on what had been said in confidence among the Gallic leaders:

> Dumnorix was the man: highly audacious, extremely influential with the people – thanks to his open-handed generosity – and ambitious for revolution. ... He maintained a large cavalry force at his own expense, which he always kept at his side. He had influence even among neighboring states, as well as among the Aedui. To consolidate this powerful position he had given his mother in marriage to a powerful aristocrat of the Bituriges [Gallic tribes west of the Aedui, their chief stronghold Avaricum (Bourges)]; he himself had

> taken a wife from among the Helvetii, and he used his maternal half-sister and other female relations to make marriage alliances with other states. Because of this connection he was a strong supporter of the Helvetii, but he also hated Caesar and the Romans on his own account because their coming had weakened his own power, while his brother Diviciacus had been restored to his old place of influence and respect (I.18; Hammond 2008, 12–13).

The machinations of Dumnorix – so they appear to Caesar, whose own such plottings were simply considered strategy – are a hallmark of the Celts and Germans as they appear in classical accounts: Caesar grants that they had a love of liberty, if enjoyed in a society less developed than that of Rome. Indeed, when Dumnorix falls, as he must in the drama Caesar casts, liberty is upon his lips:

> If he [Dumnorix] offered armed resistance and would not obey, he [Caesar] told them to kill him: for he judged that a man who had disregarded Caesar's command when Caesar was actually present would certainly not behave like a sensible man in Caesar's absence. As might be expected, when he was summoned to return Dumnorix began his resistance, defending himself by force and appealing to his supporters' loyalty: he continually cried that he was a free man and a citizen of a free state. Caesar's men surrounded and killed him, as ordered (V.7; Hammond 2008, 93).

That Caesar allows Dumnorix his say is commendable – even given the number of reasons it may have been to his advantage to ennoble his enemy (though have him killed nonetheless). Indeed, with regard to the types of reported speech in Caesar, direct discourse (*oratio recta*) and indirect discourse or reported speech (*oratio obliqua*), Caesar himself never speaks directly in *De Bello Gallico* (cf. Hammond 2008, xxxv); the great speeches belong to the Gauls and Germans. This is not to say that there is a simple dichotomy between Roman civilization and 'barbarians': Romans drew distinctions between Gallia Togata ('citizen Gaul,' that of the *toga*; i.e., Cisalpine Gaul, that on 'our' [i.e., the Roman] side of the Alps) and Gallia Comata, 'long-haired' Transalpine Gaul, less Romanized, with some exceptions: Provincia, the Province' (Provence), especially Massilia, was much more fully within the classical Mediterranean orbit. Greek Massalia, Roman Massilia, an entrepôt with Celtic, Greek, and Punic influences, a center for the trade in wine and slaves, had been issuing high-grade coinage for centuries; a common, prolific issue was the silver obol (minted since at least 200 BC) with (normally) a left-facing artistically sophisticated bust of a youthful Apollo on the obverse, a wheel on the reverse dividing the flan into quadrants with the monogram 'MA.' Nor is it to say that there was an equivalency between less-civilized Celts and Germans; when the Aedui and other Gallic tribes come under pressure from Ariovistus's Germans, the tribal leaders come back to meet Caesar:

> They asked permission to discuss with him in secret both their own welfare and the good of all. When he agreed, they all wept and threw themselves at Caesar's feet. They were as anxious, they explained, to ensure that their discussion would not become public, as they were to obtain what they

> wanted. For if it were made public they foresaw for themselves a terrible punishment. Their spokesman was the Aeduan Diviciacus, and he explained that within Gaul as a whole there were two factions, one led by the Aedui, the other by the Arverni. For many years the two had been fighting fiercely for supremacy; then, he said, it came about that the Arverni and Sequani hired some German mercenaries. Initially about 15,000 of them crossed the Rhine, but once these wild and savage men had conceived a passionate desire for the lands of the Gauls, their way of life, and their wealth, more of them had crossed the river. There were now about 120,000 of them in Gaul (I.31; Hammond 2008, 19).

For the Gauls, there is a difference, and it was the Germans, not the village-dwelling farmers that many of the Gauls had become (and who had to pay corn in tax to Caesar), who were the uncivilized threat: "In a few years they would all be driven out of Gaul, and in turn the Germans would cross the Rhine. After all, there was no comparison between Gallic land and German, nor was there any contest between the two ways of life" (I.31; Hammond 2008, 20). One cannot but bear in mind what would happen some four and a half centuries later, as recounted by Gildas and Bede, in that appeal from Celtic tribes in conflict for help from Germanic auxiliaries who would decide to keep coming; the circumstances are not exact in their similarities, but the Belgae, Atrebates, Iceni, and tribes of Britain must have shared the sentiment of the Aedui in 58 BC.

Before his first invasion of Britain in 55 BC, Caesar had tried to obtain information about the island, without much success (IV.21); nonetheless, late in the campaign season, he set out. During the account of his second campaign of 54 BC, he pauses to add an ethnographic note:

> The inland regions of Britain are inhabited by people whom the Britons themselves claim, according to oral tradition, are indigenous. The coastal areas belong to people who once crossed from Belgium in search of booty and war: almost all of these inhabitants are called by the same national names as those of the states they originally came from. After waging war they remained in Britain and began to farm the land. Population density is high, and their dwellings are extremely numerous and very like those of the Gauls. They have large herds of cattle. They use either bronze or gold coinage or, instead of currency, iron rods of a fixed weight. ... They consider it wrong to eat hare, chicken, or goose, but still they look after them for pleasure and amusement. ... Of all the island's inhabitants, by far the most civilized are those who live in Kent, a region which is entirely coastal. Their way of life is much the same as that of the Gauls. Inland, the people for the most part do not plant corn-crops, but live on milk and meat and clothe themselves in animal skins (V.12–13; Hammond 2008, 95–96).

Caesar notes in Books IV–V that the Britons still use chariots in battle, quite adroitly, trained up from youth – alone among the Celts of Europe at that time, as the custom had died out on the continent. His emphasis on the cultural similarities between Gaul and Britain is especially noteworthy. Indeed, we read in Caesar of two men named Cingetorix (the last element *-rix* the Celtic reflex of the IE term for 'king'): one is a leader of the Gallic Treveri, whom Caesar cultivates over the more rebellious Indutiomarus (V.3–4), the other, one of the four kings of Cantium (Kent; the others being Carvilius, Taximagulus, and Segovax) whom Cassivellaunus enlists in a failed attack on the Roman camp (V.22).

In Book VI Caesar turns "to give an account of the customs of Gaul and Germany and the differences between these two nations," and singled out for praise is Gallic leadership, as "No leader allows his own people to be oppressed and cheated, for if he does he cannot maintain his authority among them" (VI.11; Hammond 2008, 124–125). The role of Fortune, and of course Caesar too, in the operations of this maxim is illustrated by the account of the challenge to Aedui supremacy by the Sequani, who had enlisted the aid of Ariovistus and his Germans; the Sequani rise as the Aedui decline, until Diviciacus's embassy to Rome, at first rebuffed, is answered by Caesar himself, upon which the fortunes of the Sequani fall, and they are replaced by the Remi (VI.12). Gallic society is divided between the great mass who exist as little better than slaves and the 'men of distinction,' the druids (*druides*) and knights (*equites*). The matter of the druids and Gallic religion is worth relating here, as they bring Britain back into focus:

> The druids are involved in matters of religion. They manage public and private sacrifices and interpret religious customs and ceremonies. Young men flock to them in large numbers to gain instruction, and they hold the druids in great esteem. For they decide almost all disputes, both public and private: if some crime has been committed, if there has been murder done, if there is a dispute over an inheritance or over territory, they decide the issue and settle the rewards and penalties. If any individual or group of people does not abide by their decision, the druids ban them from sacrifices. This is their most severe punishment. ... A chief druid rules over all the rest and has supreme authority among them. When such a man dies, if there is an outstanding druid among those remaining he succeeds to this position, but if there are a number of equal ability, they decide the leadership by a vote of all the druids, and sometimes even in armed combat. At a certain time of year they sit in judgement in a sacred spot in the territory of the Carnutes, in an area right in the middle of Gaul. Everyone who has a dispute comes to this place from every region, and submits to their decisions and judgements. It is believed that this institution was discovered in Britain and transferred to Gaul; and nowadays those who want to understand these matters in more detail usually travel to Britain to learn about them (VI.13; Hammond 2008, 126–127).

The replacement of the chief druid by vote or combat recalls, in the latter method of selection, the survival of the archaic Roman *Rex Nemorensis* (the 'king of the wood' or 'grove'), the slave-priest of Diana at Aricia who gained his position by slaying his predecessor and served until slain in turn by his successor (famous in English prose as the opening episode to Sir James George Frazer's *The Golden Bough*; Frazer 1912–1930). Caesar, among other classical writers, emphasizes the reluctance of the druids in recording their learning in writing: "Nor do they think it proper to commit this teaching to writing, although for almost all other purposes, including public and private accounts, they use Greek characters" (VI.14; Hammond 2008, 127). The corpus of Gallic and Gallic-Latin bilingual inscriptions certainly testifies to literacy among the Gallic tribes (Delamarre 2007; Lambert 2002). The use of the Greek alphabet was common in the south, especially but not exclusively in Massalia/Massilia; Greek-influenced scripts of course abounded west of Greece: Etruscan, Oscan, (Celt-) Iberian – indeed Runic may have been derived from such Greek-influenced scripts. The numismatic corpus too offers abundant evidence of literacy; this is significant as Celtic numismatic activity often involved the striking or casting of imitative issues, as of drachmai and tetradrachmai of Philip II and Alexander III of Macedon or of Roman Republican issues: compare the highly stylized electrum stater of the Bituriges dating to 60–50 BC, the era of Caesar's campaigns (de la Tour 1991–1992, no. 3399; see also Grasmann et al. 1984, pt. ii: 494ff. and plates), very often executed in the more abstract Celtic artistic style and with blundered legends. But Gallic and British issues of the 1st century BC and later are often epigraphically competent.

A great debate in Romano-British studies has centered upon the extent of literacy (in Latin) in Roman Britain; there is of course evidence – from coins and pottery stamps (upon terra sigillata jars and amphorae in which wine and olive oil were shipped cross-Channel) – of literacy pre-conquest (pre-AD 43). The views on the subject have ranged from acceptance of a knowledge of Latin that was relatively common but restricted to the villas (as administrative headquarters and town-centers) and military forts (Evans 2001), to a 'Latinization' of much greater degree that saw literacy spread beyond the forts and villas to more rural areas (Cooley 2002). Correspondence of soldiers serving abroad, such as preserved in the Vindolanda tablets, shows varying degrees of literacy, some of it high; letters home may have spurred at least a limited literacy in Rome's Celtic and Germanic territories supplying legionnaires (Derks and Roymans 2002 studied the case of Batavian legionnaires). That Latin was used as a means to Romanize the British élites and their families is well known; we have the authority of Tacitus on this matter (*Agricola* XXXI). The figure usually turned to in evidence of this Roman policy is Tiberius Claudius Cogidubnus, whose *floruit* spans the AD 40s to perhaps the late 70s or 80s (Barrett 1979). The name itself is a Romano-British hybrid: the *praenomen* Tiberius and *nomen gentilicium* Claudius are fully Roman, the *cognomen* Cogidubnus is the Latinization of a British Celtic name (Tacitus had recorded Cogidumnus; *Agricola* XIV; another reading is Togidumnus, cf. Salway 2003, 748–752). Cogidubnus appears in historical accounts as the ideal client-king: he was one of Rome's native *socii*, friendly allies, loyal to Rome during the turbulent early settlement (the *turbidae res* is Tacitus's phrase; *Annales* XII.31) – notably the revolt of Boudica of AD 60/61 (following the form espoused in LHEB, rather than the geminate *Boudicca*). Cogidubnus's value as client-king was appreciated by the Romans, for their own purposes of course, as Tacitus freely admitted:

> quaedam civitates Cogidumno regi donatae (is ad nostram usque memoriam fidissimus mansit), vetere ac iam pridem recepta populi Romani consuetudine, ut haberet instrumenta servitutis et reges.

> Certain *civitates* [likely 'settlements' or 'towns' rather than 'cities' in the Roman sense] were given to Cogidubnus (he remained most loyal down to our own times) according to an old and long accepted Roman tradition of using kings also as instruments of slavery (*Agricola* XIV; Barrett 1979, 227).

The use of the superlative adjectival form *fidissimus* ('most loyal' or 'faithful') is telling; Caesar had recorded much vacillation among the British kings and chieftains a century earlier in his dealings with them (and so the frequent demand for corn and hostages). Our Cogidubnus appears also in the Chichester temple inscription, a Purbeck marble slab over 5′ × 2′ made for the dedication of the Temple of Neptune and Minerva at the Reg(i)ni *civitas* at Chichester (or *Noviomagus Reg[i]norum*; the appellative *noviomagus* 'new market' was not uncommon with Romano-Celtic place-names; Rivet and Smith 1979, 427). The inscription is important for, as famous as Cogidubnus may be as a historical example, we know relatively little about him for certain: he seems to have been of the Atrebates, had perhaps been taken to Rome as a youth and educated (see Bogaers 1979, 253 and refs.); the kingdom of the Reg(i)ni was apparently among those added to his realm, though it is believed that this kingdom did not survive his decease, which is placed anywhere from the late 60s to around the reign of Vespasian, which emperor had once served as a military commander in Britain (Shotter 2004). The monumental slab is damaged, though it was fortunately recorded by early antiquarians such as William Stukeley in his *Itinerarium curiosum* ('A Curious Journey'; Stukeley 1724/1776) and John Horsley (Horsley 1732). The fifth line of the inscription has vexed interpreters; traditionally, the obscure passage is seen as referring to Cogidubnus as a 'legate of Augustus' (*legatus Augusti*), though this is an honor known only to have been conferred upon Roman senators. A new appraisal of the line by J.E. Bogaers reads rather *rex magnus* ('great king') for the honor bestowed; the inscription is given here minus some of the conventions of epigraphic transcription:

> NEPTVNO ET MINERVAE
> TEMPLVM
> PRO SALVTE DOMVS DIVINAE
> EX AVCTORITATE TI CLAVD
> COGIDVNI REG MAGN BRIT
> COLEGIVM FABROR ET QVI IN EO
> SVNT D S D DONANT AREAM
> [ ]ENTE PVDENTINI FIL
>
> (To Neptune and Minerva, for the welfare of the Divine House by the authority of Tiberius Claudius Cogidubnus, great king in Britain, the guild of smiths [or shipwrights] and those therein give this temple from their own resources, [...]ens, son of Pudentius, presenting the site; RIB 91; Bogaers 1979, 243, with adaptation of translation to reflect the emendation).

Whether a *rex magnus* of (or in) Britain (modeled on the eastern honorific βασιλεὺς μέγας [*basileùs mégas*]; Bogaers 1979, 253) or *legatus Augusti*, it is clear that Cogidubnus was a 'model' client-king and that the process of Romanization had been carefully developed: as Tacitus had observed, in "an old and long accepted Roman tradition of using kings also as instruments of slavery."

The Germanic invaders themselves would come from Germania Inferior and Magna Germania (that largely beyond the Roman 'Pale,' modern Netherlands, and parts of Germany, Poland, and Denmark); nonetheless, it is from one of the Belgic tribes, the Menapii, that the two great usurpers of Roman Britain, Carausius and Allectus, would hail. Marcus Aurelius Mausaeus Carausius had begun his military career under emperor Maximian's campaigns to suppress rebellion and brigandage in Gaul (both recurrent in the AD 3rd century) and was given charge of the *classis Britannica* (the 'British fleet' of the Roman army) to suppress German (largely Frankish and Saxon) pirates in the Channel. He was accused of embezzlement, even collusion with the German pirates (whose descendants would be among the 5th-century settlers of Britain); sentenced to death by Maximian, in 286–287 he declared himself emperor of Britain and Northern Gaul and managed to hold on to power until assassinated by his purser and fellow Menapian Allectus. Carausius's position had already been weakened by the loss of Northern Gaul; Constantius Chlorus had retaken the vital port Bononia (Boulogne), and Constantius I set out in September 296 to suppress Allectus. The fighting was over quickly (Allectus killed in battle, perhaps at Silchester, likely before Constantius had landed), and the remaining troops in the pay of Allectus were killed at London in the autumn of 296. What is of interest with the reign of these two British usurpers is the relatively prolific coinage they left behind, and the relatively high quality of the issues themselves. A recurrent reverse theme is of a Roman galley (an allusion to the *classis* and the system of forts along the 'Saxon shore'), such as the *quinarii* of Allectus (the bronze revived quinarius was typical of Gaul in the later period, and revalued variably) struck at London with the exergue notation Q <uinarius> L<ondinium> or Q C (the mint here is uncertain: Cirencester, Clausentum, Colchester or Gloucester have been suggested; RIC V, 55, 128–130; Clausentum may be Bitterne or Wickham, Hampshire; Rivet and Smith 1979, 308–309). The many numismatic issues of Carausius are noteworthy for their propagandistic energy: of interest is a denarius of Carausius with the usual portrait obverse (the facing-right busts of Carausius and Allectus are normally radiate, i.e., wearing a crown rather than a wreath of victory, and bull-necked) and the common, often commemorative, she-wolf suckling Romulus and Remus reverse bears the legend RENOVAT<OR> ROMAN<ORVM> ('Restorer of the Romans') and RSR in the exergue. The latter has caused some curiosity as to the mint-mark: a recent suggestion (de la Bédoyère 1998; RIC V, 571–572) is that Carausius, as part of his propaganda program, sought to emphasize both his legitimacy and Roman-ness (he was a Menapian, a Belgic Celt) and was quoting Virgil's *Eclogue* IV, 6–7 on this issue and on two medallions in the British Museum (which include the acronym INPCDA [= line 2 below]):

redeunt Saturnia regna,
iam noua progenies caelo demittitur alto

[The Age of Saturn has returned,
a new generation now is descended from the heavens high.]

The denarius itself is in restored form, of 90% silver content; that such fine coinage (in weight and purity, if not artistic design) should appear in Roman Britain may say something of the durability of *Romanitas* in a seemingly far-flung province; the allusion to Virgil on these denarii and medallions give us some indication of the state of literacy in late Roman Britain. And that, culturally, we do not necessarily see a state of decline in the 3rd and 4th centuries, a collapse into that transitional period which archaeologists were first to call 'sub-Roman' Britain.

Billon antoninianus of Carausius, London mint, ca. 288.
Source: Sam Moorhead / Wikimedia commons / CC BY 2.0.

3.5 DOWNFALL: SUB-ROMAN BRITAIN

The very term 'sub-Roman Britain' suggests the difficulty in assigning any end date to Roman Britain, apart from the withdrawal of the legions in AD 410 (it is possible that reinforcements were sent in 417, but the result was soon the same). Insofar as the Roman Church is concerned, there is little need to make such a distinction: continuity is to be found in practices, liturgy, ecclesiastical organization (the influence this had on social and political geography, and therefore place-names, is difficult to underestimate), and writing in Latin. Though historians may speak of a transitional period of the 5th and 6th centuries (through to Augustine's mission to Britain in AD 597), archaeologists of the types of pottery produced in the latter days of Roman and Romano-British Britain (usually in terms of degeneration of types), linguists may keep silent. To be sure, writing continued throughout the transitional period in Latin – at times with some further qualification such as British Latin or Cambro-Latin – and likely also in Welsh, perhaps in Pictish – at least insofar as Church administration required, and likely too with regard to glossary traditions preserved from the later 7th through 9th centuries but evidencing earlier transmission and compilation histories. Roman traditions of language study, as brought to Romano-British schools in the late Republican and early Imperial periods, indicate not only a presence of literacy but of a meta-linguistic approach to letters, likely more or less continuous in that transition from late Roman Britain to early Anglo-Saxon England. Traditions of Latin writing were in evidence not just from the epigraphic evidence that survives still, or a named progenitor of British Latin such as Pelagius or Patrick (Patricius was a Briton taken to Ireland as a captive), but also from Hiberno-Latin as brought to Britain by Irish teachers; their role in the conversion of Northern Britain is of signal if underrated cultural significance; the *Hisperica Famina* and vogue in Latin octosyllabic verse in the 8th century are indications of the influence.

That British Latin is one of the vectors for literacy in early Anglo-Saxon England (for the purpose here, roughly AD 597–700) seems entirely plausible. There is some debate over whether Britons, native as well as Romanized, spoke 'proper' Latin as well as Vulgar Latin; in fact, it has been suggested Latin was in some parts of Britain not just one of the daily spoken languages but the primary one. Though the earliest Germanic-speaking peoples in Britain were likely illiterate, this is an assumption nonetheless: in that first generation or two, some of the former legionnaires, auxiliaries, and mercenaries would have achieved rank and literacy, diplomas and land-holding status, and the children of such men, and of former local Roman and Romano-British officials and other élites, should have achieved some degree of literacy. We can safely assume a certain degree of bilingualism, perhaps some multilingualism. How else might a British king have invited (hired, that is, no doubt on specified terms) Saxon and other Germanic mercenaries to Britain but through intermediaries speaking at least two tongues (given that the medium of Latin would not suffice in the case of some of the mercenaries). The matter has far-reaching implications and has not been given, traditionally, all that much consideration. The earliest literacy in Germanic, inscriptions in early Runic and Roman script (e.g., the Negau legionnaire's helmet inscription of the AD 2nd century) is concordant with service in Rome's armies or along its frontiers, activity one would expect in Britain pre-400. One thinks of the Tungrian cohort serving at Vindolanda (Bowman and Thomas 1984; Bowman 1994; McGowan 2001), which is, in fact, evidence of one Germanic-speaking group in Britain before the *adventus Saxonum*. The debate over the extent of literacy in Roman Britain is relevant also to that of literacy in the transition to early Anglo-Saxon England – in brief, whether literacy in Roman Britain was widespread or limited to *oppida* and *civitates*, that is, the military forts (administrative use) and town-centers and villas (administrative, commercial, religious use). The public uses of literacy in Roman Britain, from inscriptions to pottery stamps to coins, has a bearing on the later linguistic picture: the dedications of altars by Germanic auxiliaries suggest that some of them were literate enough to have inscriptions made accurately, presumably also that they might be read by their fellows and successors at the posts. The religious use of the Latin language – for non-Christians, the frequent oaths to gods and votive offerings, for Christians liturgical and administrative, parochial purposes – would ensure its survival: if it can be said to have disappeared from those regions settled by Germanic-speakers in the mid-5th century, which seems an overstatement, it would be revived from those where Church administration survived in the island (as it did in Wales). Roman building materials were often reused; early Anglo-Saxon coinage frequently imitated the Roman (particularly Constantinian issues; unlike 'barbarous' issues with blundered legends, Anglo-Saxon coinage could often be of a fairly high grade); many Anglo-Saxon place-names have *-cester* as the second element, from Roman *castrum* 'fort.' Bede tells us of Germanic tribesmen reporting home the richness of Britain's land and its weak defenses: they knew of the Roman system, no doubt more than a few of them had worked within it (as legionnaires) or up against it (as pirates of the 'Saxon shore').

The matter of who the component tribes were to Bede's Angles, Saxons, and Jutes (and Frisians) is vital to an understanding of the linguistic pedigree of English as a

West Germanic language. We can speak of 'before English' and, approximately, by the mid-7th century or so, of *Englisc* (and thereabouts or somewhat later the Latin manuscript annotation, as in bilingual glossaries, *anglice* 'in English,' though we also find *saxonice*, 'in the Saxon tongue'), but it is only speculatively that we can speak of the period of the formation of English. Delineating the period is troublesome enough, though its general outlines appear by default: AD 449 is given as the traditional date for a larger-scale invasion of Germanic-speakers (presumably not just warriors but also their families in what was a settlement of eastern England). The process likely began earlier, in the 420s, and continued throughout the 5th century. Just when the Germanic dialects as spoken by these settlers from what are now Germany, the Low Countries, and Denmark were substantially dissimilar from the home-country speech patterns is unknown, as we lack sufficient written records on either side of the Channel and North Sea to form any basis for judgment. But we are likely looking at the 6th century as the crucible of change. Perhaps a third-generation hypothesis is applicable also to language creation (or dissimilation), as it has generally been applied to the loss of the heritage languages for more recent immigrants to America. This at least would lend some plausibility to a tentative chronology for the 'birth of English': perhaps by the second generation born to the settlers of the mid-5th century, enough actual changes had occurred in pronunciation (at least) that there was either some attenuation of the mutual intelligibility between existing ('Anglian' [i.e., of Angeln, and land to the west of Southern Denmark inhabited by the Angles], 'Saxon,' 'Jutish') and emerging dialects or a sense on the part of the speakers themselves that they spoke 'island' or Insular varieties distinct from the Continental dialects. In this latter case, we do find evidence of later dissimilation as Anglo-Saxons came to refer to Continental Saxons and their tongue as 'Old Saxon' (compare the ecclesiastical writer John the 'Old Saxon').

Of the dialect and culture groups, to put 'tribes' into modern parlance, contributing to what would become Old English or Anglo-Saxon (the latter still the more common English designation, the former much more commonly the North American term), Frisian is traditionally seen as the closest linguistically, as, in the West Germanic branch of the Germanic languages of the Indo-European family, Modern Frisian is seen as the closest sibling to Modern English. A matter deserving closer examination is that of the implications of this genetic linguistic relationship, namely, whether the relatedness indicates a linguistic primacy to Frisian groups in the *adventus*, if not likely a numerical primacy, as traditional accounts and sheer control of territory argue for a much larger Saxon and Anglian presence, smaller Jutish (Kent and Wight), and an undefined or at least unclear Frisian presence. What is intriguing from the outset is the relative stability, geographically speaking, of the dialects of early Old English and their continuity with the tribal and administrative (under the Romans, perhaps even the road system) divisions of early Britain – so much so that one can speak of their persistence, with modifications of course, to this very day (but see the caveat in Sims-Williams 1990, 10–11 and n. 35 at 10). The Germanic place-names given the land by the first waves of settlers, the tribal divisions, and later hidage (though the Anglo-Saxon hide as a unit of land measurement has defied precise quantification, the hidage system involved the assessment of tribal lands for tax purposes), bear out what would become familiar patterns too, of 'Anglian' groups from the Midlands to the northernmost reaches of the Germanic settlement (Mercians, Northumbrians, Deirans), Saxons in what would be the south-central and southwestern counties, and 'Jutes' in the southeast (Kent in particular, the *Cent-wara*) and on the Isle of Wight (a territorial separation curious at first glance). To speak of an *Engla-lond* in the period of formation of *Englisc* is another matter entirely and, despite much critical and theoretical notice given to 'the making of English,' likely an anachronism in historiographical terms.

Nonetheless, the evidence preserved on Continent for early Old English is arguably the more abundant – in the main, bilingual Latin-Old English glossaries such as the Épinal-Erfurt, Brussels, Leiden, and Corpus Glossaries of roughly the late 7th through 9th centuries -- and it suggests what looks to eyes accustomed to later West Saxon texts as at the least a strong orthographical diversity, likely indicating diversity phonological and dialectal. One inevitably encounters at the outset the question to what extent early texts of Old English record in their orthography the actual sounds of OE; it is a question often passed over silently, as the consensus is an affirmation of the scribes' presumed fidelity in recording their own pronunciation of the language or that of their authors they were tasked with copying. In part, this axiomatic scribal accuracy is unavoidable to any investigation of the earlier stages of the language; but it is also borne out by comparison with the early written records of cognate Germanic languages (Old Saxon, Old Frisian, Old High German) and by the evidence of diachronic sound change and dialectal survivals into the modern era: vestigial forms that persist in areas isolated, geographically or socially, from changes to the mainstream or acrolectal standard form (a number of examples of these will be encountered along the way: whether the Scots pronunciation [hu:s] for [haʊs] *house* preserving that used by Chaucer, or those of the Hoi-Toiders [from [hɔɪ tɔɪd] for [haɪ taɪd] *high tide*] of North Carolina's Outer Banks or Smith and Tangier Islands in the Chesapeake Bay suggestive of 'Shakespearian' West Country forms). While the Middle English period has generally been thought of as the more heterogeneous dialectally, an observation largely if not totally true (one must factor in the weaker survival of OE texts, particularly those preserved in multiple copies), what does survive from early Old English suggests a diversity in dialect geography in broad terms – northern (Anglian) vs. southwestern (Saxon) and southeastern (Kentish) – if not also socially. The latter is largely unrecoverable for the period, though, in late Old English, Ælfric's *Colloquy* is perhaps the rare written record of spoken (West Saxon) OE – if a grammatically purified version of it – apart from some occasional passages of direct discourse in the prose, such as the OE version of the *Apollonius of Tyre*, of the 11th century, which may in its rendering of the Latin original dialogue give us a taste of OE discourse dramatic and treacly. These are matters to the future (Chapter 4), but a sample of how people spoke in this transitional period, at least how their speech would be recorded in Latin, we do have from writers such as Gildas, 'Nennius,' and Bede.

The history of late Roman Britain and sub-Roman Britain may be divisible to the contemporary historian (the disciplinary and departmental divide between the classicist and medievalist), but it was part of the same story of wonder-working providence, of decline and back-sliding along the course of salvation history to a Gildas and Nennius or Bede. If Bede's name is indeed Celtic, he is a transitional figure in several ways, and a personally ironic one. Gildas writes of the 'Fall of Britain' (*De excidio Britanniae*), 'Nennius' of the *History of the Britons* (*Historia Brittonum*), and Bede of the *Ecclesiastical History of the English People* (or 'people/*gens* of the Angles'; *Historia ecclesiastica gentis Anglorum*). The three Churchmen have history in their sights as patristic writers such as Augustine and Orosius did, but along the way they fill in the picture of the making of a *gens Anglorum* and the fall of a *gens Brittonum*. The very use of Latin *gens*, the Roman sense of which ('race, stock, family, clan, tribe,' Roman *tribus* rather than 'tribe' as among Germans or Celts) was to be broadened and altered as used in Medieval Latin, seems indicative of both a concern with Church history (its extension to 'heathen' tribes and lands, not dissimilar to the extension of Roman *imperium* by her legions) and with a kind of *urbanitas* and *ciuitas* or *Romanitas*: that Britain had known such refinement, civilization, and sense of belonging to something larger than the island before. It had lost it with the 'Fall,' not just by the withdrawal of the legions, but by the wickedness of its rulers (British [Celtic] kings, a point of particular animus with Bede). If the displacement of Celtic by Germanic in sub-Roman Britain is a form of disruption, the renewal of the role of Latin with the conversion of these Germanic tribes to Christianity (starting in Kent) represented a consoling continuity and a link, through Roman *litteras* ('letters,' literacy), with that *urbanitas* and, now, *Christianitas*. Though Bede was a partisan, as in the Easter Controversy, and particularly hostile to the Irish, he was also capable of thinking in terms of 'the Church': and it is *Ecclesia*, its organization, schooling, with Latin as the unifying language of Western Christendom, that play a central role in much of what survives from Roman and sub-Roman Britain to early Anglo-Saxon England. The earliest organization of the Church in Britain was Roman, and there is a direct link in its sense of organization and language of administration (Latin) to Roman Britain – it is a profound legacy that will shape English in the coming centuries. But Germans were not foreigners to this earlier Britain; we find them throughout the period AD 43–410 among the people of Roman Britain.

3.6 'THE PEOPLE OF ROMAN BRITAIN'

Among the early kingdoms of Anglo-Saxon England was that of Kent in the southeast, settled by Jutes in the traditional account (there seems to have been some Frisians and Franks in the settlement also). *Kent* has a long history in historical record, first occurring in Caesar at V.13.1:

> Insula natura triquetra, cuius unum latus est contra Galliam. Huius lateris alter angulus, qui est ad Cantium, quo fere omnes ex Gallia naves appelluntur, ad orientem solem, inferior ad meridiem spectat (Du Pontet 1988).
>
> The natural form of the island is triangular, one side of which faces opposite Gaul. One angle of this side, which is Kent [lit. of the *Cantii*], to which practically all ships from Gaul call into, faces the rising sun, the lower angle beholds the noon sun [faces south].

The very literal rendering of Caesar here is to point out that the first mention of Kent in history likely derives from a tribal name, the *Cantii*, who appear in Ptolemy's

Geography as the Κάντιοι (*Kántioi*); the plural tribal name appears elsewhere in Latin in *Cantici, Cantiaci*, in the Ravenna Cosmography as *Cantuarii* (gen. pl. *Cantuariorum*; a Latinization of OE *Cantware). Cantium* would then be, as Caesar has it, the land where the *Cantii* dwell (< British **Cantịon*). As the name appears in the *Anglo-Saxon Chronicle* as *Cantware,* it must have been a very early loan into Old English (late 5th–early 6th century), for the form does not exhibit expected Gmc *i*-mutation: PrOE **Cantiware* should produce *Centware*, which is found in OE texts and does occur in the simplex forms *Cent* and *Cœnt* (forms that do exhibit umlaut). Kenneth Jackson suggested that the British form was borrowed as **Canti-* and the *i* was syncopated before Old English *i*-mutation occurred (LHEB 600–601). Various proposals have sought to explain *Kent* (*Cantium*) as a topographical place-name: 'border land,' 'coast district' (Ekwall ODEPN), 'corner land, land on the edge' (CDEPN), though Mills (ODBPN) glossed: "An ancient Celtic name, often explained as 'coastal district' but possibly 'land of the hosts or armies'" following Jackson and other Celticists. Jackson called attention to an inscribed stone dating to the late 5th to early 6th century from Penmachno, Conwy, Wales, the inscription to which begins CANTIORI HIC IACIT ('Cantiorix here lies'), the first word the name of the fallen being memorialized that should likely be read *Cantio-rix*, a British name (*-rix* the common Celtic onomastic element for 'king') and interpreted as meaning 'King of Hosts' (CIIC no. 394; Jackson 1948, 55; Sims-Williams 2003, 358, 372).

Rivet and Smith prefer for *Cantium* a descriptive toponym meaning 'corner land, land on the edge' in their extensive discussion of **Cantia*, *Cantiaci*, and *Cantium* (297–300), but support *Cantiaci* as an 'ethnicon' (or ethnonym, name for a people or tribe) with reference to *Segontiaci*, a British tribe mentioned only in Caesar's account (*De bello Gallico* V.21.1) as among the five Southeastern British tribes who joined the Trinovantes in allying with Rome and against Cassivellaunus of the Catuvellauni. The Roman fort Segontium, built to support the Roman campaign against the Ordovices of Wales, is apparently not connected to the tribal name Segontiaci (though there were two Roman sites in Spain named Segontia; Rivet and Smith 1979, 454); it is now Caernarfon (Gwynedd), from the Welsh *Kaer yn Arfon*, 'the fort in Arfon,' Arfon itself < *ar Fôn*, literally 'in Môn' (that is, Mona, the name first occurring in Caesar for Angelsey), meaning 'opposite Man.' The old name Môn for Angelsey apparently just means 'mountain,' or 'high island,' and derives from the British root **mŏn-*, which also lies behind the name of the Isle of Man, known from Pliny as *Monapia*, and though Pliny located the isle properly *inter Hiberniam ac Britanniam* ('between Ireland and Britain'), the name is thought more properly to derive from **Manavia* (Rivet and Smith 1979, 410–411). That the onomastic if not etymological connection between Môn (Angelsey) and Manau (the Middle Welsh form for Isle of Man; the modern Welsh is *Ynys Manaw*) was understood in the past is apparent from Bede's reference to the *Mevanias* (or **Menavias*, with metathesis of the *n* and *v*) when he mentions the Northumbrian king Edwin's expansion of English rule over the 'two Môns' at II.5: *necnon et Mevanias Brettonum insulas, quae inter Hiberniam et Britaniam sitae sunt, Anglorum subiecit imperio* ("and also the Mevanian islands of the Britons, which are located between Ireland and Britain, he subjected to the power of the English").

A variety of proposals have been made for the origin to the name of the Isle of Wight, all of them Celtic; Mills ODBPN echoes the CDEPN in seeing 'division' or 'fork' as the original sense (referring to its dividing the Solent), the latter offering the most complicated analysis of the toponym: with early attestations in Ptolemy (Οὐηκτίς [Ouēktís], Latin *Vectis*), Diodorus Siculus, Pliny, Suetonius, and a number of early entries in the *Anglo-Saxon Chronicle*, the form is from British **Uexta* (it appears in the Antonine Itinerary as *Vecta*). The Welsh form *Gueith* (as found in the *Historia Brittonum*; MdW *Ynys Wyth*) exhibits the Brittonic sound change *χt* > *i̯th* (cf. LHEB 81, 282, 407–411 and n. 2 at 411). Like a number of British place-names, it was borrowed into early Old English (PrOE **Weoht* > *Wieht* > *Wiht*, 'Wight'). Wight seems to have been inhabited by the Durotriges down to the 1st century BC – at least its western half, on the basis of the Shalfleet Hoard (discovered August 2009); Caesar reports that the Belgae took the island ca 85 BC (the Belgae lived on both sides of the Channel, in Britain and the Low Countries – and gave their name to Belgium [Gallia Belgica]). The Belgae had as their neighbors the Durotriges to the east, the Atrebates to the north (a tribal name also found in Gaul), and the Regnenses to the east. During the Roman period, the *civitates* ('cities,' in some cases Romano-British towns for 'settled' Celtic tribes) of the Belgae included *Clausentum* (Southampton; or Bitterne or Wickham, Hamps.; Rivet and Smith 1979, 441–442) and *Portus Adurni* (or *Portus Ardaoni*; Portchester). Their capital was *Venta Belgarum*, 'Venta of the Belgae,' the first element of which is found in other Romano-British place-names and has been difficult to explain.

Other Romano-British place-names with this element include *Venta Iceni* ('Venta of the Iceni tribe,' Boudica's people), *Venta Silurum* ('Venta of the Silures,' a tribe of southeast Wales), *Bannaventa* (the Roman walled town at Whilton Lodge, Northamptonshire; British **banna* < Proto-Celtic **bando-* 'peak, horn, tip,' was a fairly productive place-name element in Britain and Gaul; Rivet and Smith 1979, 261–266, 511–512; Matasović 2009, 54), *Glannoventa* (Roman fort at Ravenglass, Cumbria; Rivet and Smith 1979, 367), and possibly *Derventio* (a river-name given to a Roman settlement along it in Yorkshire). The place-name element has been variously interpreted as related to Latin forms for 'sale, toll on goods for sale' (compare Modern English *vend*; Rivet and Smith 1979, 262), 'hill' (from a pre-IE **vin-*; Rivet and Smith 1979, 264), or just 'place' or 'town,' as in Welsh *cad-went* 'battlefield' (Matasović 2009, 413 s.v. **wentā*). At any rate, the form was borrowed during the early Anglo-Saxon period in hybrid form, *Uintan-cæstir* (Bede *HE* III. vii) and *Wintan-ceaster* (the *Anglo-Saxon Chronicle* for the year 744), the Northumbrian and West Saxon forms, respectively. And compare Romano-British *Derventio* (*Deruuentio* in Bede) > Old English *Deorwent* > *Derwent*; CDEPN is hesitant about accepting 'oak' river' (< British **dervā*) for the many river-names generated by the Old British form, thinking it may rather fit in with a variety of 'Old European' river-names deriving from PIE **dreu-* ('to run'), though Jackson's phonological argument still seems to hold. Thus, the names of the Derwents of Cumbria, Derbyshire, Northumberland, and North Yorkshire may have a common origin with the river-names Darent, Darwen, Dart (CDEPN, 185; LHEB 282).

As mentioned earlier, traditional histories of the language have found the Celtic inheritance in English to be meager, and it was suggested then that that may have more to do with almost nobody looking for it. As to the onomastic inheritance of Celtic, the personal names, toponyms, hydronyms, and theonyms, the evidence piles up fairly quickly – we can add Winchester and Derwent (and related hydronyms) to those seen so far. The legacy of these forms in Present Day English is a function of those people of Britain who lived and interacted with those who invaded and settled Britain and what would become England (Romans, then Germanic-speaking Angles, Saxons, Jutes, Frisians, and Franks). Some of the tribes of Celtic Britain have left their mark on English – the Cantii with Canterbury and Kent, and, of course the Britanni as the inhabitants of Britain were collectively called by classical writers (as the Caledonii, beyond the wall, came to stand in for the Scots, especially Highland Scots, down to the present day – Highland Football League Caledonian FC is now Inverness Caledonian Thistle). The legacy is complicated by reformations and hybrid forms: *Dorchester* < *Durnovaria*, the Romano-British form perhaps < **durno-* 'fist' (referring to 'fist-sized pebbles' as part of a hydronym), and found in OE as *Dorn* in the ethnonym *Dorn-sæte* (the 'Dorn-inhabitants,' whence *Dorset*). Behind Edinburgh, the English form of which can be dated back to 1126 (*Edenburge*; ODBPN, 173), and Scots Gaelic *Dùn Èideann*, lay Cumbric *Din Eidyn*, the name for what is now Edinburgh and environs in the age of *Y Gododdin* ('The Gododdin,' the Votadini from Iron Age Celtic and Roman times or their descendants). *Din* and *dùn* (Irish *dún*) mean 'fort,' but *Eidyn* has eluded explanation (as has the *-fermline* of *Dunfermline*). *Votadini* by a series of sound changes in British (as ancestor of Welsh and Cumbric) became *Gododin* (the *-dd-* is [ð] as in Welsh; LHEB 653), and they escaped the fate of other peoples of Roman Britain by surviving into sub-Roman and medieval times, commemorated in Aneirin's cycle of poems (their heroic but tragic fight at Catraeth [Catterick] ca. 600, until the fall of Din Eidyn to the Angles in 638). One of their heroes, Cunedda, son of Edern son of Padarn Beisrudd (Paternus Red-Robe), who was the son of Tegid ap Iago (Tegid [possibly the Roman name Tacitus] son of Iago), in his genealogy, takes us back to Roman times, indeed with his grandfather and great-grandfather perhaps to Romano-Britons, and into sub-Roman times in the Hen Ogledd (the 'Old North'). If Cunedda's father may have commanded Votadini troops in Roman service (under Magnus Maximus, the Maxen Wledig [Prince or Lord Maxen] of the *Mabinogion*), Cunedda himself is said to have led Votadini troops in resisting incursions into their territory by the Picts and Irish, and then to have moved (or been sent, as *foederati* – in treaty with Rome) to Wales to push out the Irish who had been settling there (perhaps since as early as the 4th century – ogam inscriptions are found through the 6th). The movement of Cunedda, with eight of his sons, from the 'Old North' to Wales may be mostly, or entirely, a fiction (Dumville 1977, 181–182), serving as an etiological myth for the foundation of the kingdom of Gwynedd, his sons giving their names to its cantrefs, and cementing a link between the Welsh of Wales and the Old or North Welsh of Cumbria, Northumberland, and the Southern Scottish lowlands. The rise of the Anglian kingdom of Bernicia and the fall of Din Eidyn will be returned to in the next chapter, as English spread into the 'Old North.'

The Silures of Wales mentioned above had as their neighbors to the west the Demetae, and though it may not be transparently evident, another people of Roman Britain lived on in the place-name Dyfed, the largest of the 'preserved counties' of Wales. Their capital was Moridunum ('fort by the sea'; Carmarthen < Middle Welsh *cair* + *Mirdin*), and the Latin term for Dyfed into the medieval period was *Demetia*. The Welsh genealogies in British Library, MS Harley 3859 mention a *Dimet map Maxim gulecic* (= *guletic*, i.e., *gwledic*, *wledig*, 'lord, ruler'), that is, a 'Dimet son of Maxen Wledig' who appears among the early kings of Dyfed (cf. Sims-Williams 2003, 93 and n. 481). The form *Dimet* exhibits the expected British sound change /e/ > /i/ before a nasal, which may date it to the 6th century; *Demetae* (tribal name) > *Dimet* > Old Welsh **Dɪµed* > *Dəvəd* sees the lenition of the intervocalic *m*. The former vowel raising is seen with the name of a king of Dyfed on the Castelldwyran (Pembrokeshire) memorial stone to King Voteporix of Dyfed, now in the Carmarthen Museum; a tall standing stone, six feet high, it is inscribed on its front with a legend in Roman script, and the dedicatee's name is repeated along the top edge in ogam:

MEMORIA
VOTEPORIGIS
PROTICTORIS
(Macalister CIIC no. 358; Sims-Williams 2003, 346–47)

The ogam rendering of the British (Welsh) name is VOTECORIGAS, and the P-/Q-Celtic split can be seen in the two renderings of the king's name: -CORIGAS/-PORIGAS: the actual division comes with -RIGAS/-RIGIS, genitive of VOTEPORIX; **rix* < Proto-Celtic **rīg-* 'king' is particularly well attested from Gaul: Ambiorix, Cantiorix, Dumnorix ('world king'), Magurix, Orgetorix, Uonatorix, Vercingetorix ('high warrior king'), while *rig-* is also fairly common: *Rigomagus* the old Roman name for Remagen (Rhineland-Palatinate, Germany), Mars Rigisamus (Mars 'king of kings,' known from two dedications, one from Gaul in the territory of the Bituriges, the other from West Coker, Somerset: RIB 187, a dedication on a small bronze plate reads DEO MARTI | RIGISAMO | IVENTINVS | SABINVS | V S L L M: 'To the god Mars Rigisamus, Iventius Sabinus discharged his vow happily, freely, deservingly'). And there is Mars Rigas: Malton, North Yorkshire, RIB 711, DEO MAR(TI) | RIGAE...'to the god Mars Rigas.' One might add also the mysterious figure of R(h)iannon) from the *Mabinogion*, perhaps originally an equine goddess, her name from British **Rīgantonā* 'great queen.' The name of our king of Dyfed ('Voteporix the Protector') is preserved on this ogam-stone in two scripts, one a legacy of Roman Britain and Christianization, the other from the Irish who invaded and then settled Western Britain and Wales from about AD 360 onward. Vortipor(ius) appears here in a form that preserves old British */u-/* ([w]), which indicates either that the change /u/ > /gw/had not yet been fully effected, or a conservatism on the part of the stonemason, who was perhaps Irish as the ogam inscription is in Goidelic Q-Celtic form (the stone, if it is indeed the same Uortipor, would date to ca. 540; LHEB 385–394). The Primitive Irish form VOTECORIGAS exhibits delabialization of $/k^w/$ > /k/ (in Ogam Q > C; compare early MAQ(Q)I with MAC(I) in patronymic formulas; McManus 1997, 90), the lack of expected British raising (-RIGIS instead of -REGIS) and of vowel affection and apocope (here the loss of final *-s*) in -RIGAS may also indicate a mid-6th century dating (McManus 1997, 99, 119). British monk Gildas chastises Vortipor (*Demetarum tyranne Vortipori*,

'Vortipor, tyrant of the Demetae') in his *De excidio Britanniae* ('On the Fall of Britain') as one of the five bad kings of sub-Roman Britain, for whose sins God sends the Saxons as punishment. One more inscription seems to mention the Demetae, here in a personal name, in the patronymic formula to HOGTIVIS [HOGTINIS?] FILI DEMETI ('Hogtivis/Hogtinis son of Demetus [Dimet]'); this occurs on the tall (six-foot) standing stone at St. Dogwell's (Pembrokeshire), which includes a partial ogam version reading OGTENAS. But is this an Irish or British name? – it may be a British *hogi-* name (there is a [V]ENDOGNI FILI [H]OCIDEGNI on the nearly seven-foot tall Brawdy pillar-stone; Pembrokeshire; Macalister CIIC no. 422; Sims-Williams 2003, 374), or an Irish *Ócht-* name (Sims-Williams leans to the latter at Sims-Williams 2003, 184 n. 1116).

The *Sprachraum* in which English would develop had, in the recorded half-millennium before the 'coming of the Saxons,' been one already rich in linguistic interaction – Brittonic and Goidelic, Latin classical, vulgar, and ecclesiastical. Two of the earliest writers born in Britain who used Latin as their primary medium did so with a sufficient (even proficient) competence: St Patrick, whose life spans the 5th century (432 is the traditional date for his return to Ireland as a missionary) and Faustus of Riez, whose life also spans the 5th century. Pelagius was born in the mid-4th century, possibly in Roman Britain, though Jerome believed he was from Ireland. Though the early medieval concept of *natio* is less like that expressed in MdE *nation* (at least in senses employed since the 19th century) and more in line with 'people, race,' as Bede in his ecclesiastical history of the English nation used the term *gens* ('people, stock, race'), nonetheless *Britannia* was seen by the Romans as a distinct *natio*, a number of whose tribes they found similar to those of Gaul (i.e., fellow Celts). And though there are some traces of pre-IE substrate(s) in the Celtic languages of Britain, for the purposes of describing the speech area for English, it is sufficient to say that it was a Celtic-speaking island where Germanic-speakers at first found themselves in the minority. The population of Britain may have been as much as 4 million by the late Roman period, of which something over 100,000 were soldiers, merchants, administrators, and their families. The Germanic-speaking settlers of Britain in the 5th and 6th centuries would find themselves in a situation not entirely dissimilar from that AD 43–410. Recent work has suggested that the level of Latinity in early Britain was higher than previously thought; that use of Vulgar Latin as a spoken language survived the withdrawal of Roman legions for some years; that there was some level of bilingualism between Brittonic and Goidelic in Northern Britain and Wales; and that Vulgar Latin exerted significant influence on Brittonic (see Russell 2011 in the special issue of *TPS* 'Languages of early Britain'; Sims-Williams 2012; Mullen and Tomlin 2019 on a possible metrical inscription on a pot-base from a Roman building in Kent dating from about the mid-4th century).

The creation of the ogam 'signary' to write Primitive and Old Irish, often in inscriptions that were bilingual or repeated the inscription or parts of it in two scripts, is a matter of as much contention as that of the runes; though some accounts have pushed for very early dates a more conservative estimate is the AD 3rd or 4th century (McManus 1997, 40); ogam inscriptions in Britain have generally not been dated earlier than the 5th century (Sims-Williams 2003, 354, 369), the one exception being the controversial Silchester stone (Hampshire), with the name EBICATO[S (or TEBICATOS) MAQ]I MUCO[I] (Sims-Williams 2003, 375 [no. 496]); Fulford, Handley, and Clarke translate "(The something) of Tebicatus, son of the tribe of N"; Fulford et al. 2000, 11). Thus, we do not have just a native writing system in Britain, but perhaps also writing in the local Celtic languages, examples of which include curse tablets (see Mullen 2007; Mullen 2013; Arbabzadah and Zair 2019).

Literacy in Roman Britain is more abundantly in evidence in the 3rd and 4th centuries when it can be said to have been fairly widespread. Latin was not just the language of forts, towns, and trading-ports, but also of the countryside in the many villas of Roman Britain (including such luxury villas as the Fishbourne 'palace'). Occasional inscriptions in Greek have been found in Britain, and the onomastics of Roman Britain suggest, as for other parts of the empire, a wide-ranging, if not cosmopolitan, origin to the troops, merchants, functionaries, and their families who served and lived in Britain. Re-use and re-occupation of sites was common, such as the sacred site at Hayling Island (Hampshire): coin deposition evidence shows continuous use from the late Iron Age wooden Celtic shrine, to the Roman temple, to Saxon shrines (Briggs et al. 1992; King and Soffe 2013). Numismatic evidence is particularly useful in that it provides names of rulers and, at times, moneyers, and offers one strand of evidence for the people of Roman Britain, a line that includes Germanic peoples well before the 'coming of the Saxons.'

Roman Villas. The Ordnance Survey map for Roman Britain (2010/2016) lists over 270 Roman villas in Britain; it lists another 285 rural sites with "other substantial buildings [that] may have been villas" (OS 2010/2016; and see Scott 1993, vi). These private residences of the Roman provincial and Romano-British élite boast such luxuries as mosaic floors and hypocausts (a subfloor hot-air circulation system for heating a house or bath), as at the Bignor villa (Sussex), Borough Farm villa (West Sussex), Brading villa (Isle of Wight), the famous Chedworth site (Gloucestershire), the Fishbourne 'palace' (West Sussex), and Lullingstone villa (Kent) among others. While many villas give evidence of traditional Roman religious practices (shrines, altars, lararia), Lullingstone's pagan shrine was re-purposed as a Christian chapel with its famed Chi-Rho fresco. Lullingstone boasted a massive granary and was occupied from the AD 1st through 5th centuries; it may have served as a country residence for Roman governors (Scott 1993, 104). The villas and other fine homes (the *mansiones*) indicate a high standard of living for the provincials and select natives raised to élite status: imported goods, silver table service (the Mildenhall treasure perhaps the finest example), Samian ware, dining-rooms and suites, and, eventually, private bathrooms (Black 1994) testify to Roman Britain's trade connections with the empire, as well as the wealth extraction of Britain's resources (grain, furs and animal hides, tin). The contrast with sub-Roman Britain, the *Sprachraum* of English, will be striking, though the wealth of Britannia does explain the attraction to Saxon and other Germanic settlers.

Following the numismatic evidence, the earliest minting of coins in Britain dates to around 80 BC with the Cantii of the southeast (Kent); other tribes minting coins, in gold, silver, bronze, and potin (or billon, a base-metal alloy of copper and tin or lead), include the Atrebates, Belgae, Catuvellauni, Corieltauvi/Coritani, Dobunni, Durotriges, Iceni, and Trinovantes; curiously, no tribes from the north of Britain are known to have minted coins. The Celtic issues of Britain resemble those of Continental Celts, especially of Gaul – many are imitative of Greek and Roman issues, but employ the Celtic penchant for stylization: obverse portraits are often more abstract than the classical lifelike ruler busts; reverses often include iconic animals or designs such as the triskeles. Tincomius – considered by Augustus *rex amicus et socius* of the Romans: a client-king, friend and fellow of Rome – Epaticcus, Caratacus, Verica, Cunobelinus, Prasutagus, Boudica, Addedomarus, and others appear in the legends of British Celtic coins, some 70,000 of which have been found so far, with new discoveries every year. Numismatic evidence allows for attempts at absolute chronology, and the native appropriation and stylization of Roman issues will be seen again in early Anglo-Saxon coinage. The remains of Roman Britain allow us to meet a wider range of people than just kings and queens and those who struck or cast their coins, and it might be useful to look briefly to the "people of Roman Britain" (the title is taken from Anthony Birley's seminal study; Birley 1980).

Two queens of Roman Britain figure prominently in AD 1st century politics, Boudica and Cartimandua, though Tacitus only dignifies the former with the title *regina*. Cartimandua, queen of the Brigantes in the north, provides a scandalous note in Tacitus's *Historiae* ('Histories') for having cast off her husband Venutius in favor of his *armiger* 'armor-bearer' Vellocatus: *spreto Venutio (is fuit maritus) armigerum eius Vellocatum in matrimonium regnumque accepit* (*Historiae* III.45). She was loyal to Rome, handing Caratacus over to the Romans after he had sought refuge with her following his defeat in Wales in AD 51 (he had fled there after the defeat of his Catuvellauni and led the Silures against Rome). But Venutius would cause trouble as he sought to regain the throne of the Brigantes; with Roman support, Cartimandua held off an invasion by Venutius with his new allies, but in 69, the turbulent 'Year of Four Emperors,' Rome was able to offer only limited support, and Venutius was successful in forcing her to vacate the throne (Richmond 1954). The rebellion of Boudica of the Iceni was such that the queen has become perhaps the most pre-eminent figure from Roman Britain in the popular imagination. The rebellion was certainly the largest and most destructive of the era (until perhaps the 'Great Conspiracy' of AD 367); Camulodunum (Colchester), Londinium (London), and Verulamium (St. Albans) were destroyed. But her defeat also led, in a colonial pattern to be followed later by the English, to a major rebuilding and pacification campaign by the Romans. The lines of tribal divisions in Britain, and the Roman road system, and the Anglo-Saxon kingdoms that followed, can now be recognized, often, in the current dialect divisions of England. It seems remarkable to imagine that such lines were to an extent fixed more than a thousand years ago, and perhaps not just linguistically, though the picture is quite complicated (see the genetic study in *Nature* by Leslie et al. 2015; but also the caveat in Sims-Williams 2012 about the perils of conflating genetic and linguistic evidence).

Another set of patterns was being established in Roman Britain, a template for linguistic and cultural interchange, even hybridization. The pathways of advancement offered by cooperation with (or co-option by) the Roman system led to intermarriage, as of Roman and provincial troops with British women, bilingualism (which may have survived the withdrawal of the legions in 410), and assimilation and hybridization of British onomastics (as elsewhere in the empire). A number of Romano-Britons bear Latinized Celtic names, while evidence of religious practice in Roman Britain points toward Celto-Roman influence (to be considered below). A Lousius Suavius was a centurion in Legio XX (Valeria Victrix), the legion that built Deva, its station (now Chester; Malone 2006), and worked on both Hadrians's Wall and the Antonine Wall, and whose cashiered veterans were settled at Camulodunum (Colchester; the Roman name derives from the Celtic Iron Age *Camulodunon*, the fort of British war-god Camulos); he is known from several inscriptions from Roman Britain (RIB 1499, 1506, 1681, 1859, 1861; Birley 1980, 12, 77, 180). RIB 22 is the famous London tombstone for Grata, who had perished aged 40, and was memorialized as the 'dearest wife' (*coniugi karissimae*) of Solinus; she is the British wife of a Roman, as she is said to be *Dagobiti filia*, the daughter of Dagobitus, her father clearly a Briton. Many Britons adopted Roman names, wholly or in hybrid form, to commemorate when they were granted citizenship – the name Javolenus in Britain may honor Javolenus Priscus, a *iuridicus* (Roman provincial legal officer who heard civil cases) from the Flavian era (Birley 1980, 17). Tiberius Claudius Cogidubnus received citizenship under Emperor Claudius, and this client-king with the hybrid Romano-Celtic name has been associated with either the palatial villa at Fishbourne or another at Silchester (Salway has entertained the idea that he may have been a client ruler brought in from Gaul; Salway 2003, 748–752). M. Ulpius Longinus and M. Ulpius Novanticus, the latter of the Corieltauvi/Coritani, have wholly Roman names. Agricola in his governorship led campaigns that took him from subduing the Ordovices of north Wales in 78 to working his way north to the largest engagement with the Caledonii at Mons Graupius in 83 in northeastern Scotland: a Roman victory, but as the majority of Calgacus's Caledonians escaped to fight another day with guerilla tactics, walls would be the solution (the narrower Antonine Wall, begun in AD 142, stretching from the Firth of Forth to the Firth of Clyde had the Caledonians particularly in mind). Agricola rounded the top of Scotland by ship, espied Hibernia (Ireland), then crossed the Firth of Forth by ship, set up troops in northwestern Scotland facing Ireland, and with further successful battles subdued tribes that had to this moment been unknown to Romans (...*nave prima transgressus ignotas ad id tempus gentis crebris simul ac prosperis proeliis domuit; eamque partem Britanniae quae Hiberniam aspicit copiis instruxit*...; Tacitus, *Agricola* XXIV). Despite Severan campaigns in 209 against the Caledonii and Maeatae (both confederations of smaller tribes, the latter were still known in the 7th century, appearing in Adomnán's *Life of St. Columba* as *Miathi*; Rivet and Smith 1979, 404), and the *barbarica conspiratio* of 367 (the 'barbarian' or 'Great Conspiracy') and punitive campaigns of Flavius Theodosius in response, the far north of the island still remained outside the empire. The latter affair began with a revolt by the Roman garrison on Hadrian's Wall, which allowed incursions by Picts while apparently well-organized troops of Scot(t)i

(Irish), Picts, Caledonians, and Saxons attacked the west and southeast coasts. That Romans referred to it as a *conspiratio* seems to have merit, as the *miles areani* mentioned by Ammianus Maercellinus in his *Res gestae* ('Deeds,' i.e., 'Histories,' XXVIII. iii.8), essentially native British scouts who reported on the movements of hostile native troops, seem to have withheld vital intelligence (the *areani* were native rural troops, the term a *hapax legomenon* perhaps meaning 'people of the sheep-folds'; Stevens 1955). Roman Britain was in its late stages, first the Severan reforms from 197 to 214 (under Septimius Severus and his son Caracalla) had divided Britain into two provinces, Britannia Superior (the south and Wales, with Londinium as its capital) and Britannia Inferior (the Midlands and north, with the capital at Eburacum [York]), then those of Diocletian in 296 introduced a diocesan system of four then five provinces under *duces* – hence the title *dux Britanniarum* in the *Notitia dignitatum*, a list of titles of the thousands of Roman officials in the late Empire, among which also were the *comes Brtanniarum* and *comes littoris Saxonici*, the 'count of the Britains' in charge of the field army of Roman Britain and 'count of the Saxon shore' in charge of the coastal defense forts along the east and south coasts. Mentioned among the conspirators in the *barbarica conspiratio* of 367 are the Attacotti; both Ammianus and St. Jerome mention them as distinct from other ethnicities (namely the Scotti [Irish] and Picti [Picts] and Caledonii [Caledonian Britons]); they raided Roman Britain and were later recruited as soldiers by Rome and served in units on the continent. Though usually identified as a Brittonic (P-Celtic) tribe, attempts have been made to identify them as Goidelic (Q-Celtic) speakers from Ireland, perhaps the *aithechthúatha* (Old Irish 'peasant' or 'rent-paying peoples,' i.e., a vassal or rent-paying tribe, like the Déisi; cf. Rance 2001).

By this point in late Roman Britain, the major players in the development of the English language are present: the Scots (Irish) of the northwest (what will become the Dál Riata), the Irish settlers of Western Britain and Wales (especially Dyfed), the Picts and Strathclyde Britons of the north, and the various Germanic-speaking soldiers (and sometimes also their families) who served in Roman Britain and their fellows who raided the 'Saxon shore.' The aforementioned Legio XX, renamed Valeria Victrix after its role in the victory over Boudica, would serve in campaigns in Germania (as against the Cherusci). Units of Britons would be recruited to serve both in Britain and elsewhere in the empire (they were frequently put to use in Pannonia, which is now part of Austria, Hungary, and the Balkans). Many of the troops recruited to pacify Britain came from Gaul, and later from the Rhineland (a common pattern of Roman imperial policy). Roman military diplomas, copies of grants of citizenship for service in the Roman army or navy (generally for terms of 25 or 26 years respectively), record Britons who had received their honorable discharge and grant of citizenship by the emperor. A recent evaluation of one such diploma, found in Gherla, Cluj, Romania, and dated to AD July 133, issued to a veteran of *cohors I Britannica milliaria*, a unit raised in Britain to serve in the British garrison (soldiers who have the ethnics *Britanni* and *Brittones*), indicates that the recipient was *Sepenesto Rivi filio Cornovio*, 'Sepenestus son of Rivus, of the Cornovii' (Dana 2017, 292). The Cornovii were a people of the West Midlands, and a few other Cornovians were known to have served in the Roman army; Sepenestus, if correctly identified as a Cornovian, served far from home in Dacia Porolissensis

(Northern Dacia, in what is now Romania), and his term was with a unit that had earlier served during the brutal Dacian war, perhaps the conflict ending the reign of the last Dacian king Decebalus (whose name means 'strong as ten men'). Other Britons known from Roman military diplomas include:

Lucco Trennus of the Dobunni	cohors I Britannica	in Pannonia and Moesia Superior
M. Ulpius Adcobrovatus, Corieltauvi	cohors I Brittonum	Pannonia, Moesia Superior, and Dacia
M. Ulpius Saccus, Belgae	cohors I Brittonum	Pannonia, Moesia Sup., Dacia
Bollico Iccus, Brittones (a Briton)	ala I Claudia Gallorum	Moesia Inferior, Dacia Inferior
Ivonercus Molacus	cohors I Vlpia Brittonum	Dacia Superior
[...] Saturninus of Glevi (Gloucester)	cohors I fida Vardullorum	Britannia (Camulodunum)
(name)	(unit)	(area of service)

(Dana 2017, 294)

Many others who served in Roman armies in Britain, or in Roman units abroad, bear Celtic names, or have partially or fully Romanized names to which are attached Celtic ethnonyms (as above with Corieltauvi, Belgae, etc.). There seems to have developed a distinction in Roman nomenclature between *Britanni*, the Britons of 'Roman' Britain, and *Brittones*, Britons of frontier and unconquered regions. Three of the veterans listed above (M. Ulpius Adcobrovatus, M. Ulpius Saccus, and Saturninus) apparently served in units drawn from these 'frontier' peoples; Saturninus served in a larger military unit that was also classed *equitata* (one-fifth of it was cavalry). His unit was raised in what is now the Basque country in Spain, among the Varduli, who were either Celtic or Aquitanian (later Basques) as the region was mixed Celto-Vasconic. We have two inscriptions that bear the name of a commanding officer of *cohors I Vardullorum* from Bremenium (High Rochester, Northumberland), a Roman fort above Hadrian's Wall along Dere Street north of the Risingham (Habitancum) Roman fort. An altar was dedicated to the god Silvanus Pantheus (Silvanus 'all-divine') for the health (*pro salute*) of the commander Rufinus and his wife Lucilla (RIB 1271; Salway 1967, 235); Silvanus is god of the woodland and uncultivated land, and that latter attribute makes good sense of his appearance on this altar north of Hadrian's Wall (there are a number of dedications to Silvanus throughout Roman Britain), and his worship indicates, in a Romano-British context, the importance of sacred groves in Celtic belief systems. The altar was set up by Rufinus's freedman Eutyches, who need not be Greek, as Greek names were popular with freedmen (*liberi*); fuller details of Rufinus's career can be found on the tombstone set up by his wife Julia Lucilla: cohor(tis) I Vardul(lorum) [...] | [...praef(ecto)] coh(ortis) I Aug(ustae) | Lusitanor(um) item coh(ortis) I | Breucor(um) subcur(atori) viae | Flaminiae et aliment(orum)

| subcur(atori) operum public(orum)...(Rufinus had also been prefect of the *cohors I Augusta Lusitanorum* [raised in what is now Portugal; the Lusitanians seem to have been Celtic or para-Celtic], and of *cohors I Breucorum* [the *Breuci* were an Illyrian tribe in what is now Bosnia and Herzegovina], sub-curator of the Via Flaminia and food supply, and sub-curator of public works (RIB 1288; Salway 1967, 235–236). The latter two offices were in the civil administration of Italy, while Rufinus's military service involved quite some experience among Celts or in Celticized regions. His wife Julia appears in the inscription as IVLIA LVCILLA C F, that is, *clarissima femina* ('most splendid woman,' i.e., from a family of senatorial rank). As difficult as the assignment on the British frontier may at times have been, it could still form part of an ambitious Roman's *cursus honorum*, the 'course of honors' for Romans to make their way in society, politics, and government. A Titus Haterius Nepos eventually became prefect of Egypt AD 120–124, but spent some years in the period 90–120 in Roman Britain as *censitor* (a registrar and tax official) of the *Brittones Anavaionenses*, the Britons of Anava (Annandale, Dumfries and Galloway, and the area along the River Annan in southwest Scotland). T. Haterius Nepos is known in Britain additionally from the wooden tablet Vindolanda letters (Tabulae Vindolandenses): no. 611 is a fragmentary letter from Nepos to Flavius Genialis, prefect of Vindolanda, mentioning a Coria, which may be Corbridge (Roman Coriosopitum) though seven place-names in total have the *Coria/Corio-* element (of the Dobunni, Dumnonii, Selgovae, and Votadini; it occurs also in Gaul, as in the tribal name Coriosolites; Rivet and Smith 1979, 317–321); no. 594 is very fragmentary but seems to mention the ethnic *Anavaionenses*, among whom Nepos was stationed; and no. 292 is a personal letter between two sisters: Severa, wife of Brocchus (likely a Celtic name), writes her sister Sulpicia Lepidina, wife of Cerialis, that she has asked her husband if she might visit her, and that Brocchus had replied that she should always visit her in whatever way she might (*quomodocumque possim*). Brocchus may be the successor to Nepos as prefect of the *ala Petriana*, an auxiliary unit raised in Gaul that had served in Germany and was transferred to Britain in 98 (and on the evidence of military diplomas remained there at least until 135; RIB *Tab. Vindol.* 292, 594, 611). The river-name Anava, along which Nepos served as *censitor* for the people who lived near the border between Novantae and Brigantes territory (Rivet sees them as part of the Brigantes; Rivet 1982, 321–322), is British, **anau*, cognate with early Welsh *anaw* 'riches,' and may have broader Celtic connections with Irish goddess Anu (Ana), who, with prothetic *d-* appears as Dana/Danu, and is the principal goddess of the eponymous 'people of Danu' the Tuatha Dé Danann (Rivet and Smith 1979, 249–250). At the Roman fort Brocavum, a fragmentary tombstone depicts a small barefoot boy in a cloak; the epitaph reads:

ANNAMORIS PATER
ET RESSONA MATER
F C

"Annamoris (his) father, and Ressona (his) mother, took care that this be made." (F C = *faciendum curaverunt*; RIB 784, Brougham stone epitaph)

The date of the memorial cannot be placed any more precisely than AD 43–410, or the whole span of Roman Britain; the parents whose young son is here remembered have Celtic names, very likely British (Holder 1896, I, 44, took the husband's name as < **Adnamo-rīx*). They are likely natives attached to the fort, their single names typical of a 'barbarian nomenclature' (Salway 1967, 214; Birley 1980, 113). If indeed Britons, Annamoris and Ressona were part of the subject population living at a Roman outpost in Cumbria just south of Hadrian's Wall. Their memorial for their son is simple, and not out of keeping with similar Roman memorials in Britain and the broader empire. Rome was not able to finally subjugate the far north of Britain, and Cumbria would be a troublesome region for the Angles, who carved out kingdoms in the north. But they would not be the first Germanic-speakers to settle in Britain; their kin, with their gods, had been in Britain likely since the AD 1st century. Two more sections remain in drawing the picture of the pre-English speech area: evidence for religious practice, pagan and Christian, in Roman Britain, and the presence of Germanic peoples in the island before the *adventus Saxonum*.

3.7 'AMONG DEAD KINGS AND FORGOTTEN GODS'[5]

Wrætlic is þes wealstan, wyrde gebræcon;
burgstede burston, brosnað enta geweorc.
Hrofas sind gehrorene, hreorge torras,
hrungeat berofen, hrim on lime,
scearde scurbeorge scorene, gedrorene,
ældo undereotone. Eorðgrap hafað
waldend wyrhtan forweorone, geleorene,
heardgripe hrusan, oþ hund cnea
werþeoda gewitan.

[Wondrous is this wall-stone, broken by fate; / town-steadings burst, the work of giants falls to pieces. / Roofs have fallen in, the watch-towers in ruins, / the bolted gate asunder, hoar-frost on the mortar, / broken roof-tops gaping, collapsing, / eaten away by age. Earth's grip holds / the mighty builders gone, departed, / that hard-grasp of ground, until a hundred generations / of children of men have passed on.]

("The Ruin," ll. 1–9a; the Exeter Book of Old English verse; Exeter Cathedral Library MS 3501)

That an Anglo-Saxon poet could speak so mournfully and movingly of ruins at Roman *Aquae Sulis* (Bath, the usual identification of the poet's attention), describe them as *enta geweorc* (the 'work of giants'), is indicative of a 'fall' of Roman Britain; the image may be a willfully distorted one, but the sense that such stone-work was 'of

[5] Kapuściński 2007, 145.

old' and its manufacture such as to have required giants is telling. Had the 5th-century German arrivals in Britain forgotten the works of Roman monumental architecture? Or is it a poetic conceit? So many Germans had served in Britain, not to speak of elsewhere in the empire (nor to mention the German bodyguard retained by emperors of the AD 1st century, the *numerus Batavorum*), that it seems unlikely Roman baths, theaters, or certainly garrisons could have struck them as inexplicable except as the work of giant-builders (such as the giant mason in the story of Loki and Svaðilfari in Snorri Sturluson's *Edda*), even in the late 5th–6th centuries. But the mention of *enta geweorc* calls to mind the mythico-religious world of Germanic-speaking peoples, which had long interacted and been in exchange with the Celts on the continent. The encounter in Britain would involve displacement to be sure, but it would be a centuries-long process as English encroached upon the Celtic languages of Britain. Loan-words can be useful in pointing out the long sacrality of wells, springs, groves, and hilltops, but it is helpful to look also to the larger context of the beliefs and practices the place-names and other loans allude to.

The rich archaeological ruins at Roman Bath, Aquae Sulis (the 'waters of Sulis' – Sul or Sulis is the nominative form of the British theonym), are particularly to be valued for what they can tell us of Romano-Celtic religious practices. The fate of Romano-Celtic gods is uncertain: some would likely have reverted to their Celtic names and modes of cultivation, some may have sunk into obsolescence, and others disappeared in the face of Christianization. Romano-British Christians, such as St. Patrick, came from a Christianizing and Romanizing milieu (Patrick's father was a pagan, his mother a Christian convert); what could be termed an *interpretatio Celtica*, of identifying indigenous Celtic gods with what the Romans saw as their equivalents (in the manner that the equations made between Greek gods and Roman was termed *interpretatio Romana*, and so forth), produced such pairings as Lugh-Mercury, the 'triple mothers,' or Silvanus Callirius, known from an inscription upon a bronze votive plate discovered in Colchester in 1946: DEO SILVANO CALLIRIO D(ONUM) CINTVSMVS AERARIVS V(OTVM) S(OLVIT) L(IBENS) M(ERITO) ("To the god Silvanus Callirius, Cintusmus the coppersmith willingly and deservedly fulfilled as a gift his vow"; RIB II, Collingwood and Wright 1965). Callirius had provisionally been identified with the hazel, a tree with magical associations in early Celtic cultures, but also more recently as simply the Celtic equivalent of Silvanus, a woodland god (Old Irish *caill*, 'woodland, forest' < Celtic **kalli*; Breeze 2004). Traces, perhaps traces only, of these practices survive of course in folk tradition; a Celtic element may be discernible in Old English charms and 'folk magic' (as preserved in the *Leechdoms*), and in place-names and place-name elements.

Hydronyms represent a significant portion of the known Celtic borrowings into early English. The 'sacred waters' at Aquae Sulis were joined by another such site in Roman Britain: Aquae Arnemetiae, now the Buxton Baths complex (Derbyshire). Embedded in the apparent theonym *Arnemetia* (apparently something like 'the goddess before the grove') is the highly productive Celtic naming element **nemet*, referring to a 'sacred grove' or 'sanctuary.' *Afen* and *Avon* are simply Celtic for 'river,' the original sense perhaps forgotten by English-speakers in such hybrid place-names as Stratford-upon-Avon; Celtic too are the Exe (whence Exebridge, Exeter, Exminster, Exmoor), Mon- (the hybrid Celtic-Old English form *Monmouth* < Celtic **mon-* + OE *muða*), Tern (Shrops.). Dover and Andover are a doublet; both have the British form **Dobrā*, plural of **dubro-* 'water.' Font- forms may derive from Celtic or Latin; the seemingly transparent Fonthill (Wilts.) is probably Celtic **funt* + **(j)ol* 'spring place' (ODBPN, but cf. Gelling 1997), while Fovants (Wilts.) is likely an OE formation < *Fobbe(s)* + **funta* (first occurring in a charter of 901 as *Fobbefunte*, in the Domesday Book [1086] as *Febefonte*). Fontmell too is likely a Celtic formation (Fontmell Magna and Parva, with the Latin affixes for 'big' and 'little,' Dorset), meaning 'spring by the bare hill' (ODBPN). To return to the two Romano-British *Aquae* place-names, an altar from Bath (Aquae Sulis) was dedicated by Peregrinus, *civis Trever* ('citizen of the Treveri,' Trier; the Treveri were a Celtic subtribe of the Belgae), to Mars Loucetius and Nemetona. The former theonym is a Romano-Celtic hybrid, the Loucetius epithet shows Latin *eu* > British *ou* (LHEB 306–307, 312–317); thus Mars Leucetius means 'Mars the bright' or 'Mars the shining,' and the form appears in a few place-names from Roman Britain: the river-name *Leuca* means 'the shining one,' it is now the River Loughor/Afon Llwchwr (Carmarthenshire-Swansea), and *Leucarum* is thought to refer to the Loughor Roman fort; *Leucomagus* combines *leuco-* 'bright' with the Celtic place-name element *magus* (compare Irish *magh/maigh* 'field, plain,' though *magus* later came to mean 'market' and served as an equivalent to Latin *forum*) and may be the Roman site near East Anton (Hamps.); and *Leucovia* is likely the fort built by Agricola on the River Dee (now Glenlochar, Kirkcudbrightshire; Glen-lochar is perhaps a Goidelic-Brittonic hybrid < *gleann* 'valley' + *luch* [**leuco*] 'bright, shining').

***nemet-* 'sacred grove'** Celtic *nemet-* is found in Britain in the Romano-British sites Aquae Arnemtiae (the 'waters of Arnemetia'; Roman spa at Buxton, Derbyshire; Rivet and Smith 1979, 254–255), Medionemeum (the place 'in the middle of the sacred grove'; perhaps the shrine or tropaeum or victory memorial found in Stirlingshire; Rivet and Smith 1979, 416–417), Nemetobala (if the emendation of the Ravenna Cosmography's *Metambala* is correct, perhaps to be identified with the shrine complex at Lydney, Gloucestershire; Rivet and Smith 1979, 424), Nemeto Statio (emended to **Nemeto-totatio* and connected with the Celtic god Toutatis/Teutatis, a god of the 'people,' and cognate with Germanic Teutonic; Rivet and Smith 1979, 424–425), and Vernemetum (perhaps 'great sacred grove'; Roman site at Willoughby on the Wolds, Nottinghamshire; Rivet and Smith 1979, 495). At the Roman fort Navio (Brough-on-Noe, Derbyshire) we find an altar dedicated to the goddess Arnomecta (= Arnemtiae, the goddess 'before the sacred grove') by an Aelius Motio (RIB 281). The goddess Nemetona was worshipped in Gaul and Britain; she is apparently the consort of Mars Loucetius in an altar dedication from Bath made by Peregrinus, son of Secundus of the Treveri (Aquae Sulis; RIB 140). A Quintus Neratius Proximus made a dedication to Mars Rigonemetus, 'king of the sacred grove,' at Nettleham, Lincolnshire (just a few miles northeast of Lincoln, Roman Lindum Colonia). The *nemet-* place-names and theonyms connect Celtic Britain to the wider Celtic world, with the Drunemeton ('sacred oak grove') found in Spain and Galatia (central Anatolia, now Turkey), Nemetodurum in Gaul (now Nanterre, France), and Nemetobriga ('sacred grove' at the 'hill' or 'fort'), which Ptolemy mentioned as a town of the Tiburos subtribe of the Astures in Gallaecia, Spain (Salway 2003, 673).

Romano-British temples generally involve a box-like, square or rectangular space (the *cella*) around which was often an ambulatory or veranda (of stone or wood, some, but not all, covered) and all this may be within a marked-off sacred space (or *temenos*), where this can be recognized by archaeologists; examples include the West Hill temple complex at Uley, Gloucestershire, or that at Springhead, Kent; the ambulatory is missing from the Jordan Hill complex in Dorset, but this may have been due to later plundering of the site. While the pre-Romano-British Celtic shrines were nearly all circular, some wooden huts or open structures, the Romano-British temples are generally rectangular, though smaller than those in the classical world (or in Roman Gaul). A number of the religious sites were built upon, or alongside (as at Maiden Castle, Dorset), earlier Iron Age sanctuaries and shrines such as at wells or springs (Lewis 1966; Salway 2003, 670–677; Cunliffe 2018, "Groves, Springs, and Shrines," 291–307). It is interesting to note that a number of religious sites were open to the sky, and that the enclosed space may have been designed to recall the sacred grove – both would have been familiar elements of druidic practice. Those sanctuaries at which dedications have been identified involve Roman gods, gods from elsewhere in empire (Mithras, Attis, Cybele, Isis), Romano-Celtic gods (the aforementioned Mars Loucetios and Mars Rigisamus, or Sulis Minerva at Bath), Celtic gods known also from Gaul or further afield (Epona, Mogons – Mainz in Germany, *Castrum Mogontiacum*, seems to be named for this god – Nemetona, Sucellus), and those Celtic gods known only from Britain.

The gods of Britain Inscriptions from Roman Britain record worship of Roman gods, gods from other parts of the empire, syncretic Romano-British pairings (Mars Loucetius, Mars Rigonemetus, Mars Toutatis, Sulis Minerva), and Celtic gods. The cults of Celtic gods may at times be imports – as from Gaul, the Rhineland (with the *matres* 'mothers' cults found also among the Germans), the Danube frontier and Balkans, Hispania and Lusitania (Spain and Portugal), the Alpine Celtic region, and Central Europe. A Quintus Sittius Caecilianus, prefect of the First Cohort of Aquitanians (a unit raised in Gallia Aquitania, a region that spoke Aquitanian, an extinct language believed to have been related to Basque), dedicated an altar *Deo Marti Braciacae*, to 'Mars Braciaca' (RIB 278, from Bakewell, Derbyshire); Braciaca may be an import, or a local 'god of malt' or 'brewing god' (Birley 1980, 67). Besides the *genii* ('geniuses,' local spirits), nymphs and other water deities, and spirits and shades of the imperial household worshipped in Roman Britain, a fairly significant roster of local Celtic gods is known from British inscriptions. The classic study is Eric Birley's "The deities of Roman Britain" (Birley 1986), who listed some 49 deities known only from Britain, among them Maponus (known in later Welsh tradition as Mabon), Cocidius (Mars Cocidius; Birley 1980, 84 85), Belatucadrus (perhaps 'bright shining one,' Birley 1980, 113), Matunus, Nodens, Verbeia, as well as the tutelary goddesses Brigantia and Britannia (and see, more recently, Webster 2015).

While the gods could be honored and beseeched in the earlier sacred groves and Roman-British temples, it is evident that sacred waters (rivers, springs, wells, lakes, bogs) offered another way to reach the gods – deposition hoards, such as at Llyn Cerrig Bach on Angelsey, yield abundant evidence of votive offerings sent into the waters as offerings to the gods. The practice especially of depositing weapons as votive offerings spans the Celtic regions, with particularly rich finds in the Balkans; many of these weapons have been bent or otherwise rendered unusable, perhaps in thanksgiving for having survived battle (not unlike the classical practice of making offerings at temples of Ares/Mars). Animal sacrifices are found as well, as of horses, dogs, and ravens, and there is some continuity here with Indo-European practice (the horse-sacrifice was a marker of the warrior/ruler caste, from the *aśva-medha* of Vedic India to similar practices in Ireland, and even early Anglo-Saxon England). Though highly controversial, there is some evidence of human sacrifice in the British Iron Age, as at Danebury hill-fort. Caesar had alluded to head-taking and human sacrifice in Gaul, so too had Poseidonios, Diodorus Siculus, Strabo, and Lucan (Rudd 1999; Cunliffe 2018, 283 and plate 11.17, the famous portico of the Gaulish sanctuary at Roquepertuse with niches for decapitated human skulls); and Tacitus records that the Germans who had destroyed Varus's three legions in AD 9 at the Battle of Teutoburg Forest had sacrificed Roman prisoners, including centurions and other officers, nailing decapitated heads to trees and raising altars in groves (*Annales* I.6). The former Roman officer Arminius led his Cherusci and other Germans at Teutoburg; he was said to have been an inspiration for the *barbarica conspiratio* of 367 in Britain.

The term 'Romano-British' can indicate not simply a period but a synthesis, as of temple sites built in the rectangular Roman fashion, as at Bath, Corbridge, or that of the deified Emperor Claudius at Colchester, but with dedications also to Celtic gods in their native form or matched with a Roman equivalent by *interpretatio Romana*. The Carrawburgh complex in Northumberland on Hadrian's Wall included a mithraeum (the covered or subterranean meeting space for the mystery rites of Mithras), 'Coventina's Well,' and shrines to the nymphs and *genius loci* (the 'spirit of the place'). Two other religious traditions will have enormous consequences on the history of the English language: Christianity came to Roman Britain with Roman converts from elsewhere in the empire, especially Gaul; there is evidence for its practice among the soldiers (at Richborough, Kent, and at Housesteads, Vindolanda, and other sites on Hadrian's Wall) and among private citizens (the Romano-British villa at Lullingstone, Kent), and the legacy of 'British Christianity' will be considered in the next chapter. German soldiers serving in Britain brought their own ancestral faith traditions with them, as altars dedicated to Germanic *matres* provide evidence. And this last example sets the stage for the beginnings of English.

3.8 SONS OF WODEN

Eight units of German auxiliaries, of the Batavi tribe, were attached to Legio XIV Gemina and fought at the Battle of the Medway under Aulus Plautius in AD 43 during the Claudian invasion of Britain; Cassius Dio reports that they swam the Medway and Thames in full armor (Cassius Dio LX.20.2). Germans would be in Roman Britain for its duration AD 43–410 and, of course, beyond. In the volume to the Oxford History of England on *The English Settlements* (that between those on Roman Britain and Anglo-Saxon England), J.N.L. Myres observed: "It is perhaps best to start this enquiry by considering what indications there may be of Germanic infiltration into Romano-British society before the political collapse of Roman rule" (Myres 1986, 75). The legions that served in Roman Britain would be drawn from Italy and elsewhere across the empire – the fabled Legio IX Hispana was not raised in Spain but named from its participation in Augustus's Cantabrian campaign 29–19 BC (the Cantabri, a Celtic tribe in Northern Spain). The auxiliary units attached to the legions, some 70 or so of which served in Britain, were often raised on a tribal or ethnic basis. Of these, a simple majority were raised in other Celtic regions: *cohors I Alpinorum peditata* (an infantry unit drawn from Celtic mountain tribes in Northern Italy); the *cohortes Gallorum* and *Lingonum* were drawn from Gaul, those of the Nervii from a partially Germanized Celtic people, that *Raetorum* was from the Rhaeti of the Italian Alps (a people believed to have spoken a language related to Etruscan, but who were subsequently Celticized); the Celtiberian cohort was drawn from Celtic tribes in Eastern Spain such as the Arevaci and Lusones, while the Morini and Menapii were from Gallia Belgica. Classical writers did not share the 'Celtoskepticism' of a number of modern historians, and they freely grouped peoples by ethnic origin and reported affinities between Celtic groups, culturally and linguistically. Indeed, this formed one of the bases for Roman imperial policy, as Celts from other provinces in the empire were transferred to deal with Celts in another: here, Celts from Spain, Gaul, and what are now the Low Countries were sent to subdue Celts in Britain. Mutiny, of course, was one risk the policy ran.

But in addition to these Celtic auxiliaries, and units drawn from much further afield, such as *cohors I Hamiorum*, a detachment of 500 Syrian archers from Hama, a fairly large number of units were made up of Germans: two cohorts of Tungrians served in Britain (and are better known more recently from the Vindolanda letters); the Baetasii, Cugerni, and Sunuci were drawn from Germania Inferior; the Vangiones were transferred after the Roman disaster at Teutoburg Forest in AD 9 to Britain (no doubt to avoid such banding together of German compatriots); the aforementioned Batavi (the Betuwe region in Eastern Netherlands corresponds approximately with their territory) included a cavalry detachment, and, from what is now the Netherlands, the Frisiavones and, in a smaller unit, Frisians. We also know of Saxons serving in Britain, and settling in Britain with their families in some numbers (as did other German veterans). Add to them the increasing problems with Saxon piracy from the early 3rd through 4th centuries (thus the 'Saxon Shore' forts of Eastern and Southern Britain, Brancaster, Reculver, Richborough, Dover, Lympne, Pevensey, among others) and the picture of events in AD 449, the *adventus Saxonum*, seems less a moment than a process of, as Myres suggested, 'infiltration.' That the use of German auxiliaries by Rome could be problematic was in evidence in the mutiny of the cohort of the Usipii (or Usipetes); the cohort was raised in the Rhineland and accompanied Agricola to the north of Britain ca. AD 82; there, in perhaps northwest Scotland, they killed their centurion and other officers training them, then commandeered three ships and sailed back around the north of the island and down the east coast sparring with Britons along the way until hunger allegedly drove them to cannibalism. They eventually, according to Tacitus, landed back near home and the survivors were enslaved by the Suevi and Frisii, able to boast some fame for their exploits (*Agricola* XXVIII; Birley 1980, 157).

A *numerus*, the Roman unit for native troops not normalized into a legion or auxilium, consisting of Frisians, was stationed at Vercovicium (Housesteads) on Hadrian's Wall. Two *cunei Frisionum* or *Frisiorum* are known to have served on the Wall (*cuneus* is literally 'wedge,' and was used like *numerus* for a foreign unit of allied 'barbarians'), the one at Housesteads, another at Brough-by-Sands in the early 3rd century. Though *cuneus* can refer to a massed infantry formation, we know that Frisian cavalry was valued by the Romans and served in Britain. Two inscriptions from Housesteads record the presence of the Frisians, both found within the temple of Mars there. One is an inscribed pillar just over six feet in height inscribed DEO | MARTI | THINCSO |ET DVABVS | ALAISIAGIS |BEDE ET FI|MMILENE | ET N AVG GER|M CIVES TV|IHANTI | V S L M ("To the god Mars Thingsus and to the two Alaisiagae, Beda and Fimmilena, and to the divine presence (*numen*) of the Emperor, the Germans, citizens [members] of the Tuihanti, have fulfilled their vow freely and deservedly"; RIB 1593). Mars Thingsus has been connected to Old English and Old Norse *þing*, 'legal assembly' or 'legal proceeding, case' (Shaw 2011, 38), though one wonders whether the association might also be between the field where such assemblies were held (the Icelandic *Þingvellir* for example) and the 'field of Mars' (Campus Martius) and its temple of Mars Ultor and ritual role in declarations of war and festivals such as the *Equus October* ('October Horse'). The Alaisiagae, the paired goddesses Beda and Fimmilena, are known from the other altar stone pillar from Housesteads, this just over four feet high, with a similar but fuller inscription that adds after the dedication to Mars and the two goddesses: CIVES TVIHANTI | CVNEI FRISIORVM | VER SER ALEXAND|RIANI ('the citizens of the Tuihanti of the *cuneus* of Frisians of Vercovicium of (the unit of) Severus Alexander'; RIB 1594). The Tuihanti is a tribal name perhaps to be associated with the Germanic god Tiw (whence OE *Tīwes-dæġ*, 'Tiw's day,' Tuesday) and with the Twente region of the eastern Netherlands (Overijssel province). That the second Housesteads inscription associates the Frisian *cuneus* with Emperor Severus Alexander may indicate a dating of 222–235.

Another Frisian unit stationed on Hadrian's Wall at Housesteads dedicated an altar stone to the Alaisiagae and the emperor's 'divine spirit'; this, just over three feet high, names the Alaisiagae as Baudihillia and Friagabis; it was set up by the *numerus Hnaudifridi*, or Notfried's unit (RIB 1576). As the goddesses are twice connected with Mars Thincsus (Thingsus), an attempt has been made to extend the 'thing' (legal assembly) notion to the Frisian legal terms *Bodþing* ('summons') and *Fimelþing* ('sentence'), that is, with Beda and Fimmilena respectively (cf. Simek 1993, 5–6, 33, 83, 93, 203). This does not explain their other names Baudihillia (the first half to the evidently compound name seems to be Gmc **badwa-* 'battle') and Friagabis (which might be < **frija-* + **gebōn* as 'giver of freedom,' or perhaps 'friendly giver'; Orel 2003, 114). A tombstone at Corbridge on Hadrian's Wall records the sad memorial for Ahteha: D M | AHTEHE | FIL NOBILIS | VIXIT ANIS V ('to the divine shades, for Ahtehe, daughter of Nobilis, she lived 5 years'; RIB 1180); Ahtehe (the dative form, nominative Ahteha) is evidently Germanic, and may be a hypocoristic or pet-name form of a compound Germanic personal name (on the notion that the pet or diminutive name being formed not along Latin but Germanic morphology may indicate the family spoke German in their household, cf. Salway 1967, 228). A memorial from Great Chesters (Roman Aesica) is now only partially legible, having been later reshaped for re-use, but it records the Germanic name of Dagualdus, who served in a cohort of Pannonians (perhaps the First) whose wife had the stone set up; her name is Pusinna, which has been taken as Rhaetian (Salway 1967, 232). And a *Maduhus Germanus* ('Maduhus the German') dedicated an altar to Coventina at Carrawburgh at Coventina's Well.

We know of other groups of Germans settling or being settled in Roman Britain: Marcus Aurelius settled defeated Marcomanni in Britain in the 2nd century, while in the 3rd century, Vandals and Burgundians were sent to the island. The proclamation of Constantine as imperator at York in 306 involved a chief of the Alemanni named Crocus; another chief of the Alemanni, Fraomar, was sent to Britain in 372 as a tribune, apparently to have authority over other Alemanni soldiers in Britain or removed there to reduce population pressure on the continent (Myres 1986, 79–81). The Alemanni might be remembered in the place-name Almondbury (West Yorkshire); though a number of authorities take it as 'town of all men' (CDEPN, ODEPN), Myres held that enough evidence supports that the Anglian *Alemaneberie* (*Almenberie* in the Domesday Book) records "a tradition that it had once served as a stronghold of the Alemanni" (Myres 1986, 82). In late Roman Britain, other Germans were settled as *laeti* or *foederati*, terms for those 'barbarians' granted land within the limits of the empire in exchange for providing military recruits or those under treaty with Rome with a similar arrangement. And then there were also mercenary forces, as will be seen next chapter with Vortigern's fateful call for help from Hengest and the Saxons (as in the accounts of Gildas and Geoffrey of Monmouth).

One last simple find, dating to ca. 425–475, the last days of the Romano-British period and the early days of the sub-Roman, may be mentioned here. A Runic-inscribed ankle bone (astragalus) of a roe deer from Caistor-by-Norwich (Norfolk) consists of a single word in what would then still be either Common Germanic or Northwest Germanic: ᚱᚨᛇᚺᚨᚾ (**raïhan**, 'roe'). It may be a gaming piece, as it appears among 33 other gaming pieces, colored white or black, and some 35 other astragali, though this is the largest astragalus in the urn, and the only inscribed piece (see Page 2006, 179–180, who hedges on the 'roe' interpretation). Why it is so simply inscribed ('roe,' i.e., 'from a roe') may have to do with the magical properties Runic writing was felt to have, or it may fit in with a tradition of talking objects (as with other Runic inscriptions, or the Old English riddles). The deer bone was found in a cremation urn in an East Anglian cemetery near what had been Roman *Venta Icenorum* on the *litus Saxonicum* ('Saxon shore'). The form **raïhan** is from Proto-WGmc **raihō*, the Old English reflex *rā*; the development of the later form seems to have involved lengthening of the nuclear vowel to **ai*, then loss of the glide (cf. Ringe in Ringe and Taylor 2014, 171). If it is not an import from the continent (or Denmark), and if it may be considered pre-English or proto-English at this early date, then it is the first word written in the English language.

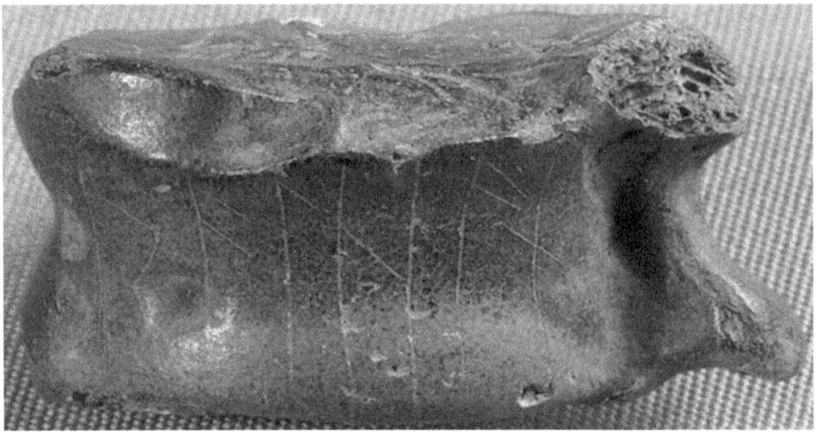

The Caistor-by-Norwich astragalus.
Source: Alexander Leischner / Wikipedia / CC-BY SA 4.0.

3.9 RETROSPECT

The language picture of English so far deals only with either a pre-English or proto-English state, that is, at a time before English would come into existence, pre-449, or during what could be called its 'embryonic' phase, ca. 449–525 or so; no precise figure can be given here, but it may be estimated that a span of at least three generations of speakers of Germanic dialects resident in Britain would be a possible framework within which one could speak of 'earliest' Old English.

Here, at this point, some generally relevant linguistic signposts pre-449 obtain. The dating of the split of Celtic from Indo-European is generally seen as 'early,' whether an Italo-Celtic phase (if not a branching) is envisioned or not, earlier than the split of Germanic from IE (roughly dated to 500 BC by historical linguists). The split of Celtic into P-Celtic and Q-Celtic branches may very well be early too (perhaps during the proto-Germanic period post-500 BC, or even earlier): it may – though there are dissenting voices – have to do with the movement of speakers of Celtic into the British Isles, namely from Britain to Ireland, or may follow an earlier split between Continental and Insular Celtic; a dating to ca. 300 BC for the spread of Celtic languages across the British Isles is probably too late. The split of Insular Celtic into Brythonic (Brittonic) and Goidelic branches is evidenced in historically recorded and surviving Celtic languages: British, Welsh, Cumbric, Cornish, and Breton (Brythonic; the position and/or affiliation of Pictish remains uncertain); Irish, Scots Gaelic, Manx (Goidelic). The relationship between Insular and Continental Celtic seems to have been close up to the AD 1st century: Tacitus records that there was little difference between the speech of Gauls and Britons (*Agricola* XI); place-names, ethnonyms (tribal names in particular), personal names, names for divinities (theonyms), and other lexical evidence seem to bear the observation out in general (though recent epigraphical and linguistic work does point to dialect differentiation, as would be expected).

The fact that Britain did not wind up speaking a Romance language tells us much of interest about the language situation in early Britain and the dynamics of language contact situations. Iberia and Gaul would develop Romance tongues (Spanish, Catalan, Portuguese in the former; French, Occitan/Provençal in the latter). The fate of the indigenous Celtic languages is a determining factor: Celtiberian appears to have faded early (perhaps the AD 1st century); Gaulish later, but perhaps before AD 400. Galician and Breton are reintroductions of Celtic by migrating Britons (likely before the *adventus Saxonum*, but accelerating with it). Basque is a non-Indo-European survival; other non-IE tongues (Tartessian?) seem to have died out in the classical period. Extent and duration of Romanization played a role also; nonetheless, Romano-British culture was a phenomenon of nearly a half-millennium. There is linguistic continuity in the use of Latin by the British Church into the Anglo-Saxon period. As simple as the observation is – that there is no 'British' Romance language – the conditions that closed off the development of a Latin-based tongue are not entirely satisfactorily explained. We have in the 5th century, or, more broadly, in late Roman Britain, one of three significant moments in which linguistic history was altered: the crucible of English itself, the 5th and 6th centuries, could have seen things develop otherwise (an indigenous Romance tongue then pitted in competition with Germanic dialects comprising Old English: the outcome may not have been much different, with a hypothetical Romance-Celtic-Germanic language situation); the Viking raids starting in 793 introduce large numbers of North Germanic-speakers into Northern and Eastern England. The linguistic consequences are felt outside the 'Danelaw'; and the introduction in 1066 of Norman French as the dominant, prestige language in England altered the history of English, but did not end it.

The *Sprachraum* in which English would develop encompasses the broader cultural reach of the Celtic tribes the Germanic-speaking mercenaries and invaders of the AD 4th and 5th centuries would encounter and then dispossess as their settlements expanded out from Britain's east and southeast, especially along river valleys. Rather than a sudden irruption in 449, the major players had been in place for centuries. Population pressures had, to some extent (precisely how much is unknown), precipitated the movement westward of Germanic-speaking tribes. But so too did the promise of plunder, good land, slaves, and the slow collapse of the expansive power of Rome (which had kept the *limes* of the Rhine more or less in place for centuries). German-Roman conflicts were hardly new: the major defeat of Varus's legions in the Teutoburg Forest had been inflicted by the Germans in AD 9. German auxiliaries and legionnaires had served for at least a few centuries in the forts of Roman Britain (Tungrians and Batavians among those named in the Vindolanda tablets).

The Roman conquest had introduced an acrolectal Latin to Britain, for use in administration (then also in the early British Church), a prestige language native élites would have their children educated in (cf. Hamp 1975 on "Social Gradience in British Spoken Latin"). But Latin was also an everyday spoken language in Roman Britain, joining, for some four centuries, the indigenous Celtic languages as a 'mother tongue.' This complicates the next stage in Britain's linguistic evolution, the dominance of the Germanic dialects of the invaders over the indigenous Celtic dialects; that there were Latin loans to the Celtic languages of Britain and early Old English may indicate that the history of Latin in Britain was not discontinuous between 410 (the withdrawal of the legions) and 597 (the conversion of Kent). The early Germanic settlements look to have been lasting in a linguistic sense as well, with the persistence to the present of some of the dialectal and linguistic boundaries of Britain. In the long view, the expansion of English in Celtic Britain is the template for the later linguistic encounters in the history of English.

The English language would develop in a predominantly Celtic-speaking island; when Celtic-speakers came to Britain is a highly, occasionally even heatedly, debated matter. Some datings range as late as the 1st century BC to even the AD 1st, which is linguistically implausible given the split in Insular Celtic into the P-Celtic and Q-Celtic languages, among other sound changes (and linguistic distance from earlier branchings of Indo-European involving Celtic, such as the proposed Italo-Celtic grouping). Epigraphic and numismatic evidence from Romano-Celtic inscriptions, especially in Gaul and Spain, also suggest a longer time depth to the separation of Celtic from Western Indo-European, to which may be added the necessary changes that separate Brittonic from Goidelic languages. The present study accepts a conventional dating ca. 350 BC as the conservative estimate, with a preference for an earlier dating (the 8th century BC). It has become increasingly accepted that the movement of Celtic-speakers into Britain may have been in waves of settlements rather than invasions, on the basis, in part, of no records of any major military campaigns being recorded by classical authors. This might be qualified by the extensive classical records of Celtic invasions of Greek and Roman territories in the Mediterranean (the sacking of Delphi and Rome by large Celtic armies, or participation of Celtic forces in the Punic War on the side of Carthage, which encompasses the period of the 4th through 2nd centuries BC); it is rather likely that Greek and Roman writers were more preoccupied with Celtic movements on their own frontier than on the edge of their maps. It is also contradicted by native oral tradition, surviving in medieval manuscripts, of waves of invasions of the British Isles and movements back and forth: of some P-Celtic-speakers in Ireland, and fairly large numbers of Irish settlers in Wales, western Britain, and Scotland; the 'pseudo-history' of the *Lebor Gabála Érenn* ('Book of the Takings of Ireland'), *Annales Cambriae* ('Annals of Wales'), *Gododdin*, and first four branches of the *Mabinogion* preserve such traditionary accounts, however challenging they may be for historians to sift. The earliest classical accounts of Britain suggest a significant time depth to the settlement, with fairly rich and entrenched tribal divisions.

The significance of the Roman period of occupation of Britain has perhaps been underplayed in earlier histories of English. Fairly widespread literacy in Latin, and occasional evidence for it in Celtic too, is present in the monuments and quotidian artifacts of Roman Britain: the Vindolanda tablets include personal letters, economic and military records, and they have now been antedated by the Bloomberg tablets of the AD 1st century found in the excavation of London's financial district during 2010–2013. Literacy was not restricted to urban centers and forts but also present in the villas of the countryside. Religious evidence suggests, as was common in the Roman system, a degree of alignment and syncretism with the native Celtic traditions, a happy circumstance that affords some of our earliest records of the Celtic gods. The accommodation worked in the other direction as well: we find native Britons adopting Roman nomenclature partially to fully, entering the ranks of the military and civil service and, in the case of significant numbers of soldiers, serving abroad. The coming of Christianity, difficult to date, but certainly present by the 3rd century, reinforced the use of Latin literacy. Clerics are among the earliest known writers of 4th- and 5th-century Britain (Pelagius, St. Patrick, Faustus of Riez); Christianity was widespread enough that British clerics attended church councils starting with that at Arles in AD 314 (and Pelagius and Faustus both had their troubles with heterodox doctrinal views). As seen in this chapter, Germans had been present in Britain the entire Roman period, AD 43–410. Saxon settlement of the 'Saxon shore' introduces the complicated matter of the Germanic presence in Britain – as soldiers stationed at Roman garrisons, as settled veterans or *laeti* and *foederati* (or as exiled or excess population from the Continent), as pirates and invaders. As Rome began to abandon Britannia, Saxons and other Germans increased their pressure on northern Gaul and came to occupy both sides of the Channel. Gaul would be returned to Roman rule for some decades longer; Britain would face a different fate in the 5th century. This of course had linguistic consequences, with a Romance language on one side of the Channel, Germanic on the other. The legions were withdrawn, British client-kings scrambled to carve out kingdoms in place of provinces or dioceses as the 'tyrants' deplored by Gildas; evidence suggests that, as elsewhere in the 5th-century Empire, some former Roman subjects made efforts at 'staying Roman' (see Conant 2012 for the example of Roman North Africa). The Roman Church remained in Wales, and was restored in the north by Irish missionaries who would labor to convert the approaching Angles in the 6th and 7th centuries. The roots of English run deeper than the 5th century, to Germans resident in Britain such as Maduhus and Ahteha and Fullofaudes and their gods, and to the native Celtic-speaking majority who gave names to hills, groves, and rivers.

REFERENCES AND BIBLIOGRAPHY

An invaluable resource for studying this period is the online version of *Roman Inscriptions of Britain*: https://romaninscriptionsofbritain.org. The website provides images of many of the objects (altars, memorials/tombstones, votive plaques, milestones, etc.) upon which the inscriptions occur, and diplomatic and critical editions with translations of all inscriptions. The online version has the additional benefit of cross-referencing of names, locations, and keywords in the corpus of inscriptions (e.g., the inscriptions mentioning Coventina, or the *cuneus Frisiorum*, or those found at Corbridge or Silchester).

The annual journal *Britannia* (Society for the Promotion of Roman Studies/Cambridge University Press, 1970–) is the pre-eminent periodical on the subject, with a particular focus on the history and archaeology of Roman Britain, and it is also a major source for recent discoveries of inscriptions.

Among the most valuable primary sources for the period are Caesar's *De bello Gallico* in eight books (ca. 49 BC; Book Eight was finished by the consul Aulus Hirtius after Caesar's death in 44 BC; he had been a legate under Caesar; the Oxford Classical Text edition by Du Pontet is still standard): besides the accounts of early Britons and the druids of Gaul and Britain, Book V is the source of the story of Lucius Vorenus and Titus Pullo (now better known from the HBO cable series *Rome*); Tacitus's *Agricola* and *Germania* (ca. AD 98) are the most valuable source for both Agricola's British campaigns (AD 78–84) and the ethnography and anthropology of the early Germanic tribes; his *Annales* (Annals) and *Historiae* (Histories) place the information in the broader imperial context (the texts are available in the Teubner [Bibliotheca Scriptorum Graecorum et Romanorum Teubneriana] and OCT [Oxford Classical Texts] series, and with translation in the Loeb Classical Library, as well as Penguin Classics and Oxford's World Classics series). Ptolemy's *Geography* (ca. 150) is a rich source for the Celtic toponyms and ethnonyms of the early Europe, especially Britain (edition of Greek text by Karl Friedrich August Nobbe, 1843–1845; for a recent translation see Berggren and Jones 2002). The *Historia Romana* of Dio Cassius (ca. AD 229) and *Res gestae* of Ammianus Marcellinus (ca. AD 378) survive in fragmentary and reconstructed form and are available in the Loeb series; the former is one of the few classical sources recounting the revolt of Boudica in AD 60/61.

Aldhouse-Green, Miranda. *Sacred Britannia: The Gods and Rituals of Roman Britain.* London: Thames and Hudson, 2018

Allen, Derek. *Catalogue of the Celtic Coins in the British Museum, with supplementary material from other British collections*, 3 vols.: vol. I, *Silver Coins of the East Celts and Balkan Peoples*, ed. J. Kent and M. Mays (1987); vol. II, *Silver Coins of North Italy, South and Central France, Switzerland and South Germany*, ed. J. Kent and M. Mays (1990); vol. III, *Bronze Coins of Gaul*, ed. M. Mays (1995). London: British Museum Press, 1987–1995

Antonelli, Luca. *Il periplo nascoto: lettura stratigrafica e commento storico-archeologico dell'Ora maritima di Avieno*. Padua: Esedra, 1998/rpt. 2009

Arbabzadah, Moreed and Nicholas Zair, "Notes on a British curse tablet from Red Hill, Ratcliffe-on-Soar (Nottinghamshire)," *Zeitschrift für Papyrologie und Epigraphik* 212 (2019), 172–179

Bailliot, Magali and Robert Symmons, "Note from the Roman Palace at Fishbourne (Sussex): A roman magic lead figurine?" *Britannia* 43 (2012), 249–260

Ball, Martin J. and Nicole Müller, eds. *The Celtic Languages*. 2nd ed. London: Routledge, 2015

Barrett, Anthony A., "The career of Tiberius Claudius Cogidubnus," *Britannia* 19 (1979), 227–242

Benson, Larry D., gen. ed. *The Riverside Chaucer*. 3rd. Boston, MA: Houghton Mifflin, 1987

Berggren, J. Lennart and Alexander Jones, trs. *Ptolemy's Geography: An Annotated Translation of the Theoretical Chapters*. Princeton, NJ: Princeton University Press, 2002

Birch, Walter de Gray. *Cartularium Saxonicum: A Collection of Charters Relating to Anglo-Saxon History*, 3 vols. London: Whiting & Co., 1885–1893

Birley, Anthony. *The People of Roman Britain*. Berkeley, CA: University of California Press, 1980

Birley, Anthony R., tr. *Cornelius Tacitus. Agricola and Germany*. Oxford: Oxford University Press, 1999

Birley, Eric, "The deities of Roman Britain," *Aufstieg und Niedergang der römischen Welt* II.18.1, in *Religion (Heidentum: Die religiösen Verhältnisse in der Provinzen)*, ed. Wolfgang Haase. Berlin: de Gruyter, 1986. Pp. 3–112

Black, E.W., "Villa owners: Romano-British gentlemen and officers," *Britannia* 25 (1994), 99–110

Bogaers, J.E., "King Cogidubnus in Chichester: Another reading of *RIB* 91," *Britannia* 10 (1979), 243–254

Boll, F. and A. Boer, eds. *Claudii Ptolemaei Opera quae exstant omnia.* 2nd ed. Wolfgang Hübner. Stuttgart: B.G. Teubner, 1998

Bowman, Alan K. *Life and Letters on the Roman Frontier.* London: British Museum Press, 1994

Bowman, Alan K. and J. David Thomas. *Vindolanda: The Latin Writing-Tablets*, Britannia Monograph Series, No. 4. London: Society for the Promotion of Roman Studies, 1984

Bowman, Alan K., J. David Thomas, and R.S.O. Tomlin, "The Vindolanda writing-tablets (Tabulae Vindolandenses IV, Part 1)," *Britannia* 41 (2010), 187–224

Bowman, Alan K. and Greg Woolf, eds. *Literacy and Power in the Ancient World.* Cambridge: Cambridge University Press, 1994

Breeze, Andrew, "The God Silvanus Callirius and *RIB* 194, from Colchester," *Britannia* 35 (2004), 228–229

Briggs, Daphne, Colin Haselgrove, and Cathy King, "Iron age and roman coins from Hayling Island temple," *British Numismatic Journal* 62 (1992), 1–62

Camden, William. *Britannia, or A Chorographicall Description of the Most flourishing Kingdomes, England, Scotland, and Ireland, and the Ilands Adioyning, Out of the Depth of Antiquitie.* London: George Bishop and John Norton, 1610 [English version of 1586 first edition]

Casey, P.J., B. Hoffmann, and J. Dore. "Excavations at the Roman Temple in Lydney Park, Gloucestershire in 1980 and 1981," *The Antiquaries Journal* 79 (1999), 81–143

CDEPN = *The Cambridge Dictionary of English Place-Names*, ed. Victor Watts, John Insley, Margaret Gelling. Cambridge: Cambridge University Press, 2004

Charles-Edwards, Thomas. "Language and society among the Insular Celts AD 400–1000," *The Celtic World*, ed. Miranda Green, London: Routledge, 1995, 703–736

CIIC = *Corpus Inscriptionum Insularum Celticarum*, 2 vols., ed. R.A.S. Macalister. Dublin: Stationery Office 1945–1949

CIL = *Corpus Inscriptionum Latinarum.* Berlin: Georg Reimer, 1863–2025 (Online). http://www.attalus.org/docs/cil/

Coates, Richard. "The significances of Celtic place-names in England," in *The Celtic Roots of English*, ed. Filppula, Markku, Juhani Klemola and Heli Pitkänen. Joensuu: Joensuun Ylipopistopainu/Joensuu University Press, 2002. Pp. 47–85

Colgrave, Bertram and R.A.B. Mynors, eds. *Bede's Ecclesiastical History of the English People.* Oxford: Clarendon Press, 1969

Conant, Jonathan. *Staying Roman: Conquest and Identity in Africa and the Mediterranean, 439–700.* Cambridge: Cambridge University Press, 2012

Cooley, Allison E., ed. *Becoming Roman, Writing Latin? Literacy and Epigraphy in the Roman West.* Journal of Roman Archaeology Supplementary Series 48. Portsmouth, RI: Journal of Roman Archaeology, 2002

Cosh, Stephen R., "A possible date for the Silchester Roman 'Church'," *Britannia* 35 (2004), 229–233

Cunliffe, Barry W. *The Ancient Celts.* 2nd ed. Oxford: Oxford University Press, 2018

Cunliffe, Barry W. and P. Davenport. *The Temple of Sulis Minerva at Bath.* 3 vols. Oxford: Oxford University School of Archaeology, 1985

Dana, Dan, "A Hitherto unrecognised Cornovian on a Military Diploma (RMD I, 35)," *Britannia* 48 (2017), 287–298

d'Arbois de Jubainville, Marie Henri. *Les Celtes depuis les temps les plus anciens jusqu'en l'an 100 avant notre ère*. Paris: A. Fontemoning, 1904

d'Arbois de Jubainville, Marie Henri. *Cours de littérature celtique*, 12 vols. Paris: E. Thorin, 1883–1902

Dauzat, Albert. *La toponymie française*. Paris: Payot, 1960/rpt. 1971

Dauzat, Albert and Charles Rostaing, *Dictionnaire étymologique des noms de lieux en France*, 2nd ed. Paris: Librairie Guénégaud, 1989

Davies, Jeffrey L. "The early Celts in Wales," in *The Celtic World*, ed. Miranda Green London: Routledge 1995, 671–700

de la Bédoyère, Guy. "Carausius and the marks RSR and I.N.P.C.D.A.," *The Numismatic Chronicle* 158 (1998): 79–88

Delamarre, Xavier. *Dictionnaire de la langue gauloise: une approche linguistique du vieux-celtique continental*. Paris: Éditions Errance, 2003

Delamarre, Xavier. *Nomina Celtica Antiqua Selecta Inscriptionum: Noms de personnes celtiques dans l'épigraphie classique*. Paris: Éditions Errance, 2007

de la Tour, Henri. *Atlas de monnaies gauloises*. Paris: Bibliothèque nationale/E. Plon, Nourrit et Cie., 1892/rpt. 1991; Scheers, S. *Un Complement à l'Atlas de monnaies gauloises de Henri de la Tour*. Paris: Maison Platt, 1992

Derks, Ton and Nico Roymans, "Seal-boxes and the spread of Latin Literacy in the Rhine Delta," in *Becoming Roman, Writing Latin? Literacy and Epigraphy in the Roman West*, ed. Allison E. Cooley, Supplement 48. Portsmouth, RI: Journal of Roman Archaeology, 2002. Pp. 87–134

DIL = *Dictionary of the Irish Language: Based Mainly on Old and Middle Irish Materials*, ed. E.G. Quin. Dublin: Royal Irish Academy, 1984/rpt. 2007

Dillon, Myles, "The Irish settlements in Wales," *Celtica* 12 (1977), 1–11

Dottin, Georges. *La langue gauloise: grammaire, textes et glossaire*. Paris: Klincksieck, 1920

Driscoll, Stephen T., Jane Geddes, and Mark A. Hall, eds. *Pictish Progress: New Studies on Northern Britain in the Middle Ages*. The Northern World, vol. 50. Leiden: Brill, 2011

Duft, Johannes. "Iromanie – Irophobie. Fragen um die frümittelalterliche Irenmission, exemplifiziert an St. Gallen und Alemannien," *Zeitschrift für schweizerische Kirchengeschichte* 50 (1956), 241–262

Dumville, David N. "Some aspects of the chronology of the *Historia Brittonum*," *Bulletin of the Board of Celtic Studies* 25 (1972–1973), 439–445

Dumville, David N. "Nennius and the *Historia Brittonum*," *Studia Celtica* 10/11 (1975–1976), 78–95

Dumville, David N. "Sub-Roman Britain: History and legend," *History* 62 (1977), 173–192

Dumville, David N. *Histories and Pseudo-Histories of the Insular Middle Ages*. Variorum Collected Studies Series, 316. Aldershot: Variorum, 1990

Dumville, David N. *Britons and Anglo-Saxons in the Early Middle Ages*. Variorum Collected Studies Series, 379. Aldershot: Variorum, 1993

Dumville, David N. *Saint David of Wales*. Cambridge: Department of Anglo-Saxon, Norse, and Celtic, 2001

Dumville, David N., ed. *The Historia Brittonum*, 3 vols. Cambridge: D.S. Brewer, 1985–1988

Dumville, David N. and Simon Keynes, general eds. *The Anglo-Saxon Chronicle: A Collaborative Edition* Cambridge: D.S. Brewer, 1983–2002

Dumville, David N., with Lesley Abrams et al. *Saint Patrick, A.D. 493–1993*. Woodbridge: Boydell, 1993

Du Pontet, René-Louis Alphonse, ed. *C. Ivli Caesaris Commentariorum pars prior et pars posterior*, vol. 1: *Bello Gallico cum A. Hirti Supplemento*; vol. 2: *Libri III de Bello Civili cum Libris Incertorum Auctorum de Bello Alexandrino Africo Hispaniensi*. Oxford: Clarendon Press, 1900/rpt. 1968, 1993

Eagles, Bruce. "Britons and Saxons on the eastern boundary of the *Civitas Durotrigum*," *Britannia* 35 (2004), 234–240

Ekwall, Eilert. *English River-Names*. Oxford: Clarendon Press, 1928/rpt. 1968

Ekwall, Eilert. *The Concise Oxford Dictionary of English Place-Names*. 4th ed. Oxford: Clarendon Press, 1960

Evans, David Ellis. *Gaulish Personal Names*. 2 vols. Oxford: Clarendon Press, 1967

Evans, Jeremy, "Material approaches to the identification of different Romano-British site types," in *Britons and Romans: Advancing an Archaeological Agenda*, ed. Simon James and Martin Millett. York: Council for British Archaeology, 2001. Pp. 26–35

Faletra, Michael A., ed. *Geoffrey of Monmouth: The History of the Kings of Britain*. Peterborough, Ontario: Broadview Press, 2008

Filppula, Markku, Juhani Klemola and Heli Pitkänen, eds. *The Celtic Roots of English*. Joensuu: Joensuun Ylipopistopainu/Joensuu University Press, 2002a

Filppula, Markku, Juhani Klemola and Heli Pitkänen, "Early contacts between english and the English languages," in *The Celtic Roots of English*, ed. Filppula, Markku, Juhani Klemola and Heli Pitkänen. Joensuu: University of Joensuu, 2002b. Pp. 1–26

Fisher, C.D., ed. *Tacitus. Annales I–VI, XI–XVI*. Oxford Classical Texts.Oxford: Clarendon Press, 1993

Fitzpatrick-Matthews, Keith J., "The xxuiii ciuitates britanni<a>e of the Historia Brittonum: Antiquarian Speculation in Early Medieval Wales," *Journal of Literary Onomastics* 4.1 (2015), 1–19

Fomin, Maxim. "Multilingual practices and linguistic contacts in Pre-Patrician Ireland and late Roman Britain," *Studia Celto-Slavica* 8 (2018), 151–172

Forster, Peter and Alfred Toth, "Toward a phylogenetic chronology of ancient Gaulish, Celtic, and Indo-European," *Proceedings of the National Academy of Sciences of the United States of America* 100.15 (2003), 9079–9084

Förster, Max. *Der Flussname Themse und seine Sippe: Studien zur Anglisierung keltischer Eigennamen und zur Lautchronologie des Altbritischen*. Munich: Verlag der Bayerischen Akademie der Wissenschaften/C.H. Beck, 1941

Forsyth, Katherine. *Language in Pictland: the case against 'non-Indo-European Pictish.'* Studia Hameliana 2. Utrecht/Münster: Stichting Uitgeverij de Keltische Draak/Nodus Publikationen, 1997

Fox, Bethany. "The P-Celtic place-names of North-East England and South-East Scotland," *The Heroic Age* 10 (2007). http://www.heroicage.org/issues/10/fox.html

Frazer, James George. *The Golden Bough: A Study in Magic and Religion*, 3rd ed., 12 vols. London: Macmillan and Co., 1912–1930

Frere, Sheppard Sutherland. *Britannia*, 3rd ed. London: Routledge & Kegan Paul, 1987

Fulford, Michael, "Nero and Britain: The Palace of the Client King at Calleva and Imperial Policy Towards the Province After Boudicca," *Britannia* 39 (2008), 1–14

Fulford, Michael, Mark Handley, and Amanda Clarke, "An Early Date for Ogham: The Silchester Ogham Stone Rehabilitated," *Medieval Archaeology* 44.1 (2000), 1–23

Galestin, M.C. "*Frisiii* and *Frisiavones*," *Palaeohistoria* 49/50 (2007/2008), 687–708

Gelling, Margaret. *The Place-Names of Oxfordshire*. 2 vols. EPNS 23–24. Cambridge: Cambridge University Press, 1953–1954

Gelling, Margaret. *Signposts to the Past: Place-Names and the History of England*. London: J.M. Dent & Sons, 1978

Gelling, Margaret. *The Place-Names of Shropshire*, 6 vols. (Parts 1–6). EPNS 62-63, 70, 76, 80, 82, 89. Nottingham: English Place-Name Society, 1990–2012. 3 vols. (Parts 7–9), ed. John Baker, Jayne Carroll, and Paul Cavill. EPNS 92, 95–96. Nottingham: English Place-Name Society, 2018–2020

Gover, John Eric Bruce, A. Mawer, F.M. Stenton, with collaboration of Arthur Bonner. *The Place-Names of Surrey*. EPNS 11. Cambridge: Cambridge University Press, 1934

Grasmann, G., W. Janssen, and M. Brandt, eds. *Keltische Numismatik und Archaeologie/ Numismatique celtique et Archéologie*, 2 vols. London: BAR International, 1984

Green, Miranda. "The gods and the supernatural," in *The Celtic World* ed. Green, Miranda. London: Routledge 1995, 465–488

Green, Miranda, ed. *The Celtic World*. London: Routledge, 1995

Guerra, Amílcar. "Novos monumentos epigrafados com escrita do Sudoeste da vertente setentrional da Serra do Caldeirão," *Revista Portuguesa de Arquelogia* 5.2 (2002), 219–231

Hammond, Carolyn, tr. *Julius Caesar: Seven Commentaries on The Gallic War, with an Eighth Commentary by Aulus Hirtius*. Oxford World's Classics. Oxford: Oxford University Press, 1996/rpt. 2008

Hamp, Eric P. "Social Gradience in British Spoken Latin," *Britannia* 6 (1975), 150–162

Harden, D. B. "The Phoenicians on the West Coast of Africa," *Antiquity* 22 (1948), 141–150

Heather, Peter. *Empires and Barbarians: Migration, Development and the Birth of Europe*. London: Macmillan, 2009

Higham, N.J. *The English Conquest: Gildas and Britain in the Fifth Century*. Manchester: Manchester University Press, 1994

Hind, John. "Pyrene and the date of the Massiliot sailing manual," *Rivista storica dell'Antichità* 2 (1972), 39–52

Hogg, Richard. "Introduction: Political history and language history," in *The Cambridge History of the English Language*, vol. 1: *The Beginnings to 1066*. Cambridge: Cambridge University Press, 1992. Pp. 1–10

Holder, Alfred Theophil. *Alt-celtischer Sprachscahtz*, 3 vols. Leipzig: Akademische Druck- und Verlagsanstalt, 1891–1913

Horsley, John. *Britannia Romana, or the Roman antiquities of Britain*. London: John Osborn and Thomas Longman, 1732

Hough, Carole. “The (non?)-survival of Romano-British Toponymy,” *Neuphilologische Mitteilungen* 105 (2004), 25–32

Hübner, Emil. *Inscriptiones Britanniae latinae*. Berlin: G. Reimer, 1873

Jackson, Keneth Hurlstone. “On some Romano-British Place-Names,” *Journal of Roman Studies* 38 (1948), 54–58

Jackson, Kenneth Hurlstone. *Language and History in Early Britain: A Chronological Survey of the Brittonic Languages, First to Twelfth Century A.D.* Edinburgh: Edinburgh University Press, 1953/rpt. Dublin: Four Courts Press, 2000 [= LHEB]

Jarrett, M.G. and J.C. Mann. “The tribes of Wales,” *Welsh Historical Review* 4 (1969), 161–171

Kapuściński, Ryszard. *Travels with Herodotus*. New York: Random House, 2007

Kennedy, David, “The *ala I* and *cohors I Britannica*,” *Britannia* 8 (1977), 249–255

Kerlouégan, François. *Le De Excidio Britanniae et Gildas: les destinées de la culture latine dans l'île du Bretagne au vie siècle*. Paris: Publications de la Sorbonne, 1987

King, Anthony and Graham Soffe. *A Sacred Island: Iron Age, Roman and Saxon Temples and Ritual on Haying Island*. Winchester: Winchester University Press/Hayling Island Excavation Project, 2013

King, J.E., tr. *Bede. Historical Works*, 2 vols. Cambridge, MA: Harvard University Press, 1954/rpt. 1999

Kitson, Peter R., “British and European River-Names,” *Transactions of the Philological Society* 94.2 (1996), 73–118

Koch, John T., “A Welsh Window on the Iron Age: Manawydan, Mandubracios,” *Cambrian Medieval Celtic Studies* 14 (1986), 17–52

Koch, John T. “Gallo-Brittonic *Tasc(i)ouanos* ‘Badger-slayer’ and the Reflex of Indo-European g^w*h*,” *Journal of Celtic Linguistics* 1 (1992), 101–118

Koch, John T. *Tartessian 2: The Inscriptions of Mesas do Castelinho,* **ro** *and the Verbal Complex, Preliminaries to Historical Phonology*. Aberystwyth: Centre for Advanced Welsh and Celtic Studies, 2011

Koch, John T. *Tartessian: Celtic in the South-west at the Dawn of History*. 2nd rev. ed. Aberystwyth: Celtic Studies Publications, 2013

Krahe, Hans. *Die Struktur der alteuropäischen Hydronomie*. Akademie der Wissenschaften und der Literatur, Mainz. Geistes- und Sozialwissenschaftliche Klasse, 1962, 5. Wiesbaden: F. Steiner, 1962 (1963)

Krahe, Hans. *Unsere ältesten Flussnamen*. Wiesbaden: Harrassowitz, 1964

Laker, Stephen and Paul Russell. “Languages of early Britain: Introduction,” in *Languages of early Britain*, ed. Laker and Russell, Special Issue, *Transactions of the Philological Society* 109.2 (2011), 109–199 at 109–112

Lambert, Pierre-Yves. *La langue gauloise*, 2nd ed. Paris: Éditions Errance, 2002

Lapidge, Michael and David N. Dumville, eds. *Gildas: New Approaches*. Woodbridge: D.S. Brewer, 1984

Leslie, Stephen, et al., “The fine-scale genetic structure of the British population,” *Nature* 519 (2015), 309–314

Lewis, M.J.T. *Temples in Roman Britain*. Cambridge: Cambridge University Press, 1966

LHEB = *Language and History in Early Britain: A Chronological Survey of the Brittonic Languages, First to Twelfth Century A.D.* (see Jackson 1953 above)

Lindsay, W.M., ed. *M. Val. Martialis Epigrammata.* Oxford: Clarendon Press, 1922/rpt. 1993

Macalister, R.A.S. *Corpus Inscriptionum Celticarum I–II.* Dublin: Stationery Office, 1945–1949/ vol. 1 rpt. with preface by Damian McManus, Dublin: Four Courts Press, 1996

Mac an Bhaird, Alan. "Varia II: Tadhg mac Céin and the Badgers," *Ériu* 31 (1980), 150–155

McCone, Kim. *Towards a Relative Chronology of Ancient and Medieval Celtic Sound Change.* Maynooth, 1996

MacDonald, George. *The Roman Wall in Scotland.* Glasgow: James MacLehose and Sons, 1911

McGowan, Joseph P. "An introduction to the Corpus of Anglo-Latin literature," in *A Companion to Anglo-Saxon Literature*, ed. Phillip Pulsiano and Elaine Treharne. Oxford: Blackwell, 2001. Pp. 11–49

Mack, Richard Paston. *The Coinage of Ancient Britain.* London: Spink, 1953

Mackie, Euan. "The Early Celts in Scotland," in *The Celtic World*, ed. Miranda Green London: Routledge 1995, Pp. 654–670

McManus, Damian, "Ogam: Archaizing, Orthography and the Authenticity of the Manuscript Key to the Alphabet," *Ériu* 37 (1986), 9–31

McManus, Damian. *A Guide to Ogam.* Maynooth: An Sagart, 1997

Maier, Bernhard. *Lexikon der keltischen Religion und Kultur/Dictionary of Celtic Religion and Culture*, tr. Cyril Edwards. Woodbridge: The Boydell Press, 1998

Malone, Stephen James. *Legio XX Valeria Victrix: Prosopography, archaeology, and history.* BAR International Series 1491. Oxford: BAR Publishing, 2006

Mann, J.C. "Spoken Latin in Britain as evidenced in the Inscriptions," *Britannia* 2 (1971), 218–224

Matasović, Ranko. *Etymological Dictionary of Proto-Celtic.* Leiden: Brill, 2009

Mette, H.J. *Pytheas von Massilia.* Berlin: De Gruyter, 1952

Meyer, Kuno. "Sanas cormaic: An Old Irish glossary," in *Anecdota from Irish Manuscripts*, vol. 4, ed. Osborn J. Bergin, R.I. Best, Kuno Meyer, and J.G. O'Keeffe. Dublin: Hodges, Figgis & Co., 1912

Miller, Konrad. *Itineraria Romana: Römische Reisewege an der Hand der Tabula Peutingeriana.* Stuttgart: Strecker und Schröder, 1916/rpt. 1964

Mills, A.D. *The Place-Names of Dorset.* EPNS 52–53, 59–60, 86–87, 94. Nottingham: English Place-Name Society, 1977–2020

Mullen, Alex, "Evidence for Written Celtic from Roman Britain: A Linguistic Analysis of Tabellae Sulis 14 and 18," *Studia Celtica* 41 (2007), 31–45

Mullen, Alex, "New thoughts on British Latin: A Curse Tablet from Red Hill, Ratcliffe-on-Soar (Nottinghamshire)," *Zeitschrft für Papyrologie und Epigraphik* 187 (2013), 266–272

Mullen, Alex. *Southern Gaul and the Mediterranean: Multilingualism and Multiple Identities in the Iron Age and Roman Periods.* Cambridge: Cambridge University Press, 2013

Mullen, Alex and R.S.O. Tomlin, "More from the Romano-British Poets? A Possible Metrical Inscription from East Farleigh, Kent," *Britannia* 50 (2019), 367–374

Myres, J.N.L. *The English Settlements.* The Oxford History of England IB. Oxford: Clarendon Press, 1986

Nobbe, Karl Friedrich August, ed. *Claudii Ptolemaei Geographia.* 3 vols. Leipzig: Tauchnitz, 1843–1845

Ócathasaigh, T. "The Déissi and Dyfed," *Éigse* 20 (1984), 1–33

ODBPN = *A Dictionary of British Place Names*, A.D. Mills. Oxford: Oxford University Press, 2011

ODEPN = *The Concise Oxford Dictionary of English Place-Names*, Eilert Ekwall. 4th ed. Oxford: Clarendon Press, 1960/rpt. 1991

Ogilvie, Robert Maxwell, ed. *Titi Livi Ab urbe condita*, vol. 1 Books I–V. Oxford Classical Texts. Oxford: Clarendon Press, 1974

Okasha, Elizabeth. *Corpus of Early Christian Inscribed Stones of South-West Britain.* Leicester: Leicester University Press 1993

Oppenheimer, Stephen. *The Origins of the British: The New Prehistory of Britain.* London: Robinson Publishing, 2007

Ordnance Survey. *Ancient Britain.* Southampton: Ordnance Survey, 2016

Ordnance Survey. *Roman Britain.* Revised ed. Southampton: Ordnance Survey, 2010/2016 rpt.

Orel, Vladimir. *A Handbook of Germanic Etymology.* Leiden: Brill, 2003

Padel, O.J. *Cornish Place-Name Elements.* EPNS 56-57. Nottingham: English Place-Name Society, 1985

Page, R.I. *An Introduction to English Runes.* 2nd ed. Woodbridge: Boydell and Brewer, 2006

Parsons, David N. "Sabrina in the thorns: Place-names as evidence for British and Latin in Roman Britain," in *Languages of early Britain*, ed. Laker and Russell, Special Issue, *Transactions of the Philological Society* 109.2 (2011), 109–199 at 113–137

Pedersen, Holger. *Vergleichende Grammatik der keltischen Sprachen.* Gottingen: Vandenhoeck & Ruprecht, 1976

Plummer, Charles, ed. *Two of the Saxon Chronicles Parallel (787–1001 A.D.).* Oxford: Clarendon Press, 1920

Pogatscher, Alois. *Zur Lautlehre der griechischen, lateinischen und romanischen Lehnworte im Altenglischen.* London: Trübner & Co., 1888

Price, Glanville. *The Languages of Britain.* London: Edward Arnold, 1984

Price, Glanville. *Languages in Britain and Ireland.* Oxford: Wiley-Blackwell, 2000

Prontera, Francesco, ed. *Tabula Peutingeriana: le antiche vie del mondo.* Florence: L.S. Olschki, 2003

Rance, Philip, "Attacotti, Déisi and Magnus Maximus: the case for Irish Federates in Late Roman Britain," *Britannia* 32 (2001), 243–270

Rankin, David. *Celts and the Classical World.* 2nd ed. London: Routledge, 2002

Ravenna Cosmography. *Ravennatis Anonymi Cosmographia et Gvidonis Geographica*, ed. M. Pinder and G. Parthey Berlin: Nicolaische Verlagsbuchhandlung, 1860

Redknap, Mark. "Early Christianity and its Monuments," in *The Celtic World*, ed. Miranda Green London: Routledge 1995. Pp. 733–778

Reeve, Michael D. and Neil Wright, eds. *Geoffrey of Monmouth. The History of the Kings of Britain: An Edition and Translation of the De gestis Britonum (Historia Regum Britanniae).* Woodbridge: Boydell Press, 2007

RIB = *The Roman Inscriptions of Britain*, 3 vols. Oxford: Clarendon Press, 1965–2009. Vol. I: *Inscriptions on Stone*, ed. R.G. Collingwood and R.P. Wright (1965). Vol. II: *Instrumentum*

Domesticum, ed. S.S Frere and R.S.O. Tomlin (1990–1995). Vol. III: *Inscriptions on Stone*, ed. R.S.O. Tomlin, R.P. Wright, and M.W.C. Hassall (2009)

RIC = *The Roman Imperial Coinage*, ed. Harold Mattingly and Edward A. Sydenham (London: Spink, 1923–); rev. ed. C.H.V. Sutherland and R.A.G. Carson. London: Spink, 1923–1994

Richmond, I.A., "Queen Cartimandua," *Journal of Roman Studies* 44 (1954), 43–52

Richmond, I.A. and O.G.S. Crawford. "The British section of the *Ravenna Cosmography*," *Archaeologia* 93 (1949), 1–50

Ringe, Don. *From Proto-Indo-European to Proto-Germanic*. A Linguistic History of English, Volume I. 2nd revised ed. Oxford: Oxford University Press, 2017

Ringe, Don and Ann Taylor. *The Development of Old English*. A Linguistic History of English, Volume II. Oxford Linguistics. Oxford: Oxford University Press, 2014

Rivet, A.L.F. "The British section of the Antonine itinerary (appendix by Kenneth H. Jackson on place-names)," *Britannia* 1 (1970), 34–82

Rivet, A.L.F., "The Brittones Anavionenses," *Britannia* 13 (1892), 321–322

Rivet, A.L.F. and Colin Smith. *The Place-Names of Roman Britain*. London: Batsford, 1979

Rudd, C. "The Head Hunters," *Coins & Antiquitues* (April 1999), 42–49

Russell, Paul. *An Introduction to the Celtic Languages*. London: Longman, 1995

Russell, Paul. "Latin and British in Post-Roman Britain: methodology and morphology," in *Languages of Early Britain*, ed. S. Laker and P. Russell, Special Issue, *Transactions of the Philological Society* 109.2 (2011), 109–199 at 138–157

Salway, Peter. *The Frontier People of Roman Britain*. Cambridge: Cambridge University Press, 1967

Salway, Peter. *Roman Britain*. The Oxford History of England IA. Oxford: Clarendon Press, 1991/rpt. 2003

Schmidt, K. H., "On the reconstruction of Proto-Celtic," in *Proceedings of the First North American Conference of Celtic Studies, Ottawa 1986*, ed. G.W. MacLennan. Ottawa: Chair of Celtic Studies, University of Ottawa, 1988, Pp. 231–248

Schnetz, Joseph, ed. *Ravennas Anonymus, Cosmographia: eine Erdbeschreibung um das Jahr 700*. Uppsala: Almqvist & Wiksell, 1951

Schrijver, Peter. "The rise and fall of British Latin: Evidence from English and Brittonic," in *The Celtic Roots of English*, ed. Filppula, Markku, Juhani Klemola and Heli Pitkänen. Joensuu: Joensuun Ylipopistopainu/Joensuu University Press, 2002. Pp. 87–110

Scott, Eleanor. *A Gazetteer of Roman Villas in Britain*. Leicester: University of Leicester School of Archaeological Studies, 1993

Seeck, Otto. *Notitia dignitatum*. Berlin: Weidmann, 1876

Seel, Otto, ed. *C. Iulii Caesaris Commentarii rerum gestarum*. Leipzig: B.G. Teubner, 1961

Shaw, Philip A. *Pagan Goddesses in the Early Germanic World: Eostre, Hreda and the Cult of Matrons*. Studies in Early Medieval History. London: Bristol Classical Press/ Bloomsbury, 2011

Shiel, N. "The coinage of Carausius as a source of Vulgar Latin forms," *Britannia* 6 (1975), 146–149

Shotter, David. "Vespasian, *Auctoritas* and Britain," *Britannia* 35 (2004), 1–8

Simek, Rudolf. *Dictionary of Northern Mythology*. Cambridge: D.S. Brewer, 1993

Sims-Williams, Patrick. "Celto-Mania and Celto-Skepticism," *Cambrian Medieval Celtic Studies* 36 (1998), 1–35

Sims-William, Patrick. *The Celtic Inscriptions of Britain: Phonology and Chronology, c. 400–1200*. Publications of the Philological Society, 37. Oxford: Blackwell, 2003

Sims-Williams, Patrick. "Bronze- and Iron-Age Celtic Speakers: What don't we know, what can't we know, and what could we know? Language, genetics and archaeology in the twenty-first century," *The Antiquaries Journal* 92 (2012), 427–49

Skene, William Forbes, ed. *Johannis de Fordun Chronica gentis Scotorum*. Edinburgh: Edmonston and Douglas, 1871

Skene, William Forbes, tr. *John of Fordun's Chronicle of the Scottish Nation*. Edinburgh: Edmonston and Douglas, 1872

Smith, A.H. *English Place-Name Elements*. EPNS 25-26. Cambridge: Cambridge University Press, 1956

Smith, Colin. "Vulgar Latin in Roman Britain: Epigraphic and Other Evidence," *Aufstieg und Niedergang der römischen Welt II* 29/2 (1983), 893–948

Soverini, Paolo, ed. *Cornelio Tacito. Agricola*. Alessandria: Edizioni dell'Orso, 2004

Stevens, C.E., "Hadrian and Hadrian's Wall," *Latomus* 14 (1955), 384–403

Stukeley, William. *Itinerarium curiosum, or, an account of the antiquities, and remarkable curiosities in nature or art, observed in travels through Great Britain*, 2nd London: Baker and Leigh, 1776

Thévenot, Émile. *Divinités et sanctuaires de la Gaule*. Paris: Fayard, 1968

Tierney, J.J. "The Celtic Ethnography of Poseidonios," *Proceedings of the Royal Irish Academy* 60 (1960), 189–246

Toorians, Lauran. "No badger in the bag," *Zeitschrift für celtische Philologie* 62 (2015), 199–211

Tristram, Hildegard L.C. *The Celtic Englishes II*. Heidelberg: Carl Winter, 2000

Untermann, Jürgen. *Monumenta Linguarum Hispanicarum, Band 4: Die tartessischen, keltiberischen und lusitanischen Inschriften*. Wiesbaden: Reichert, 1998

Ureland, P. Sture and George Broderick, eds. *Language Contact in the British Isles: Proceedings of the Eighth International Symposium on Language Contact in Europe, Douglas, Isle of Man, 1988*. Berlin: DeGruyter, 1988

Van Arsdell, Robert D. *Celtic Coinage of Britain*. London: Spink, 1989

Van Arsdell, Robert D. *The Coinage of the Dobunni: Money Supply and Coin Circulation in Dobunnic Territory*. Oxford: Oxford University School of Archaeology, 1994

van de Woestijne, Paul, ed. *Rufius Festus Avienus. Descriptio orbis terrae*. Bruges: De Tempel, 1961

Wagner, Heinrich. *Das Verbum in den Sprachen der britischen Inseln:. Ein Beitrag zur geographischen Typologie des Verbums*. Buchreihe der Zeitschrift für Celtische Philologie 1. Tübingen: Max Niemeyer, 1959

Watkins, Calvert. *How to Kill a Dragon: Aspects of Indo-European Poetics*. New York: Oxford University Press, 1995

Watson, William J. *The History of the Celtic Place-Names of Scotland.* Edinburgh: William Blackwood & Sons, 1926/rpt. Edinburgh: Birlinn, 2005

Webster, Graham. "The Celtic Britons under Rome," in *The Celtic World*, ed. Miranda Green London: Routledge. 1995. 623–635

Webster, Jane, "A Dirty Window on the Iron Age? Recent Developments in the Archaeology of Pre-Roman Celtic Religion," in *Understanding Celtic Religion: Revisiting the Pagan Past*, ed. Katja Ritari and Alexandra Bergholm. New Approaches to Celtic Religion and Mythology. Cardiff: University of Wales Press, 2015 Pp. 121–154

Werle, Georg. *Die älteste germanischen Personennamen*. Strassburg: K.J. Trübner, 1910

Whatmough, Joshua. *The Dialects of Ancient Gaul, Prolegomena and Records of the Dialects.* Cambridge, MA: Harvard University Press, 1970

Wiik, Kalevi. "On the origins of the Celts," in *The Celtic Roots of English*, ed. Filppula, Markku, Juhani Klemola and Heli Pitkänen. Joensuu: Joensuun Ylipopistopainu/Joensuu University Press, 2002. Pp. 285–294

Williams, Ifor, ed. *Pedeir Keinc y Mabinogi*. Caedydd/Cardiff: Gwasg Prifysgol Cymru/University of Wales Press, 1978

Winterbottom, Michael, tr. *Gildas. The Ruin of Britain, and Other Works.* London: Phillimore, 1978

CHAPTER 4

Adventus Saxonum

The Coming of the Saxons – Engla-lond

4.1 THE 'FALL OF BRITAIN' – THE SAXON SHORE – THE WITHDRAWAL OF THE LEGIONS – ANGLES, SAXONS, AND JUTES (AND FRANKS, FRISIANS, FLEMINGS?)

The Strasbourg oaths were sworn on 14 February 842 by Charles the Bald and his half-brother Louis the German, sons of Carolingian emperor Louis the Pious, against the passing of the throne to their older brother Lothair I. The oaths are of particular linguistic value as Louis swore the oath in what may be the earliest recorded form of French (in an undetermined northern dialect, before the *langue d'oïl / langue d'oc* split), while Charles swore the oath in the West Germanic Ripuarian Frankish language ('Ripuarian' is from Medieval Latin *ripuarius*, 'of/along the river bank,' here indicating the Franks of the Rhineland). The episode and oaths, in three languages (Latin the third), were recorded by the Frankish chronicle Nithard, abbot of St. Riquier (Somme; in the former Austrasia province of the Merovingian and Carolingian kings) in his *Historiarum libri IIII* ('Four Books of Histories'). Nithard's mother was Bertha, daughter of Charlemagne, whom Offa of Mercia had once asked to marry – the offer was rejected and strained relations between Anglo-Saxon England and Charlemagne's Frankish realm. His father was the Frankish poet Angilbert, who had been tutored in the royal court at Aachen by Alcuin of York (ca. 735–804). The oath reads:

> In Godes minna ind in thes Christianes folches ind unser bedhero gealtnissi [gehaltnissi], fon thesemo dago frammordes, so fram so mir Got geuuizci indi mahd furgibit, so hald ih tesan minan bruodher, soso man mit rehtu

sinan bruodher scal, in thiu thaz er mig sosoma duo, indi mit Ludheren in nohheiniu thing ne gegango, zhe minan uuillon imo ce scadhen uuerhen (Müller 1907, 36).

For the love of God and of Christian folk and our shared keeping [salvation], from this day henceforth, so far as God give me wisdom and strength, so I keep this my brother [Charles], just as a man by right should his brother, insofar as he do the same for me, and with Lothair in no thing will I enter into, lest by my will harm unto him may come about.

The oath in Ripuarian Frankish of 842 will look surprisingly familiar to anyone who has studied Old English, particularly earlier Old English texts. Old English would more likely formulate the oath with *For Godes lufu*; Old Low Franconian *minna* may be compared with Old High German *minne*, 'love, loving memory (of),' as in the medieval *Minnesang* 'love song' tradition. Frankish *thes Christianes folches* would find a very close match in Old English *þæs Cristenes folces*. Frankish *unser* 'our' is the same as OHG and Modern German *unser*; the Old English was *ūre*, which, like Old Norse *várr* (< **usárr*), had lost the *-n-* as had Old Frisian: Proto-Germanic **unseraz* 'our' > Proto-West Germanic **unsar* > **ūsær* > *ūser* (the form in Old Frisian and Old English). The syncopation of the *-e-* must have occurred before the *sr* > *ss* assimilative change; in Northumbrian Old English, one finds the basic form *ūser* and accusative singular masculine *ūserne*, but genitive plural *ūsra* (with syncopation; cf. Campbell OEG §§ 484, 705–706; Ringe and Taylor 2014, 339; Ringe calls the change 'startling'). With the assimilative change, one finds gen. sing. *ūsses*, dat. pl. *ūssum*.[1] Frankish and Modern German preserve the more conservative form (compare the opening to the 'Our Father' in Gothic, *Atta unsar*) compared to the Anglo-Frisian or North Sea Germanic grouping (the latter includes Old Saxon; cf. Old Saxon *Fadar ūsa* from the epic poem *Heliand*). Frankish *bruodher* 'brother' looks significantly different in comparison to Old English *brōðor* (or with voiceless allophone *brōþor*); and in comparison to Latin *frāter*, which has /f/ from Proto-Indo-European aspirated stop /b^h/, and which by Grimm's Law became the voiced stop /b/ in Germanic; PIE /a:/ underwent a merger with /o:/ in Germanic. This /o:/ remains in the OE form, but in Old High German and other Continental dialects broke (diphthongized) to /uo/. By the changes of the High German Consonant Shift medial *ð* > *d* (*dh* < **þ*), preverbal *ge-* (in *ge-altnissi*, *ge-uuizci*, and *ge-gango*) is produced as a stop /g/ in Frankish, as a glide or semi-vowel by lenition in Old English *ġ* /j/. Placing Old English back in this West Germanic textual context helps sharpen a sense of the language's 'West Germanic-ness,' that it was part of

[1] Hogg and Fulk 2011 (7.92, 296) suggest the assimilation of /sr/ > /ss/ must be early or by voicing assimilation it would have produced /zr/, then /zz/. Old English does not generally use <z> in its orthography (except in Latin loans such as *zizania*, 'weeds,' or the Biblical sense 'tares'). Such a geminate fricative /zz/ would be unusual in OE phonology and /ss/ may have been the natural result; <ss> would have likely been the spelling form /zz/ would have taken anyway ("Hence the facts must remain uncertain"; Hogg 2011, 296).

a geographically and linguistically defined sub-grouping of the Germanic branch of Indo-European, a grouping given definition also by continuing cultural contacts (here, cross-Channel).

We know of contacts between Franks and Germanic settlers in Britain from the earliest settlements (finds of Frankish coins in England, trade contacts), and most historians of the *Adventus* include Franks and Frisians among the Germanic invaders of Britain. There was sustained contact between the Jutes of Kent and Francia. The marriage of pagan King Æthelbert of Kent in 580 to Bertha, daughter of Merovingian King Charibert I, brought an important change to early Anglo-Saxon England, for Bertha was a Christian and would bring the faith to Kent, to Canterbury. Her chaplain Liudhard established the first Germanic-era church in England (there had been churches of course in the Romano-British period), dedicated to St. Martin of Tours. A Liudhard gold coin or medal (with a loop added to the coin so that it might be worn as a medallion) was found with other Frankish gold coins in 1864; the church, made from an existing building of the Roman era, still stands (with subsequent additions). On the heels of this entrée into one of the pagan kingdoms of Anglo-Saxon England, Pope Gregory I sent a mission to Kent under Augustine of Canterbury (likely of Italian birth) in 597. Canterbury was the *byriġ* or *burg* (originally a fortified dwelling or town) of the *Centwara/Centware* 'Kent dwellers': this is preserved in Latinized British Celtic forms *Cantium*, *Cantiaci*, perhaps meaning 'of the coasts,' or 'of the hosts' (Mills 2003, s.v. *Kent*).

The matter of Frisians in the *adventus* has been given considerably more attention than that of the Franks – for one, *Frysk* (West Frisian) is still very much alive as a spoken language (the figures for number of speaker vary widely, but generally 400,000 and up) and Frisian identity is cultivated by Frieslanders and recognized by the governments of Germany and The Netherlands (which had not always been the case). A second reason is that many Frisian and Dutch scholars, like their German colleagues, have been major figures in the study of Old English. The matter of Frisians and the *adventus* may be divided into Frisians in England and Frisians and England. As further refinements have been made to the West Germanic subbranch of the Germanic branch of the Indo-European family of languages the idea has been advanced of an Anglo-Frisian branching of North Sea Germanic (or, an older term, Ingvaeonic), comprised of a Frisian grouping (West Frisian, North Frisian, and East or Saterland Frisian or Seeltersk) and an 'Anglic' grouping (English, Scots, early Middle Hiberno-English dialects such as Fingallian). The fullest treatment of the development of Northwest Germanic is by Donald Ringe (in Ringe and Taylor 2014, 10–40); Ringe places Proto-Germanic in the Schleswig region and to its southern environs to not before 500 BC, and, based on sound changes, sees Northwest and West Germanic as coherent groupings (Ringe 2017, 241–242; Ringe and Taylor 2014, 41–81). The idea currently held by many historical linguists is that the East Germanic languages can be seen as having broken away from Proto-Germanic with the southern migration of Goths, Vandals, and other East Germanic tribes (Burgundians usually included among them, though there is scant attestation of Burgundian apart from some personal and place-names; on the idea of 'East Germanic' as a clade, with a generally positive view, and the complex position of Vandalic as East Germanic, see Hartman 2020, 7–13).

This left, in the Germanic ancestral homeland (German *Urheimat*), the languages that would later branch off into West and North Germanic. The coherence of the North Germanic group is asserted by a good many shared changes in the respective languages; the same has been argued for West Germanic, with the number of shared innovations high enough that, in the view of historical linguist Ringe, "it leaves no doubt that there was for some generations a unitary PWGmc language, though it seems equally clear that there were always minor dialect divisions within it" (Ringe in Ringe and Taylor 2014, 41; see also Ringe 2017, 241). Within West Germanic, some linguists have argued that one of these 'dialect' divisions could be called North Sea Germanic/Ingvaeonic, "a grouping within West Germanic from which Old English, Old Frisian, coastal Old Saxon and coastal Dutch is assumed to have developed. Ingvaeonic is generally seen as a dialect continuum from Flanders along the coast to the German Bight, sharing a number of conspicuous linguistic features" (Bremmer 2009, 22 n. 2). 'Ingvaeonic' derives from the *Germania* of Roman historian Tacitus (Publius Cornelius Tacitus, of the AD 1st century), in a famous passage worked over ever since by historians and linguists:

> Celebrant carminibus antiquis, quod unum apud illos memoriae et annalium genus est, Tuistonem deum terra editum, et filium Mannum, originem gentis conditoremque, Manno tris filios assignant, e quorum nominibus proximi Oceano Ingavaeones [variant reading: Inguaeones], medii Herminones, ceteri Istaevones vocentur (II.2).

> They celebrate in their ancient songs, which is among them their only manner of memory and historical records, a god Tuisto who issued forth from the earth, and his son Mannus, as the progenitor and founder of their people, to which Mannus they ascribe three sons, from whose names they call those [tribes] nearest Ocean [the North Sea] the Ingvaeones, those mid-coast the Herminones, and the rest the Istaevones.

Attempts have been made to connect Tuisto (or Tuisco) to **Tīwaz* (whence *Tues-day*; see below Section 4.5), while the names of the sons of Mannus have been applied to groupings of the West Germanic languages (Old English, Old Saxon, Old Frisian, Old Dutch to 'Ingvaeonic'). The Ingvaeones might plausibly be applied to the legendary Germanic ancestor Ingwi/Yngvi (whose name was given to the Ing/*Ingwaz-rune ᛝ; see Section 4.6), and the Herminones (or Irminones) to the proposed Germanic god Irmin (to whom the sacred pillar Irminsûl was dedicated; see 4.11).[2] Such legendary thinking about linguistic prehistory can be found with the application of the names of the sons of Noah to major language families, Semitic, Hamitic, Japhetic (Shem, Ham/Cham, Japheth), of which Semitic is still in use as a branch of the Afroasiatic family of

[2]There has been suggested a sort of Gothic-Vandalic 'Dioscuri' (the mythic pattern of 'divine twins,' especially in founding myths) of Ing-Irmin, and that Ermanric's name was theophoric (from earlier Gothic **Irmin-reiki*; cf. Wolfram 1988, 111, 421–422 n. 481; the second element to the name < PGmc **rīkją*: cf. Ringe 2017, 250).

languages ('Hamitic' was folded into Afroasiatic as well; 'Japhetic' was once applied to pre-IE and pre-Semitic languages such as Basque but is no longer in use).

The linguistic arguments are based upon the comparative method and the regularity of sound change, primarily, though there is also the interesting innovation in Proto-WGmc of the invariant relative particle **þē*, which under weak stress went to **þe* as found in OE (and Old Frisian and Old Saxon *thē*, Old High German *de*); though Ringe does not see the process by which this occurred as fully reconstructible, its development in the proto-era of WGmc seems more likely than an innovation that arose in each of the cognate languages (Ringe and Taylor 2014, 81). That there ever was an 'Anglo-Frisian' grouping, much less a stage of Northwest (or North Sea) Germanic, has been disputed (for a negative view, see Bremmer 1990, esp. 366–371). But that there were Frisians among the Germanic settlers of Britain is borne out by linguistic, numismatic, archaeological, and toponymic evidence, as 'tenuous' as some of that may be (again, for a negative assessment, namely that the number of Frisians in the *adventus* was probably low, see Bremmer 1990). *Frisby*, 'farmstead or village of the Frisians' (e.g., Frisby on the Wreake, Leicestershire), with the likely form < ON *Frísir* + *-by*, dates to the Viking Age (it is first recorded 1086 in the Domesday Book), while *Friston* (Suffolk) < OE *Frīsa-tūn* (compare *Freiston*, Lincolnshire and *Freston*, Suffolk; ODBPN, s.vv.) with the same meaning and first recording may refer to the settlement period. An early study, Lyons 1918, found many more Frisian-related place-names, generally recording Frisian settlement and ownership of land and towns, though some of the examples have since been reanalyzed as referring to English personal names (see Ekwall 1974; Bremmer 1981 reviews the proposed place-names skeptically, but nonetheless adds to Ekwall's total). As seen in the last chapter, Frisians and other Germanic peoples were among the auxiliary units the Roman army sent to Britain in the four centuries of Roman rule – such units were stationed all over the country, up to Hadrian's Wall. Considering the persistence of tribal and personal names in toponyms, perhaps some of these 'Frisian' place-names preserve traces of early Frisian settlement in Britain.

Perhaps even more elusive than the Frisians in Britain are the Jutes, though they are named in Bede's account of the conquest. In generally accepted terms, the Kentish dialect of Old English has been seen as 'Jutish,' or, if that term is now rarely used, the distinctiveness of Kent and Kentish is attributed to the settlement of Kent (and Wight) by the Jutes in the Bedan scheme. As 'Jutisch' is not otherwise recorded, phonological investigation by the comparative method has little to go on. German linguist Elmar Seebold (Seebold 1990) attempted to see Kentish (and behind it, Jutish) influence on the vocabulary usages of the Canterbury school, in contradistinction to that of the West Saxon Winchester school, drawing on the work of the 'Munich school' of vocabulary analysis (see Hofstetter 1987). This is a product of the German *Wörter und Sachen* ('Words and Things') philological movement, namely that words should be studied in conjunction with what they denote (if material, then with archaeological finds of material objects), as well as the German concern with *Schriftsprache* ('written language,' or written standard variety), the development of a standard written form. The late Helmut Gneuss of Munich began this movement of sorts with a careful, programmatic study of Latin loans in Old English with his 1955 monograph *Lehnbildungen und Lehnbedeutungen im Altenglischen* ('Loan Formations and Loan Meanings in Old English'); a number of his students at Munich expanded his studies of loan-formation and the development of 'standard Old English' at the school of Winchester (the late West Saxon associated with Winchester is the dialect all students of Old English first become acquainted with). Seebold drew on Hofstetter 1987 for Winchester 'words' and made vocabulary comparisons with Canterbury school texts and manuscripts that highlight patterns of difference in word choice and form that at least point to Canterbury and Kent as differing not just in terms of dialectal features (smoothing, unrounding, etc., to be seen below) but word choice and translation preferences (matching Latin with Old English equivalents; Seebold 1990, 351–352). Who else came with the Angles, Saxons, Jutes, Frisians, and Franks? No doubt smaller tribal divisions whose names are not now preserved or recognized in place-names; the Chauci lived to the east of the Frisians and likewise felt the pressure of the advancing Saxons; there is evidence of Saxon and Frisian *Terpen* ('villages') being abandoned mid-5th century. The pottery and other material objects excavated at the Saxon settlement at Mucking (Essex) match fairly closely those of the abandoned Saxon *Terp* of Feddersen Wierde on the Weser estuary. The likely Frisian *Terp* Wijster (Drenthe, Netherlands) seems to have been abandoned about the same time, and its inhabitants may have made the move to Britain (Myres, 1986, 51–52; see also Homans 1957, Hines 2017, esp. 27–33 on the matter of linguistic and Runic parallels). Some of the Runic-inscribed bracteates found in Frisia seem indeterminate as to whether the language is Old Frisian or Old English (these objects were often trade goods and made their way into graves on either side of the Channel and North Sea see Section 4.6). Were speakers of Old Low Franconian among the settlers of 449 and later? Flemings proper we do not hear of until the Norman Conquest; in a late copy of the Anglo-Saxon Chronicle (in British Library, MS Cotton Tiberius B.1, of the mid-12th century), an entry for the year 1066 mentions that *Harold...michil wel geslogon, ge Norweis ge Flœming*, 'King Harold...slew well many, whether Norsemen or Flemings.' In the Middle English translation (dating to 1385) of Ranulf Higden's *Polychronicon* by John of Trevisa (Trevessa, Cornwall) one finds the interesting linguistic tidbit that: *Þe Flemmynges þat woneþ in þe west side of Wales haueþ ileft her straunge speche and spekeþ Saxonliche inow* (MED, s.v. *Fleming*). This apparently refers to the Flemish merchants of Mailros who had been brought to Wales by Henry I around 1110, who now dwelling in West Wales "have left their strange speech" (Oksanen 2012, 178). "And speaketh Saxon-like enough" would indicate that by the Conquest of 1066, the conquest of 449 was a linguistically distant memory, if speakers of an Old Low Franconian-descended dialect could be said to speak English well enough, and in Wales.[3] In his volume for the Oxford History of England, in a section entitled "Change and Decay," J.N.L. Myres had noted that, outside of those early

[3] The brief poem 'Hebban olla uogala' ('All the birds have their nest begun': from the first line *Hebban olla uogala nestas hagunnan*) has sometimes been identified as Old Flemish, indeed as its first recording. The poem is found as a pen-trial (*probatio pennae*), a sort of doodle or marginal test of the quill, in Oxford, Bodleian Library MS Bodley 340 of the second half of the 11th century (at fol. 169v); this is a late Anglo-Saxon manuscript of homilies mainly from Ælfric, written in Rochester. A recent study suggests that the poem, perhaps in what should be described as Old Dutch, is heavily influenced by Kentish Old English forms (Kwakkel 2005).

areas in which the Anglo-Saxons had consolidated their territorial gains, "the British population in all these western regions managed for long to retain their cultural individuality, their social organization and settlement patterns, even their legal systems and the language used to express them. In Wales, to a large extent, they retain them to this day" (Myres 1986, 218). By the 6th century these newcomers to Britain had built tribal kingdoms (some with the suffixes *-ingas* and *-sǣtan*, the former a patronymic suffix, the latter indicating 'settlers, land-holders') into much larger rival kingdoms of Northumbria, Mercia, East Anglia (Angles), Wessex (Saxon; with minor Saxon kingdoms in Essex and Sussex – that is, kingdoms of the West, East, and South Saxons), and Kent (Jutes). And by this time, the West Germanic dialects these settlers spoke had become distinct enough from those of their relatives across the sea that Anglo-Saxons could speak of their kin back home as *Ealdseaxan*, 'Old Saxons' (DOE, s.v. *eald* sense I.E.2 'as an element in tribal names'; *Ealdseaxe*).

4.2 THE SOUNDS OF OLD ENGLISH

Presumably, the speech of the 'Old Saxons' was also distinct enough that the 'new' Saxons in what would become England should call their tongue *Englisċ* (or, *Englisċ ġe-reord*, that is, the 'Anglian' tongue). The earliest Runic inscriptions, being mostly very brief, give us just a few indications of what earliest Old English sounded like; for the most part, we are reliant upon the reconstructions of Proto-West Germanic and Primitive Old English that historical linguists make, abstracting back from recorded Old English, Old Saxon, and other West Germanic languages, and forward from Proto-Indo-Euopean to Proto-Germanic. Old English inherited the Proto-Germanic sound system with the developments that occurred in the stages some linguists label Proto-Northwest Germanic and Proto-West Germanic (these are approximately datable to the last centuries BC through to about AD 5th century). The phonemic inventory of Proto-Germanic has been reconstructed as:

Consonants

	V–	V+
bilabial:	p	b
	f	
		m
dental:	t	d
	þ	
		n
		l
alveolar:	s	z
		r
velar:	k	g
	h	
labiovelar:	k^w	g^w
	h^w	

nonsyllabic vocalics (semi-vowels): j w

vocalics:

short	long	trimoric
i	ī	
e	ē	ē̄
a	ā	
u	ū	
	ō	ō̄

(adapted from Ringe 2017, 242)

The inventory of sounds is arranged here rather more in the manner of handbooks of Old English, in terms of the basic distinctive features. For consonants, voicing (V− voiceless, V+ voiced), place of articulation (bilabial, labiodental, alveolar, alveolo-palatal/palato-alveolar, palatal, velar, glottal, etc.), and manner of articulation (stop, fricative, affricate, nasal, liquid). For the vowels: length (short/lax, long/tense); simple vs. diphthong (these are the two-part vowel sounds that form a single phoneme); rounding (pursing of the lips, from unrounded, e.g., /æ/, to rounded, /ʌ/, /ʊ/, /u/ in terms of increasing roundness among back vowels); height, with reference to relative elevation of the tongue in articulation (low, mid, high); and frontness/backness, in terms of which part of the tongue is elevated/lowered in the articulation of the vowel (front, central, back). Historical linguists, when using the comparative method for the reconstruction of proto-forms and proto-phonemic inventories, will need to use a much more elaborate set of terms and symbols as the evidence requires. Thus, in reconstructing back from Proto-Germanic to Proto-Indo-European, the inventory of sounds must take account of not one branch of the language family but all of the branches of the overall family of some 440 languages, the branches themselves having been reconstructed as far as the data allows. Thus, for Proto-Indo-European (ca. 3500 BC is a common estimate):

obstruents (consonants):

	V−	V+	V+ aspirated	
bilabial:	p	b	b^h	
coronal:	t	d	d^h	s
palatal:	ḱ	ǵ	ǵʰ	
velar:	k	g	g^h	h_2
labiovelar:	k^w	g^w	g^{wh}	h_3
glottal:	h_1			

sonorants 1 (semi-vowels):

y (~ i) (~ = in allophonic variation with; here the non-syllabic semi-vowel with the syllabic allophones underdotted)

r (~ r̥)

l (~ l̥)

n (~ n̥)

m (~ m̥)

sonorants 2 (high vowels, short & long):
i ī
u ū

sonorants 3 (non-high vowels, short & long):
e ē
a ā
o ō
(adapted from Ringe 2017, 8)

What stand out are the non-high /e/ (in Old through Modern English it is a high-mid vowel; /ɛ/ is mid) and the palatal /k/ and /g/, which have been said to have existed, in some accounts, in Old English. Their articulation is uncertain, beyond being further forward from the hard palate (where velars are made; Ringe 2017, 9). Outside of linguistics *sonorant* and *sonority* may not be familiar terms, and the latter is fairly nebulous even in linguistic use; essentially the distinction being drawn is between some sort of frictive (friction-like) obstruction of the airflow in the articulation of the sound (as with stops, fricatives, and affricates) versus those without such friction (semi-vowels and vowels, also together called *resonants*). Sonority has sometimes been equated with the 'loudness' of a sound, with the scaling of sounds in a 'sonority hierarchy' with vowels at the peak and obstruents at the bottom, with glides, liquids, and nasals in between. While 'loudness' seems at least partly perceptual, common sense has long pointed out that vowels are more 'important' than consonants in the sense that one can have an independent morpheme consisting solely of a vowel (the interjection *O!*), while the same is not true of a consonant (the interjection *Psst!* might seem a good counterexample). There is also the common dictum that consonants turn vowels off and on, which is true for *closed* syllables (e.g., *sit* [sɪt]), but not for the *open* (which are not closed off or blocked by an obstruent/consonant; e.g., *see* [si:]). One will also see *vocalic* and *vocoid* used in the specialist literature, which can also be disheartening; in their defense, one is again trying to draw a distinction between sounds vowel-like in their resonant, non-frictive articulation, and consonants which involve some obstruction of the airflow (on 'sonority,' see Parker 2011 in the massive 4-volume *The Blackwell Companion to Phonology*).

An attempt will be made here, in the following, to sketch in simplified form what is available in the specialist treatments. The subject of Old English phonology is rich in resources, from more traditional Neogrammarian handbooks (Campbell 1959/1987; Sievers-Brunner 1965) to more modern linguistic approaches (Lass 1994; Smith 2007, 2009) to the comparative work of historical linguists (Hogg and Fulk 2011; Fulk's *A History of Old English Meter* also offers a wealth of information about sound changes, particularly with reference to the dating of OE poems by sound changes, as well to OE dialectology; Fulk 1992). A major windfall for OE specialists is Donald Ringe's work with the two volumes of Oxford's *A Linguistic History of English* (Ringe and Taylor 2014; Ringe 2017); in the two volumes' nearly 1,000 pages, Ringe reconstructs the roots of English from Proto-Indo-European through Proto-Germanic to Proto-Northwest Germanic and Proto-West Germanic. Ringe is one of the foremost historical linguists of the day, an Indo-Europeanist who has previously worked especially with Greek dialects, Tocharian, and linguistic reconstruction and cladistics (delineating the Indo-European languages' 'family tree'). The sheer mass of detail, new observations, and reinterpretations of phonological and morphological changes and their relative chronology will take some years to be fully appreciated and worked into Old English scholarship, and, though daunting to the nonspecialist, the place of English in the Indo-European family of languages has its fullest treatment to date (Ann Taylor in volume II offers an overview of OE syntax within the framework of modern [Chomskyan and post-Chomskyan] linguistic theory; Taylor in Ringe and Taylor 2014, 392–509).

Moving forward in time, the phonemic inventory for Proto-West Germanic has been reconstructed as:

obstruents		
	V−	V+
labial:	p	b
dental:	t	d
velar:	k	g
(stops)		
labial:	f	
dental:	þ	
alveolar:	s	
velar:	h	
(fricatives)		
labial:		m
dental:		n
(nasals)		
retroflex(?)		z
dental:		l
retroflex:		r
(liquids)		
palatal:		j
labiovelar:		w
(semi-vowels)		

(adapted from Ringe in Ringe and Taylor 2014, 105–106)

The usual consonant class rubrics from the handbooks have been added in parentheses, though there is quite some debate about how some of these sounds should be classified in their development from proto-stages to Old English (and other Germanic dialects). PGmc *z is one such sound, which by the earliest Runic inscriptions (in the Common Germanic era) had undergone rhotacism (in the earlier inscriptions Ʀ is usually transcribed <R>); for example, in nominal inflection, the nom. sing. and pl. in *-*iz*/*-*īz* (PGmc **gastiz*, nom. sing., **gastīz*, nom. pl.; OE *ġiest* 'guest'), nom. sing. **sunuz* (OE *sunu* 'son'), nom. pl. **manniz* (ON, in North Germanic, saw rhotacism [z/s > r], Gothic retained *s*). To arrive at the OE forms, **sunuz* underwent a change limited to West Germanic by which PGmc **z* was lost "when the preceding syllable nucleus was unstressed" (Ringe in Ringe and Taylor 2014, 43; compare OE, OS, and OHG *sunu*); for example, PGmc nom. sing. **sunuz*, gen. sing. **sunauz* developed into Gothic *sunus* and *sunaus*, Old Norse *sunr* ~ *sonr* (probably by a-mutation) and *sonar* (the -*r* in the ON forms by rhotacism). The forms **gastiz* and **manniz* underwent i-mutation in WGmc, thus OE *ġiest* (with palatalization of **g* before high front vowel) and *mann* (nom. sing.) and *menn* (pl., by i-mutation). Lost by the first centuries of the present era are the PIE laryngeals and class of labiovelars unaspirated and aspirated (k^w, g^w, etc.). The MdE speaker will notice the missing voiced fricatives [v ð z], which are indeed found in OE, under certain conditions, though not generally reflected in the OE spelling system, excepting, with some inconsistency, earlier use of <þ> for the voiceless dental or 'interdental' fricative and <ð> the voiced. These fricatives were in complementary distribution despite the spellings; <f> was /f/ when initial, adjacent to another stop (even when a geminate: /s/ is voiceless in *cyssan* 'to kiss'), and final; when preceded by a stressed vowel, or stressed vowel + /l, r/, or followed by an unaccented vowel (e.g., inflectional endings): thus OE *wulf* (sing.) has /f/, *wulfas* (pl.) /v/ (i.e., we find in OE, despite the spelling <f> in both singular and plural, the contrast /f/ ~ /v/ as in MdE *wolf* ~ *wolves*). OE *ofer* would have /v/ as it is intervocalic; it derives from PGmc **uber/*ubar* from PIE **úper(i)* (compare Greek ὑπέρ [*hupér*], borrowed into English as the highly productive prefix *hyper-*), with the p > f by Verner's Law (with the curious exception of Gothic *ufar*, which retained voiceless /f/; Ringe 2017, 123; Ringe in Ringe and Taylor 2014, 33, 333; Lass 1994, 71–74).

For the vowels:

simple (short, long)

i ī	e ē
	a ā
u ū	o ō

diphthongs

eu (~iu)	ai	au

The status of long /e:/ is uncertain: it may have been an unstressed allophone of PGmc *ai as PGmc *ē had undergone lowering and backing to *ā in PNWGmc, unstressed *ai merging with *ē in NWGmc dialects; it may be a 'new' vowel in strong class 7 verbs such as **haitanę̨* (the underhook indicates a nasalized variant of the vowel), with reduplicating preterite **heheit*; compare OE *hātan*, *hēt* (~ *heht*, mainly in Anglian dialects, likely contracted from an originally reduplicated preterite; Lass 1994, 160; Ringe in Ringe and Taylor 2014, 10–11, 89–91, 106).

And so, coming to Old English:

	V−	V+
stops		
labial:	p	b
dental:	t	d
palatal:	k	g
velar:	k	g
fricatives		
labiodental	f	v
labial	hw	
dental:	þ	ð/þ
velar:	x	ɣ
glottal:	h	
sibilants		
dental-alveolar:	s	
palatal:	ʃ	
palato-alveolar		z
affricates		
alveolar	tʃ	dʒ
nasals		
labial:		m
dental:		n
velar:		ŋ
liquids		
lateral:		l
retroflex:		r
semi-vowels		
palatal:		j
labiovelar:		w

(see especially Hogg 2011, 10–51 and references)

The classification of some of the consonants is uncertain and can vary by account. Ringe's section on "The separate prehistory of Old English: sound changes" is extensive and approaches the subject with an Indo-Europeanist's perspective (Ringe and Taylor 2014, 167–341), and it is very interesting to see his departures – and a good many confirmations – of what the OE specialists have done on the subject. For example, a metathesis of *r* well-known to modern-day speakers is **brænnan* > *bærnan* (*a* > *æ* by i-umlaut), the causative form of OE *beornan* 'to burn'; this is known from the modern reflexes *burn*, *burnt/burned* (< *bærnan*; PWGmc **brannijan*, 'burn' in transitive sense), and *brand*, *brent*, and *Brent-* – especially in place-names: *Brentwood* (Essex) is found in the early Middle English form *Brendewode*, 'burnt wood' (ME *brennen*, past ptc. *brenned/ i-brent*, etc.) making a clearing by fire for a town settlement. Did the metathesis in Mercian OE *bernan* and Northumbrian OE *berna* (*-n* lost at times with infinitive forms in Northmubrian) occur at the same time as the further i-umlauting of *æ* > *e* as a feature of Anglian dialects of OE, as E.G. Stanley supposed in his study of *r*-metathesis in OE? (Stanley 1952). Perhaps the development was simply **brǫnnj-* > **brænn-* > **brenn-* > *bern* (the metathesis following i-umlaut; Ringe in Ringe and Taylor 2014, 341). The broader significance is that despite the wealth of scholarship on OE phonology the matter of the relative chronology of sound changes is enormously complicated and unsettled – and that despite the great emphasis given to it also by generations of German scholars who pursued the subject as part of 19th- and 20th-century *Germanistik* curricula (on this particular case of *r*-metathesis, see Luick 1921, I, 141). The voiced velar nasal /ŋ/ does not occur initially in OE (and does not in MdE, excepting personal names and a few loanwords from, for instance, Vietnamese, Tagalog, Niger-Congo languages); accounts of the pronunciation of OE sometimes stress that *singan* 'sing' was realized like [sɪnˈgən] though the syllable divide was likely [sɪŋˈgən]. The affricates /tʃ/ and /dʒ/ involved dental stop + palatal sibilant, voiceless and voiced respectively, with the former often represented by <c> (as in the classical loan, Greek via Latin, *ċiriċe* 'church'), and represented by the symbol *ċ* in modern texts; the voiced affricate /dʒ/ could appear as <cg> or <cʒ> (*eċġ* 'edge, sword,' *seċġan* 'say, tell'). The velar stops were historically 'fronted' (from velar to palatal) before front vowels (short and long *æ*, *e*, *i*, as simple vowels or as the first element of diphthongs; Campbell OEG §§427–431), following short or long *i*, /g/ intervocalically if involving front vowels (/k/ only if the preceding vowel were short or long *i*), and /g/ when preconsonantal or final when preceded by front vowel (/k/ in these environments when preceded by short of long *i*, though /k/ does not seem to have palatalized preconsonantally; Ringe in Ringe and Taylor 2014, 203). The process seems to have involved palatalization to /kj/ and /gj/ that was felt to be contrastive by speakers of OE ("apparently native learners misinterpreted automatic coarticulation effects as the results of a phonological rule"; Ringe in Ringe and Taylor 2014, 203), and assibilation (here, change of the inserted glide /j/ from fronting of the velars > /s/) of [tj] and [dj] to [tʃ] and [dʒ] (Ringe in Ringe and Taylor 2014, 203–204).

In short, Old English inherited from Proto-Germanic many of the consonants still seen in Present Day English: the complement of stops was a bit fuller with the palatal allophones of /k/ and /g/ and the nasal /ŋ/ was realized as /ŋg/, thus the infinitive form *singan* 'to sing' was pronounced [siŋgɑn]; MdE lost infinitival *-an* but an approximate modern pronunciation would be [ˈsɪŋˌən], though one can hear in some dialectal and non-native forms of MdE [ˈsɪŋˌgɪŋ], that is *sing-ging*, for *singing*. There was some variation with velar /x/ and glottal /h/, as in OE *hliehhan* 'to laugh': an original PGmc *hlahjaną underwent gemination and palatalization in PWGmc (> *-hʲhʲ-) causing the vowel to diphthongize: PGmc *a > PWGmc *æ, then by palatal umlaut to *ea*/*ie*, thus OE *hliehhan* 'to laugh' and *hleahtor* 'laughter' [xleaxtor]/[*xlæɑxtor] (Ringe in Ringe and Taylor 2014, 176–177; on the latter form *hleahtor* see Hogg 2011, 5.82). The influence of vowels on neighboring consonants is of course of paramount importance, and could produce interesting changes through time: for example, MdE *cold* – BrE [kəʊld], AmE [koʊld] or [ko:d] and other variants – was Old English *ċeald* [tʃeald]/ [tʃæɑld] with palatalization of /k/, deriving from PGmc *kaldaz (before fronting, palatalization, and breaking). In that long view, in the history of Germanic 'cold,' /k/ > /tʃ/ > /k/. The 'why' of the change has much to do with vowels.

Vowels and diphthongs:

short/lax and long/tense
simple vowels:

i i:	y y:	u u:
e e:	œ œ:	o o:
	ɛ?	
	æ æ:	ɑ ɑ:

i i:	high front unrounded
y y:	high front rounded
e e:	mid front unrounded
œ œ:	mid front unrounded
æ æ:	low front unrounded
u u:	high back rounded
o o:	mid back rounded
ɑ ɑ:	low back unrounded

The pairs /i, i:/ - /y, y:/ and /e, e:/ - /œ, œ:/ are distinguished by the more rounded pronunciation of the latter member. The digraph <oe> is found in early OE texts, especially those in Anglian dialects: *doemid* 'was judged/should be judged,' the past passive participle of weak class I verb *dēman*, from the Northumbrian version of *Bede's Death Song* (5b); from the 9th century the vowel is found also in Kentish, and occasionally in late WS texts (Sievers-Brunner 1965, §27); it is rounder than /e/ but fronter than /o/ and its pronunciation may have been like similar vowels found in contemporary Germanic languages (hence the IPA symbols /ø, ø:/ used for it). The value of *æ* is generally thought to be /æ/, the vowel in MdE *cat*, though some accounts have seen *æ* as representing a vowel between /æ/ and /a/, that is, between the near-low or mid-low front unrounded /æ/ and low front unrounded /a/ (Campbell OEG §36; Hogg and Fulk 2011, 14). The mid-front *œ* is sometimes described as the rounded allophone of /e/; it was likely more rounded early on, unrounding in later OE – just as *y* unrounded in later dialects, especially in Kentish (Schlemilch 1914).

diphthongs:

short and long

ea ēa (OE ēa < early OE ǣo < PWGmc *au; PGmc *auk > OE ēac 'also'; Ringe in Ringe and Taylor 2014, 171–172)
eo ēo (< PGmc *eu)
io īo (< PGmc *iu)
ie īe (< PGmc *au, *iu + i-mutation)

There were of course other sources for these diphthongs in OE, where they are true diphthongs, and not simply digraphs for long monophthongs: *ea*, *eo*, *io* could be produced by the influence of palatal consonants on front vowels: **kerl-* > *ċeorl* 'freeman farmer, layman,' whence *churl*, but compare Old Norse *karl* 'freeman' (or the male given name *Carl*, of the same meaning). A curious feature in the development of OE diphthongs is that they were contrastive (short and long), whereas in earlier Germanic they were not (the three were: ai, au, and eu ~iu, which had the same value as long vowels). There was the breaking of short front vowels before **h* in the patterns **a* > **æ* > *ea*, **e* > *eo*, **i* > *io*: **ahslō* > OE *eaxl* 'shoulder' (with apocope of the final short high vowel; Ringe in Ringe and Taylor 2014, 285), **flahs* > OE *fleax* 'flax,' **wīhaz* 'consecrated, holy' > OE *wīoh/wēoh* 'idol' (besides monophthong forms *wīġ*, *wīh*); of PGmc **a* > Proto-OE **æ* breaking to *ea* before *l* + another consonant (or geminate *ll*): **allai* 'all' (pl.) > **ællǣ* > *ealle*, **halsaz* 'neck' > **hæls* > *heals* (but with retraction of *æ* to *a* in Anglian dialects: WS *ealle* – Northumbrian *alle*, *heals* – *hals-*; Ringe in Ringe and Taylor 2014, 184) – there was later retraction of *æ* to *a* before single or geminate consonants or *s* + consonant clusters: dat. pl. **dagum* (*dæġ* 'day') > *dægum* > *dagum*, PGmc (with trimoric/overlong ō̄) **nabulō̄* > **næbulā* > *nafola* 'navel' (Ringe in Ringe and Taylor 2014, 190–191); of **e* and **i* before **w* and **lw*: PGmc **knewa-* > OE *cnēow* 'knee,' **gelwaz* > *ġeolu* 'yellow' (Ringe in Ringe and Taylor 2014, 187).

It may be seen as a curiosity of Old English in comparison to Modern English, with its falling (and occasionally rising diphthongs: the Southern California /iæ/, /iæ:/ and /ɛu/, /ɛu:/); but at some stage OE had the diphthongs /æɑ/, /æɑ:/, as in *eall* and *bēam*, and /eo/, /eo:/, as in *bēon* (> ME *bē(n)* with smoothing/monophthongization in the late OE – early ME period) with the vowels even in height (low in the former, high in the latter). By late OE, there is evidence of a nearly diphthong-free vowel inventory of long and short front vowels /i:/ /i/, /e:/ /e/, and /ɛ:/ /ɛ/, and back vowels /u:/ /u/, /o:/ /o/, and /ɑ:/ /ɑ/ (Lass 1987, 121–126); Richard Hogg argues in favor of using IPA /ɑ, ɑ:/ for this vowel rather than /a, a:/, as it was in OE a low-back unrounded vowel (Hogg and Fulk 2011, 14); see Lass 1994 for the path of changes from WGmc proto-forms to OE *eald* 'old,' *eolh* 'elk,' *bēam* 'tree, piece of wood,' *nēah* 'near,' *bēodan* command,' *lēoht* 'light,' with **a* > *ea*, **e* > *eo*, **au* > *ēa*, **aa* > *ē*, **iu* > *ēo*, and **ii* > *ēo* (Lass 1994, 51). An innovation in the OE vowels system, in contrast with other Germanic languages, was the development of rounded front vowels /y/ /y:/ and /ø/ /ø:/(oe /œ/ /œ:/), as by the *i*-umlaut of /o/ and /u/ in athematic nouns – that is those without the *theme* or *thematic* vowel, in daughter languages of Proto-Indo-European **e* or **o* (> Gmc **a*) added after the suffix and before the inflectional or other ending (in the pattern: root + thematic vowel [= stem] + ending): for example, PIE **wVr-t* (< PIE root **wer-* 'to turn') produces OE *weorþan* 'happen, become' and Modern German *werden*; the OE infinitive underwent breaking/diphthongization of *e* before /rC/, here **rt-*, /t/ > /θ/ <þ> by Grimm's Law.

There are a number of other OE nouns like *mūs* that undergo *i*-umlaut, producing forms recognizable today:

PGmc **brūdiz* > OE *brȳd* 'bride' (which shows the working of the Great Vowel Shift post-1400 by which unrounded /y:/ > /i/ > /aɪ/)
PGmc **hūdiz* > OE *hȳd* 'skin, hide'
PGmc **fuliþu* > OE *fȳlþ* 'filth' (OE adj. *fūl* with the noun form derived by addition of PGmc suffix *-iþ(u)*)

Proto-Northwest-Gmc **þrūþiz* > OE *þrȳð* 'might, power, glory' (chiefly a poetic word, as in such kennings as *þryðbord* 'strong-shield,' *þrȳðcyning* 'glory-king,' or 'King of glory' as epithet of God, *þrȳðærn* and *þrȳðġesteald* both 'glory/high-dwelling' = 'royal residence, palace')
(Ringe and Taylor 2014, 224)

Among the earlier changes were the 'first fronting' (Ringe speculates that this may have been as early as the 5th century; Ringe in Ringe and Taylor 2014, 283); diphthongization/breaking due to various factors; retraction of front vowels; palatalization (most historians of OE posit palatal allophones of the velars /k, g/); West Saxon palatal diphthongization; *i*-umlaut; syncope; and 'three-consonant shortening' (the shortening of tense/long vowels before a consonant cluster (*nēahst*, variant of *nīehst* 'nearest, closest [next],' > *nēhst* > *nehst*); rounding of **ā* before a nasal to ō (Hogg and Fulk 2011, 55–56; Ringe in Ringe and Taylor 2014, 142–146): PGmc *a unstressed was nasalized before nasal consonants in the coda (*a* > *ą/ã*). With the stressed vowel one has OE *þōhte* < **θã:xte:/þanhtē* (3rd sing. pret. OE *þenċan/þynċan* 'think' – the original PGmc **aŋx* >*ã:x* with the loss of the nasal and compensatory lengthening (Campbell OEG §119).

Velar consonants, noninitial, underwent palatalization when a high front vowel (*i*, *e*) followed: c (/k/), g > *ċ*, *ġ*, and geminates likewise underwent the change on the basis of the Obligatory Contour Principle (Ringe in Ringe and Taylor 2014, 207–215)– that languages resist two identical sounds in succession: thus if VV involve identical vowels, there will either be coalescence into one long vowel or dieresis (the vowels pronounced separately); so, in this example, **-kk-* when palatalized by a preceding high front vowel (long or short *i*, *eo*, *ea*) > **-ċc-* > *-ċċ-* (or, in an older formulation, the change 'spread' from the affected segment to the geminate – an assimilative change).

PGmc *skōhaz 'shoe' > PWGmc *skōh > OE sċēoh, sċōh (with loss of intervocalic *h and contraction of vowels into diphthong (here *ēo*) or a long vowel (*ō*; Ringe in Ringe and Taylor 2014, 207, 314)
PGmc *mēkijaz 'sword' > PNWGmc *mākijaz > PWGmc *mākī > OE *mēċe* (the poetic term for usual OE *sweord*, it occurs also in the kennings *beado-mēċe* and *hilde-mēċe* 'battle-sword,' and *hæft-mēċe* 'hilted-sword')
PGmc *sōkijaną 'seek' > *sōkijan > *sōkjan [syncopation of *kija > *kja in northern WGmc dialects; Ringe in Ringe and Taylor 2014, 156–157) > OE *sēċan* (see Ringe in Ringe and Taylor 2014, 207ff. for copious examples)

The 'Old' period of English is of half a millennium in duration, and the sound changes in the course of those five centuries are many and various enough as to make any absolute chronology of sound change very difficult. Sound change in later Old English is less studied to present, and some of the changes seem to overlap with morphological change: for example, the shifts /m/ > /n/, such as in nominal dative forms (*dagan* or *dagon* for *dagum*, dat. pl. of *dæġ* 'day'), or /θ/ > /s/ in Northumbrian 3rd sing. and pl. present indicative verb forms, which resulted in a confusion of the endings *-es*, *-eð*, *-að*, etc. (these are the two last sound changes in OE considered in Hogg 1992, §§ 7.101–103); the latter shift seems indicative of inflectional attrition, though both may be a result of morphological changes to late OE. Vowel changes can begin to look cyclical, though they are dependent rather on conditions specific to the respective periods of OE; seen above is the pre-English fronting of PGmc *a > OE /æ/ (e.g., PGmc *fadēr > OE *fæder*; Ringe in Ringe and Taylor 2014, 146–147); common in late OE texts was the shift /æ/ to /a/ (or to /e/ in late Kentish OE). But environment is everything: PGmc *a > Primitive OE *æ would be raised to /e/ by i-umlaut in a form like *betera* 'better' (*batiz > *bætirā > *betirā; Ringe in Ringe and Taylor 2014, 236). Much more study is needed of sound change in this transitional era (ca. 1000–1150), as the most thorough treatment of sound change in late Old English remains Schlemilch 1914 (on some of these later changes, see Section 4.7).

4.3 WORDHORD: OLD ENGLISH MORPHOLOGY AND WORD-FORMATION

'Word-formation' of course is encompassed in the modern linguistic term *morphology*, in the branch *derivational morphology*, but Old English word-formation, compounding in particular, is one of the areas of the language in which a modern reader still can see a certain 'Germanic-ness' in English: while not as free in at-will compounding as Modern German is, English is still quite prolific in word-formation from the native stock of morphemes (English is also a rather porous language when it comes to loanwords and loan formations, such as calques or loan translations, readily accepting what may be new, useful, or trendy). But this distinction blurs a similarity between Modern English and German with technicalities: if Modern English is hesitant to form single-unit compounds (two or more words written as one, and considered morphologically and semantically a 'word'), it nonetheless forms compounds at least as readily through collocation and punctuation, the former including semantic or 'invisible' compounds (two- or multi-word formations written with the original morphological boundaries: *The White House*, *10 Downing Street*). English has what might be called a more hesitant path to full compounded form: words collocated into a 'unit' may be written separately (*high tech[nology]*), then hyphenated (*high-tech*), then as if a simplex (*hightech*). One of the key morphological traits of the English language throughout its history is *inflectional decay*, a loss of inflections (word endings, affixes) and, often but not always, replacement by periphrastic constructions: for example, loss of the genitive case marking in *-es* (singular), *-a*/*-ena*, etc. (plural) with *'s/s'* or periphrastic *of* ______ formations (there is also the *Jonson his book*-type formation that persisted into Early Modern English, becoming 'antiquey' or 'obsolete' thereafter). The question of why such inflectional decay occurs has no agreed-upon answer with any level of satisfaction. Appeals to a 'laziness principle' or 'opacity' or other principle among its speakers of ease or convenience would single out English speakers among other Germanic-language speakers for 'laziness' in a way that makes little sense (much less other speakers of Indo-European languages or any language for that matter). An appeal might be made to the morphological simplifications found in Romance languages in their evolution from classical to late Vulgar Latin to the present-day vernaculars: some nouns inherited from Latin were formed from the oblique case forms (i.e., the non-nominative or base form): Spanish *cualidad* is from Latin feminine third-declension noun *quālitās* but with the final *-d* voiced from the *-t-* in the noun's oblique forms (*quālitātis* [gen. sing.], *quālitātem* [acc. sing.], etc.); *peligro* is from the Latin second-declension neuter noun *periculum* (dat. & abl. sing. *perīculō*; the Latin form had undergone metathesis and devoicing of g); this is an oversimplification of a complex morphological process ca. 400–800 during which Ibero-Vulgar Latin underwent a great many phonological and morphological changes, such that Latin third-declension accusative singular form *hominem* (< *homo* 'man') produced *hombre* (involving an epenthesis of labial and liquid that reminds one of the variant form *chimbley* for *chimney* in English).

The vocabulary of Old English is predominantly Germanic-inherited; so much of the study of the lexis of English focuses on loanwords, as English has always had a fairly porous lexical barrier (unlike many other languages), adopting loans fairly readily. It is difficult to say exactly why, and it may be a phenomenon that is, at least linguistically speaking, neutral. German, Spanish, French, and Russian, by comparison more resistant than English to large-scale importation of loanwords, supply the need – one that all languages have – often from derivational morphological processes drawing on the native stock of morphemes: compounding, affixation, semantic transfer, and extension (all of which English employs as well). Estimates of the percentage of the English vocabulary consisting of loan formations can run as high as 70–80%, leading to popular impressions that English is dependent upon other languages to some unusual or alarming degree, or that the English lexicon is no longer 'purely' Germanic (however that appeal may cut). As might be expected, most of these impressions are overstated. The simple number of loanwords sounds high, at first. The OED lists 24,088 forms in English as deriving from French; this list, however, includes a number of 'doublets,' that is, forms listed twice (or multiple times), whether by shifts in sense or variation in usage (i.e., differing registers: medical, legal, arts, etc.), or simply by word class (*abandon* is listed four times, as noun and verb) or in derivative form (*act, action, active, activity, actor*; *machine*, v. and n., *machination, machinist*). Some of these loans from French involve only the original form, the verb, or a deverbal noun, and the rest are products of English derivational morphology. For Latin, the OED lists 42,864 forms, though a number of these are affixes, and many are more 'refined' or highly technical terms. This may be shown by the old chestnut: blunt OE forms such as *flæscmettas* 'flesh-meats' versus more refined French *poultry, pork, beef(steak)*; or native stock *cooking* and *clothing* versus French loans *cuisine, (haute) couture, fashion*. There is no doubt that the Norman Conquest of 1066 would, eventually, bring with it certain refinements in administration and law, even culture; though, would this be different than any other colonial situation in which one culture's normal path of development is arrested as it is overlain by the new dominant culture? By comparison, the OED lists 3,631 loans from German (i.e., not part of the Germanic inheritance of English as a West Germanic language), 2,244 forms deriving from Italian, 1,871 forms as of Spanish origin, 1,541 from Dutch, 547 from Japanese, 535 from Arabic, 411 from Russian, 332 from Irish, 327 from Hebrew (203 more from Yiddish, though with some overlap with Hebrew), 130 from the native Algonquian languages of North America, 106 from Scots Gaelic, and 101 from Welsh. The 7,975 loans from Greek often involve forms borrowed via Latin, just as a number of the French loans may have been borrowed also from Latin. Etymology has its precision in sound changes and morphology, but it is still an art.

However, a careful sifting for 'doublets' and words where the source is uncertain, such as those attributed to 'Latin or French,' reduces this figure considerably. Deputy

Chief Editor of the OED Philip Durkin provided just such a breakdown of the figures with detailed analyses of loans on a language-by-language basis (Durkin 2014). Over against a set of 600,000 lexemes and some 275,000 headwords, with many more forms uncatalogued, the percentage of loans is somewhat less impressive. Of the 92,500 entries from the OED3 in progress (for letters *A*, *A-ALZ*, and complete letters *M*, *N*, *O*, *P*, *Q*, and *R* the percentage of loans is 32% (Durkin 2014, 24). From the OED3 data, the donor languages are essentially the same as from OED2 in terms of frequency: Latin (only), French (only), Greek, French or Latin, German, Spanish, Italian, Dutch (Durkin 2014, 22–45). From the 275,000 OED headwords, only 3.5% were traced back to Old English, pre-1150 origin (Durkin 2014, 28–29, and Figure 2.3).

A vital point often missed is frequency of use. The same 80% figure given for the percentage of loans in the vocabulary of English is often given for the percentage of words in any given utterance being from the native Germanic stock. This is, of course, a highly imprecise formulation, as speech and writing are often register-dependent, as it can matter what is being discussed, whether it is part of an occupation, pursuit, or hobby, or what the level of discussion may be (informal, formal, technical). But it is generally the case that many of the loans to English are open-class, lexical forms. 'Core' Old English vocabulary includes many of the closed-class, function words such as pronouns, articles, prepositions, conjunctions, and, with less a sense of closed-ness, interjections.

It is not a watertight truism, as there certainly are exceptions, but core vocabulary items generally seem to persist – there may be nearly synonymous additions that can be used in place of the core terms, as for elaboration, greater specification, or variety, but they are not generally that likely to replace the originals. Terms for family relationship/kinship, verbs of basic activity (motion, eating, sleeping/waking, vision, hearing and other senses), numerals (depending on the order of mathematics – English borrowed higher-order numerals, *million* and higher, from Greek), basic flora and fauna, foodstuffs, natural features, and the local built environment are generally core parts of the native stock. There are, of course, exceptions, and English interestingly has a number of basic loans from Old Norse – *window* from *vindr-auga* ('wind-eye'), *kirk* (which became more a northern and Scots variant that did not supplant the Greek loan *church*). Norse loans may have been felt to have been close to native Anglo-Saxon terms, or close enough to supplant the forms with little notice, and the source and target cultures (the donor and recipient of the lexical transfers) may have been similar enough to facilitate such loans. Among such basic 'Saxon' vocabulary elements are:

mōdor, f. 'mother' **fæder**, m 'father' **sweostor**, f. 'sister' **brōðor**, m. 'brother'

hām, m. 'home' **hūs**, n. 'house' **wudu**, m. 'forest, woods' **sǣ**, m. and f.[4] 'sea' **burg**, f. 'fortress, town'
munt, m. 'mountain'

[4] But also indeclinable (CHM, s.v.); PGmc **saiwi* > **sāwi* > **sǣi*, though the *w* was restored in less common declined forms such as dat. sing. *sǣwe* and dat. pl. *sǣwum* (more common were *sǣum* and contracted *sǣm*). The exact change the proto-form underwent is not certain for this strong (feminine) i-stem noun; it may, perhaps most likely, be an instance of loss of *w* before *i*, if that *i* had not first been lost by apocope (Campbell OEG §§ 400, 406, 610.2; Ringe in Ringe and Taylor 2014, 234, 257–259, 318).

gān, vb. 'go, walk' **habban**, III, 'have' **seċġan**, III, 'say, tell' **dōn**, vb. 'do, make' **(ge) sēon**, 5, 'see'
bēon, vb. 'be'

tōdæġ, adv. 'today' **ġiestrandæġ**, m. 'yesterday' **tōmorgen**, adv. 'tomorrow' [< *to morgenne*]

ġiese, adv. 'yes' **nā**, adv. 'no, not at all'

These are all readily identifiable to a Modern English speaker once a few sound and form changes are identified. The *ġiestran-* form produced also *ġiestranǣfen* 'yesterday evening' (archaic 'yesterneve') and *ġiestranniht* 'yesternight'; *ġiestran* could appear also as a simplex in the sense 'yesterday' and in cognate Modern German *gestern* 'yesterday' (for 'yesterday' German has also *gestrig*), OHG *gestaron/gesteron*, Gothic *gistradagis* (with a reversal in sense it denoted 'tomorrow') < PGmc **gestra-* 'yesterday' (Holthausen AEW, s.v. *ġeostra(n)*; Ringe in Ringe and Taylor 2014, 216). The spelling was fairly variable in OE, with the Vespasian Psalter (Mercian) form *ġeostran* by back umlaut (Rückumlaut; compare Modern German *brennen* > *brannte* > *gebrannt*), likewise *ġioster-* in the Lindisfarne Gospels gloss (Campbell OEG §217). In the Rushworth Gospels gloss, one finds *ġeostordæġ* with svarabhakti (parasite) vowel while late West Saxon (Ælfric) *ġyrstandæġ* exhibits metathesis of *-str-* > *-rst-* (Campbell OEG §460; for the change of Early WS *ie* >*y* see Campbell OEG §301 and Hogg 1992, 194 [section 5.167]; Hogg sees the early WS spelling <ie> as representing /i/).

By way of comparison, forms from Gothic, an East Germanic language, might be set next to those from Old English, a West Germanic language:

afar as prep 'after, subsequent to; according to' [OE *æfter*]
aftuma (comp form of adj), aftumists 'hindmost, aftermost (of two); second (hindmost) last' [OE *æfterra* (comp.), *æftermest* (superl.); cf. Ringe 2017, 317–318]
ahs 'ear of grain' [OE *ēar*]
ahva 'river, stream; flowing water' [OE *ēa*]
aina-baúr 'only-born son' [OE *ān-boren*]
ains 'one, single' [OE *ān*, *āna*]
aīrþa 'earth' (for breaking, compare proper name Enos as Aīnōs) [OE *eorðe*]
Aīwwa 'Eve' [OE *Eua*: *his wife Eua, ðæt is 'lif,' for ðan ðe heo is ealra libbendra modor* ("his wife Eva, that is, 'life,' because [lit. 'for that which'] she is of all the living mother"] (Marsden 2008, 13)
ak 'but, however' [OE *ac*]
alds 'life, lifetime' [OE *ieldo*, with also variation in the main vowel *æ* ~ *e* ~ *i* ~*y*; *ieldo* derives from the adjectival *eald* 'old,' the comparative of which is *ieldra* 'elder']
anþar 'other, another' [OE *ōðer*; as with PGmc **unseraz* 'our' > PWGmc **unsar* > **ūsœr* > *ūser* above, (4.1), with loss of nasal, here the loss of nasals before a fricative consonant, which occurred in the NWGmc phase of development (i.e., OE, OFris, OS): **anþeraz* > *ą̄þar* (nasalized tense/long /a/) > *ōþer*; Ringe 2017, 140]
bi 'by, around' [OE *be*]
brūkjan 'make use of' [OE *brūcan*, also with sense of 'to enjoy' in OE]

dags 'day' (name also of the D-rune) [OE *dæġ*, with PGmc /a/ > /æ/; PGmc *a produced three sounds in OE, which can be seen early on by the development of three runes for /æ/ ᚫ, /a/ ᚪ, /o/ ᚩ; Campbell OEG §67]

drag(g) 'drink' [noun form; OE *drinc*; the Gothic verb form's principal parts [infinitive, first preterite sing., pret. plural, past participle] were *drigkan* [driŋkan], *dragk*, *drugkun*, *drugkans*; the OE principal parts were *drincan*, *dranc*, *druncon* [in the northern Mercian gloss to the Rushworth Gospels the vowel of the present paradigm has been leveled to past forms so that one finds *drincon* for *druncon*], *druncen*]

faīhu 'goods, property' [OE *feoh*, literally 'cattle']

fōdjan 'to feed, nourish; rear' [OE *fēdan*]

fragan 'to ask' [OE *frignan*, and contract form, with compensatory lengthening, *frīnan*]

frauja 'lord' [OE *frēa*]

frei-hals 'freedom, liberty' [OE *frēols* < *frīheals*; the Gothic and OE compounds both literally mean 'free-neck,' an expression indicating freedom from a slave collar]

haban 'to have' [OE *habban*]

hails 'whole, healthy; hale' (as interjection/greeting 'Hail!') [OE *hāl* 'hale, healthy'; cf. *hælu*, *hæle* 'health'; ME *wassail(e)* is a calque on Old Norse *ves heill* 'be hale!': the OE forms were *bēo þū hāl* / *wes þū hāl*, 'be thou hale!']

*Iggws name of the *x*-rune (but originally for the ng-rune ◇, cognate with Ing [PGmc **Ingwaz*], old Germanic fertility god – possibly fused with or a doublet of Freyr – and reputed founder of Germanic lineages, such as the Ingvaeones and Ynglings; see Section 4.5)

kunnan 'to know' [OE *cunnan*, whence MdE *cunning*]

ga-laubjan 'to believe' [OE *ġe-lȳfan*, *ġe-līefan*]

maiþms 'treasure' [OE *māðum*; Gmc /ai/ preserved in Gothic, /ai/ > /a/ in this OE form]

mikils 'great, large' [OE *miċel*, Scots *mickle*]

ōþal 'ancestral homeland,' name for the *o*-rune [OE *ēþel*; Proto-NWGmc **ōþ-V-la-* (the vowel usually *i* or *e*); there was some variability in early OE forms: early West Saxon *ǣþel* ~ *ēþel* (i-mutation of ō > *ǣ*), Mercian and Northumbrian *ǣðel*, *ǣðle* (< **ǣþil*, *ǣþilǣ*); one finds also the early naming element *Ōidils-* in deuterothematic [or *dithematic*: two-part] personal names]

qiþan 'to say, speak' [OE *cweðan* – compare Middle English *queþen*, and now archaic *quoth* < *queath*; OE *becweðan* survives in *bequeath*]

saīhvan 'to see' [OE *sēon*]

saúrga 'sorrow' [OE *sorg*]

silba 'self' (as pronoun/reflexive pronoun: *is silba sunus*, 'the Son Himself') [OE *self*]

skulu 'to be obliged, should' [OE *sċulan*]

sōkjan 'to seek' [OE *sēċan*]

taīhun '100' (base-10, ten-tens) [OE *tīen* (West Saxon), *tēn*, and with loss of final *-n tēa*, *tīo* in late Northumbrian (Campbell OEG §472); PWGmc **tehuni-* with subsequent loss of intervocalic *h*; cf. Ringe in Ringe and Taylor 2014, 253]

þugkjan 'to suppose; seem' [OE *ðencan*]

ufar 'over' [OE *ofer*]

wiljan 'will, want, be willing' [OE *willan*]

The Gothic forms *gistradagis* ('yesterday') and *freihals* ('freedom; free-neck') call to mind another element of the 'Germanic-ness' English inherited: the relatively high frequency of compound formation in a number of forms of nominal composition. Well-known is the Germanic and Old English (Anglo-Saxon era) propensity for kennings, allusive poetic compounds, often of a tautological type (when both elements contain roughly the same semantic content, i.e., appositive compound formations). Interesting is their place in the broader categories of Old English compound- and word-formation, from descriptive compounds (as in Pāṇini's *karmadhāraya* class of compounds; perhaps *mæġenstān*, 'large stone,' in which *mæġen* as the descriptor seems somewhat semantically subdued), intensifying compounds (e.g., nominal *mæġenfolc* 'mighty company, large host,' adjectival *mæġenstrang* 'of great strength, mighty strong'), privative or negative compounds (*wōhhandede* 'maimed-handed,' 'bad/wrong-handed,' *unġewitnes* 'foolishness,' more literally 'un-knowing-ness') to what might be called ironic or para-litotes compounds (*mæġenlēast* 'weakness, feebleness,' but more literally 'a mighty leastness'; Carr 1939, xix, 112, 122; Bauer 1983, 201–213 gives a good overview of the types of word-formation patterns). In Charles T. Carr's classic analysis, his 'Primary' compounds include those inherited from PIE and PGmc with the first member no longer inflected; 'Secondary' compounds are those that developed in the daughter Germanic languages (Carr 1939, 309–318). Secondary compounds may consist of ADJ + N formations, such as OE *middansumer* 'Midsummer' (literally 'middle summer').

'Nominal composition' refers to the processes of compound formation in a language's lexicon and any applicable rules in the grammar; for Sanskrit, this follows the scheme of the great grammarian of classical Sanskrit Pāṇini (said to have lived in the 5th century BC). It may be of some use in examining the Sanskrit grammarian's classification system for nominal composition, as it is one of the few early such systems for any Indo-European language, and the terminology of the Pāṇinian system is still in use by linguists and has been applied, at times fairly helpfully, to Old English.

dvandva: copulative compounds
tatpuruṣa: dependent compounds
karmadhāraya: descriptive compounds
bahuvrīhi: possessive compounds
avyayībhāva: adverbial compounds
dvigu compounds: compounds with numeral as first element (Modern German *Dreieck* 'triangle'; Carr 1939, xv)

1. **dvandva** (copulative compounds, commonly in the pattern N + N, and so declined in the dual, but in the plural if involving three or more members); literally < *dva* + *dva*, the copulative compound generally involves nouns that would be in the same case and linked by *ca* 'and,' for example, MdE *bread and butter* or *peanut butter and jelly (sandwich)*. Dvandvas are normally the only compound forms in Sanskrit that can involve more than two members; however, any compound can subsequently be

included in another compound formation. This type of compounding is naturally enough highly productive, as it involves a simple copulative function: MdE *bitter-sweet* and *sweet-and-sour* are examples – both adjectives, but the former accepted as a single form and the latter still considered phrasal and so hyphenated. Nearly any pairing of forms, adjective–adjective, noun–noun, can be so compounded:

इन्द्रावरुणौ **Indrāvaruṇau** 'Indra and Varuṇa' (taken grammatically in compounded form as dual)

देवगन्धर्वमानुषोरगरक्षसास् **devagandharvamānuṣorakṣasās** (*deva-gandharva-mānuṣa-uraga-rākṣasās*) 'gods and Gandharvas and men and serpents and demons' (a **dvandva** of 5 elements, plural in inflected form)

रामकृश्णौ **Rāmakṛṣṇau** 'Rāma and Kṛṣṇa'

ब्राह्मणक्षत्रियवैश्यशुद्राः **brāhmaṇakṣatriyavaiśyaśudrās** 'brahmins and kṣatriyas and vaiśyas and śudras' (the four major castes/varṇas considered as a unit)

To be considered in this class of dvandva-compounds may be OE kennings such as *mōd-ġehygd* ('mind-thought,' the OE forms make the compound perhaps rather more reduplicative than tautological – that is, it is of a type that works in poetry) and *mōd-ġeþonc* (again, 'mind-thought'; both occur in *Beowulf* and the latter, perhaps most famously, in *Cædmon's Hymn* 2b). Collective kinship terms may be considered dvandva compounds: *āþum-sweoran* 'son-in-law – father-in-law,' *suhter-(ġe-)fædran* 'uncle-and-nephew' (Lass 1994, 195).

2. **tatpuruṣa** ('that man (of his)') These 'dependent determinative' compounds can be either nouns or adjectives, depending upon the word class of the final element; in essence, the last member of the compound is defined further by the first, and the compound can express a relationship according to all the noun cases– for example, English determinative compounds such as *homemade* and *handmade* would be expressed in Sanskrit by means of grammatical case; in English they literally signify 'made **at** home' and 'made **by** hand.'

परस्मैपदम् **parasmaipadam**, n., 'word for another' (= active voice of verbs)

गुनोपेत **gunopeta** < **guna-upeta**, adj., 'endowed with virtues/qualities'

वर्षभोग्य **varṣabhogya**, adj., 'to be enjoyed for a year' (< *varṣa*, n., 'rainy season' = 'a year' + *bhogya* future passive participle of *bhuj* 'enjoy' [2nd conjugation])

युधिष्ठिर **Yudhiṣṭhira**, 'firm in battle'

This is a fairly common type of compound formation in OE poetry, many likely nonce formations (compare *īren-byrne* 'iron-byrnie' [*Beowulf* 2986b] and the ominous sounding *īren-þrēat* 'iron-company' [*Beowulf* 330b], likely referring to a band of warriors in iron armor); from *Beowulf* also, referring to Grendel in an ironic context, *sele-ġiest* 'hall-guest' (Lass 1994, 196).

3. **karmadhāraya** (descriptive determinative compounds): here once again the latter element (**B**) is further specified or defined by the former (**A**), but adverbially or

adjectivally so and not in a case-form relationship (the case for the overall **AB**-type compound is marked on the B-form, which is usually a noun/substantive).

सर्वगुण **sarvaguṇa**, n., 'all/every virtue/quality'
हिमशिशिर **himaśiśira**, adj., 'ice-cold'
जलान्तश्चन्द्रचपल **jala-antaś-candra-capala**, adj. 'fickle as the moon reflected in water'

The OE heroic poetic kenning *eaxl-ġestealla* ('comrade, companion'; literally, 'one who stands by [your] shoulder' or 'shoulder-to-shoulder-stander') may well be an example. So too OHG *snêblanc* (*Nibelungenlied* stanza 561: *Mit snêblanken gêren* 'with white-as-snow skirt bottoms'; this word *gêren*, for the wider bottom part of a skirt or underskirt, or triangular piece of cloth added to skirts, appears in Chaucer's 'Miller's Tale' in the description of the clothing of Alisoun, the Carpenter's wife: *ful of many a goore*; I.3237, which the editors gloss as 'flounces').

4. **bahuvrīhi** ('having much rice'; possessive compounds): though these compounds end in a substantive (a noun, or other word that functions as a noun), they modify another noun and agree with it in case, number, and gender. These are generally seen as exocentric compounds, with no explicitly stated 'head,' but refer to something outside the compound to which it is applied.

तथाविध **tathāvidha**, 'of such a kind'
देवरूप **deva-rūpa**, 'having the beauty of a god'

The poetic compound *ġeolu-rand* (*Beowulf* 438a) 'yellow-shield' (or 'yellow shield-boss' or 'shield-edge'); the reference is to either a gold rim round a wooden shield or to the color of a linden-wood shield (the color is elsewhere in the poem applied to such a shield at 2610a *ġeolwe linde*). *Bahuvrihi* compounds in Old, Middle, and Modern English were the subject of a German dissertation (Last 1925; see also Marchand 1969, 42–45). Werner Last's published dissertation counted among such 'copular' compounds OE *feax-hār* ('hoary-haired, grey-haired,' in a **BA** 'umkehrte' ['reversed'] pattern) and *ierre-mōd* ('wrathful-mind'; Last 1925, 11, 21).

5. **avyayībhāva** ('conversion to an indeclinable'; adverbial compounds): these are composed of an indeclinable in the first position followed by a noun in neuter singular accusative (highly commonly in *-am*).

प्रतिदोषम् **prati-doṣam**, 'at evening'
अनुगङ्गम् **anu-gaṅgam**, 'along the Ganges'

One may arguably include Old English *tō-morgen* 'tomorrow,' an adverb grammaticalized from a prepositional phrase **tō-morgenne* ('to the morrow/morning,' 'in the morning'), comprised of the prep. *tō* (which takes the dative, and which may be unmarked in such constructions) and the masc. a-stem noun *morgen*. Similarly constructed are *today* (**tō-dæġ*, though phrasal *tō dæġe* occurs in OE; it is first found glossing Latin adverb *hodie* [< *hōc diē* 'on this day'] as the form *todæġ* in King Alfred's version of Pope Gregory's *Pastoral Care*; OED, s.v. *today*) and *tonight* (Old English *tō niht*, which seems to be attested only in phrasal form until the late Middle English *Cursor Mundi* passage *Born to night your sauueour es!* 'Born tonight your Savior is!').

The proper names of Anglo-Saxon England form another rich source for the study of nominal morphology and Old English dialects, and they follow on naturally here as so many of them were dithematic, that is, comprised of two name elements: *Cyne-wulf*, 'regal-wolf,' or *wulf-stān*, 'wolf-stone,' the latter name likely also meant to be taken rather more allusively (as combining extended attributes of each element: fierceness of the former, and perhaps also its iconic representations, and the solidity and durability or steadfastness of the latter). William George Searle's great *Onomasticon Anglo-Saxonicum* (Searle 1897) may be dated, but it has not yet been fully superseded. The names range from the earliest inscriptions (on stone, or on coin issues, in Runic and Roman scripts) to (predominantly) West Saxon forms of the late Anglo-Saxon and early Anglo-Norman periods. It was with the personal names that one of the most dramatic transformations occurred – at least at the elite and administrative levels – to the nomenclature of England.

Names of moneyers on the coins they struck, as well as names appearing in charters of land owners (or grantors), often appear in the genitive case (*-es* for strong declension forms, *-an* for weak forms). There could be significant variability in spelling, especially in the legends on coins issues, often though not always with a royal portrait on the obverse, and an iconic design on the reverse (heraldic or religious or symbolic of rule). Eadbald of Kent (reigned 616–640) was the first English king known to have had coins minted; though rare, the gold *scillingas* or *thrym-sas* of Eadbald are imitative issues, modeled after Roman and Byzantine imperial issues, with the royal portrait in profile facing rightward on the obverse, on the reverse the *globus cruciger* (an orb surmounted by a cross) within a beaded circular border with a legend around that beading. The coins are lightweight for a gold issue (usually about 1.28 g) and of lower-quality gold content. The legend on the obverse around the royal portrait with Roman diadem is AVDVARLD REG[ES (probably for Latin *regis*, 'of king'; gen. sing.); interesting is the intrusive /r/ in this early Kentish spelling of Eadbald (semi-Latinate <v> for <b>). A specimen of this gold issue was first found in the Crondall Hoard (now in Oxford's Ashmolean Museum); the Billericay, Essex, specimen found in 1997 was on a slightly concave flan (the 'blank' on which the obverse and reverse dies were hammered) reminiscent of the Byzantine 'scyphate' concave issues. In each of the specimens found the obverse die is the same, but the reverses can vary. Specimens now at Pas-de-Calais and the Hunterian Museum, Glasgow, have reverse legends that seem partially blundered but have LONDENVS decipherable – that is, London being the mint. The Crondall specimen, like the other coins of this issue, has lettering that can have characters written backwards or upside down (and the <s> often looks very much like the *sigel* or *s*-rune). The monarch's name on the Crondall coin's obverse is AVDVAʁLĐ, with the <D> struck through. This might be taken as a Latin abbreviation for either Latin *-us* (nominative *Avdvarldus*) or *-i* (genitive *Avdarldi*), the latter of which would agree with REGES if taken as *regis* (producing 'of King Auduarldus'). But it may also be an early instance of the capital *eth* <Đ> (IPA /ð/; Williams 1998, 137–138; see also Shaw 2008, Abramson 2019, and Abramson 2023, who have confirmed the issue as belonging to Eadbald). Many early issues involve 'blundered' legends, their inscriptions the work of moneyers of varying levels of literacy (and some were perhaps unlettered, and made dies imitatively). Moneyer names are especially subject to great variability in spelling, or appear in unusual forms, and that can give linguists pause in asserting their value for the inscriptions' use in recording the sounds of Old English. Two interesting points emerge: for one, literacy was not limited solely to the clergy (and could not have been in the pre-Christian period, though that raises the question of the status of early rune-carvers), and the level of lay literacy could vary widely (some moneyers may have only needed to be able to record limited forms of names); secondly, much of our knowledge of the sounds of older languages is premised upon a basic notion that early users of scripts sought to record the sound of their language with as much fidelity as their system afforded. Then again, moneyer names may not necessarily record who actually struck the coin or ran the local mint, but under whose authority, beyond the king's, coinage was made. Numismatic evidence often requires the researcher to cross-reference with other sources (e.g., for early monarch names, Bede's *Ecclesiastical History*). At any rate, here we have an early gold coin of *Audbarld (= Eadbald) of Kent. On Anglo-Saxon onomastics and nomenclature, and the suggestion that 'Name are not nouns' (but perhaps 'nominals,' or noun or determiner phrases), see Colman 2014 (esp. 51–79).

Old English inherited from Germanic its system of nominal declensions, strong, weak, athematic, and root consonant 'minor' declensions. The strong declensions included *a*-stems, *ō*-stems, *i*-stems, and *u*-stems, that is, the stem vowel is that found at the end of the stem and before any inflectional ending (if any): for example, Greek ἄρκτος (*árktos*) 'bear,' may be analyzed as **arkt-o-s** (stem + thematic vowel + masculine nominative singular ending). Old English nominals were also inflected for gender, masculine, feminine, and neuter, and for number, singular and plural, with the exception of the 'dual' pronouns *wit* 'we two' (nom. *wit*, acc. *unc*, gen. *uncer*, dat. *unc*) and *ġit* 'you two' (nom. *ġit*, acc. *inc*, gen. *incer*, dat. *inc*). The cases are only four (Sanskrit had eight, Latin five): **nominative** (subject case, agent), **genitive** (possessive), **accusative** (direct object, though also used with prepositions that 'took' the accusative, i.e., required the object of the preposition to be in the accusative), and **dative** (indirect object, recipient in ditransitive constructions, and with prepositions that 'took' the dative). Thus, for the masculine *a*-stem *stān*:

	singular	plural
nominative	stān	stānas
accusative	stān	stānas
genitive	stānes	stāna
dative	stāne	stānum

As these 'pure' *a*-stems, so the *ja*- and *wa*-stems (which are all either masculine or neuter nouns). The feminine *ō*-stems decline as does *ġiefu* 'gift':

	singular	plural
nominative	ġiefu	ġiefa, ġiefe
accusative	ġiefe	ġiefa, ġiefe
genitive	ġiefe	ġiefa, ġiefena
dative	ġiefe	ġiefum

And so also the feminine *jō*- and *wō*-stems. The *i*-stem nouns were masculine, neuter, and feminine, as masc. *ġiest* 'guest':

	singular	plural
nominative	ġiest	ġiestas
accusative	ġiest	ġiestas
genitive	ġiestes	ġiesta
dative	ġieste	ġiestum

The *u*-stem nouns were masculine and feminine, as *hand* (fem.):

	singular	plural
nominative	hand	handa
accusative	hand	handa
genitive	handa	handa
dative	handa	handum

The 'weak' declensions generally have a vocalic stem (except for *-u*) and nasal consonant oblique (non-nominative) inflections (i.e., *-an*, *-ena*), such as masculine *steorra* 'star':

	singular	plural
nominative	steorra	steorran
accusative	steorran	stoerran
genitive	steorran	steorrena
dative	steorran	steorrum

The athematic nouns decline without the thematic vowels added to the stem in the preceding paradigms of 'strong' declensions. OE *mann/monn* 'man, human being(s)' (masc.) also exhibits the influence of *i*-umlaut in its paradigm in the dat. sing. and nom. and acc. pl. (whence the MdE *man/men* root vowel distinction in number):

	singular	plural
nominative	mann	menn
accusative	mann	menn
genitive	mannes	manna
dative	menn	mannum

As *mann* so also *fōt* 'foot' (masc.) and *bōc* (fem.), which also have *i*-umlauted forms in dat. sing. (and gen. sing. for *bōc*) and in the nominative and accusative plural (*fēt*, *bēċ*, the latter with palatalization of /k/ after the front vowel). Root consonant stems end, as expected, in consonants, as with the -*nd*-stem *frēond* (masc.), or the dental stem (*mōnaþ* masc. 'month' or *mæġeþ*/*mæġþ* fem. 'maiden, woman,' the latter a syncopated form after the loss of the vowel in the unaccented second syllable).

	singular	plural
nominative	frēond	frīende
accusative	frēond	frīende
genitive	frēondes	frēonda
dative	frēonde, frīend (*i*-umlaut)	frēondum

An old *r*-stem consonant declension included core terms of family relationship *fæder*, *mōdor*, *brōþor*, *sweostor*, *dohtor* ('father,' 'mother,' 'brother,' 'sister,' 'daughter'; *sunu* 'son' was a strong masculine *u*-stem). Umlauted forms occurred in the dat. sing. of *brōþor*, *sweostor*, *dohtor*: *brēþer*, *mēder*, *dehter* (Campbell OEG §629). Adjectives in OE likewise occur in the strong and weak declensions (following the nominal stem classifications: a-stem, ō-stem, ja-stem, jō-stem, etc.), the basic rule in Germanic being that an adjective was declined as 'strong' when 'bare,' i.e., when it was used alone in modifying a noun, and 'weak' when a demonstrative preceded the adjective: *hāliġ fǣmne* 'holy woman,' *sēo hāliġe fǣmne* 'the holy woman.' A strong wa-stem adjective such as *ġeolu* ('yellow') was declined as:

singular	masculine	feminine	neuter
nominative	ġeolu	ġeolu	ġeolu
accusative	ġeolone	ġeolowe	ġeolu
genitive	ġeolwes	ġeolore	ġeolwes
dative	ġeolwum	ġeolore	ġeolwum
instrumental	ġeolwe	ġeolore	ġeolu

plural	masculine	feminine	neuter
nominative	ġeolwe	ġeolwe/-wa	ġeolwe
accusative	ġeolwe	ġeolwe/-wa	ġeolu
genitive	ġeolora	ġeolora	ġeolora
dative	ġeolwum	ġeolwum	ġeolwum
instrumental	ġeolwum	ġeolwum	ġeolwum

Thus, as *Beowulf* 2610a with *ġeolwe linde* ('yellow linden-wood shield') *ġeolu* is declined strongly as accusative singular feminine. At 438a in the same poem *ġeolorand* ('yellow-shield,' again referring to a linden-wood shield) is accusative singular masculine, but the case is borne by the second element of this *karmadhāraya* (descriptive determinative) compound formation. In general, but not without some inconsistency in what survives in the manuscripts, the adjective will be declined weakly following a demonstrative (i.e., DEM + ADJ + N): a recipe in the 10th-century Bald's *Lǣċebōc*

('Leech-book,' physician's book) against jaundice begins *wið þære geolwan adle* ('for the yellow disease'), with the adjective declined weakly in the dative singular feminine. The weak paradigm of this adjective would be:

singular

	masculine	feminine	neuter
nominative	ġeolwa	ġeolwe	ġeolwe
accusative	ġeolwan	ġeolowan	ġeolwe
genitive	ġeolwan	ġeolwan	ġeolwan
dative	ġeolwan	ġeolwan	ġeolwan
instrumental	ġeolwan	ġeolwan	ġeolwan

plural

	masculine	feminine	neuter
nominative	ġeolwan	ġeolwan	ġeolwan
accusative	ġeolwan	ġeolwan	ġeolwan
genitive	ġeolora, ġeolwena	ġeolora, ġeolwena	ġeolora, ġeolwena
dative	ġeolwum	ġeolwum	ġeolwum
instrumental	ġeolwum	ġeolwum	ġeolwum

The diphthong in *ġeolu* is etymological, rather than the product of a spelling inserting *e* between the palatal consonant and back vowel *o*, and the wa-stem origin of the form can be seen in strong oblique cases (non-nominative) and in the weak paradigm (*ġeolu* < PGmc **gelwaz*; Ringe in Ringe and Taylor 2014, 4–5, 187).

The comparison of adjectives and adverbs followed the pattern that still obtains in English: positive/absolute (base form), comparative (+ *-ra*), superlative (+ *-ost*): *glēaw* 'wise,' *glēawra* 'wiser,' *glēawost* 'wisest.' These gradable forms can likewise be declined strong or weak, and with the suffixes deriving from PGmc **-izō* (comp.) and **-istaz* (superl.) some graded forms underwent mutation (*eald – ieldra – ieldest*, 'old, older, oldest'; *lang – lenġra – lenġest* 'long, longer, longest'; Campbell OEG §658; Ringe in Ringe and Taylor 2014, 225, 267).

As 'nominals', pronouns too were inflected for case, number, and gender, though the last marking had its complications. Personal pronouns were marked for gender in addition to case in the third-person singular (as retained by MdE *he/she/it*). The interrogative and indefinite *hw-* pronouns were marked for gender somewhat inconsistently:

nominative	hwā (masc. & fem.)	hwæt (neut.)
accusative	hwone (masc. & fem.)	hwæt (neut.)
genitive	hwæs (all genders)	
dative	hwǣm/hwām (all genders)	
instrumental	hwȳ (all genders)	

These are some of the *wh-* forms familiar from MdE: *hwā* (*who*), *hwām* (*whom*), *hwæs* (*whose*), *hwæt* (*what*); the spelling reflects a generally metathesized pronunciation of /hw-/ as /wh-/, though there are a number of dialects of BrE (especially in parts of Scotland and Ireland) and AmE (mountain South) that retain the 'aspirated' pronunciation (/hw-/).

Personal pronouns:

First person

	singular	pronouns
nominative	iċ	wē
accusative	mē	ūs
genitive	mīn	ūre
dative	mē	ūs

Second person

	sing	pl
nom	þū	ġē
acc	þē	ēow
gen	þīn	ēower
dat	þē	ēow

Third-person singular

	masculine	feminine	neuter
nom	hē	hēo	hit
acc	hine	hīe	hit
gen	his	hire	his
dat	him	hire	him

Third-person plural

nom	hīe (also: hī, hēo)
acc	hīe (also: hī, hēo)
gen	hira, heora
dat	him

Demonstrative pronouns ('that, those; the')

Singular				Plural
	masculine	feminine	neuter	(all genders)
nom	sē	sēo	þæt	þā
acc	þone	þā	þæt	þā
gen	þæs	þǣre	þæs	þāra, þǣra
dat	þǣm, þām	þǣre	þǣm, þām	þǣm, þām
instr	þon, þȳ		þon, þȳ	

The instrumental case, that which expresses 'by means of,' 'with' + instrument ('by hand,' 'with a sword,' etc.), is a vestige of a larger case system found in other branches of Indo-European (e.g., Sanskrit ***aśvena*** 'by means of a horse'); in OE it could be used in adverbials such as *for þon þe*, literally 'for that which' = 'because,' with the indeclinable relative particle *þe*, or *mid þȳ* 'by means of': compare *Beowulf* 2026ff.:

hafað þæs ġeworden   wine Scyldinga,
rīċes hyrde,   ond þæt rǣd talað,
þæt hē mid ðȳ wife   wælfǣhða dǣl,
sæċċa ġesette (2026–2029b).
[had then decided   the lord of the Scyldings,
keeper of the kingdom,   and that counsel taken,
that he by means of the woman   that share of slaughter-feudings,
of battles he would settle]

Here Hrothgar, king of the Danish Scyldings, speaks of having decided that 'by means of the woman' (*mid ðȳ wife*, the old instrumental case employed here) he would settle his old feuds and hostilities – that is by marrying off his daughter Freawaru to Ingeld, son of Froda, king of the Heathobards (a neighboring Germanic tribe not securely identified, though at times associated with the Langobards/Lombards). The use of case in nominal formations in Old English poetry is evidenced in the 'appositive style' (Robinson 1985): Hrothgar is alluded to in two nominative + genitive allusive formulas: **wine Scyldinga**, literally 'friend of the Scyldings' (nom. sing. + gen. pl.) and **rīċes hyrde**, 'of the kingdom the keeper' (gen. sing. + nom. sing.) What Hrothgar seeks to settle involves gen. pl. + acc. sing. + gen. pl. : **wælfǣhða dǣl, / sæċċa**. In the glossary to their updated edition of Friedrich Klaeber's magisterial *Beowulf*, Fulk, Bjork, and Niles list *sæċċa* as the acc. pl. of fem. jō-stem *sæċ(ċ)* but query whether it is gen. pl. (Fulk et al. 2008, 425). The gen. pl. seems the likelier interpretation as it would fit in with the sort of 'elliptical' constructions Old English often favors, especially in poetry: 'a share of the feuds, (a share) of the battles.' But in Old English, a stage of the history of the English language that was much more synthetic in its morphological typology, more inflectional, these are precisely the sorts of matters of translation one expects to be settled by case – except of course when case forms, as seen in some of the paradigms above, overlap, which was no doubt one of the reasons that accelerated inflectional attrition. Reduction in forms, as by simplification or even phonological overlap, can be seen in the OE demonstrative for which PDE has only 'this, these':

Demonstrative pronoun ('this, these')

Singular				Plural
	masculine	feminine	neuter	(all genders)
nom	þēs	þēos	þis	þās
acc	þisne	þās	þis	þās
gen	þisses	þisse	þisses	þissa
dat	þissum	þisse	þissum	þissum
instr	þȳs		þȳs	

Interrogatives were *hw-* forms (MdE *wh*-words) seen above, which could be used also as indefinite pronouns, as could *sum* 'some, a certain,' declined strongly.

4.3.1 Verbal Morphology

A verb is classically defined as the part of speech (or morphological class) that expresses being or existence, action, occurrence or happenstance (something that *happens*, as a natural result from some cause, or something rather more a result of *hap* or chance); additionally, it is the part of speech that in its finite forms (those forms except the infinitive: OE *gān*, MdE *to go*) is inflected for tense, number, person, voice, mood, and aspect (see ODEG and AHD5, s.v.). These inflections for such markings of the verb are added to the verbal root or stem (if not identical with the root – i.e., what expresses the semantic content of the verb: ***go****ing*, the root in bold) in what are called by classical grammarians *conjugations* (from the Latin for 'joinings, couplings').

The Old English preverbal, or verbal prefix, *ġe-* (which can appear as *ġi-* in early non-WS texts such as the *Épinal Glossary*; see Section 4.7) is for learners of Old English one of the more maddening features of the language. The unstressed particle, prefixed before verbs, nouns, past participle-derived adjectives, and sometimes pronouns and adverbs (e.g., the adv. *ġe-dafenlīċe*, 'in a suitable or proper manner') is of very high frequency in Old English texts, prose and poetry, and is usually explained as a vestigial feature inherited from Proto-Germanic (**ga-/*gi-*; compare Gothic *ga-*, Modern German *ge-/Ge-* with past participles and derivative noun formations), and often said to be of little consequence semantically:

> Verbal *ge-* in OE is not always meaningful. In many cases it is simply coopted as a marker of the past participle (as now in German, Dutch and Afrikaans). Or a non-participial verb may appear in either form, with no apparent semantic difference: *(ge-)ādlian* 'be(come) ill,' *(ge-)campian* 'fight.' When there is a clear sense, it is usually perfective or resultative: *ge-œrnan* 'gain by running' (*œrnan* 'run, ride, gallop'), *ge-ācsian* 'gain by asking' (*ācsian* 'ask'). In other cases the sense may be quite idiosyncratic, as in *ge-standan* 'endure' (*standan* 'stand'). (Lass 1994, 204)

Students making translations of Old English passages are often puzzled as to how to translate forms with the preverbal *ġe-*; on occasion it may be taken as otiose, and left untranslated, other times it is a marker of the perfective (here an aspectual category as well as tense marking), and possibly as expressing a range of other aspects: the *ġe-standan* example cited above might actually be an instance of the **frequentative** aspect, of one standing again and again, repetitively or continuously, in such a manner as to 'endure' or 'make a stand'; *ġe-standan* occurs four times in *Beowulf*, each in a heroic formula: the first when Wulfgar approaches and stands before Hrothgar (358b, *for eaxlum ġestōd*, with the tricky, idiomatic *for eaxlum*, literally 'before the shoulders,' which Klaeber takes as 'before the face, in front'; (Fulk et al. 2008, 141) though it may reflect the heroic *eaxl-* compounds (*eaxl-ġestealla* 'shoulder companion') with the sense of 'shoulder-to-shoulder,' at the same level, as fellow warriors – the following line's *cūþe hē duguðe þēaw* (359b) 'he knew the retainer's custom' (*duguðe* is gen. sing.) seems to indicate a tribal custom and perhaps also Wulfgar's high status in the war-band; the second occurs in the same passage – Beowulf's arrival at the court of the Scyldings at Heorot – as Beowulf comes to stand before Hrothgar the king: *heard under helme, þæt hē on heo[r]ðe ġestod* (404) 'hard under helm, so that he stood at the hearth' (Klaeber's emended manuscript *heoðe* to *heorðe*), which seems another formula of a hero taking up a stand (by some custom of drawing up to a leader); the third comes in the poem's second half in the fight with the dragon as Beowulf tries to withstand its onslaught: *Stīðmōd ġestod wið stēapne rond /winia bealdor* (2566–2567a) 'Hard-spirited he stood with his upright shield / the lord of companion-friends' ('upright' for *stēapne* is the suggestion from Clark Hall-Meritt; CHM, s.v. *stēap*), and here a heroic 'taking up a stand' makes sense (as well as the need for *ġe-stōd* for the meter [*metri causa*]); and fourthly, when all but Wiglaf of his troop of Geats abandon Beowulf in this fight: *Nealles him on hēape handgesteallan / æðelinga bearn ymbe gestōdon* (2596–2597) 'Not at all about him in a heap the hand-companions (warriors) / the son of princes did they stand'; the poetic syntax has *him* (= Beowulf) described appositively as *æðelinga bearn*, and, very literally, the order has 'Not at all him in a heap the hand-companions / the son of princes about did they stand.' A recent preliminary study of the *ġe-* preverbal in OE (McFadden 2015) points to the frequent use of it in OE to express the perfect, especially in a resultative (change of state) sense, which may be tentatively linked to resultative periphrastic perfect constructions in MdE (*have* + past ptc.; McFadden 2015, 30–31; compare *Beowulf* 1196b *ġefraġen hæbbe* 'have I heard tell'). Next in frequency was the use of *ġe-* in passive constructions, which may have been significantly influenced by Latin use as Anglo-Saxon clerics and scholars made their translations: Ælfric (ca. 955–ca. 1010)[5] translated Latin 1st singular passive perfect *osculatus sum* quite literally (and correctly) as *ic eom ġecyssed* ('I am kissed'; Mitchell OES §775 fn. 196). If OE perfect forms of *habban* (sing. *hæfde*, pl. *hæfdon*) + past ptc. are not as frequent in MdE (OE instead using more frequently the simple past/preterite), where they do occur they seem to overlap with where we would opt for the perfect form (over simple past; see Taylor in Ringe and Taylor 2014, 434–435). Prefixed to nouns *ġe-* can have a "collectivizing/perfectivizing" sense (Lass 1994, 198): *ġe-brōðor* 'brothers,' *ġe-brōðru* 'brethren; fellow man' (CHM, the latter sense in OE translation of Genesis and the Gospel of John). It turns out that this vexing unstressed particle *ġe-* is a remarkably important part of OE morphology, even if its uses are not entirely understood:

1. As a marker of the past (passive) participle (Taylor in Ringe and Taylor 2014, 434)
2. As a marker of the analytic (or, periphrastic) passive participle: *beon ġeoffrode* 'be offered,' *wesan ġehaled* 'be healed' (Taylor in Ringe and Taylor 2014, 489)
3. Prefixed to collective nouns: *ġe-fēran* (nom. pl.) 'companions, fellow-farers'

[5] Ælfric of Eynsham, sometimes called 'Grammaticus' ('the Grammarian'); his literary output consists of two series of 'Catholic Homilies,' a series of Lives of the Saints (commissioned by the Ealdorman Æthelweard and his son Æthelmær), Biblical translations into Old English, the *Colloquy* (for training novitiates in Latin), a Grammar (of Latin) and Glossary (bilingual in Latin-Old English), among other writings (some of disputed attribution).

4. As an aspectual marker of verbs (perfective, possibly also frequentative, or as an intensifier or resultative: *frignan* 'ask, inquire,' *ġe-frignan* 'learn [as by having inquired]'; there may also be a quasi-causative sense here
5. Adding a sense of 'inclusivity' to indefinite pronouns: *hwa* 'someone, anyone,' *ġe-hwā* 'everyone' (Campbell OEG §719; but see caveat Mitchell OES §448)

In the broadest sense the *verb* expresses action, but action *in action* – whether this action is material, spiritual, mental, or imaginary, with an object or without, through time (the 'marked' or finite forms) or above it (the *infinitive* form: *to think*, *to walk*), in morphologically simple form (*I go*, *she goes*) or compound or complex formations (*I did go*, *she would have gone*). A preliminary distinction between nouns and verbs might be drawn by observing that though both can describe actions, the former describes them in a stative or 'walled-off' manner, as a *substantive*, that which has substance, of whatever shape or form – for example, *substantive*, *substance*, and *substantiation* are nouns, while *substantiate* (from which that last noun was derived by affixation), is a verb; the latter describes action in a dynamic fashion with much more complex markings: person (1st, 2nd, 3rd), number (singular, plural), tense (literally, 'time,' a loan to Middle English from Old French *tens*, Modern French *temps*, from Latin *tempus*, whence English *temporary*, *temporal*), voice (active, middle/mediopassive/reflexive, passive), mood (indicative, subjunctive, imperative), aspect (this last category of the verb is often missing in modern basic grammars, as it is sometimes folded into tense: perfective and progressive aspects, though there are others).

The **main verb** bears the semantic content of the action: *I did* ***go***, *she would have* ***gone*** (main verb forms in bold). An **auxiliary verb** assists the main verb in a 'helping' function. These are further subdivided into: (1) **main** (or **primary**) **auxiliaries**: *be have do*, which can assist main verbs in forming tense, voice, mood, aspect: *be* can also serve as a **linking** or **copular** verb, immediately equating subject and predicate, often in stative or existential fashion (as can *estar* and *ser* in Spanish); (2) **modal**: a group of 'helping' verbs that can express mood, modality, aspect, such as *can, could, may, might, must, shall, should, will, would*; there are also some other verbs sometimes called **semi-modals** or **marginal modals** (*dare, need, ought to, used to*), and English has long had forms of *dōn/do* functioning in this capacity, or as an emphatic form (the 'dummy auxiliary': *I went* versus *I did go*). **Participles** are finite verb forms often used in compound or complex multi-word verb phrases (what can also be called the **EF, expanded form**). The present participle has over its history in English taken forms such as *-ende* (OE) or *-ing* and can be used to indicate progressive aspect (present progressive *I am going*, past progressive *I was going*, etc.); it can also function as a deverbal adjective (*the running bear*) or as a nominal (*Running is good exercise, sometimes*; this is classically termed the **gerund**). The past participle can be used to express the perfective aspect in EF verb phrases (*We had gone*), and is also used adjectivally (*the broken chair*), with forms normatively in OE in *-ed/-de/-od* (but also *-en*) and in MdE in *-ed/-en*. So with the form *baked* one can have: (1) the past participle functioning as an adjective in *We had some baked beans*; (2) as the past participle in the passive construction *The beans were baked too long* (AHD5, s.v. *participle*, e.g.). The **infinitive** is the unmarked form of a verb as one its principal parts (infinitive, present singular, preterite singular, past participle); in Old English the basic infinitive form was *-an/-ian*, which was lost during the Middle English period (*-an* > *-en* > *-e* > Ø), and in MdE is periphrastic in form: *to* + verbal root/stem (by contrast, a synthetic language such as Spanish preserves the old Latin termination in reduced form: **cambiar, vivir, tener, reír**). The marking for time is **tense**, and generally one can speak of three *simple* tenses (present, past, future): the actuality is much more complex (e.g., the past tense is really "the marked tense, marked for separation from the speaker's 'now'" [ODEG]); this marking for time can be compounded with aspect to mark the **progressive** and **perfective**; linguists have noted other aspects of the verb, such as **inchoative/inceptive** (*It's* ***getting*** *light outside*; the vestigial Germanic inchoative/inceptive with *-n-* is found in some verbs with *-en*: *quicken*, *darken*, etc.) or **durative/continuative** (*I'm* ***still*** *reading it*; MdE marks this adverbially), **habitual** (*We* ***used to*** *go there all the time*), **terminative/cessative** (*I just* ***finished*** *reading your paper*), among others. The regional and informal AmE use of *fixin'* as a modal auxiliary may involve a sort of double-inchoative/inceptive in forms such as *I'm fixin' to get ready to go*, in the sense of 'preparing to prepare to X' or 'thinking of getting ready/preparing to X,' or it may be an instance of the **doubal modal** as found in Appalachian English (*We might could go if/iffen it don't rain*).

Modern English has a great many **phrasal verbs** that can present initial difficulties for second-language learners who look to a more literal analysis of their surface pattern, usually V + Prep, though a number of these *prepositional verbs* (or *multi-word verbs*) are not separable: for example, *Look after one another*, *look after* does not admit an Obj (such as a N/NP or Pron) to be embedded in the core V + Prep structure, whereas *look* ***it*** *up* does. In Old English it is questionable whether one should analyze co-occurrence of verbs with seemingly set prepositions as phrasal verbs: *cuman* + *tō* 'come to/toward,' *ahebban* + *up*/*on* 'lift up, raise (up),' *awendan* + *of*,' which may, literally, be directional, 'turn away/ away from,' or by metaphorical extension mean 'turn from X into Y,' 'change, alter,' even 'translate from': and with *tō* one can have 'translate from...to...'; for example, in Ælfric's Preface to Genesis, *ic cweðe nu ðæt ic ne dearr ne ic nelle nane boc æfter ðisre of ledene on englisc awendan*, very literally: 'I say now that I not dare nor I not wish (*nelle* < *ne-wille*) none book after this from Latin into English turn/translate' (DOE, s.v. *lēden*). The Old English syntax is 'freer' than that of Modern English (and the construction here is verb-final – a user of MdE would move the main verb leftward 'I dare not nor wish to translate...'), as OE was more synthetic than MdE (relying somewhat more on inflections), though Modern English does exhibit what linguists call 'P-stranding' (preposition-stranding): *She is someone you can talk to* versus *You can talk to her*, in which, in the former, the preposition has been detached from its object (on this in OE and MdE, see Taylor in Ringe and Taylor 2014, 443–446). The question of 'univerbation,' that is, the process by which such V + Prep (or in OE, Prep/Adv + V) formations become grammaticalized (to the extent that they are written as one form), is a tricky one in the history of English. In OE, prepositional prefixes could be considered separate from the verbs they were indeed modifying, or become grammaticalized (and lexicalized, in the sense of that term involving semantic change – which is what 'phrasal verbs' usually involve – a new or extended sense from the literal combination of verb + particle compoundings); for example, *tō-*, had the sense 'to, toward, besides, for the purpose that,' though as a prefixed adverbial it could be an intensifier with a sense of 'fully, completely, thoroughly'; or *æt-* usually denoted 'at, by, near, upon,' in both locative and temporal senses, but could also be used to indicate the instrumental, with nouns in the dative: *æt fēawum wordum*, 'in/with few words' (CHM, s.v.). Such forms could be considered separate from the verbs they were indeed modifying, or become grammaticalized – and lexicalized, in the sense of that term involving semantic change – which is what 'phrasal verbs' usually involve – a new or extended sense from the literal combination of verb + particle combinations. Thus we can see pairs of semantically extended or distinct unaffixed and phrasal (affixed) verbs: *breġdan* ('move quickly, pull, swing, drag') and *ætbreġdan* ('take away, carry off, escape, rescue, release'), *standan* ('stand, remain, stand first or fast') and *ætstandan* ('stand still, stand at or near, remain, resist'), *sprecan* ('speak, say, utter') and *fore-sprecan* ('to speak or answer for, be surety for, intercede for'; CHM, s.v.).

English inherited from its Germanic roots a system of seven classes of strong verbs. Verbs considered 'strong' undergo a root vowel change (or mutation or ablaut) to indicate the past/preterite tense. There are seven gradation series or patterns of root vowel change. These existed in Old English (c. 500–1100) and continue to this day. The primary parts of the verb listed are: base form (infinitive), past, past participle.

Class 1: root vowel no longer changes; generally the voiceless suffix (*-t*) indicates past; a number of verbs of this class have been remodeled as regular: burn/burnt ~ burn/burned, spoil/spoilt ~ spoil/spoiled

burn / burnt / burnt
lend / lent / lent
have / had / had
make / made / made

also includes: dwell, learn, spill, spell, spill, bend, build, rend, send, spend, have

Old English: rīdan 'ride'

rīdan	rād	ridon	riden

[infinitive, 3rd sing. pret. indic., 3rd pl. pret. indic., past participle]

Present

	singular	plural
1st	rīde	rīdaþ
2nd	rītst (rīdes)	rīdaþ
3rd	rīt(t) (rīdeþ)	rīdaþ

Preterite

	singular	plural
1st	rād	ridon
2nd	ride	ridon
3rd	rād	ridon

present participle: *rīdende*
past participle: *riden*, *ġeriden*

The paradigm is simpler in the subjunctive and imperative: *rīde* (pres. subj. sing.), *rīden* (pres. subj. pl.); *ride* (pret. subj. sing.), *riden* (pret. subj. pl.); *rīd!* (imper. sing.), *rīdaþ!* (imper. pl.). Old English had, in addition to the base infinitive form in *-an*, and the inflected infinitive form *tō* root-*enne*/*-anne*: *tō rīdenne*. The infinitive is in origin formed on the nom./acc. sing. of a neuter verbal noun (e.g., **rīdanā*); the inflected form of the infinitive, which some handbooks classify as a gerund, is likewise a verbal *ja*-stem noun in the dative (Hogg 1992, §6.8 and notes 5–6). The sense of the inflected infinitive (gerund) is one of need, expected outcome, obligation: with weak class III verb *seċġan* 'say, tell' the inflected infinitive form *tō seċġanne* has the sense 'for to tell,' 'in the telling (of)' – compare *Beowulf* 473a, where Hrothgar, king of the Scyldings said (*Hrōðgār maþelode* – the latter the 3rd sing. pret. of weak class II *maþelian*): *Sorh is mē tō secganne* ("A sorrow it is to me to have to tell"). Dialectal variation in verb forms is common in Anglian, especially Northumbrian, varieties: the 2nd and 3rd sing. forms *rīdes* and *rīde* above, or 3rd pl. pret. *riodan* (*Beowulf* 3169a), with back umlaut (Ringe in Ringe and Taylor 2014, 319–320; Fulk et al. 2008, cxxxviii, §14).

Class 2: root vowel change: ea > o, e > o, or no vowel change; the past participle form in *-(e)n* varies with the regular form in *-(e)d* (thus the p.p. of *show* can be either *shown* or *showed*, though there is also archaic and generally BrE *shewn*)
show / showed / shown

sew / sewed / sown

also includes: mow, shear, swell, saw

OE: bēodan 'command'

bēodan	bēad	budon	boden

Class 3: all three principal parts are the same, though the pronunciation of the vowel in the past and past participle forms differs from that in the present stem
keep / kept / kept
feel / felt / felt
say / said / said
*dream / dreamt / dreamt (this verb has also been remodeled to *dream / dreamed / dreamed*, which does not exhibit the change in pronunciation of root vowel)
kneel / knelt / knelt

also includes: lose, hear, lean, leap, buy

OE: bindan 'bind'

bindan	band	bundon	bunden

Class 4: root vowel change: ea > o, e > a > e, i > o > i; the past participle has the inflection *-(e)n*
break / broke / broken
speak / spoke / spoken
tear / tore / torn
write / wrote / written
see / saw / seen

also includes: hide, lie, blow, take, bite

OE: beran 'carry'

beran	bær	bǣron	boren

Class 5: the three principal parts are the same, as is the pronunciation of the root vowel (unlike strong verbs of class 3)
hit / hit / hit
burst / burst / burst
wet / wet / wet

also includes: hurt, put, cut, set, let, *fit (there is also the regular form *fit/fitted/fitted* in the causative sense 'to cause to be the proper size and shape,' for example, *She was fitted for her wedding gown*, though there is some overlap between the forms), sweat, quit, cast

OE: etan 'eat'

etan	æt	ǣton	eten

Class 6: root vowel change from the present form, with the past and past participle forms identical
find / found / found
dig / dug / dug
sting / stung / stung
hold / held / held

also includes: feed, bleed, fight, win, *get (in AmE the past participle forms *got* can be used in the sense of possessing, *gotten* in the sense of having obtained), speed, light

OE: faran 'go, fare (forth)'

faran	fōr	fōron	faren

Class 7: patterns such as i > a > u or o > a > o / u > a > u are common
sing / sang / sung
swim / swam / swum
run / ran / run

also includes: drink, ring, shrink, begin, come

OE: fōn 'seize, grab'

fōn	fēng	fēngon	fangen

The root vowel changes in the strong classes are what have led to the description 'strong'; with the three classes of 'weak' verbs (Roman numerals are customary in enumerating them, I-III), the preterite is marked by the insertion of a dental (usually *d*) rather than a gradation series of root vowel changes. For instance, weak class I *fremman* 'do, perform' has in its present forms *fremme, frem(e)st, frem(e)þ* for 1st 2nd 3rd sing., *fremmaþ* in the plural number (all persons); the preterite forms are: *fremede, fremedest, fremede* (sing.), *fremedon* (pl.), with *-d-* affixation.

fremman 'to do, make, accomplish,' weak class I

Present

	singular	plural
1st	fremme	fremmaþ
2nd	fremest	fremmaþ
3rd	fremeþ	fremmaþ

Preterite

	singular	plural
1st	fremede	fremedon
2nd	fremedest	fremedon
3rd	fremede	fremedon

Modern English calls these verbs 'regular,' though strong verbs were the commoner paradigm. Form a new verb in English, either *de novo* (new coinage) or by a suffix such as *-ize/-ise*, and its conjugation will be weak ('regular'): to use an earlier example, *to Smurf, Smurfing, Smurfed, Smurfed.* Jocular forms can be formed on the strong patterns (*Smurf – Smarf – Smurfen*), but English has in its history not only leveled paradigms but remodeled strong verbs on weak models. Additionally, Old English had six classes of preterite-present verbs in which the present forms, 1st and 3rd singular, look as if preterite: for example, *witan* 'know,' 1st/3rd sing. present *wāt*. And lastly are the anomalous verbs *dōn* 'do,' *gān* 'go,' *bēon* 'be.'

A number of high-frequency verbs in OE are from weak class I: *cennan* 'produce, beget, give birth, bring forth,' *dēman* 'judge, decide,' *herian* 'praise,' *lǣran* 'teach,' *sellan* 'give.' Weak class II *þancian* 'thank, give thanks' has present forms *þanciġe, þancast, þancaþ* (singular), and *þanciaþ* (pl., all numbers); preterite forms *þancode, þancodest, þancode, þancodon* (pl., all numbers). Weak class III *habban* 'have' in the present has the forms *hæbbe, hæfst, hæfþ* (sing.), *habbaþ* (pl., all numbers), and in the preterite *hæfde, hæfdest, hæfde* (sing.), *hæfdon* (pl., all numbers). With *habban* one can easily discern the Early Modern forms *have, hast* (*have-st), *hath* (*have-th). 'Preterite-present' verbs are those that were once strong verbs that came to be conjugated with preterite forms in the present, a shift likely semantically induced: the classic example is Greek (*oîda*), (*oîda*), 'I know,' but deriving from a sense 'Having seen therefore I know' (Sanskrit *veda*, originally 'knowledge,' < PIE **weyd-* 'see'). The Old English reflex of PIE **weyd-* is *witan* 'to know,' and its paradigm makes clear the 'preterite'-look of the present stem:

witan 'to know,' preterite-present class I

Present

	singular	plural
1st	wāt	witon
2nd	wāst	witon
3rd	wāt	witon

Preterite

	singular	plural
1st	wisse	wisson
2nd	wissest	wisson
3rd	wisse	wisson

The Old English preterite-present verbs, relatively few in number but of very high frequency in use, are generally classed as belonging to 5–7 types (Campbell OEG §767; Hogg 1992, §§6.131–140). Among these high-frequency verbs are *āgan* 'to possess' (whence MdE *own*), *cunnan* 'to know, be familiar with' (whence MdE *can*, the historical sense being 'I know how to therefore I can'), *ġe-man* 'to remember,' *mōt(an)* 'must' (from a sense 'be allowed to, need to, be compelled to'), *magan* 'to be able, to have the power to.' The present forms of *magan* were *mæġ*, *meaht*, *mæġ* (sing.) and *magon* (pl.), and the preterite *meahte* (*mihte*), *meahtest* (*mihtest*), *meahte* (*mihte*; sing.), *meahton* (pl.). This last verb has two reflexes in MdE: *may* (from *mæġ*, 1st and 3rd pres. sing.) and *might* (from *meahte/mihte*, 1st and 3rd pret. sing.); their semantic development is quite interesting: both preserve, *might* better than *may*, the original sense of 'power' or 'strength' (the Old English nominal form was *i*-stem *miht/mieht*): *may* can indicate permission, as in polite question formulations, and *might* potentiality, but both derive from a sense of 'being able to' < 'having the power/ability/strength to.' Such semantic ranges in preterite-present verbs are alluded to in the old parochial school quip that when asked, 'Can I go to the bathroom?' the nun replies, 'I am sure you *can*, but no you *may* not.'

Rounding out Old English verbs are those classes categorized as 'anomalous,' *willan* 'wish, be willing,' *dōn* 'to do,' *gān* 'to go,' and *bēon-wesan* 'to be,' all of which now function also as auxiliaries. The forms of *willan* and *dōn* are: *wille*, *wilt*, *wile* (pres. sing.), *willaþ* (pres. pl.), *wolde*, *woldest*, *wolde* (pret. sing), *woldon* (pret. pl.); *dō*, *dēst*, *dēþ* (pres. sing.), *dōþ* (pres. pl.), and *dyde*, *dydest*, *dyde* (pret. sing.), *dydon* (pret. pl.). 1st and 3rd pret. sing. can be found in a number of OE variant forms, *dede* (*y* > *e* in Kentish OE, but a feature found also in Anglian dialects), and many more in Middle English (*deude*, *didde*, *dued*, *dode*, *dude*, *gedide*), and now simply *did*. The verbs *gān* and *bēon-wesan* are **suppletive**, their paradigms filled out with forms from originally separate verbs.

Present

	singular	plural	singular	plural
1st	gā	gāþ	eom	sindon, sint
2nd	gǣst	gāþ	eart	sindon, sint
3rd	gǣþ	gāþ	is	sindon, sint

Preterite

	singular	plural	singular	plural
1st	ēode	ēodon	wæs	wǣron
2nd	ēodest	ēodon	wǣre	wǣron
3rd	ēode	ēodon	wæs	wǣron

The suppletion of *gān* with *ēod-* forms involves some uncertainty about what verbs *ēode* and *ēodon* were drawn from. The root is presumably PGmc **iij-* (PWGmc **ij-*, OE **io-*) for which the Gothic 1st and 3rd pret. sing. *iddja* 'walked, went' offers support (*iddja* itself a suppletive form to irregular Gothic verb *gaggan*). But there are difficulties in explaining the diphthong *io* as there is little evidence of the spelling in early OE (Ringe in Ringe and Taylor 2014, 371). OE has also a strong class 7 *gangan*, 'to go, walk, move,' which has the forms *gange, gengst, gengþ* (pres. sing.), *gangaþ* (pres. pl.), and *ġēong/gang, ġēonge, ġēong/gang* (pret. sing.), *ġēongon/ġīengon* (pret. pl.), with some other variants. But *gangan* could also use the suppletive *ēod-* forms (which derive from a weak verb; Ringe in Ringe and Taylor 2014, 348). The matter of *bēon-wesan*, as the verb of greatest frequency in OE, is even more complicated as it is 'multiply suppletive' (Ringe in Ringe and Taylor 2014, 372–372; Ringe 2021, 37–38). A speaker of MdE can recognize that the *am, are, is* forms, *was* and *were*, and *be* forms must be from originally distinct verbal roots. Indeed, the MdE verb 'to be' in its principal parts may derive from four sources: PIE *$h_1$es- 'to be,' 1st sing. *$h_1$esmi 'I am' and 3rd sing. *$h_1$esti 'he/she is' gave us the *eom* and *is* forms (though the former not without some complication: *eom* a reflex of PGmc *immi? See Ringe in Ringe and Taylor 2014, 373); *er- or *h_1e$h_1$óre 'he/she arrived/is there' may be ultimately behind *eart* (Hogg 1992, §6.146; Ringe 2017, 178); PIE *b^huH- (perhaps *b^huh_2-) 'become, be' is behind the *bēon* forms; and PIE *$h_2$wes- 'to stay, remain; be,' PGmc *wesaną are behind the strong class 5 verb *wesan* in OE, with /s/ ~ /r/ alternation in *wæs* and *wǣre* by Verner's Law. Lastly, the original *sind/sint* form in the pres. pl. were remodeled on the plural forms in preterite-present forms and derive ultimately from the optative forms of PIE *$h_1$es- (see especially Hogg 1992, §§6.146–150). The *bēon* forms are as close as Old English comes to a synthetic or inflectional future tense in OE: *bēo* 'I be' but also 'I shall be' (Campbell OEG §768; Hogg 1992, §6.146). These *be*-forms could express consuetudinal (habitual) aspect (not entirely unlike AAVE *be-* aspectual usages such as *I be/bees goin'*), and were also seen as constituting 'perfective present' expressing "statements which are always true" (Ringe 2021, 38): perhaps the sense that 'having (always) been so, I am.' The *be* and *have* forms were used as well to mark the perfective aspect (*had gone, had been reading*): *hæfde ġecoren* ('had chosen'), *ġedon habban wolde* ('would have done'; Taylor in Ringe and Taylor 2014, 434–439).

Adverbs could be formed in a number of ways: the commonest method was *-līċe*, the adverbial form of the adjectival suffix *-līċ*; this survives in MdE in *suchlike, childlike*, and is highly productive in the reduced form *-ly*. The suffixes *-inga* and *-unga* could function similarly, *eall* 'all' > *eallunga* 'entirely, altogether'; rarer was adverbial suffix *-a*: the adj. *til* 'good' > *tela* 'well'; the accusative and dative cases of adjectives could be used adverbially: the acc. sing. neut. (*efen* 'even'), gen. sing. (*dæġlanges* 'day-long, for a day'), dat. sing. (*ǣne* 'alone,' < *ān* 'a, one, each'; adj.), and dat. pl. (*hwīlum* 'at times,' < *hwīl*; noun). The adverb *wēl(l)* 'well,' from *gōd* 'good,' seems to be a suppletive form. While the adverb in PIE may have been more an inflectional marking, and could still be formed this way in OE (e.g., by the dative singular *-e*), in English, the processes of formation seem rather more derivational; the main patterns of adverb formation were:

1. Affixation of *-e* to the adjectival suffix *-līċ*

    beorht-līċe 'brightly'

    ġielp-līċe 'boastfully'

    samod-līċe 'together' ['together-ly'] (here the adverbial suffix has been added to an adverb, *samod* 'together, simultaneously,' in what may seem a tautological formation but is perhaps rather more an intensifying one)

2. Inflectional *-a* (from a PIE *o*-stem ablative in some instances; Lass 1994, 207) and *-e* (< a vestigial ablative as well, but dat. sing. in OE)
   hearde 'firmly, severely' (a sort of doublet formed as more frequent was the adv. *heard-līċe*)
   ēaþe 'easily'
   hraðe 'hastily, quickly, immediately'
   ġeāra 'formerly, of yore' (this is from the gen. pl. of *ġēar* 'year'

3. Inflectional *-es* (gen. sing. neut.)
   dæġes 'by day' ['of the day']
   ealles 'wholly, entirely' ['of all']
4. Inflectional *-um* (dat. pl.)
   furðum 'even, already, at first' [another adv. derived from an existing adv, *furðor*, 'later, further']
   hwīlum 'sometimes, once' ['at times']

Comparison of adverbs was normatively by suffixation of *-or* (comp.) and (superl.); comparative *-licor* and superlative *-licost* appear with short /i/; cf. Hogg and Fulk 2011, §4.77)

4.4 THE FATE OF BRITISH LATIN – CELTIC LANGUAGES IN SAXON BRITAIN – CELTIC LOANS TO OLD ENGLISH – THE CELTIC QUESTION: EARLY CONTACT SITUATIONS

To turn back to the cultural context of the development of Old English, the historical and political consequences of the Battle of Chester in AD 616 are more evident, as they are the more documented (in the *Anglo-Saxon Chronicle* and Welsh sources such as the triads and *The History of the Kings of Britain* of Welshman Geoffrey of Monmouth), than the linguistic repercussions. But the severing of Cumbric-speaking lands by the Northumbrian victory had its consequences for both Old Welsh and Cumbric and Old English. While Welsh would remain actively spoken in Wales, beyond Offa's Dyke, despite a decline in the numbers of speakers and loss of prestige with the advance of English power westward in Britain and the passage of discriminatory measures against the Welsh language in its future, Cumbric would find itself surrounded by Old English, specifically the Anglian Northumbrian dialects. Handbooks have the tendency to refer to as 'Northumbrian' such early texts as the glosses to the Lindisfarne Gospels or northern copies of poems such as "Cædmon's Hymn," though there were of course dialects in so broad a region as Northumbria (with local variants marking Deira and Bernicia, perhaps with some Celtic influence). Presumably, Cumbric-speakers would undergo a language shift, some relatively quickly, many within a few generations. But there is evidence for the persistence of Cumbric into the later medieval period, with extinction perhaps only in the 13th century.

Bernicia and Deira, two kingdoms carved out of what is now Southeastern Scotland and Northeastern England in the 6th century by the Angles, and absorbed into Northumbria in the 7th, can be seen as linguistic borderlands in the transitional sub-Roman and early Anglo-Saxon periods. Both territories have likely p-Celtic names (i.e., of the Brythonic Celtic languages: here, Cumbric), and recent work has suggested that the extent of p-Celtic place-names preserved in Bernicia in particular is much greater than previously thought (Hough 2004; Fox 2007). Place-name studies in Scotland had perhaps a tendency to concentrate upon the Gaelic (Q-Celtic) rather than the Brittonic/Brythonic (P-Celtic), a matter also of greater ease in corroboration as the former survives as a minority community language in Western Scotland and the Isles, while the latter went extinct in either the 12th or 13th century. But Cumbric is a bridge between eras: from the sub-Roman to early Anglian, with the interactions of British (Cumbric), Gaelic (Dal Riadic), and Anglian/Northumbrian Old English, and from late Anglo-Saxon England to the Norman period, with the interactions of fading Cumbric, Gaelic, Old Norse, Old English/northern Middle English, and Norse-Gaelic mixtures that were even more prevalent further north, such as in the 'northern isles' (Orkneys and Shetland), with the additional factor of Hiberno-Norse.

References in English, Scots, and Irish sources to Strathclyde Britons, Cumbrians (David I of Scotland had as one of his titles 'Prince of the Cumbrians,' a principality over which he ruled 1113–1124), and 'Brets' continue beyond the Conquest and one can see in Southern Scotland a relatively complex language picture emerge: minority populations of Cumbric-speakers (the last generations of such), increasing and encroaching Gaelic speakers from further north, relatively limited numbers of Norman French speakers, and speakers of what were Northumbrian varieties of Old English that were being reshaped in the post-Conquest period into Northern varieties of Middle English. Interesting is that at least the last three groups show significant influence from Scandinavian. Norman French was, of course, the variety of French spoken by descendants of the *Norðmanna*, Vikings who has besieged Paris and Orléans and other French cities and settled in Northern France, Normandy bearing witness to their legacy with its very name. But the Normans had already undergone a language shift before their invasion of England in the 11th century. It is an example highly relevant to the history of the English language if seldom applied: a conquering group settles into a permanent occupation in the position of a ruling minority population; the language of the subject population is adopted perhaps within generations, certainly within a couple of centuries. The scenario of the Gallicized Vikings anticipates some of the linguistic consequences of 1066. At any rate, Northern England and Southern Scotland in the first few Norman centuries were linguistic sites abounding in contact situations.

The career of the aforementioned King David, first Prince of the Cumbrians, then King of Scotland (1124–1153), provides some detail to the processes of change. Dabíd mac Maíl Coluimb, son of Máel Colum mac Donnchada (Duncan, Donnchad mac Crínáin) – these are Scots Gaelic names and one sees how close the forms and nomenclature still were with the Irish – upon the death in 1124 of his brother Alaxandair mac Maíl Coluimb, Alexander I of Scotland (Alba), fought a decade-long struggle against his nephew Máel Coluim mac Alaxandair for control of the Kingdom of Alba. Gaining that, his long rule over Scotland witnessed a number of reforms to Church and state, some of them patterned after Norman and Anglo-Norman models. During the struggle over succession in Scotland,

1093–1097, David was in England with his brothers, allegedly given safe passage by Edgar Ætheling of the House of Wessex. When Henry Beauclerc, the fourth of William the Conqueror's sons, married David's sister Matilda (baptismal name Edith), David became connected to the English court and, according to William of Malmesbury in his *Gesta regum Anglorum* (*History of the Kings of the English*), he was greatly influenced by Norman ways. William's petulant observation that residence in England at the Norman court wore off David's 'Scot barbarity' sounds early on in English history a triumphalist note and betrays well-developed ethnic anxieties: William himself was the son of a Norman father and English mother, and spent years as a monk at Malmesbury Abbey (founded by Aldhelm in the 7th century, the place-name is a Celtic-English hybrid, Maildubh's stronghold < OIr. *Maeldub* + OE *byriġ* [dat. sing of *burh*]). Henry Beauclerc, as Henry I of England, continued to patronize David, setting up his marriage to Matilda of Huntingdon, daughter of Waltheof, Earl of Northunbria and last of the English earls, who took part in the Revolt of the Earls against William and, despite confessing his guilt, was nevertheless beheaded at St Giles's Hill the last day of May 1076. And so David came into the Honour of Huntingdon, land in the shire of that name and in Bedford and Northampton. He would name his own son Henry in honor of his patron but wind up while *rex Scottorum* fighting King Stephen of England as he sought to extend his control southward into Northern England. Besides time spent in England and at its Norman court, David had been also to Normandy proper. The cultural upshot would follow on the political reforms and the direction of influence that produced them; Anglo-Norman England's cultural and linguistic reach pushed northward, even if its territorial advances were rebuffed and its borders unstable in early Norman England. David's name itself is worth considering: Gaelic Dabíd, Mael Coluimb/Maíl Coluimb, i.e., 'Malcolm,' was only later to be used as a surname (ODES records the Domesday Book 1066 Norman form *filius Malcolumbe* for Lincolnshire and Yorkshire), here following the Irish system with the patronymic mac Maíl Coluimb, literally 'son of a servant/follower of Columba,' Columcille, the Irish 'apostle of the Scots' venerated to this day as such in Scotland. David had absorbed the languages and norms of the Anglo-Norman world; he would be King of the Scots in a Britain becoming increasingly English. If an analogy to the sciences might be made, English had begun to exert a gravitational pull within Britain, the center of attraction being the court, and later London, when its seat had moved to the City.

Place-names, once again, offer stable evidence for the varieties of speech that would be written into the landscape: Snaith < ON *sneið(r)* 'piece of land cut off' (East Riding of Yorkshire), not far from Carlton (North Yorkshire; there is also a Carleton in Cumbria and in North Yorkshire) < Old Norse *karl* 'carl, freeman' + Old English *tūn*, while Carlisle in Cumbria, recorded in Latin in the 4th century as *Luguvalio*, is a hybrid, the Latinized Celtic name **Luguvalos* (linking it to a complex of place-name associated with the Celtic god Lugh) prefixed with Cumbrian *cair* (compare frequent Welsh place-name element *caer* 'fort') to produce 'fortified town of Luguvalos' (**Luguvalos* and other Celtic and Romano-British place-names were seen in Chapter 3). Indeed, the number of surviving Celtic place-names in Anglo-Saxon England is larger than previous estimates (see especially Coates 2002, 47–85), and the processes here had deep roots, stretching back to that early conquest of Britain in AD 449. The 'conquest of Britain' would work its way rather more slowly northward and westward than would the Norman Conquest of Anglo-Saxon England of 1066, but there are similarities in the types of contact situations.

4.5 THE GODS OF THE DAYS OF THE WEEK: PRE-CHRISTIAN ENGLAND

The early Celtic-Old English contacts of the 5th–7th centuries saw a supplanting not just of language but religion – a sort of 're-paganizing' of Britain as it became England. Early programs of conversion emerged in Kent (beginning in 597) and with Irish missions in the North (beginning with St. Columba's mission to Alba/ Scotland in 563). The linguistic consequences of each of these programs, across the north and in the southeast, were profound and long-lasting. The school of Theodore and Hadrian at Canterbury, founded early in the archiepiscopate of Theodore 668/669–690, would establish the study of Latin, and Greek (to some extent) in an ecclesiastical center that would remain among England's most important until the Reformation (the school survived the purges that saw the destruction of the shrine of Thomas Becket in 1538). The work of Michael Lapidge in particular has shown how extensive an intellectual program was established at Canterbury: the study and generation of Biblical commentaries, the drafting of bilingual Latin-Old English glossaries that would remain in circulation for centuries, the training of a clerical bureaucracy that would aid in uniting, eventually, an England that began as warring kingdoms (see, for instance, the studies in Lapidge 1995a). Perhaps less celebrated is that program, begun somewhat earlier, in the North: the Irish missionaries, Columba, Columbanus, Aidan, and others, would found such important monastic communities as Iona (in 563 by Columba) and Lindisfarne (in 635 by Aidan), where too Latin and Greek were studied, Biblical commentaries generated, and some of the great manuscript masterpieces of the Anglo-Saxon era were written, rubricated and illustrated, glossed and added to over centuries (the Lindisfarne Gospels, the earliest complete Vulgate Bible in Codex Amiatinus). Indeed, it was in the North that the most famous of Anglo-Saxon clerics lived and wrote, whose novitiate and early career were shaped in that Irish monastic milieu that spanned Kells, Derry, Iona, Lidisfarne, and Jarrow. But, with perhaps a few exceptions among the Franks, the Germanic-speaking invaders were 'pagan,' and would remain so for some time into the establishment of the Anglo-Saxon Heptarchy of the 6th through 8th centuries.

Mōnandæġ, m. 'Monday' [Day of the Moon]
Tīwesdæġ, m. 'Tuesday' [Day of Tīw]
Wōdnesdæġ, m. 'Wednesday' [Day of Woden]
Þūr(e)sdæġ/Þūresdæġ, m. 'Thursday' [Day of Thunor/Thor]
Frīġedæġ m. 'Friday' [Day of Frigg]
Sæternesdæġ, m. 'Saturday' [Day of Saturn]
Sunnandæġ, m. 'Sunday' [Day of the Sun]

The Old English, and, more broadly, Germanic days of the week have traditionally been taken as late classical loans from Latin, translations of the Roman planetary-based names: *diēs Solis* (day of the Sun'), *diēs Lunae* ('day of the moon'), *diēs Mārtis* ('day of Mars'), *diēs Mercurii* ('day of Mercury'), *diēs Iouis* ('day of Jove/Jupiter'), *diēs Veneris* ('day of Venus'), *diēs Saturni* ('day of Saturn'). The traditional dating of the calquing (borrowing by translating from source to target language) is the late Roman period, the milieu the Romano-Germanic provinces and frontier (possibly the Rhine delta region – for the names's passage into what would then be Proto-West-Germanic); another view is that the loan translations occurred in a scholarly Christian milieu (Shaw 2007, 393–401). There are apparently no securely datable signs of when the importation of the Roman names for days of the week occurred; the name for Friday (one of two days in the week bearing the name of a goddess, Monday the other) exhibits having undergone a rare sound change in Proto-Germanic: the geminate **ijj* simplified to **ij*, thus **Frijjōz*, genitive singular of the name for a goddess of love and marriage and the wife or consort of **Wōðanaz/Wōden/Óðinn* (the PGmc, OE, and ON forms for 'Odin'), what would become, in the nominative form, *Frigg* in ON, *Frīġ* in OE. This simply indicates that the change occurred in the later Roman era, and it was also the period for which we have information regarding linguistic exchange by *interpratio germanica*: the 'Germanizing' of Latin loans and concepts – here the Roman gods as Germanic 'great gods.' As did the Celts, the Germans venerated Mercury perhaps most of all (at least in terms of votive altars and inscriptions), then Mars and Hercules (see Shaw 2007, 386–387, 394–395). The fit of Frigg/Frīġ with Venus may not seem so close, at least when considering her Hera/Juno role as wife of the father of the gods, but the name is etymologically connected to ON *frjá* and OE *frīġe* 'love' (de Vries 1077, s.v. *frjá*). A goddess of love and marriage then does make sense as an *interpretatio germanica,* and that the day named in her honor follows that for Jove may allude to the position Thor (ON *Þórr*, OE *Þunor*, with the etymological sense 'thunderer') occupied in the earlier Germanic pantheon as he is usually equated with Jupiter (Jove). In the Indo-European context, only Tīw, Odin, and, to a somewhat lesser extent, Thor, seem to have evidence for their roots in the earlier tradition; many of the Germanic theonyms, or 'god-names,' have etymological counterparts, but their functions, even gender, can shift across the branches of the language family's mythic traditions.

Though we still have the day that bears his name, Tuesday, Tīw seems to have faded in prominence in later Germanic tradition though there was a tradition, running from Roman historian Tacitus (ca. 55–ca. 120) to Icelandic lawyer and author Snorri Sturluson (1179–1241), that Tīw (OE) / Týr (ON) was a god of war (a function later associated more with Thor, but also with Odin). This is borne out in part by his *interpretatio romana* as Mars (see Osborn 2003, who also notes the similarity between the *týr*-rune and the symbol for the planet Mars). While E.G. Stanley's *The Search for Anglo-Saxon Paganism* (1975) and the runological work of R.I. Page were highly (at times even severely) skeptical of all types of 'pagan' interpretations and readings of Old English and other Germanic texts, this may be a natural consequence of shifting trends in cultural history, and history itself. Page, of Cambridge (serving as the Elrington and Bosworth Professor of Anglo-Saxon), and Stanley, of Oxford (as the Rawlinson and Bosworth Professor of Anglo-Saxon), had both seen service in WWII and thus witnessed some of the more disturbing (and dangerous) effects of the long tide of nationalistic, even monomaniacal, *Germanistik* in the universities. What is called *Indo-European* in English (*indo-européen/ne* in French, *indoeuropeo/a* in Italian and Spanish) is in German *Indogermanisch* ('Indo-Germanic'). There is a vast literature on the subject of the appropriation of runes by the Third Reich, and of organizations such as the Deutsches Ahnenerbe (German Ancestral Heritage, founded by Heinrich Himmler in 1935), which used a Runic font in some of its communications, and one of the after-effects of the war was a decline in runological studies (see, for instance, the essays in *Runica – Germanica – Mediaevalia*, Heizmann and Nahl 2003). A recoiling from the horrors of the war had a chilling effect on the study of 'ancestral' Germanic culture, and those whose professional obligation it was to study runes often reflected a renewed skepticism of all things runological and 'Germanic.' This trend has, as all trends do, moderated in the past few decades (though of course there are other forms of misappropriation of the past in political and popular culture that continue). But runic finds have continued apace, as have the cataloguing and interpretation of early Roman inscriptions from the Germanic homelands and their newer homeland in Britain.

An early votive inscription in Britain sheds important light on the Tīw-Mars pairing; RIB 1593, an altar from Housesteads (Roman Vercovicium) on Hadrian's Wall, dates to perhaps the AD late 2nd or early 3rd century and was illustrated on its lintel with figures of Mars (with sword and shield, spear, and a goose) and a pair of goddesses holding palms and wreaths in outstretched hands. The goddesses are the *Alaisiagae*, known from two other inscriptions in Britain (RIB 1594, dated to AD ca. 223–235, and RIB 1576, date uncertain). The pairs are named as Beda and Fimilena (or Baudihillia and Frigabis), and the names may be Celtic and Germanic variants of the theonyms. RIB 1593 and 1594 are dedicated also to Mars, in 1594 *Deo Marti et duabus Alaisiagis et Numini Augusti* ('to the god Mars and the two Alaisiagae and the divine presence of the Emperor'), in 1593 *Deo Marti Thincso et duabus Alaisiagis Bede et Fimmilene et Numini Augusti* (added here is the epithet *Thincsus* to Mars, likely Proto-Germanic **þingsaz* with devoiced /g/). This is 'Mars of the Thing,' the 'thing' the old Germanic legal assembly well-known from the laws and other early records, such as the *Alþing* ('All-Thing') held annually at the *Þingvellir* ('Thing-Field') in Iceland some 30 miles north-northeast of Reykjavík (and famous in the sagas for the wrangling and haggling – and insults – that could lead to violence). In Old English, the term survives as an obsolete form in *Black's Law Dictionary* and was of high enough frequency that the *Beowulf*-poet could use it metaphorically: *ond nu wið Grendel sċeal, / wið þām āglǣċan āna ġehēġan / ðinġ wið þyrse* (Fulk et al. 2008, ll. 424b–426a): 'and now against Grendel shall I / against this giant alone raise [settle, resolve] / thing against thurse [giant]'). The form *þing* is used elsewhere in *Beowulf* in the sense 'matter, affair' (l. 409b: *Grendles þinġ*, 'the matter of Grendel' that reached Beowulf's ears back home in Sweden) and, in the derivative noun form with the preverbal, *ge-þinge* (from *þingian*, '[to] compound, settle, make arrangements') with the senses 'agreement, compact; terms; result, outcome' (Fulk et al. 2008 glossing; there is still quite evident the legal sense of the *thing*-form in these uses in the poem as well). In the particular passage at lines 424–426, the use is collocational: *ðinġ ġehēġan*, 'hold a meeting,' or assembly or proceeding. The verb *hēġan* alone means 'perform, achieve' (CHM, s.v.), and in the collocation *ðinġ ġehēġan* is more of a legal formula; this raises a number of interesting points in the poem: Grendel is a *thurse* (the obsolete Modern English form), OE *þyrs*, which along with *eoten* denoted 'giant' in Old English.

Þyrs also had extended senses and collocations, Holthausen in AEW glosses 'Riese, Dämon; Zauberer' ('giant, demon; enchanter/wizard'), and in the glossaries the term was stretched further afield: it was the go-to OE equivalent to the Marsi, an Italic tribe of the Lake Fucinus region who had been loyal to Rome until rebelling with other tribes in the Social War (91–87 BC), and who were also known for magic and snake-charming (see McGowan 2009b). Grendel and his mother in the poem are trolls, though in the poem the main terms used to refer to them are terms for 'demon, fiend' and 'wretch, attacker' (*āglǣċa* and *āglǣċa-wif*; i.e., 'troll' and 'troll-wife' in some translations). Grendel is referred to by name some 40 times in the poem, and that the most frequent means of referring to the 'monster' in the poem is his personal name must be of some significance. It is an ancient commonplace that naming and names have a power to them; that Beowulf could 'raise a thing' against Grendel emphasizes at least his quasi-human status (he is of large stature, has nails like iron, the strength of 30 men in his grip, but stalks the moor as a bipedal; he also understands human speech, feels pain, and employs magic). In the semi-Christianized world of the text as we have it, he is 'Cain's kin,' and in his lair, beneath a mere (pool), is an ancient sword carved with runes telling the story from Genesis of the flood (on the wider significance of this sword and giants and other progeny of Cain – or Cham – see Neidorf 2015, 613–614). That runic-inscribed sword might be a good analogy for the matter of the names of days of the week in English, combining the pagan, Biblical, and para-Biblical. It is very difficult to sort out the reasons for and chronology of the loan translations. But that there is a pagan element to them is highly likely. Tīw of the Thing was honored on that altar at Housesteads, as a god of war, and apparently also of the assembly (which would work well, semantically, as a pair of opposites: plunder and parley). The founders of this altar were members of a Frisian cavalry *cuneus* ('wedge'); in the dedication, they are said to be *cives Tuihanti* (the citizens of the Tuihanti or Tubantes Germanic tribe), likely modern Twente in northeastern Netherlands (RIB 1593–1594); in RIB 1576, the unit at Housesteads dedicating an altar to the Alaisiagae, likely the same unit as with the other two inscriptions, is led by a Hnaufridus, a patently Germanic name. Frisia has had a long association with horse-breeding and the Romans raised cavalry units there and deployed them up north to Hadrian's Wall. As discussed last chapter, these earlier deployments of Germanic troops to Roman Britain served as a likely enticement to conquest and settlement once Roman authority collapsed.

Our Germanic gods occupy Tuesday, Wednesday, Thursday, and Friday – it is unclear whether Sunday and Monday are to be taken as Germanic equivalents either natively or by *interpretatio germanica* – and if the weeks preserved the old ways, so too did other Old English measurements of time. OE *ġēar* 'year' and *missere* 'half-year' are the larger units, the seasons are *winter*, *ēastre* (an originally pagan term; also used was a Latin-OE hybrid *lenctentīd* 'Lenten-tide'), *sumor*, and *hærfest* (with voicing of the medial fricative in the modern form *harvest*), and *mōnaþ* 'month' has a mixture of OE and Latin-OE hybrid names for the months of their lunisolar calendar:

se æftera ġēola ('the after-Yule'): January
solmōnaþ ('mud-month,' a 'wet' month): February

hrēþmōnaþ ('Hretha/Rheda's month,' named for a pagan goddess): March[6]
ēastermōnaþ ('Ēostre's month,' also named for a pagan goddess): April
þrīmilċemōnaþ ('three milch-/three milkings-month'): May (according to the Bede in his *De Temporum Ratione*, 'On the Reckoning of Time,' so named as cows were milked thrice daily in this month)
līþamōnaþ ('mild month'): June–July (under the sub-forms *se ǣrre lȳþa* ['the earlier,' June] and *se æftera* ['the after,' July])
weodmōnaþ ('month of weeds/grasses/tares'): August
hāliġmōnaþ ('holy month,' likely referring to pre-Christian offerings and rituals): September
winterfyllaþ/winterfylledmōnaþ ('winter-ful month'): October
blōtmōnaþ ('blood-month,' referring to animal sacrifices of the pagan seasonal festival): November
ġēola/ġēolmōnaþ ('Yule month'): December

A later list is given in the *Manual* (or *Enchiridion* [*Encheiridion*]) of Byrhthferth of Ramsey (ca. 970–1020) in late West Saxon: *Giuli* (Yule-January), *Solmonð* (February; with contraction of the unstressed vowel in *monaþ*), *Hreðmonð* (March), *Eastermonð* (Easter-month/April), *Þrymilce* (May), *Lyða* (June), *Lyða* (July), *Weodmonð* (August), *hāliġmōnaþ* (September), *Winterfilð* (October), *Blodmonð* (November), *Giuli* (Yule-December; Baker and Lapidge 1995a, 24).

Yule, of course, is very much a part of current Christmastide celebrations, and as *Jul* in North Germanic languages has become interchangeable with Christmas. So too have the 12-day and -night traditions, Yuletide to Christmastide: the Twelve Days of Christmas were a religious season, its Octave the Feast of Circumcision (in the *Novus Ordo* of the Roman rite it has been replaced by the Solemnity of Mary, Mother of God). The Twelfth Night was often counted as the Eve of the Twelfth Day (a system of counting found in OE: *Tīwesniht* = Monday night, and so forth; on the range of expressions of measurement of time, see TOE, I, 301–321); its Yuletide ancestor involved feasting, while its Christmastide descendant came to involve (or subsume) more boisterous celebration (Shakespeare's play of the name was likely meant as a Twelfth Night entertainment). The re-purposing of words with originally pagan senses or contexts is natural enough, and Anglo-Saxon clerics did not seem overly fussy about some of the usages – though not with the Easter Controversy, settled at the Synod of Whitby in 664; in the Northumbria of the time some ecclesiastical matters, such as the calculation of the date of Easter, and proper clerical tonsure, had seen a division between Irish-influenced Northumbria and the South, where was followed the Roman practice on the *computus*, the text that guides calculation of the date for the moveable feast of Easter: in brief, the first Sunday following the paschal (Passover)

[6] Later ecclesiastical writer Ælfric of Eynsham used the term *hlydan monðe* (*hlydanmōnaþ*), which seems to mean 'the loud month,' with reference to the gusty winds of March. It may be a regional form, from the Southwest (Shaw 2011, 94), as four of the five attestations of its Middle English descendant *lide* ('month of March') cluster in the SW or West Midlands (the *South English Legendary* of the later 13th century, and Robert of Gloucester's *Metrical Chronicle* of around the mid-12th century; MED, s.v. *lide*).

full moon, in practice two weeks into the lunar month. The conversion of England had begun in earnest with Pope Gregory's mission to Kent in 597. The consecration of Theodore of Tarsus as Archbishop of Canterbury in 668 (reaching England in 669, holding the ecclesiastical office until his death in 690) and his founding, with Hadrian of North Africa (who accompanied him) of an educational program at the school in Canterbury set England firmly within the fold of Christendom and Christian Mediterranean culture (in Latin texts produced in the British Isles, what was called 'hisperic' [i.e., 'western' < *Hesperus*] style). The intellectual program of Theodore and Hadrian established an Anglo-Saxon literary culture and educational program that continued through the medieval cathedral schools and scriptoria at monastic centers, from Bede's Wearmouth-Jarrow in the north to Winchester, Salibury, and Exeter in the south and southwest to the establishment of Oxford and Cambridge in the later middle ages (traditionally placed at 1096 for the former, 1209 for the latter). Michael Lapidge has, over four decades of publication, filled out the signal achievement of the Canterbury School, from the teaching of Latin and Latin poetics (Lapidge 1995c), and some Greek, to Biblical exegesis, basic sciences (as of the *computus*, and meteorology), and liturgical text and practice (Lapidge 1995a, 2023). Theodore and Hadrian were native Greek-speakers, and the former may have known some Syriac, and seems to have explicated Scripture at Canterbury from an 'Antiochene' exegetical framework (that is, of the school of Antioch, the Syriac Eastern tradition; Lapidge 1995a, 8). From the north, the Irish and Dál Riadic Scots (the Irish of Western Scotland, though *Scot(t)i* refers to any of the Irish who settled in Northern Britain from the 3rd century on) evangelized Northumbria southward to Mercia (Penda of Mercia remained pagan to his death in 655).

All did not ever go forward with Christianization. While Æthelberht of Kent was then still pagan, though amenable to the Gregorian mission in 597 led by Augustine (an Italian monk from Rome, later known as Augustine of Canterbury), which landed at the Isle of Thanet, Kent, his wife Bertha, daughter of the Merovingian king Charibert I, was Christian and eager to support the conversion activity. Æthelberht's father was Eormenric, a somewhat unusual name in England at the time, though one of some frequency in the Frankish kingdom (this recalls the idea that Franks were among those first waves of settlers in the 5th century). But the name (originally Gothic), broken into its constituent parts became part of the nomenclature of kings of Kent: *erman-* + *-ric*, 'strong' or 'all ruler/king,' it was the name of the 4th-century Eastern Gothic king who battled the Huns and entered into legend – mentioned or appearing in the Old English poems *Beowulf*, *Deor*, and *Widsith*. In the Oiscingas line of Kent, that is, the descendants of Oisc, one finds successors such as **Eormen**rēd, Ēad**ric**, Al**ric** (Oisc was the son or grandson of Hengest and reigned ca. 488–516; *-ingas* is a tribal line suffix: e.g., the Wuffingas of East Anglia, or the Wǣgmundigas of *Beowulf*, that is, the line of Geats to which Beowulf and Wiglāf belong). Sæberht of Essex (the East Saxon kingdom) had been receptive to the Gregorian and Augustinian mission and was kindly toward Mellitus (who had baptized him in 604); Mellitus was either born in England or from abroad, Francia or Italy, but he became the third archbishop of Canterbury and first bishop of London. Sæberht's sons Sexræd and Sæward (and a third whose name is not recorded) did not convert, however, and following the death of their father in 616, they drove Mellitus out of London (he would return to

Canterbury). Sæward died fighting the West Saxons, and his son Sigeberht the Little remained pagan; Essex would not be re-evangelized until under his son Sigeberht the Good in the 660s. Sigeberht the Little had allied for a while with Penda of Mercia at a time when Oswald of Northumbria (the kingdoms of Deira and Bernicia) extended the northerners' reach to the southern kings. At Oswald's death, Penda became 'overlord' of the southern kings (Stenton 1989, 83). Thus, a doggedly pagan king held sway and Mercia and Essex reverted to paganism; but Oswald's brother Oswiu was a Christian and encouraged Sigeberht (the Good) to accept baptism. Oswiu had led the fight back against the brief conquest of Northumbria by King of the Britons Cadwallon ap Cadfan, who had coerced Penda of Mercia into joining him. Victorious at the Battle of Hatfield Chase in 633, Cadwallon would fall later that year at the Battle of Heavenfield (Northumberland). Pagan Penda would in turn fall in 655 at the Battle of the Winwæd (a small stream somewhere around Leeds; Stenton 1989, 84). This marked, in Bede's scheme of his *Historia ecclesiastica gentis Anglorum* ('Ecclesiastical History of the English People'), the last days of Anglo-Saxon paganism. Not that there did not occur further instances of reversion and backsliding (that English clerics would rail against) through the 7th century, but kingdom after kingdom, from those in Northumbria through Mercia to East Anglia and the East, West, South Saxons, saw Christianity grow and ecclesiastical centers founded. But the vocabulary of Old English shows that pagan survivals did occur, perhaps at times just as folk customs.

Some Old English words seem to evince this dual religious culture of the early period; *frēols* as a noun meant both 'freedom' and 'feast-day, festival,' as an adjective 'free, festive' (CHM, s.v.). It was productive of a number of derivative and compound forms: *frēolsbōc* 'charter of freedom,' *frēolsmann* 'freedman,' *frēolsnīht* 'eve of a festival,' *frēolsstōw* 'place of a festival' (see TOE, II, 992–993). While the forms had clearly been extended to include Christian feast-days, the original sense 'festival' – as in pagan and popular local festivals – seems intact; enough so that an Anglo-Saxon glossator rendered *Lupercalia* as *gālfrēols* 'revel' (CHM; the first element *gāl-* could refer to 'luxury, wantonness'). The seeming simplex *frēols* is a contraction of compound *frī-heals*, literally 'free-neck,' with contraction of /iː/ before a back vowel with loss of /x/ (Campbell 1959, §§ 238.2, 468; on the OE vocabulary of slavery, see Pelteret 1995, 41–49). The theophoric days and months offer a kind of pagan survival – to this day. The goddesses of the months, Eostre and Hreda/Hreða, have been viewed as dubious survivals, but more recent work sees them as more substantial: the former a goddess of the dawn, the latter some sort of battle goddess (her name in the traditional explanation might mean 'famous, illustrious' or 'victorious,' or 'swift'; Simek 1993, 159; Shaw 2011, 84–97, who leans toward an explanation in the personal name element *hræd-/hreð-* [Northumbrian *hrœð-*]). They may be survivals of the ancient cult of matrons found in the Rhineland among early Germans and Celts and in Britain (see Chapter 3; Shaw 2011; and the recent full study by De Bernardo Stempl 2021). The royal genealogies boast of divine sanction – Woden is the progenitor of the Anglian dynasties from Northumbria to East Anglia, and Seaxnēat (Saxnot) of the East Saxons (*seax-ġenōt* is a common analysis, which seems to mean 'blade-companion' or 'friend of the Saxons'; Simek 1993, 276), with Saxnot as the 'national god' and eponym of the Saxons. Strictly speaking, the English monarchy still does ultimately trace its origins to Woden. Stranger figures inhabit mountains, wells and springs, moors, and woodlands.

We have mention of dwarves and giants – the latter figure prominently in local lore and native mythology (and in Biblical literature and extrabiblical lore). Dwarves do not figure anywhere near as prominently in what we know of Anglo-Saxon mythology as in the Norse; giants fare a bit better, as that sword in Grendel's lair with the runic account of the Flood is called *enta ǣrġeweorc̄* ('ancient work of giants'; l. 1679a) when Beowulf presents its hilt (what remains of the sword) to Hroðgar. Later in the poem, the entrance to the dragon's barrow and the hoarded treasure therein are both called *enta ġeweorc* ('the work of giants'; ll. 2717b and 2774a, where it is *eald enta ġeweorc* 'old work of giants,' paralleling the first use at 1679a). *Þyrs*, *eoten* (cognate with ON *jǫtunn*), and *ent* all seem to describe human-like beings of great stature and strength – and skill. The OE formula *enta ġeweorc* is applied also to the Roman ruins at Aquae Sulis (Bath) in the Old English elegy "The Ruin" (l. 2b), presumably as the great stone buildings of Roman architecture seemed to the poets to be beyond human ability to the poets (though this must be an early or archaizing poetic formula as they surely recognized Roman ruins, and from the 7th century on Anglo-Saxons made pilgrimages to Rome). One may add to the native Germanic giants the Biblical Nephilim, Anakim, and Rephaim, and their appearance in Biblical glossaries (the account of the Flood, in runes, on that sword in Beowulf's lair might indicate a fusion of the traditions). But perhaps the most prolific of the mythological races were the elfin-kin. Though elves do not make an appearance in *Beowulf*, or in the other heroic verse by and large, they do appear in the folk remedies and glossaries. They are distinguished by habitation (mountain, field, wood, and water; TOE, I, 658), and noted for both their radiant beauty and mischievousness: they are associated with causing a variety of ailments, from coughing to skin conditions such as erysipelas to epilepsy (see McGowan 2009a), as through the means of 'elf-shot' (there is a folk tradition of small cherts or arrowheads being taken as evidence of elves's malignant activity). And elves have received much more critical attention of late, including two full-length studies of elf-charms and a history of elves in Anglo-Saxon England (Jolly 1996; Hall 2007). These studies are much needed as the last comprehensive study of the mythological vocabulary of Old English was Richard Jente's 1921 monograph *Die mythologischen Ausdrücke im altenglischen Wortschatz: Eine kulturgeschichtlich-etymologische Untersuchung* ("The mythological expressions in Old English Vocabulary: A culture-historical-etymological Investigation"; Jente was a professor of German at a number of American universities, latterly of the University of North Carolina, Chapel Hill). Jente's study is programmatic and thorough and gives a sense of how important a subset of the OE lexicon the mythological terms occupied: he examines over 500 words, from the elf terms to those for dwarves, giants, and goblins (these are only vaguely described in Old English texts), terms for enchantment (*ġealdor/galdor* terms, having to do with 'songs' of enchantment), and various types of magic.

The two families of pagan Nordic gods seem to have been syncretized and harmonized during the early North Germanic or Common Germanic eras. The pattern is a familiar one, mythologically: gods could be adopted or imported into divine families, sometimes with the displacement or reduction in status of gods in the inner circle (or divine triad – a common Indo-European pattern); Śiva may have been an indigenous fertility god (perhaps going back to the Indus Valley civilization) whose grafting onto the Old Indic triad Brahmā-Indra-Viṣṇu displaced Indra, an atmospheric god of thunder with his divine weapon the *vajra* ('thunderbolt'), and there may be a long-distance Indo-European correspondence between Indra and Thor with his hammer Mjǫllnir. Some members of divine pantheons may have been adopted by substrate influence, or adopted by a conquered or colonized people from the superstratum, or adstratum influence from neighboring peoples. The general arguments advanced for the fusion of the two pantheons are what might be termed the mythological and the anthropological. The anthropological argument holds that the Vanir were the fertility gods of the indigenous pre-Germanic population, and the Æsir were the pantheon of Migration Age Germans who vaunted rather more gods of atmosphere and war; Tīw/Týr seems to have been of greater importance for his battle associations, while Thor may have had the role as head of the table so to speak before Odin ascended to that role. Having settled in Scandinavia, the Germans became farmers and livestock breeders, and the gods of fertility naturally assumed increased importance. The mythological argument follows the relatively brief account in Snorri Sturluson's *Prose Edda* and cryptic references in the poetry (the *Vǫluspá*, 'Seeress's Prophecy') to a war of the gods (the familiar theomachy pattern), which may have been precipitated by attacks on Gullveig – which involve her being assaulted with spears and then, in the usual triadic fashion, burnt to death three times and reborn three times: the last as Heiðr – in a common renaming pattern – who practices *seiðr*, ritual magic, especially soothsaying, that was usually restricted to women; Odin later commit an offense by practicing it. The upshot was that the war was settled by parley: in the *Skáldskaparmál* story of 'The Mead of Poetry' the Æsir and Vanir spit into a vat, the commingled saliva a sign of their pledge (and a common mythic trope of the power of language, here concretely manifested in saliva). Kvasir the Wise will eventually rise from their spittle, an all-knowing poet, but is then murdered by the covetous dwarves Fjalar and Gjalar; from Kvasir's blood comes the 'mead of poetry,' and glib of tongue will be anyone who tastes of it. There are references also to the exchange of hostages, with varying accounts of the terms, but Hœnir is sent to Vanaheim and Njǫrðr and Freyr are sent to Ásgarðr (Puhvel 1987, 189–221, offers an overview of this mythic tradition and the interpretation of an Indo-Europeanist).

The Vanir include Njǫrðr and his twin children Freyr and Freyja, and Yngvi/Ing, who later becomes merged in identity with Freyr, likely in the function of a fertility god. And these theonyms bring us to more concrete Old English 'pagan' vocabulary. Ing/Yngvi appears in the Old English "Rune Poem," as a rune-name (ᛝ 'Ing') and as the progenitor of the Ingvaeones (speakers of North Sea Germanic, and among those tribes who came to Britain in the conquest of 449 and following). His brief appearance only in this stanza is mysterious:

ᛝ (Ing) wæs ǣrest mid Ēast-Denum
gesewen secgun, oþ hē siððan ēst
ofer wǣg gewāt; wǣn æfter ran;
ðus heardingas ðone hæle nemdun (stanza XXII; Halsall 1981, 90).

Ing was first among the East-Danes
said to have been seen, until he later east
over the waves went; after [him] ran [his] chariot;
thus the fierce ones [or Heardingas] this hero called.

The brutally literal translation tries to give a sense of the almost incantatory rhythm of the "Rune Poem". The poem is known to have survived in only one manuscript copy, British Library, Cotton Otho B.x, with contents from the early to mid-11th-century. Much of this manuscript did not survive the fire at Ashburnham House, where the Cotton collection was then housed, including the folio (fol. 165) on which the *Rune Poem* was written. The poem and list of rune-names were copied by the antiquarian Rev. George Hickes and published in his compendium *Linguarum veterum septentrionalium thesaurus grammatico-criticus et archæologicus* ("A Grammatical-Critical and Archaeological Thesaurus of the Ancient Northern Languages"; Oxford, 1705). The text of the poem is in primarily late West Saxon, with a few Kentish forms; the list of rune-names contains more Kentish features, though the variability of these features – /eo/ can appear unsmoothed or smoothed/monophthongized to /e/, *wynn* 'joy' and the name of the *w*-rune appears in expected West Saxon form within the poem but as *wen* in the rune list (/y/ in later OE unrounded and lowered to /e/ in Kentish) suggested to its modern editor Maureen Halsall that there was "a long and chequered history of transmission for the rune names" published by Hickes (Halsall 1981, 28–30; Page 2006, 69). The mention of Ing's 'chariot' (the OE is literally 'wagon') calls to mind the sacred wagon or chariot of earth-goddess Nerthus used in her processions (recounted in Tacitus's *Germania*), and a similar ritual was associated with fertility god Freyr (Page 2006, 73–74). Nerthus is cognate with ON Njǫrðr, father of Freyr and Freyja. Njǫrðr's descent from Nerthus involves an interesting gender-shift between Proto-Germanic and North Germanic traditions, which may have been grammatically induced, or the god-name derived from proto-forms in Germanic referring to 'strength, power' and also to 'man, male,' or from an IE root having to do with 'procreation' and fertility (de Vries 1977 details yet other proposals at 410–411). Or there has been the suggestion, based on varying cults of Njǫrðr in Scandinavia – by the coast, as expected for a god whose hall is Nóatún, 'enclosure of ships,' though, in Sweden, in the interior – that Njǫrðr was female and paired in another brother-sister divine twins device with the god Ullr (associated with duels and oaths; Simek 1993, 234). The ceremonial cart, chariot, or wagon calls to mind that of Freyja drawn by two male cats. These mythic vehicles were given some substantive grounding with the excavation of the Oseberg Ship site 1904–1905 (Vestfold, Norway). The ship of the burial was a smaller-class longship (*karve*), and it was accompanied by a large trove of grave goods dating to the 9th century. Among them was a wooden wagon with elaborate carvings, including cats on the back panel, and it may be older than the ship it was buried with. The Oseberg tapestry fragments from this find site include woven depictions of women in horse-drawn carts. The type of goods, their ornamentation, and deposition together seem to suggest a ritual function paralleling the literary and epigraphic evidence. Though it has been semi-mythologized, in the story of Fróði III of the Skjǫldungar (the Danish Scyldings of *Beowulf*), he was said to have been drawn about in a ceremonial cart (and continued to be even after his death, seemingly in some sort of sacred royal circuit; cf. Puhvel 1987, 207–208).

The broader question is, why did the English not preserve more of their mythic traditions? Their neighbors in Britain (Welsh, Britons, Cumbrians) and in Ireland were Christianized early on, and led the conversion of Northumbria and the establishment of centers of learning at Iona, Lindisfarne, and Wearmouth-Jarrow that might be said to rival Canterbury, especially if we consider the achievements of Bede. The German neighbors of the English, particularly in Scandinavia, preserved much more of the tradition, though there was longer resistance to adopting Christianity in those realms (especially Sweden). The preservation of English mythic lore would not likely have threatened the English church, certainly not after the 7th century. Giants appear in Old English literature, but there are no specific references to frost-giants such as Ymir, who plays a fundamental role in the Norse cosmogony. Ymir is the 'Urreise,' a proto-/cosmogonic frost-giant, and his name might be etymologically connected to Sanskrit *Yama*, a god of death in Vedic tradition: de Vries connects it to the PIE root **yemH-*, 'twin' (de Vries 1977, s.v.). There is nothing like either the Old Norse *Poetic Edda* or Snorri Sturluson's *Prose Edda* for Old English, and one can see why J.R.R. Tolkien (who was Rawlinson and Bosworth Professor of Anglo-Saxon at Oxford 1925–1945) set out to re-create the 'lost mythology' of England with his novels, from *The Silmarillion* (begun in 1914 but not published until 1977), *The Hobbit* (1937), and *The Lord of the Rings* (1954–1955, intended to be a single volume, it was published in three parts as *The Fellowship of the Ring*, *The Two Towers*, *The Return of the King*). Tolkien's work became rather less a re-creation of that lost English mythology and rather more a universe unto itself, but it is especially in the names that one sees the interests of a professor of medieval languages. Dvalinn and Dalinn are among the dwarf names preserved in Norse (the former is Dwalin in Tolkien's Middle Earth); in fact, the Norse tradition boasts a poetic sequence of dwarf names (*Dverga-tál*, 'count/reckoning of dwarves'), though for such a roster of dwarves one has to turn to Tolkien and not Old English literature. The word itself, OE *dweorh/dweorg* (ON *dvergr*), is of uncertain origin and seems a Germanic formation with no clear cognates in other branches of Indo-European. The conception of dwarves as small in stature but immensely strong, ill-tempered, meddlesome, and in Snorri's account of Ragnarok, awaiting the final battle by their doors of stone (to their subterranean mountain homes), may all be later associations (the fullest discussion of the term and supernatural beings is Liberman 2008, 46–64). A number of their names are associative, named after animals or colors, or sharing a name with other supernatural creatures (such as giants). One hint about their stature comes from the dwarf name *Nóri*, which in Modern Icelandic means 'tiny' (Liberman 2008, 48 col. a). Their reputation as workers in metal, as fabricators of treasures and mythical weapons for the gods, does seem of some antiquity; there is also the 'smith of the gods' figure in West Germanic: *Weland*, 'Wayland,' in OE, *Vǫlundr* in ON. And this in turn has links in other branches of Indo-European to a mythic complex of a divine smith – Greek Hephaistos, Roman Vulcan, Irish Goibniu (Gaibhne), Welsh Gofannon – who is sometimes described as lame (with an etiological story of his hamstringing) and whose skills are sought after, and at times jealously monopolized, by the gods.

The association of dwarves with mountains, their subterranean passages, and mining for metals is also apparently ancient, and it persists in English in the etymological senses of *cobalt* and *nickel*; the former derives from Middle High German *kobold*, a class of goblins who deceive miners by swapping in cobalt for silver, the latter from German *Kupfernickel*, 'copper-nickel,' again that one ore is deceptively left in place of another of less value by such mischievous creatures (here nickel instead of copper). The words point to longstanding miners' traditions of treacherous beings leading them astray, jealously guarding veins of ore they seem to view as their own. In that sense, dwarves are connected to a territorial mythic complex, in the celestial-terrestrial-chthonic Indo-European triadic scheme they belong to that subterranean (chthonic) realm, though poetic tradition has them venture out from their 'halls of stone,' squabbling with giants or even gods (compare the story of how Odin acquired the mead of poetry from dwarves in Snorri's *Skaldskaparmál*). Anatoly Liberman settles on a sense of 'mad, foolish,' for *dwarf*, and if his idea of rhotacism at work between *dweorh* and *dwǣs* is correct, then the OE word *ġe-dwǣsmann* 'fool' may carry with it the extended Germanic sense of 'insane, driven mad' (even 'possessed'), as the latter word occurs in Ælfric's *Lives of the Saints* (Liberman 2008, 54–55; CHM, s.v.). But there are some survivals if one looks for them: *Wyl on eowe meolce Fornetes folm*, 'Boil in ewe's milk Fornet's palm.' The best attempt to explain whose palm, or hand, is involved in this OE plant name has looked toward the Nordic evidence, with the likeliest candidate being the giant Fornjǫtr, whose name might simply mean 'proto-giant': (though there have been other attempts at etymology (de Vries 1977, 138–139, "Unsichere etymologie," 'of uncertain etymology'). Fornjǫtr appears at the head of a family of giants in the *Orkneyinga saga* ('Saga of the Orkneymen') and *Flateyjarbók*. His sons were said to be Hlér ('sea'), Logi ('fire'), and Kari ('wind'), and Kari's sons and grandsons include Jǫkull ('glacier'), Frosti ('frost'), Snær ('snow'), and, in other sources, Fǫnn ('snow drift'), Drífa ('snow drift'), Mjǫll ('powder snow'), and Þorri (the name of a winter month; Simek 1993, 88). The family nomenclature makes it clear that these are frost-giants. The application of ON Fornjǫtr/ OE Fornet to a plant may have to do with the resemblance between the plant's tubers and the fingers of the giant (Bierbaumer 1974, 1979, who suggests it is a type of orchid). But in these OE herbal remedies, which often include magical formulas and rituals, the name of a frost-giant is invoked, which at least points toward some of what has been lost of the old tradition in early England.

Times would change with the coming of Christianity, as would its reckoning. In the lunisolar system of the early Anglo-Saxon period, the reckoning of time ranged from physical observation of heavenly bodies (the phases of the moon, the course of the sun) and the seasons to the difference between the lunar and solar year – which amounts to 11 days (an *epact*); when the *epact* reaches 30 days a month is intercalated (a 'leap month,' from Latin *saltus*; our *leap day* a descendant of this process of intercalation). This naturalistic method began to change with the 'Hours' of Christian liturgy and monastic time-keeping, and Old English vocabulary adjusted accordingly: prime (Latin *prima*, the first of the liturgical hours of the Divine Office: 6 am) could be rendered *primsang* or *dægrēdsang* ('daybreak-song,' though this latter form was apparently also used for matins). And these terms for the liturgical hours – *undernsang*, 'terce' (third hour after sunrise, 9 am, *undern* was dialectally used for with this or midday), *ǣfensang* 'evensong' – would be joined by many other loans from Latin (borrowed whole or relatively so as Latinate additions, or as calques or semi-calques). The whole apparatus of the new faith would require hundreds of new terms, as would the intellectual and educational system Christianization brought, to early Northumbria and Kent (on this shift in time reckoning see especially Liuzza 2020).

4.6 THE EARLIEST ATTESTATIONS OF ENGLISH – RUNIC – ANGLO-LATIN

ᚠ ᚢ ᚦ ᚩ ᚱ ᚳ ᚷ ᚹ ᚻ ᚾ ᛁ ᛄ ᛇ ᛈ ᛉ ᛋ

f u th o r c g w h n i j ɨ p x s

ᛏ ᛒ ᛖ ᛗ ᛚ ᛝ ᛞ ᛟ ᚪ ᚫ ᚣ ᛠ ᚸ ᛣ ᛤ

t b e m l ŋ d œ a æ y ea ḡ k k̄

The Anglo-Saxon *fuþorc* (Page 2006, 43; see also Elliott 1989, 43–49)

The word *rune* derives from Old English or Old Norse *rūn*, 'mystery, secret, counsel, runic character, letter.' The runic alphabets were in use from approximately the AD 2nd century until about the 13th. The word 'rune' persisted in use for some time later in English (AHD5, s.v. *rune*). Its ultimate origin is not certain; the word appears also in Old Irish (*rún*) and Gothic (*rūna*), and the best source on the matter is still Jan de Vries' *Altnordisches Etymologisches Wörterbuch* (de Vries 1977, s.v.), which simply says that the origin of this 'Celtic-Germanic' word is unclear ('Die etymologie dieses nur kelt.-germ. Wortes ist nicht klar'; s.v. *rún*). Comparison with Lapp/Saami *rudna* ('murmur, noise') has been made, and Old Norse texts report the fame of the Laplanders/Saami as seers and magicians. A root for the word has been traced back to Sanskrit *ravati* ('roars, howls') or to the Hindu god Varuṇa (in the Vedas, the king of the gods, upholder of earth and sky) and the Greek god Οὔρανος (Ouranos).

At any rate, the word connotes the mysterious and connects writing with specialized, uncommon, even magical practice. Where runes first arose and why are not clear either: the earliest inscriptions are clustered around Southern Scandinavia (the Danish province of Jutland, the Schleswig-Holstein region of Northern Germany bordering on Denmark); the controversial inscription on the Negau helmet (dating to about AD 50, on a helmet of earlier origin) comes from much further south: the Styria/Steiermark region of Eastern Austria bordering on Slovenia. It was thought to be proto-Runic; it is now generally seen as written in a North Italic script, strengthening the link posited between Etruscan and other North Italic alphabets and Runic. The helmet is believed to have belonged to a German soldier serving in the Roman army, and the inscription is taken as a mark of ownership (of a Harigast, son of Teius, in the XVIII-II unit). Whoever first developed the Runic script seems to have modeled it after a North Italic script, although this explanation is complicated by recent research into Palaeo-Hispanic scripts such as the alphabeto-syllabic (characters representing either a single sound or a syllable, often CV) Iberian scripts. These scripts were used to record the Iberian language (non-Indo-European, possibly an early relative of Basque), Celtiberian (a Continental Celtic language), Tartessian (possibly a Celtic language; Koch 2009, 2013), and perhaps the Proto-Basque of the 'Hand of Irulegi' inscription dating to the 1st century BC (an inscribed bronze votive hand). In these Palaeo-Hispanic scripts, in the northeastern variety ϒ can represent *m* and ↑ *u* and ᛚ *l* (only this last character overlaps with Germanic Runic use). The Iberian scripts may derive from Phoenician, Greek, or Old Italic sources; there are other correspondences between Palaeo-Hispanic scripts and Runic writing that, if not sharing an origin in Old Italic scripts, make the question of origin and transmission of such writing systems baffling. The presumed course of transmission of Italic script (whether Etruscan or an Indo-European Italic source) to Germanic tribes in the Alpine and Northern Italian regions is of course, as with so much about runes, conjectural; the movement of an Italic-based script to Spain in the case of Celtiberian (and perhaps also Tartessian) may have been facilitated by the movement of Celtic tribes from the Alpine region through Gaul to the Iberian peninsula (but the early date of some of these inscriptions – to at least the 4th century BC – makes this idea seem less likely). One thing that may make Runic writing systems less mysterious is that while literacy among the early Germanic tribes has been seen as exceptional rather than widespread, exposure to writing systems of neighboring peoples (some of whom the Germans conquered) does seem to have been fairly common. Adding just one more complexity to the origin of runes is the appearance of a few Runic-looking characters among very early *hällristningar* (the Swedish term) or *hellerristninger* (the Danish), 'petroglyphs' or 'rock carvings' (ca. 1600–500 BC, or the Scandinavian Iron and Bronze Ages); some of these carvings are pictographic, or as yet undeciphered ideographic writing. Others look very much like the *týr* (ᛏ) and 'stacked' *týr* runes (Elliott 1989, 84–85). Once again, we can at least say that early Germanic tribes moved into regions in which writing was to be found, and may have imitated local scripts or even developed certain signs if not writing from earlier petroglyphic 'writing.'

Runic alphabets are carving scripts: they were made for carving primarily on wood, though many of the surviving inscriptions are found on metal and stone. The inscriptions could follow left-to-right order, or appear in retrograde order (right-to-left), or *boustrophedon* (Greek for 'turning as the ox plows,' an order of rows alternating between right-left and left-right), in either straight-line arrangement or curving or scrolling or other patterns, contingent upon the type of monument and the artistic composition in which the inscription featured or to which it was added. The Gripholm Runestone (Södermanland, Sweden, runestone U 644) is one of 26 of the Ingvarr or Varangian runestones carved to commemorate the voyages east (to Constantinople, and eventually to Georgia and the Caspian) by Swedish Vikings under Ingvarr *víðfǫrli* 'the far-travelled' (d. 1041); it is one of many runestones with the familiar iconographic representation of a scrolling Midgard serpent (*Miðgarðsormr*) on the body of which have been carved the runes. Runic inscriptions often exhibit archaic forms, whether in Common, Northwest, or West and North Germanic; there are relatively few East Germanic Runic inscriptions: the 'ring of Pietroassa,' a large gold torc (neck-ring) found in Southern Romania, bears the brief inscription **gutaniowihailag** (Krause and Jankuhn 1966, V.41, and plate 20).

ᚷᚢᛏᚨᚾᛁᛟᚹᛁᚺᚨᛁᛚᚨᚷ **gutaniowihailag**

ᚷᚢᛏᚨᚾᛁ **gutani** is the genitive form 'of the Goths,' while **wi** is likely Proto-Gmc **wīhaz* 'consecrated, holy,' PWGmc **wīh*, 'sacred object' or 'consecrated place' (Ringe in Ringe and Taylor 2014, 178); one can compare Gothic *weihs*, OHG *wīh*, and Old English *wēoh* 'idol,' with clear semantic extension from 'holy, consecrated' to an object or place so hallowed. The OE reflex occurs twice in *Beowulf*: in the famous passage in which despairing Danes, then heathens as the poet says, ordered temple-sacrifices to be made to ward off Grendel's depredations: *Hwīlum hīe ġehēton æt hærgtrafum / wīġweorþunga* ('At such times they ordered at the old temples / holy offerings'; ll. 175–176b). And it occurs as the first element of the name of Wiglaf's father Wīhstān/Wēohstān 'consecrated stone' (perhaps referring to a runestone or one on which offerings were made, or one consecrated to a god; the ON equivalent is Vésteinn).

Runic alphabets are usually called *fuþarks* or *fuþorcs* after their first 6 letters (f-u-þ-a-r-k). Early use of the alphabet can be dated to perhaps no earlier than AD 150–200 (date of the Øvre Stabu spearhead inscription **raunijaz**, 'tester,' from Oppland, Norway). Use of the scripts continued through the medieval period, concentrated particularly in Scandinavia, Northern Continental Europe, and the British Isles, though runic inscriptions have also been found in Iceland, the Faroe Islands, Shetland Islands, Orkneys, France, Russia, Poland, Rumania, Hungary, Austria, Yugoslavia (two of the more far-flung inscriptions are: the Piraeus lion from Athens – runic graffiti was carved into its shoulder –, later moved to Venice; the personal name *Hálfdanr* [Halfdane] carved into a balustrade in the Hagia Sophia in Constantinople/Byzantium/Istanbul).

A number of *futhark* sets survive, including the older Germanic futhark (in which the earliest inscriptions from the continent and Southern Scandinavia were written, dating to approximately the late AD 2nd century) and the younger futhark (inscriptions in which have been found across Scandinavia, the British Isles, Iceland, and Greenland). Early inscriptions often indicate ownership of an item, though a group of inscriptions seems to indicate sacred use: the word ᚨᛚᚢ (**alu**), connected to 'ale' (OE *ealu*), is often found in seemingly ritualistic formulas; an early inscription on a large gold neck-ring found in Pietroassa, Romania, has the inscription: ᚷᚢᛏᚨᚾᛁᛟᚹᛁᚺᚨᛁᛚᚨᚷ (**gutaniowihailag**). English runologist R.I. Page reads this as 'hereditary possession of the Goths, holy and inviolate' (Page 2006, 78). The interpretation depends upon reading the ᛟ (**o**-rune) ideographically as its rune-name *ōþal*, 'property, inheritance, native land' < PrWGmc **ōþil* (Ringe and Taylor 2014, 270); this may be compared with OE *ǣðel* (Anglian) and *ēþel* (West Saxon) < the pre-form **ǣþil* exhibiting *i*-umlaut of Gmc ō. In OE, the rune-name usually means 'homeland, native land, one's own land,' as in its two occurrences in the "Rune Poem":

ᛇ **(ēoh)** byð ūtan unsmēþe trēow,
heard hrūsan fæst, hyrde fȳres,
wyrtrumum underwreþyd, wynan on ēþle (ll. 35–37).

['yew' is on the outside a rough tree,
hard and fast in the ground, a holder of fire,
with root-stalks undergirt, a joy on one's own land.]

ᛟ**(ǣþel)** byþ oferlēof ǣghwylcum men,
gif he mōt ðǣr rihtes and gerysena on
brūcan on bolde blēadum oftast (ll. 71–73; Halsall 1981).

['homeland' is preciously dear to each of men.
if he may there of right and by what is fitting
partake of in his dwelling oftenest his riches.]

One can note with the *ēþel*-rune a lexeme that shows the durability of a Germanic concept: from its phonological history, with its earlier and (usually) non-West Saxon form *ǣþel* evidencing early Germanic sound change (*i*-umlaut), to its semantic development, from the act of hallowing to thing hallowed to a broader range of cultural if not religious significance in the sense 'homeland, one's own possession.' The coming Viking Age in England, beginning in earnest with the sack of Lindisfarne in 793, was another Germanic invasion of Britain (which was then, especially in the west and north, still in good part Celtic), or perhaps re-invasion by Germanic-speakers. How closely they could understand each other in speech at that time is obscured by our records of Old Norse (which generally are later by a century or two), but that they shared a pre-Roman script was no doubt a reminder to them of a shared heritage. That, of course, did not stop the early kingdoms from their claims and squabbling, nor the Heptarchy its larger wars, nor the Anglo-Saxons their attempts to roll back the Scandinavians of the Danelaw. If the 'antiquarian' interest often seen in, for instance, the *Beowulf*-poet's recounting of Germanic history of the 4th through 6th centuries is any indication (and the West and North Germanic versions of a 'rune poem'), the linguistic awareness of 'Germanicness' likely matched the historical. Runic writing in England was not so prolific as in Scandinavia, but the corpus of extant inscriptions spans standing high-crosses to hog-back stones (among Christian monuments), to inscribed sundials and the Thames scramaseax (a short sword with a single edge) with a full *fuþorc* of Anglo-Saxon runes and the personal name **bēagnoþ**, either the owner of the sword or the inscriber.

Among the earliest runic-inscribed objects from Anglo-Saxon England is the Chessell Down bronze pail from a woman's grave on the Isle of Wight of the 6th century (from grave 45; the dating of square-headed brooches from other graves at the site has been placed at approximately to 520–570; Hines 1990, 438; the dating holds up in Hines 2023). The pail seems to have travelled from the Eastern Mediterranean to England and could have been inscribed on the journey in Continental Germanic territories though an English provenance for the inscription has been tentatively accepted; the worn-down runes occur among incised hunting scenes and may have been of ritual significance as the sequence is not otherwise interpretable; Hines 1990 interpreted the first rune as **b**, a reading accepted by Page 1999 who transcribed the inscription as ***b*** **w s [.] e c c c æ æ æ** (the ***b*** in bold italic is a conjectural reading; Page 2006, 158–159). At the same early Anglo-Saxon cemetery (grave 76) is an Runic-inscribed scabbard mouthpiece reading **æco : sœri** dating to 525–550 (Hines 2023, 69). Ralph W.V. Elliott interpreted this two-word inscription as 'increase to pain' or 'increase to sorrow' (Elliott 1989, 104–105), that is, a non-West Saxon dialectal form of *ēaca sorge*, nom. sing. of weak masc. noun *ēaca* 'addition, increase' (compare adv. *ēac* 'also' < PGmc **auk*) and the dat. sing. of fem. ō-stem *sorg*. The *æ* of *æco* derives from Proto-WGmc **au*, lengthened and fronted to *ǣo*, or *ǣu*, as in the Great Urswick or Tunwini Cross inscription (Cumbria), which has **bæurnæ** for the dat. sing. of *bearn* 'child' (Campbell §276), the glide of the diphthong then lowered and unrounded producing *ǣa*, then raised to *ēa* (Ringe and Taylor 2014, 172). The dative form *sœri* exhibits i-umlaut of Primitive OE *o* (with "scribal anticipation of *æ* in the following syllable"; Pheifer 1974, §53) and vocalization of g in the adjectival suffix *-ig* (Elliott 1989, 105) – the form usually appealed to for the umlaut of *o* is the gloss *soærgændi* to Latin *anxius* ('anxious, worried') in the early Épinal Glossary (Pheifer 1974, entry 79). This would be W-S *sorgende* (literally 'sorrowing'), the present participle of weak class II *sorgian*; *soærgændi* exhibits unstressed **a* > *æ* before nasals in *-ændi* (Pheifer 1974, §65.2). The corresponding gloss in the Erfurt and related 'Second' Corpus Glossaries is *sorgendi*, with these three glossaries dating to the 7th–8th centuries. Pheifer and Ringe both characterize the form as 'early Mercian' in a glossary that exhibits relatively few non-Anglian forms (Pheifer §§ 89–90; Ringe and Taylor 2014, 367).

The Chessell Down scabbard Runic inscription 'increase in sorrow/pain' fits in with a pattern of named weapons in early Germanic culture, many with ominous or boastfully threatening names; there are from *Beowulf* the swords: *Hrunting*, Unferth's sword that he loans to Beowulf, whose name may mean 'thruster' (compare OE *hrindan* and ON *hrinda* 'to thrust'); and *Nægling*, which fails Beowulf in the final fight with the dragon (it may mean 'of/from nails,' or 'descendant of nails,' referring allusively to its fabrication). These weapons are often prized heirlooms, sometimes of great antiquity; Hrunting is said to be *ān foran ealdgestrēona* [1458], 'the foremost of ancient treasures,' but literally, with *ān* with partitive genitive and the adverb *foran* 'before,' 'one before [all] of the ancient treasures.' In the Icelandic *Vatnsdœla saga* ('Vatnsdal saga') Ingimundr Thorsteinsson covets the elaborate sword of the Norwegian ship captain wintering with him; by a ruse, invoking a taboo on weapons in the temple of Freyr, he acquires the sword, which becomes a family heirloom *ok kǫlluðu Ættartanga* ('and they called [it] Ættartangi' [poison-tongue]; Sveinsson 1939, 49). The Chessell Down scabbard may be a composite piece, of English and Scandinavian origin, dating to the 5th and 6th centuries (and thus in the earliest Anglo-Saxon era), though the silver strip with the Runic inscription may be a later repair (Page 2006, 22). In parallel to this are the linguistic complexities: the early Runic inscriptions and texts such as the Épinal-Erfurt, Leiden, and Corpus Glossaries are invaluable witnesses to the earliest English (Lapidge 2023 has gone so far as to declare the 7th-century Leiden Glossary a product of the school of Theodore and Hadrian at Canterbury, and thus at the head of the entire Old English glossary tradition). But they can be maddeningly difficult to pin down in terms of dating, provenance, and dialect. The Chessell Down scabbard Runic inscription exhibits early Mercian features, but it was found on Wight, where one expects early Kentish (if Bede's settlement scheme is followed, Jutes landed in Wight). A general point here is that the corpus of early Runic inscriptions in England may still hold valuable comparative information to the early dialect picture of Old English; like the early glossaries, the inscriptions are often brief or detached enough to offer less help on early syntax – but with phonology and morphology they are an important early witness to the earliest development of English.

The language of the Épinal-Erfurt Glossary its editor found in accord with certain features of early Mercian (such as in the gloss to the Vespasian Psalter, of the later 8th century), perhaps even East Mercian, such as found in the glosses to Matthew in the Rushworth Gospels. But that would be 'Rushworth 1,' the individual glosses and at times interlinear continuous gloss added to the late 8th-/early 9th-century Irish Gospel book by the scribe Farman at least a century later; 'Rushworth 2' are the glosses added by the scribe Owun, who bore a British name, in a southern Northumbrian dialect (there is quite some literature on this subject: see Brown 1892, Coates 1997, and Kotake 2023). That some features from other dialect areas could appear in a Mercian text might indicate the work of later copyists; with regard to Runic inscriptions, one may be talking of the provenance of the object – if portable. Rather more fixed were the great standing crosses of the Irish mission area, which served also as 'beacons' on monastic pilgrimage routes; and these generally exhibit Northumbrian features (Runic inscriptions of the Ruthwell, Bewcastle, Urswick Crosses). But the two lines of evidence can reinforce one another in some useful ways: that dialectal forms found in Runic inscriptions appear also in 'learned' texts would argue for their utility in dialect geography, as well as register the reliability of the rune-carvers – there are indeed examples of uninterpretable or 'blundered' legends on objects in stone, metal, and wood, but one gets a general sense that this epigraphical evidence from early England was relatively competent (certainly in the longer inscriptions). Anglo-Saxon England did not see – so far as the finds to date indicate – use of Runic writing as widely as some of their Scandinavian neighbors (and ancestors) did. Nonetheless, the early finds help reinforce also the usefulness of the comparative method in linguistic reconstruction – one feels greater confidence in proto-forms when early inscriptions exhibit the very features reconstructed for early phases of Germanic.

The first of the Tjurkö (Blekinge, Sweden) bracteates discovered in 1817, along with a solidus of the emperor Theodosius II, is of Type C. The gold disc with top loop (so that it might be worn as a pendant or sewn onto clothing) was likely made from gold solidi coins melted down; its particular Type C iconography features the galloping horse with a human head above it in profile and a bird above the male head (it is not clear whether this is a stylized horse-and-rider icon, with bird hovering above, or some sort of zoomorphic figuration). The Germanic bracteates, like earlier Celtic coinage issues of Gaul and Britain, were often modeled on Roman coinage (the aureus, then its successor the solidus) but with crude to elaborate stylization of the more life-like Roman designs. Tjurkö 1 has along its rim a two-part Runic legend in retrograde (right-to-left) script dating to the period ca. 450–650 (the Theodosius solidus dates to AD 443): **wurte runoz an walhakurne | ·· heldaz kunimudiu ···** ('Wrought [these] runes on [the] foreign-grain, Heldaz for Kunimunduz'; Antonsen 2002, 260). The personal names are usually interpreted as 'battler, hero' (*Heldaz*: compare OE *hild* 'war, battle,' and Modern German *Held* 'hero') and 'kin-protector' (*Kuni-munduz*; compare OE *mund* 'hand, palm; trust, security, protection'). The language of the Tjurkö inscription, which likely dates to after the breakup of Northwest Germanic (generally placed before the start of the Migration Age), can easily be translated word for word into Old English: *wrohte rūne on wealh-corne, Hild Cynemunde* (in attested OE *rūnstæfas* 'rune-staves' would be the more likely term for 'runes').

Some of the earliest Runic inscriptions are cryptic for a variety of incidental, unintentional reasons: the letter-forms are rare, or record linguistic forms that are archaic, or difficult to decipher because weathered or lacking enough context. Other inscriptions were deliberately cryptic, as cryptographic systems developed especially in Scandinavia: here the 24-letter rune group could be divided into *ættir* (ON *ætt*, pl. *ættir*, can mean 'family') of 8 characters, and various codes derived from substitution or alphanumeric codes (assigning a character a number as to their place in the *ætt*). Perhaps the simplest of these codes was merely replacing a vowel with the nearest consonant that followed it in the *fuþark*. One of the rare Anglo-Saxon monuments to use of a cryptographic system is the fragmentary Hackness Stone of the 8th or 9th century, much of which remains undeciphered, but of what can be made out is the name Oedilburga, an abbess of **Hacanos** (Hackness; Page 2006, 83–84). The stone seems to employ *hahalruna*, ogham-like vertical strokes with multiples of downward left and right short strokes. These look something like the 'stacked' runes found on some early Runic monuments, such as the vertically stacked *týr*-rune (which may indicate an invocation of the god's name); there is also the mirror-image forward-and-retrograde pairing of ᚨᛚᚢ **alu** (OE *ealu*, found in a number of compound formations), which denotes 'ale' but more broadly connotes 'good fortune, luck,' perhaps even 'magic.' The right panel of the whale-bone Franks Casket employs a vowel-symbol substitution system not yet fully understood (Page 2006, 86–87).

Runic inscriptions ca. 250–800

Værløse fibula. Værløse, Denmark (Copenhagen capital region). AD 3rd century

ᚨᛚᚢᚷᛟᛞ **alugod**. This may be a proper name 'Alugod' as there are a number of examples of *Alu-* and OE *Ealu-* as the first element in dithematic names (*Ealuberht*), or it could be a truncated expression – such as of good luck, well wishes (Krause and Jankuhn 1966, 34).

Möjbro stone. Uppland, Sweden. AD 300

ᚨᚾᚨᚺᚨᚺᚨᛁᛊᛚᚨᚷᛁᚾᚨᛉᛃ ᚠᚱᚨᚹᚨᚱᚨᛞᚨᛉᛃ **anahahaislaginaz frawaradaz** = *ana hahai slaginaz frawaradaz* 'Slain on his steed, Frawaradaz' (the inscription appears on the stone in retrograde order)

Gallehus gold horns. South Jutland, Denmark. AD 400

ᛖᚲ ᚺᛚᛖᚹᚨᚷᚨᛊᛏᛁᛉ ᚺᛟᛚᛏᛁᛃᚨᛉ ᚺᛟᚱᚾᚨ ᛏᚨᚹᛁᛞᛟ **ek hlewagastiz holtijaz horna tawido** 'I, Hlewagastiz, son of Holtagastiz, made the horn.' The pair of golden drinking horns was discovered between 1639 and 1734, but was stolen in 1802 and apparently melted down. Reproductions of them on display in the Nationalmuseet (National Museum, Copenhagen, Denmark) are based on drawings made of the horns. They must have been high-status objects, perhaps for oath-swearing ceremonies, at about 2-1/2 feet in length and richly decorated in repoussé fashion (hammered from the reverse side). A number of the figures depicted resemble some of those human and apparently divine figures from the famous Gundestrup Cauldron from a bog find in Northern Denmark, generally identified as of Celtic La Tène style.

Franks casket. c. AD 700 (all panels but one on display in the British Museum, London; the remaining panel is in Florence, in the Bargello/Museo Nazionale). The Franks casket is one of three runic-inscribed boxes of whale ivory found on the continent (the Gandersheim box and Mortain coffer are the others); they were all likely reliquaries, holding saints' relics or other sacred relics. The Franks casket is a remarkably executed carved whale-bone box depicting the journey of the Magi (ᛗᚫᚷᛁ front panel) as well as scenes from Germanic lore on its panels; over 260 runes in relief appear on the box. The top panel or lid features an archer named ᚫᚷᛁᛚᛁ (**Ægili**) defending his home against raiders. The right-side panel includes a runic inscription of three lines of Old English verse:

Her Hos sitiþ   on harmberga
agl[.] drigiþ   swa hiræ Ertae gisgraf
sarden sorga   and sefa torna.

['Her Hos sits on the sorrow-mound; / she suffers distress as Ertae had imposed it on her, / a wretched den (wood?) of sorrows and of torments of mind'; the translation is uncertain, as is the story alluded to.]

(*continued*)

(continued)

The main inscription does not pertain to any of the scenes illustrated but consists of these lines of verse:

fisc.flodu ahof	**on fergenberig.**
warþ gasric grorn	**þær he on greut giswom.**
hronæsban.	

The verse is taken as a riddle explaining the origin of the box's material: 'The flood lifted up the fish onto the cliff-bank; / the whale became sad, where he swam on the shingle' (translation from Elliott 1989). The final word, *hronæs-ban*, provides the solution: whale-bone.

Anglo-Saxon coinage

ᛈᚪᛞᚪ **pada**. Name of the moneyer of *sceat* coinage from Mercia; the issues, in gold and electrum (gold-silver alloy), number about 20 specimens and date from c. AD 660 and later.

ᛖᛈᚪ **epa**. Name of the moneyer of silver *sceattas* from East Anglia area (the name of the moneyer seems to be in the Kentish dialect), dating to the end of the 7th century through the first quarter of the 8th century.

ᚪᚦᛁᛚᚱᚪᛞ ᛒᚱᚩᚦᛖᚱ/ᛒᚱᚪᚦᛖᚱ ᚹᛁᚻᛏᚱᚪᛞ **aþilrad. broþer/braþer. wihtrad**. Moneyers who minted *sceattas* in Southern England (Canterbury and Reculver) and the Netherlands (Walcheren) c. AD 730–740.

ᛒᛖᚩᚾᚪ ᚱᛖX **beona reg (rex).** Name of the monarch under whom were issued early silver pennies in Southern and Eastern England in the late 8th century (the second word is a Romano-Runic version of the Latin word for 'king').

Runic inscriptions are a tricky source of dialectal information, though the *fuþorc* given at the outset of this section includes 'additional' characters such as ᛇ (i), which could be a mid-front vowel (more retracted than /i/) but in the Thornhill inscription (Yorkshire) it is used for the palatalized g (Page 2006, 47), while ᚸ (ḡ) and ᛤ (k̄) seem to have been used in the Northwest for the 'back' velar consonants /k/ and /g/ (i.e., versus their 'fronted' allophones, though the latter rune may have been used for the velar consonant /k/ following front vowels; Page 2006, 46–47). One would expect some regional variation not just in character-forms but also in their phonetic values, and the dialectal evidence from Runic bears further study. The use of runes for epigraphic purposes was not limited to plastic media (stone, wood, metal); there was an interest as well in *runica manuscripta*, of the use of runes in medieval manuscripts, singly or in *fuþorcs* (Derolez 1954). Runic sets could be found alongside other 'secret' or fantastic scripts, and it may be that as the script fell into disuse epigraphically, and rune-smiths presumably forgot or lost their trade, its preservation in manuscripts was felt to be of value. Some of this interest was no doubt antiquarian, but the use of runes in poetic manuscripts, in which the phonetic value of the rune and its rune-name could be simultaneously employed (literally or as a form of paronomasia), suggests that runes may have been seen as part of poetic and broader cultural heritage (on the rune-names see Elliott 1989, 62–63). The "Rune Poem," in Old English and Old Norse, is perhaps the finest example of the tradition. Runes were not just cryptic but also gnomic, lending a pithiness to poetic diction with their double significance; late in the Old Norse "Rune Poem" one reads:

ᛘ (maðr) er manns gaman
ok moldar auki
ok skipa skreytir (Halsall 1981, 186).

['Man' is of man the delight
and earth's increase
and of ships the adorner.]

In very brief form, the poet has summed up what 'man' is: a joy and companion unto others, an increase of the earth (an allusion as well to the Creation story in Genesis), a fashioner and adorner of ships (in that nautical culture of the English and Scandinavians). All that, but for 'man' only the rune is given, a single stave.

4.7 THE BEGINNINGS OF ENGLISH DIALECTOLOGY: LONG-RANGE PATTERNS FOR THE HISTORY OF THE LANGUAGE

There is nothing of the kind for the Old English period as there is for Early and Late Middle English with the projects *A Linguistic Atlas of Early Middle English* (LAEME) and *A Linguistic Atlas of Late Middle English* (LALME; see Chapter 5), and some scholars might say there cannot be. Old English spans the longest linguistic era of English: some 600 years from what might be called the beginnings of Old English (the earliest Runic and coin evidence in 'Pre-Old English') to the first generations after the Norman Conquest (as discussed below, Old English did not disappear in 1066 – a political system did, but the language persisted for at least a century into the new regime). Hogg 1988 had spoken of the "impossibility of Old English dialectology" (Hogg 1988), but this was a caution about types of evidence and constraints upon their interpretation rather than a literal despairing of the matter (and Hogg set out much of what is needed in analyzing Old English dialects in Hogg 1992, 67–167). Thomas Toon (also in CHEL I, 409–452; see also Toon 1983) also demurred that "[t]here is, unfortunately, no full-scale study of Old English dialects such as exists for Middle English and present-day English" (Toon 1992, 451). Nonetheless, it is standard editorial practice in the production of critical editions of medieval English texts to include a section on 'Language' in the introduction, often after a description of the manuscript(s) in terms of dating, provenance, and, where relevant, interrelations between surviving copies of the text, a tradition that derives from the production of critical editions of classical texts, such as for the Bibliotheca Teubneriana series (from German publisher B.G. Teubner, of Leipzig, then of Leipzig and Stuttgart during the DDR period, now of Berlin) or the Oxford Classical Texts series (blue dust jackets for Greek, light green for Latin).

Thus, there is a chronological range, somewhat disjointed, and a geographic range span (as 'England' grew at Britain's expense) to consider in an attempt at describing the dialect picture of Old English.

The commonest presumption is that Old English dialect boundaries follow, at least broadly, the tribal boundaries of the settlement period (approximately 450–650), a period of near-constant fighting between Germanic tribes and native Britons (and in the north, Scotti [Irish of the Dál Riada], Strathclyde Britons, and Picts), or among the tribes themselves as they made their land claims. In general, the picture given in Gildas and Bede (seen in Chapter 3) has some validity: the Angles, being from more northerly Continental homelands (Angeln, Schleswig-Holstein) settled in East Anglia (hence the eponymous *Anglia*) and pushed northward into what would be the later 'Anglian' kingdoms of Mercia and Northumbria; the Saxons, whose name derives from *seax* a shorter-blade sort of stabbing knife (thus something like 'People of the Blade'), divided into West, East, and South Saxons, and would lend their name to the regions Wessex, Essex (a kingdom that was never fully independent), and Sussex; the Jutes, from what is now the Jutland peninsula, or 'Continental Scandinavia,' (mainland Denmark), about whom less is known than the Saxons or Angles, were the northernmost of the tribes who invaded Britain, but they settled primarily in the old Celtic kingdom of Kent (a usual explanation is that the number who came over was less than that of Saxons and Angles). Bede had placed Jutish settlements in Kent, the Isle of Wight, and Southern Hampshire, for which there is some archaeological evidence in terms of "shared culture" (Nielsen 1998, 65–66). Frisians are mentioned by both Procopius and Bede as having been part of the *adventus*, and there is some place-name and archaeological evidence in support (Nielsen 1998, 66, with caveats). Franks are believed to have been among the settlers, perhaps also settlers from what is now Flanders and the Netherlands. But it is the traditional triad of Angles, Saxons, and Jutes who will form the 'Anglo-Saxon Heptarchy' of the 5th–9th centuries, through periods of Northumbrian and Mercian power to the rise of Wessex. And despite misgivings about overlapping tribal settlement patterns with dialectal regions, it is the best basic explanation we have for the origin of the dialects of Old English.

The Old English prosimetrical version of *The Benedictine Office* (Ure 1957; see also Klein 2012) survives in two later manuscript copies: Oxford, Bodleian Library MS Junius 121 (given the siglum B), and Cambridge, Corpus Christ College MS 201 (with the siglum C), both dating to the mid-11th century. B is a Worcester product and its language is a late West Saxon; the provenance of C is uncertain, and it exhibits a number of non-West Saxon features. While for *a* before a nasal consonant B has the expected late West Saxon raising to /e/, C has /æ/; C fairly consistently has lWS /y/ - /y:/ unrounded to /i/, or /e/ for /y/ (*alēsde* for *alȳsde* 'redeemed, absolved'; this is generally an Anglian, Mercian or Northumbrian, feature, but common also in lWS texts; Ringe in Ringe and Taylor 2014, 262; Schlemilch 1914); /eo/ in B can appear as /o/ in C (as in *scolde* for *sceolde* 'should'; a feature that begins to look like Middle English *sholde*; Ure 1957, 67–69). The non-West Saxon forms have been associated with a Southeast Saxon *patois* (Ure 1957, 69), but some features also look to be Kentish (useful for these late changes to OE is Schlemilch 1914). In short, we see in one manuscript a standard late West Saxon of Worcester, and in the other a dialectal admixture that points southeastward, that is, toward London and Kent, where in the early Middle English period Southern and Southeastern forms would meet in an emerging London dialect. This is by no means a certain matter, but it may show some signs of what was to happen in the next phase of the history of English, and help explain the rise of the London dialect, which had not been a major dialectal area for most of the Anglo-Saxon period. We look instead to major ecclesiastical and intellectual centers such as Winchester and Worcester for a sort of dialectal clout. Despite the relatively restricted range of Kentish Old English, this Southeastern dialect was buoyed by the ecclesiastical power of Canterbury.

Old English dialectology is also complicated by the often long transmission history of texts of liturgical and ecclesiastic use, such as psalters and saints' lives. The Old English *Life of St. Chad* might presumably be associated with Lichfield, to which see Chad (Ceadda) was appointed as Bishop of the Mercians (Lichfield was in the heart of Mercia). Chad would also later be Bishop of York, closer to home as he was, along with his brothers Cedd, Cynibil, and Caelin, Northumbrian-born. The names of the four brothers are British, not Anglo-Saxon, and this adds to that difficult picture of the fate of the Britons – that they did not simply 'disappear.' Chad had been fostered as a monk at Lindisfarne, then under the Irish abbot Colmán, who, when he returned to Ireland, set up one of the monasteries there for Anglo-Saxon monks (Maihgh Eo na Sacsan, 'Mayo of the Saxons'), as the conversion and monastery-building program in Northumbria had been dominated by Irish missionaries. Chad is believed to have been at another of these Irish monasteries for Anglo-Saxons, Rath Melsigi in County Carlow. The Old English version of his life is preserved in Oxford, Bodleian Library MS Hatton 116 of the mid-12th century, though the text is believed to be some two centuries or so older, and it shows signs of having been composed in a Mercian dialect and then transmitted in a late West Saxon copy; one telltale feature is the replacement of *io* with WS *eo* (Vleeskruyer 1953, 62–67; useful too is his list of other probable Mercian texts 50–61, which includes the Royal Psalter, the prose life of St. Guthlac, the *Læcebōc* and *Lacnunga*, early medical tracts including what might be called folk medicine charms and recipes, and the prose texts of the *Beowulf* manuscript). Spellings such *Ongenðio* (dative singular) and *Ongenðiowes* for the name of the king of the Swedes Ongentheow in *Beowulf* are among the Mercian and other non-West Saxon forms that have set scholars looking for where and when the epic may have been composed; the split between 'late daters' and 'early daters' is based partly on palaeography, internal evidence of the poem's possible political resonance with one Anglo-Saxon court or another, and the dialectal features (for the preeminent 'late dating' study see Kiernan 1997; in favor of an earlier date Fulk 1992 is the most thorough treatment of the dialectal features; on one particular vocabulary test, and in favor of an early dating, see Pulsiano and McGowan 1990). The prize in this case is locating the masterpiece of Old English literature, one of the world's greatest epics, a poem of 3,182 lines of perhaps the finest literary merit of anything – that has survived and we know of – composed in the Old English period. But much about the origin and composition of *Beowulf* remains a mystery; the poetic formulas or 'runs' point toward a once oral tradition, while the language of the poem is 'mixed' dialectally, and both can only tell us so much about the history of the poem.

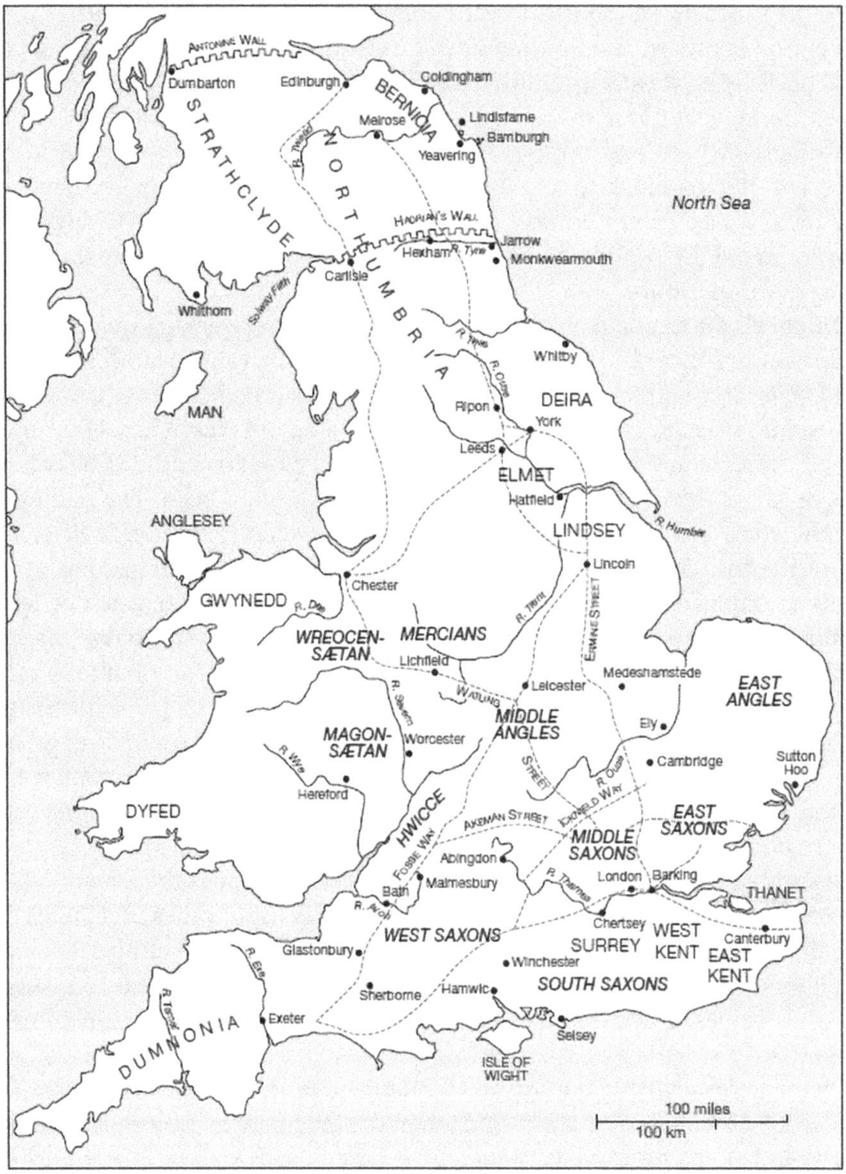

Anglo-Saxon England, from *A Guide to Old English*, Mitchell and Robinson (2011)

The most pervasive language contact situation post-597 (the arrival of the Gregorian mission in Kent) is the sustained Latin-Old English contact in the religious and intellectual sphere of the monastic centers founded with Christianization. The long arc of this spiritual and academic transformation spans the whole of the British Isles; Canterbury would retain its early prominence as the seat of the English Catholic and then Anglican church, though Kent, politically and dialectally, would not. Northumbria would be an early powerhouse, tethered to the pilgrim and *peregrini* routes from Kells, Clonmacnoise, Derry, and other Irish monastic centers to those founded by Irish monks and their students in the north, Iona and Lindisfarne notably, the former by St. Columba in 563 and the latter by St. Aidan in 634 (who had been a pupil of Senán of Munster). The milieu of Northumbria and its Christianization was not simply Celtic because of these Irish missionaries (and the many who followed and educated their successors as abbots as well as kings of Northumbria); the old kingdoms of the north bore Celtic names: Bernicia (Brythonic *Berneich* or *Bryneich* or other variants), Deira (ultimately from Proto-Celtic **daru* 'oak,' as is Derry in Ireland) were Anglian kingdoms, while Rheged was a Brittonic kingdom; its name is of uncertain etymology, though the *-ged* likely means 'wood' and like Welsh *coed* derives from Proto-Celtic **kayto-*; that it is a likely place-name element is supported by the Roman military post along Watling Street at *Letocetum* 'gray [ash] wood,' in Staffordshire (Matasović 2009, 198). The great double-house at Monkwearmouth-Jarrow was founded by Benedict Biscop, at, successively, Monkwearmouth in 674 and Jarrow in 682, upon land granted by King Ecgfrith of Deira (and from 670 King of Northumbria). Benedict was earlier on a nobleman in the Northumbrian royal house, *þegn* to Oswiu of Bernicia; his founding of the two establishments marked a turning point in the English church of Northumbria, though he too was raised in an Irish and British milieu. Like a number of Northumbrian nobles, Oswiu had been educated by the Irish and spoke Irish (Bede, *HE* III.xxv); amid the internecine and cross-kingdom struggles of the era (war against the Britons, raids and counter-raids involving Picts), Oswiu had spent a period of exile with his brothers in the Dál Riata, the Gaelic kingdom spanning Western Scotland – Argyll, 'coastland of the Gaels,' recalls this kingdom (Mills DBPN, s.v.). The grantor of lands, King Ecgfrith, would fall in battle against the Picts of Fortriu at Nechtansmere in 685. His successor, Aldfrith, was the son of Oswiu and an Irish princess (said to be Fín of the Northern Uí Néill), and Aldfrith's Irish education and affiliations may mark the peak of Irish influence in Northumbria. Aldfrith was bilingual in Irish and English, and a collection of wisdom sayings has in Irish literature been attributed to him, the *Bríathra Flainn Fhína maic Ossu* (Ireland 1999), 'the words of Flann Fína mac Ossu' (Aldfrith's Irish name: Flann of Fín, son of Ossu [Oswiu]). Oswiu's first wife was said to be Rhiainfellt, a princess of Rheged of Yr Hen Ogledd ('The Old North'), whose name meant either 'lightning queen' or 'lightning maiden' (Modern Welsh *fellten*, 'lightning,' is the lenited form of *mellten*; on *rhiain* 'queen; maiden,' cf. Matasović 2009, s.v. **rīganī*). Amid the parleys, negotiations, treaties, and threats between Anglian rulers of Bernicia and Deira and the Britons, Picts, and Gaels, there must have been a good many interpreters; Aldfrith and others spoke Irish, but we find little mention in this period of knowledge of British and Pictish.

Such was Oswiu's role as patron of the English church that Theodore of Tarsus, archbishop of Canterbury and, with Hadrian of North Africa, founder of the great school at Canterbury, came to Northumbria to visit the king. And this meeting of the two brought together the two great spheres of Christian learning in England: the immensely influential Canterbury school and the Hiberno-English culture of the north that produced a golden age of Northumbrian scholarship and manuscript making – it was under Oswiu's son Aldfrith that the Lindisfarne Gospels, with its magnificent 'Insular' (Irish-influenced) illumination, and Codex Amiatinus (the earliest surviving complete copy of the Vulgate) were produced. And common to all of this activity, from south and southeast to northeast, was the Latin language.

A quick view of dialectal differences between early Northumbrian (Anglian) OE and late 'early' to mid-West Saxon, that is Northumbrian of the 8th century and West Saxon of the 9th, may be gained from the relevant dialectal versions of "Cædmon's Hymn" in manuscripts of Bede's *Ecclesiastical History*, which may itself be dated to a few years or so before or after AD 737. Four Northumbrian versions of this short poem survive, two of them from the earliest copies of Bede's text: the 'Moore Bede,' Cambridge, Cambridge University Library Kk.5.16, and the 'Leningrad Bede,' now the

'St. Petersburg Bede,' St. Petersburg, National Library of Russia lat. Q. v. I. 18. The West Saxon version is given here in the right column from the copy found in Oxford, Bodleian Library Hatton 43 (late 10th–early 11th century):

Nu scylan hergan	hefaenricaes uard	Nu we sculon herian	heofonrices weard
metudaes maecti	end his modgidanc	metudes myhte	⁊ his modgeþanc,
uerc wuldurfadur	sue he uundra gihuaes	wurc wuldorfæder,	swa he wundra gehwilc,
eci dryctin,	or astelidae;	ece drihten,	ord astealde;
he aerist scop	aelda barnum	he ærest gesceop	ylda bearnum
hebe til hrofe,	haleg sceped,	heofon to hrofe,	halig scyppend,
tha middungeard	moncynnes uard;	middangearde	mancynnes weard;
eci dryctin,	æfter tiædæ	ece drihten.	Æfter tida
firum foldu,	frea allmectig.	firum on foldum,	frea ælmyhtig.

(Smyth 1968, 38–41; Bodleian Library digital facsimile[7])

Here, for the sake of convenience, manuscript <ȝ>, the *yogh*, has been transcribed as <g>, <ƿ> (lower-case *wynn*) as <w>; the *yogh* could represent the palatal glide or semi-vowel (or approximant) /j/ (especially in 'classical' West Saxon), the voiced velar fricative /ɣ/ (this is likely value in the Northumbrian versions), and also the voiced velar stop /g/ (and perhaps also a palatal g allophone), likely only in later texts (Hogg and Fulk 2011, 30–31, 47, who notes that the carver of the Ruthwell Cross runic inscription did not distinguish between initial and medial g, the latter most likely a fricative). Anglian dialects Northumbrian and Mercian regularly employ *u-* and *uu-* for *w-*; the form *siunhuurful*, 'rounded,' from the Corpus Glossary (*sinuurbul* in the Épinal Glossary) looks quite unfamiliar beside West Saxon *sinhwyrfel*. The early Anglian glossary forms, dating to the 8th century, here also exhibit the retraction **wir* + C > **wur* + C, as in *uuiurthit* 'becomes' in 1b of the Northumbrian version of *Bede's Death Song* (likely dating, in this dialect, to the 8th century as well) for 3rd sing. pres. of *weorðan* (strong class 3): the West Saxon form would be *wierðeð*, *wierþ* with syncopation. Compare *weorðeð* from a Kentish charter of the 9th century from Surrey, unsyncopated and not exhibiting the effect of *i*-umlaut as would WS forms; Ringe has noted that these verb forms usually do undergo syncopation (better than 90% of the time) in Kentish, and *weorðeð* may more likely be Mercian (Ringe in Ringe and Taylor 2014, 352).

The complexities of OE dialectology are apparent in such cases, where a feature might be interpreted as Kentish (southeastern) or Mercian (midlands-northern), distinctions that would be easier to determine and catalogue in Middle English. Broadly, Anglian dialects are the most distinctive in their early form – that is, in contrast with the West Saxon of the classical (Alfredian to early Benedictine Reform, that is, the 9th and 10th centuries) and late (Æthelwoldian: Æthelwold of Winchester, whose episcopacy was 963–984) and transitional West Saxon periods (11th century, and continued use in some 12th-century manuscripts). Late West Saxon texts can often exhibit some Kentish features: *ǣ* raised to *ē*, short and long *io* for *eo*, monophthongization of short and long *ea* as *e* (*ġelēfan* for *ġelēafan*, WS *ġe-lēafa* 'belief'), *eo* > *u* between *w* and *r* (*wurðian* for *weorðian* 'worship, honor'; Pulsiano and McGowan 1994, 194–198). If it was the early tribal squabbles in the settlement era, then the establishment of kingdoms in the Heptarchy era (6th to 8th centuries) that first drew dialectal boundaries among

[7] https://digital.bodleian.ox.ac.uk/objects/7850a308-0dd6-4d9a-b5b5-cbd6085b18dd/surfaces/dc5dcf3c-455a-47bf-beb4-06c04fb85433/

descendants of Angles (in Northumbria, Mercia, and East Anglia), Saxons (East, West, and South Saxon kingdoms), and Jutes (if that is indeed who settled Kent and Wight), then it was the ecclesiastical centers, from Iona, Lindisfarne, and Wearmouth-Jarrow in the north, to Canterbury to Winchester and Exeter in the southeast to southwest that helped reinforce dialectal differences in the standard forms of written Old English that emerged in early English schools: the *Schriftsprachen* (forms of a 'written standard') of Northumbrian schools, Theodore and Hadrian and their successors at the school of Canterbury, and the Benedictine reformers at Winchester. Indeed, it is that last center that has been credited with 'standard Old English' (Gneuss 1972; Gretsch 1999 and others of the 'Munich school'; Hofstetter 1988 focuses on 'Winchester vocabulary'). The caveat is that one is speaking about a *Schrftsprache*, a 'written standard' in use among ecclesiastical writers, who wrote what was not necessarily more broadly spoken. And while a *Schriftsprache* can involve written norms grammatical and syntactic, much of the work so far on 'standard Old English' at Winchester has focused largely upon vocabulary, and even more closely upon glosses – for Gretsch 1999, the Royal Psalter gloss, glosses to Aldhelm's *De Virginitate*, an *opus geminatum*, that is, one in prose and verse, and Æthelwold's translation of the *Regula Sancti Benedicti* ('Rule of St. Benedict'). Glossary words are useful especially to readers, and do not always reflect everyday speech, of which we have relatively little to go by in Old English. Ælfric's *Colloquy*, ca. 995–1000, is a type of *magister et discipuli* ('teacher and students') dialogue in which the cleric master has young novitiates ask questions of various tradespeople: *yrþlincgas/ierþlingas* ('earthlings,' farmers), *sċēphyrdas* (sheepherders), *oxanhyrdas* (oxherders), *huntan* (hunters), *fisċeras* (fishermen), *fugleras* (fowlers), *ċȳpmenn* ('cheapmen,' merchants), *sċēwyrhtan* (shoemakers), *sealteras* (salters), *bæceras* (bakers; Garmonsway 1991); the text here is in a late OE with Winchester affinities (Ælfric had been a student of Æthelwold).

Hwæt seġst þu, ierþling?
What sayest thou earthling?

Hu begæst þu þinne cræft?
How be-goest thou thine craft?

Lā lēof, þearle ic swince! Ælce dæġe iċ sceal on dæġræd ūtgān.
  Lo dear, hardily I work! Each day I shall [must] on day-break go out.
  [*þearle:* 'strongly, vigorously'; *swince* < *swincan* 'to labor, work,' Chaucer's *swinken*]

Þonne sceal iċ þā oxan tō felda drīfan and tō þære sylh ġocian.
  Then shall I the oxen to field drive and to the plough yoke [them].

Nis nān winter swā stearc þæt iċ dyrre æt hām lūtian:
  Not is there none winter so stark that I dare at home lurk.
  [*lutian*: 'to lie hidden, hide, lurk'; cf. OE *lūtan* 'to bend, stoop, decline; lay down,' which survives in BrE *lout* = 'to bend or stoop' which is possibly behind the noun form *lout* 'oaf']

ne dearr iċ for mines hlafordes ege.
  Nor dare I for my lord's terror [for fear of my master].

Ac þonne iċ þā oxan ġeġeocod hæbbe, and þæt scear and þone culter on þære sylh
  But then I the oxen have yoked, and the share and the culter on the plow

ġefæstnod hæbbe, þonne sceal iċ fulne æcer erian oþþe māre.
fastened have, then shall I a full acre plow or more.

Hwæt māre dēst þū? Hæfst þū ġīet māre tō dōnne?
What more doest thou? Have you yet more to do?

Ġiese lēof, miċel iċ hæbbe tō dōnne! Iċ sceal þāra oxena binne mid hīeġe āfyllan,
Yes dear, much I have to do! I shall the oxen bin with hay a-fill,

and hīe wæterian, and hira steall feormian.
And water them, and their stall cleanse.

In this extract from Ælfric's *Colloquy*, in its Old English version (the colloquy texts were usually part of instruction in Latin), here with a very literal rendering, one senses the language of young novitiates (boys, really) asking simple questions of their classroom guests – the conceit of the dialogue is that practicing members of the professions have visited the classroom to field questions about what they do, and of what value it is (the salter and baker are especially insistent on the value of their work). This is one of the few instances in Old English where we get a sense of 'common speech,' here because the novitiates are young, though they are being trained to join an intermediate educated class. Then, as even now, families from all ranks sent off some of their children to enter religious orders; for those from more modest backgrounds, there was a certain status conferred by the family member who was a priest or nun, or even an abbot or abbess (the bishops generally came from the higher social classes). The students in Ælfric's dialogue are building their vocabulary – a number of the words for types of fish, or plants, or parts of the plow appear also in Ælfric's *Glossary* (Zupitza-Gneuss 2003). They are also learning a lesson in Christian compassion and humility; though they are preparing to advance into an intermediate class (second in status to the ruling class), not a 'middle' class as that does not yet really exist, they are being nudged, interview by interview, into a respect for labor, for the interconnected society whose religious and spiritual needs they were one day to minster to. Many of the early Latin loanwords to Old English involve Greek and Latin terms from the new faith introduced into 6th-century England that, by fits and starts, became the dominant faith (with occasional backsliding, and a pagan re-infusion in the Viking Age). Here, the students learn the basic native terms for the *realia* of their physical world, and they are subtly encouraged to develop a respect for the trades and their fellow English people. The language of the *Colloquy* might be seen as part of the common register, a daily dialect, and, in the voices of the children speaking, youth speech – simplified, direct, given to exclamations. The use of *leof* ('dear') by the respondents from the trades seems the tender speech of elders, and is perhaps also marked by a degree of deference to these future scholars.

Though we have much more evidence from Middle English of 'low' vocabulary – in Langland's *Piers Plowman* or Chaucer's *Canterbury Tales* – there are still some glimpses in Old English, mainly from the glossaries. 'Arse' words are to be found in Old English, *earsgang* ('latrine, outhouse'), *earsendu* ('buttocks,' *earslīra* has the same meaning), *earsling* ('arse-wise' – MdE vulgar *ass-backwards* and taboo deformative *bass-ackwards* come to mind), *earsode* ('arsed, having an arse'), *earsþyrel* ('arse-hole'), and Old English had at least two words for farting, *feorting,* the immediate ancestor, and *fisting*, which may or may not have differed semantically based on volume (see McGowan 2003). It is difficult to reconstruct for OE the tone and vocabulary level of such 'low' words; they are evidently informal, perhaps more forceful by being direct and non-evasive (non-euphemistic); *earsode* 'arsed' glosses *tergosum* ('backwards') in the Paris Psalter; the glossator had more neutral glosses available, adverbs *bæcling* and *hinderling* ('backwards,' 'hinder-ly'), and *earsode* occurs only in this manuscript among the 14 or so glossed psalters from Anglo-Saxon England. Perhaps this was a more direct and vivid choice to gloss the Latin, but *earsode* and kin seem to be examples of informal OE if not slang or 'low' or vulgar language.

The early Northumbrian 3rd sing. pres. form *uuiurthit* (*Bede's Death Song* 1b) might be compared with the 3rd sing. pres. subjunctive form *uueorthae* in line 5b of the poem (West Saxon *weorðe*). Such variability, even within the same text, within mere lines of each other in this instance, is to be expected in many of the surviving OE texts. This may in part be due to an orthography that was still to an extent regional, even local (based on monastic center or cathedral school), but also to the variability in origin of scribes. As seen earlier, Irish and English monks trained German scholars at monastic centers on the continent, such as Fulda and St. Gallen; at the latter one finds in the early manuscripts glosses in Old Irish, Old English, and Old High German (some of the Old English glosses partially 'Germanized' by the High German-speaking students). The caveat mentioned earlier as to the 'impossibility' of Old English dialectology (Hogg 1988) was not prescriptive; it may be more a matter that the results will be less refined or detailed as the monumental work of the Middle English dialect atlases (LAEME, LALME), which had a much larger corpus of texts to work with. Nonetheless, from the earliest Runic inscriptions and bilingual glossaries, the latter with some their at times bewildering early dialectal forms and spelling conventions, to the later texts in multiple copies (homilies, saints's lives), and those whose tradition spans the entire Anglo-Saxon era (the glossed Psalters), enough likely awaits future researchers in drawing somewhat more definitively the dialect picture of Old English.

4.8 AD 793 – CONTACT SITUATION: THE VIKING AGE

As will be seen in the next chapter, along with the 'Middle English as Creole' debate, provocative questions have been raised and suggestions made about whether English in its development pidginized then Creolized with either Old Norse or Anglo-Norman French, or even whether Old English should more properly be classified as a North Germanic language. That Old English may have formed contact varieties with Old Norse is not unlikely. Some sort of *ad hoc* for-the-moment simplification of the languages likely occurred – in the contact situation. The "Rune Poem" cited above is one instance of a shared poetic tradition, though the versions certainly have their differences; while all extant Old English poetry was composed in the Germanic accentual system of five basic types (A-E verses), what the Norse called *fornyrðislag* ('old tale-meter') was one of a number of their poetic meters. It is conventional in histories of English to suggest that West Germanic Old English and North Germanic Old Norse were similar enough to make basic communication feasible; given some simplification in forms, on the part of the Old English or Norse speaker or both, this is likely true. But a brief passage from the Old Norse *þáttr* ('short story' – literally, 'a single strand of a rope'; Zoëga 2004, s.v.) "Auðun and the Bear" (*Þáttr Auðunar Vestfirzka*, 'Tale of

Authun of the West-Fjords'; Gordon 2009, 129–135; here, 130, ll. 36–38) makes clear that there were enough differences to hinder initial mutual intelligibility:

Auðun: nom. sing. masc. (proper name)
svarar: 3rd sing. pres. indic. < *svara*, weak II
Herra: nom. sing. masc. (this seems likely equivalent to a vestigial vocative case – the case of direct address – with sense of 'O lord/my lord')
þat: neuter nom. sing. of demonstrative pronoun 'that'
er: 3rd sing. pres. < *vera*, 'to be'
á: prep. + dative 'on, to, in' (here 'in')
yðru: dat. sing. masc. of 2nd person personal pronoun *yðarr* 'your'
valdi: dative sing. of neuter noun *vald* 'power' (compare Old English *weald* and Modern English verb *wield*)
en: conjunction 'but'
engu: pronoun < *engi*, 'none,' dat. sing. neuter – here a sense of 'nothing'
játum: 1st pl. pres. < *játa*, II ' to say "yes" [*já*] to,' 'agree to' plus dative – here, 'dative of the thing,' i.e., with a verb of agreement, what is being agreed to will be in the dative case: *engu*, *ǫðru*, and *þessu* are governed by *játum*
vér: 1st plural nom. of 1st person personal pronoun, 'we'
ǫðru: dat. sing. neut. < *annarr*, 'other,' of the strong adjective declension
en: conjunction 'than'
þessu: dat. sing. neuter of demonstrative pronoun
er: here the relative pronoun ('which,' or 'that which')
vér: 'we'
hǫfum: 1st plural pres. < *hafa*, III (here used as an auxiliary verb with following past participle form)
áðr: adv. 'before, first'
ætlat: past participle neuter < *ætla*, III, 'intend' (thus *hǫfum ætlat* = 'had intended')

[very literally: Authun answers, 'Lord, that is in your power, but nothing agree we to other than that which we had before intended.']

In the first instance, there are significant phonological differences, particularly with rounded vowels, that obtain to this day between English and North Germanic languages (and between Modern English and Modern Dutch and German). Old Norse had a more complicated vowel inventory than OE with rounded vowels *y* and *ý*, *ǫ* and *ǫ́* (/ɔ/ and /ɔ:/), *œ* (the open-mid front rounded vowel), *ø* (the mid to open-mid front rounded vowel), and diphthongs *au* (/ɔu/), *ei* (/ei/), and *ey* (/ɛy/). The velars /k/ and /g/ underwent palatalization (/k/ before /i/ and /j/), and a number of Old English–Old Norse correspondences can be deciphered by recognizing assimilative changes in ON – for example, strong verb class 3 OE *drincan* 'to drink,' ON *drekka* (Gothic *drigkan* < PGmc **drinkaną*; Ringe 2017, 269). ON lost the *n* in final position in unaccented syllables, as here in the infinitive form (compare also OE *in* 'in, on' and ON *í* with compensatory lengthening; Gordon 2009, 280). As with the contact situation between Celtic and Old English, there were likely a good many bilingual speakers (and in Wales, Scotland, and Ireland in the Viking Age, multilingual). Indeed, some level of bilingualism was necessary to serve as a vector of transmission for the relatively large number of loans from Old Norse to Old English. A perennial question regarding Norse-OE contact is that, apart from fully bilingual speakers – of which there were perhaps a good many within and bordering the Danelaw and the northern islands – is whether there were pidgin and Creole varieties, either Norse- or English-based. As to the former, the answer is likely affirmative (once again, it is a potential vector for the transmission of Norse loans to OE); as to the latter, the question is much more difficult. A first question as to the 'Norse Creole' matter is to what extent, in their development ca. 793–1066, these North and West Germanic languages differed – was it enough to hamper mutual intelligibility – which is usually seen as the primary linguistic test in any language vs. dialect distinction. A second question is to what extent populations in Britain were multilingual before the Viking Age: prior to the establishment of the Danelaw there would have been, in the Welsh borderlands, the Southwest (the 'greater' Cornwall region out to Exeter), parts of the Midlands, and most especially in the North a good many Celtic speakers and families of mixed heritage. Indeed, some of the early kings of Wessex bore British names (Cerdic, Ceawlin, Cedda, Ceawlin, and possibly also Cynric, of the 6th and 7th centuries), and the 'conquest of Britain' was a longer process than is sometimes thought (see Chapter 3).

The *Anglo-Saxon Chronicle* records for the year 891 that "three Scots" came in a hide boat to Cornwall and thence to visit King Alfred before departing on pilgrimage – the boat a *curragh* and the visitors learned monks named Dubslane, Macbeth (MacBeatha), and Maelinmun (Irish *máel*, 'servant,' a common name element). Such a visit echoes earlier contacts and associations between Irish scholars and English kings (notably Aldfrith of Northumbria, who reigned 685–704, was educated by Irish monks, and was a speaker of Irish) and may have been part of an intellectual exchange generated by Alfred's revival of learning. The 'Danelaw' was where Danish law obtained in the eastern half of England from the Thames to the Tees (at least a third of Anglo-Saxon England). The term 'Danelaw' itself is a blend, OE gen. pl. *Dena* + Old Norse *lagu* 'law'; the OE fem. noun is derived from an ON neuter plural form *lǫg* 'laws,' and the loan must have been early (pre-950 or so) as the final *-u* (< **w*) lost by ON is still preserved in the OE form. Most of the ON loans to OE belong to the 12th and 13th centuries, and Norse seems to have continued to be spoken in England up until then; the Norse loans such as *lagu*, however, seem to show archaic or conservative forms, perhaps indicating that Norse remained largely an intra-community language (and that the language shift was entirely unidirectional – toward English). A brief example of noun paradigms and a list of ON-OE prepositions may give a glimpse into the closeness and distance between the Germanic languages:

PGmc. **mánus-* ('man, human being') < Proto-Indo-European **man-*, **manu-*
Old English *mann*
Gothic *manna*
Old Norse *maðr*

PGmc. **fingraz* ('finger' = 'one of five') < Proto-Indo-European **pénkʷe* ('five')
Old English *finger*
Gothic *figgrs*
Old Norse *fingr*

singular	**Old Norse**	**Md. Icel.**	**ON**	**Md. Icel.**
nominative	maðr	maður	fingr	fingur
accusative	mann	mann	fingr	fingur
genitive	manns	manns	fingrar	fingurs
dative	manni	manni	fingri	fingri
plural				
nominative	menn, meðr	menn	fingr	fingur
accusative	menn, meðr	menn	fingr	fingur
genitive	manna	manna	fingra	fingra
dative	mǫnnum	mönnum	fingrum	fingrum

á: + dative 'on, in, to, towards,' + accusative 'to, towards, on to' [OE *on*]
af: + dative 'out of, of' [OE *of*]
at: + dative 'to, at' [OE *æt*]
eptir: + dative, + accusative 'after' [OE *æfter*]
frá, fram, um fram: + dative 'from' [OE *fram, from*]
fyrir, fyr: + dative, + accusative 'before, in front of, for, because' [OE *for*]

í: + dative 'in, within,' + accusative 'in, into' [OE *in*]
með: + dative, + accusative 'with, along, among' [OE *mid]*
of: + dative 'over,' + accusative 'over, across, through' [OE *of*]
undir: + dative, + accusative 'under, below, beneath' [OE *under*]
við: + dative 'against, towards,' + accusative 'with' [OE *wið*]
yfir: + dative 'above, over,' + accusative 'over, across' [OE *ofer*]

Perhaps the most signal Scandinavian influence on Old English was the introduction of *þ*- forms of the third-person plural personal pronouns (MdE *they*, *their*, *them*). Though some of the forms likely developed in spoken Old English, they do not appear until early ME (the *Ormulum* of the 12th century); *þæġe* apparently is not an early form of *they* though it is borrowed from Old Norse *þeir* 'they,' rather it was a demonstrative (in nom. and acc.) and occasionally a relative pronoun (nom.), with ON *-ei-* appearing as OE *æġ*- (Campbell OEG §713). The *th-/þ*- forms were borrowed in the 10th century, though there is little evidence of them in late OE written texts; this has led to the explanation that the forms may have been 'suppressed' by written standards at the monastic scriptoria and schools (e.g., the Winchester 'standard'; Morse-Gagné 2003 is the fullest discussion). A highly detailed study of Norse loans in the works of Wulfstan of York (bishop of London 996–1002, then of Worcester and York, latterly York to 1023), namely the *lagu*- ('law') and *grið*- ('truce') word-fields, looked to terms such as *utlah* and *utlagu* in the former (< ON *útlagr*, which likely does mean 'outlaw' rather than 'laying outside of'), and in the latter *ċiriċgrið*, 'church truce or peace,' 'right of sanctuary,'), which competed with the native blend, Greek (via Latin)-OE *ċiriċfrið* 'church peace,' 'right of sanctuary.' Naturally enough, ON loans and 'Norsified vocabulary' found in Wulfstan's works had much to do with Viking concepts of law, treaties, and truces; there are also the loans *healfmarc* ('half-mark') and *ōra* ('ore,' but also a Danish monetary unit, Modern Danish *øre*: 100 *øre* to a *krone* 'crown' in the current Danish monetary system). Some of these legalistic loanwords would not be long in use, as half a century later brought French terms with the Norman Conquest, displacing some of the Anglo-Scandinavian ones (Pons-Sans 2007, 80–84, 125–143, 258–260).

The most obvious vector of transmission for Norse loans to Old English is that such wranglings and truce-making, the striving for, getting, and losing kingdoms, had to have involved trusted translators, perhaps even Anglo-Scandinavian native bilinguals. The Danelaw had become fractured by the campaigns of Alfred and other kings of Wessex, the Kingdom of York by Norwegian and Danish settlements and control, for a time, by the Viking kings of Dublin. Briefly, and violently, the throne of York was taken by Eiríkr blóðøx ('Eirík Blood-axe'), who held it twice, 947–948 and 952–954. Eiríkr was one of 9 sons (the most likely figure; other sources list as many as 20) of Harald Fair-hair (Haraldr hárfagri), King of Norway (who reigned sometime between 860–880 and 930–940 and lived to be in his 80s); Harald, according to Snorri Sturluson in his *Heimskringla* ('Circle of the World,' an account in 16 sagas of the kings of Norway), divided his kingdom among his sons and appointed Eirík as high-king. Eirík, like his father, had his power base in Vestfold in the Oslofjord region and sought other territories and trade opportunities. Eirík was Harald's son by Ragnhild, daughter of a Danish king Eirík in Jutland (Denmark); he would himself marry a Danish queen (Gunnhild). Eirík's younger brother Hakon the Good (Hákon góði) was being fostered in England by the Anglo-Saxon King Athelstan; though aged only 15 at the time of Harald's death, he had powerful backers who supported his claim to the throne over Eirík's; when he landed in Trondheim ca. 940, Eirík left Norway for England. In 948, he was ruling over the Kingdom of York in Northumbria. At the urging of Anglo-Saxon King Eadred, he was then driven from York. He retook the kingdom in 952, but was driven out again in 954, dying at the Battle of Stainmoor (Stainmore) in 954, along with five other kings. The poem *Eiríksmál* ('Eric's speech,' or 'tale,' 'poem'), commissioned by his widow Queen Gunnhild, commemorates the death of Eirík in battle; Óðinn (Odin) asks about his dream, and adds that he had planned to rise before daybreak to prepare a feast for the newly slain to be welcomed into Valhalla; there is a loud noise, and Bragi, god of eloquence and poetry, believes that Baldr is coming back, but it is Eiríkr, chosen now as one of the Einherjar (the elect 'single warriors' who await Ragnarök), and Sigmundr (the dragon-slayer of the *Vǫlsunga saga*) and Sinfjǫtli are assigned the task of greeting him. Eirík arrives and speaks of those five kings (*konungar <e>ru fimm*, 'kings are there five'), who had fallen with him in battle at Stainmoor:

Eiríkr:
Konungar ru fimm,   kennik þér nafn allra:
   Ek em inn sétti sjálfr.

Eirík:
Kings there are five,   I would make known to you the name of all:
I am the sixth himself.

Those who fell alongside Eiríkr were said to be Gottormr and his sons Ívarr and Hárekr, Sigurðr, and Eirík's own brother Rǫgnvaldr. Not a century later, other descendants of Norse war-band leaders and kings, 'sons of Rollo,' the Normans, would also invade England. Amidst the workaday loan formations and other influences of linguistic contact in the history of English, it can be easy to forget that some of these contacts were rather more spectacular.

4.9 THE MAKING OF ENGLAND? WESSEX AND WEST SAXON

King Alfred, the only English monarch given the epithet 'the Great,' was so often a king at war that it is remarkable he had much time for his educational and intellectual reform program. At *Ethandune* (Edington, Wiltshire) in 878 Alfred won a major victory against the Viking Great Army that had occupied York in 868 and made its way back and forth across the country, down even to Exeter in 876. Alfred had launched a series of attacks on Danish bands from the Great Army, raised by the sons of Ragnar Lothbrok, from a defensive position at Athelney: 'the princes' island,' *æþelinga ēġ*, Somerset; the first mention of the place-name is in phrasal *Æt helingaeigge* from 878; apparently this should be *Æt æthelinga eigge*, with *æþelinga* truncated by haplography. Terms were reached with the heathen Guthrum, with Alfred standing in as godfather at the Dane's baptism; taking up the faith did not dissuade Guthrum from breaking their compact and raiding once again, and now East Anglia was occupied. With Northumbria and Mercia also beset by occupying forces, there remained only Wessex to lead the fight over the next 14 years (Stenton 1989, 246–262). Nonetheless, Alfred pursued his campaign of education on the national (Wessex and Western Mercia) and personal level. Among the texts attributed to Alfred are Old English translations of St. Augustine's *Soliloquies*, Pope Gregory the Great's *Cura pastoralis* ('Pastoral Care'), Boethius's *De consolatione Philosophiae* ("On the Consolation of Philosophy"), Orosius's *Historiarum adversum paganos libri vii* ("Seven Books of Histories against the pagans"), a prose version of the first 50 Psalms, Bede's *Historia ecclesiastica gentis Anglorum* ("Ecclesiastical History of the English People"), and an *Encheiridion* ("Handbook"), which last text may be the small book Alfred's biographer Asser claims the king carried with him, with wise sayings or commonplaces. Alfred had collected to his court scholars from Mercia and abroad; the four native scholars from Mercia were Wærferth or Werferth, Bishop of Worcester, Plegmund, Werwulf, and Athelstan; from outside England came Grimbald the Frank, John the Old Saxon (the house of Wessex reached back to the conquest of 449, but their cousins in Saxony were 'Old Saxons'), and from Dyfed the Welsh priest Asser. It was Asser who served the king most closely it seems, writing a biography of Alfred to 893, at which point Alfred had made some progress in his study of Latin – a subject he did not begin until 39 years of age (having learned to read English at 12). The storied picture of the philosophically-minded king has given way, somewhat, to a more realistic picture of a busy monarch who selected the best group of scholars he could for an educational renewal program. As the translations attributed to Alfred would have to come in the last years of his life, 893–899, the scale of work completed seems too great a task for a king with other matters to hand (and who had also initiated legal reforms, including the issuance of his own law code). Malcolm Godden made plain the unlikelihood of the traditional narrative in his study "Did King Alfred Write Anything?" (Godden 2007), as working through the texts of Gregory and Boethius was no easy matter, not to mention the extensive glossing, in Latin, the Latin texts received in the extant manuscripts. It has also been noticed that the translations at times seem to offer advice to a monarch, in addition to advice on clerical reforms (what the *Pastoral Care* aimed at), and that we may be seeing a group of clerics in an intellectual and moral advisory role to a king they viewed as sympathetic to their aims and eager to learn.

In the preface to the translation of Gregory's *Pastoral Care* attributed to Alfred is his remark that when he ascended to the throne in 871 England was in a terrible state of intellectual decline:

> Swæ clæne hio wæs oðfeallenu ón Angelcynne ðæt swiðe feawa wæron behionan Humbre ðe hiora ðeninga cuðen understondan ón Englisc, oððe furðum án ærendgewrit óf Lædene ón Englisc areccean; <ond> ic wene ðæt[te] noht monige begiondan Humbre næren. Swæ feawa hiora wæron ðæt ic furðum anne ánlepne ne mæg geðencean besuðan Temese ða ic to rice feng (Oxford, Bodleian Library, MS Hatton 20 text [ca. 890–897]; Sweet 1871, I, 2)

> So clear was the decline among the English people that very few there were this side of the Humber who their service could understand in English, or, furthermore, a letter from Latin into English could translate; and I imagine that not many beyond the Humber were there either. So few of them were there that I not a single one can recall to the south of the Thames when I took power. [OE *rīċe to feng* (< *fōn to rīċe*) – literally 'kingdom to take' – is formulaic in describing either the accession of a king – rightfully – or the grabbing of power, by whatever other means.]

Alfred's program, whatever his role in the translations – guided translator, sponsor – was important in not just the consolidation of the power of Wessex as its monarchs came to claim, as Alfred first did, to be kings of Saxon and Angles, or of the English (*rex Anglorum*) as his grandson Æthelstan did (he reigned 927–939 as 'king of the English'), but in the rise of West Saxon as the standard dialect of Old English. Standard Old English, that is, as the history of the development of standard contemporary English is a discontinuous one: it would not be West Saxon but the Southeastern and Southern varieties associated with London that would in the Middle English period become standard English. Nonetheless, the period 871–1011, from the reign of Alfred to the episcopate of Æthelwold of Winchester, would see a flowering of intellectual activity in West Saxon, not least the preservation of what survives of Old English verse in the major poetic codices that are in the main West Saxon compositions or copies. The study of Old English, revived in the later Early Modern period by antiquarians such as William Camden (1551–1623) and Franciscus Junius (1591–1677; he had for a time been owner of the 'Cædmon manuscript' of OE verse, now Oxford, Bodleian Library, MS Junius 11) and others, would codify this 'classical West Saxon' as the dialect of Old English approached by students ever since.

The Corpus of Old English Poetry

The 'corpus' (or 'body') of Old English includes approximately 33,000 lines of surviving poetry (3,182 of which belong to *Beowulf*). Somewhat more substantial, though not necessarily more representative, is the body of surviving OE prose, comprised of: Ælfric's *Colloquy*, *Homilies*, and exegetical works; Wulfstan's

(*continued*)

(*continued*)

sermons, *Canons of Edgar*, legal and other writings; the texts of the *Anglo-Saxon Chronicle*; translations by King Alfred the Great and his school, including those of Augustine's *Soliloquies*, Boethius's *Consolation of Philosophy*, Gregory the Great's *Pastoral Care*, Orosius's *History*, Bede's *Ecclesiastical History*; translations of parts of the Old Testament and the Gospels and other NT works; interlinear translations, glosses, and commentaries to the Psalms; translations of the *Benedictine Rule*; Byrhtferth of Ramsey's *Encheiridion*; the ever popular *Distichs of Cato*, *Alexander's Letter to Aristotle*, *Wonders of the East*, and *Apollonius of Tyre*; Lives of the Saints and the Martyrology; a number of other religious texts and prayers; texts on various subjects (the calendar, the ages of the world, royal genealogies, charters, laws, wills, manumissions, etc.).

Often overlooked but particularly valuable in telling us the range of knowledge in the period (and often assisting us in the decipherment of difficult words and passages in the poetry) is the collection of glosses and word-lists from the period. This includes major bilingual glossaries (or proto-dictionaries) such as the Épinal-Erfurt, Corpus, Cleopatra, Leiden, Harley, Brussels, and Plantin-Moretus Glossaries and thousands of other glosses scattered in small batches and bundles.

The only full edition of all Old English poetry to date is *The Anglo-Saxon Poetic Records* (Krapp and Dobbie 1931–1953):

ASPR I: *The Junius Manuscript* (Genesis, Exodus, Daniel, Christ and Satan)

ASPR II: *The Vercelli Book* (Andreas, Fates of the Apostles, Soul and Body I, Homiletic Fragment I, Dream of the Rood, Elene)

ASPR III: *The Exeter Book* (Christ, Guthlac, Azarias, The Phoenix, Juliana, The Wanderer, The Gifts of Men, Precepts, The Seafarer, Vainglory, Widsith, The Fortunes of Men, Maxims I, The Order of the World, The Riming Poem, Physiologus: The Panther, The Whale, The Partridge, Soul and Body II, Deor, Wulf and Eadwacer, Riddles 1–95 (in three bundles), The Wife's Lament, Judgement Day I, Resignation, The Descent into Hell, Alms-Giving, Pharaoh, The Lord's Prayer I, Homiletic Fragment II, The Husband's Message, The Ruin)

ASPR IV: *Beowulf and Judith* (the two poems occur in the British Library manuscript Cotton Vitellius A.xv)

ASPR V: *The Paris Psalter and Meters of Boethius*

ASPR VI: *The Anglo-Saxon Minor Poems* (The Battle of Finnsburh, Waldere, The Battle of Maldon, Chronicle Poems, Durham, The Rune Poem, Solomon and Saturn, The Menologium, Maxims II, A Proverb from Winfrid's Time, Judgement Day II, An Exhortation to Christian Living, A Summons to Prayer, The Lord's Prayer II, The Gloria I, The Lord's Prayer III, The Creed, Psalm fragments, The Kentish Hymn, Psalm 50, The Gloria II, A Prayer, Thureth, Aldhelm, The Seasons for Fasting, Cædmon's Hymn, Bede's Death Song, The Leiden Riddle, Latin-English Proverbs, Metrical Preface and Epilogue to the Pastoral Care, Metrical Preface to Gregory's Dialogues, Metrical Epilogue to Cambridge MS Corpus Christi College 41, Ruthwell Cross metrical inscription, Brussels Cross inscription, Franks Casket inscription, Metrical Charms)

The student of Old English generally approaches the language from a late form of West Saxon – much of the poetry mentioned above is preserved in West Saxon, or West Saxon copies (though often, as with *Beowulf*, with numerous non-West Saxon features); one estimate noted that "of 189 significant manuscripts, 160 date from *c.* 1000 or later" (Gneuss 1972, 64, drawing on Ker's great *Catalogue* [Ker 1957]). It was Helmut Gneuss's seminal "The origin of standard Old English and Æthelwold's school at Winchester" (Gneuss 1972) that began the push, largely by the 'Munich School' of Gneuss and his students, to locate a 'standard Old English' in the English Benedictine Reform, in the major houses at Glastonbury, Abingdon, Winchester (all of which Æthelwold was associated with), and elsewhere, and especially with the scholarly circle of Bishop Æthelwold of Winchester (ca. 904/905 x 909 – 1 August 984). In proposing a shift in the origin of standard Old English to Winchester and the Benedictine Reform in the later 10th century, Gneuss sought also to rule out Alfred's program in the 9th as the source. Gneuss's work on a standard West Saxon Old English associated with Winchester was pursued by a number of his former doctoral students, most notably by Mechthild Gretsch in her 1999 study *The Intellectual Foundations of the English Benedictine Reform*, which mines the evidence provided by psalter-gloss interrelations (in particular, the *Regius/Royal Psalter*, London, British Library MS Royal 2.B.v, of the mid- to later 10th century) and the Old English translations of the *Regula Benedicti* ("Rule of St. Benedict"). Gretsch's study is an important and highly detailed analysis of lexis, especially of loan translations and the matching of Latin lemmata (the source language tokens to be interpreted) and Old English glosses – as, for instance, the rendering of Latin *ecclesia*, in its senses 'church,' 'faithful community,' and 'Church,' by OE equivalents such as *ġetreowful ġesomnung*, *haligu ġesomnung*, or *ġelaþung* ('faithful gathering,' 'holy gathering,' 'congregation/assembly'), but, curiously, not by *ċiriċe* ('church') when referring to 'the Church' as an institution (Gretsch 1999, 107–108). The ecclesiastic word-field studied may at first seem narrow, but the great expansion of English vocabulary in the 9th and 10th centuries was very often Latin-derived (whether loan translations or Anglicizations of Latin forms). As such, Gretsch's study is also about Old English lexis in general, as it was the educational programs of Canterbury, Lichfield, Worcester, Winchester, York, and other centers that influenced Anglo-Saxon fields of inquiry as diverse as law, botany, musicology, architecture, and geography. The evidence from glossography – the study of glosses and glossaries – can have interesting yields despite its humble nature. Psalm verse 17:51 begins *Magnificans salutare regis ipsius et faciens misericordiam christo suo Dauid*, '[The Lord] making great the salvation of His king and granting mercy to His anointed David,' and it was Latin *christus* 'anointed' that Gretsch focused on; the readers and glossators of the time understood the primary reference of *christus* (*Christus* was generally rendered in the glosses by the loan form *Crist*), but for this adjectival usage 'anointed' some glossators chose *cyning/cynincg/ciningе* 'king' over *criste(s)* 'anointed' or *ġecorenum* 'chosen' (see Pulsiano 2001, 216–217). Gretsch connects the use of the gloss *cyning* for *christus* by the Royal Psalter glossator (though the same was done by those of the Vespasian, Junius, Cambridge, Tiberius, and Salisbury Psalters) to a change in the *Ordo* (the 'order' of coronation) for royal consecrations in Anglo-Saxon England in the course of the 9th and 10th centuries that saw increasing importance placed upon the 'anointing' of a king (as Edward the Elder at his coronation in 900 was anointed by Plegmund, Archbishop of Canterbury;

Gretsch 1999, 74–75). Gretsch's linking of interpretive glosses with *realia* reminds one of the enduring influence of the German linguistic *Wörter und Sachen* approach, of 'words and things,' of, more broadly, the close, at times even exact or precise, linkage between words and their meanings.

But there are caveats here: the corpus of psalter glosses is among the largest corpora of Old English vocabulary, psalter-gloss interrelations are still being worked out, and the ecclesiological wranglings over a specifically religious register do not necessarily extend far beyond the ecclesiastic centers into everyday speech. Despite Gneuss's opinion that "the belief that King Alfred was the founder or at any rate the harbinger of standard Old English becomes not only dubious but downright unlikely" (Gneuss 1972, 68), there is still much to recommend the notion, and publication of new editions of texts from the Alfredian program of the 9th century, such as the massive two-volume edition of the Old English Boethius (Godden and Irvine 2009), offers some support to the idea that Alfred's scope of linguistic formation and reform was broader than Æthelwold's monastic reform – Alfred was thinking on a national level, of countering a general decline in education in what he saw as not simply a people but a nation (at least those lands outside the Danelaw). The subject will bear much further analysis, though the 'Munich School' has set rigorous standards for any lexical test of 'standard Old English.'

With the matter of 'standardization' in West Saxon Old English, one is usually dealing with phonological, morphological, or lexical criteria – for example, the division of Old English phonological features into West Saxon and 'non-West Saxon.' Syntax is nonetheless one of the great barometers of linguistic standardization, and a number of advances have been made in analyzing OE poetic syntax (Robinson 1985; Donoghue 1988) and even the syntax of one OE particle, the adverb and conjunction *swa* (MdE 'so' is the reflex, though the range of senses and functions of *swa* in OE was much more complex; Schleburg 2002). An example from syntax, from the latest assessment of OE syntax by Ann Taylor (Taylor in Ringe and Taylor 2014, 392–509), involving 'small clauses' (SC) in Old English may be cited: that is, constructions involving "a constituent made up of a subject and predicate, where the predicate lacks tense inflection" (Taylor in Ringe and Taylor 2014, 498), particularly in later West Saxon prose. One sub-species of the SC involves 'participial predicates with verbal force':

> heo gesawe þone scinendan æncgel **cumende of heofenum to þam halgan wære**
> [she saw the shining angel **coming from the heavens to the holy man**]
>
> he gemette swiþe manige on þæm folce **wepende**
> [he encountered very many among that people **weeping**]
> (Taylor in Ringe and Taylor 2014, 498–501; emphasis added)

The caveat here, as with 'Winchester Standard Old English,' is that the two passages with present participles with 'full verbal force' are translations from Latin: the former from Ælfric's *Lives of the Saints* ("Life of St. Sebastian"), the latter from a homily on the Feast of the Assumption of Mary (15 August) from the *Blickling Homilies*. Both texts date to the late 10th century or very early 11th, the Blickling texts showing some Mercian forms. As with the lexical tests of 'Winchester words' in Gretsch's great study of a West Saxon *Schriftsprache* to be associated with the circle of Bishop Æthelwold (Gretsch 1999), the particular lexis and semantic range are ecclesiastical and 'scholarly,' and deeply 'Latinate': that is, under the influence of medieval Latin as taught in the schools and religious houses of Anglo-Saxon England. The examples above of participial usage show also that when considering clerical translation from Latin originals the influence of Latin on Old English could extend to syntax as well. One constraint on deriving anything beyond a 'literary standard' from Alfredian or Æthelwoldian 'standard Old English' is that the promotion of such a scholarly *Schriftsprache* to a national standard would only obtain with the literate strata of Anglo-Saxon England, which was still overwhelmingly clerical – and it may very well tell us relatively little about any spoken standard. Another constraint upon such a *Schriftsprache* as 'Winchester Old English' is that Latin nevertheless remained the primary means of communication that connected England to the Continent, and to the Western Catholic Church (cf. Bullough 2001, 45). And this was to be of great importance to the continuity of an intellectual tradition with the linguistic disruption that ensued in 1066.

4.10 LATE OLD ENGLISH, THE EVE OF 1066: SAXON, VIKING, NORMAN

If "Anglo-Saxon England ceased to exist as a political entity on 14 October 1066," it nonetheless may come as a surprise that a surprising number of texts in late Old English survive from the Conquest era and later, and though "usually regarded as faint echoes of dying shouts of an Old English literary heritage, [they] clamour to be heard, both because they survive in such numbers, and partly because of their persistence – a persistence that lasts at least into the thirteenth century" (Treharne 2012, 9, 93). What sort of persistent texts were these? Some 80 manuscripts of Old English were produced post-Conquest, including lives of Sts. Giles and Nicholas that were composed in Old English after 1066 (Swan 2006, 152); interestingly, many of these are liturgical and ecclesiastical texts:

—homiletic and hagiographical works: manuscripts written in or deriving from: Rochester and Christ Church, Canterbury, from the Southern region; others from Hereford or Worcester in the West Midlands (some 8 manuscripts dating to the range of 1150–1225;

—the Christ Church, Canterbury, Gospel Books in London, British Library MS Royal I.A.xiv (middle of the 12th century) and Oxford, Bodleian Library MS Hatton 38 (12th or 13th centuries);

—the famous Eadwine Psalter, Cambridge, Trinity College MS R.17.1 from the mid-12th century (ca. 1155–1160 at Christ Church, Canterbury; Pulsiano 2001, xxii); the particular significance of the Eadwine Psalter is that it is a 'triple psalter,' providing in its de-luxe format three Latin texts of the Psalms with three sets of glosses: the Hebraicum text (deriving from St. Jerome's translation of the Psalms from Hebrew into Latin) is glossed interlinearly in Anglo-Norman; the Gallicanum Latin version with Latin glosses (i.e., 'of Gaul,' which may derive from St. Jerome's Latin translation of the Psalms in the Greek Hexapla version – the 'sixfold' version of the Hebrew Bible attributed to Origen); and the Romanum version with Old English glosses (the 'Roman' version of the Psalms, deriving perhaps also from St Jerome, this time translating the *Vetus Latinus* Latin version of them – i.e., the 'old' versions of the Latin Bible in that these translations pre-date the Vulgate of Jerome); one study of the Old English gloss to the Eadwine Psalter sees evidence that the gloss had undergone a process of "modernisation...into early Middle English" (Pulsiano 2000, 193);

—Ælfric's late OE version of Bede's *De temporibus anni*, "On the Times of the Year," a text that is broader than the chronological and computistical (texts for calculating the date of Easter) title would suggest, as it covers also matters of astronomy and biology; provenance is either Rochester or Christ Church, Canterbury, of the mid-12th century;

—and a disparate group of texts not yet located in their provenance that includes copies of Anglo-Saxon laws and the *Anglo-Saxon Chronicle*, prognostications and 'wisdom literature' ("Debate of Solomon and Saturn," "Debate of Adrian and Ritheus," various apothegms [maxims, wise sayings]), and other texts dating to 1150–1200 (Swan 2006, 153–154).

As this material is concentrated in the period 1150–1200 it offers an opportunity to see how Old English texts could be written (and rewritten) at a time when many phonological and morphological changes were underway. This raises the perennial question of when did Middle English begin, not just as a question of periodization (though that too raises all sorts of questions; Lass 2000), but as a simple matter of language: presumably these Old English texts were in a language still quite familiar enough to English speakers (native or bilingual Norman speakers) to be read, excerpted, and reworked. But, presumably again, scribes and authors must have noted as well that these late OE texts were in a form new texts now would not take – that Middle English had begun perhaps in that period 1100–1150.

Often called the 'earliest Middle English text' is a homily for the Feast of the Assumption of Mary (15 August) by Archbishop of Canterbury Ralph D'Escures, written ca. 1100 in Latin and translated into English (in British Library MS Cotton Vespasian D.xiv). D'Escures was Norman by birth and studied at the Benedictine foundation of Our Lady of Bec (modern Le Bec Hellouin, Normandy), and in 1179 entered the Abbey of St-Martin-de-Séez (Orne département, Normandy). In England, he rose through the ecclesiastical ranks, being appointed to the episcopate of Rochester in 1108 (succeeding Gundulf, also Norman), and then that at Canterbury in 1114. It is not certain whether the homily was delivered at Rochester or Canterbury, but it was considered important enough to be very soon after copied into another manuscript at Worcester (Worcester Cathedral Library MS F.94; Treharne 2006, 182 n. 4). The English translation, and here it requires a distinction to be made – late

OE or early ME? – seems to have been faithful but at some points interpretive as it "bears witness to the Ælfrician homiletic tradition, rhetoric and diction, while simultaneously fully participating in twelfth-century developments in Marian devotion" (Treharne 2006, 181). To place the Englishing of D'Escures homily in the context of changes to English, here are two versions of Psalm 3: 3–4 in English, the first from ca. 1050 or so, the other from ca. 1300 or a bit later, that is, late Old English and mid-late Middle English.

> Late Old English: The Paris Psalter, that is the first 50 Psalms in Old English, in a translation traditionally ascribed to King Alfred (871–899), Paris, Bibliothèque nationale, MS Fonds latin 8824, dating to around the middle or second half of the 11th century (O'Neill 2001, 21) and to be plausibly localized to Canterbury, perhaps even St. Augustine's Abbey. The dialect is late West Saxon, with some trace elements of Kentish (as might be expected if the manuscript originated in Canterbury).
>
> Mid-Late Middle English: London, British Library MS Additional 17376 contains a complete copy of the Psalms in West Midlands Middle English, this copy perhaps of the earlier 14th century (thus approximately 200–250 years later than Alfred's prose psalms).

Ps 3: 3–4

3. Mid minre stemne ic cleopode to Drihtne and he me gehyrde of his þam halgan munte.	4 (3). Ich cried to my Lord wyþ my uoyce, ⁊ he herd me fram hys holy heuen.
4. Þa ongan ic slapan, and slep, and eft aras, for ðam þe Drihten me awehte and me upparærde (O'Neill 2001, 101).	5 (4). Ich slepe and slomered and a-ros; for our Lord toke me (Bülbring 1891, 3).

Both translate the Vulgate's Latin:

> *Voce mea ad Domini clamavi, / et exaudivit me de monte sancto suo* (3).
> *Ego obdormivi et soporatus sum, / exsurexi, quia Dominus suscepit me.*
> ["With my voice I cry out to the Lord, / and he has heard me from His holy mount. / I had fallen asleep and soundly slept, / but I have arisen, because the Lord supports me."]

Literal translations of the two English versions -- and perhaps only that for the Old English, is needed -- make clear that the vernacular versions are not overly literal:

> Old English: "With my voice I called out to the Lord and he me heard from His holy mount. Then I began to sleep, and I slept, and rose again, because the Lord me awakened and me reared up."
>
> Middle English: "I cried out to my Lord with my voice, and he heard me from His holy heaven. I slept and slumbered and arose; for our Lord took hold of me."

Old English preterite *cleopode* from *clipian* 'to call out, cry' has been replaced in the Middle English by *cried* from French loan *crier*; its first occurrence is ca. 1225 in the *Ancrene Riwle* (in the present form *crieð*; OED, s.v. *cry*, v.). OE *stefn/stemn* 'voice' has also been replaced by the French loan *voyse/voice*, via Anglo-Norman (first attested ca. 1300 in the early *South English Legendary*). OE phrasal *for ðām þe* (very literally, 'for that which' = 'because, for') has become simple ME *for*. The OE version follows the Vulgate *monte* more literally with *munte*; the Middle English translator reads it allegorically as *heuen* 'heaven.' The ME *Ich slepe and slomered and a-ros* trips off the tongue but does not sound quite so 'Biblical' as the OE *Þa ongan ic slapan, and slep, and eft aras* with its perhaps more dramatic pacing. Both the OE and ME employ the strong 3rd singular preterite form of OE *slǣpan* / ME *slēpen*, i.e., that with root vowel mutation; even in later OE (10th–11th centuries, especially Ælfric) the strong verb was being remodeled on the weak paradigm and we also find *slēpte*, which we have inherited.

D'Escures's early 12th-century homily (ca. 1100 × 1122) opens:

> SE godspellere Lucas sæigð on þyssen godspelle, þ<æt> se Hælend com into sumen cæstele, ⁊ sum wif hine underfeng into hire huse, þære wæs to name Martha (Warner 1917, 134, text XLIII)
>
> ['The 'Gospeller' Luke sayeth in this Gospel, that the Lord came into a certain village, and a certain woman brought him into her house, to whom [the dat. sing fem. of the demonstrative, so literally 'to the one (feminine)'] was to name Martha [to whom was the name Martha]]

Intact here are a number of OE forms, the masculine singular demonstrative *se* (as the OE equivalent of 'the'), the neuter dative singular demonstrative adjective *þyssen* (in 'classical' West Saxon it would have been *þissum* 'this'), as OE *godspel(l)* is a neuter noun (< *þæt gōd spell*, 'the good story/news,' likely deriving from entries in Latin-OE bilingual glossaries such as *bona adnuntiatio* or *bonus nuntius* 'good announcement, news' glossing *euuangelium*, a Latinized version of the Greek original; OED, s.v. *gospel*). Here *cæstele* is a loan from Latin *castellum* or Old French *castel* (Modern French *château* derives from this); the former, the Latin route, is for late OE appearances of *castel* in the West Saxon Gospels to translate Latin *castellum* 'village,' while the latter, via the Old French route, is in the current sense 'castle' (its earliest appearances are in post-Conquest continuations of the Anglo-Saxon Chronicle, for the years 1075 and 1154; OED, s.v. *castle*, sense I.i, II.3). Interesting here is the form *sæigð,* 3rd sing. pres. of OE *seċġan* or developing ME *seggen*; the OE form *sægeð* varied with contracted *sægð*, and with the diphthongized form here *sæi* and an epenthetic vowel in the consonant cluster one is not far from Early Modern English *sayeth*. The *sai-/sæi-* forms are indeed found in the West Midlands, but also in Kent, with a curious gap in the central Midlands in use (see LAEME, Maps 12332501–12332502, 14581404, which includes also *se(i)C(-)* forms, i.e., *sei-g/ʒ-* forms). When does Middle English begin? Perhaps here. The English version of D'Escures homily is clearly no great distance from the 11th-century copy of Alfred's prose psalm, chronologically or linguistically. But reading through all three texts, patterns emerge and the conventional wisdom regarding the Middle English period, that the language develops fairly quickly a syntax resembling that of Modern English and 'modernizes' (i.e., moves closer to us) with loss of grammatical gender and inflectional decay, is borne out fairly well. Why would a homily of ca. 1110–1120 show such signs of change?

For one, many of the changes were already underway in Old English; but others, such as a rapid influx of French loanwords, only follow the Conquest. Some guidance might be offered by having a look at contemporary language change and language shift. The 'third-generation hypothesis' of language acquisition and loss might be relevant. This idea developed from the immigration of non-English speakers to the United States (and more recently Britain): the first generation, the immigrants, will generally maintain the heritage L1 for their lifetime and speak English non-natively (as will be seen later, there are factors that complicate this, forces of language attrition); the children of these immigrants, the second generation, generally learn English at school as their L1 or as one of their L1s (in the case of native bilinguals) and for them maintenance of the heritage language can occur relatively easily in a household in which the parents actively use it; the children of this first generation to use English natively (a good many of whom may be bilingual), often have English as their L1 and some to no grasp of their grandparents' heritage language. There are, again, many, many factors that complicate the picture, but one can see the pattern broadly in the history of immigration to the United States, with language loss among successive generations of German, Irish (many of whom could already speak English), Italian, Polish, and other immigrants. Even among Mexican Americans of the second generation one sees language attrition of heritage Spanish – despite large Spanish-speaking communities always having been present in the Southwest. The factors influencing language shift in the 18th–21st centuries of course differ from those that can be reconstructed for the 11th through 13th (the period that came to see a decline in use of French in England). But the general notion being appealed to, as with the beginnings of English ca. 449–500 or so, is that 60–75 years might be the timeframe in which one could expect language change in a contact situation to manifest itself. One might notice changes as they occur, but the broader patterns might only be more readily discerned in the second or third generation. When did Angles, Saxons, Jutes, Frisians, and Franks notice that their dialects were becoming less intelligible to relatives back home? It was suggested earlier that certainly by 600 this must have been the case, at least by Runic and other epigraphic evidence, but likely the Germanic settlers must have had some sense of drift of the Insular versions from the Continental. The late 9th-century abbot at Athelney (Somerset), John the Old Saxon, was recruited by King Alfred from the Continent to participate in his educational reform program; the Old English term for such Continental 'cousins' was *Eald-Seaxe* 'Old Saxons.' Fairly quickly, or within three generations, there is plenty of evidence of Norman settlers who were either bilingual (Anglo-Norman and English) or, if in administration civil or ecclesiastic, multilingual (Latin as well); one of the key vectors for the large-scale importation of French loanwords into English is that French vocabulary became necessary in certain registers (law and government, but also architecture, cookery, clothing); another is that as language shift occurred, formerly native Anglo-Norman speakers brought many of their words with them to English. One sees examples of this in the trilingual glossaries of the period (the Eadwine Psalter above), of contact situations in the monasteries. It certainly occurred at the level of port and market and manor. So it may not be too implausible to suggest, insofar as any number might be suggested, that within 75 years of the Conquest we are now looking at the earliest 'Middle English.'

The place-name of Thurstable Hundred, Essex, offers an intriguing look at continuities amid the widespread changes of the early Middle English period. The generally accepted explanation of Thurstable is that it derives from Old English *Þunres-stapol*, the 'Thunderer's [Thor's] pillar,' likely marking a sacral site from long ago in English history – though not replaced or forgotten. The *Survey of English Place-Names* lists its earliest attestations as from the Westminster *Domesday Book* (1066–1087) and Assizes Rolls and other early legal and bureaucratic documents (1255 and later). The assize courts were those held in English counties by visiting judges, and the term derives from Old French *assise*, an act of 'sitting down,' and, by extension, a 'setting down,' 'settlement,' 'assessment' (i.e., a shift from the intransitive to transitive sense, though the OED notes that "perhaps both were equally early"; s.v. *assize*); in the sense of 'a thing settled,' 'statute,' the OED cites English legal historian William Stubbs (1825–1901) and his three-volume *The Constitutional History of England in its Origin and Development* (1874–1878) for the suggestion that the Old French term rendered Old English *ġesetnis* (*ġesetnes*; Middle English *isetnesse*), a feminine abstract noun with the literal sense of 'that which has been set down' and whose semantic range could extend to 'construction,' 'law,' 'sentence,' 'narrative,' 'record.' The last senses are present in the opening to the Old English *Letter of Alexander the Great to Aristotle* from the *Beowulf* manuscript (London, BL MS Coton Vitellius A.xv): *HER IS SEO GESETENIS Alexandres epistoles* ("Here is the account/record of Alexander's letter"). In his work on English legal and ecclesiastical history (he was a High Church Anglican, and had served as bishop of Chester and Oxford) Stubbs also provided Anglo-Saxon and Norman prose texts (in Latin, and Old and Middle English) of great importance to the study of the vocabulary of medieval English, particularly that having to do with political and ecclesiastical governance.[8] Thurstable Hundred was one of the land divisions into which English counties were divided (the Welsh near equivalent is the *cantref*, pl. *cantrefi*, a unit of 100 farmsteads), and, with the Domesday Book, an object of assessment and taxation.

An alternative explanation offered for Thurstable is that it is one of those English place-names with the Scandinavian personal name *Þúr-* (*Þor-*, i.e., *Þórir*, Thorir) as the first element, thus 'Thorir's column/pillar.' This has been discounted at times mainly as the place in question is in Essex, in the center of historical Thurstable Hundred, which did not have the Scandinavian presence found further north in territories longer under the Danelaw. There are place-names from within the Danelaw further north that have been interpreted as representing Norse *Þúr-*/*Þórir*,

[8] Besides his influential *Constitutional History*, he edited *Select Charters and Other Illustrations of English Constitutional History from the Earliest Times to the Reign of Edward the First* (Oxford: Clarendon Press, 1870), and, with Arthur W. Haddan, the three volumes (vol. II in two parts) of *Councils and Ecclesiastical Documents Relating to Great Britain and Ireland* (Oxford: Clarendon Press, 1869–1878).

such as Thursby (Cumbria), 'Thori or Thuri's village or farm' (*Thoresby*, ca. 1165, both place-name elements clearly Scandinavian), or Thurston (Suffolk), 'Thur's estate' (*Thurstuna*, *Thorstuna* [1086; Domesday]; CDEP, s.vv.). Old English *stapol/stapul* can encompass 'tree trunk,' 'post,' 'prop,' 'pillar,' or 'column' as a place-name element in first or second position in compound formations: *Staple/Stapel* 'the post' (Kent; 1205, 1240 the first attestations); *Staplefield/Stapelfeld* 'The field with a post' (West Sussex; 1315); *Stapleford* 'A ford marked by posts' (a common place-name, with Domesday attestations for Cambridgeshire, Leicestershire, Lincolnshire, Nottinghamshire, Wiltshire); *Staple Sound*, Northumbria, apparently refers to the cliffs known as 'The Staples' ('the columns') at the southern end of Staple Island (CDEP, s.vv.). A phonological objection to taking Thurstable as *Þunres-stapol* 'Thor's pillar' is the early loss of medial *n*; however, this we know of already from late Old English *Þunres* > *Þūres* in late West Saxon (as with *Þūres-dæġ*, 'Thursday'; Campbell, OEG §§ 393, 474). That a similar phonological process is at work with the Domesday forms *Turesstapla*, *Thur(e)stape(l)*, *Thur(e)stapl(e)* (to list the several variants) seems likely; the *Survey of English Place-Names* mentions the suggestion that a possible location of such a pillar or column was a tumulus near the church of Tolleshunt Major, "almost exactly in the centre of the hundred." This gets the anthropological or mythic brain going; as suggested in the preceding two chapters, myths, legends, and (former) religious practices have a habit of becoming embedded linguistically in the landscapes those who held them inhabited. Such a raised monument to Thor (Thunor), sited nearly dead center in the local community and near to which a later Christian church was placed, at least looks like a known pattern. What was the pillar raised to Thor/Thunor?

In his contribution to the J.R.R. Tolkien Festschrift (Davis and Wrenn 1962), 'Thurstable,' Gabriel Turville-Petre had suggested, after a wide-ranging consideration of saga evidence and Indo-European mythico-religious traditions of gods and demi-gods of pillars as 'sustainer'-figures, that: "While the *Irminsul* supported the world of the Saxons, Þórr, with his *ǫndvegissúlur* [high-seat pillars], upheld the house of the Icelandic farmer, and with his *stapol* he assured the security of the Essex hundred" (Turville-Petre 1962, 248). Speculative though this may be – but fascinating – a monument to a god on a raised height is a common cultic practice; for the language situation in the first two centuries post-Conquest what is interesting is the persistence of a place-name quite possibly reflecting not Scandinavian 'heathen' practice post-793 but that of the original Germanic invaders and settlers of Essex, the territory of the East Saxons. Thurstable Hundred was assessed in the Norman Domesday survey; it had passed from Wessex to control of Guthrum the Danish King of East Anglia (by the Treaty of Alfred and Guthrum, ca. 878 × 890), but only briefly so as Edward the Elder brought it back into the fold ca. 910; Maldon was close nearby, site of the famous battle 11(or 10 in some sources) August 991 between Ealdorman Byrhtnoth of Essex and a Viking army under Olaf (perhaps Óláfr Tryggvason of Norway); the area is bounded on the West by the River Lea, which flows into the Thames, both river-names (as seen in Chapter 3) likely of British origin (the Lea perhaps to be connected to **lug-* and meaning 'bright river' or 'bright water'); but a few miles north of Maldon is Colchester, known to the Romans as *Camulodunum*, the 'fort of Camulos' (a Celtic god equated by the Romans with

Mars), the capital of the Trinovantes where Cunobelinus of the Catuvellauni held sway until ca. AD 40 (Cunobelinus being Shakespeare's Cymbeline). The story of the local toponyms and hydronyms reflects that of the language to this point: from original Celtic, to the Roman and Romano-British periods, to an East Saxon smaller kingdom, to Mercian, then West Saxon dominance, to the encroachment of the Danelaw, back to Wessex, and now to the Norman era. The Lea and Colchester, Celt and Roman; Thurstable and Maldon: Saxon, Viking, Norman.

But Conquest had come, though an Anglo-Saxon Lincolnshire thegn (*þeġn*) Hereward ('army-guard'), called 'the Wake' (like the surviving surname it likely indicated a 'watchman'; Hanks et al. 2016, 2815), took up the cause of the resistance, taking to the woods at Bruneswald (along the fen at the border of Huntingdonshire and Northamptonshire), and then the island monastery at Ely, joined by others such as Earl Morcar. The Conqueror laid siege to the island, though the Anglo-Saxon Chronicle says that Hereward and a few others escaped, Hereward disappearing into legend, perhaps to Scotland (Stenton 1971/1989, 285, 605–606).

REFERENCES AND BIBLIOGRAPHY

Abramson, Tony, "England's Earliest Coinage, With Particular Reference to the York Group of Gold Shillings," *British Numismatic Journal* 89 (2019), 1–18

Abramson, Tony, "A Second Canterbury Gold Shilling of Eadbald of Kent: A new and unique find that augments the corpus of rare coins of this monarch," *British Numismatic Society Research Blog* 20th April 2023 (online)

Amos, Ashley Crandall. *Linguistic Means of Determining the Dates of Old English Literary Texts*. Cambridge, MA: The Medieval Academy of America, 1980

Antonsen, Elmer H. 1967, "On the Origin of Old English Digraph Spellings," *Studies in Linguistics* 19 (1967), 5–17

Antonsen, Elmer H. *Towards a Grammar of Proto-Germanic*. Tübingen: Max Niemeyer, 1972

Antonsen, Elmer H. *A Concise Grammar of the Older Runic Inscriptions*. Tübingen: Max Niemeyer, 1975

Antonsen, Elmer H. *Runes and Germanic Linguistics*. Trends in Linguistics, Studies and Monographs 140. Berlin: De Gruyter, 2002

ASPR. *The Anglo-Saxon Poetic Records*, edited by George Philip Krapp and Elliott Van Kirk Dobbie. 6 vols. New York: Columbia University Press, 1931–1953

Baker, Peter S. and Michael Lapidge, eds. *Byrhtferth's Enchiridion*. Early English Text Society, Supplementary Series 15. Oxford: Oxford University Press, 1995

Ball, C.J.E., "Mercian 'Second Fronting.'" *Archivum Linguisticum* 14 (1962) 130–145

Ball, C.J.E., "The Language of the Vespasian Psalter: Two Caveats," *Review of English Studies* 21 (1970), 462–465

Ball, C.J.E., "Problems in early Northumbrian phonology," in Kastovsky, Dieter and Gero Bauer, eds. *Luick Revisited: Papers read at the Luick-Symposium at Schloss Liechtenstein 15.-18.1985*. Tübingen: G. Narr, 1988. Pp. 109–117

Bammesberger, Alfred, ed. *Old English Runes and their Continental Background*. Anglistische Forschungen 217. Heidelberg: Carl Winter, 1991

Bammesberger, Alfred and Alfred Wollmann, eds. *Britain 400–600: Language and History.* Anglistische Forschungen 205. Heidelberg: Carl Winter, 1990

Bammesberger, Alfred and Gaby Waxenberger, eds. *Das fuþark und seine enizelsprachlichen Weiterentwicklungen: Akten der Tagung in Eichstätt vom 20. bis 24. Juli 2003.* Ergänzungsbände zum Reallexikon der Germanischen Altertumskunde, Band 51. Berlin: Walter de Gruyter, 2006

Barber, P.J. *Sievers' Law and the History of Semivowel Syllabicity in Indo-European and Ancient Greek.* Oxford Classical Monographs. Oxford: Oxford University Press, 2013

Bauer, Laurie. *English Word-Formation. Cambridge Textbooks in Linguistics.* Cambridge: Cambridge University Press, 1983

Bennett, W.H., "The southern English development of Germanic initial [f s þ]," *Language* 31 (1955) 367–371

Bierbaumer, Peter, "Altenglisch *fornetes folm* – eine Orchideenart," *Anglia* 92 (1974), 172–176

Bierbaumer, Peter. *Der botanische Wortschatz des Altenglischen.* 3 vols. Frankfurt: Herbert Lang, 1975–1979

Birkett, Tom. *Reading the Runes in Old English and Old Norse Poetry.* London: Routledge, 2017

Bischoff, Bernhard and Michael Lapidge, eds. *Biblical Commentaries from the Canterbury School of Theodore and Hadrian.* CSASE 10. Cambridge: Cambridge UP, 1994

Björkman, Erik. *Scandinavian Loan-Words in Middle English.* Part I. New York: Haskell House, 1969

Boehler, Maria. *Die altenglischen Frauennamen.* Germanische Studien 98. Berlin: Ebering, 1930

Brandl, Alois. *Zur Geographie der altenglischen Dialeckte.* Berlin: Georg Reimer, 1915

Bremmer, Rolf H., Jr., "Frisians in Anglo-Saxon England: A Historical and Toponymical Investigation," *Fryske Nammen* 3 (1981), 45–94

Bremmer, Rolf H., Jr., "The Nature of the Evidence for a Frisian Participation in the *Adventus Saxonum*," in Bammesberger, Alfred and Alfred Wollmann, eds. *Britain 400-600: Language and History.* Heidelberg: Carl Winter, 1990, pp. 353–371

Bremmer, Rolf H., Jr., "Hermes-Mercury and Woden-Odin as Inventors of Alphabets: A Neglected Parallel," in Bammesberger, Alfred, ed. *Old English Runes and their Continental Background.* Heidelberg: Carl Winter, 1991, 409–419

Bremmer, Rolf H., Jr., "The *Gesta Herewardi*: Transforming an Anglo-Saxon into an Englishman," in *People and Texts: Relationships in Medieval Literature. Studies Presented to Erik Kooper*, ed. Thea Summerfield and Keith Busby. Costerus New Series 166. Leiden: Brill, 2007. Pp. 29–42

Bremmer, Rolf H., Jr. *An Introduction to Old Frisian: History, Grammar, Reader, Glossary.* Amsterdam: John Benjamins, 2009

Brooks, Nicholas. *The Early History of the Church at Canterbury.* Leicester: Leicester University Press, 1984

Brown, Edward Miles. *The Language of the Rushworth Gloss to the Gospel of Matthew and the Mercian Dialect.* Part II. Göttingen: Dieterich'schen Universitäts-Buchdruckerei, 1892

Brunner, Karl. *Altenglische Grammatik.* (*Nach der angelsächsischen Grammatik von Eduard Sievers*/After the Anglo-Saxon Grammar of Eduard Sievers = Sievers-Brunner). 3rd rev. ed. Sammlung kurzer Grammatiken germanischer Dialekte. A: Hauptreihe, Band 3. Tübingen: Max Niemeyer, 1965/rpt. 2014

BT = Joseph Bosworth, *An Anglo-Saxon Dictionary*. Edited and enlarged by T. Northcote Toller. Oxford: Clarendon Press, 1898/rpt. 1989.

BTS = *An Anglo-Saxon Dictionary. Supplement*. T. Northcote Toller. Revised and enlarged by Alistair Campbell. Oxford: Oxford University Press, 1921/rpt. 1980

Bullough, Donald A. Review of Gretsch 1999. *Notes and Queries* 48.1 (2001), 44–45

Campbell, Alistair. *Old English Grammar*. Oxford: Clarendon Press, 1959

Carr, Charles T. *Nominal Compounds in Germanic*. London: Humphrey Milford/Oxford University Press, 1939

Cavill, Paul and George Broderick, eds. *Language Contact in the Place-Names of Britain and Ireland*. Nottingham: English Place-Name Society, 2007

CHM = Hall, J.R. Clark. *A Concise Anglo-Saxon Dictionary, With a Supplement by Herbert D. Meritt*. 4th ed. Toronto: University of Toronto Press, 1960/rpt. 1984

Claridge, Claudia and Birte Bös, eds. *Developments in English Historical Morpho-Syntax*. Amsterdam: John Benjamins, 2019

Clark, Cecily, "Onomastics," in CHEL I (1992), pp. 452–489

Coates, Richard, "On Some Controversy Surrounding *Gewissae/Gewissei*, *Cerdic* and *Ceawlin*," *Nomina* 13 (1989–1990), 1–11

Coates, Richard, "The Scriptorium of the Mercian Rushworth Gloss: A Bilingual Perspective," *Notes and Queries* 44 (1997), 453–458

Coates, Richard. "The significances of Celtic place-names in England," in *The Celtic Roots of English*, ed. Filppula, Markku, Juhani Klemola and Heli Pitkänen. Joensuu: Joensuun Ylipopistopainu/Joensuu University Press, 2002. Pp. 47–85

Colman, Fran. *Money Talks: Reconstructing Old English*. Trends in Linguistics, Studies and Monographs 56. Berlin: Mouton de Gruyter, 1992

Colman, Fran. *The Grammar of Names in Anglo-Saxon England: The Linguistics and Culture of the Old English Onomasticon*. Oxford Linguistics. Oxford: Oxford University Pres, 2014

Cook, Alber S. *A Glossary of the Old Northumbrian Gospels*. Halle: Max Niemeyer, 1894. Rpt. Hildesheim: Georg Olms, 1969

Crowley, Joseph P., "The Study of Old English Dialects," diss., University of North Carolina at Chapel Hill, 1980.

Crowley, Joseph P., "The Study of Old English Dialects," *English Studies* 67 (1986), 97–112

Dahl, Ivar. *Substantival Inflexion in Early Old English*. Lund: Gleerup, 1938

Dance, Richard. *Words Derived from Old Norse in Early Middle English: Studies in the Vocabulary of the South-West Midland Texts*. Medieval and Renaissance Texts and Studies Volume 246. Tempe, AZ: Arizona Center for Medieval and Renaissance Studies, 2003

Davis Norman and C.L. Wrenn ed. *English and Medieval Studies: Presented to J.R.R. Tolkien on the Occasion of his Seventieth Birthday*, London: George Allen & Unwin, 1962. Pp. 241–249

De Bernardo Stempel, Patrizia. *Muttergöttinen und ihre Votivformulare. Eine sprachhistorische Studie*. Indogermanische Bibliothek. Heidelberg: Universitätsverlag Winter, 2021

Denison, David, Ricardo Bermúdez-Otero, Chris McCully, and Emma Moore, eds. *Analysing Older English*. Studies in English Language. Cambridge: Cambridge University Press, 2012

Derolez, René. *Runica Mansucripta: The English Tradition*. Bruges: De Tempel, 1954

Derolez, René, "Cross-Channel language ties," *Anglo-Saxon England* 3 (1974), 1–14

Dietz, Klaus, "Die südaltenglische Sonorisierung anlautender Spiranten," *Anglia* 108 (1970), 292–313

di Paolo Healey, Antonette and Richard L. Venezky, eds. *A Microfiche Concordance of Old English*. Toronto: University of Toronto Press/Pontifical Institute for Mediaeval Studies, 1980. Online version: *Dictionary of Old English Web Corpus*. https://tapor.library.utoronto.ca/doecorpus/

DOE = *Dictionary of Old English*. Ed. Antonette diPaolo Healy et al. https://doe.artsci.utoronto.ca/ [fascicles A-Le, 1986 – present]

Donoghue, Daniel. *Style in Old English Poetry: The Test of the Auxiliary*. Yale Studies in English. New Haven, CT: Yale University Press, 1988

Dresher, Bezalel Elan, "The Mercian Second Fronting: A Case of Rule Loss in Old English," *Linguistic Inquiry* 11/1 (1980), 47–73

Dresher, Bezalel Elan. *Old English and the Theory of Phonology*. New York: Garland, 1985

Dumville, David N., "The Anglian Collection of Royal Genealogies and Regnal Lists,"*Anglo-Saxon England* 5 (1976), 23–50

Dumville, David N., "The West Saxon Genealogical Regnal List and the Chronology of Early Wessex," *Peritia* 4 (1985), 21–66

Dumville David N., "The West Saxon Genealogical Regnal List: Manuscripts and Texts," *Anglia* 104 (1986), 1–32

Dumville, David N. *Three Men in a Boat: Scribe Language and Culture in the Church of Viking-Age Europe*. Inaugural Lecture, Professor of Palaeography & Cultural History, University of Cambridge (13 May 1996). Cambridge: Cambridge University Press, 1997

Durkin, Philip. *Borrowed Words: A History of Loanwords in English*. Oxford: Oxford University Press, 2014

Ekwall, Eilert. *Contributions to the History of Old English Dialects*. Lund: Lund University, 1917

Ekwall, Eilert. *English River-Names*. Oxford: Clarendon Press, 1928

Ekwall, Eilert, "A problem of Old Mercian phonology in the light of West Midland place-names," *Namn och Bydg* 51 (1963), 16–48

Ekwall, Eilert. *The Concise Oxford Dictionary of English Place-Names*. 4th ed. Oxford: Clarendon Press, 1974

Elliott, Ralph W.V. 1989. *Runes: An Introduction*. 2nd ed. New York: St. Martin's Press

Feilitzen, Olof von. *The Pre-Conquest Personal Names of Domesday Book*. Uppsala: Almqvist & Wiksells, 1937

Filppula, Markku, Juhani Klemola, and Heli Pitkänen, eds. *The Celtic Roots of English*. University of Joensuu, Faculty of Humanities. Studies in English 37. Joensuu: Joensuun Yliopistopaino/Joensuu University Press, 2002

Fischer, Olga, Ans van Kemenade, Willem Koopman, and Wim van der Wurff, eds. *The Syntax of Early English*. Cambridge Syntax Guides. Cambridge: Cambridge University Press, 2004

Fisiak, Jacek, "Old East Anglian: a problem in Old English dialectology," in *East Anglian English*, ed. Jacek Fisiak and Peter Trudgill. Cambridge: D.S. Brewer, 2001. Pp. 13–38

Flohrschütz, Armin. *Die Sprache der Handschrift D. der angelsächsischen Annalen im Ms. Cotton. Tib. B IV*. (Inaugural-Dissertation, Universität Jena). Hildburghausen: Druck von Dr. L. Nonnes Erben (Druckerei der Dorfzeitung), 1909

Förster, Max. *Keltisches Wortgut im englischen: eine sprachliche Untersuchung*. Halle: Max Niemeyer, 1921

Förster, Max. *Der Flussname Themse und seine Sippe: Studien zur Anglisierung keltischer Eigennamen und zur Lautchronologie des Altbritischen*. Munich: C.H. Beck, 1941

Fox, Bethany. "The P-celtic Place-Names of North-East England and South-East Scotland," *The Heroic Age* 10 (2007). http://www.heroicage.org/issues/10/fox.html

Fulk, Robert D. *A History of Old English Meter*. Philadelphia: University of Pennsylvania Press, 1992

Fulk, R.D., Robert E. Bjork, John D. Niles, eds. *Klaeber's Beowulf and The Fight at Finnsburg*. 4th ed. Toronto Old English Series. Toronto: University of Toronto Press, 2008

Garmonsway, G.N., ed. *Ælfric's Colloquy*. Exeter Medieval Texts and Studies. Exeter: University of Exeter Press, 1991

Gelling, Margaret, "Latin loan-words in Old English place-names," *Anglo-Saxon England* 6 (1977), 1–13

Giffhorn, Jürgen. *Phonologischen Untersuchungen zu den altenglischen Kurzdiphthongen*. Munich: Wilhelm Fink, 1974

Gneuss, Helmut. *Lehnbildungen und Lehnbedeutungen im Altenglischen*. Berlin: Erich Schmidt, 1955

Gneuss, Helmut. *Hymnar und Hymnen im englischen Mittelalter*. Buchreihe der Anglia 12. Tübingen: Max Niemeyer, 1968

Gneuss, Helmut, "The origin of standard Old English and Æthelwold's School at Winchester," *Anglo-Saxon England* 1 (1972), 63–83

Gneuss, Helmut, "*The Battle of Maldon* 89: Byrhtnoð's *ofermod* Once Again," *Studies in Philology* 73 (1976), 117–137

Gneuss, Helmut. *Language and History in Early England*. Variorum Collected Studies Series. Aldershot: Ashgate Publishing, 1996

Gneuss, Helmut, "A newly-found fragment of an Anglo-Saxon psalter," *Anglo-Saxon England* 27 (1998), 273–287

Gneuss, Helmut, "Ælfrics Grammatik und Glossar: Sprachwissenschaft um die Jahrtausendwende in England," in *Heilige und profane Sprachen. Die Anfänge des Fremdsprachenunterrichts im westlichen Europa*, ed. Werner Hüllen and Friederike Klippel. Wiesbaden: Otto Harrassowitz, 2002. Pp. 77–92

Gneuss, Helmut, "The Study of Language in Anglo-Saxon England," in *Textual and Material Culture in Anglo-Saxon England: Thomas Northcote Toller and the Toller Memorial Lectures*, ed. Donald G. Scragg. Cambridge: D.S. Brewer, 2003. Pp. 75–106

Gneuss, Helmut. *Ælfric of Eynsham: His Life, Times, and Writings. Old English Newsletter* Subsidia 34. Kalamazoo, MI: Medieval Institute Publications, 2009

Gneuss, Helmut and Michael Lapidge, eds. *Anglo-Saxon Manuscripts: A Bibliographical Handlist of Manuscripts and Manuscript Fragments Written or Owned in England up to 1100*. Toronto Anglo-Saxon Series 15. Toronto: University of Toronto Press, 2014

Godden, M.R., "Did King Alfred Write Anything?", *Medium Ævum* 76.1 (2007), 1–23

Godden, Malcolm and Susan Irvine, eds. *The Old English Boethius: An Edition of the Old English Versions of Boethius's De Consolatione Philosophiae*. 2 vols. Oxford: Oxford University Press, 2009

Gordon, E.V. *An Introduction to Old Norse*. 2nd ed. Oxford: Oxford University Press, 2009

Grant, Raymond J.S. *The B Text of the Old English Bede: A Linguistic Commentary*. Amsterdam: Rodopi, 1989

Gretsch, Mechthild. *The Intellectual Foundations of the English Benedictine Reform*. CSASE 25. Cambridge, 1999

Haan, Germen J. De. *Studies in West Frisian Grammar: Selected papers by Germen J. de Haan*. Ed. Jarich Hoekstra, Willem Visser, and Goffe Jensma. Linguistik Aktuell/ Linguistics Today 161. Amsterdam: John Benjamins, 2010

Hall, Alaric. *Elves in Anglo-Saxon England: Matters of Belief, Health, Gender and Identity*. Anglo-Saxon Studies 8. Woodbridge: The Boydell Press, 2007

Hall, J.R., "The Sword Hrunting in *Beowulf*: Unlocking the Word *hord*," *Studies in Philology* 109.1 (2012), 1–18

Halsall, Maureen, ed. *The Old English Rune Poem: A Critical Edition*. McMaster Old English Studies and Texts 2. Toronto: University of Toronto Press, 1981

Hanks, Patrick, Richard Coates, and Peter McClure. *The Oxford Dictionary of Family Names in Britain and Ireland*. 4 vols. Oxford: Oxford University Press, 2016

Hartman, Frederik. *The Vandalic Language*. Indogemanische Bibliothek. Dritte Reihe: Untersuchungen. Heidelberg: Universitätsverlag Winter, 2020

Heizmann, Wilhelm and Astrid van Nahl, eds. *Runica – Germanica – Mediaevalia*. Ergänzungsbände zum Reallexikon der Germanischen Altertumskunde 37. Berlin: De Gruyter, 2003

Herbert, Máire. *Iona, Kells, and Derry: The history and hagiography of the monastic familia of Columba*. Dublin: Four Courts Press, 1988

Hines, John, "The Runic Inscriptions of Early Anglo-Saxon England," in Bammesberger, Alfred and Alfred Wollmann, eds. *Britain 400–600: Language and History*. Heidelberg: Carl Winter, 1990, 437–455

Hines, John, "The Anglo-Frisian Question," in *Frisians and their North Sea Neighbours: From the Fifth Century to the Viking Age*, ed. John Hines and Nelleke IJssennagger. Woodbridge: The Boydell Press, 2017. Pp. 2–42

Hines, John, "The Archaeological Dating of the Early Finds: How Certain are the Results?", in Waxenberger, Gaby, Kerstin Kazzazi, and John Hines, eds. *Old English Runes: Interdisciplinary Perspectives on Approaches and Methodologies with a Concise and Selected Guide to Terminologies*. Ergänzungsbände zum Reallexikon der Germanischen Altertumskunde, Band 134. Berlin: De Gruyter 2023, 59–80

Hofstetter, Walter. *Winchester und der spätaltenglische Sprachgebrauch. Untersuchungen zur geographischen und zeitlichen Verbreitung altenglischer Synonyme*. Munich: Wilhelm Fink, 1987

Hofstetter, Walter, "Winchester and the standardization of Old English vocabulary," *Anglo-Saxon England* 17 (1988), 139–161

Hogg, Richard M., "The chronology and status of 'Second Fronting,'" *Archivum Linguisticum* 8 (1977), 130–145

Hogg, Richard M., rev. of Toon 1983. *Journal of Linguistics* 21.1 (1985), 245–250

Hogg, Richard M., "On the impossibility of Old English dialectology," in Kastovsky, Dieter and Gero Bauer, eds. *Luick Revisited: Papers read at the Luick-Symposium at Schloss Liechtenstein 15.-18.1985*. Tübingen: G. Narr, 1988. Pp. 183–203

Hogg, Richard M. *A Grammar of Old English. I: Phonology*. Oxford: Basil Blackwell, 1992

Hogg, Richard M. *An Introduction to Old English*. Edinburgh Textbooks on the English Language. Edinburgh: Edinburgh University Press, 2002

Hogg, Richard M. and R.D. Fulk. *A Grammar of Old English. II: Morphology*. Oxford: Wiley-Blackwell, 2011

Holthausen, Ferdinand. *Altenglsches etymologisches Wörterbuch*. 3rd ed. Heidelberg: Carl Winter, 1974

Homans, George C., "The Frisians in East Anglia," *The Economic History Review n.s.* 10.2 (1957), 189–206

Hough, Carole. "The (non?)-survival of Romano-British Toponymy," *Neuphilologische Mitteilungen* 105 (2004), 25–32

Hough, Carole, ed. *The Oxford Handbook of Names and Naming*. Oxford: Oxford University Press, 2016

Insley, John, Review of Colman 2014. *Anglia* 135.3 (2017), 573–580

Ireland, Colin A. *Old Irish Wisdom Attributed to Aldfrith of Northumbria: An Edition of Bríathra Flainn Fhína maic Ossu*. Medieval and Renaissance Texts and Studies, Volume 205. Tempe, AZ: Arizona Center for Medieval and Renaissance Studies, 1999

Ireland, Colin A. *The Gaelic Background of Old English Poetry before Bede*. Publications of the Richard Rawlinson Center. Berlin: de Gruyter, 2022

James, Alan G. Review of Cavill and Broderick 2007. *The Journal of Scottish Name Studies* 3 (2009), 135–158

Jente, Richard. *Die mythologischen Ausdrücke im altenglischen Wortschatz: Eine kulturgeschichtlich-etymologische Untersuchung*. Anglistische Forschungen 56. Heidelberg: Carl Winter, 1921

Jolly, Karen Louise. *Popular Religion in Late Saxon England: Elf-Charms in Context*. Chapel Hill, NC: University of North Carolina Press, 1996

Kastovsky, Dieter and Gero Bauer, eds. *Luick Revisited: Papers read at the Luick-Symposium at Schloss Liechtenstein 15.-18.1985*. Tübinger Beiträge zur Linguistik. Tübingen: G. Narr, 1988

Ker, N.R. *Catalogue of Manuscripts Containing Anglo-Saxon*. Oxford: Clarendon Press, 1957

Kiernan, Kevin S. *Beowulf and the Beowulf Manuscript*. Ann Arbor: University of Michigan Press, 1997

Kitson, Peter, "The nature of Old English dialect distributions, mainly as exhibited in charter boundaries," in *Medieval Dialectology*, ed. Jacek Fisiak. Trends in Linguistics, Studies and Monographs 79. Berlin: De Gruyter Mouton, 1995. Pp. 43–135

Klein, Thomas, "Dialect and Word Choice in Old English: Two Case Studies WITH Old English Perception Verbs," *Anglia* 130.4 (2012), 471–498

Klingenberg, Heinz. *Runenschrift – Schriftdenken – Runeninschriften.* Germanische Bibliothek. Heidelberg: Carl Winter, 1973

Knappe, Gabriele. *Traditionen der klassischen Rhetorik im angelsächsischen England.* Anglistische Forschungen 236. Heidelberg: Universitätsverlag C. Winter, 1996

Koch, John T., "A Case for Tartessian as a Celtic Language," *Palaeohispánica* 9 (2009), 339–351

Koch, John T. *Tartessian: Celtic in the South-West at the Dawn of History.* Celtic Studies Publications 13. Aberystwyth: Celtic Studies Publications, 2013

Kopaczyk, Johanna and Hans Sauer, eds. *Binomials in the History of English: Fixed and Flexible.* Studies in English Language. Cambridge: Cambridge University Press, 2017

Kortlandt, Fredrik, "The origin of the Old English dialects," in *Linguistics across Historical and Geographical Boundaries: In Honour of Jacek Fisiak on the Occasion of His Fiftieth Birthday.* Ed. Dieter Kastovsky and Aleksander Szwedek. Vol. 1: *Linguistic Theory and Historical Linguistics.* Berlin: Mouton de Gruyter, 1986. Pp. 437–442

Kotake, Tadashi. *Rushworth One: An Edition of Farman's Old English Interlinear Gloss to the Rushworth Gospels (Oxford, Bodleian Library, MS Auct. D.2.19).* Medium Ævum Monographs 44. Oxford: Society for the Study of Medieval Languages and Literature, 2023

Krause, Wolfgang. *Schriften zur Runologie und Sprachwissenschaft.* Ed. Heinrich Beck, Klaus Düwel, Michael Job, and Astrid von Nahl. Ergänzungsbände zum Reallexikon der Germanischen Altertumskunde, Band 84. Berlin: De Gruyter, 2014

Krause, Wolfgang and Herbert Jankuhn. *Die Runeninschriften im älteren Futhark.* Göttingen: Vandenhoeck & Ruprecht, 1966

Kuhn, Sherman M., "The Dialect of the Corpus Glossary," *PMLA* 54.1 (1939), 1–19

Kuhn, Sherman M. *The Vespasian Psalter.* Ann Arbor: University of Michigan Press, 1965

Kwakkel, Erik, "*Hebban olla uogala* in historisch perspectief," *Tijdschrift voor Nederlandse Taal- en Letterkunde* 121 (2005), 1–24

Lapidge, Michael, tr. *Aldhelm: The Poetic Works.* Cambridge: D.S. Brewer, 1985

Lapidge, Michael, ed. [= Lapidge 1995a] *Archbishop Theodore: Commemorative Studies on his Life and Influence.* CSASE 11. Cambridge: Cambridge University Press, 1995

Lapidge, Michael, [= Lapidge 1995b] "The career of Archbishop Theodore," in Lapidge, Michael, *Archbishop Theodore: Commemorative Studies on his Life and Influence.* Cambridge: Cambridge University Press, 1995a, pp. 1–29

Lapidge, Michael, [= Lapidge 1995c] "Theodore and Anglo-Latin octosyllabic verse," in Lapidge, Michael, *Archbishop Theodore: Commemorative Studies on his Life and Influence.* Cambridge: Cambridge University Press, 1995a, pp. 260–280

Lapidge, Michael, "Aldhelm and the 'Épinal-Erfurt Glossary,'" in *Aldhelm and Sherborne: Essays to Celebrate the Founding of the Bishopric*, ed. Katherine Barker and Nicholas Brooks. Oxford: Oxbow Books, 2010. Pp. 129–163

Lapidge, Michael, "St. Gallen and the 'Leiden Glossary,'" *Anglia* 133 (2015), 634–655

Lapidge, Michael, ed. *Bede's Latin Poetry*. Oxford Medieval Texts. Oxford: Oxford University Press, 2019

Lapidge, Michael, ed. *Canterbury Glosses from the School of Theodore and Hadrian: The Leiden Glossary*. 2 vols. Publications of the Journal of Medieval Latin. Turnhout: Brepols, 2023

Lapidge, Michael and Michael W. Herren, trs. *Aldhelm: The Prose Works*. Ipswich: D.S. Brewer, 1979

Lass, Roger. *The Shape of English: Structure and History*. London: J.M. Dent & Sons, 1987

Lass, Roger. *Old English: A Historical Linguistic Companion*. Cambridge: Cambridge University Press, 1994

Lass, Roger, "Language Periodization and the Concept of 'Middle,'" in *Placing Middle English in Context*, ed. Irma Taavitsainen, Terttu Nevalainen, Päivi Pahta, and Matti Rissanen. *Topics in English Linguistics 35*. Berlin: De Gruyter, 2000. Pp. 7–41

Last, Werner. *Das Bahuvrihi-Compositum im Altenglischen, Mittelenglischen und Neuenglischen*. Greifswald: Hans Adler, 1925

Law, Vivien A., "The Transmission of the *Ars Bonifacii* and the *Ars Tatuini*," *Revue d'histoire des textes* 9 (1979), 281–288

Levison, Wilhelm. *England and the Continent in the Eighth Century*. Oxford: Clarendon Press, 1946

Liberman, Anatoly. *An Analytic Dictionary of English Etymology*. Minneapolis, MN: University of Minnesota Press, 2008

Lindsay, William M., ed. *The Corpus, Épinal, Erfurt and Leyden Glossaries*. Publications of the Philological Society VIII. London: Oxford University Press, 1921

Liuzza, R.M., ed. *The Old English Version of the Gospels*. 2 vols. Early English Text Society O.S. 304, 314. Oxford: Oxford University Press, 1994–2000

Liuzza, R.M., "Island time: the English Day and the Christian Hours," in *Old English Lexicology and Lexicography: Studies in Honor of Antonette DiPaolo Healy*, ed. Maren Clegg Hyer, Haruko Momma, and Samantha Zacher. Cambridge: D.S. Brewer, 2020. Pp. 186–198

Lloyd, Albert L. *Anatomy of the Verb: The Gothic Verb as a Model for a Unified Theory of Aspect, Actional Types, and Verbal Velocity*. Studies in Language Companion Series 4. Amsterdam: John Benjamins, 1979

Lockwood, W.B. *Historical German Syntax*. Oxford: Clarendon Press, 1968

Luick, Karl. *Historische Grammatik der englischen Sprache*. 1 vol. in 2 parts. Leipzig: Christian Hermann Tauchnitz, 1914–1921

Lyons, Jessie M., "Frisian Place-Names in England," *PMLA* 33.4 (1918), 644–655

Marchand, Hans. *The Categories and Types of Present-Day English Word-Formation*. 2nd ed. Handbücher für das Studium der Anglistik. Munich: C.H. Beck, 1969

Marsden, Richard, ed. *The Old English Heptateuch and Ælfric's Libellus de Veteri Testamento et Novo*. Volume 1: Introduction and Text. Early English Text Society O.S. 330. Oxford: Oxford University Press, 2008

Matasović, Ranko. *Etymological Dictionary of Proto-Celtic*. Leiden Indo-European Etymological Dictionary Series, Volume 9. Leiden: Brill, 2009

McFadden, Tom, "Preverbal *ge-* in Old and Middle English," *ZAS Papers in Linguistics* 58 (2015), 15–48

McGowan, Joseph P., "An Introduction to the Corpus of Anglo-Latin literature," in Pulsiano, Phillip and Elaine Treharne, eds. *A Companion to Anglo-Saxon Literature.* Oxford: Blackwell, 2001a, pp. 11–49

McGowan, Joseph P., "Anglo-Latin Prose," in Pulsiano, Phillip and Elaine Treharne, eds. *A Companion to Anglo-Saxon Literature.* Oxford: Blackwell, 2001b, pp. 296–393

McGowan, Joseph P., "Praefanda Anglosaxonica," *Studia Neophilologica* 75 (2003), 3–10

McGowan, Joseph P., "Elliptical Glossing and Elliptical Compounds in Old English," in *Beatus Vir: Studies in Early English and Norse Manuscripts in Memory of Phillip Pulsiano*, ed. A.N. Doane and Kirsten Wolf. Medieval and Renaissance Texts and Studies 319. Tempe, AZ: Arizona Center for Medieval and Renaissance Studies, 2006. Pp. 359–381

McGowan, Joseph P., [= McGowan 2009a] "Elves, Elf-Shot, and Epilepsy: OE *ælfādl*, *ælf-siden*, *ælfsogeða*, *bræccoþu*, and *bræcsēoc*," *Studia Neophilologica* 81 (2009), 116–120

McGowan, Joseph P. [= McGowan 2009b] "Giants and Snake-Charmers: OE *Þyrs*," *Notes and Queries* 56.4 (2009), 487–490

von Mengden, Ferdinand, "How myths persist: Jacob Grimm, the Long Hundred and duodecimal counting," in *Englische Sprachwissenschaft und Mediävistik: Standpunkte – Perspektiven – Neue Wege*, ed. Gabriele Knappe. Frankfurt: Peter Lang, 2005. Pp. 201–221

Mills, A.D. *A Dictionary of British Place-Names.* Oxford: Oxford University Press, 2003

Mitchell, Bruce and Fred C. Robinson. *A Guide to Old English.* 8th ed. Oxford: Blackwell, 2011

von Mengden, Ferdinand. *Cardinal Numbers: Old English from a Cross-Linguistic Perspective.* Topics in English Linguistics. Berlin: Mouton de Gruyter, 2010

Mertens-Fonck, Paule. *A Glossary of the Vespasian Psalter and Hymns.* Paris: Société d'Édition 'Les Belles Lettres'. 1960

Middeke, Kirsten, "'Subsumed under the dative'? The status of the Old English instrumental," in Claridge, Claudia and Birte Bös, eds. *Developments in English Historical Morpho-Syntax.* Amsterdam: John Benjamins, 2019, pp. 35–56

Middeke, Kirsten. *The Old English Case System: Case and Argument Structure Constructions.* Brill's Studies in Historical Linguistics, Volume 12. Leiden: Brill, 2022

Minkova, Donka. *The History of Final Vowels in English: The Sound of Muting.* Topics in English Linguistics 4. Berlin: Mouton de Gruyter, 1991

Minkova, Donka. *A Historical Phonology of English.* Edinburgh Textbooks on the English Language. Advanced. Edinburgh: Edinburgh University Press, 2014

Mitchell, Bruce. *Old English Syntax.* 2 vols. Oxford: Clarendon Press, 1985

Morse-Gagné, Elise E. "*Viking Pronouns in England: Charting the Course of THEY, THEIR, and THEM,*" diss., University of Pennsylvania, 2003.

Motherwell, George McCormick, "Old English Morphemic Structures: A Grammatical Restatement," diss., Indiana University, 1959.

Müller, Ernst, ed. *Nithardi historiarum libri III.* Monumenta Germaniae Historica, Scriptrores rerum Germanicarum 44. Hannover: Hahnsche Buchhandlung, 1907

Murray, Alexander Callander. *Germanic Kinship Structure: Studies in Law and Society in Antiquity and the Early Middle Ages.* Studies and Texts 65. Toronto: Pontifical Institute of Mediaeval Studies, 1983

Myres, J.N.L. *The English Settlements.* Oxford: Clarendon Press, 1986

Neidorf, Leonard, "Cain, Cam, Jutes, Giants, and the Textual Criticism of 'Beowulf,'" *Studies in Philology* 112.4 (2015), 599–632

Nielson, Hans F., "Old Frisian and the Old English Dialect," *Us Wurk* 30 (1981), 49–66

Nielsen, Hans F.*The Continental Backgrounds of English and its Insular Development until 1154.* Odense: Odense University Press, 1998

ODEG = *The Oxford Dictionary of English Grammar.* Sylvia Chalker and Edmund Weiner. New York: Oxford University Press, 1994

ODES = *A Dictionary of English Surnames.* P.H. Reaney and R.M. Wilson. 3rd ed. Oxford: Oxford University Press, 2005

Oksanen, Eljas. *Flanders and the Anglo-Norman World, 1066–1216.* Cambridge: Cambridge University Press, 2012

O'Neill, Patrick P., *ed. King Alfred's Old English Prose Translation of the First Fifty Psalms.* Medieval Academy Books, No. 104. Cambridge, MA: The Medieval Academy of America, 2001

Osborn, Marijane, "*Tir* as Mars in the Old English *Rune Poem,*" *American Notes and Queries* 16.1 (2003), 3–13

Padel, Oliver James. *Cornish Place-Name Elements.* English Place-Name Society Vol. 56/57. Nottingham: English Place-Name Society, 1985

Page, R.I. *Runes.* London: The British Museum, 1987

Page, R.I., "Two runic notes," *Anglo-Saxon England* 27 (1998), 289–294

Page, R.I. *An Introduction to English Runes.* 2nd ed. Woodbridge: The Boydell Press, 2006

Parker, Steve, "Sonority," in *The Blackwell Companion to Phonology.* 4 vols. Malden, MA: Wiley-Blackwell, 2011. Vol. 2, 1160–1184

Parsons, David, "British **Caraticos,* Old English *Cerdic,*" *Cambridge Medieval Celtic Studies* 33 (1997), 1–8

Pelteret, David A.E. *Slavery in Early Mediaeval England: From the Reign of Alfred until the Twelfth Century.* Studies in Anglo-Saxon History VII. Woodbridge: The Boydell Press, 1995

Pheifer, J.D. 1974. *Old English Glosses in the Épinal-Erfurt Glossary.* Oxford: Clarendon Press, 1974

Pons-Sans, Sara. *Norse-Derived Vocabulary in Late Old English Texts: Wulftsan's Works, A Case Study.* North-Western European Language Evolution Supplement, 22. Odense: University Press of Southern Denmark, 2007

Pons-Sanz, Sara. *Norse-Derived Vocabulary in Late Old English Texts.* North-Western European Language Evolution, Supplement, vol. 22. Amsterdam: John Benjamins/ University Press of Southern Denmark, 2012

Puhvel, Jaan. *Comparative Mythology.* Baltimore: The Johns Hopkins University Press, 1987

Pulsiano, Phillip. *Old English Glossed Psalters: A Collective Edition.* Vol. 1: *Pss. 1-50.* Toronto Old English Studies. Toronto: University of Toronto Press, 2000

Pulsiano, Phillip and Joseph McGowan, "*Fyrd, Here,* and the Dating of *Beowulf,*" *Studia Anglica Posnaniensia* 23 (1990), 3–13

Pulsiano, Phillip and Joseph McGowan, "Four Unedited Prayers in London, British Library Cotton Tiberius A.iii," *Mediaeval Studies* 56 (1994), 189–216

Pulsiano, Phillip and Elaine Treharne, eds. *A Companion to Anglo-Saxon Literature*. Oxford: Blackwell, 2001

RIB = *The Roman Inscriptions of Britain*. 3 vols. Oxford: Clarendon Press. Vol. I: *Inscriptions on Stone*, ed. R.G. Collingwood and R.P. Wright (1965). Vol. II: *Instrumentum Domesticum*, ed. S.S Frere and R.S.O. Tomlin (1990–1995). Vol. III: *Inscriptions on Stone*, ed. R.S.O. Tomlin, R.P. Wright, and M.W.C. Hassall (2009)

Ringe, Don, "Levelling and Rule Restructuring in Old English Adjectives," *Indo-European Linguistics* 3 (2015), 73–83

Ringe, Don. *From Proto-Indo-European to Proto-Germanic*. A Linguistic History of English, Volume I. 2nd revised ed. Oxford: Oxford University Press, 2017

Ringe, Don. *A Historical Morphology of English*. Edinburgh Textbooks on the English Language. Advanced. Edinburgh: Edinburgh University Press, 2021

Ringe, Don and Ann Taylor. *The Development of Old English*. A Linguistic History of English, Volume II. Oxford Linguistics. Oxford: Oxford University Press, 2014

Robinson, Fred C. *Beowulf and the Appositive Style*. Hodges Lectures. Knoxville, TN: University of Tennessee Press, 1985

Sauer, Hans, "The Old English Suffix *-el/-il/-ol/-l* (> ModE *-le*, cf. *beetle, girdle, thistle*) as Attested in the *Épinal-Erfurt Glossary*," in *Innovation and Continuity in English Studies: A Critical Jubilee*, ed. Herbert Grabes. Bamberger Beiträge zur Englischen Sprachwissenschaft Band 44. Frankfurt: Peter Lang, 2001. Pp. 289–313

Schabram, Hans. *Superbia. Studien zum altenglischen Wortschatz, I: die dialektale und zeitliche Verbreitung des Wortguts*. Munich: Wilhelm Fink, 1965

Schleburg, Florian. *Altenglisch swa: Syntax und Semantik einer polyfunktionalen Partikel*. Spracheissenschaftliche Studienbücher. Heidelberg: Universitätsverlag Winter, 2002

Schlemilch, Willy. *Beiträge zur Sprache und Orthographie spätaltenglischer Sprachdenkmäler der Übergangszeit, 1100–1150*. Studien zur englischen Philologie xxxiv. Halle: Max Niemeyer, 1914

Schramm, Gottfried. *Namenschatz und Dichtersprache. Studien zu den zweigliedrigen Personennamen der Germanen*. Ergänzungshefte zur Zeitschrift für vergleichende Sprachforschung 15. Göttingen: Vandenhoeck & Ruprecht, 1957

Scragg, Donald G. 1970. 'Initial *h* in Old English.' *Anglia* 88: 165–196

Scragg, Donald G., "A ninth-century Old English homily from Northumbria," *Anglo-Saxon England* 45 (2016), 39–49

Searle, William George. *Onomasticon Anglo-Saxonicum: A List of Anglo-Saxon Proper Names from the Time of Beda to that of King John*. Cambridge: Cambridge University Press, 1897

Seebold, Elmar, "Was ist jütisch? Was ist kentisch?", in *Britain 400-600: Language and History*, ed. Alfred Bammesberger and Alfred Wollmann. Anglistische Forschungen 205. Heidelberg: Carl Winter, 1990, 335–352

Sharpe, Richard, tr. *Adomnán of Iona, Life of St. Columba*. London: Penguin Books, 1995

Shaw, Philip A., "The origins of the theophoric week in the Germanic languages," *Early Medieval Europe* 15 (2007), 386–401

Shaw, Philip A., "Orthographic Standardization and Seventh- and Eighth-Century Coin Inscriptions," *Studies in Early Medieval Coinage 1: Two Decades of Discovery*, ed. Tony Abramson. Woodbridge: Boydell Press, 2008. Pp. 97–112

Shaw, Philip A. *Pagan Goddesses in the Early Germanic World: Eostre, Hreda and the Cult of Matrons*. Studies in Early Medieval History. London: Bristol Classical Press/ Bloomsbury, 2011

Shaw, Philip A., "Adapting the Roman alphabet for writing Old English: evidence from coin epigraphy and single-sheet charters," *Early Medieval Europe* 21 (2013), 115–139

Simek, Rudolf. *Dictionary of Northern Mythology*. Cambridge: D.S. Brewer, 1993

Sisam, Kenneth. *Studies in the History of Old English Literature*. Oxford: Clarendon Press, 1953

Smith, A.H. *English Place-Name Elements*. 2 vols. Cambridge: Cambridge University Press, 1956

Smith, A.H., ed. *Three Northumbrian Poems: Cædmon's Hymn, Bede's Death Song, and The Leiden Riddle*. Methuen's Old English Library. London, Methuen & Co, 1968

Smith, Jeremy J. *Sound Change and the History of English*. Oxford Linguistics. Oxford: Oxford University Press, 2007

Smith, Jeremy J. *Old English: A Linguistic Introduction*. Cambridge Introductions to the English Language. Cambridge: Cambridge University Press, 2009

Smyth, A.H., ed. *Three Northumbrian Poems: Cædmon's Hymn, Bede's Death Song, and The Leiden Riddle*. London: Methuen, 1968

Snyder, Lee Lamar, "The Old English Dialect Boundaries: Some Place-Name Evidence," diss., University of Pennsylvania, 1969.

Sprockel, C. *The Language of the Parker Chronicle*. Vol. I: *Phonology and Accidence*. The Hague: Martinus Nijhoff, 1965

Stanley, E.G., "The chronology of *r*-metathesis in Old English," *English and Germanic Studies* 5 (1952), 103–115

Stenton, Frank M. *Anglo-Saxon England*. 3rd ed. Oxford: Oxford University Press, 1971/rpt. 1989

Stevenson, W.H., ed. *Asser's Life of King Alfred, together with the Annals of Saint Neots*. Oxford: Clarendon Press, 1904

Stockwell, R.P., "The Old English short digraphs: some considerations," *Language* 31 (1955), 372–389

Sveinsson, Einar Ólaf, ed. *Vatnsdœla saga*. Íslenzk fornrit VIII. Reykjavík: Hið íslenzka fornritafélag, 1939

Swan, Mary, "Old English Textual Activity in the Reign of Henry II,"in Ruth Kennedy and Simon Meecham-Jones, eds., *Writers of the Reign of Henry II: Twelve Essays*. The New Middle Ages. New York: Palgrave Macmillan, 2006. 151–168

Sweet, Henry, ed. *King Alfred's West-Saxon Version of Gregory's Pastoral Care*. Early English Text Society O.S. 45. 50. 2 vols. (as one). Oxford: Oxford University Press, 1871

Symons, Victoria. *Runes and Roman Letters in Anglo-Saxon Manuscripts*. Ergänzungsbände zum Reallexikon der Germanischen Altertumskunde, Band 99. Berlin: De Gruyter, 2016

Tacitus, *Germania*. P. Cornelius Tacitus. II.2. *Germania, Agricola, Dialogus de oratoribus*. Ed. Erich Koestermann. Leipzig: B.G. Teubner, 1970

TOE. *A Thesaurus of Old English*, ed. Jane Roberts and Christian Kay, with Lynne Grundy. 2 vols. Costerus New Series 131–132. Amsterdam: Rodopi, 2000

Toon, Thomas E. *The Politics of Early Old English Sound Change*. New York: Academic Press, 1983

Toon, Thomas E., "Old English Dialects," in CHEL I (1992), pp. 409–451

Toswell, M.J. *The Anglo-Saxon Psalter*. Medieval Church Studies, vol. 10. Turnhout: Brepols, 2014

Treharne, Elaine, "The Life of English in the Mid-Twelfth Century: Ralph D'scures' Homily on the Virgin Mary," in Ruth Kennedy and Simon Meecham-Jones, eds., *Writers of the Reign of Henry II: Twelve Essays*. The New Middle Ages. New York: Palgrave Macmillan, 2006. Pp. 169–186

Treharne, Elaine. *Living Through Conquest: The Politics of Early English, 1020–1120*. Oxford Textual Perspectives. Oxford: Oxford University Press, 2012

Turville-Petre, Gabriel, "Thurstable," in *English and Medieval Studies: Presented to J.R.R. Tolkien on the Occasion of his Seventieth Birthday*, ed. Davis and Wrenn. Pp. 241–249

Ure, James M., ed. *The Benedictine Office: An Old English Text*. Edinburgh: Edinburgh University Press, 1957

Vleeskruyer, R., ed. *The Life of St. Chad*. Amsterdam: North Holland, 1953

Vries, Jan de. *Altnordisches etymologisches Wörterbuch*. Leiden: E.J. Brill, 1977

Warner, Rubie D.-N., ed. *Early English Homilies, from the Twelfth Century MS. Vesp. D. XIV. Part I: Text*. Early English Text Society, O.S. 152. London: Kegan Paul, Trench, Trübner & Co., 1917

Waxenberger, Gaby, "The Representation of Vowels in Unstressed Syllables in the Older English Runic Corpus," in Bammesberger, Alfred and Gaby Waxenberger, eds. *Das fuþark und seine enizelsprachlichen Weiterentwicklungen: Akten der Tagung in Eichstätt vom 20. bis 24. Juli 2003*. Berlin: Walter de Gruyter, 2006, 272–314

Waxenberger, Gaby, Kerstin Kazzazi, and John Hines, eds. *Old English Runes: Interdisciplinary Perspectives on Approaches and Methodologies with a Concise and Selected Guide to Terminologies*. Ergänzungsbände zum Reallexikon der Germanischen Altertumskunde, Band 134. Berlin: De Gruyter, 2016

Wenisch, Franz, "Kritische Bemerkungen zu Angaben über die Verbreitung einiger angeblich westsächsischer Dialektwörter," *Anglia* 96 (1978), 5–44

Wenisch, Franz. *Spezifisch anglisches Wortgut in den nordhumbrischen Interlineargglossierungen des Lukasevangeliums*. Anglistische Forschungen 132. Heidelberg: Karl Winter, 1979.

Wenisch, Franz, "*(ge)fægnian*: zur dialektalen Verbreitung eines altenglischen Wortes," *Problems of Old English Lexicography: Studies in Memory of Angus Cameron*. Ed. Alfred Bammesberger. Regensburg: Friedrich Pustet, 1985. Pp. 393–426

Williams, Gareth, "The Gold Coinage of Eadbald, King of Kent (AD 616-40)," *British Numismatic Journal* 68 (1998), 137–140

Wilson, R.M., "The provenance of the Vespasian Psalter gloss: the linguistic evidence," in *The Anglo-Saxons: Studies in some aspects of their history and culture presented to Bruce Dickins*, ed. Peter Clemoes. London: Bowes and Bowes, 1959. Pp. 292–310

Wischer, Ilse, "Old English *wolde* and *sceolde*: A semantic and syntactic analysis," in Claridge, Claudia and Birte Bös, eds. *Developments in English Historical Morpho-Syntax*. Amsterdam: John Benjamins, 2019, pp. 111–127

Wolfram, Herwig. *History of the Goths*. Berkeley, CA: University of California Press, 1988

Wollmann, Alfred. *Untersuchungen zu den frühen lateinischen Lehnwörtern im Altenglischen. Phonologie und Datierung*. Texte und Untersuchungen zur englischen Philologie 15. Munich: Wilhelm Fink, 1990

Wrenn, C.L., "'Standard' Old English," *Transactions of the Philological Society* 32 (1933), 65–88

Wynn, J.B., "An examination of the language of the Corpus, Épinal, and Erfurt Glossaries," diss., University of Manchester, 1956.

Yorke, Barbara, "The *Bretwaldas* and the origins of overlordship in Anglo-Saxon England," in *Early Medieval Studies in Honour of Patrick Wormald*, ed. Stephen Baxter, Catherine Karkov, Janet L. Nelson, David Pelteret. Aldershot: Ashgate, 2009. Pp. 81–96

Zoëga, Geir T. *A Concise Dictionary of Old Icelandic*. Toronto: University of Toronto Press, 2004

Zupitza, Julius, ed. *Aelfrics Grammatik und Glossar: Text und Varianten*. 4th ed. Ed. Helmut Gneuss. Berlin: Weidmann, 2003

CHAPTER 5

Conquest, and After

The study of Middle English has profited immensely in the past 60 years from the development of large-scale parsed corpora (such as the Penn-Helsinki Parsed Corpus of Middle English; PPCME2) and major dialect atlases for early and late Middle English (both housed in Edinburgh), resources all now available online. The Linguistic Atlas of Early Middle English (LAEME, version 3.2) covers the chronological range 1150–1325, while the Linguistic Atlas of Late Middle English (LALME) covers 1325–1450. The LAEME has comparatively fewer texts to work with, particularly in the North-Northern Midlands and in the Central Midlands (which can clearly be seen on LAEME's 'Map of Survey Points,' with heavier concentration of points in the further West Midlands and East Midlands and a scattered range across the South), and the number of text skews higher toward the second half of its chronological period. It nonetheless follows the model of the LALME, on which LAEME's original principal researcher Margaret Laing had worked. By comparison, the LALME had an embarrassment of riches with the proliferation of surviving texts 1325 onward, though this is balanced by, to the student, a bewildering range of dialectal forms.

Great benefits may be derived also from recent studies on the historical phonology of English (Minkova 2014) and the morphology of the period (Ringe 2021). Studies on the syntax of individual texts enhance the diachronic perspective on a period in which the English language moved closer to the syntax recognizable to modern readers; it is difficult to say with any precision, but by ca. 1350, Middle English texts are 'easier' to read in terms of their syntax.

The major developments of the period resist any simple tabulation but include:

— Loss of grammatical gender, excepting the third person singular of the personal pronouns, where it remains [*he* / *she* /*it*]; in earliest ME texts nouns may still be marked by grammatical gender: e.g., feminine abstract nouns in *-nesse/-nisse/-nysse* in the Southern ME "Homily on the Annunciation of the BVM" in British Library, MS Vespasian D.xiv; grammatical gender is missing completely in the *Ormulum* by the

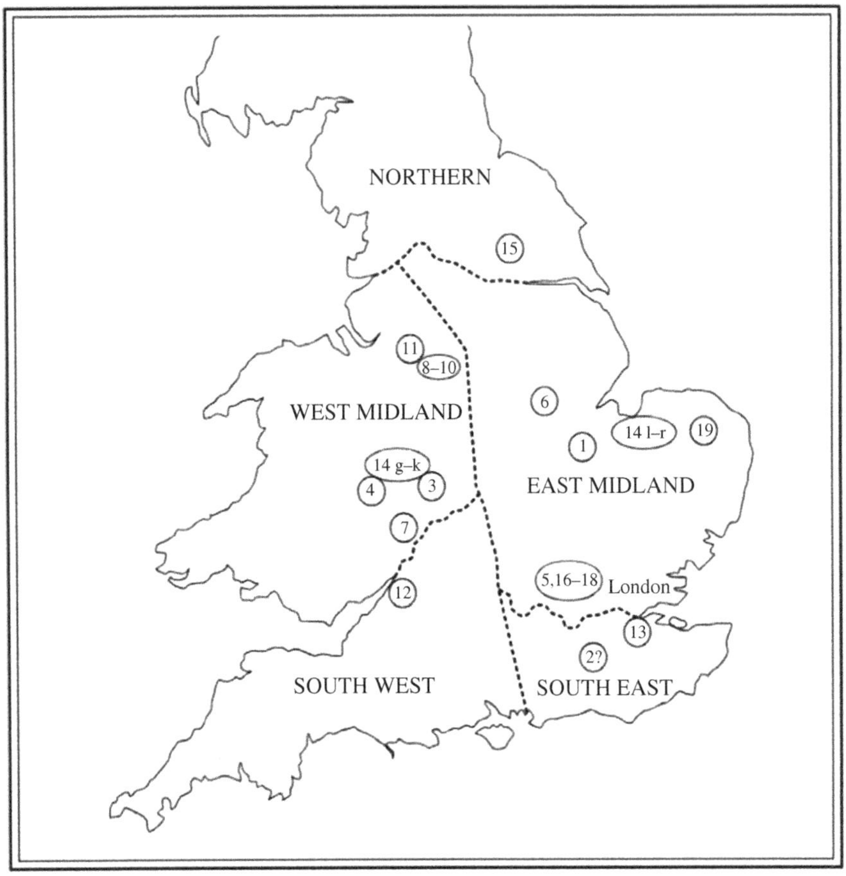

The five major Middle English dialect areas (figure with numbered representative texts from Turville-Petre and Burrow 2020). 1) The Peterborough Chronicle, Middle English continuations (one set for the years 1122–1131, another for 1132–1154) in an early East Midlands dialect (possibly localized further to the monastery's Cambridgeshire) to the Old English *Anglo-Saxon Chronicle* (that in a West Saxon dialect, perhaps Winchester): an early witness to earliest Middle English prose, the Peterborough continuations exhibit already significant grammatical changes to the language (see pp. 263–264 below; see also Bergs and Skaffari 2007); 2) *The Owl and the Nightingale* (a Southern dialect, variably localized: Southern Midlands, Southeastern; see pp. 263–265, 268–271, 288, 294–295); 3) Laȝamon, Brut (early West Midlands ME, Worcestershire; see pp. 265–266, 294); 4) *Ancrene Wisse/Ancrene Riwle* (the 'AB-language" of a number of other poems in 13th-century West Midlands dialect; see pp. 292, 303); 5) *Sir Orfeo* (Southern-Southeastern; see pp. 276–277); 6) *The Cloude of Unknowyng* (northern East Midlands); 7) William Langland, *Piers Plowman* (Langland, 1332–1386, is associated with the Malvern Hills, his dialect perhaps can be localized to southwestern Worcestershire); 8) *Patience* (Northwest Midlands, ca. 1400; LALME localizes to Cheshire-Staffordshire border); 9) *Sir Gawain and the Green Knight* (like *Patience* and *Pearl*, from the same manuscript, British Library, Cotton Nero A.x, with same localization of language); 10) Pearl ; 11) *St. Erkenwald* (ca. 1400; Cheshire); 12) John Trevisa, *Dialogus inter dominum et clericum* ("Dialogue between a lord and a clerk"; Trevisa, ca. 1342–1402, was born in Cornwall and his is a later Southwestern ME dialect); 13) John Gower, *Confessio Amantis* (Gower, ca. 1330–1408, had family roots in Kent and Suffolk, that is, Southeastern Midlands and Kentish dialect regions, but is associated with an emerging London-Southeastern standard); 14) lyrics by Franciscan friar John of Grimestone (ca. 1372, Norfolk dialect); 15) York Play of The Crucifixion (15th-century late Northern ME); 16–18) works of Geoffrey Chaucer (ca. 1342/1343–1400; Chaucer's language is most closely associated with the emerging 'London standard'); Julian of Norwich, *Revelations of Divine Love, Shewed to a Devout Anchoress* (ca. 1343 to sometime after 1416; Mother Julian of Norwich's text is actually in a late ME dialect localized to Lincolnshire). Many other texts could be added to the dialect picture (to Lincolnshire could be added the romance *Havelok the Dane* of the 13th century; see pp. 287, 295–297; on emerging Hiberno-English dialects of Leinster and Munster, see pp. 309–310). For further refinements to the mapping of ME dialects, see Fulk 2012.

Augustinian canon regular Orm, a text dating to the last quarter of the 12th century (Ringe 2021, 66). While it is customary to speak of a 'loss' of grammatical gender in late OE to early ME, the process is rather more complicated, involving a number of 'gender shifts,' as of feminine nouns to masculine or neuter, as perhaps intermediary to 'loss' (Mustanoja 1960, 43–52; Curzan 2003). One early example of such morphological change may be seen in a line from *The Owl and the Nightingale* from the late 12th to very early 13th century:

> Hit ware þare Hule eardingstowe (line 28; Stanley 1972).
> [It was the dwelling-place of the Owl.]

Early Middle English *Hule/ule* ('owl') was originally a feminine n-stem noun in Old English (*ūle*), and *eardingstowe* was originally a feminine noun as well (OE *eardungstôwe*); the poem's *þare Hule eardingstowe* would have been Old English *þǣre (h)ūlan eardungstôwe*, the genitive singular feminine. The gender or 'concord class' for 'owl' – OE *(h)ūle*, ME *(h)ule* – had been reassigned (likely to masculine) or lost by the early Middle English stage; but the definite article form *þare* (OE *þǣre*, gen. sing. fem., 'of the') retains marking for number, case, and gender. There may be some conservatism in function words at play – pronouns, articles – versus lexical morphemes; but the attrition of gender-marking in late Old English to Middle English is evidenced by reassignment of loanwords to different concord classes/declensions, more commonly out of feminine and neuter and into the masculine classes (though there were also shifts into feminine and neuter classes, as among Latin loans to Old English; see Ringe 2021, 57–58). The loss of gender and original case marking with *Hule* is counterbalanced by its retention in *þare*. It is not certain whether the movement of nouns out of other gender or concord classes to the masculine was a step along the way to loss of grammatical gender overall; an early Middle English text such as *The Owl and the Nightingale* indicates that the process was gradual.

— The consequent rise of an invariant *þe* 'the' as definite article, the *þ-* by levelling from the non-nominative forms; in OE, we saw the paradigm m/f/n *sē / sēo / þæt* in the demonstratives, with *þ-* in the accusative, genitive, and dative and instrumental, e.g., masculine *þone* (acc.), *þæs* (gen.), *þǣm/þām* (dat.), *þon/þȳ* (instr.), etc. This is a signal development in the history of English as one might say the grammatical concept of the 'definite article' has developed out of the demonstratives. This change seems to have been effected most thoroughly in the North, in somewhat more staggered fashion in the South and West Midlands, but it was overall an early change. It can be found even in an early Southwestern (or Southwest Midlands) poem like the gnomic debate poem *The Owl and the Nightingale*, dating to by or before the accession of Henry III and in a Southern/Southwestern dialect with forms deriving in part from late Kentish. That the invariant definite article had taken hold even in the London area is evidenced by its appearance in the Proclamation of Henry III of 1258 (Mossé 1968, §68). Thus in *The Owl and the Nightingale* we find the invariant *þe* as definite article (e.g., its correlative comparative use at line 448 *Þe more ich singe þe more i mai*; Stanley 1972). As might be expected, so significant a morphological change, spread over so disparate a range of local dialects, saw the persistence, in the South and West Midlands, of some of the older forms into the 12th and 13th centuries:

South-West Midlands		
m. *þes* (gen.) *þan, þēne* (dat.)	m.f.n. (plural)	*þā*
n. *þet, þat* (nom., acc.) *þe* (instr.)		
f. *þā, þat* (acc.) *þer, þāre* (dat.) *þe* (instr.)		
London/Southeastern		
m. *þane* (acc.) *þan* (dat.)	m.f.n (plural)	*þō* (nom., acc.)
n. *þæt* (nom., acc.)		*þan* (dat.)
f. *þǣre* (dat.)		
Kent		
m. *sē* (nom.) *þane* (acc.) *þā* (dat.)	m.f.n (plural)	*þō* (nom., acc.)
n. *þet* (nom., acc.)		
f. *si* (nom.) *þō, tō* (acc.) *þō* (dat.)	(Mossé 1968, §67)	

An invariant plural form *þā* appears in the early ME continuations of the *Peterborough Chronicle* (1122–1154) and the *Ormulum* (ca. 1154–1180), and a plural *þō* appears as late as in *The Travels of Sir John Mandeville* (ca. 1371).

— Large-scale loss of nominal inflection to such a point that by the late period we may think of case as we do with MdE: largely vestigial (marking mainly for case, number, and gender with the singular of the personal pronouns [*he/him.him, she/her/her*]). For instance, even in the early ME *The Owl and the Nightingale* the adjectival declensions have been reduced: with the exception of the masculine accusative singular of strong declension adjectives (which add the termination-*ne*), all other forms, in all cases and genders, end in *-e*. The noun declensions are similarly if not quite so drastically reduced: in the strong declensions, masc. and neut. gen. sing. in *-es*, plural masc. and neut. nom./acc. in *-es/-e* with the dative occasionally also in *-es*. In the paradigm for the weak nouns (all genders) all forms are with *-e* with the exception of fem. gen. sing. in *-es/-e* for the strong fem. from OE, masc. and neut. nom./acc. in *-es* (with some neuter forms in *-e*), and neuter weak declension nouns with *-en(e)* in the nom. and acc. plural (Stanley 1972, 15). This seemingly inconsistent morphological variation is why readers of early Middle English texts often have to consult the 'Language and Dialect' section in editions of the texts.

— A profound shift in nominal declension would occur between these early ME texts and the poetry of Chaucer (ca. 1343–1400) with the zero-form singular nominative and accusative (e.g., *sto(o)n, fader, herte*), genitive singular in *-es* (*sto(o)nes, faderes/fadres, hertes*), a dative singular in *-e* (though this was gradually being lost also), and extension of the *-es* to all plural endings (grammatical gender having largely collapsed by Chaucer's day in the nominal system; Horobin and Smith 2002, 104–105). Though not without some complication, as there were *r*-declension plurals such as *sustren* ('sisters'), *mōdren* ('mothers'), and *brethren(e)/bretherene/brotheren(e)* ('brothers'). Case marking declined in the same dialectal areas where gender was lost (one exception being the Southeast; Ringe 2021, 84).

— Simplification of the conjugation of verbs: a process already underway in later Old English the Germanic classes of verbs in OE underwent profound remodelling among the strong and weak conjugations (the 7 classes of strong verbs, 3 classes of weak verbs, and preterite-present verbs, seen last chapter); in *The Owl and the Nightingale* the inherited strong and weak conjugations in the present tense have $1^{st}/2^{nd}/3^{rd}$ singular forms in *-e, -st/-est, -eþ* and plural in *-eþ* (with four distinct forms in the present). An OE anomalous verb such as *dōn* appears in ME as *do / dest, dost / deþ* (singular), *deþ* (plural) in the present, and in the preterite *dude* and **dude(n)* (compare OE *dyde* and *dydon* and Chaucerian *do / dost, doost, doist / doth, doith,* and *dide / dide(n).* Typical strong, *binde(n)* 'to bind,' and weak, *loue(n)* 'to love,' paradigms from Chaucer's poetry in the present indicative are given below (cf. Ringe 2021, 115–116):

	SING		PL
1st	binde	1st	binde(n)
2nd	bindest	2nd	binde(n)
3rd	bindeth	3rd	binde(n)
1st	loue	1st	loue(n)
2nd	louest	2nd	loue(n)
3rd	loueth	3rd	loue(n)

In the subjunctive, the forms are *binde* and *loue* for $1^{st}/2^{nd}/3^{rd}$ singular and plural *binde(n)* and *loue(n).* The verb 'to be' (ME *bēn*, OE *bēon*) is of course anomalous and, apart from a core of *am / art/ is* in the present singular and competing *be(e)n* and *are(n)* in the plural, there are a bewildering number of variants forms in the written record; preterite forms *was* and *were(n)* too have their variants: *wast* (2nd sing.), *wore* (3rd sing., a form not unlike what is heard in the Ozark American English for *were*), *wuren* (3rd pl.; MED, s.v. *bēn*). New verbs were borrowed from French, and existing verbs underwent semantic extension and reassignment, or passed into obsolescence. A study of verbs of motion in the two manuscript copies of Laȝamon's *Brut* (Ogura 2002) noted increasing use of *wenden* (< OE *wendan*, which survives in collocational use as *wend one's way*) and *turnen* (< OE *tyrn(i)an*), as *liðen* (OE *līðan*, 'go, travel') and *fūsen* (< OE *fȳsan*, 'send forth; hasten, hurry') faded in use, while the Middle English reflexes of OE *būgan* ('bend; change direction, turn'), *tēon* ('draw, pull, drag,' but here in its sense 'betake oneself to, go, roam'; CHM, s.v.), and *hweorfan* ('turn, move, come, depart') were replaced by *wenden* and *turnen.* The two surviving manuscript copies of Laȝamon's 16,000-line 'Matter of Britain' poem, dating to ca. 1200, are both from the West Midlands, London, British Library MS Cotton Caligula A.ix and Cotton Otho C.xiii, and both dated to the 13th century with the Caligula copy believed to predate the Otho by some 25–75 years. Ogura's study of frequencies in the choice of verbs of motion in this early Middle English text did not find much that was probative in the dating of the copies, which may be more contemporaneous than thought, but the lexical choices may be evidence rather more of synchronic than diachronic change (unless comparing OE to early ME). The Caligula manuscript copy tended to prefer *faren/feren,* where Otho used *wenden* (the two most common verbs of motion in the text) and Otho was somewhat more likely to drop the *i*-preverbal: *iwende* versus *wende*, which may be an early indicator of the fate of OE *ȝe-*/ME *i-* over the course of the next two centuries; the prefix persists in Chaucer's past participle forms *ihote/icleped* 'named, called,' but would soon become increasingly rare. Verb/auxiliary + infinitive combinations with *gan/bigan* give a sense of this transitional period of English grammar: *he wolde...faren (in)to Rome* ('he would/wished to go to Rome'), *ich wolle/wulle faren/we<n>de min(n)e wœi/way* ('I will go my way')[1]; the line *þe king him gon to slæpen: and Brien gon to wepen* (Caligula) / *þe king him gan sleape: and Brian gan wepe* (Otho) still has that reflexive-like *him* (literally, 'the king him 'gan/went to sleep') but one sees the use of verbs of motion in idioms expressing the onset of sleep: *go to sleep, fall asleep* (Ogura 2002, 213–214, 222–225). Unstressed vowels tended toward /ə/ – final *-e* would eventually be lost entirely, though in the usual pronunciation guides to Chaucer, for instance, a form such as *dide*, 3rd sing. pret. of *dōn* 'to do,' is to be realized [didə], MdE *did.*

That said, there was considerable dialectal and free variation throughout the Middle English period; with this last example, the *Middle English Dictionary* (MED) records early preterite forms *did(e)* and *gedid(e)* (with the preverbal inherited from Old English that would lose the initial glide and reduce to *y-* or *i-* before disappearing); *dit* and *didde*, the latter with the geminate after the short vowel; and *deude* among other forms (MED, s.v. *dōn*). What are now fully modal auxiliaries *shall* and *may/might* were preterite-present verbs, the present form resembling a strong-class preterite with umlaut (*i schal*), the preterite form a weak-class past form with dental suffix (*-d, -t*): *shold(e), shuld(e), shild, isceolde* and a great many other variant forms (the last form is closest to Old English *ġe-sċeolde*, preterite of *sċulan*; MED, s.v. *shulen*). The category 'modal auxiliary' might more rightly be applied during this period of the language; as seen earlier, these auxiliaries (or 'verbal auxiliaries') in Old English (*āgan, cunnan, durran, magan, mōtan, sċulan, þurfan*, and *willan*) could function as independent or simplex forms: *willan* in the sense 'wish, want,' *durran* 'dare, venture, presume,' and so forth (see Mitchell, *Old English Syntax* §§990ff.; see also Ringe 2021, 36–37). Genuine modality can be seen with ME *shulen*; the MED lists for its sense as a modal auxiliary: 'expressing what is appropriate, reasonable, right, prudent' (should do something); 'expressing duty, responsibility, or secular obligation' (ought do something); 'expressing moral or spiritual obligation or compliance with religious belief or practice'; 'expressing an order, a commandment, direction'; or as a 'hortative auxiliary expressing advice, counsel, suggestion'; 'expressing certainty, belief, assertion, intention, determination,

[1] The verb of motion (*faren/feren, wenden*, etc.) + *way* idiom is new; compare the idiomatic use of *woll/wyll* + ADV *wel(le)* in Malory's *Le morte D'Arthur/Morte Darthur* (ca. 1470, published by Caxton 1485): *'I woll welle,' seyde kynge Arthure*, literally 'I wish/would well' = 'readily agree' (Vinaver 1971, 25, 811).

assurance'; 'expressing prophecy, prediction, annunciation'; expressing 'fate, destiny'; 'expressing consuetudinal or iterative action, action under normal circumstances or resulting from natural inclination'; 'expressing imminence'; 'expressing action or event expected, set, or appointed'; among the 28 senses the MED gives for *shulen* are those expressed in MdE with *should*, with greater or lesser frequency. In fact, one finds in this period the multivalence, or synchronous polysemy (that the word could be seen as employing several of its senses at once), of *shall/should*; the early Vespasian Homilies (of the 12th century), in Homily 10 on the *Decalogum Moysi* (the 'Ten Commandments' or 'Decalogue of Moses'), says about the Eighth Commandment: *⁊ se þe specð leasunge, he sceal losigen sylf* (Warner 1917, 10): "and he who speaketh lies, he shall lose himself." The sense of *shall* (*sceal*) here clearly encompasses futurity and rightful outcome, prediction and certainty (in outcome and belief), and what ought to be (in a religious sense, and likely also by common sense or proverbial wisdom). No doubt the far greater corpus of extant Middle English texts allows for such refinement in definitions, but it is likely too that in this period there was a rich expansion in semantic content and nuance; there certainly was in terms of forms (the most comprehensive account of ME verbal inflection is Fulk 2012, 71–90).

— Syntactic change is less noticeable to students of Chaucer, for example, as they encounter an English syntax more like their own than in Old English or early Middle English (until 1150, say, early ME syntax is still very much like that of late OE); the general idea that a loss of inflections led to a more fixed order is often repeated because in its broad outline it is true – and it points to a larger structural or 'deep' change in English from a more synthetic to analytic language (Los 2015, 48–49). The expanded form of the verb existed already in OE (e.g., *willan, sculan, habban* + infinitive for compound tense formation and to express aspect [durative, progressive]), and the periphrastic *do*-form would rise in use and prominence in Middle English – for example, the OE homiletic *and treowa he deð færlice blowan*, literally 'and trees He [God] doeth suddenly to bloom' = 'He [God] makes the trees suddenly bloom' still has the original sense of OE *dōn* 'make, do'; in a 13th-century rhyming verse *þe sonne: / In winter does a-rise* 'the sun in winter does arise,' though a nonemphatic use that does not, generally, occur in MdE, one can seem grammaticalization underway (the fuller uses of periphrastic *do* await the 15th and 16th centuries; Los 2015, 109–111). In periphrastic verbal constructions *be* forms would displace OE *weorðan* in the Middle English period (Los 2015, 84); it was not a simple change as it is difficult to tell whether the decline in use of *wurthe* (infin. *worthen* < OE *weorðan*) led to its replacement by *be*-forms or that *be* and the periphrastic use of other verbs such as *become, come, turn* helped effect the change (Mustanoja 1960, 617).

— Advances in dialectology and historical phonology: a number of these signal developments will be outlined below. The two great dialect atlases of Middle English, the LAEME and LALME, have just begun to pay dividends, while a recent diachronic history of English phonology has taken up every single sound change 1100–1500 (Minokva 2014). One of the critical developments of the Middle English era was the 3rd person singular personal pronoun *she*; OE *hēo* in its variant forms had apparently given rise to some ambiguity, at least in speech, and a *s*- pronominal form would have helped disambiguate the gender-bearing singular forms. But the explanation of its development has been problematic; the dialect atlas data provides information about distribution of competing forms and some idea of the chronology of displacement of the *hēo* forms by the *she/scho/sche/shee* forms. Don Ringe recently suggested that the form *schō* 'she' (*ȝhō* in the *Ormulum*) likely does not follow a pattern of *hēo* > **hjō* > /ço:/ (/ç/ the voiceless palatal fricative), rather as OE preterite *ēode* 'went' by monophthongization and glide insertion > ME *yēde* ~ *yōde*, so an OE **hjēo* > /hjo:/ or /ço/: then the rarer phoneme /ç/ > /ʃ/ (*schō*; Ringe 2021, 74–76; see also Jordan 1974, 112 at §, 149 at §151); thus Orm's *ȝhō* and his use of the yogh initially, in his idiosyncratic spelling system, represented word-initial *j-*. Of the 280 tokens used in the questionnaire to the LALME, from *the, these/those* to *world, other*, and *thousand* (high-frequency words, most of them function words; Vol. I, 552–553), *she* generated among the most complex maps in the atlas (see Dot Maps 10–20, Vol. I, 307–309; and Item Maps 4.1–6, Vol. II). The County Dictionary of LALME lists the variant forms from the maps by survey point and county; here one can see the full range of forms of ME 'she': *che, cheo, cho* (Buckinghamshire to Staffordshire to Lincolnshire and Lancashire from the Midlands to the North); *he, hee, heo, ho* and other *h-* forms (East Anglia and the Southeast all the way across the South to Exeter); and the *sche, she, scho, sho* forms that would predominate and survive in MdE *she* (Vol. IV, 7–8).

These morphological and syntactic changes, among others, lend credence to the perceptual notion that English was modernizing – that is, drawing 'closer' to the language as spoken at present. This is of course a retrospective view, from the perspective of speakers of a language that became more analytic than synthetic in its syntactic typology, reliant less on inflections and more on periphrastic constructions (from *þare hūlan* to 'of the owl'). But to a reader of earlier English texts, the poetry and prose of later Middle English is much 'easier,' more familiar with its thousands of French loans, and Old English more distant, more 'Germanic.' In terms of word frequency by usage, this is a superficial notion, as the words of highest frequency in use are mainly from the native stock of morphemes of English. In the list of the Oxford English Corpus of the OED of the 100 most common words in English, the vast majority are function words and core verbs (*the* and *be* the two most frequent in use); at number 61 in the list, *people* is one of the very few loans to make the list (a borrowing from medieval French). As much distance as there may *seem* to be between Modern English and German, as many and significant as were the changes wrought by the Norman Conquest, English, linguistically speaking, remains a Germanic language.

5.1 WHEN DOES MIDDLE ENGLISH BEGIN?

An important collection of essays at the turn of the millennium (Swan and Treharne 2000) set out a course of study and re-interpretation of the Old to Middle English transition that has borne fruit in the two decades since; focused on a seemingly narrow range of manuscript production, English manuscripts of the 12th century, the attempt to fill in one picture (manuscript and text production) added to the mosaic of intellectual history under the Norman and Angevin kings. And to the history of the English language. Statements of England becoming a land of two tongues, Latin and French (which the Normans did promote in their cultural program), have always been too broad, and begged the question of how then did English survive? Counter-intuitive as it may at first seem, Old English played a great role in this survival. Elaine Treharne points out that English in the 11th century survived two conquests (Cnut in 1016, William in 1066) and remained "a political, intellectual, religious, and ideological tool" (Treharne 2012, ix; 1–4, 9–12). It might be said that the conquest of 1016 began in 793, a point that will be of value in the discussion in 5.7 with regard to the "Middle English as Creole" hypothesis. The Viking conquest was never total, though raids struck all along the coasts of the British Isles, 793–1066; Alfred's campaigns and the growing power of Wessex (which had linguistic consequences for Kentish and Mercian Old English) checked the Danes and other Scandinavians to within the Danelaw. The Norman Conquest spelled the end of Anglo-Saxon England, but the Normans would survive barely a century in power – the ethnonym derives from Old Norse *Norðmaðr*, pl. *Norðmenn*, via Medieval Latin *Normannus*. Supplanted in 1154 by the Angevin monarchs, the Normans fairly rapidly lost others of their far-flung possessions (Sicily and parts of the Maghreb by 1194). Angevin is a French loan and simply means 'of Anjou,' and its first attestation in English was in Henry Watson's ca. 1508–1511 romance *The Noble History of King Ponthus*: "Ponthus made a maundement of brytons poyteuynes, normans & angeuynes for to go to galyce to conquere his countre th<at> the sarasynes helde." Watson's Early Modern English is perhaps still difficult enough to contemporary readers that it requires translation: "Ponthus made a command of Britain's Poitevins, Normans and Angevins that they should go to Galicia to conquer his country that the Saracens held." Watson's language is interesting too in that one faces here, some four and a half centuries after the Norman Conquest, a similar question at the outset of this chapter – what are the borders of the periods of the history of English? This section takes up the matter of "When did Middle English begin?"; the natural next question is, when did it end? The Great Vowel Shift (Chapter 6) is the usual signpost for the Late Middle English to Early Modern English transition. In this line from Watson's Early Modern English romance is the ME-sounding construction *for to go* – compare *Som man desireth for to han richesse* ("Some men desire to have riches") from Chaucer's "Knight's Tale" (I. 1255). The *for to* infinitive construction survived in dialectal English and made its way to the United States – it may seem curious at first, but regional use is especially common in the mountain regions (Appalachians, Great Smoky Mountains, Ozarks), but these regions have long been repositories of more archaic forms of English, as well as ballads and folk tales.[2] A number of the Middle English attestations of *maundement*, as 'commandment,' not surprisingly come from the early 'Wycliffite' Bible (MED, s.v.).

The early ME debate poem *The Owl and the Nightingale* was likely composed in the range of 1189 × 1216, that is, following the death of Henry II and by the reign

[2] There is a very good discussion of the construction at the Yale Grammatical Diversity Project (English in North America), website: https://ygdp.yale.edu/phenomena/for-to-infinitives.

of Henry III, and is preserved in two surviving manuscript copies, British Library, MS Cotton Caligula A.ix and Oxford, Bodleian Library, MS Jesus College 29. Both manuscripts date to the second half of the 13th century and seem to derive from the same exemplar. The Cotton manuscript contains contemporary works on Latin and Anglo-Norman as well as early Middle English, and the language of the Caligula copy is of interest for its Southern and Southwestern features (which may match the references in the poem to Guildford, Surrey, and Portesham, Dorset) – and for those that seem to derive rather from Kentish, that is Southeastern features (some of the end-rhymes work better when converting the manuscript spelling into corresponding Kentish form; Stanley 1972, 18). The Caligula manuscript was written by a single scribe, but in two different spelling systems: lines 1–900 and 961–1183 (Ci in Stanley's scheme; Stanley 1972, 7–8), and lines 901–960 and 1184–1794 (Cii; e.g., for the 3rd singular fem. personal pronoun Cii has *heo*, as in OE, Ci *ho*). Like many other medieval English texts, *The Owl and the Nightingale* is preserved not in an autograph manuscript in the author's own dialect but in copies that show some signs of dialect admixture, though in the case of this early ME 'talking animals' debate poem the transmission history seems to be within the range of 50–75 years of composition (whereas, as seen last chapter, that of *Beowulf* may involve 200–300 years between composition and sole surviving manuscript). The charm to the poem is of course in the framework story of an owl and nightingale sparring verbally, invoking proverb literature and folk traditions to illuminate and, at times, castigate, human behavior, in language that is by turns charming, overwrought (*'Abid! Abid!' þe Ule seide, 'Þu gest al to mid swikelede'* ["'Abide! Abide!' the Owl said, 'you go on wholly in deceit'"; ll. 837–838]), even vituperative. The two birds present arguments for, and themselves represent, two modes of being, two ways of life, the Owl a more serious, contemplative, sober way, the Nightingale a more active, light-hearted and cheerful one; as the poem's editor E.G. Stanley has observed: "The reader who strives to follow the poet's meaning will remember, as he reads the Nightingale's case, that it is not enough, and as he reads the Owl's, that it is not everything" (Stanley 1972, 22). As with many of these medieval debates and beast fables there is not so much a solution offered as the presentation of contrasting views seriously considered; the Owl and Nightingale at the poem's end submit to the advice of the Wren (all three birds are female, as marked by the pronoun *ho/heo*) to avoid breaking 'the king's peace' and submit to the judgement of *Þat Maister Nichole* (1746). The cleric Nicholas of Guildford is one of a number of associations of the poem with Guildford; the language of the poet might originally have been of the Surrey-Dorset Southern variety, though one cannot be much more definitive as no other local texts of the period are known. The reference to the 'king's peace' (*grith*, OE *cyninges griþ*, '[king's] peace, protection,' is still listed in *Black's Law Dictionary* as one of the legalisms deriving from the 'Saxon' era) is made with both Middle English and Old English terms:

Hwat! wulle ȝe þis pes tobreke ("What! Would you this peace destroy?"; *pes* 'peace' a loan to Middle English from Old French) [1730]

Ȝef ȝe doþ griþbruche on his londe ("If you make breach-of-the-peace in his [the king's] land"; both elements of the compound *griþbruche* derive from Old English) [1734]

At the level of grammar, syntax, and orthography, one can see the development of English into its early 'Middle' phase; so also, for the history of English poetry, the versification. *The Owl and the Nightingale* employs rhyming couplets with octosyllabic lines of four stressed elements, often in what would in later English verse be termed 'iambic':

x′ x′ x′ x′ (with inversions of weak and stressed elements, or substitution of unstressed for stressed)

An Hule and one Nightingale (4)
Þe Nightingale bigon þe speche (13)
Ac pipest also doþ a mose (503; "As pipes also does a titmouse")
To Portesham þat heo bicome (1791)

What is striking in *The Owl and the Nightingale* is the persistence of Old English vocabulary: besides the aforementioned *griþbruche* one sees:

boȝe (15; 'bough,' < OE *bōg*, masc. *ā*-stem)
segge (18; 'sedge,' < OE *seċġ*; ME *-gg(e)* = [ʒ])
eardingstowe (28; 'dwelling place,' < OE *eardungstōw*)
fnast (44; 'breath, blast,' < OE *fnǣst*; OE <fn-> with the initial preconsonantal *f-* pronounced (i.e., [fn]) would not survive the 14th century)
al toslit (694; 'all rent asunder, slit open' < OE *eal(l)* + *tōslītan*, the prefixed *tō-* has an intensifying emphasis)

The examples could be multiplied in the hundreds, though the survival of Old English vocabulary in an early Middle English poem dating to ca. 1189 × 1216 is not remarkable in and of itself, what is worth noting is the 'antique-y' feel to scores of Old English forms that would be replaced over the next two centuries and the place of the poem in the history of lexical expansion and displacement in English. The modern student of Middle English generally finds texts such as *The Owl and the Nightingale*, the *Ormulum*, or *Havelok* 'harder' than Chaucer's poetry, and that is of course a function of the distance between Old English and *Havelok* and Havelok and *The Canterbury Tales*. English was simply developing, not necessarily from 'Old' to 'Middle,' which are from our perspective; much can be made of these labels, 'Old,' 'Middle,' and 'Modern' in current theoretical approaches in terms of being arbitrary – 'Old English' speakers might have seen their language as 'Middle' in the sense of the Germanic continuum, that is, as 'younger' than the forms of speech of their Continental forebears pre-449 – or 'presentist.' But as the study of the history of the English language is a 'Modern' pursuit of the universities in the Early Modern English and later periods, the labels are useful. There is something 'harder,' more Old English-like, to poems, collected, for instance, in Carleton Brown's *English Lyrics of the XIIIth Century* (Brown 1932/1965):

Þu þad madist alle þinc,
Mi suete fadir, hewene kinc,
Bi-sue to me þad am þi sone,
þad for monkine habe fles ynomin (Brown, no. 33, p. 61).

Thou that made every thing,
My sweet Father, heaven's King,
Look upon me that am your Son,
that for mankind has taken on flesh.

The verse is preserved in a Cambridge manuscript of the 13th century (Trinity College MS 323 [B.14.39]); a moving religious verse of Christ upon the Cross addressing God the Father, it is an example of early West Midlands ME (perhaps Hertfordshire) of a kind early enough that the passage of the language from OE to eME is readily apparent, as are a number of sound changes:

þad	*OE þæt* [vowel lowering, voicing of final stop]
alle	*OE ealle* [monphthingization > *a*]
þinc	*OE þing* [devoicing of final velar stop]
kinc	*OE cyning* [syncopation of final velar stop, syncopation – both changes could already be found in late West Saxon OE]
Bi-sue	*OE besēon* (early ME *biseon*; 2nd sing. imperative; unrounding of eME *bysy* < OE *beseoh*
þi	*OE þī(n)ne* [acc. sing. masc.; compare ME *þin sone*; a general pattern emerges in ME whereby *þi* (pronoun > pronominal adjective) would be used before words beginning with a vowel or *h*, and *þin* before words beginning with consonants; this can be seen too in Early Modern English (cf. Nevalainen 2006, 78), e.g., KJV Genesis 22:2 *Take now thy son, thine only son Isaac*
monkine	*OE monncynne* [degemination and unrounding of *y* to *i*]
fles	*OE flǣsċ* [the ME form here may be [flɛ:š] or [flɛ:s]
ynomin	*OE ġenumen* [OE preverbal *ġe-* > ME *i-/y-*, lowering and unrounding of main vowel *u* to *o*, raising of weakly stressed *-en* to *-in*]

There were a great many internal changes to English underway in this transitional age that were in evidence before 1066; but that signal historical development brought with it a new era of language contact and change, between Germanic and Romance.

5.2 NORMAN FRENCH; ANGLO-FRENCH, ANGLO-NORMAN

Anglo-Norman French, the dialect of Norman French spoken in England, had a relatively brief lifespan, at least under that rubric, roughly from the time of the Conquest to about 1225, the aftermath of the taking of the Duchy of Normandy by Phillip II of France in 1204. French continued to be spoken in England, and one might consider the period 1225–1450 to be post-Norman Anglo-French (the history of 'English' French a subject that needs further study). French was – along with Latin, it should be stressed – the language of governance and civil administration, while Latin continued as the language of ecclesiastical administration. Latin also continued as a language of national and international scholarship. While the Renaissance/Early Modern era has often been noted for an efflorescence of classical scholarship, it was not exactly a revival. Latin had never disappeared.

The laments of an Alfred or Æthelwold over the decline in learning in the Anglo-Saxon period were no doubt genuine, but quite different circumstances obtained; there seem to have been no 'pagan revivals' post-Conquest, and the status of ecclesiastical centers and bishops only grew, until the Reformation era. Even the very language of law and governance was shaped by Norman French and Anglo-Norman: *Parliament* itself is a loan, from Old French *parlement* via Anglo-Norman. The first dated use of the term in the OED is from ca. 1300 in the early *South English Legendary*, a large collection of the *vitae* of saints recast in versified form. These versified lives of the saints, taken together with the prose lives from Middle English, could be seen as an extension of an earlier tradition in the British Isles of the *opus geminatum*, the 'twinned work,' in prose and verse, made of lives of saints such as Cuthbert and Guthlac or the roster of lives and occasional verse-homilies or exhortations on holy days (Feasts of the Circumcision, Epiphany, Annunciation, Septuagesima [Shrovetide, or the 70-day period of pre-Lenten observance, Lent, and Easter and Easter week], etc.). The early *South English Legendary* seems to date to the last quarter of the 13th century and is written in a Southern West Midlands-Southwestern dialect; the later collection grew through the 14th and 15th centuries and, combined, the texts have served as a highly useful diachronic archive of phonological and morphological change in Middle English. In the life of Thomas Becket (or, in later forms, Thomas a/á Becket; ca. 1118–1120 – 29 December 1170) one reads that:

> Þo heo comen to þe parlement [to clarindone]: þe king axede heom a-non
> ȝweþur heo wolden holde þe lawes: ase heore Auncestres heolden (Horstmann 1887, ll. 531–532, following Horstmann's punctuation for caesura, with *to Clarindone* [*In wilte-schire*] supplied from line 530).

The reference is to the calling of Thomas to Clarendon after he and his fellow bishops had rejected the 'constitutions of Clarendon' issued by Henry II in 1164 at Clarendon Palace, Wiltshire, to check ecclesiastical power. And there is, apparently, for the first time in English, *þe parlement* 'the Parliament.' The forms in the passage are worth some brief analysis:

Þo 'Then' < Old English *þā*

heo 'they,' the Southern form of the 3rd plural nominative of the personal pronoun (elsewhere the Scandinavian-derived or -influenced *th-* forms had taken hold; e.g., *þei*; Mossé 1968, §65)

comen 'came,' 3rd plural preterite of infinitive *come(n)*

þe 'the': by inflectional decay, one is on the way to an invariant definite article/demonstrative; the French noun *parlement* is a masculine abstract noun (with the Latinate derivational suffix *-ment*); in Old English the form would have been *þam/þæm*

axede 'asked,' 3rd singular preterite of ME *asken* (< OE *âscian*); the form here shows the unmetathesized /ks/

heom 'them,' accusative plural masculine (*heo* above is the subject and so in nominative, *heom* here the direct object and so in the accusative; a simple point, but the inflectional collapse observed with the OE demonstrative (to an invariant *the* unmarked for case, gender, or number) was not happening with the third-person personal pronouns, which today are still marked, in the singular forms, for case and, one of the only remaining instances in English function words where this is true, for gender

a-non 'at once,' from Old English phrasal *on ānum*, 'at one' ('at once, right away, immediately'), prep. *on* (+ dative) + dat. sing. masc. of pronoun *ān* 'one'

ʒweþur conj. 'whether' < OE *hwæðer*; the spelling with <ʒ> is a Southwestern form, the yogh here representing apparently the voiceless glottal fricative /h/

wolden holde 'would hold/wished to hold,' auxiliary *wolden* 3rd plural past indicative or subjunctive of *wille(n)*, though in this sense of 'wished to hold' may be the better translation in that it makes transparent the underlying *willen*

lawes 'laws,' accusative plural < OE fem. *lagu* 'law'; in OE the /g/ in *lagu* was a voiced velar fricative [ɣ] that, between back vowels, underwent lenition to [w] in late OE / early ME (Minkova 2014, 83, 205)

Auncestres 'ancestors,' a loan from Old French that, with *parlement*, makes its first appearance in English in this text according to the OED (s.vv. *parliament, ancestor*)

heolden 'they held,' 3rd pl. preterite of *hōlde(n)*

och-on 'each one,' a variant form of the pronominal phrase *ēch-ōn* 'each one, everyone,' appearing often elsewhere in the text as *ech-on*; the word *each* has an enormously complicated and contested etymology. If via OE *ǣlċ* the form has lost /l/ after velarization (to [ɫ]) as *ase* above did (OE *ealswa* > ME *as(e)*) when "in high-frequency words of low prosodic prominence" (i.e., the stress placed on a word in comparison to the words around it; Minkova 2014, 130). LAEME records a wide range of dialectal variants of *ech* 'each' forms: *uch/vch* forms are chiefly West Midlands, especially Herefordshire (Map 00728920); *euch/which* forms are found in far Southern Shropshire, but predominantly in Herefordshire and Worcestershire (as likely reflexes of OE *ǣġhwilċ*; Map 00728919), but also in early Anglo-Irish (the Middle English as used in early colonial Ireland; McIntosh and Samuels 1968); forms ending in *-k(-)* are found in the East Midlands and especially through the North (Map 00728914); in all LAEME has 36 maps for the forms of 'each' in early Middle English 1150–1325.

One may compare the later versions of this Life of Thomas Becket, from ca. 1300 to 1325, in the Harley (British Library, MS Harley 2277) and Cambridge copies (Corpus Christi College MS 145), which are, dialectally, of the West Midlands and Hampshire (central Southwestern ME, that is, a descendant of late West Saxon OE):

Þo hi bigonne þis parlement þe kyng hom esste anon
War hi wolde þe lawe holde þat is auncestres hulde echon (D'Evelyn and Mill 1967–1969, vol II, 627, ll. 523–524).

The Eadwine Psalter (Cambridge, Trinity College MS R.17.1), a *de luxe* format 'triple psalter' with glosses to three Latin versions of the Psalms, in Anglo-Norman, Latin, and Old English, was not the only manuscript of the period to pair up Anglo-Norman and Old English: London, British Library 7.D.ii, of the 12th century, has, following a selection of the works of patristic writer Cassiodorus, a brief trilingual glossary, letters A-C (at fols. 18v-19v), with lemmata (the words being glossed, headwords in proto-dictionaries in a sense) in Latin and interpretations in Anglo-Norman but also, within the text, 14 words in Old English (Pulsiano 2000, 192–193, who lists 6 further trilingual manuscripts). A 12th-century roll of charters from Holme St Benets (St. Benet's Abbey, Norfolk) includes another trilingual glossary, in the main Latin glossed by French on the dorse of the roll (Oxford, Bodleian Library, Norfolk Rolls 81); about a dozen Old English words are found in the glossary, and there are traces of more, the ink on the dorse of the membrane roll having been partly rubbed away in places (McGowan 1998, 167–168). In a manuscript of miscellaneous contents from about the last quarter of the 13th century (British Library MS Additional 32085) can be found copies of the Magna Carta (1215, though there are later versions with later editions, abridgements, and additions) in Latin and Anglo-Norman; the latter begins at fol. 112v *Icy comence la chartre le Rey Johan done a Renemede* ("Here begins the charter the King John gave at Runnymede"); there is a copy of *Le lapidaire du roi Philippe*, "The Lapidary of King Philip," either Philip III or IV of France (whose reigns cover the period 1245–1314); and there are two collections of recipes – one of the imports with the Conquest was a new cuisine – in Anglo-Norman (British Library, MS Additional 46919 contains a Middle English version of them). An interesting collection it is as it gives evidence of the sort of linguistic activity in an era of language contact: texts imported from France are found alongside a French version of the Magna Carta (which had been written in Latin) alongside an apparently homegrown Anglo-Norman composition *Seneschaucie*, a handbook for the *seneschal*, a loan from Old French and title of the chief officer employed by the lord of a manor to manage the various other officials and workers.

In what could be called a kind of 'twinned' work, the English cleric Laȝamon (rendered as Layamon or Lawman[3]) 'Englished' Wace's *Roman de Brut* (1155) as the *Brut* (ca. 1200). As part of the 'Matter of Britain' cycle, Wace and Layamon joined the chronicles of Geoffrey of Monmouth (*Historia regum Britanniae*, "History of the Kings of Britain," ca. 1135), in the company of William of Malmesbury (his *Gesta regum Anglorum*, "Deeds of the Kings of the English," 1125), Henry of Huntingdon (*Historia Anglorum*, "History of the English," 1139), and Geffrei (Geoffrey) Gaimar (*Estoire des Engleis*, "History of the English," ca. 1135–1140). Here in Latin, Anglo-Norman, and Middle English are names and places familiar from the 'Matter of Britain' in the three languages in use at the time in England for literary and intellectual activity: "[t]he higher literary culture was essentially trilingual" (Lass 1987, 58).

Quant cil d'Irlande venu furent
E li altre ki venir durent,
Artur, de jurnee en jurnee,
Ad Normendie trespassee;
Chastels et viles trespasça,
E sa gent crut e espeisça;
Tuit aloent en sa busuine (Weiss 2002; ll. 11609–11615).

[3] Or even Laghamon, as the /ȝ/ represented the OE voiced velar fricative [ɣ], which was in late OE–early ME undergoing lenition ('softening') to [w]; [ɣ] in OE was always preceded by a back vowel and the same process that saw the shift OE *lagu/lage* > ME *lawe* influenced MdE *gnaw* and *bow* (Minkova 2014, 205).

["When those of Ireland had come, / And those others who were to come, / Arthur, day by day, / To Normandy he pressed on; / Castles and vills he went past, /And his men [in number'] grew and increased; / All helped in this business."]

Here in Anglo-Norman is a story British and English in names: *Engleterre* (England); *Escoz/Escoce* (Scotland); *Tamise* (Thames); *Henguist* (Hengest); *Cornuaille* (Cornwall). The prose Lancelot cycle, namely *Le livre de Lancelot del Lac* (*Lancelot du Lac*, 'Lancelot of the Lake'), was once attributed to Walter Map (ca. 1130 × 1135–1210); the attribution was popular enough that a number of manuscripts of the Old French text bear the name 'Gautier Map' (e.g., Paris, Bibliothèque nationale, MS français 1430, of the first quarter of the 13th century; at the top of fol. 1r is the added rubric: *hystoire du Roy Artus, & de la table ronde* ["History of King Arthur, and of the Round Table"]). Map was perhaps born in Hereford, though he described himself as hailing from the Welsh marches; the surname 'Map' may actually be a nickname from the Welsh name element *uab/fab/mab/ap* 'son of' – that is, we have only the introductory part of his Welsh name (not unlike the later practice of Irishmen being called 'Mac' as a generic; James, Brooke, Mynors 1983, xiii). His one work of certain attribution is the *De nugis curialium* ('On the Trifles of Courtiers'), a collection of anecdotes, historical and contemporary, sometimes satirical, at other times in the *exemplum*-tradition (modelling what is 'exemplary,' in Chaucer's English *ensamples*), of noteworthy events and personages (collected into five *distinctiones*, 'divisions, parts'). Map's Anglo-Latin prose style is fairly straightforward, of interest for its various vignettes and character studies – as of the rise of Godwine, son of a cowherd, to an earl of King Æthelred (at V.3) – and for the Latinization of various English names and words (the *Dictionary of Medieval Latin from British Sources* [DMLBS] is the major resource for the Latin in use in the medieval British Isles, and a resource not yet brought to bear upon study of the history of the English language). The Arthurian tradition Walter Map was popularly, if erroneously, linked to is also another largely untapped resource for the history of the language: here, Celtic, Germanic, and Romance traditions became intertwined over the course of the late Old English through Middle English periods. The 'Arthur of the Welsh' became the Arthur of the English and French (Bromwich et al. 2008; Burgess and Pratt 2009; Barron 2012); *Et quant il vint a karlion* ('And when they came to Caerleon'; Sommer 1908–1916, 429): Caerllion, Wales, once was Roman Isca Augusta, named after the river Wysg (Roman Isca, English Usk), which was part of Logres in the French version, a Gallicization of medieval Welsh Lloegyr, which refers to Southern and Southeastern Britain below the Humber. And the fruits of this meeting of three traditions (Celtic, Germanic, Romance) can be seen in the Middle English romances.

The copy of the romance *Sir Orfeo* from the Auchinleck manuscript (Edinburgh, National Library of Scotland, Advocates MS 19.2.1) was produced in London ca. 1330 (1331 × 1340), in a southern-southeastern dialect: *Orfeo* was written by Hand A (i.e., scribe 1), and the LALME has localized the scribe's language to the London-Middlesex border. The five or six scribes who wrote out the forty-four pieces in poetry and prose (there are also a number of leaves missing from the manuscript) did not all hail from the same dialect areas, though the mansucript itself is viewed as likely a London product (e.g., the romance *Sir Beves of Hamtoun* [Bevis of Hampton] was written by scribe 5 and is localized to Essex; the verse *Speculum*

Gy de Warewyke [Guy of Warwick] was copied by scribe 2 and localized to the Gloucestershire-Worcestershire border). The Middle English romances are a product of French influence in the centuries after the Conquest, though the matter of influence and sources is quite complicated: Norman French of course is also the product of conquest, that of the Vikings under Duke Rollo and successors, and so a Germanic-Romance contact situation. The romance literature of Old French and Anglo-Norman was also deeply influenced by the Celtic literature of Brittany and 'old Britain.' *Guy of Warwick* was a figure equally popular in French and English literature (and localized, in romance fashion, in an Anglo-Saxon England fading into legend). *Sir Orfeo* recasts the Orpheus and Eurydice myth through Celtic and Romance lenses: Orfeo loses Heurodis (Eurydice) not to Hades but to the 'land of faery'; Orfeo is not the singer from Thrace, but a king with his throne in Winchester of Wessex. When Orfeo returns to Winchester with Heurodis, having won her back from the king of fairy (in an Otherworld reminiscent more of the Welsh Annwfn), he goes unrecognized and finds a place to rest *with a begger y-bilt ful narwe* ('a beggar of narrow means'; l. 483; Shepherd 1995, 187). And he asks *tidinges* of this beggar:

> The povre begger in his cote
> Told him everich a grot –
> Hou her Quen was stole owy
> Ten yer gon with fairy.
> And hou her king en exile yede
> (Bot no man nist in wiche thede)
> And hou the Steward the lond gan hold –
> And other mani thinges him told (ll. 489–496).
>
> [The poor beggar in his hut / Told him every little bit – / How their Queen was stolen away / Ten years gone in fairy. / And how their king was in exile led / (But no man knew into which land) / And how the Steward the land gained hold – / And many other things him told.]

Povre is a French loan, and *en exile* may be a calque of the French expression (Shepherd 1995, 187 n. 1), but the rhyming pair *cote...grot* are from Old English. But the particular romance frame used in reworking the classical myth is French-influenced, suffused as it is, also, with Celtic myth. These three layers of the linguistic and cultural history of Britain, the original Celtic (pre-449 British), the Germanic (post-449), and Norman French (post-1066) shaped Middle English romance, in its language, imagery, and symbolism.

5.3 SOCIETAL CHANGE, LINGUISTIC CONTACT: A NEW INSULAR ORDER

William of Malmesbury (ca. 1085/90–1143), of Wiltshire, embodied the legacy of Conquest; he was the son of a father from Normandy and an English mother, and his *Gesta regum Anglorum* ('Deeds/History of the kings of the English') was completed in February of 1126, based on his note in Book II (Thomson 2003, 6). But his tone seems stridently anti-Norman at times, and he was proud of his education at Malmesbury abbey and felt himself to be the heir and defender of an intellectual tradition that stretched from King Alfred through Benedictine reformers such as Æthelwold of Winchester (ca. 909–984), which, in his native Southwest of England, formed, in R.M. Thomson's view, a sort of "distinctive culture within the Anglo-Norman world of the twelfth century...ecclesiastical and Latin, focused on a group of ancient cathedral and monastic foundations" (Thomson 2003, 4; Thomson 2016).

William noted in his *Gesta Pontificum Anglorum* ("Deeds/History of the Bishops of England"), completed around 1125, that the speech of Northumbrians, particularly those of York, was "inharmonious and uncouth" (Winterbottom and Thomson 2007, 326–327 [III.99.4]). The translation may underplay slightly the animus of this Wiltshire native (son of a Norman father, English mother) as William wrote *Sane tota lingua Nordanhumbrorum, et maxime in Eboraco, ita inconditum stridet ut nichil nos australes intelligere possimus*: "Indeed the overall language of the Northumbrians, and especially in York, thus crudely squeals so that we southerners are able to understand nothing." What is translated as two adjectives, 'inharmonious and uncouth' in William's Anglo-Latin, is actually an adverb and verb pairing: *inconditum stridet.* A minor point to be sure, but William is following standard classical Latin in the ways of forming adverbs in the language, here employing the accusative singular neuter of the adjective adverbially. Latin *inconditus* means 'rough, uncouth, irregular, disordered, confused,' deriving from the verb *condere* and privative prefix *in-*; William's use of the adverbial *inconditum* is its first attestation in the *Dictionary of Medieval Latin from British Sources* (for the adj. they gloss 'unpolished, rough, crude'). The earliest use of the adjective form seems to be from Ælfric's *Grammar*, dating to about 998, in his description of the interjection as a part of speech, *interjectio est pars orationis significans mentis affectum voce incondita*, "the interjection is a part of speech signifying a state of mind [affection, or emotion] in a rough voice." For *voce incondita,* the Old English version of Ælfric's *Grammar* has *mid unġesċeapenre stemne.* The definition of interjection Ælfric borrowed from the 4th-century Roman grammarian Aelius Donatus (his *Ars minor* on the parts of speech) and the OE rendering *ungesceapenre* (literally 'unshapened,' 'poorly formed or made') shows how closely matched medieval English could be with Latin (and such matchings seem to be one of the vectors of transmission of Latin loanwords to English). The sense is of course a little more figurative though the MdE translation 'uncouth' has an etymological rightness, coming as it does from OE *uncūð*, 'unknown,' though it had already in the early Middle English period extended to a sense of 'unknowing, ignorant' (ME *Bestiary*, ca. 1220; OED, s.v. sense 7). The first attestation of *uncouth* as applied to language the OED lists as William Penn's *A brief account of the rise and progress of the People called Quakers* (1693, some dozen years after Penn had founded Pennsylvania): "Though that side of his understanding which lay next to the world, and especially the expression of it, might sound uncouth and unfashionable to nice ears." And *inconditus* itself found its way from Latin into English. Richard Taverner (1505–1575) writes in his *The Garden of Wysdome* "to pardon mine incondite and grosse phrase" (OED, s.v. *incondite*); Taverner had been a protégé of Thomas Cromwell at the court of Henry VIII (Starnes 1956), though that did not protect him from falling afoul of Henry.[4] One might be tempted to say that Ælfric is saying the same thing (via Donatus) with *unġesċeapenre stemne/voce incondita* – that both are referring to informal speech versus formal. The interjection is in the classical formulation a part of speech that expresses a (heightened) emotion in a nonstandard voice (one that may be louder, less restrained, more informal). And if that has been a perennial concern of grammarians and writers about language, so too was a sense of the superiority of Latin to the vernacular, or at least a bit of smugness about the level of education of the 'literate' (and in the Western Middle Ages that often meant 'Latin letters') versus monoglot speakers of the vernacular. Add to this a regionally specific Southern-Northern divide that sharpened in England in the early Middle English period.

stefen, steuen, steven 'voice': The form *stemne* 'voice, speech' < *stefne* by assimilation, is common in West Saxon (Campbell OEG §484); the later 10th-century gloss by scribe Farman to the Rushworth Gospels, in Mercian, has *stæfn* (unassimilated) alongside *stemn*. The apocope of PGmc *-ō (PGmc **stebnō* has the Continental Germanic reflexes Old Saxon *stemna*, Old High German *stimna*, Old Frisian *stemme* (unassimilated *stifne* is an earlier change). The matter is one of why there was no epenthesis here with the consonant cluster *-Cn* (word-final consonant + /n/): compare OE *faþm* > MdE *fathom* with vowel epenthesis. Ringe attributes this to variation in words with *Cn*-clusters, that "[a]pparently epenthesis did not occur after a light syllable" (Ringe and Taylor 2014 6.9.5, at 330). Another question is what happened to Old English *stefn/stemn* and Middle English *stefne/steven/steuen/steven*? The OED labels the form *steven* as "Obsolete exc<ept> dialect," and that in surviving dialectal use, the sense is mainly 'A loud voice.' Wright in his EDD lists the form as northern and Scots, with many of the attestations from Yorkshire; Wright's collections bear out the surviving sense of 'A loud shout or noise; an

(*continued*)

[4] Taverner is known also for Taverner's Bible (1539), a revision of Matthew's Bible, which had included the Tyndale New Testament; this latter text was actually published by John Rogers in 1537 under the name Thomas Matthew. Like Rogers, Taverner was of a reformist mind in such matters. He was, in a pattern that marked the 16th century in England, a wit, a writer of overlong periodic sentences, and an ardent advocate of a classical education; the fuller title of his other 1539 work was *The garden of wysdom wherein ye may gather most plesaunte flowres, that is to say, proper wytty and quycke sayenges of princes, philosophers, and dyuers other sortes of men. Drawen forth of good authors, as well as Grekes as Latyns, by Richard Tauerner, 1539. Solde in Lomberd Strete at the signe of the Lamb by John Haruey.* Edward I had expelled the Jews from England in 1290 and Lombard Street reflects the new bankers who took over the lending-at-interest trade. The street became famous for its 'hanging signs,' a tradition that continues to this day. John Harvey, stationer, had such a sign of "the Lamb" (Duff 1905, 68). The OED reference to this first appearance of *incondite* is difficult to find; they cite only the signature 'A.ij.' The passage is from the preface to Book II of *The Garden*, 'Rycharde Tauerner to the gentle readers'; a version is available at the University of Michigan's *Early English Books Online* project website: https://quod.lib.umich.edu/cgi/t/text/text-idx?c=eebo;idno=A13401.0001.001.

(continued)

uproar, outcry; a ranting,' such as, from Northeast Yorkshire, *He gav oot sikan a stevn* (*sikan* is a Northern, and Scots and Irish, form of regional *suchan*, 'such a,' with Northern /k/ for /tʃ/). By conversion, *steven* appears also as a verb, as in phrasal *steven oot*; from North Yorkshire, *He did steven oot, yo' mud a heard him iver so fahr. Yon beos wants foddering, they deu steven oot* (EDD V.755): "He did cry out loudly, you might have heard him ever so far [away]. Yonder beasts need feeding, they do cry out [so much]" (*mud* is widely attested in the North and Scotland as a form of the auxiliary *might*). But *steven* had other senses and could be applied to the wind (*It stevvons and stoors*, '[the wind] makes a great noise and stirs about,' North Yorkshire) and *to steven and to stand to a thing*, 'to protest and to stick to one's word.' Which last sense seems to be extended to putting your voice, your word, to something, as in *steyvened*, 'to pay a sum on deposit on making a bargain for purchase of anything': *We hae no steyvonin' here; they all pay for 't when they come, an' tak' it wi' 'em when they goa* (recorded in Leeds, 1898). But *steven* was about to be crowded out by French loan *voice* in this period; around 1300, in the life of St. Francis of Assisi in the early *South English Legendary*, one finds:

> Bi a churche of seint Damian: a day he cam gon,
> Þat ope þe poynte was to falle a-doune: In he wende a-non
> And kneolede a-doun bi-fore þe croix: ase he dude wel ofte.
> Þo spac a voix þare-inne: wel Mildeliche and softe
> And seide, "Fraunceys, go þe forth: and a-rer up min hous an heiȝ,
> Þat, thou sixt, fallez to grounde: and al destruyd is neiȝ" (Horstmann 1887, 55 ll. 51–56).

This is the famous miracle of St. Francis at San Damiano: in our early ME version Francis came one day a-going by a church of St. Damian, that was up to the point of falling down, and in he went at once; and kneeled down before the cross (the French loan is from Old French *croiz, croix* and variants), as he had so often done before; then spoke a voice therein, full mild and soft, and it said: "Francis, go thee forth, and rear up my house on high, that, thou seest (with *sixt* compare OE *siehst*, or Modern German *Du siehst*), falleth, and is near to all destroyed (ME *neiȝ* < OE *nēah* 'near'). Almost jarring is the contrast between the OE- and French-derived forms in *spac a voix* ('spake a voice'). But *voice* was crowding into the vocabulary (as OE *rōd* 'rood' was to be largely displaced by *cross* from Latin and French), and by Chaucer we can see the result; in his works Chaucer uses forms of *steven(e)* a dozen times; he uses *voys* some five and a half times more frequently (the spelling *voys* predominating over *vois*). A similar displacement would happen with another OE word for 'voice, speech' *reord*, which, too, would become dialectal up North and survive mainly in Scots (*reird, reerd, reard*).

One senses the rivalries between the former kingdoms of Anglo-Saxon England and, post-1066, what might be some resentment of the former power of the old Kingdom of Northumbria and Durham and its diocese (see 5.5). An old linguistic dictum is that the primary *linguistic* difference between language and dialect is the test of mutual intelligibility (if undertaken honestly). William of Malmesbury is one of the first of a number of English writers who would complain of difficulty in understanding Northerners. Some three centuries later, Geoffrey Chaucer famously engaged in what may be among the earliest 'dialect fictions' in English literature. Chaucer's reeve Osewold (Oswald) of Norfolk, a *sclendre colerik man* ('slender, choleric man'; I.587) seeks to 'quit' (requite) the miller Robyn's bawdy (and brilliant) send-up of the Knight's opening tale of courtly love from afar; as the miller had included a reeve in his tale, so the reeve, choleric and revenge-minded, places a miller in his own and the bawdiness is redoubled with *yonge povre scolers two* (I.4002), John and Aleyn (Alan), who *Of o toun were they born, that highte Strother. / Fer in the north; I kan nat telle where* (I.4014–4015). With *ik* for *y/I* (first-person singular pronoun) and other forms in the speech of John and Alan, Chaucer the southerner (and Londoner) is clearly having fun with the 'oop north' linguistic divide (Epstein 2008); if William of Malmesbury could, ca. 1125, complain of difficulty in understanding the speech of Northumbrians, Chaucer can trade on that 'Northern-ness' for humor with a London and courtly southern audience.[5]

5.4 THE TRANSITIONAL TWELFTH CENTURY

At the Benedictine foundation of St. Mary and St. John the Baptist at Godstow, Oxfordshire, Prioress Alice of Eaton in 1403/4 compiled a cartulary (a loan from Medieval Latin *c(h)artularium*), or monastic register, comprising the various charters, grants of rights and privileges, and especially documents in witness to the endowing of the monastery with lands by the crown or local nobles. Such collections grew as additional documents bearing witness to local land grants (and disputes) were copied into the manuscripts as a means of permanent record, which had a sort of religious sanction to them in that they were housed in ecclesiastic centers (Amt 2014). The latter benefit was particularly evident in the Old English period with the tradition of

[5] There is some evidence that Chaucer may have known whereabouts a Strother was: Benson 1987 mentions that there was a 13th-century recording of a *Lange Strothere*, with *strother* indicating 'a place overgrown with brushwood' (note to I.4014); the ME form, recorded ca. 1300 in the *Feodarium Prioratus Dunelmensis*, a 15th-century compilation of the holdings of the priory and convent of Durham and feudal duties of tenants enfeoffed (*feud/feod*, *feodatus*, *(en)feoffment* have entered English from French and Latin in this period and are found in *Black's Law Dictionary*); the form occurs twice in a note formerly held in the convent concerning the boundaries of Elvet and Houghall in Yorkshire (Co. Durham), while the form *del Estrother* occurs also in the *feodarium* (Surtees Society, vol. LVIII, at 10 and 203). The place-name referring to a marsh, and one covered in brush, was apparently extended to owners of estates built on such a stretch of land in the North, such as the surname *Langstroth* (West Riding of Yorkshire, Lancashire) and *Strother* (Northumberland, Durham, West Riding of Yorkshire, Cheshire; Hanks, Coates, McClure 2016, s.vv.). Smith in the EPNS volume for the East Riding of Yorkshire sees the place-name *Strowood* < *Stort(h)wayt(e)*, with early forms *Stortheweyt* (1281), *Storwhait* (1303), *Strothwayth* (1309), among others, with common metathesis of *str-* and epenthetic *-e-* (*-theweyt* < *þveit*, whence the common place-name element *-thwaite*) as deriving from Scandinavian *storð* 'brushwood' + *þveit* 'enclosure' (Smith 1970, 236). In fact, there is even more evidence of *Strother*-related place-names and surnames from Yorkshire (McGowan, forthcoming); this does not change the effect of Chaucer's *I kan nat telle where*, which, from a Londoner, referring to a town *Fer in the north*, may have the force of a New Yorker, referring to an industrial (now post-industrial) Ohio city, saying, "Toledo, wherever that is."

copying manumissions into Gospel books (as with the Bodmin manumissions in the St Petroc Gospels, British Library, MS Additional 9381 of the 10th century) or other manuscripts in ecclesiastical collections; the formulas of the manumissions were often explicitly religious, with the manumittor freeing slaves 'for love of God' and the 'need of [their] soul' – *for Godes lufa ⁊ for heora sawle þearfe.*[6] This particular formula is from a late Old English manumission recorded in the Durham *Liber Vitae*, literally the Latin for 'book of life,' a record of the benefactors of and pilgrims to the diocese of Durham who would be remembered in the prayers and Masses said by the members of the congregation (a tradition still very much alive in the Roman Catholic church). The diocese of Durham had begun as that of Lindisfarne in 635, then was translated to Chester-le-Street ca. 882; the old Anglo-Saxon church at Durham was called the *Alba Ecclesia*, or 'White Church,' after the whitewashed wattle-and-daubed walls. A stone church followed in 998 (the 'Great Church,' *Ecclesia Major*) and the cathedral proper belongs to the Norman era. According to Symeon of Durham Bishop William de St-Calais of Durham ordered this church to be razed (*ecclesiam...destrui precepit*) and, on 11 August 1093, with Turgot the Prior who was second to him in authority in the diocese, he and other members of the community laid the first stones of the new church (*Eo enim die episcopus et qui post eum secundus erat in ecclesia prior Turgotus cum ceteris fratribus primos in fundamento lapides posuerunt* ("Tract on the Origins and Progress of This The Church of Durham," iv.8; Rollason 2000, 244). Symeon was himself from Normandy, and seems to have been in the service of Bishop William de St-Calais there, returning with him from the bishop's exile in 1091 (Rollason 2000, xlv). St-Calais's fortunes mirrored to an extent those of the Conquest. Though William the Conqueror himself had visited St-Calais in Durham and had him appointed bishop late that year (or in early 1081), in 1088, early in the reign of William Rufus, the Conqueror's third son, he either joined the rebellion of Odo of Bayeux against the king or remained strategically on the sidelines (in Durham Castle). St-Calais was put on trial at Salisbury, and the case on behalf of the king was pursued by Lanfranc, the Archbishop of Canterbury (it was a civil procedure, as would be the case pursued against Thomas Becket in 1164 at Northampton Castle). Following exile back in Normandy, relations with William Rufus improved and St-Calais was restored to his bishopric in 1091, and in 1093 he oversaw the building of what would become Durham Cathedral. A recent study of the architecture of Durham Castle Chapel and Durham Cathedral has suggested a tension between senses of 'Normanness' (or *Normanitas*) and 'Englishness' that found some accommodation in the architectural styles of the two buildings. The castle's chapel was private, within the castle building, and "[t]he unfettered expression of Normanitas effected by Bishop William in the castle's chapel suggests that the patron was disinterested in assimilating to his new homeland and still considered Norman visual language to be superior" (Bernstein 2018, 268). The cathedral begun at roughly the same time, in 1093, however, was in more of a hybrid Norman-English style. Similarly, Bishop William's handling of the 'cult of St. Cuthbert' was a difficult matter; the Anglo-Saxon saint was a symbol of the monastic communities of the north, and of the power of the Bishop of Durham, and the translation of the saint's remains and relics to the cathedral in 1104 was an act both religious and political. It also led to the discovery of the saint's pocket-Gospel book, a small-format copy of the Gospel of John made in Northumbria, perhaps at Wearmouth-Jarrow, ca. 710–720,

[6] From the Durham *Liber Vitae*, London, British Library, MS Cotton Domitian A.vii, fol. 47r.

which had been placed later in the saint's coffin following his death in 687 (the manuscript was purchased from the British Province of the Jesuit order in 2012 and is now British Library, MS Additional 89000).

Symeon's account of these events in the 'origins and progress' of the church in Durham is of course, for an ecclesiastical text, written in Latin, not Norman French or late Old English. As seen earlier, the widespread use of Latin in the Old English period for religious matters led to its adoption for matters of government, law, finance, and record-keeping. The various periods of Latin loans to Old English reflect this expansion in use of Latin: from more purely religious use, especially catechetical in the conversion period (from AD 583 on), to the work of chroniclers and royal record-keepers (still largely clerics), to that of educated lay persons (including a number of Anglo-Saxon kings, such as the Irtish-educated Aldfrith of Northumbria [ruled 684–704/5] and Alfred of Wessex [871–899], both of whom sponsored educational reform programs). The vocabulary of the faith (*eucharist/communion, confession, baptism, font, chrism, bishop*) entered English via Latin; the study of Latin opened up for novitiates a whole new world of classical learning from the Continent; the spoken use of Latin provided an international medium of communication (as witnessed by pastoral letters and constitutions and consecrations from Rome, or treaties among rulers). As seen earlier in the previous chapter, the effects of Latin upon the lexis (vocabulary) of English were profound and continue to this day. The influence of Latin, as through reception of these loans, upon phonology, morphology, and syntax is more contested – admittedly not so profound, but not negligible. In the passage from Symeon, some sense of the linguistic interaction and legacy of contact can be seen in miniature:

> **Eo** enim **die** episcopus et *qui* post eum secundus erat in ecclesia *prior Turgotus*
> For **on that day** the bishop and *he* who after him second was in the church *the Prior Turgot*
>
> cum **ceteris fratribus** *primos* in fundamento *lapides* posuerunt
> with **several brothers** the *first stones* in the foundation placed

Bold face and italic have been added to give a sense of grammatical governance and syntax in the Latin; *eo die* is the ablative of time in Latin, and it has been borrowed into English legal vocabulary to indicate something as occurring 'on that day' or 'on that same day' (and so appears in *Black's Law Dictionary*), and the conjunction *enim* can mean 'for,' 'indeed,' 'truly,' or even just 'and,' and normatively appears in second position in a sentence (whereas the conjunction *nam* is placed first). *Qui* and *prior Turgotus* are in the nominative (subject) singular case referring to the Norman Prior of Durham Turgot (later Bishop of St. Andrews); *eum*, like *eo*, is a form of the Latin pronoun and demonstrative *ea*, and is the object of the preposition *post*, and it refers back to *episcopus* 'bishop,' that is William of St-Calais; *secundus* is nominative singular as it too refers to Turgot. The fellow brothers of Durham Priory (founded in 1083) are in the ablative because governed by the preposition *cum* 'with' (ablative of accompaniment), and *primos lapides* 'first stones' is in the accusative plural as the direct object of the main verb (in common verb-final position) *posuerunt*. This analysis of the Latin grammar and syntax, what is called **parsing**, will bring back terrible memories for some readers of compulsory exercises in Latin grammar. But it became a bedrock of English education from the time the school at Canterbury was established in AD 597 by Augustine of Canterbury, and from Ælfric's *Grammar* and *Glossary* onward, students have been drilled in Latin (and at times Greek) declensions and conjugations. Education in Latin had as its primary purpose the understanding of Scripture and the liturgy of the church, the training of clerics in service to the church, and broader aims in understanding the grammar and structure of Latin for access to the wider literature in the western church and the use of Latin as a *lingua franca* medium of communication. As one of the languages of this period, along with English (transitioning from its late Old English form to early Middle English), Norman French, and Anglo-Norman (a dialect of French particular to England; see in 5.2), Latin could serve as an intermediary among competing vernaculars, and perhaps for the same reason we do not see it undergo creolization in England: it was no one's first tongue. Clerics might use it in saying Mass, in the Liturgy of the Hours, and in monastic and ecclesiastical administrative communication and find that most of this communication involved Latin, but as the grammatical texts of the era make clear it was not their mother tongue (there are other factors involved that will be considered in 5.8). It did, however, connect its Northern French and English users with the culture of the past and the culture of the Mediterranean.

Theodore of Tarsus (in Cilicia, Anatolia – now modern Turkey) and Hadrian, a Berber from North Africa, brought to the Anglo-Saxon school at Canterbury the Greek language and learning of Eastern Christendom. That tradition of learning in Greek and Latin became a mark of erudition, and often of prestige, in England's medieval universities (one thinks of the prestige of the professorships in those languages at Oxford and Cambridge). As that primary language of the liturgy and education, Latin was the vector of transmission of whole classes of vocabulary (science, medicine, law, literary criticism), and French, as a Romance language (developing in a Gaul that had been more thoroughly Romanized than Britain), was often the intermediary for many of those loans. This is the subject of Section 5.6, but one brief example from Symeon might be mentioned: *posuerunt* 'they placed' or 'set down.' This is the third plural perfect active indicative of Latin third conjugation *pōnere*, 'to put, place.' The word, however, came to English from Old French *poser* via Anglo-Norman likely in the 12th century, though the OED's earliest attestation is from a Middle English statute book (*Statutes of Realm*) dating to ca. 1325: *ȝif ani posez excepcion of seisines defendede*: 'if anyone raise an objection to seisin defended'; *seisin* in medieval use differed from modern 'ownership' in that it involved 'possession' by showing evidence of use of the land (the MED has *any* for *ani* for the reading from Oxford, Bodleian Library, MS Rawlinson B.520). The passage is a Middle English legalism heavily influenced by Anglo-Norman, with the French-inflection *posez* and the loans from Anglo-Norman (*excepcion* 'exception'), Old French (*seisines*, 'seisin, and act of taking possession of something'), and French and Latin (*defendede*, Old French *defendre* and Latin *dēfendere* likely reinforcing each other, though the loan is conjugated as Middle English). Record of early French loans to English are dependent upon the survival of early Middle English texts; as we have fewer of these texts ca. 1150–1300 – both verse and prose records become prolific 1350–1500 – we are often left presuming that a number of French loans first attested ca. 1325–1375 likely entered the language earlier (especially items from the legal and governance lexicons). At any rate, in one of the senses of Old French *poser*, 'to suppose or assume (a proposition) for argument's sake' (OED dates this to the late 13th century), we find Palamoun and Arcite arguing over who has been struck most deeply with love for the fair Emelye in "The Knight's Tale" of Geoffrey Chaucer's *Canterbury Tales* (ca. 1387–1400); Arcite now rebuts Palamoun's argument in a passage replete with French loanwords, chivalric sentiment, and, at times, comical legalisms:

> I pose that thow lovedest hire biforn;
> Wostow nat wel the olde clerkes sawe,
> That 'who shal yeve a lovere any lawe?'
> Love is a gretter lawe, by my pan,
> Than may be yeve to any erthly man;
> And therefore positif lawe and swich decree
> Is broken al day for love in ech degree.
> A man moot nedes love, maugree his heed;
> He may not fleen it, thogh he sholde be deed,
> Al be she mayde, or wydwe, or elles wyf (I.1162–1171).

> [I suppose that you loved her before; / Know you not well the old clerk's saying, / Love is a greater law, by my head/noggin (*pan* = 'skullpan,' i.e., head, mind), / Than may be given to any earthly man; / And therefore manmade law and such decree / Is broken each day for love in every degree. / A man needs love, despite it all; / He cannot escape it, even if he should be dead, / Whether she be maid, or widow, or otherwise wife.]

Arcite's *I pose* follows the earlier French sense of *poser*, which with its prefixed derivatives formed a *-pose* complex in English deriving from Old French and Anglo-Norman (following the post-classical and medieval senses of *pōnere*, 'to place, put' > 'to put [declare, affirm, assert, claim],' with the influence of Medieval Latin *pausâre*,[7] which supplanted it in Romance); *compose* and *impose* (earlier Old French forms *enposer* and *emposer*) are from 12th to 13th-century French (though both have their earliest attestations with printer William Caxton in the late 15th century), while *oppose* is fairly straightforwardly from Middle English *oppōsen* (Anglo-Norman *op(p)oser* < Old French *oposer* of the 12th century).

The case of *depose* is more complex, and more interesting: *depose(n)* 'to put down,' is from Old French *deposer*; in medieval French the form became associated with senses of *dépondre*, which it came to replace; *deposit*, verb and noun, do not seem to be attested before the 17th century, and came via French *depositer*, which derived

[7] The OED entry for *pose* as a verb (sense 1) gives an exceptionally detailed history of the forms in Romance (Old French, Old Occitan, Catalan, Spanish, Italian) and the various senses of classical, post-classical, and Medieval Latin *pōnere* and *pausâre* that influenced each other and their Romance reflexes. English did not inherit the sense of French *poser* 'to bury, to lay to rest,' though that is found in another *pōnere*-derived formation *repose* (as in 'eternal repose'). The expression is still known among Catholics in the prayer for the souls of the departed from the Liturgy of the Hours *Requiem aeternam* ("Eternal repose grant unto them, O Lord, and let perpetual light shine upon them"), which is now made more transparent in contemporary use as 'Eternal rest grant unto them....' Chaucer's *pose* = 'suppose' bears a sense from the French no longer in English use but for which *suppose* would come to serve (French *supposer* < Latin *suppōnere* < *sub-pōnere*, which could have the literal sense 'to place below,' as it did in Anglo-Norman through the 12th century).

from Medieval Latin *dēpositāre*, the frequentative form of *depōnere* (that is, a verb form indicating repetitive action). Senses 1–2 in OED indicated a 'putting down,' or 'laying (something) down' into a 'position of rest'; by the late 17th century it formed a collocative use with *eggs*: hens could *lay eggs*, or, in a somewhat more 'scientificky' manner (a concern in the 17th and 18th centuries for the developing scientific prose of English), *deposit eggs*. The depositing of money, into a bank to earn interest, or into the hands of another, dates to the early 18th century. The OED's figurative sense 3c is religious or spiritual; the earliest attestation is Matthew Wilson's *Mercy and truth* (1634): "The Apostles haue...deposited in her [the Church], as in a rich Storehowse, all things belonging to truth"; later that century John Milton would write "To violate the sacred trust of silence / Deposited within thee" (*Samson Agonistes*, ll. 428–429). Though the OED does not mention a source for this figurative use, it is from the Catholic tradition of the *fidei dēpositum* ('the deposit of Faith,' the substance of the faith), deriving from *O Timothee, depositum custodi* ("O Timothy, guard what has been entrusted to you"; 1 Timothy 6:20), and developed by Church writers such as the 5th-century Vincent of Lérins of Gaul – latterly in the dogmatic constitution *Dei verbum* ['The Word of God'] of Pope Paul VI in 1965, and the apostolic constitution *Fidei depositum* of Pope John Paul II in 1992; the Vulgate *depositum* translates the original Greek παραθήκη [*parathēkē*] 'deposit, something entrusted to one's keeping.' Milton likely knew the Catholic origin of this usage (it is a term used in the Anglican communion as well), and may have been claiming it in his own idiosyncratic theology in this Biblically based 'closet drama' (those originally meant to be declaimed not performed on stage). He was, to put it as charitably as it might be phrased, decidedly 'anti-Papist' and deeply involved in the religious partisanship of the time; if the older Catholic claim to the term did not bother him, he might have been upset at least to have been beaten to its first use by Matthew Wilson the recusant. Recusants were those who in the wake of the Act of Uniformity of 1558 refused to move (or 'convert' in the view of many of the 'refusers') to the rite of the Church of England. The term derives from *recūsāns*, the present participle of Latin *recūsāre*; the Latin present participle was declined for most of its forms as a third-declension adjective (thus *recūsāns* [nom. sing.], *recūsāntis* [gen. sing.], etc.). In a common pattern of formation – whether directly borrowed from Latin, or from a Romance language such as French – the form adopted was minus the oblique case endings: so with such other Latinate borrowings as *dependent*, *fragrant*, *lambent*, *mendicant*, *pendant* (noun) and *pendent* (adjective; via Anglo-Norman), *penitent* (via the Middle French form), *resplendent* (via Middle French), *tangent*, and *urgent* among others.[8]

We might see here in this one passage from his 'Knight's Tale' the legacy of early Middle English in Chaucer's later Middle English. There are as would be expected a number of French loans in the passage, including the Anglo-Norman formation *maugre(e)* < *mal gré*, meaning 'ill will, spite,' when taken as a noun phrase; it

[8] As with *recusant*, which dates to the Reformation era, *intransigent* was not a loan to Middle English but, via Modern French *intransigeant*, derives from Spanish *los intransigentes*, a term for the Republicans during the Cantonal Rebellion (1873–1874) and in the Spanish Civil War (1936–1939), which ultimately derives from a Latin present participle.

can also function adverbially in the sense 'nonetheless, in spite of everything' (though this is rare: the MED lists only two occurrences, from the *Ayenbite of Inwyt* [ca. 1340] and *Kyng Alisaunder* [ca. 1425]; see also Mustanoja 1960, 392); and as a preposition, having at least partly grammaticalized (like Modern English *in spite of*). Chaucer uses *maugree* (and less frequently in the spellings *maugre* and *mawgre*) some 28 times in his poetry, several times in nominal form, but in a majority of instances as a preposition, 9 times in the formula *maugree X heed/hede* (with X a possessive adjective: *his, hir, thy/thyn/thyne/youre, my*), 'in spite of X's heed.' The MED records 82 instances of the nominal form of *maugree* and 92 of the prepositional, so Chaucer's 28 uses of the Anglo-Norman loan are a not insignificant share of the total. Most of the attestations of the form are from late to very late (ca. 1500) Middle English; about the earliest attestation of *maugree* is from the second-oldest Middle English romance *Havelok the Dane,* which its editor G.V. Smithers places between ca. 1295 to 1301 and 1310. The language of the only complete copy of the 3001-line romance, Oxford, Bodleian Library MS Laud misc. 108, is localized to Norfolk, the dialect of the poet to Lincolnshire (Smithers 1987, lxix, lxxxix). Chaucer uses the simplex *gre(e)* some 18 times in his works, often in prepositional phrases used adverbially, *in/at(te)/of gre(e)*, 'graciously, pleasingly.' English *agree* (*a-gree*) is also from Anglo-Norman; an older now obsolete sense of the word was 'to please, be pleased,' 'to accept something gracefully' (OED senses I.1.a, I.2.b). But Old English is there in Chaucer's *wostow* – 2nd sing. pres. of ME *wite(n)* < OE *witan* + enclitic pronoun *thow* < OE *þū* – and *moot* (3rd sing. pres. of ME *mot* 'must' < OE *mōtan*). The successive couplets rhyming on *decree* – *degree* and *heed* – *deed* give a sense of what had happened to English since the Conquest; the first pair are French loans, the second native English words (*heed* in noun form a conversion from the OE verb from *hēdan*, *deed* from OE *dǣd*). The early ME romance *Havelok the Dane*, as might be expected, exhibits some Scandinavian influence as to morphology and vocabulary (e.g., *are-dawes*, 'days of yore,' < Old Norse *ár-dagar*; *Havelok* will be returned to in 5.7; compare this with the Old English *in ġēardagum* in the opening line to *Beowulf* ['in days of yore']).

The aphoristic text *The Proverbs of Alfred* seems to date in composition (by its language) to about 1150, though its manuscript tradition is up to a century later. As it purports, in an antique-y way, to be the wisdom of the great West Saxon king, Alfred the uniter of kingdoms, the early Middle English text is perhaps self-consciously transitional, paying respect to an English monarch in an age of Norman kings and employing a language and script archaic in appearance. The text employs the OE characters *ƿ*,*ȝ*, *þ*, and *ð* (with the ð used medially and finally; Arngart 1955, 12). The voiced velar stop /g/ is retained initially and following *n*, thus *king* is pronounced [kiŋg]; final -*g* > -*h* or -*ch* [χ] as in *inoh/inoch* [ɪnɔχ] < OE *ġenōg/ġenōh* 'enough.' The value /j/ is represented in the manuscripts either by ȝ or *y* (*ȝiuen* and *yeue*, from *ȝife(n)/yēue(n)* 'give'). Grammatical gender is preserved in the nouns: *þene tyme* 'the/that time' (masc.), *þire heorte* 'the heart' (fem.), *þat lond* 'the/that land' (neut.; Arngart 1955, 213–214). Case is preserved with OE functions, though the endings are becoming more uniform: singular nominative in -Ø or -*e*, dative in -*e* most commonly (*mid felde, on golde*), genitive in -*es*; nom. and acc. pl. largely in -*es* (< OE -*as*), apart from those with -*(e)n* (in *honden* [fem.] and *cweðen* the final -*n* is by analogy; neut. *eren* 'ears' seems to be the only genuinely vestigial weak OE noun [< *ēaran*]; Arngart 1955, 214–217). Orthography in particular is what varies among the manuscript copies of the *Proverbs*:

> AT Seuorde (siforde, sifforde)
> séte þeynes monye. (kinhis monie)
> fele Biscopes.
> and feole. bok-iléred. (booc-lerede, boclered)
> Eorles prute. (herles prude)
> knyhtes egleche.
> þar wes þe eorl Alurich.
> of þare lawe swiþe wis.
> And ek Ealured (alfred)
> englene hurde.
> Englene durling: (derling)
> on englene lond he wes kyng (Arngart 1955, 70–71).

[At Seaford (East Sussex) / sat many thanes (var. kings) / many a bishop / and many book-learned men, / earls proud, / knights fearsome. / There was the earl Ælfric, / of the law very wise. / And also Alfred, / of the English the guardian, / of the English the darling: / over England was he the king.]

The dialect of the text in the main points to Sussex, its inherited forms from West Saxon and Kentish, but for the concluding sections 30–34 of the text (known as 'Father's Advice'), it seems to be more northerly (East Midlands) and of a later composition date. Dialectal and thematic parallels connect the *Proverbs of Alfred* with *The Owl and the Nightingale*. This latter poetic wisdom dialogue has been localized to Surrey; the word *cliure* 'claw' ([klifrə] from OE *clifor*) occurs only in these two texts, and both credit Alfred with a tradition of wise sayings (Arngart 1955, 57–64).

In the early sections of the Godstow Latin Cartulary (there was also a late Middle English version from the 1460s), one can see in the list of Abbesses of the Benedictine establishment at Godstow a clear form of transition in the names. The earliest abbesses bore Norman names for the most part, though many seem to have been children of Norman-English marriages:

Ediva of Winchester (Edith of Launceleve [or Launcelene]), founder, abbess ca. 1115–ca. 1166
E., second abbess, ca. 1167–ca. 1181 (identified only by the initial in the manuscript, perhaps Ediva's daughter Emma; Amt 2014, xxxix)
Agnes, ca. 1181–1195/6
Juliana, ca. 1196–ca. 1219
Felicia de Bade (Bath), ca. 1219–1225
Amfelicia 1225–1241
Flandrina de Braose (Brewes), 1241–1248 (the given name is 'of Flanders'; Dauzat 1977, 258)
Emma Bloet, 1248–1269
Isolda of Durham, 1269–1278

Rose of Oxney, 1278–1283
Mabel Wafre, 1283–1295
Alice de Gorges, 1295–1304
Matilda of Upton, 1304–ca. 1316
Margery de Dyne, 1316–1335
Matilda Beauchamp, 1335–1349 (Amt 2014, xxxix–xl)

By comparison one sees a greater number of English (or at least more Anglicized) names among the abbesses of the century before the establishment's dissolution under Henry VIII: Elizabeth Pytte (1430–1434), Elizabeth Felmersham (1435–1446), Alice of Henley (1446–1470), Margaret More (1471), Alice Nunny (1471–1480), Katherine Field (1480–1494), Isabel Braynton (1494–1517), Margaret Tewkesbury (1517–1535), and Katherine Bulkeley (Bewmaris, 1535-November 1539; Amt 2014, xlii–xlii). One can see across the entries of the cartulary the onomastic (personal name-related) effects of the Conquest and post-Conquest eras – of course these names refer to people and we see in the English, French (Norman, and other regional forms), and other names indications of the continuities and changes in the peopling of Britain; interesting as well can be the Latinization of names in the official documents of the period, which, in the earlier ME period, are still predominantly in Latin.

One finds in the Godstow records an Agnes, daughter of Payn fitzJohn (ca. 1185–1189), *Agnes filia Pagani filii Johannis* (document 132), with the Norman name-element *fitz*, from the dialectal form *fiz* of *fils* 'son,' ultimately from Latin *fīlius*; the convention seems to be Anglo-Norman (rather than Norman), and increased in frequency as the use of family surname identity grew in the 12th century. The pattern spread to Wales and Ireland during this century (as Wales was a base for the Norman invasion of Ireland). *Fitz* survived as a simplex in the surnames Fitz, Fice, Fis, Fitch, with early attestations from Warwickshire (Reginald le Fiz; 1193), Yorkshire (Robert Fiz; 1212), and Oxfordshire (William le Fiz; 1374). Fitzroy, *fiz de roy* = *fils de roi*, 'son of the king,' may have been used by 'royal bastards' (e.g., Henry FitzRoy, 1519–1536, son of Henry VIII and his mistress Elizabeth Blount), but it also became a surname (mainly in London; there was record of a Charlotte Fitzroy of Westminster in 1688; Hanks et al. 2016, 928). A Richard FitzGilbert accompanied William the Conqueror in 1066, and his great-grandson Robert FitzWalter was one of the guarantors of the Magna Carta in 1215. Surnames such as Fitzgerald, Fitzgibbon(s), Fitzhenry, Fitzmartin, and Fitzpatrick are more common in Ireland, deriving from names of the Anglo-Norman (and Cambro-Norman) aristocracy of the initial conquest period (Hanks et al. 2016, 927–929).

And there is a Ralph de Cheindut and Agnes his wife, daughter of Ralph de Scaccario (24 March 1259) (45); *scaccārium* is the 'exchequer' (treasurer); Richard fitzNeal, the natural son ('bishop's nephew') of Nigel, Bishop of Ely (likely born in Normandy, but his political and ecclesiastical career is known to have been primarily in England), was commissioned by Henry II to write the *Dialogus de scaccario* ("Dialogue on the Exchequer") in 1177; a head for finances and taxes apparently ran in the family as Nigel had served as exchequer under Henry I before being elevated to the see at Ely in 1133. An interesting mix of names, English and Norman, is found among the witnesses to an agreement of Abbess Margery de Dyne and to lease Godstow land (two acres) to Richard de Bachiler

(1 November 1322): *Hiis testibus Elya de Espele, Waltero Mauncel, Willelmo Sperlynge, Petro le Heyward, Henrico le Zouge,*[9] *et aliis*; "[witnessed] by these witnesses Elie de Espele, Walter Mauncel, William Sperling, Peter Heyward, Henry le Zouge, and others" (document 46). Naming traditions could include the use of geographic identifiers (*de Fernham, of Garsington, de Quency* from the Godstow records) and hypocoristic epithets such as *rūfus* ('red,' of the hair or complexion), as with William Rufus, the second Norman king of England; *ruadh*, usually referring to red hair, was a not uncommon epithet in Ireland (compare Italian surnames Rossi, Rosso, Rossetti, Rossino, Rossini). Another common naming convention is a trade byname, as with *scaccario* ('exchequer') above; in the Godstow cartulary, we find these tradespeople, often among the witnesses to agreements to land leases:

John the: barber (*Johanne le barbour*: document 497 [from 29 September 1307]), goldsmith (*Johanne aurifabro:* 497 [the same]; and *Johanne filio Waltri aurifabri*, 'John the son of Walter the goldsmith': 548 [26 October 1315]), baker of the archdeacon of Winchester (*Johanne pistore Wintoneiensis archidiaconi*: 504 [ca. 1180 × 1195]), as well as butler, cook, draper, dyer, fisherman, franklin, gatekeeper, glover, mariner, mason, plumber, porter, scribe, smith, spicer, and weaver.

Matilda the haymonger (*Matilda la Heymonger*: 519 [mid-13th century]) and weaver (438 [24 June 1235])

Richard the: barber (*Richard le Barbur* and his wife Matilda: 14 [3 February 1233]), cowman, franklin, mercer, miller, seneschal (steward), tawyer (dresser of hides), vintner, and weaver.

Robert the: brewer, chamberlain, cornmonger (*Robertus cornmonger*: 698 [1225 × 1237]; an interesting mixture of Latinized given name with the trade name in Middle English), cutler, farrier (worker on horses' hooves and shoes), fletcher (arrow maker), hostler, reeve, tailor (Amt 2014, by document number; on these and other medieval professions, see Fransson 1935).

All such records of the legal and economic past are also social records; in a document recording the return by Stephen Agoth (the surname *Agot* is Norman, of Scandinavian origin) of a tenement (in its earlier sense, a land-holding) to Godstow and Abbess Matilda of Upton, dating to 1304 × 1316, we see that the holding was in *Irelaundes Lane* and was witnessed by *Gervasio le bakere* (document 711). Geoffrey le Brocher of Bletchingdon made two grants of land to Godstow Abbey (sometime around 1236 to later in the century; documents 59, 61), and among the witnesses to the larger grant (9-½ acres, one headland, ½ an acre of meadow; Amt 2014, document 61) were two Knights Templar, Osebert Templar and Robert le Templer. Geoffrey 'le Brochere' is perhaps a maker of brooches, or

[9] This somewhat unusual surname is of French origin, with attestations in Anglo-Norman and Anglo-French including: Alanus de Zuche (1175; from the Pipe Rolls, the financial records of the Exchequer); Roger la Zuche/de la Suche/de la Soche (1212); Esseby la Zusche (1241); Alan la Sutche (1243); Thoma le Zouge (1402 for 1347, from an assessment during the reign of Edward III; MED, s.v. *zŏuche*). The ME form *zouche* (with many variant forms: *zouge, souche, soche*, and others) derives from Old French *soche/chuche* and means 'a tree trunk of large log' (MED, s.v. *zouche*, noting that the form may be Anglo-French) and seems to have extended from use in place-names to personal names, perhaps indicating geographical origin.

other sharp implements (a Roger le Brochere appears in the early Letter-Books of London, in 1281; Hanks et al. 2016, 348). One more worker of a craft might be mentioned from these documents: one of the witnesses to the grant by John Ponchard of Over Kiddington of a *messuage* in Afterleghe and Over Kiddington (Oxfordshire) to Robert de Badington, parson of Nether Kiddington (Amt 2014, document 76, dated 5 April 1316).[10] The grant was witnessed *Petro dicto le Gigur*: "Peter, called The Fiddler." Old French *gigur* is not a particularly common word (it can refer to a player of the fiddle or lute), and its modern equivalent *gigeur* as 'fiddler' (not to be confused with *gigueur/gigueuse*, dance of a *gigue* and automaton wood figures of such a dance) is found in the French of Canada's Atlantic Provinces (l'Acadie), especially the Gaspé coast, where Norman, Picard and other French musical traditions mixed with the Celtic (as on Cape Breton Island).

If such records of land grants and quitclaims bore the modern reader with their repetitiveness and formulaic language, it is a salutary reminder of the daily uses of a language, that by dint of repetition, access to a standard register and official vocabulary, something happens; illocutionary acts, a pragmatic function of language by which things can be done with words (pledge an oath, curse someone or something, make a promise, bear witness, have someone speak up ["I can't hear you"]), can be fixed in memory, set to parchment. Record-keeping was not just to survive better in the Middle English period, but to expand greatly with the professionalization of (secular) scribes and chancery clerks, which is not to suggest that the output of clerics in any way decreased – that is certainly not the evidence borne out by Orm, the *Ancrene Wisse*, or the outburst of preaching from the 12th to 14th centuries, to say nothing of the religious ferment – Wycliffe and the Lollards – from 1381 to the Reformation. The *Onomasticon Anglo-Saxonicum* of William Searle cautiously offered in the introduction that "this Onomasticon aims at being a fairly complete list of Anglo-Saxon names and of the men and women who bore those names" (Searle 1897, I.vii). While for the linguist and lexicographer the names and forms come first – and one notes in this period a decline setting in of the Old English dithematic names (compound names in which each element is a noun: *Ælf-wine*, 'elf-friend') – without "the men and women who bore those names," there would of course be nothing to study. Our Johns and Richards, Roberts and Matildas from the Godstow cartulary are often from ordinary walks of life, and they would have spoken ordinary words in their local dialects. Godstow sat not quite three miles north of Oxford, at the old juncture of Wessex and Mercia; the locals associated with the Abbey can be expected to have spoken Midlands varieties of early to late Middle English, though religious houses often drew members from other regions. The Godstow records show how quickly Norman and Anglo-Norman clerics supplanted the English, only to yield to those with more English-sounding names in the late Middle English period.

[10] A *messuage* is a 'Dwelling-house with the adjacent buildings and curtilage' (*Black's Law Dictionary*, s.v.); it is a loan from Anglo-Norman, and one of a number of Chaucer's Anglo-Norman legalisms. It occurs in Chaucer's "Reeve's Tale," *Bothe of his catel* [chattel] *and his mesuage*; I. 3979, with reference to the plans of the miller Symkyn (the diminutive form of Symond, Simon) to marry his daughter well and keep his property intact with her (the Reeve is going to quit the miller Robin from the pilgrim company in rather nasty fashion with his Symkyn stand-in). *Curtilage*, another Anglo-Norman loan to early ME, is the court enclosing the outbuildings and land of a messuage, and the concept was transferred in part to *courtyard*.

That their names and speech have survived to this day, given the flux and, quite often, brutality of history, is extraordinary. In looking at this period as 'transitional,' it is customary now to question every label and term students of the subject apply to it. English did survive, and English was still and would remain English – not a simple point as the sections on the 'Creole hypothesis' and dialect diversity of Middle English hope to show. But compared to the changes in the course of Old English ca. 500–1100, it might be said that the pace of changes 1150–1300 or so may have quickened, or, at least, that these changes would alter the shape of English more dramatically, bringing it closer to our own speech, and further from that of Ælfwine, Leofgyth, Offa, and Uhtred.

5.5 THE BEGINNINGS OF FRENCH LOANS TO ENGLISH (1100–1400)

The first attestation of the French loan *sire*, as a 'title of distinction,' the OED records is ca. 1225 *leoue sire* in the early Middle English *Ancrene Riwle*, "Rule for Anchoresses" (Millett 2005, 21 line 45); the text usually goes by the title *Ancrene Wisse* – the nominal form *wisse*, from OE *wīsian* ('instruct, guide'), occurs only in this text. It also occurs in the Anglo-Norman translation of Henry III's 1258 Proclamation: *Henrí par la grace deu Rey de Englet<er>re Sire de Irelande. Duc de Normandie de Aqui<t>en et Cunte de Angou. a Tuz ses feaus Clers et Lays saluz* (Ellis 1868, 18; "Henry by the grace of God King of England, Sire of Ireland, Duke of Normandy, of Aquitaine, and Count of Anjou, to all his subjects clerical or lay, greetings"). Not only is *sir/sire* in evidence here in the salutation to Henry's proclamation, but so too is a form that will also make the journey to English: *ses feaus*, 'his subjects,' but also, more literally, those who have pledged *fealty* to him (a loan via Old French *feauté*; Löfstedt 2014, 322). Anglo-Norman *siute/siwte/suite*, as in *suit/lawsuit*, is another legalism English adopted in the early Middle English period (Löfstedt 2014, 322–324). Scores more would enter from Anglo-Norman, naturally enough, as the Conquest had brought a new legal order. And French legalisms are a source for formations with postmodifiers, that is, those following the Romance pattern of N + Adj (the postpositive modifier) rather than normative English syntax of Adj + N: *fee simple*, or archaic *socage fieu*, a 'fief held on socage' – *socage* itself is an Anglo-Norman loan for services due for land tenure not including knight-service (OED, s.v. *socage*; *Anglo-Norman Dictionary*, s.v. *sokage*, a use dating to 1215). The work of scribes – eventually, chancery clerks as the period develops – officers of the realm (and of manors – *seneschals*, an Anglo-Norman loan), and ecclesiastical and lay authors will serve as major vectors of transmission of French loans to English. The path could at times be a bit circuitous – the 'trial scene' in Marie de France's *Lai de Lanval* (ca. 1170, part of the Arthurian cycle) seems to exhibit contemporary Anglo-Norman legal language, some of it found in other texts with Latinate endings: that is, Old French and Anglo-Norman loans to Latin, which, as a legal, administrative, and scholarly language could then also serve as a secondary source of French loans (Schauwecker 2017, 483–486). An analysis by William Rothwell expanded to a set of other Anglo-Norman texts – *Le Mystère d'Adam*, the Anglo-Norman version of the *Navigatio Sancti Brendani* (the Irish *Voyage of St. Brendan*), Geoffrey Gaimar's *L'estoire* *des Engleis*, and others – and found a set of central legal terms, here given in their MdE form: *abet, accuse, appeal, argument, assise, brief, count, court, defend, establishment, guarantee/warrant* (< *guarant*), *plea, plead, plaintiff, pledge, response, retire, seisin* (Rothwell 2000, 24, 31–36).

The classic study of loan formations in English is Mary Serjeantson's *A History of Foreign Words in English* (Serjeantson 1961); as Middle English is the period in which it might be said the lexical floodgates opened to French (and the flood of Latin would swell for the next several centuries), Serjeantson's history of loanwords gives pride of place to "The French Element" (104–212). Indeed, one of the earliest French loans to English apparently was *prūt/prūd* 'proud,' which entered later Old English through glosses to Defensor's *Liber scintillarum* ('book of sparks,' a collection of 2500 wise sayings from the Bible and patristic writers) and to colloquies of Ælfric Bata, an early 11th-century student of Ælfric of Eynsham, in both cases glossing forms of Latin *arrogantia* (OED, s.v. *proud*). An entry from Ælfric of Eynsham's *Glossary* (ca. 990s) matches Old French *capun* 'capon' with the Latin lemmata *cāpō* and *gallinaccus* (Serjeantson 1961, 105). The flow would increase of course with the Conquest, and Serjeantson arranged these chronologically, dated by earliest appearance where possible: *gingifer* 'ginger,' *bacun* 'bacun,' *prisun* 'prison,' *castel* 'castle,' *market* from the 11th century; *cancelere* 'chancellor' and *capelein* 'chaplain' are Anglo-Norman, but the forms that remain in English were 're-borrowed' from the Central/Île-de-Paris dialect which had *ch-* [ʃ] for Northern/Norman *c-* [k]; along with *prior* (monastic use, head of a priory or chapter), *curt* 'court,' *rent, tresor* 'treasure,' *acorden* 'to come to an accord' ('come to terms'), *miracle, clerc* 'cleric, clerk,' and *pilegrim* 'pilgrim' (by dissimilation from Old French *pelegrin*, itself by dissimilation from Latin *peregrīnum*) are from the first half of the 12th century (Serjeantson 1961, 106–110). As French was the language of government, civil and ecclesiastic, French words were borrowed to entitle the new order of administration in England: *gouvernement* 'government' itself is a French loan, appearing for the first time apparently in Geoffrey Chaucer's *Boece* (his prose rendering of Boethius's *De consolatione Philosophiae* "Consolation of Philosophy"). The pace of French loans quickened during the 13th century as Anglo-Norman faded in the wake of the loss of the Duchy of Normandy in 1259; if the Norman ruling class might have until then been somewhat more insular socially, so now they were geographically and politically. In sociolinguistic terms, there was greater need for broader social contact and communication with the native English-speaking majority, and a growing reliance on them for "the development of professional administrative classes in institutions relating to justice, administration and representation" (Lusignan 2009, 25).

An interesting point to be added to the story of the English language is the development of French in England during the 300 years following the Conquest. Anglo-Norman literature was produced in England; Wace, born on the isle of Jersey, produced the *Roman de Brut* on the 'matter of Britain,' whose links, forward and back, between British, French, Breton, Welsh, and English literature are as enormously convoluted as anything in the *Breuddwyd Rhonabwy* ("Dream of Rhonabwy," ca. 1300), which combines the *awen* (the 'inspiration' of the bards) with the 'Arthur of the Welsh.' Wace's Jersey French is often classed with Guernésiais as Channel Islands French: Guernésiais and Jèrriais are descendants of Norman French, the former more influenced by English than the latter, and still spoken by a small percentage of the population on the respective islands. Anglo-Norman was different enough from Standard Central French that scribes of the latter (Central French) could correct the grammar of scribes of the former (Anglo-Norman); the morphological and syntactic history of Anglo-Norman seems to show that it developed in parallel to Central French (that French links were maintained despite political separation; Ingham 2009 and the other essays in Wogan-Browne 2009 are the most thorough recent appraisal of the 'French of England'). As seen throughout this chapter, French borrowings were never an isolated phenomenon, but continuous, and increase in number even in the transitional 15th century.

5.6 EARLY MIDDLE ENGLISH LITERATURE

The literature of early Middle English is not nearly as plentiful as that for later ME, but it does include a mixture of prose and poetry, some of it rather long-winded (the *Ormulum* in particular). Among the earlier texts are the anonymous early Middle English versions of the first two books of the Bible, which, unlike the Old English poems *Genesis* and *Exodus* from the Junius manuscript of Old English verse (Oxford, Bodleian Library, MS Junius 11), are nearer paraphrases, and rougher verse ("doggerel in which the more dreadful lines afford comic relief" in one estimate; Cottle 1970, 164). Occupying 81 folios in the smaller format Cambridge manuscript Corpus Christi College 444, the 4162 lines of verse (longer than the Old English versions, and the epic *Beowulf*) are at least of interest linguistically. The manuscript dates to around 1250, written by a single scribe, the language that of West Norfolk early Middle English, or, more broadly, early East Midlands. One salient feature of the language of the Middle English *Genesis and Exodus* is the low rate of French loanwords in the vocabulary, such that one editor, the remarkably prolific Rev. Richard Morris (1833–1894),[11] described the poems, along with Laȝamon's *Brut* (ca. 1200) and the *Ormulum* (ca. 1180s), as "semi-Saxon works" (Morris 1865, xiii); the early ME *Genesis and Exodus*, however, is in a Southern dialect, Laȝamon's in West Midlands (Worcestershire), and Orm's in East Midlands (Lincolnshire). The Southern dialect of the *Genesis and Exodus* is more 'conservative' in that it preserves more of the features of late Old English – for example, dual pronoun forms, and a somewhat fuller verb paradigm (e.g., present forms *singe / singest / singeð* [sing.], *singen* [pl.]; preterite forms *sang / sunge / sang* [sing.], *sungen* [pl.]). There are relatively few Norse loans in the *Genesis and Exodus* – especially in comparison with the Northern *Ormulum* (from a region that had been within the Danelaw). Wace's *Roman de Brut*, in Anglo-Norman, dates to ca. 1150, the eME *Proverbs of Alfred* to later in the 12th century. Like the *Genesis and Exodus*, *The Owl and Nightingale* is a Southern-Southern Midlands text that might also be described reasonably

[11] London-born of Welsh parents, Morris edited a dozen volumes for the Early English Text Society, including *Sir Gawayne and the Green Knight* (Original Series 4 [1864]), the Middle English *Story of Genesis and Exodus* (O.S. 7 [1865]), and a 7-volume edition of the nearly 30,000 lines of verse in the *Cursor Mundi* (O.S. 57, 59, 62, 66, 68, 99, 101 [1879–1893]).

accurately enough by Morris's 'semi-Saxon' label; it too maintains, to an extent, the Old English dual pronouns, as the Nightingale says to the Owl:

So bo hit euer in unker siþe
Þat þu bo sori, & ich bliþe! (ll. 993–994)

So be it ever in our [i.e., 'of us two'] case,
That thou be glum, and I be glad!

Southern also, with some Southern Midlands forms, is what may be the earliest chivalric romance in English, *King Horn* of the mid-13th century; *Horn* is a fairly wild combination of 'matter of Britain' material, Anglo-Saxon, Norse, and Irish, as well as 'Saracens' (who may rather in earlier versions of the story have been Viking invaders). There are some similarities between *King Horn* and *Havelok the Dane*, which, in somewhat convoluted (and not yet fully understood) fashion parallel the multilingual nature of medieval Britain in their 'macaronic' story tradition: inherited Anglo-Saxon traditions, Norse, Danelaw Norse and Hiberno-Norse, Celtic (the relationship between the medieval Welsh tales collected under the title *Mabinogion* and Arthurian tradition would be one example), and Romance (French and Anglo-Norman).

Havelok or, *The Lay of Havelok the Dane*, belongs to what might be called Period 2 of early Middle English, likely later than 1275 but written before 1310 (Smithers 1987, lxix–lxxiii); though the scribe is dialectally of Norfolk, the poet is from Lincolnshire, perhaps Lincoln itself (Smithers 1987, lxxxix). It is a story of dispossession and restoration, as a young princess of England, Goldeboru/Goldeborw, daughter of Aþelwold, is entrusted to Earl Godrich of Cornwall who breaks his word and, in a pattern found across Celtic and Germanic myth, imprisons her in a tower (in this instance, at Dover). In Denmark, a similar situation obtains for young Havelok, prince of Denmark, who, after his father Birkabeyn's death, is given over to Grim the *þral* 'thrall' (l. 527), a fisherman by trade, with instructions from Denmark's wicked regent Godard to drown the lad. Grim, in another common mythic pattern, will flee with Havelok to England, and then, in yet another common pattern – the origin story to a place-name – found in the Humber-mouth the town of Grimsby, whose medieval seal features three of the main figures mentioned here:

SIGILLVM COMMUNITATIS GRIMSBYE
HAB[UE?]LOC GRYEM [i.e, GRYME] GOLDEBVRGH
[The seal of the community of Grimsby
Havelok Grim Goldeboru; Smithers 1987, frontispiece]

The table is then set for restorations to come to two kingdoms, and the eventual marriage of a princess of England and a prince of Denmark.

Though dating to later in the literature of early Middle English, *Havelok* has a ring to it as being between Old and Middle English. The language is early ME, in which "there is no longer a true system of inflexions" (Smithers 1987, lxxix); most nouns mark plural case forms in simple *-es* (< OE *-as*), and *-es* marks also the genitive singular of nouns. If the romance is part of the 'matter of Britain,' it might also be said to be part of a 'matter of Denmark' (*Hamlet* of course comes to mind): it is a story out of the old Danelaw and the tale may in origin have sought to legitimate the rule of Cnut as king of England (1016–1035; Smithers 1987, lvii). There is an earnestness to the narration, and its theme is "about the triumph of right over wrong, and of the lawful right of succession to a kingdom; the importance of law and order in feudal England of the thirteenth century; the power of goodness, and the governance and the protection of the good man by God" (Smithers 1987, lix). Some early Middle English forms may be seen in the following passage from the poem:

> **Herknet** to me, gode men –
> Wiues, maydnes, and all men –
> Of a tale þat **Ich** you **wile telle**...
> Þe tale is of Hauelok **imaked** (ll. 1–3, 5)

herknet = 2nd pl. of eME *herk(e)nen* < OE *heorcnian* (the form here in OE would be *heorcniað*, which could be either the present plural form [all numbers] or the present imperative plural, which is likely the form here in *Havelok*). The OE verb could be either intransitive ('to listen, to give ear to'), or transitive, that is, with an object ('listen to somebody/thing, pay attention'). The contrast can be found in a Homily on the Assumption of the Blessed Virgin Mary from Ælfric (ca. 955–ca. 1010) *Martha wæs swiðe bysig ymbe Drihtnes ðenunge, and hire swuster Maria sæt stille æt Drihtnes fotum, heorcnigende* ("Martha was very busy about her service of the Lord, and her sister Mary sat still at the Lord's feet, hearkening"; intransitive); *heo [Maria] gesæt æt Godes fotum, his word heorcniende* ("Mary sat at God's [the Lord's] feet, hearkening to His word"; transitive). Curious is that though OE *heorcnian* and ME *herk(e)nen* are, with *hark* (AmE prefers the form *harken* over *hearken*), inherited from Germanic, the earliest attestations are from later OE (Ælfric, the prose *Life of St. Guthlac*; or for *hark*, from early ME, the *Lambeth Homilies* ca. 1175). Later phrasal verb *hark back*, or *hearken/harken back*, in the sense 'To have origin in or be reminiscent of a past event or condition; recall or evoke' (AHD5, s.v. *hark*) may derive from the hunt with the hunter's cries to the hunting dogs, 'Hark! Forward! Hark! Back!' (*Hark!* still meaning 'Listen!'). *Hearken/harken back* the panel of the *American Heritage Dictionary* labeled a 'usage problem' (AHD5, s.v. *hearken*). The Christmas hymn "Hark! The herald angels sing" maintains the imperative form of the verb ('Listen!') and is traditionally attributed to Charles Wesley, dated to 1739, with the melody by Felix Mendelssohn. The form *terkne* is a contraction of *to herkne*; interesting is the development of the infinitive form in Middle English, from its inflectional (e.g., OE *-an*, *-ian*, etc., and ME *-en*) form to a periphrastic *to X* form (this development has a complex history, with significant changes in later ME in the 15th century; Ringe 2021, 112; Los 2005).

Ich: the first-person singular personal pronoun form, in its stressed form (*I*, *Y* were the unstressed forms); this is quite common through the poem but varies with *Hic* [hɪtʃ] (twice, at lines 304 and 305) and *Ic* (once at line 298).

wile telle: 1st pres. sing. *wile* 'want, be willing' + *telle* infinitive; the sense, at the opening of a heroic verse romance such as *Havelok* is 'I wish to tell'; but in a number of lines *wile* is also used as an auxiliary verb + infinitive to form the future tense (Old English did not have inflectional future forms): *Al Denemark I wile you yeue* ("All of Denmark will I give you"; l. 485). Or the aux + infinitive could indicate mood (e.g., subjunctive at l. 575 *wolde him dere* 'would him injure').

imaked: past participle of *make(n)*, in the expanded verb form *is...imaked.* Middle English *make(n)* is a relatively high-frequency verb in the sense of 'create, construct, build, fashion,' deriving from Old English *(ġe)macian*, past participle form *ġemacod*. Both the OE and ME would have been trisyllabic, but the usual vocalization has occurred with the preverbal *ġe-*. OE *(ġe)macian*, whence MdE *to make*, was rare enough in Old English, occurring mainly in West Saxon texts, for Sherman Kuhn to suggest that the verb was a loan from Old Saxon, and thus our modern form *make* may not be inherited from Old English (Kuhn 1986; the OED mentions this study in its etymology, s.v. *make* v.). On the fate of OE preverbal *ġe-*, see 5.1.

There are some Northernisms in *Havelok*, many of them of Norse origin, which is not surprising as Lincoln had been one of the 'Five Boroughs' of the Danelaw along with Derby, Leicester, Nottingham, and Stamford: *coupe* 'to buy' (at ll. 1801, 2006) < Old Norse *kaupa* and *teyte* 'cheerful, merry' (1842, 2332) < ON *teitr* are found surviving into eMdE in Northern dialects and Scots (e.g., in the poetry of makars Robert Henryson, William Dunbar, and Gavin Douglas). The past participle form *yat* 'yielded to' (1675, emended from MS *þat* or *wat*, the initial graph could be a thorn [voiceless *th*] or wynn [w]; the form does occur elsewhere, e.g., *ȝatedd* in the *Ormulum* l. 154, and especially in early 13th-century poetry) seems to derive from ON *játta* via OE or eME. The auxiliary verb *mone* < ON *munu* (841) 'must, shall,' is still heard in Northern English dialects and Scottish English. The idiomatic expression *gouen hem ille* (164) 'were distressed' involves a reflexive usage of *giue* in the sense that 'they gave themselves (presented themselves) to be ill'; it may be a calque (loan translation) from ON *giva* [i.e., *gefa*] *sik illa* ('give off oneself being ill/bad,' 'be distressed'; Smithers 1987, 87). The loan of idioms and expressions does occur;[12] what would be significant here to the Lincolnshire provenance is that the expression entered early East Midlands Middle English. Such more 'extended' loan formations are among the evidence adduced at times for the 'Creole hypothesis' of Middle English.

[12] The famous Mardi Gras invocation *laissez les bons temps rouler* ('let the good times roll') used in Louisiana (and marketed and spread nationwide) might not be a genuine Acadianism – Louisiana French may be more likely to used *quittez* in place of *laissez* in the sense of 'let.' The direction of the loan may actually be English to French, though Louisiana musician Clarence 'Bon Ton' Garlow recorded in 1949 the zydeco-blues song 'Bon Ton Roula/Roulet,' a phonetic rendering of *bons temps rouler*.

5.7 THE CREOLE HYPOTHESIS; LANGUAGE CONTACT OR DISPLACEMENT?

To return to the vexed matter of the voicing of initial (and final) fricatives in eME, the question of lenition comes up again. The term *lenition* itself may be one of the particular sticking points among historical phonologists of English; the German equivalent is *Erweichung*, simply 'softening,' and may not carry the freight of English *lenition* (a Latin loan also simply meaning to make *lenis*, 'soft'), which very often refers to one of the common phonological processes of consonant mutation in Celtic languages. And this has at times been one of the features those who espouse more 'Creolist' views of contact between early Celtic and Germanic (here, early English) hold out as possible substrate influence of the former on the latter. The Celtic languages moved, as did English in its history, from more synthetic morphology toward more analytic constructions: e.g., periphrastic verb forms (such as the periphrastic DO; Filppula et al. 2002, 12–20). The theory of possible Old English–Old Norse creolization during the era of Viking conquests (ca. AD 793–1066) was seen earlier (section 4.8); the idea of 'Middle English as a Creole' is similarly not entirely new, but likely spurred on by recent advances in contact language linguistics (to be dealt with in more detail in chs. 10 and 11). Manfred Görlach had seemingly dispensed with the idea of Middle English as a Creole in a 1986 essay "Middle English - a creole?" in the Jacek Fisiak Festschrift: "Unless simplification and language mixture are thought to be sufficient criteria for the definition of a creole or creoloid...then Middle English does not appear to be a creole" (Görlach 1986, 335). More recently Don Ringe echoed Görlach's assessment, specifically on the matter of an Old Norse–Old English Creole, and the question of the vector of transmission of Norse influences on English - especially function forms (e.g., the third-person plural forms *they / their / them*) - and whether this indicates either mutual intelligibility between ON and OE or a pidginized/Creolized/*koiné* form of the languages in contact (Ringe 2021, 95–98). It is debatable, as seen in the last chapter, to what extent ON and OE were mutually intelligible, the one a North Germanic language and English a West Germanic language. Interestingly, this matter has been provocatively addressed by Emonds and Faarlund 2014, who suggest that English was a North Germanic language. The morphological and lexical evidence they adduce is tantalizing, as these are areas of English over which Scandinavian exerted an influence (there is no doubt that ON brought many words into English; French, however, brought far more); but they avoid almost entirely phonological matters, and the Scandinavian morphological and syntactic examples seem less convincing when one considers, and sounds out, the phonological level of the proposed influences (in a contact situation, one would have expected far more phonological influence than seems in evidence). Similarly, the idea of a Norman French or Anglo-Norman contact situation as a staging ground for pidginization, then, within a generation or two, the formation of a Creole, seems contrary to the documented fate of Anglo-Norman in the century after the loss of the Duchy of Normandy in 1259. It appears that Anglo-Norman developed in parallel to Central French of the Paris region (Ingham 2009), and that Anglo-Norman phonological influence was relatively limited, e.g., Old French *clergie* > *clergy* with the /dʒ/, yet we do see anglicization in the French sound patterns of loans: Old French *garant/ guarant* becomes *warrant* in Middle English, though the word is an earlier loan to French from Germanic. There may be some sense of unease about contemporary language matters that motivates an English-as-Creole argument, namely, the global spread of English and the perception that there is a sort of triumphalism attached to that status.

But a contact situation presumes that with pidginization an immediate communicative need be filled by radical simplification of the languages in contact, usually with one of them serving as the base for the contact or 'mixed' form (there are exceptions to this, such as Michif in Chapter 7); the base language usually supplies the majority of the grammatical and syntactic rules, the lexifier or donor language vocabulary (but also some phonological influence). Sustained contact and expanded communicative needs can lead to a pidgin undergoing Creolization, especially if for a second generation of users it becomes a primary means of communication; then, the contact variety increases in complexity and may indeed, over time, become what speakers (and linguists) consider a separate language. It is not clear to what extent late Old English speakers in the century after the Conquest needed to learn Norman French; it is usually presumed that for proper functioning of the manorial system, some feudal administrative officials had to use English with their workers and serfs. A good many Norman knights married English women, and the onomastics of Norman, Angevin, and Plantagenet England bear witness to such familial mixing. Interesting is how relatively quickly French given names appear among tradespeople in charters and other land documents of the period (as seen with the Godstow cartulary above). Given names may follow fads and trends, but the persistence of Anglo-Saxon names argues against the idea of wholesale adoption of French names by the English working classes and seems rather to point to children of mixed Norman and English heritage who came to identify with their 'mother country.' Particularly with the loss of the Duchy of Normandy, there may have been a sense even for descendants of the Norman nobility in England that ties had been weakened but not severed, as continued Anglo-French and French contact in the 14th and 15th centuries indicates. The result of this sociolinguistic situation is that there may not have been the sort of contact situation one sees in other colonial encounters. As Anglo-Saxon identity became subsumed under the English after 1066, so eventually did the Norman. By comparison, there is some regional pride, much of it humorous, in the North about Viking heritage (York has made a cottage industry out of it). No doubt there occurred in the Danelaw and post-1066 contact situations that produced *ad hoc* local varieties that would look like Norse-English or Norman French-English pidgins to contemporary observers. But evidence of resultant structural change (as with later contact varieties such as Gullah or Tok Pisin or Kriol) seems wanting for medieval English as a Creole. The vast majority of developments in Middle English are explicable by comparison with Old English. But in the relatively near future, in the 16th and early 17th centuries, such situations as give rise to contact varieties would occur, in the colonial endeavors of the English nation, and a number of resulting English-based pidgins and Creoles are still with us.

5.8 A PANOPLY OF TONGUES: THE EMERGING COMPLEXITY OF THE DIALECTAL PICTURE

Led by Simon de Montfort, the Sixth Earl of Leicester, Anglo-Norman barons extracted from Henry III a number of privileges set down in letters patent 18 October 1258 in what are known as *The Provisions of Oxford*. Relations between the barons and Kings John and Henry III had been pitched between accommodation and open rebellion since Magna Carta (1215). The First Barons' War erupted in 1215–1217, and the Provisions came after various struggles to reassert the checks on royal power Magna Carta had set out. Montfort like his father Simon de Montfort, Fifth Earl of Leicester, had been born in France, and like his father's father became lord of Montfort l'Amaury near Paris. Simon de Montfort, Sixth Earl of Leicester, was a leader of the opposition to Henry III, and he rallied them, and to some extent the general populace, with his campaigns; in 1264, he cancelled debts owed to the Jews of Leicester, while his son Henry participated in the massacre of the Jews of Worcester. Welsh forces also allied with Simon and the other rebellious barons, and they were there with him at the Battle of Evesham (Worcestershire) in 1265 when he was defeated by Edward Longshanks (later Edward I), stabbed with a lance by loyalist baron Roger Mortimer, then brutally mutilated. In 1258, the 'provisions' granted by Henry III were recorded in Latin and French, and also in early Middle English, perhaps to appease a rebellious native population (on the purposes, and audiences, of Henry's proclamation and letters see Machan 2003, at "The Barons' War and Henry's Letters," 21–69). The document is one of the few royal proclamations from the era in the English language; the copy from the Public Record Office (now The National Archives) was apparently sent to Huntingdonshire (the other copy, sent to Oxfordshire, is in the Bodleian Library):

> Henri, þurȝ Godes fultume King on Engleneloande, Lhoauerd on Yrloande, Duk on Normandi, on Aquitaine, and Eorl on Aniow, send igretinge to alle hise holde, ilærde and ileawede, on Huntendoneschire (Dickins and Wilson 1951, 8).
>
> [Henry, through God's help King in England, Lord of Ireland, Duke of Normandy, of Aquitaine, and earl of Anjou, sends greetings to all his kingdom, learned and unlearned, in Huntingdonshire.]

Much here is from Old English: *fultum* 'help, aid, protection' must have begun to sound archaic (the MED records 14 instances of it ca. 1150–1325, all but 3 before 1300); *holde* (dative of *hōld*), from OE *heald* 'protection, keeping,' had a newer sense of 'kingdom, realm'; *ilærde and ileawede* < OE *ġelǣred and ġelǣwed* ('learned and lewd' [the latter in its original sense 'unlearned']). But there is the French loan *duc*. The proclamation is apparently the first instance of the London dialect in Middle English, then Southern/Southeastern in forms, but which would, over the next century, increasingly feel the influence of the East Midlands. Curiously, *igretinge* 'greetings,' from OE *grētan*, is the only occurrence of this form in Middle English. The at first somewhat jarring spelling <oa> in *Engleneloande*, *Lhoauerd*, and *Yrloande*, apparently represents [ɔ:] (Minkova 2014, 191). The spelling <ou> for [u:] derives from Anglo-Norman and, when word-final, English scribes used <ow>; <i> for <j> is common in medieval Latin manuscripts (and would continue with the use of Latin in England through to the modern era in the printing of Latin texts and use of lower-case Roman numerals in typography – e.g. <iij> for <iii> '3'); here <i> in *Aniow* represents /ʒ/, and so, in this Proclamation, a pronunciation approximating the current French one [ãʒu] or [ɔ̃ʒu]. A short text, but one of some historical and dialectal importance.

A wealth of resources have become available in the past two decades or so to assist in one of the more obscure periods of the history of English. The companion (or 'daughter' as its founders call it) of the great *A Linguistic Atlas of Late Medieval English* (LALME), *A Linguistic Atlas of Early Middle English* (or LAEME; Laing 2013) is an online project that enables large-scale searches of eME by form or string, county or feature map. The LAEME, like other electronic corpora, is not easy to use (*user-friendly* is one of the fictions of the computer age), and one misses the ability to use all 4 volumes of the print LALME at once. Compiler Laing herself demonstrated the type of study enabled by corpus linguistics with a study of the 'Jespersen Cycle' of negation in early ME (Laing 2002); the 'Jespersen Cycle' (after Jespersen 1917) is the idea of a sort of life cycle of negative constructions found, such as in French and English, in which one may have at first simply a negative marker (e.g., OE and ME *ne*) placed before the verb, then preverbal *ne* and an adverb meaning 'not' (e.g., OE *nāht/nōht*, ME *nowt/naʒt* and variants), then a 'not' form alone placed after the verb.

OE *ne habbe*, or contracted form *nabbe*, '(I) not have'

eME (ca. 1200) *Ðarof sade ðe apostele...ðanne ne habbe ic naht kariteð, and swa ic habbe all forloren* (*Vices and Virtues*, 'Of witte,' cited from the Michigan Corpus of Middle English Prose and Verse)
("Thereof said the apostle [Paul]...then not have I naught/not charity, and so I have all lost"; the Vulgate proof-text 1 Corinthians 13:3 has *caritatem non habuero, nihil sum*, "If I have not charity/love, I am nothing")

late ME–Early Modern English *I have not*

References in the *Middle English Dictionary* ca. 1400–1450 seem to bear out the transition to the third phase of the 'Jespersen Cycle' of negation in English:

ca 1386 (to 1430 for posthumous copies) *dar I nat for drede* (Chaucer, *Legend of Good Women* 2216)
ca 1425 *Nature was nat my frende* ("Dialogue between Reason and Adversity"; the ME version of Petrarch's *De Remediis*)
ca. 1450 *I Wot Not Who is hys name, for he hym nowt knowe* (*Castle of Perseverance*, one of the three plays dating to the 15th century from the Macro MS; Folger Shakespeare Library MS V.a. 354)

Modern linguists often use electronic corpora to identify patterns and look for constraints, particularly syntactic. Following George Jack's work on this matter of negation in ME (especially Jack 1978), Laing suggested 'Jack's Law' for a seeming constraint in use of adverbial negation in early Middle English in constructions *ne* + *bute(n)* – the latter with the sense 'only': that in such constructions, seemingly without exception, single negation was preferred over double negation (Laing 2002, 306–309).

While much modern work on the corpus data of early English is done by computer, at times with machine-read texts – a somewhat worrying trend – three volumes from Swedish linguist Gillis Kristensson (Kristensson 1967, 1987, 1995) made use of personal and place-name evidence from examination of the medieval Lay Subsidy Rolls of The National Archives (UK)[13] to try to refine dialect boundaries for early Middle English beyond the main five seen already (Northern, West Midlands, East Midlands, Southern/Southwestern, Kentish). The data assembled over some three decades (from the original dissertation published as Kristensson 1967) made use of the Lay Subsidy Rolls now held in the National Archives of the United Kingdom; and from that data, place-names and then personal names (onomastic evidence) were the primary focus. Kristensson's approach was different from, but ran parallel to, that of the *Linguistic Atlas of Late Middle English* (LALME, 1986). Begun in 1952,[14] LALME was headquartered at the University of Edinburgh and resulted in the publication of four large-format volumes with their 'dot maps' indicating the location of the linguistic tokens being mapped. Work on the *Linguistic Atlas of Early Middle English* began in the following year (1987), with the main compiler Margaret Laing, who had worked on LALME. LAEME is also based at the University of Edinburgh, which now has an Angus McIntosh Centre for Historical Linguistics. Kristensson (1995) in working through the Lay Subsidy Rolls for the East Midlands counties looked to the old tribal settlement zones (and later kingdoms) of the Saxons and Angles and saw Northamptonshire as a dialectal dividing line between Saxons in the south of the county and Angles in the north. In the southern extremity of the county, one finds Aynho, < *Æga* + *hōh*, 'Æga's hillspur' (ODBPN), with the proper name looking Saxon. In the north of the county are the tribal names Kettering and Oundle, the latter where St. Wilfrid expired in 709 at his Middle Anglian monastery (Stenton 1989, 144–145). Corby, north of Kettering, is Scandinavian, another layer of complexity to the inheritance of Anglo-Saxon era Northamptonshire in eME. Yet the *Survey of English Dialects* did not record the Scandinavian form *beck* for small stream in the county, which was found in Norfolk just to the east, though common term *brook* was not (SED 3. 2, 421; Poussa 1997, 429). And Kristensson 1967 on the northern counties and Lincolnshire looked to the dialectal meeting of Northumbrian (subdivided into northern and southern varieties) and Mercian, with Lincolnshire, the West Riding of Yorkshire, and Lancashire belonging more to the Midlands in the early 14th century (241, and Maps 1 and 17). This Kristensson attributes to natural geographic barriers (Witham and marshes, Trent and fens, hills west of Bardsey, Yorkshire), but also to the methods of the Domesday Survey: "In Domesday, Lancashire south of the Ribble was surveyed with Cheshire, Lancashire north of the Ribble with Yorkshire.... The Ribble in its lower reaches was thus

[13] These are available online from The National Archives website in the E 179 Database (records relating to lay and clerical taxation): http://www.nationalarchives.gov.uk/e179.

[14] In the Preface to the print volumes, Angus McIntosh notes that an inspiration for the project was fieldwork with modern dialects (LALME 1986, I: vii).

a time-honoured border between administrative units whereas in Eastern Lancashire, the steep Longridge Fell served the same purpose" (241–242).

An article by Kristensson (Kristensson 1986) offered a new look at the West Midlands *wæll(e)*-group of words, that is, those that vary in the realization of i-umlauted /a/ before *l* + C (/a/ > /æ/ in words such as *cælf* 'calf,' *wǣll(e)* 'well, stream' [OE *wǣl(l)*], *wælm* 'spring') and sought to more precisely identify the area in which /æ/ appears as /a/ in early Middle English, while it appears as /e/ in the rest of the West Midlands (Kristensson 1986, 443–445). Turning once again to the evidence of place-names and personal names in the taxation records from the Lay Subsidy Rolls, Kristensson first determined that the not uncommon geographic surname element *atte Walle/Welle* was indeed referring to a stream or well and not a 'wall' (from OE *weall*, which also could have given rise to the *walle* forms). Old English /æ/, under the influence of /l/, had raised to /ɛ/ in the OE Second Fronting and then to /e/ in late OE, thus giving rise to early ME *welle* (and Modern English *well*) – except in West Mercian (a dialect area previously loosely defined). Here, unlike other OE dialects, there was already an /ɛ/ phoneme (the product of /æ/ to /ɛ/ by the Second Fronting); this, however, in West Mercian was lowered to /æ/ in the later OE period and thence to /a/ in early Middle English (producing the place- and personal names in *walle*). What was the area within the West Midlands in which this change took place? Middle English "*walle* prevailed in Lancashire south of the Ribble, the western half of Derbyshire, Shropshire, Staffordshire, Herefordshire, and Gloucestershire west of the Severn" (and, with a few exceptions, Cheshire; Kristensson 1986, 450). If so, and like all attempts to further specify the dialect boundaries of OE, this is a tenuous matter; the range corresponds with the Anglo-Saxon period dioceses of Hereford and Lichfield, and would be one of those instances of quite interesting continuity between OE and ME. This recalls as well attempts to link West Mercian OE (such as found in the Vespasian Psalter gloss; British Library, Cotton Vespasian A.i) with the AB-language of early ME (that of the *Ancrene Wisse* and *Katherine*-group of texts).

There is some debate, however, whether this Second Fronting involved /æ/ to /ɛ/ or /æ/ to /e/ and whether /ɛ/ was an allophone of /æ/ or a new phoneme (/ɛ/) in late OE and early ME (Jack 1990 thought it did exist as a separate sound that arose during the OE period). Richard Hogg in the first volume of his *A Grammar of Old English* offered a more detailed and cautious explanation of and chronology for the changes: the Second Fronting seemed to occur in all sound environments except for when velarized *l* [ɫ] followed (that is, the 'dark' or 'back' *l* in MdE *full* or *elk*; Hogg 1992, at 135–136; §5.87); whether it is an early or later change in OE is a matter of debate – as is the relative chronology of this fronting of /ɑ/ to /æ/ and the raising of /æ/ to /e/ in West Mercian texts (many of which are glosses, though there is also a *Life of St. Chad*; Vleeskruyer 1953, and now Donnelly 2022). A more recent account by Donka Minkova (Minkova 2014) accepts that there is a phoneme /ɛ/ in OE and that while OE [æ:] "appears to have been raised a notch to [ɛ:] in most dialects" (Minkova 2014, 201, §7.3.2), with relevance to short OE [ɛ], ME [ɛ:] may 'in open syllables' come from the tensing of OE [ɛ]: OE *stelan* 'to steal' with [ɛ] develops into ME *stēle(n)* with [ɛ:] (Minkova 2014, 201–202). Forms such as *feder* (compare West Saxon *fæder*, 'father') and *fet* (for *fæt* 'vessel, cup' = MdE *vat*) are found in the interlinear gloss to the Vespasian Psalter, which presents its own difficulties: the manuscript was written ca. 825–850 at Canterbury (where the Kentish dialect of OE was predominant) but the glosses that were added up to a century later exhibit Mercian features – that is, the dialect of OE spoken in the Midlands, in the Kingdom of Mercia, which with Northumbrian formed the set of Anglian dialects of Old English (the Vespasian Psalter gloss also exhibits the effect of the Second Fronting). This has led to the suggestion that the scribe at Canterbury may have hailed from Mercia, or that the gloss is a copy made at Canterbury by a Kentish scribe from a Mercian original of some monastic center in the Kingdom of Mercia (Ball 1970, 464–465; see also the introduction to Pulsiano 2001).

Broader questions arise of how to determine the dialect of a text that is not an autograph (i.e., in the author's own hand), especially as there are more examples than the Vespasian Psalter that point to texts recorded in manuscripts in which there is an admixture of dialectal features, which suggests a text that has gone through stages of copying in which author or compiler spoke a dialect different than that of the copyist(s) – and there are a good many texts, glossaries and glossed texts such as Psalters – that involve a number of hands: main scribe, contemporary or later correctors, glossators. At any rate, there is the natural desire to draw more lines on a dialect map, to further subdivide the large regions so far determined for Old and Middle English, and it may be that the dialect region of the West Midlands may be divided on the basis of the *wæl(l)* group of words. Then again, some boundaries on the dialect map seem to work rather well; Kristensson's Northern Counties survey (Kristensson 1967) found a fairly solid county correspondence in place-name second element forms in *-cester* [sɛstər]/-cestre/-chester and related variants (which are found in Northumberland and Durham) and those in *-caster*/*-castre* (found in Cumberland, Westmorland, Lancashire, and Lincolnshire), which he found to be another line of evidence "that the Mercian area extended as far as the Ribble" (246 and Map 32).

There are several salutary reminders for early dialectology in this work: (1) Everything is local, that the 'big picture' always consists of quite local data points. This can be seen in contemporary urban dialectology, where one must continue to ask for the most local identifier of a speech community – a neighborhood of a city, a section of a neighborhood, even a street that may serve as a dividing line between smaller speech communities or enclaves (ethnic, racial, religious). (2) People: a speech community consists of people, and people are not just users of a language but have forms of association and markers of identity that are extralinguistic (though language nearly always in some way gives expression to those other identifiers). (3) Geography: human beings live in a physical environment, and this has shaped settlement patterns and historical events. As seen in Chapter 3, the Germanic tribes that invaded Celtic Britain often proceeded in ways that made sense on the ground (such as bypassing some of the Celtic *oppida* [hill-forts] and taking valleys); we still do not understand what happened to the original tribes, and their rate of survival and numbers have perhaps been underestimated. Early transport was heavily dependent on sea and navigable rivers; an island nation is subject to different settlement patterns than one that has a limited littoral or is landlocked. Occupation, trade, arable land, and natural resources also shaped human settlement patterns. Some geographic barriers could seem insurmountable and became natural boundaries linguistically; others, such as the Ribble in Kristensson's 1967 study, were not so much a natural barrier as customary or administrative. (4) Data: dialect atlases, maps with their isoglosses, and electronic corpora can be too neat, and miss the nature of language as a complex system (referring here to 'complex system' ideas in Kretzschmar 2015 and Burkette and Kretzschmar 2018); this is certainly the case with the early ME period, with the complex legacy of Old English dialects, the continuing role of Latin as a liturgical and ecclesiastical and civil administrative language, the Scandinavian legacy, and the varieties of French in use in England 1066–1350.

The relatively limited scope of the data in Kristensson's studies – the taxation records of the Lay Subsidy Rolls – nonetheless produced a wealth of returns, much of which is still being worked out with regard to Middle English dialects of the survey period 1290–1350. How much more complex is the data of the LAEME project: the early Middle English sections of the Helsinki Corpus of English Texts consist of 113,010 words (Period I, 1150–1250) and 97,480 words (Period II, 1250–1350, while LAEME, covering the period 1150–1325, consists of over 600,000 words (the Helsinki Corpus for all periods currently stands at over 1.5 million forms).

The North is different, and seemingly always has been. Some reasons for this have been seen in chapters 3–4, the Celtic-Anglian interaction zone among them and, after 793, Scandinavian influence from the waves of Viking settlements. Yet in the ME period, "[t]here is a large corpus of literary materials which, though strongly northern and richly dialectal in character, has thus far proved impossible to localise," as "the Middle English of the North admitted much less internal variation than did the Middle English of comparably large areas of the Midlands and the south"; this may be due to some as yet undetermined extent upon the Viking settlements' influence upon the Anglian OE dialects of the region and "the discontinuous character of settlement, whether English or Scandinavian in origin, over those extensive regions where barren uplands are variously dissected by habitable dales" (LALME 1986, IV:x). Lurking in there somewhere is another influence; mention of Cumberland, Westmorland, Lancashire, and the Ribble brings to mind that until the 12th-century Cumbric, a Brythonic Celtic language, was spoken in the area. Most of Scotland still spoke Scots Gaelic in the Early Middle English period. And then there was the Auld Alliance, formed in 1295 by the Council of Twelve that had replaced John Balliol ('Toom Tabard' he was called, 'empty coat') after he had been deposed, and was ratified at Dunfermline on 23 February 1296, which formalized a mutual defense pact between Scotland and France that likely had already existed (Bonner 1999). Edward I would invade in 1296 and inflicted a defeat on the Scots on 27 April 1296 at the Battle of Dunbar. Edward had just concluded a 22-year campaign of conquest in Wales, bringing in English settlers who often lived separated from the Welsh. Trouble was just beginning with the Scots, and names such as William Wallace (ca. 1270–1305) and Robert the Bruce (1274–1329) would loom large in the next few decades; the name Wallace is the Scots form, deriving from Anglo-Norman *le Waleis* 'the Welsh,' and apparently refers not to Strathclyde Britons but was "brought from the Welsh March by a family of tenants of the Stewarts in the 12th century" (Hanks et al. 2016, 2823). Robert le Brus's ancestors came from Normandy, from Brix commune, in Manche; early bearers of the name make clear its place-name origin: Robert de Bruis (1086, listed as of Yorkshire in the Domesday Book); another Robert de Bruis of Lincolnshire listed in the Templars Records (1185); and the earliest bearer of the name from Scotland, Robert de

Brus 1175–1178 in the Glasgow Register (the *Registrum episcopatus Glasguensis*, the register of the diocese of Glasgow; Hanks et al. 2016, 361). It was Edward I who removed the Stone of Scone to Westminster and commissioned the coronation chair beneath the seat of which the stone has been placed for subsequent coronations; minus the various twists and turns to the Stone of Destiny (Stone of Scone) story, it was returned to Edinburgh Castle in 1996 and most recently made the trip to Westminster for the Coronation of Charles III and Camilla 6 May 2023. More than dialectal boundaries were to be complicated in the dawning 14th century.

5.9 THE DIALECT PICTURE FROM 1300

A carol or dance song preserved among other songs on a parchment leaf bound into a manuscript now at Oxford (Bodleian Library, MS Rawlinson D.913) has the *incipit* 'Icham of Irlaunde,' by which the poem has since been known. The songs in this part of this manuscript miscellany (sometimes called the 'Rawlinson lyrics') were written in the early to mid-14th century in the south of England. The 'Icham of Irlaunde' etc., apparently was the refrain, while a (female) soloist sang the stanza, and it has been speculated that this is both a dancing song and the first mention in English of Irish dance.

Icham of Irlaunde
Ant of the holy londe
Of Irlande.

Gode sire, pray ich þe
For of saynte charité
Come ant daunce wyt me
In Irlaunde.

1] *Icham* = *Ich* + *am*. *Ich*: First-person singular personal pronoun, nominative case (from Old English *iċ*); variant spellings/forms in the ME period: *ic*, *ik*, *ih*, *ihc*, and reduced form *i*, which survives today; compare Modern German *Ich*, Icelandic *ég*, etc. *Am*: first-person singular present indicative of the verb 'to be,' for which there are a good many variant (and at times competing) forms throughout Middle English.

The form is < infinitive form *bēn*, *bee(n)* (uncontracted – though also an orthographical variant), *bie(n)*, *beo(n)*, *bī(n)*, *benne*. The forms of the Middle English verb 'to be' were in some flux throughout the period, and nearly every text edition of early to late ME gives information on the particular forms in the verb's paradigm for the text:

1st singular present indicative: *am*, *œm*, *em*, *bē*, *beo*, *eom*, *es*, *is*
2nd singular: *art*, *œrt*, *ar(e)*, *bę̄th*, *beoth*, *beost*, *bist*, *biest*, *hart*, *hert*, and others, as well as the V + enclitic PRON forms *artow* (with *-ow* for *-ou* [u]; 'art thou') and *hertou*; the *h-* forms *hart*, *hert*, etc. show aspiration: the 'silencing' (Jordan 1974, 178) of [h] was already underway in the third-person singular neuter personal pronoun *hit* ('it') in later OE but there was some volatility, especially in the north, as to

spellings with or without <h>. See LAEME map 00079406 on these forms with *h-*; the occurrences are mainly in the North, West Midlands, and Wiltshire. Maps 0079401–0079407 in LAEME plot the dialectal forms of (singular) 'are.' In LALME see dot maps 118–130 (Volume I) for the various *ar/er/be/beth* forms and the item 17 ('are') maps in Volume II (81–86).

3rd singular: *is, es, bith*

plural (all numbers): *āre(n), ern, bēth, beoth, buth, bueth, sinden, sonden* (and others; MED, s.v. *bēn*)

Irlaunde: one of the names of Ireland/Éire, found in this lyric in two spellings (such orthographic variation is common in pre-modern English texts); the form *Irlaunde* in the first and last lines (but *Irlande* line 3) derives from OE *Īra-lond* ('land of the Ir-ish,' the *Īra* deriving from Old Irish *Ériu*, a mother-sovereignty goddess, whence the modern nation-state name *Éire*); *-launde* is a variant of ME *lond* (and a realization of [ɔ]), though see *daunce* below

2] *Ant* = 'and,' from Old English *ond*; here the final dental consonant has been devoiced; *londe*: preserves what was originally an inflectional *-e* (the case here is genitive)

5] *charité*: ultimately from Latin *caritas* ('affection, Christian love'), the form in this lyric was borrowed directly from Old French *charité*

6] *daunce*: from Old French *danser; daunce/daunse* is a borrowing from French but not with the *-an-* of Île de Paris/Central French but Anglo-Norman variant *-aun-* (this is found also with other A-N borrowings such as *gaunt, haunt, laundry*; Minkova 2014, 241); *wyt*: from Old English *wið*, the ME form *wiþ* has undergone a change in the final consonant from fricative to stop (still a common change in Modern English).

This poem, or carol, from the first leaf of the Rawlinson D.913 manuscript follows two Old French lyrics, one of which, "chanson de mal mariée" ("Song of Her Badly Married"), may be a 'chanson à danser' ("song for dance," one meant to be performed with a dance; Hirsh 2014, 104–111); before the French verse, the leaf begins with a Middle English lyric or carol in a Southern dialect (Southwestern, but also with some Southeastern features; Heuser 1918, 178–179):

> Of euerykune tre,
> of euerykune tre,
> þe haweþorne blowet suotes,
> of euerykune tre.

> ["Of every kind of tree, / of every kind of tree, / the hawthorn blooms the sweetest, / of every kind of tree."]

Evidently, this is the burden (refrain, chorus) of the carol (Robbins 1942); interestingly, the next stanza repeats *My lemmon sse ssal boe* ("My darling she shall be"), which is also replete with Southern forms, the *sse(o)* form of *she* localized to Gloucestershire (LALME, Vol. II, 10). The manuscript context of 'Icham of Irlaunde' raises the question of composition; the leaf has been added to a manuscript with contents ranging from the 14th to 16th centuries; dialectally, the Middle English lyrics on the leaf show strong Southern affiliations, though with some Northern and Southeastern (i.e., late Kentish) forms. But perhaps the strongest affiliation is with Southwestern England, an area from which a number of settlers to Norman Ireland hailed. In an important study that has not received enough follow-up investigation, "Prolegomena to a Study of Mediæval Anglo-Irish" (McIntosh and Samuels 1968), LALME editors Angus McIntosh and M.L. Samuels outlined the texts and manuscripts written in or affiliated with Ireland in the Middle English to Early Modern English period (some 45 items, ca. 1365–1527; McIntosh and Samuels 1968, 1–4). In examining the language of the documents, they tried to determine what features seemed to belong to authors originally from England and which genuinely belong to a local Anglo-Irish dialect (especially in the Dublin records), that is, the beginnings of Hiberno- or Irish English. Among the dialectal forms they found were:

ham ('them') and *har* ('their), which appeared later as *tham*, *thar* (which call to mind later Scots, Ulster Irish, and Appalachian and Ozark American English dialects)
streinþ 'strength'
hit, *hyt* ('it,' with *h-* forms predominant)
sill, *syll(e)* 'sell' with vowel raising
woddis 'woods,' *commyng* 'coming' and other geminates
i-/y- preverbal retention in past participles
(McIntosh and Samuels 1968, 4–5)

Indeed, McIntosh and Samuels note that the Southwestern dialect found in the Rawlinson D.913 carols shares similarities with developments in early Anglo-Irish. Might 'Icham of Irlaunde' be one of the first verses in Anglo-Irish?

Ireland under the Normans. One particular area of toponymic, dialectal, and language contact data still largely untouched is that from Norman Ireland and Hiberno-(Middle) English. One small sample of place-names and place-name elements that would undergo anglicization – and enter the English language – as English spread through continuing conquests in Ireland may be found in the *Triallam timcheall na Fodhla* ("Let us journey around Ireland") of John O'Dugan (d. 1371, Roscommon; Carney 1943); Seaán Mór Ó Dubhagáin was of the O'Dugans who had been traditional historians to the O'Kellys (Ua Ceallaigh) of Ui Máine (a kingdom of southern central Connachta/Connaught). O'Dugan's topographical poem of 916 lines (likely incomplete as it devotes fewer lines to Leinster), is a valuable source of tribal and place-names from medieval Ireland. Among the place-name elements recorded that remain productive in Irish toponymy:

baile 'town, village; townland'
normally appears in anglicized place-names as *Bally-*
carraig 'rock':
Carraig-na-Siúire (Carrick-on-Suir [sʊər]; Co. South Tipperary); Carrick-on-Shannon (Co. Leitrim) is actually from *Caradh-Droma-Rúisc* ('weir of marsh ridge')

crích 'boundary, territory; boundary furrow; limit; end' (NG *críoch*) [kri:χ]

Crích na gCédach: the territory of the Cédach sept of Leinster, ultimately said to be descended from AD 2nd-century king Cathaoir Mór

Crích *Conaille* (Co. Tipperary); *críoch* of Conaill (Connel)

Críoch Leachta (Anglicized *Creelaghta*; Co. Longford ('boundary monument')

lios 'rampart,' 'a small circumvallation or ring-fort; a fairy-fort, rath or liss' (Dinneen). Dinneen notes further that: "an ancient Irish steading (dún) might consist of a walled enclosure (urlann) followed by a circular palisaded earthwork (ráċh), the last of which enclosed the lios in which stood the buildings" (s.v. lios).

Lismore (Co. Waterford) ('great/big ringfort')

sliabh 'mountain'

Sliabh Guaire > Slieve Gorey (Co. Cavan) ('mountain of Guaire,' a king of Connachta; in the medieval Irish annalistic tradition, the mountain was the site of a disappearing lake)

To which may be added: *achadh* 'field, plain' > *Agha-*; *áth* 'ford' > *Ath-*; *cathair* 'city' > *Caher-*; *ceathramhadh/ceathramha* 'quarter (of a townland)' > *Carrow-/-carrow*; *clochan/cloghan* 'row of stepping stones at ford of a river' > *Clogh-*; *cluain* 'meadow' > *Cloon-/Clon-*; *cúl* 'back; corner' > *Cool-*; *dair* 'oak,' *doire* 'oak wood/grove' > *Derry-*; *dún* 'fort' (Downpatrick: *dún* + *Pádraig*); *eanach/eanagh* 'watery place, marsh' > *Anna-*; *magh* 'plain' > *-moy/Moy-*; *sean* 'old' > *Shan-*; *tulach* 'small hill, hillock' > *Tulach-/Tullagh-*; e.g., Tullymore (*tulach* + *mór*).

McIntosh and Samuels noted the similarity between the Southwestern pronoun form *ȝeo* 'she' to *ȝho* as found in the Hiberno-Middle English Kildare lyrics in British Library, MS Harley 913 (Turville-Petre 2015); this dialectal variant of the ME 'she' pronoun we saw at the outset of the chapter as it involves one of the cardinal morphological developments of Middle English (Northern forms such as *schō* and Orm's *ȝhō*; Ringe 2021, 74–75). The small-format (essentially *vade mecum* or pocket Gospel-book sized) manuscript dates to ca 1330 and is localized to a Franciscan establishment at either Kildare (by 1210 the Norman 'Liberty of Kildare') or Waterford; it contains 16 poems in what could variously be called medieval Anglo-Irish, early Anglo-Irish or Hiberno-English, or a Leinster dialect of Middle English. Most famous of the poems in the Kildare manuscript is the verse satire "The Land of Cokaygne"; though the 'Cokaygne' of the poem is a recurrent folkloric 'land of plenty,' this ME version is a rather wild ecclesiastical satire: far less sober than Langland's *Piers Plowman*, there is a level of slapstick humor and unbridledness that is almost Swiftian (who was with his own satirical output following an Anglo-Irish tradition).

Fur in see bi west Spayngne
Is a land ihote Cokaygne.
Ther nis lond vnder heuen riche
Of wel, of godnis hit iliche.
Thoȝ paradis be miri and briȝt,
Cokaygn is of fairir siȝt (ll. 1–6).

["Far in the sea west by Spain / is a land a-called Cokaygne. / There is no land under heaven-kingdom / Of soundness, of goodness unto it alike. / Though Paradise be merry and bright, / Cokaygne is of fairer sight."]

Here at the abbey in Cokaygne, roasted geese all dressed with plenty of garlic fly off the spit to the abbey and cry out *Gees al hote, al hote!* (ll. 102–104), while larks well-seasoned with cloves and cinnamon fly into the monks' mouths. The monks say their Masses by windows that turn from glass to crystal to give them more light, and back to glass when done. The monks then play, taking to the air by their sleeves and hoods until their abbot, seeing they do not answer his call, resorts to a stratagem that would offend postmodern sensibilities but involves a pivotal use of ME *toute/towte* 'buttocks' (though in this context the colloquial 'butt cheeks' would be more in line with the satire).

The overly literal translation above is very nearly unnecessary; many of the changes that mark this period in the history of the English language, 1100–1400 or so, have made the jangling satirical verse familiar to us in the way that the more colloquial, cruder Elizabethan 'low' comedies are. The link of course is there, and perhaps always had been in English. The anonymous friar, or lay brother perhaps, whose wild – and crude – imagination came up with this satirical verse ca. 1330 evinces a number of features of an Irish dialect of Southern Middle English: retention of the *i-* preverbal (*ihote, iseeth*), raising of /e/ to /i/ (*godnis*), 3rd singular and plural verb inflection in *-eth*. The biting satire of lax monastic discipline is part and parcel of the times, and looks forward to the next two centuries of calls for reform and the Reformation: that is not quite here yet, as Chaucer's *Canterbury Tales* Host Harry Bailly teases the Parson *I smelle a Lollere in the wind* (II.1173): Lollards and Lollardy, *lollard* a loan perhaps from Dutch, for the itinerant preachers and proto-Protestants. In "'The Land of Cokaygne," the anonymous poet aims low, and accesses a level of the vocabulary seldom seen in OE, which may be a case of a greater abundance of data, and the better survival rate of ME verse. Or perhaps the language indicates a change in the sense of humor, and the insane vision of our satirist is meant to shock as a corrective. The low frequency of *towte/toute*, 'buttocks' – the MED lists 14 occurrences of the word for the entire period – may very well indicate a sort of 14th-century 'street language.' Inappropriate in the higher verse forms, but of use here in poking fun not just at the monasteries and orders, but at the verse-form and language itself, the dream-vision genre, and perhaps also the Irish *immrama* (voyage, especially Otherworld voyage) tradition. Perhaps, the contact situation here in Kildare or Waterford is not just dialectal, but literary, and we have evidence of the emergence of Hiberno-English and the 'low' register of Middle English.

5.10 CHAUCER AND THE ENGLISH LANGUAGE

Geoffrey Chaucer (ca. 1343–1400) is a figure of such importance to the history of the English language, and to the writing of the history of the language, that few other poets since – perhaps Shakespeare only – receive such acclaim in the sort of cottage industry (especially in book subtitles) that has grown up around the 'making of English' (on this and other critical and mythico-critical concerns see Cannon 1998, 179–220). It is not without some *felicitee* (one of the many, many French loans in the Chaucerian vocabulary) that one might say there is something to the myth after all. There had of course been poets before Chaucer, many fine and great, but it is Chaucer, Gower, and Lydgate whom Scottish poet William Dunbar (ca. 1457–ca. 1530) names first among the *makar(i)s* ('makers; bards, poets') in his ca. 1508 'Lament for the Makaris' (*noble Chaucer, of makaris flour* ['the flower of makers']). Dunbar and Scottish Chaucerians such as Robert Henryson belong to the next chapter, as does Dunbar's own language: is it Middle Scots or early Modern Scots? (Kopaczyk 2014). But Chaucer arrives on the literary, and linguistic, scene in the second half of the 14th century and changes nearly everything, not so much in terms of phonology, morphology, or syntax, as these had already undergone many of the major changes of what is called Middle English, but as a poet and 'makar' of poetic language. Chaucer's mastery was one of vocabulary to be sure (see the useful 'Chaucer's Words' in Cannon 1998, 226–416, and Davis et al. 1981), but equally so of voice. Like Shakespeare, he had an ear for dialogue and dialect, from boorish to elite, and one gets a picture of London in language in both poets. Chaucer of course was not the dramatist, genre-wise, but much of his poetry involves a dramatic architecture of character and what those characters say to each other, to themselves, and to his audience (like Langland, Chaucer made great use of direct discourse). In comparison to *The Owl and the Nightingale* discussed earlier (5.1), Chaucer's diction is replete with French loans; indeed his vocabulary is *saffroned* with French words – *saffron* is a loan from medieval Arabic that entered Middle English from Old French *safran*; Chaucer was the first to use the word as a verb (Chaucer, like Shakespeare after him, was fond of new coinages by conversion, or zero-affixation – e.g., here, *saffron* > *to saffron*), placing it in the mouth of his wily Pardoner: *And in Latyn I speke a wordes fewe, / To saffron with my predicacioun* (VI. 344–345).

One example of the interplay of languages, and of employing and interchanging vocabulary from both the native stock of English and the newer French loans, is the brilliant satirical tale Chaucer gave to the Nun's Priest in the *Canterbury Tales*. The Monk's preceding tale of the 'fall of princes,' of those of 'high degree' who fall low (*I wol biwaille in manere of tragedie / The harm of hem that stoode in heigh degree*; Benson 1987, VII.1991–1992) is interrupted by the Knight: *Heere stynteth the Knyght the Monk of his tale* ("Here stops the Knight the Monk of his tale," with the interesting syntactic pattern VSOO). And this is likely as the Monk's relentless repetitive theme of those on high brought down low, usually of their own accord, of figures from the Bible and classical antiquity through to more recent medieval kings who fall crashing down, comes a little too uncomfortably close to the Knight's own station and class. The Monk feels slighted enough by the Knight's request for a lighter tale to pass off the rest of his turn, which goes to a fellow cleric, about whom we know little from Chaucer's Prologue to the *Tales*. But the Nun's Priest's Tale is a *tour de force*, and it continues on the Monk's tale while satirizing it, clothing a *tragedie* (later averted just in time) in the fabliau tradition. The source of the tale is ultimately Marie de France's *Del cok e del gupil* ('The cock and the fox'); French-born, as her *nom de plume* suggests, Marie (d. 1215 in Shaftesbury) may be counted among those English writers who composed mainly in French (standard French and Anglo-Norman; she composed also in Latin, and was proficient in English and perhaps also Breton, in which many of the originals of the fabliaux tradition circulated (the 'Breton *lais*'). The principals of this satirical fable, which is also a brilliant allegorical tale, are Chauntecleer, 'sing-clear,' from the *Roman de Renart* and his *dame* Pertelote, 'confuses/mars lot (fate)' – there are other interpretations, though Chauntecleer likely plays on her name when he cites the anti-feminist proverb *Mulier est hominis confusio* 'Woman is the ruin of man,' which Chauntecleer diplomatically translates *Womman is mannes joye and al his blis* (VII. 3166). And of course the fox who steals into the farm and flatters Chauntecleer to his peril, Renart (with the obvious French pun on *renard* 'fox'), who is here called Russell. The tale's title reflects the interplay of English and French set up in the Prologue to the tale: *Heere bigynneth the Nonnes Preestes Tale of the Cok and Hen, Chauntecleer and Pertelote* (the particular barnyard animals are in English, their proper names are French). The Knight begins to express his unease at the Monk's tale in largely English form, *That ye han seyd is right ynough, ywis* ('That which you have said is right enough, indeed'), before switching to more French-laden rhyming vocabulary:

> I seye for me, it is a greet **disese**,
> Whereas men han been in greet **welthe** and **ese**,
> To heeren of hire **sodeyn** fal **allas**!
> And the **contrarie** is **joye** and greet **solas**,
> As whan a man hath been in **povre estaat**,
> And clymbeth up and wexeth **fortunat**,
> And there abideth in **prosperitee** (French forms in bold; VII.2771–2777).

The staple literary interjection *allas* is from Old French *helas*, literally 'ah, am I tired' (Medieval Latin *lassus*, 'tired, fatigued'). And the tale is shot through with linguistic interplay, courtly and clerical: the Nun's Priest is chaplain to nuns educated in Latin and French, in the latter language likely also in popular and romantic tales; the manners and bearing of cock-and-hen Chauntecleer and Pertelote mimic those of the French-speaking court Chaucer attended. Chauntecleer's disturbing (and, it turns out, prophetic) dream of a threatening creature very like a fox, and his wife Pertelote's dismissive interpretation of it (she accuses him of cowardice, attributes it to an imbalance in the humors or indigestion, and recommends a laxative), lead to a wildly satirical overview of ancient and medieval dream theory, spanning Latin *exempla* (the *exemplum* an instance, example, or exemplary literary passage) and French *ensamples*. The treachery of *daun Russell* ('master,' Latin *dominus* through Old French) is compared, hyperbolically, but also, on Chauntecleer's part, movingly, to the great betrayals of history, from Homer's Sinon onward. All this mock epic tragic machinery, with its classical and medieval allusions, its Latin and French literary ancestors, is of course cast in a barnyard. It is an Englishing of the French fabliau tradition, but also clever folk preaching of the Nun's Priest, steeped in the clerical Latin tradition. But, in the end, the moral of the story is cast in English: *Beth war*, 'beware.' In this one tale from the *Canterbury Tales*, one can see, in miniature – just as one saw tragedy in miniature in Chauntecleer's barnyard – the story of English, French, and Latin in Chaucer's day.

Chaucer's English is given some detail when Chaucer the pilgrim observes at the conclusion of the Miller's Tale that *folke hadde laughen at this nyce cas / Of Absolon and hende Nicholas / ...But it were oonly Osewold the Reve*, that is, all the company laughed at the Miller's tale of a foolish reeve but for Osewold the Reeve (I. 3855–3856, 3860). As

Osewold in his prologue prepares his return on the Miller's tale he twice uses the Northern form of the first-person pronoun: *But ik am oold; me list not pley for age* (I.3867), *And yet ik have alwey a coltes tooth* (I.3888), directly contradicting himself: he is old and cares not to engage in such play because of age...and yet he has always had a colt's tooth (the same wants and desires of his youth), which no doubt is a first salvo in rebutting what happened in the Miller's Tale with John the Reeve, Alisoun, and *hende Nicholas*. This last adjective, *hende*, derives from OE *ġehende* 'at hand, near' and Chaucer (through the Miller and his Chaucer-the-pilgrim narrator) applies it 11 times to *swiving* clerk Nicholas. ME *hende* had primary senses of 'courteous, gracious, pleasant,' 'noble, courtly, well-bred, refined, sportsmanlike' (Benson 1987 and the MED, s.v.), and it has been suggested that it may very well still carry its original OE sense (see note in Benson 1987 at I.3199). The sheer dint of repetition of *hende* by the Miller and narrator is a usual giveaway that Chaucer is having fun with words (and what Nicholas gets up to in the tale would fit the case of the OE original 'at hand'). An interesting point, semantically, is to what extent Chaucer and other speakers of Middle English were aware of the original sense of 'Saxon' words that had undergone semantic change. Someone as well-read as Chaucer, who drew on earlier alliterative romances, imitating and satirizing them, no doubt had an even sharper grasp of 'antique-y' vocabulary from earlier in the language. The third instance of Northern *ik* by Chaucer is not so immediately discernible to the modern reader:

> 'So theek,' quod he [Osewold], 'ful wel koude I thee quite
> With bleryng of a proud milleres ye...' (I. 3864–3865)

The form *theek* is a contracted form of the verb *thēn* ('thrive, prosper') with enclitic Northern pronoun form *ik*. It begins the sequence *theek* (3864), *ik am* (3867), *ik have* (3888) that fairly thunders home Oswald the Reeve's 'Northern-ness'[15] and double-quits the Miller by aligning himself with his two *swiving* Northern scholars – as the present participle of *swīven* the form only occurs once; *swīven*, 'to engage in intercourse' (though most its contexts would suggest its force is 'fornicate') is actually a rare word in ME, as it is mostly associated with Chaucer. Of the 15 instances of the verb recorded by the MED, 8 are from Chaucer's works – all 8 from the *Canterbury Tales*. Its other occurrences are from secular verse, but like *swinken* (usually meaning 'to work, labor') in the sense of 'copulate' (two out of three occurrences in the MED are from the *Canterbury Tales*) the 'swiving' and 'swinking' in Chaucer may, because so humorously memorable, actually give a false impression of the word's frequency. Or, the rare use in the *Canterbury Tales* and secular verse may give some indication of its force, not necessarily vulgar, but perhaps more roughly colloquial than would normally appear in medieval verse. It was used often enough by Chaucer that Alexander Pope, in 'Chaucer,' the first of his *Imitations of*

[15] See Section 5.4; Tim William Machan had questioned "why did Chaucer, apparently for the first time in English literature, use extended writing in dialect in this *Tale* for both the narrator and some of its characters, and why did he use it here alone?" (Machan 2003, 117). Machan reads Chaucer's use of dialect here sociolinguistically, perhaps so that the Reeve might "dissociate himself from the other pilgrims" (Machan 2003, 125); another possible answer was mentioned above that Chaucer was also setting up a Northerner's speech for ridicule by a London audience – a first instance, perhaps, at least in English literature, of such a linguistic bias against 'the North.'

English Poets (first printed in 1727, but dating to ca. 1713–1718), could write "WOMEN ben full of Ragerie, / Yet swinken not sans secresie" (Ault and Butt 1954, 41–42). These forms in Chaucer's Middle English are still rather close to the OE: *thēn/thene/thee(n)* are from OE *þēon*, 'thrive, prosper, flourish; grow, increase, ripen' (CHM, s.v. *ðēon*), *ythe/ithēn/ithe/ithi/ʒeðeon* are from OE *ġeþēon*; there is the ME collocation *bet ithoʒen* 'better off' (*ithoʒen* from OE *ġeþogen*).

Chaucer's profound influence on the English language lay not simply in his essential promotion of English as a vital (and soon predominant) literary language but in a literary legacy that grew over the following two centuries. His imitators, in style and meter (the 'rime royale' stanza of seven lines ABABBCC), and humor, span the late Middle English period to the Early Modern English and Scots periods, that is, from 'the monke of Bury' (John Lydgate of the Benedictine house at Bury St Edmunds) to 'Scottish Chaucerians' such as Robert Henryson (ca. 1420–ca. 1506) and William Dunbar (ca. 1457–ca. 1530).

A collection of 247 letters from 1472–1488 from the Cely (Sely) family of staplers (wool wholesalers) housed in the Public Record Office, London (now part of the National Archives, Kew), may, as well as any documents of the later 15th century, demonstrate the shift that century from late Middle to Early Modern English. Richard Sely the elder, his sons Robert, Richard the younger, and George, and the younger Richard's godfather William Maryon, were London staplers involved in the cross-channel trade (a number of their letters were sent from Calais and Bruges). The letters are of the formally courteous style one thinks of with Early Modern English, though tempered with touches of the personal and, of course, the practical. Most noteworthy in the language of the letters is the evolving orthography of 15th-century English, the 'business' or commercial loanwords from Latin and occasionally from Flemish and Middle Dutch (*gruff*, *inship* 'embark,' *wrack*; Hanham 1975, xxii). One sees in the language of the letters a form of English between two worlds, medieval and Early Modern:

> I grete the wyll, and I haue resayuyd a letter from the, wryte at Caleys the xxiiij day of Jun, the weche I haue wyll understand, that ye [haue] solde youre fellys the sopesans, for the weche I am wyll plesyd....
>
> [I greet thee well, and I have received a letter from thee, written at Calais the 23rd day of June, the which I have well understood, that you have sold the wool sheepskins the substance [perhaps, 'the greater part of which'; Hanham 1975, 250], for which I am well pleased....]
>
> [Richard Cely the elder at London to Robert Cely at Calais, 5 July 1474; Hanham 1975, 3]
>
> I wos at Auvelay, and I departyd from London on Estryn Ewyn, and I cowd not get frome my Loord of Sent Jonys not paste iij days togyddyr syn Estyr Ewe. iij days afor the wrytyng of thys I departyd from my Loord, and come to se my father and my mother, and the morow after thys I pwrpos be grasse of God to goo ageyn. Syr, our father and mother ys in good heyll and myrry in Essex, thankyd be Good....

[I was at Aveley [Essex], and I departed from London on Easter Eve, and I could not get from my Lord of St. John [Sir John Weston, Prior of the Knights of St. John of Jerusalem] not past three days together since Easter Eve. Three days before the writing of this I departed from my Lord, and came to see my father and my mother, and the next day after this I purpose by the grace of God to go again. Sir, our father and mother are in good health and merry in Essex, thanked be God....]

[Richard Cely the younger in Essex to George Cely at Calais, 26 May 1479; Hanham 1975, 51]

The Cely letters are a treasure trove of evidence of later 15th-century English, a neglected transitional period in the language's history. There is tremendous variability in spelling, as between generations, and, quite interestingly, between Richard the younger and other family members. Richard the elder's wife Agnes was of the Andrews of Adderbury, Oxfordshire, though her family had lands also in Northamptonshire; Richard the younger seems to have been educated in the north rather than London. His maternal uncle Richard Andrew had been Dean of Newarke College, Leicester in 1450 (*Laysetter* in Richard's spelling), then Dean of York (1452; Hanham 1975; xiv–xv). Richard wrote to his brother George in 1481: "Syr, ȝe know whell that I haue bene in the Northe Contre, and ther I haue had grette scheyr [cheer] of my nowlde [old] aqweyntans" (Hanham 1975, 106). This may explain Richard's spelling *heyll* ('health; hale') as a northernism in his 1479 letter to George Cely above. Spellings in the Cely letters have the expected geminates, *harttely* (for *hertley*, 'heartly, cordially'; Hanham 1975, 106) and *worchepffull* ('worshipful'; 56), which can indicate preceding short vowels (*halfe a doson quysschyns*; 56) or be 'ornamental,' or, with vowels, indicate long vocalics. But these geminates are used with remarkable inconsistency, even within individual letters. Initial /hw/ and /wh/ can be difficult to discern in the variable spelling of the 40 correspondents in the Cely letters: *weche* for 'which' in the 1474 letter above, though one finds also in the letters the spellings *whyche*, *whyhch*, *wysche*, *qwich*. But in these letters of wool factors, staplers, and their representatives one sees distinctly Middle English forms persist: *sche* for 'she,' *Estryn Ewyn* (*Estryn* apparently a vestigial genitive singular of the OE weak fem. n-stem), *þe* for 'the,' and retention, occasionally, of the preverbal *y-*, especially in past participles (Middle English *i-*, Old English *ġe-*): *y-yeven*, 'given,' *y-deyed* and *y-beryd*, 'died' and 'buried,' *i-closed*, *y-dysscharged*, *y-served* (Hanham 1975, 6, 54–55, 223). The correspondent here is William Maryon, the godfather of the younger Richard, likely a peer of the senior Richard, a member of the Merchants of the Staple, the letters from which the forms derive dating to 1476–1484. Though George of the younger generation uses *y-clowsyd* in a letter of 1480 (in the sense of 'securely wrapped up'; Hanham 1975, 101), the use of the preverbal, though not common in the letters, is found more among correspondents of the older generation: Maryon, or William Cely, apprentice to the elder Richard and a family 'dependant.' Great changes were coming to the English language, especially those to the vowels in what is now known as the Great Vowel Shift, but medieval English lingered a little while longer, into that 'age of new Discoverie.'

REFERENCES AND BIBLIOGRAPHY

Amt, Emilie, ed. *The Latin Cartulary of Godstow Abbey*. Records of Social and Economic History, New Series 52. Oxford: The British Academy/Oxford University Press, 2014

Arngart, Olof, ed. *The Proverbs of Alfred. II: The Texts Edited with Introduction, Notes and Glossary*. Acta Regiae Societatis Humaniorum Litterarum Lundensis XXXII: II. Lund: Gleerup, 1955

Arngart, Olof, ed. *The Middle English Genesis and Exodus: Re-edited from MS. C.C.C.C. 444 with Introduction, Notes and Glossary*. Lund Studies in English 36. Lund: C.W.K. Gleerup, 1968

O.D. ed., *Of Arthour and Merlin*. Ed. O.D. Macrae-Gibson. 2 vols. EETS, O.S. 268, 279. London: Oxford University Press, 1973–1979

Ashe, Laura, "Language," in *A Handbook of Middle English Studies*, ed. Marion Turner. Oxford: Wiley-Blackwell, 2013. Pp. 379–395

Ault, Nicholas and John Butt, eds. *Alexander Pope: Minor Poems*. The Twickenham Edition VI. New Haven: Yale University Press, 1954

Bailey, Charles-James N. and Karl Maroldt, "The French Lineage of English," in *Langues en contact: Pidgins, Creoles*, ed. Jürgen Meisel. Tübinger Beiträge zur Linguistik 75. Tübingen: Gunter Narr, 1977. Pp. 21–53

Ball, C.J.E., "The Language of the Vespasian Psalter Gloss: Two caveats," *Review of English Studies* 21 (1970), 462–465

Barber, Charles. *The English Language: A Historical Introduction*. Cambridge Approaches to Linguistics. Cambridge: Cambridge University Press, 1993

Barron, W.R.J., ed. *The Arthur of the English: The Arthurian Legend in Medieval English Life and Literature*. 2nd ed. Cardiff: University of Wales Press, 2012

Bartlett, Robert. *England under the Norman and Angevin Kings, 1075–1225*. The New Oxford History of England. Oxford: Clarendon Press, 2000

Bennett, J.A.W. and G.V. Smithers, eds. *Early Middle English Verse and Prose*. Oxford: Clarendon Press, 1968

Bense, Johan Frederik. *The Anglo-Dutch Relations from the Earliest Times to the Death of William the Third, Being an Historical Introduction to a Dictionary of the Low-Dutch Element in the English vocabulary*. The Hague: Martinus Nijhoff, 1925

Bense, Johan Frederik. *A Dictionary of the Low-Dutch Element in the English Vocabulary*. The Hague: Martinus Nijhoff, 1939

Benson, Larry D., gen. ed. *The Riverside Chaucer*. 3rd ed. Boston: Houghton Mifflin, 1987

Bernstein, Meg, "A Bishop of Two Peoples," *Journal of the Society of Architectural Historians* 77 (2018), 267–284

Bergs, Alexander and Janne Skaffari, eds. *The Language of the Peterborough Chronicle*. Studies in English Medieval Language and Literature. Frankfurt am Main: Peter Lang, 2007

Bonner, Elizabeth, "Scotland's 'Auld Alliance' with France, 1295–1560," *History* 84 (1999), 5–30

Brett, Martin and David A. Woodman, eds. *The Long Twelfth-Century View of the Anglo-Saxon Past*. London: Routledge, 2016

Bromwich, Rachel, A.O.H. Jarman, and Brynley F. Roberts eds. *The Arthur of the Welsh: The Arthurian Legend in Medieval Welsh Literature*. Cardiff: University of Wales Press, 2008

Bülbring, Karl D. Ed. *The Earliest Complete English Prose Psalter*. EETS, O.S. 97. London: Kegan Paul, Trench, Trübner & Co., 1891

Burgess, Glyn S. and Karen Pratt, eds. *The Arthur of the French: The Arthurian Legend in Medieval French and Occitan Literature*. 2nd ed. Cardiff: University of Wales Press, 2009

Burkette, Allison and William A. Kretzschmar Jr. *Exploring Linguistic Science: Language Use, Complexity, and Interaction*. Cambridge: Cambridge University Press, 2018

Burnley, John David, "French and Frenches in Fourteenth-Century London," in Kastovsky, Dieter and Arthur Mettinger 2003, pp. 17–34

Brown, Carleton, ed. *English Lyrics of the XIIIth Century*. Oxford: Clarendon Press, 1932/rpt. 1965

Cable, Thomas. *The English Alliterative Tradition*. Philadelphia, PA: University of Pennsylvania Press, 1991/rpt. 2016

Cannon, Christopher. *The Making of Chaucer's English: A Study of Words*. Cambridge: Cambridge University Press, 1998

Carney, James, ed. *The Topographical Poems of Seaán Mór Ó Dubhagáin and Giolla-na-naomh Ó hUidhrín*. Dublin: Dublin Institute of Advanced Studies, 1943

Chewning, Susannah Mary, ed. *The Milieu and Context of the Wooing Group*. Religion and Culture in the Middle Ages. Cardiff: University of Wales Press, 2009

Claridge, Claudia and Birte Bös, eds. *Developments in Historical Morpho-Syntax*. Amsterdam: John Benjamins, 2019

Clark, Andrew, ed. *The English Register of Godstow Nunnery, Near Oxford, Written about 1450*. Early English Text Society, O.S. 142. London: Kegan Paul, Trench, Trübner & Co., 1911

Clark, Cecily, ed. *The Peterborough Chronicle, 1070-1154*. Oxford: Oxford University Press, 1958

The Concise Scots Dictionary, ed. Mairi Robinson. Aberdeen: Aberdeen University Press/2nd ed. London: Chambers, 1996

Concise Scots Dictionary, 2nd ed. Scottish Language Dictionaries. Edinburgh: Edinburgh University Press, 2017

Cottle, Basil. Review of Arngart 1968. *JEGP* 69.1 (1970), 163–165

Curzan, Anne. *Gender Shifts in the History of English. Studies in English Language*. Cambridge: Cambridge University Press, 2003

Dalton-Puffer, Christiane. *The French Influence on Middle English Morphology*. Topics in English Linguistics 20. Berlin: Mouton de Gruyter, 1996

Dance, Richard. *Words Derived from Old Norse in Early Middle English: Studies in the Vocabulary of the South-West Midland Texts*. Tempe, AZ: Arizona Center for Medieval and Renaissance Studies, 2003. Medieval and Renaissance Texts and Studies Volume 246

Da Rold, Orietta, Takako Kato, and Elaine Treharne. *The Production and Use of English Manuscripts 1060 to 1220*. Leicester: University of Leicester, 2017. https://www.le.ac.uk/ee/em1060to1220/

Dauzat, Albert. *Dictionnaire étymologique des noms de famille et prénoms de France*. Paris: Larousse, 1977

Davis, Norman, Douglas Gray, Patricia Ingham, and Anne Wallace-Hadrill. *A Chaucer Glossary*. Oxford: Oxford University Press, 1981

Dean, Ruth J. and Maureen B.M. Boulton. *Anglo-Norman Literature: A Guide to Texts and Manuscripts*. Anglo-Norman Text Society, Occasional Publication Series 3. London: Anglo-Norman Text Society, 1999

Denison, David, Ricardo Bermúdez-Otero, Chris McCully, and Emma Moore, eds. *Analysing Older English*. Studies in English Language. Cambridge: Cambridge University Press, 2012

D'Evelyn, Charlotte and Anna J. Mill, eds. *The South English Legendary*. 3 vols. EETS O.S. 235–236, 244. Oxford: Oxford University Press, 1956–1959/rpt. 1967–1969

Dickins, Bruce and R.M. Wilson, eds. *Early Middle English Texts*. London: Bowes and Bowes, 1951/rpt. 1965

Diensberg, Bernhard. *Untersuchungen zur phonologischen Rezeption romanischen Lehnguts im Mittel- und Frühneuenglischen: die Lehnwörter mit mittelenglisch oi/ui und ihre phonologische Rezeption*. Tübinger Beiträge zur Linguistik 268Tübingen: Gunter Narr, 1985

Dietz, Klaus. *Die Rezeption des vorkonsonantischen L in romanischen Lehnwörtern des Mittelenglischen und seine Reflexe im neuenglischen Standard*. 2 vols. Munich: Wilhelm Fink, 1968

Dobson, E.J. *English Pronunciation 1500–1700*. 2 vols. 2nd ed. Oxford: Clarendon Press, 1968

Domesday Book: A Complete Translation. Alecto Historical Editions, ed. Ann Williams and G.H. Martin. London: Penguin Books, 2005

Donnelly, Kiera. "Dating the *Life of St. Chad*: Reviewing the Evidence and Approaches". Diss. University of Sydney, 2022

Duff, E. Gordon. *A Century of the English Book Trade: Short Notices of All Printers, Stationers, Book-Binders, and Others Connected with it from the Issue of the First Dated Book in 1457 to the Incorporation of the Company of Stationers in 1557*. London: The Bibliographical Society, 1905

Dunham, William Huse, Jr., "The Chronology of Hengham's Dismissal," *The English Historical Review* 47 (1932), 88–93

Ellis, Alexander J. *The Only English Proclamation of Henry III, 18 October 1258*. London: Asher and Co., 1868

Emonds, Joseph Embley and Jan Terje Faarlund. *English: The Language of the Vikings*. Olomouc: Palacký University Press, 2014

Epstein, Robert, "'Fer in the north; I kan nat telle where': Dialect, Regionalism, and Philologism," *Studies in the Age of Chaucer* 30 (2008), 95–124

Evans, D. Simon. *A Grammar of Middle Welsh*. Dublin: Dublin Institute for Advanced Studies, 2006

Feodarium Prioratus Dunelmensis: A Survey of the Estates of The Prior and Convent of Durham Compiled in the Fifteenth Century, ed. William Greenwell. Publications of the Surtees Society, vol. LVIII. Durham: Andrews & Co., 1872

Filppula, Markku, Juhani Klemola and Heli Pitkänen, eds. *The Celtic Roots of English*. Joensuu: Joensuun Ylipopistopainu/Joensuu University Press, 2002

Fisiak, Jacek, "The voicing of initial fricatives in Middle English," *Studia Anglica Posnaniensia* 17 (1984), 3–23

Flermoen Stenbrenden, Gjertrud, "Why English is not dead: A rejoinder to Emonds and Faarlund," *Folia Linguistica Historica* 37 (2016), 239–279

Fransson, Gustav. *Middle English Surnames of Occupation, 1100–1350*. Lund Studies in English 3. Lund: C.W.K. Gleerup, 1935

Fulk, R.D., "Conditions for the voicing of Old English fricatives I: Phonology," *Interdisciplinary Journal for Germanic Linguistics and Semiotic Analysis* 6 (2001), 55–77

Fulk, R.D., "Conditions for the voicing of Old English fricatives, II: Morphology and syllable structure," *English Language and Linguistics* 6.1 (2002), 81–104

Fulk, R.D. *An Introduction to Middle English: Grammar, Texts*. Peterborough, ON: Broadview Press, 2012

Gaşiorowski, Piotr, "*Zounds!* – Middle English Voiced Fricatives Revisited," in *Mostly Medieval: In Memory of Jacek Fisiak*, ed. Hans Sauer and Piotr P. Chruszczewski. San Diego, CA: Æ Academic Publishing, 2020. Pp. 305–314

Geoffrey of Monmouth. *The History of the Kings of Britain, Geoffrey of Monmouth*, ed. Michael A. Faletra. Peterborough, ON: Broadview Editions, 2008

Görlach, Manfred, "Middle English – a Creole?," in *Linguistics Across Historical and Geographical Boundaries: In Honour of Jacek Fisiak on the Occasion of His Fiftieth Birthday*. Vol. 1: *Linguistic Theory and Historical Linguistics*. Ed. Dieter Kastovsky and Aleksander Szwedek. Trends in Historical Linguistics. Studies and Monographs. Berlin: Mouton de Gruyter, 1986. Pp. 329–344

Greimas, Algirdas Julien. *Dictionnaire de l'ancien français*. Paris: Larousse, 2001

Hahn, Thomas, ed. *Sir Gawain: Eleven Romances and Tales*. TEAMS Middle English Texts Series. Kalamazoo, MI: Medieval Institute Publications, 1995

Hanham, Alison. *The Celys and their World: An English Merchant Family of the Fifteenth Century*. Cambridge: Cambridge University Press, 2002

Hanham, Alison, ed. *The Cely Letters, 1472–1488*. Early English Text Society, O.S 273. Oxford: Oxford University Press, 1975

Hanks, Patrick, Richard Coates, and Peter McClure. *The Oxford Dictionary of Family Names in Britain and Ireland*. 4 vols. Oxford: Oxford University Press, 2016

Helsinki, Corpus. *The Helsinki Corpus of English Texts*, 2018. http://icame.uib.no/hc/

Herzman, Ronald B., Graham Drake, and Eve Salisbury, eds. *Four Romances of England: King Horn, Havelok the Dane, Bevis of Hampton, Athelston*. TEAMS. Middle English Texts Series. Kalamazoo, MI: Medieval Institute Publications, 1999

Heuser, W., "Fragmente von unbekannten Spielmannsliedern des 14. Jahrhunderts, aus MS. Rawl, D. 913," *Anglia* 30 (1918), 173–179

Hickey, Raymond, "Lenition in Irish English," in *Paper from the International Conference on Language in Ireland. Belfast Working Papers in Language and Linguistics*. Belfast: University of Ulster, 1996. Pp. 173–193

Hirsh, John C., "The Rawlinson Lyrics: Context, Memory and Performance," in *Middle English Texts in Transition: A Festschrift Dedicated to Toshiyuki Takamiya on his 70th Birthday*, ed. Simon Horobin and Linne Mooney. Manuscript Culture in the British Isles. Woodbridge: Boydell & Brewer, 2014. Pp. 104–115

Hogg, Richard M. *A Grammar of Old English. I: Phonology*. Oxford: Basil Blackwell, 1992

Honeybone, Patrick, "Lenition in English," in *The Oxford Handbook of the History of English*, ed. Terttu Nevalainen and Elizabeth Closs Traugott. Oxford: Oxford University Press, 2012. Pp. 773–787

Horobin, Simon and Jeremy Smith. *An Introduction to Middle English*. Oxford: Oxford University Press, 2002

Horstmann, Carl, ed. *The Early South-English Legendary, or Lives of Saints. I: MS. Laud, 108, in the Bodleian Library*. EETS O.S. 87. London: N. Trübner & Co., 1887

Ingham, Richard, "The Persistence of Anglo-Norman 1230-1362: A Linguistic Perspective," in Wogan-Browne, Jocelyn et al. 2009. Pp. 44–54

Isaac, G.R., "Diagnosing the symptoms of contact: some Celtic-English case histories," in *The Celtic Englishes III*, ed. Hildegard L.C. Tristram. Heidelberg: Universitätsverlag Carl Winter, 2003. Pp. 46–64

Jack, George, "Negative adverbs in Early Middle English," *English Studies* 59 (1978), 295–309

Jack, George, "The reflexes of second fronting in the AB language," *English Studies* 71.4 (1990), 289–306

James, M.R., ed. *Walter Map: De nugis curialium, Courtiers' Trifles*. Rev. by C.N.L. Brooke and R.A.B. Mynors. Oxford Medieval TextsOxford: Clarendon Press, 1983

Jespersen, Otto. *Negation in English and Other Languages*. Copenhagen: Bianco Lunos Bogtrykkeri, 1917

Johannesson, Nils-Lennart and Andrew Cooper, eds.*The Ormulum. Volume I: Text and Glossary*. EETS O.S. 360–361. Oxford: Oxford University Pres, 2023

Jordan, Richard. *Handbuch der mittelenglischen Grammatik: Lautlehre*. 3rd ed. Heidelberg: Carl Winter Universitätsverlag, 1968

Jordan, Richard. *Handbook of Middle English Grammar: Phonology*. Tr. and rev. Eugene Joseph Crook. Janua Linguarum, Series Practica, 218. The Hague: Mouton, 1974

Kastovsky, Dieter and Aleksander Szwedek, eds. *Linguistics across Historical and Geographical Boundaries*. 2 vols. 1: *Linguistic Theory and Historical Linguistics*. 2: *Descriptive, Contrastive and Applied Linguistics*. Trends in Linguistics: Studies and Monographs, 32. Berlin: Mouton de Gruyter, 1986

Kastovsky, Dieter and Arthur Mettinger, eds. *Language Contact in the History of English*, 2nd rev. ed. Studies in English Medieval Language and Literature 1. Frankfurt am Main: Peter Lang, 2003.

Kay, Christian J. and Jeremy J. Smith, eds. *Categorization in the History of English*. Amsterdam Studies in the Theory and History of Linguistic Science. Servies IV – Current Issues in Linguistic Theory, Volume 261. Amsterdam: John Benjamins, 2004

Kennedy, Ruth and Simon Meecham-Jones, eds. *Writers of the Reign of Henry II: Twelve Essays*. The New Middle Ages. New York: Palgrave Macmillan, 2006

Ker, N.R. *Facsimile of MS. Bodley 34: St, Katherine, St. Margaret, St. Juliana, Hali Meiðhad, Sawles Ward*. Early English Text Society, O.S. 247. London: Oxford University Press, 1960.

Kibler, William W. *An Introduction to Old French*. New York: The Modern Language Association of America, 1984

Kopaczyk, Joanna, "The Language of William Dunbar: Middle Scots or Early Modern Scots?" *European Journal of English Studies* 18.1 (2014), 21–41

Kretzschmar, William A., Jr. *Language and Complex Systems*. Cambridge: Cambridge University Press, 2015

Kristensson, Gillis. *A Survey of Middle English Dialects 1290–1350: The Six Northern Counties and Lincolnshire*. Lund Studies in English 35. Lund: C.W.K. Gleerup, 1967

Kristensson, Gillis, "A Middle English Dialect Boundary," in Dieter Kastovsky and Aleksander Szwedek 1986. Pp. 443–457

Kristensson, Gillis. *A Survey of Middle English Dialects 1290–1350: The West Midland Counties*. Publications of the New Society of Letters at Lund 78. Lund: Lund University Press, 1987

Kristensson, Gillis. *A Survey of Middle English Dialects 1290–1350: The East Midland Counties*. Publications of the New Society of Letters at Lund 88. Lund: Lund University Press, 1995

Kuhn, Sherman, "Old English *macian*, Its Origin and Dissemination." *Journal of English Linguistics* 19 (1986), 49–93

LAEME. Laing, Margaret. *A Linguistic Atlas of Early Middle English, 1150–1325*. Version 3.2. Edinburgh: The University of Edinburgh, 2013. http://www.lel.ed.ac.uk/ihd/laeme2/laeme2.html

Laing, Margaret, "Corpus-provoked questions about negation in early Middle English," *Language Sciences* 24 (2002), 297–321

Laing, Margaret and Keith Williamson "The Archaeology of Medieval Texts," in Kay, Christian J. and Jeremy J. Smith 2004a. Pp. 85–107

Laing, Margaret and Keith Williamson 2004b, eds. *Speaking in Our Tongues: Proceedings of a Colloquium on Medieval Dialectology and Related Disciplines* Cambridge: D.S. Brewer

LALME. McIntosh Angus, M.L. Samuels, and Michael Benskin. *A Linguistic Atlas of Late Middle English*. 4 vols. Aberdeen: Aberdeen University Press, 1986

Langland, William. *Piers Plowman: The Prologue and Passus I-VII of the B text as found in Bodleian MS. Laud 581*. Ed. J.A.W. Bennett. Clarendon Medieval and Tudor Series. Oxford: Clarendon Press, 1972/rpt. 1989

Laskaya, Anne and Eve Salisbury, eds. *The Middle English Breton Lays*. TEAMS Middle English Texts Series. Kalamazoo, MI: Medieval Institute Publications, 1995.

Lass, Roger. *The Shape of English: Structure and History*. London: J.M. Dent & Sons, 1987

Lass, Roger, "Phonology and Morphology," CHEL II, 1992, pp. 23–155

Lass, Roger, "Language Periodization and the Concept of 'Middle'" in *Placing Middle English in Context*, ed. Irma Taavitsainen, Terttu Nevalainen, Päivi Pahta, and Matti Rissanen. Topics in English Linguistics 35. Berlin: De Gruyter, 2000. Pp. 7–41

Legge, Mary Dominica. *Anglo-Norman Literature and its Background.* Oxford: Clarendon Press, 1963

Liddy, Christian D. and Richard H. Britnell, eds. *North-East England in the Later Middle Ages.* Woodbridge: The Boydell Press, 2005

Löfstedt, Leena, "Notes on the Beginnings of Law French," *Romance Philology* 68 (2014), 285–37

Lomas, Richard, "St Cuthbert and the Border, *c.* 1080–*c.* 1300," in Liddy, Christian D. and Richard H. Britnell 2005, pp. 13–28

Los, Bettelou. *The Rise of the To-Infinitive.* Oxford: Oxford University Press, 2005

Los, Bettelou. *A Historical Syntax of English.* Edinburgh Textbooks on the English Language – Advanced. Edinburgh: Edinburgh University Press, 2015.

Lusignan, Pierre, "French Language in Contact with English: Social Context and Linguistic Change (mid-13th–14th Centuries)," in Wogan-Browne, Jocelyn et al. 2009. Pp. 19–30

Macdonald, Alastair J., "John Hardyng, Northumbrian Identity and the Scots," in Liddy, Christian D. and Richard H. Britnell 2005, pp. 29–42

McGowan, Joseph, "More Glosses in Early Medieval English Manuscripts," *Notes and Queries* 243.2 (1998), 166–168

Machan, Tim William. *English in the Middle Ages.* Oxford: Oxford University Press, 2003

McIntosh, Angus and M.L. Samuels, "Prolegomena to a study of mediæval Anglo-Irish," *Medium Ævum* 37 (1968), 1–11

Malone, Kemp, "When Did Middle English Begin?", in *Curme Volume of Linguistic Studies.* Language Monographs, 7. Ed. James Taft Hatfield, Werner F. Leopold, and Andreas Johannes Friedrich Ziegelschmid. Philadelphia: Linguistic Society of America, 1930. Pp. 110–117

The Works of Sir Thomas Malory, ed. Eugène Vinaver. 3 vols. Oxford: Clarendon Press, 1967. One volume ed. with revised glossary, *Malory, Works.* Oxford: Oxford University Press, 1971

Sir Thomas Malory, Le Morte Darthur: The Original Text edited from the Winchester Manuscript and Caxton's Morte Darthur, ed. P.J.C. Field. Cambridge: D.S. Brewer, 2017/rpt. 2019

Millett, Bella, ed. *Ancrene Wisse: A Corrected Edition of the Text in Cambridge, Corpus Christi College, MS 402, with Variants from Other Manuscripts.* (Drawing on the uncompleted edition by E.J. Dobson, with a glossary and additional notes by Richard Dance). 2 vols. EETS O.S. 325–326. Oxford: Oxford University Press, 2005–2006

Minkova, Donka. *The History of Final Vowels in English: The Sound of Muting.* Topics in English Linguistics 4. Berlin: Mouton de Gruyter, 1991.

Minkova, Donka, "Phonemically contrastive fricatives in Old English?", *English Language and Linguistics* 15.1 (2011), 31–59

Minkova, Donka. *A Historical Phonology of English.* Edinburgh Textbooks on the English Language – Advanced. Edinburgh: Edinburgh University Press, 2014.

Minkova, Donka, "Preference theory and the uneven progress of degemination in Middle English," in *Linguistic Preferences*, ed. Patrizia Noel Aziz Hanna and Laura Catharine

Smith. Trends in Linguistics, Studies and Monographs 358. Berlin: De Gruyter Mouton, 2021. Pp. 265–292

Morris, Richard, *ed. The Story of Genesis and Exodus.* Early English Text Society, O.S. 7. London: Trübner & Co., 1865

Morse-Gagné, Elise E. "Viking Pronouns in England: Charting the Course of THEY, THEIR, and THEM." Diss., University of Pennsylvania, 2003

Mossé, Fernand. *A Handbook of Middle English.* Baltimore: Johns Hopkins University Press, 1968

Mustanoja, Tauno F. *A Middle English Syntax. Part I: Parts of Speech.* Mémoires de la Société Néophilologique de Helsinki, XXIII. Helsinki: Société Néophilologique, 1960

Nevalainen, Terttu. *An Introduction to Early Modern English.* Oxford: Oxford University Press, 2006

Nykiel, Jerzy, "'Thone vpon thother': On pronouns *one* and *other* with initial *th-* and *t-* in Middle English," in Claridge, Claudia and Birte Bös 2019, pp. 57–75

Ogura, Michiko, "Verbs of Motion in Laȝamon's *Brut*," in *Laȝamon: Contexts, Language, and Interpretation*, ed. Rosamund Allen, Lucy Perry, and Jane Roberts. London: King's College London, Centre for Late Amtique and Medieval Studies, 2002. Pp. 211–225

O'Neil, David, "The Middle English Creolization Hypothesis: Persistence, Implications, and Language Ideology," *Studia Anglica Posnaniensia* 54 (2019), 113–132

O'Neill, Patrick P., ed. *King Alfred's Prose Translation of the First Fifty Psalms.* Medieval Academy Books 104. Cambridge, MA: The Medieval Academy of America, 2001

Otter, Monika, "1066: The Moment of Transition in Two Narratives of the Norman Conquest," *Speculum* 74.3 (1999), 565–586

Palmatier, Robert Allen. *A Descriptive Syntax of the Ormulum.* Janua Linguarum. Series Practica 74. The Hague: Mouton, 1969

Penn-Helsinki, Corpus. *Penn-Helsinki Parsed Corpus of Middle English.* 2021. https://www.ling.upenn.edu/hist-corpora/PPCME2-RELEASE-4/index.html

Plag, Ingo. Review of Dalton-Puffer 1996. *Language* 74.2 (1998), 392–395

Poole, Austin Lane. *From Domesday Book to Magna Carta, 1087–1215.* 2nd ed. The Oxford History of England. Oxford: Clarendon Press, 1958

Pons-Sanz, Sara M. *Norse-Derived Vocabulary in Late Old English Texts.* North-Western European Language Evolution, Supplement vol. 22. Odense: University Press of Southern Denmark, 2007

Poussa, Patricia, Review of Kristensson 1995, *Neuphilologische Mitteilungen* 98 (1997), 427–430

Prestwich, Michael. *Plantagenet England, 1225–1360.* The New Oxford History of England. Oxford: Clarendon Press, 2007

Pulsiano, Philip, "A Middle English Gloss in the *Lambeth Psalter*," *ANQ: A Quarterly Journal of Short Articles, Notes and Reviews* 10.1 (1997), 2–9

Pulsiano, Phillip, "The Old English Gloss of the *Eadwine Psalter*," in Swan, Mary and Elaine Treharne 2000, pp. 166–194

Pulsiano, Phillip, ed. *Old English Glossed Psalters:* Volume I: *Psalms 1-50*. Toronto Old English Studies. Toronto: University of Toronto Press, 2001

Reaney, P.H. *The Origin of English Surnames*. London: Routledge and Kegan Paul, 1967/rpt. 1980

Ringe, Don. *A Historical Morphology of English*. Edinburgh Textbooks on the English Language – Advanced. Edinburgh: Edinburgh University Press, 2021

Ringe, Don and Ann Taylor. *The Development of Old English. A Linguistic History of English,* Volume II. *Oxford Linguistics*. Oxford: Oxford University Press, 2014

Ritt, Nikolaus, "The Spread of Scandinavian Third Person Plural Pronouns in English: Optimisation, Adaptation and Evolutionary Stability," in Kastovsky, Dieter and Arthur Mettinger 2003, pp. 279–304

Robbins, R. H., "The Burden in Carols," *Modern Language Notes* 57 (1942), 16–22

Roffe, David. *Domesday: The Inquest and the Book*. Oxford: Oxford University Press, 2000

Rollason, David, ed. Symeon of Durham. *Libellus de Exordio atque Procursu istius hoc est Dunelmensis ecclesie. Tract on the Origins and Progress of this the Church of Durham*. Oxford Medieval Texts. Oxford: Oxford University Press, 2000

Rothwell, William, "The Trial Scene in *Lanval* and the Development of the Legal Register in Anglo-Norman," *Neuphilologische Mitteilungen* 101 (2000), 17–36

Rusch, Willard James. *The Language of the East Midlands and the Development of Standard English: A Study in Diachronic Phonology*. Berkeley Insights in Linguistics and Semiotics 8. New York: Peter Lang, 1992

Russom, Geoffrey. *The Evolution of Verse Structure in Old and Middle English Poetry*. Cambridge: Cambridge University Press, 2017

Samuels, M.L., "Some applications of Middle English dialectology," *English Studies* 44 (1963), 1–6, 81–94

Schauwecker, Yela, "The origin of the medieval French legal register revisited," *Neuphilologische Mitteilungen* 118 (2017), 469–488

Schlemilch, Willy. *Beiträge zur Sprache und Orthographie spätaltenglischer Sprachdenkmäler der Übergangszeit (1000–1150)*. Halle, Max Niemeyer, 1914

Scragg, Donald G. *A history of English spelling*. Manchester: Manchester University Press, 1974/rpt. 2011

Serjeantson, Mary S. *A History of Foreign Words in English*. London: Routledge and Kegan Paul, 1961

Shepherd, Stephen H.A., ed. *Middle English Romances*. Norton Critical EditionsNew York: W.W. Norton, 1995

Smithers, G.V., ed. *Havelok*. Oxford: Clarendon Press, 1987

Smith, A.H. *The Place-Names of The East Riding of Yorkshire and York*. English Place-Name Society, Volume XIV. Cambridge: Cambridge University Press, 1970

Smith, Jeremy J. *Sound Change and the History of English*. Oxford Linguistics. Oxford: Oxford University Press, 2007

Smith, Jeremy J., "The spellings <e>, <ea> and <a> in two Wooing Group texts (MSS London, Cotton Nero A.xiv and London, Lambeth Palace 487)," in Chewning, Susannah Mary 2009, 84–95

Smyser, H.M., "The List of Norman Names in the Auchinleck MS. (Battle Abbey Roll)," in *Mediaeval Studies in Honor of Jeremiah Denis Matthias Ford*, ed. Urban T. Holmes, Jr., and Alex J. Denomy. Cambridge, MA: Harvard University Press, 1948. pp. 259–287

Sommer, Oskar, ed. *The Vulgate Version of the Arthurian Romances*. 8 vols. Washington, DC: The Carnegie Institution of Washington, 1908–1916/rpt. New York: AMS Press, 1979

Stanley, E.G., ed. *The Owl and the Nightingale*. Old and Middle English Texts. Manchester: Manchester University Press, 1972

Starnes, D.T., "Richard Taverner's *The Garden of Wisdom*, Carion's *Chronicles*, and the Cambyses Legend," *The University of Texas Studies in English* 35 (1956), 22–31

Stenton, Frank M. Anglo-Saxon England. *Oxford History of England*. 3rd ed. Oxford: Oxford University Press, 1989

Stevick, Robert, ed. *One Hundred Middle English Lyrics*. Rev ed. Urbana, IL: University of Illinois Press, 1994

Swan, Mary, "Old English Textual Activity in the Reign of Henry II," in Kennedy, Ruth and Simon Meecham-Jones 2006. Pp. 151–168

Swan, Mary and Elaine Treharne, eds *Rewriting Old English in the Twelfth Century*. CSASE 30. Cambridge: Cambridge University Press, 2000

Thompson, W. Meredith, ed. *Þe Wohunge of Ure Lauerd and other pieces*. Early English Text Society, O.S. 241. London: Oxford University Press, 1958

Thomson, R.M. *William of Malmesbury*. Rev ed. Woodbridge: The Boydell Press, 2003

Thomson, R.M., "William of Malmesbury's Diatribe against the Normans," in *The Long Twelfth-Century View of the Anglo-Saxon Past*, ed. Martin Brett and David A. Woodman. London: Routledge, 2016. pp. 113–121

Thorn, Caroline and Frank Thorn, eds. *Domesday Book 10: Cornwall*. Chichester: Phillimore, 1979

Thurneysen, Rudolf. *A Grammar of Old Irish*. Revised and enlarged ed. D.A. Binchy and Osborn Bergin. Dublin: Dublin Institute for Advanced Studies, 1975/rpt. 2017

Treharne, Elaine, "The Life of English in the Mid-Twelfth Century: Ralph D'Escures's Homily on the Virgin Mary," in Kennedy, Ruth and Simon Meecham-Jones, 2006. Pp. 169–186

Treharne, Elaine. *Living Through Conquest: The Politics of Early English, 1020–1120*. Oxford Textual Perspectives. Oxford: Oxford University Press, 2012

Tristram, Hildegard L.C., "The Politics of Language: Links between Modern Welsh and English," in *Of dyuersitie & chaunge of langage: Essays Presented to Manfred Görlach on his 65th Birthday*, ed. Katja Lenz and Ruth Möhlig. Heidelberg: Universitätsverlag Carl Winter, 2003. Pp. 257–275

Turville-Petre, Gabriel, "Thurstable," in *English and Medieval Studies: Presented to J.R.R. Tolkien on the Occasion of his Seventieth Birthday*, ed. Norman Davis and C.L. Wrenn. London: George Allen & Unwin, 1962. Pp. 241–249

Turville-Petre, Thorlac, ed. *Poems from BL MS Harley 913 'The Kildare Manuscript'*. Early English Text Society O.S. 345. Oxford: Oxford University Press, 2015

Turville-Petre, Thorlac and J.A. Burrow. *A Book of Middle English*. 4th ed. Oxford: Wiley-Blackwell, 2020

Upward, Christopher and George Davidson. *The History of English Spelling*. Oxford: Wiley-Blackwell, 2011

Vleeskruyer, Rudolf, ed. *The Life of St. Chad: an Old English Homily. Edited with Introduction, Notes, Illustrative Texts and Glossary*. Amsterdam: Noord-Holland Publishing Company, 1953

Wace. *Roman de Rou. The History of the Norman People: Wace's Roman de Rou*. Tr. Glyn Burgess. Woodbridge: The Boydell Press, 2004

Waldef: A French Romance from Medieval England. Tr. Ivana Djordjević, Nicole Clifton, and Judith Weiss. Leeds: Arc Humanities Press, 2020

Walkden, George and Donald Alasdair Morrison, "Regional Variation in Jespersen's Cycle in Early Middle English," *Studia Anglica Posnaniensia* 52 (2017), 173–201

Warner, Anthony, "English-Norse Contact, Simplification, and Sociolinguistic Typology," *Neuphilologische Mitteilungen* 118 (2017), 317–404

Warner, Rubie D.-N., ed. *Early English Homilies, from the Twelfth Century MS. Vesp. D. XIV*. Part I: *Text*. Early English Text Society, O.S. 152. London: Kegan Paul, Trench, Trübner & Co., 1917

Weiss Judith, ed. Wace. *Roman de Brut*. 2nd ed. Exeter: University of Exeter Press, 2002

Wells, John E. *A Manual of the Writings in Middle English, 1050–1400*. New Haven, CT: Connecticut Academy of Arts and Sciences, 1916. Subsequent expanded edition ed. J. Burke Severs, Albert E. Hartung et al. 11 vols. New Haven, CT: Connecticut Academy of Arts and Sciences, 1967–2005

Whitelock, Dorothy, ed. *English Historical Documents I, c. 500–1042*, 2nd ed. London: Eyre Methuen, 1979

William of Malmesbury. *Gesta Pontificum Anglorum: The History of the English Bishops*. 2 vols. Ed. and tr. Michael Winterbottom and Rodney M. Thomson. Oxford Medieval Texts. Oxford: Clarendon Press, 2007

Wogan-Browne, Jocelyn, et al., eds. *Language and Culture in Medieval Britain: The French of England c. 1100–c. 1500*. New York: York Medieval Press, 2009

Zimmer, Stefan, "A medieval linguist: Gerald de Barri," *Études celtiques* 35 (2003), 313–350

Zimmer, Stefan, "Gerald of Wales's alleged Greek *mis, tis* again," *Cambrian Medieval Celtic Studies* 50 (2005), 73–76

CHAPTER 6

Early Modern

6.1 FORMES OF SPECHE

As was the 12th century, the 15th century has been considered a pivotal transitional era in the history of the English language. Perhaps more than any other change, the 15th century marks the onset of what is known as the Great Vowel Shift (GVS); the term was first applied to the series of major changes in the long vowels of late Middle English–Early Modern English by Danish linguist Otto Jespersen in the first volume of his *A Modern Grammar of English on Historical Principles* (Jespersen 1909, I.VIII, 231–247); the exact chronology is not settled, but the diphthongization (breaking) of high vowels (/i:/ and /u:/) and raising of the long vowels reshaped the phonemic inventory space of English resulting in pronunciations we consider 'Modern.' Most simply stated, the GVS is the series of shifts in the long vowels and breaking of high vowels /i:/ and /u:/ of Middle English that produces the PDE long-vowel forms (in square brackets is the longer series of changes along the chronological scale 1400/1500/1600/PDE; after Lass 1999, 72)

bite	i > ai	[i	ei	ɛI	aɪ]
meet	e: > i:	[e:	i:	i:	i:]
meat	ɛ: > i:	[ɛ:	ɛ:	e:	↗]
mate	a: > eɪ	[a:	a:	ɛ:	eɪ]
house	u: > aʊ	[u:	ou	ɔʊ	aʊ]
boot	o: > u:	[o:	u:	u:	u:]
boat	ɔ: > əʊ	[ɔ:	ɔ:	o:	əʊ]

The classic, and perhaps neatest, graphic formulation of the GVS is Jespersen 1909 (here with [:] to mark vowel length in place of Jespersen's raised dot):

ai ← i:	u: → au
↑	↑
e:	o:
↑	↑
ɛ:	ɔ:
↑	
a:	

The common view was that the change began with the raising of /i:/ and /u:/, which, as the highest vowels in the phonemic inventory of English, broke/diphthongized as they could be raised no higher without becoming (stop) consonants: if one keeps raising the front of the tongue in articulation of the /i:/ or *ee*-sound one touches the roof of the mouth in the frontal hard palate – alveolar region and winds up saying something like *it* or *eat*. Thus the raising and breaking of /i:/ and /u:/ produced diphthongs /ai/ and /au/ (/aʊ/) that 'cleared' phonetic space for /e:/ and /o:/ to be subsequently raised (to /i:/ and /u:/), producing a 'drag-chain' effect that saw /ɛ:/ and /ɔ:/ raised to /e:/ and /o:/, and /a:/ raised to /ɛ:/. The chronology of these long-vowel shifts is generally given as ca. 1400–1750, that is, the chronological range of development from Middle English through Early Modern English (see Minkova 2014, 252–256). There are a number of caveats to the traditional model, of course, which is, inevitably, with so complex a system as human language, a little too neat. The focus has primarily been upon the output: contemporary English, namely, Standard Southern (i.e., London) British English. Some changes did not take place in some regions; for example, in the north and Scotland, the back rounded vowels /u:/ and /o:/ did not participate in the shift (in Scotland [hu:s] remained undiphthongized, compare also Dougal [du:gəl] / [du:gʌl] < Scots Gaelic *dùbh-gall* [duhgəl] / [du:əlˠ] 'dark-stranger/foreigner/non-Gaelic speaker'). For the Northern Great Vowel, Shift Smith (2007) gives the schematic:

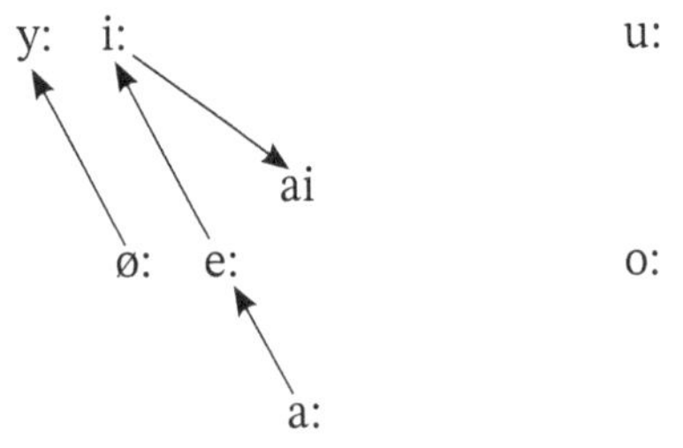

(Smith 2007, 128)

In Smith's view, the Northern GVS was actuated by the disturbance to the three long-vowel system of Scots (/i:/ and its allophone /y:/, /e/, and /ǣ:/) by the new long front vowel /ɛ:/ (Smith 2007, 149–153). The shift, or chain-shift, in Middle Scots seems also to overlap with the rise of the variety as a sort of standard, for use in day-to-day and literary registers (Smith 2007, 152). If so, it may parallel the complex of factors Smith sees as actuating the Southern GVS, as in his model:

front	a:	→	æ:, ɛ:
	ɛ:	→	e:
	e:	→	i:
	i:	→	ɪi, əɪ
back	ɔ:	→	o:
	o:	→	u:
	u:	→	ʊu, əʊ

(Smith 2007, 128)

This is still fairly close to the standard model (since Jespersen 1909) except for the realization of the breaking of high vowels /i:/ and /u:/ (with /i:/ breaking to a diphthong that seems a little closer to Cockney pronunciation of *nice*, and /u:/ with a sort of *oo-uh* or *ew-uh* realization). The shift, or in Smith's view 'shifts,' may be the result of sociolinguistic processes: (1) the rise of a standardized variety in London by the early 15th century; (2) the further decline of French – though French loans, which proliferated from Central French in the 14th and 15th centuries, may have continued to have been pronounced in accord with French norms (as seen in Chaucer), the onrush of French loans into English might be seen as the phenomenon of 'language death'; (3) standardization of spoken and written varieties seems to co-occur with the Southern GVS, and it is the London forms that are found in PDE; (4) as London in the Middle English period has grown economically through trade, especially but not limited to the wool trade – as with the Celys last chapter (Chaucer's father had been a vintner, Caxton was a member of The Mercers' Company) – new immigrant communities arrived (Flemings are mentioned a number of times in Chaucer); this growth of London had a sort of 'gravity effect' drawing people in from neighboring regions, and this would presumably have had a dialect levelling effect on the newcomers and their children as they adopted London/Southeastern forms; (5) the loss of final *-e* seems to coincide with the changes of the Southern GVS; the loss changed the pronunciation of English (increasing the number of monosyllables) and made *-e* otiose, for poetic use (*metri causa*, 'for reason of meter'), or as a marker of preceding vowel length (*mill* versus *mile*, *dot* versus *dote*); that the vowels tensed by the Middle English Open Syllable Lengthening became phonemicized, that is, distinctive, not allophonic, for the more prestigious London dialect: OE *mete* 'food, meat' [mɛtə] > [mɛ:tə], OE *nama* 'name' [nɑmə] > [na:m] (see also Minkova and Lefkowitz 2021).

The chronology of the changes has always been problematic; Karl Luick in his *Historische Grammatik der englischen Sprache* ("Historical Grammar of the English Language," 1914, 1921–1940/rpt. 1964) had posited that the mid-high/mid-close long vowels /e:/ and /o:/ had begun to raise first, pushing into the phonemic space of /i:/ and /u:/ causing them to diphthongize in a 'push-chain'; Jespersen had thought this diphthongization began first, opening up the space for the other long vowels to be raised in a 'drag-chain' (Minkova 2014, 248–260 is the most thorough recent treatment). A recent study, based upon spellings (Stenbrenden 2016), has suggested that in West and East Midlands Middle English, the raising of ME [e:] and [o:] and diphthongization of [i:] and [u:] began earlier, and simultaneously.

Stenbrenden's study of long-vowel shifts found that a number of changes were underway earlier and persisted longer: the unrounding of OE */ȳ:/* began ca. 950 and its diphthongization to MdE /aɪ/ began ca. 1250; the diphthongization of /u:/ to /aʊ/ began ca. 1250 (see Table 9.2 in Stenbrenden 2016, 316). Stenbrenden also cautions against seeing phonemes as points in the usual trapezoidal representation of the vocal space, as a phoneme such as mid-high unrounded /e:/ with its allophones occupied more phonetic space than in traditional diagrams (Stenbrenden 2016, 315–316; this is similar to the idea of 'peripherality' of phonemes as employed in the ANAE, Labov et al. 2006; see also Labov 1994, 145–154).

Among the others changes from 1450 on were a number of short vowel shifts, the lowering of /i/ to /ɪ/ (ME *sitten* > *sit*), /a/ raised to /æ/ by 1650 and then backed and tensed to /ɑ:/ later that century (only to move forward again in AmE); a split in realizations of ME /u/ produced the split between the rounded /ʊ/ in *full* and the unrounded /ʌ/ in *but* (Nevalainen 2006, 114–126). Some sign of things to come with regard to rhotacism in English can be seen in 15th-century *passell* for *parcel* and 16th-century *skasely* for *scarcely* (Nevalainen 2006, 127–127); a number of diphthongs in Middle English (and in French loans) monophthongized: /iw/ in *new* and /ew/ in *dew* merged as /ju:/ or /u:/; /æj/ in ME *day/daie* and /ɛj/, /ej/ in *þei/they* merged as /eɪ/; /au/ in *aunt* split into /ɑ:/ and /æ(:)/; /oi/ in *joy* > /ɔɪ/ and /ui/ in *boil* shifted to /əi/ (still heard dialectally; there is also Irish English /ai/ ~ /aj/ 'bile' for *boil*) then /ɔɪ/ (Minkova 2014, 267–270). Palatal /ç/ and velar /x/ disappear, though they persisted long enough into the Early Modern period to be recorded in spelling and to produce the *though*/*tough* split: in words such as *though* and *bough* <h> (/ç/, /x/) > /-Ø/, while in forms such as *tough, rough, enough* [-x] > [-f] (Minkova 2014, 112–114). The reduction of /hw-/ to /ʍ/ (the voiceless labiovelar fricative), in those dialects that maintain the *whine-wine* distinction, or /w/ does not occur in Northern dialects and Scots, for which the grapheme <qu(h), qw(h)> was developed (*quilke* for *which*, from OE *hwilc(e)*, with /k/ for /tʃ/ (Minkova 2014, 109–110). A number of other consonants are lost:

> [mb] > [b] by assimilation in *dumb, thumb, lamb*
> [ln] > [l] by assimilation; OE *elnboga* > *elbow*; OE *myln* > *mill*, but *mylne, milne* forms persisted into the early 17th century; *kiln* can be found in the forms *kill/kell* 1500–1700, though *kiln* persists (and in compounds like *lime-kiln* and *brick-kiln*)
> [nd] and other final consonant clusters underwent reduction; [ŋg] > [ŋ] > [n], [ɪŋg] > [ɪŋ] > [ɪn] can be found as early as the 14th century, and is widely known in contemporary English as the *g-dropping* phenomenon (*going* > *goin,*' though this has also been interpreted as the substitution of the alveolar nasal [n] for the velar [ŋ])
>
> (cf. Dobson 1968, II, 960–1004)

Initial consonant cluster /kn-/ is reduced to /n/ much later, in the 18th century; through the 16th and 17th centuries the pronunciation [kn] was maintained, though there may have been an 'intermediate' stage of <hn-> [xn-], as [gn-] may have gone through [χn-] (Dobson 1968, II, 976–977); with the fortunes of *knight* 1400–1700 we see a number of the changes ME to eMdE: initial consonant cluster reduction, [-xt] reduction, and GVS [iː] > [aɪ].

To transition from phonology to morphology, in Chaucer's own 'Tale of Melibee,' with which Chaucer the pilgrim entertains, in a manner of speaking, the Canterbury-bound company after his doggerel-verse 'Sir Thopas' is cut short by Host Harry Bailly, he quotes a series of old *sawes*. The Old English feminine strong noun *sagu* 'story, tradition, saying' (hence MdE *saw* as in 'old saw' or 'wise saw') had first undergone fortition (strengthening) of /ɣ/ to /g/ (i.e., from the voiced velar fricative to the velar stop, or 'hard g'); in late Old English and Middle English the /g/ underwent lenition (softening) to [w] when between back vowels: thus OE *dragan* 'to drag' > ME *drawen*, OE *sagu* > *sawe* (Minkova 2014, 103). The 'old saw' Chaucer cites here is from Seneca's *De ira* ('On Wrath'):

> Forthermoore, ye knowen wel that after the comune sawe, 'it is a woodnesse a man <for> to stryve with a strenger or a moore myghty man than he is hymself, / and for to stryve with a man of evene strengthe – that is to seyn, with as strong a man as he is – it is peril, / and for to stryve with a weyker man, it is folie' (*Canterbury Tales* VII.1480–1482).

Here one can find transitional uses of the infinitive, in the "infinitive as subject (or nominal)" (e.g., *to be called a kniȝte is faire* in *Piers Plowman*, B-text, Passus XIX.28; Mustanoja 1960, 523) and "infinitive after a copula" constructions:

> it is a woodnesse a man <for> **to stryve with a strenger or a moore myghty man than he is hymself** ["it's madness for a man to strive against a stronger or more mighty man than he himself is"; cf. Visser II.912]

This belongs to a chiastic (X-formed, syntactically criss-crossing) parallel arrangement:

> *it is a woodnesse* a man **<for> to stryve with a strenger or a moore myghty man than he is hymself,** and **for to stryve with a man of evene strengthe...** *it is peril*

This, in Chaucerian English ca. 1386–1390 (Benson 1987, 923), looks forward to the periodic sentences and balanced 'contrarieties' of Elizabethan 'golden' (i.e., Latinate, classically influenced, Ciceronian) prose style. The construction *for* + *to* + infinitive (e.g., Visser II.916.c), so common in Middle English after the early period (ca. 1300 on), would fade in frequency during the 16th century. Patterns that had been in development since Old English would gain a certain fixity, no doubt encouraged by the introduction of the printing press to England by William Caxton ca. 1476. The use of the infinitive included nearly every grammatical function and syntactic position available: as an adjunct to a noun phrase (adjectivally), *lean times* ***to come***, *ability* ***to learn***; adjunct to an adjective (in postposition), *eythe* ***to bigyle*** ('easy to beguile'), *fair* ***to behold***; as an adverbial, *Se kyng hit dide* ***for to hauen sibbe*** ('the king did it so as to have peace'; *Peterborough Chronicle*, entry for year 1127), *Now in order* ***to tell the difference****...we have manufactured* (Ian Fleming, *Casino Royale* [1953]; Visser II.926–966). The 'plain infinitive,' that is, the 'bare infinitive' without *to*, which had already been grammaticalized in this position from the preposition (Los 2005), and *to*-infinitive in Middle English seem to have been employed depending upon the auxiliary used (the plain infinitive was used with *can*, *may*, *must*, *shall*, and *will*) or the syntactic position of the finite verb and infinitive: the *to*-infinitive was used if a word or group of words was interposed, for example, *And he* ***hath levere talken*** *with a page / Than* ***to comune*** *with any gentil wight* (Chaucer, *Canterbury Tales*, "Squire's Tale," V.692–693): "he would prefer/he would rather **talk** with a page/ Than **to converse** with a gentleman").

Though perhaps not so profound as with what occurred in the Middle English period, there were other morphological and syntactic changes in the 15th and 16th centuries. The development of *do* as an auxiliary with a number of functions dates back to Old English; for instance, its use in elliptical verbal constructions (in place of repeating the main finite verb form):

> þæt he **wunode** butan worunge on Godes þeowdome þær on mynstre a, and he swa **dyde** siððan of þam dæge (Ælfric, *Lives of the Saints*, St. Maurus; Los 2015, 109).
>
> [...that he **dwell** [literally, *dwelt*] without wandering away in the service of God there in the monastery ever forth, and so he **did** henceforth from that day]

The emphatic *do* – with its 'dummy' auxiliary status – appears in the 15th century, and *do* in interrogative constructions belongs to the 16th century (Los 2015, 110).

Among other verbal changes, there is apparently an implied imperative in 2nd person forms in *-est*, for example, Christopher Marlowe, *Edward II*, *Nephue* [nephew], *I must to scotland, thou staiest here* (Visser II.719). And the further specification of *shall* as an auxiliary is seen more clearly through this period, as between what Visser called 'predictive' *I shall* and 'promissory' *I shall.*:

Predictive

Surely can we al tel that die we shal (St. Thomas More, ca. 1522)
if it please you to accept of a poore gentleman, I shall be bound by det & dutie to be yours for euer (Robert Greene, 1583)
the longer we liue, the more wee shall learne (Thomas Nashe, 1600)

Promissory

Bi god, I hard [heard] *masse ȝistirdaie...bi God, I schal heere masse to morewe* (Welsh cleric Reginald Pecock, ca. 1445)
We shall rekene to morow And shall paye also (William Caxton, 1483)
This now shall I alway kepe surely in memory (William Cunningham, 1559)

[Visser III.1, 1501]

The great influx of Romance vocabulary in the Middle English period had affected as well the lexis of English in its stress-patterning. The older native or Germanic Stress Rule (GSR), by which stress fell on the lexical root of a word, had developed in the Proto-Germanic period; in Proto-Indo-European, stress was 'free' and could fall on affixes. The Germanic innovation was the removal of stress from prefixes and suffixes, with some exceptions; we see this now in words such as *ánswer* < Old English *and-swárian*, as the prefix was stressed since it had been lexicalized – the form was seen more as a compound of two lexical elements than simply prefix + root. The many French and classical (Greek and Latin) loans followed the Romance Stress Rule (RSR; CHEL II, 82–90 is an excellent guide), though there was subsequent re-analysis of many of them according to the native system of accentuation. But in Chaucer, we can see the many French loans following the RSR: *charité, pitée, prédicácioūn*. The last Middle English form was borrowed from Latin *praedicātiō* via Anglo-Norman *predicaciun* in the sense of 'preaching, sermon.' As a Latinate loan, the stress-patterning follows the classical three-syllable set model for polysyllabic words (as do continued scientific, medical, and other loans from Greek and Latin today):

ultima (final syllable): _́ (monosyllable with long vowel or diphthong stressed)
penultima (next-to-last syllable): _́ _ (accent moves 'forward' [i.e., leftward] in the word; *fídēs*)
antepenultima (the next to next-to-last syllable): the stress rests on the penultima if it is long, or upon the antepenultima if it is short, thus *amīcus* 'friend' versus *dómĭnus* 'lord') _ _́ _ or _́ _ _

Thus, one can see the sort of cyclic stress-patterning at work in polysyllabic loans and classical derivative formations that abound in scientific, medical, literary, and other technical registers: *a-PO-si-O-pe-sis*, *bi-FUR-ca-tion*, *CON-ta-MIN-a-tion*, *ma-TUR-a-tion*). There can be of course exceptions (and mispronunciations that become standard), but the 'counting forward' from the end of a classical loan formation can aid in pronouncing an unfamiliar term. This will be of use in reading the more classically minded of the Elizabethan and Jacobean writers, with their at times ornate Latinate formations and 'ink horn' scholarly neologisms. The diplomat-scholar (and lexicographer) Thomas Elyot (ca. 1496–1546) is famous for his *The Boke named the Governour* (1531), a handbook in the medieval tradition of guides for princes that he dedicated to Henry VIII (such as medieval Augustinian canon Giles of Rome's *De regimine principum*, "On the governance of princes," ca. 1277–1280, written for Philip the Fair of France). Elyot also compiled a dictionary (*The Dictionary of syr Thomas Eliot knyght* [1538]; see Bately in Cowie 2009, I, 41–49]) and, among other works, a popular medical treatise *The Castel of helthe* (1539). The following examples are from the 1541 printing of Elyot's medical treatise by Thomas Berthelet (the "royal printer and bookbinder to Henry VIII, king of England"; Davenport 1901) with select variants from his 1539 printing:

> Galen the most excelle<n>t phisition fearyd, that in wrytynge a compendiouse doctryne for the curing of syckenes, he should lose all his laboure, for as moche as no man almoste dyd endeuoure hym selfe to the fyndynge of truthe, but that all men dyd so moche esteme ryches, posssessions, authority, and pleasures, that they supposed theym, which were studiouse in any parte of Sapyence, to be madde or distracte of theyre wittes: for as moch as they demid the chife Sapience (which is knowlege of thynges belongyng as wel to god as to man) to haue no beyng ('The Proheme' ['The Preface'], signature A.ii.).

Thinges Naturall be .vii. in number.

Elementes.	Powers.
Complexions.	Operations and
Humours.	Spirites.
Members. [Membres (1539)]	

Thynges not naturall be syxe in number.

Ayre.	Emptinesse and re=
Meate and drinke.	pletion, and
Slepe and watche.	Affections of the
Meuinge [Meuyng] and rest.	mynde (Treatise, 1R).

From the preface, Latin and French loans include *phisition* ('physician'), *compendiouse*, *doctrine*, *curing*, *laboure*, *endeuoure* ('endeavor'), *esteme*, *ryches*, *posessions*, *authority*, *pleasures*, *supposed*, *studiouse*, *Sapience*, *distracte*, *chife* ('chief'). *Sapience* first appears in the poetry of Chaucer and Langland in the 1370s, and here, in medieval and Renaissance fashion, may also indicate the personified *Sapientia* ('Wisdom,' as *Philosophia* was 'Lady Philosophy' in Boethius and the many medieval versions of his *Consolation of Philosophy*). The preponderance of Latinate and classical loans, especially as conveyed through French (Old French, Anglo-Norman, and Middle French) is nothing unusual for the era; nearly any prose treatise on any subject would contain as high or higher – especially John Lyly (1553–1606) with his *Euphues: The Anatomy of Wit* (1578) with its eponymous *euphuistic* style, that is, 'graceful, pleasing,' but also a bit bombastic with its deliberate Latinisms – not terribly unlike the 'hisperic' style of Aldhelm's Latin from the Old English era (Thomas Carlyle apparently was the first to use the coinage *euphuistic*, in 1828; OED, s.v.). The OED records 130 words that have their first attestation in John Lyly's works, including, from *Euphues*, *axiom* ('A proposition that commends itself to general acceptance'), *barbarism* ('The use of words or expressions not in accordance with the classical standard of a language'), *brinish* (as of tears), *conscive* ('fellow citizen,' a nonce-word in *Euphues*), *contemplature* ('an act of contemplation'), *content* (as a noun, 'in a contented condition'), *fading* (as a noun, 'a gradual dying out'), *overwarm* (as verb), *quipping* (as a noun), *slipshod* (here, meaning 'wearing slippers'), *strictness* (noun), and *trifold* ('threefold, triple'). Though much of his language can seem fussily learned, all was not *fustian* with Lyly – a term for a coarse cloth of cotton and flax, first used by Christopher Marlowe in his *Faustus* (ca. 1593) for '[i]nflated, turgid, or inappropriately lofty language' (OED, s.v.).

When Elyot mentions *thinges naturall* – the geminate <l> was by this time ornamental, not indicating preceding vowel quantity, which was unstressed – he employs a number of loans (*elementes*, *complexions*,[1] *humours*, *members*, *powers*, *operations*), yet when he lists *thynges not natural* (*ayre*, *meate*, *drinke*, *slepe*, *watche*, *rest*, *mynde*) he is

[1] The spelling the French loan *connexion* was standard in BrE from its first appearance in the early 17th century; Noah Webster in his *An American Dictionary of the English Language* (1828) notes that "For the sake of regular analogy, I have inserted *Connection* as the derivative of the English *connect*, and would discard *connexion*"; OED, s.v. *connection*; cf. Upward and Davidson 2011, 167–168).

employing native words from Old English. As a maker of a dictionary and arbiter of linguistic use, it is difficult to imagine that irony is not deliberate.

6.2 POWER OF THE PRESS

The original 'power of the press' has to do of course with the printing press (Scragg 1974, 64). The importation of the press to England by William Caxton in 1476 (or very near thereabouts) has been taken traditionally as a fair enough signpost for the "end of Middle English" (Lass 1994, CHEL III, 90). Caxton had printed the first book in English, a translation he had made of Raoul Lefèvre's *Recueil des histoires de Troye* (1464) in Cologne, and set to press ca. 1473 in Ghent under the title *Recuyell of the Historyes of Troye* – *recuyell* a French loan for 'literary collection,' first used in nominal form here by Caxton; the verb form *recueil* first appears in the Middle English metrical romance *Sir Ferumbras* (Fierbras is the fictional Saracen opponent to Charlemagne in the *chansons de geste* tradition; he is, in the earlier versions, son of the Saracen king Balan and a giant). There too Caxton published his English version of Jean de Vignay's French version of Italian Dominican Jacopo de Cessole's Latin treatise *Libellus de moribus hominum et officiis nobilium ac popularium super ludo scachorum* ("Book on the morals of men and duties of nobles and commoners or On the Game of Chess," dating to the later 13th century); his *The Game and Playe of Chess* is the first dated work of his press (31 March 1474). Caxton set up his press in The Almonry section of Westminster on Tothill Street (the neighborhood so named from *eleemosynary*, referring to the alms the abbey distributed there). His enterprise passed to his assistants Wynkyn de Worde and Richard Pynson in 1491, who were both from abroad (the former from Alsace, the latter from Normandy) but they, quite importantly, hired compositors (typesetters) from England (Scragg 1974, 67). The arrival of the printing press, however, did not at first help stabilize English spelling, not to the level monastic scriptoria or scriveners' workshops could in developing what would now be termed *house style*. Whereas professional scribes had settled on the spelling <v> for /v/ by the time Caxton printed *The History of Jason* (1477), Caxton's use of <v> and <u> for the sound is variable in that printed work (and would be in other printings of the late 15th century; Scragg 1974, 66). But the printing press would eventually encourage more stability in orthography, though printers at times set the text they had in hand or printed from manuscripts, which could include spellings not reflecting contemporary pronunciation: "if a letter or digraph was pronounced at the time it first came to be printed, it is likely to have been preserved in Modern English even if it has since fallen silent (hence *gnat*, *know*, *ought*, etc.)" (Upward and Davidson 2011, 174). It is during the 14th and 15th centuries that the -*e* in spellings of *name* and *time* came to mark the preceding vowel length when the -*e* had been largely lost: this being one of the effects of the Great Vowel Shift in the spelling of English: OE *nama* [na:mə] > [neɪm], OE *tīma* [ti:mə] > [taɪm].

John Stanbridge (1463–1510) of Heyford, Northamptonshire, would come to New College, Oxford, in 1480 and remain associated with the university the rest of his career, from 1486 on as the headmaster of Magdalen College's associated school (founded in 1480 by Bishop William [Patten] Waynflete). A major grammarian of the era, his works such as the popular Latin grammar *Accidence* (ca. 1495) went through multiple editions, many printed by Wynkyn de Worde (the colophon to the Oxford, Bodleian Library Arch. G.e.4 reads: "Prynted at westmynstre In Caxtons hous by wynkyn de worde"[2]). The tradition of longer and shorter versions of these grammars of Latin, the 'Longer' and 'Shorter Accidence,' came to be associated with Stanbridge as either author or compiler/editor, with the incipit, "Here begynneth the Accidens of maister Stanbridges awne makynge" (Gwosdek 1991, 11–12). Based ultimately on the *Ars maior* and *minor* of 4th-century Roman grammarian Donatus, Stanbridge's grammatical work is of interest for the application of a Humanist educational program and the passages in English ca. 1500 explaining Latin or English grammar. The variability, even flux, of the orthography (and punctuation) in the early printed versions is noteworthy:

> How knowest a nowne for al maner thyng þat a man may see fele. Here. or vnderstonde þat berith þe name of a thynge is a nowne.
>
> How knowe ye a nowne / for al þat I may fele see here or vnderstand þat berith þe name of a thyng is a nowne.
>
> How knowe yow a nowne? for he is a part of reson declined with case. and the name of euery thynge that may be felt. sene. hard or vnderstonde. is in latyne a nowne propur or appellatyue (Gwosdek 1991, 9–10; in a 1529 printing the last clause reads: *euery thynge that may be felte/seen/herde or understande, is in latyn a nowne p<ro>pre or appellatyue*).

The 1525 printing, with the Caxton Gothic typeface, of the version of Jean Froissart's *Chronicles* by John Bourchier, 'knight lorde Berners,' which, as the title page notes were *Tra<n>slated out of Frenche into our maternall Englysshe tonge*, was made by Caxton's former assistant Richard Pynson, *printer to the kynges noble grace*, the press now located in Fleet Street. In the lurid tale of Gaston, young son of the Earl of Foix, who suffers treachery at the hands of the King of Navarre, we find <ȝ> employed to represent /ks/ or /z/ (e.g., *the erle of Foiȝ*); Bourchier's is a fairly dramatic rendering of Froisssart: *Than the chylde wente to Panpylone* [Pamplona] *to take his leaue of the kyng his uncle. The kyng made hym great chere and taryed hym there a ten dayes / and gaue to him great giftes and to his men: also the last gyfte that the kyng gaue hym was his dethe* (The English Experience facsimile 1970; III.xxvi). Of note is the distributive syntax in *and gave to him great giftes and to his men*: V + IO + DO + IO, the double indirect object *to him and to his men* being split or cleft.

The 1640 printing by Richard Meighen in London of Ben Jonson's *The English Grammar* (1640), was made the same year as Stephen Daye printed *The Bay Psalm Book*, the first book set to press in North America, at Cambridge, Massachusetts Bay Colony. Daye's printing was a major event for American bookmaking, while Jonson's grammar was bound up in an edition of his collected works a few years after his death

---

[2] Alston 1969, [38]; the digital Bodleian version (which they date to 1499) is available at: https://digital.bodleian.ox.ac.uk/objects/7ae0f420-beff-45e0-9cfc-7ccbb20671d1/

(the *Grammar* in vol. II, along with masques and plays such as *Bartholomew Fair*). As would be expected with Jonson, the *Grammar* is Latinate in its terminology (he uses the spelling *præposition*) and tenor (the work is alternatively titled *Grammatica Anglicana*). As Jonson and the *Bay Psalm Book* have been set together here, the matter of 'English' English and emerging 'American' English will be turned to again in the next chapter with the early days of the English language in the Americas.

6.3 THE RENAISSANCE COMES TO ENGLAND – NEW LATIN AND NEW LEARNING

Stephen Hawes's influential if modest poetic output gives us a glimpse into an age that, if neglected in comparison to its preceding and succeeding eras in terms of literature and politics, was vital to the development of the English language. While the Stationers' Company had been established in 1403 as a guild of manuscript makers and sellers, the trade association took on ever greater significance with the introduction of the printing press in 1476. The term *stationer* (and in turn *stationery*) derives from Latin *stationarius* and in the medieval period referred to the booksellers, binders, and illustrators who set up shop outside old St. Paul's in London. One such publisher who set up outside St. Paul's was the German Wynkyn de Worde (d. 1534), that is 'little Wynand' of Wörth; de Worde was publisher of all of Hawes's poetic works, furnishing his *The pastyme of pleasure* with twenty-four woodcut engravings (completed by 1506, published 1509, reprinted later under the title *The Historie of graunde Amoure*; Lewis 1954, 652). Hawes's verse has never been treated particularly kindly by the critics; C.S. Lewis began his appraisal remarking, "Of the bad poets who wrote at this time I shall first mention Stephen Hawes, not because he is necessarily the oldest (his dates are uncertain), but because he is the most completely medieval" (Lewis 1954, 128). More recent appraisals have been somewhat more positive, agreeing that Hawes looked back to the medieval poets for his inspiration (Chaucer, Langland, and especially Lydgate) but noting that his engagement with print was forward-looking (Edwards 1983, 25). Of linguistic interest is that 'transitional' element to be found in his verse; though not as deliberately archaizing as Skelton (ca. 1463–1529), Hawes's language, his orthography and vocabulary in particular, offers insight into early Tudor English and perhaps the earliest form of East Anglian Early Modern English.

The Stationer's Company, or Worshipful Company of Stationers and Newspaper Makers was founded in 1403, chartered in 1557; it is 47th among the 100 'livery companies' of London (*livery* here referring to the uniform that was typical of – or came to be associated with – a given profession). The first attestation for the form in the OED seems to be from Anglo-Norman: a financial reference from 1311 to Robert de Watlington as a *stacioner* (likely of the Watlingtons of Norfolk). The 'vocabulary' or 'thesaurus for children' (*Promptorium parvulorum*) from ca. 1440 has the entry

(*continued*)

(continued)

Stacyonere, or he þat sellythe bokys (the work is attributed to the cleric Geoffrey the Grammarian, of Lynn, Norfolk). The first occurrences of the word in its modern spelling seems to be from poet George Wither (1588–1667), in his *The schollers purgatory discouered in the Stationers common-wealth, and discribed in a discourse apologeticall, asvvell for the publike aduantage of the Church, the state & vvole common-vvealth of England, as for the remedy of priuate iniuryes* (1625). Wither was an interesting figure whose career spanned the Elizabethan to Commonwealth eras; he had served in Charles I's army but came round to more Puritan views, and was a noted satirist of his day – 'Wither's Motto' an example of the wit that allegedly led to a brief imprisonment: *Nec habeo, nec Careo, nec Curo. Nor Haue I, nor Want I, nor Care I. Livery*, in the sense of 'a characteristic garb or covering' (OED, s.v., sense III.10) first seems to occur ca. 1335 in the medieval Anglo-Irish expansion of the famous *Erþe toc of erþe* verse from the Kildare manuscript (British Library, MS Harley 913): *Whan erþ makiþ is liuerei, he grauiþ vs in grene* (poem 48, line 52 in Turville-Petre 2015): "When Earth makes his livery, he graves (buries)/robes us in green," the play on *grauiþ* indicating that Earth dresses us in its green and also under that green (Turville-Petre 2015, 136). These London *liveries* would come to have their distinctive (often ceremonial) costumes, and coats of arms and headquarters, as of the Stationers, Grocers, Fishmongers, and various other 'Worshipful Companies'; the motto of the Stationers' Company is 1 Peter 1:25: *Verbum Domini manet in aeternum*, 'But the word of the Lord endureth forever.' *Livery* in its development came to encompass the *livery cab* (horse and carriage for hire), *livery stable* (and by extension and narrowing a horse kept for such purpose in such a stable), to, by technological advance, *livery car* (and *livery service*, which in AmE often indicates *limo service*). And where AmE may use *logo* for a commercial enterprise's branding emblem or symbol (and particular color scheme), BrE can still use *livery*. Increasingly archaic, but still recognizable from literature and television dramas, are the *footmen in livery*.

Hawes likely hails from Norfolk, the Haugh/Hawes/Haws name common there (Reaney and Wilson 2005, 221; ODFN 2016); he may have been at Oxford, at Magdalen College, in 1493, and is known to have held the title of *valet de chambre/sometyme grome of <th>e honourable chambre of our late souerayne lorde kynge Henry <th>e seuenth* (Edwards 1983, 2). Hawes as poet was, by his own admission, following on the medieval tradition of English poetry, and thus a transitional figure in the history of English verse; his very Early Modern English strikes the reader as transitional also linguistically. In his *Example of Vertu* he acknowledges his debt to three great figures of Middle English verse, Geoffrey Chaucer, John Gower, and John Lydgate:

O prudent Gower in langage pure
Without corrupcyon moost facundyous
O noble Chauser euer moost sure
Of frutfull sentence ryght delycyous

O vertuous Lydgat moche sententcyous
Vnto you all I do me excuse
Though I your connynge do now vse (Edwards 1983, 10–11).

In brief, a number of phonological and orthographical features are typical of what might be seen as the transitional period of late Middle English to earliest Early Modern English ca. 1475–1510. The orthographical details of *v/u*, *-ion/-yon*, *-ious/-yous*, and *i/y* more broadly may be minor, but they are indicators of changes in pronunciation and spelling in the dawning age of print, and of the legacy of medieval English, an age of manuscripts. Hawes's *in langage pure / Without corrupcyon moost facundyous* ('eloquent'; 1–2) no doubt recalls Lydgate's *Of speche ryght facundious* from his *Troy Book* (1430), and *ryght* itself – pronounced [riːχt], but soon to undergo diphthongization to produce EMdE [raɪt] by the Great Vowel Shift – preserves by its orthography the Old and Middle English forms (*ryght*, *right*, *riht*). Adjectival *moche* is as found in Chaucer (*muche*, *moche*, *myche*), and not a *mickle*-form as found in the North or in Scots (from OE *miċel/myċel*), though in Chaucer the adverbial form *muchel/mochel* is found. The French loan *vertuous* would maintain its Anglo-Norman spelling, as found in Middle English texts to Caxton (1490) to the King James Bible (1611), until displaced by *virtuous* in the 18th century. Indeed, the legacy of French influence is readily apparent in even this brief extract from Hawes: *prudent* (first attestation the early Wycliffite Bible, ca. 1382), *corruption* (Langland's *Piers Plowman*, ca. 1377), *facundyous*, *noble* (*Ancrene Riwle*, early 13th century), *sure* (the Middle English romance *Of Arthour and of Merlin*, ca. 1330), *frutfull* (also first occurring in *Arthour and Merlin*), *sentence* (*Ayenbite of Inwyt*, ca. 1340, a Middle English version of Laurent d'Orléans's *La Somme le Roi*), *delycyous* (in the Life of St. Patrick from the early South English Legendary, ca. late 13th century[3]); *sentencyous* has a parallel in Old French but was borrowed directly from the Latin, and *vse* 'use' (its first attestation seems to be from early West Midlands ME, in the rhythmical prose prayer *On Lofsong of ure Lefdi* ("A Love-Song of Our Lady," a translation of the French original of Marbode of Rennes [ca. 1035–1123]). The most obvious, and important, French borrowing in the extract from Hawes's verse is of course *langage*, first attested in the metrical life of St. Thomas Becket from the early South English Legendary. Born in Cheapside, London, this English saint and martyr was of Norman stock, his parents Gilbert and Matilda of families from Thierville and Caen in Normandy. The 'language' situation in the metrical life itself is interesting; the rubric is in Old French: *Ici poez oyer coment seint Thomas de Kaunterbures nasqui. e de quev manere gent de pere e de Mere* ("Ici pouvez-vous entendre comment Thomas de Canterbury est né; et quelle sorte de gens étaient son père et sa mère"; "Here may you hear of how Saint Thomas of Canterbury was

[3] *Delicious* originally meant 'Extremely pleasing to the senses, esp. taste or smell' (OED), then underwent semantic narrowing to taste particularly; in 21st-century English, the word has broadened to encompass all the senses, often in a cloying and trendy fashion: one can now apply 'delicious' to furniture, clothing, etc. The current broadening of the adjective's range of applicability is not entirely new: it had earlier been applied to personal appearance/beauty, in a somewhat obvious semantic extension, as had the truncated informal *delish*.

born; and of what manner of people were his father and mother"; Horstmann 1887, 106). But the tale itself is in characteristically Middle English verse form:

> Wolle ʒē nouþe i-heore þis englische tale.... / Of londone is fader was... / Gilbert bekat was is name.... / Ake is Moder was of heþenesse....
>
> Þoruʒ godes grace heo was i-lad With men þat onder-stonde hire langage, ... Ake euere heo axede In hire langage to londone for-to go (Horstmann 1887, 106–108).
>
> [Would you now wish to hear this English tale.... / Of London his father was... / Gilbert Beket was his name.... / But his mother was of heathendom....
>
> Through God's grace was she accompanied By men that understood her language,... But ever she asked in her language "To London for to go."]

The interesting details of Thomas Becket's parentage are that his mother Matilda was born pagan, and christened only upon her settling in England; father Gilbert's story is fantastical if not fanciful: captured by the Saracens, held for a year and a half, he is the object of affection of the Saracen admiral's daughter (who will follow him later to England). If there is anything to this, it is in the time of the First Crusade; *admiral* is, ultimately, via French and Latin, from Arabic *amīr* (likely Arabic definite article *al-* + *amīr*; compare Anglo-Norman *almiral*; the origin of this word occasions one of the more complex etymologies in the *OED*). Here, in the midst of the story of Thomas Becket and his parents, his father Gilbert's imprisonment by the Saracen emir and rescue by his daughter, French *langage* enters into the English language for the first recorded time. The Norman origins of the Bekets, and alleged Crusades experiences of Gilbert Beket, are a reminder that the Early Modern period was not the first period of English history to witness far-flung travels. But it is in this Renaissance, with its intellectual ferment and changes, that we witness also the Age of Exploration: both would shape the development of English profoundly, apart from the internal changes the language was already undergoing.

Hawes's epic-length allegorical poem *The Passetyme (Pastime) of Pleasure* (about 6,000 lines long), often reprinted through the 16th century under the title *The Historie of graunde Amoure*, sees Grand Amour on a medieval dream-quest – an even Arthurian one: dame Fame in chapter 43 adds Graund Amoure's name to those of heroes past, Arthur among them; he visits the Tower of Doctrine, where seven daughters, figures of the Seven Liberal Arts (of the medieval trivium and quadrivium: "Howe he was receyved of Logyke...Howe he was receyved of Rethoryke;" Chapters 6–7), set him on the path to wisdom; he battles a giant with three heads, and another with seven (chapters 33, 35); and then a dragon made "of seven metalles" ("His necke silver.../ His breste stele"; chapter 37); and then he eventually comes to La Belle Pucelle (The Beautiful Maiden), marries her, and lives his life until Aege (Age) and Deth (Death) inexorably come for him: "But whan I thought longest to endure, / Deth with his darte arest me sodenly; Obey! he sayd..." (chapter 41).

The 'Passetyme' with its dream vision and mystery play-like and allegorized moral figures – Dames Confession, Contricion, Mercy, and Charite, then Remembraunce [personified as male] and Dame Fame come to visit him at the point of death (chapters 41–43) – sits, literarily, between the medieval and Early Modern, between the medieval mystery plays of vices and virtues, Langland's stern and satiric moralizing, and Chaucer's *The House of Fame*, and, from *The Canterbury Tales* (ca. 1386–1400), the tales of Melibee, The Pardoner, and The Parson, and Edmund Spenser's *Faerie Queene* (1590–1596). It does so also linguistically; at the very opening, La Grande Amoure meets Fame in a meadow:

> Whan Phoebus ent'red was in Gemine,
> Shining above in his fair, golden spere,
> And horned Dian than but one degree
> In the Crab had ent'red fair and clear,
> Whan that Aurora did well appear
> In the depured air and cruddy firmament,
> Forth than I walked without impediment... (Chapter 1; Mead 1928; Rollins and Baker 1992).

> Whan Phebus entred was in Geminy,
> Shynyng above in his fayre golden spere,
> And horned Dyane then but one degre
> In the Crabbe had entred fayre and cleare;

> When that Aurora did well appeare
> In the depured ayre and cruddy firmament,
> Forth then I walked without impediment (Percy Society ed. 1845).

The first seven-line stanza from Hawes's *Passetyme* is based on Wynkyn de Worde's second edition of the poem (with woodcuts) from 1517; the second copy of the opening stanza is from the Percy Society's reprint of the 1555 edition printed by Richard Tottel and John Waley. In both we see the relatively free variation in the spelling of vocalic *i/y* with *y* predominating in the 1555 edition (*shynyng*, *fayre*). The variation between *i* and *y* is one of the legacies of Middle English (Blake 1992, 14), and was found also in English editions of Latin texts (and in English spelling of classical forms: *Dian* and *Dyane*, *Gemini* and *Geminy*). There was a growing preference in the age of printing to employ *-y* or *-ie* in the final position (thus *only* or *onlie* rather than *onli*; Salmon 1999, 28). The spelling *spere* for *sphere* likely indicates the continued Latinate or 'learned' pronunciation of Latin *sphaera* (from Greek σφαῖρα, *sphaîra*); Medieval Latin *spera* is common in early English writers such as Bede, as in his computistical works and the sources he consulted for them (such as Dionysius Exiguus; as in the Basel, Öffentliche Bibliothek des Universitäts F.III.a manuscript, glossed in Old English; McGowan 2012, 6). The pronunciation likely maintains the stop /p/ in [sp-], as it was pronounced through to late Middle English and into the 16th century; the OED lists attestations from the Northumbrian *Cursor Mundi* to Richard Rolle to Chaucer in the 14th century (*the spere solide* in Chaucer's *Treatise on the Astrolabe* and *þe seuenþe spere* in *Troilus and Criseyde*).[4] But toward the end of the century, one finds in Spenser *vnto the starry sphere* (*Faerie Queene* Book I), by which point the fricative /f/

[4] The form *speir* in Gavin Douglas's Scots translation of Virgil's *Aeneid* (1513) is likely not a diphthong but an indication that the preceding vowel was long (Görlach 1991, 59).

gives the modern [sfɪə] in BrE and [sfɪ(ə)r] or [sfi:r] in AmE. Hawes's opening clearly echoes Chaucer's to *The Canterbury Tales* with the seasonal and astrological allusions, though Hawes's opening salvo fairly thuds in the modern ear with *cruddy firmament.* This of course means something like 'starry,' and is the metathesized form of *curdy*, 'curd-like,' here describing the heavens, while in Spenser's Book I of *Faerie Queene* it refers to congealed blood (*His cruell wounds with crudy bloud congeald*).

When Age (*Age* or *Aege* in Hawes's poem) visits 'Graunde Amoure,' one hears again a Chaucerian echo and finds an adverbial construction from Old and Middle English:

> Thus as I lived in such pleasure gladde,
> Into the chamber came full prively
> A fayre olde man, and in his hand he hadde
> A croked staffe; he wente full wekely:
> Unto me than he came full softely,
> And with his staffe he toke me on the brest,
> Obey! he sayd, I must you nedes arreste.
>
> My name is Age... (Percy Society ed, chapter 40).

And while the device of geminate consonants to indicate preceding vowels as short is complemented with that other Early Modern English device of *-e* (*gladde, hadde, staffe*), of particular interest is the modal auxiliary + *need(s)* construction: *I must you nedes arreste*. While *must needs* is now archaic, the construction *need(s)* with a modal such as *must* or *mote* has a long history in English. It occurs with the modal *sċulan* ('have to, must, shall') in the *Anglo-Saxon Chronicle* (the Peterborough continuation) for the year 1131: *Hi scolden nedes, on fif <ond> twenti wintre ne biden hi næfre an god dæi* ('They had need, for in five and twenty years they had never experienced a single good day'). If the orthography looks haltingly modern, the punctuation is nearly that of Present Day English. There is relatively little variation in the use of punctuation in the two printings of the first stanza from Hawes above: punctuation is light, and largely a legacy of medieval manuscript practice. Printers looked to texts such as John Hart's *The opening of the unreasonable writing of our Inglish toung* (1551) and the *Interpungendi ratio* (found also under variations of the title such as *De ratione interpungendi* and *De usu et ratione interpungendi*, 'On the rationale of punctuation,' 'On the use and rationale of punctuation'; 1561) by the Italian Humanist Aldus Manutius (Salmon 1999, 21–23).

What changes that can be observed in the 16th century, the first full century of printing the English language, involve the adaptation of the medieval *per cola et commata* ('by colons and commas,' i.e., by clauses and phrases) system and somewhat more frequent use of punctuation marks. The medieval tradition of organizing the logical, rhetorical, and semantic content of speech by constituent clauses and phrases, by 'pointing' it with relatively spare use of such notations as semi-colon, colon, dash, virgule (/), and period, saw the introduction of the question mark (or 'asker' or 'wonderer'; Hart 1551) and exclamation point (this would come into near over-use the next century and a half – only 21st-century text and social media hyper-overuse would surpass the Early Modern use of exclamation mark). The *period*, from classical Latin *peri(h)odos/periodus* (< Greek περίοδος [*perīodos*]), 'A group of words organically related in grammar and sense' (OLD, s.v. *perihodos*), underwent semantic extension so that the term for a syntactic unit formed from related clauses and phrases came to refer to the pause after such a complete unit and then the sign (.) that was used to mark it off (OED senses III.16.a, III.17.b). The first recorded uses of *period* in these senses are to be found in Spenser's *Shepeardes calender* (1579; "The whole Periode & compasse of speache"), in Robert Greene's tract *Penelopes Web* (1587, referring to the pause at the end of a sentence), and in Richard Mulcaster's *Elementarie* (1582, the period as punctuation mark). Robert Greene was a dramatist (*Friar Bacon and Friar Bungay* [1590]) pamphleteer, and wit; his *Greenes Groats-worth of witte* [1592]) often figures in discussions of Shakespeare (the *Groats-worth* pamphlet for the presumed reference to Shakespeare as the 'upstart Crow'). Greene's *Penelopes Web*, a tract extolling and illustrating female *vertue* in the *exemplum* tradition (Penelope as the prime example of virtue and fidelity, though Greene ranges widely, even wildly across the centuries for examples), is interesting with regard to the foregoing matters of orthography and punctuation. Greene, rarely found other than tongue-in-cheek, seems earnest in his encouragement of feminine virtue, particularly in marriage, though the tract often borders on farrago, with a sort of heaping up of examples, and leaping between and among them, that can also seem satirical.

To the right Honorable and vertuous his very good Ladie and *Mistresse, the Ladie Margaret Countesse* of Cumberland: and to the no lesse *Honourable and vertuous the Ladie Anne* Countesse of Warwicke: *Robert Greene* wisheth encrease of Honor and Vertue....

For if trueth be the daughter of tyme, and tyme the Heralt that best emblazeth affections: the report that the Gretians made of the Princesse of Ithaca, may seeme but a fiction compared with that fame of your Ladiships vertuous resolutions: which are such and so rare, as your very enemies (if you have any) are forced maugre their teeth to bee true discouerers of your vertues.

TO THE GENTLEMEN READERS HEALTH. So oft (Gentlemen) have I relyed vpon your courtesie, and found you so fauorable, that still I aduenture to present what I write to your iudgementes, hoping as my intent is to please all, if it might be without offence, so I shal be pardoned of al, though presuming to farre.... But considering that *Mars* wil sometime bee prying into *Venus* papers, and gentlemen desirous to heare the parlie of Ladies, I thought rather to write a lyne to much, and so be counted forward, then by leauing out one title, incurre your displeasures, and so be iudged froward: but whatsoeuer I haue done or written, I onely desire for my paynes your fauorable acceptance, and so wish to you, as to my selfe, to liue fortunate, and dye happy.

...whereas there is no greater perswasion to allay the chollericke humour and froward disposition of men, then Obedience: for sayth *Theocritus*, a good wife should vse the custome in her house that the *Persians* did in the warres: for when their enemies made any inuasion either by skirmish, Camizado, or maine battell, if they rusht vpon <the> (y^{e}) pykes with any clamours, the *Persians* receiued them with silence, but if they assaulted with furie they ioyned forces with lowde Alarums: so should a wise woman when she sees her Husband in choller, appease him with patience, and when he is quiet then seeke to perswade him with reasons (Grosart 1881–1883, 141–143, 144–145, 164–165).

Greene uses here the offset colon (:) not so much, as now, to introduce a series or list as to introduce a clause of result or a concessive or suasive clause that might now be offset by the semi-colon (;) or introduced by an adverbial *namely*. Throughout the Early Modern era one sees the great influence of a classical curriculum on English writers: Horace especially upon lyric verse, Virgil, Homer (at first in Latin translations, but with Ben Jonson and other classically trained authors in Greek with increasing frequency), Lucan on epic verse, Seneca in particular upon tragedy; with the rise of Humanistic Latin, which saw the extension of use of Latin as a scholarly language to studies of politics, society, the humors (and various other para- and pseudo-scientific investigations), music, art, and manners, the 'old language' found new use in not just the scriptorium or chancery but in the universities.

The classical tripos of Cambridge was still formally some years away (it would be established in 1822), and Ben Jonson was disappointed in his hope of studying there; he did attend Westminster School until 1589 (one of his masters the anti-quarian William Camden, a figure in the 'rediscovery' of Old English), and gained a knowledge of the classics worthy of a classical philologist. Jonson's oft-repeated quip that Shakespeare had 'Smalle Latin and Lesse Greeke' is a typically grouchy Jonson-ism; Jonson had his humours (in the 16th-century sense of the term), and his rivals, but his admiration of Shakespeare is abundantly clear even in *Timber; or, Discoveries* (1641), his observations on many topics, but particularly valued for those on drama, poetry, and the theater world, wherein Jonson lobbed another of his famous quips about Shakespeare – *sufflaminandus erat* ('it was needed [at times] he should be stopped'); or, told that the Bard had not ever blotted a line out in his writing, "My answer hath been, would he had blotted a thousand." Jonson's Latinate quip would make its way into James Joyce's *Ulysses* (*sufflaminandus sum*, 'would that I had been stopped'), another author deeply steeped in the classics (at Dublin's Clongowes Wood College by the Jesuits); and, by simply being in Latin, gives some sense of the currency of the language in Renaissance England. The expectation was that his literary peers and any former pupils of a grammar school might understand him in Latin; *grammar school* itself is a name for that primary level of education (in AmE it is still in use, varying with *elementary school*, *K-8*, and *primary school*), and indicates the rudiments of Latin: the very language needed to explain grammar (nouns, verbs, adjectives, adverbs; comma and colon; sentence and paragraph, all of these are Latin loans), while Greek (often in Latin 'garb,' i.e., in Latinized form) provided many of the terms of rhetorical figures (aposiopesis, apostrophe, congeries, ekphrasis, and so forth). The first instance of *grammar school* in the language is from John of Trevisa's translation of Ranulf Higden's ca. 1352 *Polychronicon*, a 'universal history' (a medieval genre of history-making, often starting with Creation through Biblical chronology to one's own times). Trevisa's Middle English translation of 1387 was printed in 1480 by William Caxton, and at V.51 one reads *At Alexandria he heeld a gramer scole* (V.51; OED, s.v. *grammar school*); the reputation of the institution was such that in *Henry VI, Part 2,* Shakespeare has rebel Jack Cade say *Thou hast most traiterously corrupted the youth of the Realme, in erecting a Grammar Schoole* (IV.vii.31). Printed and glossed by Caxton, that is. Trevisa provided a translation into the English of his day of Higden's Latin chronicle; Caxton printed Trevisa with his own insertions and clarifications of 'older words' in the Middle English. Higden himself, a monk at the Benedictine Abbey at Chester, worried that traces of the history of England and its poets and writers could be lost:

> Writing of poetes is more worthy to preisynge of emperoures þan al þe welþe of þis worlde, and riches þat þey welde while þey were alyue. For storie is wytnesse of tyme, mynde of lyf, messager of eldnesse [Caxton: *oldnesse*]; story weldeþ passyng doynges, storie putteþ forþ hire professoures. Dedes þat wolde be lost storie ruleþ [Caxton: *reneweth*]; dedes þat wolde flee out of mynde, storye clepeþ [Caxton: *callith*] aȝen; dedes þat wolde deie, storye kepeþ hem euermore....I haue y-kast and y-ordeyned, as I may, to make and to write a tretes, i-gadered of dyuerse bookes, of þe staat of þe ylonde of Britayne, to knowleche of men þat comeþ after vs (Babington 1865, Vol. I, 7).

Nearly a century later, Caxton's glosses to Trevisa's translation of Higden are relatively minor; he even corrects, at times, what he sees as errors in Trevisa's English. Orthographically, thorn (*þ*) and yogh (ȝ) are familiar enough still to Caxton and his readers, but not quite a century and a half later, in the age of Shakespeare and Jonson, they have disappeared. The old case marking with *-e* for dative (prepositional) case (*of mynde*) had by Caxton's day ceased to be a grammatical distinction, and demonstrative *þat* and *þe* have become invariant *that* and *the* (the latter now fully the definite article). The main vowel in *dedes* [de:dəs] 'deeds' has been raised to /i:/ in the series of changes grouped under the heading the Great Vowel Shift.

Farrago, 'a medley, mixture, hotchpotch,' mentioned just above with *Greenes Groats-worth of witte*, is first attested in Ben Jonson's late comedy *The Magnetic Lady*, performed by the King's Men company at Blackfriars Theatre in 1632, a work of his 'declining' powers, with a cast of characters with allegorical and satiric names: Lady Loadstone and Master Compass, the former's niece Placentia Steel (who will go into labor on stage) and the ill-matched suitors who pursue her including Parson Palate and Sir Diaphanous Silkworm. The word derives from the Latin *farrago,* denoting 'mixed fodder for cattle,' spelled *farragoe* in Jonson, and often degeminated in the 17th and 18th centuries (*farago*). The Renaissance preoccupation with codifying grammar, spelling reform, proper diction, and erudite allusion to the classics not only presages the 'Age of Reason' application of logic to language use and learning, but also a sharpening of distinctions between varieties of English. London-Southeastern was in the ascendant, on its way to literary and spoken standard status (later 'RP'); this development saw a loss of prestige in Midland varieties, even a drawing down of what constituted 'Northern': the tradition of seeing Watford Gap, Northamptonshire, as the dividing line between Southern and Northern English varieties brought down that border from Northumbria to central Mercia (in the Old English timeframe), or down to the southern East Midlands (in the Middle English timeframe). The 'speech area' of standard English became more circumscribed around Greater London, such that the Southwest and West Country, and even Essex, became more 'regional' in their dialects. All the more so with Chaucer's *Fer in the north* (from the 'Reeve's Tale,' *Canterbury Tales*), and perhaps no more so than with Scots and Scottish English.

6.4 ENGLISH AND SCOTS

A parallel development had been emerging in the North in the Old English period, at first as part of Northumbrian (Anglian) dialects of OE, then, more divergently, as the beginning of Middle Scots, a Northern Middle English-derived variety spoken mainly in southeastern Scotland, with a literary dialect often consciously cultivated (especially from the 18th century onward). The division between the Lowlands (Lallans) and Highlands was a linguistic one, with Middle Irish used in the central and northern regions and spoken at the medieval court; sometime in the 13th century, one can point to an emerging Scots Gaelic still spoken today in the Western Isles and north of Scotland as a minority language. Though the development of Scots and Scottish English is usually associated with a form of Northern Middle English, this picture may be a little more complicated than previously thought, as the dialect picture of the North and Scottish Borders may have involved a set of varieties of Northern ME (see, most recently, Gilbert 2021). That Lallans should be the variety that engendered a 'national' literature in Scotland may have been first made apparent by Gavin Douglas's *Eneados*, the poet's 1513 rendering of Virgil's *Aeneid* in Lowland Scots: "It must have occurred to him that if [William] Wallace and [Robert the] Bruce had not, as *pius Aeneas* had done, founded a kingdom, they had at least, and with as great pains, re-established one: and that they had felt the compulsion of duty or destiny no less than the Trojan hero" (McDiarmid 1983, 12; see also Aitken 1983, vii).

The Middle Scots Arthurian romance *Golagras and Gawane* is usually dated to the later 15th century (though it may belong to an earlier part of that century) and is known from the 1508 printed edition by Walter Chepman and Androw Myllar, who had established the first printing press in Scotland that year (the Chepman and Myllar Press of Edinburgh). Relatively few products of the Chepman and Myllar Press survive; the alliterative verse *Gologras and Gawane* appears as the second chapbook in the bound volume of Chepman and Myllar Prints in the National Library of Scotland, Edinburgh.

> In tyme of Arthur, as trew men me tald,
> The King turnit on ane tyde towart Tuskane,
> Hym to seik ovr [variant: our] the sey, that saiklese was [wes] sald,
> The syre that sendis all seill, suthly to sane;
> With banrentis [knights banneret], barounis, and bernis [fighting men] full bald,
> Biggast of bane and blude bred in Britane (Hahn 1995, ll. 1–6).

Arthur's knights are making the pilgrimage to Jerusalem, 'one time turned toward Tuscany, / Him [Christ] to seek over the sea, that soke-less [blameless] was sold [by Judas]'; here are the familiar forms of later Scots in Middle Scots: *tald* ('told') and *sald* ('sold'), 3rd sing. pret., though these involve a fairly complicated matter of phonological development. The **a* in Anglian OE *ald* (WS *eald* 'old') and *salde* (< **salða*; WS *sealde*, 3rd sing. pret. of *sellan* 'to sell' < weak I verb **saljan*, originally with the sense 'to give, offer up [as for money, for sale]') underwent breaking in West Saxon (**a* > **æ* > *ea*) and perhaps somewhere around 1200 (early ME) had undergone homorganic cluster lengthening to /aː/ (i.e., vowel lengthening before a cluster of consonants with the same, or nearly same, place of articulation – in this example, alveolars). The later development of this /aː/ by the GVS produced *sold*. OE *sellan*, like other verbs of weak class I underwent i-umlaut, while the preterite form did not (WS pret. *sealde* involves breaking before *l* plus consonant, though the chronology of the breaking and i-umlaut is uncertain; Campbell, OEG §§139, 249ff.; Lass 1994, 70; Ringe and Taylor 2014, 218–222): the upshot is present-day *sell/sold* (Minkova 2014, 162–163). The Scots form comes from late Northumbrian OE /Early Middle English /aː/ forms, though there are a bewildering number of ME variants of the preterite: *sōld(e), soulde, sēlde, sellid, sillide, ʒialde, sælde, cēlde, saulde*, among others (MED, s.v. *sellen*). Whereas in England /aː/ > /ɔː/ > /oː/ (thus *old, sold*) was the outcome of later developments, in the Scottish Lowlands /aː/ seems to have remained unrounded until the 14th century, then diphthongized to /ɑᵘ/ or /aᵘ/ (DSL, "History of Scots to 1700," Phonology 6.13). Compare Middle Scots *sauld* ('sold'), *tauld* ('told'), or *doun-tauld* ('down-told,' i.e., 'paid down'; DOST, s.vv.). Breaking is to be observed in *seik* ('seek') and *seill* (*sele*, from the Middle English, 'happiness, prosperity, good fortune'; DOST, s.v.; MED, s.v.); *suthly to sane*, 'truly to say' (compare OE *sōþlice tō seċġanne*): *suthly* (compare MdE *forsooth*) is the outcome of the GVS in Scotland, /oː/ raised to /uː/ (vowel 6 in DSL's Phonology section [6.25]; so with *blude* 'blood'); *sane* occurs also in variants *sain* and *sayen*.

Hector Boece (or Boyce; 1465–1536), born in Aberdeen, was one of the leading Scottish academic figures of his day; trained at the University of St. Andrews, then at the University of Paris, he was the first head of the newly established University of Aberdeen, and a friend of the leading humanist Erasmus. His *Historia gentis Scotorum* (1527, "History of the Scottish People") appeared in a metrical version in 1535 (*Buik of the Croniclis of Scotland*) and a Scots version published in 1536 by John Bellenden (*Heir beginnis the hystory and croniklis of Scotland*); the following is from the allegorical prologue of the Scots version made by makar William Stewart, begun in 1531 but not published until edited for the Rolls Series (Turnbull 1858):

> The quhilk contenis mony nobill storie,
> Lang tyme befoir tynt [lost] out of all memorie,
> Of eldaris deidis preceidand him [James IV of Scotland] beforne (Turnbull 1858, 1–2).

'The which [*quhilk*]' was Boece's work (*Ane noble buikhis princeheid for to pleis*), and the sentiment is a common one in Scots literature: that which has been lost, some of it for good, and now the province of *makaris*. In a way, it is in Scots that Middle English enjoyed an afterlife: *quhilk*, and its many variant forms (*queilk, qwylke, wealk*, etc.), descends from Northern Middle English *whilk(e)*, in turn from Old English *hwilċ(e)*, with the stop /k/ for affricate /tʃ/. And the past participle *tynt*, from Older Scots *tyn(e)*, is a loan from Old Norse *týna* 'lose, destroy.' The periodization of Scots has been the subject of recent work by Johanna Kopaczyk of the University of Glasgow (Kopaczyk 2013, 2014), with a view toward seeing Scots of this period as rather more 'Early Modern' than 'Middle' Scots, one determinative feature, as seen in the poetry of *makar* William Dunbar, being the loss of the inflectional marking of the infinitive. This had been a process underway in late Northumbrian Old English and as Northern

ME infinitives in *-en* were reduced to *-e* (and that to the schwa /ə/), periphrastic forms with *for to/to/til* + verb developed (Kopaczyk 2014, 15); in this case Early Scots **tynen > tyne > to/for to tyn*: DOST *sal tyne* 'shall lose' (15th century), *sal tyn* (1440), *sal he his gudis tyne* 'shall he his goods lose' (14th–15th-century breviary), *sall tine his swerd* 'shall lose his sword' (Bellenden's Boece 1536), *to tyne the said fals money* (Act, Parliament of Scotland 1567).

The poet or *makar* William Dunbar (1459–1530) may straddle the linguistic dividing line between Middle and Early Modern Scots, with a recent study in support of the latter classification (Kopaczyk 2014). *Makar*, with variant forms *makkar*, *mackar*, *maikar*, *maikkar*, is a loan from Middle English and, broadly, simply a 'maker' of any number of trades; but in early literary Scots, it also meant a 'maker of verse' or other literary endeavors, a bard, a versifier. The earliest attestation of *makar* in the DOST is from *The Actis and Deidis of the illustere and vailȝeand Campioun Schir William Wallace, Knicht of Ellerslie* (ca. 1475) by Blind Harry (Henry the Minstrel, 1440–1492; Moir 1889): *Quhen guid makaris rang weill in to Scotland* (Bk. XI, 1455). *Quhen*, 'when,' involves the Early Scots outcome of Old English *hw-*, thus OE *hwæt* > EScots *quhat* 'what.' The 'Phonology' section *History of Scots to 1700* of the DSL, which is the fullest treatment, in concise form, of the historical phonology of Scots to date, cites the Northumbrian Old English form *chwa* from the Lindisfarne Gospels gloss as a source to EScots *quha*, which is much more familiar as *wha* 'who' (Robert Burns's *Scots Wha Hae*). The development may have been from a Northumbrian */xw-/ to early Scots /x^w-/ or /ʍ-/, the voiceless labiovelar fricative (DSL, 'Phonology,' sect. 6.31.1).

Some debate still goes on about the 'naturalness' of Scots and the classification of dialects of Scots versus those of Scottish English, the former seen as archaic, regional (and dying out), or artificially maintained or revived for literary use. And, also, about reference to a 'Scots language' (see Millar 2018, 1–3, who argues for 'language'). This artificiality of literary Scots was no doubt to be found in Dunbar's day, if not so much as in that of Hugh MacDiarmid (*nom de plume* of poet Christopher Murray Grieve, 1892–1978). Often less acknowledged is that the question of naturalness is no less relevant to literary Elizabethan English. A work such as *Buchan Claik: The Saat an the Glaar o't* ('Buchan Gossip/Talk: the salt and mud of it') by Peter Buchan and David Toumlin (Buchan and Toumlin 1998) may answer to these concerns, as this glossary records both the more performative and more natural everyday talk of Buchan, Aberdeenshire. Poets of North-Eastern Scotland compose still in Doric – the name for this variety of Scots is of uncertain origin, and the first attestation in the SND, from 1809, refers more broadly to the Scots language (the narrowing to the Scots of Aberdeenshire is much more recent). But to some extent, this is not unlike the language and culture revivalism of the Eisteddfod of Wales (*eisteddfod* literally a 'sitting' or 'session') or the Comórtas Filíochta in Ireland ('tournament of poetry/poetry competition'; both are national poetry competitions, respective 'chairings of the bard'). The *claik*, 'gossip,' a term that originally referred to the shrill noise of birds (SND, s.v.), of Buchan is both performative and natural, as Toumlin acknowledges in the introduction to *Buchan Claik*: "Doric 'spik' [speak] is sometimes the comic relief in the drama of our lives, in print and on the concert platforms, though I must admit that some of the performers excel in their burlesque imitation of what was natural, instinctive behaviour within my own life span" (Buchan and Toumlin 1998, 7). Doric in the northeast and Gàidhlig in the northwest were the roots and remains of a long period of language contact in Scotland. And Scots, however volatile a category of 'language,' and Scottish English have started to receive their linguistic due. Among the 16 guides to 'Pronunciation for World Englishes' of the OED is one for 'Scottish English'[5]; it is rather simpler than those of the Dictionaries of the Scots Language (DSL), as it outlines standard varieties, with only /x/ (with the usual 'as in ***loch***') of note among consonants, but with a much longer section on vowels, notably, from the Wells lexical set: *mouth* [mʌʊθ], *goat* [got] (versus BrE [gəʊt]), *pride* [prʌid](versus BrE and AmE [praɪd]), and a split between *birth* [bɪrθ] and *berth* [bɛrθ] (versus BrE [bəːθ] for both). Scottish English and Scots are rhotic, though it is noted that the /r/ is more an approximant or tap rather than an actual trill. For instance, the trill in the Highland Scottish English of BBC weather forecaster Calum MacColl (also a speaker of Gaelic) in a phrase such as *per hour* is usually classified as an alveolar trill, though it can sound closer to a dental trill (or like the 'slender' /r/ following a front vowel in Gaelic).

That Scottish Englishes will persist is no less certain than the fate of other markedly distinctive varieties of English, from African American English to Caribbean Englishes, Irish Englishes to South Asian Englishes. The question 'why?' is not entirely a linguistic one: geographic isolation plays an important role in dialect divergence and persistence, as does social isolation. The Scottish Borders as a linguistic zone predates the era of the *reivers*, the border raiders of the 14th century – *reifer* is from Old English *rēafere* 'robber' (*robber* is a loan from Anglo-Norman, of late Latin origin).; so, strife and separation between Scotland and England supplies some, but not all, of the rationale for the linguistic divergence. The long persistence of Gaelic in the west and north through this critical period – from late Middle to Early Modern English – no doubt left its imprint on Scots and Scottish Englishes. And the social and cultural import of the contact likely makes the persistence of these varieties not simply a linguistic matter, but one of identity and heritage.

6.5 AN ENGLISH CHURCH: THE BIBLE IN ENGLISH TO 1611

The 'old saw' of the Chruch prohibited of vernacular translations of Scripture, as one of the foundational grievances of the Protestant Reformation, is, like many another sweeping generalization, not quite true. The Church did restrict preaching on Scripture to clerics in the pulpit; but daily religious life was filled with readings and quotations from Scripture, the Psalms in particular were integral to the Liturgy of the Hours; illustrated folio and de-luxe Biblical manuscripts permitted instruction in Scripture to parishioners who could neither read nor write: British Library, MS Cotton Claudius B.iv of the 11th century, the 'Old English Illustrated Hexateuch' (the first six books of the Bible: Genesis, Exodus, Leviticus, Numbers, Deuteronomy, Joshua), was commissioned by abbot Ælfric of Eynsham, who made the translation of Scripture and wrote the Old English prefaces: the manuscript has over 400 illustrations of episodes

[5] https://www.oed.com/information/understanding-entries/pronunciation/world-englishes/scottish-english/?tl=true

from the Bible. Churches, and quite often public spaces, were filled with paintings, sculptures, friezes, tapestries, altar cloths, and other plastic art forms illustrating the same. In the Order of the Mass, the Gospel reading is followed by the homily in the Liturgy of the Word; here the priest explained the reading in the vernacular, often by quoting the *sermo* ('reading') extensively, at times in word-by-word fashion (the *pericope* for a homily, or *pro-thema* for a sermon, was a Biblical passage then expounded upon). That Biblical episodes worked their way into popular culture, into popular humor (as Chaucer's Miller, Reeve, and Wife of Bath, among others, show), suggests that the bar had as much or more to do with the low level of literacy, a bar that had been raised as much or even more so by civil authorities and the class system. For the history of the English language, there is no doubt about the lasting religious, literary, and cultural influence of the English translations of the Bible in the Reformation era, which begins in England a decade after Martin Luther's 1517 Ninety-Five Theses with Henry's failed appeal for an annulment of his marriage to Catherine of Aragon in 1527. The King James Bible is perhaps the greatest of all the English translations in influence: the acronym KJV has a nearly totemic power, especially in American English. The original printing by Robert Barker, Printer to the King, in 1611 is a landmark in book publishing, with its famous title page by Flemish engraver Cornelis Bol:

THE
HOLY
BIBLE,
Conteyning the Old Testament,
AND THE NEW:
Newly Translated out of the Originall
tongues: & with the former Translations
diligently compared and reuised, by his
Maiesties speciall Co<m>mandement.

Appointed to be read in Churches.
Imprinted at London by Robert
Barker, Printer to the Kings
most Excellent Maiestie.
ANNO DOM. 1611.

The authorization for the new Bible 'to be read in Churches' was made presumably by James's Privy Council; it does not survive. Here, the ornamental spellings *originall;* and *speciall* with geminate <l> are balanced by *maiestie,* still showing its French origin in its spelling. A signal trait of the English Reformation – which began as a movement as political as it was theological, with nationalist leanings thrown in – is that the word *Commandement* should appear on the title page: not the Ten Commandments of the Lord God, but *his Maiesties speciall Commandement.*

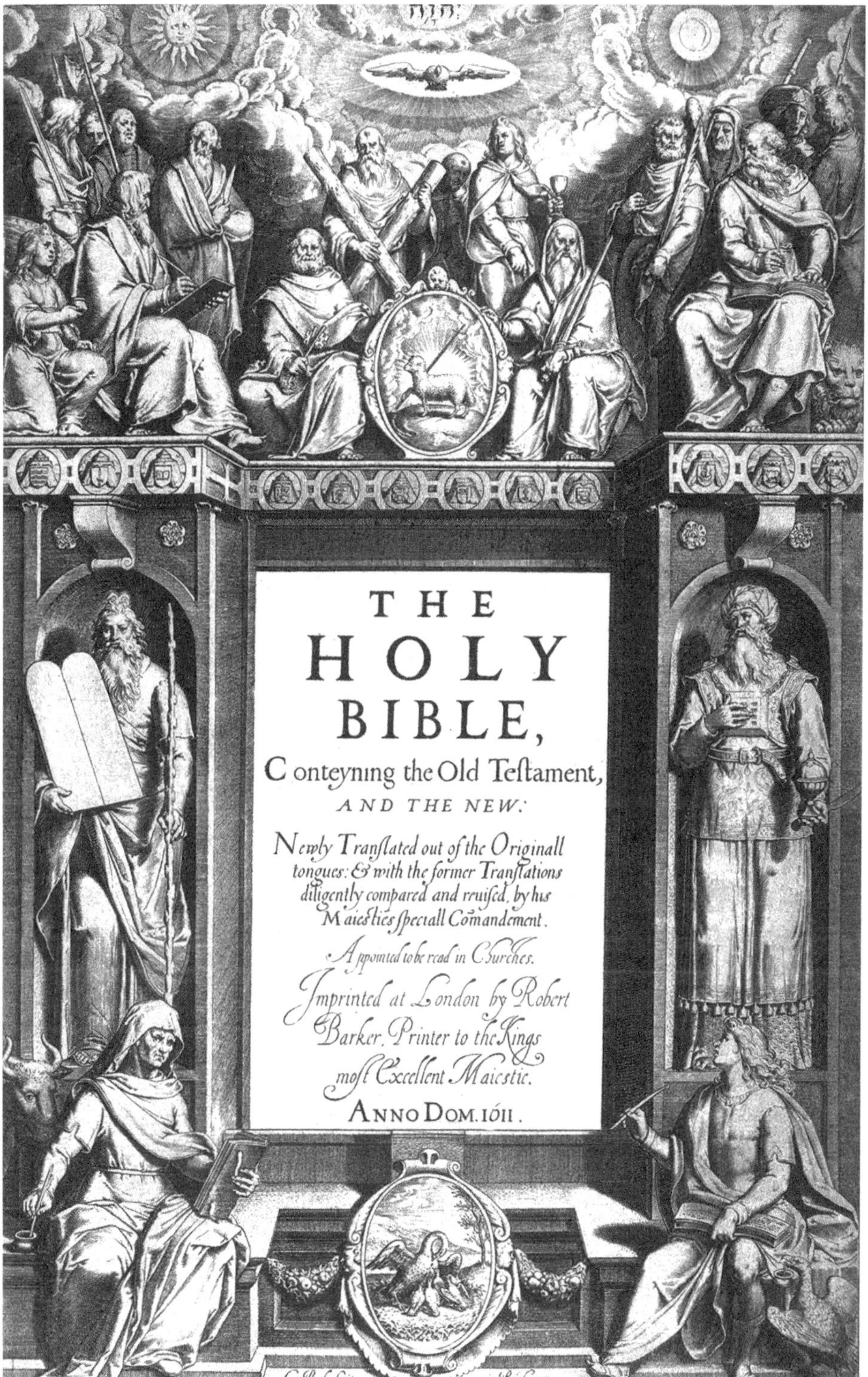
THE
HOLY
BIBLE,
Conteyning the Old Testament,
AND THE NEW:
Newly Translated out of the Originall
tongues: & with the former Translations
diligently compared and reuised, by his
Maiesties speciall Comandement.
Appointed to be read in Churches.
Imprinted at London by Robert
Barker, Printer to the Kings
most Excellent Maiestie.
ANNO DOM. 1611.
C. Boel fecit in Richmont.

Often overlooked is the linguistic character of the Protestant Reformation: the Reformation began, took root, and remained largely confined to areas of the West and North Germanic languages. Martin Luther, Andreas Rudolph Bodenstein von Karlstadt, Phillip Melanchthon, Joachim Westphal, Huldrych Zwingli, and many others were native German speakers (or associated with German-influenced milieu like the Geneva of Jehan Cauvin [John Calvin]); in the British Isles, Yorkshireman John Wycliffe (ca. 1328–1384) was an important precursor of the Reformation in England and, like West Countryman William Tyndale (ca. 1494–1536; Stinchcombe, Gloucestershire), he produced an important translation of the Bible into English. Hugh Latimer (ca. 1487–1555) and Thomas Cranmer (1489–1556) were of the East Midlands (Leicestershire and Nottinghamshire), and Matthew Parker (1504–1571) of East Anglia (Norwich). A pattern emerges here that is seen in the 'Great Migration' of Puritans from England in the latter part of the 16th and early 17th centuries. They, too, would predominantly not be from the London region. There are no doubt theological and academic-intellectual trends in Germanic-speaking countries that led to the Reformation's association primarily with these linguistic areas (Lutheranism spread to North Germanic countries, or those under their sway, e.g., Finland).

The signal failure of the Reformation to take hold in any significant way in Romance-speaking countries (French Huguenots notwithstanding) no doubt has its theological and academic reasons too. One consideration is indeed linguistic: the distance between the Latin of the liturgy and the Romance vernaculars was far smaller than that between the Romance Latin-derived languages and the Germanic branch of Indo-European. Latin was associated with *Popery* (Cranmer used the term in 1551) and the move was on toward the vernacular, with the Bible now available, to those who could afford it, in English translation. All vestiges of the *Papist* menace were to be extirpated, the altars stripped, the frescoes whitewashed; as Tyndale uncharitably observed in his Prologue to his translation of St. Paul's Epistle (a Latin-derived form in competition with *Letter*, which also comes from Latin): *If wilfull blindnes and malicious malyce were not the cause this epistle onlye were ynough to wede oute of the heartes of the Papistes that cankred heresye* (1534; OED, s.v. *papist*). A whole new anti-Catholic vocabulary developed in this period, and it survives, with some elaboration, in the United States and Northern Ireland: *Papist*, *Taig/Teague* (eponymous generic from Irish male-given name *Tádhg*), *Mick* (same type of formation as *Taig*), *Romish/Romanist*, *mackerel snapper*, etc. And yet the move away from Latin was still some two centuries distant, or, in academic circles, was a mid-20th-century phenomenon (the 'death of the classics'). Latin maintained its scholarly cachet at least for some of the reasons it had been the language of the Western Church: it worked as a *lingua franca* for theologians and Biblical scholars, and many of the scholarly resources for the study of Biblical Hebrew and Greek were in Latin.

Almost immediately, the English Reformation generated its own Dissenters, who had their intellectual roots in the Lollards of the mid to late 14th century; *Lollard* is a Dutch loan, *lollaerd* meaning 'mumbler, mutterer' – once again, at least on the linguistic level, a Germanic phenomenon. One reads, at the foot of the central tablet Cornelis Bol engraved for the King James Bible, not *In the yeare of oure Lord 1611*, but, in Latin, *Anno Dom<ini> 1611*.

The following passage, given in English translations ranging from ca. 1000 to 1611, has long elicited much commentary from patristic and later writers. Jacob wrestles with a mysterious stranger until daybreak, usually interpreted as an angel (compare Hosea 12:4 KJV 1611: *Yea, he had power ouer the Angel and preuailed*); the mysterious stranger realizing Jacob's strength strikes him on the hip socket and dislocates the hip. "Let me go, for the day is breaking," the stranger says; "I will not let you go, unless you bless me" Jacob responds. The stranger asks Jacob his name: "Jacob," to which the stranger replies, "You shall no longer be called Jacob, but Israel, for you have striven with God and with humans, and have prevailed." Six centuries of English are represented in the renderings of this passage below:

Genesis 32: 22–27 Jacob wrestles with an angel

Old English, attributed to Ælfric of Eynsham (ca. 955–1010); text of the Illustrated Old English Hexateuch, London, British Library MS Cotton Claudius B.iv (ca. 1025–1050), fol. 49v-50r

he aras ða on dægred, <ond> na<m> his wif mid heora endleofan sunu, <ond> oferfor þone ford ðe man iacob nemð; þa he ealle ða þing ofer gebroht hæfde ðe hys wæron. he ana belaf þær bæftan. ða wraxlode an engel wið hyne on mergen. ða he geseah þ<æt> he hyne oferswyðan ne mihte, ða æthran he hys sine on hys ðeo, <ond> heo þær rihte forscranc. ða cwæð se engle to iacobe, forlæt me, nu gæð dæg steorra up. he <ond>swarode <ond> cw<æð> ne forlæte ic ðe ær þu bletsige me. þa cw<æð> se engel hwæt is þin nama. Iacob cw<æð> he; Þa cw<æð> he ne byð þin nama nateshwon iacob genemned, ac israhel, for ða<m> þe ðu wære strang ongean god, <ond> þu byst strengra ongean men.

[Very literal translation: He arose then on day-break, and took his wife with their eleven sons and fared over the ford which the man Jacob named; then he all the things brought over he had which his were. He alone remained there behind. Then he wrestled an angel against him until morning. The he [the angel] saw that he him overcome might not, then he struck his sinew on his hip, and it there right was shrunken. Then said the angel to Jacob, let me go, now goeth the day star up. He answered and said, I will not let you go before you bless me. Then said the angel, What is thine name? 'Jacob' said he. Then he said, not be your name any longer Jacob called, but Israel, for that you were stronger against God, and you be stronger against men.]

'Wycliffe Bible' (1382–1395; earlier version printed in Forshall and Madden 1850, vol. I)

And whanne sobirly he was arysun, he toke his two wyues, and as feel seruantis with elleuen sones, and he ouerpasside the foorth of Jaboth. And, ouerladde alle thingis that to hym perteyneden, he dwelte aloon, and loo! a man wristlide with hym vnto the morwe. The which whanne he sawȝ that he myȝte not ouercome hym, he towchide the synwe of his hip, and anoon it wexe drye. And he seide to hym, Leeue me, forsothe now vpsteyeth the morwetide. He answeride, I shal not leeue thee, but if thow blisse to me. Thanne he seith, What is the name of thee? He answeride, Jacob. And he, No more, he seith, Jacob shal be clepid thi name, but Israel; for if anentis God thow hast ben strong, myche more anentis men thow shalt haue the maystri.

[*feel* ‘many’; *foorth* ‘ford’; *towchide* ‘touched’; *vpsteyeth* < *upstīen* ‘to rise upward’; *clepid* ‘called’; *anentis* ‘against’; *maystri* ‘mastery’]

Tyndale Old Testament (‘The fyrst Boke of Moses called Genesis,’ 1530 printing)

...a<n>d rose vp the same nyghte a<n>d toke his .ij. wyves and his .ij. maydens <and> his .xi. sonnes <and> went ouer the foorde Jabok. And he toke them a<n>d sent the<m> ouer the ryuer a<n>d sent ouer that he had a<n>d taried behinde him selfe alone.

And there wrastled a man with him vnto the breakynge of the daye. And when he sawe that he coude not prevayle agaynst him, he smote hi<m> vnder the thye and the senowe of Jacobs thy shranke as he wrastled with him. And he sayde: let me goo for the daye breaketh. And he sayde: I will not lett the goo excepte thou blesse me. And he sayde vnto him: what is thy name? He answered: Jacob. And he sayde: thou shalt be called Jacob nomore but Israell. For thou hast wrastled with God and with men a<n>d hast preuayled.

The Coverdale Bible (1535)

...and rose vp in <th>e night, and toke his two wyves and the two maydens and his eleuen sonnes, and wente vnto the foorde of Jacob, toke them and caried them ouer the water, so that all that he had came ouer, and taried him self alone on this syde.

Then wrestled there a man with him vntyll the breake of <th>e daye. And whan he sawe <tha>t he might not ouercome him, he touched the senowe of his thye, and <th>e senowe of his thye shrancke in wrestlinge with him. And he sayde: Let me go, for <th>e daye breaketh on. But he answered: I will not let <th>e go, except thou blesse me. He sayde: What is thy name? He answered: Jacob. He sayde: Thou shalt nomore be called Jacob, but Israel, for thou hast stryuen with God and with men, and hast preuayled.

The Great Bible (1539)

...and rose vp the same nyghte, and toke hys two wyves and hys two maydens, and his eleuen sonnes, and went ouer the foorde Jabok<.> And he toke the<m> and sent the<m> ouer the ryuer, and sent ouer that he had, and taried behinde hym selfe alone.

And there wrastled a man wyth hym unto the breakynge of the daye. And when he sawe that he coulde not preuayle against hym, he smote hym under the thye, and the senowe of Jacobs thye shra<n>ke, as he wrastled wyth hym. And he sayde: let me goo, for the daye breaketh. Which answered: I wyll not let the goo, excepte thou blesse me. And he sayde unto hym: what is thy name? He answered: Jacob. He sayde: thou shalt be called Jacob nomore, but Israell. For as a prynce has thou wrastled wyth God: and wyth man, and hast preuayled (Edward Whytchurche printing, 1540).

The Geneva Bible (1560)

And he rose vp the same night, and toke his twio wiues, and his two maides, and his eleue<n> children, & went ouer the forde Iabbók.

And he tooke them, & sent them ouer the riuer, & sent ouer that he had.

Whe<n> Iakkób was left him selfe alone, there wrestled a man with him vnto the breaking of the day.

And he sawe that he colde not preuaile against him: therefore he touched <th>e holowe of his thigh, & the holowe of Iakkobs thigh was loosed, as he wrestled with him.

And he saide, Let me goe, for <th>e morning appeareth. Who answered, I wil not let thee go except thou blesse me.

Then said he vnto him, What is thy name? And he said, Iakkób.

Then said he, Thy name shal be called Iakkób no more, but Israél: because thou hast had power with God, thou shalt also preuaile with men.

King James Bible (1611)

And hee rose vp that night, and he tooke his two wiues, and his two women seruants, and his eleuen sonnes, and passed ouer the foord Jabbok.

And he tooke them, and sent them ouer the brooke, and sent ouer that hee had.

And Jacob was left alone: and there wrestled a man with him, vntill the breaking of the day.

And when he saw, that he preuailed not against him, he touched the hollow of his thigh: and the hollow of Jacobs thigh was out of ioynt, as hee wrestled with him.

And he said, Let me goe, for the day breaketh: and he said, I will not let thee goe, except thou blesse me.

And he said vnto him, What is thy name: and he said, Jacob.

And he said, Thy name shall be called no more Jacob, but Israel: for as a prince hast thou power with God, and with men, and hast preuailed.

Revered English hymnodist Charles Wesley (1707–1788), younger brother of John Wesley with whom he established the Methodist movement, took up the episode in his hymn "Wrestling Jacob" (hymn no. 136 from his *A Collection of Hymns for the Use of the People Called Methodists* [1747]; Marks 2012, 2140–2142), which he treated allegorically (with Christ as "the man" in Genesis 32, that is, the angel Jacob wrestled through the night). Perhaps not the finest of his hymns ("Contented now upon my thigh / I halt, till life's short journey end"; stanza 10), it is interesting for setting up 'love' in rhyming couplets with 'move,' 'strove,' and 'above.' By 1747, only 'above/love' would fully rhyme, even for someone from Wesley's North Lincolnshire (Epworth); *above* is from Old English *bufan, beufan* < **be-ufan*, while 'move/love' only became closer as the main vowel of Anglo-Norman loan *mover* underwent raising and rounding; for a time, in some dialects, *love* would have retained its historical /u/ perhaps long enough for the two forms to have been near rhymes. *Strove* as from *strive* is a Middle English form deriving from Old French *estriver*; though past forms occur in ME such as *striuede* and *striueden*, that is, as regular or weak inflectional forms, the OED notes that, as would be expected with a loan from French, the strong forms seem to be earlier; *strove* increased in frequency in the 16th century (it is the form used consistently in the KJV Bible [1611]), and, though now nonstandard, was also used as the past participle (*strived* and *striven* the usual forms; s.v. *strive*).

And so, some 800 years of trying to understand, in English, the mystery of Jacob wrestling the angel through the night.

6.6 THE ENGLISH STAGE – SHAKESPEARE AND THE ENGLISH LANGUAGE

What more can be said – *quid plura*? the Latin phrase that may ultimately be behind this phrasing – about Shakespeare and the English language? Perhaps only Chaucer, in an even more critical century of change (the 14th) can be said to rival The Bard's influence on English. The First Folio of Shakespeare's works is without question a landmark in English literature as well as publishing. The title page engraved portrait of Shakespeare by Martin Droeshout is less celebrated, if valuable nonetheless as one of the few representations of The Bard. The engraving sits below the title: *Mr. William SHAKESPEARES / COMEDIES, / HISTORIES, & / TRAGEDIES. Published according to the True Originall Copies* (Folger Folio no. 68). Below the portrait is the imprint: *LONDON / Printed by Isaac Iaggard, and Ed. Blount. 1623.* In smaller italic type below the bottom left of the portrait is the inscription: *Martin Droeshout sculpsit* [Latin: carved, engraved] *London*. Droeshout, as the family name indicates, was of Flemish descent. There was long a Flemish presence in London; Chaucer refers to Flemings in the *Canterbury Tales*; notable is the allusion to the Peasant Rebellion of 1381 and resentment of Flemish merchants and tradespeople: *Certes, he Jakke Straw and his meynee / Ne made never shoutes half so shrille / Whan that they wolden any Flemyng kille* ("Indeed, Jack Straw and his mob / Never made shouts half so shrill / When they wished any Fleming to kill"; "Nun's Priest's Tale," VII.3394–3396). By 1635, he had wound up in Madrid, partially anglicized his name to Droeswoode (Dutch *hout* given its English equivalent), and apparently converted to Catholicism (his family having once fled to England to escape persecution as Protestants). Isaac Jaggard and his father William were noted printers of the day, their shop located in Barbican (the name for the neighborhood referred to the *barbecana* 'fortified gate-tower' located in the northwest section of Roman London); William Jaggard (1568–1623) has been in poor health and passed shortly before the edition's appearance (known to have been in readers' hands by December of 1623), while publisher Edward Blount (1562–1632) was a member of the Stationers' Company. In a reversal of the frontispiece tradition (in which the portrait 'faces' the title page), Droeshout's engraving dominates the title page while fellow dramatist Ben Jonson's commemorative verse serves as the frontispiece:

To the Reader.
This Figure, that thou here seest put,
It was for gentle Shakespeare cut;
Wherein the Grauer had a strife
with Nature, to out-doo the life:
O, could he but haue dravvne his vvit
As well in brasse, as he hath hit
His face; the Print would then surpasse
All, that vvas euer vvrit in brasse.
But, since he cannot, Reader, looke
Not on his Picture, but his Booke.

Not Ben Jonson's finest verse – did he dash it off, or was its clunkiness meant to match that of Droeshout's portrait of Shakespeare? By contrast, there is Jonson's commemorative verse for his daughter Mary, lost as an infant in 1593 (at six months of age):

Here lyes to each her Parents ruth,
MARY, the Daughter of their youth:
Yet, all heauens gifts, being heauens due,
It makes the father, lesse, to rue.
At sixe moneths end, shee parted hence
With safetie of her innocence;
Whose soule heauens Queene, (whose name shee beares)
In comfort of her mothers teares,
Hath plac'd amongst her virgin-traine:
Where, while that seuer'd doth remaine,
This graue partakes the fleshly birth.
Which couer lightly, gentle earth (Jonson 1616, 774; *Epigrammes* XXII).

Jonson's two poems offer a snapshot of Early Modern English 1616–1623. At the level of typography and orthography, we see the usual patterns of use: the colon (and occasionally the semi-colon) is usually separated by a space from its preceding text, the comma flush with the preceding text. The apostrophe marks vowel contraction in *-ed* regular past tense forms, but is not used to mark the possessive of nominals. Geminates can still mark vowel length (*looke*, *Booke*, *shee*, *Queene*), while inflectional *-e-* marking nominal plurals (*teares*) or third singular present verb forms (*beares*) would fade from use later in the 17th century; *-e* to mark preceding vowel length continues in use for some time still (*traine*, *remaine*) and had in this period been extended to words where it had not occurred in the base and nominative singular forms: compare Chaucerian *cas/caas* ('situation, case') with *case*, or Old English *līf* with *life* (the latter had undergone raising and breaking with the Great Vowel Shift, from [li:f] to [lɑɪf]/[lʌɪf]); this is to be distinguished from inflectional *līfe* (dative singular) and *līfes* (genitive singular) in Old English (Görlach 1991, 47).

The function of final *-e* in Early Modern English – when it was not otiose (no longer needed or of any function) – is often a source of confusion, all the more so given the inconsistency and ambiguity in the practice of early printers. In general, *-e* was employed to distinguish: (1) vowel length, namely that a preceding vowel was long (*see*, an open syllable, or *name*, closed); (2) to distinguish the values of consonants where there was graphemic variation: that is, where *c* had its historical OE value /k/ but under the influence of Latin and French could also represent /s/; thus OE *mys*, plural of *mus* 'mouse,' came to be spelled *mice*; (3) to distinguish *-s* use: as word-final, that is, organically part of the word, from inflectional – that is, word-final *-s* etymologically part of the word versus a grammatical marker such as the *-s* plural.

In the First Quarto edition of *Hamlet* (1603), the soldiers Barnardo and Francisco are simply called 'two Centinels' ('sentinels') until named in the dialogue; fairly quickly, in just the first scene, one can see the many differences between the First Quarto (1603) and First Folio (1623) much less modern printed editions. The ghost of King Hamlet appears and disappears, and appears and disappears again:

> 2. [Barnardo]: See, it stalkes away.
> Hor[atio]: Stay, speake, speak, by heauen I charge thee speake.
> Mar[cellus]: Tis gone and makes no answer.
> [Barnardo]: How now *Horatio*, you tremble and looke pale,
> Is it not something more than fantasie?
> What think you on't?
> Hor[atio]: Afore my God, I might not this beleeue, without
> the sensible and true auouch of my owne eyes.
> Mar[cellus]: Is it not like the King?
> Hor[atio]: As tho art to thy selfe,
> Such was the very armor he had on,
> When he the ambitious *Norway* combated.
> So frownd he once, when in an angry parle
> He smot the sleaded pollax on the yce,
> Tis strange.

Though Quarto *sleaded pollax* (Folio *sledded Pollax*) has occasioned some proposals for emendation (more radically to *leaded pole-ax*), that of famed early Shakespeare editor Edmond Malone (1741–1812) to *Polacks* has held place ever since. Though now an ethnic slur for Poles and, especially, Polish Americans, the first attestation in the OED is Sir Thomas Hoby's translation of *The courtyer of Count Baldessar Castiglione* (1561: "and saw the Moscouites, which for suspicion of warr were in doubt of the Polakes, were on the other side"), the second from a letter of Sir Philip Sidney (1574: "The Polakes hartily repente their so fur fetcht election"), and the third is this Quarto edition of *Hamlet* (1603). That 'Polacks' (Poles), is likely meant here is clearer by Act IV with references to battles involving Poles and Fortinbras of Norway leading an army through Poland. And likely too is that Shakespeare's use of *Pollax/Polacks* does not have the semantic force of the later slur; this seems first attested in AmE by 1898 in Finley Peter Dunne's Mr. Dooley character. Chicago native Dunne (1867–1936) was the son of Irish immigrants, and his 'Mr. Dooley' character, Martin J. Dooley, was an Irish barkeep in the working-class Bridgeport section of Chicago whose witticisms appeared in newspaper columns for the *Chicago Herald* and *Chicago Evening Post* (1893–1915, 1924–1926). Dooley's Irish-brogue monologues evince the American working-class world of ethnic rivalries and humor; in this first AmE instance, "'Well, said Mr. Dooley, 'ye'er thoughts on this subject is inthrestin,' but not conclusive, as Dorsey said to the Pollack, that thought he cud lick him'" (OED, s.v. *Polack*), the original ethnonym is from Polish *Polak*, and perhaps transmitted to English through 16th-century Italian *polacco*. The pejoration of the term in AmE mirrors the period of increased Polish and other East European immigration to the States (the same era that produced *hunk/hunky* < *Bohunk*). Here, at least, we can say Shakespeare meant it as no slur.

To some extent, Shakespeare's Hamlet had a forebear in Thomas Kyd's Hieronimo in the latter's *The Spanish Tragedy* (after 1582, ca. 1587–1592); Kyd may have written an earlier drama about Hamlet, though it has not survived (Neill 2014, xiii). Kyd had a short and turbulent life (1558–1594): the son of a London scrivener, he was educated at Richard Mulcaster's Merchant Taylors' School, and landed in the service of either the Earl of Sussex or Earl Strange, which afforded him the support and, if serving the latter, the theater-world connections an aspiring dramatist required. He shared lodgings with fellow dramatist Christopher Marlowe, whom he denounced when 'atheistical' papers were found in their room, though this did not save him from torture (Neill 2014, xii). Kyd's *Spanish Tragedy* exhibits a wildness not just in its dramatics but its language, its rhetorical flourishes, and consciousness of English as one among several important languages of the day, not to forget the languages of antiquity one would study at Mulcaster's school (Greek and Latin). While the Spaniards of Kyd's tragedy are suitably Mediterranean in their passions, the great speeches are products of that 'new learning' of the English Renaissance; for instance, Hieronimo's opening soliloquy to Act III, Scene ii:

O eies! no eies, but fountains fraught with teares;
O life! no life, but liuely fourme of death;
O world! no world, but masse of publique wrongs,
Confusde and filde with murder and misdeeds;
O sacred heauens, if this vnhallowed deed,
If this inhumane and barberous attempt,
If this incompatible murder thus
Of mine, but now no more my sonne,
Shall unreueald and vnreuengéd passe,
How should we tearme your dealings to be iust,
If you vniustly deal with those that in your iustice trust? (III.ii ll. 1–11)

The juxtaposition of contrarieties (with *no*-phrases and negative prefixes *mis-*, *in-*, *un-*), use of *polyptoton* (*just...unjustly...justice*), and *amplificatio* (from *eyes* to *life* to *world* to *heavens*) are no doubt what led contemporary dramatist Thomas Nashe to hail Kyd as an 'English Seneca' (Neill 2014, xii-xiii). And Kyd was not done as he capped Hieronimo's plangent speech with the congeries, "Eies, life, world, heauens, hel, night, and day, / See, search, show, send some man, some meane, that may!"

(III.ii ll. 22–23). When the ghost of Don Andrea and the figure of Revenge take the stage again at the play's end, one has heard mention of names Spanish, French, Italian, Turkish, Greek, and Latin. The subject itself was timely, in the buildup to the Armada of 1588, and Spain's long-anticipated fall, the play alludes to. Shakespeare and contemporaries could send up the wildness and excess of Kyd's Don Andrea and Hieronimo (the original title was *The Spanish Tragedie: OR, Hieronimo is mad againe*), but they were nonetheless deeply influenced by the play – it was performed some 29 times during 1592–1597 at a number of theaters, including the original Globe (Mulryne 1989, xxx–xxxi).[6]

Kyd's bouts of rhetorical excess were offset by a rhetorical dexterity, his Latinate vocabulary by an impassioned use of plain English (in the mouths of Spaniards). And Kyd's linguistic, dramatic, and classical learning facility help temper debates over Shakespeare's like facility. Neither was a college graduate, both expanded their dramatic canon beyond English subjects and characters, and each of them was well enough grounded in classical rhetoric to deploy it with aplomb or excess. The Latin-based education system did not, apparently, in any way inhibit linguistic experimentation with the English language. The use of rhetorical figures such as *figura etymologica* and *polyptoton*, by which one conjoins, in the same line or series, words from the same root or sharing the same etymological origin, suggests an increasingly complex semantic awareness in Elizabethan writers; for Shakespeare, *satisfaction* in its semantic range was "personal, civic, and honour-based (as in fighting a duel) and which also had religious overtones"; Mote (or Moth), the page to Don Adriano de Armado in Shakespeare's *Love's Labour's Lost*, bore a name that "with dancing polysemy means *word* (*le mot*, motto, motty), *winged insect*, *speck* (as in mote and beam [with reference to Matthew 7: 3–5]), and probably *scruple*" (Kerrigan 2016, 147, 92). Shakespeare's semantic innovations, like those of Chaucer, are such that one may say that he, like the author of *The Canterbury Tales*, genuinely shaped the English language.

And Shakespeare could also be innovative with morphology. Conversion, or zero-derivation, is not uncommon in his verse (e.g., deriving a noun from a verb, or a verb from a noun, the latter often termed *back-formation).* New words were being coined for new things, or being brought back from a 'Newe World,' and traces of this might be found in Shakespeare's *Bermudas* and Prospero's island in *The Tempest* – although, as with Thomas Hariot's *A briefe and true report of the new found land of Virginia* (1588), with, in John White's illustrations, its analogizing of the Algonquian natives of the Powhatan Confederacy with Britain's ancient Celts, there may be some of the 'European wild man' in Shakespeare's vision of Caliban (Kermode 2000, 291).

> *Cymbeline* I.iv.14–16 Iachimo: ...wherein he must be weighed rather by her value than his own, **words him**, I doubt not, a great deal from the matter (Wells and Taylor 1986).

---

[6] Printings of these dramas often boasted of where they played, such as the 1623 printing of John Webster's *The Duchess of Malfi*: *The Tragedy of THE DVTCHESSE OF Malfy. As it was presented privatly, at the Black-Friers; and publiquely at the Globe, By the Kings Maiesties Seruants. The perfect and exact Coppy, with diuerse things Printed, that the length of the Play would not beare in the Presentment* (London: Nicholas Okes and John Waterson, 1623).

Here, we see Shakespeare's morphological freedom, with another noun > verb conversion, with transitive *word* here meaning 'to describe' (Shewmaker 2008), or 'to speak of' (Onions 1986), with the sense of the line 'make a report of him which is remote from the fact' (Onions ibid.). The 'new' verb *to word* occurs only three times in Shakespeare's works, in two later dramas, *Antony and Cleopatra* and *Cymbeline*, both historical dramas, the one set in Roman times of Caesar and Octavian, the other in Celtic Britain of the early AD 1st century. In each case, the formation might be more properly *to word X* (where *X* is a pronoun):

words him (*Cymbeline* I.iv.15)
word it with thee (*Cymbeline* IV.ii.241)
He words me (*Antony and Cleopatra* V.ii.187)

Cleopatra speaks to Charmian and her other attendants just after Caesar's departure, the sense of her declaration "He words me, girls, he words me, that I should not / Be noble to myself" (187–188) being 'to flatter' (Onions 1986). The second occurrence in *Cymbeline* is contrastive, with *to word* set against *to sing* as Guiderius speaks with his brother Arviragus: "Cadwal, / I cannot sing. I'll weep, and word it with thee, For notes of sorrow out of tune are worse / Than priests and fanes that lie" (IV.ii.305–308). There is perhaps here another instance of Shakespeare's linguistic matching of 'enveloping' plot detail: some two decades earlier, King Cymbeline has exiled treacherous lord Belarius, who had taken away Cymbeline's two young sons, Guiderius and Arviragus, to Wales. Belarius now goes by the name Morgan, the sons renamed as well (Guiderius > Polydore, Arviragus > Cadwal). Filtered through Raphael Holinshed's *Chronicles of England, Scotland, and Ireland* (first ed. 1577, second ed. 1587) and what other knowledge Shakespeare had of the 'Matter of Britain' (Geoffrey of Monmouth, and perhaps local oral traditions), Cymbeline is the Catuvellauni leader Cunobelinus (British for 'dog-strong,' or 'strong as a dog,' seen earlier in Chapter 3) and Cadwal, a British name that occurs in Holinshed (and recalls the tribal name Catuvellauni).

With *A Midsommer Nights Dreame* (ca. 1595), it is difficult not to imagine Shakespeare returning to the Warwickshire of his youth, the old territory of the Dobunni tribe of Iron Age and Roman Britain. It is set in a fairyland that is the imagined ancient Greece of Chaucer's 'Knight's Tale' on the one hand, on the other, the old forests and woodlands of an earlier Britain – such as his own Forest of Arden, left unspoiled by the Romans. The various strands of Shakespeare's subjects, the history of his England, the Romans of his grammar schooling whose roads and ruins still dotted the British landscape, the Italianate comedies of his Renaissance dramatic career, and the 'Celtic' plays of the furthest British past (see, for instance, Loughnane and Maley 2013), these all seem to lead back home in this comedy, to his Warwickshire youth. The play is in its way childish, the language often quite simple – how else would fairies talk, but earnestly and simply, when not up to their tricks. As it is one of the more difficult of his plays to find sources for; one supposes, if only by default, to look to local legend and folk tradition. The cadences of even the *dramatis personae* (a classical convention dramas in English ever since have inherited) have the incantatory rhythm of nursery rhyme and children's song – there are the fairies Peasebottom and Cobweb, Mote and Mustardseed, Robin Goodfellow the puck, a carpenter (Peter Quince) and a weaver (Nick Bottom), a bellows-maker (Francis Flute) and a joiner (Snug), a tinker (Tom Snout) and a tailor (Robin Starveling), and of course the King and Queen of the fairies, Oberon and Titania. Among the many stagings of the play, the variously hazy and glittering compositions of the 1935 film version by Max Reinhardt and William Dieterle (with the seemingly odd ensemble of Olivia de Havilland, Dick Powell, Mickey Rooney, and James Cagney) captured some sense of the wavering world of faery Shakespeare evokes from rural Britain. The vocabulary has its loans from French and Latin, but, perhaps because of its simplicity, from the mouth of a puck (a word of uncertain etymology, appearing in both Germanic and Celtic) or fairy-queen, it is often preponderantly of English stock.

Titania:
And **th**orough **th**is **d**istemperature we **see**
The **seasons** alter: **h**oary-**h**eaded **fr**osts
Fall in the **fr**esh lap of the crim**son** ro**se**,
And **on o**ld Hiems' [Winter's] thin **an**d icy crown
An odorous chaplet of **s**weet **s**ummer buds
Is, a**s** in mockr'y, **s**et. The **s**pring, the **s**ummer,
The **ch**ilding **au**tumn, **a**ngry winter **ch**ange
Their **wo**nted liveries, and the mazèd **wo**rld
By their increase **now kn**ows **no**t **which** is **which** (II.i.106–114).

The alliterative effects roll back English poetry too, to those earlier alliterative traditions of Old and Middle English verse. The effect is actually staggering, as the lines are laden with repeated sounds in close and embracing patterns (***ch**iding*...***ch**ange*).

The 'puck' Robin Goodfellow is given the task of closing the play; he appears, broom in hand:

Now the hungry lion roars,
        And the wolf behowls the moon,
Whilst the heavy ploughman snores,
        All with weary task fordone.

...And we fairies that do run,
        By the triple Hecate's team
From the presence of the sun,
        Following darkness like a dream,
Now are frolic. Not a mouse
Shall disturb this hallowed house.
I am sent with broom before
To sweep the dust before the door (V.ii.1–4, 12–20).

Oberon says, before he and all the fairy-retinue depart:

Now until the break of day
Through this house each fairy stray....

With this field-dew consecrate
Every fairy take his gait
And each several chamber bless
Through this palace with sweet peace;
And the owner of it blessed
Ever shall in safety rest.
Trip away, make no stay,
Meet me all by break of day (V.ii.31–32, 45–52).

Though *chamber*, *palace*, and *peace* are French loans, and *several* derives from Latin via Anglo-Norman, Latinate *consecrate* is followed by English *bless* and *blessed* – and much of all the rest is of English stock.

And Robin at the last, with sound-patterning in the plays' close that slows down the cadence with heavier consonantal sounds, nasal and dental clusters: offe**nded**, **mended**, slu**mb**ere**d**, repreh**end**, **mend**, frie**nd**s, a**mend**s.

If we shadows have offended,
Think but this, and all is mended:
That you have but slumbered here,
While these visions did appear;
And this weak and idle theme,
No more yielding but a dream,
Gentles, do not reprehend.
If you pardon, we will mend.
And as I am an honest puck,
If we have unearnèd luck
Now to 'scape the serpent's tongue,
We will make amends ere long,
Else the puck a liar call.
So, good night unto you all.
Give me your hands, if we be friends,
And Robin shall restore amends (Act V, Epilogue).

If Robin begs the indulgence of the audience to consider it all a dream – however half-hearted that request may be – one senses in this overtly simple and earnest early comedy, Shakespeare putting away the Warwickshire of childhood, as many of the great dramas, and tragedies, lay ahead.

REFERENCES AND BIBLIOGRAPHY

Aitken, A.J., "The Language of Older Scots Poetry," in McClure, J.D., ed. *Scotland and the Lowland Tongue. Studies in the Language and Literature of Lowland Scotland in Honour of David D. Murison*, 1983, pp. 18–49. Aberdeen: Aberdeen University Press

Alexander, Catherine M.S., ed. *Shakespeare and Language*. Cambridge: Cambridge University Press, 2004

Babington, Churchill, ed. *Polychronicon Ranulphi Higden Monachi Cestrensis; together with the English Translation of John Trevisa and of an Unknown Writer of the Fifteenth Century*. Vol. I. *Rerum Britannicarum Medii Aevi Scriptores*. London: Longman, Green, Longman, Roberts, and Green, 1865

Bately, Janet, "Bilingual and Multilingual Dictionaries of the Renaissance and Early Seventeenth Century," in *Cowie* 2009, vol. I, pp. 41–64

BCP = Book of Common Prayer *The Booke of the Common Prayer and Administracion of the Sacramentes, and Other Rites and Ceremonies of the Churche: After the vse of the Churche of England*. London: Edward Whitchurch, 1549

Benson, Larry D., gen. ed. *The Riverside Chaucer*. 3rd ed. Boston: Houghton Mifflin, 1987

Bergin, Osborn. *Irish Bardic Poetry: Texts and Translations, Together with an Introductory Lecture*. Foreword by D.A. Binchy. Ed. David Greene and Fergus Kelly. Dublin: Dublin Institute for Advanced Studies, 1984.

Biblia. The Byble, that is the holy Scrypture of the Olde and New Testament, faythfully translated in to Englysh. [The Coverdale Bible. Compiled by Myles Coverdale.] [Zurich?], 1535

The Byble in Englyshe [The Great Bible, 1539]. London: Edward Whitchurch, 1540

The Holy Bible, Conteyning the Old Testament, AND THE NEW [King James Bible]. London: Robert Barker, 1611

Blake, Norman F., "Spelling and Standardisation," in *The Cambridge History of the English Language*. Volume II: 1066-1476. Cambridge: Cambridge University Press (1992), pp. 9–15

Boethius, Hector. *Chronicle of Scotland*. Edinburgh, 1540. The English Experience, Number 851. Amsterdam: Theatrum Orbis Terrarum, 1977

Brown, John Russell, ed. *John Webster: The White Devil*. Manchester: Manchester University Press, 1996

Buchan, Peter and David Toulmin. *Buchan Claik – The Saat an the Glaar o't: A Compendium of Words and Phrases from the North-East of Scotland*. Edinburgh: Gordon Wright Publishing, 1998

Campbell, Alistair. *Old English Grammar*. Oxford: Clarendon Press, 1959

Cowie, A.P., ed. *The Oxford History of English Lexicography*. 2 vols. Oxford: Clarendon Press, 2009

Danielson, Bror, ed. *John Hart's Works on English Orthography and Pronunciation 1551, 1569, 1570*. Uppsala: Almqvist & Wiksell, 1963

Davenport, Cyril. *Thomas Berthelet: Royal Printer and Bookbinder to Henry VIII, King of England. With Special Reference to his Bookbindings*, Chicago: The Caxton Club, 1901

Dobson, E.J. *English Pronunciation 1500-1700*. 2nd ed. 2 vols. Oxford: Clarendon Press, 1968

Edwards, A.S.G. *Stephen Hawes*. Boston: Twayne Publishers, 1983

The English Bible: King James Version. Volume One: *The Old Testament*, ed. Herbert Marks; Volume Two: *The New Testament and Apocrypha*, ed. Gerald Hammond and Austin Busch. New York: W.W. Norton & Company, 2012

Forshall, Rev Josiah and Sir Frederic Madden, eds. *The Holy Bible, Containing The Old and New Testaments, with the Apocryphal Books, in the Earliest English Versions, Made from the Latin Vulgate by John Wycliffe and his Followers.* 4 vols. Oxford: Oxford University Press, 1850

Froissart, Jean. *The Thirde and Fourthe Boke of Sir Johan Froyssart.* 1525. The English Experience Number 250. Amsterdam: Da Capo Press/Theatrum Orbis Terrarum, 1970

Gilbert, Jay. *Dialect Variation in Northern Middle English: Scribal Language and Dialect in Northern Manuscripts of The Pricke of Conscience.* Medium Ævum Monographs, New Series XLI. Oxford: Society for the Study of Medieval Languages and Literature, 2021

Görlach, Manfred. *Introduction to Early Modern English.* Cambridge: Cambridge University Press, 1991

Grosart, Alexander B. *The Life and Complete Works in Prose and Verse of Robert Greene, M.A.* The Huth Library. Vol. X: *Prose.* London: [privately printed], 1881–1883

Gwosdek, Hedwig, ed. *Early Printed Editions of the Long Accidence and Short Accidence Grammars.* Heidelberg: Carl Winter Universitätsverlag, 1991

Hahn, Thomas, ed. *Sir Gawain: Eleven Romances and Tales.* TEAMS Middle English Texts Series. Kalamazoo, MI: Medieval Institute Publications, 1995

Halle, Morris and Samuel Jay Keiser. Rev. of Danielson (1963). *Language* 43.3 (1967), 773–787

Gerald Hammond and Austin Busch. See *The English Bible: King James Version*, 2012

Hart, John. *The Opening of the Unreasonable Writing of our Inglish Toung, wherin is shewid what necessarili is to be Left, and What folowed for the Perfect Writing thereof.* 1551. London, British Library, MS Royal 17.C.vii. Ed. Danielson 1963

Hart, John. *An Orthographie [1569].* Ed. R.C. Alston. English Linguistics (1500-1800). No. 209. Menston: The Scolar Press, 1969

Hickscorner [c. 1497-1512]. The Tudor Facsimile Texts, ed. John S. Farmer. London: T.C. & E.C. Jack, 1908

Horstmann, Carl, ed. *The Early South-English Legendary, or Lives of Saints. I: MS. Laud, 108, in the Bodleian Library.* EETS O.S. 87. London: N. Trübner & Co., 1887

Jespersen, Otto, ed. *John Hart's Pronunciation of English (1569 and 1570).* Anglistische Forschungen Heft 22. Heidelberg: Carl Winter, 1907

Jespersen, Otto. *A Modern English Grammar on Historical Principles. Part I: Sounds and Spelling.* Heidelberg: Carl Winter's Universitätsbuchhandlung, 1909

Jonson, Benjamin. *The English Grammar Made by Ben. Iohnson. For the Benefit of all Strangers, Out of His Observation of the English Language Now Spoken, and in Use.* London: Richard Meighen, 1640

Jonson, Benjamin. *The Workes of Beniamin Jonson.* London: William Stansby, 1616

Kastovsky, Dieter, ed. *Studies in Early Modern English.* Topics in English Linguistics 13. Berlin: Mouton de Gruyter, 1994

Kermode, Frank. *Shakespeare's Language.* New York: Farrar, Straus and Giroux, 2000

Kerrigan, John. *Shakespeare's Binding Language.* Oxford: Oxford University Press, 2016

Kopaczyk, Joanna, "Rethinking the traditional periodisation of the Scots language," in *After the Storm: Papers from the Forum for Research on the Languages of Scotland and*

Ulster triennial meeting, Aberdeen 2012, ed. Janet Cruickshank and Robert McColl Millar. Aberdeen: The Forum for Research on the Languages of Scotland and Ulster, 2013, 233–260

Kopaczyk, Joanna, "The Language of William Dunbar: Middle Scots or Early Modern Scots?" *European Journal of English Studies* 18.1 (2014), 21–41

Labov, William. *Principles of Linguistic Change*, 3 vols. Volume 1: *Internal Factors* (1994); Volume 2: *Social Factors* (2001); Volume 3: *Cognitive and Cultural Factors* (2010). Language in Society vols. 20, 29, 39. Malden, MA: Blackwell/Wiley-Blackwell

Labov, William, Sharon Ash, Charles Boberg. *The Atlas of North American English: Phonetics, Phonology and Sound Change*. Berlin: Mouton de Gruyter, 2006.

Lass, Roger 1994. *Old English: A Historical Linguistic Companion*. Cambridge: Cambridge University Press

Lass, Roger Ed. *The Cambridge History of the English Language*. Volume III: *1476-1776*. Cambridge: Cambridge University Press, 1999

Lewis, C.S. *English Literature in the Sixteenth Century, Excluding Drama*. Oxford: Clarendon Press, 1954

Loewenstein, David and Janel Mueller, eds. *The Cambridge History of Early Modern English Literature*. Cambridge: Cambridge University Press, 2002

Los, Bettelou. *The Rise of the To-Infinitive*. Oxford: Oxford University Press, 2005

Los, Bettelou. *A Historical Syntax of English*. Edinburgh Textbooks on the English Language. Advanced. Edinburgh: Edinburgh University Press, 2015

Loughnane, Rory and Willy Maley. *Celtic Shakespeare: The Bard and the Borderers*. London: Routledge, 2013

McClure, J.D., ed. *Scotland and the Lowland Tongue. Studies in the Language and Literature of Lowland Scotland in Honour of David D. Murison*, ed. J.D. McClure. Aberdeen: Aberdeen University Press, 1983

McDiarmid, Matthew P., "The *Gododdin* and Other Heroic Poems of Scotland," in J.D. McClure *Scotland and the Lowland Tongue. Studies in the Language and Literature of Lowland Scotland in Honour of David D. Murison*, Aberdeen: Aberdeen University Press, 1983, pp. 1–17

McGowan, Joseph P. *Manuscripts in Switzerland*. Anglo-Saxon Manuscripts in Microfiche Facsimile Volume 20. Medieval and Renaissance Texts and Studies Volume 412. Tempe, AZ: Arizona Center for Medieval and Renaissance Studies, 2012

Marks, Herbert, ed. See *The English Bible: King James Version*, 2012

Mead, William Edward, ed. *The Pastime of Pleasure by Stephen Hawes. A Literal Reprint of the Earliest Complete Copy (1517) with Variant Readings from the Editions of 1509, 1554, and 1555, together with Introduction, Notes, Glossary, and Indexes*. EETS O.S. 173. London: Published for the Early English Text Society by Humphrey Milford, 1928

Millar, Robert McColl. *Modern Scots: An Analytical Survey. Edinburgh Textbooks on the English Language. Advanced.* Edinburgh: Edinburgh University Press, 2018

Minkova, Donka. *A Historical Phonology of English*. Edinburgh Textbooks on the English Language. Advanced. Edinburgh: Edinburgh University Press, 2014

Minkova, Donka and Michael Lefkowitz, “Middle English Open Syllable Lengthening (MESOL) or Middle English Compensatory Lengthening (MECL)?”, *English Language and Linguistics* 25.1 (2021), 15–180

Moir, James, ed. *The Actis and Deidis of the Illustere and Vailȝeand Campioun Schir William Wallace, Knight of Ellerslie, by Henry the Minstrel*. Edinburgh: William Blackwood and Sons, 1889

Mugglestone, Lynda, ed. *The Oxford History of English*. Oxford: Oxford University Press, 2006

Mulryne, J.R., ed. *Thomas Kyd: The Spanish Tragedy*. The New Mermaids London: A & C Black/New York: : W.W. Norton, 1989

Mustanoja, Tauno F. *A Middle English Syntax. Part I: Parts of Speech*. Mémoires de la Société Néophilologique de Helsinki, XXIII. Helsinki: Société Néophilologique, 1960

Neill, Michael, ed. *Thomas Kyd: The Spanish Tragedy*. A Norton Critical Edition. New York: W.W. Norton, 2014

Nevalainen, Terttu. *An Introduction to Early Modern English*. Oxford: Oxford University Pres, 2006

Norbrook, David and H.R. Woudhuysen. *The Penguin Book of Renaissance Verse*. London: Penguin Books, 1992

ODFN. *The Oxford Dictionary of Family Names in Britain and Ireland*, ed. Patrick Hanks, Richard Coates, and Peter McClure. 4 vols. Oxford: Oxford University Press, 2016

Onions, C.T. *A Shakespeare Glossary*. Oxford: Clarendon Press, 1911/rpt. 1986

Percy Society. *The Pastime of Pleasure: An Allegorical Poem, By Stephen Hawes*. London: Printed for The Percy Society by T. Richards, 1845

Reaney, P.H. and R.M. Wilson. *A Dictionary of English Surnames*. 3rd ed. Oxford: Oxford University Press, 2005

Ringe, Don and Ann Taylor. *The Development of Old English*. A Linguistic History of English, Volume II. Oxford Linguistics. Oxford: Oxford University Press, 2014

Rollins, Hyder E. and Herschel Baker, eds. *The Renaissance in England: Non-Dramatic Prose and Verse of the Sixteenth Century*. Prospect Heights, IL: Waveland Press, 1992

Salmon, Vivian. “English punctuation theory,” *Anglia* 106 (1988), 285–314

Salmon, Vivian, “Orthography and Punctuation,” *The Cambridge History of the English Language*. Volume III: *1476–1776*. ed. Lass Roger Cambridge: Cambridge University Press, 1999, pp. 13–55

Salzman, Paul, ed. *An Anthology of Elizabethan Prose Fiction*. Oxford: Oxford University Press, 1987

Scragg, Donald G. *A History of English Spelling*. Manchester: Manchester University Press, 1974

Shewmaker, Eugene F. *Shakespeare's Language: A Glossary of Unfamiliar Words in His Plays*. 2nd ed. New York: Checkmark Books, 2008

Shakespeare, William. *The Complete Works*. Ed. Stanley Wells and Gary Taylor. Oxford: Clarendon Press, 1986

Smith, Jeremy J. *An Historical Study of English*. London: Routledge, 1996

Smith, Jeremy J., "From Middle to Early Modern English," in Mugglestone, Lynda *The Oxford History of English*. Oxford: Oxford University Press, 2006, pp. 120–146

Smith, Jeremy J. *Sound Change and the History of English*. Oxford: Oxford University Press, 2007

Stanbridge, John. *Accidence* [1496]. Ed. R.C. Alston. English Linguistics 1500–1800, A Collection of Facsimile Reprints No. 134. Menston: Scolar Press, 1969

Stenbrenden, Gjertrud Flermoen. *Long-Vowel Shifts in English, c. 1050–1700: Evidence from Spelling*. Studies in English Language. Cambridge: Cambridge University Press, 2016

Turnbull, William, ed. *The Buik of the Croniclis of Scotland; or, A Metrical Version of the History of Hector Boece; by William Stewart*. 3 vols. Rerum Britannicarum Medii Aevi Scriptores: or, Chronicles and Memorials of Great Britain and Ireland During the Middle Ages [Rolls Series] 6. London: Longman, Brown, Green, Longmans, and Roberts, 1858

Turville-Petre, Thorlac, ed. *Poems from BL MS Harley 913 'The Kildare Manuscript'*. Early English Text Society O.S. 345. Oxford: Oxford University Press, 2015

Tyndale 1530. Old Testament. *The fyrst boke of Moses called Genesis*. Tr. by William Tyndale. Antwerp: Hans Lufft [Johan Hoochstraten (Michiel Hillen van Hoochstraten)], 1530

Tyndale 1526. *The New Testament*. Tr. William Tyndale. Ed. W.R. Cooper. London: The British Library, 2000

Upward, Christopher and George Davidson. *The History of English Spelling*. Oxford: Wiley-Blackwell, 2011

Visser, Fredericus Theodorus. *An Historical Syntax of the English Language*, 3 vols. in 4 pts. Leiden: E.J. Brill, 1963–1973

Wells, Stanley and Gary Taylor, eds. *William Shakespeare: The Complete Works*. Oxford: Clarendon Press, 1986 [1st ed.], 2005 [2nd ed.]

'Wycliffe Bible' [1382–1395]. In Forshall, Rev Josiah and Sir Frederic Madden 1850.

CHAPTER 7

In the New World

7.1 A NEWE DISCOVERIE: THE BEGINNINGS OF NORTH AMERICAN ENGLISHES

The frontispiece engraving of Thomas Hariot's *A briefe and true report of the new found land of Virginia* (1588), the work of Dutch engraver Theodor de Bry (1528–1598), depicts a stylized entrance to a building in neoclassical style, with five of the native Algonquian Virginian figures from his report. The pediment is surmounted by *[t]her idol Kiwasa*, a squatting divinity, with hands resting on the splayed knees, carved of wood and placed in the temple of the town of Secota(m).

> yt is carued of woode in lengthe 4. foote whose heade is like the heades of the people of Florida [Seminoles], the face is of a flesh colour, the brest white, the rest is all blacke, the thighes are also spottet with whitte. He hath a chayne abowt his necke of white beades, betweene which are other Rownde beades of copper which they esteeme more then golde or siluer. This idol is placed in the temple of the towne of Secotam, as the keper of the kings dead corpses (Hariot 1588/1590, cap. XXI).

The Early Modern English of Hariot's *Briefe and true report* is typical of the era and of an Oxford-born author such as Hariot. The variability in orthography is to be expected, the [e:] of *esteeme* and *keper* likely not yet raised to [i:], the final *-e* largely otiose (perhaps in prepositional phrases such as *with whitte* and *in the towne* there is the vestigial dative). What is remarkable about Hariot's text, and John White's illustrations (he produced watercolors de Bry made into engravings), is their ethnographic content and the natural means of introducing native vocabulary to an English-speaking readership – the formula, though not new, would become standard: *which they call....* This would be matched by the reverse naming ritual *which we call*:

> The they brougt vs to their village in the iland called, Roanoac, and vnto their Weroans or Prince, which entertained vs with Reasonable curtesie, althoug the wear amased at the first sight of vs. Suche was our arriuall into the parte of the world, which we call Virginia... (Hariot 1588/1590, cap. II).

English had already undergone major morphological changes in the period 1100–1500, changes not to be matched in the subsequent half-millennium of development; the sound changes grouped under the rubric of the Great Vowel Shift seen in the last chapter were underway but would take some two centuries to reach the vowel and diphthong inventory we recognize as that of Present Day English. The major changes to come would particularly involve the lexis of English, but in this long period of overseas exploration and empire-building, the loanwords were to come from not just scores but a couple hundred languages around the globe (we often neglect to note that English in its colonial expansion brought English words to these languages as well). The territories acquired, nearly all but a few small islands inhabited, would expand the toponymy of English tremendously (for the contemporary speaker, there is nothing remarkable in mentioning place-names of English, Norse, French, Spanish, Dutch, Native American, African, or Asian origin).

Hariot is writing from his own experience on the 1584–1590 Roanoke voyages commissioned by Sir Walter Raleigh (Raleigh had been granted the patent in 1584, Sir Richard Grenville led the settlers; Raleigh never himself went to the 'new found land'). The first Roanoke venture (in territory now part of North Carolina) was a failure, and there is the enduring mystery of what happened to this first company of settlers: the word *Croatoan* carved onto a tree trunk the only message left behind; it could refer to an Algonquian-speaking local people, or their assembly or tribal council. But settlement would continue and John Rolfe (1585–1622, b. Heacham, Norfolk) would bring seeds from a South American strain of the tobacco plant; the word itself was transferred to English via Spanish from an indigenous language (perhaps Carib [OED] or Taino [AHD5]); Rolfe is chiefly known for his marriage in 1614 to Pocahontas (or Amounte), daughter of the Virginia *sachem* ('chief'; a loan from the Algonquian Massachusett language), a relationship emblematic of the English-native exchanges to follow. Their son Thomas Rolfe (1615–1680) spent much of his youth in England; he lived, it might be said, primarily as an Englishman, marrying Jane Poythress, the daughter of Captain Francis Poythress, an English landowner in Virginia. Early colonial regulations discouraged children of 'mixed marriages' from re-establishing contact with their native families, though Thomas apparently applied to the governor of the Virginia colony to continue contact with his uncle Opechancanough, who succeeded to the chieftaincy of the Powhatan confederacy after the death in 1618 of his brother Powhatan (relations between the confederacy and the colony, which had broken out into conflict in 1609, would deteriorate after Powhatan's passing). The 17th century was filled with settler-native conflicts: the English-Powhatan Wars (1609–1649), the Pequot War (1636–1638), Kieft's Rebellion (1643–1645, between the Dutch settlers of the greater New Amsterdam region and the Lenape), and King Philip's War (1675–1678).

These and many other smaller, regional conflicts and trade disputes, fed largely by the expansion of the original colonies, would occasion, along with regular colonial administrative records and correspondence, a flood of documentation by which one can chart the adoption of native terms, the varying levels of contact varieties, and the attrition of native languages. Alliances could be as fluid as they were unpredictable; European powers often allied with native confederacies at one time or another, in one combination or another as fortunes and frontiers shifted.

William Strachey (1572–1621) had survived shipwreck on Bermuda – then uninhabited – in 1609 and some ten months later made it to the Virginia colony in boats made on that island (his misadventures are thought to be one of the inspirations to Shakespeare's *The Tempest* [1611]); in his account *The Historie of Travell into Virginia Britania* (1612), he records that Thomas Hariot had become conversant in (Carolina) Algonquian:

> Our country of *Virginia* hath no want of many Marchandizes, (which we in *England* accomplish in *Denmark, Norway, Prusia, Poland, etc.*, fetch far, and buy deare,) which advaunce much and assured Increase, with lesse exchaung of our owne, with as few hazardes by Sea, and which would mayntayne as frequent, and goodly a Nauy, as what runs the Leuant Stage; and those by divers treatyes, both in Latin, and English, private, and publique, haue bene in their particuler names and values oftentymes expressed, especially that which hath bene published by that true Lover of vertue, and great learned professour of all arts and knowledges, *Mr. Harriotts*, who lived there in the tyme of the first Colony, spake the Indian language, searcht the country and made many proufes [proofs] of the richenes of the soyle, and Commodities thereof; besydes, many Planters from thence, and right worthy Marchants, and those well knowne to be men of much belief and Creditt, haue witnessed as much to the worlde, in these latter tymes; yf men will giue them Stoage [stowage], and welcome, in their good opinions; and sett asyde, their owne overweenunges and singularity, to entertayne a Truth: and out of those great plentyes, and havinges, which God hath lent them (to be his Stewardes here) be pleased to heare themselues entreated, to spare but a little little Portion, to the raysing, and buylding vp of a Sanctum Sanctorum, a holy howse, and a sanctuary to his blessed name, among Infidells, placing those therein on whome yt hat now pleased him both to be sufficiently revenged for their forefathers Ingratitude and Treasons, and to descend in mercy, to lighten [them] that sate in darkness, and in the Shadowe of Death, and to direct their Feet in the way of Peace (Wright and Freund 1953, 21–22).

Strachey was not simply a voyager to the west and sometime settler, but a traveler in literary circles of London in the early years of the 17th century; he was a shareholder in the theater company Children of the Queen's Revels, which had taken over from Richard Burbage's Blackfriars Theatre. Dramatist John Marston was a fellow shareholder, and Ben Jonson wrote for the company; Strachey wrote 'an uninspired sonnet' in praise of Jonson's *Sejanus His Fall* (1603) and attended plays at Blackfriars one to three times a week (Wright and Freund 1953, xix). One gets a sense of the stylings, pretensions, and, it might be said, failings of prose of the era in his long periodic sentence above. Anglo-Norman loans *Marchaundizes, advaunce*, and *exchaung* (< *eschaunge*) still show their origin in the orthography; *marchandise* was the predominant spelling from the mid-13th through mid-16th centuries, while *merchandise* grows in frequency from 1585 onward (OED, s.v. *merchandise* 1.a). The interchange of *i/y* and *v/u* (and *ai/ay* and, more interestingly, *ui/uy*) are typical, as are the occasional geminate (*Infidells*) and capitalization for proper nouns and for emphasis. One can see quite clearly the influence of classical rhetoric from the 'grammar scoles,' a spelling of the era, here borrowed from *The Boke of Husbandrie* (1532) of Anthony Fitzherbert (1470–1538; b. Norbury, Derbyshire). The balancing of things contrary and complementary (*both in Latin, and English, private, and publique*), and organization of series show the influence of readings in Latin in the schooling of the Renaissance – as with the verbal series referring to Hariot *who lived there...spake the Indian language... searcht the country...and made many proufes* or the tricolon (rhetorically balanced unit of three elements) *which we in England accomplish...fetch far...and buy deare*. In terms of argument, Strachey pivots from *marchaundizes* and *much and assured Increase* to the spiritual benefits to be offered the natives in sparing *but a little little Portion* of that increase in building up a 'Holy of Holies' in the New World (language echoing in diction if not quite in spirit the Puritan fathers of New England); this Strachey does by redeploying the economic vocabulary of his 'pitch': *men of much belief and Creditt, yf men will give them Stoage, out of those great plentyes, and havinges.*

Who *spake the Indian language*: Hariot was said to have learned the Algonquian dialect of the Roanoke settlement area, while Raleigh was known to have brought back to England some 20 or so Native Americans and sponsored their study of English. One of Raleigh's interpreters was the first native to be baptized in the Anglican communion, Manteo (b. ca. 1564), of the ruling caste of the Croatan tribe (perhaps part of the larger Roanoke Algonquian people). Another, Wanchese, the last sachem of the Roanoac (Roanoke) people, worked with Manteo in teaching Hariot the local Algonquian dialect; he and Manteo traveled to England and remained there as guests of Raleigh 1584–1585. Raleigh's sponsorship of his 'Indian interpreters' had the ulterior motive of encouraging the loyalty of the natives to the English. Manteo would remain a loyal friend to the English of the Roanoke voyages; Wanchese, though he visited England once more in the later 1580s, left the English for the Secotan people and warned against the encroachment of the English settlers (Vaughan 2002). A number of these interpreters were praised by Raleigh's associates and contemporaries for their proficiency in English; on his 1595 voyage to Guiana, Raleigh had employed some of these native interpreters, one of whom, John Provost (known also as 'Indian John' and 'John of Trinidado'), assisted Raleigh's friend and fellow explorer Lawrence Keymis on his 1596 Guiana voyage. Provost spent some years in England with Raleigh's nephew Sir John Gilbert and is likely the 'Indian John' who received Robert Harcourt in Guiana in 1609 (Vaughan 2002, 363; another benefit of this 'interpreter corps' was that, returned to their peoples, they could serve as liaisons for future venturers). The recruitment of native interpreters could be matched with the selection of English voyagers to be trained in the native languages. On that 1595 Guiana voyage, Raleigh met with Topiawari, cacique of Arromaia in Guiana, *cacique* a word for 'chieftain' that enters English via Spanish or French, deriving from an indigenous language of Haiti; he left in Arromaia his young servant Hugh Goodwin and a Frauncis Sparrow, a servant of Captain George Gifford, to study the local language (Vaughan 2002, 361–362). Cayowaroco, son of Topiawara, left for England with three other Arromaia natives to study English, staying likely at Durham House (where Raleigh received Manteo and Wanchese).

Though Raleigh and other English explorers and planters were mindful of the long-term advantages of such exchanges in linguistic training, there were more pressing immediate concerns. The Roanoke settlement was in need of food, and what had at first been a generous arrangement of supply of corn and other food to the struggling English by Powhatan became a burden on the Virginia natives as the English demanded more and more assistance; Captain John Smith had suspected that chief Powhatan, a "subtell owlde foxe," was well aware that corn could be used as a lever on the English (Kupperman 2007b, 174). Ralph Lane's *An Account of the Particularities of the imployments of the English men left in Virginia* (1586) spelled out the perilous state of the young Virginia colony: "For at that time wee had no weares [weirs] for fishe, neither could our men skill of the making of them, neither had wee one grayne of corne for seede to put into the ground" (qtd. in Kupperman 2007b, 174, 351 n. 71). For these newcomers, an awareness of flora and fauna, the food sources to be derived from them, weather, topography, and ethnography were not simply scientific or scholastic matters; even in the first part of his *Briefe and true report* (1588), "Of Marchantable commodities," Hariot lists the Algonquian term *wapeih*, apparently a type of white clay: "very like to terra sigillata: and hauing beene refined, it hath beene found by some of our Phisitio<n>s and Chirurgeons to bee of the same kinde of vertue and more effectuall. The inhabita<n>ts vse it very much for the cure of sores and woundes" (Hariot 1590, 8). The second part concerns "of svche commodities as Virginia is knowne to yeelde for victual and sustena<n>ce of mans life, vsually fed vpon by the naturall inhabitants," and here there is a proliferation of Algonquian terms, as might be expected: *Okindigier* ('called by vs. *Beanes*'); *Wickonzówr* ('called by vs. *Peaze*'); *There is an herbe which is sowed a part by itselfe & is called by the inhabitants Vppówoc...The Spaniards generally call it Tobacco* (the loan did enter English via Spanish by the late 16th century, though the Spanish explorers seem to have transferred the Haitian Carib term for the pipe used to smoke tobacco – or a roll of the leaves smoked cigar-like – to the plant itself); *Openauk* ('a kind of roots of round form' – identified as saw greenbriar); *Okeepanauk* ('also of round shape'; giant puffball mushroom); *Kaishúcpenauk* ('a white kind of roots about the bigness of hen egs'; duck potato); *Tsinaw* ('like vnto the which in England is called the *Chinaroot* brought from the East Indies'; possibly laurel greenbrier [*Smilax laurifolia*]); *Coscúshaw* ('some of our company tooke to bee that kinde of roote which the Spaniards in the West Indies call *Cassauy*'; green arrow arum [*Peltandra virginica*]); *Habascon* ('a roote of hoat taste almost of the forme and bignesse of a Parseneepe'; Jack-in-the pulpit [*Arisaema triphyllum*]); types of berries and acorns are given their native names, but relatively few native forms for animals (land and water) are given. Here, Hariot generally gives English equivalents, with a few exceptions: *Sacquenúckot & Maquówoc* (likely muskrat and mink: 'We neuer took any of them ourselues, but sometime eate of such as the inhabitants had taken

& brought vnto vs'); and, as edible riverine and sea life was more familiar, the lone shellfish example was *Sekanauk*, 'a kind of crustie shell fishe which is goode meate, about a foote in breadth, hauing a crustie tayle, many legges like a crab; and her eyes in her backe' (Hariot 1590, 13–21; this is the horseshoe crab, of which today usually only the roe is eaten).

If one vector for the transmission of loans from Native American languages was the description of the natural world, on the basis of simple survival needs or, in better times, with a naturalist's eye, another involved ethnographic and linguistic interests. While it is impossible to separate these proto-anthropological interests from their colonial adjuncts (just as the naturalistic descriptions nearly always overlapped with interests in 'marchandizes'), and one might parallel them to texts the explorers read in grammar schooling (such as Caesar's descriptions of Celts and Germans), nonetheless 'true reports' from a Hariot or Strachey show how linguistic exchange occurred. Hariot's interest in bringing the light of the faith to the Virginia natives is expressed with much less fervor than by New England Puritan ministers to 'praying Indians,' and it is difficult to tell how seriously it is meant – and whether it served also as a cover for his interests in native faith traditions, which seem genuine (if at times syncretic – a sort of *interpretatio Anglicana* that saw native religious expression through western Christianity – in this instance, western Protestantism). It is difficult to sort to what extent his recording of Secotam views of the afterlife accurately reflects native views or suggests those views were proximate enough to Christian ones to make conversion easier:

> They beleeue also the immortalitie of the soule, that after this life as soone as the soule is departed from the bodie according to the workes it hath done, it is eyther carried to heaue<n> the habitacle of gods, there to enioy perpetuall blisse and happinesse, or els to a great pitte or hole, which they thinke to bee in the furthest partes of their part of the worlde towarde the sunne set, there to burne continually: the place they call *Popogusso*.
>
> For the confirmation of this opinion, they tolde me two stories of two men that had ben lately dead and reuiued againe, the one happened but few yeres before our comming in the countrey of a wicked man which hauing beene dead and buried, the next day the earth of the graue beeing seene to moue, was take<n> vp againe; Who made declaration where his soule had beene, that is to saie very neere entring into *Popogusso*, had not one of the gods saued him & gaue him leaue to returne againe, and teach his friends what they should doe to auoid that terrible place of torment (Hariot 1590, 26).

Conversion to Christianity was an aim of these European ventures in the New World, though the manner and pace of conversion varied according to the colonizing power (conversion in New France to Roman Catholicism was often a process of longer discernment and duration). The adoption of a new baptismal name was (and can still be) the norm, Pocahontas of course perhaps the most famous example (christened Rebecca at her baptism in 1613, she married John Rolfe the following year). The Bideford (Devon) parish register records the christening of a 'Wynganditoian' (an

Algonquian of the Virginia region[1]) named 'Raleigh' on Sunday 26 March 1588; the origin of his name is readily apparent, and he had been brought back to England a captive of the Anglo-Powhatan strife by Sir Richard Grenville, a native of Bideford. He was perhaps one of the 'Indian interpreters'; the same parish register records his burial the following year on 7 April (Quinn 1955, I, item 71). Christopher Newport, who had been captain of the *Susan Constant* on the 1607 Jamestown voyage, was entrusted by Chief Powhatan with Namontack, who had in 1605 been sent by the sachem to live with the English Virginia settlers to learn their language and customs. The exchange of youths between the peoples occurred in these early years of the settlement; from the English the natives received Thomas Savage, Samuel Collier, and Henry Spelman – the last of whom would witness the major events of the Anglo-Powhatan encounter (including the taking and ransoming of Pocahontas by the English) while he lived among the Powhatan and the Patawomeke of the Potomac and write his own *Relation* of the Virginia settlement ca. 1613 (Bailyn 2012, 58, 107) A number of these English youths were indentured; Raleigh had been granted the power to impress crewmen, among whom was the Irishman Darby Glavin (Kupperman 2007a, 33).

Early linguistic information from these *Relations* has been traditionally viewed skeptically, with many materials incomplete or lost (such as Hariot's dictionary of Algonquian). But advances in historical linguistics of Native American languages have shown that there were more than a few capable linguists among the early voyagers (especially among the Jesuits of New France). The early mariners were often knowledgeable in at least the rudiments of one or more other languages, as well as various forms of nautical pidgins. The 'gentleman' explorers could be multilingual, and educated in a program back home with an increasingly metalinguistic focus, as treatises on orthography and grammar, and rhetoric proliferated through the 16th and 17th centuries (see for instance Salmon 1988). William Strachey's 1612 *The Historie of Travell into Virginia Britania* included "A Short Dictionary, added vnto the former Discourses of the Indian Language, vsed within the Chessiopiock Bay" of Virginia Algonquian-English and English-Algonquian in batches arranged alphabetically (Wright and Freund 1953, 174–207). One of the longer native vocabularies from the early colonial era, at over 800 words, Strachey's sought to record in his English spelling (which itself is variable) what he heard from native informants (and we are not sure of the particular dialects they spoke of Virginia Algonquian); but among the forms we see an early attestation of that famous loan from Virginian Algonquian, *moccasin*: 'shoos – Mawhcasuns' (Wright and Freund 1953, 201; this attestation is not recorded in the OED). Hariot had attempted to solve the problem of English-native phonological representation by the creation in 1585 (possibly with the help of Manteo) of "An vniversall Alphabet conteyninge six & thirty letters, whereby may be expressed the lively image of mans voyce in what language soeuer; first devised vpon occasion to seeke for fit letters to expresse the Virginian speche," which survives in two manuscript copies

[1] There is a 'Wingandekoa' at the cape (Cabo de arenas; Sandy Cape) below the inlet usually thought to be the first cartographic depiction of Chesapeake Bay on Abraham Ortelius's 1587 map of the Americas. The name does not appear on de Bry's 1590 map in his printing of Hariot's *Briefe and true report*, perhaps indicating its disuse.

(Westminster Library MS 2 and British Library, MS Additional 6788). The cursive characters sought to represent 12 vowels in Algonquian (for two of which Hariot could give no English equivalents), only two of them diphthongs (/eɪ/, /aɪ/), and 24 consonants (the Westminster copy is reproduced at Vaughan 2002, 349, and Salmon 1992, 37). In dealing with the problems of writing down an 'oral' (i.e., heretofore unwritten) language such as (Carolina) Algonquian Hariot may have been influenced by works such as John Hart's *An Orthographie* (1569; cf. Jespersen 1907), part of the 'orthoepist' (literally Greek for 'correct diction') spelling reform movement of the 16th and 17th centuries. For Hart, the problem was dealing with how to write down, non-natively, 'indigenous' languages such as Welsh and Irish:

> If anye man of one or another nation, would gladly learne to pronounce any straunge speach which is accustomed to be written so confusely,[2] as it were (of necessitie) only to be learned by the liuely voice, and not able to be red by any order of their writing, as maye be sayde of the Welsh and Irish.... As by the way of pastime, I haue done [written Welsh...] from a Welshmans mouth, though I vnderstode no worde thereof, and did reade it againe to him, and diuers others...so as one amongst them...sayde vnto the rest in Welsh, that I coulde speake Welsh so well as he.... The like haue I done of the Irishe, and may as easily doe of the Barbarian, or Russian speaches, or any other so straunge as they (Hart in Salmon 1992, 31).

This anticipates, though imperfectly, what Henry Sweet and others would attempt some 300 years later with the founding of the International Phonetic Association and the International Phonetic Alphabet (IPA) currently in use.

A briefer but more sophisticated word-list was compiled by James Rosier, who had written *A True Relation of the most prosperous voyage made this present yeere 1605, by Captaine George Waymouth, in the Discovery of the land of Virginia* (Quinn and Quinn, 1983, 248–311). Rosier records some native words and names from the Eastern Abenaki encountered in New England during the Waymouth voyage in 1605 in his *Relation* – *Tabacco* (280), *canoa* ('canoe,' 277 *et passim*), *sagamo* (*sagamore*, 'chief, commander'; 309ff.) – and his word-list was appended to the text by Samuel Purchas in his printing, (which also included a list of the *sagamores* of the New England Eastern Abenaki). Appearing also in Rosier's word-list are *coribo* ('caribou') and *Moosur* (= Abenaki *mŵs* 'moose'; Quinn and Quinn 1983, 481–493; on these and other early word-lists see Goddard 1996, 17–21).

Captain John Smith (1580–1631), of Jamestown fame and notoriety, plays a significant role in the linguistic history of English in the New World; a more dashing and difficult character than a Strachey or Rosier (and perhaps more colorful than even Raleigh), Smith's recordings of the English exploration and settlement of Virginia and New England, including his *A true relation of such occurrences and accidents of noate as hath hapned in Virginia since the first planting of that colony* (1608), his *A Map of Virginia* (1612), and the lengthy *The Generall Historie of*

2 A rare form for *confusedly*, which is found in use ca. 1500–1750 ("now obsolete"; OED, s.v.).

Virginia, New England, and the Summer isles (1624), preserve some 150 native terms, corroborating a number of times those in other 'true relations' (which may described as a genre of English prose writing ca. 1580–1625). In the first book of *The Generall Historie,* Smith directs the reader to Hariot's account in his *Briefe and true report* (1588) of the flora and fauna of the new land ("Let those briefes suffice, because I would not trouble you with one thing twice"; Barbour 1986, II, 77), but nonetheless confirms a number of native terms other writers had recorded, such as *cassavia* (the *cassava* root; Smith's is the second attestation of the term for the plant in the OED), *manitou* ('a spirit,' in the spellings *manito, mantoac*), *sachem* ('chief, paramount chief'), *sagamore* ('chief,' also spelled *sagamo*), *tomahawk* (*tomahacks*; Strachey's *Historie of Travell* [1612] is the first attestation of the term for this battle-axe), and *weroance* ('king, governor').

In late 1607, Smith was captured by a band of Powhatan under Opechancanough, Chief Powhatan's younger brother, while scouting for food supply along the Chickahominy River. The term *chickahominy* may mean 'cleared place' (Barbour 1986, I, 101 n. 85), though the natives of the Chickahominy tribe are described as the 'coarse-ground corn people,' and it is the clipped form *hominy* (from Algonquian *uskatahamen* or, in Smith's texts, *ustatahamen*) that has entered English for the ground kernel corn (maize) boiled in milk – and been borrowed from native Virginian cooking as a staple of America cuisine of the Southeast. It is possible the sense 'cleared space' may refer to land cleared for the cultivation of maize, while *uskatahamen* means 'grounded while raw.' In the explanatory text to his *A Map of Virginia,* Smith describes the various dishes the natives make from corn, either roasted kernels, rough-ground, or smooth-ground into a powder: *...or else boyle them in water eating the broth with the bread they call* Ponap. *The grouts and peeces of the cornes remaining, by fanning in a Platter or in the wind, away, the branne they boile 3 or 4 houres with water, which is an ordinary food they call* Ustatahamen (Barbour 1986, I, 158; the same passage appears in the second book of Smith's *Generall Historie*; Barbour 1986, II, 113). The *ponap* bread mentioned is the *apone* in Strachey and Hariot, that is, *pone* or *cornpone* (the latter an English-Algonquian blend), which also has entered Southern American cooking (see DARE, s.vv. *corn pone, pone, hominy,* the last of which is now labeled 'esp[ecially] S[outh] Atl[antic]'). The "Description of the Covntrey, the Commodities, People, Government and Religion" that accompanied his *Map of Virginia* (1612) gives a brief word-list ("Because many doe desire to knowe the maner of their language, I have inserted these few words"; Barbour 1986, I, 136), including '*Mockasins.* Shooes,' appended to which is a set of 8 sentences in Virginia Algonquian, the last of which is:

> *Kekaten pokahontas patiaquagh ningh tanks manotyens neer mowchick rawrenock audowgh.* Bid Pokahontas bring hither two little Baskets, and I will give her white beads to make her a chaine (Barbour 1986, I, 139).

Though it was with Rolfe that Pocahontas would travel to England, it was Smith's 12-year-old pageboy, Samuel Collier, who was sent to Powhatan as one of the English interpreters of 'Indian speche,' voyages that would have been extraordinary for such young people.

Smith was also a naval officer, with experience in the Turkish wars; in 1602–1604, he fought the Ottomans, was captured and sold into slavery, and made his way back to England through Russia and the Baltic lands. All this before Virginia. His 1626 primers for young sailors, *A Sea Grammar* and *Accidence for young Sea-men* (Barbour 1986, III, 39–121), are valuable for their account of ships and seamanship in an era when England would build an empire upon the seas, and in the margins are over 300 nautical terms listed as they occur with explanation in the text ('a Guy, which is a rope brought to it from the fore mast, to keepe the weight upon it steady, or from swinging to and againe'; Barbour 1986, III, 72). But in taking to the sea-lanes, other types of nautical and trade jargons emerged.

An early and curious record gives evidence of an indigenous-based contact variety from this early colonial period, the Delaware Trade Jargon. Though other indigenous-based pidgins and Creoles from North American existed, only a few have been studied in any detail: Michif, Chinook Jargon, and Mobilian Jargon. The Semitic language scholar and sometime professor and politician (and occasional archaeologist) J. Dyneley Prince had published in 1912 a record entitled 'The Indian Interpreter' found within a deed dating to 1684 in the New Jersey Department of State archives (Prince was at the time Acting Governor of the State). Though there are other sources for Delaware Trade Jargon (including a letter of William Penn from 1683), Prince's list of 261 items includes as well phrases of two or more morphemes (many early lists of native languages offer just single-morpheme vocabularies, with the indigenous lemmata glossed by Latin or English). Prince's evidence for the trade jargon has most extensively been studied by native language expert Sarah Thomason (Thomason 1980). The jargon was apparently used in the Delaware Valley between Europeans and speakers of Munsee, Unami, and Unalachtigo Lenape languages; though *mink* is generally seen as deriving from a Scandinavian loan to Middle English, one finds the curiously similar *miningus* 'mink' in the jargon (unless that is a nativized loan from English), as well as *squatid* ('little squaw, girl'; *squaw* + diminutive suffix *-tit*), *tomohickan* ('axe, tomahawk'), *brandwyne* (for 'rum'; *brandy-wine* is from Dutch *brandewijn*; the Brandywine Creek tributary of the Delaware was first settled in 1638, which the Lenape called Wauwaset), *pone* ('bread'), *kecko gull une* ('how many guilders for this?'; *gull* from Dutch *guilder*), *manitto* ('the manitou; spirit'), *anna* ('mother,' likely a pidginized form), *papouse* ('a suckling child'; the English form *papoose* 'cradleboard' is borrowed from the Narragansett language; Prince 1912, 509–522).

As the English, Spanish, French, and other European colonizers kept coming (as native interpreter Wanchese and Chief Powhatan had feared), New World encounters increased in intensity and duration (from skirmish to protracted warfare, to mutual capture and enslavement). The vocabulary that was once exotic or impenetrable became embedded in the lexicon of English over the next few centuries, some of high frequency, some more regional (or part of Native American Englishes). Hundreds of native terms were borrowed (Cutler 1994 examines over a thousand), and besides those that named bird or plant or lake or stream, others came along with the things (foods, footwear, weapons) and concepts (of the spiritual and religious, or of parley, treaty, and peacemaking) borrowed. As will be seen in the following chapter, American English, like the broader American culture, borrowed from and co-opted native language and culture, and elevated it to iconic status just as the young nation pushed continuously westward over native lands. The general pattern was one of dispossession (as it had been centuries earlier in Wales, Cornwall, Scotland, and Ireland); in its particulars, there was great complexity. In early American literature, there developed a genre of 'captivity narratives,' especially of women's captivity narratives such as that of Mary Rowlandson, *The Soveraignty and Goodness of God: A Narrative of the Captivity and Restoration of Mrs. Mary Rowlandson* (1682); on the morning of 10 February 1675 the town of Lancaster, Massachusetts colony, was attacked by a raiding party of Nipmuc (Nashaway), Narragansett, and Wampanoag under the leadership of Nashaway sachem 'One-Eyed' John Monoco; Mary's husband, the Puritan minister Joseph Rowlandson, was away down the coast appealing to Massachusetts Bay officials for more security for Lancaster during the raids and battles of Metacom's (King Philip's) War. Members of the extended family and neighbors had sought refuge in the Rowlandson homestead, which was attacked by gunfire for two hours, then set afire; Rowlandson herself was wounded, and her 6-year-old daughter Sarah seriously wounded by gunfire (she would die on the subsequent forced march). Rowlandson would be sold into slavery by a Narragansett warrior to *Saggamore* Quannopin and his wife Weetamoo, who was the sister of Metacom's wife and the *squaw sachem* of the Pocasset band of Wampanoags (Derounian-Stodola 1998, 340, nn. 27–28). Mary Rowlandson was eventually ransomed, with funds from a subscription taken up by Puritan women of Boston, and her time among the Narragansett and Wampanoag February–May 1675 offers some insight into the changing linguistic and cultural situation in colonial New England. For one, native words were still often capitalized and italicized in colonial narratives, but those of higher frequency were no longer glossed – the English-speaking readers, at least of New England, could be expected to be familiar enough with them to require no explanation: Rowlandson mentions *sachem*, *squaw*, and *sagamore* of course (the first two from Massachusett, the third from Eastern Abenaki), but also *wigwam* (Eastern Abenaki) and *papoose* (Narragansett or Pequot): "When my master [Quannopin] came home, he came to me and bid me make a shirt for his Papoos of a Hollandlaced Pillowbeer" (Derounian-Stodola 1998, 40; that is, a shirt for his child made of a Holland-lace pillow case). *Papoose* underwent semantic transfer in extending from a term for a native child to the cradleboard used to carry native children (a backpack-like carrier). When referring to a native child, the term is labeled as 'Offensive' (OED) or 'Often Offensive' (AHD5), though this usage is largely historical, as the cradleboard is what is overwhelmingly meant by AmE usage. As the wife of a Puritan minister, and herself a devout Protestant Christian, the fear of being in the hands of the 'savages' is matched by that of being sold on to the French – that is, to the Catholics. This was a fear realized by the author of another famous captivity narrative, John Williams's *The redeemed captive, returning to Zion* (1707).

On 29 February 1704, just before daybreak, a raiding party of about 50 Canadian French soldiers and some 300 Abenaki, Maqua,[3] and other natives attacked the village of Deerfield, Massachusetts, killing 47 townspeople outright and carrying off 122 others

[3] Mohawks of Caughnawaga, upstate New York, converted to Catholicism by French Jesuits, who then migrated to the Kahnawake Mission near Montreal, on the south bank of the St. Lawrence.

into captivity (a number of whom, injured or straggling, were killed on the 300-mile march). One of the homes attacked belonged to the Reverend John Williams:

> ...the Enemy immediately brake into the Room, I judge to the number of Twenty, with *Painted Faces*, and hideous Acclamations. I reach'd up my hands to the Bed-tester [the vertical of the bedboard that supported the canopy (i.e., *tester*)], for my Pistol, uttering a short Petition to God.... The Enemies who entr'd the House were all of them *Indians* and *Macqua's*, insulted over me a while, holding up Hatchets over my head, threatning to burn all I had; but yet God beyond expectation made us in a great measure to be Pityed: for tho' some were so cruel and barbarous as to take, & carry to the door, Two of my Children and Murder them, as also a Negro Woman; yet they gave me liberty to put on my Clothes.... About Sun an hour high, we were all carryed out of the house, for a March, and saw many of the Houses of my Neighbours in Flames, perceiving the whole Fort, one house excepted, to be taken. Who can tell, what Sorrows pierced our Souls, when we saw our selves carryed away from Gods Sanctuary, to go into a strange Land, exposed to so many Trials? the journey being at least Three hundred Miles we were to Travel; the Snow up to the Knees, and we never inur'd to such hardships and fatigues; the place we were to be carryed to, a Popish Country (Williams 1707, 4–5).

The Reverend Williams would be returned to his Zion, but attempts to ransom his 7-year-old daughter Eunice were unsuccessful, and complicated in subsequent decades as Eunice was assimilated into the Kahnawake Mohawk band (a not uncommon fate of Europeans and Africans captured on such raids), converted to Roman Catholicism (with the baptismal name Marguerite), learning to speak Mohawk and French; she married the Mohawk man François Xavier Arousent (Arosen) and though she visited her Puritan family in Deerfield through the years she refused to return permanently. Yale historian John Demos traced the efforts of her father Reverend Williams and her brother Samuel to 'redeem' her over the following decades (a word of some religious and spiritual freight in Puritan parlance) in his *The Unredeemed Captive* (Demos 1994). His Epilogue presents an interesting coda to the story of Eunice and her two families, some 130 years after the raid. On 27 August 1837 Deerfield minister John Fessenden (1804–1881) preached a sermon to the First Congregational Society, "and in the Hearing of Several Indians of Both Sexes, Supposed to be Descendants of Eunice Williams" who had visited the graves of Rev. Williams and family and attended services: "I would recognize with pious humility...the workings of that mysterious providence, which has mingled your blood with ours, and which...admonishes us that God...hath made of one blood all nations of men, and hath determined the times, the places, and circumstances in which they should live, in order to accomplish his designs of impartial benevolence and general good" (Demos 1994, 246, 252). During the time of Queen Anne's War (1702–1713), the French of *Quebeck* and the disputed Maine region[4] had

[4] Perhaps named since 1622 for the region in France, but this is uncertain; it may derive from the nautical use *the main* to refer to the mainland of the coast; the French had included it in their *Acadia/l'Acadie*.

established alliances with native tribes, especially the Abenaki, as a buffer to the more populous English colonies to the south. The divide was linguistic, cultural, and religious, and native tribes were often caught on, and divided by, these lines. The five-novel series of American author James Fenimore Cooper's *Leatherstocking Tales* – the most celebrated two of the series were *The Last of the Mohicans* (1826) and *The Pathfinder* (1840) – attempted to employ, with some success, the Anglo-French-native patois of the northeast and developing midwestern frontiers. To the south of New England, there was another contact zone in the 17th and 18th centuries: Anglo-Dutch.

Sandwiched between two major English colonial ventures were the Dutch settlements of the Mid-Atlantic seaboard. With its opportune situation at the mouth of the Hudson, Nieuw Amsterdam, which encompassed what would later be the greater New York City, Long Island, and Northern New Jersey region, looked always to be in a perilous state, a prize England and the English would eventually take. But language traces often remain long after memory of their active use can fade. On Nicolaes Visscher's map of *Nova Belgica/Nieuw Nederlandt* ('new Belgium' the Neo-Latin form; Visscher 1655) one finds the Latinate form *Pennsylvania* (William Penn's eponymous compound 'Penn's Woods' in Neo-Latin) but also the simply descriptive *'t Lange Eylandt* ('the Long Island'; *'t* is the clipped form of *het*, formerly the neuter dative form of the Dutch article). Cartographers of the era knew the work of fellow map-makers, and often freely borrowed details and features (Visscher borrows heavily from the 1651 New Nederlandt map of Jan Janszoon, who used the Latinized *Janssonius* in his published work). Visscher's map extends southward to Virginia in its bottom-left corner: there is *Pouhatan* (Powhatan) of Hariot's *Report*, and *Iames Town* and *Chesapeack Bay*, the latter two brought over with the second element intact from English – in a not uncommon pattern, Dutch and other European settlers (excluding the French) were more likely to understand and employ English place-name forms than the English were to preserve non-English forms. One sees Anglicization, partial to full, in many of the place-names from New Netherland: *Breuckelen* > 'Brooklyn,' *ten Bronck/Broncks* [land/river] > 'The Bronx,' *Roode Hoek* 'Red Point' > 'Red Hook'; Hempstead, Long Island, was established in the early 1640s by English settlers from the Connecticut Colony and Dutch of New Netherland; the name is either from Hemel Hempstead (Hertfordshire), home of John Carman, one of the town founders, or Heemstede (Noord-Holland); it may also be a Dutchified rendering of the English name (it appears as *Heemstee* on Visscher's 1655 map). By the time of Visscher's map – the Dutch gave up New Netherland with the Treaty of Breda 1667 – there was a new name to lay over the territory: *Niew Jorck*, with Long Island also labeled *Jorck Shire*. Visscher nevertheless preserves many of the older Dutch forms or variants for English and French place-names: *Roode Eylandt* (Rhode Island), *Adriaens Blocks Eylant* (Block Island, RI, named for Dutch trader Adriaen Block [1567–1627]), and *Hendrick Christiaenss Eylant al<iter> Marthaes Vyneard* ('otherwise Martha's Vineyard'). *Nieuw Hollant* (Cape Cod) is at its Provincetown extremity labeled *Staaten hoeck* ('States Point'; like *Staten Eylandt* [Staten Island] it is named for the Dutch *Staten-Generaal*, 'States-General,' the Dutch Parliament), with the additional gloss *ook* (Modern Dutch *ook*, 'also') *Cape Cod, Witte hoeck* ('White Point'), *Cape Iames.*

Consistent across the English, French, and Dutch maps of the period is a careful recording of native names – in the early period, the 16th and 17th centuries, most of the names were of course indigenous. But the early cartographers and ethnographers seemed keenly interested in native languages and traditions. This did not stop European encroachment upon native lands, as these were, in historian Bernard Bailyn's view, the 'barbarous years' of the settling of America by European colonists (Bailyn 2012), in which the peopling of America was an enormously complicated matter. The Europeans who encountered the hundreds of native tribes along the Eastern seaboard were themselves a highly disparate group. In 1621, a group of French-speaking Huguenot Walloons from the Spanish Netherlands led by Jesse de Forest petitioned the Virginia Company of London for permission to establish their own community in the new Virginia colony. The Walloon Protestants had met and been influenced by English Puritan refugees in Leiden, Rotterdam, and other Dutch cities and had heard there might be refuge in the new English settlements. The Virginia colony was of a different character than the New England plantation, more *cavalier* – a term more characteristic of the reign of Charles I, but which describes accurately enough the royalist character that was encouraged in Virginia. James deprived the Virginia Company of its charter in 1624, and Virginia became a royal colony thereafter. Trouble had been brewing with increasing Puritan influence on the company, as well as with an independent Puritan community in Nansemond County (Bailyn 2012, 159). Perhaps fearing trouble of a similar kind, the petition of de Forest's Walloons was denied in 1621. Some of the Walloons and other religious exiles would land along the Hudson in Nieuw Nederlandt, others in the Dutch Caribbean, and some in Dutch Brazil (territory seized from the Portuguese in the northeast, in the area of Pernambuco to Natal to Fortaleza; Dutch Brazil would last 1630–1661). Like these itinerant Dutch settlers, some English arrivals in America had first been elsewhere in the developing empire, and they brought with them knowledge of other colonial European languages, contact varieties (nautical pidgins, West African Pidgin English, Caribbean contact varieties), and native languages.

The types of 'contact situations' in the New World were likewise complex. The English language had already shown itself to be porous when it came to borrowing or accepting new words during the Middle English period (Latin had already been established as a major contributor to the lexicon in the Old English period). The Early Modern period would see a rapid expansion in the roster of languages from which it would borrow words; though the OED lists about 130 loans from the Algonquian family of native languages in the Eastern United States and Canada, when taken together with place-names and ethnonyms of Algonquian origin the total multiplies to several hundred. Though the work of these Early Modern linguists – Dutch traders, French Jesuits, English explorers – has been approached with some caution, subsequent work with native language revival programs has shown the value of their recordings. There were different purposes to be sure between the trader, trapper, and missionary, but the linguistic interaction opened the way for new loan formations, for a broadening of the toponymy and hydronymy of English (not just of native place-names, but geographic features); for a wider lexicon of flora and fauna; and, in encountering non-Indo-European languages beyond the British Isles, metalinguistic skills. Latin would still form the basis for their construction of grammars and primers of 'native tongues,' but these New World linguists became more acutely aware of the diversity in sound and structure as they grappled with transcribing what their informants told them of this world.

One such student of native languages was New Amsterdam trader Govert Loockermans (1616–1671). Born in Turnhout, he came to New Amsterdam, to Manhattan, in 1633 having served as a cook's mate (Bailyn 2012, 223). He worked at first for the Dutch West India Company, trading with natives along the Hudson, studying native languages. Acquisitive in other ways, Loockermans began to build his fortune, at times in partnership with English New Englander Isaac Allerton (1586–1659), who had arrived in Massachusetts in 1620 aboard the *Mayflower*. Loockermans seems to have locked horns with some local native leaders among the Raritan and Lenape, possibly violently. He seems to have been quarrelsome with his fellow Dutch, as well as running afoul of the West India Company and Director-General of New Amsterdam Petrus (Pieter) Stuyvesant. Whether it was maturity, rising financial fortunes, or a sudden civic sense, Loockermans became involved in New Amsterdam politics, on the Board of Nine that raised grievances against the company and the lack of representative government in the colony, and he helped draft the Vlissingen (Flushing) Remonstrance of 1653 (Middleton 2010). In what is now Flushing, in the borough of Queens (New York City), a growing community of English Quakers had settled, who had felt their religious freedom restricted by the Dutch Reformed Church; the Remonstrance is thought to be one of the inspirations for the provision for religious freedom in the Bill of Rights to the US Constitution. Loockermans eventually left an estate valued at 520,000 guilders (Bailyn 2012, 528), as well as his correspondence from his New Amsterdam years. Though the correspondence is in Dutch, Loockermans was apparently proficient also in English. Here in a letter to his cousin Seth Verbrugge and his father Gillis Verbrugge of Amsterdam (undated, but perhaps ca. 1649) he makes mention of the nautical term *skipper*, first borrowed into Middle English in 1390, but a rare word that we see used with increasing frequency in New Amsterdam – New York records of the 17th century (no doubt the loan being reinforced by contact with the Dutch usage): *de* ***schipper*** *vande Posthoorn die na Angola gaet die heeft bij ons noch niet geweest doch sulle in Compagnie gaen soo Kroon seyt* ("the skipper from the *Posthorn* going to Angola is not here with us yet, but we will go out with the Company as Kroon tells us"; Loockermans, *Correspondence*; emphasis added). Through the 1650s to early 1660s, Loockermans could refer to *Niew Nederlant* and *Niew Amsterdam*. In a notice of a sale of 2000 roofing tiles from his estate in 1671, however, we find the subscription: *in New Yorck...10 Junij 1671*. Two years later, the Dutch would very briefly regain control of the colony, but English was in the future of *Niew Yorck*.

7.2 PROVIDENCE: PURITANS AND PILGRIMS

For the Pilgrims of Plymouth, and the Puritans of the Massachusetts Bay Colony, the *Newe World* was to be a world apart – not *Cavalier* as the later colonies of Virginia or Carolinas, much less *Catholicke* as Maryland in part would be – but a more *Select* group of churches that would grow slowly; Puritan and Nonconformist (Separatist, i.e., separating from the Church of England) leader Robert Browne (ca. 1550–1633, born in Northamptonshire) had written in 1584 that "the kingdom off God was not to be begun by whole parishes, but rather off the worthiest, were they never so fewe" (his *A True and Short Declaration, both of the Gathering and Joyning Together of Certaine Persons*, Morgan 1987, 17).

John Cotton (1585–1652), one of these early Puritan fathers, exhibits a conservatism in not just religious but also grammatical and orthographical matters (*begetteth* with old 3rd singular verbal inflection *-eth*), and seems to anticipate Jonathan Swift in his section "Some offences in English parish Churches," minus the humor of course:

> It is a publick offence, that in their parish Communion, (which not *communion of spirit*, but *co-habitation* begetteth) they partake with all *ignorant* and *scandalous* persons, not excluding drunkards, whoremongers, profane swearers, covetous wordlings, Atheists, Papists, and the like; whereby it cometh to passe, that not a *little leaven*, but a *great masse of leaven* hath deeply leavened the whole lump (Cotton 1645, 80).

Cotton's congeries "drunkards, whoremongers...Papists, and the like" is echoed some 70 years later in Captain Lemuel Gulliver's envoi in Book IV of Swift's *Gulliver's Travels* (1726):

> My Reconcilement to the *Yahoo*-kind in general might not be so difficult, if they would be content with those Vices and Follies only which Nature hath entitled them to. I am not in the least provoked at the Sight of a Lawyer, a Pick-pocket, a Colonel, a Fool, a Lord, a Gamester, a Politician, a Whoremonger, a Physician, an Evidence, a Suborner, an Attorney, a Traytor, or the like. This is all according to the due Course of Things (Swift 2005, 276).

The 'heaping up' rhetorical device congeries can occur naturally in speech and writing wherever a list may seem suitable – for emphasis, or to express outrage, or drawn out long enough, for satirical purposes. Cotton, the Puritan divine, was expressing earnest (if self-righteous) outrage at lax discipline and disorganization among the churches of the Massachusetts Bay Colony (1630–1691), as he had expressed outrage at similar failings back in England among parishes of the Anglican Communion. Cotton led a relatively colorful life for a Cambridge-trained cleric; born in Derby, he had attended first Trinity for the bachelor's, then Emmanuel for the master's (the latter much more receptive to Puritan theology). His association with St. Botolph's, Lincolnshire, which saw Cotton return to his native East Midlands, began in 1612; Cotton was able to negotiate fairly successfully his own nonconformism and attachment to Puritan circles while serving in the Church of England. But during the reign of Charles I the bargain became more difficult; some of Cotton's peers went into hiding, or fled, even to America, as Cotton himself soon would. In 1630 Cotton delivered a sermon in Southampton to the party of John Winthrop embarking on a journey to the Massachusetts Bay Colony aboard the *Arbella* (one of 11 ships in the flotilla that left in April 1630); entitled 'Gods Promise to His Plantation,' the sermon struck, in England, many of the notes that would become characteristic of the religious writing of Puritan New England.

In the section 'The forme of Gods publick Worship' Cotton alludes to the origins of the Bay Psalm Book:

> Before Sermon, and many times after, wee sing a Psalme, and because the former translation of the Psalmes, doth in many things vary from the originall,

> and many times paraphraseth rather then translateth; besides divers other defects (which we cover in silence) wee have endeavoured a new translation of the Psalmes into *English meetre*, as neare the originall as wee could expresse it in our *English* tongue, so farre as for the present the Lord hath been pleased to helpe us, and those Psalmes wee sing, both in our publike Churches, and in private (Cotton 1645, 67).

And from the Preface to that first book printed in America:

> ...we have therefore done our indeavour to make a plaine and familiar translation of the psalmes and words of David into english metre, and have not soe much as presumed to paraphrase to give the sense of his meaning in other words; we have therefore attended heerin as our chief guide the originall, shu<n>ning all additions, except such as even the best translators of them in prose supply, avoiding all materiall detractions from words or sence....
>
> As for our translations, wee have with our english Bibles (to which next to the Originall wee have had respect) used the Idioms of our owne tongue in stead of Hebriasmes, lest they might seeme english barbarisms.
>
> Synonimaes wee use indifferently: as *folk* for *people*, and *Lord* for *Iehovah*, and somtime (though seldome) *God* for *Iehovah*....
>
> Lastly. Because some hebrew words have a more full and emphaticall signification then any one english word can or doth somtime expresse, hence wee have done that somtime which faithfull translators may doe, *viz.*, not only to translate the word but the emphasis of it; as אל [El] *mighty God*, for *God*, כרך [barak] *humbly blesse* for *blesse*....
>
> ...and soe have attended Conscience rather then Elegance, fidelity rather then poetry, in translating the hebrew words into english language, and Davids poetry into english meetre
>
> that soe wee may sing in Sion the Lords;
> songs of prayse according to his owne
> will; untill hee take us from hence,
> and wipe away all our teares, &
> bid us enter into our masters
> ioye to sing eternall
> Halleluiahs.
>
> (*The Whole Booke of Psalmes* 1640, [9–12])

Just over a century later, Americans such as Benjamin Franklin (1706–1790) and Noah Webster (1758–1843) would encourage the drift in orthography (reflecting as well the phonology), punctuation, and prose style away from British models that had been underway in the late Early Modern English in use in the American colonies. Here in 1640–1645 we see relatively little of that 'drift' toward 'Americanisms'; Cotton and *The Bay Psalm Book* are still thoroughly English in prose style, diction, and orthography – hardly unexpected at this early date in colonial history. But in Cotton's tract and the translators' introduction to the *Bay Psalm Book*, one sees that option for 'plainer' style and unadorned forthrightness; and while this is in the main reflective of Puritan theology, it seems also to indicate the direction 'American English' would take.

Of course, the text itself of King David's 'Psalmes' was the main work of the translators; one may compare these translations with those of the long Early Modern period in the previous chapter. The *Bay Psalm Book* may seem a simpler, even homelier version; plainness in style and a literal, faithful directness in the 'Englishing' was not just a theory of translation but a religious mandate:

Ps 1:3

And shall be like to a tree
    Planted by water-rivers:
that in his season yeilds his fruit,
    And his leafe never withers.

Ps 23

The Lord to mee a shephearde is,
    want therefore shall not I.
Hee in the folds of tender-grasse,
    doth cause mee downe to lie:
To waters calme me gently leads
    Restore my soule doth hee:
he doth in paths of righteousnes:
    for his names sake leade mee.
Yea though in valley of deaths shade
    I walk, none ill I'le feare:
because thou art with mee, thy rod,
    and staffe my comfort are.
For mee a table thou hast spread,
    in presence of my foes:
thou dost annoynt my head with oyle,
    my cup it over-flowes.
Goodnes & mercy surely shall
    all my dayes follow mee:
and in the Lords house I shall dwell
    so long as dayes shall be.

Ps 102:11

My dayes as shadow that decline:
    & like the withered grasse am I.

The earnestness of these Englished psalms – the rendering of Psalm 23 is rather homely with some forced rhymes – was matched, however, by the reformer's zeal, and subsequent disagreements about whose *covenant* was the more authentic soon led to the formation of more churches. Crises in the Massachusetts churches came to a head in 1636, the year in which the General Court of the colony blocked an attempt at establishing a new church at Dorchester, Massachusetts Bay Colony; the law they set down, in part in reaction to fears that local church members were motivated by a ‘covenant of works’ rather than one of ‘saving faith,’ enjoined that:

> Forasmuch as it hath bene found by sad experience, that much trouble and disturbance hath happened both to the church and civill state by the officers and members of some churches, which have bene gathered within the limitts of this jurisdiccion in a undue manner, and not with such publique approbacion as were meete, it is therefore ordered that all persons are to take notice that this Court doeth not, nor will hereafter, approve of any such companyes of men as shall henceforth joyne in any pretended way of church fellowshipp, without they shall first acquainte the magistrates and the elders of the greater parte of the churches in this jurisdiccion, with their intencions, and have their approbacion herein. And ffurther, it is ordered, that noe person, being a member of any churche which shall hereafter be gathered without the approbacion of the magistrates, and the greater parte of the said churches, shalbe admitted to the ffreedome of this commonwealthe (Morgan 1987, 99–101).

In this 1636 document, the orthography gives some sense of changes that had been underway since Middle English: *bene* (line 3) is likely the ‘short ” of the orthoepists (the Early Modern writers on spelling) and so *bene* would be pronounced [bɪn] (Dobson 1968, I, 169); *meete* (4) was since 1500 pronounced [mi:t]; *publique* in *-que* and the abstract nouns with *-tion* as *-(c)cion* show the influence of their French origin *(jurisdiccion, approbacion, intencions)*. Geminates can still mark preceding short vowels: *civill, limitts, fellowshipp*. But the semi-retention of etymological spellings of French loans and Early Modern periodic style (the long sentences of multiple clauses) suggests a writer still more at home in England – or one arguing with an English audience.

Trouble too had been brewing with the separatist tendencies of Roger Williams, whose departure from the church at Salem, Massachusetts, would lead to the establishment of Rhode Island that year; Williams was granted a large parcel of land at the top of Narragansett Bay by the sachem of that tribe, Canonicus (ca. 1565–1647), who had been on friendly terms with the Pilgrims who had landed at Plymouth in 1620. Williams renamed the Narragansett land Providence, of the Providence Plantations, which was joined by settlements nearby at Newport and Portsmouth (the original name was Algonquian: Pocasset) in the Colony of Rhode Island and Providence Plantations in 1644.

A roster of some of the other significant Puritan figures shows some interesting patterns:

Thomas Shepard (1605–1649): born in Towcester, Northamptonshire (East Midlands), had been schoolmaster from 1627 at Earls Colne Grammar School (Essex); Archbishop Laud (Canterbury) barred him from preaching for doctrinal reasons. He boarded the *Defence* for Massachusetts in 1635 and became minister at Cambridge, MA (Congregationalist), then Harvard College (founded 1636). He was involved in the Antinomian Controversy 1636–1638, and, like a number of other ministers of New England, preached among the natives. He died in 1649 of quinsy.

Anne (Marbury) Hutchinson (1591–1643): born in Alford, Lincolnshire (East Riding of Yorkshire), she was the daughter of an Anglican minister with Puritan sympathies; she was banished in 1638 from the Massachusetts Bay Colony and settled with other dissenters at Pocasset on Narragansett Bay (renamed Portsmouth 1639). Her husband William Hutchinson (1586–1641), also born in Alford, hailed from a prominent family in Lincoln. The Hutchinsons were among those who purchased Aquidneck Island from the Narragansett tribe, which the English called Rhode Island (the name would be extended to the larger Colony of Rhode Island and the Providence Plantations).
John Eliot (1604–1690): born in Widford, Hertfordshire (Home Counties), he is the most famous of the 'Indian preachers,' establishing the *Praying Indian* town at Natick (Massachusetts Bay Colony) in 1651.
Henry Vane the Younger (1613–1662): born in Debden (Essex), and educated at the Westminster School, then Magdalen Hall, Oxford, Vane had been on the Parliamentarian side of the Civil War, and though an associate of Oliver Cromwell, he had refused to take the oath approving the execution of Charles I. He offered Anne Hutchinson and fellow 'Antinomians' support during that theological crisis in the Massachusetts Bay Colony, and support also to Roger Williams's colony in Rhode Island (Vane was also one of the fathers of Harvard College). Served as the fifth Governor of the Massachusetts Bay Colony, 1636–1637. He would return to England in 1639, and was returned to Parliament as MP for Kingston upon Hull (1640–1650; he would serve several terms in Parliament: MP for Whitchurch for five months in 1659, then for Kingston upon Hull again 1659–1660). He was imprisoned in the Tower of London in July 1660 (clemency had not been extended to those believed involved in 'regicide'), then was moved to the Isles of Scilly in 1661 to forestall any attempts to break him out; he was returned to the Tower in April 1662, tried for treason, and convicted. He was beheaded at Tower Hill on 14 June 1662.

Vane is the rather more 'aristocratic' figure in the Puritan and nonconformist Bay Colony region; had he stayed in New England, he might have been a moderating influence on the controversies that ensued; nonetheless, he it was who achieved a sort of *martyrdom* – a word of great value in the developing Puritan vocabulary:

> Mention being made to him of the cruel proceedings against him;
> Alas (said he) what ado they keep to make a poor creature like his Sa|viour!
> In discourse he said, If the shedding of my Blood, may prove an
> occasion of gathering together in one, the dispersed Interests and Rem|nant
> of the Adherers to this Cause (of whatever differing perswasions)
> I should think ten thousand Lives (if I had them) well spent in such
> a service.
>
> He was much pleased in this consideration, That he was hastening
> to a place where God nor none of his, would be ashamed to own and re|ceive
> him. Here is nothing in this world (saith he) but reproaching
> and despising God's precious Saints; but in Heaven there is a good
> reception for them, where are Mansions prepared from the beginning
> of the world.

> After his Sentence, he said to some Friends, God brought him up|on on three stages, (to wit, before the Court) and was now leading him to the fourth (his Execution-place) which was far easier and pleasanter to him than any of the other three.
>
> *The TRYAL of Sir Henry Vane Knight, at the Kings Bench, Westminster, June the 2d. and 6th. 1662 together with what he intended to have spoken the day of his sentence (June 11) for arrest of judgment (had he not been interrupted and over-ruled by the court) and his bill of exceptions: with other occasional speeches, &c.: also his speech and prayer, &c. on the scaffold* (London, 1662). [Early English Books Online, University of Michigan]

The heroic language drafted for recounting (and to some extent recasting) the *tryal* of Sir Henry Vane (the title *Knight* figures proudly in the account, not without some irony) is of the same tenor as that applied to the Puritan accounts of God's 'wonder-working Providence' in the New World, a world of epic battles between the godly and evil spirits literal and figurative, and it anticipates that of John Milton in his epics (*Paradise Lost* especially). Compared to the more 'Puritan' documents above – the Colony General Court declaration of 1636, *Bay Psalm Book* of 1645, Cotton's 1645 tract – Vane's 1662 testimony seems more 'modern' – and perhaps more 'royalist.' The political and religious divisions that were solidifying both sides of the Atlantic seem to have had some linguistic effects.

For the language of American Puritanism was quite simply that: a language, not just a vocabulary, though it was indeed one of a *visible church*, *visible saints*, *wonder-working*, *God's Providence*, *City on a Hill*, *sanctification*, *freemanship*, *covenant*, *Antinomianism* (those who held they were 'freed by grace from the obligation of observing the moral law'; OED, s.v. *antinomian*; from the Greek *anti-* 'against' + *nomos* 'law'). The earlier senses of *goodman* and *goodwife*, as head of a household and his wife, or such a householder of some property and status (found in Middle English and Scots; OED, s.v. *goodman*, senses 2–3) were extended in Puritan New England to those who were also noted for their *godliness*, and the use of the terms as a form of respectful address was also a way to inculcate and reinforce such godliness (as with Nathaniel Hawthorne's 1835 short story 'Young Goodman Brown'; Hawthorne's great-great-grandfather John Hathorne [1641–1717] had been one of the magistrates who presided over the Salem Witch Trials 1692–1693). Modesty in speech was encouraged, and there were modelled forms of testifying and witnessing to God's grace (adult baptism was generally the norm where practiced). A whole rhetoric of exhortation to godliness and away from sinning developed, and as the movements splintered, dozens of names were coined for the new denominations. A 'churche' was, in the definition of English Puritan John Field (1545–1588), *a company or congregatione of the faythfull called and gathered out of the worlde by the preachinge of the Gospell, who followinge and embraceinge true religione, do in one unitie of Spirite strengthen and comforte one another, dayelie growinge and increasinge in true faythe, framinge their lyves, governmente, orders and ceremonies accordinge to the worde of God* (Morgan 1987, 14). Besides the shifting tides of orthography, the later Early Modern English of New England religious controversialists is to be noted especially for the register developed – a vocabulary, speech, and prose style fitted to a purpose and pursuit: the religious experiences of Reformation-era nonconformist Protestants. It might also be considered one of the early registers of an emerging *American* English, along with that of the early explorers and colonists.

Roger Williams (1603–1683), the dissenting Puritan minister and founder of Rhode Island (with the joining of Aquidneck and the Providence Plantations into a single colony), was also a highly capable linguist and, with John Eliot, an early figure in the recording and preservation of native languages in the colonial period. Williams had a knowledge of the *tres linguae sacrae* ('three sacred languages,' Hebrew, Greek, and Latin) as well as the modern European languages French and Dutch; of particular note was his learning of Narragansett, an Algonquian language (perhaps part of the larger Algic grouping) related to, or a dialect of, Massachusett-Narragansett (or 'Massachuset'). It is from Narragansett that English borrowed *askútasquash*, retained in English in the clipped form *squash*, and, once added, it admitted of modifiers: *summer squash, butternut squash*; *Italian squash* is a name for *zucchini* (in AmE) or *courgette* (BrE).

The Natick dialect of Massachusett-Narragansett was the variety fellow minister John Eliot used for his Massachusett translation of the Bible (1663), in which Eliot introduced English words in Massachusett form: the imprint for Cambridge, MA, printer Samuel Green is a hybrid of English and Narragansett: *Printeucop nashpe Samuel Green*. *Nashpe* [našp^{h}i:] is the preposition 'with,' used to translate English 'for,' *print +eucop* is a hybrid, the equivalent of *print-er*. There is evidence of multilingualism among natives of the Americas in the early colonial period, and known cases of pidgins that formed among native languages, then between native and European languages. A pidgin Massachusett was spoken in Eastern New England from Maine to coastal islands (Martha's Vineyard) down to Long Island. Pidgin Delaware was fairly widely used in the Mid-Atlantic region, some words of it appearing in a 1683 letter of William Penn (Goddard 1996, 18–19). The lands of the Delaware had been a zone of tribal interaction before the European arrival; then the English, French, Dutch, and Swedish settlements were established in the PA-NJ-DE region. Thomas Hariot's *A Briefe and true report of the new found land of Virginia* (1588) records some words, perhaps as many as 80 or so, of Carolina Algonquian from his work on the 1585–1586 voyage Raleigh sponsored to what is now Virginia and North Carolina; he had reportedly collected more materials on the local language that have not survived (Goddard 1996, 18). William Strachey (1572–1621) compiled *A Dictionarie of the Indian Language, for the Better Enabling of Such Who Shalbe Thither Ymployed* (1612) of Tidewater Virginia Algonquian, in which Strachey records Algonquian *apones* 'bread,' from which American English regional *pone* and *cornpone* derive (maize cake, thin maize cake or loaf cooked in ashes).

One of the editors of the aforementioned *Bay Psalm Book* was Governor Thomas Mayhew of the Massachusetts Bay Colony; he led the first settlements on Martha's Vineyard, Nantucket, Chappaquiddick, and the Elizabeth Islands south of Boston Harbor and the near Cape in 1641. Through shrewd land deals, he expanded settlement into traditional Wampanoag lands; the Wampanoag were speakers of a dialect of the Algonquian Massachusett language. By 1681, documents in the Dukes County Registry of Deeds make clear that the Wampanoag were under some pressure to sell off more holdings, and that sachems were trying, at times unsuccessfully, to stem independent sales of land by members of the tribe. A document of 11 September

1681, in Wampanoag, Massachusett, with contemporary English translation, gives a sense of the quandary sachem Muttask faced:

> [in Wampanoag:]
> neen muttask Sachim ut kuhtuhquehchuet kah nashaquetesset weque...
> [Document 22, facsimile and transcription, Goddard and Bragdon 1988, Part I, 94–95]
>
> [English:]
> Muttask Sachem att Kuhtuhquetuut and Noshauaquetset as far as wanummusit Know ye all people that I Muttask and my principall men my Children & people are owners of this, this our Land for ever. They are for ever ours and our offspring for ever shall enjoy thereof: I Muttask and we Principall men together with our Children and all our people are agreed that no person shall sell any Land but if any person will steallingly sell any Land: take yee your Land because it is for ever yours; butt if any one will not performe this Covenant he shall fall to, to have any of this Land, att Kuhtuhquehtuut & Nashaouquetset for ever I Mutask and we principal men and our Children say this shall be for ever....
>
> I Mattask sachem and my cheife men speake this in the presence of God it shall be thus for ever: I muttask this in my hand Sep^{t}. 11th 1681
> [Goddard and Bragdon 1988, Part II, 775]

Witnesses to the 1681 document include John Keeps (Keps), possibly the John Keeps whose daughter married John Leonard of Agawam (killed during King Philip's War), Puttuhquannon, and Sasauapinu; the latter two bear Massachusett names. Documents from this period do not always figure prominently in the history of earliest American English, but they offer a wealth of information about language contact, particularly with personal and place-names. The prosopography – the study of the shared character of a people, from names to ranks to social connections – of the early colonial period in America is hampered by differences in personal name nomenclature, English and native. But what is clear is that native chiefs and their 'principall men and [their] Children' were very much aware that the settlers wanted more of their land, and would keep trying to acquire it, by deed or war. Clear too is that even on Nantucket or Martha's Vineyard, there remained an extensive native toponymy that had been transmitted by oral tradition and now made its way into colonial records. Much of the naming of the New World was simply renaming.

7.3 NEW ENGLAND, LA NOUVELLE-FRANCE: ENGLISH, FRENCH, MOHAWK, HURON – CONTACT SITUATIONS

Native American ethnonyms in what is now the United States and Canada appear frequently in French and English forms, and not a few were transmitted to English via French, by the explorers, cartographers, missionaries (and ethnographers), and *coureurs des bois*; this last group were the 'wood runners,' 'runners in the woods,' French Canadian fur traders and trappers who often lived out in the 'woods' for extended periods of time and at times married native women. They were the Franco-Canadian counterpart to the Anglo-American (and often Scots Irish) *woodsmen*, with their moosehide, deer- or buckskin outerwear, fur hats, and long rifles (one thinks of the nickname *La longue carabine*, 'the long rifle,' given to Hawkeye in James Fenimore Cooper's 1826 novel *The Last of the Mohicans*, part of his Leatherstocking Tales five-novel sequence). While French *congé* has been borrowed in the sense of 'dismissal,' and Anglicized in pronunciation with final [e] > [i] thus the alternative spelling *congee*, its original sense was an '[a]uthoritative or formal leave or license to depart,' and such were the writs issued by the French government to fur trappers in a system established by First Minister of State Jean-Baptiste Colbert in 1681. Trappers and adventurers who had issued out of Québec City (Ville du Québec, established 1608) in the days of Governor Samuel de Champlain had become a problem for the subsequent governors, or *gouverneurs*; Gouverneur, NY, in St. Lawrence County, is named for Founding Father Gouverneur Morris, author of the Preamble to the US Constitution; his given name derived from his mother's maiden name (she was of French Huguenot descent). The new system of permits or licenses for the fur trade brought a gradual end to the wilder days of the *coureurs des bois*, whose ranks were often filled with young indentured male servants (*engagés*) and ex-soldiers. Their legacy lives on, however, in the *métis* ('mixed,' i.e., of mixed European and indigenous ancestry) of the Great Lakes and Canadian prairie regions. The term *métis* may have first been applied to Euphrosine-Madeleine Nicolet, daughter of French *coureur des bois* Jean Nicolet, sieur de Belleborne (1598–1642) and his native wife of the Nipissing tribe (Ontario Province). As this mixed French-native population increased, so too did the sense of identity of the people, and *Métis* is an ethnonym of one of the largest indigenous (First Nations in Canadian English usage) populations in modern Canada (more than 600,000 people).

The *congé* system ushered in the age of the *voyageur*, the canoe-borne traders who pushed further westward, through the Great Lakes, the *Pays d'en-Haut* ('Upper Country'). The American city Detroit was in this new territory, its name a clipping of French *le détroit du Lac Érié*, 'the strait of Lake Erie'; the lake is named for the local Iroquoian Erie people; other variants of the ethnonym include the French-transmitted *Eriez* and *Riquéronon*, or *Nation du Chat*, 'People of the Cat,' perhaps after the raccoon tails used in their dress, or it may have been an endonym meaning 'People of the Panther.' The settlement began with the founding of Fort Pontchartrain du Détroit in 1701 by Antoine de la Mothe, sieur de Cadillac (1658–1730); he would later be governor of La Louisiane (1710–1716) and Captain Alphonse de Tonty, Baron de Paludy (1659–1727). And Cadillac, of course, became part of the heritage of American automobile-making centered in Detroit: Henry M. Leland had founded the Cadillac Automobile Company in 1902 (from 1909 part of General Motors) in honor of le sieur du Cadillac (he would go on to found the Lincoln Motor Company in 1917). Memory of the *voyageurs* survives in Voyageurs National Park in upper Minnesota.

To an extent, the extent of Nouvelle-France has been forgotten in modern memory, in large part because of a series of territorial losses to England and Spain. At its height New France stretched from Labrador (named after Portuguese explorer João

Fernandes Lavrador) to the Lake Winnipeg region across its northern frontier, south along the courses of the Missouri and Mississippi rivers (both names of native origin transmitted in French form) down to Louisiana and the Gulf coast, then back north along the Appalachians to Fort Duquesne at the junction of the Allegheny and Monongahela rivers (hydronyms also of native origin; the fort would be taken by the British in 1758 and the settlement named Pittsburgh in honor of William Pitt) to the Québec heartland along the Saint-Laurent (St. Lawrence). Tourists know New Orleans and the 'parishes' of old La Louisiane, but the American place-name register of this vast tract is filled with French forms: Ste-Geneviève, Missouri, on the Mississippi opposite Kaskaskia, Illinois (the Kaskaskia people were part of the Illiniwek Confederacy) in what was then known as *Haute-Louisiane* or *Pays des Illinois* (the French form *Illinois* with *-ois*, a suffix used to derive ethnonyms and national and linguistic terms, is believed to derive from *Illini*, the singular of *Illiniwek*). Joliet, Illinois, is named for Louis Jolliet, who traced the upper reaches of the Mississippi; accompanying him was the French Jesuit Jacques Marquette (1637–1675), who had established the first European settlement in Michigan at *Sault-Sainte-Marie*, contemporary Sault Ste. Marie (English-speakers have raised the original pronunciation of French *sault*, 'rapid(s),' from [o] to [u]). Marquette's legacy in the upper Great Lakes region is preserved in the town of Marquette, WI (Green Lake County), and the Jesuit-founded Marquette University in Milwaukee (there is a 'Pere Marquette Park' in Ste. Genevieve, Missouri). The trader Jean Baptiste Point du Sable (d. 1818) of African and perhaps French Canadian descent (though possibly born in Haiti) and his Potawatomi wife Kitihawa (baptismal name Catherine) are considered the first permanent residents of what would become Chicago. The period of trade, religious, and linguistic interaction in early American English is of much longer duration than commonly thought; du Sable's stay at the mouth of the Chicago River was some two centuries after Raleigh's Roanoke venture.

It was the Jesuits who preserved one of the greatest archives of this period of native-European contact in their reports to the order's Superior General back in Paris in what have come to be known as the 'Jesuit Relations' (*Relations des Jésuites*). These reports of Jesuit missionaries in New France 1632–1673 were collected and printed in 73 volumes by Reuben Gold Thwaites (Thwaites 1896–1901/1959); many of the relations give assurance to the order's leadership that conversion efforts were yielding results; the French Jesuits in North America took a slower approach to conversion of the natives, as it was a process of discernment and catechetical formation that could take years, as it did for St. Kateri Tekakwitha (1656–1680) of the Kahnawake Mission in Mohawk territory on the south shore of the St. Lawrence, who had been baptized by the Jesuit Jacques de Lamberville. These relations tell of the missionaries' struggles with the harsh winters and hot, humid summers, the difficulties of travel by canoe and portage (a loan from Anglo-Norman), the friendships with and animosities of local tribes, the successes and setbacks in establishing missions and building communities of converts. They also include eminently valuable ethnographic and linguistic information, as a number of the French Jesuits were able linguists, especially Fr. Jean de Brébeuf (1593–1649). Brébeuf spent years studying the Wendat (Wyandot) or Huron language and made a translation of the catechism from French to Wyandot in 1630, and a celebrated Christmas carol in that language, 'Jesous Ahatonhia' ('Jesus, He is born') ca. 1642. It was at St.-Ignace

(Ontario) that Brébeuf, along with his younger fellow Jesuit Gabriel Lalemant, was tortured and killed by the Iroquois who had attacked the nearby Huron mission village at Saint-Louis.

What is striking in the Jesuit relations is how often they parallel the records of Puritan missionary work with the 'praying Indians' (such as those for whom John Eliot founded Natick, Massachusetts, in 1651). The missionary work is now seen as highly controversial, but, in that timeframe, the Catholic missionaries of New France and Puritan missionaries of New England saw their work as part of the Gospel mandate, an act not just of 'civilizing,' but of mercy and love. Whatever contemporary writers may think of their motives and actions, the language of the period is suffused with their faith (in the salutations of letters, forms of address, Biblical allusions).

from the relation of Jean de Brébeuf (1636)

François Sangwati: Huron convert: "L'vn d'iceux no*m*mé François *Sangouati* estoit Capitaine de nostre village" ["one of them named François *Sangouati* was Captain of our village"] (Thwaites X: 10). There is a pattern in these texts to italicize the native surname, the given name a baptismal one, in French, usually with religious association (often of a saint or Biblical personage). French *ou* for *w* in transcription of native names is very commonly found (*Outaouais* for Ottawa, *Potaouatomi* for Potawatomi; Missouri is from the Illinois language rendering, in French orthography, of the Siouan ethnonym *ouemissourita*, 'people of the dugout canoes.'

Marie Aoesioua: young Huron convert: "Nous auons vne petite fille entre autres no*m*mee Marie *Aoesioua*, qui n'a point sa pareille; vous diriez que tout son contentement soit de faire le signe de la Croix, & de dire son *Pater* & *Aue*" ["We have a young girl among us named Marie *Aoesioua*, who has no equal; you could say her whole contentment is to make the sign of the Cross, and to say the Our Father and Hail Mary"] (Thwaites X: 22).

En bon François: Visiting Huron country in summer, Brébeuf relates the trials of Canada's seasonal insects: "& de plus vous arriuerez en vne saison où de miserables petites bestioles, que nous appellons icy *Taouhac*, & pulces en bon François" ["moreover you will arrive in a season of miserable little creatures, that we call here *Taouhac*, 'fleas' in proper French"] (Thwaites X: 90).

Valuable as the Jesuit relations are to a picture of language contact in the early colonial Americas, priests such as Fr. Brébeuf were not the only observers of the linguistic interactions. The date of birth of Baron Lahontan (Louis-Armand de Lom d'Arce de Lahontan; 1666–1716) is according to a record from the Archives municipales de Pau, "Le neufvieme de juin mil six cents soixante six nasquit et receut l'eau du sacreme*nt* de baptesme en la paroisse de Lahontan..." ("the 9th of June 1666 born and received the water of the sacrament of baptism in the parish of Lahontan"; Ouellet and Beaulieu 1990, vol. 1: 211), though he himself gave at times conflicting information (1: 211 n. 4). The name Lahontan (printed also as *de la Hontan*) is of the Pyrénées-Atlantiques region, or Bas-Pyrénées (Dauzat and Rostaing 1978, s.v.; they cite the 13th-century form *Lafontac* and 17th-century *Fontano*, as well as the variant *Hontanx* as < late Latin **fontanum*, Latin *fons* in sense 'spring,' as found in toponyms). As with the *Jesuit Relations*, Lahontan's work originates in dispatches home, the *Nouveaux voyages* consisting in 25 letters dated between 8 November 1683 and 31 January 1694 "supposément addressées à un vieux parent de France" ("supposedly addressed to an elderly relative in France"; Ouellet and Beaulieu 1990, 1: 25). Lahontan enjoyed a vogue of sorts in English translation for the next half-century: the first edition of the 'New Voyages' appeared in English in 1702–1703, followed by those of John Harris (1705), Daniel Coxe (1722), and Cadwallader Colden (1747; Colden was a Scots-Irish physician who served twice as Governor of colonial New York). Three of Lahontan's works provide some insight into French-English-native colonial and linguistic interrelations in the period: *Nouveaux Voyages de Mr. Le baron de Lahontan dans L'Amérique septentrionale* ('The New Voyages of Monsieur Baron de Lahontan in North America'; 1703), which includes the *Petit Dictionnaire de la langue des sauvages* ('Brief dictionary of the language of the savages'; Ouellet and Beaulieu 1990, vol. 1: 732–771), *Mémoires de l'Amérique septentrionale* ('Memoirs of North America'; 1703), and *Suite du voyage de l'Amérique* ('Continuation of the Voyage to America'; 1704), in the first part of which were the *Dialogues*.

The *Nouveaux Voyages* was dedicated to Frederick IV, King of Denmark and Norway, who was at the time of publication (1702–1703) engaged in the alliance against France in the War of the Spanish Succession. The extended subtitle of the work, 'Qui contiennent une rélation des différens Peuples qui y habitent...' ('which contains a relation of the different people who live there...') continues with a further allusion to the adversarial position Lahontan came to hold toward the French enterprise in North America, "L'intérêt des François & des Anglois dans le Commerce qu'ils font avec ces Nations; l'avantage que l'Angleterre peut retirer dans ce Païs, étant en Guerre avec la France" ("the interest of the French and English in the trade they make with these [native] nations; the advantage that England might gain in this country, being at war with France"; Ouellet and Beaulieu 1990, 1, 243, 245). Lahontan, as a *lieutenant du roi* ('king's lieutenant'), defended New France ably during King William's War (1689–1697), but wound up deserting after the Battle of Placentia, Newfoundland (1692). He fled first to Portugal, then Holland and Spain, and spent his remaining years writing accounts of his time in America and, more controversially, in the France he was unable to return to, advocated for Britain to take New France. The tragic turns Lahontan's life would take, the position he finds himself in at the publication of this work (composed during a second stay in Amsterdam), set against the country of his birth, no doubt have their presence in the *rélations* of his *Nouveaux Voyages*. Of concern here, too, with Lahontan's conflicted loyalties and sentiments, is their influence on the recording of events, of attitudes toward French and English (and French and English to native), the competing colonial powers and their languages in a formative period that would settle, eventually, with some fluctuation, language divisions that hold to the present in Canada.

Lahontan's glossary *de la langue des sauvages* ('on the language of the savages') is in the main a brief series of observations and select vocabularies arranged, in medieval fashion, in bilingual glossary format, on Algonquian and Iroquoian (especially Huron) languages (see, in general, Trigger 1987/2000 and other studies by Trigger in the References). Though subsequent linguistic work has clarified matters markedly, Lahontan's observations are often precocious (one sees the early comparative method at work), and his recordings at times, and for the time, are quite accurate – one example, his note concerning the labials in Iroquoian languages:

> Je dirai de la Langue des *Hurons* & des *Iroquois* une chose assez curieuse, qui est qu'il ne s'y trouve point des lettres *labiales*; c'est à dire de *b, f, m, p*. Cependant cette Langue des *Hurons* paroît être fort belle & d'un son tout à fait beau; quoi qu'ils ne ferment jamais leurs levres en parlant.
>
> I will speak about a quite curious thing about the language of the Hurons and Iroquois, which is that one does not find the labial consonants, that is to say *b, f, m, p*. This language of the Hurons, however, seems quite lovely and with a beautiful sound to it; though they never close their lips in speaking (Ouellet and Beaulieu 1990, 1: 766).

Lahontan's remarks may seem strange from a contemporary perspective, but we see the beginnings of modern linguistic analysis. In his glossary, Lahontan includes the terms French and English, his *François* for *français*, and *Anglois* for *anglais*):

> Anglois, *Ouatsakamink dachirini*. (That is, The Men from Across the River)
> France, Païs des François, *Mittigouchiouek endalakiank*
> François, appellez constructeurs de Vaisseaux, *Mittigouch*. ['The French, what are called builders of ships']
> Roi de France, grand Chef des François, *Mittigou, Kitchi Okima* ['the King of France, the Great Chief of the French']
> (Ouellet and Beaulieu 1990, 1: 737, 747, 758)

For comparison with the Dutch-English interactions in Nieuw/New Amsterdam (7.1 above) are place and personal names from Lahontan's *Nouveaux Voyages*:

Manat: "Manhattan," on map facing "Lettre I" in *Nouveaux Voyages*, in "Pais des Anglois" (Ouellet and Bealieu 1990, 1: 256) ['country of the English']
Monreal: "Lettre II" (1: 267; post 1759 one sees the calque *Mount Royal* in English records)
Algonkins: "Lettre IV" (1: 279)
Nouvelle Yorc: "Lettre V" (1: 288, 296, 304): "Lettre VII": "Gouverneur de *Nieu-Yorc*" (Dutch-French version; 1: 305); "Gouverneur de la *Nieu-Yorc*" (1: 306); "de la *Nouvelle Yorc*" (1: 375); "la *Nouvelle York*" (1: 454)
Calumet (Le Calumet de paix): "Lettre VII" (1: 303): "le grand *Calumet* de paix" (1: 305); "Ici finit le credit & l'autorité du *Calumet de Paix*" (1: 412) ['the Calumet of Peace/peace pipe'; 'the great Calumet of Peace'; 'here ends [about] the value and authority of the Calumet of Peace']; the OED lists its first attestation as 1638, from the *Jesuit Relations* for this native clay pipe, often used ceremonially (as in professions of friendship)
la Virginie: "Lettre VII" (1: 304)
les Ilinois: "Lettre VII" (1: 305)
Iroca: Latinized form of *Iroquois* (1: 310)
Missisipi: "Lettre VIII" (1: 313)

Kitchi Okima: "Lettre VIII" (1: 317); in Lahontan's "Explication" of terms in the *Nouveaux Voyages* he glosses: "C'est ainsi que tous les Sauvages, dont les langages se rapportent à celui des *Algonkins*, nomment les Gourverneurs Généraux de *Canada*, du mot de *Kitchi*, qui signifie *Grand* & de *Okima*, qui veut dire *Capitaine*. Les *Iroquois* & les *Hurons* les appellent *Onnontio*" ["this is how the Savages, whose languages are related to those of the Algonquians, refer to the Governors-General of Canada, with the word *Kitchi*, which means 'Great,' and *Okima*, which is to say 'Captain.' The Iroquois and Hurons call them *Onnontio*"]; (1: 516); compare *Kitchi Manitou*, "Grand Esprit" (1: 662) ['Great Spirit']

Raquettes: illustration facing opening of "Lettre X" (1: 325; description at 325–326); the form is not in the OED, though heard in Canadian English; there is a *Raquette River* in upstate New York that may derive from this term for native snowshoes; these deer sinew wooden-framed "kinde of shooes a yard long, fourteene inches broad, made like a Racket" appear in Samuel Purchas's *Pilgrimages* in a 1607 entry on the North Virginia voyages (Quinn and Quinn 1983, 350)

Caribous: also at "Lettre X" (1: 329–330); first attestation is the 1609 English translation of Marc Lescarbot's *Nova Francia* ('New France')

Carcajoux: "Lettre XI" (1: 333); first attestation of the wolverine-like *carcajou* is 1709, from the English translation of Lahontan's *Nouveaux Voyages*

Porc-épi: "Lettre XI" (1: 334), i.e., the *porc espin*, 'spiny pig' (*porcupine* entered Middle English via Old French)

Major Gregori: "Lettre XIII" (1: 348); a partial Gallicization of English *Gregory*, instead of the equivalent *Grégoire*

Lac Herrié: "Lake Erie" in "Lettre XIII" (1: 355; as Lahontan signs it, this letter was dispatched from Niagara 2 August 1687); often elsewhere *Lac Errié* (as at 1: 486)

Poissons blancs: here, in "Lettre XIV," written from Missilimakinac (on the strait between Lakes Erie and Huron) a reference to the Great Lakes whitefish (the contemporaneous Algonquian form is given as *attikamek*; 1: 367); in his discussion of the *poisson blanc* in his *Mémoires de l'Amérique septentrionale* (1: 593), Lahontan mentions the affinity of Great Lakes natives for fish broth

Saut Sainte Marie, Lac Supérieur: "Lettre XV" (1: 372), now Sault Ste. Marie, MI, and Lake Superior

Ouisconsinc (la Rivière de): "Wisconsin" in "Lettre XVI" (1: 393): the usual French *ou(i)-* for native and English *w(i)-*

Cacique ("ce grand Chef ou *Cacique*")['the Great Chief' or *Cacique*']: "Lettre XVI" (1: 417); *cacique* is a loan from Spanish, a Hispanicization of Taino *kasike* for a local chieftain; its first attestation in English is from Richard Eden's 1555 translation of Gonzalo Fernández de Oviedo y Valdés's *La historia general de las Indias* in epitome form; it is attested next in Sir Walter Raleigh's *Discoverie of Guiana* (1596); this is a good example of the interchange of indigenous loanwords from one colonial sphere to another (here, from the Spanish Empire of the Caribbean and South America to the French and English of North America; OED, s.v.)

Missouris ("la Rivières des *Missouris*" and "Village des *Missouris*"): "Lettre XVI (1: 426)

Crocodile: "Lettre XVI" (1: 430; and cf. 1: 567–568): a transfer in use to not just New World crocodiles but the more common alligator; *crocodile* has a long history in the European languages, deriving ultimately from κροκόδειλος (*krokódeilos*) in Herodotus; *alligator* is also attested for the first time in Eden's translation of Oviedo's treatise, and derives from the fusion of Spanish definite article + noun *el lagarto* > *alligator* (OED, s.v.); Spanish use of 'the lizard,' which could be seen as a form of understatement (or litotes), may actually involve a sort of taboo deformation (the alligator as '*the* lizard,' i.e., one to be feared)

Kenébeki ("situé sur les Côtes maritimes de la *Nouvelle Angleterre*") ['situated along the maritime coasts of New England']: Fort Loyal, Casco Bay, ME; compare Kennebec(k), 1: 453: "la Rivière de *Kenébeki*" ['Kennebec River'] (1: 480)

ces Bandits: from Ital. *bandito*, Le Robert gives the first appearance in French as 1663; the 1703 English version has "these Bandito's"; (letter dated to 1690; 1: 454); "ces Bandits" (1: 485) in the 1703 version "these *Banditi's*"

Baston: Boston (1: 455)

Indians, Indians: from Lahontan's account of Sir William Phips's unsuccessful attack on Quebec City ("Ville de Kebec" on the accompanying plate of the battle in Lahontan's account) in late 1690; Phips was born in Pemaquid, ME, in 1651 and had gained his title from the salvage of Spanish wrecks in the Caribbean in 1687; here his men (and their native auxiliaries) are retreating from Quebec after an unsuccessful assault and, "ils se sauverent pêle et mêle, en criant *Indians, Indians*" ['they saved themselves [running away] pell-mell crying out "Indians, Indians"'] (1: 464)

In his *Mémoires de l'Amérique septentrionale*, we read Lahontan in English, on the English. Of the five government reports attributed at present to Lahontan, one is in English: *Brief Remarks concerning the Cod-Fishery, the Beaver Trade, and the Limits of New England and New France*, a product of Lahontan's later years in Hannover, which, as it mentions events of 1709–1710 but not that the conflict had concluded, was apparently written during the War of the Spanish Succession (Lahontan, *Brief Remarks*, ed. Towle and Rawlyk 1963–1965). Of interest in particular is his discussion of Niagara ('the Lake Errié') and the Great Lakes. A good many of the settlers in the respective colonial ventures spoke more than one language, and many were familiar with nautical pidgins and early varieties of American Indian Pidgin English (AIPE); Père Brébeuf and Baron Lahontan are noteworthy among the early recorders of contact varieties for their metalinguistic skills: a consciousness of recording not just language data, but data about language itself (as a human faculty).

There is yet one more part of the story of language in the Americas in the colonial era. John Rolfe, husband of Pocahontas, father of Thomas Rolfe, had brought tobacco cultivation to the Virginia colony in 1612; it quickly grew into a lucrative and expansive trade in the Virginia and Carolina colonies. The first attestation of the loan to English, in William Harrison's *The Description of England* (1577), attests to its great popularity: *In these daies* [1573] *the taking-in of the smoke of the Indian herbe called Tabaco, by an instrument formed like a litle ladell, wherby it passeth from the mouth into the hed & stomach, is gretlie taken-vp & vsed in England* (OED, s.v. *tobacco*). The demand for tobacco back in Europe sent bales and bales of tobacco leaves into a trade network of gold, rum, and furs. Gold from the 'Gold Coast' in West Africa had set off a first scramble to explore along the Bight. This European exploration of Africa began in what was still the European Middle Ages, most famously under Prince Henry 'the Navigator' of Portugal (1394–1460). The Portuguese capture of Ceuta on the North African side of the Strait of Gibraltar in 1415 allowed the small, recently unified, kingdom to launch a challenge to Muslim Arab domination of the slave and spice trade. The latter, especially for clove, mace, and nutmeg, from India and the Moluccas, was under an Arab monopoly and were the first lure for Portuguese and then Spanish ventures along the western coast of Africa. Once the feared, stormy Cape Bojador had been passed (in what is now Western Sahara) in 1434, the Portuguese continued down the African coast until Bartolomeu Dias in 1488 sailed round the Cape of Good Hope. By 1510, the Portuguese empire of sea routes stretched from Brazil to the Malabar coast of India. Somewhat more soberingly, the Papal bull *Romanus Pontifex* (issued 8 June 1455 by Pope Nicholas V) encouraged the Portuguese ventures provided that they would also bring the Catholic faith to these new lands and challenge Muslim conversion programs in Africa (Dille 2021, 5–9); the bull also mentioned Prester John, the elusive Christian priest-king who maintained a Christian realm somewhere in the East amidst the pagans and Muslims. One foot was placed firmly in the future in an age of navigation and exploration; the other remained in the old world of medieval legend (Prester John figures in the Middle English *Travels of Sir John Mandeville*).

John Rolfe witnessed a new trade in late August 1619 with the arrival of a 'Dutch man of Warr' *The White Lion*, which brought with it some of the enslaved African people who had been on their way to Mexico aboard the Portuguese vessel *São João Bautista*; *The White Lion* sold off the 20 or so African men and women (perhaps from Angola) as indentured servants. As will be seen in the following chapter, the consequences of this arrival were profound and altered the course of the colonial Americas to the present day. The linguistic consequences were also profound and were to be felt in the English colonies in the development of West African English-based contact varieties whose 'creole-like' features (Makoni et al. 2002) survive to this day in African American English.

7.4 THE PLAINS OF ABRAHAM (1759): ENGLISH AND FRENCH IN CANADA

Benjamin West's Quaker family moved from Springfield, Pennsylvania territory, in 1738, to Newtown Square, 12 miles west of Philadelphia, where they owned an inn that still stands (The Square Tavern, which houses some of West's paintings). Patronized by wealthy Philadelphians, West embarked in 1760 on a tour of Italy to see the works of Italian masters; a stay in England in 1763 became permanent, though West became one of the great painters of colonial American history. His masterpiece was *The Death of General Wolfe* (1770), exhibited at the Royal Academy in 1771, and, since 1918, part of the permanent collection of the National Gallery of Canada in Ottawa[5]. The large-scale composition has the dying General James Wolfe (b. 1727, Westerham, Kent) just to the right of bottom center, a fellow officer holding a handkerchief to the fatal wound

[5] Figure: Benjamin West, The *Death of General Wolfe* [1770] https://www.gallery.ca/collection/artwork/the-death-of-general-wolfe-0

to Wolfe's chest; Lieutenant Henry Browne of the Louisbourg Grenadiers – a temporary unit Wolfe had formed after the earlier siege of the French Fortress of Louisbourg on Cape Breton Island – holds a flag over Wolfe in the cluster of five British officers surrounding the fallen general. To the right, two other officers stand looking on, hands clasped in prayer. To the left of the center of the composition, another cluster of British officers, one from a local militia clad in green, with native deerskin boots decorated in beadwork, stands looking toward Wolfe. Beneath them is a native ally, seated, head resting on his right closed hand, right elbow on his thigh; he is bare-chested, various tattoos visible (geometric leather-stocking-like pattern on the right leg, claw on right shoulder, scrolling serpent over right shoulder blade), rifle resting over the right leg, hatchet on the ground beneath his left leg, a shoulder bag resting on his right hip with Algonquian beadwork. West was of course not present at the Battle of the Plains of Abraham, 13 September 1759, in Quebec City on the heights overlooking the St. Lawrence. But he had insisted on some fidelity in detail of the figures and uniforms. The native ally looks on at the dying young general (Wolfe was 32 at the Plains of Abraham; he had been 19 when he fought at the Battle of Culloden); his head is mostly shaved, a zigzag tattoo rises along his left temple. His expression shows some of the concern of the other witnesses, perhaps also some admiration (for a 'noble death'), and something more stoic: perhaps some curiosity as he watches an Englishman die. The details of dress and characteristic features are all the more striking seeing the large canvas (5 × 8 feet) in person in Ottawa. The Battle in Québec in 1759 would change the political and demographic picture of Canada: the deportations of French Acadians to Louisiana had begun in 1755 and would continue through 1764 – whence, eventually, the Cajuns (*Acadien* > *Cajun* in aphetized form). So too the linguistic.

The English ascendancy in Québec would last into the 20th century when French Canadian birth rates would outpace the English (*La revanche des berceaux*, 'the revenge of the cradles') and a Québecois ethno-nationalism would lead to political power (the *Parti Québecois,* founded in 1968, and *Bloc Québecois*, founded 1991) and *séparation* referenda in 1980 and 1995 (with *Oui* graffiti in blue, *Non* in red across Montréal). Québec City/ Ville de Québec and environs are the old Québecois heartland where French is the majority tongue; the battle was for Montreal/Montréal, the largest city in the Province of Québec and the center of English administration and financial clout. The coat of arms of the Ville de Montréal honors the complicated ethnolinguistic history of the city post-1759: in the upper left corner is the French fleur-de-lis, then, clockwise, the English rose, the Irish shamrock, the Scottish thistle; in local Anglophone lore the coat represents the French founding, English conquest, the Irish labor that dug the canals (including the miserable labor on Lachine Canal[6]), and the Scots who did the banking – such as John Redpath: born in Earlston, Berwickshire, in 1796 in a Scotland that had been wracked by the Lowland Clearances, he

[6] The name is borne by the Lachine rapids of the St. Lawrence and the town that once stood there (razed in a Mohawk raid in 1689), allegedly named by René-Robert Cavelier, sieur de La Salle (1643–1687), who had supposedly sought a passage through America to China (hence *La chine*); he had made a number of other discoveries, and is credited with naming the lower reaches of the mouth of the Mississippi *La Louisiane*. The Irish canal diggers had their own lore, that it felt as if they had been digging their way to China. In the 19th and early 20th centuries, the Irish formed the lowest stratum of Montréal society.

emigrated to British Canada at the age of 20; Redpath eventually made his fortune in banking (Bank of Montreal), sugar from the West Indies, and construction (employing cheap Irish immigrant labor). By the 1970s and 1980s, Montréal was virtually an Anglophone city, as the city's largest and most prestigious university (McGill) was Anglophone and young Francophones increasingly spoke English, for a variety of reasons that were by then more sociolinguistic than political. The erosion of French in Montréal and environs was in part due to the region's settlement history: the 'western townships' of Montréal had always been a mixture of English and French, often on a town-by town basis: Dorval, Valois, Pointe-Claire and Dollard des Ormeaux, Cedar Park and Kirkland, heading westward, then Beaconsfield, Baie-d'Urfé on the western end of Île de Montréal; then the Île-Perrot and the Vaudreuil, Dorion, and a cluster of French towns for the last few miles left of Québec; at Pointe-Lalonde on the 401 highway one crosses into Ontario and the town names are English and Scots: Bainsville, Glen Gordon, Lancaster, Glen Roy, MacGillivray Bridge, Camerons Point, Glen Walter, Cornwall. The 401 will follow westward along the St. Lawrence to the shores of Lake Ontario and on to Toronto, Canada's largest city, the Anglophone financial, academic, and political capital. But north from Cornwall is the federal capital, chosen by Queen Victoria on a map back in England and named after the Ottawa/Odawa people, a large Algonquian-speaking tribal grouping whose territories had spanned large swathes of what is now Ontario and Michigan.

Canada is officially bilingual at the federal level, in English and French – though the English monarch appears on Canadian currency and postage stamps, a sore point, rather understandably, for Québecois nationalists – with recognition also of indigenous/First Nations languages such as Ojibwe/Ojibway, Inuktitut, Cree, and others. In the National Capital Region, English is predominant in the capital city, but across the Ottawa River in Hull (named for Hull in Yorkshire), the vast majority of the residents are Francophone. The bilingual situation in Canada can be town-by-town, as in the western and eastern townships of the Montréal region, but at the national level, French is largely found in Québec and parts of the Atlantic Provinces. One finds along the western shore of Cape Breton Island, in the route northward to the Highlands, a series of Francophone towns such as Cap Le Moine, Grand Étang, and Chéticamp. Visit a local supermarket in this region and one hears a different sort of French from the standard Québecois or Montréalais (though even here, there are regional differences between urban and countryside); this is what is left of the old Acadian French (*le français acadien*), and there is heavy influence from neighboring English. Across Cape Breton, one can hear Francophones code-switching between French and English (in combinations different from the *franglais* of Québec). In New Brunswick, with its English-speaking majority, there is the *Chiac/Chi'aq* patois, a variety of Acadian French with significant English lexification. The *Joual* of Montréal is a working-class French variety, a source of local pride and more of a social variety than a contact variety.

The primarily lexical exchange between French and English is bidirectional, though unequal in terms of influence and borrowing. *Anglos*, English-speaking Québecois/Quebeckers (a term distinct from Spanish loan *Anglos* for English-speakers in the American Southwest), will all know the common French loans and local terms, from *poutine* (the twice-fried French fries then heated up with a vinegary brown gravy and cheese curds), to *dep* (a clipped form of *dépanneur*, 'corner store'), to *CÉGEP* (*Collège d'eneignement général et professionel*, pronounced [seɪdʒɛp]), a pre-college degree program required for university admission in the province. The 'language wars' in Quebec of the 1970s to present led to a movement of over 200,000 English-speakers out of the province, mainly to Toronto, Calgary, and other Anglophone cities. At the national level, official Canadian bilingualism works rather better for the Anglophone than the Francophone Canadian. Most young Québecois speak English well, even if there may be some reluctance to use it in some situations (as when an Anglophone is perceived as expecting English to be spoken); Francophones in English-speaking majority provinces west and east of Québec do not readily find the same linguistic accommodation. This perceptual sense of a language and tradition (and by extension, people) under siege fed a linguistic nationalism in Québec that resulted in Parti Québecois-led language legislation: the *Loi 101* or *La chartre de la langue française* (Charter of the French Language) of 26 August 1977. The Charter sought not just to establish the French Language as the official language of Québec but to stem the tide of what the French variously term Anglo-American cultural imperialism or *Coca-Colonialism.* It has always been a controversial legislative move by René Lévesque and other Québecois nationalists – and *nationalists* is the term as the 'language laws' (as Anglophone Quebeckers call such measures) have gone hand-in-hand with the separatist movement (the main library in Montréal is not the *Bibliothèque municipale* as in French cities, but the *Bibliothèque nationale*, now the *Bibliothèque et Archives nationales du Québec*). Not provincial, national. The promised third referendum on *la séparation* has not yet been held, and a number of matters have changed since the second in 1995, in which the *Non/No* vote won by a razor-thin margin, 50.58% vs. 49.42% for *Oui*, which some nationalist politicians blamed on the *allophone* vote (in Québec language politics this refers to speakers, generally new immigrants to the province, of languages other than French or English). The First Nations of Northern Quebec overwhelmingly voted *Non/No.* Demographics have seen increased immigration of these allophones to Québec, which had previously had policies favoring Francophones (thus immigration patterns in the province differed from those of the rest of Canada, with the Francophone immigrants hailing from the Maghreb, the Levant, Haiti, West Africa, and the former Indochine). *Loi 101* and subsequent language legislation, most recently Bill 96 of the Assemblée nationale du Québec/National Assembly of Québec of June 2022, which regulates matters ranging from business signage (signs must have French spellings – i.e., no apostrophes – and have the French letterings twice the size of the other language, with only one other language in addition to French permitted) to language use in education and the workplace. The latter area has caused the most consternation among Anglophones and allophones: businesses with (currently as of 2022) 25 or more employees must conduct all business primarily in French; thus Montreal's largest newspaper, the English-language daily *The Montreal Gazette*, must conduct its business and meetings in French. It is easy to see how such restrictions, as restrictions they are, cause resentment among English-speakers in the province; somewhat unusually, given the power and prestige of English globally, the language here is on its back foot, and *Loi 101* in its uneven and sometimes heavy-handed enforcement certainly *felt* at times discriminatory; this is complicated by the somewhat tricky Québecois formation *pure laine* ('pure wool') borrowed into Quebec English. Ostensibly, it refers to the old core of French settlers in Québec, but it was seen as referring more specifically to white Francophones in distinction to Francophones from West Africa, the Caribbean, or the Middle East.

On the other hand, the shoring up of French in the province of Québec may be counted as a successful language revival program: Montréal is secure, for now, as the largest Francophone city in the Americas (the picture for Francophones in other provinces is not so salubrious). But it is also worth noting that resentment of the encroachment of the English language in what had been Nouvelle-France and its financial and fur-trade capital Montréal was part of a larger series of resentments of France's loss of vast tracts of its overseas territories, and the depopulation of Acadia under British rule. Francophones number about 8 million out of Canada's 38 million people; French speakers had been a quarter of the population, but that percentage has been dropping the last two decades with new waves of allophone immigration. Their sense of threat might seem exaggerated, but French Canadians could worry by looking at the fate of other linguistic and cultural minorities in Canada. The Inuit people with the recognition of Nunavut ('our land' in the Inuktitut language) made significant territorial and financial gains (with gas and oil rights, enough that other Canadians made joking reference to the *United Inuit Emirates*); but many First Nations face continued economic and social hardships, with the same fears of language attrition as Native Americans in the United States (in the Canadian example, by English and French). Cape Breton Scots Gaelic is a threatened language and tradition, despite the efforts of Colaisde na Gàidhlig/Gaelic College of St Anns, Cape Breton Island. The 'Newfie' dialects suffer from outmigration of younger generations; an old joke in Newfoundland is that every high school graduate there gets the same graduation gift: a suitcase. Newfoundland has a long cultural and linguistic history, with Canada's most distinctive English dialects (see Boberg 2006 in general on Canadian Englishes). The folk story tradition is heavily influenced by Irish and Scots stories and forms: *un* for *one*, *goina* for *going*, *nar* for *neither* (see, e.g., the "Hard Head" folk stories in Halpert and Widdowson 1996, I, 388ff.).

The expulsion of the Acadians 1755–1764, *Le grand dérangement* ('The Great Trouble' or 'Upheaval'), was not, like the 'Great Migration' of Puritans to New England, a major population shift in contemporary terms. The 10,000–11,000 Acadians deported to other territories of the British Empire (then, for many of them, migration to Louisiana that in 1762 came under Spanish control) were, however, some two-thirds of Acadia's populace. The cultural and linguistic loss compounded the historical memory. With the American Revolution, some 15,000 loyalists from the American colonies were deported 1783–1785 by the new American government to New Brunswick (which had once been part of l'Acadie/Acadia; Saint John became instead a Loyalist city). One legacy of these shifts in fortune and language is that New Brunswick, at the provincial level, has French and English as the official languages. But another is a sense of French loss, the major loss being that of 1759. Two generals lost their lives at that battle on the Plains of Abraham: General Wolfe on the British side and, having been shot in the back while leaving the field of battle for the city, and General Montcalm, Louis-Joseph de Montcalm-Grozon (1712–1759), commander of the French forces. The defeats Montcalm had inflicted on the British in the French and Indian Wars (1754–1763) had encouraged the Americans in their ambitions for independence. For the Québecois, the defeat on the Plains of Abraham was the beginning of a long disaster; that sense of defeat and second-class status fed a culture of resentment and defiance. The motto on automobile license plates in Québec is *Je me souviens*, the French reflexive construction literally 'I to myself recall' = 'I remember.' What is to be remembered is left unsaid, but the Battle on the Plains of Abraham is a common suggestion. In West's rendering of the moment of death of General Wolfe, one sees the uniforms and dress of the British Army, the Louisbourg Grenadiers, and native and colonial auxiliaries. In the distance, the French have left the field, and the English have captured the heights. In New England and Nouvelle-France, the contact situation is already of some two centuries' duration, as even before Jamestown (1607) linguistic contact had occurred, evidenced by nautical pidgins and American Indian Pidgin English (AIPE); a new linguistic world was taking shape, English, French, African, and native.

REFERENCES AND BIBLIOGRAPHY

Bailey, Richard W. *Speaking American: A History of English in the United States.* New York: Oxford University Press, 2012

Bailyn, Bernard. *The Barbarous Years: The Peopling of British North America: The Conflict of Civilizations, 1600–1675.* New York: Alfred A. Knopf, 2012

Baker, Emerson W., "Finding the Almouchiquois: Native American Families, Territories, and Land Sales in Southern Maine," *Ethnohistory* 51.1 (2004), 73–100

Bakker, Peter, "'The Language of the Coast Tribes is Half Basque': A Basque-American Indian Pidgin in Use between Europeans and Native Americans in North America, Ca. 1540-ca. 1640," *Anthropological Linguistics* 31 (1989), 117–147

Barbour, Philip L., ed. *The Complete Works of Captain John Smith (1580–1631).* 3 vols. Chapel Hill, NC: University of North Carolina Press, 1986

Batchelder, Samuel F., "Some Sea Terms in Land Speech," *The New England Quarterly* 2.4 (1929), 625–53

The Bay Psalm Book: A Facsimile of the First Edition of 1640. Ed. Zoltán Haraszti. Chicago: University of Chicago Press, 1956

Boberg, Charles. *The English Language in Canada.* Cambridge: Cambridge University Press, 2006

Bonvillain, Nancy. *A Grammar of Akwesasne Mohawk.* Ottawa: National Museum of Man/ Musée National de l'Homme, 1973

Brandt, Elizabeth and Christopher MacCrate, "'Make Like Seem Heep Injin': Pidginization in the Southwest," *Ethnohistory* 29 (1982), 201–220

Burkette, Allison, "'Stamped Indian': Finding history and culture in terms for American 'cornbread'," *American Speech* 86.3 (2011), 312–339

Campeau, Lucien. *La mission des Jésuites chez les Hurons, 1634–1650.* Bibliotheca Instituti Historici S.I., vol. XLVI. Montréal: Les Éditions Bellarmin/Rome: Institutum Historicum Societatis Iesu, 1987

Canny, Nicholas, *ed. The Oxford History of the British Empire*, vol. 1: *The Origins of Empire: British Overseas Enterprise to the Close of the Seventeenth Century.* Oxford: Oxford University Press, 1998

Cartier, Jacques. *Voyages au Canada, suivis du Voyage de Roberval.* Ed. Marie Hélène Fraïssé. Montréal: LUX, 2002

Cotton, John. *The Waye of the Churches OF CHRIST in New England. Or, THE VVAY OF CHURCHES walking in Brotherly equalitie, or Co-ordination, Without Subjection of one Church to Another.* London: Matthew Simmons, 1645

The Complete Works of Captain John Smith (1580–1631). 3 vols. Ed. Philip L. Barbour. Chapel Hill, NC: University of North Carolina Press, for The Institute of Early American History and Culture, Williamsburg, VA, 1986

de Champlain, Samuel. *Des sauvages.* Ed. Alain Beaulieu and Réal Ouellet. Montréal: Éditions TYPO, 1993

Dauzat, A. and Charles Rostaing. *Dictionnaire étymologique des noms de lieux en France,* 2nd ed. Paris: Librairie Guénégaud, 1978

Demos, John. *The Unredeemed Captive: A Family Story from Early America.* New York: Alfred A. Knopf, 1994

Derounian-Stodola, Kathryn Zabelle, ed. *Women's Indian Captivity Narratives.* New York: Penguin Books, 1998

Dillard, Joseph L. *A History of American English.* London: Longman, 1992

Dille, Glen F., ed. *Spanish and Portuguese Conflict in the Spice Islands: The Loasa Expedition to the Moluccas 1525–1535. From Book XX of* The General and Natural History of the Indies *by Gonzalo Fernández de Oviedo y Valdés.* The Hakluyt Society, Third Series Volume 38. London: The Hakluyt Society, 2021

Dobson, E.J. *English Pronunciation 1500–1700.* 2 vols. Oxford: Clarendon Press, 1968

The English Bible: King James Version. Volume One: *The Old Testament,* ed. Herbert Marks; Volume Two: *The New Testament and Apocrypha,* ed. Gerald Hammond and Austin Busch. New York: W.W. Norton & Company, 2012

Goddard, Ives, "Some Early Examples of American Indian Pidgin English from New England," *International Journal of American Linguistics* 43.1 (1977), 37–41

Goddard, Ives, ed. *Handbook of North American Indians,* Volume 17: *Languages.* Washington, DC: Smithsonian Institution, 1996

Goddard, Ives and Kathleen J. Bragdon. *Native Writings in Massachusett.* 2 vols. Philadelphia: American Philosophical Society, 1988

Grund, Peter, "The Nature of Knowledge: Evidence and Evidentiality in the Witness Depositions from the Salem Witch Trials," *American Speech* 87.1 (2012), 7–38

Hakluyt, Richard. *Voyages and Discoveries: The Principal Navigations, Voyages, Traffiques and Discoveries of the English Nation.* Ed. Jack Beeching. London: Penguin Books, 1972

Halpert, Herbert and J.D.A. Widdowson. *Folktales of Newfoundland: The Resilience of the Oral Tradition.* 2 vols. Publications of the American Folklore Society, New Series. World Folktale Library, Vol. 3. New York: Garland Publishing, 1996

Haraszti, Zoltán. *The Enigma of the Bay Psalm Book.* Chicago: University of Chicago Press, 1956

Hariot, Thomas. *A briefe and true report of the new found land of Virginia.* Frankfurt am Main: Johann Wechel/Theodor de Bry, 1590

The Heath Anthology of American Literature, ed. Paul Lauter et al. 7th ed. Volume A: *Beginnings to 1800.* Boston: Houghton Mifflin Company, 2013

Hennepin, Louis. *Nouvelle découverte d'un très grand pays situé dans l'Amérique entre le Nouveau Mexique et la mer Glaciale (1697) [the English edition extends the title: ...both parts illustrated with maps and figures, and dedicated to His Majesty K. William...to which is added, several new discoveries in North-America, not publish'd in the French edition].* London: M. Bentley, J. Tonson, H. Bonwick, T. Goodwin, and S. Manship, 1698a

Hennepin, Louis. *Nouveau voyage d'un pais plus grand que l'Europe*. Utrecht: Marchand Libraire, 1698b

Jespersen, Otto. *John Hart's Pronunciation of English (1569 and 1570)*. Anglistische Forschungen 22. Heidelberg: Carl Winter, 1907

The Jesuit Relations and Allied Documents Ed. Reuben Gold Thwaites. 73 vols. Cleveland: The Burrows Brothers Company, 1896-1901; rpt. New York: Pageant Book Company, 1959

The Jesuit Relations and Allied Documents: Travels and Explorations of the Jesuit Missionaries in North America (1610–1791), ed. Edna Kenton. New York: The Vanguard Press, 1954

Kupperman, Karen Ordahl *Roanoke: The Abandoned Colony*. 2nd ed. Lanham, MD: Rowman & Littlefield, 2007a

Kupperman, Karen Ordahl *The Jamestown Project*. Cambridge, MA: The Belknap Press of Harvard University Press, 2007b

Lahontan (Louis-Armand de Lom d'Arce, Baron de Lahontan). *Œuvres complètes*, 2 vols. Ed. Réal Ouellet and Alain Beaulieu. Montréal: Les Presses de l'Université de Montréal, 1990

Lahontan. *Brief Remarks concerning the Cod-Fishery, the Beaver Trade, and the Limits of New England and New France*. Ed. Edward L. Towle and George A. Rawlyk in: "Baron de Lahontan: Memoir concerning the economic and strategic importance of Placentia, Newfoundland," *The Newfoundland Quarterly* 62.4 (1963): 5–10; "A New Baron de Lahontan Memoir on New York and the Great Lakes Basin," *New York History* (July 1965): 212–229.

Leclerc, Chrestien. *Nouvelle relation de la Gaspésie (1691)*. Ed. Réal Ouellet. *Bibliothèque du noveau monde*. Montréal: Les Presses de l'Université de Montréal, 1999

Leechman, Douglas and Robert A. Hall Jr., "American Indian Pidgin English: Attestations and Grammatical Peculiarities," *American Speech* 30.3 (1955), 163–171

Lescarbot, Marc. *Nova Francia (Histoire de la Nouvelle-France)*. London: George Bishop, 1609; rpt. Amsterdam: Theatrum Orbis Terrarum/Walter J. Johnson, Inc., 1977. The English Experience: Its Record in Early Printed Books Published in Facsimile, Number 877

Loockermans, Govert. *Correspondence and Papers, 1647–1700*. Stuyvesant-Rutherford Papers, Box 23. New York Historical Society

Makoni, Sinfree, Geneva Smitherman, Arnetha F. Ball, and Arthur K. Spears, eds. *Black Linguistics: Language, Society and Politics in Africa and the Americas*. London: Routledge, 2002

Mather, Cotton. *Magnalia Christi Americana, Books I and II*, ed. Kenneth B. Murdock. Cambridge, MA: The Belknap Press of Harvard University Press, 1977

Middleton, Simon, "Order and Authority in New Netherland: The 1653 Remonstrance and Early Settlement Politics," *The William and Mary Quarterly* 67.1 (2010), 31–68

Miller, Mary Rita, "Attestations of American Indian Pidgin English in Fiction and Nonfiction," *American Speech* 42.2 (1967), 142–147

Morgan, Edmund S. *Visible Saints: The History of a Puritan Idea*. Ithaca, NY: Cornell University Press, 1963/rpt. 1987

Oberg, Michael Leroy, "Gods and Men: The Meeting of Indian and White Worlds on the Carolina Outer Banks, 1584–1586," *The North Carolina Historical Review* 76.4 (1999), 367–390

Ouellet, Réal and Alain Beaulieu. See Lahontan, *Œuvres complètes* above, 1990

Prince, J. Dyneley, "An Ancient New Jersey Indian Jargon," *American Anthropologist n.s.* 14.3 (1912), 508–524

Quinn, David B., ed. *The Roanoke Voyages 1584-90.* 2 vols. The Hakluyt Society, Second Series, Part II, Volumes 104–105. London: The Hakluyt Society, 1955

Quinn, David B. and Alison M Quinn, eds. *The English New England Voyages, 1602–1608.* The Hakluyt Society, Second Series, Part II, Volume 161. London: The Hakluyt Society, 1983

Salmon, Vivian. *The Study of Language in 17th-Century England.* 2nd ed. Amsterdam Studies in the Theory and History of Linguistic Science. Series III – Studies in the History of the Language Sciences, Volume 17. Amsterdam: John Benjamins, 1988

Salmon, Vivian, "Thomas Harriot (1560-1621) and the English Origins of Algonkian Linguistics," *Historiographia Linguistica* 19 (1992), 25–56

Swift, Jonathan. *Gulliver's Travels.* Ed. Claude Rawson and Ian Higgins. Oxford World's Classics. Oxford: Oxford University Press, 2005

Thomason, Sarah Grey, "On interpreting 'The Indian Interpreter,'" *Language in Society* 9 (1980), 167–193

Thwaites, Reuben Gold. See *The Jesuit Relations and Allied Documents* above, 1896–1901/1959

Towle, Edward L. and Rawlyk, George A. See Lahontan, *Brief Remarks concerning the Cod-Fishery, the Beaver Trade, and the Limits of New England and New France* above, 1963–1965

Trigger, Bruce G. "Trade and Tribal Warfare on the St. Lawrence in the Sixteenth Century," *Ethnohistory* 9 (1962), 240–256

Trigger, Bruce G. "The Mohawk-Mahican war (1624-28): The establishment of a pattern," *The Canadian Historical Review* 52 (1971): 276–286

Trigger, Bruce G. *The Children of Aataentsic: A History of the Huron People to 1660.* Montreal: McGill-Queen's University Press, 1987/rpt. with a new preface 2000

Trigger, Bruce G. "Early Native North American Responses to European Contact: Romantic versus Rationalistic Interpretations," *The Journal of American History* 77.4 (1991): 1195–1215

Vaughan, Alden T., "Sir Walter Ralegh's Indian Interpreters, 1584–1618," *The William and Mary Quarterly* 59 (2002), 341–376

Visscher, Nicolaes. *Novi Belgii Novæque Angliæ: nec non partis Virginiæ tabula multis in locis emendata ([Map] of New Belgium [Netherland] and New England: as well as with parts of Virginia updated in many places).* Amsterdam, 1655 [second printing 1685]

The Whole Booke of Psalmes, Faithfully Translated into English Metre. Cambridge, Colony of Massachusetts Bay: Stephen and William Daye, 1640

Williams, John. *The Redeemed Captive, Returning to ZION. A Faithful HISTORY OF Remarkable Occurrences, IN THE Captivity AND THE Deliverance OF Mr. John Williams; Minister of the Gospel, in DEERFIELD, Who, in the Desolation which befel that Plantation, by an Incursion of the French & Indians, was by Them carried away, with his Family, and his Neighbourhood, unto CANADA*. Boston: B. Green, for Samuel Phillips, at the Brick Shop, 1707

Wright, Louis B. And Virginia Freund, eds. *The Historie of Travell into Virginia Britannia (1612), by William Strachey, gent.* The Hakluyt Society, Second Series, Part II, Volume 103. London: The Hakluyt Society, 1953

CHAPTER 8

Imperium

8.1 A 'MODERN' ENGLISH

In "The Plan of a Dictionary of the English Language" (1747), Samuel Johnson pursued a line of seriocomic modesty – glossing *lexicographer* as 'a harmless drudge' in the finished project (1755) – that belied his efforts to see it through, and get paid: "No one but a blockhead ever wrote, except for money" (James Boswell, *The Life of Samuel Johnson*, 5 April 1776; Womersley 2008). And to fulfill a great passion of his, even if there was some reluctance, as ever with Johnson, to express it earnestly: to describe, and even rationalize to some extent, the history and lexicon of English, with a view toward concision, clarity, and pithiness:

> When I first undertook to write an English Dictionary, I had no expectation of any higher patronage than that of the proprietors of the copy, nor prospect of any other advantage than the price of my labour; I knew, that the work in which I engaged is generally considered as drudgery for the blind [unlearned], as the proper toil of artless industry, a task that requires neither the light of learning, nor the activity of genius, but may be successfully performed without any greater quality than that of bearing burthens with dull patience, and beating the track of the alphabet with sluggish resolution (Kolb and DeMaria 2005, 25–26).

The theme he continued in the preface to his great *Dictionary*, published in two large volumes in 1755:

> Among these unhappy mortals is the writer of dictionaries; whom mankind have considered, not as the pupil, but as the slave of science, the pioneer of literature, doomed only to remove rubbish and clear obstructions from the paths of Learning and Genius, who press forward to conquest and glory, without bestowing a smile on the humble drudge that facilitates their progress.

> Every other authour may aspire to praise; the lexicographer can only hope to escape reproach, and even this negative recompense has been yet granted to very few (Johnson 1755, I, [A.i]).

By *pioneer*, Johnson is holding both to the sense he gives it in his *Dictionary*, 'One whose business is to level the road, throw up works, or sink mines in military operations,' and to extended senses he knew of but chose not to include as he held to historical principles still observed in the great *Oxford English Dictionary*. The word derives ultimately from Latin *pēs* 'foot,' through Old French *peonier* 'foot soldier'; but Johnson seems aware of an emerging sense of 'trailblazer, frontiersman,' a sense further developed in the New World (and an America Johnson would not exactly sympathize with in 1776).

comedy: A dramatick representation of the lighter faults of mankind.
leveller: 1. One who makes any thing even. 2. One who destroys superiority; one who endeavours to bring all to the same state of equality.
oats: A grain, which in England is generally given to horses, but in Scotland supports the people.
pirate: 1. A sea robber. 2. Any robber; particularly a bookseller who seizes the copies of other men.
popular: 1. Vulgar; plebeian. 2. Suitable to the common people. 3. Beloved by the people; pleasing to the people. 4. Studious of the favour of the people. 5. Prevailing or raging among the populace: as, a *popular* distemper.
sept: A clan; a race; a generation. A word used only with regard or allusion to Ireland, and, I suppose, Irish.
Scotch *Hoppers*: A play in which boys hop over lines or scotches in the ground.

Even in so small a sample from the over 2,300 pages of Johnson's *Dictionary,* one might get a sense of Johnson's usual historical and etymological rendering of entries, and of what then-current senses predominated at publication in 1755. *Popular* follows the usual usages of later Early Modern English, the gloss 'Studious of the favour of the people' hints at instances in the entries where Johnson indulges a certain forthrightness and irritability. Our *hopscotch* as a children's game is localized to its etymological sense, involving scotching or scoring the ground and as a pastime once mainly for boys. *Comedy* is a rather narrow definition but reflects Johnson's literary sensibilities, *sept* exhibits Johnson's usual skeptical distemper about things Irish, and *oats* is one of those wry insertions in an otherwise eminently sober dictionary aimed no doubt at his friend and biographer, the Scotsman James Boswell.

The hunt for flashes of Johnsonian wit among the many thousands of entries in the *Dictionary* might belie the scholarly nature of the overall enterprise. In his "Plan" (1747), Johnson wrote perceptively about the inclusion and 'naturalization' of technical terms and loanwords into the language. As to the former, "all are not equally to be considered as parts of our language, for some of them are naturalized and incorporated, but others still continue aliens, and are rather auxiliaries than subjects" (Kolb and DeMaria 2005, 31). He includes 'words in the common law,' such as *habeas corpus*, *præmunire* ('to fortify or safeguard in advance': here against any foreign usurpation of English sovereignty), *nisi prius* ('unless before'), all of which are to be found in a specialized dictionary such as *Black's Law Dictionary*, as well as a term 'of controversial divinity' (i.e., Roman Catholic) *hypostasis* (Kolb and DeMaria 2005, 32). Though Johnson was not the first dictionary-maker of English, he was likely its most comprehensive surveyor to date, a task he freely admitted was daunting: "...I am frightened at its extent, and, like the soldiers of Caesar, look on Britain as a new world, which it is almost madness to invade. But I hope, that though I should not contemplate the conquest, I shall at least discover the coast, civilize part of the inhabitants, and make it easy for some other adventurer to proceed farther, to reduce them wholly to subjection, and settle them under laws" (Kolb and DeMaria 2005, 58). In short, that he should be a *pioneer*.

Included also in the *Dictionary* of 1755 were Johnson's treatises *A History of the English Language* and *A Grammar of the English Tongue*. The preceding century and a half had produced many such tracts, a good many of them in Latin, but Johnson's *History* is notable for the many illustrative passages he included from Old and Middle English: King Alfred's *Boethius*, the West Saxon Gospels, the early Middle English *Poema morale* (which Johnson had copied from antiquarian George Hickes's *Linguarum veterum septentrionalium thesaurus grammatico-criticus et archaeologicus* ['Thesaurus Grammatical-Critical and Archaeological of the Old Northern Languages'; 1705]), later entries post-Conquest from the *Peterborough Chronicle*, *The Land of Cockaygne* (from the Harley 913 manuscript, written in Ireland, in what is an early Anglo-Irish dialect of Middle English), and, among others, passages from Sir John Mandeville's *Travels* and the poetry and prose of Geoffrey Chaucer. In fact, Johnson's *History* is rather more a reader of illustrative passages (to fill out his etymological notes in the *Dictionary*) than a history *per se*:

> Thus have I deduced the *English* language from the age of *Alfred* to that of *Elizabeth*; in some parts imperfectly for want of materials; but I hope, at least, in such a manner that its progress may be easily traced, and the gradations observed, by which it advanced from its first rudeness to its present elegance (Kolb and DeMaria 2005, 263).

Though Johnson was influenced by works on Latin grammar such as those of John Colet (1467–1519), Dean of St. Paul's, and William Lily (ca. 1468–1522), who was the first 'high master' at St. Paul's School (founded by Colet in 1509), he broke from the tradition of trying to harmonize classical Latin grammar with the English, which could be seen as "imposing ideal, non-empirical categories upon it" (Kolb and DeMaria 2005, xli). English would, with its own peculiarities, require its own sort of grammar. Johnson preferred the written form over the spoken, formal over colloquial, and made it abundantly clear that he viewed the 'American dialect' as a debased form of the British; in a review of a geographical work by Lewis Evans (ca. 1700–1756), Johnson railed that Evans had written with "some mixture of the *American* dialect, a tract of corruption to which every language widely diffused must always be exposed" (Romaine 2001, 168). Evans had been born in Wales and came to America in perhaps his early 30s; his surveying of the Philadelphia and greater Mid-Atlantic region produced a number of important maps, such as "A map of Pensilvania, New-Jersey, New-York, and the three Delaware counties" (1749, in the collection of the American Philosophical Society, Philadelphia). Johnson felt rather much the same about Americans themselves; in his entry for 15 April 1778 in his *Life of Samuel Johnson*, James Boswell recounts a conversation on Christian virtue and friendship with Mrs. Knowles, who counters Johnson's irritable dismissal of counting everyone as a friend by alluding to Christ having twelve Apostles, "yet there was *one* whom he *loved*." Boswell is at a loss to explain Johnson's ensuing outburst: "I am willing to love all mankind, *except an American*." So Boswell "diverted his attention to other topicks" (Boswell 1791, vol. II, 226–227). This was the work on grace by the *American* Puritan theologian Jonathan Edwards (1703–1758). Edwards was a major figure in the spiritual revivalism of The Great Awakening in America, which had a charismatic tenor Johnson did not like. But Johnson could hardly slight Edwards's English, as it was that of a New Englander from British America largely untouched by the changes and reforms to come with Noah Webster and others in the Revolutionary period.

The orthography of Johnson and other writers of the 18th century is not quite that of contemporary Modern English, but the trailing edge of later Early Modern English. Edwards, in his early tract *A Faithful Narrative of the Surprizing Work of God in the Conversion of Many Hundred Souls in* Northampton, *and the Neigbouring Towns and Villages of New Hampshire in New England* (published in London in 1737), still uses the <our> spellings (*neigbouring, endeavoured*); preterite and past participle forms in <-ed> can appear as <'d> (*subjoin'd, appear'd, seem'd, labour'd*); for *show* the infinitive form used is *to shew*. Most notably, the style of Edwards's writing and public speaking (sermonizing) is still closer to British English than that of Revolutionary-era American writers. The sentence structure and syntax is marked by an education in the classical languages – use of tricolons, balancing of contrarieties in two major clausulae. And this is natural enough as Edwards was educated at Yale College (later university) and would later serve as President of Princeton University – schools of the 'Ivy League' founded on the British model (in curriculum and architecture). And they would produce an academic elite that was Anglophilic rather more than cosmopolitan, and that academic elite would in turn fill the ranks of the economic and political class – an American Oxbridge (though this blend dates to William Makepeace Thackeray's novel *The History of Pendennis* [1850]). One example of Edwards's hortatory, classical prose style may suffice:

> I think the main ground of the Doubts and Fears that Persons, at their Conversion, have been exercised with about their own State, has been that they have found so much Corruption remaining in their Hearts. At first **their Souls seem to be all alive**, **their Hearts are fixed** and **their Affections flowing**; they seem to live quite above the World, and meet with but little Difficulty in religious Exercises; and they are ready to think it will always be so: Tho' they **are truly abused** under a Sense of their Vileness by reason of former Acts of Sin, yet they **are not then sufficiently sensible** what Corruption still remains in their Hearts; and therefore **are surprized** when they find that they begin to be dull and dead Frames, to be troubled with wandering Thoughts in the time of publick and private Worship, and to be utterly

> unable to keep themselves from 'em; also when they find themselves **unaffected** at Seasons in which, they think, there is greatest Occasion to be **affected**; and when they feel worldly Dispositions working in them, and it may be Pride, and Envy, and stirrings of Revenge, or some ill Spirit towards some Person, that has injured them, as well as other workings of indwelling Sin: Their Hearts are almost sunk with the Disappointment:; and they are ready presently to think that all they have met with is nothing, and that they are meer Hypocrites (Edwards 1737, 83–84).

Edwards's sermonizing here consists of two sentences: the first a direct assertion, *I think...has been that* with an embedded restrictive clause *that Persons...their own State*; the second a long periodic flourish that builds to the pessimistic state that such sinners find themselves in. The latter sentence is a set-piece of rhetorical flourishes that in its ornateness seems a little decadent given the sober subject; an initial tricolon (in bold) is balanced by another in the middle and one more at the end (*Hearts are almost sunk...they are ready...that they are meer Hypocrites*). Between the first and second tricolons and second and third are modal-plus-infinitive constructions (underlined). And following that second set of infinitive constructions is the pair of contrarieties *unaffected...affected.* The long Latinate tradition of composition in English schooling through the Renaissance and Enlightenment persists now into the American Great Awakening; Edwards's religious zeal is not so strict that he keeps to a plain style puritanically. The form *publick* is a remodeling based on Latin: the French loan had been spelled *publique* from the 15th through the mid-17th centuries, and the French adjectival suffix *-ique* was replaced with the English form truncated from Latin *-icus* (Salmon 1999, 45). The era saw also the rise of <gh> for <g> (<ȝ>, <g>, <h>, <gh> in Middle English) in final position, so too with <ck> for <k> in that position. The spellings, with some inconsistencies, represented outcomes of sound changes that had been underway since Middle English:

> <gh>: this spelling is another Middle English realization of /-χ/, /-h/, which in Modern English orthography presents some confusion about the sound represented: in *light* and *high* the final consonant (coda /-h/, /-χ/ – Old English *hēah* [he:aχ]. [he:æχ]) is lost (or "fully lenited"; Minkova 2014, 113). With *enough* and *tough* the voiceless labiodental fricative /f/ was the outcome. The process depended on the original input, whether earlier Middle English /ç/ or /χ/was involved (with the former, OE *niht* > Modern English *night* with vocalization of <h> ~ <gh> thus the pronunciation 'nite'; with the latter /χ/ > /f/ in forms such as *enough* ('enuff') and *dwarf* (from Old English *dweorh* [dweɔrχ]). *Enough* had a convoluted orthographical history, from Old English *ġe-nōh* / *ġe-nōg* to Middle English forms such as *i-now* (the <w> an orthographical variant of <ȝ>). The change /ç/ > Ø (complete loss) occurred whether the preceding vowel was front or back; but there was a constraint on the change /χ/ > /f/, as this occurred only with preceding back vowels (thus MdE *caught* and *thought*); *daughter*, from OE *dohtor*, had a regional pronunciation *dafter* with /-f-/ beside the now predominant form [dɔ:tər] (Minkova 2014, 113–115; Nevalainen 2006, 128). In some dialects of MdE,

New England-Canadian English (Atlantic Provinces) and BrE (northern and Scots), there seems to be a vestigial lenited /χ/ in forms such as *daughter, thought, slaughter*: [dɔː$^{\chi}$tər] or [dɔː^{h}tər].

What stands out in Edwards's tract to modern readers is his use of capitalization – this was extended to many categories of nouns in English, though not as a rule, as in Modern German, to all nouns. The usual proper nouns and names and titles are capitalized, as are names for subjects, conditions, actions, states, qualities, sensations, and so forth: thus *Conversion* and *Worship*, *Doubts* and *Fears*, *Difficulty*, *Acts of Sin*, *Pride* and *Envy* (Salmon 1999, 46–48). 1776 is the turning point in the development of Modern English, usually appealed to by historians of the language; the political rupture between Britain and its American colonies, despite the attempt to return the Americans to the fold in the war 1812–1815, would set the British and American varieties of English on divergent paths. The great growth of empire, by sea power, commerce, and a sort of linguistic commonwealth, would see the spread of English to the far corners of the globe and set the stage for the rise of World Englishes in the postcolonial period. Although it has been remarked that "it is probably true that no radical changes took place in English dialects in the post-1776 period until the second half of the twentieth century" (Ihalainen 1994, 205, who proceeds to demonstrate the complexities of the observation), dialects of English have persisted in the face of increasingly powerful forces of convergence. Public education is certainly, in the pre-modern media age (i.e., before radio and television), among the most powerful forces; the 1870 Education Act of Parliament was inspired in part by the National Education League's push for "free, compulsory and non-religious education for all children."[1] As was public discourse, the press most obviously, but so too the recording of political proceedings – from 1803 in the Hansards, records of all speeches in Parliament (named after the publisher Thomas Curson Hansard [1776–1833]). The digital Hansards have become one of a number of large-scale corpora of actual English usage – admittedly that of professional or hereditary political figures trained in speechifying – used in corpus linguistics to study features and their distribution diachronically and synchronically. In that War of 1812, in which Great Britain dispatched forces that unceremoniously burned official Washington, DC, 24 August 1814 – Capitol, White House, and other Federal buildings – Parliament was as often concerned with more pressing matters on the Continent (Napoleon) or matters more in the pockets of Members (Corn Laws, the importation of spirits from Ireland). The Hansard for 6 June 1814 records that "Lord Castlereagh presented a copy of the Treaty of Peace and Amity, signed at Paris the 30th of May 1814, between his Britannic Majesty and his Most Christian Majesty" (a sticking point in the treaty was France's reluctance to abolish the slave trade); it ends on the note that "The Treaty was then ordered to be taken into consideration on Friday se'nnight," that is

[1] https://www.parliament.uk/about/living-heritage/transformingsociety/livinglearning/school/overview/1870educationact/ (which includes the Hansards of the readings of the bill in Parliament 17 February and 25 July 1870).

a week, seven days and nights, later.[2] The 'high style' or even fustian of Parliamentary debate – once it moved into the light in 1803 (not having been public before) – was a product of the 'public school' and university education system and writers such as Dr. Johnson who preferred the formal written standard over the colloquial.

It is apparent in American English of the 18th century that norms were becoming more democratized in the colonies and young nation; when it occurred in British English is more difficult to pin down, but one author in particular – the Victorian era's most popular writer – has been singled out: Charles Dickens. His great novelistic output, extended, or, depending upon one's view, bloated by serial publication, generated more first instances of new coinages, including slang, than any other author of the 19th century. Dickens's own style and preoccupations – journalistic and drawn with a social realism – had a democratizing sensibility: Dickens wrote for a mass audience, often of issues of a broader society than had been portrayed in the English novel, from the workshop to the poorhouse. Dickens had an ear for common speech, and he introduced perhaps a greater number of slang and informal terms to English speakers than any other writer of the 19th century: *whizz-bang* and *butterfingers* from his first effort, 1837's *The Pickwick Papers*. The current online OED lists 9,232 citations of Dickens's works, 1,286 of them 'first in meaning' usages (first attestation of the word in that particular sense), 629 of them as the first attestation of a word's use (by comparison the OED has 32,567 citations of William Shakespeare's works, 7.072 as first in meaning, 2,276 first attestations). These 'first attestations' are not necessarily the first use of the form, but the first *recorded* use editors at the OED have found; and the 629 words that first occur in Dickens are not by and large new coinages by the author, rather forms Dickens heard and employed for the first time in print. And that Dickens likely *heard* many of these forms is apparent in a quick survey of them: *a-buzz* (*A Tale of Two Cities* [1859]), *arse-head* (*Barnaby Rudge* [1841]), *beef-faced* (*Oliver Twist* [1838]), *fancy-dressed* (*The Pickwick Papers* [1837]), *flummoxed* (*Pickwick Papers*), *gonoph* (*Bleak House* [1852]; i.e., 'thief,' which OED traces to the Hebrew, though one wonders if Dickens heard it through Yiddish *ganef/gonef*), *jowled* (*great-jowled* from *Great Expectations* [1861]), *kidney pie* (*Sketches by Boz* [1836]), *nohows* (*Dombey and Son* [1848]), *passenger-list* (*Martin Chuzzlewit* [1844]), *pimpled-faced* and *pimply-faced* (*The Old Curiosity Shop* [1841] and *Pickwick Papers*), *slangular* (i.e., 'slangy'; *Bleak House*), and *tousled* (*Dombey and Son*). Perhaps a journalistic element of Dickens's word-play and word-creation

[2] Robert Stewart (1769–1822), Second Marquess of Londonderry, Viscount Castlereagh, was born in Dublin, from an Ulster Scots lineage; he led a remarkably eventful life that ended tragically in suicide. The attack on the American capital was led by Major-General Robert Ross, whose troops had been landed by Admiral Sir Alexander Forrester Inglis Cochrane, and advised and assisted by Rear-Admiral Sir George Cockburn. Ross too was born in Ireland, of Scots stock; Cochrane was born in Scotland, of the Earls of Dundonald, and Cockburn was born in London as his father was MP for Lanark Burghs, West Lothian. It was not unusual for the ranks of the British army and navy to be filled with Scots, of Scotland or Ulster; but they would have heard familiar accents on the American side as their forces also boasted many of the same extraction. The American Ulster Scots would be famous as frontiersmen (and Indian fighters); a number of them fell at the Battle of the Alamo in 1836.

is his nearly profligate use of the hyphen, especially in the generation of descriptive compound nouns and adjectives: *Tom Smart beat him in the drinking by about half a salt-spoon-full* (*Pickwick Papers*); *The doctor was amazingly shabby, in a torn and darned* ***rough-weather sea-jacket*** (*Little Dorrit* [1857]; bold added). That Dickens was at least somewhat more in tune with the 'vernacular' seems certain, and in that he was preparing the way for other 'modern' novelists in a break with tradition: "The style of Dickens's novelistic career begins in pure derivation, a sustained send-up not only of the Johnsonian high style of journalistic and parliamentary claptrap in the eighteenth-century Age of Rhetoric but of Sir Walter Scott's editorial aliases and their prefatory paraphernalia – and then finds its true quasi-oratorical tone amid the cleared debris of tradition" (Stewart 2001, 136). Then again, Dickens was quite fond of the tricolon, as with *Little Dorrit*'s "stifled, choked, and blinded by the dust" (Stewart 2001, 146), which is a classical rhetorical flourish and a mark of traditional composition and oratory. What may be newer was Dickens's focus on the lives, and language, of the working class and poor, their thoughts and inner lives. And that did pave the way for a James Joyce or William Faulkner.

Dickens's earliest literary efforts canvassed many of London's neighborhoods: *Sketches by 'Boz': Illustrative of Everyday Life and Everyday People* (serial publication 1833–1836), 56 of them in all, ranged from Bloomsbury to Seven Dials (a former slum, now part of much tonier Covent Garden), Drury Lane to Finsbury Park, to Islington, Vauxhall Gardens, Walworth – and Newgate (this likely conjured up painful memories for Dickens; his father John had been sentenced to Marshalsea Prison in Southwark as a debtor). *The Pickwick Papers* (1836–1837) has Samuel Pickwick and three other members of his Pickwick Club travel round London, its suburbs and environs. Dickens, born in Portsmouth, had come to London for work like many other young people; others, in a common pattern, arrived following a reversal of fortune, as would the titular character of his *Nicholas Nickleby* (1839). His early years in journalism saw him make Pickwickian journeys. Dickens, perhaps as much or more than any other Victorian writer, helped draw a 'Literary London.' And the great growth of the metropolis further cemented London as the dialectal standard of British English, though that is a distinction not without complication, especially in terms of class (BrE settles higher on the social class scale than does AmE, a little more firmly toward the upper strata of Southeastern England). The first formal census of the city was by order of the Census Bill passed by Parliament 3 December 1800, with census day Monday 10 March 1801. The population then ascertained was just over a million, making it the second largest city in the world (what was then Peking, Beijing, was the largest). By the time he had completed *A Tale of Two Cities* (1859) and *Great Expectations* (1860) London's population had crested over 3 million, with nearly 4 out of 10 residents born outside the city (the largest population born outside England was of the Irish). London had long been at the nexus of major dialect groupings, Southeast, Essex, Sussex, and Kentish, that dated to the Middle English period (though the names of these broad groupings derive from Anglo-Saxon times). It was in the Middle English period that London Southeastern had dislodged – for good it would turn out – previous claimants for standard English (Winchester had held a claim in the late Anglo-Saxon period, as had West Saxon more broadly; but in the early Anglo-Saxon eras it had been Northumbria and

Mercia). By the eve of World War I, London proper, 'Inner London,' could boast of 7 million inhabitants (after the population declines in the 1980s and 1990s, it would not reach 7 million again until 2001).

The density of population in higher-density settlements can be productive of both linguistic convergence (higher-density communication networks) and divergence (formation of enclaves by class, religion, ethnicity, race, regional or national origin). Like New York City, a short physical distance geographically can be mapped to a greater distance in terms of speech communities. Isoglosses in an urban environment can arise from transecting by a river, freeway/motorway, park, industrial vs. residential zoning, or simply a street or block (and that in turn might mark an enclave by any one or more of a number of determiners). To use an example from popular culture, a recurring guest on *The Jonathan Ross Show* (on ITV 2011 to present) is East End actor Ray Winstone, raised in Homerton (Borough of Hackney); Ross was born in St. Pancras, north London, but raised in Leytonstone (Borough of Waltham Forest). Both Winstone and Ross were raised 'within sound of Bow Bells' (the church of St. Mary-le-Bow, Cheapside) and so are within the Cockney region proper. Ross's speech has been noted for his apparent substitution of /w/ for /r/ (enough that a nickname is 'Wossy'), which has been explained at times as a speech impediment (also called, somewhat confusingly, *rhotacism*) – though it is also a feature of some English dialects (such as that of Norwich, Norfolk – and also Estuary English, considered in Chapter 12). The particular sound change is a fronting of /r/ to the voiced labial (or labiodental) approximant /ʋ/ – that is, an articulation of /r/ pushed forward from the alveolar or apical pronunciation to the labiodental, which is that of /f/ and/v/. Or, to describe it from the direction of the articulation of /w/, the voiced labiovelar approximant (or 'semi-vowel'), as it involves pronouncing /r/ as an unrounded or less rounded /w/. The articulation of /r/ sounds in English is enormously complex, with English having 6 types of the sound (including the alveolar tap /ɾ/ and uvular fricative /ʁ/ in Scots and in the Northumbrian 'burr'; see Minkova 2014, 115–132). Apart from this particular change with /r/ in Ross's accent, the two East Enders do not sound so similar as might be expected; some of this is due to demographic factors: Leytonstone has an average income lower than the London average (but higher than that for England at large), but rather higher than Homerton (Hackney overall has a much higher poverty level). Homerton and Leytonstone are about four miles apart, less 'as the crow flies,' but Homerton is in the much more densely populated Hackney and closer to the inner core. It is a general truism that North and South London accents are generally distinguishable by Londoners, which may for Southwark, Lambeth, and Brixton also be class- and ethnic- or racially marked, and more 'far-flung' regions approaching or beyond the Metropolitan Green Belt may have their distinctive features as well (Metropolitan London is now so vast that its outer reaches do in fact extend into other dialect regions, such as Essex and Kent).

That said, a variety such as Estuary English is rather more a social phenomenon than a regionally bound variety (beyond being originally Southeastern): its origins lay in a British version of 'downspeak,' of speakers from relatively privileged backgrounds trying to sound less 'posh' (see Chapter 12). Multicultural London English (MLE) is a rather more problematic designation, as it seems more a catch-all term, and one that would not be applicable to American Englishes (as diverse as London is, the United States is much more diverse at the national level). As distinct from affective varieties such as 'Mockney' or 'Jafaican,' especially as spoken by 'posh' or middle-class white British youth, respectively, MLE seems contingent upon the source variety – that is, Caribbean English, Asian Englishes (Bengali is the second-most spoken language in London after English), East African Englishes, and so forth. As every word has its own history, so too may every accent, speech community, or neighborhood. Slavic-accented British English varieties (source influences such as Polish and Ukrainian) are quite different from those influenced by Nigerian and other West African Englishes. The subject will bear more study in the future, but for the moment New York may offer an interesting comparison: multicultural for much longer and at a higher rate and scale than London, New York City Englishes are often borough- and class-marked (Bronx and Brooklyn accents), but the particular ethnolinguistic influences have remained distinct: Puerto Rican (Nuyorican), Dominican, Italian, Irish, Russian, Yiddish. Borough Park and Crown Heights, Brooklyn, are the largest Orthodox Jewish neighborhoods in the United States, home to Yiddish newspapers and other media, and the demographic influence can be heard in the local Brooklyn accents (the same sort of influence on accent does not seem to obtain in quite the same way in, for instance, Golders Green in North London). But another great distinction was developing with the movement to big cities, in Britain and America, through the 19th and 20th centuries – that between urban and rural dialectology. The great *Atlas of North American English*, a project initiated by preeminent American sociolinguist William Labov and collaborators (Labov 2006), depends primarily upon the evidence from mid to large cities; by contrast, Joseph (and Elizabeth) Wright's *English Dialect Dictionary* (1898–1905) and the *Survey of English Dialects* (1950–1961) were focused more at the town and village level. The Wrights had believed they were recording ways of speech fated to disappear; Labov and co-researchers came to a different conclusion: that though there are, to be sure, forces of convergence at work, dialects of American English in certain major urban areas (such as Philadelphia, Baltimore, Birmingham, AL, Chicago, Kansas City, etc.) were becoming less intelligible to one another. That is, despite common wisdom about the apparent genericization of culture and resulting dialect levelling, less noticed forces of divergence were more powerful (which is the subject of section 8.5). Great changes overall were coming, to society at large, and its demographic makeup, in the late Imperial period. And it was, as so often happens in human history, a great war that spurred many of these changes.

8.2 THE GREAT WAR

"If I should die, think only this of me," Rupert Brooke wrote in "The Soldier" (1915), "That there's some corner of a foreign field / That is for ever England." Brooke was one of the early British poets of note of the Great War; his sonnet 'The Soldier' had the distinction of appearing in the *Times Literary Supplement* and of being read out during Easter service from the pulpit at St. Paul's Cathedral in 1915. His vision of his own death was youthfully heroic, patriotic, and classically cast (he had attended Rugby, then read classics at King's College, Cambridge). "There shall be / In that rich earth a richer dust concealed... / A body of England's, breathing English air.... / Gives somewhere back the thoughts by England given; / Her sights and sounds; dreams happy as her day; / And laughter, learnt of friends; and gentleness, / In hearts at peace, under an English heaven." Brooke died on the way to Gallipoli with the Mediterranean Expeditionary Force, 23 April 1915, on a French hospital ship off the Greek isle Skyros, not by bullet or shell but of septicemia from a severely infected mosquito bite. Shropshire-born Wilfred Owen came from more modest circumstances and fell in combat 4 November 1918 in Northern France, just one week before the war's end. Owen's poetry, however, is a number of orders removed from Brooke's in language, sentiment, and form. Change had been on the way to English versification and poetic form before the Marne, Verdun, Ypres, and the Somme, but the war changed poetry as it changed culture irrevocably. The first stanza of Owen's "Anthem for Doomed Youth" (1917) gives some indication of the transition from classicizing verse forms that had predominated since around 1550:

> What passing-bells for these who die as cattle?
>   – Only the monstrous anger of the guns.
> Only the stuttering rifles' rapid rattle
> Can patter out their hasty orisons.
> No mockeries now for them; no prayers nor bells;
>   Nor any voice of mourning save the choirs, –
> The shrill, demented choirs of wailing shells;
>   And bugles calling for them from sad shires.

The octave of this sonnet in irregular rhyme returns in some ways to the Germanic accentual verse of Old English (and a subject Owen had studied at University College, Reading). Owen's experiments with assonance have been frequently remarked upon, and here, coupled with the frequent alliterations, the effect is of a sonnet breaking out of form and returning to the tradition of the Old English elegy (the *ubi sunt* ["where are..."] motif of an elegy such as 'The Ruin' from the Exeter Book). Other than Latinate *monstrous*, *orisons* (a word also jarringly medieval and ecclesiastical), *choir*, *demented*, and *bugle* (borrowed via Anglo-Norman, ultimately from Latin *buculus*, diminutive form of *bos* 'ox' as the early form of the musical instrument was an ox horn), the vocabulary is Germanic, from Old or Middle English. The aural effects of the words chosen are striking: ***bell****s...****c****a****ttle*** toll in the repetition of the liquid consonant; ***on****ly...****an****ger* and ***ang****er...****g****uns* in the second line link by assonance heavy nasal and velar consonants; ***st****u****tt****ering...****ra****ttle* work by onomatopoeia, and are echoed in the following line's *patter*, while the ***r****ifles'* ***r****apid* ***r****attle* gives an alliterative effect that might seem a bit heavy, but the repetition in three not two gives an auditory sense of the firing of rifles by massed infantry and of that terrible weapon emblematic of the war, the machine gun – iconic of the gangster era in the United States, and sounded out with the onomatopoeic expression *rat-tat-tat*; the correlating *no...no.../Nor...nor* in lines 5–6 echo again the repeating sound and build a congeries of what will be withheld from the 'doomed youth'; for them only the ***shrill...shells*** and 'bugles calling for them from **s**ad **sh**ires' (***shires*** looping back to the *shrill...shells*). One obvious reason such auditory effects may have been deployed, besides their poetic efficacy, was that the Great War, unlike the succeeding conflict that would begin some two decades later, was largely not broadcast – it appeared in the papers. Lord Kitchener, the British Secretary of State for War, sensed the impact newsreel footage (like the *actualités* of the Lumière and Pathé Brothers, a French invention barely a decade old) might have on morale and war footage was heavily censored. Commercial radio broadcasting would not get going until the 1920s; film is still in the silent era, so one could see but not usually hear the war when one went to the movies (the pattern of showing war newsreels before the main features continued through World War II[3]).

Owen's famous "Dulce et Decorum Est" (published 1920, posthumously) upends traditional citation of the line from Horace *Odes* III.ii *dulce et decorum est pro patria mori* ('sweet and fitting it is to die for the fatherland') as 'The old Lie.' The poem draws a haunting picture of one of the soldiers caught out in a gas attack without the mask on in time ('As under a green sea, I saw him drowning'). The soldiers had been marching as if asleep, "Drunk with fatigue; deaf even to the hoots / Of tired, outstripped Five-Nines that dropped behind" – the specific World War I-era reference is to the German 15cm (5.9-inch) artillery shells, 'Five-Nines.' That the young men had been lied into dreams of glory by Horace's ode is implied, with a nod to British classical education and the *gravitas* Greek and Latin had in British education since the Anglo-Saxon period (the school of Theodore and Hadrian at Canterbury of the late 7th century is a conventional benchmark). The long tradition of English classical scholarship and dedication to the classical languages, in elite grammar schools and with the major professorships in the universities, was reaching a peak in this period (contemporary poet A.E. Housman was at the time Kennedy Professor of Latin at Trinity College, Cambridge). Many of the wartime poets were steeped in the classics, their poetry in classical allusion; here Horace's Augustan patriotic verse is branded the 'old Lie' for the use it has been pressed to in pro-war propaganda. The term 'Augustan' itself had been appropriated in English tradition for the 'golden age' of literary production in the first half of the 18th century as equivalent to the golden era under Roman emperor Augustus of Virgil, Horace, and Ovid. Though England and Germany in particular would strive to maintain their traditions of classical scholarship, the study of the classics began its decline following the war. The 'shock of the new' (borrowing art critic Robert Hughes's phrase) was felt across the culture; old paradigms and conventions had already been under assault by the turn of the century, and the profound pessimistic effects

[3] An exception to the avoidance of combat photography was the War Office-sponsored silent film *The Battle of the Somme*; Geoffrey Malins and John McDowell filmed the preparatory British bombardment of German positions and early stages of the battle between 26 June and 9 July. The battle would last until 18 November. In the United States, the Office of War Information (OWI) continued the policy of 'military review' of newsreel footage for movie theater audiences, producing a 'lag time' in their appearance.

of the shock of the war would change many forever (though the blame laid at Horace's feet may not entirely be fair[4]).

Owen's allusion to 'Five-Nines' directs attention to the profoundest effect the war had on the English language: its vocabulary. Some 70 million soldiers of the Allied and Central Powers served in the war 1914–1918, at least 10 million of whom died; some 8 million civilians died in occupations and outrages such as 'The Rape of Belgium': the human toll of rape and murder in the German occupation of Belgium was propagandized in the British and American press (the burning of the library at the University of Louvain/Leuven was one of the material outrages in the occupation); the very slogan 'The Rape of Belgium' itself helped galvanize popular support for the entry of the United States into the war 6 April 1917. Such slogans, and the posters publicizing them, became a hallmark to the First World War. The word *slogan* is a loan to English from Irish or Scots Gaelic *sluagh ghairm*, the 'cry of the host' (or 'war cry'), the sense in which it is used in its first appearance in Gavin Douglas's 1513 *Eneados*, his Middle Scots translation of Virgil's *Aeneid* (in the form *slogorne*); well into the 19th century the use of the term is mainly in Scotland (it appears in its modern spelling in Thomas Macaulay's *The History of England from the Accession of James II* [vol. V, 1861]). With some semantic narrowing and loss of intensity, the term now means a 'motto associated with a political party or movement or other group' or, somewhat more crassly, 'a short and striking or memorable phrase used in advertising' (OED, s.v.). It may be that during World War I one can begin to take account more accurately, in terms of documentation and social impact, of slang; perhaps fitting, *slang* is a word of unknown origin, though the 'feel' of the word (and derivatives such as adjectival *slangy*) might suggest some role for onomatopoeia. The milestone in the study of slang was the publication of Eric Partridge's *A Dictionary of Slang and Unconventional English* in 1937; the fourth edition of H.L. Mencken's *The American Language* in 1948 (Mencken 1960) expanded the author's briefer consideration of American slang in earlier editions and a markedly more positive assessment of slang could be discerned among researchers (Lighter 1972; CHEL VI, 219, 238). Out ahead of the scholars was American poet Walt Whitman, who had observed in his essay 'Slang in America': "Slang, profoundly consider'd, is the lawless germinal element, below all words and sentences, and behind all poetry" (Whitman 1885). The US wartime 'Liberty Bonds,' established by four

[4] That Horace could state so bluntly and unquestioningly Roman patriotic virtue has been chalked up to pressure from the Augustan propaganda campaign to which Horace presumably succumbed. Discomfort at the line *dulce et decorum est pro patria mori* has been enough that one classicist proposed emending *dulce* to *dulci* so that it should be the adjectival form and modify *patria* ("fitting it is to die for the sweet fatherland"; Nisbet 1988). Curious is how seldom critics have continued to read what follows in Horace's ode: *mors et fugacem persequitur virum / nec parcit inbellis iuventae / poplitibus timidove tergo* ("and death pursues men in flight / nor are spared those unwarlike youths / in their timid knees or back"). Poet James Michie perhaps captured the sense best with his translation "The young coward, flying, gets his quietus in the back and knees" (Michie 2002). In *Odes* II.vii Horace had alluded to his poor showing at Philippi, having fled the scene of battle without his shield. It is difficult not to see Horatian irony at *Odes* III.ii: sweet and fitting it is to die for the fatherland – flee and you'll get it anyway in the back turned on battle or the back of your knees. Horace so frequently tempers statements of conventional Roman pieties with undercutting irony; it is difficult not to see the same here.

Liberty Loan Acts April 1917-September 1918, were promoted by Silent Era movie stars Charlie Chaplin, Mary Pickford, Douglas Fairbanks, Sr., and Al Jolson, and a historic advertising campaign of poster art and slogans, parallel to those in support of the general war effort, often employing more colloquial language (including 'slang'); perhaps the most famous of these was J.M. Flagg's 1917 recruitment poster with Uncle Sam 'I Want You for U.S. Army,' which was based on the 1914 British poster of Field Marshal Lord Kitchener pointing at the viewer with the slogan 'Britons. Join Your Country's Army!'.

The use of sloganeering in World War I was not a new phenomenon, but it was sharpened into an efficacy not seen before, and would continue during the World War II era with posters in support of the war effort, such as the oft-imitated Rosie the Riveter 'We Can Do It!' poster, originally produced for Westinghouse Electric in 1942. Many of the slogans were of the 'do your bit' type: 'If You Can't Enlist, Invest! Buy A Liberty Bond'; 'Lend Him a Hand, Buy Liberty Bonds'; 'Back Up Our Boys With Your Liberty Bond.' An interesting legacy of these propaganda efforts birthed by corporate advertising culture (and advances in mass psychology) was the frequent use of the exclamation point (!). The point, or mark, which likely derives from medieval manuscript pointing, had been declining in frequency of use since its introduction in the late 15th century and highwater mark the following century (it is called the 'wonderer' in John Hart's *An Ortographie* [1569]; Salmon 1999, CHEL III, 22–23, 30). It may be a mixed legacy of 16th-18th-century verse and novels (and pamphlets) and later advertising culture that gave rise to the emphatic exclamation pointing of World War I-era posters; the widespread use of slang seems a more recent development. The old adage has it that old men send young men to die in wars they started – the most cited formulation is that of US President Herbert Hoover in 1944, "Older men declare war. But it is the youth that must fight and die," but the sentiment goes back to the Greeks. It is the theme of Erich Maria Remarque's *All Quiet on the Western Front* (1928; the original German title is *Im Westen nichts Neues*, 'In the West Nothing New') and Wilfred Owen's 'Dulce et Decorum Est'; both writers deplore the propaganda that urged young men into the trenches.

Propaganda has always been a part of warfare; its role in shaping public sentiment was broadened and accelerated by mass media in the 20th century. The tenor of war propaganda has likewise always been, by turns, crude and bigoted – it was for the Romans, as it was for the Allied and Central Powers in World War I. As Germany was the most feared Central Power (Ottoman Turkey perhaps in second – dubbed 'The Sick Man of Europe,' an expression perhaps deriving from Tsar Nicholas I), caricature and stock portrayal of 'The Hun' was particularly crude (and historically inaccurate – the Huns had actually besieged the early Germanic peoples): ape-like, snarling, topped by the Pickelhaube (spiked helmet). Of course, every combatant nation had its cartoons and satirical magazines: Germany's often irreverent weekly satirical magazine *Simplicissimus* had long satirized German (especially Prussian) militarism but took a patriotic turn in the war; one of its inspirations had been Britain's *Punch* (Demm 1993). The term *Hun* for the Germans in World War I was used both sides of the Atlantic and likely derives from Kaiser Wilhelm's mention of Attila the Hun in his *Hunnenrede* ('Huns speech') 27 July 1900 that sent off German soldiers to help put down the Boxer Rebellion in China; the British in particular employed *Jerry* (*Jerries*) and *Fritz*, the French and other Allies *the Boche* ([bɔːʃ], meaning something like 'blockhead'), and

Americans and Canadians were partial to *Heinie*. While *Kraut* occurred with greater frequency in World War II (and was a staple of fiction of the era), it derived from a 19th-century American clipping of *sauerkraut* and fits in with ethnic epithets that derive from the ethnic group's typical cuisine; most of these are now taboo slurs: *Beefeater* (British), *beaner/rice and beaner* (Mexican), *chopsticks, chop suey* (Chinese), *curry muncher* (South Asian/Indian), *pea souper, Pepsi* (French Canadian). In the poster battles of World War I *Hun* was the favorite term: 'Beat Back the Hun with Liberty Bonds,' 'Halt the Hun!,' 'Always Huns AD 451–1915, Protect Our Women and Children, Join the Australian Army.'

The use of ethnic epithets was of course much more commonplace than at present – at least in open speech. Such epithets were long considered a staple of working-class speech and thus 'slang,' and their frequency derives in large part from the frequency of contact between new immigrant groups and the local native working class: areas of more affordable housing were long areas of contact between immigrant groups in the United States and, more recently, in London and other British cities. Wartime extended use of such epithets to the broader public as war fever loosened linguistic taboos. Such epithets were naturally a part of the solder's lexicon – which was largely slang, often vulgar or obscene – as modern war training sought to inculcate hatred of the enemy, and battlefield experience, during which soldiers could see each other sympathetically as unfortunate peers, each under compulsion to kill, could also sharpen this hatred as soldiers lived in fear of the enemy and saw the carnage their opponents wrought up close.

In his seminal study of the cultural and literary impact of World War I, *The Great War and Modern Memory* Paul Fussell traced the impact of trench warfare and mass, industrial-scale carnage upon 'sensitive people,' such as writers on the home front or battlefield. From Thomas Hardy's 'prescience' to the war poets who "survived to experience what the war had turned into" (Fussell 1977/2013, 3, 302), Fussell traced the devastating impact the war had not just upon the lives and towns and nations it destroyed, but upon the modern world's sense of itself, the belief in progress and technology, the confidence (even hubris) of a modern age that was soon, and irrevocably, in the British expression, 'knocked for six.' "One reason," Fussell writes, "the Great War was more ironic than any other is that its beginning was more innocent," and once young soldiers experienced "what the war had turned into" there would be, in Philip Larkin's phrase, "Never such innocence again" (Fussell 1977/2013, 18). The effect of the war upon 'bodies and minds' is a central focus in *The Great War and Modern Memory*, as is the broader destruction it caused upon the national psyche, the arts, and the ability of language to adequately describe reality. In a lengthy consideration of Robert Graves's early memoir *Good-bye to All That* (1929), he quotes Graves on some of the long-lasting effects of the war: "I still had the Army habit of commandeering anything of uncertain ownership that I found lying around about; also a difficulty in telling the truth" (219). If poetry and society and civility were never to be the same again, so too language. Again, among the poets, David Jones's *In Parenthesis* (1937) registers the shock of war upon the language and form of poetry; ostensibly an epic poem in "seven parts" (Jones 1937/1955), the 'books' of the epic are introduced by quotations from the 7th-century Old Welsh *Y Gododdin* of Aneirin ('The Gododdin,' a Brittonic tribal name descended from the Roman-era Votadini British tribe): Jones's father was from a Welsh-speaking Flintshire family, and *In Parenthesis* interlaces the experiences of the British army unit that heads to the Battle of the Somme with mournful monuments of Welsh legendary history (such as the Battle of Catraeth, a catastrophic defeat of the Old North Britons by the Angles in what is now Yorkshire). The epic's form has sometimes been described as a 'deconstructed' or 'destructured' novel (Jones was also a noted painter and engraver), and it bears comparison to stream-of-consciousness forms used by James Joyce, T.S. Eliot, and Ezra Pound. Though Jones's poem does not push language as far as Joyce would with *Finnegan's Wake* (1939), in which stream-of-consciousness narrative encroaches upon morphology itself in creating macaronic (multilingual) blends and word boundaries shatter with truncations, infixes, and *ad hoc* formations, it is part of a Great War reckoning of a language inadequate to the task of expressing the war experience. In that respect, with the wars that followed, there has been no recovery.

One register of the personal and popular impact of the Great War is the effect it had on lexis: vocabulary, more so than one's accent or grammar and syntax, allows for greater personal choice – idiosyncrasy in word choice is generally more tolerated than in those other aspects of language. The room for innovation in lexis too allows one to put a personal stamp on one's use of the language; or, following the innovation of others can create a sense of inclusion, of being in-the-know, or up-to-date. Two of the most common descriptors for the war itself now seem terribly dated, or even naive: the Great War was indeed so in contrast to the Franco-Prussian and others (though to the historian the Napoleonic conflicts and Punic Wars might be rivals); the 'war to end all wars' (or 'the war to end war') derived from H.G. Wells's 1914 tract *The War That Will End War*. English writer Wells was a visionary in science fiction, fantasy, and dystopian fictions (*The Time Machine* [1895], *The Island of Doctor Moreau* [1896], *The War of the Worlds* [1898]), but his vision did not extend to politics and war. Indeed, the optimism and enthusiasm of the young recruits and general public came to bitter disappointment after the mass slaughters of Verdun (21 February-20 December 1916), the First Battle of the Somme (1 July-18 November 1916), Passchendaele (31 July-10 November 1917), or the Kaiserschlacht ('The Kaiser's Battle,' 21 March-18 July 1918). In a pattern found throughout history the names of battles themselves became rallying cries and lexified as generics or stand-ins for other battles of that type (such as in the pattern 'another X'): Camlann, Catraeth, Maldon, Hastings, Agincourt, and many more. *Passchendaele* in particular seems to cast an ominous semantic (even phonological) shadow; this tremendously costly campaign on the Western Front ended with the capture of Passchendaele in West Flanders by the Canadian Corps. It is memorialized by the nearby Tyne Cot Commonwealth War Graves Cemetery set on the section of the Ypres Salient – the largest – captured by the New Zealand Division and 3rd Australian Division. Its name derives from the resemblance of the German pillboxes to workers' cottages in the Tyneside (*Tyneside cots*). The somber memorials of World War I cemeteries, and particular shock of the scale of loss of life in the war, generated a commemorative tradition and language in observations of the 'war dead' and the Armistice 'elevens' (the eleventh hour of the eleventh day of the eleventh month of 1918). In the Commonwealth, the formal 11 November observation is Remembrance Day, in the US Armistice Day (since 1954, Veterans Day); the laying of wreaths and bouquets at memorials, such as the Cenotaph in Whitehall, and parades of veterans in uniform have been a familiar sight in the century since the Great War's end. Remembrance Day is also known in Britain as 'Poppy Day,' from the wearing of red poppies that grew over the graves of fallen soldiers in Flanders – it has a specific origin in Canadian veteran John McCrae's 1915 poem "In Flanders Fields" ("In Flanders Fields, the poppies blow, / Between the crosses, row on row").

The cultural impact of the war, in newspapers and magazines, and, increasingly, in photography was such that many terms we associate with World War I have earlier origins but were *popularized* during 1914–1918. *Tommy* and *Tommies* for British soldiers, deriving from *Tommy Atkins* as a generic for 'A British private soldier,' may date ultimately to the 18th century (the first attestation in the OED dates to 1850). While *Blighty* derives from the days of The Raj (from Urdu *bilāyatī/vilāyatī* meaning 'foreign'), it was popularized in the cynical *Blighty wound*, an injury at the front serious enough to send one back home to 'Blighty'; its AmE equivalent was *million-dollar wound. Poilu*, 'hairy' (perhaps by extension 'manly, virile') was a generic for the French infantryman in the war (it may also refer to their characteristic facial hair). The term *doughboy* for the American infantryman is of uncertain origin but was originally used 'derisively' (RHHDAS, s.v.) or 'frequently somewhat depreciative' (OED, s.v.); it dates to before the American Civil War (the attestations are extensive in the RHHDAS entry), but, again, was popularized in World War I. As soldiers are often known and characterized by their uniform and headgear, the eponymous *Brodie helmet* marked the doughboy and other infantrymen of the war. Designed in 1915 by Englishman John Leopold Brodie, the saucer- or washbowl-like steel helmet was an icon of war photography; the American issued M1917 Helmet remained in US Army use until 1942, when it was replaced by the M1 Helmet (itself iconic of World War II films and photographs), which proved durable enough to be standard issue until 1985. Another eponym was the *Zeppelin airship* (after the German general who designed the aircraft, Ferdinand Adolf Heinrich August Graf von Zeppelin); colloquially known as *zeps*, the *Zeppelin raid* was particularly feared (the airship would, by semantic extension, give its name in AmE as one of the terms for a sandwich served on a long roll[5]). Wartime propaganda on the German side gave English *strafe*, most commonly referring to an attack by machine-gun fire from low-flying aircraft; it derived from the subjunctive verb form in the expression *Gott strafe England!* ('God punish England!'). Though *ack-ack* for the anti-aircraft gun and its fire seems onomatopoeic, in the first instance, it was an initialism *a-a* = *anti-aircraft* from the British military signal use of *ack* for the letter *A* (OED, s.v.). *Whizz-bang* for high-velocity small shellfire was partly onomatopoeic in that the sound of the shell flying (*whizz*) would be heard before the report of the gun firing it (*bang*; OED, s.v.).

As in all wars, the language of the soldiers themselves was largely slang, and much of that invective was directed against conditions, food, commanding officers, and the war itself – the Battle of the Somme was known in soldier-talk as "the Great Fuck-Up" (Fussell 1977/2013, 12). One imagines there were many other *f-word* combinations and derivatives in active use in the war (as they had been in working-class speech in general), but our records for the war seem to have been more heavily censored than for World War II (to which belong *fubar* and *snafu*). Nonetheless, the RHHDAS does record 1918 American uses of the expression *fuck 'em/'im* (these are repeated in Sheidlower 2009, s.v. *fuck*, sense 4a).

[5] Like the *hoagie*, the *zep* (usually with cold or cooked salami) is said to be a Philadelphia area Italian American invention (the *zep* localized to the metro-area city of Norristown).

[**slang of the American Expeditionary Force 1917–1920**; Lighter 1972 *ace*: a term that, with reference to pilots, can be antonymous: it can refer, in complimentary fashion, to a skilled pilot, especially a fighter pilot (thus the 'flying aces' of World War I, such as Manfred von Richthofen, the 'Red Baron'), or in deprecatory fashion, to 'a pilot or student pilot who has destroyed five or more friendly aircraft'; RHHDAS, s.v. sense 5.B). The positive *ace* in sense of 'A person who or thing which stands out, excels, or represents perfection in any field, activity, or occupation' (OED, s.v. *ace* sense 4.a) and negative senses derive ultimately from a history of gambling by dice or cards: medieval French *as*, the side of a die marked with a single dot or spot and marking the 'lowest' score possible; this extends forward in time to card-playing in which the value shifts to the 'highest' card. The broader semantic history of *ace* is incredibly rich and complex and the modern student who *aces an exam* (scores very well, often easily so) employs a term that as noun refers to the letter grade 'A' (highest mark) and as verb to the ability 'to manage (a difficult situation) successfully,' to 'ace it' (first attestation in the RHHDAS dates to 1955–1957); behind this success achieved with relative ease is the earlier sense 'to resist (interrogation or cross-examination) tenaciously and successfully' and 'to maneuver (someone) into (something), esp. through the use of flattery or deceit' (RHHDAS, senses 1–2, 4). Which may indeed put the college slang use in its proper context.

Big Bertha: the massive German siege howitzer or M-Gerät, a 42-ton field artillery piece with a range of nearly 6 miles.

bird: an aircraft, a term in use still in military jargon for planes, and by 'plane-spotters' (aviation enthusiasts).

blimp: the 'barrage balloon,' without a rigid skeleton or internal structure (and thus distinct form the Zeppelin and dirigible; this battlefield balloon lives on in David Low's cartoon military man 'Colonel Blimp,' who debuted in the *Evening Standard* in April 1934, and with the 'Goodyear Blimp,' which includes also dirigibles in the fleet of airships launched since 1925 by the Goodyear tire company emblazoned with the company's logo (and appearing, in particular, over major sporting events such as the Indy 500 and Super Bowl).

Chew one's ass out, *chew out*: Though the OED lists the first occurrence of this imaginative phrasal verb for being severely reprimanded as from 1948, and labels it 'colloquial' and chiefly an Americanism, the RHHDAS attestations point to World War I usage; *chew* throughout the history of the language could be used metaphorically (*chew the cud*); an early usage in the sense 'to worry with reproaches,' 'to jaw,' is from the early Middle English alliterative homily *Hali Meidenhad* ('Holy Maidenhood') of the early 13th century: *Chit te & cheoweð þe & schent te schomeliche* ('he chides thee and chews thee and puts thee to shame disgracefully'). This being soldiers' usage, other parts of the anatomy could get chewed off (ears or 'balls'), and to this day one can, metaphorically, and colorfully, have one's 'ass chewed out/off.'

pillbox: concrete or stone/brick low fortification and gun emplacement (of the Germans in the first attestation from 1917) normally with small slits or windows for firing; like the bunkers of World War II (first attestation for *bunker* in this sense in the OED is from 1939) these were targets of hard-fought frontal assaults to knock out machine guns; a semantic extension from the smaller *pillbox* 'case for pills.'

vinegar blink: vin blanc, a comic deformation of the French; one of a number of such formations, like *toot sweet*, *tooter sweeter* (< Fr. *tout de suite* 'right away, at once'), indicate a perennial Anglo-American attitude toward the French (though allies in this war): a sense of French snobbishness and condescension, felt even in the sounds of their language; an attitude that takes the French down a peg, but simultaneously makes the user seem unsophisticated, rude (ironic in that the very qualities imputed to the French were rudeness and a superciliousness about their sense of being more sophisticated than their English and American partners).

Vodka: a Russian, Russian soldier.

war baby: an officer advanced because of the war's urgent needs, generally viewed as 'green' or incompetent; the term saw subsequent use in later conflicts, such as the World War II use *war baby* for the generation born during 1939–1945, or, when coupled with *baby boom* and *Boomer* (a term that can also be used snidely or derisively in contemporary AmE – e.g., the retort, *OK, Boomer*), can refer to the generation that came of age in the 1960s (the *Woodstock Generation*, *Baby Boomers* or just *Boomers*, in contradistinction to the following *Generation X/Gen X*, *Millennials*, and *Zoomers/Zers*).

webfoot: an infantryman, with the idea of the clumsiness of having to walk the trenches (or the idea that one would develop webbed feet from walking in wet trenches).

whistling Willy/Willie: incoming heavy artillery shell (from the sound in flight); one of a number of terms for enemy artillery shells, often descriptive of the sound made in air incoming overhead; *trolley car* was one of these terms, and indicated the 'rumbling' sound made by some heavy shells in flight; *whistling Willie* indicates another characteristic sound, and was used also by Canadian and British troops and dates to at least the Boer War (which would indicate transfer of the term from British to American soldiers). The German 240mm shell was dubbed the *ashcan*.

Wooden Cross: sarcastic allusion to an imagined military decoration consisting of one's death and burial with a grave marked by a usual wooden cross (also called *Croix de Bois*, 'wooden crosses'; Raymond Bernard's 1932 film *Les Croix de Bois*, based upon Raymond Dorgelès's novel, makes a similar bitter point).

Yanks Are Coming: This is from the chorus 'That the Yanks are coming, the Yanks are coming' from American popular composer George M. Cohan's 'Over There' (1917); *Yank* the clipped form of *Yankee* (as a designation for an American, it might derive ultimately from Dutch diminutive *Janke* 'little John').

The Yanks of course were coming, late to the fray, following the sinking of the Lusitania (7 May 1915) and the Zimmerman Telegram (January 1917), which entered the lexicon of the American experience in the Great War, and again in World War II. It is a popular tradition among Americans, when they feel they have been 'high-hatted' by Brits and other Europeans, to remind them that they would be speaking German today were it not for 'the Yanks' – though the Yanks have since eclipsed the Europeans in military and financial power, in part from the great run-up in war production in the Second World War. In the 'Cold War' that followed, the Americans took the lead role, but still felt anxious about the view of them held by the 'Old Powers' (Britain and France in particular). As seen earlier, this 'anxiety of influence' may have contributed to overt and subconscious shifts in American English away from British English, such as the spelling reform proposals of Benjamin Franklin (1768) and Noah Webster (1783). The changes to the language in the Great War era were most pronounced in the lexicon, but there were pragmatic concerns as well. As reportage and memoirs of the war were still fairly heavily censored (officially, and by self-censorship, which may at times be a subspecies of the former), we only get occasional glimpses of how soldiers actually spoke – for full-blown profanity and invective, we await World War II: there is no World War I exact match to Joseph Heller's Yossarian and other World War II squadron members in *Catch-22* (1961), a phrase that entered the language for the novel's presentation of problems whose resolution is impossible because of inherent contradictions, conditions, and, especially, absurdities. But a preliminary shot had been fired from the trenches, redoubts, and prisoner-of-war camps: real speech from extraordinary circumstances was leaking out, slang expressions and invective were shared among the troops (British to American English, sometimes through Canadian, Australian, or New Zealand intermediaries – *whistling Willie* may be one example), as was a way of speaking: bitter, profane, direct, hard-bitten, cynical. If World War I was remarkable – and the last such conflict to be so in this way – for the number of aristocratic enlistees and junior officers who fought (and, in many cases, died) in the conflict, the bulk of the infantry came from the working class. And the societal barriers and taboos that walled off 'low speech' from the 'refined' weakened in the wake of shared experiences and suffering in the war – a democratizing effect in the trenches (a social class parallel to the World War II-era saying, of uncertain attribution, 'There are no atheists in foxholes').

8.3 COMMONWEALTH AND DECOLONIZATION: 'SO-CALLED ÉIRE,' CELTIC REVIVALS (IRISH – SCOTS GAELIC – WELSH – MANX – CORNISH – CUMBRIC)

The neutrality of Ireland in the Second World War under Taoiseach Éamon de Valera irked no less than the First Lord of the Admiralty Winston Churchill, who, in speaking to the naval staff, referred to the "so-called neutrality of so-called Eire."[6] De Valera had been born in New York City in 1882 in a charity hospital on Lexington Avenue, the son

[6] 5 September 1939, in the Churchill Papers (CHAR 19/3), Churchill College Cambridge Archives; cf. O'Halpin (2008), p. 1 n. 2.

of Irishwoman Catherine Coll (from Bruree, Co. Limerick) and Spaniard Juan Vivion de Valera; he was christened Edward (Éamon is the usual Irish equivalent for English Edward and Edmund) and lived for a time in Brooklyn and Manhattan's East Side. His father headed out to the Western U.S. because of a respiratory condition when Éamon was 2 years old; Juan never returned, and upon news of his death in 1885, Éamon was taken back to Ireland by his Uncle Ned and raised by his grandmother and other relatives in Bruree. He was educated in the National School in Bruree, then the Christian Brothers School in Charleville, Co. Cork, and Blackrock College, Dublin. He began a career as a mathematics teacher, and returned at various points to university-level instruction; he also became seriously involved with the Irish language movement, joined the *Conradh na Gaeilge* (the Gaelic League), and became more politically minded joining the Irish Volunteers (*Óglaigh na hÉireann*, 'warriors/volunteers of Ireland,' a name used after the Irish War of Independence by the IRA [Irish Republican Army] and various splinter groups such as the Provisional IRA, the 'Provos,' Continuity IRA, and 'Real IRA'). The evolution of de Valera from the New York City-born child returned to Co. Limerick to young teacher and *Gaeilgeoir* (Irish-speaker) to nationalist, revolutionary, and independence leader and statesman of the Irish Free State (1922–1937), then Taoiseach of independent Éire (after 1948 the Republic of Ireland), is precisely the pattern feared by Churchill and other 'Unionist' (in the broadest sense of that political sentiment – i.e., preserving the United Kingdom) politicians: heritage identity can lead to language revival which leads to (Celtic) nationalism and rumblings of independence. And, of course, this pattern has occurred in the case of Ireland (for 26 of Ireland's 32 counties; 6 of 9 of Ulster's traditional counties remain in the United Kingdom as Northern Ireland), and occurs in Wales, Scotland, Cornwall, and even with faint rumblings in Cumbria (Yr Hen Ogledd, the 'Old North' of the early medieval period). One should mention here the fate of Breton: a 'British' (Brythonic) language after all, descended from dialects of British brought by Britons fleeing the Saxon advance through Southern and Western Britain in the 5th to 6th centuries. Some 1 million people in the broader region of Brittany spoke the language in 1950, though the number of native speakers may have reached as low as 170,000–200,000 in recent years. Recent attempts at language revival are showing some promise, as have efforts in Wales, where some 800,000 people can speak Welsh as their L1 or L2 (the counties with the highest numbers of speakers are Angelsey, Carmarthenshire, Ceredigion, Conwy, Gwynedd, and Rhondda Cynon Taf). The language revival movement for Cornish (Kernowek/Kernewek) once thought of as a local oddity (like the flying of Saint Piran's flag) is now more seriously linguistically grounded; there is a Cornish Language Board (Kesva an Taves Kernewek) that offers competency exams – a Cornish equivalent to the Irish Foras na Gaeilge, until 1999 the Bord na Gaeilge with its publications organ An Gúm ('plan, scheme'), or Inverness-based Bòrd na Gàidhlig (established in 2005), or Cardiff-based Bwrdd ar Iaith Gymraeg (Welsh Language Board).

On the part of the 'English' English, there can be a sort of popular dualism in attitude with regard to the Celtic languages of Britain: a taunting of those 'who cannot speak their own language' in referring to monolingually English Welsh or Scots (the Irish have compulsory Irish language lessons in their schooling), balanced with an irritation at hearing the languages being used beyond the *cúpla focail* as the Irish say ('a few words,' i.e., not fluent). A similar irritation can be witnessed in the United States at hearing languages other than English spoken in public, particularly Spanish. In both situations, English is hardly under threat: the Celtic languages had been in retreat since the late medieval to Early Modern periods, the revival movements a slow outgrowth of 18th-century Romantic movements and 19th-century 'linguistic nationalism' and separatist and independence politics (postmodern critics often ignore Celtic language revivals, but they were early forerunners of anti-colonial struggles in the wider Empire); in the United States, at no period in its history has the nation ever been so thoroughly monolingual nor the pace of linguistic assimilation so rapid than at present. In the former case, the real irritant, or fear, is that language revival sharpens identity, and identity sharpens separatism – a not entirely unfounded alarm: the Scottish National Party (SNP) has an independence platform and held a Scottish Independence referendum in 2014 (defeated 55% to 44%, though the 'yes' or 'aye' vote may have been dampened by worry over Scotland's relationship with the EU). The SNP, currently the largest party in Scotland, has even floated the idea of a 'Bord fir the Scots Leid' ('Board for the Scots Language,' *leid* or *leed*, a Scots form deriving from Old English *lēden/lœden*, literally 'Latin,' but secondarily, 'any tongue, language'[7]). Plaid Cymru ('Party of Wales'), a much smaller party at Westminster (but with a bigger share of seats in the Senedd Cymru [Welsh Parliament]) also has a platform of independence (and membership in the EU and UN for Wales/Cymru) and bilingualism. Of course, such linguistic nationalism (or separatism) is not unusual in the broader linguistic context. The Catalan independence movement made international news with independence referenda in 2014 and 2017, a declaration of independence in October 2017, then a swift and fairly heavy-handed crackdown and assumption of direct rule by the central government in Madrid; the Catalan President Carles Puigdemont i Casamajó and other independence leaders were charged by Madrid with sedition and other offenses and fled into exile (as Spain continues to seek his extradition). The pro-independence parties strengthened their position in the 2021 elections. Language, of course, plays a major role in the Catalan independence movement in that a distinct linguistic identity can galvanize other senses of distinctiveness. The 'linguistic nationalisms' of Britain do not have the economic clout of the Catalans (though enough to upset Westminster nonetheless), but they do explain the persistence of dialectal distinctiveness in Ireland, Scotland, Wales (and to some extent in Cumbria and other parts of the north and Cornwall). The dialects of Irish English have been influenced by the dialects of the Irish language; the influence is embedded in Irish English and persists whether the speaker is fluent in Irish or not. So in Wales with Welsh Englishes (south and north); the dialectal situation in Scotland, with its traditional linguistic Lowland (Lallans)-Highland boundary is complicated by the historical role, self-conscious revival, and literary use of Scots (Scots English descended from Northumbrian Old English and early Middle English).

The roots of 'Celtic Englishes' go well back in history: to the 5th century for contact with Welsh, British, Cornish, Irish (to the 4th century in Dyfed and south

[7] The *Scottish National Dictionary* (online: Dictionaries of the Scots Language) has an early attestation from Alexander Ross's 1768 poetic 'pastoral tale' *The Fortunate Shepherdess*: "Speak my ain leed, 'tis guid auld Scots I mean" (s.v. *leed*).

Wales especially, though there is the evidence of ogham inscriptions from north Wales and in the 5th century from Cornwall also) and Cumbric (and perhaps also Pictish, though it is not securely classified as a Brythonic Celtic language); to the 6th for contact with Dál Riada Irish Gaelic; and from 627 Gaelicized Isle of Man after the conquest by King Edwin of Northumbria. 'Celtic Englishes' is of course a contested term as Hiberno-English, Scots English, Welsh English and other varieties might also be considered markedly distinct 'ethnic' dialects of English, or, like African-American English, dialects that exhibit features deriving from earlier pidginization. Or the level and intensity of heritage (Celtic) language influence on the production of English by Celtic speakers may be such that it is of a higher order than regional English dialects, which themselves often show the legacy of second-language influence, for example, the historical influence of Scandinavian in the former Danelaw (influence that is even more marked in the Orkneys and Shetland Islands – the end of Yuletide Up Helly Aa, 'Up Holy [Day] All,' festival one revivalist example). Though the 'extinction' of Pictish and Cumbric likely dates to the 12th century or so, enthusiasts have proposed reviving Cumbric (as has been undertaken for Manx and Cornish), either from medieval materials (essentially reviving 'Old Cumbric') or plotting its anticipated subsequent development (reviving a reconstructed Modern Cumbric or 'Cumbraek'), or adopting Old or Modern Welsh. The last speaker of Cornish is said to have been Dolly Pentreath, who died in 1777, while the last native speaker of Manx was fisherman Ned Maddrell (d. 1974). Cornish has, as mentioned above, its Language Board for the revival of the language, and for Manx there is Yn Çheshaght Ghailckagh (Manx Gaelic Society, founded in 1899), which promotes the revival of the language through the publication of grammars and primers of Manx (Gaelg) and a language policy that reintroduced the language to schools (adopted as government policy in 1992). The Cooneil ny Gaelgey (Gaelic Council) handles a task that often arises in the Celtic-speaking parts of the British Isles conquered by England: rendering names for streets, titles, government offices, and creating neologies for things for which there are no modern Manx equivalents (similar difficulties arose with 'modernizing' Irish and Welsh[8]).

In Wales and Ireland, official language policies and language planning schemes are designed to maintain and expand the number of speakers of the languages and, of signal importance, increase primary subject schooling in the native languages. The language planning takes place across a spectrum of nongovernmental organizations (NGOs), quangos (quasi-autonomous nongovernmental organizations: taxpayer-funded but not entirely under control of the central government), and official governmental bodies. Wales has a Commissioner of the Welsh Language (Coisiynydd y Gymraeg, since 2023 Efa Gruffudd Jones; the Irish equivalent is An Coimisinéir Teanga, 'The Language Commissioner'); one of its most telling functions is "Sicrhau bod cyrff cyhoeddus yn cydymffurfio â safonau'r Gymraeg" ("Ensure that public bodies are in compliance with Welsh language standards"[9]). A goal of both the

[8] A similar task is undertaken by the Vatican's Office of Latin Letters in producing Latin terms for modern concepts and things for papal documents. The successfully revived language Modern Israeli Hebrew also required the generation of new terms for things of the modern world.

[9] https://www.welshlanguagecommissioner.wales/cymraeg.php

Commissioner of the Welsh Language and Ireland's Official Languages Act of 2003 (Acht na dTeangacha Oifigiúla 2003, amended 2021) is to ensure that governmental and public services be available in both languages, and, indeed, that a native speaker should be able to conduct one's life in the native tongue (this latter goal may not quite have been achieved yet, though Article 8 of the Constitution of Ireland had declared Irish the 'first official language'). The "Language Scheme 2019–2022" of the Official Languages Act 2003 from the Roinn an Taoisigh (Department of the Taoiseach), effective 1 July 2019, sought in particular to enhance 'Irish language services' from the government, including publication in Irish, signage in Gaeltachtaí (officially recognized native Irish-speaking areas), and face-to-face counter service in Irish at government offices. The Addysg Cymru/Education Wales "Welsh in education, Action Plan 2017–21" (issued 2017) focuses particularly upon education and the inclusion of Welsh language as a compulsory GCSE (General Certificate of Secondary Education) subject. The plan seeks to increase both the number of learners in 'Welsh-medium education' and primary teachers teaching in Welsh, and to return to 1 million speakers of Welsh by 2050 (the last time there had been a million Welsh speakers was in the census of 1911; Plaid Cymru had been founded in 1925 in part to promote the use of Welsh). Welsh devolution referenda in 1997 and 2011 have furthered the push toward independence (and that sense of 'nationhood'), and the Welsh language and Welsh English have given it sharper expression (Lewis 2019; Williams 2019): indeed the Welsh National Assembly, the English term for the government in Wales, is known separately as the Senedd Cymru in Welsh, while 'Senedd' ('senate, parliament') is the joint term for the body.

In the 2016 Irish census, some 1.7 million people claimed to speak Irish as their L1 or L2, a figure that means as an L2 for the majority of the respondents. The Irish (Gaeilge) that many people in Ireland learn in school and speak is the *An Caighdeán Oifigiúil* ('the official standard'), a composite of Gaeltachtaí dialects from the provinces of Connachta, Munster, and Ulster (Leinster was the most heavily Anglicized of the provinces); there was not a little debate about which dialects should be used, and speakers of Ulster Irish or Munster Irish dialects naturally hewed to their own speechways (see "Which dialect?" in Doyle 2015, 227–230). As a composite 'standard' variety the 'school Irish' is at variance with 'living dialects' of Irish in Gaeltachtaí and there may be some developing difficulty in comprehension between the urban 'official' Irish and the traditional rural dialects (the sort of traditional 'Heartland' encompasses Cos. Donegal, Mayo, Galway, Kerry, and Cork; see Hickey 2011, especially his survey of dialects 105–133). The Irish 'Language Scheme 2019–2022' comes in the wake of debates in Ireland about compulsory Irish in secondary schooling; former Taoiseach Enda Kenny of Fine Gael, an Irish speaker who had once himself taught Irish at the primary school level, had sided with those arguing for a reduction in years of compulsory Irish in the secondary school years on the view that compulsion was actually making the learning of the language more unpopular. The goal of the language programs is not entirely clear since the Constitution's declaration was that Irish is to be the primary official language of Ireland; it is a long project on which the Irish government has spent considerable sums of taxpayer money: the current Fianna Fáil government has increased the language budget for 2021 by an additional €14.8 million to a total of €78 million (and now to €107million in 2025). Ireland is the rare case in Europe of a nation in which the majority of its people does not speak the national language as their

L1; if the intention had been, as with Israel and the project to revive modern spoken Hebrew, to restore Ireland's national language and place English in the role of the country's useful even vital L2 (England is Ireland's largest trading partner), then this has not happened. Even the goal of making modern Ireland a fully bilingual state has not quite been reached. Wales has set out an ambitious but quite achievable plan to have some one-third its population be Welsh-speakers by 2050. But in both cases, English remains the primary language for most of the population. That both governments have concentrated their focus on primary and secondary education shows that their eyes are on the future.

But where to place Ireland and Wales in the scheme of Global English is not easy to determine. Though they are placed by Kachru (Kachru 1992) within the 'Inner Circle' of Englishes, the 'norm-providing' varieties, Irish and Welsh Englishes are not quite a neat fit in this model; proximity and time depth are factors that distinguish these varieties from younger Commonwealth postcolonial varieties such as Canadian, New Zealand, Australian, and South Asian Englishes. In the case of colonies abroad such as these, the English arrived with settlers and displaced the indigenous/Aboriginal languages in place for centuries, even millennia. Ireland is England's first external colony proper, and the occupation (here in the neutral sense, though the Irish Nationalist use of 'the occupation' extends from it) has lasted nearly 900 years. The Celts of Britain were indigenous, and the displacement was largely internal (some Britons fled or were driven out to Brittany in France and Gallaecia in Spain [Britonia/Bretoña]). Schneider's comprehensive "dynamic model" (Schneider 2007) does not consider either Ireland or Wales as test cases, and the grid developed in classifying postcolonial Englishes really fits external colonies of shorter duration better. The data for Irish English has recently benefited from the research of Raymond Hickey on the varieties of Irish English and the position of Irish English among British (and World) Englishes (see Hickey 2007 in particular); for example, the development from the 1980s of a 'Dublin 4' accent, and a Dublin Vowel Shift (see Hickey 2005). Dublin 4 is a postcode encompassing trendier neighborhoods in central Dublin such as Baggot Street Upper, Ballsbridge, Donnybrook, Merrion; the 'middle-clarse' accent might be understood, at least socially, as parallel to Estuary English in England, an accent that consciously sought to dissociate itself from the established patterns (and so it was given the nickname 'Dortspeak,' reflecting, to an extent satirically, pronunciation of the name of the train line DART [Dublin Area Rapid Transit]). Yet, as Hickey noted from recordings of Dublin speakers, some elements of the accent did survive, such as the raising of non-rhotic back vowels and retraction of /aɪ/ to /ɑɪ/ or /əɪ/ (*time* and *kind* as *toim* and *koind*) and fronting of /aʊ/ (*now* sounding more like [næʊ]). And the characteristic pronunciation of Cork as 'cark' ([kɒːɹk] saw the vowel raised and shortened to /o/ and a trill [voiced retroflex approximant] /ɻ/ for the alveolar approximant /ɹ/; Hickey 2005, 45–91).

A formation in older Irish American speech (recorded in New England) may evidence interference, direct or inherited, from Irish: *Are you coming over the Friday? Will you be here the Saturday?* The locution 'the [day of the week]' may preserve the use of the definite article *an* in Irish with the demonstrative: *an bhean seo*, literally 'the woman this' = 'this woman'; *An bhfuil tú ag teacht an Aoine seo*, 'Are you be coming over this Friday?, *an Aoine seo*, 'the Friday this.' But the matter of Irish-English contact in American English, that is of Irish Gaelic and American English, is still awaiting fuller study.

8.4 AN 'INNER CIRCLE' OR 'INNER CIRCLES'?

An interesting legacy of long-term contact between Celtic and English speakers, and Brythonic and Goidelic, is the history of forms of the 'North Country Score' or *yan tan tethera* and other alternative counting systems used in Northern England (Cumberland, Lancashire, Yorkshire, Derbyshire, Lincolnshire) and Wales. The sets of numerals, generally up to 20, were apparently borrowed during the early contact period with Old English and persisted in use into the 20th century, mainly for sheep-counting and counting out stitches in knitting. The northern English varieties are called *yan tan tethera* 'one, two, three' and seem, based on closeness to Modern Welsh, to derive from Cumbric, the Brythonic language of the 'Old North' (*Yr Hen Ogledd*), spoken until about the 12th century (the Strathclyde Britons had been absorbed into the Kingdom of Scotland by the mid-11th century); one example from the north, of the dozens recorded, is given here (Greene 1992, 551):

1 *yan* (Welsh *un*)
2 *tan* (W *dau* [m.], *dwy* [f.])
3 *tethera* (W *tri*)
4 *pethera* (W *pedwar*)
5 *pimp* (W *pump*)
6 *sethera* (W *chwech*)
7 *lethera* (W *saith*)
8 *hovera* (W *wyth*)
9 *covera* (W *nau*)
10 *dik* (W *deg*; compare Irish *deich*)
11 *yan-a-dik* (W *un ar ddeg*; probably a literal sense 'one on ten'; Greene 1992, 499)
12 *tan-a-dik* (W *deuddeg*; Modern Welsh uses the compound numeral, literally 'two-ten'; compare Irish *a dó dhéag* 'the two ten')
13 *tethera dik* (W *tri ar ddeg*)
14 *pethera dik* (W *pedwar ar ddeg*)
15 *bumfit* (W *pymtheg*)
16 *yan-a-bumfit* (W *un ar bymtheg*)
17 *tan-a-bumfit* (W *dwy ar bymtheg*)
18 *tethera bumfit* (W *deunaw*) [the North Country form is a composite numeral literally meaning 'three-fifteen' = 'three and fifteen,' while the Modern Welsh is a compound numeral meaning 'two-nine' = 'two nines']
19 *pethera bumfit* (W *pedwar ar bymtheg*) [literally 'four-fifteen' and 'four on fifteen']
20 *figgit* (W *ugain*) [for the North Country form compare Irish *fiche*, for the Welsh Latin *uiginti*]

[There is great variety in the forms for 'twenty' in counting scores; just a few would include: *jigget* (SW border of West Riding, Yorkshire); *iggan* (clearly Brythonic, from Yorkshire, used in counting stitches in knitting; *giggot/gigget* (recorded in: Borrowdale, Keswick, Lake District; Wasdale, Lake District; Eskdale, Coniston and other Lake District regions;[10] the Lincolnshire forms *fixit* and *figgit* are interesting in that they seem rather to be Goidelic; Barry 1969, 88–89.]

Celtic seems to have been decimal, but was influenced early on by the vigesimal ('twenty'-based) system; compare Modern Welsh *deugain* (< *dau* + *ugain* 'two-twenty' = 'two twenties'). An echo of the system is found in English in counting by scores, 'four score' = '80' as in U.S. President Abraham Lincoln's famous opening to his "Gettysburg Address" (19 November 1863): "Four score and seven years ago our fathers brought forth on this continent a new nation, conceived in Liberty, and dedicated to the proposition that all men are created equal"; in earlier English was the 'long hundred' (120), a vestige of duodecimal counting (base-12) as found in Old Norse. The rhyming series *tethera* - *pethera* - *sethera* - *lethera* - *hovera* - *covera* (3-4-6-7-8-9) likely bears the influence of counting games and rhymes and deforms some original Brythonic forms; a number of other such 'scores' exist down to Dorset in the Southwest. The cadence of the series of rhyming 'numerals' apparently appealed also to James Joyce, who worked it into Book III, Chapter 2 of *Finnegans Wake* (1939): "If any lightfoot Clod Dewvale was to hold me up, dicksturping me and marauding me of my rights to my onus, yan, tyan, tethera, methera, pimp, I'd let him have my best pair of galloper's heels in the creamsourer" (Joyce 1939/1976, 457). Of course, *yan* for 'one' may also be the form heard still in Northumberland as a development from Old English *ān* 'one' (also 'a certain one, some one'; Leith 1997/2005, 45). From Cardiganshire, Wales, comes a counting score in a Brythonic-speaking area that derives from Goidelic (Old Irish): *în* 'one' (Old Irish *óen*, Modern Irish *haon*), *tô* 'two' (OIr *dá*, MdIr *dó*), *târ* 'three' (OIr and MdIr *trí*), *câr* 'four' (OIr *cethair*, MdIr *ceathair*), *cŵi* 'five' (OIr *cóic*, MdIr *cúig*), *nochde* 'nineteen' (MdIr *naoi déag*), *wichi* 'twenty' (likely from an early initial mutation of OIr *fiche*; Greene 1992, 551–552). The sets of 'counting scores' likely have their ultimate origins in the early medieval period: the Brythonic > English *yan-tan-tethera* set to the 6th century or so as the Kingdom of Northumbria pushed further northward; the Irish > Welsh *în-tô-târ* to the Irish settlements in Wales starting in the 3rd–4th centuries. That the sets are 1–20 likely points to their practical use in counting sheep and counting off stitches, but it may also show the influence of vigesimal systems on early Celtic (e.g., how Old Irish could express larger numbers in 'twenties': *da fhicit* 'two score'; *tri fichit* 'three score'; *secht fichit* 'seven score'; Thurneysen 2017, 245).

There are two other points of interest concerning 'counting scores' and *score* itself. One is the path of transmission and preservation of these alternative sets of numbers 1–20, from sheep- and stitch-counting to counting games and children's rhymes: the rhyme in the *yan-tan-tethera* was no doubt mnemonic (it made memorization of the

10 Interesting too are these place-names from Cumbria, all of Scandinavian origin or influence: *Borrowdale* < ON *borgar-dalr* ('stronghold-valley'); *Coniston* < ON *konungs-tūn* ('king's-homestead/manor'), probably the Scandinavianized form of OE *cynings-tūn* (early attestations of this place-name include *Koningeston* from 1196 and *Kunyngston* from 1336; CDEPN, 155); *Eskdale*, 'valley of the Esk' (*Esk* a British river-name), perhaps understood by Scandinavians in the area as 'ash-valley' (*eski-dalr*; CDEPN, 218).

set easier), but also playful: an element of 'fun' in what could otherwise be tedious. The pattern can be found in various 'counting-off' or 'out' games, by which one is 'out' or 'it' having reached a certain number in a count (forward or backward ['counting down' in that case]). Children's game rhymes such as *Ip dip* or *Eeny, meeny, miney, mo/Eena, meena, mina, mo* employ 'nonsense' words set in 'doggerel' verse, in the traditional analysis, and they can vary considerably across region; *Ip dip* as a 'counting-out rhyme' in the British Isles has its profane varieties ('Ip dip dog shit' known from Northern Ireland), though its purpose remains the same: to count 'out' one of a group of children arranged in a line or circle, sometimes with a foot placed forward as the counted item (the last line often some variant of 'Out goes you' or 'O-U-T spells out'). If *Ip dip* may be 'nonsense' words, their rhyme and rhythm are their point of being; the *eena/eeny* of *Eeny meeny*, which the OED holds to be a "nonsense word" (s.v. *eeny*; see also Liberman 2008, s.v. *eena*, 62–64) may echo Brythonic words for 'one' – the Cornish version is *Ena, mena, mona, mite* (Jago 1882, 160): Old Welsh, Breton, and Cornish *un*, Old Irish *óen* (< Proto-Celtic **oyno-*; Matasović 209, 304–305). An alternative view was proposed by the late Creolist Derek Bickerton, who felt that the only support for the 'Celtic' explanation was that no other had been offered, and that the opening line may have come from the São Tomense Creole (Portuguese-based) *ine mine mana mu* 'my sister's children' and heard by children in the United States from enslaved São Tomeans sometime in the later 18th to 19th centuries (Bickerton 1982, 226). Bickerton admitted that he had found no evidence of the São Tomense Creole being spoken in the United States, and the phonological resemblance of the particular phrase may be a result of chance, or of Celtic English speakers influencing the Creole, and why it would be fitted into the first line of a counting-off rhyme is not clear. A larger point here is the traditional resistance in Anglophone scholarship to any proposed Celtic origins for English words, phrases, and other features. Opie and Opie 1997 (*The Oxford Dictionary of Nursery Rhymes*, 156–158) had noted examples from Scotland and Ireland (citing Bolton 1888) and the tradition of "Anglo-Cymric" (Ellis 1879) and other scores points to Celtic-speaking regions and borderlands in Britain (in Cumbria and the north, Southern Scotland, Wales, Cornwall; Ellis 1879, 324–325 provides a comprehensive list of locations from which scores were collected). That a number of such scores, as preserved in children's rhymes, appeared also in the United States should come as no surprise and likely has British origins (Barry 1969, 81, maps out where Celtic numerals survived in the United States). The more difficult question is how these Celtic numerals survived in English: one view would see them as the product of early contact between Angles and Scots and Cumbrians and other Celts from the 6th century onward; another view sees later importation from Scotland and Wales (Barry 1969, 81–87). The remoteness of the sheepherding occupation might explain the survival of such an archaism in the regional English of the border zones.

A second point of interest is the role of children's rhymes and games in both linguistic innovation and the preservation of vestigial forms. The role of *Lallwörter*, the German term for babble-words or 'babytalk' expressions, has been significant in the creation of popular child language forms – *eeny meeny miny moe* and *Tic-Tac-Toe* exhibit the rhythmical patterns of much child language. Reduplication, rhyme, and nonce- and nonsense-forms are common; common too is the connection to play. Onomatopoeia and a simple (childlike) delight in the sounds of words seem a part of this tradition of 'nursery rhymes,' play songs, and counting scores. Though the origin of Lewis Carroll's Tweedledum and Tweedledee has often been located in a 1725 satiric poem on the composers Handel and Bononcini by John Byrom (1692–1763), 'Strange all this Difference should be / 'Twixt Tweedle-dum and Tweedle-dee,' Byrom may have been drawing on an earlier nursery rhyme tradition; Ellis in his 'Anglo-Cymric Score' mentions a children's rhyme from Sussex and one of its variants:

> Eena deena dīna dust
> kakla weela wīla wust
> spit, spat, mus' be done,
> tweedlum, twoddlum, twenty one.
>
> Igdum, digdum, didum, dest,
> Cot-lo, wel-lo, wi-lo, west;
> Cot-pan, must be done,
> Twiddledum, twaddledum, twenty-one![11] (Ellis 1877–1879, 366)

The first version begins with the Brythonic 'one-two-three' from counting scores, and plays with verbal form by alternating root vowels – indeed, the verses sound like mnemonic devices for grammatical forms (declensions, conjugations). The development toward nonsense forms in child's play rhymes is evident with 'Igdum, digdum, didum,' but both end with an echo of counting scores on 'twenty-one.' Both verses employ heptasyllabic lines, an echo perhaps of early medieval Celtic verse form, or another form of counting, this of syllables. That children's games and rhymes could be fairly complex should not be surprising; their traditional nature helped preserve a number of archaisms in verse and vocabulary. *Tic-Tac-Toe* (British *Tit-tat-toe* or *noughts and crosses*, Irish and Welsh *X'y Osies* or *Exy Ozy's*) likely derives from ancient board games; the name for the game (now played on paper or notepads or online) is first recorded in the 19th century and occurs in a counting-rhyme from Southern Scotland and Northern England:

> Tit, tat, toe
> Here I go,
> And if I miss
> I pitch on this (Bolton 1888, 3).

In this particular 'counting-out' tradition, boys would place a finger in a school cap and the counter would go round, pointing at fingers for each monosyllable called out, with the last word 'this' landing on the one being counted out or 'titted out.' Many of these games of being 'it' or, in Britain more commonly, 'out,' have broad affinities; the

[11] The variant "Twiddledum Twaddledum Twenty One" appeared in the "Numbers – 1" episode of *Teletubbies* (Season 1, Episode 9 [1997]).

game of 'musical chairs' is one of them (here the objective is inverted, the goal being to be the last one seated when the music stops rather than the one selected when the count ends). Rhymes that serve to commence a game, or race, or work activity can often use the counting device; one 19th-century example found in the United States and Britain re-entered popular culture in Elvis Presley's "Blue Suede Shoes" (written by Cal Perkins in 1955): "One for the money, two for the show, / Three to make ready, and four to go!" A game of equal antiquity, *three men's morris* (and its more complicated variants with greater numbers of 'men' or pieces, *six men's morris, nine men's morris*) involves a board, originally incised, with lines in a cross pattern and diagonals (looking like an *X* over a cross) with pieces at the start of the game lined up at rest opposing each other with the objective being to move them into a another straight line of three 'men' called a *mill*. As *morris* is thought to be a corruption of *merels* (or *merrils* or other variant spellings), from Old French *merele/merelle* ('token,' 'counter'), *mill* as the line formed by a winning formation of pieces in the game is also used for the name of the game itself by semantic extension; in Ireland it is often used in the plural *mills*, and an attestation for this use the OED took from P.W. Joyce's *English as We Speak It in Ireland* (Joyce 1979): "A few years ago I saw two persons playing mills in a hotel in Llandudno; and my heart went out to them" (sense 9a). Joyce, from Co. Limerick, had learned the game there as a child, aware that it was an import from England, and was delighted later in life to see it still being played in North Wales. The death and emigration of so many native Irish speakers 1845–1852 (*an Gorta mór*, 'the Great Hunger') and 1879 (*an Gorta beag*, 'the little Famine') depleted whole villages in the former 'Congested Districts' in areas that were majority Gaelic-speaking. The shift to English was seen as one of survival, then modernization; adding insult to injury was the great rise in 'stage Irish' dialect in cartoons and satirical articles about Ireland and the Irish. The stereotypical forms and expressions did at times have grounding in actual use, and some of them may have in turn entered Irish English as 'Irishisms' – J.M. Synge's dramas and travel memoir *The Arans Islands* (1907) are sometimes knocked for 'stagey' renderings of the islanders' manner of speaking English (or for Synge's attempts to render the force of their Gaelic), and are one of the bitter targets of Martin McDonagh's 1997 play *The Cripple of Inishmaan* ('Inishmaan' the Anglicization of *Inis Méain/Meadhóin*, the 'middle island'):

> "I have seen Frenchmen, and Danes, and Germans," said one man, "and there does be a power of Irish books along with them, and they reading them better than ourselves. Believe me there are few rich men now in the world who are not studying the Gaelic" (Synge 1911/1998, 11)
>
> "Bedad," he said, "this is the greatest wonder ever I seen." (73)
> "And is there any great wonder in the world at this time?" (73)

Synge's recording of the old man's observation that "there are few rich men in the world who are not studying the Gaelic" recalls the European scholars who had come to Aran and the mainland to study Irish, such as the German Kuno Meyer (1858–1919) and the Dane Holger Pedersen (1867–1953), in preparation of studies of Old Irish and comparative Celtic and Indo-European grammar. These men in their suits, with their books, would, like Synge, have seemed rich to the islanders – this before Irish government policies of resettling islanders on the mainland or electrifying the islands, policies that, ironically, further hurt traditional Irish-speaking reserves (the 'evacuation' of the Blasket Islands off the coast of Co. Kerry in 1953 reduced an Irish-speaking treasury, the home of the traditional storyteller Tomás Ó Criomthain [1856–1937], and the place of Peig Sayers's memoirs of her youth *Machtnamh Seana Mhná* [*Reflections of an Old Woman* (1962)]). The use of the periphrastic *do* and invariant or nonstandard *be* forms are characteristic of Irish English, as is the expression 'a power of X' ('there be a power of wonders in it,' i.e., 'a lot,' an expression in decline but still heard in rural Ireland). *Bedad* is first attested by the OED in the letters of Jonathan Swift in 1710, and was common and typical enough to appear in Thackeray's *Vanity Fair* (1848; in the mouth of Major O'Dowd's wife Peggy; Thackeray let the Irish have it in fuller force in *The Luck of Barry Lyndon* [1844]); it is a contraction of *by dad* (with smoothing the diphthong in *by* [baɪ] to /ɛ/ or /ɪ/) as standing for, like *begad*, 'by God.' As such, it is either a euphemistic form (Share 1997, 17) or a taboo deformation by which an oath becomes an asseverative (like Irish English *begob* and *begorrah*, or the reduplicative and stagey *begosh and begorrah*, all of which stand in for 'by God'). The formulation 'And is there any great wonder' is typical, and likely mirrors Irish *agus an bhfuil* ('and' + interrogative particle + 'be'). Seen already are the Irish English verbal constructions *There be/bees*, *Is it X you're after* ('Is it tea [teɪ] you're after?'), or *There is to me X* (= 'I have/am X'). The last example has persisted in Irish English, and is one of the constructions influenced by Irish *tá mise* ('[there is to me'); e.g., *tá mise tinn*, 'there is to me sickness/soreness' = 'I am sick'). Perhaps the *reductio ad absurdum* of Irish English 'stagery' is James Joyce's *Finnegans Wake* (1939), the great harbinger of the postmodern novel (if not the thing itself), a pretentious puzzle of macaronic linguistic obscurantism. And yet much of the novel is more easily understood if read in a Syngean Gaeltacht Hiberno-English, Dublin jackeen-speak, or broad Ulster accent: 'Naw, yer maggers, aw war jist a cotchin on thon bluggy earwuggers' (*earwuggers* = Irish English *earwiggers*, 'eavesdroppers, meddlers'; Joyce 1939/1976, 31). Though Joyce had spoken of his exile from Ireland as one of his weapons, as the cliché goes he wrote of nothing but Dublin and Ireland. The short stories in *Dubliners* (1914) range across the Insular world of Christian Brothers schools to the intellectual putdown Molly Ivors delivers to Gabriel Conroy in 'The Dead': *West Briton*. The idea behind the term is, at one level, jocular, that the furthest Britons are found out west, not in the West Country or Wales even, but across the Irish Sea in 'John Bull's Other Island'; at this level, it can seem a 'bit of blarney,' a piece of characteristic Irish bluster and exaggeration, self-satirical. At a more serious political and intellectual level, it directs criticism at a perceived shame at Irish ways and a desire to 'ape' British ways – the sort of 'Ta now!' language of Ascendancy Trinity College, Dublin (to be contrasted with the Catholic 'National' university, University College Dublin).

Many of the British/Protestant – Irish/Catholic distinctions are said to have been muted in the modern Republic; the North is another matter altogether. But at the level of language, one sees a marked difference between the Irish English of Irish writers and the British English of the Anglo-Irish gentry: *Me & Nu: Childhood at Coole* (1970), the memoir by Lady Gregory's granddaughter Anne (de Winton), is entirely free of such 'Irishisms,' and those that appear in the 'Big House' novels of Mary Nesta Skrine (Molly Keane) are stagey. Keane's novels were hailed for their satiric wit and observations of the life – and language – of the 'Big House' Anglo-Irish. What is remarkable, at least in the south (within The Pale) is the preservation of near-RP forms:

> Mummie said: "My dear child – what *can* this mean?"
> "Only Hubert's been sick in his bed and he has a dreadful pain. I'm frightened."
> "And Mrs. Brock?" she asked.
> "She's at choir practice."
> "What a good word for it," Papa said.
> "Everybody's out. There's a dance in the gate lodge. Oh, do come quickly, he may be dead now."
> "Extraordinary, people are," she said (Keane 1981, 16).

The question arises of how Anglo-Irish speechways could remain so distinct from the speech of the majority of Irish people, and some of the likely explanations have been seen before in the history of the English language. A smaller class of people in the ruling position (or, as it was called in colonial Ireland, 'the [Protestant] Ascendancy') can naturally enough in less democratic systems become isolated from 'the masses'; they can also self-isolate, marrying within the group to preserve land and title, and affiliating with others of the group only in pursuance of that goal and to preserve their culture, which can often entail, bluntly speaking, a sense of superiority (as much could be said of the Anglo-Norman aristocracy in England post-Conquest). Language becomes a marker of belonging and not-belonging, indicating the language of peers and, in the 'Big House' tradition, that of the servants and peasants.

The title of P.W. Joyce's survey of 19th- to early 20th-century Irish English, *English As We Speak It in Ireland* (Joyce 1979), nods in the direction of an important point about non-native Englishes that has since been borne out in the rise of 'World Englishes': that what could be called 'extramural' Englishes (i.e., those spoken outside of England) have been significantly shaped by the local speech communities and their particular L1 or heritage language. One might say, with some justification, that some Welsh, Scots, and Irish speakers of English speak it non-natively. This is a simple fact for the smaller, generally elderly communities of native Celtic speakers (a dwindling population at the close of the 20th and start of the 21st centuries); but it is true in an extended sense for those whose English is so markedly shaped by the legacy of their grandparents' native tongues. Varieties of even Dublin English, which developed within the crucible of The Pale (Leinster seeing the most significant language loss during British rule), are sometimes considered nearly unintelligible by speakers of what are considered more standard varieties. All the more so with rural varieties of Irish and especially Scots English (though the 'Wedgie' of Glasgow qualifies as an urban entrant). Even the Irish national broadcaster RTÉ (Raidió Telefís Éireann, a good example of a Hibernicization, here of English 'Radio [and] Television of Ireland') has subtitled rural Irish accents; a minor YouTube sensation was the interview by video reporter Seán Mac an tSithigh (McSheehy or Sheehy are common Anglicizations of the surname) of rural Mount Brandon, Co. Kerry, farmer Mikey Joe O'Shea.[12] Mac an tSithigh begins the report "Last Saturday Mikey Joe O'Shea brought his flock of Scotch sheep down from the mountain commonage ahead of lambing"; O'Shea then recounts the loss of sheep he believes to have occurred: "Well, there was forty-five sheep missing like" (*forty-five* showed characteristic Kerry Gaeltacht English features, with aspiration of the initial fricative and a trilled /r/: [fʱɔɹti fɑɪv][13]). Mikey Joe O'Shea's West Kerry accent is indeed difficult to decipher at points; West Kerry is a significant Irish-speaking region, the Dingle and Iveragh Peninsulas being Gaeltachtaí. The reporter Seán Mac an tSithigh is himself a native of Kerry, from Baile an Fheirtéaraigh (Ballyferriter).

The onomastics of modern Ireland, Scotland, and Wales are interesting in the fluctuation between more Anglicized and Celticized names. It was not uncommon for Gaeltachtaí Irish – from Donegal, Mayo, the Arans, Galway, or Kerry – to have Anglicized names if born before independence or to make the acquisition and use of English in the modernizing nation easier (it can also be a matter of personal choice, or religious or ethnic identity as with the Anglo-Irish). The famous seanchaí ('shanachie,' traditional storyteller) John Henry was born Seán Ó hInnérighe (Ó hEiniri after the spelling reform in 1945); he was one of the last monolingual Irish speakers. Fashion in naming trends can reflect attitudes of students toward learning compulsory Irish in schools in the Republic. Kate and Mary and Bridget and Agnes in one generation can be replaced by Éilís and Nuala and Saoirse and Maire in another; present trends are toward more Gaelic or Gaelicized names, some being revivals of rare Gaelic names. No longer limited to the Gaeltachtaí are the more formal traditions of Irish nomenclature, with *mac* and *Ó* before the surname for males, *Ní* for females; the use of Gaelic forms of names was once a telltale marker of writers employing the Irish language primarily or solely, though the association is not as certain given the popularity of Gaelic names in recent decades. Novelist Éilís Ní Dhuibhne (the name could be Anglicized as Elizabeth or Alice Deeney/Denny) writes in English and Irish; Irish-language poet Nuala Ní Dhomhnaill (Nuala/Fionnuala is a name from Irish mythology, the surname usually Anglicized O'Donnell) was born in Lancashire but moved to the Dingle Peninsula as a child. In Scotland overtly Gaelic names can be associated with Gaelic-speaking regions (the Western Isles, Lewis, Harris, North Uist, Benbecula, South Uist, Barra;

[12] The 'viral video' itself then provoked 'reactions' to it such that the 'best reactions' themselves become viral in social media. The original RTÉ report from its Twitter/X feed and reactions to it can be found, for instance, in Aoife Kelly, "'Oh For flock Sake, some Farmer's been fleeced' – Best reaction to RTE news story about Kerry farmers' missing sheep," *Independent.ie* 10 April 2017 (online).

[13] As mentioned in chapter 1, IPA practice has here been reversed for the alveolar liquid /r/ and alveolar trill ('trilled' /r/). Following OED practice, [r] has been employed for the usual initial *r* in English (as in *red* [rɛd]); the IPA uses the symbol /r/ for the trill, and /ɹ/ for the English alveolar liquid /r/. As the trill is absent in many varieties of English (exceptions, as here, are some varieties of Irish English, or of West African English), the 'regular' English *r* is transcribed as [r], and the rarer trill is transcribed as [ɹ]. The IPA was conceived of and designed by speakers of English (such as Henry Sweet), Danish (Otto Jespersen), and French (Paul Passy) for whom [r] would make more sense as representing the common initial *r* sound in their languages; but in seeking to be 'international' it sometimes made choices that make the transcription of English more difficult. A number of major American dictionaries of English and the ANAE project do not employ the IPA in their transcriptions.

Skye; Argyll Islands); the Gaelic place-names of the Western Isles and Highlands attest to how much more widely spoken Scots Gaelic once was. Wales has always been known by a relatively smaller set of native surnames: Jones and Evans are from 'John' (the former via Ioan, the latter from Ieuan/Ifan, 'John,' which with the patronymic ap/ab [< *mab*], in aphetic form, produced the surname Bevan); Davies (the usual association is with Dyfed/Dafydd, 'David'); Williams (the name is originally Germanic, popularized in Britain with the Conquest; Gwilym is the Welsh form, e.g., the famous 14th-century Welsh poet Dafydd ap Gwilym, David son of William, or David Williams); Thomas, Roberts, Lewis, Hughes, Morgan, and Griffiths round out the most popular family names. To encourage Welsh given names, the Welsh Government (Llywodraeth Cymru) even has a webpage of 'Welsh Names for Children/Enwau Cymraeg i Blant,' with popular forms for girls (Alys, Angharad [from 'Peredur fab Efrawg,' 'Peredur son of Efrawg,' in the *Mabinogion*], Carys, Ceri, Ffion, Gwen, Heledd, Rhian, Rhiannon, Siân, Sioned) and boys (Aled, Cai, Carwyn, Dafydd, Dylan [*Dylan eil ton (ail don)*, 'Dylan Second Wave' from the *Mabinogion*], Emyr, Gareth, Gruffudd, Ieuan, Owain, Rhodri, Rhys).[14] Scotland has always maintained certain given names that draw on Scots history, and among the popular Gaelicized names are Catrìona (Catherine), Curstaidh (Kirsty), Eilidh (Helen), Màiri (Mary), Sìne (Jane); Alasdair (Alexander), Aonghas (Angus), Calum (Columba, 6th-century Irish missionary saint to Scotland), Domhnall (Donald, MacDonald), Iain (John), Niall (Neil), Risteard (Richard), Ruairidh (Rory), and Seumas (James, Hamish). Interestingly, with a few exceptions (namely *Richard* from Germanic 'strong-king' < **rīk-* + **harduz*; cf. Ringe 2017, 123, 328), these names are overwhelmingly monothematic (having one naming element). The Scots surname Aitken is a fairly common one and, for some reason, borne by a number of footballers, as well as the linguist A.J. Aitken (1921–1998), who formulated the 'Scottish Vowel-Length Rule' or Aitken's Law. The surname is actually derived from a hypocorism (pet-name form) on *Adam* (*Ad* + diminutive suffix *-kin*), with Early Scots /a:/ undergoing diphthongization during the Great Vowel Shift. The operation of Aitken's Law, by which a number of vowels in Scots and Scottish English are long by environment (as before /r/, voiced fricatives /v/, /ð/, /z/, /ʒ/, or a word-final open syllable or morpheme boundary [e.g., end of the first element of a compound formation]), was seen earlier in the development of Early Scots and the complexities of the Great Vowel Shift in Scotland. The vowel length shift has marked the Northern, Central, and Southern accents of Scotland (and to an extent Geordie also).

8.5 CONVERGENCE AND DIVERGENCE: MODERN DIALECTOLOGY, METHODS AND RESOURCES

Mentioned earlier in this chapter was the split in dialectology between urban and rural dialects. This is in some way a natural disciplinary division of labor: the study of rural,

[14] https://llyw.cymru/cymraeg-i-blant/enwau-cymraeg-i-blant. These are of course suggestions; the Icelandic government goes further with their *Mannanafnanefnd*, literally 'people-names-committee,' which regulates that children's names maintain Icelandic tradition and rules on admission of new names.

more 'conservative' dialects was often seen as an aid to the earlier pronunciation of English, and its evidence is used in that manner: as an aid to reconstructing, in part, in addition to the tools of historical linguistics, the sounds of Old and Middle English. The preservation, and perseveration, of archaic features in rural dialects has been of great help to diachronic approaches to the history of English. Joseph Wright's *English Dialect Dictionary* (EDD; 6 vols., 1898–1905) is one of the great repositories of 'folk' and 'common' British speech; it looks back over the centuries of English in the speech of people whose lives remained fairly close to the villages, hamlets, and farms of their ancestors, and to the foods, customs, tasks, and – especially, and most engagingly – humor of British folkways. Wright was born in Bradford, West Riding, Yorkshire, in 1855, the son of a weaver (like his father, Wright found work at a very young age in a quarry). The family moved to Middleborough, North Yorkshire, where Wright attended a factory school, though Wright was also an assiduous autodidact. At 21, his implausible but dogged pursuit of education saw him finance the first of two stints at the University of Heidelberg; during the second stint there, he studied under the Indo-Europeanist Hermann Osthoff. Oxford Professor of Comparative Philology F. Max Müller, renowned as a Sanskritist, found work for Wright at Oxford (and Wright would later succeed Müller in the Comparative Philology chair). Two of Wright's great passions were the earlier Germanic languages (his *Grammar of the Gothic Language* is still in print) and local dialects (he began, naturally enough, with the study of his native Yorkshire). Wright had, along the way, worked as a bobbin doffer at the mill in Saltaire (Yorks.); and, sure enough, *bobbin* appears in the EDD: 'A wooden tube or cylinder upon which yarn is wound in weaving and spinning.' It is in the attestations collected for the EDD that the folk dialects come alive; the first for *bobbin* is from Lancashire: *He'd ha' done mooar wark wi' a bobbin-gun* ['a toy gun made out of a weaver's wooden bobbin'] *nur* [nor] *they'd ha' done wi' a sixty-eight peawndhur* [sixty-eight pounder cannon]. Wright's phonetic renderings of regional British speech are as entertaining as they are important: he was working at recording speech at a time when the International Phonetic Alphabet was just being introduced. Among those working on the alphabet was Henry Sweet, whose particular interest was Old English, though his first academic position was as Reader in Phonetics at Oxford (he was also a longtime President of the International Phonetic Association and an inspiration for George Bernard Shaw's Professor Henry Higgins). One of the sponsors of the publication of the EDD was another Anglo-Saxonist, the Rev. W.W. Skeat, the first Elrington and Bosworth Professor of Anglo-Saxon at Cambridge. Wright's system is an approximation of the IPA system, and he tended to add glosses to his phonetic renderings not so much because of the limitations of his transcriptions as the nature of his informants' speech. For the slang term *bobby-dazzler* ('Anything striking or excellent of its kind; a fine, handsome woman'), he included, from a Staffordshire informant, *You mun kum ən sei ar nəu os; its ə reglər bobi-dazlər* ('You must come and see our new house, it's a regular bobby-dazzler'). But there were two Wrights working on the EDD – Joseph's wife Elizabeth Mary Wright (née Lea; 1863–1958), who had attended Wright's lectures on Old English (Elizabeth was a student at Lady Margaret Hall and Wright was lecturing through the AEW, the Association for the Education of Women). Elizabeth published a number of articles on Old and Middle English literature and assembled much of the EDD's raw data. Her interests in dialects and folklore of Britain came together in her 1918 book

Rustic Speech and Folk-Lore. And there one can see her interests in the Northumbrian dialect of Old English and its Yorkshire and other northern descendants; in her Northumberland sample *gan through the yet, and swin the field wi' the beass in't,* 'go through the gate and traverse diagonally the field with the cattle in it,' one can see OE *ġeat* [jeət] 'gate' behind *yet.* And a form *heeaf-hod* recorded from North Yorkshire clearly derives from OE *hēafod* 'head.' The 6 volumes of the EDD are a treasury of English folk speech and tradition and northern studies, and the partnership of the Wrights in producing the work helped illuminate the legacy of Old English at a time when academic study of the earliest English was being more formally established at British universities (in competition with the German state-funded system).

One descendant of the EDD is the *Dictionary of American Regional English.* Also in 6 volumes (1985–2013), the massive project began under the auspices of the American Dialect Society; the ADS was founded in 1889, and desired for American English an equivalent to the Wrights's EDD. Fieldwork was conducted from 1965 to 1970 with 82 researchers visiting 1002 communities, interviewing a total of 2777 informants. This data was augmented, as with the OED, by a reading program of print sources. The informants were recruited by the field workers and tended toward older generations (the project at the time classified 60+ as 'old'; DARE, vol. 1, 'List of Informants,' lxxxvi-cli), and from 'rural' or 'village' habitation. The questionnaire assembled a total of 1877 questions under the usual semantic headings: time, weather, topography, etc. (DARE, vol. 1, lxii–lxxxv), though, given the generational and community types, with an emphasis on terms more likely to elicit vocabulary tokens from more rural life (thus categories for domestic animals, farm animals, farming, farm buildings, as well as 'fishing, hunting, wildlife' and 'wildflowers, weeds'). While the citations and attestations may not include as colorful dialect speech as the EDD, the DARE project shows the advances made in the century since the EDD was conceived. The dictionary includes also over 1,700 dot maps of the United States plotted according to population density (there is a location map at vol. 1, xxxi, that serves as a sort of master map): thus New York has an elongated Hudson Valley leading eastward to an exaggerated metro area of the Five Boroughs; a number of Mountain West states, more lightly populated, appear as thin slivers. The volumes began under the general editorship of Frederic G. Cassidy, known also for his work with Jamaican Creole and Old English, and then proceeded to conclusion under Joan Houston Hall (who had been associate editor). There are some 60,000 headwords, which is a remarkable number for a lexicon of regional English, that is, of variant or nonstandard terms. A good many terms are slang or 'folksy' regionalisms. Slang proper (here in the sense of cruder terms rather than the 'folksy') was addressed in the *Random House Historical Dictionary of American Slang,* which remains incomplete at two volumes (A-G [1994], H-O [1997]); though Oxford University Press was reported to have taken up the project, no further volumes have appeared. The sixth volume of DARE, at over 1000 pages, offers the raw data of responses to the questionnaire, maps of lexical isoglosses from the responses (e.g., the distribution of *frosting* [northern tier states and CA] vs. *icing* [Mid-Atlantic, Midlands, South] for what is placed on cakes and cupcakes), and a listing of the dialectal regions, with maps, DARE helped refine (including such subdivisions as Delmarva [DE, MD, VA] in the Mid-Atlantic, and the Desert Southwest [this is useful for such topographical terms as *arroyo* and *bajada*]).

The index by 'Region, Usage, and Etymology' allows one to find entries by source language, as with Canadian French (missing is *poutine*) or Louisiana French, or region (e.g., New England, at 493–502). As with the OED, attestations are supplied in chronological order; thus the term *belly wash* (or *belly washer*) for 'soft drink' first appears in 1900 in college slang, then in 1931 in 'Loggers' argot' (s.v., *belly wash*); though the term can also apply to any diluted or weak drink (as of coffee or alcohol), contemporary use seems to bear out the soft drink sense, especially as an accompaniment to a snack or meal.

The DARE project offers much more than a lexical-based dialect atlas; its focus upon folkways – foodways, music, children's games, pastimes – and regional vocabulary (everything from describing the weather to nuisance insects to social gatherings) serves as a cultural atlas, a register of the *community* part of 'speech community.' The prefatory matter to the *Dictionary of Southern Appalachian English* (Montgomery and Heinmiller 2021) takes that approach one step further with profiles of the informants themselves and historical photographs of 'Appalachian folk' (xiv–xxviii). Much of the informant material for the DSAE comes from interviews conducted by Joseph Sargent Hall (1906–1992), who had been hired by the US National Park Service to record the speech and folkways of people of the Great Smoky Mountains. As with the DARE project, DSAE conducted extensive readings of earlier print sources (these sources, in the range 1774–2018, are helpfully given in a "Chronological List of Works Cited with Abbreviated Titles," 1139–1186). The list of speakers (xxxvi–xlii) has one column of information that is quite telling – 'Education.' There are some college graduates among the interviewees, but one sees with greater frequency figures such as '2–3 years,' '3–4 years,' 'some grade school,' and 'prob<ably> illiterate.' Mountain speech has often been ridiculed as ignorant – and racist; many, but not all, of its speakers are white, many quite impoverished; much of it involves folk wisdom, prognostications, wry humor. Some of it is quite straightforward, blunt (like Huck Finn's language); *big* as a verb can mean 'impregnate,' as in *he bigged her* (heard by the author in the Ozarks in the early 2000s). Other terms conjure up pastimes and traditions now fading away or known only in the region; *Belsnickle* is 'A person in masquerade who goes from house to house at the Christmas season sometimes to play pranks, beg for treats, but especially to query the good behavior of children and make them behave' (from the German, the attestations are from WV, PA Appalachians, the Shenandoahs). Of great utility, in a work otherwise preoccupied with lexical data, is the "Grammar and Syntax of Southern Appalachian and Smoky Mountain English" (xliii–lxvi). Many of the features described are well known: *a*- prefixing (*slipping and a-falling and a-pitching*; lvi), use of objective case of pronoun for nominative/subject (*My daughter and me went over there*; xliv), alternative pronoun forms (*you'un, you'uns, we'uns, y'all*; xlv), *yon* and *yonder* as demonstrative adjectives (*on yon side of Cumberland Gap*; *yonder way right there*; xlvi), alternative strong verb forms, some of which might be seen as retentions of earlier forms or unlevelled variants (*arrive: arrove, catch: cotch/cotched, creep: crope, drive: driv: druv, give: gin: gin, rake: roke/ruck, shine: shun, swell: swole*; l–lii), and anomalous or ungrammatical/alternate forms of the verb *to be* (*They's about six or seven guitar players here*; liii), and double modals (*If you give me thirty minutes, I mighta coulda thought of some names*; lv). Appalachian English also has a variety of alternate forms of negation: *I hain't seen nothing of him*; *Hit didn't scare me nary a speck nor a spark*; *We ain't starvin' none*; *I never did go hardly any* (lvii). Adverbs and adverbials can be formed with *-s* affixation: *long time beforehands*; *everywheres up there*; *put it somewheres else*; *Well if you was anyways near to a bear, he could charge you*; lviii–lix). Redundant formations are also common: *worser* (double comparative); *drounded* (pleonastic past marker; this form is used by Huck Finn in Twain's novel 1885) – Appalachian and Ozark mountain speech share a great many features grammatically, a legacy in part of settlement patterns east to west; *folkses* (double nominal plural); *firstest, bestest* (double superlatives); *speechify, argufy* (redundant *-ify* suffix to denominal verbs; lxiii–lxiv); the conjunction *iffen*. In his poem cycle "Elegy for the Southern Drawl," Rodney Jones (native to Northern Alabama) records some of these very forms:

> The old people in the valley where I was born
> Still hold to the brogue, elisions, and coloratura
> Of the Scotch-Irish, and brandished
> Like guns the *iffens*, *you'ns*, and *narys*
> That linked by the labyrinthine hollers
> Of the foothills of the Appalachian Mountains
> The remnants of a people whose dominion
> Obtained no less from unerring marksmanship
> Than their spiritual resolve never to learn
> Any tongue as remote as Greek or Latin,
> Much less the Cherokee or Sequoya
> That still haunted, like mist, the names of rivers (Jones 1999, 48).

An early attestation of the use of the pronoun *one* correlatively raises an interesting matter with the study of regional dialects; in a letter of William T. Martin, of Pickens County, SC, dated 31 October 1861 occurs the passage: *I don't thank* [think] *that thear will be Mtch mrry untill times changes far the beter orr wors one* (Martin's letters are part of the collection at the Stuart A. Rose Manuscript, Archives, and Rare Book Library, Emory University, Atlanta, GA). This is not a case of a fieldworker recording an informant's speech in rough phonetic form, but the written form, rough and ungrammatical as it may be, of the writer's spoken dialect of English. Assumptions about levels of general literacy are a modern concern: in general, the further back in time, the rarer it is. Many of us can find letters of forbears written in rough, ungrammatical, even semi-literate form, or possess documents in which a previous generation of relatives simply signed with an 'X' to which the literate registrar affixed the notation 'his/her mark.' What one has here is rather more the 'common' or 'folk' rather than 'cultivated' speech of earlier times, as recorded by writers who may have had relatively little formal education. A study by Edgar Schneider and Michael Montgomery (editor of the DSAE) of Antebellum Southern working-class white speech from the Southern Plantation Overseers Corpus, consisting of letters written between 1794 and 1876, offers examples of this less 'cultivated' speech: *the potatos also is not as good*; *the two last weeks has bin the bissiest time*; *tha have de Stroied thirty or forty barrels*; *So tha say I will Let yo no* (Schneider and Montgomery 2001, 399). These letters offer also an interesting look at the social and caste stratification of the system of slavery in the Antebellum period; like the Cely and Paston letters for British English, they offer evidence of 'everyday English' of the past – or as close to it as we can get in the diachronic study of dialects.

On the other hand, synchronic variation is easier to study in populations that undergo the sorts of changes one sees in urban centers: the formation and re-formation of enclaves; movement away from first-generation immigrant neighborhoods by second- and third-generation children and grandchildren of immigrants; the availability of white-collar professions and ensuing upward mobility (and overall greater wealth in the big cities); high-density and multiplex networks that entail more frequent verbal and social interaction on a daily basis; higher-density population over shorter distances allowing innovations to spread more quickly. That said, the urban environment, which held out the promise of greater opportunities for work and wealth, has proven no less riven by social stratification than the rural. This was one of the findings of William Labov's landmark study *The Social Stratification of English in New York City* (1966, 2nd ed. 2006). Besides the famous department store study ("The social stratification of (r) in New York City department stores"; Labov 2006, 40–57), the book set out a number of principles for the emerging field of sociolinguistics (or, "The study of language in its social context"; Labov 2006, 3–17). Labov is essentially the 'godfather' of sociolinguistics in the United States, though he had credited the inspiration and work of Uriel Weinreich, his thesis advisor at Columbia University. Weinreich, born in Vilnius, Lithuania, was, like his father Max, a linguist specializing in Yiddish and language contact; he passed away at a young age (40), having just completed his *Modern English-Yiddish, Yiddish-Modern English Dictionary* (1968; Weinreich 2012), still a standard reference work. As a Creole, Yiddish has proven a fertile ground for language contact study, all the more so as many of its speakers moved to the United States, particularly East Coast cities such as New York and Philadelphia. Labov had begun his early sociolinguistic and dialectal work in New York City (but also in Martha's Vineyard), and began a long-range study of Philadelphia's regional dialect upon moving to the University of Pennsylvania. That university had an early prominent role in the development of linguistics, as Noam Chomsky, under the influence of Penn linguists such as Zellig Harris (whose work spanned structural to generative linguistics), obtained his B.A. and M.A. there with a thesis on *Morphophonemics of Modern Hebrew* (1951; Chomsky 2011). While Chomsky's ever-shifting program of increasingly abstract approaches to language, informed more by logic and mathematics, moved in a direction that anticipated some of the interests of computer science, the work of Labov and other sociolinguists looked rather more to the social sciences.

Labov's major 3-volume *Principles of Linguistic Change* considers linguistic variation in terms of *Internal Factors* (Labov 1994), *Social Factors* (2001), and *Cognitive and Cultural Factors* (2010; the three volumes are dedicated to Weinreich). The *Internal Factors* volume can now be seen as preparatory to *The Atlas of North American English* (Labov 2006), especially its concentration on chain shifts, and general principles for such (115–121; there is also a lengthy discussion of proposed models of the Great Vowel Shift, 145–154). Labov's long-term Philadelphia studies were highly detailed; a contrastive study was made on King of Prussia, a working- to middle-class suburb of Philadelphia that sits as the western terminus of the Schuylkill Expressway.

The tensing of /æ/ among young speakers was analyzed in both locations, downtown and outside, with the result that tensing of /æ/ was most frequent in *planet* (among a sample set of *Sally, Allen, alligator, planet, Janet, animals, hammer, camera, giraffe*; Labov 1994, 436–437). Tensing was found to be much more common with *planet* than *hammer* or *giraffe*. But things of course change: the present author is native to the area and can attest that not only is *hammer* tensed among younger speakers as highly as *planet*, but likely even more so (with what might be an overlong /æ:/ – *haaaaaaaammer*). And this pronunciation can be found through the greater western and northern suburban regions – out toward King of Prussia along the Schuylkill (from the Dutch, but locally pronounced [sku:kʌl], 'skoo-kul'), then further west-southwestward along Route 202, and west-northwestward along Route 422 to Phoenixville and Collegeville (i.e., along routes of high-density suburban development since World War II for the inner suburbs, the 1980s for the exurbs). Volume 2 of Labov's *Principles, Social Factors* (Labov 2001), presents many of the fundamental sociolinguistic concepts regarding the *speech community*, especially in Part B (147–322) 'Social Class, Gender, Neighborhood, and Ethnicity.' Once again, much of the specific data employed is from his longitudinal neighborhood studies of Philadelphia, and his concept of 'leadership' in the neighborhood and 'socioeconomic hierarchy'; his Section 10.6, "Who leads the leaders?" (363–365), points to "interpersonal sources as well as mass media" (363), to which one would now naturally (and inevitably) add social media. Volume 3 of *Principles, Cognitive and Cultural Factors* (Labov 2010), investigates the 'why' of sound change, the "Driving Forces" (Chapter 9), and models and patterns of diffusion of change (chapters 15–16). That the ANAE should have a more urban-centered focus seemed predestined by the 1966 study on social stratification of English in NYC: that one of the great factors for transmission and diffusion of sound change (and presumably also its generation) is the density of the city environment: "that people who talk to each other the most tend to resemble each other in their forms of speech" (Labov 2006, 403).

The major dialect atlas projects for American English are profiled at the Linguistic Atlas Project website at the University of Georgia (https://www.lap.uga.edu/) and a sister site at the University of Kentucky (https://linguisticatlasproject.org/); where available, data sets are to be found at the Georgia site's Data Download Center (as is always the case with online projects, not all of the links work, and the sets can be quite cumbersome to read). Coverage of the United States ranges from early projects in New England (*Linguistic Atlas of New England*, LANE), the Atlantic coastal region from New York to northeastern counties of Florida (*Linguistic Atlas of the Middle and South Atlantic States*, LAMSAS), data from Lorenzo Dow Turner's pioneering work with Gullah speakers on the Sea Islands (SC and GA; Turner 1949), to early data collected by Claude M. Wise on Hawaiian English and Pidgin while at the University of Hawaii 1949–1950 (hosted on the Kentucky website). The Hawaii data includes 830 scans of notes with IPA transcription of informant responses on terms and expressions for weather, dwellings, animals, flora, and so forth. Under the rubric 'Religion and superstition,' one finds Hawaiian loans such as *akua* 'god, spirit,' *kepalo(a)* 'evil spirit, ghost.' The *Linguistic Atlas of North-Central States* involved data collected 1933–1978 from OH, KY, IN, IL, MI, WI, a broad section of the 'Midlands,' and, interestingly, data also from Southern Ontario; the *Linguistic Atlas of the Gulf States* presented data from 914 informants collected 1968–1983 in a region (TN, GA, FL, AL, MS, LA, AR, TX) with abundant language contact (Spanish from the Gulf shores into TX, French of course in Louisiana but throughout the region to East Texas; on this project and Lee Pederson's work see Montgomery and Nunnally 1998); the *Linguistic Atlas of the Upper Midwest* collected data 1949–1962 from 208 informant interviews and also by mailed-in worksheets; the single-state *Linguistic Atlas of Oklahoma* collected data in two sets, 1959–1963 and 1980–1984 – Oklahoma is a sort of 'keystone' state dialectally, situated between the South, Midlands, and West and with a significant original Native American population expanded by government resettlement programs to the 'Indian Territory' as well as new migrations from the state's oil and natural gas booms. The *Linguistic Atlas of the Western States* (begun in 1988 under Lee Pederson as the *Linguistic Atlas of the Rocky Mountain States*) is an ongoing project with completed interviews from Colorado, Utah, and Wyoming, but also data from California to El Paso, TX – in the far west of Texas the border city forms a metroplex with Ciudad Juárez, Chihuahua, which has its own distinctive *norteño* dialect of Mexican Spanish, and in terms of English dialects fits in with West Texas and Mountain New Mexico. The *Linguistic Atlas of the Pacific Coast* and *Linguistic Atlas of the Pacific Northwest*, covering California and Nevada and Washington, Oregon, and Idaho, respectively, are somewhat smaller projects covering what is usually considered the least studied dialect region of the United States (The West). There are a number of reasons for this, from institutional funding to cultural identity (the South is fairly extensively documented, in part, due to a strong regional identity bound up in history), as well as settlement patterns and time depth: English came to the West later, and the rapid growth in population in an otherwise lightly settled region came, for California, with World War II, and in the Northwest with more recent tech booms and Asian immigration (in the case of Seattle, and, on the Canadian side, Vancouver and Victoria). But the gap has been partially filled by three volumes on *Speech in the Western States* in the PADS (Publications of the American Dialect Society) series of the American Dialect Society, to whose organ of publication, *American Speech* the volumes serve as supplement. The three volumes cover *The Coastal States* (vol. 1; PADS 101; Fridland et al. 2016), *The Mountain West* (vol. 2; PADS 102; Fridland and Wassink 2017), and *Understudied Varieties* (vol. 3; PADS 105; Fridland et al. 2020); the third volume of 'understudied varieties' covers an interesting range of Native American (the Yakama of Washington state) and Native and white speech (in Nevada), AAVE (Black speakers in Bakersfield, CA), Nisei-generation Japanese English in Merced County, CA, the English of Mormons in Southwest Washington, and the vowels of the broader Anchorage, AK, region. In the *Coastal States* volume only one study touches upon that most elusive of dialects, Southern California (Dan Villareal's "'Do I Sound Like a Valley Girl to You?' Perceptual Dialectology and Language Attitudes in California," Fridland et al. 2016, 55–75). SoCal raising has been productive of new diphthongs, including rising diphthongs; as pervasive as the dialect is in popular media, systematic study of it remains a *desideratum*.

There is fairly strong consistency in method among the American English dialect atlas projects, as well as continuity with the types of forms and questionnaires used in

Britain with the *Survey of English Dialects*. These original notes are being digitized on both sides of the Atlantic, which greatly aids in visualizing the overall interviews conducted (one sees the results for an individual person, rather than a linguistic token). The *Dialect and Heritage Project*, based at the University of Leeds (and supported by the National Lottery Heritage Fund), offers samples from the University Library collection of SED materials, such as notes and photographs; highlighted is informant James 'Jimmy' Marsden of Thropton, Northumberland, interviewed 28 January 1953. Marsden was the village tailor, a veteran of World War I, and a breeder of dogs and ferrets (he is pictured on the website with some of his ferrets); among the forms recorded from his Northumberland speech are [kle:z] *clothes*, [se:ks] *six*, [stjupɪd] *stupid* (with glide insertion), and [jə na:] *you know*.[15]

The LAMSAS project conducted dialect interviews over the period 1933–1972 with 1162 informants (by 9 field workers); the bulk of the interviews were conducted in the years 1936–1941(688), and the vast majority were made by two linguists: Guy Lowman (826; the principal field worker, he was only 32 when he died in a car accident) and Raven McDavid (278). LAMSAS follows LANE fairly closely in its methodology, as University of Chicago linguist Raven McDavid, Jr. (1911–1984) was involved in much of the work that gave rise to the individual projects (including Kurath and McDavid 1961; Kurath was the director of LANE). The *Handbook* to LAMSAS (Kretzschmar et al. 1993) provides introductory chapters on the choice of informants (chapters 2–3, 5–57) in the atlas's northern (NY, NJ, PA), central (WV, DE, MD, DC, VA, NC), and southern zones (SC, GA, and northern Atlantic counties of FL). The 787 worksheet items are grouped by semantic field (geography, topography, numerals, time, etc.; 102–112); sections on dialect areas and settlement patterns (147–164) are followed by a long, richly detailed last chapter – that occupies more than half the volume – on "Community Sketches and Informant Biographies" (165–454) that serves as a salutary reminder that in the end dialects are about people, their speech communities, and where they live. On that note, the *Handbook* details classification of types of speech that might make some postmodern readers uncomfortable, though it is of a longstanding tradition in dialectology: that is, classification of speakers as: *Folk speakers*, those of the oldest generation whose speech is "subject to a minimum of education and other outside influence"; *Common speakers*, whose speech is "subject to a moderate amount of education (generally high school), private reading, and other external contacts"; and *Cultivated speakers*, "representing wide reading and elevated local cultural traditions, generally but not always with higher education" (Kretzschmar et al. 1993, 11). Frequent reference is made in handbooks of BrE dialectology to 'cultivated' and 'common' distinctions. As detailed a guide as the *Handbook* is, the mass of data in the individual fascicles can still be overwhelming – see, for instance, the varying pronunciation of the geographical token *New England* in fascicle 1 (McDavid and O'Cain 1980, 69–80): the variation from an essentially standard [nu ɪŋglənd] is remarkable, from forms that insert a glide in *New* [nju] to those where the /d/ in *England* is weakly articulated or lost. In Fascicle 2 one finds variation in the pronunciation of the initial

[15] https://dialectandheritage.org.uk/about/the-survey-of-english-dialects/#1

consonant in *Virginia*, with the devoiced pronunciation (/v/ > /f/) occurring much more frequently in the Carolinas (McDavid and O'Cain 1980, 125–132). These dialect projects produce large datasets, and as fieldwork progressed from pencil and notebooks to wax discs to reel-to-reel, then cassette tapes for field recordings, surveys sent out and returned by post progressed to telephone interviews (such as the TELSUR of the ANAE). And now there are smartphones, and fieldwork is often not in the field any longer.

Large datasets are the raw materials for corpus linguistics, and though a number of dialectologists are aware of the dangers of stripping phonological and lexical data of spoken context (whether that be for an hour, or over days, weeks, months, or longer), postmodern linguists seem bound to their tech, to which the First Law of Computing applies: garbage in, garbage out. Surprising to nonspecialists is how relatively few informants are contacted: the Labov-directed *Atlas of North American English* is the largest project of its kind, attempting to survey every significant urban area of the United States with 50,000 or more inhabitants. The plan was that such a method would encompass the speech patterns of 68% of the US population during the survey period (1992–1999, with some interviews conducted until 2001). Each city with a population of at least 1 million would have at least four informants contacted, in cities in the ranges 200,000 upward to 1 million (divided between those with metro area larger or less than 5,000 square miles) and below 200,000 at least 2 informants would be interviewed (Labov, Ash, Boberg et al. 2018, 9, 21–22). Some 145 urban concentrations were deemed 'central' cities (Appendix 4.1, 30–31). In all, the project selected 762 informants, and the results from 439 of the 762 "TELSUR speakers" were subjected to acoustic analysis (9, 36–40). Two major alterations to traditional dialect atlases of AmE were made by the ANAE project: the new nationwide atlas overwhelmingly sampled the urban over the rural, and the phonological over the lexical (the ANAE's subtitle is *Phonetics, Phonology and Sound Change*; the atlas, rather maddeningly, does not use IPA transcriptions and employs *upgliding* and *ingliding vowels* to describe rising and falling diphthongs) – there is a nod toward lexical and grammatical variation with tried-and-true isoglosses such as terms for carbonated beverage (*soda*, *soda pop*, *pop*, *tonic*, *cool drink*, *Coke* as a generic, etc.), the vowel in *roof* ([ruf] vs. [rʌf]), positive use of *anymore*, construction of *needs* + past participle (*floor needs swept*, etc.; 289–296). This very brief treatment of the sort of variation that was a mainstay of earlier atlases and projects like DARE and RHHDAS seems intended to serve mainly as an overlay corroborating the dot maps for phonological features (and there is good concord between them). The number of TELSUR informants is surprisingly low for a national population that was 282 million in 2000, 335 million at a minimum in 2024 (not counting those born abroad and in the United States documented or undocumented; the Yale-MIT study reached a figure as high as 22 million for those in the United States undocumented as of 2016: Fazel-Zarandi, Feinstein, Kaplan 2018; the actual figure is certainly even higher, perhaps as high as 30 million or more). Many of the great regional atlas projects described above began in the 1930s, and so are 'historical,' providing a snapshot of the language at that time, and surviving among elderly speakers. One criticism of earlier atlases, which applies also to the ANAE, is the skewing of informant sampling toward primarily white ethnicities or national origins; the Mid-Atlantic section of LAMSAS did not originally sample Black speakers, and ANAE had only 45 African American informants (out of the 762 overall), and 13 who identified as Hispanic.[16] This is a significant omission in an atlas that is primarily urban-centered, though the interviews date to the 1990s and recruited informants on their 'representativeness' in the local speech community. On the other hand, the shift to an urban focus corrected an oversight in the earlier regional atlases that focused overwhelmingly on English and Ulster Scots Protestants: in the ANAE German Americans were most heavily sampled (according to their proportion of the population in the Midland, North, South, and West groupings; 23–24); Italian Americans were the largest group sampled in the Mid-Atlantic group (surprisingly, the Irish were sampled at a low rate in the Mid-Atlantic region though they outnumber Italians).

But there is nothing quite like the *Linguistic Atlas of North American English*. The project corroborates many of the findings of earlier dialect atlases of AmE and plots out sound changes *in-process*, with a strong emphasis upon mergers and splits: the Northern Cities Shift, low back vowel merger (see now also Becker 2019); vowels before /r/ and /l/ and before intervocalic /r/ – the *merry*, *Mary*, *marry* merger resulting in /e/ in all these forms that is complete in regions such as coastal California, and a great many of the sound changes tracked by the ANAE involve raising: the maps plot out the relative height of vowels such as the /ɪ/ in *bit*, /ɛ/ in *bet*, /ʌ/ in *but*, the diphthong /aɪ/ in *wide* (Chapter 10, Maps 10.1–27), as well as the relative fronting or backing of /oʊ/ in *boat*, corroborating earlier studies that the diphthong is being fronted in Midland and South, but fronting is resisted in a northern tier from Canada's Atlantic provinces across New York, upper Pennsylvania through to Michigan, the Chicago area, and Wisconsin (105, Map 10.28). Canada is oddly given short shrift (216–224), particularly the matter of French-English interaction in the Ottawa-Hull capital region, Québec, and the Atlantic Provinces: one can hear on the north side of Cape Breton Island, in towns such as Chéticamp, frequent code-switching between French and English – with significant raising of vowels before /r/ and further rounding of back vowels /ɔ/, /ʌ/, /ʊ/, and /u/ before /r/ or before intervocalic /r/: e.g., *sure* sounding more like [ʃœr]); or the English of the Maritimes, especially 'Newfie' and Labrador English (on Cape Breton English[17] see Clarke 2010; on Prince Edward Island English see Pratt 1996). A comparison may be made to Kurath and McDavid's *The Pronunciation of English in the Atlantic States* with its highly detailed studies of vowels – for example, their mapping of the pronunciation of /ʊ/ in *wool* [wʊl], which can vary between a nearly diphthongized /ʊᵊ/ (almost as *wuh-ull*) to variants of /u/ (Kurath and McDavid 1961, Map 6). At the time, Philadelphia fell within the range of use of the former

[16] African American English is a subject Labov has written about since the 1960s, in professional and popular format; see, for instance, "The Growing Divergence of Black and White English" and "The Politics of African American English" in Labov 2012, 38–97.

[17] The dialects of Cape Breton are roughly divided among the French-influenced north (western, that is, facing Les Îles-de-la-Madeleine and PEI), the Gaelic central (around Bras d'Or Lake) and Highlands regions, and the English Canadian urbanized zone of Sydney to Glace Bay (cf. Davey and MacKinnon 2016). The picture is, of course, more complicated than this, as evidenced by place-names: The Margarees, Dunvegan, Craigmore, Creignish, Ingonish, Skir Dhu, Beinn Scalpie, all of them of Gaelic origin (Cape Breton Gaelic is still spoken, mainly by older speakers but being revived by Colaisde na Gàidhlig/Gaelic College at St Anns).

(partially diphthongized) /ʊ/; but since at least the 1980s the pronunciation [wul], even [wu:l] is increasingly common (and perhaps class-marked, found among working-class and lower-middle-class speakers). And this is what one finds in the relevant maps in ANAE, that this raising of /ʊ/ is now associated with the Philadelphia area (Maps 10.13–14). It is not uncommon in that region – again it is a pronunciation that is class-marked (working to middle) – to hear *pool* for *pull*, *fool* for *full* (conversely, in a number of regions in Texas, one hears the opposite: *pool* lowered to *pull* – 'swimmin' pull').

The resources for the study of Spanish and English in the United States are growing, but much more needs to be done. The main zones of interaction were spread through the Southwest in the colonial era, and in those states deriving from lands ceded by the Treaty of Guadalupe Hidalgo (1848). Among those states, New Mexico stands out as an interesting case with the Spanish and English of the *manitos*. In New Mexican and Mexican Spanish the term *manito*, deriving from the diminutive of *mano* 'hand,' with the sense 'Amigo, compañero' (DdM [2023], s.v.), 'friend; neighbor' (Cobos 1983, s.v.), has been used by newer Mexican immigrants to New Mexico to refer to the 'old' Spanish New Mexicans (one can see the Spanish flag flown on ranches in more northerly counties around Santa Fe). The *manitos* look to their heritage as part of New Spain rather than the brief rule under Mexico 1821–1848 (and even briefer tenure under the First Mexican Empire 1821–1823). Manito Spanish is now an endangered variety, restricted to New Mexico and Southern Colorado: a range, in Southern Colorado, from Durango in the west to Trinidad in the east, and across New Mexico, but especially a northern swathe from Raton south-southwestward through Taos, Chimayó, and Abiquiu to the Santa Fe region. The 'Old Spanish' of 'Nueba México' – the Early Modern Spanish from the 1598 colonization of the region under Juan de Oñate – was closely related to *norteño* Mexican Spanish in phonology in terms of *yeísmo* (realization of /ll/ phoneme), initial /j/ as /x/ (*joyo* [xojo]) (Cobos 1983, vi–vii). Rubén Cobos's *A Dictionary of New Mexico and Southern Colorado English* (Cobos 1983) provides etymologies that demonstrate just how complex the language contact situation in the region has been over 400 years: there are a great many *Nahuatlismos* 'Nahuatlisms,' loans from Nahuatl and other indigenous languages, some brought with the Spanish explorers from the Central Valley of Mexico, others from contact with the Pueblos in New Mexico (speaking languages such as Hopi, Zuni, Jemez, Tewa; cf. Goddard 1996, 224–228). Of interest to later New Mexican Spanish-English contact are the many *anglicismos*: *balún* ('balloon'), *curvear* ('to curve, throw a curve ball' among other meanings), *chequers* ('checkers'), *chipe* ('cheap'), *choque* ('chalk'), *estiquer* ('sticker'), *estrechar* ('to stretch'; this and the preceding form with prothetic *e-*), *jaiguaras* ('high waters,' i.e., American English slang *floods* – pants worn high enough above the ankles as to provoke ridicule), *nacho* (here not the food, but an adverb from English *naturally*), *tanape* ('turnip'); as seen in other Spanish-English contact situations (Chapter 12 below), English /wV/ > Spanish /guV/: *guato* (< *wad*, slang term for 'bundle of money'), *güinchil* (< *windshield*), *güique* (< *weak*; Cobos 1983, s.vv.). In their *The Spanish Language of New Mexico and Southern Colorado: A Linguistic Atlas* (2008), Garland D. Bills and Neddy A. Vigil present one of the fullest treatments of any variety in the United States: the project involved 366 informants from the region, their ages spanning from 15 to 96. Even though the 'Anglo' (English-speaking, Anglo- or other non-Hispanic Euro-American) population did not reach a simple majority until the mid-20th century, "a shift to English as the dominant or only language is characteristic of the overwhelming majority of native-born Hispanics in our survey area as well as in the U.S. Southwest more generally" (Bills and Vigil 2008, 165). Color-dot maps plot out the atlas by thematic 'variables': 'retentions' (from Peninsular Spanish), New World forms ('maritime' and Caribbean), Nahuatlisms, independent developments, Anglicisms, and Mexicanisms. Among the Anglicisms is *torque* from *turkey*, which varies in use with *gallina de la tierra, ganso, guajolote, cócono*; the English loan forms – *torque, terque, turkey* – are in more common use with speakers in the age groups 15–40 and 41–64 (Bills and Vigil 2008, 33, 46–47, 216, and Maps 4.1–4, 4.6–7). The significant number, and advance in usage, of Anglicisms indicates also that New Mexican-Coloradan Spanish is suffering from language attrition: for 'pickup truck' *camión* competes with *troca* and *troque*; *galleta*, a loan to Spanish from French *galette*, is being replaced by the 'integrated' English loan-forms *craque* and *craca*, even in a hybrid formation such as *craque salado*, 'salted cracker' (Bills and Vigil 2008, 180–183, Map 10.9). Individual loan forms are one type of exchange, and one indicator of language shift in the Southwest; another is the frequent code-switching among their informants: ***And I bet you*** *que en un diccionario* ***that there's not such a word*** (Bills and Vigil 2008, 167).

The distinctiveness of this community was reinforced mutually, between older *manitos* and newer arrivals from Mexico, which can be reflected in the nomenclature of *españoles* (descended from the Spaniards of New Mexico) and *chicanos* (*chicano/as* who arrived later, especially in Albuquerque and the lower Rio Grande valley). A commonly heard distinction is that these 'original' New Mexicans are not 'Mexicans': *La comida mex – de nojotros* [= *nosotros*]. *No quiero decir que mexicano, porque no semos mexicanos nojotros. Dicemos mexicanos, pero no semos. México está otro lado* ("The food of us Mex – of us. I don't mean Mexican, because we're not Mexicans. We say Mexicans, but we're not. Mexico's over there on the other side (of the border)"; Bills and Vigil 2008, 12–13). This is a point frequently impressed upon visitors with regard to 'New Mexico cooking,' with its *(carne) adobada* (red-chile marinated pork), *sopapillas* (puffed fry-bread, often served with honey and butter), *posole* (hominy-based soup), *piñon* (pine nut), and, most of all, chiles ('red or green?' is the usual question). The cuisine is a blend of Old World Spanish, Native American, and other European groups. The distinction is social as well as cultural and linguistic, as between more prosperous highland ranchers and laborers in the Rio Grande Valley, for whom there are a number of terms: *Surumato*, probably the same as Pachuco *surrumato*, indicates 'Southerner' and 'immigrant' (i.e., from Mexico) and may also be related to Texas Spanish *zurumbático* ('slightly crazy,' 'ignorant'), all with a sense of 'unsophisticated, countryfied.' Another term is *chúntaro*: *Todos nos dicen manito y nosotros shúntaro* ("They all call us Manito and we [call them] Chúntaro"; Bills and Vigil 2008, 13); this term is found in use in Northern Mexican Spanish as well, deriving from a native ethnonym, and applied originally to natives by Spanish-speakers, with the sense of lower-social standing and lack of sophistication/education ('persona de baja extracción social o de poca instrucción'; DdM, s.v.). The Northern-Southern distinction within the New Mexican Spanish zone (which extends into Southern Colorado) has produced a host of isoglosses in both languages. The broader dispersal of Anglicisms in Mexican American and Mexican Spanish can be found in the *Diccionario de Mexicanismos* (DdM) of the Academia Mexicana de la Lengua (a corresponding academy with La Real Academia Española of Madrid); the latest edition (2023) contains ever more English loans and hybrid forms; the Anglicisms undergo varying levels of Hispanicization: while *lonchería* ('lunch counter') is found in Mexican Spanish in border cities such as Tijuana, *lunch* as a simplex is found in the DdM; *manicure* has been borrowed, as has the agentive form *manicurista*; the computer slang term *spam* has simply been reformed according to Spanish phonological norms as *espam* (with prothetic vowel *e-*; DdM, s.vv.).

Turning to another set of colonial and postcolonial varieties, dictionaries of Anglo-Indian varieties have two popular treatments with rhyming titles, Nigel Hankin's *Hanklyn-Janklin* (Hankin 2003) and the venerable *Hobson-Jobson* of Henry Yule and A.C. Burnell (Yule and Burnell 2015; originally published 1886). 'Anglo-Indian' is a dated term, and it may be noted that *Asian* in BrE is *South Asian* in AmE (*Asian* in AmE is a hypernym, with hyponyms such as *East Asian, South Asian, Southeast Asian, Asian and Pacific Islander*). Many of the terms in these two lexica are restricted in use to the Indian subcontinent and derive from not just Sanskrit and Hindi but Urdu (the most frequent source after Hindi), Tamil, Tibetan, Bengali, and Arabic. The scope of the glossaries includes flora and fauna of the subcontinent, the Islamic conquest, the Mughal period, the British colonial era, foods, literature, street vending, bazaars, dress, place-names, modes of conveyance, caste, and religions. The OED has recently added phonological information about Indian English pronunciations for loanwords from South Asia (as part of an effort to expand past standard RP notation, which also includes Canadian, Australian, and other varieties of World Englishes). With a span of coverage like that of the OED and DARE, that is, of standard vocabulary historically treated and regionalisms, *The Australian National Dictionary* (2nd ed. 2016) in its 1854 pages is a remarkable treasury of not just Australian English but Australian life and folkways (such as the earlier observation of *Sheelah's Day*, the day after St. Patrick's feast; s.v. *sheila*).

Rodney Jones's "Elegy for the Southern Drawl" cited above brings up the matter of *dialect maintenance* for dialectologists (see Picone 1997 on Louisiana French, Maguire 2020 on Mid-Ulster English). This section began with the EDD of Joseph and Elizabeth Wright, a late Victorian omnibus of English folkways, customs, and humor that the compilers feared would disappear. Most of the atlases profiled serve also as conservators of traditions and ways belonging to the elderly. Two important studies in the PADS series that took up this matter of dialect loss and maintenance, the one with the 'Ocracoke Brogue' of the Outer Banks of North Carolina (Wolfram et al. 1999), the other looking at just one county in that state (Warren County, in the state's northeastern Piedmont region; Hazen 2000), both held out some hope for programs to interest younger speakers in their communities' linguistic heritage. Music of course is one of the folkways by which a region's linguistic heritage finds expression and life; Stephen Wade's *The Beautiful Music All Around Us* (Wade 2012) was clearly a labor of love, based on decades of recording and researching Amcrican music, from folk to jazz to bluegrass to gospel – Wade cites African American composer and musicologist John Work III: "He told of a Nashville churchgoer who exhorted a vocal quartet during an especially long song: 'Keep on singing, chillun,' she called out, 'I ain't near tired yet'" (7). Foodways are another expression of regional culture and, as the dialect atlases show, highly productive of regional terms. Nearly every tourist stop in rural regions will offer a cookbook of local cuisine. Ella Mae Tucker's *High on the Hog – Hillbilly Recipes* (Tucker 1966) introduces her selection of Ozark recipes, noting that "Hill folk, of necessity as well as of desire, were a self-sufficient people. And their recipes reflect this characteristic. In this book, you will find a collection of recipes which demonstrates deliciously how the hillbilly lived off the land, yet lived very HIGH ON THE HOG." And therein are recipes for huckleberry muffins, hush puppies (see Chapter 9), persimmon cake, peach leather, golden-good fried chicken, burnt sugar icing, rabbit pie with hot biscuits, squirrel pie, corncob jelly, hominy, sassafras tea, and 'pot likker' (i.e., the 'liquor' or liquid left over from boiling greens). And Ozarks locals are known for their wry, deadpan humor (see Harkins 2004); a *Hillbilly Calendar* is published in Forsyth, Missouri (in Taney County, in Southern Missouri Ozark country) that has its own recipes at the end ("Ma's cookin' notes By ma herself") and each month illustrated with photos of the hillbilly family, and their shack and still, that takes us through the year: "Sweetater's barthday" (1 January 2005); "Pa's winter vacation" (7 February); "Look fer Pa" (19 February); "Ma plant taters, Pa go fishin" (24 March); "Ma sleep in" (May: Mother's Day); "make shine," "Pa not well" (10–11 June). And each month has its bit of folk wisdom: "When its fer shore an accident, putting yore shirt on wrong side out will bring you good luck" (November); and for when the year begins: "Opening yore winders a little on New Year's night lets bad luck out an good luck in." The calendar notes are written in the shaky scrawl of one of Pa's younger boys; it's just for fun, and the phonetic renderings are exaggerated, but not wholly inaccurate, and they can be a mark of what might be seen as a defensive pride for a variety often denigrated by outsiders. And Mark Twain would have a young 'Missouri hick' narrate his own story in one of the greatest dialect fictions of all time, which will be taken up in the next chapter.

REFERENCES AND BIBLIOGRAPHY

The Australian National Dictionary. 2nd ed. Bruce Moore. 2 vols. Melbourne: Oxford University Press, 2016

Barry, Michael, "Traditional Enumeration in the North Country," *Folk Life: Journal of Ethnological Studies* 7.1 (1969), 75–91

Becker, Kara. *The Low-Back-Merger Shift: Uniting the Canadian Vowel Shift, the California Vowel Shift, and Short Front Vowel Shifts Across North America. PADS 104*. Durham, NC: Duke University Press, 2019

Bickerton, Derek, "An Afro-Creole Origin for Eena Meena Mina Mo," *American Speech* 57.3 (1982), 225–28

Bills, Garland D. and Neddy A. Vigil. *The Spanish Language of New Mexico and Southern Colorado: A Linguistic Atlas*. Albuquerque: University of New Mexico Press, 2008

Boberg, Charles, John Nerbonne, and Dominic Watt, eds. *The Handbook of Dialectology*. Oxford: Wiley-Blackwell, 2018

Bolton, Henry Carrington. *The Counting-Out Rhymes of Children: Their Antiquity, Origin, and Wide Distribution, A Study in Folklore*. London: Elliot Stock, 1888

Boswell, James. *The Life of Samuel Johnson, LL.D*, 2 vols. London: Charles Dilly, 1791

CHEL III = *The Cambridge History of the English Language*, Volume III: 1476–1776, ed. Roger Lass. Cambridge: Cambridge University Press, 2000

CHEL IV = *The Cambridge History of the English Language*, Volume IV: 1776–1997, ed. Suzanne Romaine. Cambridge: Cambridge University Press, 1998

CHEL V = *The Cambridge History of the English Language*, Volume V: *English in Britain and Overseas: Origins and Development*, ed. Robert Burchfield. Cambridge: Cambridge University Press, 1994

CHEL VI = *The Cambridge History of the English Language*, Volume VI: *English in North America*. Cambridge: Cambridge University Press, 2001

Chomsky, Noam. *Morphophonemics of Modern Hebrew* [1951]. New York: Routledge, 2011

Clarke, Sandra. *Newfoundland and Labrador English*. Dialects of English. Edinburgh: Edinburgh University Pres, 2010

Cobos, Rubén. *A Dictionary of New Mexico and Southern Colorado Spanish*. Santa Fe, NM: Museum of New Mexico Press, 1983

DARE = *Dictionary of American Regional English*, 6 vols. ed. Frederic G. Cassidy and Joan H. Hall. Cambridge, MA: The Belknap Press of Harvard University Press, 1985–2013

Davey, William John and Richard P. MacKinnon. *Dictionary of Cape Breton English*. Toronto: University of Toronto Press, 2016

Davies, Janet. *The Welsh Language: A History*. Cardiff: University of Wales Press, 2014

Davis, Lawrence M. *English Dialectology: An Introduction*. University, AL: University of Alabama Press, 1983

DdM. Academia Mexicana de la Lengua *Diccionario de Mexicanismos: Propios y compartidos*. Mexico City: Planeta, 2023

Demm, Eberhard, "Propaganda and Caricature in the First World War," *Journal of Contemporary History* 28.1 (1993), 163–92

Doyle, Aidan. *A History of the Irish Language: From the Norman Invasion to Independence*. Oxford: Oxford University Press, 2015

EDD = *The English Dialect Dictionary*, ed. Joseph (and Elizabeth) Wright. 6 vols. London: Henry Frowde, 1898–1905

Edwards, Jonathan. *A Faithful Narrative of the Surprizing Work of God in the Conversion of Many Hundred Souls in Northampton, and the Neigbouring Towns and Villages of New Hampshire in New England*. London: John Oswald, 1737

Ellegård, Alvar. *The Auxiliary do: The Establishment and Regulation of Its Use in English*. Gothenburg Studies in English vol. 2. Stockholm: Almqvist & Wiksell, 1953

Ellis, Alexander J., "The Anglo-Cymric Score," *Transactions of the Philological Society* (1877–1879), 316–72

Evans, Geraint and Helen Fulton, eds. *The Cambridge History of Welsh Literature*. Cambridge: Cambridge University Press, 2019

Fazel-Zarandi, Mohammad M., Jonathan S. Feinstein, Edward H Kaplan, "The number of undocumented immigrants in the United States: Estimates based on demographic modeling with data from 1990 to 2016," *PLOSOne* 201813 e0201193. https://journals.plos.org/plosone/article?id=10.1371/journal.pone.0201193

Filppula, Marku. *The Grammar of Irish English: Language in Hibernian Style*. Routledge/ESA Studies in Germanic Linguistics. London: Routledge, 1999

Fridland, Valerie, Tyler Kendall, Betsy E. Evans, Alicia Beckford Wassink, eds. *Speech in the Western States.* Volume 1: *The Coastal States. PADS 101.* Durham, NC: Duke University Press, 2016

Fridland, Valerie, Alicia Beckford Wassink, Tyler Kendall, Besty E. Evans, eds. *Speech in the Western States.* Volume 2: *The Mountain West. PADS 102.* Durham, NC: Duke University Press, 2017

Fridland, Valerie, Alicia Beckford Wassink, Lauren Hall-Lew, Tyler Kendall, eds. *Speech in the Western States.* Volume 3: *Understudied Varieties. PADS 105.* Durham, NC: Duke University Press, 2020

Fussell, Paul. *The Great War and Modern Memory.* Oxford: Oxford University Press, 1977/rpt. 2013

Goddard, Ives. *Languages. Handbook of North American Indians,* Volume 17. Washington, DC: Smithsonian Institution, 1996

Greene, David, "Celtic," in *Indo-European Numerals*, ed. Jadranka Gvozdanović. Trends in Linguistics, Studies and Monographs 57. Berlin: Mouton de Gruyter, 1992. Pp. 497–554

Hanklin, Nigel. *Hanklyn-Janklin: A Stranger's Rumble-Tumble Guide to Some Words, Customs, and Quiddities, Indian and Indo-British.* 4th New Delhi: Tara Press/India Research Press, 2003

Harkins, Anthony. *Hillbilly: A Cultural History of an American Icon.* New York: Oxford University Press, 2004

Hazen, Kirk. *Identity and Ethnicity in the Rural South: A Sociolingustic View through Past and Present Be.* PADS 83. Durham: Duke University Press, 2000

Hickey, Raymond. *A Sound Atlas of Irish English.* Topics in English Linguistics. Berlin: Mouton de Gruyter, 2004

Hickey, Raymond. *Dublin English: Evolution and Change.* Varieties of English Around the World. Amsterdam: John Benjamins, 2005

Hickey, Raymond. *Irish English: History and present-day forms.* Studies in English Language. Cambridge: Cambridge University Press, 2007

Hickey, Raymond. *The Dialects of Irish: Study of a Changing Landscape.* Trends in Linguistics Studies and Monographs 230. Berlin: De Gruyter Mouton, 2011

Hickey, Raymond, ed. *The Oxford Handbook of Irish English.* Oxford: Oxford University Press, 2024

Genuine Hillbilly Calendar. Forsyth, MO: Hillbilly Calendars, 2005

Hughes, Arthur, Peter Trudgill, and Dominic Watt. *English Accents and Dialects: An Introduction to Social and Regional Varieties of English in the British Isles.* 5th ed. London: Routledge, 2012

Ihalainen, Ossi, "The Dialects of England Since 1776," CHEL V (1994), ed. Robert Burchfield, pp. 197–274

Jago, Frederick William Pearce. *The Ancient Language and the Dialect of Cornwall.* Truro: Netherton & Worth, 1882

Johnson, Samuel. *A Dictionary of the English Language: in which The WORDS are deduced from their ORIGINALS…* 2 vols. London: W. Strahan, 1755

Jones, Rodney. *Elegy for the Southern Drawl.* Boston: Houghton Mifflin, 1999

Joyce, James. *Finnegans Wake*. London: Faber and Faber, 1939/New York: Penguin Books, 1976

Joyce, P.W. *English as We Speak It in Ireland*. Dublin: Wolfhound Press, 1979

Kachru, Braj B., "World Englishes: approaches, issues and resources," *Language Teaching* 25.1 (1992), 1–14

Keane, Molly. *Good Behaviour*. London: Abacus, 1981

Kolb, Gwin J. and Robert DeMaria, Jr., eds. *Johnson on the English Language*. The Yale Edition of the Works of Samuel Johnson, Volume XVIII. New Haven, CT: Yale University Press, 2005

Kretzschmar, William A., Jr., Virginia G. McDavid, Theodore K. Lerud, and Ellen Johnson. *Handbook of the Linguistic Atlas of the Middle and South Atlantic States*. Chicago: University of Chicago Press, 1993

Kurath, Hans. *Linguistic Atlas of New England*. Linguistic Atlas of the United States and Canada. Providence, RI: Brown University, 1939

Kurath, Hans and Raven I. McDavid, Jr, *The Pronunciation of English in the Atlantic States: Based Upon the Collections of the Linguistic Atlas of the Eastern United States*. University, AL: The University of Alabama Press, 1961

Labov, William. *Principles of Linguistic Change,* Volume 2: *Social Factors*. Language in Society vol. 29. Malden, MA: Blackwell, 2001

Labov, William. *The Social Stratification of English in New York City*. 2nd Cambridge: Cambridge University Press, 2006

Labov, William. *Principles of Linguistic Change*, 3 vols. Volume 1: *Internal Factors* (1994); Volume 2: *Social Factors* (2001); Volume 3: *Cognitive and Cultural Factors* (2010). Language in Society vols. 20, 29, 39. Malden, MA: Blackwell/Wiley-Blackwell

Labov, William. *Dialect Diversity in America: The Politics of Language Change*. Charlottesville, VA: University of Virginia Press, 2012

Leith, Dick. *A Social History of English*. 2nd ed. London: Routledge, 1997/2005

Liberman, Anatoly. *An Analytic Dictionary of English Etymology: An Introduction*. Minneapolis, MN: University of Minnesota Press, 2008

Lighter, Jonathan, "The Slang of the American Expeditionary Forces in Europe, 1917–1919: An Historical Glossary," *American Speech* 47.1/2 (1972): 5–142

Lewis, Llŷr Gwyn, "'Amlhau Lleisiau'n Llên': Birth and Rebirth in Welsh Language Literature, 1990–2014," in *The Cambridge History of Welsh Literature*, ed. Evans, Geraint and Helen Fulton (2019), pp. 669–695

McDavid, Raven I., Jr. and Raymond K. O'Cain. *Linguistic Atlas of the Middle and South Atlantic States*. Chicago: University of Chicago Press, 1980. Fascicle 1 = McDavid and O'Cain 1980a, Fascicle 2 = McDavid and O'Cain 1980b

Maguire, Warren. *Language and Dialect Contact in Ireland: The Phonological Origins of Mid-Ulster English*. Edinburgh: Edinburgh University Press, 2020

Mencken, H.L. *The American Language: An Inquiry into the Development of English in the United States*. 4th ed. New York: Knopf, 1960

Michie, James, tr. *Horace. Odes: With the Latin Text*. Modern Library Classics. New York: Random House, 2002

Minkova, Donka. *A Historical Phonology of English*. Edinburgh Textbooks on the English Language – Advanced. Edinburgh: Edinburgh University Press, 2014

Montgomery, Michael B. and Thomas E. Nunnally, eds. *From the Gulf States and Beyond: The Legacy of Lee Pederson and LAGS*. Tuscaloosa. AL: The University of Alabama Press, 1998

Montgomery Michael B. and Jennifer K.N. Heinmiller. *Dictionary of Southern Appalachian English*. Chapel Hill, NC: University of North Carolina Press, 2021

Nevalainen, Terttu. *An Introduction to Early Modern English*. Oxford: Oxford University Press, 2006

Nisbet, Robin, "The Old Lie: Dvlce et Decorvm Est," *Omnibus* 15 (1988), 16–17

O'Halpin, Eunan. *Spying on Ireland: British Intelligence and Irish Neutrality during the Second World War*. Oxford: Oxford University Press, 2008

OHBE IV = *The Oxford History of the British Empire*, Volume IV: *The Twentieth Century*, ed. Judith M. Brown and William Roger Louis. Oxford: Oxford University Press, 1999/rpt 2004

Ó Muirithe, Diarmaid, ed. *The English Language in Ireland*. Cork: The Mercier Press, 1977/1985

Opie, Iona and Peter Opie, eds. *The Oxford Dictionary of Nursery Rhymes*. New ed. Oxford: Oxford University Press, 1997

Picone, Michael D., "Enclave Dialect Contraction: An External Overview of Louisiana French," *American Speech* 72.2 (1997), 117–153

Pratt, T.K. *Dictionary of Prince Edward Island English*. Toronto: University of Toronto Pres, 1996

Romaine, Suzanne. *Language in Society: An Introduction to Sociolinguistics*. 2nd ed. Oxford: Oxford University Press, 2001

Salmon, Vivian, "Orthography and Punctuation," in CHEL III (1999), ed. Roger Lass, pp. 13–55

Sayers, Peig. *An Old Woman's Reflections/Machtnamh Seana Mhná*, tr. Séamus Ennis. Oxford: Oxford University Press, 1962

Schneider, Edgar W. *Postcolonial English: Varieties around the world*. Cambridge Approaches to Language Contact. Cambridge: Cambridge University Press, 2007

Schneider, Edgar W. and Michael B. Montgomery, "On the Trail of Early Nonstandard Grammar: An Electronic Corpus of Southern U.S. Antebellum Overseers' Letters," *American Speech* 76.4 (2001), 388–410

Share, Bernard. *Slanguage – A Dictionary of Irish Slang*. Dublin: Gill & Macmillan, 1997

Sheidlower, Jesse. *The F-Word*. 3rd ed. Oxford: Oxford University Press, 2009

SND/eSND = *Scottish National Dictionary* (10 volumes, 1931–1976), in the online *Dictionaries of the Scots Language* (DSL) project; included also is the *Dictionary of the Older Scottish Tongue* (12 volumes, 1931–2002): https://dsl.ac.uk/

Stewart, Garrett, "Dickens and language," in *The Cambridge Companion to Charles Dickens*, ed. John O. Jordan. Cambridge: Cambridge University Press, 2001. Pp. 136–151

Synge, John Millington. *The Aran Islands*. Mineola, NY: Dover Publications, 1911/1998

Thomas, Alan R., "English in Wales," CHEL V (1994), pp. 94–147

Thomas, Dylan. *Under Milk Wood*. New York: New Directions Publishing, 1954

Thurneysen, Rudolf. *A Grammar of Old Irish*. Tr. D.A. Binchy and Osborn Bergin. Dublin: Dublin Institute for Advanced Studies, 2017

Tucker, Ella Mae. *High on the Hog – Hillbilly Recipes*. Cassville, MO: Asher Creek Publications, 1966

Turner, Lorenzo Dow. *Africanisms in the Gullah Dialect*. Chicago: University of Chicago Press, 1949

Upton, Clive and J.D.A. Widdowson. *An Atlas of English Dialects*. 2nd ed. London: Routledge, 2006

Wade, Stephen. *The Beautiful Music All Around Us: Field Recordings and the American Experience*. Urbana, IL: University of Illinois Press, 2012

Weinreich, Uriel. *Modern English-Yiddish Yiddish-English Dictionary*. New York: Yivo Institute for Jewish Research, 2012

Whitman, Walt, "Slang in America," *The North American Review* 141, no. 348 (November 1885), 431–435

Williams, Kevin, "The Dragon Finds a Tongue: Devolution and Government in Wales Since 1997," in *The Cambridge History of Welsh Literature*, ed. Evans, Geraint and Helen Fulton (2019), pp. 655–68

Wolfram, Walt, Kirk Hazen, Natalie Schilling-Estes. *Dialect Change and Maintenance on the Outer Banks*. PADS 81. Tuscaloosa: The University of Alabama Press, 1999

Womersley, David P., ed. *James Boswell: The Life of Samuel Johnson*. London: Penguin Books, 2008

Wright, Elizabeth Mary. *Rustic Speech and Folk-Lore*. London: Humphrey Milford/Oxford University Press, 1913

Yule, Henry and A.C. Burnell. *Hobson-Jobson: The Definitive Glossary of British India*. Oxford World's Classics. Oxford: Oxford University Press, 2015

CHAPTER 9

An American Century

The three-decade span that saw the publication of Nathaniel Hawthorne's *The Scarlet Letter* (1850), Herman Melville's *Moby-Dick* (1851; publication title: *Moby-Dick; or, The Whale*), and Mark Twain's *Adventures of Huckleberry Finn* (1884) can be plausibly said to have witnessed the emergence of a distinctly American canon of literature, in an increasingly distinct American English. That is, to British audiences, whom earlier American writers had striven to please. In the span between Hawthorne and Melville, natives of, respectively, Salem, Massachusetts, and New York City, to Mark Twain (the pen-name of Samuel Langhorne Clemens), a native of Northeastern Missouri, the American literary canon had moved westward. The distinctions in taste, speech, setting, plot, and character that had begun to increasingly distinguish British and emergent American literature were then found to be distinguishing an increasingly broad and diverse American canon. American literature developed in an age of printing, and the printing press had played a pivotal role in the forging of the Republic itself. What would not change so quickly was the British attitude toward things American; for all the brashness, headiness, openness of the upstart republic's culture, its vaunting of the new over the traditional, there was after all an Old World condescension. One that Americans, in their early centuries of formation, sought to allay, writing for London rather than Philadelphia (at least in the literary sphere) – a sense of inferiority that looked to British models as a safe harbor. But that word Americans now spelled *harbor*, not *harbour*, since Noah Webster's spelling reform introduced first in his *A Compendious Dictionary of the English Language* (1806).[1] The subtitle to Webster's Dictionary had made clear the challenge to British linguistic dominance with its subtitle: *In Which FIVE THOUSAND Words are added to the number found in the BEST ENGLISH COMPENDS.* Webster's *Dictionary* has ever since been a byword for correctness in American English, and 'Webster's Dictionary' itself a collocation, shorthand for anything authoritative. It was in his

[1] The first edition of Webster's *Dictionary* is available in digital facsimile on the Internet Archive: https://archive.org/details/compendiousdictionaryoftheenglishlanguage1806/mode/2up

Preface that Webster traced the history of English orthography and pronunciation, pointing out disparities even among authorities in Great Britain itself, and intimating that standardization was unlikely given not just habits of spelling and speaking, but habits of mind:

> That a complete standard, to which all the polite and learned of a nation will conform, is, in its own nature, impracticable, may be satisfactorily proven from the structure of the human mind; from the various modes in which different men view the same subject; the different effect of the same degree of evidence on different minds; the different impressions made by education, which become the ground-work of uncontrollable prejudices; and the extreme reluctance which men feel in relinquishing their peculiar notions, and yielding to the opinions of others. The same consequence may be deduced from the variableness of pronunciation among the leading characters of a nation. So far is the present pronunciation of the court and stage in England from being fixed, that no two writers are yet agreed what it is; and if the case were otherwise, there is no probability that it would remain the same for any considerable time (Webster 1806, xi).

Though Webster admired Samuel Johnson and his own *A Dictionary of the English Language* (1755), he did not always accept his judgments (especially as to etymologies):

> It is evident that Johnson supposed *comptroller*, to have a different original from *control*; than which nothing can be more false. It is simply a combination of two French words *contre*, and *rolle* – which are from the Latin *contra-rotula*. The ancients *rolled* their parchments into the form of a wheel; hence a register or record, obtained, in the middle ages, the name of *rotula,* a little wheel, which the French softened into *rolle*.... That such a blunder should ever have been made by a man of letters, is not easily accounted for; but that it should still hold its place in dictionaries and in practice, would be incredible, if our laws, records and constant practice were not evidences of the fact (Webster 1806, xvii).

Webster, a Hartford, Connecticut, native, was descended from old Yankee stock, with two colonial governors in his family tree: John Webster (1590–1661), Governor of the Connecticut Colony, and, on his mother Mercy's side, William Bradford (1590–1657), of Plymouth Plantation. He may be making, to an extent, a 'national' point here among 'British' peoples – that is, pointing toward 'American' progress in linguistic science.

Webster had already set his *compendious* dictionary against the *best English compends*, and now corrects Dr. Johnson (though the etymology, broadly correct, belongs not to Webster but earlier lexicographers). Webster might not be pleased to see the subsequent fate of *comptroller*: in the latest edition of the *American Heritage Dictionary of the English Language* (AHD5 2018) the form does not merit its own entry but a cross-reference to *controller*; but there one reads in the Usage Note that though the spelling *comptroller* arose ca. 1500 by a false association with *compte*, a Middle English alternative form of *counte/cownte*, "evidence suggests that the spelling pronunciation (kŏmp-trō'lər) and (kŏmp'-trō'lər) may now be used by a majority of speakers. In our 1995 survey, 43 percent of the Usage Panel indicated that they pronounce *comptroller* like *controller*, while 57 percent pronounce it with *mp*, as it is spelled, with stress either on the first or second syllable. And half of those Panelists who pronounce *comptroller* like *controller* indicated that they also consider the *mp* spelling pronunciations acceptable" (AHD5, s.v. *controller*). Not the sort of progress Webster might have hoped for, but consider the fate of AmE and BrE pronunciations of *lieutenant*. Webster's 1806 *Dictionary* proper is rather more an A-Z glossary in 355 pages not unlike the medieval bilingual Latin-English glossaries from the Épinal-Erfurt Latin-Old English glossary (Chapter 4) to the *Medulla grammatice* (Latin-Middle English, with a number of lemmata from Greek and Hebrew). But in a tradition that would endure in American dictionaries Webster included a number of appendices of 'useful information,' the first of which involved a "Money Table": this began with the familiar American silver monetary measures *dollar*, *half dollar*, *quarter dollar*, *dime*, and copper *cent*; the *nickel* would be introduced in 1866 and was in circulation concurrently with the *five-cent piece* (the 'Shield Five Cents,' in circulation 1866–1883) or earlier *half-dime* (or *half-disme* [di:m], first minted in 1792). At the lower end of denominations was the *mill*, a 1/10 cent unit – the *mill* is still found in contemporary use as a unit of property tax assessment (one dollar per one thousand dollars of the assessed value of a property). At the upper denomination end were the gold coins *eagle*, *half eagle*, and *quarter eagle* (valued at 10, 5, and 2-1/2 dollars). The American currency table was followed by the British and Scots system – this has continued in American dictionaries and handbooks as, unlike the English system of measurement in yards and furlongs and so forth that was retained in AmE, American readers grew less familiar with *farthing*, *tuppence*, *shilling*, *guinea*. Monetary tables for a number of other countries follow, then tables of "Weights and Measures" (measures of length, cloth and square measure, ale and beer, and dry measure). Population figures for the states were inserted after tables of Hebrew and Athenian months, with separate columns for Black and total populations (as of the 1790 and 1800 censuses, Virginia had the largest Black population in the United States at just over 41% of the total population: 367,465 Black Virginians out of a state population of 886,149; Webster does not specify the status of the Black population). This rather vital statistic is followed, oddly enough, by a table on the Roman calendar (which Webster spells here *calender*, but in the dictionary *calendar*). Chronological tables follow, the third of which is "A chronological Table of the most remarkable Events, in or respecting America, intended as the outline of American History"; the entry for 1775 begins, "Battle at Lexington began war April 19 / Ticonderoga seized by Col. Allen, May / George Washington appointed commander / in chief of the army, June 15, took com/mand of the troops investing Boston July 2" (405; *siezed* here, but *seize* within the dictionary).

In his two-volume 1828 *An American Dictionary of the English Language* Webster returns to "orthoepy" (correct pronunciation) and orthography in his lengthy introduction (some 81 pages). But in this much more elaborate preface to the dictionary, he covers such matters as "Origin of Language," "Affinity of Language" (he outlines the Indo-European and 'Shemitic' families, and notes the affinity of Cornish and Armoric

[Breton] in the Brythonic branch of Celtic). He also provides "A Philosophical and Practical Grammar of the English Language" (vol. I, [52 ff.] in the unpaginated text). Here one gleans some interesting bits of information on a period of American English not so well described to date. He surveys the gradation series of strong verbs, now termed 'irregular verbs,' and in noting that English suffers from a dearth of inflections and so has to rely upon auxiliaries he strikes a Johnsonian note: "But as we have no more than about half a dozen different terminations, and are therefore obliged to form our modes and tenses by means of auxiliaries, the combination of these forms a part of the business of learning the language, which is extremely difficult and perplexing to foreigners. Even the natives of Scotland and Ireland do not always surmount the difficulty" (Webster 1828, I, [72]).

The "Grammar" itself is comprised of 45 "Rules," of "Agreement or Concord," which solidified the perception of Webster as a prescriptivist, though this assessment may be tempered by his partiality toward, and tolerance of, 'Americanisms'; for Webster this could include Native American loans, or those from other colonial languages of the Americas, or words given new senses in America (see Cassidy and Hall 2001, 200). Webster's markings of the English verb are not those of contemporary handbooks, but of interest for AmE usage ca. 1780–1830: I was / Thou wast / He was // We were / Ye or You were / They were (his 'past subjunctive mode'); I were / Thou wert or You was or were / He were // We were / Ye or You were / They were ('hypothetical tense'; I, [68]). For future tense marking, Webster allows *shall, will, should* as options (a collapse in the *I shall / you will* pattern). Perhaps most interesting to modern dialectologists is his brief "Directions for the Pronunciation of Words" (I, [86–87]): <-e>, final *-e*, "indicates the preceding vowel is long"; "*ti* after a consonant have the sound of *ch*" – thus Webster records that *bastion* is pronounced *baschan* and *digestion* apparently as [daɪʤɛstʃɪn] *dye-jess-chin*; while *w* is silent in *who, whom, whose*, and, he says also, *whoop*, "When *wh* begins a word, the aspirate *h* precedes *w* in pronunciation, as in what, whiff, whale, pronounced hwat, hwif, hwale; *w* having precisely the sound of *oo*, French *ou*" (I, [86–87]). The value assigned by Webster to /w/ in /hw-/ is not entirely clear, but that in certain environments /wh/ was still aspirated, or pronounced more like original /hw/ allows one to tentatively date the progress of the change /hw-/ > / wh-/ (at least in his New England dialect). Somewhat more curious is Webster's note on vowels before /r/; while the development of non-rhotic English is the major phonological change dated to the 18th century, linguists have been hesitant to draw many other conclusions from the evidence of American texts of the 18th and early 19th centuries. In Webster's scheme in the 1828 *Dictionary*, the low back vowel merger (or *cot-caught* merger) seems in evidence, as does the /ɔ/ - /o/ or *horse-hoarse* merger (see Fisher 2001, 75–77). Rather more curious is his assertion that "Before the letter *r*, there is a slight sound of *e* between the vowel and the consonant. Thus bare, parent, apparent, mere, mire, more, pure, pyre, are pronounced nearly baer, paerent, appaerent, me-er, mier, moer, puer, pyer. This pronunciation proceeds from the peculiar articulation *r*, and it occasions a slight change of the sound of *a*, which can be learned only by the ear" (I, [87]). Of immediate interest is that the New Englander Webster is recording rhotic pronunciations for these forms, since as a Hartford native Webster's local dialect placed him on the Western (rhotic) New England side; though most of the Eastern seaboard colonial cities were non-rhotic until the mid-20th century – the great and persistent exception being Philadelphia – the ANAE found the restoration of postvocalic /r/ to be occurring outside the Boston-Providence Eastern New England, NYC, and Charleston-Savannah Southeastern non-rhotic zones (ANAE, 47–48, Map 7.1, 226–227, Map 16.1). Interestingly, African American speakers from Southern non-rhotic zones tended to be more conservative in its preservation, even in regions further inland from the coastal plain (e.g., Durham, NC, Columbia, SC, or Atlanta, GA), or brought the pronunciation with them (as to New Orleans, Chicago, Gary, IN, or Flint and Detroit, MI; ANAE, Map 7.1). Webster, from a modern linguistic viewpoint, may be lumping together a few phonological phenomena, which would not be unexpected for the time of publication. *Mire* as [maɪɚr] or [maɪɛr] would not be unexpected (the same going for *pyre* as *pyer*); the pronunciations of *bare, parent, apparent* seems to involve tensing of /e/ or near diphthongization of /a/ or /ɛ/ (it is difficult to tell what vowel Webster means in his notation <ae>). The pronunciations *moer* and *puer* for *more* and *pure* do seem to indicate diphthongization, and loss of glide/glide deletion with *pure.*

Webster's own writing style, its elaborate periodic sentences and parallelisms, could strike the modern reader as quite British. When one looks at his sample passages in the "Grammar" and in the attestations to entries in the *Dictionary* – the 1828 version is greatly expanded and offers full entries – they are overwhelmingly from British authors. But Webster was sketching an American tongue with his dictionary-making, and the spellings he encouraged would be increasingly adopted over the course of the following century. The writers mentioned at the outset, Hawthorne, Melville, and Twain, all set their major fictions in the 1830s and 1840s. And that century from about 1845 to 1945 might well be called an 'American Century': the eminent historian of American English Richard W. Bailey traced the emergence of this American tongue, the 'cultural cringe' American and British speakers might feel about one another's variety, the "American reaction and British counter reaction," and, as unfashionable as the pronouncement may now be, "The triumph of American English" (Bailey 2001, 486–495).

9.1 HUCK AND JIM

The familiar story of the adoption of the name 'Mark Twain' by Samuel Langhorne Clemens (1835–1910) has often been seen as part of the author's ironic, folksy humor. His earlier writings about working on Mississippi riverboats describe instead a young leadman or sounder, then a cub-pilot terrified of the responsibilities. He trained for two years as a Mississippi riverboat pilot, was granted a license in 1859, and served as a pilot until the outbreak of the Civil War in 1861. He had been advised by an older pilot that to be successful he would have to memorize the thousand miles plus of the river's course, aware of every sandbar, hidden island, and shoal. Twain dedicated a chapter in *Old Times on the Mississippi* (1876) to "Sounding"; he writes of the sort of conversation pilots had at the change of watch, here taking a sounding with the leads (plumb-lines with lead weights) at Hale's Point, Tennessee, on the stretch down the river between New Madrid and Memphis: "I judge the upper bar is making down a little at Hale's Point, had quarter twain with the lower lead and mark twain with the other" (DeVoto 1977, 77). North of New Madrid was the call-in at *St. Looy* (St. Louis), and on the passage from Baton Rouge to New Orleans, he saw sugar plantations and the leftover crushed stalks – for which English borrowed the French term used by Twain, *bagasse* (DeVoto 1977, 98). Twain also provides in his *Old Times* reminiscences an early recording of the front vowel raising /ɛ/ to /e/ in the insult *aig-suckin'*: "Cain't you see nothin', you dash-dash aig-suckin', sheep-stealin'..." (*egg-sucking*, 'sneaking or contemptible'; RHHDAS, s.v.; *dash-dash* a contemporary print form for expletives); the earliest attestation is from North Carolinian humorist Johnson Jones Hooper (1815–1862) in his: "You sassy, aig-suckin', roguish, gnatty, flop-eared vermint!" (with re-raising of /a/ to /ɛ/ in *varmint*). Hooper would become Secretary of the Provisional Congress of the Confederate States of America, succumbing to tuberculosis in Richmond in 1862.

Twain's 'homespun,' wry, and at times bitter even angry sense of humor no doubt had much to do with his upbringing and family. He was born in 1835 in Florida, Missouri, in Monroe County, NE Missouri, due west of the Mississippi; at four years of age, his family moved to Hannibal, MO, in Marion County, on the Mississippi River. And that move proved formative, as in Hannibal Twain began his early career as a printer's devil (apprentice), then took to the river in his early 20s. One of seven children, only his older brother Orion and sister Pamela lived to old age. His Hannibal, and his boyhood home there (206–208 Hill Street – the home is now part of a National Park site), would have been relatively comfortable with father John an attorney (Hannibal becomes the St. Petersburg of the Tom Sawyer and Huckleberry Finn novels). But Samuel lost his father to pneumonia in 1847, and at 13 he was a printer's apprentice and went to work setting type for his brother Orion's newspaper, the *Hannibal Journal*. He left home at 18 to pursue work as a printer in St. Louis and cities in the East (NYC, Philadelphia), returning to Missouri at 22, then served as a riverboat pilot on the Mississippi until the outbreak of the Civil War. Twain encouraged his younger brother Henry to take to the steamboat trade; Henry would perish at 20 years of age in 1838 when the boiler on the *Pennsylvania* exploded near Memphis, Tennessee. The family tragedies no doubt shaped Twain's outlook on chance and fate, while the down-home-ness of a number of his relatives gave him a similarly sharp sense of humor with a turn for self-criticism and deflation (as Huck says, "Thinks I, this is what comes of my not thinking"; Twain 1885/1996, 124).

His famous *nom de plume* 'Mark Twain,' a river depth mark of two fathoms, or 12 feet, comes from this Mississippi experience; the novel *Huckleberry Finn* follows the river's course, from Hannibal/St. Petersburg, through Pike County, Missouri (20 miles south), south toward Cairo, Illinois (where the Mississippi and Ohio Rivers meet – and which holds out a dream of freedom for Jim) – the river is a looming presence: literally, with its floodings, and figuratively. It is also a source of freedom, both real and lasting (a crossing from slave to free states), and temporary ("and it *did* seem so good to be free again and all by ourselves on the big river and nobody to bother us"; 1885/1996, 260). For riverboat navigation, *soundings* were taken either with a marked *sounding pole* (most commonly used on the Ohio River, which is a shallower river) or by a rope with a lead weight by the *leadman* who called out the soundings: 'mark twain' (two fathoms) meant *safe water*. The other measurements were whole or fractional marks: *half (twain)* was 3 feet, *quarter* 1-1/2 feet, *quarter less* 4-1/2 feet, *mark one* or *half twain* 6 feet, *quarter twain* 13-1/2 feet, *quarter less three* 16-1/2 feet, and so on until *mark four* (24 feet), after which *no bottom* would be called. The Eastern Missouri journey down from St. Petersburg (Hannibal) through St. Louis and Ste. Genevieve (whose French character is still preserved in the town's architecture) was meant to head to Cairo, Illinois, Jim and Huck miss Cairo in the night and when Huck comes ashore on the east bank of the river he is in the Old Kentucky world of the Grangerfords and Shepherdsons, who impress Huck – still going under the name George Jackson – enough that it affects his speech. Colonel Grangerford in particular impresses Huck:

> He [Colonel Grangerford] was a gentleman all over; and so was his family. He was well born, as the saying is, and that's worth as much in a man as it is in a horse, so the Widow Douglas said, and nobody ever denied that she was of the first aristocracy in our town; and pap he always said it too, though he warn't no more quality than a mud-cat [catfish], himself (Twain 1885/1996, 97).

To express his admiration for the genteel 'high-toned' Grangerfords, Huck appeals to the social authority of the Widow Douglas from St. Petersburg, and contrasts the Colonel with his own "Pap" in a disparaging tone – Huck siding here more with 'townfolk' such as the Widow and the Sawyers than with his 'backwoods' Pa. The infatuation with the Western Kentucky 'aristocracy' doesn't seem to last very long, however:

> I don't want to talk much about the next day. I reckon I'll cut it pretty short. I waked up and was agoing to turn over and go to sleep again, when I noticed how still it was – didn't seem to be anybody stirring. That warn't usual. Next I noticed that Buck was up and gone. Well, I gets up, a-wondering, and goes down stairs – nobody around; everything as still as a mouse. Just the same outside; thinks I, what does it mean? Down by the wood-pile I comes across my Jack, and says.... (Twain 1885/1996, 104).

Here, it sounds as if Huck has, in retrospect, recognized that he already wants to leave the feuding world of the Grangerfords and Shepherdsons, and in his speech pattern has already left, as he seems to have gone back to his out-of-school, outside-town nonstandard grammar and syntax. Huck is also reluctant to talk as the Grangerford-Shepherdson feud will take the life of Buck Grangerford, a boy, like Huck, of about 13. An out from this madness is provided once more by the river: "I went off down to the river, studying over this thing, and pretty soon I noticed that my nigger was following along behind" (Twain 1884/1996, 150). Jack, the enslaved man from the Grangerford household – Kentucky, a slave state – follows Huck toward the river under the pretense of showing him some *water-moccasins* (the *water moccasin*, or *cottonmouth*, a venomous snake): "Mars Jawge, if you'll come down into de swamp, I'll show you a whole stack o' water-moccasins" (150). *Master* syncopates to *mars*, *George* is pronounced non-rhotically with tensing of /ɔ/, and there is the usual substitution of stop for fricative with *de* for *the*. The man leads Huck a mile through the swamp to an overgrown dry patch of land: "You shove right in dah, jist a few steps, Mars Jawge, dah's whah dey is. I's seed 'm befo', I don't k'yer to see 'em no mo'" (150). The glide insertion with *k'yer* [kɟɛr] for *care* is characteristic of Southern mountain speech, and Southern AmE more broadly (Williams 1992, 59, s.v. *care*), and likely derives from Irish and Scots-Irish English; so too is the fronting and raising of *just* to *jist*. Presumably, Jack comes originally from Eastern Kentucky or Western North Carolina. Here he is leading Huck to a reunion:

> I poked into the place aways, and come to a little open patch as big as a bedroom, all hung around with vines, and found a man laying there asleep – and by jings it was my old Jim! (150).

Huck's *by jings* is a mild oath, likely from dialectal BrE or Scots; the original form *by jingo* might be a taboo deformation of *by Jesus*, with variant forms such as *by jingle, by jing* (DARE, s.vv.), and perhaps also *by-ginneys* (DSAE, 153), and so related to a variety of other taboo-deformation religious oaths (*by gonnies, by juckers, bedad/bydad, begad, by gum/Dam gum it*; DSAE, s.v. *by*). Huck's use of the 'n-word' is so jarring to contemporary readers that it has led to the banning of the book, or the use of expurgated versions. The use of the racial epithet (arguably the most offensive word in the language at present) was meant to be jarring then (1884) and now. Huck's casual use of it seems to be one of a number of things he comes to regret by the novel's end, and his use of it occurs especially in slave-holding states (Missouri, Kentucky, Arkansas). Jack's ruse to bring Huck to Jim is interesting in that we can sense a clandestine communication system among those who are enslaved (or, like Jim, on the run from slavery): the system is outside the main discourse, and coded. Huck had just been used by Sophia Grangerford as a clandestine go-between for the messages between her and her forbidden beau Harney Shepherdson; the means of conveyance is the copy of the New Testament she leaves in the church the two clans attend, seated apart. Huck suspects the ruse innately: "Says I to myself something's up – it ain't natural for a girl to be in such a sweat about a Testament" (149). So when Huck sees Jack following him from the Grangerford residence with the announcement that he wanted to show him some water moccasins, Huck is once again suspicious: "Thinks I, that's mighty curious; he said that yesterday" (150). That the system of coded communication has its shortcomings is plain in the pathos of Huck's unaware "he said that yesterday." The reunion with Jim is also laden with pathos: "I waked him up, and I reckoned it was going to be a grand surprise to him to see me again, but it warn't. He nearly cried, he was so glad, but he warn't surprised"; Jim had tried to stay close to Huck in the river, but he knows what fate could await him on either bank: "I 'uz off too fur to hear what dey say to you – I wuz 'fraid o' de dogs – but when it 'uz quiet agin, I knowed you's in de house, so I struck out for de woods to wait for day" (150–151). The pairing of Huck and Jim has often been seen as an unlikely one, but the runaway outcast boy and runaway slave are not so odd a pairing, as their linguistic parallels show. It is, sadly, a temporary pairing given the historical moment of the novel, and being on that river suspends that painful reality, at least for a time:

> 'Why didn't you tell my Jack to fetch me here sooner, Jim?'
> 'Well, twarn't no use to 'sturb you, Huck, tell we could do sumfn – but we's all right, now. I ben a-buyin' pots en pans en vittles, as I got a chanst, en a patchin' up de raf', nights,
> when --'
> '*What* raft, Jim?'
> 'Our ole raf.'
>
> I was powerful glad to get away from the feuds, and so was Jim to get away from the swamp. We said there warn't no home like a raft, after all. Other places do seem so cramped up and smothery, but a raft don't. You feel free and easy and comfortable on a raft (151, 156).[2]

9.2 AMERICAN VOICES

That distinctive American 'voices' had not only developed but become increasingly recognizable is apparent in satirical references to one's literary predecessors. Alexander Pope's *Imitations of English Poets*, said to have been written in his youth and published in the 1717 edition of his *Works* performed a similar function for English poets such as Edmund Spenser (1553–1598, according to his memorial in Westminster Abbey's Poets' Corner), Edmund Waller (1606–1687), Abraham Cowley (1618–1667), John Wilmot, Earl of Rochester (1647–1680), Thomas Sackville, Earl of Dorset (1643–1706), and Jonathan Swift (1667–1745). Pope's admiration for and envy of these poetic predecessors manifests itself in various ways: Pope at times uses crudities, but Swift comes off easy in his imitative treatment "The Happy Life of a Country Parson," as Swift had been known to use crudities aplenty. His send-up of Spenser may have been triggered by Pope's own epic ambitions, translating Homer's *Iliad* (most notably) and *Odyssey*, though through Latin translations of Homer's Greek, and Spenser's daring to write an "English epic" with *The Faerie Queene* (1590–1596). Here, Pope has Spenser reduced to describing an English alley:

> In ev'ry town where Thamis roll his tyde,
>   A narrow pass there is with houses low;
> Where, ever and anon, the stream is eyed,
>   And many a boat, soft sliding to and fro.

[2]The *k'yer* (*care*) in Jack's speech is perhaps the voiced palatal fricative /ʝ/, or it is simply the approximant/glide /j/. It is heard also in Jamaican and other Caribbean varieties of English (e.g., *careful* as [kjerfʌl] or [kʝɚfʌl]). One can sense Twain detected in Jim's *en a patchin' up de raf* the sort of intonation patterning found in Gullah or Caribbean English Creoles.

There oft are heard the notes of infant woe,
The short thick sob, loud scream, and shriller squall;
How can ye, mothers, vex your children so?
Some play, some eat, some cack against the wall,
And as they crouchen low, for bread and butter call.

Pope's imitations of English poets are not merely based on style, meter, and diction, but on imitations of the contemporary form of the English language in each poet's lifetime. They are not always purely accurate in linguistic terms, but echoic, imitative, like theatrical dialects. Here antique-sounding forms such as *Thamis* for *Thames* and *tyde* for *tide* (a genuine Renaissance/Early Modern English spelling) are complemented by the vestigial Middle English 3rd plural present form *crouchen. Cack* stands out in tone and sound and drives home that Spenser is removed from his shepherds and royal courts and now surveys an impoverished English lane (not without a touch of sympathy). Pope then turns to the personified Envy and Malice, linking our imitation of Spenser to that poet and his literary forebear William Langland (his Middle English *Piers Plowman*, ca. 1362–1380s, in the A-, B-, and C-texts versions). Arguably, Pope's funniest imitation is that of Chaucer, which presents a brief bawdy folk tale as if a dislodged Canterbury Tale (from one of the lower-ranking members of the pilgrimage):

Women ben full of ragerie,
But swinken nat sans secresie.
Thilke moral shall ye understond,
From schoole-boy's tale of fayre Irelond....

This is not as close to the Middle English as it could be, but it does not need to be: it sounds "Chaucerian" enough with 3rd plural form *swinken*, 'to labor, toil' (but with its usual *double-entendre* from Chaucer's Miller's and Reeve's tales from *The Canterbury Tales*), and with the rhyming pair *ragerie* and *secresie*, whose root forms *rage* and *secret* were in fact loans to Middle English from Old French. Pope may be adding a more contemporary jibe by attributing the naughty story – to be brief, the gag involves a duck – to Ireland. Linguists try, in the pre-recording technology centuries, to reconstruct phonological data from written texts, especially those recorded in multiple copies and, ideally, in multiple dialects (the Old English glossed psalters, Northumbrian and West Saxon versions of Bede's poems, the great many Middle English texts whose provenance can be reasonably localized). Or, with somewhat less certainty, from the use of dialect in the authors' fictions (Geoffrey Chaucer is often cited as the first writer in English to do so). Less precise an instrument, but still of quite some value, is the assessment and imitation of earlier writers by their successors. Mark Twain wrote rather caustically about the novels of James Fenimore Cooper (1789–1851); to an extent there was no doubt some professional rivalry at work, perhaps even some begrudging tongue-in-cheek admiration of Cooper's success, but Twain let Cooper have it for the perceived "unnaturalness" of Cooper's seemingly Anglocentric prose – that is, that Cooper was writing to impress a British audience and writing more in a British manner. His bestselling "Leatherstocking Tales" irritated Twain, especially *The Last of the Mohicans: A Narrative of 1757* (1826):

> When a person has a poor ear for words, the result is a literary flatting and sharping; you perceive what he is intending to say but you also perceive that he doesn't *say* it...its English is a crime against the language. Counting these out, what is left is Art (DeVoto 1977, 354, 356).

Less charitably, Twain seemed to bristle at native names in Cooper's five "Leatherstocking" novels such as that of the last Mohican chief: "Chingachgook (pronounced Chicago I think)" (DeVoto 1977, 545). Cooper never tried to imitate as fully as Twain would later the dialects of his characters, and his upstate New York figures, from Fort Ann northward through the Adirondacks to New France, would have spoken English, Dutch, French, Mohican (or Mahican, an Eastern Algonquian language; Goddard 1996, 23, 740), Huron, Sauk, Fox, Iroquois, Oneida, Lenni Lenape, Iroquois (called the Mengwe or Mingo by the Delaware) and other native languages; additionally, Cooper gives glimpses of the many pidgins and trade jargons and Creolized forms of native–native and native-European contact varieties spoken in colonial New York. Our main (Anglo-)American figure Natty (Nathaniel) Bumppo, also known as Hawkeye or La Longue Carabine, was raised among the Delaware and is companion to Mohicans Chingachgook and his son Uncas and knows their languages; Major Duncan Heyward is able to negotiate in French with General Montcalm's forces; Magua is a Huron chief, allied, at first secretly, with the French who speaks French or a French-based patois (the French call him *Le renard subtil*, 'the sly fox'). The novel's action takes place during the French and Indian War (1754–1763), and the various parleys and captive exchanges would have been polyglot affairs (Schachterle 2011). Cooper often does not specify how the speakers were understood at these polyglot assemblies, such as the great mourning ritual that closes the novel, at which the elderly sagamore Tamenund of the Lenni Lenape speaks:

> Go, children of the Lenape; the anger of the Manitto is not done. Why should Tamenund stay? The pale faces are masters of the earth, and the time of the red-men has not yet come again. My day has been too long. In the morning I saw the sons of Unâmis [one of the three constituent tribes of the Lenape] happy and strong; and yet, before the night has come, have I lived to see the last warrior of the wise race of the Mohicans (Cooper 1826, III, 295).

But Cooper's works do provide attestations for a number of Native American loans to English in this 'middle' period of the development of American English. The earliest colonial Englishes belong to the first quarter of the 17th century, and a traditional dating for the transition from Early Modern English is somewhere around 1750–1800 – in the American context, the period of increased immigration to America from the 1750s onward, the passage of the Stamp Act in 1765, Declaration of Independence in 1776, and War for Independence (1775–1783), ratification of the US Constitution in 1788, completion of first elections in 1789. The long 19th century saw dramatic historical changes that bore a signal imprint on the development of American English. To use one example, and follow on from Cooper's portrayals of Algonquian and other Native Americans of the Northeast, the vector of transmission for native loans to American English would be altered and pushed further westward. The Indian Removal Act of 1830, passed by the 21st Congress of the United States under President Andrew Jackson, designated lands "west of the river Mississippi, not included in any state or organized territory, and to which the Indian title has been extinguished, as he [the President of the United States] may judge necessary, to be divided into a suitable number of districts, for the reception of such tribes or nations of Indians as may choose to exchange the lands where they now reside, and remove there" (Twenty-First Congress, Session I, Chapter CXLVIII, Statute I, Section 1, May 28, 1830). The critical word *removal* is understood now quite differently than as used in the 1830 act (as in transitive 'removing oneself from somewhere/something,' or intransitive, 'to move, go away, depart'); its sense is rather that of a *forcible removal*, as of a number of tribes to the Indian (Oklahoma) Territory or many of the Delaware (such as the Unami and Munsee of Cooper's novels) to Kansas, Oklahoma, and Wisconsin (the removal of natives from the Cherokee Agency in 1838–1839 is an infamous disaster, the "Trail of Tears"). That the Act was unlikely to operate well as a voluntary measure might be gauged in its last provision: "the sum of five hundred thousand dollars is hereby appropriated" (Section 8).

The Acts of Congress are of course statutes, the product of legalistic writing, with long sentences consisting of multiple periods, often attached to one another by semicolons and *wherefores* and *herebys*. A significant addition to American English was the nomenclature whereby native affairs (since 1824 the purview of the Bureau of Indian Affairs) would be discussed. This Act concerned the lands "of such tribes or nations," and early use seemed to distinguish population size and affiliation or confederacy by a rough ascending order of *clan*, *band* (smaller groups of subtribes of perhaps 10–50 individuals), *tribe*, *nation*. The use of *nation* for larger or confederated groups of natives (*Iroquois Nation*, *Cherokee Nation*, *Navajo Nation*) gave some strength to larger native groups for sovereignty and land and water rights (reservations in the United States are legally *sovereign nations*, often with their own governing councils or legislatures and police administration). The terms are applied from European languages, as are *warrior*, *brave*, and *chief*, though *clan* is from Scots Gaelic and Old Irish *clann* (in the sense 'offspring,' in turn from Latin *planta* 'plant,' a seemingly unusual sound change explicable in that Irish is a q-Celtic language in which initial /p/ > /k/; see Chapter 3). And the application of Scots Gaelic *clan* to native peoples offers some perspective on the English outlook toward the groups of indigenous Americans: that they saw some similarity between the native family and suprafamilial kinship structures that reminded them of the sept and clan systems in Ireland and Scotland, which had earlier been colonized by the English. There is likely in the term's use also a semantic force of 'wildness' (see Cutler 1994, 32–43), which is certainly a characteristic attributed to the Irish in John Derricke's *The image of Irelande, with a discouerie of woodkarne* (1581). The *wood-kerne* were Irish foot-soldiers who had, in fact and lore, taken to the woods after the Anglo-Norman conquests; the term is an Anglo-Irish hybrid of *wood* (a calque of Irish *coille*) and *kerne* < Irish *ceithern* (Middle Irish *cethern*, 'four, quatrain'). Like the Irish and Scots Highland *gallowglass* (Irish *gallóglaigh*) they often became mercenaries. One can detect both the colonial and semantic ('wild, savage') context for the application of *clan* to Native Americans, and the comparison between the colonized groups was made abundantly clear in Thomas Hariot's *Briefe and true report of the new found land of Virginia* (1588; see Chapter 7): following the illustrations of the Virginia Algonquian natives and their villages is a section "Som picture, of the Pictes which in the olde tyme dyd habite one part of the great Bretainne" with John White's rendering of tattooed Picts and neighboring Celts. At the opening of Shakespeare's *Macbeth* King Duncan is informed that rebellious Macdonald "from the Western Isles / Of kerns and gallowglasses is supplied" (I.ii.12–13). The sort of interchange between native and European on the East coast that occurred in the early years of settlement led to a number of early loans: native flora and fauna, culinary, cultural, or of weaponry and governance. As native populations were reduced, by war and sickness and relocation, the vector of transmission narrowed in the East and moved west (Cutler 1994, 53–78). And the new settlers pushing westward met new native peoples, and their terms for the new flora and fauna and customs. Cutler (1994) dated the native loan *wapiti* (large elk) to the decade 1800–1809 from the Shawnee language, *mackinaw* forms (from Ojibwa *michilimachinak*, 'island of the large turtle'; with reference to places-names such as Lake Mackinaw and Mackinac Island, Michigan, and mackinaw cloth, blankets, boats, and trout) to the decades 1810–1819 and 1820–1829, and from 1840 to 1849 *cayuse*, named after the Cayuse people of the Pacific Northwest – applied here to a breed of horse and, by pejoration, because of the horse's temperamental reputation, to the mustang, and thence used in Western jargon as a cowboy insult (Cutler 1994, 88–91; Adams 1993, 59). Many of these loans involve names for plants, and of course the largest corpus of native loans involves toponyms. Many of these loans are regional, known primarily to locals, and some are now historical or obsolete and encountered only in early records. The range of native loans to American English still awaits further discoveries as, in parallel to Celtic loans to early English, there can be some debate about whether an English or other Germanic source is more likely – there has been some historical resistance to crediting Celtic and Native American origins to English vocabulary items – and the route of transmission from source to target language can at times be convoluted. A good many native loans from the Northeast, Upper Midwest, and Canada passed into English via French, and many native loans passed through Spanish in the Southwest. Popular ideas can also alter or obscure the origin of some native loans: the *tomahawk* is often associated in the popular imagination with the Plains Indians, but it is a loan from Powhatan Virginia Algonquian – and thus among the earliest native loans to English.

Indeed the earliest attestation for *tomahawk* is ca. 1612, from William Strachey's *The Historie of Travaile Into Virginia Britannia* (Oxford, 1612; Wright and Freund 1953); Strachey led a colorful life in later Elizabethan and Jacobean London, in the company of dramatists such as Ben Jonson and George Chapman and other literati at the Mermaid Tavern, in diplomatic service (to Turkey), and then as part of the Virginia Company. He was stranded when the *Sea Venture* ran aground off Bermuda for a year and, making it then to Virginia, became Secretary of the Jamestown colony (Major 1849, xx–xxii). Two other 17th-century attestations are recorded by the OED and, among attestations in the following century, a reference to "The wampum and tomahawks I have purchased" in a letter of George Washington (the spelling *tomahawk* by now standard; Strachey recorded *tamahauke*, while also recorded are *tamahawks* [1674] and *tomhog* [1716]). *Wampum*, the strings of cylindrical beads whittled from sea shells, was most famously used as a form of currency by colonists trading with Native Americans; natives used it for a variety of purposes, such as in elaborately beaded belts, for ceremonial and official purposes: it was famously used to ratify treaties, such as the alleged *kaswentha* (mutual accord, as symbolized in the Two-Row wampum belt) of 1613 between the Dutch of New Amsterdam and the Hodensaunee Confederacy[3] or the Great Treaty of Shackamaxon (1682 or 1683) between the Lenni Lenape and William Penn. These early accounts of the colonies of Massachusetts Bay, Rhode Island, Pennsylvania, Virginia, and others, the treaties, land surveys and divisions and claims, and other documents record the vector of transmission of loans from Native American languages to English (and, more specifically, the earliest American English). Strachey had appended to his *Historie* one of two accounts of the Powhatan Algonquian language, his *A Dictionarie of the Indian Language*. The bilingual glossary is not unlike those Latin-English glossaries of the medieval period, arranged in two columns of Powhatan-English or English-Powhatan forms: *apones* 'bread' (whence *pone, corn-pone*), 'A hatchet, *taccahacan, tamahaac*' (which also glosses 'A morter' [mortar]), 'Monowhauk, *a sword*,' 'Suckquohana, *water*' (compare *Susquehanna/Susquehannock*, an Algonquian river-name that may mean 'muddy' or 'crooked river'), 'Virginia, *Tsenahcommacah*,' 'Winggapo, *my beloved friend*,' 'A woman queene, *wironausqua*' (apparently Virginia Algonquian *weroan* 'leader, chief,' as recorded in Thomas Hariot's 1588 *Briefe and true report*, + *squaw*).

The various early forms of *(ap)pones* mark the development of a loan from Native Americans, not just linguistic but culinary and cultural. *Pone* or *corn-pone* became a staple of especially Southern American cooking, as the extensive entry for *pone* in the *Dictionary of American Regional English* records; following the first attestation in Strachey's 1612 *Virginia Britannia* is a 1796 entry from Benjamin Henry Latrobe's *Journal* of his travels 1796–1820: *A few biscuits, and pones of Indian and wheat bread* (DARE vol. IV, s.v. *pone*). Latrobe was born in England, the son of a Moravian minister, and is principally known for his architectural works, including the U.S. Capitol, the Baltimore Basilica (the first Roman Catholic cathedral in the United States), Nassau and Stanhope Halls at Princeton University, and, in collaboration with Thomas Jefferson and Irishman James Hoban, the White House. The Moravian church presence in colonial America (the church at Lititz, PA, dates to 1787, the community established there to 1749) also had a culinary effect: the *Moravian cookie*, a sort of very thin rolled version of the German *Lebkuchen* associated with Christmas markets (the Nürnberger Christkindlesmarkt or American counterparts), a spiced molasses cookie.

---

[3] The Dutch document is said to be a fake, partly on linguistic grounds: the Dutch of the purported original text anachronistic, as is the use of *Seewant* for *wampum*, though the term interestingly derives from Delaware Pidgin; Charles T. Gehring and William A. Starna, "Revisiting the Tawagonshi Treaty of 1613," *New York History* 93.1 (2012), 95–101. The first attestation of the Massachusett or Narragansett loan *wampum* in English is from a 1636 entry in John Winthrop's *The History of New England from 1630 to 1649* (Cambridge, MA, 1649).

The next attestation in DARE for *pone* comes from Joel Chandler Harris's *Nights with Remus* (1883), the second of nine total volumes of Southern Black folk tales, aphorisms, songs, and trickster stories (notably those of Br'er [Brother] Rabbit) Georgia native Harris collected. The recording of the Black speech of Uncle Remus and other figures by Harris, a white man, in what was then termed the 'Negro dialect,' has long been controversial. The *pone* citation is typical: *She tuck'n fry 'im up a rasher er bacon, en bake 'im in a pone er bread*. The afterlife of Harris's Uncle Remus stories, including the popular Walt Disney mixed live-action-and-animated film production *Song of the South* (1946), has been controversial enough to throw doubt upon the value of Harris's dialect renderings. There is no doubt that Uncle Remus, in popular fiction and film, has been painfully associated with 'Uncle Tom' figures in American popular culture, which in turn recalls the controversial role of Harriet Beecher Stowe's antebellum novel *Uncle Tom's Cabin* (1852). Stowe's renderings of 'Negro speech' in her 'sentimental novel' are likely the most controversial examples of dialect fiction in all of American literature, rather less because they are exceptionally bad or offensive (in the context of 19th-century American fiction of or about the South) as that *Uncle Tom's Cabin* enjoyed a popularity greater than any other American novel of the latter half of the 19th century. None of the linguistic appraisals of Stowe's ear for dialect can undermine the social force of her abolitionist novel – few works of fiction have had so great an influence on historical events. And despite the stereotypical nature of the Black speech as written by Harris or Stowe, there is value in what they did record as we are in an age before mechanical recording devices. The great archive of ex-slave recordings in the Library of Congress's *Voices Remembering Slavery: Freed People Tell Their Stories*[4] begins in 1932 with recordings of Gullah men and women from the Sea Islands of South Carolina and Georgia made on discs by linguist Lorenzo Dow Turner. Turner was a pioneer in the study of Gullah and its West African origins and vital role in writing the history of African American English (notably his *Africanisms in the Gullah Dialect* [1949]). He was also a leading figure at several Black universities: Howard University, Fisk University, and Roosevelt University (what are now known as HBCs, 'Historically Black Colleges'). The recordings begin nearly 60 years after the interviewees' emancipation from slavery, and span Virginia and the South Atlantic coast, the Bahamas, Alabama, and Texas (these last recordings made by father-and-son musicologists Alan and John Lomax and John's wife, the folklorist Ruby Lomax). The recording made by Alan Lomax and others of George Johnson of Mound Bayou, MS, in 1941 gives a sense that the dialect renderings made by late 19th-century novelists missed many of the Africanisms in speech that was decreolizing – features that would only be noted more clearly by linguists such as Turner – but that they did record some salient features of Black speech from the later period of enslavement to the early post-Emancipation decades. George Johnson's speech exhibits *l*-vocalization ([saɪdwo:k] for *sidewalk*) and front vowel /ɛ/ >

4 https://www.loc.gov/collections/voices-remembering-slavery/about-this-collection/

/ɪ/ raising ([ʤɪnrʌl] for *general*). Compare this sample of speech from Uncle Tom's wife Aunt Chloe in the chapter "An Evening in Uncle Tom's Cabin":

> 'So I did,' said Aunt Chloe, – 'I may say dat. Good, plain, common cookin', Jinny'll do; – **make a good pone o' bread**, – **bile her taters** *far*, – her corn cakes is n't extra, not extra now, Jinny's corn cakes is n't, but then they's far, – but, Lor, come to de higher branches, and what *can* she do? Why, she makes pies – sartin she does; but what kinder crust? Can she make your real flecky paste, as melts in your mouth, and lies all up like a puff? Now, I went over thar when Miss Mary was gwine to be married, and Jinny she jest showed me de weddin's pies. Jinny and I is good friends, ye know.... Lor! to think of some of our dinners! Yer mind dat ar great chicken pie I made when we guv de dinner to General Knox? I and Missis, we come pretty near quarrelling about dat ar crust. What does get into ladies sometimes, I don't know; but, sometimes, when a body has de heaviest kind o' 'sponsibility on 'em, as ye may say, and is all kinder *'seris'* and taken up, dey takes dat ar time to be hangin' round and kinder interferin'!... And de Gineral, he knows what cookin' is.... Bery nice man, de Gineral! He comes of one of de bery *fustest* families in Old Virginny! He knows what's what, now, as well as I do – de Gineral (Stowe 1852, vol. I, 43, 45–46; bold added).

Aunt Chloe's *fustest*, a non-rhotic form of double superlative of *first*, is paralleled by the *fust* ('first') in Hanna Jenkins's Gullah 'seeking' religious testimonial below. Her *pone o' bread* is an example of an expression of some frequency in regional AmE: *DARE* cites a number of attestations, from Virginia (*pone of corn-bread*) to SE Missouri to NW Arkansas (*three pones of baker's bread*), West Texas to Eastern Tennessee to the Gulf Coast (a variety of *pone of X-* collocations from the *Linguistic Atlas of the Gulf States*). The semantic extension seems to range from the native Algonquian cornmeal loaf or cake to the form of the handmade cake/loaf/fritter made from other grains, though competing with this more general *pone = loaf/cake* was the narrower *corn-pone* (that the cake or loaf or fritter is *pone* if made from cornmeal). A whole host of other culinary forms gathered about the original native food: cakes or loaves, either hand-formed or pan-shaped, fritters, flat cakes (that would be even thinner than fritters, more flapjack-like), and *corn-dodgers*: hand-shaped, usually circular, cornmeal cakes griddled, baked, or even boiled: Twain refers to *corn-dodger* in his *Autobiography* (DeVoto 1977, 625); when Huck is reunited with Jim, "he got out some corn-dodgers and buttermilk, and pork and cabbage, and greens" (Twain 1885/1996, 155). The general ingredient was cornmeal, though the fritter or dodger can include whole kernels; in Pennsylvania Dutch cooking, toasted dried sweet corn crushed into granular form. It can be made from scratch on the quick, or on the road, over a campfire or cooked in ashes (e.g., *ash pone*, a form DARE records as belonging primarily to Virginia). Cooking by the latter means, in the ashes of a fire also gave rise to the terms *ash bread* (South to Midlands), *ashcake* (Virginia to Georgia), *ashdog* (a New England term, Connecticut and New Hampshire, for an Indian meal [corn meal] ball-like fritter – it is also a term for the *hushpuppy*; DARE s.v.v. *ashdog, dogbread, hush puppy*), *ashnan* (or *ashnanny*, made from biscuit dough, chiefly from South Carolina; see Burkette 2011), and *fire cake* (Massachusetts to Pennsylvania, the term attributed to General Washington's encampment at Valley Forge during the

Revolutionary War; DARE marks the term as possibly obsolete). The geographic distribution of *corn pone* is, according to DARE, "now widespread exc[luding]" New England, having previously been a Southern and Midland term; the DSAE adds that *pone* forms, such as *pone bread*, *pone of [corn]bread*, are found in greater frequency in South Carolina and Georgia in the Appalachians rather than the Piedmont or coastal regions, which accords well with the general tripartite dialect division of South Atlantic states: or quadripartite when including the Ocracoke Brogue of the Outer Banks and Gullah of the Sea Islands; *cornmeal bread* is the term found across the northern tier of states, New England, upstate New York, Pennsylvania to the Great Lakes Region (and thence to California – one of the terms brought by internal migration from the MW to California). *Corn muffin* had originally been a Mid- to South Atlantic term but is now in general use. And so also the *hush puppy*, 'A dollop of cornmeal batter, sometimes seasoned, fried in deep fat' (DARE, s.v.). The *hush puppy* has become particularly associated with fish or seafood meals, likely as it can be fried in the same fat or oil as the battered fish; the South Carolina term *redhorse bread*, 'cooked at fish fries' ... 'about the same as hush puppies' (DARE, s.v.) is named after the mullet-like *redhorse*, and cooked in the same oil as the fish as an accompaniment. The *hush puppy* is widely known across the United States, often as a side with fried fish (such as catfish, or in seafood 'fish and chips'-style combinations), though the distribution map in DARE shows that it is still highly concentrated in use from Georgia to Texas. A term limited mainly to New England is *Indian pudding*, a dish of baked or boiled cornmeal soaked in molasses and served usually as a dessert; the term seems to be declining in usage (it was on the menu of the fabled Durgin-Park restaurant at Faneuil Hall, Boston Harbor, from its founding in 1827 until its closing in 2019). From William Strachey's 1612 glossary of Algonquian terms to Stowe's 1852 novel *Uncle Tom's Cabin*, and from Harris's Uncle Remus stories to present, American English has seen four centuries of *(corn) pone* – enough that *corn pone* (or *cornpone*) can mean 'corny,' 'cornball,' or 'cloyingly folksy'; this is a mild pejoration of the term's associative extension from the food item, from a rustic food to 'a rustic Southerner,' to a sort of bumpkin-ness (RHHDAS, s.v. *corn pone*; and cf. Twain, *Europe and Elsewhere*, "corn-pone opinions"; DeVoto 1977, 572).[5]

If Stowe's Black characters are all rather overdrawn, stagey, melodramatic – so too are all of her white characters (especially slave trader Haley and the notorious Simon Legree, on the villainous end, or the angelic young proto-abolitionist Eva St. Clare). As would Twain and Harris, Stowe quietly noted the influence of Black speech on Southern white speech. Here are early attestations of features found in the 1941 recording of former slave George Johnson (Aunt Chloe's *Gineral* for *General*), as well as a host of other features characteristic not just of Black speech of the later 19th century but found in contemporary AAVE: stop for fricative in *de*, resumptive pronouns (*de Gineral, he*), resolution of final consonant clusters (the clipped *Lor'* for *Lord*), substitution of /b/ for /v/ (*bery*), 'linking' or intrusive /r/ and non-rhotic forms (*fustest* for double-superlative *firstest*), as well as turns of phrases still familiar not just in Southern Black speech but in forms of AAVE wherever AAVE speech communities may be found. The influence of Black speech on the white was profound enough for one scholar to suggest that Twain may have even modeled Huck

[5] As *corn pone* can now indicate a rube-ish quality to person or character or speech (or place: *cornpone town*, DSAE, s.v.); in AAVE *cornbread* can function similarly: RHHDAS records the nominal form, 'an unsophisticated Southern black person,' though this has extended also to adjectival use.

Finn not just on the real-life Hannibal, MO, "poor-white outcast child" Tom Blankenship, but on a 10-year-old Black child Twain wrote about in his 1874 *New York Times* story "Sociable Jimmy" (Fishkin 1993, 3, 14–16). Shelley Fisher Fishkin's *Was Huck Black?* proposed a thesis that was groundbreaking for literary critics and theorists: "For Twain's imaginative blending of black voices with white ones (whether conscious or unconscious) effectively deconstructs 'race' as a meaningless category.... How will Americans respond to the news that the voice of Huck Finn, the beloved national symbol and cultural icon, was part black?" (Fishkin 1993, 144). To the linguist Twain's "imaginative blending" is rather more naturalistic; like many others raised in the Southern Midlands and South, Twain knew of the interchange of influence of Black and white speech, and he consciously, and carefully, deployed the nuances – racial, social, class-based – in the dialogue of his varied characters. Fishkin (1993) mentions briefly in the notes Pederson's important 1967 study of "Mark Twain's Missouri Dialects" but the aim of her study is more theoretical (about race as a category, and canon-formation), as Pederson's study had answered many of the linguistic questions raised in the later study's theoretical musings. If Huck was "part black" in his speech it was to some extent an inherited feature of Pike County speech (and the counties, such as Marion, that were carved out of Pike after 1820), likely reinforced and perhaps expanded by Jim's influence; and Jim's influence likely extended beyond the linguistic, as he fills in a paternal role abandoned by Pap.

A somewhat more complex example of literary recordings of Southern Black speech can be found in the short stories of Louisiana writer Kate Chopin (1850–1904). Chopin, *née* Katherine O'Flaherty, was born in St. Louis in an Irish and Louisiana French household; upon marriage to Oscar Chopin in 1870 she moved to her husband's native New Orleans, then after business misfortunes, to Cloutierville, Natchitoches Parish, Louisiana; Natchitoches (pronounced [nækətəʃ] or [nækətɪʃ], or Les Natchitoches ([nakitoʃ] or [nakitɔʃ]), was then a center of cotton plantations, and Oscar managed some of the smaller holdings in the parish. The Cajun and Creole culture, and languages and dialects, of the region provided the setting for Kate Chopin's two great short story collections, *Bayou Folk* (1894) and *A Night in Acadie* (1897). Chopin employed various eye dialect forms to try to capture the range of local speech forms, from Cajun (Acadian) and Creole speakers of Louisiana English to speakers, free and enslaved, of forms of Southern Black English and the more high-toned speech of characters addressed as Mademoiselle (or Mamzelle), Madame, or Monsieur (or P'tit Maître, 'little master,' for a boy). In "Mamouche" from *A Night in Acadie* in Natchitoches, the elderly Doctor John-Luis (the local partial Anglicization of Jean-Louis as the main white characters are Acadian) comes to adopt the raggedy boy who shows up on his doorstep; the boy at first goes by the mononym Mamouche, but then divulges that he is the son of Mathurin Peloté and grandson of Théodule Peloté, who had married John-Luis's lost love Stéphanie Galopin. The sometimes fluid or uncertain linguistic and racial categories of old Louisiana are invoked at the story's start when John-Luis's "old negro" Marshall opens the door to Mamouche:

> G'long back on de gall'ry an' drip yo'se'f! W'at Cynthy gwine say tomorrow w'en she see dat flo' mess' up dat away?
>
> Is you wi'te o' is you black? Dat w'at I wants ter know 'fo' I kiar' victuals to yo in de settin'-room (Chopin 1999, 285).

Mamouche's speech is that of an Acadian boy, but one whose family has apparently fallen on hard times, and the boy's speech shows clear signs of the influence of Black speech forms in addition to the expected French influence:

> I'm wi'te, me....
>
> I come from Cloutierville this mo'nin'. I been try to git to the twenty-fo'-mile ferry w'en de rain ketch me.
>
> Why, yas! Théodule Peloté it was my gran'pa.... Yas, that who was my gran'ma. She die two year ago down by Alexandria (Chopin 1999, 285–286).

The vowel lowering in *yas*, for *yes*, is still heard in some varieties of AAVE, and has become something of a speech 'meme' in contemporary youth English (as in the intensive form *yaaasss*); the vowel raising in *ketch* (for *catch*) is found also in the speech of Jim in Twain's *Huckleberry Finn*. The influence of Black English on Mamouche's speech is also grammatical: the missing copula in *that who was*, the resumptive pronoun use (*I'm wi'te, me*), the alternative auxiliary forms (*I been try*), and the absence of past tense marking (*She die*). The influence can be seen too in the speech of the unmarried Acadian plantation owner Mamzelle Aurélie in "Regret" from the same collection: "I tell you, Aunt Ruby...me. I'd manage a dozen plantation' than fo' chil'ren. It's terrassent! [overwhelming] Bonté! [goodness!] Don't talk to me about chil'ren" (Chopin 1999, 243). If some of Chopin's renderings of Black speech seem as exaggerated as Stowe's, the range of varieties she sought to capture was wider; in "A Dresden Lady in Dixie," the haughty Madame Valtour interrogates her Creole maid Viny about who had been in her room in her absence; Viny responds, "Pa-Jeff comed in yere wid de mail.... On'y Agapie w'at brung you some Creole **aigs**. I tole 'er to sot 'em down in de hall. I don' know she comed in de settin'-room o' not" (Chopin 1999, 255–256; emphasis added). Of interest are the past tense forms *comed* and *brung* (the latter common throughout Southern speech), *yere* the variant form of adverb *here*,[6] and the non-rhotic forms *sot* ('sort') and *o'* ('or'). Chopin can with her Acadians indicate also class and gender differences in speech, as with the various rivals in "At the 'Cadian Ball" from *Bayou Folk*; and so with Bobinôt to Calixta, "*Bon Dieu*! You know that makes me crazy, w'at you sayin'. You mean that, Calixta? You ent goin' turn roun' agin'?" or Clarisse to Alcée Laballière, "Ah Dieu sait! [God knows] It's only something that happen' to me" (Chopin 1999, 150). Louisiana is a particularly complex zone of language interaction, and, whether in the city of New Orleans, the Cajun 'capital' of Lafayette, or the smaller parishes, racially and linguistically diverse peoples lived together. In the folktale tradition of French Louisiana,

[6] Compare Twain's *thish-yer*, 'this here,' with /s/ > /ʃ/ substitution and glide /j/ insertion; the process is likely even more complicated, with [ðɪs hi:r] > [ðɪs jɛr] > [ðɪʃjɚr], though the second vowel could also be /ɛ/ or /ʌ/ or some other unrounded mid-back vowel lower than /ə/; this occurs, along with intrusive and linking /r/ forms *feller* and *kinder sad-like*, in his short story "The Celebrated Jumping Frog of Calaveras County" (1865; DeVoto 1977, 39, 41). Calaveras County is in central Northern California, and had drawn hopefuls and 'tramps' to the region for placer-mining (gold mining in stream beds) during the Gold Rush. The frog's name in the story is Dan'l Webster.

Acadian (Cajun) and Creole, there seems to have been a sense that English was the language of authority figures or outsiders (Ancelet 1994, xlix, 71).

In the short tale "La vieille fille qui voulait se marier" ("The Old Maid Who Wanted to Marry"), the titular *vieille fille* asks her grandmother for advice on how to find a husband; *grand-mère* tells her to pray at night by an oak tree and await an answer. A first try yields no response, so she prays harder and an old owl (*vieil hibou*), as God's messenger, cries out *Hou houou!*, which she interprets as "Who, who!" – she is not picky as to the suitor, just that he be sent *tout de suite* 'right away' (Ancelet 1994, 70–71). The tale's teller, Clotilde Richard of Carencro, Lafayette Parish, apparently heard the story in English and kept the pun in the owl's response in English (rendered in phonetic French as *hou houou*) rather than using *kee* (*qui, qui*, which occurs in tales for the cry of the sparrow or kildeer [plover]). Barry Jean Ancelet, who collected these stories, notes, "For Mme Richard, it is not surprising that God speaks in English, just like any other person in power" (71). A number of tales concern Lapin and Bouki, Rabbit (the Br'er Rabbit in Joel Chandler Harris's Uncle Remus stories) and Bouki ('hyena' in Wolof), tales that have West African origins and have also been found in Maritime Acadien tradition, and down the Mississippi in Missouri and Louisiana French. In *Dans la grosserie* ("In the Grocery") Lapin tells Bouki *C'est l'heure on* gone" ("it's time to go"), *Mais Bouki voulait pas* gone ("Bouki didn't want to go"); here, the expected French infinitive (*partir, aller*) is replaced by the English past participle *gone*. This may be an influence of Creole grammar, as a number of the transmitters of these animal fables were Creoles; one such Creole storyteller, Wilson 'Ben Guiné' Mitchell of Parks, St. Martin Parish, in a version of the famous "tar man" story, speaks a Creole French interspersed with occasional English words and phrases: *et fait un petit n-homme en* coal tar *dans le milieu du jardin. Ah*, well, *Bouki vient, li gardé comme ça-là. Lapin vient, li gardé comme ça-là. Li hélé li, li dit, 'Qui c'est ça, cil-là*, "...and made a little tar man in the middle of the garden. Ah, well, Bouki came and looked at him like this. Lapin came and looked at him like this. He yelled to him, he said, 'Who is this?'" (*Le petit bonhomme en* coal tar ?, "The Little Tar Man"; Ancelet 1994, 7). English *go on* can be used in place of French *avance* in the stories, presumably as a high-frequency English expression everyone would have known; it seems to also be used at times reduplicatively, as in this Creole tale from Carrie Charles of Cade, St. Martin Parish:

> Ça fait, li joue une autre danse. Ça té so troisième danse. Quand li joue l'autre danse, li – yé continué après danser, pi après *brag on* li, li dit yé "*Go ahead*, avance là-bas toujours! Li dit, "Avance!" li dit. Tout d'une escousse, li jette banjo-là par terre, li dit yé, "*Good-bye*" li dit, "*I'm gone*."
>
> So he played another tune. That was his third tune. When he played another tune, he – they continued to dance and to brag on about him. He says to them, "Go on!" he says. All of a sudden, he threw the banjo down and said to them, "Good-bye!" he says, "I'm gone!" ("Lapin joue banjo", "Lapin Plays the Banjo"; Ancelet 1994, 15).

The matter of influence, and its direction, is enormously complex: one feature noted by Pederson 1967 may illustrate just how complex the linguistic picture may be. Glide insertion after initial velars was reported by Pederson's oldest Marion County informants as being "exclusively" used in "Negro speech" – for example, *garden* as [gjɒrdɪn] or *cards* as [kyardz] or [kyɔrdz] (Kurath and McDavid 1961, 175; Pederson 1967, 177). In the American South the glide insertion after /g/ or /k/ is found in both 'common' and 'cultivated' speech, clustered most heavily from Virginia to South Carolina, and occurs in British English throughout the Midlands but also in East Anglia and the Southwest, though only in 'common' speech (Kurath and McDavid 1961, 175 and map 167). In two extended discussions of language matters in Twain Fishkin notes features of Black English (especially Southern Black speech) that influenced General Southern AmE – for instance the use of sequential verb forms (Huck's "first one hound and then another *got up* and *went for me*, and of course *I stopped*, and *faced them*, and *kept still*"; Fishkin 1993, 47) – and the stigmatization by white speakers of Black influence on their speech and a supposed resistance among linguists in "recognizing the influence of African-American speech patterns on both Southern speech and American speech in general" (Fishkin 1993, 131). But Southern writers had long remarked on the influence of Black speech on white, and the stigmatization (as of *ain't*) was also deeply class-marked; the use of sequential verbs is also a hallmark of childhood narrative style, as it is of Irish and Scots-Irish speech (another great influence on Southern and Midland speech). In the postmodern moment there has been a de-emphasis upon if not erasure of Huck Finn's identity; it is instructive to note that Twain, upon seeing F.W. Kemble's illustration for the cover of the first edition of his novel (1884), had remarked, "All right and good, and will answer, although the boy's mouth is a trifle more Irishy than necessary" (David and Sapirstein in Fishkin 1996, 35). Irish and Ulster Scots speech exerted a strong influence on Black speech in the Caribbean (especially in Jamaica and the Barbados) and the American South and Midlands. In the passage from Stowe above Aunt Chloe's *bile her taters* is one such example of the influence: [baɪl] for [bɔɪl] is commonly found in American caricature of 'stage Irish' speech; the pattern of influence was recognized enough that it appears in exaggerated form in Victor Fleming's 1939 film version of *Gone With the Wind.*

Mark Twain (Samuel Langhorne Clemens) was himself of part Scots-Irish descent; he was born in Florida, MO, in Monroe County, until his father, a lawyer, moved the family to Hannibal some 35 miles away, on the Mississippi in what was then Pike County. Pike County had been settled by Cumberland Gap emigrants or those who took that route westward, with most of its population hailing from Virginia, the Carolinas, and Kentucky (Pederson 1967). Pike County speech was identifiable enough as 'rustic' that during the California Gold Rush, "Pike countyans" became a generic term for other such 'hick' varieties (originally a hypocoristic form, from *Richard*, *hick* made the journey across the Atlantic with the sense of 'bumpkin, yokel'[7]). Twain's father's occupation placed the Clemens family more solidly in the middle ranks of Pike County,

[7] Illustrative quotations in the RHDAS are interesting for the range of collocations that early on attached to *hick*: "merry hick" (1676); "Richard Bumpkin! Ha! A Perfect Country Hick!" (1702); "the Country Hick" (1720); "Gang of Hicks" (1904); "hick towns" (1908; s.vv., *hick*, n. and adj.). *Hick* is one of a number of disparaging terms for (poor) whites that are only roughly synonymous (*buckra, cracker, redneck, hillbilly, po' white, white trash, Tobacco Road, ape* – the last term was usually applied to the Irish); like a number of these terms it has become auto-antonymous among people it has been applied to: *Missouri hick* can be used with ironic or defiant pride in the broader Ozark region.

though they were like many of the county's denizens from the South (his father, John, was from Virginia, mother Jane from Kentucky). The settlement pattern of Pike County is critical as Hannibal is not quite 120 miles N-NW of St. Louis, a city whose demographics would change significantly 1830–1920: the early Native and French population would be overwhelmed by a Southern migration from the mid-Southern states Virginia, North Carolina, Kentucky, and Tennessee; a large wave of German immigrants began in the 1830s, followed by Irish and Italian immigrants and Southern Blacks from the Delta in the Great Migration. This led to St. Louis becoming once again a Catholic-majority city, as it had been under the French; in a campaign fraught with ironies, leading Presbyterian abolitionist Rev. Elijah P. Lovejoy (1802–1837), martyred for the cause by a pro-slavery mob in November 1837 in Alton, IL (across the river from St. Louis, in the free state Illinois), railed vociferously (and viciously) against Catholics and Catholic doctrine (as, along with slavery, one of the twin perils endangering the United States). Fellow abolitionist and Presbyterian minister Lyman Beecher (1775–1863), father of novelist Harriet Beecher Stowe, had warned that St. Louis and the Mississippi Valley would be "the scene of the death struggle between Protestantism and Catholicism" (Duerk 2015, 105). Cross-state, Kansas City was similarly shaped by the immigrants following the French foundation; but many of these came from Midland states such as Ohio and Illinois, followed by the Germans and Irish, then Southern Blacks (some of whom were from New Orleans and made Kansas City a second home for jazz music), and, more recently, Mexican internal migrants from the Southwest. The two major metropolitan areas of Missouri are distinct from the rest of the state, demographically and dialectally (seen, for instance, in the *soda* [urban] - *pop* [rural] isogloss). Though part of a Midland dialectal band, St. Louis and Kansas City have their differences; while Kansas City does exhibit the low-back vowel merger (or *cot-caught* /ɑ/ - /ɔ/ merger, both realized as /ɑ/), Indianapolis and St. Louis have resisted the merger (ANAE 121–124, Map 11.1). Within the broader Midland dialect band, Pike County is to be located in the Central Mississippi Valley region. Besides the salient phonological features of the dialects of the region, the lexical and grammatical features seen above with *Adventures of Huckleberry Finn* help draw a general picture of an unusual dialect continuum along the Mississippi: Twain's "Explanatory" that he employed among the dialects represented "the ordinary 'Pike County' dialect" and "four modified varieties of this last" likely refers to class-marked variants in a town such as Hannibal, and the various mid-South origins of "Pike countyans." While "the extremest form of the backwoods South-Western dialect" has Pap as its most natural exponent, Huck likely can also be said to be a speaker of the variety, tempered by the "sivilizing" effect of life with the likes of the Sawyers and the Widow Douglas. Though our modern critical focus gravitates naturally toward Jim and the novel's presentation of the personal, social, and national sins of slavery, de-emphasized has been just who Huck Finn is: white trash, shanty Irish, son of an absent Irish drunk, a category of 'po' white' looked down upon by most other strata of society (for how this system of social stratification could work, more recently, in Warren County, Eastern North Carolina, see Hazen 2000, 33–52). The affectionate bond that develops between Huck and Jim operates at the level of surrogate father and son, at the level of dialect interaction and difference ("Negro" and "backwoods"), across a generational and racial gap that, in the end, for all its bonding and affection, remains unequal.

As so much depends critically, for literary interpreters and theorists, upon the language represented by the 'eye dialect' of authors such as Stowe, Harris, and Twain, the question remains about the accuracy of representations of Black speechways by white authors. The charge that these authors reduced their Black characters to 'minstrelsy' has long been lodged – though Pap, the Duke and Dauphin are caricatures of types of lower-class whites – and one might look to recordings of Black speech by Black authors for some sense of the linguistic value of late 19th- and early 20th-century American fictions to the dialect picture. James Weldon Johnson (1871–1938), poet, novelist (*The Autobiography of an Ex-Colored Man* [1912]), major figure of the Harlem Renaissance and the Civil Rights Movement, was also an important collector of Black hymns from the South. Born in Jacksonville, Florida, his mother from the Bahamas, Johnson published in 1925 the collection *The Book of American Negro Spirituals*. Here are found such well-known Spirituals as "Go Down Moses" ("Tell ole Pharaoh, / Let my people go"), "Swing Low, Sweet Chariot," "Roll Jordan, Roll," "Nobody Knows the Trouble I See," "Up on de Mountain" ("Walkin' / 'long – Lord, Wid hung down head – Lord! / Chillun, – an' achin' heart"),"O Wasn't Dat a Wide River?" ("Dere's one mo' river to cross"), "Keep Me F'om Sinkin' Down." Johnson records the hymns in eye dialect and sheet-music form – these are records of how the songs were actually sung in Black churches: characteristic stop for fricative substitution of /b/ for /v/ (*ribber* for *river*), or /d/ for /ð/ or /θ/ (*de* for *the*, *dere* for *there*, *dem* for *them*, *wid* for *with*), final consonant clipping and consonant cluster reduction (*roun'*, *boun'*, *han'*, *clim'in'*, *jus'*), and the auxiliary forms, as were found in Jim's speech in Twain, *gwine* ('going,' 'goin') and *gwinter* ('going to': "Oh, I'm a gwinter sing"). These and like features are found in other recordings of the Spirituals: in "Done Found My Lost Sheep," the second stanza begins "In that Resurrection Day / Sinner can't find no hiding place" (Marks/Hammond and Busch 2012, vol. 2, 1338). The use of forms of *a*, from the verbal prefix *a-* to intensifying *a-* ("a-plenty") to emphatic *-a/-a-* can be found in the Spirituals: "The soldiers there a-plenty, / Standing by the door" ("The Angel Roll the Stone Away"), "I Got a home in-a that rock," "The trumpet sounds within-a my soul," "Green trees a-bending, / Poor sinner stands a-trembling" ("I Got a Home in-a That Rock," "Steal Away to Jesus"; Marks/Hammond and Busch 2012, vol. 2, 1349–1341). The pioneering work of Black linguist Lorenzo Dow Turner (1890–1972) preserved a record of the Gullah of older speakers as the younger generations saw increased decreolization of the variety accelerate; the stories Dow presented in *Africanisms in the Gullah Dialect* (1949) are often in a "deeper" variety of the Creole, more basilectal. Dow employed a number of IPA phonetic symbols to render the sounds of Gullah, but also relied on a form of 'eye dialect' too:

> unə pɪk ə bascɪt ə bin fə fɒɪw n wʌn sɛnt. tu bascɪt – wɒt ɪt kʌm tu?
> You pick a basket of bean for five and one cent. Two basket – what it come to?
>
> yɛs, mam! mi nə gwɒɪn gɒn, fə mi na dat bʌkrə fɐɪt.
> Yes, mam! Me not going go, for me and that white man [will] fight.
>
> an dɛn, yu si, en dɛ no sɛf-rɐɪzɪn. dat flat flɒwə. ɒɪ ha fə bɒɪ ʃoda; ɒɪ ha fə bɒɪ lad. yu si?. ɒɪ ha fə bɒɪ ʃʊgə, fə ɪf ɒɪ had dɪ flɒwə, ɒɪ had tʊ pe.

And then, you see, ain't there no self-rising. That flat flour. I['d] have to buy soda; I['d] have to buy lard. You see? I['d] have to buy sugar; for if I had the flour, I['d] have to pay.

(Diana Brown, "had tɒɪm ɒn ɛdɪsto/Hard Times on Edisto"; Turner 1949, 260–261)

ɑn wɛn ɒɪ fʌs kʌm tru bɪfo de dɑt mɒnɪn, ɒɪ kʌm əʃɐʊtɪn.
ɑn dɛn ɪt pye lɐɪk ɒɪ rɐɪz, n ɒɪ rɐɪz ɐʊt mɒɪ slʌmbə. ɪt pye lɐɪk ɒɪ rɐɪz ɒn ə ʃɪp lodɪd wɪd pipl gwɒɪn tʊ dɪ si.... mi on sɪn we ɒɪ had in dɪs wʌl, dat we mɪ dɒʊŋ fo ɒɪ kəmɛns tʊ si gʊdnɪs. ɒɪ had tʊ pʌnɪs tru dɪ wɑlɪ fo ɒɪ kʊd si lɐɪt.
And when I first come through before day that morning, I come ashouting.
And then it appear like I rise, and I rise out of my slumber. It appear like I rise on a ship loaded with people going to the sea.... Me own sin what I had in this world, that weigh me down before I commence to see goodness. I had to punish through the valley before I could see light.

(Hanna Jenkins; Waccamaw, South Carolina; Turner 1949, 272–275)

The second selection from Hanna Jenkins was of the *sikɪn* type of testimonial, a personal testament of spiritual breakthrough or revelation, characteristic of charismatic Black Christian expression. The 'seeking' testimonials are interesting for the light they can shed on life under slavery, their scheme of allusions (as with the Spirituals) ranging from Exodus to Psalm 23 to Christ's suffering, death, and Resurrection. The language is direct, personal, colloquial, and one finds many of the features recorded by Stowe, Harris, and Twain. Turner was a linguist and better able to record the phonological features of a Creole such as Gullah or the decreolized dialects of AAVE of the Antebellum through post-Reconstruction periods; novelists naturally are more concerned with making dialogue intelligible to readers. But two points emerge in comparing the data on early Black American speech from white and Black recorders: the features that correspond between a Twain and Johnson, and given scholarly backing by linguist Turner (*a*-prefixing, use of serial verbs and cleft-sentences – see also Mufwene and Gilman 1987), would seem to suggest that the earlier novelists were not simply reducing Black speech to minstrelsy – not primarily. Twain, in particular, was altering the American novel for good, with both a boy narrator (and a lower-class, even outcast one at that) and a foregrounding of colloquial speech – namely, *American speech*, detaching to an extent the American novel from the standards, diction, and canon considerations of British literature. Johnson sought to preserve and ennoble Black religious life with his recording of the Spirituals; Turner sought to preserve a vital part of Black American linguistic heritage that was fading by the time of his major work's publication in 1949. The correspondences found across their works would seem to suggest there is value still in literary recordings of the 19th and early 20th centuries. That said, just as Twain had lit out for new territory with his great American novel *Huckleberry Finn*, when Huck Finn takes his leave of us in his story one senses something foreboding in his farewell: "But I reckon I got to light out for the Territory ahead of the rest, because Aunt Sally she's going to adopt me and sivilize me and I can't stand it. I been there before. THE END. YOURS TRULY, HUCK FINN" (Twain 1884/1996, 366). The novel is set in the mid-1840s, so perhaps Huck can make a go of it in the Kansas Territory by the time its eastern portion is admitted to the Union as a free state in January 1861. But Kansas would have a bloody road to statehood. Perhaps Huck would push on further west, strike it rich with a silver lode or gold vein, but Twain was a master ironist and a darker fate may have awaited Huck in the coming "Bloody Kansas" struggle, Civil War, and Indian Wars. Then again, Huck's voice and his intense dislike of *stretchers* ('lies') might see him drift forever onward each time he is disgusted by what he sees.

/æg/ and Pre-velar Raising

Twain's *aig-suckin'* taunt calls to mind another regional development of this vowel raising; long noted as a characteristic – even stereotypical - feature of the Pacific Northwest, raising of /æ/ before /k/ and /g/ is part of a larger NW and Western raising shift involving front vowels /æ/, /ɛ/, /e/ (and perhaps may be analyzed as a vowel merger; Swan 2020, 47). The *bag* [bæg] > *beg* [bɛg] raising may be the most remarked upon change ("Would you like a 'beg' for that?"), and can be heard in other environments with front vowel + velars /k, g/: *flag* as *fleg*, *back* as *beck*. The raising is complicated by what may be a related lowering of /e/ to /ɛ/ in *bagel* (i.e., *bagel* to something more like *behgel* or *beggle*), though this may also be analyzed as a three-way merger of /æ/, /ɛ/, /e/ as /ɛ/ (or variants closely peripheral to /ɛ/). The change is especially associated with the Seattle, WA, region, and speakers who are older and more rooted in the region (as contrasted with newer arrivals as the region saw an infusion of 'tech money,' especially from Northern California [Bay Area]). It is likely, as with many regional features of AmE, significantly class-marked. It is a change that crosses the border, having been noted also in the greater Vancouver, BC, region. Swan 2020 proposed even more detailed refinements in the demographic profile of raisers and non-raisers in the two metro regions – identification as 'native' residents as opposed to more recent arrivals with the tech boom in the case of Seattle, or 'heritage' Canadian (English or other European origin) vs. Chinese Canadian in the case of Vancouver (Mandarin and Cantonese native speakers in the first generation; Swan 2020 47, 49–51) with, in each case, the former group likelier to be 'raisers.' The range of raising might even involve 'hyper-raisers' (for whom *beg* raises to *bayg/beyg*, i.e., /æ/ to /e/; Swan 2020, 60–68). One of the interviewees in Swan 2020, a male Seattle native with strong regional identification (his residence dating back to before "all the people from California moved north and 'ruined it'"; Swan 2020, 62), also exhibited the Southern and Western raising of /ɛ/ to /e/ ~ /eɪ/ in words such as *measure* and *treasure* (so that they sound like *maysure* and *traysure*); this is a pronunciation heard, for instance, among older Southern Californians whose families a generation or two earlier had moved out west from Texas and Oklahoma (see, for instance, ANAE section 20.4, 279). Though no further details about the respondent were given, it would have been interesting to have heard whether his parents or grandparents, on one side of the family or the other (or both), had moved to the Northwest from Texas or the Southern Midlands. The lure of Southern California was touted in the 1930s and 1940s in advertisements in magazines aimed at readers in the Midwest and South with promises of orange groves, year-round-recreation, and a 'romantic' Spanish Renaissance/mission architecture (this at a time when Helen Hunt Jackson's 'Old California' historical romance novel *Ramona* [1884] was a staple on school reading lists). The 'twang' that travelled with this internal migration faded after the first few generations but may be heard still in inland regions (East County San Diego, where the town of Ramona is located, the 'Inland Empire' of Riverside County and environs). Interestingly, the /ɛ/ > /e/ or /eɪ/ raising brought to Southern California from Western Mountain and Plains and Southern Midland regions spread to local Mexican Americans and newer immigrants from Mexico – the pattern of immigration from Mexico has shifted further southward, from speakers of norteño Mexican Spanish dialects, from Baja to Sonora to Chihuahua, to Altiplano-Central Valley dialects (San Luis Potosí to Puebla), to the southerly Pacific coast band of Jalisco-Michoacán-Guerrero-Oaxaca. This raising is noted, in general form, in the major *Atlas of North American English* project (Labov et al. 2006): in the West, the southernmost instance of /æ/ raising is Fresno, CA; in the Pacific NW it ranges from Eugene and Portland, Oregon, Seattle to Spokane, Washington, to Vancouver, British Columbia, and most northerly to Anchorage, Alaska (ANAE Map 13.3, 175–177). These were the general findings in an earlier major lexical project: the "Pronunciation Guide" to the *Dictionary of American Regional English*, section 3.I.6 (Vowels before /g/, /ŋ/), where the editors succinctly noted:

> a. egg, leg, keg, etc. /ɛ/ predominates, but /e/ is also frequent, sometimes alternating with /ɛ/ even within the speech of individuals. Across the North /ɛ/ dominates, becoming mixed with /e/ in the rural West; from the South Midland into the Southwest, /e/ is most frequent; in the South and the lower Ohio Valley, both vowels occur. Cag, with /æ/, was once very common for keg (DARE vol. I, lii).

As has been occurring throughout North American English in the last generation, more well-to-do suburban youth lack a number of these characteristic regional features, exhibiting instead more supra-regional class-marked speech patterns that are often labeled 'generic,' though these features are often Western and often, again, of Southern California middle to upper-middle-class origin.

9.3 BIG CITIES OF THE EAST

The earlier, pre-Famine waves of Irish immigration reshaped the cities of the Eastern seaboard, and Baltimore, Maryland, was a natural destination as Maryland had been founded as a *proprietary colony* (a type of colony arguably somewhat more independent than the *charter* or *crown colonies*) observing religious tolerance by Cecil Calvert (1605–1675), Second Baron of Baltimore (Second Lord Baltimore), a Roman Catholic from English recusant stock. Though not a "Catholic colony" as such, its policy of religious toleration ended with the Protestant Ascendancy of 1689 in the colony. Cecil had clashed with the Society of Jesus (Jesuits) over land tenancy matters (Sutto 2009), but the Catholic character of the future state was one of Calvert's legacies (the Baltimore Basilica, now the Basilica of the National Shrine of the Assumption of the Blessed Virgin Mary, was established in 1821 as the first Basilica in the United States). As with every immigrant group to the Americas, the Irish brought with them the political issues from the homeland – in this case, for the Irish-speakers (predominantly though not exclusively Catholic), the matter of the emancipation of Ireland. In the ledger of the Irish Emancipation Society of Maryland covering 1828–1835,[8] one finds information on the chapter's proceedings, rules, and membership, with notes throughout made by a D.J. Foley; a note from the proceedings records that, "In pursuance of a notice in the Papers of this City for a meeting of the friends of Civil & Religious Liberty to be held at MP Reilly's Hotel on the 8th of May – Robert Armstrong was called to the Chair and Maurice Fitzgibbon appointed to act as Secretary," and a list of the members of the rules committee follows: Rob<er>t Armstrong, Luke Victory, Charles C. Harper, Doctor Roach, Charles S. Walsh, Doctor Coskery, John McMullin. The Preamble to the society's Constitution is written in the contemporary legalistic British English of such documents:

> The object of the Catholic Association in Great Britain and Ireland is, to elevate the Irish People by healing the dissentions that prevail among them by educating the Children of the poor by providing employment for industry, and by enabling the voters to maintain their independence against such land-lords as would exert over them an improper influence. These purposes are sought to be effected by collecting voluntary contributions from all classes and denominations, and many of the most distinguished Protestants of England and Ireland are members of the Association. The cause of the Irish Catholics is the cause of freedom both civil and religious and every friend of political liberty must acknowledge that whatever may have been the wrongs mutually inflicted upon each other by our ancestors in the blindness of religious zeal at

[8] Baltimore, Maryland Historical Society MS 1830, "A List of Members of 'The Associated friends of Ireland in the city of Baltimore' who have paid for the following years, commencing on the first Monday in May each year"; cols. for 1831, 1832, 1833, 1834, 1835.

> this enlightened period of the world difference of worship and belief is no reason or excuse for oppression....
>
> In a free country like our own nothing is more becoming than to feel and evince an interest in those who struggle for liberty in other regions. The emotion is spontaneous and wholesome. It were shameful indeed if we who have set the example and afford the model of perfect freedom should withhold our applause and assistance from those who are endeavouring as far as their condition will permit to imitate us.... From peculiar circumstances of situation from similarity of language and in many instances a common descent we justly cherish a kind feeling for Ireland. Under the influence of these motives we have formed the Society of which the following is the Constitution and we are actuated by the hope that although our pecuniary aid may be small the moral effect of our exertions will be great and useful (1r-2v).

The spellings *dissentions* and *endeavouring* stand out, and signatories to the document include a Campbell of Co. Armagh as well as a Rayburne (and the aforementioned Robert Armstrong), which indicates Ulster Scots Presbyterians among the membership, though most of the names are generally seen as Irish Catholic (though a vexing matter for contemporary audiences, the identification of ethnicity and religious affiliation by surname and region is still very much in force in Ireland and the diaspora – as it is for many other immigrant groups). A significant proportion of the membership hailed from just two counties: Cork and Donegal, the latter among what would be called the 'congested districts' under British colonial administration that would be hardest hit by the famines 1845–1852. And it is in the decade following the founding of this Baltimore Irish Emancipation Society that would see an explosion in Irish immigration to the United States, with the poorest Catholic emigrants the largest single group. The earlier migration patterns saw as many as 200,000–400,000 Ulster Scots move to the colonies in the 18th century, to Virginia and the Carolinas especially (Fischer 1989, 608–612), and the Scots-Irish influence on American culture and American English has been profound. A number of the Ulster Scots and Irish came to America by contracts bought and sold, as indentured laborers or convicts (Ekirch 1987, 83–94; in the latter case, essentially as slave labor). The subsequent waves of primarily landless Catholic famine emigrants came especially from the southwest, west, and northwest (Cos. Cork, Kerry, Galway, Sligo, Leitrim, Donegal); a great many were Irish-speaking monoglots, others spoke a rudimentary English lampooned in the British and American press. But there were features of this emigrant Hiberno-English borne out in more sober records, or used for literary effect. In Brian Friel's *Philadelphia, Here I Come!* (first performance 1964) when Gar (Gareth) O'Donnell of tiny Irish-speaking Ballybeg (Baile Beag, 'small town'), Donegal, is set for America the locals are convinced that there will be great danger there; fellow townsman Ned removes his great-buckled belt to give to Gar: "By the way, Gar, since I'll not see you again before you go.... If any of them Yankee scuts try to beat you up some dark night, you can...you know...there's a bloody big buckle on it...manys a get I scutched with it" (Friel 1965, 57–58). Not to be confused with Hebrew *get* or *ghet* (divorce decree), which passed into American

English through Yiddish, *get* and *git* (the latter in the frequent collocation *old git*) are from the slang of the British Isles. Originally *get* referred to 'progeny, offspring' in general, though it has narrowed in this sense to animals only (OED, s.v.; AHD5, s.v., sense 1). It then pejorized to 'A foolish or contemptible person' (AHD5), and seems to have been primarily a Northern and Scots usage – which would explain its appearance in DARE as largely 'rural,' with a North Carolina attestation, the vector likely Scots-Irish.

The first great age of mass migration to the United States was that span from the Irish famines of 1845, 1847, and later, until the immigration acts of 1921–1924: the Emergency Quota Act of 1921 limited immigration to 3% of each foreign-born group's population at the time of the 1910 Census; the 1924 Johnson-Reed Act reduced that quota to 2% of each immigrant group's population at the 1890 Census, with the proviso that immigration be halted from an "Asiatic Barred Zone" (Filipino and Japanese immigrants were not affected by this restriction). The National Origins Formula that was developed to set such quotas was in response less to immigration from China so much as to stem rising numbers from Eastern and Southern Europe: 1.7 million from Czechoslovakia, 3.8 million from Poland, 1.6 million from Russia, 500,000 from Hungary, 500,000 from Yugoslavia, and some 370,000 from Latvia and Lithuania; in the 1920 Census, there were only 85,000 Chinese immigrants in the country; and though Chinese immigration has increased dramatically in the past few decades, the overall Chinese population is still only 1.2%, the overall Asian population 6–7%. By contrast, the three large non-English immigrant waves, in order of peak arrival in America, were the Germans (15.4 million), Irish (10.6 million), and Italians (3.4 million). German immigrants have generally been seen as easily assimilating into American society, though that is an oversimplification. While many German immigrants were Protestant (especially Lutheran), nearly 40% were Catholic, and they faced the usual anti-Catholic sentiment and discrimination. German immigrants assimilated fairly quickly to English, though continued use of German left its imprint on the vocabulary of American English (obvious examples being *hamburger* and *frankfurter*); a large number of German-language newspapers were founded in the United States, perhaps the most significant was "The Staats," *New Yorker Staats Zeitung und Herold* founded in New York City in 1834 (and this is not to consider the remarkably active publishing industry in that city in Yiddish: *Idishe gazeṭen* [Yiddish/Jewish Gazette], *Der Yudisher herold* [The Yiddish/Jewish Herald], *Der Teglikher Herold* [The Daily Herald], founded, respectively, in 1874, 1890, 1894). Italians faced discrimination as Southern Europeans, as well as religious and ethnic discrimination (a majority of Italian immigrants during 1890–1920 were from Sicily). Like the Irish, many Italians were rural farmers who wound up in the big cities in America; the Italian influence on American English is seen especially in cuisine (Romaine 2001, 178; after the *hamburger* and *hot dog/frankfurter*, *pizza* is a staple American food). The general notion is that the Irish, like the Scots and Scots Irish, arrived "largely already English-speaking peoples" (Romaine 2001, 178). This may be qualified by where the majority of the Irish famine immigrants hailed from: densely populated western counties, which were also majority Irish-speaking. There may have been as many as 200,000–250,000 native Irish-speakers in New York City alone by the 1880s;

in 1881 the first Irish-language newspaper in the world was founded in the Bedford-Stuyvesant neighborhood of Brooklyn, *An Gaodhal* (*The Gael*). Its first issue in October 1881 began in bilingual format, with a primer of the Irish language and the *sean chló* (the 'old type/font' of the *cló gaelach* 'Gaelic script'). Founded by Micheál Ó Lócháin (Michael Logan) of Co. Galway, by the fifth issue of its first volume, more of its contents were in Irish in Gaelic script as was the new masthead: *An Gaodhal, leabhar-aithris míosamhal tabhartha chum an Teanga Ghaedhilge a chosnad agus shaorthughadh agus chum Féin-riaghla Cinidh na h-Éireann* ("The Gael: monthly journal dedicated to the defense and free-use of the Gaelic Language and to the Self-rule of the people of Ireland").[9] One of the larger Irish neighborhoods in Philadelphia was working-class Port Richmond (see Labov 2001, 467), which then became Philadelphia's "Little Poland," and home of the long-running Polish-language newspaper *Gwiazda* ('Star'). These earlier major immigrant populations had a lasting impact on the ethnic composition of the major cities, and it was from these Euro-American enclaves and speech communities that many of the interviews *Atlas of North American English* were drawn. The great growth of America's big cities was driven by these waves of immigration – as continues to be true with the second great wave following the Immigration and Nationality Act of 1965 (which ended the previous quota system) – and the growth in cities fueled America's rise to power.

In some ways, the rise of the United States to geopolitical preeminence might be traced to the long century between the Civil War (1861–1865) and the post-War standoff with the Soviet Bloc, the Cuban Missile Crisis (16–28 October 1962) serving as a salient point in that 'Cold War.' Cuba would figure significantly in the rise of America to prominence: the Spanish-American War (21 April–10 December 1898) had its *casus belli* in the sinking of the USS Maine in Havana harbor 15 February 1898 (by an explosion of munitions aboard the ship – variously, and still inconclusively, attributed to accident, mine, or even a 'false flag' attack). The squaring-off between old (Spanish) and new (American) empires was a media affair in the newspapers, with alarmist coverage that was strikingly modern in the pre-cable television era. The term *concentration camp* has often been dated to the Second Boer War (1899–1902) with the internment camps for Boers the British military established to stem guerilla warfare by clearing out local support in the veldt (or *veld*, often found in compound formations such as *bushveld* or *grassveld*, a Dutch loan to English from South Africa); it has earlier occurrences, and the real origin may be in Spain's policy of *reconcentración* in Cuba during the Ten Years's War (1868–78) and the camps set up for Cuban rebels and their families (the *reconcentrados*) by General Valeriano Weyler y Nicolau. The Spanish policy had many descendants, the Boer concentration camps among them; tens of thousands of Boer men, women, and children died in the camps; hundreds of thousands of Cubans in General Weyler's

[9] Issues of the journal are being transcribed by a joint project of New York University and the University of Galway, and are available in digital facsimile from the University of Galway: https://digital.library.universityofgalway.ie/p/ms/categories/an-gaodhal.

camps. These two examples of such camps are the first attestations recorded for the compound *concentration camp* in the OED:

> 1897 *Orleans (Indiana) Progress* 20 May issue: American citizens must not be starved or otherwise executed in Spanish concentration camps in Cuba.
>
> 1901 *Parliamentary Debate* (UK Hansards) 4th series 90 (180): The policy of placing the women and children confined in the concentration camps in South Africa, whose husbands and fathers are in the field, on reduced rations.

The often inflammatory newspaper coverage of such conflicts, especially but not limited to the United States, led to the label *yellow journalism*. The origin of the term is disputed, but early attestations point to Richard F. Outcault's "The Yellow Kid" as the source. Outcault's innovative cartoon work (including early multi-panel work and the first use of speech balloons) was boosted by the newspaper circulation wars and early use of color inserts – such as for the comics sections. "The Yellow Kid" was a shaven-headed boy in a yellow nightshirt several sizes too large who appeared in Outcault comics such as "Hogan's Alley" and "McFadden's Flats." Outcault's "Yellow Kid" first appeared in Joseph Pulitzer's *New York World* and then in William Randolph Hearst's rival *New York Journal*, and it was the New York City circulation war between Pulitzer and Hearst that often was labeled 'yellow' or 'yellow kid' journalism. Both publishers fed the public outrage that helped launch the Spanish-American War after the USS Maine sinking. Outcault's cartoon figures focused on poorer American internal migrants and immigrants, the Black people of "Possumville" and the Irish tenement slumdwellers of New York City. The "Yellow Kid," whose name was Mickey Dugan, belonged to the latter group, and his 'lingo' was often imprinted comic by comic on the front of his oversized nightshirt. The Kid's ethnic origins are made clear by his slogans:

> Every t'ing is fun wit' me.
>
> Gee dis puts me in remind of de time when Napoleon crost de Alps, only de Alps wuzn't in it wit Fift Avenue.
>
> Wot kind of woik wud I do if I had te earn me own livink.... I ain't so worse at trowin dice.... Aint no money in art no more people only wants frames now a days.... Say! Great Scott! I didnt come out fer a fish story – I cud lie jist as well wit out it. Chee I am tired (from "A Few Things the Versatile Yellow Kid Might Do for a Living," *The New York Evening Journal* [1896])
>
> Listen te de woids wot de phonograff will give yer. Say dats dead straight an on de level an I kin stand fer it – See! Tanks awfully (from "The Yellow Kid and His New Phonograph: A Farce, A Comedy and a Tragedy, All in One, Showing How, in Every Case, Murder Will Out, and Virtue is its Own Reward" [*New York World* 25 October [1896])
>
> I am playin dis game and I dont want no fresh mug te gimme any tips see. Dis gang tinks dey kin queer me but wait an see. Dats one two tree ("The Yellow Kid Takes a Hand at Golf" [1897]; cf. Olson 1993)

Richard F. Outcault's "The Yellow Kid". Richard Felton Outcault / Wikimedia commons / Public Domain

Many of the hallmarks of Hiberno-English are present, as well of those of stereotypical 'stage Irish' speech and caricatures of Irish American speech: the substitution of dental stop for fricative [θ]/ [ð] > [t]/[d] (*with* to *wit'*, *think* to *tink*, *three* to *tree*, *thanks* to *tanks*, etc.), devoicing of final [g] > [k] (*living* to *livink*) and of [dʒ] to [tʃ] (*gee* to *chee*), vowel fronting (*just* to *jist*, *for* to *fer*), vowel lowering and fronting (*to* to *te*), and vowel raising (*can* to *kin*). Morphologically, one finds the usual grammatical solecisms parodied in Irish use of English (verbal concord), and the emphatic *see* can be positioned finally as a discourse marker. Interesting are the emerging NYC features of hypercorrect /r/ (*you* to *yer*) and breaking of the central vowel in *work* [wərk] to *woik* [wɔɪk], characteristic of Brooklyn English (Flatbush namely, made most famous by another cartoon character, Bugs Bunny). The use of the objective pronoun *me* as possessive adjective too is a hallmark of Irish English. At the sociolinguistic level, the informal and, by turns, boastful and blarney-esque tone and expressions fit in with 19th-century satire of Irish English, and the shiftlessness and dullness of intellect (offsetting the sharpness in wit was the 'Irish thick' stereotype) were common in views of the Irish on both sides of the Atlantic. Indeed, though Outcault produced also crude caricatures of Black Americans (especially of children) and Chinese immigrants, there is a particular vitriol in his caricature of the Irish (in early Vaudeville, 'bogtrotter' Irishry and Pat-and-Bridey antics were the most popular form, followed by 'blackface' performances). Hogan's Alley and McFadden Flats could be equated with the infamous Five Points of lower Manhattan of the mid-19th century, but by the turn of the century, mass Irish immigration had spread to the Bronx, Queens, and Brooklyn.

The tag exclamation of The Yellow Kid was "hully gee,"[10] deriving ultimately from "Holy Jesus," a typical Irish and Irish American religious interjection, of a type with "Jesus, Mary, and Joseph" ("Jaysus, Mary, an' Chosef"). The satire of Irish speechways in America could be tinged with cruelty also. In the "Hogan's Alley" strip "An Untimely Death" two of the tenement's denizens, Jimmy McManus and The Kid's dear friend Liz, discuss the death of Liz's brother Patsey Clinchey:

> CHIMMEY M'MANUS: Say, Liz, is yer brutter Patsey dead?
> ELIZABETH CLINCHEY: Sure he is, an' he died a terrible det, too. Dat poor kid couldn't eat nuthink fer two days afore he croaked, an' he had ter die hungry right here within a stone's trow of Tanksgivink.

While Outcault was seen as shining a light on the dire lives of children of the tenements in NYC (as Jacob Riis had with his photojournalism), we are invited to laugh at these Irish kids, yet with the unsettling specter of the Great Hunger looming in the background. The Kid and Liz and other Irish characters from Hogan's Alley and McFadden Flats often have the simian features found in 19th-century *Punch* caricatures of the Irish; anti-Catholicism fused with racialized notions of the Irish as subhuman in American newspaper cartoons as well (particularly the brilliant Thomas Nast lampoons of the Tammany Hall Irish Democratic machine) and persisted until the 1960s (and dogged the presidential

[10] The expression is found in the work of several American writers, such as in Stephen Crane's *Maggie: A Girl of the Streets* (1893) and O. Henry's "A Little Local Colour" (in his collection *Whirligigs* [1910], in which it is seen as belonging to "The Bowery").

campaign of John F. Kennedy, Jr.). The slur 'ape' (likely a truncation of *Irish ape*) for an Irish person could still be heard in NYC within living memory.[11]

By late 1896 The Yellow Kid was enlisted, well before the sinking of the USS Maine, in ginning up war with Spain; Hearst's *New York Journal* in the Monday 30 November 1896 edition printed "A Leaflet from The Yellow Kid's Journal" in which The Kid takes up the matter of "Cuber" (the hypercorrected non-rhotic form later used by JFK): "The sitchaution in Cuber is like dis – if Wiler [General Valeriano Weyler] sends me anudder box o' dem lalla perfecktoes [Cuban cigars] he kin have de use o' me yot [yacht] w'en 'e wants t' chase back t' Spane an' say I'll tell ye wot, if dey try t' give me de rinky dink I'll rite a tellygram t' me old side partner, Yoolaylee [the Infanta María Eulalia] say you didn't know me an' Yooly wuz frends did je?" Once again, The Kid's lingo makes sense when sounded out in a stereotypical Irish accent (*did je* [dɪd dʒə] for *did you*) and put in the context of what was seen then as typical Irish exaggeration and bluster (e.g., *Irish hurricane* 'a flat calm at sea'[12]). The scope of The Kid's antics has expanded past New York's Lower East Side to mirror the growing role of the still young United States in international affairs, and here the new coinage 'yellow journalism' begins with "Yellow Kid" locutions. The earliest OED attestations include:

Galveston Daily News (Texas) 14 November 1896: The 'yellow kid' fad is about to submerge the football interest in New York City.
Macon Telegraph (Georgia) 13 December 1896: The public is bound to respect such employment of the forces and facilities of journalism. There is no appeal made to low taste...there is no catering to an alleged 'demand' for the spice of lubricity; there is no concession to the 'yellow kid' abomination.
New York Press 31 January 1897: Victory for the yellow journalism.

By 1898, with the start of the Spanish-American War, collocations such as 'yellow press' and 'yellow journalism' become set; unclear in the semantic development of the terms is what role The Yellow Kid plays in its course: as a reinforcing intermediary of the earlier references starting in the 1840s to 'yellow literature' (of a sensational, poor quality), or as the source reinforced by earlier senses of 'yellow' ('sensational,' 'lacking in courage,' etc.). But set was the within-the-pressroom criticism of fellow publishers

---

11 Despite the evidence from Nast's cartoons the term does not appear in the *Random House Historical Dictionary of American Slang* (RHHDAS; Lighter 1997); Ignatiev's *How the Irish Became White* (Ignatiev 1995) has been tremendously influential and controversial, if highly selective in the evidence considered (see for instance Pearl 2009).

12 RHHDAS, volume II (Lighter 1997), s.v. Interesting is The Kid's early use of *rinky dink* as a noun (it is now in use only as the adjective); the earliest OED attestation is from the Philadelphia publication *The North American*, 10 December 1895 issue: "Von Koeller gets what, in the chaste language in use under the lindens, is termed the rinky dink." The reference is to Ernst-Matthias von Köller, the German (Pomeranian) conservative politician and Kaiser Wilhelm loyalist who was forced to resign his ministerial position; "under the lindens" refers to the popular song of the day (in a number of versions, such as G.W. Warren's 1874 "Under the Lindens," deriving ultimately from Walther von der Vogelweide's Middle High German verse "Under der linden" ["Under the lime tree"]), as well as to Unter den Linden boulevard in Berlin's Mitte district. Here, the sense is that von Köller was done in or had; the OED has: 'A deception, a swindle; ill-treatment' (s.v. *rinky-dink*).

and journalists as 'yellow' and popular backlash against the incitement and propaganda of the 'yellow press' (in that sense, *yellow journalism* may be an ancestor of 21st-century *fake news*). Set too was the rise to international prominence of the United States (on the conjunction of these, see Spencer 2007). Had the United States not risen so spectacularly (and perhaps inevitably) to such prominence and power in the 20th century, the focus on Britain and British English would have remained as central as it has been for the preceding 13 centuries of the language's history. The rise of an 'American Century' is perhaps to be taken less as displacement than succession and partnership. By the dawn of the 21st century, the Anglo-American alliance is still dominant, as is the New York-London financial axis (the one change being that in 1900 one would have said 'London-New York'). To be sure, the British Empire declined and entered a postcolonial era, though the Commonwealth maintained economic and linguistic ties – and the latter have been, as with French in Africa, perhaps most significant. The Spanish-American War gave the United States the spoils of empire: newfound dominance in the Caribbean, greater involvement in other former Spanish colonies (especially in Central America), and a foothold in the Pacific with the Philippines for the projection of power (and another *casus belli*, this time on the part of Japan, for another war). It would be American English that spread to Guam, the Philippines, Palau, the Caroline and Marshall Islands. The annexation of Hawaii by the United States in 1898 established the base for westward expansion across the Pacific; statehood would follow in August 1959, a linguistic consequence of which would be the shift from Maritime Polynesian Pidgin to English-based pidgins (Dreschel 2014; Alaska had been voted statehood in Congress in January of that year, which at admission still had speakers of some two dozen native languages).

The 20th century saw both the dissolution of empires and the maintenance and spread of former colonial languages. In the case of English, postcolonial growth was remarkable, extending even to nations not formerly part of the British Empire or traditional American spheres of influence (to Kachru's 'expanding circle' of Englishes). If the seeming rate of change in morphology and syntax had slowed in the major varieties, the pace of change in lexis accelerated. Forces of convergence too accelerated, with firmer policies of universal compulsory education, a genericizing corporate economic model, and development from the computer to the digital age. But the picture from the major dialect atlas projects of the 20th century suggests that the phonology of English continues to witness significant change and variation. Indeed, the major work of William Labov suggests that the forces of divergence are increasing dialectal differences and affecting comprehension cross-dialectally, though in systematic ways in accord with Labov's variationist approach. The regular sound changes of the Neogrammarians seem to be continuing apace, though nonvariationist models suggest, alternatively, that many, many factors are at play in the complex system that is language (Kretzschmar 2015). If Britain saw a reordering of the dialect map by the continued movement to an ever-expanding metropolitan London, class as well as region continued to be major determinants. In the United States, the picture was more complex as territories became states (five states were admitted to the Union in the 20th century); the urban vs. rural divide blurred with movement to the cities then solidified again with the Great Migration northward of Southern Blacks as cultural differences between city and small town sharpened; mass immigration crested and paused with legislation: the Immigration Act of 1924 stringently reduced immigration quotas; that of 1965 opened up the most prolific era of mass immigration to the United States in simple numbers of arrivals.

The complexity of the American picture is perhaps best encapsulated by its largest city, and financial capital, New York City. Far and away the most diverse city in the world, it has always been one of sharp elbows, a boom-and-bust dynamic, gilded hyperbole and gruff even bitter sarcasm, dialectally distinct, emblematic of America yet also resented or loathed by many Americans. The "city in slang" (Allen 1993) allows for an appreciation of the ethnic mixture – perhaps composite is the better term for a metropolis of enclaves – that waves of immigration and the voracious demands of capital wrought. Somewhat counterintuitively, given present preoccupations, 'ethnic' can trump racial or religious or gender or other categories in NYC, a city of tribes and nations; but a metropolis such as NYC can only begin to be understood by multivariate analysis (there are a number of variables in Latino/a New Yorker communities, race a vital one especially among Puerto Rican and Dominican residents). Irish-born William Russell Grace served twice as the city mayor (1881–1882, 1885–1886); the first Catholic mayor of the city, he opposed the Tammany Hall that many of his fellow Irish had built into a potent political force. Italian American Fiorello Laguardia, son of a Catholic father and Jewish mother (he would himself be a practicing Episcopalian), served three terms as mayor (1934–1945), like Grace in opposition to 'the machine.' The one constant in American big-city politics of the 20th century was the dominance of the Democratic machine, which generated its own vocabulary. The perennial corruption of machine politics engendered caricature in the ever-popular political cartoons of the daily broadsheets and tabloids, and the caricature of the cartoon relies very often upon broad ethnic and racial stereotypes (officially repudiated in the 21st century, they have simply been recoded). The evolution of the ethnic epithet *dago*, originally applied to Spaniards and others of Iberian descent and by later in the 19th century applied primarily to Italians (especially Sicilians), or the increase in terms of abuse for African Americans with the migration of Southern Blacks to northern cities from 1877 (the collapse of Reconstruction) to the early 1960s provide a window into the complex tensions of America's growth: projection of power abroad, internal migration, and reshaping, even unrest domestically.

German-born Rudolph Dirks produced the comic *The Katzenjammer Kids* for William Hearst's *New York Journal* starting in 1897 to compete with *The Yellow Kid* in rival Joseph Pulitzer's *New York World*. The "Katzenjammer ['caterwauling'] Kids" featured mischievous twins Hans and Fritz, their long-suffering Mama, and adventures with pirate captain John Silver; the pranking twins derived from Wilhelm Busch's illustrated storybook *Max und Moritz – eine Bubengeschichte in sieben Streichen* (1865; "Max and Moritz: a Boys'-Story in Seven Pranks"). Dirks's Katzenjammer Kids belonged more to a folkloric, fantasy world of pranks and treasure hunts and was in some ways the German American rival to if not equivalent of the Irish American tenement kids of Richard Outcault's Hogan's Alley (both stories presented crudely stereotypical Black characters – in Dirks's strip a tropical island inhabited by black natives ruled by King Bongo). As with *The Yellow Kid*, *The Katzenjammer Kids* speak with their stereotypical ethnic accent: "Vun t'ing iss sure – if ve find a island mit cannibals on I send you ashore – you little skallywaggers!" says Captain Silver in one early strip. The Germans and Irish were the two largest groups of immigrants to the United States in the 19th century, and they form the two largest national-origin groups in the nation to date (there is some controversy in how Latinos are counted, and whether all immigrants hailing from Ireland should be counted as one group – i.e., Irish and Scots Irish together – but, quite interestingly, the two largest national-origin ethnic groups in the United States have remained the same for over a century). The respective comics reflect to an extent the different experiences of the two major non-English immigrant groups: the prank-pulling German twins range over the countryside and high seas in slightly demented Brothers Grimm fashion; the Kid, Liz, Chimmie ('Jimmy'), and other slum children inhabit a narrow slice of NYC's Lower East Side. Both are identified and lampooned by their ethnically marked dialects of American English. The pattern can be multiplied in portrayals of Yiddish-speaking Jewish immigrants, the Southern-inflected AAVE of Blacks arriving in northern cities, the 'hunkies' of Upton Sinclair's *The Jungle* (1906; the Poles, Lithuanians, and other Eastern Europeans employed in Chicago's meatpacking industry) or the Mexican, Irish, and Italian miners in his *King Coal* (1917).[13] The ferment and flux of America's history of immigration shaped the culture and economic growth of America profoundly; the rise in American power found expression, as such things so often do, in a war. The Great War would announce the arrival of a younger player on the geopolitical stage, as it would mark the decline of some of the older players. The cultural and linguistic impact of the Great War was also profound: upon vocabulary, upon reading and writing (poetry still had a literary prominence it would not match in the Second World War), and in the balance of power among Englishes.

9.4 THE MELTING POT – PERCEPTUAL DIALECTOLOGY – SUBURBANIZATION

The sillier side of 'perceptual dialectology' was online blog *Gawker*'s 'bracket challenge' user-poll-driven "America's Ugliest Accent Tournament" that ran September–October 2014. Based on the 'brackets' for the annual NCAA men's and women's basketball

[13] Sinclair's sympathies lay with the miners in the Colorado Coalfield War (1913–1914) he fictionalizes in *King Coal* (1917), and though his 'labor novels' helped spur reforms in working hours and child labor regulation his touch was not always light with the portrayal of American 'ethnics' – a not uncommon trait among more well-to-do and -bred progressive writers. Heroine Mary Burke, daughter of a miner, uses the asseverative *sure* in abundance as well as pronominal *a body* ("And what were ye doin' up there, if a body might ask?" [Sinclair 1994: 27], "Sure, the good old pertaties is good enough for me" [28], "Sure, he'd not know it if they could!" [111]); while the German, Italian, Mexican and Greek miners fare reasonably well on the 'eye dialect' scale, the Slavic miners do not: "Said Rusick, the Slav, slow-witted and slow-spoken, 'Them fellers get mighty damn sore if they lose their job and don't get no strike'" [380]). In his earlier novel-cum-exposé *The Jungle* about the Chicago meatpacking industry, Lithuanians such as protagonist Jurgis Rudkus are the put-upon virtuous nascent socialists, while the Chicago Irish (Mike Scully, Buck Halloran, Judge Pat Callahan, and the primary villain Phil Connor) are corrupt Democratic pols and thugs. This likely reflects resentment of the rise of the Irish Democratic machine in Chicago, parallel to that of NYC's Tammany Hall, and a general sense that the Irish were becoming 'uppity.' Sinclair's *The Jungle* infuriated President Teddy Roosevelt but did lead to significant reforms in working conditions in the industry and in food safety.

championship tournaments (the men's bracket is the one that draws the heaviest betting traditionally), the 'March Madness' that caps the very long college basketball season in the United States. The stuff of 'office pools' (off-record bets), *Gawker* established a 'Sweet Sixteen' field of 'ugly' American accents (skipping the earlier rounds that whittle down the field of 64 teams); the original brackets pitted Boston vs. Baltimore, LA vs. Chicago, Pittsburgh vs. Atlanta, Memphis vs. "Philly" (Philadelphia, a pet-name once used rather more by outsiders than natives, like "Beantown" for Boston), Scranton vs. New Orleans, Tallahassee vs. Minneapolis, NYC vs. Charleston, and Louisville vs. Providence. Front-loaded with this field by the staff, and adjudged egregiously ugly enough to skip any earlier rounds, the mantra "No matter who you are, you all sound disgusting" kicked off voting. The initial field begged a few questions: Do people nationwide really know a Scranton (Pennsylvania) accent? The American version of the television show *The Office* was set in Scranton, but it was, like most television, rarely 'spot on' with the accent (a charge leveled in Britain about the 'Brummie' in *Peaky Blinders*). And is 'ugly' the same as 'annoying' or 'irritating' (in which case LA would carry the field). Some of the 'teams' were given snarky profiles of their uglier stereotypical features in eye dialect (*Bastan*, *Shi-cah-go*), often with links to YouTube (and one gets a sense of how influential film and viral videos are in informing and misinforming Americans about how other Americans speak). But amidst the snarky fun and trolling (the entire enterprise was designed to set off flame wars and trolling among dialectal partisans), an interesting linguistic note could be heard: "American accents are changing and flattening. The brash Philadelphia accent, the distinct Texas twang, and even the ballsy New York squawk could soon disappear, mating with blander vocal patterns in neighboring regions." While error-hunting and triumphant dismissal are hallmarks of academics commenting in public media, not everything is wrong here. While the largest survey of American dialects ever undertaken (the *Atlas of North American English* of William Labov and team; Labov et al. 2006) found just the opposite, that dialectal divergence was increasing and that respondents from different regions (e.g., Philadelphia, PA, and Memphis, TN) were having more difficulty understanding each other, the judgments about comprehensibility of American dialects need to be qualified by class. Certainly, powerful forces of convergence have leveled some dialectal differences: upper-middle- to upper-class younger generations do not seem to have the same regionally marked ways of speaking as their parents and grandparents (especially if they came from less privileged backgrounds). But there are other factors at work than simply sound change (which is still occurring): many of the third- to fourth-generation children of immigrants live now in the suburbs rather than the inner-city or rural ethnic enclaves their grandparents did.

Just a few miles make for a world of difference, as between, say, Harlem and Westchester County. Two recent NYC-specific examples might suffice. Lin Manuel Miranda, creator of the enormously popular hip-hop musical *Hamilton* (2015), also wrote the musical *In The Heights* (2005) about the Washington Heights neighborhood in the far upper west side of Manhattan, now the largest Dominican American neighborhood in the U.S. Fans of the shows seem to have presumed that Puerto Rican American Miranda was a denizen of "the Heights," but he actually grew up in Inwood at the northern tip of Manhattan, the son of a political fixer, and attended primary and secondary schools affiliated with Hunter College and then private Wesleyan

University. Inevitably, success in the United States is usually media-crafted as a 'rags-to-riches' story, then the postmodern trend of debunking kicks in and childhood 'in the hood' turns out to be tonier (a peril many hip-hop artists have faced). A parallel trend in Britain would be the 'Mockney' (e.g., Lily Allen) and 'Jafaican' (Sting and many other British musicians of the 1980s and 1990s, David Byrne and Gwen Stefani in the United States) accents. The desire for 'authenticity' is nothing new, and the interrogation of neighborhood affiliation often results in actual or alleged exposure of fraud (perhaps of a 'regional' or 'linguistic appropriation' akin to 'cultural appropriation'). The tremendous success of Miranda's musicals, and the racial and ethnic content of their plots (America's racial history in *Hamilton*, the Dominican enclave of *In the Heights*), made criticism inevitable as media adoration grew. More serious charges involved the casting of both musicals, the 'erasure' of The Heights's Jewish residents (who had once been the majority), and 'whitewashing' of Alexander Hamilton's involvement in the slave trade (the subject of Ishmael Reed's caustic play-in-response, *The Haunting of Lin-Manuel Miranda* [2019]).

A second, perhaps more divisive example involves Representative Alexandria Ocasio-Cortez of New York's 14th District, a wildly gerrymandered district that even looks like the original *gerrymander*.[14] Ocasio-Cortez, of Puerto Rican heritage, generated both interest and controversy with a now-famous election campaign television advertisement that intoned, "Women like me aren't supposed to run for office. I wasn't born to a wealthy or powerful family – mother from Puerto Rico, dad from the South Bronx. I was born in a place where your zip code determines your destiny." It was a slick and effective political ad for a 'safe' Democratic seat in which Ocasio-Cortez ousted Irish American fellow Democrat Joe Crowley. Crowley was raised in the Irish enclave of Woodside, Queens (once known as "Irishtown," the demographics have, as with so many other NYC neighborhoods, changed), son of an Irish American father who was a Korean War veteran and NYPD officer and an Irish immigrant mother from County Armagh. Crowley was part of the 'old guard' of the NYC Democratic party and Ocasio-Cortez (rebranded as 'AOC,' an acronym of the 'Twitter Age' that seemed to irk as many as it inspired) would be part of 'The Squad' upon assuming office in January 2019, a term said to have been inspired by hip-hop terminology, and meant to lend a sense of 'cool' to a decidedly 'uncool' profession (the original membership in 'The Squad' included Rep. Jamaal Bowman of New York's 16th District, Rep. Cori Bush of Missouri's 1st, Rep. Ocasio-Cortez of New York's 14th, Rep. Ilhan Omar of Minnesota's 5th, Rep. Ayanna Pressley of Massachusetts's 7th, and Rep. Rashida Tlaib of Michigan's 13th). Now in her third term in Congress, AOC's original campaign ad and crafted identity spoke of 'outsidership' if not actual oppression, and the voiceover "Women like me aren't supposed to run for office" overlay a visual of AOC riding the elevated train in The Bronx. Soon

[14] The political term derives from Massachusetts Governor Elbridge Gerry's redrawing of the South Essex district to favor the Democratic-Republican (Jeffersonian Republican) Party. The blend is an eponymous one, combining *Gerry-* with *salamander*. The resemblance of the South Essex district to the amphibian was most famously pointed out in a political cartoon that ran 26 March 1812 in the *Boston Gazette*. Such redistricting has continued apace, by both major political parties, ever since in American electoral politics.

enough, a discordant note was struck, and not just in 'conservative media,' about just what 'zip code' formed AOC's destiny. Ocasio-Cortez's mother was born in Puerto Rico, her late father a Bronx-born architect of Puerto Rican descent who moved the family when AOC was five years old from the Parkchester neighborhood of the central Bronx (a planned community set out by insurers Metropolitan Life that was once 'whites-only') to tony suburban Yorktown Heights, Westchester County, one of the wealthiest counties in America. Critics leapt not just upon the age at which AOC left The Bronx but also that she was known as Sandy Cortez at well-regarded Yorktown Heights High School. Such carping is inevitable in politics, but it did point out a glaring conflict with the media-crafted persona AOC had projected. A denizen of Westchester County and product of Yorktown Heights High School and private Boston University is indeed the sort of person who could run for office and expect to be funded; part of the promise of good schools is that they open up such opportunities. And it is an age-old tradition in the American class system for parents to make financial sacrifices to move their children to better school districts. The bitter irony for Crowley in his political defeat by AOC was that he was the candidate with genuine working-class credentials; those of AOC are solidly middle.[15]

And this is most evident in AOC's accent, which almost completely lacks any traditional NYC features. Missing is the standard regional marker [ɔ:] (*kawfee*), [æ:] usually breaks/diphthongizes, and AOC's English is fully rhotic. These are stunning features for anyone claiming working-class NYC origins, but unremarkable for one having spent the formative years in upper-middle-class Yorktown Heights. The most distinctive features of AOC's accent are the rising non-interrogative tone at the end of clausular units ('Upspeak,' or 'rising terminals'), vocal fry, and diphthongization/breaking of [æ] to [iæ], features one usually associates with Southern California. In a press conference 20 April 2021 at the National Mall in Washington, DC, Rep. Ocasio-Cortez, Rep. Ed Markey of Massachusetts, and other Congresspersons spoke in support of the 'reintroduction' of the 'Green New Deal' (GND) after its failure to advance in the Senate during the term of the 116th Congress (the term ending January 2019). Remarkable in Rep. Ocasio-Cortez's portions of the 'presser' were instances of the California Vowel Shift (CVS) and front vowel tensing and raising[16]:

> [08:16 and following]: ...because for so long our [ɑ:r] movement towards a sustainable future [fjɛu tʃər'] has been divided with really [ri:ɪłli] just this false notion [nɛʊʃın] that we have to choose between our planet [pli:æ:nɛt] and our economy.

---

[15] Heather Schwedel's "Why Conservatives Are So Obsessed With Alexandria Ocasio-Cortez's High School Nickname 'Sandy,'" *Slate* 4 January 2019 (online) is an ardent *apologia* for AOC's apparent refashioning of her Westchester upbringing, but concedes that "The uproar fuels the bigger narrative that Ocasio-Cortez is an invention, a performer of oppression and even of her ethnicity." An even bigger narrative is the role the major media play in such performances of identity; most political use of accent/dialect is performative, as it can be in the daily lives of most people (to enact authenticity, gain trust, seem truthful, and various other sociolinguistic strategies).

[16] Video of the presser conference is widely available on news sites; used here is NBC's coverage of the event. A transcript is available at https://www.rev.com/blog/transcripts/green-new-deal-reintroduction-press-conference-transcript-april-20

[09:24] And we decided to come together in sweeping legislation [lɛdʒɪsleiʃɪn] that not only rejects that notion [nɛuʃɛn] but creates a plan [pli:æ:n] for 20 million union jobs [dʒɑ:bs] in the United States of America [əme:rɪkə] to rebuild our infrastructure [ɪnfrəʃtrʌktʃjɛr], to restore public housing, to make sure that we expand [ɛkspi:æ:nd] our access [æ:ksɛs], not only to EV [electric vehicles] and EV infrastructure [ɪnfrəstrʌktʃɛr] but mass transit [tri:æinsɪt], everything from coast-to-coast chargers to making sure [ʃɛr] we have a resilient Amtrak [i:æmtræ:k] infrastructure to the New York subway system [sɪstʌm].

The most distinct prosodic features are those of Southern California English: the tensing of final consonants with vocal fry (especially prominent with final /r/ in *future* and *sure*), and the rising tone at phrase/clause boundaries (in non-interrogative positions). The tensing of /æ/ is of high frequency (as in *access*) and can be found in Mid-Atlantic English (especially NYC and Philadelphia) but here it seems part of a continuum of tensing and breaking that also sees the insertion of (and even further tensing of) the glide vowel /i/ to produce [iæ] and variants (the SoCal pronunciation *eeeand*, *Speeanish*, and so forth); this is distinct from the /æ/-raising characteristic of NYC English, such as in *can* or *stand* for which the transcription /ɛe/ has been used (/æh/ has also been employed in Labov's major study *The Social Stratification of English in New York City* (originally published 1966; Labov 2006). In the case of *expand*, the phonological environment is important: tensing of /æ/ before nasals seems a more general phenomenon in North American English (ANAE 84 and Map 10.7). The ANAE notes that in the Mid-Atlantic region "the raised vowels are re-assigned to the tense phoneme /æh/" (87) – the concentration of this 'reassignment' runs from Baltimore to NYC (the Five Boroughs and western Long Island), but is also, quite interestingly, clustered in Southern California and its frequency there seems to be much greater than recorded in the ANAE map. This is to be expected as the data for ANAE was collected primarily in the 1990s; the shift was already underway in Southern California and has accelerated over the past two decades. The sheer scale of the ANAE is remarkable, but the data is already dated for some shifts in-progress and the reliance upon telephone surveying (Telsur) for the data is not ideal (no project of this scale could be completed in any reasonable span of time relying upon the old-fashioned field work of the earlier dialect atlas projects of the 20th century, which produced richer detail in data collected). The shift of /s/ to /ʃ/ before stops and consonant clusters with initial stop consonant(s) occurs here sporadically (*infrashtructure*), and is a general pattern in a number of US dialect regions; it had once been more characteristic of AAVE, as in the pronunciation *shtreet* for *street* but was also heard in the speech of former President George W. Bush (*shtrength* for *strength*). Of SoCal origin too is the pronunciation *Amairica* (i.e., [əme:rɪkə]) for *America*, which seems part of the western /ɛ/, /e/, /æ/ > /e/ merger (i.e., the loss of distinction in pronunciation of *merry*, *Mary*, *marry* so that all are pronounced as *Mary* in the western region – not universally, but predominantly in the coastal states; see Figure 2.5 in D'Onofrio et al. in Fridland et al. 2016). The changes noted in AOC's accent seem to have originated primarily in Southern California since the 1980s (the present author has charted the diphthongization of /æ/ > /iæ/ for some 20 years in San Diego, Orange County and Los Angeles north to about San Luis Obispo), but they have since migrated cross-country and become a more generalized suburban middle-class feature (and, at first and primarily, one found in the speech of young females). Insofar as these changes are in-progress, it might be said that AOC's speech patterns resemble those of general middle-class suburbia rather than more working-class NYC patterns. And this is a critical point – the class-marking of traditional dialect patterns. If dialect atlases such as the ANAE have found increasing divergence among dialects in the United States, the constraint seems to be one of class; at the same time, a levelling trend has spread from suburban to suburban region, the primary movers of some of the changes being younger female speakers (as with 'vocal fry' and 'Upspeak'). Thus, the traditional speech patterns seem more the preserve of working-class speech communities, a phenomenon with a number of plausible and historically grounded explanations (group solidarity, regional pride, sense of authenticity, contradistinction to the suburbs).

The phenomenon can now be heard nationwide as Southern California English has spread to suburban communities and, particularly among middle to upper-middle-class suburban younger female speakers, levelled regional features. It can be heard in suburban college students from the Boston area who exhibit rhotic speech, or Midwestern suburbanite students who sound 'Californian' (but hail from La Grange, Hinsdale or Napierville, IL [Chicago's western suburbs] or from Lenexa or Olathe, KS [western suburbs of Kansas City, MO]). Or, in this instance, it can explain why AOC's speech is heavily rhotic (unlike most New Yorkers, and therefore lacking hypercorrections such as *lore* for *law* or *idear* for *idea*) and lacks the tense /ɔː/ so characteristic of NYC English (*cawl* for *call*) – compare for instance the more typical New Yorker accent of Brooklyn-born Senator Chuck Schumer, or Brooklyn-born Rep. Jerrold Nadler of the 10th District, former Senator Alfonse D'Amato of Brooklyn and Long Island, or former mayor Rudy Giuliani born in Brooklyn's East Flatbush neighborhood.

Of course, politicians have always turned accents on and off based on audience or occasion: Bill Clinton could play up or underplay his Hot Springs, Arkansas, accent; Barack Obama, more controversially, could be criticized for using, or, in some views, appropriating a non-native AAVE or for not sounding "Black enough" (Alim and Smitherman 2012). Perhaps the finest American orator of the postwar period, Dr. Martin Luther King, Jr., could shift dramatically in accent and register, from a calm, more secular register for middle- to upper-class white audiences to the more rousing evangelical (in its broadest sense) tones of the 'preacher man' in his most soaring speeches. If FDR did relatively little to temper his 'aristocratic Northeast' (or, New York 'Old Dutch money') accent, and JFK his non-rhotic accent (his early years were spent between Brookline, MA, and Hyannis Port on the Cape), the question of 'inauthenticity' began to rise with George W. Bush. His stump-ready 'Texas Rancher' persona and accent were at odds with his New England formative years: born in new Haven, CT, raised in Midland and Houston, TX, for the years of primary education, "W" returned to New England for the next eight years attending elite Phillips Academy in Andover, MA, and then back to New Haven with Yale University. A factor in the changing fortunes of political accents has been the mobility of the American political class like England with Oxbridge and France with "Sciences Po" (the École libre des sciences politiques in Paris, now the Institut d'études politiques de Paris, the matrix for French political élites), the United States does indeed have a political class. The American *cursus honorum* (after the Roman 'course' or 'curriculum of honors' by which one ascended the rungs of the political ladder) can include elite private preparatory schooling, or boarding or military school, study abroad (Europe mainly), internships and clerkships, much of which takes the young person away from the original dialect region. The question can then become: where is one from? And, as with many things modern and postmodern, this can be as much a matter of fact as of choice and self-fashioning. Donald Trump's brash 'New York tycoon' speech style was an anomaly, a throwback to an earlier era of the 'business Democrat' (which Trump had been) throwing their hat in the political arena. So the question of why AOC does not have a typical NYC (much less working-class Bronx) accent is one to be answered by social factors: the move to the suburbs at so young an age, the privilege of good schooling, shifts in the concept of 'authenticity,' and a change in the demographics of the Democratic Party – once again, one might say, as the party had changed before in the 19th century when it gained a stronghold in the Eastern big cities while the Southern base was more rural. New prized demographics of the party are 'suburban women,' the 'college-educated,' Silicon Valley 'tech entrepreneurs,' liberal 'venture capitalists' as the party becomes less working class, more technocratic. A somewhat more difficult question to answer is why so few noticed the very un-Bronxlike accent. Mere mention of a tough Bronx upbringing conjures up an immediate roster of pronunciations and speech characteristics to a New Yorker; that none were to be heard may have gone largely unremarked in the media (if not on the street) as so many in the media now come from a similar suburban, college-educated background. Since so much of the crafting of language in politics has been about making the voter feel that the candidate is not just "someone like me" but "someone who sounds like me," the media miss on AOC's missing NYC accent may have been because she sounds like so many of them.

Returning to *Gawker*'s bracket challenge of "America's Ugliest Accent," it might be questioned to what extent perceptual dialectology influences dialect migration and switching, if these terms might be used: that is, if the suburban de-regionalization (here meaning the decline or absence of expected regional dialectal features) of the past 20 years is a conscious process and a product of motivation rather than systematic subconscious changes, and one that can to an extent be 'controlled' as in cases of code-switching: this is not an apparent or obvious matter – code-switching certainly seems to be motivated by matters of register, occasion, audience/interlocutor, but it can also seemingly be subconscious too – as when speakers who employ the strategy are asked why they do it and simply cannot explain it or say they did not realize they were doing it. Does the perceptual (or even folkloric) undesirability of an accent encourage migration away from it? Is the rate of migration influenced by class?

The *Gawker* tournament of "ugly accents" presupposes popular conceptions of a number of major and not-so-well-known regional dialects. The bracket pairings are meant to accentuate the ridiculousness (and ridicule) of the satirical challenge, but they do involve a shorthand of well-worn cliches that can have some broad validity: Boston vs. Baltimore is an 'Eastern regional' that pits America's most harshly non-rhotic city with the curiosities of Baltimore, 'Charm City,' often called America's southernmost Northern city/northernmost Southern city (the city that uses the affectionate 'hon' as an all-purpose greeting, and, like Philadelphia, can say *woder/warder* for *water* and, uniquely, *am-byue-LANCE* for *ambulance*). The Chicago-LA big-city pairing (America's second- and third-largest metropolitan regions) is class- as well as regionally marked: brash Windy City nasality and vowel fronting and raising (*Chicaaaahgo, lack your door*) vs. perceived Left Coast snootiness and condescension and self-delusion: the "we're just as good as New York" angst, not to mention the rising 'Valley Girl' non-interrogative intonations and other features mocked in the fake soap opera "The Californians" on *Saturday Night Live.* Mid-majors Pittsburgh (once a bigger player in the Industrial Age) and Atlanta (a rebuilt major Southern city) are as stark a contrast as any in the tournament; similarly, less well-known Memphis (at least at the national level) was doomed to 'one and done' status in its pairing with the reviled "Philly" accent. Scranton vs. New Orleans was an 'annoying' pairing, with grating Pennsylvania coal country nasality pitted against perhaps the most performative accent in the nation, that of the 'Big Easy.' Tallahassee vs. Minneapolis was a meeting of nonstarters unlikely to make it far in the tourney, both lesser known (Minneapolis being conflated with the more general associations of Minn-eh-SO-ta speech, Canadian raising and 'Scandinavianisms,' while Tallahassee stood in for the Deep South speech of the Florida Panhandle). NYC and Charleston was a lopsided pairing – general American revulsion at NYC itself and how New Yorkers "tawk" left Charleston's aristocratic "Suthin" (non-rhotic) tones no chance of advancing. And, finally, a more even match-up of Providence and Louisville traded on two smaller-city regional accents that are distinct from their larger regional grouping: Little Rhody's small capital is quite distinct in its form of non-rhotic speech from better-known northern neighbor Boston, and in the [ɔ] vowel shows the influence not of its closer neighbor but NYC to the south (Rhode Islanders can say [ðɔt] *thought* and [hɔd] *hard* rather than Boston-area [ðɑ:t] and [hɑ:d]), while Louisville is distinguished by the divergent pronunciation its own residents have for the city's name ("Lou-uh-vull" or "Lou-ee-vill" or "Luhvul" or "Loo-ah-vill" among a few others). Interestingly, the Pittsburgh vs. Scranton final emphasized Pennsylvania's pride of place (with Philadelphia another of its entrants) as the state with the "ugliest" accents; it also localized this "ugliness" with cities that had ugly industrial pasts: Pittsburgh in the western part of the state once enshrouded with smog from its steel mills (thus the nicknames 'Iron City' and 'Steel City,' their NFL team the Pittsburgh Steelers), Scranton in the northeastern part famous for anthracite coal-mining. Both are predominantly working-class, and both drew in large numbers of Poles and other Slavic immigrants (including one of the largest surviving Ruthenian communities outside of Europe in the broader Scranton area); old stereotypes about Slavs seem to have remained an acceptable prejudice in the United States and made it easier to mock the "ugliness" of the Pittsburgh and Scranton accents.

9.5 DIALECTAL DIVERSITY IN AMERICAN ENGLISH AND THE STUDY OF AFRICAN AMERICAN ENGLISH

The *Gawker* mock tournament had as its premise a sense of nostalgia for "ugly accents" that might soon disappear, but it seems clear that de-regionalization is more a suburban phenomenon, and class-marked middle class to upper-middle class, and likely to be distinguished from existing regional class differences – for example, the upper-class dialects of Boston Brahmins or elite New Yorkers distinguished from the working-class varieties. Labov 1966/2006 had studied rhoticity as class-marked in NYC in the famous Saks/Macy's/Klein's experiment ("The Social Stratification of [r] in New York City Department stores"; Labov 2006, 40–57). The three department stores were chosen to study an occupation-specific subset of the New York City speech community (salespeople, cashiers, floorwalkers, 'stockboys'; Labov 2006, 45) at stores that often hired staff with a view toward accommodating, at the upper end of the scale, the store's prestige (namely, Saks Fifth Avenue); Labov had noted the interesting detail that staff at higher-end stores accepted lower wages at establishments of higher prestige, and that management "take many unusual measures to ensure that the sales people feel that they share in the general prestige of the store" (Labov 2006, 44). The survey sought to elicit responses in natural speech (i.e., not in an interview format) with the token *fourth* (in the phrase "fourth floor") in 'casual' and 'emphatic' speech (Labov 2006, 46). The results indicate that rhoticity–non-rhoticity in NYC can be described as scalar, and class-marked or -conditioned. Rhotic pronunciations are of higher prestige, and those with greater 'security' in their dialect (the Saks employees) exhibit "a shift between casual and emphatic pronunciation, but it is much less marked" than that found among Macy's employees (who aim for the rhotic pronunciation in emphatic use, but who use the non-rhotic pronunciation more frequently in 'natural' use; Labov 2006, 47–48). The Klein's employees did at times use the rhotic pronunciation, but at a lower rate: from 5% in casual use to 18% in emphatic (Labov 2006, 48). The clearly greater ease with which Klein's employees used their native form (the general non-elite pronunciation of *fourth* as sounding like *foth* or *fawth*) reflects the nature of the store and the 'image' it projects and relations staff and customers were expected to have: working-class, discount-minded, unpretentious (one thinks of the popular if condescending 'memes' about "Walmart shoppers be like" in the United States; there are similar "Tesco shoppers" memes in the United Kingdom). Macy's, as a brand, had always projected the image as a comprehensive department store offering a more upscale shopping experience than discounter competitors such as Klein's (S. Klein Stores), J.C. Penney (now JCPenney), Sears, or Korvettes (like the Klein stores, now defunct). But Macy's had always been a more middle-class destination offering frequent sales and significant discounts that Saks Fifth Avenue, as an elite retailer, did not. To this day, staff are selected and trained to cater to the particular customer experience, and speech style is part of that presentation and experience. While race was factored into the analysis, Black employees at Macy's and Klein's especially tended toward more r-lessness in pronunciation (although this is also *class-dependent*); more telling for the time, the 1960s, was the lower number of Black employees at Saks than at Macy's or Klein's (Labov 2006, 49–50). A study like this could be constructed for any major city – Philadelphia had its more upscale John Wanamaker Store (1300 Market Street), mid-range Gimbels (Gimbel Bros.) Strawbridge & Clothier (Strawbridge's, absorbed by Macy's in 2006), and Lit Bros. Class-marking can be made with the Philadelphia area /iu/ ~ /ɛu/ shift (i.e., *Tuesday* pronounced not *Toosday* but *Tewsdee* with smoothing of /eɪ/ to /i/ in *-day*).

Beyond the NYC department store survey, which looked at one particular variable (treatment of /r/), Labov's broader study of linguistic social stratification on the city included four other variables: /æ/ as in *bag*, a sound treated very confusingly as /æh/ in Labov 2006 and in the ANAE (what is being referred to is the tensing of /æ/, but also its breaking/diphthongization to an /ɛe/ or even /æi/ /or /iæ/ sound – i.e., *bag* as *beeeag* or *bayg* or *baaahg*, but not the *bag* > *beg* raising found along the northern tier of states); the /ɔ/, represented rather inscrutably in the studies as /oh/, the "aw" sound in *caught*, *talk*, *dog* (NYC does not participate in the *cot-caught* merger found in various regions of the United States, especially as one moves west; rather, one hears *cawt*, *tawk*, and *dawg* with a tensed /ɔ/ open-mid back rounded vowel); and the treatment of /θ/ and /ð/ (Labov's /th/ and /dh/, which look like they should be the notation for aspirated dental stops but represent the interdental fricatives, voiceless and voiced respectively): these sounds seem to be articulated in a scalar way, from 'proper' fricatives /θ/ and /ð/, to mid-range affricates /tθ/ and /dð/, to the more working-class substitution of the stops /t/ and /d/ (thus the stereotypical Brooklyn *tree* for *three*, or general NYC *wit* for *with*; Labov 2006, 35–37, 405). All attempts at describing the complex phenomena of the articulation of human speech are approximate; as impressive as spectrogram information, Herz figures, and formant analysis may seem, they tell one little about how to make the sounds in question. For this, one needs native informants or recordings of them. Labov 2006 admitted the particular difficulties in recording and analyzing the NYC /ɔ/ vowel, not just in terms of height (Labov 2006, 35–36), but in terms of rounding: "it is a sound nearly unique in American dialects. It is raised and centered beyond (oh-2) [ɔ with a ə glide, a sort of *aw-uh* sound] level with most pronunciations of *sure* and is rounded with what appears to be considerable tension. The rounding is quite different from that observed in British tense [ɔ:]: it is actually a pursing of the lips, in women; in men, a similar but distinct phonetic quality is imparted by what seems to be a hollowing of the tongue" (Labov 2006, 36). The "hollowing of the tongue" may be a slight retraction and raising of the tongue, and may not be as gender-marked as in the 1960s observations; it is a more typically working-class New Yorker pronunciation, one especially associated with Brooklyn, in which the characteristic articulatory feature is indeed that "pursing of the lips," the /ɔ/ in Brooklyn *dog* ([dɔ:g] or *dawg*) is not so much raised as much more rounded and tensed (*dawwwg*). The value of the focus on NYC in Labov 2006 and other studies is that the city is indeed the 'great cosmopolis' of North America, and it is fascinating to see the power of dialectal constraints that have produced remarkable dialect maintenance (most notably at the working-class level, and most New Yorkers are working-class).

The broader sociolinguistic observations of studies of the urban dialects of NYC and other major American cities are of great importance: Labov (2006) had noted that: "The evidence of this survey as a whole reinforces the idea that the social group of peers in which a speaker spends his pre-adolescent years is the main force in establishing his linguistic pattern" (131), an idea corroborated by the "critical age hypothesis" of education researchers. The notions that "[w]hile parents may be the primary source for the basic language pattern which is common to all English speakers, they have little influence as a rule on the child's native speech or social dialect variations" and that "a child's native speech pattern is determined by his immediate friends and associates" (131, and examples at 131 note 2) may elide some other factors of note – the differences in parenting styles between new immigrants (and this also requires noting what country and culture are part of the heritage) and American-born residents, and the role of compulsory schooling: that a child whose parents were from Waco, TX, should pick up the dialect of where his/her family has moved to is not necessarily solely a register of the influence of the child's peers, but may also include the dialect modeling of teachers and adult neighbors; the peers certainly play a role in reinforcing the adoption of the local norms.

The massive Labovian project that came to fruition in 2006 with the publication of the large-format print volume of the *Atlas of North American English* was complemented by Labov's immense 3-volume *Principles of Linguistic Change* (Labov 1994, 2001, 2010). Volume 2, *Social Factors*, is most immediately relevant to the urban dialects mentioned in this section. Here, Labov distills the core findings and principles and theoretical implications of decades of dialect and neighborhood surveys (the NYC and Philadelphia studies are among his most comprehensive, but the Telsur and other projects considered many other cities). A great theme throughout Labov's work has been a concern with the diversity of dialects; the *Social Factors* volume begins with a consideration of "The Darwinian Paradox" (Labov 2001, 3–34), in which Darwin's observations of "the parallels between linguistic and biological evolution" (from his *The Descent of Man* [1871]) are fairly roundly rejected: "The general consensus of 20th-century linguists...finds no evidence for natural selection or progress in linguistic evolution" (9). Indeed, "the major agent of linguistic change – sound change – is actually maladaptive, in that it leads to the loss of the information that the original forms were designed to carry" (10). The major findings of the ANAE, from the Northern Cities Vowel Shift to the Southern Vowel Shift, the /æ/-tensing in the Philadelphia-to-Baltimore Mid-Atlantic region (which is even more complex than the ANAE found in its Telsur data), the *cot-caught* merger found in New England and other regions to the West (but not the larger part of the Mid-Atlantic), and Midland to North Midland fronting of back vowels (the *lock-lack* shift in Chicago) may indeed indicate an increase in dialect divergence in North America (here including as well Canadian raising and the Canadian Vowel Shift). While Labov's National Science Foundation-supported "Project on Cross Dialectal Comprehension" (Labov 2010, 21–85) pointed up seeming problems in comprehension among speakers from cities such as Chicago, Philadelphia, and Birmingham, AL, many of the examples seem rather to involve *mondegreens*, the term for mishearings of words or phrases that produce seeming new ones: *mondegreen* derives form a mishearing of *layd him on the green* as *Lady Mondegreen* from the ballad "The Bonny Earl of Murray." Thus, the misunderstanding of a Philadelphia speaker's "That's a great shirt!" by a Montreal speaker who replies "What do you mean, 'grapefruit?'" seems rather occasioned by vowel harmony of /e/ in *great/grape* than any cross-dialectal problem (Labov 2010, 24, example 8, which involved Labov's own family). The experiment involved hearing a speaker pronounce a word in isolation, then in a phrase, then in the fuller context; naturally the rate of misunderstanding was highest on the word in isolation, but what was interesting was that there were still misinterpretations when heard in larger contexts: thus it was not surprising that Philadelphia and Birmingham speakers interpreted a Chicagoan's pronunciation of *block* as *black* (the common Chicago fronting of /a/ to /æ/); miscomprehension in isolation occurred at a rate of 90%, but dropped to 21% when the context "senior citizens living on one block" was restored (Labov 2012, 18). Less plausible is that non-Chicagoans mistook a Chicagoan's pronunciation of *that* as *theater*, *Fiat*, or *Peter* (Labov 2012, 19). That the Northern Cities Shift has made the personal names *Ann* and *Ian* homophonous might require some qualification: from Philadelphia to Chicago, one can hear *Ann* pronounced like *eean* [ɛæin] or [æin] but still mainly as a monosyllable (occasionally starting to break to *ee-an*), but *Ian* almost always retains the 'un' or 'in' in the second syllable [iˈʌn]/[iˈɪn], that is, *ee-un* or *ee-in* (Labov 2012, 20).

A "Summary Statement on African American Vernacular English" (Labov 2012, 141–150) submitted to the Curriculum Commission of the California State Board of Education 10 February 2008 signed by nine linguists, including William Labov and John Baugh,[17] sought to assert that use of AAVE as the home language was not necessarily a bar to the acquisition of standard 'academic' AmE, and that, in the terminology of bilingual education applied in this instance to bidialectal education, the process can be additive rather than subtractive: "All students (regardless of linguistic, social, and economic background) should be taught standard academic English in a way that respects the richness, legitimacy, and vitality of their home language" (Labov 2012, 149). The key point the linguists were trying to make to the educationists was that AAVE is a "rule-governed system," and they laid out systematically the major characteristic features of the variety: the shift of /θ/ and /ð/ to /t/ and /d/ in demonstrative adjectives and pronouns *this, that, these, those* (and adjectival and pronominal forms of *either* and *other*), and the shift of 'th' sounds to /f/ in word-final or syllable-final position (*with* > *wif, bathroom* > *bafroom*) and of the voiced fricative /ð/ to /v/ in forms such as *brother* and *breathe* (Labov 2012, 143); the vocalization of liquid consonants /l/ (*help* > *he'p*) and /r/ (*Florida* > *Flo'ida, Carolina* > *Ca'olina*), though the assertion that "African-Americans use the vowel-like pronunciation of /r/ more than Whites" (143) likely needs some regional qualification (this would not seem to be the case in New England); the reduction of consonant cluster and /t/-dropping (*that's* or *dat's* > *thass* or *dass*); that "speakers of AAVE do not make a difference between /ɪ/ and /e/ before the nasal consonants /m/ and /n/, so that *pin* and *pen*, *him* and *hem* sound the same" (145), though this might be refined as the raising of /ɛ/ to /ɪ/, a characteristic feature of much of the South (especially large parts of Texas) and likely the legacy of the 'Great Migration' of Southern Blacks to northern cities. The grammatical features included, briefly: matters of verb-subject agreement (*we goes there*; *they gots it*); alternative tense marking, alterative use of auxiliaries in complex tenses (*done gone, been gone*); invariant *be*; lack of marking the possessive or alternative forms such as *mines* (one could add an example such as *they got they bike*); zero-plural formations (*fifty cent, five dollar*); use of double and multiple negation (145–148). Many of these features have been discussed in the previous chapters on earlier stages of the history of English; their persistence raises a number of interesting and at times disturbing questions. While a number of non-native accents of English have persisted as a result of political or religious isolation or 'walling off' (Irish English, Scots English, Welsh English), in the United States many of the 'ethnic' Englishes fade over time as generations born in the United States assimilate and integrate and – perhaps just as importantly – climb the social ladder at least into the middle class. Where they persist is usually in working-class neighborhoods, the constraints being economic and class-based (while in Belfast or Derry Irish English, one has to add the religio-ethnic factor). If ethnic enclaves themselves persist through continued immigration from the

[17] The full list of signatories was: William Labov, H. Samy Alim, Guy Bailey, John Baugh, Anne H. Charity, Lisa J. Green, John R. Rickford, Tracey Weldon, and Walt Wolfram.

particular country of origin (e.g., in "Little Italy" or "Chinatown" neighborhoods), the features of the 'ethnic dialect' (here an imprecise traditional 19th-century term for non-Anglo-American varieties of AmE) may endure with continued influence or reinforcement from speakers of the heritage language. This would be one of the exceptions to the 'third-generation hypothesis' of linguistic assimilation of non-English-speaking immigrant groups in the United States (that by the third generation, the grandchildren of the original immigrants, English is the L1, and the heritage language may not be spoken at all or only haltingly as an L2).

By and large, linguistic assimilation has accelerated in the United States despite popular perceptions to the contrary: about 93–94% of US residents speak English as their L1 or L2. Of course, how well is always a matter of perception and self-reporting in surveys; the US Census Bureau American Community Report on "Language Use in the United States: 2011" found that only 9% of some 37 million people reporting speaking Spanish in their home said that they could not speak English at all (the 2020 estimate is 41 million Spanish-speakers, though the decline in use of Spanish among US-born Latino/as is increasing). This figure is only surpassed by the 9.7% of residents who spoke Chinese (Mandarin, Cantonese, and other varieties) at home who reported not being able to speak English (in third were 7.6% of Armenian speakers). These are usually the older relatives of the family; younger immigrants learn English remarkably quickly, or already speak it as a second language before arrival, compared to immigrants from earlier periods of American history. One indicator of the pattern of more rapid linguistic assimilation (or integration) of non-English-speaking immigrants in the United states is the expansion of offerings in "Heritage Spanish" in American universities, a sort of third track for Spanish-learners: not the introductory courses for non-Hispanic Americans and others learning 'from scratch,' nor the more advanced or 'academic' offerings for those who speak it at least a bit in the home, but courses designed to salvage the 'heritage' language for those Hispanic or Latino/a (or Latinx or Latine) students of the third or even second generation who did not learn it in the home proficiently.[18] Bold predictions from 20 years ago had foretold that Univision or Telemundo would be the first Spanish-language network to dislodge one of the English-language 'Big Three' (ABC, NBC, CBS) from their perch in viewership. While Univision is the most watched Spanish-language broadcaster in the United States, it has never reached a higher ranking in viewership than 5th place, and despite boasting gains in overall viewership, Spanish-language television has been losing younger viewers to English-language television and streaming services (the latter have siphoned off young viewers from all of the major networks); Univision began in 2012 to offer English subtitling to its primetime programming. After a number of setbacks and

[18] While the number of immigrants from Latin America continues overall as the largest share of new arrivals to the United States (about 40% if one places together Mexico, Central America, and South America), and 25% of immigrants come from just Mexico, since 2018 China and India have passed Mexico in numbers of new immigrants and Asia is expected to overtake Latin America in the next two decades (with the caveat, as always: if present trends continue). Recent data from the Pew Research Center suggests that the decline in use of Spanish in the home is occurring in every metro center studied in the period 2006–2015: Jens Manuel Krogstad and Mark Hugo Lopez, "Use of Spanish declines among Latinos in major U.S. metros," Pew Research Center 31 October 2017 (online).

miscalculations (including a failed move into English-language programming), Univision merged with Mexico's Televisa in April 2021 and is now headquartered in New York City.[19] In refocusing on Spanish-language programming, Univision is banking on what will likely continue as the second largest programming market in the United States by language well into the 21st century; and though Asian immigration now outpaces that from Latin America in California, the linguistic diversity of Asian immigrants does not present a similar linguistic bloc. Patterns, as always in US immigration history, can change, but Spanish seems likely to remain the second-most spoken language in the country for the next few decades despite the more rapid shift to English among Latino/as and the need for "Heritage Spanish" classes. The question to be returned to is the persistence of AAVE as the most distinctive and distinct variety of American English. Why have more general assimilative patterns that have affected Irish, Italian, Korean, Armenian, German, Russian, Filipino, and other immigrants not affected African Americans in a similar manner? Why, as the 20th century drew to a close, was AAVE still controversial enough to warrant appeals from linguists asserting its cultural, community, and educational validity? The distance toward linguistic assimilation would seem on the surface shorter for a speaker of a dialect of English (albeit one likely descended from a Creole) than for speakers of other languages.

A simple, and controversial, answer would be that the African American experience simply has been different, the origins of the variety and culture inextricably bound up with slavery, Reconstruction, the Great Migration north, and continued segregation and discrimination in the "free" north (Chicago has often been cited as the most segregated city in America). Linguists know that isoglosses, varying features by which lines on a dialect map of occurrence/nonoccurrence may be plotted, can be formed on the basis of geographical or social barriers – a river, or a street demarcating one racial or ethnic enclave from another. Lower frequency of interaction between different groups – Black and white speakers, for instance – can raise up such a barrier, between people who do not want to speak to each other, or do not wish to be seen speaking to each other, or have not found ways to speak to each other naturally (the barrier can of course have been raised unilaterally). A speech community that feels walled off can turn inward and self-perpetuate, as can one that wishes to remain separate (as for religious reasons – Pennsylvania Dutch has survived where the religious community maintains cohesion in parts of Pennsylvania, New York, Ohio, and Indiana). The *pin/pen* raising mentioned above (by which AAVE *ten* can sound like *tin* or, in a further step, *kid* like *keed*) is a Southern feature, but one heard frequently in AAVE in Philadelphia or Chicago. Its preservation for several generations in the north speaks to community cohesion, voluntary or compulsory: pride in and attachment to a way of speaking and the community that speaks that way, or defensiveness and entrenchment at being labeled for the way one speaks (broader matters of identity can involve forms of voluntary and involuntary association, and for the latter, race in particular). And a second great factor is identity: a way of speaking that intimately expresses individual

[19] Meg James, "Spanish-language media giants Univision and Televisa to merge," *Los Angeles Times* 13 April 2021 (online); "Univision sells the Onion, Gizmodo and other websites to private equity firm," *Los Angeles Times* 8 April 2019 (online).

and communal identity is more likely to be preserved in the face of pressure to assimilate. Certainly a number of African Americans have assimilated to standard varieties of AmE – this can be celebrated as "success," or "having arrived," or derided as "sounding white" or 'bougie.' But as many of these considerations can be extended to 'accents' of non-native AmE, the unique case of AAVE may point to structural as well as cultural factors, and these 'structural' factors may not be well understood. In the coda to his revised version of *The Social Stratification of English in New York City* William Labov questioned what "competing explanation may there be for the maintenance of linguistic stratification?" (he had just mentioned the "balance of opposing forces" between overt and covert prestige; Labov 2006, 402–403); how might, he wondered, the Northern Cities Shift proceed "in the same way for 34,000,000 people across the entire Inland North"? And one could as well ask how might the features of AAVE persist for many of the nation's 47 million African Americans? Labov concluded: "To understand such phenomena, we may have to turn to structural factors that are independent of social stratification, or social factors of a wider scope than we have considered before" (403).

A different approach with, on occasion, some differing results was H. Samy Alim's *You Know My Steez* (Alim 2004), a study of AAVE from the later 1990s to early 2000s with examples from West Philadelphia and, at the core of the study, the West Coast. The researcher had taught at two secondary schools, a middle school in West Philadelphia (John P. Turner Middle School on Baltimore Avenue), and the anonymized "Haven High" in "Sunnyside." As the study engaged in a form of anthropological linguistics, which the author occasionally termed "Hiphopology," some degree of anonymization of subjects would be standard in social research; that it was extended also to school and place made interpretation of results more difficult as AAVE (the author employed the term "Black Language") is also regionally marked though classified as a social dialect. The distinction, seen before, is more complicated with AAVE, as features of the supraregional super-variety preserve Southern forms wherever a speech community remains cohesive (whether it is Detroit or Chicago, the Bay Area or Albany, NY). But there is regional variation among speech communities of social dialects, variation that is inevitable, however much a community may be isolated or deemed inward-looking. A curious pattern of the later 19th and 20th centuries is the arrival or movement to the big cities of immigrants and internal migrants from rural areas (Irish 'peasants,' rural Sicilians, Southern Black sharecroppers). The popular notion of 'countryfied' Black speech has some linguistic rightness in the Great Migration, which saw, in two major waves, some 6–7 million Southern Blacks move to northern cities. In the beginning of the first wave, from 1916 to the early WWII period, some 60,000 Blacks from the South (the Delta region, Mississippi in particular), moved to Chicago's South Side in just a few years, to be followed by tens of thousands more. The 'Black Belt' developed along the south-north axis of State Street, traditionally from 79th Street north to 12th (including the historic Bronzeville section; the greater Chicago area Black community extends east into Indiana, to East Chicago, Hammond, and Gary). Alim's 2004 study enlisted native informants, young students trained in ethnolinguistic methods, but the collection of data from speakers of AAVE has sometimes been controversial (a parallel is the writing of 'ghetto fiction' by white writers, and television programs such as David Simon's HBO-produced *The Corner*

[2000, based on his 1997 book] and *The Wire* [2002–2008], both set in Baltimore, MD). The 1993 program *Ghetto Life 101* by radio producer David Isay aired on National Public Radio (NPR) in the United States in 1993, and was controversial within the broadcaster among Black staffers and nationally, perhaps nowhere more so than in Chicago.[20] In the original half-hour program (there were two succeeding follow-ups) two teenagers for the South Side of Chicago, LeAlan Jones, 13, who lived in the family home next to the Ida B. Wells Homes housing project, and his friend Lloyd Newman, 14 ([fɔ:ti:n yi:əz o:l, "fawteen yee-uhz ole"]), from the Wells Homes in the Bronzeville neighborhood, documented the local "ghetto life" with their taperecorders (LeAlan: [tɛp ri:kɔrdəz], with smoothing and lowering of the /eɪ/ in *tape*). The Wells Homes were named for the famous African American journalist and civil rights advocate Ida Bell Wells (1862–1931), who was born in Mississippi and left Memphis, TN, for Chicago when her newspaper, the *Memphis Free Speech and Headlight* was attacked because of its investigations into lynchings. The homes were constructed 1939–1941 as part of the Public Works Administration, and the large project spanned four city blocks (39th down to 35th). The Wells project as well as the notorious Cabrini-Green Homes housing project were both completely razed by the city by 2011. The device of the young "reporters" canvassing their South Side "ghetto world" was effective in getting 'real' stories and especially real voices, from their young peers to grandparents (who had made the move from the South); it was also seen, at times, as exploitative, offering yet again a sort of 'ghetto tourism' for the college-educated, white liberal NPR audience. Most striking in the voices recorded are the Southern forms that persist in the AAVE even of the second generation born in Chicago: *dog* is [do:g] not [dɔ:g], *walk* is more like *wawk* [wɔ^{w}k]. And the particular variety of Southern (more toward the Mississippi Delta and Gulf Coast) includes more non-rhotic forms: *corner* [kɔrnɑ], *sisters* [sɪstʌz].

Alim's "Sunnysidaz," as he calls his young informant-researchers, also provide the perspective of a young generation's experience of "ghetto life." Though the pseudonyms Sunnyside and Shadyside are applied to the poorer and richer communities divided by a major highway, with no mention of state or region at all, the community profiled is clearly East Palo Alto, CA, a lower-income (working to lower-middle class) section of the larger Palo Alto-Menlo Park area, even then at the time of the study rapidly gentrifying and expanding into the Bay Area tech corridor and Stanford University research complex (the highway is US 101). East Palo Alto is a small suburban community, population 28,000 (2021; 20,000 at the time of the study), lower-income in an area of spectacularly high incomes, and now has as its neighbor on its north end Meta/Facebook's massive corporate campus. Alim's researcher-informants are presented through reported speech, from their field notes or the author's; perhaps somewhat controversially, Alim himself 'style-shifted' in the study between AAVE and standard academic prose (the Preface "Respect Da Dialect" is in a standard academic register, while the

---

20 Michael Miner, "Ghetto Life 101: Was It Exploitive?," *Chicago Reader* 17 June 1993 (online); Howard Kurtz, "NPR Staff Split Over 'Ghetto Life 101,'" *The Washington Post* 1 July 1993 (online).

"Acknowledgements" section appears as "Shout Outs" in a somewhat over-the-top youthful hip-hop register; Alim 2004, xiii–xxv, xxvii–xxxii). The title is derived from a line by the late rapper Guru from the Gang Starr track "You Know My Steez" (*steez* often explained as a blend *style* + *ease*). There has been no rush to follow in Alim's footsteps in presenting a study of AAVE in AAVE, but the study's core interest is the presentation of a corpus of youth-reported speech (from "semistructured conversations"):

> 'Don't you like Gospel?' And I'm like, 'Weeell, kinda, sorta, but...'
> ...so like, I love hearing, you know, positive messages, but like, if the music's wack, it's just hard....
>
> Yeah, like, sometimes they be rappin rhymes, like I don't get it. Like, they be cool, but I'm like....
>
> The neighborhood just like...
> White!
> Yeah, you know how like, like they be having like million dollar houses that be hella BIG and beautiful and shit. They don't be like our houses, you know....
>
> My mom useta go to high school – this whole area, right here....
>
> I'ma use a fake name....
>
> Yeah, it was like, I mean, he poseta be one of the pioneers of Hip Hop.... (Alim 2004, 23, 35, 104–105, 216, 251, 252)

The major features Alim noted his young informants employing are those found in many studies of AAVE earlier in the century – zero copula (*neighborhood just like*), absence of third person singular marker (*-s*), invariant *be* (*they be rappin, they be having*), zero possessive marker, absence of *-s* plural (Alim 2004, 35). Here too are contracted forms *useta* (*used to*) and *poseta* (*supposed to*), both with epenthetic /ə/. There are telltale markers here not just of California English – use of the 'narrative present' *like* (*but I'm like*) – but of 'NorCal' English: the young informants live above the "*hella*-line" (approximately the San Luis Obispo region on the Central Coast): *hella BIG*. The premodifier *hella* belongs to the Bay Area, perhaps originating in Oakland in the 1970s, and may very well come from *hell of a* /*helluva*; it serves as an intensifier, an ambivalent one (*hella bad, hella good*) and, like *hyphy* [haɪfi:] (< *hyperactive*, describing Bay Area hip-hop style and attributed to Keak da Sneak in the mid-2000s) is viewed possessively by NorCal residents (it should not be used by outsiders), and often derisively by SoCal speakers (who view it as jarring and irritating). It is the stuff of youth language, which is often exaggerative, performative (a function of 'cool'), self-pitying (*They don't be like our houses*), and exclusionary (enforcing group membership or exclusion).

The 'mystique' (as it has become) of the 'hard life,' which to older speakers can indeed seem self-pitying (compared to their own memories – or their parents' – of the Great Depression), has greatly influenced younger generations, especially under the sway of the valorization by some hip-hop artists of 'street cred' and 'the hood'; talking tough can be a register of being tough (a pragmatic function), and it can be difficult at times, at least initially, to differentiate natural or genuine working-class speech from the performative varieties. If earlier generations sought to consciously alter their speech upward on the class scale to cover up working-class origins and speak 'proper English,' younger generations reach for the covert prestige of 'down-talk,' of trying to sound from rougher circumstances than one was really raised in – as with the examples earlier of Lin-Manuel Miranda and AOC, or the countless hip-hop artists, country music singers, athletes, politicians, academics and others who have been caught in the trap of being exposed as hailing from more comfortable backgrounds than their performative personas. In a way, this is an odd postmodern phenomenon: the proof is in the speech, though 'faking it' is often readily detectable, which would suggest that such self-fashioning can be a participatory act, in which the faker (perhaps an overly harsh term) and the admirer both know that the article, however desirable (even expected), is not genuine.

'Appropriation' of AAVE by non-Black speakers (or Black speakers from middle- to upper-class backgrounds who did not grow up in a native speech community) has for some decades been ridiculed (Vanilla Ice, Iggy Azalea), or, more seriously, classed 'linguistic blackface' when the motive seems to be financial gain from Black culture. President Barack Obama faced criticism on the language front for employing the 'rhythms' of Black speech, being subject at times to charges of opportunism. And he was criticized as a product of elite schools, fast-tracked by the Chicago Democratic machine and powerful backers in the Democratic National Committee: a law professor, skilled orator, "community organizer" (this term itself became a touchstone for political divisions), professionally ambitious politician. Linguist John McWhorter referred to President Obama's use of a 'blaccent' as part of the 'double consciousness' phenomenon W.E.B. DuBois described as indicative of the Black experience in America, and noted that "there's nothing at all surprising in the fact that the President talks, worships, and even thinks in different ways depending on who he's around."[21] Alim and co-author Geneva Smitherman, whose seminal *Talkin and Testifyin: The Language of Black America* (Smitherman 1986) placed Black English in its broader Afro-Caribbean and African context, saw rather Obama's "mastery of Black cultural modes of discourse" and an orator "'hyper-aware' of his audience" (Alim and Smitherman 2012, 3, 5). The slight hedging here in both assessments may be that of the linguist who holds on principle that one's speech patterns are determined early, before a "critical age," that is, in one's formative years. Barack Obama spent his formative years in Hawaii, Jakarta (Indonesia), and Hawaii again, his parents academics; his own university and postgraduate years were spent in Los Angeles (Occidental College), New York City (Columbia University), and Cambridge, MA (Harvard Law). Until the years of community work and teaching law at the University of Chicago, the formative experience was largely outside any native AAVE speech community – and the Chicago years were

[21] John McWhorter, "The Perpetual Failure to Understand Obama's Double Consciousness," *The New Republic* 3 October 2012 (online).

post–college. In that sense, AAVE is not his 'native' variety, thus the use of 'style-shifting' by Alim and Smitherman is critical, and they had noted that Obama's 'shifting' had been criticized at times by Black politicians and activists: "There are some who read his 'chameleon-like' speaking skills as not quite authentic, or as slightly patronizing."[22] By contrast, First Lady Michelle Obama (née Michelle LaVaughn Robinson) is a Chicago native, raised in the predominantly Black South Shore neighborhood (67th–79th Streets along Lake Michigan), and seems much more at ease in AAVE use; she met Barack Obama after joining the prestigious Chicago law firm Sidley Austin having attended Princeton University and Harvard Law. A recent study by Nicole Holliday examined 'coronal stop deletion' in formal and informal speech contexts for Barack and Michelle Obama; the corpus sampled is small, speeches each gave to the 2012 and 2016 Democratic National Conventions (as representations of their formal speech patterns), and joint interviews with the ABC talk show *The View* in 2012 and a pre-Super Bowl edition of *CBS This Morning* in 2016 (for informal patterns). Political speeches are of course quite formal, scripted (often by teams of writers), and thoroughly rehearsed; television interviews on talk programs are more relaxed, but they may still not quite be 'informal' occasions as they too involve plenty of media 'prepping' with the topics of conversations and even questions submitted beforehand. Some 635 tokens were collected and the overall result was that loss (deletion) of the phonemes /t/ and /d/, in final or syllable-final position mainly (e.g., *-ed* of past tense or past participle verb forms, or *-t* in words such as *best* or *first* [*bes'*, *firs'*]) was markedly more frequent with Michelle than Barack Obama and that Michelle Obama "may be engaging in more marked style-shifting than Barack is" (Holliday 2017, 476). This can be seen with other features of AAVE in their speech and accords well with their different upbringings and familiarity with AAVE in a native speech community. Once again, the local variety of where one grows up, the speech community in which ones spends the formative years, is critical. Actors, politicians, newsreaders, and others professionally trained in shifting their accent or adopting another (usually more standard) accent may be able to pass as members of another speech community (or at least 'style-shift'), but there are always traces of the imprint of the original, formative speech community variety.

Alim and Smitherman's *Articulate While Black* derived its title from loaded references to Obama as 'articulate' by fellow politicians such as President George W. Bush and Senator then President Joe Biden; in fact, it was Joe Biden's assessment in particular, first reported in the *New York Observer*, that laid bare ingrained American assessments of AAVE and African Americans: "I mean, you got the first mainstream African-American who is articulate and bright and clean and a nice-looking guy. I mean, that's a storybook, man" (Biden apologized for the remark, and supporters chalked it up to his long history of verbal gaffes[23]).

[22] H. Samy Alim and Geneva Smitherman, "Obama's English," *The New York Times* 8 September 2012 (online).

[23] "Biden's description of Obama draws scrutiny," *CNN* 9 February 2007 (online).

Mayor Richard J. Daley of Chicago

Daley (1902–1976) was born to a working-class Irish family in the Bridgeport neighborhood on Chicago's South Side; the Bridgeport section was known as the "Back of the Yards," in reference to the slaughterhouses of the city's meatpacking industry. In a city that had grown heavily Catholic with waves of Irish, Italian, Lithuanian, and Polish and other Slavic immigrants, the local parish was a ready identifier – for the Daleys it was Nativity of Our Lord Parish at 37th and Union (Cohen and Taylor 2001, 14–27). Loyalty to parish and neighborhood – and the Irish Catholic culture of the Bridgeport enclave – marked Daley's rise and career, most notably his long tenure as Mayor of the city (1955–1976). His education from primary school through university was at Catholic schools (the Christian Brothers' De La Salle Institute and the Vincentians' DePaul University). Daley's use of and control over the Democratic machine in Chicago could be seen by critics and admirers as autocratic. To his credit, Daley helped guide Chicago away from the fate of other 'Rust Belt' American cities (Pittsburgh, Cleveland, Cincinnati, Dayton, Toledo, Detroit, Flint, Gary, St. Louis), keeping the downtown vibrant and occupied with major building and transportation projects. Daley is also famous, or infamous, for presiding over a city that was heavily segregated, and for his handling of protests at the 1968 Democratic Convention held in the city. Daley maintained the working-class speech patterns of his upbringing – he was a mayor of shi-cah-go [ʃɪca:go], and noted for frequent malapropisms and gaffes.

By the end of the 20th century and early years of the 21st, a 'double linguistic consciousness' with regard to AAVE might be said to have developed: judgements about articulateness of course presuppose earlier ideas about a variety of American English considered not just nonstandard but unacceptable, even 'uneducated'; and yet, simultaneously, Black English, through the register of the pulpit and oratory of Dr. King and other civil rights leaders and politicians, on the one hand, and the vehicle of hip-hop culture, on the other, had not just entered the mainstream but come to dominate popular culture – a popularity that brought fame and wealth, but also commodification and genericization. This had happened before with the blues, jazz, R&B, gospel, and soul earlier in the century – Black art forms that generated hundreds of vocabulary items that entered the lexicon of American English and reshaped American slang and popular expression indelibly. If the American neology *cool* may indeed be attributed to Jazz Age tenor saxophonist Lester "Pres" Young (1909–1959), then it is Black English that gave the modern English-speaking world that most influential, fluid, and elusive concept that has shaped younger generations globally under an oxymoronic cover term (that what is 'cool' is what is 'hot'), a form that is adjective, noun, adverb, discourse marker, and interjection (*Cool!*).

The long 20th century by and large saw an English language that had stabilized to a great extent structurally; as compared to the 12th–14th centuries, English morphology and syntax had settled into patterns that had developed over the preceding few centuries and obtain still (there are variations, but they are, historically speaking, less dramatic). Despite popular conceptions about language standardization and dialect levelling, the work of the major dialect atlases in the United States and the United Kingdom (and the major phonological ANAE project) indicates that dialects of English may be experiencing continued drift, at least in pronunciation, perhaps even in cross-dialectal comprehension (Labov 2010). Vocabulary (lexis) has witnessed the greatest change: the great earlier periods of Latin loanword introduction and formation (in various stages in the Old English period, and especially in the Early Modern period), and even the great influx of French loans post-1066 might be dwarfed by the rapid expansion of the English lexicon in the 20th and 21st centuries, in both the formal and informal parts of the lexicon. Science, medicine, technology, and politics on the formal side, and popular culture on the more informal, have added thousands of new words to English. The global empires that matured and then faded in the 19th and 20th centuries opened up avenues for the expansion of English and paths that led foreign loans into the vocabulary of the English language. If there is one exception to the core stability of English in this period, it is Black English (in the United States, Caribbean, and United Kingdom): a look at Gullah or Caribbean Creoles in the first decade of the 20th century and subsequent forms of AAVE or Jamaican English (in Jamaica or London, and as distinct from Jamaican Creole) gives evidence of movement from the Creole and pidgin origins of Afro-European contact varieties toward what might be called 'dialectalization,' that is, further decreolization of already decreolizing varieties and the formation of dialects of Black English. Forces of convergence have been powerful in the 20th century: the rise of compulsory education and widespread literacy, the accessibility and influence of printed and now digital matter, and the global reach of English have 'incentivized' the use of standard varieties of the language. But there seem to be a number of constraints upon these forces of convergence: the 'Celtic Englishes' remain distinct, especially phonologically, an interesting variation to the pattern in Britain of linguistic assimilation to a standard variety by second-generation immigrants; in the United States, where such a pattern is perhaps weaker (lacking any single equivalent to RP), one can still hear characteristic forms in Italian American or Asian American Englishes in the second and third generations. Identity is certainly one of these constraints. Alim 2004 recorded the view of a Black teacher in Philadelphia: "The reason why Black students continue to speak their language is because, really, if you think about it, it's the ONE THING that they own in this world. It's the one thing that NOOOOBODY can take away from them. NO-body" (246).

Looking back at a century that witnessed major changes to the world order, the decline of empires and birth of new nations, spectacular technological development (from first flight by the Wright Brothers in 1903 to the 'Space Race') and communication on a scale unimaginable in earlier centuries, a salutary reminder of human vanity is the acknowledgement of how much of this was birthed by war: "There seems to be no doubt that World War II was a punctuating event for the development of the English language. The large scale movement of population involved – primarily among men – was certainly one factor. Another is the radical shift in the relative power and status of Britain and the U.S." (Labov 2006, 225). The focus moves now to the global turn in English, a development spurred on by involuntary and voluntary association of hundreds of millions of people, of the 'English language' and 'Englishes.'

REFERENCES AND BIBLIOGRAPHY

Adams, Ramon F. *The Cowboy Dictionary: The Chin Jaw Words and Whing-Ding Ways of The American West*. New York: Perigee Books, 1993

Alim, H. Samy. *You Know My Steez: An Ethnographic and Sociolinguistic Study of Styleshifting in a Black American Community*. PADS Number 89. Durham, NC: Duke University Press, 2004

Alim, H. Samy and Geneva Smitherman. *Articulate While Black: Barack Obama, Language, and Race in the U.S*. New York: Oxford University Press, 2012

Allen, Irving Lewis. *The City in Slang: New York Life and Popular Speech*. New York: Oxford University Press, 1993

Ancelet, Barry Jean. *Cajun and Creole Folktales: The French Oral Tradition of South Louisiana*. Jackson, MS: University of Mississippi Press, 1994

Apple, R.W., Jr., "G.I.'s vocabulary in Vietnam is beaucoup exotic," *The New York Times* 3 November 1965.

Atwood, E. Bagby. *A Survey of Verb Forms in the Eastern United States*. Ann Arbor, MI: University of Michigan Press, 1953

Bailey, Richard W., "American English abroad," in CHEL VI, *The Cambridge History of the English Language, Volume VI: English in North America*. Cambridge: Cambridge University Press, 2001, pp. 456–496

Bailey, Richard W. *Speaking American: A History of English in the United States*. Oxford: Oxford University Press, 2012

Baranowski, Maciej. *Phonological Variation and Change in the Dialect of Charleston, South Carolina*. PADS Number 92. Durham, NC: Duke University Press, 2007

Batz, Bob, Jr., "Poll Says Pittsburgh Accent is 'America's Ugliest,'" *Pittsburgh Gazette* 20 October 2014 (online).

Becker, Kara, ed. *The Low-Back-Merger Shift: Uniting the Canadian Vowel Shift, the California Vowel Shift, and Short Front Vowel Shifts across North America*. PADS 104. Durham, NC: Duke University Press, 2019

Boas, Hans C. *The Life and Death of Texas German*. PADS Number 93. Durham, NC: Duke University Press, 2009

Boberg, Charles, John Nerbonne, and Dominic Watt, eds. *The Handbook of Dialectology*. Oxford: Wiley-Blackwell, 2018

Burkette, Allison, "'Stamped Indian': finding history and culture in terms for American 'cornbread,'" *American Speech* 86.3 (2011), 312–339

Carver, Craig. *Americsan Regional Dialects: A Word Geography*. Ann Arbor, MI: University of Michigan Press, 1989

Cassidy, Frederic G. and Joan Houston Hall, "Americanisms," in CHEL VI, *The Cambridge History of the English Language*. Cambridge: Cambridge University Press, 2001. pp. 184–218

CHEL VI = *The Cambridge History of the English Language, Volume VI: English in North America*. Cambridge: Cambridge University Press, 2001

Chopin, Kate. *Bayou Folk and A Night in Acadie*. Ed. Bernard Koloski. New York: Penguin Books, 1999

Cohen, Adam and Elizabeth Taylor. *American Pharaoh: Mayor Richard J. Daley: His Battle for Chicago and the Nation*. Boston: Little, Brown and Company, 2001

Cooper, James Fenimore. *The Last of the Mohicans: A Narrative of 1757*. 3 vols. London: John Miller, 1826

Cutler, Charles L. *O Brave New Words! Native American Loan Words in Current English*. Norman, OK: University of Oklahoma Press, 1994

Dannenberg, Clare J. *Sociolinguistic Constructs of Ethnic Identity: The Syntactic Delineation of an American Indian English*. PADS Number 87. Durham, NC: Duke University Press, 2002

DARE = *Dictionary of American Regional English*. 6 vols. Ed. Frederic G. Cassidy and Joan H. Hall. Cambridge, MA: The Belknap Press of Harvard University Press, 1985–2013

David, Beverly and David Sapirstein, "Reading the illustrations in *Adventures of Huckleberry Finn*," in Twain 1996, ed. Fishkin, pp. 33–40.

Dawson, Hugh, "The Ethnicity of Huck Finn – and the Difference it Makes," *American Literary Realism, 1870–1910* 30.2 (1998), 1–16

DeVoto, Mark, ed. *The Portable Mark Twain*. New York: Penguin Books, 1977

Dillard, J.L. *A History of American English*. London: Longman, 1992

D'Onofrio, Annette, Penelope Eckert, Robert J. Podesva, Teresa Pratt, and Janneke Van Hofwegen, "The low vowels in California's Central Valley," in Fridland, Valerie, Tyler Kendall, Betsy E. Evans, and Alicia Beckford Wassink, eds. *Speech in the Western States*, Volume 1: *The Coastal States*. Durham, NC: Duke University Press, 2016, pp. 11–32

Dreschel, Emanuel J. *Language Contact in the Early Colonial Pacific: Maritime Polynesian Pidgin before Pidgin English*. Cambridge: Cambridge University Press, 2014

Duerk, John A., "Elijah P. Lovejoy: Anti-Catholic Abolitionist," *Journal of the Illinois State Historical Society* 108.2 (2015), 103–121

Ekirch, A. Roger. *Bound for America: The Transportation of British Convicts to the Colonies, 1718–1775*. Oxford: Clarendon Press, 1987

Evans, Dayna, "America's ugliest accent has come down to Pittsburgh vs. Scranton" [America's-Ugliest-Accent-Tournament] *Gawker* 15 October 2014 (online).

Fischer, David Hackett. *Albion's Seed: Four British Folkways in America*. New York: Oxford University Press, 1989

Fishkin, Shelley Fisher. *Was Huck Black?: Mark Twain and African-American Voices*. New York: Oxford University Press, 1993

Fishkin, Shelley Fisher, ed. *Mark Twain. Adventures of Huckleberry Finn*. The Oxford Mark Twain. New York: Oxford University Press, 1996

Fridland, Valerie, "Network Strength and the Realization of the Southern Vowel Shift among African Americans in Memphis, Tennessee," *American Speech* 78.1 (2003): 3–30

Fridland, Valerie, Tyler Kendall, Betsy E. Evans, and Alicia Beckford Wassink, eds. *Speech in the Western States*, Volume 1: *The Coastal States*. PADS 101. Durham, NC: Duke University Press, 2016

Fridland, Valerie, Alicia Beckford Wassink, Tyler Kendall, Besty E. Evans, eds. *Speech in the Western States*, Volume 2: *The Mountain West*. PADS 102. Durham, NC: Duke University Press, 2017

Fridland, Valerie, Alicia Beckford Wassink, Lauren Hall-Lew, Tyler Kendall, eds. *Speech in the Western States,* Volume 3: *Understudied Varieties.* PADS 105. Durham, NC: Duke University Press, 2020

Friel, Brian. *Philadelphia, Here I Come!* New York: Samuel French, 1965

Fussell, Paul. *The Great War and Modern Memory.* Oxford: Oxford University Press, 1977/rpt. 2013

Fussell, Paul. *Wartime: Understanding and Behavior in the Second World War.* New York: Oxford University Press, 1989

Glowka, A. Wayne and Donald M. Lance, eds. *Language Variation in North American English: Research and Teaching.* New York: The Modern Language Association of America, 1993

Goddard, Ives. *Handbook of North American Indians.* Volume 17, *Languages.* Washington, DC: Smithsonian Institution, 1996

Gordon, Matthew J. *Small-Town Values and Big-City Vowels: A Study of the Northern Cities Shift in Michigan.* PADS Number 84. Durham, NC: Duke University Press, 2001

Hazen, Kirk. *Identity and Ethnicity in the Rural South: A Sociolinguistic View through Past and Present Be.* PADS Number 83. Durham, NC: Duke University Press, 2000

Hazen, Kirk, ed. *Appalachian Englishes in the Twenty-First Century.* Morgantown, WV: West Virginia University Press, 2021

Holliday, Nicole, "'My Presiden(t) ad Firs(t) Lady were Black': Style, Context, and Coronal Stop Deletion in the Speech of Barack and Michelle Obama," *American Speech* 92.4 (2017), 459–86

Hughes, Arthur, Peter Trudgill, and Dominic Watt. *English Accents and Dialects: An Introduction to Social and Regional Varieties of English in the British Isles.* 5th ed. London: Routledge, 2012

Ignatiev, Noel. *How the Irish Became White.* New York: Routledge, 1995

Johnson, Daniel Ezra. *Stability and Change Along a Dialect Boundary: The Low Vowels of Southeastern New England.* PADS 95. Durham, NC: Duke University Press, 2010

Keiser, Stephen Hartman. *Pennsylvania German in the American Midwest.* PADS 96. Durham, NC: Duke University Press, 2012

King, Ruth. *Acadian French in Time and Space: A Study in Morphosyntax and Comparative Sociolinguistics.* PADS 97. Durham, NC: Duke University Press, 2013

Kohn, Mary Elizabeth, "(De)Segregation: the Impact of De Facto and De Jure Segregation on African American English," in *Language Variety in the New South,* ed. Reaser, Wilbanks, Wojcik, and Wolfram (Chapel Hill, NC: University of North Carolina Press, 2018), pp. 223–240

Kretzschmar, William A, Jr., "Review: A Glass Half Empty, A Glass Half Full" [review of Labov 1994], *American Speech* 71.2 (1996): 198–205

Kretzschmar, William A., Jr. *Language and Complex Systems.* Cambridge: Cambridge University Press, 2015

Kretzschmar, William A., Jr., "LAVIS: where are you going, where have you been?" in *Language Variety in the New South,* ed. Reaser, Wilbanks, Wojcik, and Wolfram (Chapel Hill, NC: University of North Caroline Press, 2018), pp. 18–41

Kretzschmar, William A, Jr., Virginia G. McDavid, Theodore K. Lerud, and Ellen Johnson. *Handbook of the Linguistic Atlas of the Middle and South Atlantic States*. Chicago: University of Chicago Press, 1993

Kurath, Hans and Raven I. McDavid, Jr. *The Pronunciation of English in the Atlantic States: Based upon the Collections of the Linguistic Atlas of the Eastern United States*. Tuscaloosa, AL: University of Alabama Press, 1961

Labov, William. *Principles of Linguistic Change*. 3 vols. Volume 1: *Internal Factors* (1994); Volume 2: *Social Factors* (2001); Volume 3: *Cognitive and Cultural Factors* (2010). Language in Society. vols. 20, 29, 39. Malden, MA: Blackwell/Wiley-Blackwell

Labov, William. *The Social Stratification of English in New York City*. 2nd ed. Cambridge: Cambridge University Press, 2006

Labov, William. *Dialect Diversity in America: The Politics of Language Change*. Charlottesville, VA: University of Virginia Press, 2012

Labov, William, Sharon Ash, Charles Boberg. *The Atlas of North American English: Phonetics, Phonology and Sound Change*. Berlin: Mouton de Gruyter, 2006

Lanehart, Sonja, ed. *Sociocultural and Historical Context of African American English*. Amsterdam: John Benjamins, 2001

Lanehart, Sonja, ed. *The Oxford Handbook of African American Language*. Oxford: Oxford University Press, 2015

Lighter, J.E., ed. *Random House Historical Dictionary of American Slang*. Volume One, *A-G* (1994). Volume 2, *H-O* (1997). New York: Random House, 1994–1997

Major, Richard Henry, ed. *William Strachey, The Historie of Travaile into Virginia Britannia*. London: The Hakluyt Society, 1849

Marks, Herbert, ed. *The English Bible: King James Version*. Volume One: *The Old Testament*. Volume Two: *The New Testament and Apocrypha*, ed. Gerald Hammond and Austin Busch. New York: W.W. Norton & Company, 2012

McDavid, Raven I., Jr., and Raymond K. O'Cain, eds. *Linguistic Atlas of the Middle and South Atlantic States,* Fascicles 1–2. Chicago: University of Chicago Press, 1980

McNair, Elizabeth DuPree. *Mill Villagers and Farmers: Dialect and Economics in a Small Southern Town*. PADS Number 90. Durham, NC: Duke University Press, 2005

Mencken, H.L. *The American Language: An Inquiry into the Development of English in the United States*. 4th ed. New York: Knopf, 1960

Montgomery, Michael B., "Review article: The Linguistic Atlas of the Gulf States," *American Speech* 68.3 (1993): 263–318

Montgomery, Michael B. and Thomas E. Nunnally, eds. *From the Gulf States and Beyond: The Legacy of Lee Pederson and LAGS*. Tuscaloosa, AL: The University of Alabama Press, 1998

Montgomery, Michael B. and Joseph S. Hall. *Dictionary of Smoky Mountain English*. Knoxville, TN: University of Tennessee Press, 2004

Montgomery, Michael B. and Jennifer K.N. Heinmiller. *Dictionary of Southern Appalachian English*. Chapel Hill, NC: University of North Carolina Press, 2021

Mufwene, Salikoko S. and Charles Gilman, "How African is Gullah, and Why?" *American Speech* 62.2 (1987), 120–139

Mufwene, Salikoko S., John R. Rickford, Guy Bailey, and John Baugh, eds. *African-American English: Structure, History and Use*. London: Routledge, 1998

Olson, Richard D., "'Say! Dis is Grate Stuff!': The Yellow Kid and the Birth of the American Comics," *Syracuse University Library Associates Courier* 28.1 (1993), 19–34

Pearl, Sharrona, "White, with a Class-Based Blight: Drawing Irish Americans," *Éire-Ireland* 44 (2009), 171–199

Pederson, Lee A., "Terms of Abuse for Some Chicago Social Groups," *Publications of the American Dialect Society* 42.1 (1964): 26–48

Pederson, Lee A., "Mark Twain's Missouri Dialects: Marion County Phonemics," *American Speech* 42.4 (1967), 261–278

Pope, Alexander. *Imitations of English Poets*. vol. I, in *The Works of Mr. Alexander Pope*. 2 vols. London: Bernard Lintot, 1717

Preston, Dennis R., "[ˈsʌðɚn], [ˈsʌðən], [ˈsʌðɹən], [ˈsʌðn̩], [sʌːn] What We/They Think/ Thought It is /Was/Will Be," in *Language Variation in the New South*, ed. Reaser, Wilbanks, Wojcik, and Wolfram (Chapel Hill, NC: University of North Carolina Press, 2018), pp. 42–61

Read, Allen Walker. *Milestones in the History of English in America*. Ed. Richard W. Bailey. PADS Number 86. Durham, NC: Duke University Press, 2002

Reaser, Jeffrey, Eric Wilbanks, Karissa Wojcik, and Walt Wolfram, eds. *Language Variety in the New South: Contemporary Perspectives on Change and Variation*. Chapel Hill, NC: University of North Carolina Press, 2018

Reed, Ishamel. *The Haunting of Lin-Manuel Miranda*. New York: Archway Editions, 2020

Reynolds, Bill, "The /z/ → [d] Variable Rule in Negative Contractions in Southern States English," *American Speech* 69.4 (1994): 361–72

Robinson, Fred C., "The Adoption of Technical Terms in Popular Discourse," *The Sewanee Review* 119.2 (2011): 308–15

Romaine, Suzanne. *Language in Society: An Introduction to Sociolinguistics*. Oxford: Oxford University Press, 2001

Schachterle, Lance, "James Fenimore Cooper on the Languages of the Americans: A Note on the Author's Footnotes," *Nineteenth-Century Literature* 66.1 (2011), 37–68

Schneider, Edgar W., ed. *Focus on the USA*. Varieties of English Around the World G16. Amsterdam: John Benjamins, 1996

Sledge, E.B. *With the Old Breed: At Peleliu and Okinawa*. New York: Oxford University Press, 1990

Smitherman, Geneva. *Talkin and Testifyin: The Language of Black America*. Detroit, MI: Wayne State University Press, 1986

Spears, Arthus K., ed. *Race and Ideology: Language, Symbolism, and Popular Culture*. Detroit, MI: Wayne State University Press, 1999

Spencer, David R. *The Yellow Journalism: The Press and America's Emergence as a World Power*. Medill School of Journalism: Visions of the American Press. Evanston, IL: Northwestern University Press, 2007

Stockwell, Robert and Donka Minkova. *English Words: History and Structure*. Cambridge: Cambridge University Press, 2001

Stowe, Harriet Beecher. *Uncle Tom's Cabin: Or, Life Among the Lowly*. 2 vols. Boston: John P. Jewett & Company, 1852

Strelluf, Christopher. *Speaking from the Heartland: The Midland Vowel System of Kansas City*. PADS 103. Durham, NC: Duke University Press, 2018

Sutto, Antoinette, "Lord Baltimore, the Society of Jesus, and Caroline absolutism in Maryland, 1630–1645," *Journal of British Studies* 48 (2009), 631–652

Swan, Julia Thomas, "*Bag* Across the Border: Sociocultural Background, Ideological Stance, and BAG Raising in Seattle and Vancouver," *American Speech* 95.1 (2020), 46–81

Tagliamonte, Sali A. and Derek Denis, "Linguistic Ruin? LOL! Instant Messaging and Teen Language," *American Speech* 83.1 (2008): 3–34

Tamminga, Meredith, "Interspeaker covariation in Philadelphia vowel changes," *Language Variation and Change* 31 (2019): 119–33

Thomas, Erik R. *An Acoustic Analysis of Vowel Variation in New World English*. PADS 85. Durham, NC: Duke University Press, 2001

Turner, Lorenzo Dow. *Africanisms in the Gullah Dialect*. Chicago: University of Chicago Press, 1949

Twain, Mark. *Adventures of Huckleberry Finn*. The Oxford Mark Twain, ed. Shelley Fisher Fishkin. New York: Oxford University Press, 1996

Webster, Noah. *A Compendious Dictionary of the English Language*. Hartford. CT: Hudson & Goodwin, 1806

Webster, Noah. *An American Dictionary of the English Language*. 2 vols. New York: S. Converse, 1828

Williams, Cratis D. *Southern Mountain Speech*. Ed. with an Introduction and Glossary by Jim Wayne Miller and Loyal Jones. Berea, KY: Berea College Press, 1992

Wolfram, Walt, "The Relationship of White Southern Speech to Vernacular Black English," *Language* 50.3 (1974): 498–527

Wolfram, Walt, Kirk Hazen, Natalie Schilling-Estes, eds. *Dialect Change and Maintenance on the Outer Banks*. PADS Number 81. Tuscaloosa, AL: University of Alabama Press, 1999

Wolfram, Walt and Erik R. Thomas. *The Development of African American English*. Oxford: Blackwell, 2002

Wolfram, Walt and Natalie Schilling-Estes. *American English: Dialects and Variation*. 3rd ed. Malden, MA: Wiley-Blackwell, 2016

Wright, Louis B. and Virginia Freund, eds. *The Historie of Travell into Virginia Britannia (1612), by William Strachey, gent*. The Hakluyt Society, Second Series, Part II, Volume 103. London: The Hakluyt Society, 1953

CHAPTER 10

A Postcolonial Era 1

Asia and the Pacific, the Antipodes

On 21 June 1948, the HMT *Empire Windrush* arrived at Tilbury, Essex, having entered the Thames mouth after its journey from the Caribbean (the last leg of an Australia to England voyage). Passengers disembarked the next day (22 June now marked in the United Kingdom as Windrush Day). The ship's 1,027 passengers included 802 passengers from the Caribbean, who had embarked at Kingston, Jamaica, Trinidad, and Bermuda (an earlier port-of-call was Tampico, Mexico, when a group of 66 Polish refugees boarded who had made their way across the Pacific from Siberia). This pioneering group of emigrants and their children came to be known as the 'Windrush Generation,'[1] and among them were soldiers who had served in the recently concluded war and calypso singers such as Lord Kitchener (Aldwyn Roberts) and Lord Woodbine (Harold Adolphus Phillips) from Trinidad, as well as shipping heiress and writer/artistic muse/activist Nancy Cunard. The story of the ship itself serves as a bridge between the subject of the previous chapter and the present: the *Empire Windrush* had been operated for the government of the United Kingdom by the New Zealand Shipping Company, but it began life as the *Monte Rosa*, which had operated under Hamburg Süd as an emigrant transport vessel for Germans headed to Latin America, then a cruise ship, then a troop transport during the war. In its last capacity, the *Monte Rosa* had been used to deport 46 Norwegian Jews in 1942 and was later bombed by British and Canadian fighters and mined by Norwegian operatives recruited by the British (the *Kompani Linge* special operations group). The *Monte Rosa* would survive the war, only to succumb to a fire during its service as a transport in the Korean War (making it as far as the Western Mediterranean, off the coast of Algeria). Transport by

[1] The lives of descendants of the "Windrush Generation" and other members of the British Caribbean population, and 2012's 'Windrush Scandal,' are among the subjects of British director Steve McQueen's five-film project "Small Axe," aired on the BBC in Fall 2020, a series of linguistic interest for the attempt to capture the accents (and popular music) of the period from the late 1960s to early 1980s.

sea was soon to give way to that by air, but the age of exploration by sail had occasioned the various and varying contact situations productive of linguistic contact, such as gave rise to the nautical jargons of those who took to sea by profession or impressment and those who met them in the Atlantic and Pacific worlds.

Some idea of the environment that gave rise to 'jargons,' and could also lead to more pidginized forms of contact languages, is given by Fr. François Norbert Blanchet; Blanchet had been sent, along with Fr. Modeste Demers, by Archbishop Joseph Signay of Québec from Montréal to be the vicar-general of the Oregon province. After an arduous journey of some 5,000 miles by canoe and portage, Blanchet arrived at the Hudson's Bay post at Fort Vancouver (established in 1825 for the fur trade) and reported that: "The real language of the Chinooks is of almost insurmountable difficulty and is entirely different from that of the neighboring tribes. But they understand a jargon by means of which the whites generally can make themselves understood by the Indians frequenting Fort Vancouver. This jargon, composed of 350–400 words borrowed from different languages and distorted in pronunciation, is of so easy a study that, three months after the arrival of the missionaries, one of them, Mr. Demers, possessed it sufficiently well to be able to explain the catechism and give instruction to the catechumens without having to force himself to write what he had to tell them" (Goddard 1996, 128; cf. Landerholm 1956, 19: the relation also records that Demers translated the Creed into Chinook Jargon). As seen earlier, colonial contact situations, at first maritime (along the coasts, on islands), then riverine (into the interior), were the crucible for the generation of pidgins and Creoles. The situation in the Northwest was made even more complicated by the arrival of Sandwich Islanders (Hawaiians) brought by Russian vessels from New Archangel (Alaska settlement), who contributed to local 'jargons'; a number of these "Sandwich Islanders" were brought further down the coast to Fort Ross, the Russian settlement north of San Francisco Bay: in December 1820, the brig *Golovin* brought to Ross the Hawaiian women Maktim (aged 38) and Karua (aged 39), while Kapisha (no age given) was left at the Farallon Islands (off the coast of San Francisco; Gibson and Istomin 2014, I, 427–428). The Jesuits and other Catholic missionaries had usually in their preaching and catechizing learned the native languages by applied study, often of some years' duration; translations of the Bible, the Our Father, Apostles's Creed, and catechism were introduced gradually in the usual French model of catechetical training. The translations were not always of the highest accuracy, as with the Quiripi Catechism of Puritan Abraham Pierson (1658; Quiripi was an Algonquian language of Southern New England and Central and Eastern Long Island). 'Trade jargons,' of course, had more temporal applications and could be more rudimentary. Though an oversimplification of an enormously complicated and variable experience of cultural and linguistic contact some half a millennium in duration, one can at times see a scalar series of jargons, pidgins, and Creoles based on need: an immediate trade or travel scenario might lend itself to a more *ad hoc* linguistic solution, while sustained contact, as with religious conversion efforts and permanent European (and other colonial) settlement, would extend the contact situation and give rise to linguistic varieties of greater complexity (thus the term 'Creole genesis'; Muysken and Smith 1986; Rickford and Romaine 1999).

The linguistic and geographic environment of 'pidgin/Creole genesis' of course shifted and altered over the course of the colonial period to the era of independence and decolonization. Language debates occurred in nearly every postcolonial Anglophone nation or territory, and were especially acute in India from 1947. Debates in India's

Constituent Assembly were particularly heated in 1948 with the proposal that while Hindi be established as the nation's official language (or Hindustani, though this name too was fraught with controversy), Hindi or English could be used in the Assembly. The debate on 6 November 1948 heard from members requesting that the choice of two languages be expanded to 8 or 9 major languages of India; Arun Chandra Guha, Member of Parliament (Lok Sabha) for Barasat, West Bengal, pleaded that: "There is no shred of doubt in the mind of any of us that Hindi is destined to be the national language and the language of the State in India; yet that should not mean that other languages which have mighty literature, mighty traditions behind them should not be allowed to be spoken in this House without the speaker declaring himself to be unable to express himself in Hindi or English. I would request that other languages should be allowed to be freely used in this House."[2] Urdu became the official language of Pakistan in 1948; the Nastaliq script used for Urdu was used in India for Hindustani by India's substantial Muslim population. But the language picture continued to be a complicated one in newly independent (and partitioned) India; in 1950, the Constituent Assembly was disbanded and replaced by the Lok Sabha ('house' or 'place of the people') and the new Constitution of India (or Bharat, from Sanskrit *Bhārata*) declared in 1950 in Article 343 (1) that "The Official Language of the Union government shall be Hindi in Devanagari script," and that official use of English was to cease 15 years after the new Constitution (26 January 1965), a proscription obviated by the Official Languages Act of 1963 that permitted continued use of English by the government. To an extent, English continued in use as it was now felt to have a 'neutral' status among post-Partition linguistic, ethnic, and religious divides, but prestige and access were also factors. Among the varieties of 'Indian English' are higher-status BrE forms, some with what has been seen as 'Victorian' coloring in lexis (e.g., "felicitations") and a preference for near-RP forms, which can be a vestigial function of caste, but also of one's sense of relationship to the 'mother country' and the large Asian, that is, South Asian, diaspora in Britain. On the other hand, continued wide use of English in the education system, especially in the higher educational sphere, and increasing numbers of Indians studying abroad in the United Kingdom and the United States, are borne out by the range of varieties of Indian English and the increasing influence of AmE – see, for instance, the study of formal vs. informal function words, such as *whilst–while*, in Sedlatschek (2009, 116–124): "the very fact that there has been no communicative need to replace *amidst* in IndE suggests a fairly high degree of independence of IndE vis-à-vis the prestige varieties in that particular instance and serves as a reminder that IndE must not be treated as a carbon copy of BrE or AmE but is to be appreciated in its own right" (120). India's more recent geopolitical pivot to the United States and growing numbers of diasporic communities in America (beyond the well-established 'Desi' communities in Northern California and Northern New Jersey) have complicated the legacy of BrE in the Indian subcontinent. The growth of India's tech sector has forged links with Silicon Valley (Bangalore/Bengaluru, the Indian counterpart), while the growing – and controversial – outsourcing of jobs to India in tech and services has been based on the use of English by many Indians.

[2] *Constituent Assembly of India Debates (Proceedings)*, Volume VII, 6 November 1948; these are now conveniently available online: https://www.constitutionofindia.net/constitution_assembly_debates

As complicated and vexed as India's postindependence relationship with the English language has been, many other Anglophone nations have had their 'postcolonial moment': in Nigeria, too, English continued in use with a sense of 'neutrality' amid a religious divide and among tribal/ethnic divisions, and as Africa's most populous nation, Nigeria, with the world's second-largest film industry (dubbed 'Nollywood' in a blend following the pattern of Mumbai's 'Bollywood') and rapidly growing economy, stands as the Anglophone giant in West Africa. The legacy of World War II is felt in nations such as the Philippines (where AmE is the influence) and Papua New Guinea (where the English-based Creole Tok Pisin has official status). To speak of 'postcolonial Englishes' is to introduce an enormously complex, truly global subject, one that depends especially upon the speakers of the varieties and the uses to which they put their postcolonial Englishes.

10.1 PIDGINS AND CREOLES, ATLANTIC AND PACIFIC VARIETIES

The Language Manuals series of the United States Armed Forces Institute (USAFI) was assembled by linguists from the Linguistic Society of America and the Intensive Language Program of the American Council of Learned Societies, starting in April 1942 and lasting until 1974; the language services are provided more in-house now with the Defense Language Institute Foreign Language Center in Monterey, CA. They were part of broader educational pamphleteering by the USAFI and War Department, including such issues as: *The Balkans: many peoples, many problems* (1944); *Can war marriages be made to work?* (1944); *Our British ally* (1944); *What shall be done about Germany after the war?* (1944); *What shall be done with the war criminals?* (1944); *How shall lend-lease accounts be settled?* (1945); *What shall be done about Japan after victory?* (1945); *Canada, our oldest good neighbor* (1946). The small grey-covered pamphlets were made to fit in the chest pocket of the soldier (the 'blouse,' field, or battle dress blouse) or sailor. The *Melanesian Pidgin Phrase-Book and Vocabulary* (1943) was "Distributed to Navy personnel by Educational Service Section" (Hall 1943). The introductory section will seem terribly dated to contemporary readers, but mixed in with some of the basic observations are others from emerging linguistic insights into pidgins and Creoles:

> If a white man wishes to understand a native or tell him something, he will have a much better chance of doing so if he knows and is able to use at least a few words of Pidgin....
>
> The Pidgin used in the Solomons differs somewhat in vocabulary (but not in grammatical structure) from that of New Guinea and the Bismarck Archipelago.
>
> Pidgin is not, as some people think, merely a 'corrupt' English; you cannot talk Pidgin just by mixing up English words any which way. The grammar of Pidgin is simple, but its rules are as firmly fixed as those of the best English.
>
> Speak slowly at all times. The natives cannot understand you if you talk too fast (Hall 1943, 1–3)

The grammatical sketch in the *Phrase-Book* is spare but relatively technical for such a brief guide and reflects the state of Tok Pisin ('talk pidgin,' or 'Pidgin Talk') during the World War II era. The contact variety seems to have roots in the 19th century with the recruitment (and, at times, abduction) of Papua New Guinea peoples for work in Queensland. British and Australian English have had a determinative influence on the contact variety, though the service of Papuan scouts in the U.S. Army would have linguistic consequences too. In the grammatical sketch meant for US servicemen, nouns are said to lack plurals, this distinction achieved by pre-modifying numerals (*two-fellow man* 'two men') or other modifiers (*plenty-fellow man* 'men'); the genitive or possessive was also achieved in periphrastic form: *house belong dis-fellow man* 'this man's house' – the preposition *belong* takes on in Tok Pisin and other Pacific/Oceanic contact varieties a wide range of duties, with the sense of 'belonging to, concerning, of, for,' and often occurs in the variant form *bilong* or contracted *blong* and clipped form *long* (Hall 1943, 3–4, 7–8). Verbs are described as lacking their principal markings (tense, person, and number), but the future tense employs an initial *bimeby* (< *by and by*; as an adverb it can mean 'soon,' and as part of the verb it indicates futurity); the past tense can be realized with a postposed (following the verb) *finis'* ('finish') as an auxiliary: *em ee-come finis'* 'he has come' (Hall 1943, 5–6). And one finds in Tok Pisin the transitivizer *em/im*, seen in earlier Native American contact varieties (as distinct from the pronoun form *'um/'im*): *Light-im fire* ('Light the fire'), *You find-im shoot-lamp belong me* ('Look for my flash-light'; Hall 1943, 14–15). An entry in the *Phrase-Book* such as *You look-im Jap soldier?* ('Have you seen any Japanese soldiers?'; Hall 1943, 25) places the language guide back in its immediate context: interaction between American soldiers and sailors and local men recruited as scouts in the Pacific campaigns of World War II – a short section (42–43) adds "Solomon Islands Terms," as scouts from neighboring regions were vital to such brutal, bitterly fought battles as Guadalcanal (7 August 1942–January 1943).

Change over time can be observed in grammars and dictionaries of Tok Pisin and in the status of the contact variety. The main island is divided between the eastern half, now the independent nation of Papua New Guinea, a member of the Commonwealth since 1975, having been under Australian administration for 60 years (Tok Pisin is now one of the official languages of this nation), while the western half had been a Dutch colony until 1962, and now forms the Papua and West Papua provinces of Indonesia. East Papua itself had been divided between a northern half under German colonial rule, and the southern British administration. A German-based Creole, Unserdeutsch ('Our German') or Rabaul Creole German, was spoken in the north and has been replaced in large measure by Tok Pisin. Only 100 or so elderly speakers maintain the variety, and linguists such as Péter Maitz have been recording these speakers to preserve the variety in what way they can (Maitz and Volker 2017).[3] Unserdeutsch is one of a handful of German-based Creoles, and it began among children at the Vunapope

[3]The Germanistik program at the University of Bern has a webpage with video samples of speakers of Unserdeutsch/Rabaul German Creole: https://www.germanistik.unibe.ch/research/projects/unserdeutsch_rabaul_creole_german/index_eng.html

Roman Catholic Mission a few miles south of Rabaul. While English is the lexifier for Tok Pisin (perhaps as much as 75–80% of the vocabulary is from English; Dutton 1985, iii), words have made their way into the variety from Malay and Unserdeutsch. The number of loans is not large, but the proposed borrowings illuminate how complex contact varieties may be; Engelberg and Stolberg estimate that "There are about 70 items in Tok Pisin that correspond to German–Dutch cognates where the Dutch cognate is mediated either by Coastal Malay or by Ambonese Malay" (Engelberg and Stolberg 2017, 46). Tok Pisin *anka* 'anchor' could be from English, or German *Anker*, or Dutch via Ambonese Malay *angkar* or Coastal Malay *djangkar*; *stiabot* 'starboard' may be from English *starboard* (Tok Pisin English forms are often non-rhotic) or German *Steuerbord* (Engelberg and Stolberg 2017, 46, 51).

The great change Tok Pisin has undergone is in status: now an official language, it has grown in use to count some 500,000 L1 and as many as 5 million L2 users. The growth and duration in use of a contact variety can produce an increase in complexity and fixity (thus, a pidgin can undergo Creolization), and this can lead to a certain level of prescriptiveness in pronunciation, grammar, and, when written down, orthography. Thus, the spelling of contemporary Tok Pisin will seem significantly at variance with late-19th- and early-20th-century recordings of use. For instance, the use of adverbial *bimeby* to indicate future tense of verbs, spelled so in the 1943 *Phrase-Book* for the US military, now appears as *baimbai* and is seen as a more fixed morphological element involving "the grammaticalization of Future from a temporal adverbial" (Winford in Schreier and Hundt 2013, 231), not unlike the use of *tomorrow* in PDE *We return tomorrow*. There can of course still be variability in spelling among users of the varieties, as with the Bislama of Vanuatu expression for 'thank you very much': *tank (y) u tumas, tangkyu tumas* (*tumas* = 'too much,' a slight semantic weakening that works better in *sori tumas*, 'so sorry,' 'very sorry'). Tok Pisin is now a broadcast standard on the Australian Broadcasting Service's Tok Pisin Service:

> ABC Tok Pisin Sevis em igat nius sevis yu ken trustim, em i save lukluk gut long ol narapela media platfom we bai ken givim yu ol niupela toktok long ol stori blong Australia na Pacific rijin.
>
> The ABC Tok Pisin Service provides trusted news, analysis, features, and multimedia content to keep you up-to-date with the stories that matter from Australia and across the Pacific region (ABC's English version).
>
> [https://www.abc.net.au/news/tok-pisin/]

More literally, the ABC Tok Pisin Service "it has news service you can trust-em"; the high-frequency prepositions *long* and *blong* and enclitic transitivizer *-im* are here, as is the conjunction *na* 'and' and the use of reduplicated forms (*lukluk* 'to look' and *toktok* 'to talk,' the latter also a noun meaning 'speech, language, talk'). As seen with the changes to English in the 15th century, with the introduction of the printing press to English, use of a variety in media inevitably pushes toward a certain degree of standardization, and this can be heard in the *Wantok* ('one-talk,' fellow speaker of Tok Pisin) radio programs on the ABC Tok Pisin Service, as one can hear more acrolectal forms (such as used by white Australian speakers or government officials in Papua New Guinea) and more mesolectal to basilectal forms from local and especially rural speakers. Papua New Guinea is the most linguistically diverse region in the world, with some 850 languages spoken, and Tok Pisin has to an extent allowed for a home-grown solution to a *lingua franca*.

The official status of Tok Pisin in Papua New Guinea, along with English and Hiri Motu, and expanded range of use thereby has led to further 'complexification' or stabilization in the contact variety; this is to be expected when change is in the direction of further creolization (an increase in complexity and/or fixity of the lexicon, grammar, and syntax). The continuing increase in English's role as the lexifier, the base for the majority of the vocabulary, has also expanded the use of Tok Pisin in broadcasting. Hiri Motu is also a contact or mixed variety (though generally described as neither a genuine pidgin nor Creole), but one based on the Austronesian language Motu, spoken by the Motu people of the southern coast of Papua New Guinea. This simplified Motu served as a regional language alongside what was called "broken" English, a term one finds describing other English-based pidgins and Creoles such as the Australian Aboriginal Torres Strait Creole 'Broken' (or 'Brokan'). The name Hiri Motu includes the Motu word for their annual trading voyages (*hiri*), though it has also been called Pidgin Motu and Police Motu, the latter in reference to its use by the police force created by Sir William MacGregor (1846–1919) while he was Lieutenant-Governor of British New Guinea. The Scot MacGregor had received medical training at Aberdeen, Glasgow (University of Strathclyde), and Edinburgh, and began work abroad in the Seychelles and Mauritius, apparently to his credit in dealing with epidemics and mental health. In 1888, he was appointed to posts in Papua New Guinea (1888–1898) and set about establishing 'law and order' with the Armed Native Constabulary in a region with its tribal disputes (Dutton 1985, 41–81). In the next decade, he was appointed Governor of Lagos Colony, Nigeria, then of Queensland, Australia. The career of MacGregor traces not only the range of the British Empire across the Pacific and West Africa, but also traces a linguistic arc of pidgins and Creoles. While Hiri Motu functioned for some time as a *lingua franca*, and serves that purpose still as a market language in the capital, Port Moresby (Chatterton 1975, 5), it has now been passed in numbers of speakers by Tok Pisin, from which it has borrowed vocabulary (e.g., *pilisi* 'please'). The aforementioned Torres Strait Creole has a role in the complicated history of Hiri Motu/Police Motu, 'Broken' English, and Papuan Pidgin English – Papuan workers returning from working in Australia, in the Torres Strait and Queensland, brought with them a pidginized version of English. Recruits to MacGregor's police force brought it with them and came into contact with other varieties, while the base for Police Motu is now seen as pre-dating the English colonial period as a "lineal descendant" of a simplified Motu trade language, then 'Broken' English and other Austronesian and Papuan languages (Dutton 1985, 40, 132–136 and Figure 7-1). Throughout the history of Hiri/Police Motu, and Tok Pisin, the common thread is *need*: trade jargons and pidgins fulfill a need on the *hiri* (trading voyage) and in the markets; recruitment of native workers (to Australia) and members of the constabulary required some way of bridging linguistic gaps in a region with some 850 languages;

missionaries needed to learn the local language to proselytize – the first missionary to the Motu was the Reverend W.G. Lawes of the London Missionary Society, who later became proficient in Motu but was first taught the simplified Motu by the locals (Dutton 1985, 36–37); then followed the colonial officials, who encourage the adoption of "official" English but must at first get by in the "Broken" or pidginized forms.

The need for simplified varieties in initial contact situations leaves its imprint on subsequent, more complex varieties (usually, Creoles). One can see this still in the bilingual introduction to the Oxford *Papua New Guinea Tok Pisin English Dictionary*:

> Tok Pisin is the official name for the largest *lingua franca* of Papua New Guinea, a country in which more than 800 local languages are spoken.
>
> Yumi long Papua Niugini i gat planti ol tok ples. Namba bilong ol tok ples bilong PNG i winim 800.
>
> We [literally *you-me*] in Papua New Guinea have plenty-languages place. Number belong plenty-languages place belong Papua New Guinea more than 800.
>
> [*i* is a particle used between subject and predicate; *ol*, 'all,' can be the pronoun *they* but here is a particle used to form the plural of nouns; *winim* is literally 'win' or 'beat,' and the literal sense is that the *numba bilong ol tok* 'beats' 800.]

The development of Tok Pisin as a national language is interesting for a number of reasons: it argues for the 'utility' principle in the persistence of English in postcolonial situations; the particular situation is one of tremendous linguistic diversity; the tendency toward decreolization has been arrested in that while a standard form of English is used in the nation, one cannot really speak of a "Papuan English"; the lack of a local variety of English as a national standard, in part a result of the aforementioned linguistic diversity (itself a product of the nation's geography and settlement patterns), has left the Creole in place as a *lingua franca*; as the Creole developed in complexity, internal constraints (and interaction with Australian English, for instance) have checked the drift away from the English base and enforced a 'systematicity' that makes the Creole maximally useful across a region of some 800 (or more) Papuan languages (often classified into 40 or perhaps as many as 60 branches), and one in which a local variety of English did not take hold as a rival (British, American, or Australian English all could have filled that role over the last 140 years). The use of Tok Pisin at the national level, and in local media (and by the Australian Broadcasting Corporation) has raised the prestige of a variety once considered 'broken English,' and local pride in the contact language seems likely to solidify its use well into the future. There are other Pacific English-based pidgins and Creoles, but Tok Pisin with some 4 million or more speakers (primarily L2) is perhaps the most vibrant of the English-based contact varieties in the Pacific region. And it serves as a complement and interesting contrast to the many established and emerging varieties of English in the wider Asian-Pacific region.

English-based pidgins and Creoles

The designation ML = mixed language is used for varieties categorized by linguists as more properly being 'mixed languages' rather than Creoles; the terminology can be confusing as some fully Creolized varieties go by local names that include variant spellings of 'pidgin': 'Pijin,' 'Pisin'.

10.1.1 Africa

West African Pidgin English continuum (Huber 2008b, 167): the historical roots of West African pidgins and Creoles stretch back to the 15th century (with, for instance, Portuguese as an early lexifying language); contemporary contact varieties include interaction with French in Francophone nations such as Senegal, Guinea, Côte d'Ivoire, Benin, and Cameroon, and local Niger–Congo languages; some 85 million or so people speak one of the varieties of West African Pidgin English (Nigerian Pidgin the giant in the continuum)
Krio (Sierra Leone; Finney 2013, 157–166)
Ghanaian Pidgin English (Huber 2013, 167–175)
Nigerian Pidgin (Faraclas 2013, 176–184)
Kamtok (Cameroonian Pidgin English; Ayafor 2008, 428–450; Schröder 2013, 185–193)
Pichi (Bioko island, Equatorial Guinea; Yakpo 2013, 194–205)
Liberian Kreyol, Kru Pidgin (Liberia)
Liberian Settler English (Liberia; Singler 2008, 395–415)
Sheng (Kenya: Kibera, Nairobi; an emergent mixed language, Swahili and English, perhaps creolizing with increasing English influence)

Caribbean–Caribbean Basin–Central America
Bahamian Creole (The Bahamas; Hackert 2013, 127–138); similarities have been noted with Gullah (Sea Islands off the coasts of South Carolina, Georgia, and Northeastern Florida; Geechee, Sea Island Creole; Klein 2013, 139–147), the last extant Atlantic Creole with mainly elderly speakers
Bajan (Barbados; Blake 2008, 312–319)
Eastern Caribbean Creole English (Turks and Caicos Islands, US Virgin Islands, British Virgin Islands, Dutch Windward Islands [St. Eustatius, Saba, St. Martin], Anguilla, Montserrat, Barbuda, Windwards [Dominica, St. Lucia, St. Vincent and the Grenadines, Carriacou, Grenada]; Aceto in Schneider 2008, 290–311)
Trini (Trinidad and Tobago; Trini Talk, Trinidadian English Creole; Mühleisen 2013, 61–69)
Vincy (St. Vincent and the Grenadines; Vincentian Creole; Prescod 2013, 70–80)
Patwa (Jamaica; Jamaican Creole; Devonish and Harry 2008, 256–289; Patrick 2008, 609–644; Farquharson 2013, 81–91)
Samaná English (Dominican Republic)

Belizean Kriol (Belize, speakers also in Mexico and Honduras; Belizean Creole, Broken; Escure 2013, 92–100)
Bay Islands Creole (Honduras; perhaps 300,000 Creole and Black African Hondurans speak either English or an English-based Creole; Escure 2008, 742–743)
Miskito Coast Creole and Rama Caye Creole (Nicaragua's Atlantic coast); many Miskito Natives speak either Nicaraguan English or the English-based Creole, especially in Bluefields and the Corn Islands; the latter Creole is spoken by about 500 Rama Indians (Escure 2008, 743–744; Bartens 2013, 115–126)
Saintandrewan (Providencia and San Andrés Island, off the coast of Nicaragua but Colombian territory; San Andres Creole English; Escure 2008, 744–745; Bartens 2013, 101–114).
Limón Creole (Costa Rica, Puerto Limón region; a descendant of Jamaican Creole brought by Jamaican laborers; also called Limonese Creole, or *Mekaytelyu*, 'make I tell you' in Jamaican Creole; Winkler and Obeng 2000; Escure 2008, 745)
Panamanian English Creole (Panama's Caribbean coast, Panama City, Colón, possibly also on Panama's Pacific coast; also called Guari Guari/Wari Wari [apparently an exonym; Herzfeld 1980, 233] and descended from Jamaican Creole brought by Jamaican laborers; Escure 2008, 745–46)

Sranan Tongo ('Surinamese Tongue,' serves as a *lingua franca* in Suriname, also spoken in Western French Guiana; Römer 2006; Winford and Plag 2013, 15–26)
Saramaccan (Suriname; like Nengee, Saramaccan derives from early colonial-era marronage; West African languages such as Gbe and Kikongo have left their imprint on the Creole; Aboh et al. 2013, 27–38)
Nengee (Suriname, some speakers in French Guiana; also called Ndyuka or Eastern Maroon Creole, influenced by West African languages, Amerindian languages, and Portuguese; Migge 2013, 39–48)
Ndyuka (Suriname and French Guiana, a 'maroon' Creole, spoken by the Aukan [Ndyuka], one of six Maroon peoples of Suriname and French Guiana; also heavily lexified by Portuguese, as well as Dutch and the Akan languages of Ghana; the paramount chief of the Maroon peoples is called *granman*, or *gaanman* in Ndyuka)
Kriyoliiz (Guyana; influence of Dutch, Hindi [Bhojpuri], and Arawakan; Devonish and Thompson 2013, 49–60)

South and Southeast Asia, Pacific Islands
(Hawaiian) Pidgin (US state of Hawaii; Hawaiian Creole; Velupillai 2013, 252–261)

Butler English (India; also called Boxwallah English, Cheechee English; Hosali 2008, 563–577)
Singlish (Singapore; Wee 2008, 593–609)

Tok Pisin (Papua New Guinea; now not simply a *lingua franca* but a national language; Smith and Siegel 2013, 214–222)
Solomon Islands Pijin (Solomon Islands Creole, closely related to Tok Pisin; Jourdan and Selbach 2008, 164–187; Jourdan 2008, 467–487)

Biche-la-mar/Bichelamar/Bêche-de-mer/Bislama (Vanuatu, also in Fiji; Crowley 2008, 142–163; Meyerhoff 2013, 223–231)

Nauruan Pidgin English (Nauru; Tok Pisin, Pijin, and Bislama can be grouped as descendants of Melanesian Pidgin English; Nauruan Pidgin is a descendant of Micronesian Pidgin English – remnants of contact varieties can be found across Micronesia/Federated States of Micronesia – and with the historical influence of Chinese Pidgin English)

Norf'k and Pitcairnese (Norfolk Island, Pitcairn Island; Ingram and Mühlhäusler 2008, 267–291; Mühlhäusler 2008, 568–82; Mühlhäusler 2013, 232–240)

Kriol (Australian Aboriginal communities in Western Australia and the Northern Territory; Malcolm 2008, 124–141, 415–443; Schultze-Berndt et al. 2013, 241–251)

10.2 MOTHER COUNTRY: ASIAN-PACIFIC VARIETIES OF ENGLISH

Asian-Pacific English-speaking countries and territories

Total number of English speakers (L1 and L2), other major languages (where applicable); figures are from Crystal 2019, 115–117, except for those marked with the asterisk.

10.2.1 East Asia

China (including Inner Mongolia, Tibet, Turkic regions): 250,000,000–400,000,000 (figure is highly uncertain; Mandarin, Cantonese, Hakka, Hokkien, and others)

Hong Kong 6,260,000 (Cantonese, Mandarin, Yue, Hakka, and other Chinese language varieties)

Japan 18,950,000 (Japanese, Korean, Ryukyuan, and Ainu)

Mongolia 916,000 (Mongolian, Oirat, and Buryat)

North Korea 508,000 (Korean)

South Korea 22,838,000 (Korean)

Taiwan 1,177,000 (Taiwanese Mandarin, Hokkien, Hakka, and indigenous languages of the Formosan family)

10.2.2 Southeast Asia

Brunei 360,000 (Malay, Brunei Malay, Hokkien, Cantonese, Hakka, and indigenous languages)

Burma/Myanmar 8,204,000 (Burmese, many other languages in the Tibeto-Burman, Tai-Kadai, Karenic, Austroasiatic, Sino-Tibetan, and other language families)

Cambodia 3,208,000 (Cambodian/Khmer, French, Austroasiatic, and Tai-Kadai languages)

Indonesia 52,737,000 (Bahasa Indonesia [Malay], Javanese, Sundanese, and Dutch)
Laos 701,000 (Lao, Hmong, Khmu, and French)
Hong Kong 7,400,000 (Cantonese, Hakka, and Mandarin)
Malaysia 31,200,000 (Malay [Bahasa Malaysia]; a large number of native languages of Austronesian, Malayo-Polynesian, Muritic, and other language families)
Philippines 103,622,000 (Tagalog, Cebuano, Ilocano, and Pangasinan)
Singapore 5,811,000 (Malay, Mandarin, and Tamil)
Thailand 6,844,000 (Thai and languages in the Kra-Dai, Austroasiatic, Sino-Tibetan, Austronesian, and Hmong-Mien language families)
Timor-Leste (East Timor) 432,000 (Tetum and Portuguese co-official, Mambai, and Makasae)
Vietnam 4,769,000 (Vietnamese, French, Khmer, Nùng, Cham, and Hmong)

Australia 24,700,000 (Aboriginal languages in Pama-Nyungan and other families)
New Zealand 4,588,000 (Māori)
Cook Islands 19,000 (Cook Islands Māori/Rarotonga, Pukapukan)
Papua New Guinea 7,920,000 (Tok Pisin, Hiri Motu, and many Papuan languages)
Indonesia 52,737,000 (Bahasa Indonesia and other regional forms of Malay)
Solomon Islands 606,000 (Pijin, native language in the Austronesian family)
Vanuatu 276,000 (Bislama and French)
Fiji 924,000 (2023, L1 and L2 speakers; Fijian, iTaukei, Hindi, and Rotuman)
Norfolk Island ca. *2100 (as of 2023; Norf'k)
Pitcairn Islands ca. 35-54 (as of 2023; Pitkern/Pitcairnese)
Guam 108,000 (Chamorro)
Kiribati 116,000 (Gilbertese/Ta taetae ni Kiribati)
Nauru 10,300 (Nauruan)
Palau 21,4000 (Palauan)
Northern Marianas 50,000 (Chamorro and Carolinian)
Samoa 196,000 (Samoan)
Tonga 107,000 (Tongan)
Tuvalu 10,000 (Tuvaluan)
Marshall Islands 55,400 (Marshallese)
Federated States of Micronesia 105,000 (Chuukese, Pohnpeian, Kosraean, Yapese, and other Austronesian languages)
American Samoa 57,000 (Samoan)
Niue ca. *1700 (Niuean)

Mauritius 1,283,000 (French and Morisien Kreol)
Seychelles 98,000 (French and Kreol)

10.2.3 South Asia

Afghanistan 3,436,000 (Pashto, Dari)
Bangladesh 30,000,000+? (Bengali, Urdu, and a number of Dravidian, Austroasiatic, and Tibeto-Burman languages)
Bhutan 750,000 (Dzongkha and other Tibeto-Burman languages)

India 150,000,000–400,000,000 (English-speaking population is growing rapidly, but reliable figures are hard to come by; India likely has the second largest English-speaking population in the world after the United States, and is likely to remain so [though China's English-learner population has grown exponentially in recent decades]; Hindi, Urdu, and many other Indo-Iranian, Dravidian, Austroasiatic, and other languages)
Maldives 338,000 (Dhivehi and Arabic)
Nepal 14,565,000 (Nepali, Maithili, and Bhojpuri)
Pakistan ca. 108,000,000 (Urdu is the national language; Punjabi, Pashto, and Sindhi)
Sri Lanka ca. 5,200,000 (Sinhala and Tamil)

10.3 AUSTRALIA

In describing a regional or national variety or set of varieties of English in a global context, one inevitably has to consider the range of varieties possible (or, in a post-colonial context, likely): from exported British dialects to contact varieties (pidgins, Creoles, and 'mixed languages' that include English) to emerging local dialects and national standards (as can be said since the mid-19th to early 20th centuries). With the case of Australia, though the lifespan of English in the continent 'down under' is relatively short (from 1788), the indigenous (Aboriginal) roots are deep, the colony's origin stark (in blunt historical terms, and enduringly so in subsequent national myth-making and popular culture – a figure such as Ned Kelly one example), and the dialectal and linguistic contact situation complex (English, Irish, Scots, Aboriginal; and later Asian and Pacific immigrants as well as those from Greece, Lebanon, and other nations in the modern period). The indigenous language picture in Australia is enormously complex as it likely is "the largest and also the longest-established linguistic area in the world" (Dixon 2002, 690). As human settlement of Australia dates back some 40,000–50,000 years before the present, one is talking about a landmass area that once also included New Guinea. The drier, more open terrain of southwest New Guinea and most of Australia, relatively easy to traverse, does not exhibit as much linguistic diversity as the more mountainous and thickly forested areas of northeast Australia and the rest of New Guinea. Dixon's classification of Australia's indigenous languages proposes 50 groupings, from the Papuan languages in the Torres Strait Group to the Pama-Nyungan (the largest Australian language family) and other Aboriginal language groupings; to this latter family belongs the Western Desert language, a group of dialects for which no endonym (indigenous name) is known now to exist – a phenomenon not unusual with indigenous languages (Dixon 2002, xxxi–xxxii, 1–2). While several Australian Aboriginal languages have a few thousand speakers, such as Djambarrpuyngu, Warlpiri, and Tiwi, nearly half of the 250–400 or so known languages (the figures vary by method of classification, and the difficulty of the language-dialect line) are no longer spoken and most of those with speakers are moribund or endangered (with only older speakers left). Despite attempts at language maintenance and revival, the state of most Aboriginal languages is parlous, a situation likewise found in the Americas. Dixon had noted that of the half of Aboriginal languages no longer actively spoken, some were known from "a sprinkling of words used within the English spoken by their tribal descendants" (Dixon 2002, 2). The encounter with English in Australia began in 1788 – a relatively recent encounter among those of the colonial era. Certainly, most of the Aboriginal linguistic influence upon Australian English is to be found in the lexicon, at least in terms of "white" Australian English (and now that of more recent immigrants to the country, from Asia, Greece, Lebanon, etc.). The native language loss stemming from this encounter is simply incalculable, from language loss to language shift.

Gurindji Kriol

Jenasis
God bin meigim ebrijing.
1:1–3 Orait, longtaim wen God bin stat meigimbat ebrijing, nomo enijing bin jidan. Imbin jis eniwei, nomo garram enijing. Oni strongbala woda bin goran goran ebriwei, en imbin brabli dakbala, en det Spirit blanga God bin mubabat ontop langa det woda.

Brom deya God bin tok, "Lait!" En streidawei det lait bin kamat.

[very literal parsing: Genesis 1: 1-3. God been make-em everything. All right, long-time when God start make-em-up everything, no anything been alive/ in existence. It been just (so) anyway, no have anything. Only powerful water go-round go-round every-way, and it been proper darkness, and that Spirit belong God been move-about on-top along that water. From there God been talk, "Light!" And straightaway that light been come-out.]

Mak 2: 3-5
Wal Jisas bin insaid langa det haus dalimbat detlot pipul det gudnyus, en fobala men bin kaman deya langa det kamp. Deibin garrimap wanbala leimbala men garram im sweig. Bat dei nomo bin go gulijap langa Jisas, dumaji detlot pipul bin jadimap det haus, en detlot fobala men bin lafta galimap ontop langa det haus, en deibin deigimat det ruf rait ontop langa Jisas weya imbin jandap, en wen deibin binij deigimatbat det ruf, deibin pudumdan det leimbala men garram det sweig.

Wal wen Jisas bin look olabat, imbin sabi deibin bilib langa im brabli, en imbin tok langa det leimbala men, "Main fren, ai larramgo yu fri brom det nogudbalawei blanga yu."

Mark 2: 3–5 Well Jesus been inside belong that house tell-em-bout that-lot people that good news, and four men been come there to that camp. They been carry-em-up one lame man got-em him belonging [on his pallet]. But they no-more been go near unto Jesus, too-much that-lot people been shut-out that house [there were too many people to get in the house], and that-lot four men been had to climb up on-top belong that house, and they-been take up that roof right on-top of Jesus where he been, and when they been finished take-em-up that roof, they been put-em-down that lame man got-em that pallet.

Well when Jesus been look at them, he been know they been believe him truly, and he been talk unto that lame man, "My friend, I let-em-go you free from that no-goodnesses [sins] belong you."
(*Holi Baibul* 2018)

Dating to the establishment of cattle stations in Kalkaringi in the Victoria River District of Australia's Northern Territory, the English–Gurindji contact situation was unusual (but not unprecedented) in that an English-based pidgin formed that led to the development of a Creole (called Kriol) without full loss of the native language (which remains endangered with 500 or so speakers, though it seems young people are not now learning the language; Meakins 2011, 13) nor complete shift to Kriol. Instead, as with Michif of Canada seen earlier, a 'mixed language' developed in which there were morphological borrowings to the 'dominant' language (generally seen as unusual in contact situations), while "[c]ode-switching between Gurindji and Kriol was a precursor of the mixed language" (Meakins 2011, 7). Not all contact situations are alike, and since the study by Peter Bakker of the Michif contact language spoken by Métis of the Canadian plains regions (Saskatchewan and Manitoba, with some speakers on the U.S. side in North Dakota; Bakker 1997), the framework of pidgin and Creole 'contact languages' has been expanded to include 'mixed languages' in which the level of exchange is more intensive than simple lexification (borrowing of vocabulary from the adstrate or substrate languages) or limited phonological exchange. In the case of contact languages, the changes appear more 'structural,' such as borrowings in inflectional morphology (pronoun system, nominal inflection, and verb markings). In the case of Gurindji Kriol, the extensive study by Meakins (2011) has shown that while Kriol supplies much of the "verbal grammar" of the mixed language (auxiliaries, tense and aspect marking, and derivational morphemes), the native language, Gurindji, supplies much of the "NP structure"; thus, in the example ***brokbrok*** *dei bin beit-im dem* ***la bingka*** – very literally, "the frogs they been bite-em them the hand," the boldface elements are from Gurindji (representing the subject [*brokbrok*] and object [*la bingka*] of the sentence), and the central VP is from the Kriol (*dei bin beit-im dem*; Meakins 2011, 11–13).

im silip langa gran (Meakins 2011, 17)
"him sleep 'long ground" ["He is sleeping on the ground"]

langa gud-wan kantri blanga im dadi (18)
"in the good-one country belong to his father"

big-wan **yawu** dei bin grab-im **jangkarni** (269)
"big-one fish they grab-em big"

i bin lib-im **nyanuny** basikul-**ma** bihain **karnti-ngka** (275)
"he been leave-em for-him bicycle [**ma** is a topic marker] behind tree [**ngka** is the locative marker]"

Being 'mixed,' specialists in contact linguistics avoid any '-based' description – though with a significant proportion of English and English-based pidgin elements in the mixed form, one can speak of Gurindji Kriol as part of the extended 'family' of varieties of the English language. This is an important point of increasing relevance in an age of 'International English' and 'Global Englishes': where and how does one draw linguistic boundaries? With what language, Canadian French or Cree, Ojibwe, and other Canadian First Nations languages, would Michif be classified? A simpler answer for the moment would be to consider Gurindji Kriol as belonging to both linguistic systems, English and Aboriginal Australian. A sample of the breakdown in origin of structural and lexical features of Gurindji Kriol in Meakins's Table 1 (Meakins 2011, 20) gives a sense of the 'mixed' nature of this variety.

> **Structural**: bound verbal morphology (Kriol; i.e., non-isolating verbal markers [e.g., those that are affixed to the verbal root]); case (nominal) morphology (Gurindji); number marking (nominal, including *paucal* [i.e., expressing 'a few' as distinct from singular, dual, and plural]; Gurindji); negation (Kriol); pronouns (Kriol); emphatic and possessive pronouns (Gurindji); interrogative pronouns (Kriol); deictics (*this/that* [Gurindji] *here/there* [Kriol]); determiners (Kriol); interjections (Gurindji).
>
> **Lexical:** stative verbs (mixed); verbs of motion (mainly Gurindji); verbs of bodily functions (Gurindji); colors, noun forms (Kriol); plants (mainly Gurindji); animals (mixed).

Modern Australia was shaped by a number of forces that had linguistic consequences; one was a change in the prescriptive/descriptive balance of assessment of varieties in English – 'Australian English,' itself stratified by class, race, ethnicity, and other factors (and as will be seen shortly with 'Bogan,' class may prove the most enduring stratifier), saw its actual and perceptual stock rise through the later 20th century and especially in the 21st century: 'Aussie' English, like Irish English before it, became popular, not just 'quaint' (as in popular perception Leinster Irish English can be seen). It is easy, perhaps facile, to chalk this up to the successful popular exports of Australia, which has an outsize presence in world cinema in terms of box office and awards; the films of Australia in particular, and the music, literature, television, sports, and iconography, have spread 'Aussie' (as a variety, as a cultural product) around the world, with the strongest impact perhaps in the United Kingdom and the United States. It may seem a trite example, but the adoption in American English of the Australian expression *good on you* (AmE "good for you," i.e., "you did good"), which like the adoption of Britishisms such as *spot on* can seem jarring, irritating, or pretentious (and now fall prey to calls of cultural appropriation), is evidence of a change in views of the "Land Down Under." And the change has certainly been an ameliorative one, especially in Britain (the picture is even rosier since the assessment of Bradley and Bradley 2001). While not an exact parallel by any means, the U.S. state of Georgia had a similar reputation as a 'penal colony' in its origins; it was neither Botany Bay nor Van Diemen's Land, even though James Oglethorpe (1696–1785) had envisioned it as a "Debtor's Colony." The sole early record of transportation of convicts to Georgia comes from the mid-1730s, when a shipment of 40 Irish convicts landed in Georgia after being turned away by Jamaica, though perhaps some 50,000 other convicts were landed in other colonies on the eastern seaboard of British America (Ekirch 1987, 113). Australia has variously buried and embraced the convict heritage; two film/television productions about Irish convict Alexander Pearce (1790–1824), who escaped multiple times from the penal colonies at Van Diemen's and Sarah Island, was accused of cannibalism, and hanged in Hobart on 19 July 1824, appeared recently within a year of one another: *The Last Confession of Alexander Pearce* (2008; directed by Michael James Rowland), and *Van Diemen's Land* (2009; directed by Jonathan auf der Heide). The general sense of Australian English, internally but especially abroad, is of a language that is plain-spoken, direct, no-nonsense, and of distinctly non-elite origins. The "First Fleet" of 11 ships transporting convicts to the Colony of New South Wales brought with them, on the whole, people charged with theft; in some cases, those charged with assault and more costly burglaries had first been sentenced to death, then had the sentence commuted to transportation to the penal colonies (no doubt there was some sense that a certain number of 'tougher' convicts would be necessary to colonize more far-flung possessions such as New South Wales).

From the records of this "First Fleet," one can get some confirmation of the dialectal origins of some of the transported convicts; while a simple majority of the convicts on the 11 ships were convicted at the Old Bailey, London, there is not always information as to their ultimate origin if not Londoners (last names give some idea of ethnic and regional origin – e.g., Scots, Irish, Welsh, and Cornish). Regional courts seem to have been particularly active in sentencing convicts to transportation: the *Charlotte* transported 107 convicts, predominantly but not exclusively males (the *Lady Penrhyn* and *Prince of Wales* transported only female convicts, 102 and 51, respectively), a large number of whom had been sentenced in Devon, with a fair number also from Wiltshire. The *Scarborough* transported a fairly large number of convicts sentenced in Cornwall (at Bodmin and Launceston),[4] and a fairly sizeable proportion of convicts hailed from or were sentenced in western and northern counties, Gloucestershire in particular. While Australian English has traditionally been seen as a mixture of English dialects, with significant influence from Irish English, its particular phonology has usually been linked to Cockney and West Country dialects; indeed, a significant component of the First Fleet generation consisted of poor Londoners and men and women from Gloucestershire, Wiltshire, Devon, Cornwall, Shropshire, Staffordshire, Dorset from the southwest, west, and West Midlands, and Durham, Lancashire, and Yorkshire from the north. With regard to Northern English dialects, there is some overlap with the vowels in *fleece* (Northern English [i:] ~ [i] ~ [ei], Australian [i:] ~ [^{ə}i] ~ [əɪ]) and *square* (Northern English [ɛ:] ~ [ɛə] ~ [ɜ:], Australian [eə] ~ [e^{ə}] ~ [e:]; Beal 2008, 130–135; Horvath 2008, 91–93).

Pronunciations usually associated with Australian English include the "broad *a*," which can confusingly refer to tensed or lengthened ('broad') /ɑ:/ and diphthongal *a* in *plate* or *today* (the characteristic 'broad' or working-class pronunciation "tuh-die") retracting from /eɪ/ to /ʌɪ/ (Peters 2008, 391), and the diphthongization of the /o/ in *so* to /əʉ/ ~ /əu/ (Horvath 2008, 92). The usual stratification of Australian English into 'broad,' 'general,' and 'cultivated' owes the origins of the first two classes (roughly the more working-class and rural and urban, middle-class groupings) to the "founder generation," while the 'cultivated' class may be connected to a "second wave" of British immigrants to Australia in the later 19th century who brought with them accents closer to British RP (Leitner 2004, vol. 1, 5–6). The social implications and associations of

[4] The State Library of New South Wales, Australia, has a useful online archive of resources about the First Fleet: https://guides.sl.nsw.gov.au/convicts-bound-for-australia/first_fleet

these "levels" of Australian English accent are wide-ranging and deeply significant, and, as elsewhere in the English-speaking world, subject to code-shifting, diglossia, manipulation, and fakery. General Australian seems to function at times as does Estuary English in Britain – it can be a means for a politician (or actor or athlete) of a somewhat (or significantly) posher background to sound more 'folksy,' common, or down-to-earth (and in the parlance of an incessantly media-driven age, more 'accessible'). As with the Estuary English of former Labour PM Tony Blair (Anthony Charles Lynton Blair) in Britain, an Oxford-educated (St. John's College) barrister, so too, to perhaps a lesser extent, the General Australian of Welsh-born former Labor PM Julia Gillard (a lawyer in the high-powered firm Slater and Gordon). As 'New Labour' in Britain and other Anglophone Commonwealth nations has evolved from its trade union roots to more technocratic lawyer–bureaucrats, and tech millionaires/billionaires, so the rising anxiety over linguistic authenticity – of parties quite simply fielding candidates who don't sound like their traditional voters. This is an enormously complicated and common phenomenon in the 21st century – the social anxiety of politicians, athletes, and musicians (particularly acute in hip-hop) who do not quite sound like the persona they have projected. It is not, however, a new phenomenon (one thinks of Renaissance 'self-fashioning'), and while easily derided and lampooned, it has shaped the language significantly, at least in its popular expression.

The main significant phonological traits of Australian English are of course in the vowels; the General and Cultivated norms are:

simple vowels: /i/, /e/, /ɜ/ (as in *serve*), /æ/, /ɑ/, /ɒ/, /ə/, /ʌ/, /u/, /ʊ/, /ɔ/ (ranging from front to central to back)

diphthongs: /eɪ/, /aɪ/, /ɪə/ (as in *cheer*), /eə/ (as in *chair*), /ɑʊ/, /ɔɪ/, /oʊ/ (as in *show*), /ʊə/ (as in *sewer*) [Peters 2007, 885]

A main consonantal difference, as can be seen from some of the diphthongs, involves rhotacism – Australian, New Zealand, and South African Englishes are in the main non-rhotic, with some dialectal exceptions (Southland on the South Island in New Zealand, and some Broad varieties in South Africa's Cape Province). There are, nonetheless, some significant variants:

linking /r/ and /intrusive /r/ do occur (as in *idea* > *idear*), a common phenomenon with non-rhotic varieties of English
vocalization of /l/ (*milk* to something like *miwk*, i.e., [mɪlk] > [mɪuk])
substitution of fricatives /θ/ > /f/ and /v/ > /ð/ (*fink* for *think* and *muvver* for *mother* as found also in Cockney)
h-dropping is more common with function words (such as personal pronouns *him* and *her*, which are clipped to *'im* and *'er*) than with content words
/ŋ/ > /ŋk/ in quantifiers such as *something*, *anything*, *everything*, *nothing* (Burridge 2010, 136–137)

The approximate values of Australian English vowels obtain for General varieties (such as used in broadcasting, education, and governance; on broadcast 'destandardization,' see Price 2012, 347–349), while the Cultivated variety may approximate RP more closely with the diphthongs and can sound therefore more 'British' (among Australian actors, Hugh Jackman's accent is classified as General, Cate Blanchett's as Cultivated). Significant differences are to be found in the Broad Australian varieties, and there are a range of these, from rural to working-class suburban. And here might be mentioned the 'Bogan' phenomenon. The etymology of *bogan* is listed as "uncertain" in the major lexica (*Macquarie, Australian Oxford Dictionary/Australian National Dictionary*) but might be connected to the river-name Bogan or associated place-names, the key factor being an association of 'bogan' culture and attitudes with either the Western Sydney suburbs or areas west of the Bogan River. Its force is something like that of the Americanism *white trash* or *Tobacco Road* (both of which derive from the American South), its range of application from external, derisive use (often class-marked and condescending) to self-application with covert prestige. Media use of the term pejorized with the Cronulla riots of 2005, which saw clashes between white Australians from the Sydney beach suburbs of Cronulla and North Cronulla and Middle Eastern youths ('Lebs' in the offensive parlance of the time, based on the Lebanese origin of many Middle Eastern immigrants to Australia), accused of harassing beachgoers and lifesavers. As is usually the case with mass media, coverage soon devolved into hysteria, race-baiting, mutual recrimination, and an eventual sifting of the narrative that blamed 'bogans' in large part for the problems (despite claims that many involved were not from the area). The name "Cronulla" has reverberated ever since in Australian culture, to the extent that it has become an eponym ('another Cronulla'), and, if not a watershed moment, it has inspired examination of modern changes in immigration patterns to the nation: the novels of Michael Mohammad Ahmad (*The Tribe* [2014] and *The Lebs* [2018]) provide some perspective on growing up Arab–Australian, while accounts from those who participated in the 2005 riots fill out the media narrative (Farrell 2015). From a semantic perspective, the term *bogan* would seem to have fewer negative entailments as AmE *white trash* and may be more amenable to ameliorative use – for example, in-group use of the term as a mark of solidarity or ironic pride. This in turn can provoke some backlash, some of it ironic, some condescending (*bogan* is an eminently useful marker in virtue-signaling by middle-class white speakers of General Australian): the emergence of the "CUB" (*cashed-up bogan*) may be one example of this, a snarky (or snide) reference to 'bogans' (such as athletes the late Shane Warne and Lleyton Hewitt) who have 'made it good' (and, by implication, risen above their station in life – in this sense it is not unlike the earlier *Mick on the make*; for the phenomenon, see "Bogans on parade," Lalo 2010, or the blog "Things Bogan Like").

If the lexical part of things 'bogan' belongs to exaggerative popular and social media culture (perhaps like 'Zef' culture in South Africa), the phonology of Broad Australian has a long documentary trail, in fact the longest of any variety of Australian English. The rest of the Anglophone world heard the vowels, especially the diphthongs of Broad Australian, from the likes of Paul Hogan ("Crocodile Dundee") and the late Steve Irwin ("The Crocodile Hunter"); that is, from Australian film and television exports. Distinctive departures from General Australian include the diphthong /æ/ or /ɔe/ in *price* (/aɪ/ in RP and General American) raising to /ɔɪ/ ("proice") or the breaking or diphthongization of /i/ and /u/ to /ɘɪ/ and /ɘʊ/ (Horvath 2008, 92). And if Canadian English is known for the raising of the diphthong in *about*, from /ɑʊ/ to /ʌʊ/ (i.e., Canadians do not pronounce the word like "aboot" but more like "aboat"), Broad Australian fronts and slightly raises to /æˈʊ/ or /ɛʊ/ (Burridge 2010, 136). There is some grammatical evidence to suggest that Australian English is now a national variety, looking to 'Australian' standards rather than British (*The Cambridge Guide to Australian English* is one such indicator; Peters 2007); there is, however, the example of 'uptalk' or 'upspeak' among young Australians (the rising non-interrogative tone at the end of clausular units) that may show more recent influence of American English (the 'Valley Girl' upspeak now endemic to the young people, in female speech more than male, throughout the United States; Burridge 2010, 139–142). Next to phonology (accent), perhaps the most distinctive area of variation to outside observers is in the lexicon:

from Australian English:

banana land (Queensland)
barbie (barbecue grill)
bathers (swimsuit)
bikie (biker, member of a biker gang)
Blind Freddy (even Blind Freddy could see that)
bogan; cashed-up bogan (CUB)
bonzer (outstanding, excellent)
boong (of uncertain etymology, an offensive term for an Aboriginal Australian or native of New Guinea; *abo* and *Jacky* are also offensive epithets for Aboriginal people)
brumby (feral horse)
budgie, budgerigar
chook raffle
cooee, coo-ee (a call to another across a distance, originally an Aboriginal traditional term)
di(d)geridoo (once thought to be from an Aboriginal language, now usually explained as onomatopoeic, or possibly from Irish Gaelic)
doctor (a cooling wind, sea breeze; e.g., Fremantle Doctor)
dole bludger
dunny (toilet)
Esky (cooler; 'Eskino' trademark name genericized)
fair dinkum (but apparently originally a Britishism, from Derbyshire; Burridge 2010, 134)
(a/the) fair go (fair, reasonable chance at something)
fair suck of the sauce bottle (be reasonable)
fairy bread (buttered bread triangles topped with 'hundreds & thousands' [sprinkles/jimmies])
far up himself
firie (firefighter)
flash as a rat with a gold tooth
flat out

Kath & Kim accent
knocked back
ocker (a boor, an aggressive lout)
punter (< BrE)
sango, sanger ('sandwich'; compare AmE, and ItalAmE 'sangwich')
sarvo (< clipping of *this afternoon*, *afternoon* > *arf* + *-o* + voicing)
saveloy/sav; sav and roll (football food)
shag (cormorant)
she'll be apples (everything will be all right)
sheila (first recorded 1832 as *shelah*, for an Irish girl or woman < proper name Sheila(gh), Síle)
shivoo (party)
sickie (sick day, day off from work)
skippy (Australian of British decent, generally derisive)
snag (sausage)
Stolen Generation
stoush (fight, brawl)
Strine (< *Australian*, as pronounced with a 'Broad' accent)
stubby (short-necked beer bottle)
swag, swagman
trackie dacks (tracksuit pants; can be seen as 'bogan' attire)
Woop Woop (long distance away)

loans from Australian Aboriginal languages:

adjigo (type of yam, from Nhanta/Nhanda)
barramundi (type of freshwater fish, now popular on menus worldwide; < an Aboriginal language of Queensland)
betong (kangaroo rat, from Dharuk)
billabong (Wiradhuri)
boomerang (Dharuk – SE Australia)
budgie/budgerigar (Yuwaalaraay/Yuwaaliyaay, Aboriginal language no longer spoken): parakeet
coolibah (type of gum tree, from Yuwaalaraay/Yuwaaliyaay, of Pama-Nyungan Aboriginal language family)
currawong (bird of passerine/songbird family; possibly from Yuggera or Dharuk)
dingo (Dharuk)
kangaroo (perhaps from Guugu Yumithirr language – in NE)
koala (Dharuk)
kookaburra (Wiradhuri – NE): kingfisher
mulga (snake; from Kamilaroi or Yuwaalaraay)
quokka (type of wallaby, from Nyungar language)
waddy (Dharuk): club
wallaby (Dharuk)
[the *Oxford English Dictionary* includes 194 words of Aboriginal origin; a detailed examination of Australian Aboriginal influence upon lexis is Moore 2001].

Australian "external territories"

Christmas Island: population nearly 2,000, one-fifth of population of Chinese descent, other ethnic origins Malay, Australian, English, Irish, and Indian from diasporic communities in Malaysia and Singapore; English, Mandarin, Malay, and Cocos Malay (a decreolized form of Malay descended from a Malay trade jargon).

Cocos (Keeling) Islands (Australian Indian Ocean Territory): population of just over 540 persons; Malay and English the main languages.

Nauru, with a population of just over 10,600 people, gained independence from Australia in 1968; Nauruan the official language, English widespread and used for government.

Norfolk Island: the former penal colony's present population is 1,750, official languages English and Norf'k (profiled above); the annual Bounty Day (8 June) celebrates the heritage of descendants of the HMS Bounty mutineers who moved from Pitcairn Island to Norfolk (not quite half the present population is made up of these descendants).

Papua New Guinea: Territory of Papua, an external territory (1902–1949); Territory of New Guinea, transferred from Germany to Australia by League of Nations mandate for the period 1920–1949, having been occupied by the Australian military (1914–1920). The territories were combined from 1949 to 1975, independence gained in 1975. Population of 9 million; English, Tok Pisin, Hiri Motu, and Papua New Guinea Sign Language are the official languages.

If the modern nation has become in its official and elite culture fairly relentlessly 'politically correct' (and New Zealand all the more so), Australians have often been known for not taking themselves too seriously. A bestseller when the original edition appeared in 1965, Afferbeck Lauder's *Let Stalk Strine* ("Let's Talk Australian") was a humorous poke at and tribute to Broad Australian speech, perhaps more affectionate than satirical. Afferbeck Lauder (= "alphabetical order" in Strine) was the pseudonym of Alastair Ardoch Morrison, writer (early dispatches on "Strine" appeared in *The Sydney Morning Herald*), graphic artist, and illustrator (under the additional pseudonym Al Terego – 'alter ego' of course). Lauder was the self-described presumptive Professor of Strine Studies at the University of Sinny (Sydney). *Let Stalk Strine* was followed by *Nose Stone Unturned* in 1967; Professor Afferbeck then turned his attention to the 'posh' (or 'plummy'; Beale 2009) tones of Sydney's "Naw Shaw" (North Shore) in *Fraffly Well Spoken* (1968) and *Fraffly Suite* (1969; *fraffly* = 'frightfully'). The author's apology for the first volume was founded on the occasional misunderstandings between British English and Strine:

> It was recently reported (*Sydney Morning Herald,* 30 November, 1964) that while the English writer Monica Dickens was autographing copies of her latest book as they were being bought by members of the public in a Sydney

> shop, a woman handed her a copy and said, "Emma Chisit." Thinking that this was the woman's name, Monica Dickens wrote: "To Emma Chisit" above her signature on the flyleaf. The purchaser, however, in a rather more positive voice, said: "No, Emma Chisit?" Eventually it became clear that she had been speaking Strine, and had used the Strine equivalent of the English phrase, "How much is it?"
>
> It is obvious that incidents such as the above must cause endless misunderstanding, discord and international friction. This little book is an attempt to fill this gap (Afferbeck 1982, 9).

Along with the silliness of some of the humor is a frank appraisal (and appreciation) of Australian working-class frankness: their bluntness, parsimony (in speech and 'quid'), and skewering of pretension. That some of the humor of *Let Stalk Strine* and its sequel is turned back on the speakers of Strine themselves would be part and parcel of the bluntness and 'piss-taking' anyone within the speech community could expect of family, friends, and neighbors. And the "dictionaries" of Strine are in broad and humorous form the outline of a speech community:

air fridge (average)
airmgunnavago (I'm gonna have a go)
air-sarts (ersatz)
ark ellery (art gallery)
bim-bye (bitten by)
chew calmer nova (you coming over?)
crairded (crowded)
egg jelly (actually)
emeny (how many)
flares (flowers)
garbler mince (couple of minutes)
Jeggoda…Nar, dingo ("Did you go to…Nah, didn't go")
money (Monday)
to mipe lice? (to my place?)
jars-chewer nigh (just you and I)
Sander's Lape (sound asleep)
sbitarsh (It's a bit harsh)
scona rine (it's gonna rain)
semmitch (sandwich)
tan cancel (town council)
water bat (what about)
yegottny (you got any?)
(Afferbeck 1982, 11–43)

One descendant of Professor Afferbeck's Strine is of course the "Kath & Kim accent," the Strine-tones of the mother and daughter pair of the ABC (Australian Broadcasting Corporation) sitcom that ran from 2002 to 2005. Set in the fictional Melbourne suburb of Fountain Lakes, *Kath & Kim* is one of the most popular Australian television series to date, and the "situational comedy" was heavily dependent upon the repartee of the titular mother and daughter and, of course, their accent: Strine.

Afferbeck and *Kath & Kim* evidence the informality that is both the reality and stereotype of Australian English – and in postmodern 'meta' culture, these two categories often merge in irony, self-parody, and subconscious affectation. Nicknames for or shortened forms of place- or personal names (hypocoristic forms) are found everywhere, but Australians seem particularly fond of them: *Oz* (Australia); *Adders* (Adelaide); *Crowie* (Crow's Nest); *Macker* (Macquarie University); *Sevvo* (Seven Hills); *Scarbs* (Scarborough); *Shep* (Shepparton; Simpson 2001, 89–96). The discourse marker *yeah-no*, used as a mild asseverative, or hedge, or polite weakening of a statement ("Yeah no, I understand"; Peters and Collins 2012, 590), usually seen as unique to Australian English, has cropped up in Southern California English in the past two decades; the vector of transmission may be "surf speak," as other links and loans between the two surf cultures have been around for some time (the Australian surfwear company Billabong has long had a strong presence in Southern California). And while the evidence for the grammatical and syntactic distinctiveness of Australian English seems slight (Newbrook 2001 offers some detail, including Australian use of *usedn't to* for the negative form of *used to*; 116), the most apparent differences are in phonology and lexis.

10.4 NEW ZEALAND

Broad similarities, particularly in phonology, have long led observers (and, latterly, linguists) to speak of 'Antipodean' Englishes, encompassing the varieties of Australia, New Zealand, and South Africa (the rationale for their appearance in this order here). But significant differences, of course, obtain, particularly in terms of the native language situation in each nation. In contrast to Australia, where some 400 Aboriginal languages in about 28 distinct language families have been spoken (many now extinct or moribund), in New Zealand, one native language, *Te Reo Māori*, that of the native Māori people, is spoken. A language in the Eastern Polynesian family, New Zealand Māori is spoken by some 125,000–150,000 or so people out of an ethnic population of some 550,000–600,000. But the figure for the number of speakers includes varying levels of fluency, and Māori, like so many Australian Aboriginal languages, is considered endangered. The national rate of Māori language use is about 23% (*The Social Report 2016*),[5] and to combat inter-generational language decline, the *kōhanga reo* ('language nest') system has sought to help revive the language at the *whānau* (extended family or kin unit, also a political unit) level. The closely related Cook Islands Māori language is spoken by some 14,000 people; it became co-official with English in 2003 (New Zealand Māori achieved that status by the Māori Language Act 1987). In simple lexical terms, Māori has had a significant influence upon the vocabulary of New Zealand English (see page 553). Reasons for this are complicated and speak to the many factors of loan word adoption and formation: level and intensity and type of contact situation (trade, colonization, military occupation); duration of contact situation: this

[5] https://socialreport.msd.govt.nz/cultural-identity/maori-language-speakers.html

may explain some differences in adoption of Native American loan words in American English, a contact situation of some four centuries' duration, and those of Australia and New Zealand that date, respectively, to 1788 and somewhat later in New Zealand (Captain Cook visited in 1769, the first Christian mission was established in 1814); size of respective populations of speakers of English and indigenous languages; the nature of topography, flora, and fauna is even a factor: the less familiar these are to the arriving English speakers, the greater the likelihood (though not without constraints from the other factors) of adoption of native "words for things."

The strong phonological overlap in the phonology of Australian and New Zealand Englishes is tempered somewhat by differences in perception of the varieties and a certain rivalry between the two national varieties (or sets of varieties). New Zealand English, like other colonial varieties, was once judged harshly, and not just by speakers from Britain but within New Zealand society and its educational establishment: "this objectionable colonial dialect," "Well educated New Zealanders speak of hospiddles" (Gordon and Abell 1990, 23; Schneider 2003, 268). Indeed, in 1910 Augustus Heine, acting Headmaster of Wellington College had observed that New Zealand English had gotten "[m]uch worse in the past ten years," while in 1924 F. Martin Renner, in a speech to the Wellington Joint Standing Committee of the New Zealand Educational Association, had noted "defects" in the developing New Zealand accent: *praise* pronounced "prise," *my* as "moi," *Mexico* as "Mexiceouw," *shout* as "sheout" (Gordon and Abell 1990, 24). While lamentations over perceived decline in spoken English are to be found anywhere English is spoken – and the lamenting of such lamentation by linguists can become just as *pro forma* and *de rigueur* – what is really being pointed out is the increasing divergence of New Zealand English from that of the 'mother country.' The observations of Heine and Renner are interesting in dating this divergence, at least to when it became much more noticeable (and, perhaps, to their ears, intolerable); Renner's phonetic representations are doubly interesting in that modern speakers will recognize their own 'broad' New Zealand pronunciations. That there is significant overlap between the phonology of Australian and New Zealand Englishes has long been known; much more contentious is the matter of why – do both sets of varieties have similar origins in London or Southeastern British English (the "Cockney hypothesis"), or is New Zealand English a species of Australian English? (An excellent overview is Gordon et al. 2004, "Previous attempts to explain the origins of New Zealand English," 66–84). Some attempts have been made to explain the distinctiveness of New Zealand English by way of language contact with Māori or other languages. While it is certainly true that Māori significantly shaped New Zealand English lexis, there has been disagreement over whether the language contact or "mixing bowl" theory of New Zealand English origins can explain the loss of rhoticity (Gordon et al. 2004, 235; Hay and Clendon 2012, 762–765). While certain features of Irish influence have been identified, only the /w/ ~ /hw/ distinction seems to have survived (but now is in decline); it is curious that New Zealand English was less influenced by Irish immigrants (who made up 20% of the population by 1871) than was Australian English (Gordon et al. 2004, 232–233). Highly significant, at least to the idea of an Australian role in the formation of New Zealand English, are the levels of Australian immigration to New Zealand and movements of peoples between the colonies for reasons of settlement, transportation, and labor opportunities (Gordon et al. 2004, 228–230).

One persistent popular distinction between 'Aussie English' and 'Kiwi' English is a preference for the latter over the former, a sense that it sounds 'better' or more 'refined.' Some of this is of course impressionistic, with some friendly rivalry and neighborly teasing, and some may be lingering stigmatization of Australia's penal colony origins. An old joke on this subject makes the point succinctly:

> A Kiwi [other variants have a Brit or American] lands in Sydney and is greeted by a customs officer.
> "You aren't carrying any drugs, are you"
> "No."
> "Knife?" ("noif")
> "No."
> "Gun?"
> "No."
> "Do you have a criminal record?" ("rekkid")
> "Erm. Do you still need one to get in?"

Nonetheless, both Aussies and Kiwis have historically been said to suffer the 'cultural cringe,' an internalized sense of inferiority in the face of RP and traditional British culture (and, to an extent more recently, American culture), and a deference to the standards of the mother country and the Queen's English (a similar sense dogged early Americans and was perhaps only shaken off by the quintessentially American novels of Mark Twain). Recent work has suggested that New Zealand and Australian English may share many of their similarities not from the flow of Australian immigrants to New Zealand so much as the similar set of shared influences, in dialect and the demography of immigration, of southeastern English (London, Cockney, and Essex), Irish, and Scots influences that by dialect mixing and leveling produced the "linguistic drift" (the concept belongs to American linguistic Edward Sapir; Sapir 1921, 147–170) that resulted in similar outcomes in Australia and New Zealand (and to an extent in South Africa also; Bayard 2000, 297–324; Hay et al. 2008, 1–13). At any rate, if the rest of the English-speaking world often has trouble distinguishing between Australian and New Zealand accents, Aussies and Kiwis do not. Frequently noted are the 'Kiwi' raising of /ɛ/ to /ɪ/ (such that *pen* sounds like *pin*) and the raising (and fronting) of the vowels in *trap* (/ɒ/ to /ɛ/) and *dress* (/ɛ/ to /e/; Gordon, Campbell, Hay et al. 2004, 205–207). Among other phonological features of New Zealand English are:

> non-rhoticity (with the exception of the Southland dialect)
> *h*-dropping
> *hw-* ~ *w-* merger
> NEAR-SQUARE merger (/iː/ and /e/ > /ɪː/)
> PULL-POOL merger (/ʊ/ and /u/ > /ʊ/)
> KIT-STRUT merger (/ɪ/ and /ʌ/ > /ʌ/, i.e., the "fush and chups" Kiwi pronunciation Australians point up as characteristic)
> vocalization of /l/ (*smile* > [smao])
> These are among a score of distinctive phonological features of New Zealand English examined in extensive detail in Gordon et al. 2004; see also Bauer and Warren 2004, 580–602. and Gordon and Maclagan 2008, 64–76.

One interesting feature of Australian and New Zealand Englishes is the claim often made of limited regional difference in varieties, one often made also about Canadian English (though one that does not obtain in the Atlantic provinces or Québec). It is a claim striking to Americans and Britons, given their rich differences in regional dialects, and one that of course does not quite hold up when combined with social factors (thus the categorization of Australian, New Zealand, and South African Englishes as Broad-General-Cultivated). Australians can make a popular distinction between Sydney and non-Sydney "occa" (*ocker*, one from the boondocks), "up North," and rural dialects, or class-marked Bogan varieties. New Zealand offers the "rolling *r*" dialect of the Southland region of the South Island (including parts of the Otago urban region). Here, indeed one finds rhotic speech in an otherwise non-rhotic island nation, and, at least among older speakers, use of /ɛ/ for the TRAP vowel in words such as *castle*, *dance*, and *chance* (Gordon and Maclagan 2008, 66–67).[6] Australians notice a New Zealander penchant for the high-rise terminal intonation contour (a necessary but pretentious linguistic term for 'upspeak'), the rising intonation at the end of clausular units, which may be of even higher frequency in Māori English (Stubbe and Holmes 2000, 251; Warren and Bauer 2008, 83). As with Australian English, in addition to phonology, distinctiveness of the variety is to be found in lexis, in "New Zealand English" words and words of Māori origin. The former can include isoglosses such as *thongs* and *Esky* (cooler) with Australians, and *jandals* and *chilly bin* for New Zealanders. Words of Māori origin are often employed with higher frequency in Māori English (or what is sometimes called "bro talk"), which is a variety of New Zealand English (and distinct from the historical Pidgin Māori; Clark 1990), and which incorporates Māori vocabulary of lower frequency in New Zealand English to express Māori traditions, concepts (such as *taonga*, which represents a wide-ranging cultural concept, from 'what is conquered by the spear' = 'land, property,' to 'inheritance,' 'heritage'), beliefs, and politics. The sidebars give examples from both vocabulary sets, and one Māori loan might be highlighted, the semantically complex (perhaps even vexed) *Pākehā*, 'a New Zealander of European descent' (*OED*, s.v. *Pakeha*; first attestation is from John Nicholas Liddiard's *Narrative of a Voyage to New Zealand* [1817]), or 'stranger' (OED), 'pale people,' 'imaginary beings resembling men,' or simply in opposition to *tangata whenua*, the 'people of the land' (the Māori). Anger over land disputes following the Treaty of Waitangi (1840) led to the New Zealand Wars (1845–1872), and the term *pākehā* could certainly have been expected to pejorize in Māori use. Modern resentment of the term by white New Zealanders, to the degree that the term can be felt to be "racist," is also to some extent understandable. Like other exonyms (terms for oneself or one's people applied by outsiders), such as Anglo, Eskimo, or Slav, tone is important. A term fairly spat out will be understood as having a stronger, and likely more malign, semantic force than one used more measuredly. The semantic range of ethnonyms and epithets is an enormously interesting and complex one, and a subject not easy to address, however dispassionately the analysis may be intended. No people on earth lack terms for others with semantic force ranging from suspicion to contempt. We have already seen terms of contempt for native Australians used by English and

[6] A 2005 tv recording by New Zealand journalist Jim Mora gives examples of this Southland "rolling *r*": https://teara.govt.nz/en/video/40141/the-southland-rolling-r

other European settlers (or 'arrivals,' as early transported convicts are not the same class of colonials as settlers). Some evolution of the term *pākehā* (or *Pākehā*, there are debates about whether it should be capitalized) can be seen in its adoption by white New Zealanders as a self-referential term, though this is often politically marked as a more left-leaning tendency – by contrast, *Anglo* as a self-referential term in the United States for non-Hispanic Americans has proven much less popular, as it is not a clipping of English *Anglo-American* but the Spanish adjective (and presumptively masculine, which offers new challenges to its adoption in the age of *Latinx* and *Latine*). Introducing and promoting a Māori term for white English-speaking New Zealanders (but now also encompassing all newer non-Māori New Zealanders) indicates a continued presence of Māori people, and reverses (or perhaps in some small measure compensates for) the usual colonial pattern of applying European exonyms to native peoples. And it is quite natural for any people to find that such terms rankle, as for some New Zealanders, *Pākehā* does. But all of these words are part of the language, and beyond their immediate semantic application and import, they record the history not just of English, but of the peoples who now speak it.

Lexis of New Zealand English

beached as (< "beached as a whale")
bodangie
breakback
cobbler
to deal to
dunny (toilet)
filled roll
fizzy
to front up
geeshed
get off the grass
gone burger ("he's goneburger," i.e., he's gone, outta here)
Gweilo (< Cantonese = 'white devil' or 'ghost,' a racial slur referring to Europeans/Westerners)
had a mare
hungry as
jandals
Nesian (for New Zealander/Zealandian)
to pink (to shear a sheep too closely)
quite nice
sand shoes
sheepie
sweet as (used adjectivally, a strong asseverative = 'really good')
togs
woolie jumpers

Māori words in New Zealand English

Aotearoa (the Māori name for the nation, now used along with *New Zealand*)
haka
hapū (subtribe or clan within an *iwi*)
hongo (nose touch greeting)
iwi (Māori largest social unit)
kaupapa (Māori world-view, philosophical-cultural outlook)
kia ora! (greeting, now used like 'Hello')
Kura Takahi Puna (Royal New Zealand Infantry Regiment II/I)
mana (life force, spiritual energy)
Mana motuhake ('self-power, autonomy')
mana whenua ('power over land, territorial right')
marae (traditional meeting-place of an *iwi*)
mere (weapon, type of stone club)
Ngapuhi (a Māori *iwi* of Northern New Zealand)
pākehā, Ngati pakeha
pepeha (Māori cultural identity)
pohutukawa (NZ Christmas tree)
pounamu (jade or greenstone; traditional Māori carvings made from it, in patterns such as the *toki* [adze], believed to have *mana*)
Tangata tiriti ('people of the Treaty'; generally, non-Māori New Zealanders)
Tangata whenua ('people of the land,' those with a traditional claim to a land district)
taonga (possession, treasure, artifact)
te reo ('the language,' the Māori language)
Tuhoe (flag)
tumeke (interj. 'awesome!')
whānau (whānau)

[The *Oxford English Dictionary* records 290 words of Maori origin; the lists above and in the OED do not always overlap, as some of the loans may be used only within New Zealand, or mainly by Māori speakers of English.]

10.5 SOUTH AFRICA

At first glance, the grouping of South African varieties of English along with the "Asian-Pacific" region seems geographically odd, but the linguistic rationale is traditional for what have been called 'Antipodean' varieties (Australia and New Zealand and their island dependencies and former territories, and South Africa). The broad similarities among these varieties are particularly striking in phonology, with of course some local variation. It is customary too to categorize South African Englishes into the grouping "White South African English," "Black South African English," and "Indian/South Asian/Asian South African English." For modern South African English, the repeal of apartheid laws in 1991 and the 1994 election that saw the African National Congress outpoll the National Party/Nasionale Party were signal events. The Afrikaans that was the language of apartheid and *baasskip* ('boss-ship,' i.e., 'white supremacy') was removed from its position as the primary official language and placed among 11 official languages (see sidebar below on the SADC) that represented a more linguistically pluralistic new South Africa. That said, the way was opened for English to replace Afrikaans in government functions and expand its appeal as a quasi-*lingua franca* within the country and with other Anglophone African nations. Additionally, English had been a vehicle of the anti-apartheid movement, part of the larger modern phenomenon of the use of English in political protest movements to garner international media attention. The growth of English in the "new South Africa" is as an L2 rather than L1 (Bowerman 2008, 168).

The phonology of "White South African English" has many of the distinctive features of other "Antipodean" Englishes: the vowel in *kit* can be raised (/ɪ/ > /i/), as can that in *trap* (/æ/ > /ɛ/), that in *goose* fronted and further rounded (/uː/ > /yː/), the diphthongs in *price* and *mouth* smoothed (/aɪ/ > /ɑː/, /aʊ/ > /ɑː/, though the latter can be realized in Broad White South African English as /æʊ/, with a fronted nucleus to the diphthong; Bowerman 2008, 169–72). One interesting development with regard to the consonants in the English of White South Africans is the use of the phonemes /χ/ (the uvular fricative of Afrikaans) or /x/ (the velar fricative) in loanwords from Afrikaans and Khoisan, such as *gogga/goggo* from Afrikaans, the "creepy-crawly" insect ([xɔxə], [xɔxɔ]) (Bowerman 2008, 173; DSAE, s.v. *gogga*, *goggo*). The variety is largely non-rhotic (excepting "linking" *r*); /r/ in initial position can be post-alveolar or retroflex, occasionally trilled (this is also found in L2 use of English by Afrikaans speakers; Bowerman 2008, 173). The trilled *r* is also found in mesolectal varieties of Black South African English, which are marked sometimes also by the shift of the dental fricatives (θ, ð) to stops (t, d) and of the voiceless affricate /tʃ/ to /ʃ/ (van Rooy 2008, 179–185; this is also a common substitution among L1 Spanish speakers in the United States with English as their L2: e.g., *chicken* > *shicken*, *watches* > *washes*). As most speakers of Black South African English employ it as their L2, their native languages (e.g., Bantu languages such as Zulu and Xhosa) would be expected to exert some influence on this variety of English, and recent work suggests that the "syllable-timed rhythm" of Black South African English may be one such prosodic product of influence (van Rooy 2008, 186). The substitution of dental stops for the dental fricatives also occurs with Indian South African English, while somewhat more curiously the voiceless stops /p t k/ remain unaspirated before a number of vowels and diphthongs (/ɑː/, /ɔː/, /ʊ/, /ɒ/, /eɪ/, /oʊ/, /ɛə/) so that articulation of *park, pork, put, pot, pay, poke, pair* (this last is also non-rhotic) does not have, as in many other varieties of English, initial aspirated *p* (/p^h/; Mesthrie 2008, 190–198). Major factors distinguishing Indian South African English include the influence, among older generations, of substrate languages from India: Bhojpuri Hindi, Gujarati, Urdu, Konkani, and the Memon dialect of Sindhi (from the Indo-Iranian branch of Indo-European), and Tamil and Telugu (Dravidian languages); the varieties of English spoken in British India were also brought with Indian workers to South Africa; contact with South African English then exerted its influence, especially with younger generations born in South Africa (Mesthrie 2008, 190–191). The particularly complicated historical and linguistic story of the Cape settlement gave rise to what is now preferably called Cape Flats English (the southeast, inland region of Cape Town), formerly known as 'Colored English' (a designation for South Africans of mixed South Asian, African, and Dutch and English origin, and a former racial category under apartheid). Cape Flats English is close to the broad form of White South African English and shows some influence of substratal Cape Dutch and Afrikaans, though the extent of influence is under debate (Finn 2008, 200–204, 217–220).

The varieties of South African English gained international recognition in the modern period in large part from the anti-apartheid struggle; just as Afrikaans was inextricably linked with apartheid (from which language the term itself derives), English became associated with the popular movements within South African and abroad against apartheid (a dichotomy that grossly oversimplifies the political issues, but popular linguistic associations can be highly influential nonetheless). For the international observer, the particular legacy of South African Englishes upon the language has been lexical. No doubt the racial complexities of apartheid and post-apartheid South Africa resonate strongly with English-speakers abroad, as racial matters have come to the fore with more urgency in 2020 (as with Black Lives Matter protests in the United States, the United Kingdom, and other nations). With the great and evolving shift in power in the "new" South Africa, as the English-speaking world heard of Robben Island and Madiba (the affectionate Xhosa soubriquet in place of Nelson Mandela's English first name),[7] newer Afrikaans loans such as *plaasmoorde* ('farm murder') and *plaasaanvalle* ('farm attacks') have presented difficulties for western mainstream media, which had come round to adopt, eventually, a strongly anti-apartheid plank. The attacks on white South African farmers and their families, which have their historical antecedent in Rhodesia/Zimbabwe,[8] have been thoroughly politicized within (in the Afrikaner community, and by Julius Malema of the Economic Freedom Fighters party) and without South Africa; the lexicographer and general student of the language note the new terms all human events generate, and the greater the controversy or polarization over an issue, the more productive the lexical result can often be (the wild proliferation of *-gate* scandal terms – and not just in the United States – but one example). There may be a sociolinguistic aspect to the appearance of *plaasmoorde* as a recent loan to English from Afrikaans: the earlier *zef* loan, and the popular subculture it encompasses, may indicate a sense of dislocation among white working-class Afrikaners. While *Zef* culture may date to the 1960s, and may derive from the souped-up Ford Zephyrs that were popular street vehicles (resulting in the simple colloquial clipping *Zephyr* > *zef*), the discontent and dislocation seem to have accelerated post-1994.

But not without complication. The 'Zef style' has been popularized by white South African hip-hop artists such as Zander Tyler (stage name Jack Parow) and Die Antwoord ("The Answer," comprised principally of Watkin Tudor Jones/Ninja and Ani du Toit/ Yolandi Visser); the latter group has had the greatest success abroad and with their music videos, television shows, artwork and merchandising have spread 'Zef' abroad.

[7] The matter of who can or should use the name "Madiba" was sufficient to warrant the not entirely un-humorous guide in Max Fischer's "A South African's guide to when it's okay to call Nelson Mandela 'Madiba,'" *The Washington Post* 9 December 2013 (online).

[8] Such as under President Mugabe's 2000–2001 "land reform" program; "Zimbabwe's white farmers: who will pay compensation?", *BBC News* 16 May 2019, https://www.bbc.com/news/world-africa-48264941

The whole 'Zef' movement has been dogged from the start by intimations that it may not just be ironic (the ironic 'cool' and covert prestige of working-class fashions and pursuits) but satirical performance art[9]; post-apartheid, about 800,000 white South Africans left the country, a number of the wealthy among them. A phenomenon seen any time there is political instability anywhere in the world (not just "white flight" but the flight of elites – as is happening in Hong Kong), one result can be the consolidation of those who cannot afford to leave, and an intransigence in those communities that feel left behind or beleaguered. A distant parallel can be seen in the "Anglo" (English-speaking) communities in Québec: in the 1970s, some one million English-speakers lived in the Montréal metro area; now there are some 600,000 province-wide. The passage of Loi/Law 101 in 1977 (*Charte de la langue française/Charter of the French Language*) by the pro-separation Parti Québécois was meant to shore up French from the English threat in the province, particularly in Montreal/Montréal, where French was in decline among younger speakers. The battle was won by the French-language advocates, but not without capital flight and a 'brain drain' as wealthier "Anglos" left for Toronto and Calgary. Left behind in neighborhoods such as Westmount, Notre-Dame-de-Grace, Sainte-Anne-de-Bellevue, Pointe-Claire, and Lachine were English-speaking minorities who felt increasingly beleaguered by language laws that sought to promote French only in the workplace. In the case of the Western Cape region in South Africa, the homeland of Afrikaans, a similar "digging in" seems to have occurred with the Afrikaans-speaking minority (some 7 million speakers, but only about 13–14% of the population of the nation now).

The 'Zef' style movement, even if self-parody and self-consciously created to an extent, has proved influential, and there are few more powerful drivers of linguistic innovation and creativity in the 21st century than popular (youth) culture. As a sort of white South African version of 'white trash' (American), 'yob' (British), or 'bogan' (Australian) culture, 'Zef' prides itself on a sort of 'un-cool' (or *dwankie* in Zef slang) so 'un-cool' that it is 'cool' – the origins of the "un-cool" fashions, the clothing, track suits, sneakers (trainers), or cars, are, of course, in the limited income and opportunities of working-class neighborhoods. The 'flash' style of 'Zef' rappers may be a counterpart to the Cashed-Up Bogan (CUB) of Australia seen earlier. In a way, the various working-class white subcultures are a sort of "return of the suppressed," demographics the mainstream media and academic elites have little interest in. And the linguistic mixing of and code-switching between Afrikaans and English seems to be increasing in colloquial speech and especially in the music, much of which derives from or has been influenced by American hip-hop (and this is paralleled in 'Zef' culture by its spread to and growth in popularity among Black and 'Brown' ['Coloured'] South Africans). In an interview about *Zef* style, Jack Parow observed that "In the Cape we've been talking like that for jarre and jarre, since I can remember.

[9] Alex Bhattacharji, "Die Antwoord: The Real Zef Rappers of Beverly Hills," *The New York Times* 29 November 2016 (online): https://www.nytimes.com/2016/11/29/t-magazine/entertainment/die-antwoord-zef-rap-hollywood.html

Both young and old use it."[10] Both Parow and Die Antwoord sing primarily in English and code-switch occasionally to Afrikaans (here Parow uses only one hybrid Afrikaans–English phrase, "for jarre and jarre," for Afrikaans *vir jare en jare*, 'for years and years'). The music style has proven popular with Black and 'Brown' South Africans as well, and collaborations with artists from these communities are frequent – and such collaborative interactions, with their linguistic products and consequences, may give a glimpse into the future of South African Englishes.

A reminder of South Africa's linguistic past comes from another of the nation's hip-hop figures, Jaak, the late Jacques Jacobs (Jaak Spraak; 1975–2017). A native of Paarl in the Western Cape, Jaak identified as a 'Brown South African' (the former apartheid-era designation "Colored") descended in part from Indian Ocean slaves brought by the Dutch to the Cape Province in the 17th century (Worden 2016). Jaak became an emissary of sorts for the use of Afrikaans by descendants of some of the Creole's original speakers: people of mixed Malagasy, Mascarene (from what are now Mauritius and Réunion), East African, Austronesian, and South and Southeast Asian and Dutch descent. The notion that Afrikaans was a "white" language was hard to shake in the wake of the Afrikaans Medium Decree of 1974, though Afrikaans is itself a Dutch-based Creole (with lexical influence of the Khoisan language Khoekhoe, Bantu languages, South African Malay, and other languages). The "Bantu Education" directive required Black schoolchildren to be instructed in Afrikaans and English, and it spurred on the Soweto uprising of 1976, which fueled the rise of the African National Congress (ANC) and helped bring about the end of apartheid policies. Jaak sang primarily in Afrikaans, with some mixing in of English, as an attempt to rehabilitate the image of Afrikaans,[11] while pointing out the continued 'apartheid' that occurs in places like Paarl, divided by the Berg River, which separates the white and Black and Brown sides of the city (majority Afrikaans-speaking, with some two-thirds of the population identifying as 'Colored'). If Jaak's musical output was the Afrikaans of the Cape Flats (his debut album was entitled *Flêtse Maniere* [2009], "Cape Flats ways," "council house ways"), its origin lay in African American culture; Jack Parow had helped put together the nine-part music/concert television series in 2016 entitled *Dis Hoe Ons Rol*, "That's How We Roll," an expression used elsewhere in contemporary colloquial Afrikaans, and a clear loan from African American Vernacular English. The sort of pop culture and linguistic hybridity in evidence in South African hip-hop music certainly seems to indicate a loosening of older divides in South African society; the somewhat freer association of younger generations of course has its own complexities in a racially pluralistic society, and their linguistic output is one measure of such. To what extent popular music can be taken as a register of the broader culture is uncertain, but the diverse linguistic background of the nation can be expected to continue to shape South African varieties of English.

[10] "The Dummies guide to Zef," *news24* (Cape Town) 16 February 2010 (online): https://www.news24.com/News24/The-Dummies-guide-to-Zef-20100216

[11] "Africa Beats: Afrikaans rapper Jaak," *BBC News* 24 May 2013 (online): https://www.bbc.com/news/av/world-africa-22635300

Loanwords from Afrikaans

The OED lists 324 loans in English deriving from Afrikaans or the Cape Dutch of the 18th–19th centuries. Many of these describe the flora and fauna or topographical features of Southern Africa; others have to do with more recent politics, especially the official apartheid period (1948–1991).

aardvark
aardwolf
Afrikaner
apartheid
assegai
baas
baasskap
bakkie (pickup truck)
berghaan (South African eagle)
biltong
Boer
boerewors (sausage)
boomslang (tree snake)
commando/kommando (ultimately from Portuguese)
dagga (hemp, cannabis)
duiker
eland
gabba (pal, mate, friend)
hartebeest (from Cape Dutch)
klipspringer
koppie (small hill)
kraal (< Dutch < Portuguese)
kudu (antelope) < Xhosa < Nama (dialect of Khoekhoe)
laager
lekker (sweet, nice)
meerkat
platteland
pronk
rand
sjambok
springbok
trek
veldt (Cape Dutch)
wildebeest (Cape Dutch)
Zef

10.6 MAURITIUS, RÉUNION, SEYCHELLES, MADAGASCAR

Uninhabited until the arrival of the Portuguese in 1507, Mauritius endured a history of colonial exchange perhaps even more complex than that of St. Lucia in the Caribbean. It was the Dutch who introduced sugar cane to the island in 1638 and, in 1639, slaves from Madagascar. The importation of enslaved people from East Africa accelerated under French rule (1715–1810), while British rule (1810–1968), with the abolishment of slavery in the Empire on 1 February 1835, saw the colonial administration turn to indentured Indian laborers – in the years following the arrival of the first 75 indentured Indian laborers in 1834, some 450,000 people were recruited from India to work in Mauritius (Allen 1999, 16). The social and linguistic history of Mauritius was made by these shifts in colonial rule and dependence upon the production of sugar and resulting labor demands. The African legacy of Mauritius was established early on, as between the 1730s and 1820s, some 75–85% of the island's population consisted of enslaved Africans (Allen 1999, 13). The later African population of Mauritius, descendants of slaves from Madagascar, Mozambique, and the 'Swahili coast,' and of 'maroons' who had fled slavery (the steep monolith Le Morne Brabant figures in Mauritian history and legend as the refuge of maroons), came to be outnumbered by the Indian indentured population and their descendants post-1910 (when the system of Indian immigration was ended). The way was set for an 'intercultural' process of Creolization (or in the Francophone Caribbean, *créolité*, a term also applied to Indian Ocean nations), such that since independence in 1968 (a republic declared in 1992), Mauritian Creole (*Kreol*) is the dominant language on the island. Some 1.3 million people speak this French-based Creole, which has also been significantly lexified by English (some 550-plus words; Baker and Kriegel 2013, 259) and Bhojpuri Hindi, the latter spoken also in other former colonies where the British employed similar indentured labor recruitment programs (Guyana, Trinidad and Tobago, Suriname, Fiji, and South Africa). The particular historical mixing of peoples, languages, and cultures on Mauritius, in particular the Indian indentured diaspora, inspired Mauritian poet Khal Torabully to coin the term *Coolitude* (Torabully 1992). Itself a hybrid term, modeled on French *négritude* and English *coolie* (as seen earlier, a word of disputed etymology, though possibly from Gujarati), *Coolitude* sought to trace *le voyage inverse*, the 'reverse journey' made by indentured laborers (to that made by the colonists), and *l'odyssée coolie* (Torabully 1992, 7; Carter and Torabully 2002, 15; Bannerjee 2013, 11–15). Torabully's father was from Trinidad, his mother's family from India and British Malaya, and his poetry is primarily francophone, leavened with Mauritian Creole, Hindi, English, Arabic, and other linguistic traces of the Indian Ocean trade; it does often employ a level of informality and familiarity found in contact languages: *Nous sommes bagasse, nous sommes mélasse, / mon frère cafre, notre peau notre trace* ("We are bagasse [sugar cane residue], we are molasses, / my Black African brother, our skin our trace"; Carter and Torabully 2002, 89).

Torabully's poetic and critical work in recovering a vital stage in the history of Mauritius, and of the development of Mauritian Creole, casts light also upon other islands and territories in the Indian Ocean and Caribbean to which Indian laborers (the *jihaji*, or 'ship traveller' generations) were sent and the racial, cultural, and linguistic legacy that has shaped Mauritius, the Seychelles, Réunion, Fiji, Trinidad and Tobago, Jamaica, Guyana, and Suriname. The contact languages in each of these lands, English-, French-, and Dutch-based, have been lexified also by Hindi as well as African languages, and descendants of Indian 'ship travellers' have been prominent in the political life of these postcolonial nations (among them Mahendra Chaudry of Fiji, Noor Hassanali of Trinidad and Tobago, and Prithvirajsing Roopun of Mauritius – a number of other Presidents of Mauritius and Suriname have also been of Indian descent). In many of these postcolonial nations, English is an official or de facto language of government and education – as in Mauritius, where Creole is the dominant first language, but English is also widely studied in school. As with the case of the 'mother country' India, English emerged as a 'neutral' variety in a linguistic or cultural or religious melting pot. Stripped of its former authority, its colonial legacy fading in the advance of a postcolonial reality, English connected these young nations not just with the Commonwealth and an Anglo-American economic and political world, but to a broader cultural exchange with other Anglophone nations and people. As has French with *Francophonie*, the continued and expanded use of English allows for a wider reach to the postcolonial nation's writers, musicians, actors, and other artists, politicians, diplomats, and activists. So many of these nations do not make the news in western "mainstream news media" until there is a crisis, but when that occurs, round much of the world, the signs of protest appear in English.

Mauritius is an example of a nation in which English is in a nondominant linguistic position; once a colonial language, it is the French-based Creole, with roots in the previous colonial administration (1715–1810), that is primary. While the study of English is growing in Mauritius, and some 200,000-plus people speak it, Creole is likely to remain the L1 as an extension also of the cultural and ethnic identity of Mauritians. A short sample from the *Gramer Kreol Morisien* (2012) gives an idea of the position of English as a (modest) lexifier of a French-based Creole:

> Kreol, Franse, Angle fer parti trwa lang ki tou Morisien bizin itilize mal-mal omwin onivo konpreansion dan bann sitiasion kominikasion ki fer parti so lavi toulezour (16).
>
> Kreol, French, English are three languages that every Mauritian needs to use at least at the level of comprehension in the communicative situations of their everyday lives.

Closely related to Mauritian Creole are those of Réunion and the Seychelles, also French-based, though with less lexification (fewer loanwords) from English. This western Indian Ocean region is rather more a part of *la Francophonie*, though historical ties were with the Portuguese, who had first settled Mauritius and held Mozambique as their colonial base.

10.7 HONG KONG, SINGAPORE, MALAYSIA

The handover of Hong Kong on 1 July 1997 was a signal political event whose consequences are being felt through to this moment, as Chief Executive of Hong Kong Carrie Lam dealt with renewed democracy protests (2019–2020) as well as the covid crisis (from late 2019). While mainland China has more recently been a focus of exponential growth in second-language learners of English (figures range as high as 250 million Chinese learners of English, or even higher), Chinese English varieties in Taiwan and Hong Kong are well-established (particularly Hong Kong, which had been under British administration from 1841 to 1997). An impressionistic curiosity is that, among world varieties of English, Chinese English (here meaning mainland China) is considered the most distant from standard BrE in terms of phonology – in popular terms, the 'accent,' with Chinese learners of English viewed as often having the 'heaviest' of non-native accents of English. This is often explained as the result of L1 interference of Sino-Tibetan languages such as Mandarin and Cantonese, and while there are significant differences in terms of respective phonemic inventories (and that Mandarin, Cantonese, Hakka, Fujian, and other Chinese languages are tone-based), the example of standard Hong Kong English can serve as a counterweight: few global varieties of English can be as close to RP as broadcast standard Hong Kong English. The salient point is that certain inevitable linguistic factors will influence non-native production of L2 learner English, but that other factors such as the education system (which has been British-based in Hong Kong), attitudes toward learning English and relative prestige of English locally, as well as contact with native English speakers (such as British Hong Kong residents) and opportunity to study and work abroad need all to be considered. Hong Kong's status as a sort of third Anglophone 'financial capital' (after London and New York City) also bolstered the use of a standard (local) English variety. Hong Kong English-language newspapers and television (*South China Morning Post*, and *The Standard* are large-circulation English-language papers) and global coverage of financial news from Hong Kong also bolster the continued use of English in Hong Kong: London and New York look to overnight news from the Hang Seng Index of the Hong Kong Stock Exchange as a harbinger of the behavior and mood of world markets.

The political developments of the Chinese Communist Party's "One China Policy" do not yet seem to have led to any great changes in the use of English in Hong Kong (whereas native Cantonese has faced pressure from government promotion of Mandarin as a "unifying" force in pursuit of that policy). The policies of the 'central government' (i.e., the CCP) of China and the matter of a 'Chinese Century' seem to be setting up not just a 'second Cold War' (between China and the West) but a new field of encounters conducted primarily in English. The "Confucius Institute" and "Thousand Talents Program" of the CCP have established academic, scientific, and economic links between China and western nations, especially through university research sponsorship and exchange (with charges also of 'economic espionage'). Modern China has long sent hundreds of thousands of its students abroad annually (it is often the largest source of 'international students' in the United States, Australia, Canada, and the United Kingdom), and western corporations are very eager to access the one billion-plus consumers in mainland China. This has led to charges of tenderfooted self-censorship on the part of Hollywood, professional sports teams (the American NBA has been accused of being especially solicitous), and major corporations, nearly all of which have taken advantage of the cheaper Chinese labor market. Indeed, "Made in China" has replaced "Made in Japan" as a term of derision in the United States for corporate policies of outsourcing. There is an interesting semantic shift involved in this last example: in the 1980s, Japanese automobile imports were viewed as a threat to the once-dominant American auto industry. As Japanese cars were synonymous with 'cheap,' 'reliable,' and 'fuel-efficient,' the desire by Japanese automakers to move into the 'luxury car' market faced a sort of 'branding' crisis: the solution for a number of them was to place the luxury line under fake Latin names that connoted 'luxury' and/or 'reliability' while distancing it from the Japanese brand (thus Honda launched the Acura division in 1986, Nissan the Infiniti Motor Company in 1989, and Honda the Lexus brand also in 1989). The rebranding and spin-off of 'luxury divisions' in the long run allowed 'economy' brands to charge much more for their cars, but was eventually outpaced by an amelioration in the original brands: Japanese goods are now associated with 'quality' in the way German brands have been. The semantic placeholder for the pejorative now seems to be 'Chinese made,' which may too eventually shift as so many consumer goods, from economy to luxury level, are made in China (there is a saying in the Philippines that one is living well when one has a German car, a Chinese house, and an American pension).

Modern migration and capital flight from Hong Kong are expanding the Chinese "circle of English," especially in Canada's Vancouver metroplex, in which Hong Kong and other Southern Chinese émigrés form the largest and wealthiest new immigrant group. The interactions that once were limited to phone calls home, and the occasional visit to relatives, have expanded greatly, and daily (if not more), with social media. It remains to be seen just how much social media platforms push linguistic 'hybridity' (this can often just mean code-switching in texts and tweets), but their allure of instant communication and social approbation has no doubt had some linguistic consequence (which is why many governments seek to censor them). As so much of social media activity is informal or at the level of slang, its half-life often seems acutely short – for example, the 'Singlish' (Singapore English) interjection or exclamation *haiyoh* (from Mandarin; it has a range of senses, 'oh,', 'and', 'also,' 'hey,' 'yeah' or can have a more negative sense like 'oh shoot') younger speakers can feel is passé, while *kiasu* (from Hokkien; also used in 'Manglish,' Malaysian English[12]), which indicates a sort of anxiety or fear of losing out on something (Wong 2020, 101), has been equated with FOMO ('fear of missing out') by young speakers (Wong 2020, 101–102, who nonetheless sees *kiasu* as "culturally more primal and contextually far more pervasive" than English FOMO [102]). The Cantonese ethnic tag (or racial slur) *gweilo(h)*, which has the force of terms like *farangi* (from Farsi, but used widely across Central and South Asia; it ultimately has a medieval origin in equating 'Franks' as the 'foreigner'), sparked a small controversy in 1999 with a program entitled *Gwai Lo Cooking* on a minor Canadian cable channel; *gweilo* may have lost some of its force as a racial epithet for 'ghost people' or 'white devils,' but the semantic force of such terms is often in how they are uttered. A signal development in these contact situations is the shift from actual to virtual space: once "you had to have been there," now you only need to have been *retweeted*.

Some three-fourths of Singapore's population of 5.9 million people (2021) is of Chinese descent, mainly from Southern China (the Malay population is some 14%,

[12] *Manglish* is also used to refer to mixed versions of Malayalam and English in India's Kerala state; there is the 2014 film by Salam Bappu entitled *Manglish* set in Mattancherry, Kerala, that features Malayalam and English in contact as part of its core plot.

the Indian population 9%). The varieties of Chinese spoken in Singapore – Cantonese, Hokkien, Teochew, Hakka, and others – led the government to promote a "Speak Mandarin Campaign" in 1979 (Deterding 2007, 3–4) to simplify the language picture for early language education in the school system (Singapore's four official languages are English, Mandarin, Malay, and Tamil). English is promoted as the primary language for Singaporeans as a unifying measure, and a common distinction is made between a more formal "Singaporean English" (as taught in schools and used in media and government) and "colloquial Singaporean English" (often called 'Singlish'). As can be expected, the phonology of Singaporean Englishes is strongly influenced by transfer and interference from the phonemic inventories of Chinese languages, Malay, and Tamil (Singaporeans have been found to identify very quickly the ethnic origin of a speaker of English in Singapore by hearing a speaker's pronunciation; Deterding 2007, 5). As found in other varieties of Chinese-influenced English, there occur in Singaporean English reduction of final consonant clusters, substitution of the glottal stop /ʔ/ for the voiceless alveolar stop /t/ (Schneider 2007, 158–159), dental fricatives replaced by dental stops (or /f/ if /θ/ is in final position, though *maths* can be realized as [mɛts]; Deterding 2007, 14), syllable-timed rhythm, and the influence of tone (rising and rise-fall; Deterding 2007, 36–39). Singaporean English is non-rhotic and /l/ is vocalized in the final position (*school* [sku]; Deterding 2007, 20–21). Morphological features characteristic of Chinese English are found as well: reduction of *-ed* (*stopped* > *stop*), irregular concord in third-person singular forms (*I like places that is quiet lah*), and loss of -s plural in some instances (*the few country that I've been to*), though this seems to involve a larger morphological pattern of marking count and non-count nouns: Singaporean English can pluralize non-count nouns (*furnitures*, *stuffs*, *clothings*; Deterding 2007, 42–47; Wee 2008, 604–606).

In colloquial Singaporean English, or 'Singlish,' the influence of the other languages of Singapore is much more overt; the 'discourse particles' *lah* (seen just above), *leh*, and *lor* abound in Singlish usage: *lah* can be a (mild) asseverative (*nothing much to buy there lah*), or indicate acceptance (and resultant resignation to what has been said), and in general seems intended to signal familiarity and even solidarity between speakers (Deterding 2007, 66–71); there has been the suggestion that *lah* may also bear the intonation in the discourse (the collocation *OK lah* follows a rise-fall pattern, while use of *lah* alone can bear low-level or mid-level tone; Deterding 2007, 67–70). The origin of *lah* is not known (Hokkien, Malay, and Cantonese have been suggested), and it is perhaps the most frequent of a number of discourse markers: *leh* is less assertive than *lah*, and *lor* even less so, while *ah* can put the topic into focus or link to further specifying information about it (*magazines, ah, magazines...all sorts lah*); *yah* can be the informal equivalent to *yes* found in many other varieties of English, but in Singaporean English it can also indicate continuation or completion (*yah, that was like a long way back, when I was in primary school, yah*; Deterding 2007, 72–73). The use of *got* as an auxiliary has been put to some alternative uses in Colloquial Singaporean English (*You got read the papers today? I got read*), while the collocation *where got?* can indicate disagreement with a statement (*This dress very red. Where got?* [= "Is it?"]; Lee, Ping, Nomoto 2009, 298–299).

There are links between elements of Colloquial Singaporean English and Malaysian English (the discourse particle *lah* appears also in Malaysian English), Brunei

English, and Indonesian English, or what could be called a continuum of Malay Englishes. It may be too soon or unclear at the moment to add Brunei English to the 'expanding circle' of English, though its introduction as a compulsory school subject since 1985 and use in teaching core subjects in primary school (from the fourth year on) have resulted in a bilingual education system and a majority of the population with some knowledge of the language. At a more informal level, "Poklen English" is a stigmatized basilectal form of Brunei English spoken in the Kampong Ayer ('water village') region of the capital Bandar Seri Begawan, used especially in online texting conversations; code-switching with Malay is common, as are nonstandard spellings and capitalizations of English words. The term *poklen* has been genericized to indicate a 'bumpkin,' an 'uneducated' or 'uncool person' (Haji-Othman and McLellan 2014). Broad similarities obtain in the phonology of these Malay Englishes, especially with Malaysian English (Baskaran 2008, 283–289).

With the longest history in the region, Hong Kong English at the formal level has been noted for its closeness to RP, while informal Hong Kong English is noted for frequent Cantonese–English code-mixing and -switching. It is this latter phenomenon that "has provided a pathway along which English comes to be used among Hong Kong Chinese speakers in more informal or intimate domains," and though English is still seen as 'foreign,' the code-switching "seems to have neutralized the 'alien-ness' or 'other-ness' of English" (Setter et al. 2010, 102). And that long history of English in Hong Kong is such that developments locally allow one to speak not just of "English in Hong Kong" but of Hong Kong English.

10.8 SOUTH ASIAN ENGLISHES

The varieties of South Asian Englishes (Pakistan, India, Bangladesh, and Sri Lanka) have deeper roots than many other world varieties of English with colonial origins (the Englishes of Scotland, Wales, and Ireland excepted). Taking the traditional dating of 1612 as the start (the East India Company victory over the Portuguese at the Battle of Swally/Suvali, Gujarat), South Asian Englishes have roughly the same chronological depth as American English. If Indian Englishes are sometimes in popular conceptions thought to be particularly phonologically distinct (i.e., the impression that Indian accents are distinctive, or more easily distinguished by their 'Indianness'), we are really talking about the influence of the native Indian languages' phonological systems and transfer and substitutions of phonemes: the /b/ ~ /v/ and especially /w/ ~ /v/ interchanges are particularly frequent in occurrence (the "welly good" and "vee vould" of Anglo-Indian dialogue fictions), and especially of note is the transfer of retroflex (or 'cerebral') consonants from the Indo-Iranian (such as Hindi, Punjabi, Gujarati, Sindhi, and Maharashtri) and Dravidian (Tamil, Telugu, Malayalam, and Kannada) languages; the retroflex consonants (ṭ, ḍ., ṭh, ḍh, ṇ, ṣ, short and long vocalic *ṛ*) are pronounced with the tip of the tongue bent back and up and tapping the hard palate in the roof of the mouth. As seen in Chapter 2, Danish linguist Holger Pedersen had explained the "retraction" of /s/ to /ʃ/ in the *satəm* branches of Indo-European (Balto-Slavic and Indo-Iranian) and thence to retroflex ṣ in Sanskrit as part of the "ruki rule" (see Fortson 2010, 414–416); it is not clear why retroflex consonants occur in Sanskrit and other Indo-Iranian languages (including the Dardic subbranch of Indo-Aryan, languages spoken in Northeastern Afghanistan, Northern Pakistan, and Indian Kashmir). Words in which they occur that have Indo-European reflexes indicate the consonants are not (in these cases) borrowed but the product of an assimilative sound change /ʃ/ > ṣ /ʂ/, while in other cases the sounds occur in loans from the Dravidian languages (Fortson 2010, 211). The appearance of retroflex consonants in South Asian Englishes is, of course, a natural transfer, and can be seen not just in Indian pronunciation of English but also in English loans to Hindi and other Indian languages (e.g., English *tennis* > Hindi टेनिस *ṭenis*). One inheritance of BrE is that standard or 'higher' forms of Indian English are non-rhotic, while nonstandard or vernacular forms are rhotic (Wells 1982/1996, 626, 629–630; Sailaja 2009, 19–20), though there is an increasing influence of rhotic forms of AmE lately, which may be the result of the use of AmE-influenced varieties in call centers, increasing numbers of Indian students pursuing university and professional degrees in the United States, and contact with the growing Indian diaspora in the United States. Substitution of dental stops for the interdental fricatives is common (/θ/ > /t/, /ð/ > d), though the voiced interdental stop can also be replaced by retroflex ḍ (as in demonstratives *these, those*); initial /t/ can be replaced by retroflex ṭ in words such as *today* and *tomorrow* (Sailaja 2009, 21–22). There is less variance between standard forms of BrE and Indian English in the vowels and diphthongs, one exception being in the fronting of the diphthong in words such as *boil* and *coin* (where /ɔɪ/ > /a:ɪ/, so that they sound more like 'bile' and 'kine'; Sailaja 2009, 26). One feature long noted in 'Anglo-Indian' or South Asian English is the rhythm, sometimes described as 'sing-songy' (as has been Irish English), but which linguists describe as more a 'syllable-timed' versus the 'stress-timed' rhythm of English. In general, the syllable-timed language gives each syllable the same duration or amount of time in articulation such that each syllable seems to take the same amount of time in being pronounced; a stress-timed language, such as standard varieties of British and American English, is one in which the unstressed syllables are "compressed" to allow for the same interval between stressed syllables, which may not be articulated with equal duration. This has been noted in particular with Sri Lankan English, which may not maintain the distinction between strong and weak forms or between primary and secondary stress (Kachru 1994, 516–517); this is only made clearer with examples: thus, in South Asian English, one might hear *mistake* as [ˈmɪstek] (i.e., more like "miss-take" rather than "miSTAKE"), or *suitable* as [suˈte:bl] (as "sue-tay-bull," with equal stress on each syllable, rather than "SUIT-uh-BULL"; Wells 1982/1996, 631).

Attitudes toward English can influence both code-switching (between English and Hindi and other Indian languages) and loanword formation (and the direction of such loan formations). The use of English in code-switching can be as a language of "nearness" or "distance" by South Asian speakers, that is, as a language of familiarity (and possible indicator of education or class) or as one of distancing (of "authority," "foreignness"):

> Tell Archna not to make that much noise, aur aap bhi Rekha se mana kar dijiye (the clause in Hindi is: "and you should tell Rekha the same").

> Just wait, we're leaving in a few minutes, nehin to gaadi chut jayegi (Hindi: "or else we'll miss the train"; Sailaja 2009, 92).

In the first example, English is actually the language of "nearness" used by a husband speaking to his wife (Archna), who was educated in English, and his cousin (Rekha) from the countryside, who was not; in the latter, the code-switching between English and Hindi serves a complementary function, and the hearer is presumed to be fluent in both languages. Code-switching is an enormously complicated matter, one not fully understood yet at all, in terms of motivation, utility, or mechanism. Speakers might report that the switch to the native language was occasioned by not remembering or knowing the English equivalent, or report that they do not consciously know why they are switching between languages. Status of the languages can undoubtedly be a factor, as English in the global context can be associated with modernity, 'class' (in its more amorphous sense of 'classy'), education, or access. Or the use of English can carry connotations of authority (political, scientific, and economic) or appeal to broader conventions (connecting the speaker to international norms). Conversely, English can bring up a contentious colonial legacy, or be an appeal to authority that is resented or seen as inauthentic or a sort of betrayal of local allegiance. The relationship between speakers of South Asian Englishes (or any other global Englishes) and that colonial legacy of course shapes the varieties and uses they may be put to – in the cases of India, the Pakistans (now Pakistan and Bangladesh), and Sri Lanka, the persistence in use of English was a sort of compromise, a shift away from original nationalist designs to abandon English. And as is so often the case with other postcolonial Englishes, local refashioning and innovation have put the local stamp on the language. And the matter is not simply one of the survival of English in Britain's former colonies, but, in the South Asian example, also the link between South Asian communities at home and abroad (older, indentured labor-based links with the Caribbean and Indo-Pacific region, and more recent movement to Britain, the United States, Canada, and Australia). These links allow one to trace the development of South Asian varieties of English and chart their influence in areas of greatest salience: in literature, film, music, cuisine, politics, and sport.

The beginning of Anglo-Indian literature – or Indian literature in English – was *The Travels of Dean Mahomet* (1794); Dean Mahomet (Sheikh Din Muhammad) had served in the army of the East India Company and accompanied an army friend home to Cork, Ireland. His marriage to a local Anglo-Irish woman and conversion to the Church of Ireland/Anglicanism from Islam were the beginnings of his adventures in the British Isles, which saw a bigamous marriage to an Englishwoman in 1806 and his establishment of London's first Indian restaurant in 1810 (The Hindoostane Coffee House in Mayfair). By Anglo-Indian literature, in this instance, is meant the tradition of writing in a standard Indian English literary form: loans from Hindi, Bengali, and a number of other Indo-Iranian (Indo-European family) and Dravidian languages can be common (and the novels, plays, and nonfiction and other literary output of Indian authors writing in English have been a vector for such loans), as well as dialogue in mixed Anglo-Indian forms ('Boxwallah English,' 'Hobson-Jobson'). 'Anglo-Indian' itself can refer to this literature in English by South Asian writers, often in a 'high' literary dialect (BrE the usual model), or to 'mixed' or contact varieties of English and Hindi or other Indian languages (Wells 1982/1996, 624). It has also been used over time to refer to English people born in India (Rudyard Kipling), to a variety of English spoken by 'Brits' in India, or 'a person of mixed British and Indian descent' (OED, s.v.). The interest here to the history of English is the variety of vectors of influence presented by the colonial and postcolonial history of India.

While the continuance of English in India was, in some quarters, an unhappy solution to the "language problem," for some Indian writers, the use of English, a colonial legacy, opened their work up to a wider readership, to literary fame, and perhaps to an academic post in the United Kingdom or another Anglophone university system. On a broader level it re-established the prominence of Indian literature, an ancient tradition spanning Vedic and classical Sanskrit to the Prakrits – indeed the study of Sanskrit in the west, at first for its vital role in reconstructing Indo-European, not only asserted Indian literature's pride of place among world literatures but also illuminated the broader contexts of Greek and Roman literature (such that one now speaks of "Indo-European epics" and themes that span the early literatures from Ireland to India, or from the *Táin Bó Cúailnge* to the *Mahābhārata*). The Indo-European connection might be dwelt on for a moment: England's foreign colonial program began with Ireland – considering, perhaps not entirely rightly, the expansion into Wales, Cornwall, Cumbria, and Scotland a continuation of conquests of Celtic-speaking regions begun in the early Anglo-Saxon period. Of the British colonies abroad that were held for lengthy periods of time Ireland and South Asia stand out as regions where fellow Indo-European languages were spoken (Celtic, in the Goidelic branch, in Ireland; Indo-Iranian in much of South Asia). It is a truism with some linguistic validity that it is often easier to learn a language from the same language family as that of one's L1; this has sometimes been invoked to explain the seemingly easier acquisition of English (or level of proficiency in pronunciation/accent achieved) in India versus China. It is an oversimplification to which exceptions attach, but there is a general sense that the greater the number of inherited similarities between the source and target language, the easier the transition. Irish English and Indian English are distinguished by their accents, even after centuries of use of English in the respective regions (and the near displacement of Irish by English), a phenomenon explicable by the influence of the sound system of the L1 or heritage language – in the latter case, one may be speaking rather of heritable phonological "interference" or influence from the L1 even if not used by second-generation learners (a common phenomenon among Hiberno-Irish speakers of the earlier 20th century, before compulsory Irish language classes were instituted by the independent Free State and Republic of Ireland).

The distinctive Indian or South Asian accent has often been the subject of satire and ridicule, as the Irish accent still is in British comedy. (For some reason, lampooning Scots, Welsh, and Irish accents is still acceptable in Britain – and to a somewhat lesser extent, regional accents of BrE – despite outrage over caricature of other accents of English.) There is a long film and television history of stereotypical Indian accents by English or Indian actors. Saeed Jaffrey's character Billy Fish in John Huston's *The Man Who Would Be King* (1975) comes off as a bit over-the-top but suggests in the film the character's subaltern status and desire to please even cast-off British soldiers (Michael Caine of Southwark playing Anglo-Irish Peachey Carnehan of "Dubling," and Sean Connery of Edinburgh as Englishman Daniel Dravot). Jaffrey had worked with and managed All India Radio and played a wide range of roles, from Deputy Prime Minister Sardar Vallabhbhai Patel (Vallabhbhai Jhaverbhai Patel; the Persian loan *sardar* is an honorific meaning 'chief, leader, prince') in Richard Attenborough's *Gandhi* (1982) to shopkeeper Ravi Desai on "Coronation Street," but was also known for his suave RP BrE accent. There is no mistaking the satiric intent of the accent of Peter Sellers's character Hrundi Bakshi in Blake Edwards's 1968 comedy *The Party*; Peter Sellers, of Portsmouth, played up a stereotypical Indian accent, one that rather more offends than amuses today's audiences, but one that also has some phonological rightness (influence of Indian retroflex consonants on production of English stops). Amitabh Bachchan's character Arjun Singh in the 1982 comic 'masala film' (mixed genre) *Namak Halaal* (literally "good/permissible salt," with the sense of "Devoted Servant") is one descendant of Sellers's Bakshi; so too is Hank Azaria's voicing of convenience store manager Apu Nahasapeemapetilon in the long-running American animated series *The Simpsons*. Apu's accent on the show (and yet, curiously, not his surname) increasingly has come to be seen as gratingly stereotypical if not offensive, and in 2020 Azaria decided to stop voicing the character (though it had been part of the show from 1990 to 2020).

Consciousness of and sensitivity toward portrayals and imitations of accents is nothing new; a sense of dialect level formed part of the repertoire of classical Sanskrit dramatists (lower-caste characters spoke more ribald Prakrit lines and usages not permitted in 'perfected' Sanskrit) as far back as two millennia ago and was the stock-in-trade of Greek and Roman comedy and satire (to say nothing of Chaucer's *Canterbury Tales*). And the objections may have as much to do with real or perceived inaccuracies or exaggerations in representing the accents as the rising clout and prominence of Indians and the Indian diaspora. The latter group and their UK- and US-born descendants have become well-known in all walks of life, from theater and music, medicine and engineering, to finance and academia – indeed, since the 2010 census Indian Americans are the wealthiest ethnic group in the United States (though only 1% of the U.S. population), and Indian Americans have become a much sought-after voting demographic by the two major political parties. Indian immigrants to the United Kingdom, the United States, Canada, New Zealand, and elsewhere have, like other immigrant groups, faced the difficulties of adaptation and acculturation, and a perceived shift in attitudes and – in the view of the immigrant (first) generation – mores, in the new home by the second generation. As Japanese Americans and Canadians speak of the *Nisei* generation (the children of the immigrant generation), and Filipinos/Filipinas of the *pinoy/pinay* generation, so Indians abroad can refer to *desis* (*desi* ultimately from Sanskrit *deśa*, 'region, land,' the second element in the compound country name Bangladesh, 'country/region of Bengalis'). Conflict between the generations is a staple of novels and films of the Indian diaspora, and a reflection of more recent trends of self-awareness and self-examination in the postmodern world (by comparison we find Irish immigrants using class-marked terms such as *lace-curtain Irish* versus *bog Irish* or *shanty Irish*; the endonymic forms are greatly outnumbered by the more hostile terms others had for the Irish: *Paddy*, *Bridey, ape, harp*, *Mick*, *bogtrotter*, *Taig/Taigue/Tadg*, *Papist, narrowback*, *mucker*). Mixed feelings about arrival into the middle class or higher is another staple of immigrant literature, film, and popular culture: ABCD 'American-Born Confused Desi' is one example, to which could be added 2018's "Crazy Rich Asians," directed by Jon Chu, which satirizes the stereotype of Asian 'success,' and the actual excesses of (Singaporean) Chinese *nouveax riches*, as well as the somewhat more low-brow YouTube series "Ultra Rich Asian Girls" (2014), with the particular experience being that of the upper-class Hong Kong Chinese of Vancouver (the *fuerdai*, the Mandarin term for 'rich second generation').

The experiences of Indian Americans and Indian/South Asian Britons (or British Indians or Asians – in BrE 'Asian' has the sense of South Asian; in AmE, it generally indicates East Asian) seem divergent on a number of counts; for one, Britain has the sense of the 'mother' or 'home country' for immigrants from the former colony (though a shift is underway, BrE is still the prestige variety in India). Movement to Britain has a sense of history to it that immigration to America does not, as the latter destination is a genuinely new one (speaking of migration routes rather than the immigrants' own experiences). In terms of vocabulary, BrE already bore the imprint of the Raj and earlier loans from trade jargons (the OED count is 937 loans from Indian languages, to which may be added more recent popular borrowings); for AmE, the influence is more recent. 'Asian' immigrants in Britain hail from Pakistan, India, and Bangladesh, and among those from India, Punjabis, Bengalis, and Gujaratis predominate (and among them are many who had once lived in other former colonies such as Trinidad, Guyana, and Uganda). In the United States, Gujaratis have become particularly prominent in franchises of motels and hotels, fast-food chains, and convenience stores, a shift from an earlier generation's business pattern of Indian-centered grocery stores and restaurants. In Britain, there seems to be for the moment greater participation and prominence in politics: Baron Noon, Sadiq Khan, and Priti Patel; significant are the number of life peers and, lately, the distribution of Asian MPs across the political spectrum and the split over Brexit. If the proverbial great passions of India have been said to be cricket and nationalism (to which Bollywood has often been added), recent loans from Indian/South Asian languages to English bear out the lexical domains of greater frequency: current politics of the region, cuisine, dress and customs, religions, and film.

10.8.1 Politics

Line of Actual Control (LAC): in the disputed Indo-Chinese/Sino-Indian border region (Ladakh-Tibet).

Demchok sector: from the disputed Indo-Chinese border region; as the dispute is ongoing, like any other international political issue, vocabulary can be expected to be generated for as long as the media pay attention.

Aksai Chin, *Siachen Glacier*: again part of the Indo-Chinese border dispute.

Lashkar-e-Taiba (LeT): Urdu for 'Army of the Good'; one of a number of Pakistan-based jihadist organizations responsible for attacks in India, including the April–May 2025 skirmishes after the Pahalgam attack; this would be one of example of many from news coverage of Indo-Pakistani affairs, especially of the Jammu and Kashmir region; names for Islamist organizations have become more prominent in global English vocabulary since September 11th, which might serve as a cover term for the *War on Terror/Global Terror* lexical domain.

ISI (Inter-Services Intelligence): the major Pakistani military intelligence organization

Kargil, Kargil War: after Kargil, Kashmir, flashpoint of 1999 military conflict between India and Pakistan; the conflict received the Bollywood treatment in a number of films to date, such as *LOC: Kargil* (directed by J.P. Dutta, 2003).

Jai Hind: Hindi for 'victory to India,' this entered press coverage in Spring 2025 with coverage of the 'Indo-Pak' cross-border strikes in the Kashmir region after the Pahalgam attack on 22 April 2025; of less frequency would be references to *Vijay* (Hindi for 'victory,' from Sanskrit *vi-jaya*; Vijay is a very common male given name in India).

10.8.2 Sports

Men in Blue: the Indian national cricket team (Team India); cricket is a national passion, India vs. Pakistan matches in particular reach international audiences with the respective diasporas. Major championship competitions include the Ranji Trophy and Devdhar/Deodhar Trophy. India has had spectacular success in Test matches, currently ranked No. 1 in Tests.

kabaddi: a native Indian sport in which two squads of seven players try to send a 'raider' across a baulk line into the defending team's area to tag as many players as possible without being tackled. The 'raid' must traditionally be conducted in a single breath; thus, the raider is to chant "kabaddi" (Tamil for 'hand-catch' or '-clasp') during the effort. The sport is popular in Northern India and Pakistan, though the name for it is from the Tamil language (OED, s.v.); a popular tradition derives it from Arjuna's raid on the camp of the Kauravas as recounted in the *Mahābhārata*.

10.8.3 Cuisine

Few others areas of the lexicon have had such an impact from South Asian languages as the culinary. The range of borrowings is so extensive as to require qualification by regional cuisine (as with Chinese cuisine: Mandarin, Szechuan, Cantonese, Hunan, etc.). Areas with large Indian diasporic communities (London, Toronto, Northern New Jersey-NYC, and Northern California) can boast of restaurants serving northern and southern Indian cuisines (the latter almost synonymous with vegetarian cuisine and *dosas*), though the type of cuisine can be even more specific (e.g., Baltistan cookery) and also include regional cuisines of Pakistan, Nepal, and Tibet (the last area is often included in South Asia in terms of cuisine, religion, and culture, even if Tibetan is in the Sino-Tibetan family of languages). *Chicken/murgh tikka masala* had even become the most popular dish in Britain, though 'fish and chips' and 'Sunday roast' seem to have reasserted their dominance more recently. The simple numbers of terms from Indian cuisine a speaker of English may know will depend on taste for and familiarity with Indian cooking: *masala, naan, paratha, samosa, raita, chutney, korma, thali, jalfrezi, gulab jamun, biryani/briyani, channa, ghee, da(a)l, aloo, lassi, makhani, mulligatawny* are all of high to fairly high frequency.

10.8.4 Music

playback singer: a hallmark of Indian cinema (the Bombay/Mumbai base now known as 'Bollywood'), the professional singer who sings on the soundtrack for the actors who may not have the necessary vocal skills, but also a device to let audiences hear favorite singers perform songs written for the film or traditional songs recast for the soundtrack; Noor Jehan (1926–2000) was one of the most revered playback singers of all time; contemporary Pakistani singer Sajjad Ali gained notice as a young singer in the 1980s by covering Jehan's famous "Banwari Chakori" (from Nandlal Jaswantlal's 1953 film *Anarkali*) on the Pakistani television program *Silver Jubilee*; Ali's 1996 hit (or in South Asian parlance, *super-hit*) "Chief Saab" mixes in some examples of Urdu slang (with occasional English forms, such as in the title: *saab* = *sahib*). Playback singers often became paired with actors, as did Mukesh Chand Mathur (who went by the mononym Mukesh) with Raj Kapoor (e.g., the 1970 Kapoor film *Mera Naam Joker*, "My Name is Joker"), and recorded songs in a number of languages for the various regional Indian film markets (Mukesh in Hindi, Urdu, Gujarati, and Punjabi, among others); the pairing of male and female playback singers was common as well, to combine well-known voices in songs and to match or play off types of voices (Kapoor's acclaimed 1951 film *Awaara* ["Vagabond"] featured the famous playback singers Mukesh, Lata Mangeshkar, Mohammed Rafi, Shamshad Begum, and Manna Dey).

bhangra: type of dance with uplifted arms associated with farm workers in the Punjab, now also the music that accompanies the singing of *boliyan* ('couplets') with playing of the double-headed drum (the *dhol*) and single-stringed *toombi*; perhaps most famous outside India is Daler Mehndi's 1998 hit "Tunak Tun" and accompanying music video; London-born and New York-based DJ Rekha (Rekha Malhotra) popularized bhangra with her "Basement Bhangra" parties in New York City; in a pattern increasingly common with all forms of popular Indian music, she mixed in American hip-hop to the Punjabi form.

Qawwali: Sufi devotional singing, traditionally delivered by males; made most famous outside South Asia by the late Nusrat Fateh Ali Khan (1948–1997).

10.8.5 Bollywood

natak: 'drama' (from Sanskrit *nataka*, which could refer to classical dramas such as those of Kālidāsa), as a genre, which can be qualified by an English modifier: for example, *natak comedy*.

item number, *item song*: the Bollywood dance numbers that are inserted into a film's narrative flow, often without perceptible interruption of the linear progress of the film; given the preponderance of female performers in such 'items,' and the strategic box office designs at work, there has been some upset more recently with reference to *item girls* (the term dates to the *item* in which Shilpa Shetty danced in the 1999 crime natak *Shool*, "Spike").

thumka: the hip-swaying dance move of female *item* dancers is a Bollywood staple, and it has spawned an exercise craze; in India and its diasporic communities, social media has accelerated the reach of such phenomena, to which might be added the popular bhangra *dance-offs*.

India is at times referred to as a 'sleeping giant,' whether in terms of geopolitical significance, sport, music, or film: the Bollywood 'dance numbers' have made appearances in western popular culture, but they do not yet command the box office or enjoy the popularity found at home or in the Middle East and elsewhere. India seems poised to surpass – or has already surpassed – China as the world's most populous nation, based on current demographic projections. It is, unlike China (with perhaps some 250–400 million English language learners), a country in which English is spoken natively, though by a relatively small percentage of the population, and used much more widely as an L2. At the level of politics, and not without controversy, India has drawn closer in recent years to the United States; the relationship with Britain, painful colonial legacy notwithstanding, has been close, drawn closer by Indians in the diaspora. Economic ties with the United States are not limited to just the well-known Indian-based call centers, or outsourcing to India of American firms, or India's major production of iron and steel, but increasingly with India's own 'Silicon Valley' in Bengaluru/Bangalore. Educational ties are strengthening: Indians abroad now study not just at British universities (joined by generations of British Asian students), but hundreds of thousands of Indian students attend American universities. Indian doctors are increasingly represented in the American health care system. Where there are such links, linguistic – especially lexical – exchange will follow, and India, and South Asia more broadly, can be expected to provide more borrowings into the lexicon of English through the 21st century.

REFERENCES

The student of contact varieties of English around the globe has the signal benefit of several major research projects recently brought to print or online. The four-volume *Varieties of English* handbook from Mouton de Gruyter (2008) covers world varieties of English and English-based pidgins and Creoles by region: vol. 1 *The British Isles* (ed. Bernd Kortmann and Clive Upton); vol. 2 *The Americas and The Caribbean* (ed. Edgar W. Schneider); vol. 3 *The Pacific and Australasia* (ed. Kate Burridge and Bernd Kortmann); vol. 4 *Africa, South and Southeast Asia* (ed. Rajend Methrie). Each volume is prefaced by two lists of features ("Phonology and phonetics," " Morphology and Syntax") compiled by Edgar W. Schneider. The four-volume Oxford University Press *Survey of Pidgin and Creole Languages*, ed. Susan Maria Michaelis, Philippe Maurer, Martin Haspelmath, and Magnus Huber offers in-depth profiles of 74 pidgins and Creoles, the majority based on European colonial linguistic encounters: Volume I *English-based and Dutch-based Languages*; Volume II *Portuguese-based, Spanish-based, and French-based Languages*; Volume III *Contact Languages Based on Languages from Africa, Asia, Australia, and the Americas*; Volume IV *The Atlas of Pidgin and Creole Language Structures*. Though English-based contact varieties are covered in the first volume, the entire series is of critical value in assessing the role of English in world contact varieties (e.g., in a Dutch-based Creole such as Afrikaans, a "mixed language" such as Michif in Canada, the interaction of English- and French-based varieties in West Africa, or the multilingual varieties found in the Caribbean). At the structural level eminently useful are: the global-in-scale Oxford University Press *The World Atlas of Language Structures* (2005), ed. Martin Haspelmath, Matthew S. Dryer, David Gil, and Bernard Comrie, which is updated online at https://wals.info/; the English-focused *The Mouton World Atlas of Variation in English*, ed. Bernd Kortmann and Kerstin Lunkenheimer (Berlin: Mouton de Gruyter, 2013); and the two-volume Mouton (2008) *A Handbook of Varieties of English* (vol. 1: *Phonology*, vol. 2: *Morphology and Syntax*), ed. Edgar W. Schneider, Kate Burridge, Bernd Kortmann, Rajend Methrie, and Clive Upton.

A full list of references is to be found following Chapter 11.

CHAPTER 11

A Postcolonial Era 2

The Caribbean, Africa, the Middles East, Caucasus, Central Asia, Latin America

11.1 CARIBBEAN VARIETIES OF ENGLISH

The current state of Caribbean Englishes can be ascertained not just in Kingston, Spanish Town, Nassau, or Port of Spain, but in cosmopolises such as London and New York City, which each boast large Caribbean communities and the cultural traditions and celebrations emigrants brought with them (Notting Hill Carnival, West Indian Carnival NYC). While London neighborhoods such as Hackney, Tottenham, Brixton, and Shepherd's Bush are associated with West Indian communities ('West Indian' is generally a BrE locution, though it has now also been transferred to NYC; AmE has generally used 'Caribbean' and 'Afro-Caribbean'), a number of other British cities have significant populations, particularly industrial cities such as Birmingham, Manchester, Leeds, Leicester, and Luton, and this Caribbean emigration has generally been Anglophone – from former colonies. In the United States, the picture of Caribbean immigration is more complexly multilingual: NYC boasts of a significant Jamaican population (as do, to a somewhat lesser extent, Boston and Philadelphia; the latter also has a well-established West African community in West Philadelphia), and there are communities of immigrants from Grenada, Guyana, Belize, and Trinidad and Tobago in the boroughs of Brooklyn, Queens, and The Bronx. Brooklyn, in particular, is home to the largest Caribbean communities in the city; the Flatbush section, in central Brooklyn, has a large Haitian community in a neighborhood that had been for much of the 20th century Irish, Jewish, and African American. The northeast end of Flatbush and adjoining East Flatbush are home to the 'Little Caribbean' neighborhood along Church Avenue. In Upper Manhattan 'Spanish Harlem' grew within the formerly Italian East Harlem, a wedge-like neighborhood with Fifth Avenue as its western boundary and 96th Street as its southern edge, while a large Dominican neighborhood has grown over several decades in Washington Heights, a neighborhood once predominantly Jewish. The ebb and flow of 'ethnic neighborhoods' in American cities is part of the life cycle of these urban centers, and is not always without controversy; in the Latino/a 'heartland' of Los Angeles, a number of traditionally Hispanic neighborhoods have shifted increasingly to newer Asian populations; in Flatbush, Brooklyn, the parish of St. Jerome on Newkirk Avenue has for the past few decades offered Mass and services in Haitian Creole ("Mes Fransè e Kreyòl, Legliz Sen Jewòm, Pawas [= *paroisse*, 'parish'] Brooklyn"), but has more recently added a Mass in Spanish. Though English becomes dominant usually by the third generation, the complex linguistic legacies of 'ethnic enclaves' have left an imprint particularly upon lexis.

In the 21st century, developments in Caribbean English revolve around some degree of decreolization of contact varieties as contact continues with standard forms of BrE (although Bermuda is often seen as an outlier, with an accent described as more American-influenced), shifts in status and prestige of Caribbean varieties, from standard local varieties of English to basilectal dialects and contact varieties (e.g., in Jamaica, high-status standard Kingston Jamaican English vs. Spanish Town Patwa), and the influence of Caribbean communities abroad as easier travel and mass communication (especially by mobile phone) keep families in closer contact than had been possible for earlier generations. The Anansi stories from colonial Jamaica served earlier as examples of West African imports to the Anglophone Caribbean; a more recent example of Jamaican popular culture in Britain might serve as an example of the influence of the diaspora and of shifting attitudes toward 'nonstandard' varieties.

Some minor controversy, though only 12 OFCOM complaints, was generated by the program *Rastamouse*; on CBeebies, the BBC channel for its youngest demographic (children up to 7 years of age). The cast of characters in the stop-motion animated series, which ran for 104 episodes from 2011 to 2015, were mice living in an imaginary Jamaican Mouseland. The sources of what controversy there was centered on the stereotypical (or, in some views, potentially racist) portrayal of the Jamaican accent and lifestyle (the rasta/reggae theme of the show), the introduction of 'nonstandard' English to so young an audience, and alleged drug references and innuendoes. The lead character was crime-fighting, skateboarding, reggae-playing Rastamouse, assisted in his detective work by members of "Da Easy Crew." Cases were called in over a walkie-talkie by an often despondent and harried President Wensley Dale (the show made persistent references to cheese, which were seen by older viewers as a proxy for marijuana – an interpretation not without merit). The basic moral to each crime-fighting episode was one of correction, redress, and redemption, or, in the show's tagline, "how to make a bad t'ing good." A number of plotlines involved the orphanage [ɑːrfənɪʤ] Rastamouse often assisted in a series that, whatever its possible double entendres (a charge lodged also against the American Looney Tunes cartoon series and the BBC's *Teletubbies*), offered an appropriately simplistic uplifting moral message every episode. More controversial, linguistically speaking, was the dialogue in more mesolectal Jamaican English (and, less frequently, Patwa). Some educational theorists and linguists have held that exposure to nonstandard forms could interfere with the 'comprehensible input,' phase of early language acquisition, an argument that parallels debates about when to introduce second-language education in school (excepted here are; 'native bilinguals,' for whom the home environment is also a language 'school'). The fear of 'interference' in language acquisition seems largely to have been unfounded – for many viewers, the Jamaican English Rastamouse, Zoomer, Bagga T, Missy D, and President Wensley Dale used was not the variety of the home environment. This was also, of course, an animated series about talking Jamaican mice: certainly not the strangest premise for a children's show on offer. But for those whose home variety was like that of "Da Easy Crew," there could be seen some validation of their speech ways. While the example of Wilfred Pickles's Northern accent on the BBC in 1941 could be seen as the start of opening the airwaves to non-RP accents, it really is only much more recently that regional British accents have been mainstreamed. While the Jamaican patterns of *Rastamouse* could be seen as a more radical departure from earlier prescriptive practice, it was also a way of introducing English-speaking children to the range of accents and varieties of English that are part of modern Britain.

English-speaking countries and territories in the Caribbean

'Anglophone' or 'English-speaking' in the Caribbean/Caribbean basin here of course encompasses a wide range of varieties and English-based pidgins and Creoles, and even within these, further stratification can be present. Jamaican patois (or 'Patwa'), like French-based Haitian (Ayisyin, Kréyòl Ayisyen [< *haïtien*]), ranges along a linguistic continuum from acrolectal varieties, those closest to the superstratum (English) – which may belong more properly to a post-Creole continuum that may result in decreolization, or a merger with the standard form of the superstrate language – [1] to the basilectal. In Jamaica, again as in Haiti, coastal and urban varieties are often more likely to range from the mesolectal to the acrolectal (Patrick 1998), while the basilectal is more likely to be found in the rural (mountainous) interior. The 'basilectal' forms in the Caribbean exhibit greater influence of the Niger–Congo languages and the various precursors of the Caribbean pidgins and Creoles: the Manding trade language, Guinea Coast Creole English, and Portuguese Pidgin. The linguistic continuum often overlaps with racial differences, from a more coastal Creole population (also to be included are British whites) to African populations in the interior (the term 'full-bloods' of former use). The linguistic and racial differences are very much to be seen in the postcolonial politics of the Caribbean (20th-century American Black Nationalist leader Marcus Garvey

[1] Or the pattern pidginization > Creolization > decreolization sometimes suggested for Black English/AAVE in the United States.

was born in Jamaica). While some six million people speak English in the Caribbean, this figure requires the qualifier 'varieties,' and, on some islands, includes second-language speakers whose native tongue may be a variety, or contact variety, of French, Spanish, or Dutch. Presented are the territories with rounded population figures current to 2021:

British English-based varieties

Anguilla 15,100
Antigua and Barbuda 100,960
The Bahamas 391,200
Barbados 287,000
Belize 390,350
British Virgin Islands 30,600
Cayman Islands 64,950
Dominica 71,800
Grenada 112,000
Guyana 782,000
Jamaica 2,940,000
Montserrat 5,900
St. Kitts and Nevis 54,800
St. Lucia 182,800
St. Vincent and the Grenadines 110,600
Trinidad and Tobago 1,395,000
Turks and Caicos 38,200

American-English based

Puerto Rico ~800,000 (Spanish and English are official, and despite moves toward greater bilingualism in the school system, Spanish is dominant in Puerto Rico and spoken in some Puerto Rican communities on the mainland)
US Virgin Islands: 105,900

Just as the 1980–1981 Hunger Strikes brought working-class Northern Irish accents (Catholic and Protestant) into English homes over the BBC nightly, so the Brixton riot in 1981 brought forward Black Caribbean voices from that Lambeth neighborhood (the fourth film, *Alex Wheatle*, in Steve McQueen's 2020 film series *Small Axe* on BBC One recreates this era). Ties with the Commonwealth have remained fairly strong in the Anglophone Caribbean: Antigua and Barbuda, The Bahamas, Barbados, Belize, Dominica, Grenada, and Guyana are the member states from the Caribbean basin. But American involvement with and influence over the Caribbean has been increasing. Large-scale migration from English-, French-, and Spanish-speaking Caribbean islands to the United States outpaces that to Britain; the US territories of Puerto Rico and the

US Virgin Islands have long been America's toehold in the region. The invasion of Grenada in 1983, the American Operation Uphold Democracy 1994–1995 in Haiti, and involvement after that nation's devastating earthquake in 2010 follow on a long tradition of US military actions (and relief work) in the Caribbean. The connections between immigrant communities in the United States (especially along the Eastern seaboard, from Miami to Boston) and their home communities in the Caribbean have expanded the reach of American-accented English in a region historically associated with British English. This is of course also a global pattern vitiated to an extent by the rise of 'global Englishes,' local Asian, African, Pacific, Caribbean, and other varieties of increasing independence from the Anglo-American axis. In the end, they are all varieties of English, and the advantages of broader communicability may serve as a constraint upon divergence, while local identity (and pride) may check forces of convergence.

Though the roots of Caribbean accents of English and the surviving English-based Creoles go back to the earliest days of colonial settlement of the Caribbean basin and to the contact varieties of West Africa, in the postcolonial era, national and literary standard varieties have made their mark on literature in English. Two Anglophone Caribbean writers have won the Nobel Prize in literature, Derek Walcott of St. Lucia in 1992 and V.S. Naipaul of Trinidad in 2001, and two have been awarded the Booker Prize (Naipaul in 1971, and Jamaican novelist Marlon James in 2015). Many Caribbean authors have accepted teaching posts in the United States and the United Kingdom (poets Walcott at Boston University and Jamaica's Claudia Rankine at Yale University), and the literary and intellectual circle of the Anglophone Caribbean has grown to encompass the English-speaking world. While most writers from the region write for the most part in local standard varieties, the prose, dialogue, and poetry of the Anglophone Caribbean is also laced with the patois, to striking literary, social, and political effect: Walcott's epic *Omeros* (1990) localizes the Greek epic – the fishermen Achille and Hector, while the blind man Seven Seas stands in for the poet of the *Iliad* himself – with the 'patois' for Homer's Ionic – "*mer* was both/mother and sea in our Antillean patois" (II.iii):

> *'Ous croire 'ous c'est roi Gros let? Voleur bomme!*
> "You think you're King of Gros let [Gros-Islet], you tin-stealer?"
> Then in English: "I go show you who is king! Come!" (I.iii)

In "The Dust" from *Rights of Passage* (1967), Barbadian poet Kamau Brathwaite (Lawson Edward Brathwaite) captures the patois of a group of women at evening in a rural grocery:

> Miss Evvy, uh wants
> you to trus; me half
> pung-a flour an' two
> cake o' soap till
> Mundee come wid de will
> o' de Lord.

One of the women blames the blight on their crops on a neighboring island's volcano and extends the observation to the linguistic differences in the Lesser Antilles:

in one o' dem islands away
where they language tongue-tie
an' to hear them speak so
in they St. Lucia patois
is as if they cahn unnerstan'
A single word o' English (Breiner 1998, 179).

Kingston and Castries, New York and London: the diffusion of Caribbean English in the later 20th and early 21st centuries offers a check, or constraint of sorts, on the idea of 'Global English': to be sure, the use of standard varieties of English has advanced the educational and economic opportunities of the island nations, but the local, the patois and Creole, has made the 'return journey' or been exported, an expression of identity in music and poetry, in the way of speaking.

11.2 AFRICAN ENGLISHES IN THE 21ST CENTURY; FRENCH AND ENGLISH IN WEST AFRICA

If there is one region of the world in which the seemingly unstoppable march of Global English is meeting resistance it is West Africa. Perhaps 100 million people in Africa speak French, mainly as an L2 or as a co-L1 with a local language, and while there may be some inflation in the figure from the Organisation internationale de la Francophonie and other French-language bodies, from the Maghreb in the northwest to West and Central Africa French has a stubborn and growing presence. About 25 African nations have significant to dominant populations of French speakers, with Algeria, Cameroon, Côte d'Ivoire/Ivory Coast, the Democratic Republic of the Congo, Guinea, Madagascar, Morocco, Senegal, and Tunisia numbering in the millions of speakers (the DRC over 40 million speakers – second only to France). The number of English speakers in Africa is more than double that for French, in large part because of Anglophone Nigeria, Kenya, and southern African countries.

English in Africa

Figures from Crystal 2019, 115–117, and Ethnologue unless otherwise noted; Mauritania has been included in North Africa because of the predominance of Arabic and historical links to the Arab Maghreb empire. Other languages given with significant numbers of speakers or with high religious or cultural influence.

(*continued*)

(*continued*)

North Africa

Mauritania 425,000 (Arabic, Hassaniya Arabic, Berber dialects, French, and Wolof)
Western Sahara 11,900 (Arabic, Hassaniya Maghrebi Arabic, Spanish, French, and Berber/Tamazight)
Morocco 4,934,000 (Arabic, Moroccan Maghrebi Arabic, Hassaniya Maghrebi Arabic, Berber/Tamzight, and French)
Algeria ca. 3,000,000 (Maghreb Arabic, French; French is officially promoted in Algeria, although some recent moves by the Ministère de l'Éducation nationale/Ministry of National Education have been meant to encourage English for "cultural independence"[2])
Tunisia 1,608,000 (Arabic, Tunisian Derja Arabic, French, and Berber dialects)
Libya 1,255,000 (Arabic, Libyan Arabic, Berber dialects, and Italian)
Egypt 28,000,000–33,319,000 (Arabic, Egyptian Arabic, Sa'idi Arabic, Coptic, and French)
Sudan 16,000,000 (Arabic, Sudanese Arabic, Beja, and Dinka)

West Africa

Benin 571,000 (French, Fon, Yoruba, and Ede)
Burkina Faso 954,000 (French, Mossi, Dyula, and Fula)
Cameroon 4,200,000 (French and English, co-official; Bulu, Ewondo, Yemba, and Ghomala; to the figure for English may be added also speakers of Kamtok/Cameroonian Pidgin English)
Cape Verde 53,200 (Portuguese and Portuguese-based Cape Verdean Creole/Kriolu)
The Gambia 1,500,000 (Mandinka, Pulaar, and Wolof)
Ghana ca. 19,000,000 (Akan and Ewe)
Guinea 662,000 (French, Fula, Malinké, and Loma)
Guinea-Bissau 60,000 (Portuguese, Fula, and Mandinka)
Ivory Coast/Côte d'Ivoire 4,000,000 (French, Dioula, and Kwa, Akan, Kru, and Mande languages)
Liberia 550,000 (Kreyol, Merico, Kru Pidgin, and native Mande and Kru languages)
Mali 928,000 (French, Bambara, Fulfulde, and Songhai)
Niger 427,000 (French, Arabic, Hausa, Songhai, and Tuareg languages)
Nigeria 115,000,000 (Igbo, Edo, Yoruba, Hausa, and over 500 other languages)
Senegal 800,000 (French, Wolof, Pulaar, and Serer)
Sierra Leone 6,700,000 (Krio, Mende, and Temne)
Togo 383,000 (French, Ewé, and Kabiyé)
St. Helena 7,000 ('Saint,' St. Helenian English variety)
Ascension Island 800–880
Tristan da Cunha 250

[2] Lamine Ghanmi, "Algeria seeks to replace French with English at university, sparks 'language war,'" *The Arab Weekly* 8 March 2019 (online).

Central Africa

Central African Republic 254,000 (French, Sango [an African-based Creole])
Chad 745,000 (French, Chadian Arabic, Mundang, Maba, Sara, and Sango Creole)
Democratic Republic of the Congo 4,088,000 (French and Arabic are co-official; many languages in the Niger-Congo, Nilo-Saharan, and Afroasiatic language families)
Gabon 179,700 (French, Fong, Mbere, and Eshira)
Equatorial Guinea 17,800 (Spanish, Portuguese, Fang, Benga, and a number of Bantu languages)
Mali 928,000 (French, Bambara, Fulfulde, and Soninke)
Republic of the Congo 242,000 (French, Kintuba, Lingala, and Bateke)
São Tomé and Príncipe 9,900 (Portuguese and Portuguese-based Creoles)

East Africa

Burundi 250,000 (Kirundi and French)
Comoros 16,500 (Comorian, French, and Arabic)
Djibouti 45,500 (Arabic, French, Somali, and Afar)
Eritrea 2,000,000 (Tigrinya, Tigray, Afar, Beja, and Arabic)
Ethiopia 10,000,000 (Amharic, Oromo, and Tigrinya)
Kenya 4,000,000 (Kikuyu, Dholuo, Kamba, and Swahili)
Madagascar 3,821,000 (Malagasy and French)
Mauritius 900,000 (French and French-based Mauritian Creole)
Mayotte 25,000 (French and Shimaore Comorian)
Réunion 44,000 (French and French-based Réunion Creole)
Rwanda 1,800,000 (Kinyarwanda, French, and Swahili)
Seychelles 35,000 (French-based Kreol and French)
Somalia (and Somaliland) 900,000 (figure is likely higher; Somali, Arabic, Swahili, and Italian)
South Sudan 5,000,000 (Dinka, Nuer, and Bari; with independence, Arabic was de-listed as an official language in the Republic of South Sudan)
Tanzania 5,000,000 (Swahili, Arabic, over 120 languages in the Niger-Congo, Nilo-Saharan, and Khoisan language families)
Uganda 20,000,000 (Swahili, co-official with English, some 40 other languages, of the Bantu family in the south and Central Sudanic in the north)

Southern Africa

(Madagascar and the Comoros joined the SADC, Southern Africa Development Community, but are included above in East Africa)

Angola 1,327,000 (Portuguese sole official language; Chokwe, Kikongo, Kimbundu, Oshiwambo, and Umbundu)
Botswana 950,000 (Tswana co-official with English)
Eswatini/Swaziland 900,000 (Swazi and English co-official)
Lesotho 550,000 (Sesotho and English co-official)

(*continued*)

(*continued*)

Malawi 900,000 (Chichewa the most widely spoken; other significant Bantu languages include Chinyanja, Chiyao, and Chitumbuka)
Mozambique 1,471,000 (Portuguese, Emakhuwa, Cisena, Xitsonga, and Elomwe)
Namibia 415,000 (Ovambo/Oshiwambo, Koekhoegowab, Afrikaans, RuKwangali, and German)
South Africa 30,000,000 (Afrikaans, Ndebele, Setswana, Northern Sotho/Sotho sa Leboa, Southern Sotho, siSwati, Tsonga, Tswana, Venda/Tshivenda, Xhosa, and Zulu)
Zambia 5,200,000 (Bemba/ChiBemba, Nyanja, Tonga, and Lozi)
Zimbabwe 8,000,000 (Chewa, Chibarwe, Kalanga, Khoisan, Nambya, Ndau, Ndebele, Shangani, Shona, Zimbabwean sign language, Sotho, Tonga/Chitonga, Tswana, Venda, and Xhosa [with English, 16 official languages in total])

The English language came to East Africa as part of the expansion of British holdings in the continent in the later 19th century; there were, however, a few distinguishing features to East Africa: English came to be used as a colonial (and now postcolonial) *lingua franca* in addition to an existing one: Swahili (Kiswahili). South Asian laborers and merchants were brought into Kenya, Tanzania, and Uganda, and more followed for the economic opportunities, with significant influence not just upon the regional linguistic situation (many were speakers of Gujarati and Punjabi; Schmied 2008, 155), but also, for instance, upon cuisine: one example is the *sambusa*, the Indian *samosa* turnover with various fillings, often with potato as the base, which has spread through Africa with Indian immigrants and beyond, to the Middle East and Central Asia, to Trinidad and Tobago and Guyana; the word is borrowed into English from Hindi, but ultimately derives from Persian. In the 21st century, East African Englishes share the *lingua franca* role in major media with Swahili, with the slight advantage to English in that major news coverage (*The Citizen* [Tanzania], *The EastAfrican* [Kenya], *Arusha Times* [Tanzania], and government-run *Daily News* [Tanzania]) and official pronouncements are often made in English (particularly if involving international affairs, or international agencies), though popular sports and entertainment coverage is often in Swahili (*Mwanaspoti*, part of the Mwananchi Communications group, Tanzania). In Kenya, the Nation Media Group publishes the Swahili daily *Taifa Leo* ("Nation Today") and the largest circulation paper in the country, *Daily Nation*, which began in 1960 as the English-language edition of *Taifa Leo*. The next highest-circulation paper is *The Standard* – mass media in Kenya has shifted more toward English since independence, a pattern not uncommon in postcolonial Africa. In Uganda, the major media are also now more in English, though the second *lingua franca* role is played by Luganda (of the Bantu family of languages) rather than Swahili.

One of the great changes since independence – 1963 for Kenya, 1962 for Tanzania, and 1962 also for Uganda – has been rapid population growth and urbanization. Kenya (population 52 million), Tanzania (58 million), and Uganda (44 million) are now mid-sized countries with a majority of their populations children and young adults.

Urbanization is genuinely a global trend, and though many African countries still have majority rural populations, a shift toward urban centers is rapidly under way: in 80 years, Nairobi has grown from 24,000 people to a metro population of 10 million (2021); Arusha has grown from 55,000 (1978) to over 400,000 (2020); Dar es Salaam had some 84,000 residents in 1950 and now boasts a metro population of 7 million. Urbanization has brought with it higher-density neighborhoods, mass transit, large urban hospitals, sports stadiums (capital cities all boast major football arenas), universities, office buildings, and government centers. The trade-offs have of course been enormous (as always, and as in 18th-century Britain), from environmental impacts to ethnic tensions and a widening gap between economic classes (all newer African cities now have expanding rings of suburbs and luxury villas). One linguistic consequence has been the rise in utility in English; in the village, the local languages suffice for day-to-day needs; in the cities, Swahili and English serve a greater role (Luganda in Uganda). An interesting, more recent development has been the arrival of a new inspiration to African popular culture: African American culture. American hip-hop and African American cultural styles have swept Africa in the last few decades, a sort of return gesture considering the great influence of African culture on African American (at the time 'Afro-American') music, art, clothing, and lifestyle in the 1970s–1990s. While certain terms from East African popular music may be more familiar to 'worldbeat' and 'Afrobeat' audiophiles, music has been one of the most productive vectors for the transmission of loanwords from East Africa. A good many are from Swahili, or are Swahili–English hybrids: the traditional *taarab* music played at weddings (and imported to Zanzibar from Oman, with South Asian influences) has been merged with modern dance music, as has female-performed *chakacha* music; the simple mix of violin and percussive instruments has added the electronic keyboard (especially cheaper models of the Casio), as has the popular Tanzanian street form *mchiriku* (as popularized by the band Jagwa Music); street bands such as Mnanda Music perform in *uswahlini*, 'Swahili (areas),' in Dar es Salaam – the term has been applied also to areas of Nairobi. Swahili *ngoma* ('song') has broadened in use from its original reference to drumming styles (and dances) to something like 'musical style,' especially in describing new hybrid street forms of popular music; *Congo rumba* (usually sung in French) and *soukous* dance music have spread from Central Africa; the latter has, in turn, been mixed in with *majika* music from Mozambique.

But everywhere, there is local hip-hop: the large Kibera [ki: berˈ ə] slum of Nairobi is the birthplace of the mixed language *Sheng* (a blend of *Swahili* and *English*), an outgrowth of the young male motorbike taxi drivers, their slang (or "Vehicular Swahili"; Githiora 2002, 165), and mobile phone culture, and now of Sheng hip-hop (performers such as Octopizzo and Kalamashaka). Exaggeration and overstatement are the province of hip-hop, and Kibera, at times said to have one million residents and the status of Africa's largest slum (of approximately 130,000 persons), has, it seems now, been the subject of such exaggeration. Figures of 700,000 to 1 million residents were made by international aid organizations and NGOs, namely UN-Habitat (the United Nations Human Settlement Programme) and the Institut français de recherche en Afrique (IFRA; the French Institute for Research in Africa); population figures for all of Africa are notoriously difficult to come by, especially for Nigeria, Africa's most populous nation (and an Anglophone country with a number of Francophone neighbors). Nigeria's last major census without serious dispute was in 1962; those of 1991 and 2006 were beset by charges of manipulation (all attempts at population counts play into rivalries between the north and south of the country and the religious and ethnic divisions). The 2006 census estimated Nigeria's population at 140 million persons; a current figure puts it at 206 million: the latter figure likely an overcount. The tensions that surround the census have to do with religion, language, and ethnicity, and point up why the use of English has continued as a relatively neutral language of federal governance. To return to Sheng, Swahili–English contact varieties in East Africa are not new; with the 'Sheng' of Kibera, one can plot the evolution in the past 20 years of what was clearly once a Swahili-based contact variety: in Githiora 2002, the variety is almost entirely African, with a Swahili base (even if what Kenyan speakers and observers considered a 'bad' form of Swahili), and borrowings from Luo, Gikuyu, Masai, Luhya, Giriama, and Taita (Githiora 2002, 159–160); there is *kam* ('come'), *Walapa!* (< "What's up!'), *Niwatize?* ('What's going on?'; Swahili *ni* 'is' + English 'What is it'), *stori* ('story'; Githiroa 2002, 166, 168). In the data collected in Githinji 2008, on sexist attitudes in Sheng, English clearly has a greater role as a lexifier: terms for 'girl' include *chik*, *dame*, *hoe*, *mama*, *siste*; those for 'boy' *bro*, *boi*, *hommie*; for father, there is the usual term *papa* but also *oldman* (an Americanism, as is *beshte* for 'bestie, best friend'; Githinji 2008, 21–22; compare also African American *oldhead*). A recent study of another Swahili–English mixed variety (McIntosh 2010) from Malindi, Kenya, a coastal town north of Mombasa, finds a 'medialect' (i.e., used in text messaging) of "rapid code-switching" between the native Kigiriama and English and Swahili, with a "condensed, abbreviated English" in which "English is almost without exception the only language subject to orthographical condensation" (McIntosh 2010, 337–338). As with Sheng of Kibera ("Sheng" has been used to refer to other Swahili-English contact varieties, such as those of Mombasa), the motivation for the Malindi Swahili–English (and Kigiriama) contact is a sense of 'persona,' 'self-fashioning' (McIntosh 2010, 337) – or, in that simple but all-pervasive formula found worldwide, what is 'cool.' Examples of the texting 'peer language' are illuminating for the form of East African contact variety and of a global English 'textspeak':

> **vidze msena** [Kigiriama in bold], y u ddnt do the trip ("What's up my friend, why didn't you go on the trip?")
> so **tukutane** mond **asabuhi**, w'out **kosa** [Swahili in bold] ("So let's meet Monday morning, without fail"; McIntosh 2010, 338, 341).

The "condensed" English may not just be a product of texting but also the influence of Sheng, and the nature of the code-switching between Swahili and English may indicate a claim to "an African yet global identity" (McIntosh 2010, 342).

Like many other African Englishes, East African English is non-rhotic, excepting pre-vocalic /r/, which can be a trill or flap (as in Nigerian English and other West African Englishes). The liquid consonants /r/ and /l/ can be interchanged, but with the tendency toward employment of the one or the other – for example, *lorry* > [loli] or [rori] (Schmied 2008, 159). Diphthongs are often smoothed, and the central vowel in *nurse* [nə:s] is more front and open [nɑ:s]; that in *kit* [kɪt] is raised [kit]. Conversely, the final vowel in *happy* is lowered, [i] > [ɪ] ("happee" > "hap-ih"; Schmied 2008, 160–61). As East African English is more syllable-timed than stress-timed, as are other African Englishes, stress patterns often vary from those of standard English, with a common shift in stress to final syllables (e.g., for CON-sti-TU-tion, con-sti-tu-SHUN).

In West Africa, Nigeria is the economic, demographic, and political giant, though one beset by religious, ethnic, and linguistic fissures – the Biafra crisis (1967–1970) in the Nigerian civil war period was one terrible consequence of colonial-era map-drawing and nation-making, though also the product of new political realities with independence in 1960. For its brief life as the Republic of Biafra, English was the national language. Over 500 languages are spoken in Nigeria, such as Fula/Fulani of the Niger-Congo family of languages (with over 65 million speakers across the Sahel) and the Ijaw languages of Niger-Congo, but the three "giants" of Nigeria are Igbo (Niger-Congo), Hausa (in the Chadic branch of the Afroasiatic family), and Yoruba (Niger-Congo). The languages are coterminous with large ethnic groupings of Nigeria and neighboring West African nations. The Hausa are concentrated in the north, from Sokoto to the old cultural center of Daura, Kano to Maiduguri (and some 11 million Hausa live in Niger), and seem to have migrated from Nilo-Saharan-speaking regions further east; the Hausa are predominantly Sunni Muslim. The majority of Yoruba are Christians (some 22 of 28 million Yoruba in Nigeria), with a significant Sunni Muslim population in areas under historical Hausa influence. The great majority of 40 million Igbo people in Nigeria are Christians; in fact, the Igbo are the largest ethnic group of Christians in Africa; the Igbo Roman Catholic Cardinal Francis Arinze was for a time a rumored papal candidate. His parents had converted to Catholicism from the native Igbo religion; traditional faiths are still practiced by some Yoruba – the loanword *orisha* (traditional guiding spirits) is from the Yoruba language, and Yoruba brought the religion with them to the Caribbean and especially Brazil in the syncretic faith Candomblé. Yoruba has also given English *juju* (for a musical style), *sekere* (a gourd-rattle), *agogo* (musical handbell), and *egus(s)i* (food made from crushed watermelon seeds) among the 26 loans listed in the OED; the OED lists 8 words of Igbo origin, among them *obeah* (the 'witchcraft' practices found in Afro-Caribbean tradition; the term has been extended to anthropological use with reference to African religious practice also in Haiti), and *okra*, a staple of Southern American cuisine (its alternative name, *gumbo*, a word deriving from an unspecified Bantu language of Angola, is also applied to the soup that can be thickened with the plant's pods, a staple of Louisiana Creole cuisine); from Hausa, the OED derives 11 loans, including the *riga*, the loose, and draped open robe (called *agbada* in Yoruba) worn by West African men. A more recent loan from Hausa is *boko* in the name of the Nigerian Islamist terrorist organization *Boko Haram*; *haram* is the familiar loan from Arabic meaning 'forbidden,' while *boko* is a Hausa form meaning 'false, fake,' the unspecified referent being 'western education' or 'culture.' The name *Boko Haram* was widely used in the media but never by the organization itself, which is formally known as *Jamā'atu Ahli is-Sunnah lid-Da'wati wal-Jihād* ("Brotherhood of the People of the Sunnah for Dawah and Jihad"). Widespread coverage of outrages such as the mass abduction of 300 Christian schoolgirls from Chibok, Borno State, has put *Boko Haram* firmly in the "War on Terror" lexicon in western media. In the lexicon of the arts and popular entertainment, Nigeria has given English 'Nollywood,' the world's second most prolific film industry after Mumbai's 'Bollywood'; the northern Nigerian Hausa-language film industry based in Kano now adds 'Kannywood' to the collection of *-wood* blend formations.

The divisions in Nigeria along ethnic and linguistic lines obtain for many if not most African nations, and those along religious lines for a good number of nations outside southern Africa. The north (Hausa)–south (Igbo) divide has been observed in minor differences between varieties of Nigerian English: the simple vowels in Hausa English are contrastive as in most varieties of English, but non-contrastive (lacking tense vowels) in southern/Yoruba–Igbo English; the front vowel [ɪ] in *kit* in standard English pronunciation is found in Hausa English, but is raised in southern/Yoruba–Igbo English to /i/ (Gut 2008, 41–42). Nigerian English is non-rhotic so the *bath* vowel /ɑ:/ in Hausa English (or /ɑ/ in southern Nigerian English) makes homophones of *march* and *match* (Gut 2008, 43). The usual "syllable-timing" found in other African Englishes obtains for Nigerian English, with the additional prosodic feature that Hausa, Igbo, and Yoruba are "tone languages" (two in Hausa and Igbo, three in Yoruba); this results in the impression that Nigerian English has two tones, High and Low (Gut 2008, 51–52). And, again, as with other African Englishes, there can be a tendency toward shift in stress in Nigerian English to the last syllable in verbs with suffixes *-ate, -ise/-ize, -fy*, or *-ish* (e.g., te-le-VIZE, pub-li-CIZE), or with nominal and adjectival suffixes such as *-day* (mon-DAY) or *-able* (cap-ABLE; Gut 2008, 48).

Two other distinctive national varieties of English bear mention in consideration of 21st-century trends, Ghanaian and Liberian English. Ghanaian English resembles closely West African and more broadly African Englishes in the treatment of RP diphthongs (most are monophthongized) and in being non-rhotic. These similarities can be encapsulated in the example from Ghanaian news-readers' pronunciation of *the news on the hour* [dɛ nius ɔn di â] (/â/ here represents /ɑ/ with a falling tone – Ga, Akan, Twi, and other languages of Ghana are tone languages; Huber 2008, 81–82). The Ghanaian pronunciation of *desire* ("deh-SAI-ah") [dɛsɑɪə] and *our* ("ow-ah") [ɑʊə] both see the diphthongs smoothed to /ɑ/ or /â/; there are distinctive consonantal features of Ghanaian English: loss of final /-n/ with nasalized vowel in place of the final consonant, and glottalization and even loss of /-t/: *got* [gɔt] (there is variation between /ɑ/ and /ɔ/ in Ghanaian English) shifts to [gɔʔ] and even [gɔ] (Huber 2008, 83–84). As with other African Englishes, there can occur final consonant cluster reduction (*hundreds* > [hɑndrɛs]; Huber 2008, 88) and the influence of spelling pronunciations, which can occur in all varieties of English, especially when a target variety, such as RP, is seen as more prestigious and desirable.

Liberian English, here referring to 'Liberian Settler English,' the dominant variety in Liberia based on the historical population of ex-slaves resettled in the territory (1822–1867), is in some ways an outlier among West African Englishes (as with the Philippines, the model is American rather than British English). Thus Liberian English alone pronounces *trap* as [træp] rather than [trɑp], following the standard AmE pronunciation. The vowel in *kit* is /e/ rather than /ɪ/, and though non-rhotic, Liberian English in general follows the AmE consonant system (the voiced interdental fricative /ð/ is replaced with the voiced stop /d/) and, perhaps also a product of its unique history, Liberian Settler English is more stress- than syllable-timed (Singler 2008, 108–112).

An interesting development with English in Africa in the late 20th and early 21st centuries is the persistence and growth of English-based Creoles – indeed, their spread from coastal regions inland and even their establishment as national varieties: Nigerian Pidgin English, Kamtok (Cameroonian Pidgin English), Krio of Sierra Leone, Ghanaian Pidgin English, and Pichi of the island of Bioko (Equatorial Guinea).

Krio (Sierra Leone)

dis wan ya na mi sista
[this one here is my sister]
"This (one) is my sister." (Finney 2013, 162)

da wan de noto mi brɔda
[that one there not is my brother]
"That (one) is not my brother" (Finney 2013, 162; *noto* is the negative copula in Krio)

a tiŋk se dɛm dɔn kam
[I think that them done come]
"I think that they have arrived." (Finney 2013, 163; *se* = 'say' in Krio and here seems to be a complementizer and so is rendered 'that': *I think* THAT *they have arrived*)

Ghanaian Pidgin English

dɛ ren i mek ful de
[the rain he make full day]
"It rained the whole day." (Huber 2013, 173)

Pichi

È fayn fɔ dring smɔl-wan
[It be fine for drink small-one]
"It's good to drink moderately." (Yakpo 2013, 197)

À dè tek mi pikin go nà hospital, claro
[I would take me little one go to/unto hospital, **surely** (Sp.)]
"I would take my child to the hospital, of course." (Yakpo 2013, 199)

Nigerian Pidgin English

ì gò pé mà mɔni
[he go pay my money]
"He will pay my fee." (Elugbe 2008, 64)

Kamtok (Cameroon Pidgin English)

Na Joseph i haus
[It is Joseph his house]
"It is Joseph's house." (Schröder 2013, 187)

I bin di kof fo wan awa
[he/she been has cough for one hour]
"He/she has been coughing for one hour." (Schröder 2013, 189)

These West African contact varieties have been listed in north to south distribution, and geography, or the geopolitical environment, is of great linguistic consequence: historically, the Gulf of Guinea was a central region to the slave trade, and the cradle of West African pidgins (with bases in the trading then settler languages Portuguese, Spanish, English, and French); another colonial legacy is the linguistic patchwork that continues to influence the language situation and language planning and policy in the postcolonial era. Sierra Leone's colonial history is particularly complex, with the role played by Krios, that is, Creoles, those of mixed ancestry: descendants of freed slaves from America, the Caribbean, and the Gulf of Guinea region who settled there from 1787 on, and the British resettlement of ex-slaves following the abolition of slavery in 1807. Sierra Leone now is surrounded on its northern and inland border by Francophone Guinea, and to the south by Liberia with its American English-influenced variety. Ghana is surrounded on all sides by Francophone nations: Côte d'Ivoire, Burkina Faso, and Togo. Nigeria is the Anglophone powerhouse of the region, but surrounded by Francophonie: Benin, Niger, Chad, and Cameroon. Bioko, renamed Fernando Pó in the colonial era by the Portuguese, was with Equatorial Guinea ceded by the Portuguese to the Spanish in 1778, though a base in the port of Malabo was leased by Britain (1827–1843) but then returned to Spanish control: the linguistic upshot is that independent Equatorial Guinea recognizes Spanish, French, and Portuguese as official languages, though Pichi (or Pichinglis or Fernando Po Creole English) is widely spoken on Bioko, while the Portuguese-based Creole Fa d'Ambô (Post 2013, 81–89) is spoken on the islands of Annobón and Bioko in the Gulf of Guinea (both provinces of the nation of Equatorial Guinea). The adoption of French and Portuguese (only in 2010) as official languages by Equatorial Guinea was also motivated by the desire to join Francophone and Portuguese-language associations – a pattern seen with other cooperative organizations in Africa such as the SADC (the Southern African Development Community, which is multilingual but gives English primacy in its functioning). Equatorial Guinea, too, is surrounded by Francophone neighbors, Cameroon and Gabon.

In Cameroon, a nation created out of a union (by a UN resolution in 1961) of the former French Cameroun and the former British colony Southern Cameroons (on the northwest side of Cameroun), an "Anglophone Crisis" has developed from charges of mistreatment of Anglophone Cameroonians by the French-speaking majority. A self-declared autonomous Amba Land (or Ambazonia) seeks to protect the Anglophone population and, in essence, revive the independence of the Southern Cameroons. The shift from the Federated Republic of Cameroon to the United Republic of Cameroon under President Paul Biya, a move that cements the dominance of the Francophone majority in the unitary nation-state, has precipitated increased calls for independence by "Ambazonia" activists, such that the 'Ambazonia Defence Forces' were created in September of 2017. The government crackdown on separatists has been bloody; the ADF since late 2017 has resorted to guerrilla tactics and allied itself with the IPOB, the Indigenous People of Biafra, in neighboring Nigeria, which seeks to re-establish the Republic of Biafra that was briefly independent during the Nigerian civil war (1967–1970). The alliance is natural in that both movements seek independence for a smaller state from its larger federal nation-state; another link for the ADF is linguistic, as both are Anglophone. The conflict is ongoing, with guerrilla tactics including the use of IEDs in 2021 by Ambazonian forces, which now include more than 50 separatist militias known collectively as "Amba Boys." Quite sadly, West Africa has a language war for the 21st century. While the violence in Cameroon is unusual, rivalry between

Francophone and Anglophone nations and regions is not. Both France and Britain seek to support the maintenance of their respective languages in former colonies, and, in that sense, the term *postcolonial* is semantically weakened: there is little *post-* about it in the language stakes.

At the local linguistic level, things are not so clear-cut: where people are in contact in multilingual societies, languages are in contact. For instance, in Camfranglais, a French-based 'mixed language' popular with Francophone youths in Cameroon's north, the sources of the variety extend from English to Cameroon Pidgin English to local languages. The unification of French Cameroun (République du Cameroun, which gained independence 1 January 1960) and English Cameroons (independent 1 October 1961 as the Federal Republic of Cameroon) in 1972 as a bilingual United Republic of Cameroon (simply the Republic of Cameroon since 1984), with official French and English, has seen the rapid rise of French- and English-based contact varieties in the Francophone north and Anglophone south. Camfranglais is often characterized as among the emerging "urban youth varieties" (such as, for instance, Sheng in Nairobi, Kenya) intimately linked to popular culture, and is itself shaped by and open to hybridity. Thus the American English (Black English/BVE/AAVE) clipping *bro* (< *brother*) and *bago* (< *Sebago*, the American shoe brand, here denoting any expensive shoe) show the increasing influence of American pop culture. The following examples of Camfranglais give a sense of the range of pidginization, or at least language mixing, that occurs in a French-based variety in active contact with Cameroon Pidgin English and Cameroonian English:

> *One day all le mot va know ce que vous faites back-back* ["One day everybody will know that you're up to no good"]
> *Courage bro, tu fais du bon boulot* ["Courage bro, you're doing a good job"]
> *ils sont go à l'hôtel* ["they are going to the hotel"]
> *Les wats exploitent trop l'Afrique* ["The whites exploit so much of Africa"]
> *Wat, c'est how?* ["white (man), how's it going?"]
> *Je work au ministère du travail* ["I work for the Ministry of Labor"]
> *Je know cook le sanga* ["I know how to cook sanga" (Cameroonian stewed dish of maize and ground cassava leaves)] (Fonkoua 2015, 77, 84, 101, 182, 243, 245, 250)

Les wats exploitent trop l'Afrique and *ils sont go à l'hôtel* are primarily (West African) French with lexical borrowing from English; *les wats* 'the whites' records the local pronunciation that has undergone monophthongization (smoothing) [waɪts] > [wɑts], while go has been inserted into the verb phrase as a zero-inflection participle *sont go* ('are go' = 'are going'). The level of borrowing from English increases in the colloquial greeting *Wat, c'est how?*, which resembles more Pidgin English, while *Je know cook le sanga* uses English for the verb phrase but marks it more in line with French usage (*savoir cuisiner* 'know how to cook' > *know cook*). The sentence *One day all le mot va know ce que vous faites back-back* is a more thorough-going mixture, and may indicate a speaker more fluent (or familiar) with the official languages of Cameroon (French and English) and pidgin: *le mot* is not French 'word' but a borrowing from local language Duala meaning 'people, crowd'; *back-back* is a local pidgin reduplicated form. A contrast can readily be made with Cameroon Pidgin English:

I di rait leta dem ["He/she is writing letters," with resumptive pronoun *dem* "them"]
A wan go fo ton ["I want to/would like to go to town"]
man we i di pas fo rot ["the man who is crossing the road"]
I bai kain-kain clus dem ["He/she bought several/many kinds of clothes"] (Schröder 2013, 188–91)

The form *di* in the first and third examples is an aspect marker, likely used to mark habituality and progressivity (SPCL I: 188): *di* in *di rait* = 'is writing' marks the progressive aspect, as it does in *man we i di pas fo rot*, which is, very literally, *man* ('the man') + *we* (relative marker, 'who') + *i* (3rd singular pronoun, 'he,' used resumptively) + *di pas* ('is passing/crossing') + *fo* ('for,' usual West African non-rhotic pronunciation) + *rot* ('road,' final consonant devoiced). The pidgin examples clearly involve greater simplification at the grammatical level while still involving internally consistent rules (within the pidgin); the Camfranglais examples are more of the 'mixed language' variety, generally involving knowledge of the standard varieties (if in colloquial forms). The contrast also serves to point out just how complicated, and *living*, these day-to-day linguistic interactions are in multilingual postcolonial societies in which globalizing popular culture meets and hybridizes on the local level.

The Portuguese-based Creole of Cape Verde/Cabo Verde, an island nation off the west coast of Africa (nearest to Senegal), has put down roots in the New England region of the United States, particularly the Boston area and Fall River, Massachusetts. Over 350,000 Cape Verdeans have emigrated to the United States since the beginning of the 19th century, many working in the former whaling and current fishery industries. With them have come their varieties of Kriolu/Kriol, which have undergone partial lexification by English in the United States, as school systems, such as the Boston Public Schools system, have employed 'dual-language' education models (and now there is the Haitian Creole Program, which has increased in numbers of learners in recent decades[3]). While Portuguese had been the sole official language of Cape Verde, the Creole was widely spoken and seen as an integral part of Cape Verdean 'Creole' identity. Constitutional reforms led to the new 2010 Constitution (Constituição da República de Cabo Verde), which re-asserts the official status of Portuguese but also "promotes the conditions for the officialization of the Cape Verdean mother-tongue [Kriolu] on par with the Portuguese language" (Article 9.1-2: "1. É língua oficial o Português. 2. O estado promove as condições

[3] Surpassing the Cape Verdean Creole programs in the city's "Dual Language/Two Way Bilingual Programs" (https://www.bostonpublicschools.org/Page/5735); the 2010 major earthquake in Haiti spurred increased immigration into the United States from Haiti during the continuing reconstruction period; Tara García Mathewson, "How Discrimination Nearly Stalled a Dual-Language Program in Boston," *The Atlantic* 7 April 2017 (online).

para a oficialização da língua materna cabo-verdiana, em paridade com a língua portuguesa"). The Santiago version of Kriolu (Ilha de Santiago, Cabo Verde) is the predominant form of the Creole spoken in the United States (Lang 2013, 3–11); as the Verdean community is relatively circumscribed geographically (mainly in New England, and mainly the Eastern Massachusetts–Boston area), interaction and bilingualism with English are high and can be expected to have more than just lexical effects on the Creole.

The ultimate African origins of Portuguese-based Cape Verdean Kriolu/Kriol and Guinea-Bissau Creole and Spanish-based Papiamentu (spoken in the "ABC islands" Aruba, Bonaire, and Curaçao in the Caribbean) link back to English with the formative influence of Upper Guinea Creole and Gulf of Guinea Creole on broader West African pidgins and Creoles in the 17th and 18th centuries, and the rise of Portuguese-based contact varieties such as Santome and Angolar (Hagemeijer 2011; Hagemeijer 2013, 50–58; Maurer 2013, 59–71). While relatively few English words made their way into these Portuguese-based varieties, English colonies and slave-trading stations were nearby, and the zone of linguistic interaction in West Africa explains the appearance of Portuguese, Spanish, and Dutch in the English-based pidgins and Creoles of West Africa and the Caribbean. The influence of English on these Portuguese-, Spanish-, French-, and Dutch-based contact varieties has been increasing in the late colonial and postcolonial periods, for the variety of reasons seen so far: the turnover in colonial administrations, transfer of colonial possessions by treaty (Saint Lucia from France to Britain, the Philippines from Spain to the United States), growth in political clout of the Anglo-American alliance, use of English as a lingua franca in international organizations, and the contemporary power of, in particular, American popular culture – American hip-hop's far-reaching appeal through the Caribbean and across Africa and beyond in a way inverts the original colonial journey. The complexity of the interactions means it is not always possible to trace the source or direction of influence; one small example from Spanish-based Papiamentu might stand in for many others: the expression *Mashá danki*, 'many thanks,' is a blend in place of Spanish *muchas gracias*: the *danki* is clearly from Germanic, and more likely English *thanks* than Dutch *bedankt* (Goilo 1997, 127).

Similar to Mauritius, the Cape Verde islands were uninhabited until the Portuguese landed (in 1456 in this instance); Cape Verde is also a Creole nation, the majority of the population descendants of European settlers and enslaved African people brought to the islands from West Africa by the Portuguese. Cape Verde looks both to Africa and Portugal, while the case of Mauritius is perhaps even more complex – succeeding waves of European colonization, importation of African slaves, then of Indian indentured laborers, so that, in a sense, Mauritius looks to Europe, Africa, and South Asia: it is a nation of the Indian Ocean between Africa and Asia in a number of senses. Mauritius joined the Southern African Development Community (SADC) in 1995, three years after the organization's founding. Its signing on with the SADC is often given as one of the reasons for the increase in the teaching and use of English in Mauritius, as Anglophone nations predominate among the 16 member states of the SADC, though the intergovernmental organization employs French, Portuguese, and Swahili in addition to English in its operations.

SADC member states and their official languages

Angola: Portuguese (Umbundu, Chokwe, and other local languages are used in broadcasting and government communications)
Botswana: English and Tswana
Comoros: Comorian (languages in the Bantu family), French, and Arabic
Democratic Republic of the Congo: French (national status was given also to Kikongo, Lingala, Swahili, and Tshiluba)
Eswatini (eSwatini/Swaziland): siSwati and English
Lesotho: Sesotho and English
Madagascar: Malagasy and French
Malawi: English and Chichewa
Mauritius: English, French, and Mauritian Creole
Mozambique: Portuguese
Namibia: English
Seychelles: French, English, and Kriol
South Africa: English, Afrikaans, Ndebele, Sepedi, Sesotho, Swazi, Tsonga, Tswana, Venda, Xhosa, and Zulu
Tanzania: Swahili and English
Zambia: English, Bemba, Kaonde, Lozi, Lunda, Nyanja, and Tonga (Chitonga)
Zimbabwe: English, Chewa, Chibarwe, Kalanga, Koisan (Tshwao/Tjwao), Nambya, Ndau, Ndebele, Shangani, Shona, Sotho, Tonga, Tswana, Venda, Xhosa, and Zimbabwean sign language

11.3 THE MIDDLE EAST, CAUCASUS, AND CENTRAL ASIA

Turkey 12,178,000 (Turkish, Kurdish, and Arabic)
Syria 3,781,000 (Arabic, Levantine Arabic, Armenian, Assyrian, Aramaic, and French)
Lebanon 2,618,000 (Arabic, Levantine Arabic, and French)
Israel 7,150,000 (Israeli Hebrew, Arabic, and Russian)
Jordan 3,621,000 (Arabic and Jordanian Arabic)
Iraq 13,527,000 (Arabic, Kurdish, Turkmen, Syriac, and Armenian)
Iran 32,384,000 (Farsi/Persian, Armenian, Azeri, and Arabic)
Saudi Arabia 3,291,000 (Arabic, Najdi Arabic, Hejazi Arabic, Gulf Arabic; large numbers of guest workers speaking Tagalog, Urdu, and Punjabi); the figure is likely significantly higher given the rapid growth in English-language private schools, American and British, in the nation
Kuwait 3,194,000 (Arabic, Kuwaiti Arabic, French, and Farsi/Persian [Ajam community])
Bahrain 1,070,000 (Arabic, Bahraini Arabic, and Balochi)
Qatar 1,838,000 (Arabic, Qatari Arabic, Farsi/Persian, and numerous guest worker languages from Pakistan, India, and the Philippines)
United Arab Emirates 8,575,000 (Arabic and Emirati Arabic)

Oman 3,931,000 (Arabic, Omani Arabic, Gulf Arabic, other dialects of Arabic, and Swahili)
Yemen 2,530,000 (Arabic, Yemeni Arabic, Mehri, Soqotri, and Razihi)

Georgia 195,200 (figure is likely higher as Georgia replaced Russian as the nation's second language with English; Georgian, Russian, Abkhaz, Mingrelian, Svan, and other Kartvelian languages)
Armenia 1,215,000 (Armenian, Russian, French, and Azeri)
Azerbaijan 1,500,000 (Azeri, Russian, and Armenian)

Kazakhstan 907,000 (Kazakh and Russian)
Uzbekistan 1,536,000 (Uzbek and Russian)
Turkmenistan 275,000 (Turkmen, Russian, and Uzbek)
Kyrgyzstan 429,000 (Kyrgyz, Russian, and Uzbek)
Tajikistan 442,000 (Tajik, Russian, and Uzbek)

English has grown in use quite significantly in many of the post-Soviet republics since 1991, and besides the usual arguments for its study, its various forms of utility, and the international connections it offers, an additional reason has emerged: it is not Russian. While Russia has since 1991 sought to maintain use of the language in its former Tsarist and Soviet domains, and not without some success (Cyrillic is still used for some of the languages of the "stans," and significant Russian populations remain in Central Asia), English has gained ground, with linguistic and geopolitical consequences (the war between Russia and Georgia in August 2008 is not unrelated, nor is the ongoing Ukraine crisis). And modern Russia has been militarily resurgent and an energy giant Western Europe (Germany in particular) depends upon for natural gas in the winter; Russia outmaneuvered the United States and NATO on several occasions in the Balkans (the Pristina airport "incident" in 1999), in Georgia in 2008 (where tensions continue), and to the great embarrassment of the Obama administration, in Syria and the Crimea. But the geopolitical context may be one of the major factors promoting the shift to English: the desire to join the EU (as on the part of Turkey and Georgia; the latter was granted candidate status in 2023, but the process was put on hold in 2024), draw close to or enlist the help of NATO, gain access to western energy markets (the list of claimants here is long, from Azerbaijan to Kazakhstan, though China is an emerging major customer), open up educational opportunities abroad, and buffer the influence of the "Russian bear." Political and territorial tensions of course lead to international negotiations and brokered deals, and, as with the UN, much of the proceedings can be conducted in English. This has, in turn, led to refusals to use English by national or other leaders as a sign of defiance or pride, or of parity with the Anglo-American alliance. Vladimir Putin, who speaks German (he was a KGB agent in Dresden, then in East Germany, 1985–1990) and English (well enough to correct translators), routinely speaks only Russian to the international press.

In the wake of its 2008 war with Russia, Georgia began to promote the teaching of English in its school system (the only official language of the country is Georgian); as one student, Tekla Iordanishvili of Tbilisi, interviewed in a *New York Times* article, noted, "English is the international language, we need it."[4] Similar sentiments can be heard across the broad region, from Turkey (with its important role in NATO, though EU membership seems unlikely: accession talks with the EU were suspended in February 2019) through the Levant to the Gulf, and from the Caucasus to the "stans" (Turkmenistan, Uzbekistan, Kazakhstan, Kyrgyzstan, and Tajikistan), the desire for economic and political integration drives a demand for English-language education. Even in Iran, with suspended relations with many nations after the deposition of the Shah in 1979 during the Islamic revolution, the demand for English is strong. The association of English with opportunity, connection, and modernization is the usual explanation; in the case of Iran, there may be a generational shift in a nation demographically young; and there is an earlier tradition of association with the west, of elite education in western universities and consumption of western luxury goods (French and English were both popular second-language objects of study in the Shah's Iran). Most of the nations in the region are Muslim-majority or Islamist (at the governmental or constitutional level), and an additional matter with the learning and use of English is to what extent the English language entails 'westernization'; the answer seems variable and dependent upon the particular nation, though a number of governments in the region have at times denounced, in their public pronouncements, or even enshrined in their constitutions or policies, 'western' influence. But another answer has been suggested in the case of Pakistan, officially Islamic, in which the use of English "represents Islamic values and embodies South Asian Islamic sensitivities" (Mahboob 2009, 188; Mahboob 2013, 9–11, extends similar observations to English use in Saudi Arabia). The use of Arabic in local production of English for religious matters is seen as asserting Islamic values; use of Arabic in a religious context while speaking English is common for Anglophone Muslims the world over: *Allah* for 'God,' the greeting *As-salamu Aleikum*. This is a natural process of contact and loan development; early loans to English deriving from Hebrew (*amen*, *Eden*, *cherub*, and *seraph*) came with the conversion to Christianity (from AD 597 onward); loans from the later medieval period on came also from English Jewry and the practice of Judaism in England. The vocabularies of Hinduism and Buddhism have brought several hundred loans to English from Sanskrit, Prakrit, and Pali; more recently, a different, popular focus on yoga has brought the Sanskrit lexicon of the 'discipline' (which is what the Sanskrit means – literally *yoga* is 'yoked') to English.

Although roughly half of the 1.1 million foreign students (pre-covid[5]) who attend American universities come from just two nations, China and India, some 80,000 come from the Middle East (the figure for the United Kingdom is 27,500). The exposure to English in these nations normally occurs in private secondary schools. Kuwait, Qatar, the UAE, and Saudi Arabia have a number of American and British English-language and

[4] Clifford J, Levy, "Memo from Tbilisi: Still Fighting Russia, This Time with Words," *The New York Times* 23 January 2011 (online). The piece was echoed by Reuters and other news agencies and the following year in the online *Voice of America* piece by James Brooke, "English Replaces Russian as Top Foreign Language of Study in Ex-Soviet Georgia," *VOA News* 17 October 2012, which may indicate a US-backed policy.

[5] Elizabeth Redden, "International Student Numbers Decline," *Inside Higher Ed* 16 November 2020 (online).

bilingual "high schools" (to use the American term) that prepare students for study abroad at Anglophone universities. An interesting detail in Saudi Arabia and the Gulf states is the number of well-regarded Indian schools offering English-language curricula; the large number of guest workers from South Asia led to the creation of schools for the children of South Asian guest workers, and a number of these schools are quite upscale, such as the highly ranked Kuwait Indian School in Kuwait City's Jeleeb al-Shuyoukh district. A number of "International" schools in the region offer instruction in AmE or BrE, where once BrE was dominant (and of higher prestige); the American International School in Kuwait City is highly ranked, while the Al-Alameen International School in Saudi Arabia receives top marks and is based on a British educational model. The English language has a mixed legacy in the region; there was British involvement in "protectorates" in Egypt (in total, a period of 1882–1956), Palestine (1920–1948), and Transjordan (1921–1946), and campaigns in and/or occupations of Afghanistan, Syria, Iraq, and Aden (Yemen). Military and colonial occupation was one vector for the introduction of English, and it remains so with British military participation in the more recent American-led wars in Afghanistan and Iraq, not to mention various other proxy and police actions (from Syria to Yemen). Trade is another, especially the tremendous growth of the oil industry in the region since the 1920s – the predominant trade link between the Middle East and not just the west but the rest of the world. The global travel networks have made study abroad much easier for university students, and it is in this area that the acquisition of English has accelerated most rapidly. Perhaps confirming the fears of more conservative Arab and Islamic leaders of the region, Anglophone pop culture has landed in the Middle East, especially American hip-hop and Hollywood. The exchange has been lopsided, with English forms being absorbed by Arabic, but there is some movement in the other direction – Arabic slang in local English is making its way (such as *obreeza* for 'police'). The linguistic influence of Muslim immigrants to Britain, the United States, and other Anglophone countries has affected mainly only the lexicon and raised the profile of existing Arabic loans to English (*al-athan/azan* [call to prayer], *burqa*, *Eid* [*Eid al-Fitr*, *Eid al-Adha*], *fatwa*, *hajj*, *halal*, and others; Mohideen 2007). Mobile/smartphone and social media culture is exceedingly popular among Middle Eastern youth, and one sees now not just code-switching, or 'linguistic hybridity,' between English and standard Arabic (Hopkyns et al. 2020), but between compressed, colloquial (often American) English and local dialectal varieties (such as Khaleeji in Kuwait and Emirati in Dubai) and their slang (Dashti 2015, 30–31). One of the least studied parts of the 'expanding circle' of Global Englishes in Kachru's model (Mahboob 2013), English in the Middle East is likely to grow significantly with the younger generations increasingly electing or being required to learn it (for the case of Jordan, see Hamdan and Abu Hatab 2009).

Unique to the region is the case of Israel. The modern state, founded in 1948, launched one of if not the most successful language revival programs in history: the use of modern Israeli Hebrew is testimony to determination in language planning. Palestinian Arabic is spoken by Israeli Arabs, while English and Russian are the next most common languages (Russian from the large-scale post-Soviet *aliyah* of Russian Jews). English is very widely spoken by Israelis, estimates running as high as 85%; no other nation in the broader Middle East has so high a figure, and some of the reasons are peculiar to Israel alone. American Jews played an instrumental role in the foundation and funding of modern Israel, and have continued vigorous fundraising campaigns (and lobbying of the American government). As with many American ethnic and religious groups, links to the homeland are shrouded in nostalgia and mythmaking; in the case of American Jews who had found refuge and success in the United States from the 1890s through the 1930s, an attachment to the Zionist cause took on a dire urgency with the Holocaust. At the linguistic level, the broad cultural impact of Yiddish on American English (not just on vocabulary, but on the American sense of humor and comedy) was felt also in Israel (with some 250,000 Yiddish speakers) as nearly a third of Israelis are Ashkenazim (from Germany, Poland, and Russia, but also from Britain, the United States, France, and other countries). For Israelis, English is not just a necessary international language of diplomacy (few nations have been as beset with negotiations and accords and cease-fires as Israel) but a link to its largest international backer, the United States. And when an Israeli politician wants to speak to the world, it is in English. Prime Minister Benjamin Netanyahu is often noted for his fluent (American-accented) English; he had lived in Philadelphia in his early years of schooling while his father, Benzion, taught at Dropsie College, and he had returned to the United States to attend the Massachusetts Institute of Technology. And when many Arab leaders wish to make an appeal to the international community, they too use English, and many of these leaders have themselves been educated at British and American universities (King Abdullah II of Jordan had attended elite Deerfield Academy in Massachusetts, Pembroke College, Oxford, and Georgetown University in Washington, DC). And while an earlier generation of Arab leaders had spoken with an RP British accent, one now can also hear American-accented English. The phonological traits of Israeli English and the "Israeli accent" (i.e., that of *sabras*, Israel-born Jews) are shared to an extent by Yiddish: the German-based Creole strongly influenced phonologically and lexically by Hebrew. The fricatives ר (*resh*), a voiced uvular fricative (but also realized as a rhotic consonant, an alveolar trill or tap), and ח (*hēth*), a voiceless uvular fricative, when transferred to the production of English, give the Israeli accent that "guttural" quality, being pronounced at the back of the throat. This is a characteristic already noted earlier for Yiddish, which has been, especially in the New York metropolitan region, a highly productive source of loanwords to American English (and thence to other varieties).

11.4 LATIN AMERICA

Mexico 32,563,000 (if including first-generation immigrants to the United States, temporary and seasonal workers, perhaps another 20–25 million speakers can be added to the total [with some inevitable overlap]; Spanish, major Mayan language populations, many speakers of indigenous languages in Uto-Aztecan and other indigenous families)

Guatemala 1,697,000 (Spanish, though population is majority indigenous, especially speakers of Mayan languages)

Honduras 829,000 (Spanish and indigenous languages)

El Salvador 616,000 (Spanish and indigenous languages)

Nicaragua 311,000 (to which could be added perhaps 30,000 speakers of the English-based Creole along the Miskito coast; Spanish and indigenous languages)

Costa Rica 640,000 (Spanish and indigenous languages)
Panama 405,000 (recent education initiatives have likely pushed this figure higher; Panamanian Spanish the dominant language, some 400,000 people speak indigenous languages)
Colombia 2,455,000 (To which may be added speakers of English-based San Andrés Creole; Spanish is the majority language, also numerous native languages in Arawakan, Chibchan, and other families)
Venezuela 1,596,000 (Spanish, native languages in Arawakan, Cariban, and other families; Italian)
Ecuador 830,000 (an indigenous/mestizo majority nation; Spanish is official though some 2.3 million or more people speak an indigenous language, especially varieties of Quechua)
Peru 1,607,000 (Spanish, Quechua, and Aymara have official status, with some 20% of the population speaking an indigenous language natively)
Suriname 510,000 (English-based Sranan Tongo may be added to the total; Dutch is official, also Bhojpuri Hindi and indigenous languages)
French Guiana 84,900 (French, French-based Kriyòl, and native languages)
Brazil 12,682,000 (Brazilian Portuguese, German, a number of indigenous languages in Macro-Jê, Tucanoan, and other families)
Bolivia 552,000 (Spanish and a large number of indigenous languages are all official; to the latter belong major native languages such as Aymara, Guaraní, and Quechua)
Paraguay 340,000 (Spanish and Guaraní are co-official)
Uruguay 345,000 (Spanish and Portuñol [term for Spanish-Portuguese mixed varieties in northeast Uruguay])
Chile 1,830,000 (Chilean Spanish, Mapuche, Quechua, and Rapa Nui)
Argentina 9,292,000 (Spanish [Rioplatense], Italian, German, Portuñol, Welsh [Patagonia], native languages of Quechuan, Tupi-Guaraní, Mataco-Guaicuru, and other families)

The war in the Falklands, April to June of 1982, might be seen as one of the last of the colonial contests between Spain and Britain, a conflict seemingly inconceivable some four decades later (if only in terms of advances in surveillance capabilities). The English-speaking islands remain under the British flag, and Argentina has weathered a number of other political crises since the fall of its *junta* (one of many loanwords from Spanish to English), and one oddity of the conflict is that the islands sit offshore Patagonia, a region of the Southern Cone nations of Chile and Argentina settled in part by Welsh and English farmers. A few thousand Welsh speakers still survive in Patagonia, and place-names (some since Hispanicized or re-Hispanicized) record the "Welsh colony" of the late 19th and early 20th centuries (Cwm Hyfryd, 'lovely valley,' Trelew, Trevelin, and others; the Río Chubut was called *Afon Camwy*, 'twisty river'). Though all of the Spanish-speaking Latin American nations – that is, most of Latin America, excepting Portuguese-speaking giant Brazil, French Guiana, Suriname, Guyana, and Belize – have Spanish-only or -primary educational systems, nearly all of them have encouraged or mandated the study of English in schooling. Though there is a long tradition of viewing the influence of English as an extension of "Yankee imperialism" (a sort of linguistic *yanquismo*), there seems to be a softening in attitudes more recently as English becomes associated with international business and education and, especially, pop culture from the "big neighbor" to the north (in one view, the study of English in Argentina and other Latin American nations may be "perceived as additive rather than hegemonic"; Porto 2014, 11). The growth in EFL teaching in Latin America reflects, in part, closer economic ties since the era of the 'Reagan Doctrine' and American interventions in Grenada (1983) and Panama (1989–1990) and operations, covert or otherwise, in Guatemala, Honduras, El Salvador, and Nicaragua in the 1980s and 1990s (the succeeding 'War on Drugs' and 'Plan Colombia' have seen involvement in Colombia, Venezuela, and other nations); and, in part, the waning of Marxist (or, in the case of Peru, Maoist) movements in Latin America has led to a political rapprochement conducive to greater cultural and educational exchange (rather than the more political and military). And there is a generational change, as younger people in Latin America have a different view of the United States and the United Kingdom, and travel and study abroad have fed a sense of English as not simply useful but desirable. The varieties of English spoken in Latin America are naturally most significantly influenced by transfers from Spanish phonology (as seen earlier with Spanish and English in 19th-century United States). The continued growth of large Spanish-speaking populations in the United States is now the primary crucible for English–Spanish linguistic interaction (some Spanish-speaking communities had always been present, others were added later by treaties such as that of Guadalupe Hidalgo [1848] at the end of the Mexican–American War): beyond the border, these Spanish-speaking communities still see the language-attrition pattern of the "third-generation hypothesis" (and it seems to be accelerating), but continued immigration has so far partly replenished the numbers of Spanish-speakers. The varieties of interactions are dependent upon the varieties themselves: of English *and* Spanish. Mexican Spanish has long been dominant in the Southwest, with the complication of the Manitos in New Mexico, whose 'Spanish' Spanish has been encroached upon by more recent Mexican Spanish-speaking arrivals; Puerto Rican Spanish was at home in the 'Nuyorican' and *Boricua* areas of Manhattan, the Bronx, and Brooklyn, though Dominican Spanish has a growing presence in 'Spanish Harlem' and Washington Heights in upper Manhattan. Mexican immigrants had through the 1990s and first decades of the 21st century moved well beyond the Southwest heartland to Chicago ("Michoachigoan," after the number of arrivals hailing from Mexico's Michoacán state), Kansas City, Pennsylvania (Lancaster and Reading), and the Carolinas, for work in agriculture, meat-packing, and construction, though there is some flow back to the Southwest in recent years. This new era of English and Spanish *en contacto* will be turned to in the next chapter as one of the signal influences upon American English in the 21st century.

11.5 VARIETY AND IDENTITY

In Africa, the postcolonial linguistic choices are made more complicated by the needs of economic development and international communication. Africa's rising profile in international business is fueled by the very same thing that set off the 'Scramble for

Africa' in 1885 (and over a millennium earlier with the Arab conquests) – the great abundance of natural resources (coltan and rare earth metals now in the scramble for the materials needed in global cell/mobile phone production). The older scramble for diamonds and gold continues unabated (the modern English collocations *blood diamond* or *conflict diamond* are used to refer to exploitative extraction of the gem from current or former war zones in such nations as Angola, the DRC, Liberia, and Sierra Leone). The United Nations has been actively involved in a number of 'peace-keeping missions' throughout the continent; the bureaucracy-heavy organization, with English and French still as its official languages, creates acronyms for its operations, and these include the following recent missions:

MINUSCA: UN Multidimensional Integrated Stabilization Mission in the Central African Republic
MINUSMA: UN Multidimensional Integrated Stabilization Mission in Mali
UNISFA: UN Interim Security Force for Abyei (Sudan–South Sudan border area)
UNMISS: UN Mission in South Sudan
MONUSCO: UN Organization Stabilization Mission in the Democratic Republic of the Congo
UNAMID: African Union–United Nations Mission in Darfur
MINURSO: UN Mission for the Organization of a Referendum in Western Sahara

The checkered career of UN peacekeeping missions around the world was exacerbated by the absolute disaster of the Rwanda mission in 1994, which resulted in actual genocide (a term whose creation was seen earlier). In fact, the Rwandan genocide, along with the charge that the Srebrenica massacre the following year in Bosnia rose to meet the definition of the term, gave new semantic life to *genocide* and the 1948 UN "Convention on the Prevention and Punishment of the Crime of Genocide" (General Assembly Resolution 260), a term freighted with the weight of its origins in the Holocaust. Hesitation to "use the term," under the US administrations of Bill Clinton, George W. Bush, and Barack Obama, was no doubt dogged by measuring up any contemporary program of killing with those in WWII for which Raphael Lemkin had created the term. There was also the matter of the "Responsibility to Protect" doctrine promoted by Samantha Power, a former member of the National Security Council and US Ambassador to the UN in President Obama's second term. The English–French linguistic duopoly of the UN overlaps very neatly with the postcolonial linguistic situation of Africa: much of the continent is still divided between Anglophone and Francophone spheres, and foreign political, economic, and military intervention, often under the auspices of the UN and its WHO, or NGOs such as Médecins sans Frontières/Doctors Without Borders, continues along a French/Anglo-American axis (France's ongoing "Operation Barkhane" in the Sahel, the US establishment of AFRICOM [United States Africa Command] in 2007). The choice of postcolonial African nations in the period 1951 to present between what has been called *endoglossic* (languages from within the nation, indigenous) and *exoglossic* (from outside, foreign, former colonial languages; Wolff 2000, 342) national language policies has had results not unlike those in other postcolonial nations – local differences certainly obtain, but sentiments about abandoning English expressed in newly independent India (with which the previous chapter began) could be heard in a number of African nations. So President Jomo Kenyatta's declaration in 1970 of Swahili as Kenya's national language in place of English; and, as *The New York Times* report dryly observed: "Last month Robert Matano, secretary general of the party and Assistant Minister of State in President Jomo Kenyatta's Government issued a directive – in English – stating that Swahili would become Kenya's national language."[6] The economic 'apron strings' of the mother country tied former colonies to organizations of states with the former colonial power at the center; hope for a 'coattail effect' to such continued association was one reason for English and French (and in a smaller scope, Portuguese, Spanish, Dutch, and German) to continue in use in African nations. The rise of the UN and NGOs reinforced both the prestige and utility of English and French; political and economic instability reinforced the need for foreign aid and even intervention. What has been, in some respects, the re-binding of former colonies to the colonial power in Africa has become at times a two-way street, with the new elites able "to control replenishment of their own ranks" by linking 'upward social mobility' to the use of 'foreign' languages such as French and English (Wolff 2000, 342). In many of these nations, French and English are the L1 of a very small percentage of the population – it is L2 use that can see millions of speakers. And most of these nations require higher education, if not also primary and secondary education, to be conducted in one of these languages (with English starting to pull ahead of French in terms of frequency of requirement in education and prestige). French and English also allow for the increasingly valued (and common) study abroad; in the colonial era, elites and future bureaucrats would be educated abroad or at French- or English-language colleges in-country. Now study abroad is nearly *de rigueur* and an important source of exchange and revenue for American and British universities (a similar pattern obtains for countries of the Middle East, especially the Gulf States).

The maintenance and expansion of French and especially English in Africa has yet other explanations. As mentioned before, English is the language of international protest, the surest way to get a sound bite-like placard on the international news, to codify a country's present political struggle officially as an "issue" in the eyes of the international community (as seen through those of the BBC or CNN). But a plurality of African governments have chosen one or another colonial language as their official or national language, and a majority have chosen a language policy of one former colonial language plus one or more local languages. As Africa is home to over 1,000 languages, bilingualism, even multilingualism, is a matter of course. If the use of French or English may be seen in some ways as an extension of the colonial past, it has also been seen by many African governments as a way forward, if not always a fully satisfactory compromise. The late Kofi Annan was the seventh Secretary General of the United Nations (1997–2006), his acrolectal Ghanaian English the hallmark of an accomplished career diplomat whose tenure at the UN was marked by successes (he was awarded the 2001 Nobel Peace Prize jointly with the UN) and failures (the UN failure in Rwanda foremost among them, though various corruption scandals surrounded the organization as well). But in a sense, African English had arrived

[6] "Swahili Declared Kenya's Language," *The New York Times* 10 May 1970 (online).

on the global stage with the advancement of Secretary General Annan. The international media has a tendency to broadcast more widely UN debates and pronouncements conducted in English, a pattern that also occurs with the Olympic Games/Les Jeux Olympiques (which, like the UN, has French and English with the host country's major language as its official languages). The use by much of Africa of French and English as *lingua francas* has obvious economic, political, and cultural applications: participation in international organizations, peacekeeping forces and disaster relief missions, and organizations of economic cooperation; the chance to be better heard in the international media (and to understand what is being said in return); broader visibility for African artists – many of the film productions in Francophone and Anglophone Africa are collaborative productions. In this last area, Africa had lagged behind much of the rest of the world; Chad's first homegrown feature-film production was Mahamet Saleh Haroun's *Abouna* ("Our Father") from 2002, in which the first voice heard in the soundtrack is a radio announcer on French shortwave radio. Now Nigeria comes third globally in the number of film productions per year – many are digital productions seen on streaming services (on television or even on mobile phones), but the rise of Nigerian film-making is such that it has garnered the soubriquet 'Nollywood.' The list of African Nobel laureates in literature tells in brief form the past century of African colonial and postcolonial history, from Francophone Albert Camus (born in Algeria; Nobel in 1957) to Egyptian Naguib Mahfouz (1988; his novels were written in Arabic, though a good part of his fame abroad was from translations into English) to Nigerian Wole Soyinka (Nobel in 1986) and South Africans Nadine Gordimer (1991) and J.M. Coetzee (2003), all of whom wrote in English. It may be pointed out that Soyinka is the only Black African writer in that group of Nobel laureates, but this is unlikely to stand long, as the eyes of the Anglophone literary world have been turned to Africa, Asia, and the rest of the world as literature curricula have broadened in the university systems and the demand for global Anglophone literature (and translations into English of other world literatures) has increased. A look at the Booker Prize awards and shortlists of recent years is one indication of future trends.

And this gets to the matter of linguistic identity. One of the signal innovations of sociolinguistics in the last 50 years has been the investigation of the role of language in expressing and shaping identity. The utility of the language variety one speaks can be a matter of good fortune (one's own variety if standard, or prestigious), or compulsion (the simple economic, educational, and social need to speak a standard variety, of one's own language or the dominant language). The link between one's identity and language variety may seem quite natural to some speakers: they may be comfortable in their own variety, as it is the standard, or it serves its purposes well enough for their particular line of work or social community. The matter of overt and covert prestige seen earlier has produced the phenomenon of 'downspeak,' employed by those of the most prestigious registers and economic strata who want to sound less privileged or to have the 'street smarts' their particular zip/post code did not naturally have on offer; a pastime of the popular and tabloid press is to expose the 'posh' backgrounds of musicians, athletes, politicians, and others whose identity is based on hard-luck stories that are the result of self-fashioning or dreamt up by promoters and publicists. Linguistic identity can be a very fluid and subjective register of a person's overall identity, which is an even more subjective register of human experience. Though it can shape linguistic expression profoundly, it is not a matter so easily treatable by theoretical linguists as can be more abstract phenomena such as syntactic representation (and this explains some of the distance, say, between a Chomskyan generative framework and socio- and ethnolinguistic fieldwork). The classification of contact varieties as acrolectal, mesolectal, and basilectal is of course not just a measure of the variety's closeness (acrolectal) or distance (basilectal) from the standard form of the base language, but a social measure too. Basilectal forms can seem more 'genuine' or 'authentic' to speakers who do not see themselves (or are not seen by others) as belonging to the acrolectal social grouping. In the case of Jamaican Creole or patois, this can be a racially as well as economically and socially stratified matter:

acrolectal	it's my book	I didn't eat any
mesolectal	iz me buk	a in nyam non
basilectal	a fi mi buk dat	mi na bin nyam non
		(Wolff 2000, 329)

In both the mesolectal and basilectal versions of the latter example, English *eat* has been replaced by the West African loanword *nyam* (Allsopp 2003, 410–411; Cassidy and Le Page 2009, s.v. *nyam*). The grammar appears more nonstandard than the acrolectal Jamaican English version, and is the product of a long history of contact varieties from West African Pidgin English to the Caribbean Creoles. The shift between varieties is of course common, and can be situationally and socially conditioned; a good deal of what speakers in their native speech communities do with such variety-shifting is intuitive, done on-the-fly (which one knows when one gets it wrong). As Cassidy and Le Page noted in the introduction to their *Dictionary of Jamaican English*, "This creole speech, or dialect, is by no means homogenous. It exists in rather archaic forms in some isolated settlements, and, being always under the influence of English as the language of prestige, adapts itself in varying degrees in the usage of communities, individuals, and social levels, to standard English usage" (Cassidy and Le Page 2009, xi). Such distinctions in 'levels' of contact varieties are to be found also in dialects: income, race, ethnicity, religion, and 'sociogeography' (rural/urban, which side of the river, and so forth down to the level of neighborhood and even which parts of a neighborhood). The scale, ranging from overt prestige, those varieties embodying or close to the standard (and thereby more widely communicative in mass media and associated with economic opportunity), to covert (those less economically or socially desirable at the standard or 'high' level), is one that encompasses a broad range of social and linguistic strategies. Most speakers of a language can be said to be 'diglossic,' that is, speaking more than one variety of their language, which can be as simple as using a more formal variety for the relevant social, work, religious, and other situations that expect its use. A more relaxed speech variety may be used among family, friends, and neighbors from the same speech community. The matter is more complex with contact varieties as the degree of contact and influence is dependent upon perhaps even more factors; one such factor that needs to be taken into consideration would be the genetic relationship of the languages involved in the contact situation.

In the Caribbean, English-based contact varieties have been in contact with other colonial languages (Indo-European languages such as Spanish, French, Dutch, and Portuguese), indigenous languages (Cariban and Arawakan languages, from which a number of loanwords to English derive), and, perhaps most enduringly, West African languages – an interaction that had begun with the West African pidgins and Creoles brought by the slave trade to the Caribbean. Some of the lexification of Caribbean Creoles by Portuguese began back on the "Gold Coast" of Africa in the late 15th–16th centuries; as seen previously, early English explorers of the North American coast encountered elements of Basque and Portuguese 'nautical pidgins' in what is now New England and Atlantic Canada. Purely economic purposes generated the various trade jargons and many of the Atlantic and Pacific pidgins, which, being used for the very specific and localized purposes of exchange of goods and services, often had limited vocabularies, perhaps only in the hundreds of words as Chinese Pidgin English may have functioned for its purpose with 700–750 words (Holm 1988, vol. I, 73). Reduction of vocabulary and simplification of grammar are the norm in the varieties used in the contact situation – a form like Tok Pisin *bilong* could "express nearly every locative relationship imaginable" (Holm 1988, vol. I, 73). Persistence in the use of the contact variety and, especially, the transmission of it to other generations of speakers normally leads to an increase in complexity. If the contact situation persists even as a Creole based on the colonial or other dominant language has developed, decreolization may occur – which has been posited for African American Vernacular English: West African Pidgin English > Caribbean plantation Creoles > Gullah/Patwa/other Creoles then decreolization to varieties such as Jamaican English and AAVE; an oversimplified outline to be sure, but one proposed historical pattern. And this can also be a vector for transmission of forms from the contact variety (or languages that have lexified it). Thus, words from AAVE or Jamaican patois can be found in AmE and BrE; the former now spread globally with the tremendous popularity of African American culture (political figures and movements as well as artists and entertainers), and the latter with the new contact situations in London and other British cities with the Windrush generations. With Edgar Schneider's 'Dynamic Model' of the evolution of postcolonial Englishes (Schneider 2007, 21–70), in each of the five phases (Foundation, Exonormative stabilization, Nativization, Endonormative stabilization, and Differentiation), the second of four conditions is "identity constructions"; in this framework, as the nation moves toward independence, from an 'exonormative' state in which the standard language variety comes from abroad (the 'settlers') to an endonormative one (in which the local variety of that language grows in prestige), a sense of national unity grows that produces the call for independence. A period of "nation-building" in the movement toward and realization of independence produces a sense of unity, with the linguistic consequence that the local variety of English (and/or English-based contact variety) increases in prestige and can serve as part of that new national identity. In Schneider's fifth and last phase of evolution of postcolonial Englishes, the "Differentiation" phase, that unificd national sense can devolve back to more localized identities (ethnic, tribal, linguistic, and religious): "The citizens of a young nation no longer define themselves primarily as a single social entity in relation to the former colonial power but rather as a composite of subgroups, each being marked by an identity of its own," as "members of smaller, sociolinguistically determined groups" (Schneider

2007, 53). Schneider's "case studies" for his 'Dynamic Model' involved the nations of Fiji, Australia, New Zealand, Hong Kong, the Philippines, Malaysia, Singapore, India, South Africa, Kenya, Tanzania, Nigeria, Cameroon, Barbados, Jamaica, and Canada. This gives a range of Caribbean, Asian, and African Englishes, though one might be tempted to group Australia, New Zealand, and Canada separately as English-majority (or European-majority) settler countries. Fiji has the interesting complexity of the development of Fijian and Indo-Fijian Englishes within the nation, a pattern that obtains in Trinidad and Tobago, Guyana, South Africa, Uganda, and other former colonies to which Indian laborers were brought by indenturing or recruitment. Nigeria is singled out as "far more advanced" in the development of a "local standard form of English" than any other African nation (Schneider 2007, 211). And the case study of Canada almost entirely avoids the effects of Loi/Law 101 the Charter of the French Language and the politics of English in Québec and the strains upon Canada's official policy of bilingualism (247–250).

As influential as the 'Dynamic Model' is, there is a tendency in postmodern linguistics to treat language as an abstract phenomenon, something capable of being walled off from its speakers for analysis, which is indeed done in corpus linguistics to an extent. But a living language does not have a life apart from its speakers, and they live by and large in societies. In the examples of Fiji and South Africa (and one can add Trinidad and Uganda), there are tensions between the native populations and the descendants of Indian laborers, often based on resentment over the actual (or perceived) prosperity of the Asian communities. This resentment boiled over with disastrous repercussions when President Idi Amin of Uganda ordered the expulsion of all Asians (South Asian people, mainly from the Indian state of Gujarat) in August 1972. There is the difficult predicament of "Colored" people in South Africa, and the case of breakaway Biafra (1967–1970) in Nigeria, and that nation's continuing tensions between the Muslim north of the country and the Christian and animist south. Language planning results in language policy, and language policy can reflect and even exacerbate the fault lines in postcolonial nations (colonies were often drawn up to use these differences to effect control). An interesting development in the postcolonial moment has been the use of English, in local and international/global varieties, as not just a national *lingua franca* but as a link to the Anglo-American sphere and beyond – to the UN, to aid and development agencies, to cultural organizations, and to international corporations globally. It may be tinged with some irony, and it may seem a bitter defeat to the many postcolonial leaders who sought to get rid of English with independence, but the national and international varieties of English have served in the postcolonial period an almost linguistic peacekeeping duty. In nations that are as remarkably linguistically diverse as Nigeria or India or Papua New Guinea, English helped negotiate the "then what else?" question when it came to national language policy (one result being the African pattern of English- or French-plus-one official language policies). In nations in that "Differentiation" phase, local languages could often entail particular ethnic and religious identity: the question of "elevating" contact varieties to national languages (Papua New Guinea has done this with Tok Pisin), the language question and riots in India and the fault lines of partition (and that of Hindi-Urdu), the official status of Irish in Éire/Ireland, even the French-English divide in Canada (which can also be realized as a Protestant-Catholic divide) are examples of the difficulties in negotiating differences at the level of governance. As the use of English at the national government level could help postcolonial nations negotiate the perils of which local languages to select as official, it also linked those national governments to global governance structures – and the early years of the 21st century have witnessed a remarkable rise in attempts at globalist association, the role of the WHO in the COVID-19 crisis one example.

In the 21st century, an expanded sense of 'utility' seems to be developing; continued language contact and mixing occurs apace on social media, in 'textspeak' (rather prolifically with Taglish), and in emails, tweets, and hashtags. As social media is driven rather inexorably by visibility, popularity, 'coolness,' fad, and fashion, the utility of English in 'cyberspace' (a term that now seems dated and may be waning) is obvious – a larger audience, more 'likes,' more peer approbation (but also the risk of negative tweets, 'tweetshaming,' even dreaded 'cancelling'). The broad reach of English in cyberspace has not cancelled or crowded out local languages to any greater degree, it seems, than spoken varieties have in past centuries. But the rapid vector of transmission for the new, the latest, and the most popular offered by social media has fed the further spread of English to areas of the globe not speaking any legacy varieties of English from the colonial era or World War II military occupation or contemporary military actions or peacekeeping operations.

The 'utility' of 21st-century Englishes can very often be bound up with matters of 'identity.' The networking, outreach, 'friending' (and 'unfriending'), and, it can be said, not unfairly, grandstanding of many young users of English on social media can certainly be not just an expression of identity, but also its creation and performance. The 21st-century growth of *virtue-signaling* and ancillary *cancel culture* (in BrE, there is the phenomenon of *no-platforming* or *deplatforming*; AmE still uses *disinvite*) is encouraged but also much deplored in major media. That much of the world of *social media influencers* (or just *influencers*) is fake should come as no surprise: advertising culture has always been largely fake. The question of identity in language is vast and one of the preoccupations of sociolinguistics (Le Page and Tabouret-Keller 1985 is an important study); at no point in the history of English has the matter of identity not been of great significance – it is simply that at no other point in its history have we had such abundant evidence of its expression. This is not simply a matter of technology and the availability of data but also a cultural phenomenon. The culture of English has developed from a medieval period in which a great share of its literature remains anonymous deliberately – a cultural trait that obtains in the earliest 'pagan' Germanic period as well as in the Christian era. If the 'pagan' conception of anonymity may have something to do at times with traditional oral poets who saw themselves as belonging almost guild-like to a chain of predecessors (perhaps ironically the Old English poem *Widsith* expresses this best, if "Widsith" is actually the name of the traditionary bard [*scop*] and not simply an epithet), the Christian conception was grounded in modesty, an aversion to vainglory, and a sense that all glory belonged to God (from whom the poetic gift derived). The story of Cædmon both supports and undercuts this notion, as we have the poet's name (a Northumbrian poet with a possibly Celtic name) and the story of the poetic gift bestowed by God upon a lowly cowherd in a dream vision.

The contrast with the Renaissance could hardly be starker – that is, until the 21st century. The celebration of and preoccupation with the self is perhaps best distilled in the *selfie* (and the *gramming* of *selfies* – something for the next chapter). And yet another simultaneous trend is more in keeping with that distant medieval past: the trend-setting and trend revivals (*throwbacks*, *retro* trending, and so forth) of social media have also pointed toward collective identities and cultural expressions. One last example might help bring the matters of variety and identity together: *John Canoe.*

The tradition of *Junkanoo* (or *Jonkonnu*) is known especially from Jamaica but is found elsewhere in the Anglophone Caribbean (including Belize). The festival has more recently been localized to the Christmas season (often sometime between Boxing Day, 26 December, and New Year's) and varies in elaboration, from small street *mus-korates* (masquerades) to the "fancy dress" mummer-like parades in the Bahamas (in Jamaica, the newspaper *The Daily Gleaner*, now *The Gleaner*, has sponsored John Canoe festivals since the 1950s). The etymology of *John Canoe/Junkanoo/Jonkonnu* ranges from an 18th-century folk hero figure "John Canoe" (or "John Connú" from Axim, Ghana) to French *gens inconnus* (with reference to the masked dancers) to Ewe *dʒoŋˈkɔnu* (Le Page and Tabouret–Keller 1985, 20), Yoruba *Egungun* masquerades in which the masked dancers chase "hooligans" called *janduku* (Allsopp 2003, 320–321), or to perhaps Ewe *dzoŋˈkɔ* + *nu* 'witch doctor' (Cassidy and Le Page 2009, s.v.). John Canoe is the name for the lead dancer in a troupe of usually 11 characters, including a king and queen, the whip-bearing "Pitchy-Patchy" who keeps order between dancers and spectators (a figure in a costume of bits of cloth, occasionally banknotes or other strips of fabric or paper), *Ku-Ku* (a male dancer with a house as a headdress), a devil figure, figures in animal head masks, a heavily pregnant woman (often portrayed by a male dancer). The simpler street forms of the masquerade involve begging for money from street spectators or from drivers and passengers in passing vehicles; the more elaborate parade forms resemble more *carnaval*-like traditions. The origins of the tradition are from West Africa, from Nigeria, Ghana, and Togo, but mixed in are a variety of European influences: the "sets" and "Set-girls" from the French Caribbean, groups of girls in matching dresses and ribbons whose dances at Christmas-New Year's would be rewarded with money ("Blues and Reds" was one rivalry of sets, based on the color of the gowns; Cassidy and Le Page 2009); the Morris dances and, perhaps more closely, mumming from the British Isles (a fairly close parallel is the Mummers Parade held New Year's Day in Philadelphia). The orderly and elegant tradition of "Set-girls" belonged to the 18th and 19th centuries and came to be blended in with the more raucous John Canoe street celebration. Like all such traditions, it was in danger of fading away in the modern era,[7] but has undergone a revival in recent years: now videos of the celebrations can be found on platforms such as YouTube and on social media, and the characters, language (deriving in part from Caribbean and West African Creoles), and music and dance reach a new generation of spectators online.

[7] Paul H. Williams, "Where has Jonkanoo gone? Traditional masquerade on steady decline," *The Gleaner* 21 December 2014 (online).

John Canoe dancers: Isaac Mendez Belisario (1837), Yale Center for British Art / Public domain.

The many varieties of English worldwide can only be touched upon here in summary form, with some attempt to place the linguistic varieties in the context of their speakers – their nations, more local affiliations, other languages and varieties, cultural, religious, artistic traditions. As many of these nations are younger, both in terms of independence and in their demographics, the future holds a number of changes in store for the 'new Englishes.' And yet, as has been seen, excepting developments among contact varieties (where we see both decreolization and Creole genesis, as with Sheng in Nairobi, Kenya), major structural changes to the language have been slowing, certainly in comparison to periods such as early Middle English (ca. 1100–1250/1300) or Early Modern English (ca. 1500–1650). Sound changes continue as they will with any living language and, as we will see in the next chapter, in a Labovian framework (here referring in particular to Labov's 3-volume *Principles of Linguistic Change* and *Atlas of North American English*), they may be increasing in number and frequency and serving to spur dialectal divergence (and not just in the United States). The emphasis upon youth is not misplaced in terms of popular speech: the engine of change in youth speech, particularly but not limited to vocabulary, is popular culture. And one of the most dynamic sources and vectors of change is the globalization of African American Vernacular English and culture – in music, speech style, cultural fads, trends, and memes, few other phenomena are so influential as African American hip-hop, from NYC to Los Angeles, London to Nairobi to Hong Kong. The phenomenon may involve both celebration and appropriation, and may express protest or commoditized 'fun.' And yet it parallels nearly exactly what has always happened to English as it expanded beyond its original base: adopted willingly, or by compulsion (economic, colonial, and educational), localized and shaped by other hands, and returned to the broader language community. We will also return to developments in the original *Sprachraum* of English, to England. Pronouncements about the 'future' of English nearly always invoke the 'global' tag, and often speak of that 'expanding circle' (in Kachru's model) of World Englishes as becoming wholly independent of English (British, or Anglo-American); or, there may be speculation about a 'family of Englishes,' generated as were the Romance languages from Latin. But there are linguistic constraints to either scenario: the rise of Global Englishes is predicated upon their communicability and utility, how they connect the local variety to the other varieties and provide the linguistic link to educational, political, economic, or communicative opportunity, how they permit the local to become global. The idea of a 'family of English languages' is fascinating, but a number of differences from the Roman model obtain. English has grown so far beyond its original geographic and ethnic base (England and the English of the Anglo-Saxon [500–1100], Norman [1066–1154], and later periods) that a collapse of the home country would have all sorts of political to psychological effects, but it would not generate the consequences that 476 produced with Rome's collapse. Nor would a shift in power away from the United States. Neither of which, despite media 'clickbait' stories forecasting doom and gloom for the major powers, seems likely any time soon if at all (ethnic, racial, religious, linguistic, or political tensions seem more likely to splinter nations such as China, Indonesia, Yemen, Iran, Iraq, Syria, Turkey, Libya, Nigeria, or even Mexico before the United States or the United Kingdom). Inasmuch as forces of divergence may be leading over those of convergence, as counterintuitive as that may seem in a globalizing world, this divergence may be occurring at the level of dialect and variety within the larger system, that system being the English language. And that system may be viewed as the superordinate set, included within which are the dialects, and attached to which, at points of intersection with other linguistic systems, are English-based pidgins and Creoles. Accepting David Crystal's estimate of perhaps 2.3 billion speakers of English (as L1 and L2; Crystal 2019, 115), or even allowing a more generous estimate of 3 billion speakers (expanding the criterion of 'speaker' to more modest levels of spoken proficiency – a standard used in figures for most other languages), one is still looking at less than half the world's population (8.3 billion, a figure impossible to calculate precisely, and likely an overestimate). For all the trendiness of the 'global' label, we are still in a world that requires subtitles and are likely to remain so for the foreseeable future.

REFERENCES AND BIBLIOGRAPHY

Abdulaziz, Mohamed H. and Ken Osinde, "Sheng and Engsh: development of mixed codes among the urban youth in Kenya," *International Journal of the Sociology of Language* 125 (1997), 43–63

Aboh, Enoch O., Norval S.H. Smith, and Tonjes Veenstra, "Saramaccan," in SPCL1, *The Survey of Pidgin and Creole Languages*. Oxford: Oxford University Press, 2013, pp. 27–38

Aceto, Michael, "Eastern Caribbean English-derived language varieties: morphology and syntax," in Schneider, Edgar W., ed. *Varieties of English 2: The Americas and the Caribbean*. Berlin: Mouton de Gruyter, 2008, pp. 439–453

Aceto, Michael and Jeffrey P. Williams, eds. *Contact Englishes of the Eastern Caribbean*. Varieties of English Around the World volume G30. Amsterdam: John Benjamins, 2003

Alim, H. Samy and Geneva Smitherman. *Articulate While Black: Barack Obama, Language, and Race in the U.S.* Oxford: Oxford University Press, 2012

Allen, Richard B. *Slaves, Freedmen, and Indentured Laborers in Colonial Mauritius*. Cambridge: Cambridge University Press, 1999

Allsopp, Richard, ed. *Dictionary of Caribbean English Usage*. Kingston: University of the West Indies Press, 2003

Ansaldo, Umberto. *Contact Languages: Ecology and Evolution*. Cambridge Approaches to Language Contact. Cambridge: Cambridge University Press, 2009

APCLS = *The Atlas of Pidgin and Creole Language Structures*, ed. Susanne Maria Michaelis, Philippe Maurer, Martin Haspelmath, and Magnus Huber. Oxford: Oxford University Press, 2013

Arends, Jacques, Pieter Muysken, and Norval Smith, eds. *Pidgins and Creoles: An Introduction*. Creole Language Library, Volume 15. Amsterdam: John Benjamins, 1994

Arnold, A. James, ed. *A History of Literature in the Caribbean*. Volume 2: *English- and Dutch-Speaking Regions*. Amsterdam: John Benjamins, 2001

Austin, Peter K. and Julia Sallaband, eds, *The Cambridge Handbook of Endangered Languages*. Cambridge: Cambridge University Press, 2011

The Australian National Dictionary: Australian Words and Their Origins. 2nd ed. 2 vols. Ed. Bruce Moore. Melbourne: Oxford University Press, 2016. https://australiannationaldictionary.com.au

Ayafor, Miriam, "Cameroon Pidgin English (Kamtok): morphology and syntax," in Kortmann, Bernd and Edgar W. Schneider, eds. *A Handbook of Varieties of English. Volume 1: Phonology*. Berlin: Mouton de Gruyter, 2004, pp. 909–928

Baker, Philip and Sibylle Kriegel, "Mauritian Creole," in SPCL2 *The Survey of Pidgin and Creole Languages*, 2013, pp. 250–260

Bakker, Peter. *A Language of Our Own: The Genesis of Michif, the Mixed Cree-French Language of the Canadian Métis*. Oxford Studies in Anthropological Linguistics, vol. 10. New York: Oxford University Press, 1997

Bannerjee, Rohini, ed. *Les espaces divers de la coolitude*. London, ON: Les cahiers du GRELCEF, 2013

Bartens, Angela, "San Andres Creole English," on SPCL2 *The Survey of Pidgin and Creole Languages*, 2013, pp. 101–114

Baskaran, Loga, "Malaysian English: phonology," in Mesthrie, Rajend, ed. *Varieties of English 4: Africa, South and Southeast Asia*. Berlin: Mouton de Gruyter, 2008, pp. 278–291

Bauer, Laurie and Paul Warren, "New Zealand English: phonology," in Kortmann, Bernd and Edgar W. Schneider, eds. *A Handbook of Varieties of English*. Volume 1: *Phonology*. Berlin: Mouton de Gruyter, 2004, pp. 580–602

Bayard, Donn, "The cultural cringe revisited: changes through time in Kiwi attitudes toward accents," in Bell, Allan and Koenraad Kuiper, eds. *New Zealand English*. Amsterdam: John Benjamins, 2000, 297–324

Beal, Joan, "English dialects in the North of England: morphology and syntax," in Kortmann, Bernd and Clive Upton, eds. *Varieties of English 1: The British Isles*. Berlin: Mouton de Gruyter, 2008, pp. 114–141

Beale, Bob, "Let stalk some more Strine," *The Sydney Morning Herald* 24 October 2009 (online).

Bell, Allan and Janet Holmes, eds. *New Zealand Ways of Speaking English*. Clevedon: Multilingual Matters, 1990

Bell, Allan and Koenraad Kuiper, eds. *New Zealand English*. Varieties of English Around the World vol. G25. Amsterdam: John Benjamins, 2000

Blair, David and Peter Collins, eds. *English in Australia*. Varieties of English Around the World vol. G26. Amsterdam: John Benjamins, 2001

Blake, Renée, "Bajan: phonology," in Schneider, Edgar W., ed. *Varieties of English 2: The Americas and the Caribbean*. Berlin: Mouton de Gruyter, 2008, pp. 312–319

Bobda, Augustin Simo, "Cameroon English: phonology," in Mesthrie, Rajend, ed. *Varieties of English 4: Africa, South and Southeast Asia*. Berlin: Mouton de Gruyter, 2008, pp. 115–132

Boberg, Charles. *The English Language in Canada: Status, History and Comparative Analysis*. Studies in English Language. Cambridge: Cambridge University Press, 2010

Bowerman, Sean, "White South African English: morphology and syntax," in Mesthrie, Rajend, ed. *Varieties of English 4: Africa, South and Southeast Asia*. Berlin: Mouton de Gruyter, 2008, pp. 168–176

Bradley, David and Maya Bradley, "Changing attitudes to Australian English," in Blair, David and Peter Collins, eds. *English in Australia*. Amsterdam: John Benjamins, 2001, pp. 271–285

Breiner, Laurence A. *An Introduction to West Indian Poetry*. Cambridge: Cambridge University Press, 1998

Broderick, George. *A Handbook of Late Spoken Manx*. 3 vols. Tübingen: Max Niemeyer, 1984–1986

Buchstaller, Isabelle, Anders Holmberg, and Mohammad Almoaily, *eds. Pidgins and Creoles beyond Africa-Europe Encounters*. Creole Language Library, vol. 47. Amsterdam: John Benjamins, 2014

Burridge, Kate, "English in Australia," in Kirkpatrick, Andy, ed. *The Routledge Handbook of World Englishes*. Abingdon: Routledge, 2010, pp. 132–151

Burridge, Kate and Bernd Kortmann, eds. *Varieties of English 3: The Pacific and Australia*. Berlin: Mouton de Gruyer, 2008

Carter, Marina and Khal Torabully, eds. *Coolitude: An Anthology of the Indian Labour Diaspora*. London: Anthem Press, 2002

Cassidy, Frederic G. *Jamaica Talk: Three Hundred Years of the English Language in Jamaica*. Kingston: University of the West Indies Press, 1961/2005

Cassidy, Frederic G. and Robert B. Le Page. *Dictionary of Jamaican English*. 2nd ed. Cambridge: Cambridge University Press, 2009

Chatterton, Percy. *Say It in Motu: An Instant Introduction to the Common Language of Papua*. Buranda, Queensland: Robert Brown & Associates, 1975

Chaudenson, Robert. *Textes créoles anciens (La Réunion et Île Maurice): Comparaison et essai d'analyse.* Hamburg: Helmut Buske Verlag, 1981

Chaudenson, Robert. *Des îles, des hommes, des langues: Langues créoles, cultures créoles, cultures créoles.* Paris: Éditions L'Hamrattan, 1992

Clark, Ross, "Pidgin English and Pidgin Maori in New Zealand," in Bell, Allan and Janet Holmes, eds. *New Zealand Ways of Speaking English.* Clevedon: Multilingual Matters, 1990, pp. 97–114

Corne, Chris. *Seychelles Creole Grammar: Elements for Indian Ocean Proto-Creole Reconstruction.* Tübingen: Gunter Narr, 1977

Crowley, Terry, "Bislama: phonetics and phonology," in Burridge, Kate and Bernd Kortmann, eds. *Varieties of English 3: The Pacific and Australia.* Berlin: Mouton de Gruyer, 2008, pp. 142–163

Crystal, David. *Language Death.* Cambridge: Cambridge University Press, 2000/2014

Crystal, David, "A global language," in Seargeant, Philip and Joan Swann, eds. *English in the World: History, Diversity, Change.* Abingdon: Routledge, 2012, pp. 151–177

Crystal, David. *The Cambridge Encyclopedia of the English Language.* 3rd ed. Cambridge: Cambridge University Press, 2019

Cummings, Patrick J. and Hans-Georg Wolf. *A Dictionary of Hong Kong English: Words from the Fragrant Harbor.* Hong Kong: Hong Kong University Press, 2011

Dashti, Abdulmohsen, "The role and status of the English language in Kuwait," *English Today* 31.3 (2015), 28–33

D'Costa, Jean and Barbara Lalla, eds. *Voices in Exile: Jamaican Texts of the 18th and 19th Centuries.* Tuscaloosa: University of Alabama Press, 1989

DeBose, Charles E., "Samaná English: a dialect that time forgot," *Proceedings of the Ninth Annual Meeting of the Berkeley Linguistics Society* (1983), 47–53

Deshors, Sandra C., ed. *Modeling World Englishes: Assessing the interplay of emancipation and globalization of ESL varieties.* Varieties of English Around the World vol. G61. Amsterdam: John Benjamins, 2018

Deterding, David. *Singapore English.* Dialects of English. Edinburgh: Edinburgh University Press, 2007

Deuber, Dagmar. *English in the Caribbean: Variation, Style and Standards in Jamaica and Trinidad.* Studies in English Language. Cambridge: Cambridge University Press, 2014

Devonish, Hubert and Dahlia Thompson, "Creolese," in SPCL1, *The Survey of Pidgin and Creole Languages.* Oxford: Oxford University Press, 2013, pp. 49–60

The Dictionary of New Zealand English. Ed. H. W. Orsman. Melbourne: Oxford University Press, 1998

A Dictionary of South African English on Historical Principles: South African Words and Their Origins. Ed. Penny Silva, Wendy Dore, Dorothea Mantzel et al. Cape Town: Oxford University Press, 1996

Dixon, R.M.W. *A Grammar of Boumaa Fijian.* Chicago: University of Chicago Press, 1988

Dixon, R.M.W. *Australian Languages: Their Nature and Development.* Cambridge: Cambridge University Press, 2002

Dixon, R.M.W., "Australian Aboriginal Words in Dictionaries – A History," in *Language at Large: Essays on Syntax and Semantics*, ed. Alexandra Y. Aikhenvald and R.M.W. Dixon. Empirical Approaches to Linguistic Theory, vol. 2. Leiden: Brill, 2011. Pp. 529–553

Drechsel, Emanuel J. *Mobilian Jargon: Linguistic and Sociohistorical Aspects of a Native American Pidgin*. Oxford Studies in Language Contact. Oxford: Clarendon Press, 1997

Drechsel, Emanuel J. *Language Contact in the Early Colonial Pacific: Maritime Polynesian Pidgin before Pidgin English*. Cambridge Approaches to Language Contact. Cambridge: Cambridge University Press, 2014

DSAE. *Dictionary of South African English*. Dictionary Unit of South African English. Rhodes University, Makhanda/Grahamstown. https://dsae.co.za/

Durrleman-Tame, Stephanie. *The Syntax of Jamaican Creole: A cartographic perspective*. Linguistik Aktuell/Linguistics Today 124. Amsterdam: John Benjamins, 2008

Dutton, Tom. *Police Motu: Iena Sivarai (Its Story)*. Port Moresby: University of Papua New Guinea Press, 1985

Dutton, Tom and Dicks Thomas. *A New Course in Tok Pisin (New Guinea Pidgin)*. Pacific Linguistics, Series D, no. 67. Canberra: Department of Linguistics, Research School of Pacific Studies, Australian National University, 1985

Ekirch, A. Roger. *Bound for America: The Transportation of British Convicts to the Colonies, 1718–1775*. Oxford: Clarendon Press, 1987

Elugbe, Ben, "Nigerian Pidgin English: phonology," in Mesthrie, Rajend, ed. *Varieties of English 4: Africa, South and Southeast Asia*. Berlin: Mouton de Gruyter, 2008, pp. 55–66

Elyas, Tariq and Ahmar Mahboob, "World Englishes in the Middle East and North Africa (MENA)," *World Englishes* 40.2 (2020), 154–158

Engelberg, Stefan and Doris Stolberg, "The influence of German on the Lexicon of Tok Pisin," in Maitz, Péter and Craig A. Volker, eds. *Language Contact in the German Colonies: Papua New Guinea and beyond*, 2017, 27–64

Escure, Geneviève, "Belize and other central American varieties: morphology and syntax," in Schneider, Edgar W., ed. *Varieties of English 2: The Americas and the Caribbean*. Berlin: Mouton de Gruyter, 2008, pp. 732–762

Escure, Geneviève, "Belizean Creole," in SPCL1, *The Survey of Pidgin and Creole Languages*. Oxford: Oxford University Press, 2013, pp. 92–110

Escure, Geneviève and Armin Schwegler, eds. *Creoles, Contact and Language Change: Linguistic and social implications*. Creole Language Library, vol. 27. Amsterdam: John Benjamins, 2004

Faraclas, Nicholas, "Nigerian Pidgin," in SPCL1, *The Survey of Pidgin and Creole Languages*. Oxford: Oxford University Press, 2013, pp. 176–184

Farquharson, Joseph T., "Jamaican," in SPCL1, *The Survey of Pidgin and Creole Languages*. Oxford: Oxford University Press, 2013, pp. 81–91

Farrell, Paul, "Cronulla was home and I understood why we rioted. Now I know we were wrong," *The Guardian* 10 December 2015 (online).

Finn, Peter, "Cape Flats English: phonology," in Mesthrie, Rajend, ed. *Varieties of English 4: Africa, South and Southeast Asia*. Berlin: Mouton de Gruyter, 2008, pp. 200–222

Finney, Malcolm Awadajin, "Krio," in SPCL1, *The Survey of Pidgin and Creole Languages*. Oxford: Oxford University Press, 2013, pp. 156–166

Fonkoua, Hector Kamdem. *A Dictionary of Camfranglais*. Duisburg Papers on Research in Language and Culture, vol. 107. Frankfurt am Main: Peter Lang, 2015

Fortson, Benjamin W. IV. *Indo-European Language and Culture: An Introduction*. 2nd ed. Oxford: Blackwell, 2010

Fyle, Clifford N. and Eldred D. Jones. *A Krio-English Dictionary*. Oxford/Freetown: Oxford University Press/Sierra Leone University Press, 1980

Gibson, James R. and Alexei A. Istomin, eds. *Russian California, 1806–1860: A History in Documents*. 2 vols. Hakluyt Society Series III, vols. 26–27. London: Ashgate/The Hakluyt Society, 2014

Githinji, Peter, "Sexism and (Mis)representation of women in Sheng," *Journal of African Cultural Studies* 20.1 (2008), 15–32

Githiora, Chege, "Sheng: peer language, Swahili dialect or emerging Creole?" *Journal of African Cultural Studies* 15.2 (2002), 159–181

Goddard, Ives, ed. *Handbook of North American Indians*, vol. 17, *Languages*. Washington, DC: Smithsonian Institution, 1996

Goilo, E. R. *Papiamentu Textbook*. Tenth edition. Oranjestad, Aruba: De Wit, 1997

Gordon, Elizabeth and Marcia Abell, "'This Objectionable Colonial Dialect': historical and contemporary attitudes to New Zealand Speech," in Bell, Allan and Janet Holmes, eds. *New Zealand Ways of Speaking English*. Clevedon: Multilingual Matters, 1990, pp. 21–48

Gordon, Elizabeth, Lyle Campbell, Jennifer Hay, Margaret Maclagan, Andrea Sudbury, and Peter Trudgill, eds. *New Zealand English: Its Origins and Evolution*. Studies in English Language. Cambridge: Cambridge University Press, 2004

Gramer Kreol Morisien, vol. 1. Ed. Daniella Police-Michel, Arnaud Carpooran, and Guilhem Florigny. Phoenix, Mauritius: Akademi Kreol Morisien/Ministry of Education and Human Resources, 2012

Gut, Ulrike B., "Nigerian English: phonology," in Mesthrie, Rajend, ed. *Varieties of English 4: Africa, South and Southeast Asia*. Berlin: Mouton de Gruyter, 2008, pp. 35–54

Hackert, Stephanie, "Bahamian Creole," in SPCL1, *The Survey of Pidgin and Creole Languages*. Oxford: Oxford University Press, 2013, pp. 127–138

Hagemeijer, Tjerk, "The Gulf of Guinea Creoles: Genetic and typological models," *Journal of Pidgin and Creole Languages* 26.1 (2011), 111–154

Hagemeijer, Tjerk, "Santome," in SPCL2 *The Survey of Pidgin and Creole Languages*, 2013, pp. 50–58

Haji-Othman, Noor and James McLellan, "English in Brunei," *World Englishes* 33.4 (2014), 486–497

Hall, Robert A., Jr. *Melanesian Pidgin Phrase-Book and Vocabulary*. Rev. ed. Baltimore, MD: Waverly Press/Linguistic Society of America, 1943

Hamdan, Jihad M. and Wafa A. Abu Hatab, "English in the Jordanian Context," *World Englishes* 28.3 (2009), 394–405

Hancock, Ian F., ed. *Diversity and Development in English-related Creoles*. Ann Arbor, MI: Karoma Publishers, 1985

Hay, Jennifer, Margaret Maclagan, and Elizabeth Gordon. *New Zealand English*. Dialects of English. Edinburgh: Edinburgh University Press, 2008

Hay, Jennifer and Alhana Clendon, "(Non)-rhoticity: Lessons from New Zealand English," in Nevalainen, Terttu and Elizabeth Closs Traugott, eds. *The Oxford Handbook of The History of English*. Oxford: Oxford University Press, 2012, pp. 761–772

Heine, Bernd and Derek Nurse, eds. *African Languages: An Introduction*. Cambridge: Cambridge University Press, 2000

Herzfeld, Anita, "Limonese Creole and Panamanian Creole: comparison and contrast," *Papers of the Mid-America Linguistics Conference* (1980), 218–242

Hickey, Raymond, ed. *Legacies of Colonial English: Studies in Transported Dialects*. Cambridge: Cambridge University Press, 2005

Holi Baibul: The Holy Bible in the Kriol language of Australia. Orlando, FL: Wycliffe Bible Translators, 2018

Holm, John. *Pidgins and Creoles*, Volume I: *Theory and Structure*. Volume II: *Reference Survey*. Cambridge: Cambridge University Press, 1988–1989

Holm, John. *An Introduction to Pidgins and Creoles*. Cambridge: Cambridge University Press, 2000

Hopkyns, Sarah, Wafa Zoghbor, and Peter John Hassall, "The use of English and linguistic hybridity among Emirati millennials," *World Englishes* 40.2 (2020), 176–190

Horvath, Barbara M., "Australian English: phonology," in Burridge, Kate and Bernd Kortmann, eds. *Varieties of English 3: The Pacific and Australia*. Berlin: Mouton de Gruyer, 2008, pp. 88–110

Hosali, Priya, "Butler English: morphology and syntax," in Mesthrie, Rajend, ed. *Varieties of English 4: Africa, South and Southeast Asia*. Berlin: Mouton de Gruyter, 2008, pp. 563–577

Huber, Magnus [2008a], "Ghanaian English: phonology," in Mesthrie, Rajend, ed. *Varieties of English 4: Africa, South and Southeast Asia*. Berlin: Mouton de Gruyter, pp. 67–92

Huber, Magnus [2008b], "Ghanaian Pidgin English: phonology," in Mesthrie, Rajend, ed. *Varieties of English 4: Africa, South and Southeast Asia*. Berlin: Mouton de Gruyter, pp. 93–101

Huber, Magnus, "Ghanaian Pidgin English," in SPCL1, *The Survey of Pidgin and Creole Languages*. Oxford: Oxford University Press, 2013, pp. 167–175

Ingram, John and Peter Mühlhäusler, "Norfolk Island-Pitcairn English: phonetics and phonology," in Burridge, Kate and Bernd Kortmann, eds. *Varieties of English 3: The Pacific and Australia*. Berlin: Mouton de Gruyer, 2008, pp. 267–291

Jacobs, Bart, "The Upper Guinea origins of Papiamentu: linguistic and historical evidence," *Diachronica* 26.3 (2009), 319–379

Jahr, Ernst Håkon and Ingvild Broch, eds. *Language Contact in the Arctic*. Trends in Linguistics, Studies and Monographs 88. Berlin: Mouton de Gruyter, 1996

Jourdan, Christine, "Solomon Islands English: morphology and syntax," in Burridge, Kate and Bernd Kortmann, eds. *Varieties of English 3: The Pacific and Australia*. Berlin: Mouton de Gruyer, 2008, pp. 467–487

Jourdan, Christine and Rachel Selbach, "Solomon Islands Pijin: phonetics and phonology," in Burridge, Kate and Bernd Kortmann, eds. *Varieties of English 3: The Pacific and Australia*. Berlin: Mouton de Gruyer, 2008, pp. 164–187

Kachru, Braj. *The Alchemy of English: The Spread, Functions, and Models of Non-native Englishes*. Champaign, IL: University of Illinois Press, 1990

Kachru, Braj [1994], "English in South Asia," in *The Cambridge History of the English Language*. Volume V: *English in Britain and Overseas: Origins and Development*, ed. Robert Burchfield, Cambridge: Cambridge University Press pp. 497–553

Kachru, Braj B. *Asian Englishes: Beyond the Canon*. Seattle: University of Washington Press, 2005

Kachru, Braj B., Yamuna Kachru, and Cecil L. Nelson, eds *The Handbook of World Englishes*. Oxford: Blackwell, 2006

Kachru, Braj B., Yamuna Kachru, and S.N. Sridhar, eds. *Language in South Asia*. Cambridge: Cambridge University Press, 2008

van Kemenade, Ans and Bettelou Los, eds. *The Handbook of the History of English*. Oxford: Blackwell, 2006

Kirkpatrick, Andy, ed. *The Routledge Handbook of World Englishes*. Abingdon: Routledge, 2010

Klein, Thomas B., "Gullah," in SPCL1, *The Survey of Pidgin and Creole Languages*. Oxford: Oxford University Press, 2013, pp. 139–147

de Klerk, Vivian, ed. *Focus on South Africa*. Varieties of English Around the World vol. G15. Amsterdam: John Benjamins, 1996

Kortmann, Bernd and Edgar W. Schneider, eds. *A Handbook of Varieties of English. Volume 1: Phonology*. Berlin: Mouton de Gruyter, 2004

Kortmann, Bernd, Kate Burridge, Rajend Mesthrie, Edgar W. Schneider, and Clive Upton, eds. *A Handbook of Varieties of English*. Volume 2: *Morphology and Syntax*. Berlin: Mouton de Gruyter, 2004

Kortmann, Bernd and Clive Upton, eds. *Varieties of English 1: The British Isles*. Berlin: Mouton de Gruyter, 2008

Kortmann, Bernd and Kerstin Lunkenheimer, eds. *The Mouton World Atlas of Variation in English*. Berlin: Mouton de Gruyter, 2012

Kouwenberg, Silvia and John Victor Singler, eds. *The Handbook of Pidgin and Creole Studies*. Oxford: Wiley-Blackwell, 2008

Lalla, Barbara and Jean D'Costa. *Language in Exile: Three Hundred Years of Jamaican Creole*. Tuscaloosa: University of Alabama Press, 1990

Lalo, Michael, "Bogans on parade," *The Sydney Morning Herald* 8 November 2010 (online).

Landerholm, Carl, ed. *Notices & Voyages of the Famed Quebec Mission to the Pacific Northwest, Being the Correspondence, Notices, etc., of Fathers Blanchet and Demers, Together with those of Fathers Bolduc and Langlois....* Portland, OR: Champoeg Press for the Oregon Historical Society, 1956

Lang, Jürgen, "Cape Verdean Creole of Santiago," in SPCL2 *The Survey of Pidgin and Creole Languages*, 2013, pp. 3–11

Lanham, L.W. and C.A. Macdonald, eds. *The Standard in South African English and its Social History*. 2nd ed. Heidelberg: Julius Groos Verlag, 1985

Lauder, Afferbeck (Alastair Ardoch Morrison). *Strine: Let Stalk Strine and Nose Tone Unturned*. Sydney: Lansdowne Press, 1982

Lee, Cher-Leng, "Motivations of code-switching in multi-lingual Singapore," *Journal of Chinese Linguistics* 31.1 (2003), 145–176

Lee, Cher-Leng, "Filling gaps or code choice? Code-switching across generations in colloquial Singapore Mandarin," *Global Chinese* 5.1 (2019), 1–24

Lee, Nala Huiying, Ling Ai Ping, and Hiroki Nomoto, "Colloquial Singapore English *got*: functions and substratal influences," *World Englishes* 28.3 (2009), 293–318

Lefebvre, Claire. *Issues in the Study of Pidgin and Creole Languages*. Studies in Language Companion Series 70. Amsterdam: John Benjamins, 2004

Leitner, Gerhard. *Australia's Many Voices*. 2 vols. Berlin: Mouton de Gruyter, 2004

LePage, Robert B. and Andrée Tabouret-Keller. *Acts of Identity: Creole-Based Approaches to Language and Identity*. Cambridge: Cambridge University Press, 1985

Li, David C.S. *Multilingual Hong Kong: Languages, Literacies and Identities*. Multilingual Education, vol. 19. Cham: Springer, 2017

Lipski, John M., "Language Contact Phenomena in Louisiana Isleño Spanish," *American Speech* 62.4 (1987), 320–331

Lipski, John M. *A History of Afro-Hispanic Language: Five Centuries, Five Continents*. Cambridge: Cambridge University Press, 2005

Litteral, Robert and Karl J. Franklin. *An Introductory Programmed Course in Tok Pisin*. 2nd ed. Ukarumpa: Summer Institute of Linguistics, 1990

Lyovin, Anatole V. *An Introduction to the Languages of the World*. New York: Oxford University Press, 1997

Macalister, John, ed. *A Dictionary of Maori Words in New Zealand English*. Melbourne: Oxford University Press, 2005

Macquarie Dictionary. 2026. https://www.macquariedictionary.com.au/

Mahboob, Ahmar, "English as an Islamic Language: a case study of Pakistani English," *World Englishes* 28.2 (2009), 175–189

Mahboob, Ahmar, "Englishes of the Middle East: a focus on the Kingdom of Saudi Arabia," in *Middle East Handbook of Applied Linguistics*, ed. R. Akbari and C. Coombe. Dubai: TESOL Arabia Publications, 2013, Pp. 1–13

Maitz, Péter and Craig A. Volker, eds. *Language Contact in the German Colonies: Papua New Guinea and beyond*. Special issue of *Language and Linguistics in Melanesia: Journal of the Linguistic Society of Papua New Guinea*, 2017

Malcolm, Ian G., "Aboriginal English: From contact variety to social dialect," in *Processes of Language Contact: Studies from Australia and the South Pacific*. Montréal: Les Éditions Fides, 2000, pp. 123–144

Maurer, Philippe, "Angolar," in SPCL2 *The Survey of Pidgin and Creole Languages*, 2013, pp. 59–71

McIntosh, Janet, "Mobile phones and Mipoho's prophecy: the powers and dangers of flying language," *American Ethnologist* 37.2 (2010), 337–353

McWhorter, John H., ed. *Language Change and Language Contact in Pidgins and Creoles*. Creole Language Library, vol. 21. Amsterdam: John Benjamins, 1999

McWhorter, John H. *The Missing Spanish Creoles: Recovering the Birth of Plantation Contact Languages*. Berkeley, CA: University of California Press, 2000

McWhorter, John H. *Defining Creole*. Oxford: Oxford University Press, 2005

McWhorter, John H. and Jeff Good. *A Grammar of Saramaccan Creole*. Mouton Grammar Library 56. Berlin: De Gruyter Mouton, 2012

Meakins, Felicity. *Case-Marking in Contact: The development and function of case morphology in Gurindji Kriol*. Creole Language Library, vol. 39. Amsterdam: John Benjamins, 2011

Menang, Thaddeus, "Cameroon Pidgin English (Kamtok): phonology," in Mesthrie, Rajend, ed. *Varieties of English 4: Africa, South and Southeast Asia*. Berlin: Mouton de Gruyter, 2008, pp. 133–149

Mesthrie, Rajend, ed. *Varieties of English 4: Africa, South and Southeast Asia*. Berlin: Mouton de Gruyter, 2008

Mesthrie, Rajend and Rakesh M. Bhatt. *World Englishes: The Study of New Linguistic Varieties*. Key Topics in Sociolinguistics. Cambridge: Cambridge University Press, 2008

Meyerhoff, Miriam, "Bislama," in SPCL1, *The Survey of Pidgin and Creole Languages*. Oxford: Oxford University Press, 2013, pp. 223–231

Migge, Bettina, "Nengee," in SPCL1, *The Survey of Pidgin and Creole Languages*. Oxford: Oxford University Press, 2013, pp. 39–48

Mihalič, Franc. *The Jacaranda Dictionary and Grammar of Melanesian Pidgin*. Melbourne: Jacaranda Books, 1971

Mohideen bin Mohamed Ali, Haja, "Islamic Terms in contemporary English," *English Today* 23.2 (2007), 32–38.

Momma, Haruko and Michael Matto, eds. *A Companion to The History of the English Language*. Chichester: Wiley-Blackwell, 2008

Moore, Bruce, "Australian English and indigenous voices," in Blair, David and Peter Collins, eds. *English in Australia*. Amsterdam: John Benjamins, 2001, pp. 133–149

Mufwene, Salikoko. *The Ecology of Language Evolution*. Cambridge Approaches to Language Contact. Cambridge: Cambridge University Press, 2001

Mufwene, Salikoko and Lioba Moshi, eds. *Topics in African Linguistics*. Amsterdam: Johns Benjamins, 1993

Mufwene, Salikoko, John R. Rickford, Guy Bailey and John Baugh, eds. *African-American English: Structure, history and use*. London: Routledge, 1998

Mühleisen, Susanne, "Trinidad English Creole," in SPCL1, *The Survey of Pidgin and Creole Languages*. Oxford: Oxford University Press, 2013, pp. 61–69

Mühleisen, Susanne and Bettina Migge, eds. *Politeness and Face in Caribbean Creoles*. Varieties of English Around the World, vol. G34. Amsterdam: John Benjamins, 2005

Mühlhäusler, Peter. *Pidgin and Creole Linguistics*. Oxford: Blackwell, 1986

Mühlhäusler, Peter, "Norfolk Island – Pitcairn English (Pitkern Norfolk): morphology and syntax," in Burridge, Kate and Bernd Kortmann, eds. *Varieties of English 3: The Pacific and Australia*. Berlin: Mouton de Gruyer, 2008, pp. 568–582

Mühlhäusler, Peter, "Norf'k," in SPCL1, *The Survey of Pidgin and Creole Languages*. Oxford: Oxford University Press, 2013, pp. 232–240

Mühlhäusler, Peter, Thomas E. Dutton, and Suzanne Romaine, eds. *Tok Pisin Texts: From the Beginnings to the Present.* Varieties of English Around the World, Text Series, vol. T9. Amsterdam: John Benjamins, 2003

Munro, Martin and Celia Britton, eds. *American Creoles: The Francophone Caribbean and the American South.* Liverpool: Liverpool University Press, 2012

Muysken, Pieter and Norval Smith, eds. *Substrata versus Universals in Creole Genesis: Papers from the Amsterdam Creole Workshop, April 1985.* Amsterdam: John Benjamins, 1986

Myers-Scotton, Carol. *Social Motivations for Code-Switching: Evidence from Africa.* Oxford: Clarendon Press, 1993

Nevalainen, Terttu and Elizabeth Closs Traugott, eds. *The Oxford Handbook of The History of English.* Oxford: Oxford University Press, 2012

Newbrook, Mark, "Syntactic features and norms in Australian English," in Blair, David and Peter Collins, eds. *English in Australia.* Amsterdam: John Benjamins, 2001, pp. 113–132

The New Zealand Oxford Dictionary. Ed. Graeme Kennedy and Tony Deverson. Melbourne: Oxford University Press, 2004

Ngonyani, Deo, "Language Shift and National Identity in Tanzania," *Ufahamu: A Journal of African Studies* 23.2 (1995), 69–92

Noor Azam, Haji Othman and James McLellan, "English in Brunei: challenges and future directions," *World Englishes* 33.4 (2014), 486–497

Orkin, Mark M. *Speaking Canadian English: An Informal Account of the English Language in Canada.* Abingdon: Routledge, 1971/2015

Oxford Papua New Guinea Tok Pisin English Dictionary, ed Craig Alan Volker et al. Victoria: Oxford University Press/Wantok Niuspepa, 2008

Patrick, Peter L. *Urban Jamaican Creole: Variation in the Mesolect.* Amsterdam: John Benjamins, 1998

Patrick, Peter L., "Jamaican Creole: morphology and syntax," in Schneider, Edgar W., ed. *Varieties of English 2: The Americas and the Caribbean.* Berlin: Mouton de Gruyter, 2008, pp. 609–644

Peters, Pam. *The Cambridge Guide to Australian English Usage.* Cambridge: Cambridge University Press, 2007

Peters, Pam, "Australian and New Zealand English," in Momma, Haruko and Michael Matto, eds. *A Companion to The History of the English Language.* Chichester: Wiley-Blackwell, 2008, pp. 389–399

Peters, Pam, Peter Collins and Adam Smith, eds. *Comparative Studies in Australian and New Zealand English: Grammar and beyond.* Varieties of English Around the World vol. G39. Amsterdam: John Benjamins, 2009

Peters, Pam and Peter Collins, "Colloquial Australian English," in Kortmann, Bernd and Kerstin Lunkenheimer, eds. *The Mouton World Atlas of Variation in English.* Berlin: Mouton de Gruyter, 2012, pp. 585–591

Poplack, Shana and David Sankoff, "The Philadelphia Story in the Spanish Caribbean," *American Speech* 62.4 (1987), 291–314

Porto, Melina, "The Role and Status of English in Spanish-Speaking Argentina and its Education System: Nationalism or Imperialism?" *SAGE Open* (January-March 2014), 1–14

Post, Marike, "Fa d'Ambô," in SPCL2 *The Survey of Pidgin and Creole Languages*, 2013, pp. 81–89

Prescod, Paula, "Vincentian Creole," in SPCL1, *The Survey of Pidgin and Creole Languages.* Oxford: Oxford University Press, 2013, pp. 70–80

Price, Jenny, "Old news: Rethinking language change through Australian Broadcast Speech," in Nevalainen, Terttu and Elizabeth Closs Traugott, eds. *The Oxford Handbook of The History of English.* Oxford: Oxford University Press, 2012, pp. 341–351

Rickford, John Russell and Suzanne Romaine, eds. *Creole Genesis, Attitudes and Discourse: Studies Celebrating Charlene J. Sato.* Amsterdam: John Benjamins, 1999

Rickford, John Russell and Russell John Rickford. *Spoken Soul: The Story of Black English.* New York: John Wiley & Sons, 2000

Roberts, Sarah Julianne, "The role of diffusion in the genesis of Hawaiian Creole," *Language* 74.1 (1998), 1–39

Römer, Ulrike. *Sranan Tongo: An English-based Creole in the Republic of Suriname.* Munich: GRIN Verlag, 2006

Sailaja, Pingali. *Indian English.* Dialects of English. Edinburgh: Edinburgh University Press, 2009

Samarin, William J., "Chinook Jargon and pidgin historiography," *Canadian Journal of Anthropology* 5.1 (1986), 23–34

Sapir, Edward. *Language: An Introduction to the Study of Speech.* New York: Harcourt, Brace and Company, 1921

Sato, Charlene J., "Linguistic Inequality in Hawaii: The Post-Creole Dilemma," in *Language of Inequality*, ed. Nessa Wolfson and Joan Manes. Berlin: De Gruyter Mouton, 1985, Pp. 255–272

Schmied, Joseph, "East African English (Kenya, Uganda, Tanzania): phonology," in Mesthrie, Rajend, ed. *Varieties of English 4: Africa, South and Southeast Asia.* Berlin: Mouton de Gruyter, 2008, pp. 150–163

Schneider, Edgar W., "The dynamics of new Englishes: from identity construction to dialect death," *Language* 79.2 (2003), 233–281

Schneider, Edgar W. *Postcolonial English: Varieties Around the World.* Cambridge Approaches to Language Contact. Cambridge: Cambridge University Press, 2007

Schneider, Edgar W., ed. *Varieties of English 2: The Americas and the Caribbean.* Berlin: Mouton de Gruyter, 2008

Schreier, Daniel. *St. Helenian English: Origins, Evolution and Variation.* Varieties of English Around the World vol. G37. Amsterdam: John Benjamins, 2008

Schreier, Daniel, Peter Trudgill, Egdar W. Schneider, and Jeffrey P. Williams, eds. *The Lesser-Known Varieties of English.* Studies in English Language. Cambridge: Cambridge University Press, 2009

Schreier, Daniel and Marianne Hundt, eds. *English as a Contact Language.* Cambridge: Cambridge University Press, 2013

Schreier, Daniel, Marianne Hundt, and Edgar W. Schneider, eds. *The Cambridge Handbook of World Englishes*. Cambridge: Cambridge University Press, 2020

Schröder, Anne, "Cameroon Pidgin English," in SPCL1, *The Survey of Pidgin and Creole Languages*. Oxford: Oxford University Press, 2013, pp. 185–193

Schultze-Berndt, Eva, Felicity Meakins, and Denise Angelo, "Kriol," in SPCL1, *The Survey of Pidgin and Creole Languages*. Oxford: Oxford University Press, 2013, pp. 241–251

Seargeant, Philip and Joan Swann, eds. *English in the World: History, Diversity, Change*. Abingdon: Routledge, 2012

Sedlatschek, Andreas. *Contemporary Indian English: Variation and Change*. Varieties of English Around the World vol. G38. Amsterdam: John Benjamins, 2009

Setter, Jenny, Cathy S.P. Wong, and Brian H.S. Chan. *Hong Kong English*. Dialects of English. Edinburgh: Edinburgh University Press, 2010

Siegel, Jeff, ed. *Processes of Language Contact: Studies from Australia and the South Pacific*. Montréal: Les Éditions Fides, 2000

Siegel, Jeff. *The Emergence of Pidgin and Creole Languages*. Oxford: Oxford University Press, 2008

Siemund, Peter and Noemi Kintana, eds. *Language Contact and Contact Languages*. Hamburg Studies on Multilingualism vol. 7. Amsterdam: John Benjamins, 2008

Simpson, Jane, "Hypocoristics of place-names in Australian English," in Blair, David and Peter Collins, eds. *English in Australia*. Amsterdam: John Benjamins, 2001, pp. 89–112

Singler, John Victor. *Pidgin and Creole Tense-Mood-Aspect Systems*. Creole Language Library, vol 6. Amsterdam: John Benjamins, 1990

Singler, John Victor, "Liberian settler English: phonology," in Mesthrie, Rajend, ed. *Varieties of English 4: Africa, South and Southeast Asia*. Berlin: Mouton de Gruyter, 2008, pp. 102–114

Smith, Geoff P. and Jeff Siegel, "Tok Pisin," in SPCL1, *The Survey of Pidgin and Creole Languages*. Oxford: Oxford University Press, 2013, pp. 214–222

Soussi, Houssine, "World Englishes in multilingual Morocco," *World Englishes* 40.2 (2020), 259–267

SPCL1 = *The Survey of Pidgin and Creole Languages*, volume I: *English-based and Dutch-based languages*. Ed. Susanne Michaelis, Philippe Maurer, Martin Haspelmath, and Magnus Huber. Oxford: Oxford University Press, 2013

SPCL2 = *The Survey of Pidgin and Creole Languages*, vol. II: *Portuguese-based, Spanish-based, and French-based Languages*. Ed. Susanne Maria Michaelis, Philippe Maurer, Martin Haspelmath, and Magnus Huber. Oxford: Oxford University Press, 2013

SPCL3 = *The Survey of Pidgin and Creole Languages*, vol. III: *Contact Languages Based on Languages from Africa, Asia, Australia, and the Americas*. Ed. Susanne Michaelis, Philippe Maurer, Martin Haspelmath, and Magnus Huber. Oxford: Oxford University Press, 2013

Stubbe, Maria and Janet Holmes, "Talking Maori or Pakeha in English: signalling identity in discourse," in Bell, Allan and Koenraad Kuiper, eds. *New Zealand English*. Amsterdam: John Benjamins, 2000, pp. 249–278

Subramaniam, Samanth, "India after English?", *The New York Review of Books* 9 June 2014 (online).

Syea, Anand. *French Creoles: A Comprehensive and Comparative Grammar*. Abingdon: Routledge, 2017

Thompson, Roger M. *Filipino English and Taglish*. Varieties of English Around the World, vol. G3. Amsterdam: John Benjamins, 2003

Todd, Loreto. *Pidgins and Creoles*. New ed. London: Routledge, 1990

Torabully, Khal. *Cale d'etoiles: Coolitude*. Sainte-Marie, Réunion: Azalées-Éditions, 1992

Trudgill, Peter and Jean Hannah. *International English: A Guide to Varieties of English Around the World*. 6th ed. London: Routledge, 2017

Van Rooy, Bertus, "Black South African English: phonology," in Mesthrie, Rajend, ed. *Varieties of English 4: Africa, South and Southeast Asia*. Berlin: Mouton de Gruyter, 2008, pp. 177–187

Velupillai, Viveka, "Hawai'i Creole," in SPCL1, *The Survey of Pidgin and Creole Languages*. Oxford: Oxford University Press, 2013, pp. 252–261

Velupillai, Viveka. *Pidgins, Creoles and Mixed Languages: An Introduction*. Creole Language Library, vol 48. Amsterdam: John Benjamins, 2015

Verhaar, John W.M., ed. *Melanesian Pidgin and Tok Pisin: Proceedings of the First International Conference of Pidgins and Creoles in Melanesia*. Amsterdam: John Benjamins, 1990

van der Wahl, Marijke and Bart Jacobs, "The discovery, nature and implications of a Papiamentu text fragment discovered in 1783," *Journal of Pidgin and Creole Languages* 30 (2015), 44–62

Walcott, Derek. *Omeros*. New York: Farrar, Straus and Giroux, 1990

Wales, Katie. *Northern English: A Social and Cultural History*. Cambridge: Cambridge University Press, 2006

WALS = *The World Atlas of Language Structures*, ed. Martin Haspelmath, Matthew S. Dryer, David Gil, and Bernard Comrie. Oxford: Oxford University Press, 2005. https://wals.info/

Warren, Paul and Laurie Bauer, "Maori English: phonology," in Burridge, Kate and Bernd Kortmann, eds. *Varieties of English 3: The Pacific and Australia*. Berlin: Mouton de Gruyer, 2008, 77–88

Wee, Lionel, "Singapore English: morphology and syntax," in Mesthrie, Rajend, ed. *Varieties of English 4: Africa, South and Southeast Asia*. Berlin: Mouton de Gruyter, 2008, pp. 593–609

Wells, John C. *Accents of English 3: Beyond the British Isles*. Cambridge: Cambridge University Press, 1982/rpt. 1996

Williams, Jeffrey P., Edgar W. Schneider, Peter Trudgill, and Daniel Schreier, eds. *Further Studies in the Lesser-Known Varieties of English*. Studies in English Language. Cambridge: Cambridge University Press, 2015

Williams, Joseph J. *Whence the Black Irish of Jamaica?* New York: Dial Press, 1932

Williams, Robert L. *Ebonics: The True Language of Black Folks*. St. Louis: Institute of Black Studies, 1975

Winford, Donald. *Predication in Caribbean English Creoles.* Creole Language Library, vol 10. Amsterdam: John Benjamins, 1993

Winford, Donald, "Re-examining Caribbean English Creole Continua," *World Englishes* 16 (1997), 233–279

Winford, Donald. *An Introduction to Contact Linguistics.* Oxford: Blackwell, 2003

Winford, Donald, "Substrate influences and universals in the emergence of contact Englishes: re-evaluating the evidence," in Schreier, Daniel and Marianne Hundt, eds. *English as a Contact Language.* Cambridge: Cambridge University Press, 2013, pp. 222–241

Winford, Donald and Ingo Plag, "Sranan," in SPCL1, *The Survey of Pidgin and Creole Languages.* Oxford: Oxford University Press, 2013, pp. 15–26

Winkler, Elizabeth Grace and Samuel Gyasi Obeng, "West Africanisms in Limonese Creole English," *World Englishes* 19.2 (2000), 15–171

Wolff, H. Ekkehard, "Language and society," in Heine, Bernd and Derek Nurse, eds. *African Languages: An Introduction.* Cambridge: Cambridge University Press, 2000, pp. 298–347

Wong, Jock Onn, "The Singlish interjection *bojio*," in *Meaning, Life and Culture: In conversation with Anna Wierzbicka*, ed. Helen Bromhead and Zhengdao Ye. Acton: Australian National University Press, 2020, Pp. 99–114

Woolford, Ellen B. *Aspects of Tok Pisin Grammar.* Canberra: Department of Linguistics, Research School of Pacific Studies, Australian National University, 1979

Woordeboek van die Afrikaanse Taal (WAT). University of Stellenbosch. https://www.wat.co.za

Worden, Nigel, "Indian Ocean Slaves in Cape Town, 1695-1807," *Journal of Southern African Studies* 42.3 (2016), 389–408

Yakpo, Kofi, "Pichi," in SPCL1, *The Survey of Pidgin and Creole Languages.* Oxford: Oxford University Press, 2013, pp. 194–205

CHAPTER 12

A World of Englishes

At the beginning of the 21st century the English language had unquestionably attained global status. But nearly everything else about this moment in its history is subject to speculation, projections, and predictions, even a sort of politico-linguistic malaise. Bold, even boastful, forecasts of numbers of speakers of a 'global English' had likely been surpassed even before 1 January 2001 (the actual starting point for any 21st-century English, notwithstanding the media-promoted Y2K phenomenon). The British Council's "English 2000" program sought to promote global adoption of the language, extending use to 1 billion speakers; its endorsement by Charles, Prince of Wales (now Charles III), at the project's launch in 1995 generated some irritation in the United States over his comments on the "very corrupting" influence of American English, issued in what might seem a linguistic manifesto: "We must act now to ensure that English, and that to my way of thinking means English English, maintains its position as the world language well into the next century" (*The Times*, 24 March 1995; see also the response of an American linguist in Baron 1995). Both matters seem to have been moot by the time the British Council moved into action: if counting L1 and L2 speakers equivalently as 'speakers of English' – and this does not always seem to be agreed upon – the one billion figure had likely already been passed some time earlier; the role of 'English' English (BrE) seems already to have been reduced from the dominant, most widely spoken standard variety at the head of 'global Englishes' to a 'prestige role' instead with the rapid rise of American varieties of English worldwide, even in former British colonies.

No doubt, as seen in the previous two chapters, the matter is best seen within a postcolonial framework. Since the end of World War II the rapid eclipsing of British military and economic hegemony by the United States has played out in the linguistic sphere as well; close allies in nearly all matters – despite some differences over Northern Ireland, the two Gulf Wars (1990–1991, Operation Desert Storm; 2003–2011, Operation Iraqi Freedom), were largely Anglophone ventures – Britain and America have nonetheless jockeyed for position in what could be termed an Anglophone sphere of influence. In all matters except, to a certain extent, prestige the Americans seem to hold the advantage. In the context of flagging imperial duties, the Soufrière volcano (la grande Soufrière) began erupting on 18 July 1995 on the "Emerald Isle of the

Caribbean," Montserrat (where a Leeward Caribbean Creole English is still spoken by several thousand islanders). Media coverage of the eruption and eventual evacuation of nearly two-thirds of the island nation's inhabitants was extensive on the BBC. The outpouring of concern for the welfare of the crown citizens of this diminutive British Overseas Territory – the island is some 10 miles south to north and 7 miles west to east with not quite 6,000 souls – was impressive, if also paternalistic. The approach of the handover of Hong Kong, slated for 1 July 1997 (at the end of a 99-year "lease"), also loomed over the inception of English 2000 in the Spring of 1995. Perception, at least, seemed to suggest both opportunity in the linguistic marketplace and threat to the language's market share. Perception, of course, but not quite reality.

Misconceptions naturally abound over all sorts of matters that are of enough interest to be treated not just in the specialist journals but popular media also. Inasmuch as the global spread of English inescapably leads back to the colonial and military ventures of Britain and America (and now to postcolonial Anglophone nations expanding their own regional spheres of influence), the future of English will largely escape attempts at guidance, legislation, and regulation. The example seen earlier of Québec's Loi/Law 101 (*La charte de la langue française/Charter of the French Language*) may provide a qualified exception – and a precarious one for French-language advocates, as the dike holding back the English tide has been shored up, but the menacing flood has not crested. Without a doubt, the 'First-World' status of English in its 'Inner Circle' use (Kachru 1988) makes the language largely immune to language planning where it is the majority L1. By contrast, English and Spanish in the United States exhibit the effects of a linguistic power (or prestige) differential (Zentella 1997); despite its growing influence, now well beyond the American Southwest and New York and Miami, it remains to be seen whether Spanish as an L2 in the United States too succumbs to the "third-generation hypothesis" of heritage language loss (as have Dutch, French, Swedish, Irish, Italian, Polish, and many other languages of immigrant groups). In an age in which members of the commentariat could speak, however simplistically, of "the end of history" (Fukuyama 1992), it is hard to imagine any great change to the core L1-grouping of speakers of English (the United Kingdom, the United States, and Canada, and the 'Antipodean' group of Australia, New Zealand, and South Africa) apart from continued (if slower) growth and continuity to the present contradictory forces of convergence and divergence in local varieties. It is another matter with L2 use of English around the world. Here the scope for innovation and change seems particularly exciting if uncertain among the 'World Englishes' (Kachru's 'Expanding Circle' of Englishes). The influence of another 'Information Age' (or 'Digital' or 'Cyber Age'), however overstated or piously deplored it may be in popular accounts, will no doubt likewise continue to produce interesting and rapidly disseminated innovations in use of the language worldwide. Even the predictions of linguists with regard to the global spread of English may have missed 'First-World' expansion within Western Europe (Mesthrie 2008: 31–32), so it can be sobering, in an age of "irrational exuberance,"[1] to think of what cannot be

[1] A phrase used by then-chairman of the Board of Governors of the Federal Reserve of the United States Allan Greenspan with regard to overvaluation of the stock market in a speech to the conservative American Enterprise Institute on 5 December 1996; see Uchitelle 1997 and Schiller 2005.

foreseen or predicted in the future of English. Nonetheless, the present moment offers a wealth of matters meriting consideration: the status of English as a global language; the matter of what is meant by 'global' or 'world Englishes' (interpretations range from national [e.g., Nigerian or Kenyan] or regional [e.g., South Asian] varieties or groups of varieties to a possible nascent English family of languages); the great cultural and linguistic impact of the growing Latino population of the United States; deregionalized regional varieties such as Estuary English and a seemingly expanded role for linguistic affectation and identity-driven self-fashioning; the "business" of English, its expanding use in the EU, continued use with the United Nations and NATO, for the Olympic Games, and across the range of governmental and nongovernmental organizations (NGOs) that have proliferated in this 'technocratic' age; the much heralded 'digital age' of texting, tweeting, podcasting, and social networking. A last section is entitled "The Queen's English/The King's English"; the rubric alludes not just to the French adage *plus ça change* but also to an observable if understudied cultural phenomenon in America and other former British colonies and territories: that the unmooring of English in its history from the 'mother country' seems to have produced a species of cultural nostalgia in the battle over prestige. Americans are not alone in their Royal Wedding frenzies (however much these are inflated and driven by the media) and other sporadic and inconsistent Anglophilic outbursts. If the role of a 'countercultural' covert prestige attached to some varieties of AmE has helped power the tremendous reach of American popular culture – arguably, American hip-hop has had a cultural impact greater than either rock 'n' roll or its American forebear jazz – then the continued inversely attractive pull of the overt prestige of high-status varieties of BrE should come as no surprise.

12.1 ENGLISH WORLDWIDE OR WORLD ENGLISHES?

In the last chapter the global spread of English in the latter half of the 20th century was discussed in the context of a post- World War II American ascendancy and the dawning of a postcolonial era. In the 21st century one signal development is the advancement of English-based pidgins and Creoles to co-official even official status at the governmental level. This is a remarkable development given the political wrangling involved in 'language planning.' As English has encircled the globe, immigration patterns have furthered ever closer bonds between English-speaking communities around the world. Caribbean English speakers in London, Brooklyn, or Toronto bring with them as well the food, music, and Carnival/Carnaval. South Asian English speakers have profoundly influenced the United Kingdom – chicken tikka masala (at one time) overtaking fish and chips or Sunday roast as the favorite British food – and, increasingly, Canada (Ontario in particular) and the United States (Northern New Jersey, Northern California, the Palo Alto area in particular). The South Bay section of San Diego is home to the largest Filipino-American community in North America; San Diego is also a home port of the U.S. Navy, a branch of the armed services with large numbers of Filipino-Americans and recent immigrants from the Philippines staffing ships and bases.

To focus on changes in the 21st century, examples from East African Englishes will be turned to. Here postcolonial national varieties of English coexist alongside

English-based pidgins and Creoles, along with pidgins and Creoles with local language bases, and, with great expansion in cell phone/mobile technology, the developments of 'textspeak' and 'medialects' (McIntosh 2010). And many of the changes seem to be occurring among younger speakers; the example of Sheng for instance (*Sheng* < *Swahili* + *English*), used among youths in Nairobi, Kenya, which seems to be driven in particular by 'street' use by *manambas*, the young men who work on the *matatus*, the private vans that serve as public transport in the capital. As such, Sheng has sometimes been classified as a 'peer language,' or as a Swahili-based pidgin or emerging Creole with syntax from Swahili, but borrowings in phonology, morphology, and vocabulary from English, Luo, Kikuyu (Gĩkũyũ), Masai, Luhya, Kigiriama, Taita, and other Kenyan languages (Githiora 2002, 159, 166–167); though it is spoken also by students at the primary and secondary levels, the subculture of the *matatu* drivers and the often rough and perilous trips they make is the original base (Wa-Mungai and Samper 2006; a similarity may be noted in the 'jeepney' subculture of the Philippines). Whereas *Engsh* is associated with better-off neighborhoods of Nairobi, *Sheng* is more working class and may have originated in the Kaloleni neighborhood (Abdulaziz and Osinde 1997; Githiora 2002, 159), though it is usually associated with the Kibera neighborhood of Nairobi. It does not at first blush seem all that indebted to English: *mimi hapana ona yeye jana* 'I did not seen him/her yesterday,' *twende nyumbani, bwana* 'let's go home, man' (Githiora 2002: 165–166) – *bwana* ('boss,' here made a familiar term for another male) and *safari* (from Swahili, ultimately Arabic, and used generally for 'journey') have made their way to English, as has *mzungu*, 'white, European,' used in Kenya condescendingly though with a satiric or comic edge at times (the first attestation in the OED is from 1844). But a form such as the "casual greeting" *Walapa!* < *what's up* (Githiora 2002, 166) may show an increasing influence of popular AmE. In studying the religious and cultural ethos of coastal Malindi, north of Mombasa, linguistic anthropologist Janet McIntosh noticed in the first decade of the 21st century the spread of cell phone/mobile use and a resulting influence of 'textspeak' on a linguistic situation that already involved code-switching and -mixing (McIntosh 2010, 350–351). The text message examples are fascinating for the picture that emerges of linguistic inventiveness and flux (here following McIntosh's convention that the Kiswahili elements appear in bold-face and Kigiriama in bold-face italics):

> **Sasa vipi mambo, jo**, da girl went. Nyevu iz here, visit me at hom.
> **So how are things, man**? The girl went. Nyevu is here; visit me at home.
>
> Jenny ni ***mkongo***, plz b hom.
> Jenny is ***sick***, please come home.
>
> ***Sidza mona*** but ***nikirira*** evening ***ninda lola kala ni*** fresh.
> ***I haven't seen him/her***, but ***pass by my place*** in the evening; ***I'll see if it's*** cool.
> [*fresh* is from Sheng, ultimately from AAVE]
>
> weh. wsup now? uhuru park is 2pm. y r u wakin me up? ya am goin. pray 4 us.
> Weh. What's up now? Uhuru park is 2pm. Why are you waking me up? Yeah, I am going. Pray for us.

[This last example refers to protests at Nairobi's Uhuru Park during the electoral disputes of 2007–2008 and is in a sort of Kenyan English textspeak.] (McIntosh 2010, 342, 346, 351).

The Sheng and Kigiriama-Kiswahili-Kenyan English examples evince the broad reach of English, especially of AmE teen texting-speak conventions and AAVE and hip-hop pop culture; and they can be seen to serve as a "symbol of group solidarity" (Schneider 2007, 196), and a connection to a wider, sometimes seemingly more desirable – at least in material terms – world.

12.2 NEW BRITISH VARIETIES

The London staked out in Martin Amis's "London trilogy," the novels *Money* (1984), *London Fields* (1989), and *The Information* (1995), is not recognizably that of *Lionel Asbo: State of England* (2012) – "In dusty Diston (also known as Diston Town or, more simply, Town), nothing – and no one – was over sixty years old" (Amis 2012, 9). Diston, *Dis-ton*, may be a dystopic exaggeration of northeast London's Dalston (Borough of Hackney), and Lionel Asbo is partly in the line of the famed 'Lotto lout' and 'King of Chavs' Michael Carroll, who won a £9.7 million lottery jackpot in 2002 on his first try and was photographed claiming his prize wearing an electronic tag for a drunkenness charge (he would later famously lose most of his fortune and ask for his binman job back: "And being a binman is great anyway. I think it's the best job going. Outside, having a laugh with people.").[2] In a setting that is an exaggerated contemporary England, Lionel (Pepperdine) Asbo sets a record with his first restraining directive at three years of age, a record he commemorates at 18 when he adopts by deed poll the then current term ASBO (anti-social behavior order) as his last name – a bit of linguistic conversion, from noun-phrase acronym to proper noun. A denizen of tower flats (Avalon Tower) and a low-end 'debt-collector' and fence, Asbo is a terror in Diston, with his pair of fighting pit bulls (Joe and Jeff) kept mean and ready on a diet of lager and Tabasco sauce. He is more than anything, in a novel by turns absurdly satirical and acidly realistic, a walking lexicon of 'yobspeak.' Lionel – or 'Loyonel' or 'Loyonoo' as Amis renders Asbo's pronunciation – did his 'bit' in a *YOI* ('Young Offender Institution') and later in *The Scrubs* (H.M.P. Wormwood Scrubs) – as he later tells his nephew Desmond Pepperdine, "All it is, Des, when you in prison, you have you peace of mind. Because

[2] There is a good deal of Carroll imported to Asbo, who offered in retrospect what he enjoyed about his lottery win: "The holidays, the hookers, the money and the fast cars"; see Hayden Smith, "'Lotto lout' Michael Carroll wants job on the bins back," *Metro* 19 May 2012 [http://metro.co.uk/2010/05/19/lotto-lout-michael-carroll-wants-job-on-the-bins-back-319980/]; he has since taken a job in a Walkers biscuit factory: Jaya Narain, "Lotto lout Michael Carroll takes £204-a-week job in biscuit factory after squandering £10m jackpot," *Mail Online* 7 July 2013 [http://www.dailymail.co.uk/news/article-2357844/Lotto-lout-Michael-Carroll-takes-204-week-job-biscuit-factory-squandering-10m-jackpot.html].

you not worried about getting arrested. That's all it is" (Amis 2012, 249). The satirist's license to exaggerate is present in Lionel Asbo's 'yobspeak,' but in its way *Lionel Asbo: State of England* is about an across-the-board decline, the English language included – not in the judgment of contemporary linguists certainly, but to the eye and ear of a contemporary novelist:

> "Dogs," said Lionel, "they descended from wolves. That's they heritage. Now *wolves*," he went on, 'they not man's natural enemy. Oh no. You wolf won't attack a human. That's a myth, that is, Des. A total myth."
>
> Des listened. Lionel pronounced "myth" *miff*. Full possessive pronouns – *your*, *their*, *my* – still made guest appearances in his English, and he didn't invariably defy grammatical number (*they was*, and so on). But his verbal prose and his accent were in steep decline (Amis 2012: 14).

The renderings are often those of a generalized working-class East London (white) accent, many accurate – "'Hypothesis,' *Hypoffesis* – and while others are not deployed exactly to a linguist's liking, they are laid out with emphatic care: "Truck: pronounced *truck-uh* (with glottal stop on the terminal plosive)" (Amis 2012, 16) – what would be [trʌʔ] with substitution of the glottal stop for final stop, or [trʌʔə] with the trailing vowel after release of the glottal stop. One does not quibble with a novelist's ear for dialect normally, as in this case the English language itself has a vivid role in the novel's "State of England" satiric landscape. Asbo litters Diston and everywhere he goes with crudities sexual and racial and his speech patterns more than those of any other characters are the novel's touchstone. His nephew Desmond, half-Trinidadian, is under Asbo's sway (when not terrified of him, there is a sort of replacement father role "Uncle Li" plays), but also determined to break free of him and Diston – through books, university, journalism, then marriage and fatherhood. While Asbo is set up to be easily loathed – in part as a caricature of "all that is wrong with Britain" – he is also the novel's Miltonic hero. Desmond Pepperdine, biracial, fatherless, quiet yet well-spoken, kindly, is the Dickensian underdog – there is even a bit of sly satire of his 'politically correct' desirability as underdog in that, in the end, Desmond's long suppressed "sin" comes back to haunt him in the form of a vengeful Uncle Lionel. All is upended when Asbo gets the news, during a stay at Wormwood Scrubs, that he has won the lottery, just 50p shy of £140 million. 'Lotto lout' Asbo runs through his money quickly, but also learns to make it from investment schemes; his accent, however, remains unchanged, part of Asbo's fierce resistance to a 'celebutante,' 'reality-tv star' media world. A letter he sends from prison to his nephew Desmond, "by far the longest literary effort that Des had ever seen from his uncle's pen...was in block capitals and unpunctuated, like a telegram without the stops":

> DES BE AT NORF GATE ON SATDEE JULY 11 TWELVEFIRTY BRING ME DRIVE-IN LICENSE ME BIRF STATIFICAT ME BLAK SELL FONE AN ME CUMPEW UH... (Amis 2012, 81).

It is a rendering perhaps less as Lionel Asbo would spell it – as an exaggerated and exaggerative character not really a point one need worry about – than for the reader's amusement and comprehension of Asbo's voice. The phonetic spelling *compew uh*, clearly meant to record Asbo's pronunciation rather than a likely spelling, is interesting for the future of literary dialect, particularly those pronunciations that seem to defy pronunciation spelling. As seen earlier, literary conventions in representation of dialect often trump linguistic accuracy, and as one cannot imagine using IPA in most literary contexts, conventional or *ad hoc* solutions will likely have to do. And in an age of Estuary English, how does one render the *l*-vocalization of *Essex girls*: [gaʊ′rs]/[gaʊʷs]?[3]

12.3 THE BUSINESS OF ENGLISH: ENGLISH AS A SECOND LANGUAGE

As the most widely used language in business, politics and diplomacy, mass media, and international organizations (treaty organizations, athletic associations, NGOs), the teaching and learning of English as a second or other language (TESOL, TESL, TEFL) is big business. Numbers are hard to come by, but growth in the numbers of programs offering training in teaching English to non-native learners, of countries to which such teachers are sent to or hail from, and of learners of English as a second or other language has been spectacular since the 1960s. The TESOL International Association (Teachers of English to Speakers of Other Languages), a professional organization for ESL teachers that offers support and training in second-language pedagogy, noted in its annual report that the 2012 convention held in Philadelphia boasted 7,333 attendees from 118 countries.[4] The for-profit Oxford Seminars program maintains a list of some 29,630 English language schools worldwide.[5] Simply within the United States, government statistics show 5.3 million limited-English proficiency (LEP) students in public schools in the country (2021 estimate; National Center for Educational Statistics), who speak over 400 different languages (though 80% of the students have Spanish as their L1). This is just in the public school systems K-12 (kindergarten through high school); excluded here are figures for adult learners: in the United States there are more than one million adult learners in government-funded programs.[6] The British Council maintains a list of accredited English-language schools with coursework for foreign learners, and estimates that 600,000 learners enter the United Kingdom each year to learn the language.[7] The British Council repeats the widely used figure of 750 million EFL speakers worldwide (as seen earlier, that figure has likely passed 1 billion).

[3] Chris Irvine, "What is an Essex Girl?", *The Telegraph* (online) 5 March 2010, http://www.telegraph.co.uk/news/uknews/7368909/What-is-an-Essex-Girl.html.

[4] http://www.tesol.org/about-tesol/annual-report.

[5] http://www.oxfordseminars.com/esl-schools-directory/.

[6] The figure is for students in US public schools (nces.ed.gov). http://www.ncela.gwu.edu/data/biennial;

[7] http://www.britishcouncil.org/d210-english-open-doors-schools-directory-july-15.pdf; http://www.britishcouncil.org/accreditation-az-list.htm.

A quick Internet search on the subject reveals how many *.coms* are involved in this "business of English," especially of *Business English*, the jargon and threshold skills viewed necessary in international business. As also seen earlier, English in its expansion benefits from no near competitors – and a near competitor is what is needed to genuinely make inroads on the status of English as a global business and scientific language. Mandarin may still have more L1 speakers, but is not yet even a hemispheric or regional language (i.e., outside the borders of China); while the study of the language has increased among foreign-language learners, many of those learners already speak English as an L1 or L2. Regionally, BrE or, increasingly, AmE is used in South Asia (Pakistan, India, Bangladesh), Indonesia and Malaysia, Southeast Asia (Burma, Thailand, Laos, Cambodia, and especially Vietnam), East Asia (Japan and the Koreas), and in the Philippines and much of Oceania. Add to that the growing interest in and esteem of regional varieties of English (Singlish, Hong Kong English, Malaysian English, etc.), English-based pidgins and Creoles, and the increasing use of English loanwords in languages of Asia ("Konglish"). Inasmuch as China and the United States compete economically and militarily not just in 'spheres of influence' such as the South China Sea, but globally, the language battle may already have been lost. While the whole "most spoken language" matter can be cast in jingoistic or stridently political terms, it is more a matter of historical moment and, to a lesser extent, utility. In part, the growth of English beyond its territorial linguistic homelands to even a "post-anglophone" extent has enabled this spread; it also loosens the fixity a language and culture and people can have as with, say, Japanese or Norwegian. That is not to say that the expansion of English for business and cultural purposes is without political scope. The Japan Exchange and Teaching (JET) Program, run in cooperation between the U.S. and Japanese governments, has as of 2024 "5861 participants from 51 countries" (mainly the United States, Canada, the United Kingdom, Australia, New Zealand, and South Africa).[8] The program's purpose is simple: "to help enhance internationalization in Japan by promoting mutual understanding between Japan and other nations. The program also aims to improve foreign-language education in Japan and to encourage international exchange at the local level by fostering ties between Japanese youth and foreign youth." Thousands of students from Anglophone countries have been immersed in Japanese culture, begun to learn or master Japanese, but lurking in the background is the postwar Japanese-American political arrangement and fears of Japanese "isolationism."

What might be called a regional projection of cultural and business power can be seen in other government-fostered schemes. The Australian Broadcasting Corporation (ABC) sponsors through its Australia Network the 15-part video series "The Business of English" aimed at its Australian neighbors – Australian foreign policy has always been concerned with Commonwealth and Anglophone ties (Australian troops served in the U.S. conflict in Southeast Asia, and in Afghanistan and Iraq), but it has become increasingly concerned with its Asian neighbors. The English instruction programs involve a fictionalized cast including Victor Tang, sales representative for Asia-Pacific region of "Oceanwide Imports Ltd," and Lin Tan, sales manager also for an imports

[8] https://jetprogramme.org/en/history/

firm. In some respects silly, nonetheless, as seen earlier, television and now the Internet play an enormous role in the acquisition of English worldwide.

This worldwide spread of English involves now nations never directly under British or American colonial rule or occupation ('sphere of influence' is another matter). In some cases, English is displacing another colonial European language (French, Spanish, Dutch). Thomas Clayton's study of English in Cambodia – a nation with colonial ties to France (as part of Indochine) and a vexed relationship with the United States (which secretly carried out 'carpet bombing' of the Southeast Asian nation during the Vietnam conflict) – made the broader observation that nations such as Cambodia may demonstrate that the learning and use of the English language may have "slipped the orbit of the United Kingdom and the United States" and led to a "post-anglophone" stage in its development (Clayton 2006, 246). In such an envisioned moment, needs or objectives outside American or Anglo-American geopolitical or cultural ('Coca-colonialism') expansion are at work, such as those of the "global infrastructure of English-language universities" or in the "international aid community *sauf* Francophonie" (Clayton 2006, 246). And while French, by its prestige and French government lobbying, maintains a foothold as a global second language at the diplomatic and international-organization level, much of this business is conducted in English.

12.4 NEW CRISES, NEW WORDS

In the wake of the horrific events of 11 September 2001, official reaction to the terrorist attacks on the United States was swift, involving as it often did measures that had been in the planning long before the 2001 attacks. The Office of Homeland Security (OHS) was rapidly constituted, former governor of the state of Pennsylvania Tom Ridge appointed as its director on 8 October 2001. On 25 November 2002 the Homeland Security Act established the Department of Homeland Security (DHS), a designation the governmental umbrella-grouping still bears. Though references to the *homeland* and *homeland security* appear in President George W. Bush's speeches and especially in the utterances of White House spokespersons, it was not an entirely new form. In a 1999 speech to the Citadel military academy in Charleston, South Carolina, then Texas Governor Bush asserted that "We will defend the American homeland by strengthening our intelligence community."[9] The collocation *homeland defense* also occurs in the address, and by late 2001 *homeland security* is fully realized as an AmE collocation that would soon be exported globally, as would the *global war on terror* (GWOT). And this new "type" of war, declared upon a technique employed by *non-state actors*[10] rather than a nation-state, asymmetrical and unconventional, 'global' in scope, would engender a vast vocabulary unto itself – in all

[9]The speech, delivered on 23 September 1999, was entitled "A Period of Consequences"; http://www3.citadel.edu/pao/addresses/pres_bush.html.

[10]A semantic extension of an existing term that refers to organizations or entities that participate in international relations, part of 'political science' or 'politics and government' jargon; the term, in referring to such entities as al-Qaeda, narrows and becomes pejorative to 'violent non-state actors.'

probability, a vocabulary nearly as prolific as that of computer technology, but given even greater dissemination beyond specialist users by mass media.

The rapid dissemination of 'milspeak' in 21st-century media is the product of a number of factors: the near dominance in the media of retired military officers, and paid promoters from 'defense institutes' and other think tanks, as well as friendly reporters (ex-*embeds*, or those wishing to keep the supply lines of information open) on news programs "to put things in perspective"; and, more broadly, a general militarization of society – something certainly seen during World War II – and language. Contemporary English is rife with sporting and military metaphors to begin with – perhaps a natural result of a competitive society – but the military and 'security-minded' metaphorical scheme has achieved a sort of linguistic *full-spectrum dominance*. Reporters and spokespeople seem even to adopt the rigidity of posture and facial set of technocratic military briefers – minus the 'plain talk' and forthrightness (even crudity and vulgarity) military officers once used in press pool interviews. The incessant drive to *stick to the script*, *stay on message*, and *control the narrative* has rendered most public proclamations semantically opaque, empty boilerplate. And the rapidity of dissemination is matched by a profligacy in coinage – for example, the U.S. *Department of Defense Dictionary of Military and Associated Terms* (March 2017 version) is 394 pages long, of which 114 pages constitute an appendix of over 4,000 acronyms in current use in the military.[11] A large, complex organization will have need of internal policy guidelines and a list if not glossary of terms currently in use, but the sheer vastness of DOD and MoD operations is nonetheless staggering: *continuity of government* (COG), *continuity of operations* (COOP); *counterterrorism* (CT), hence *CT training*, *CT exercise*, or, from a DOD job announcement: "Serve as a USSOCOM Special Operations Counterterrorism (CT) Exercise Fusion Cell member within USSCOM Force Management Directorate/J7 at MacDill AFB, Tampa, FL"[12]); *tactical air command center* (TACC); *target acquisition*, *target development*, *target of opportunity*, *target-rich environment*. The rise of a 'corporate defense industry,' an evolution of the 'military-industrial complex' (MIC; a collocation with spin-off coinages such as 'prison-industrial complex,' 'university-industrial complex'[13]), has produced all sorts of symbiotic military and defense contractor hybrids, and a 'revolving door' of military to corporate transfers – MIC can appear unexpanded, frequent enough in its usage that it joins other lexified acronyms ("the MIC" in place of the *military-industrial complex*).

The name of the DHS umbrella organization – the "Department of Homeland Security" – is itself a hypernym, or umbrella or cover term. OED2 lists as the first attestation to *homeland* its use, in an immediately religious context, a line from Scots poet (and ardent supporter of James I) Alexander Craig's "The Pilgrime and

---

[11] This is US DOD Joint Publication 1-02 http://ra.defense.gov/documents/rtm/jp1_02.pdf: https://www.tradoc.army.mil/wp-content/uploads/2020/10/AD1029823-DOD-Dictionary-of-Military-and-Associated-Terms-2017.pdf; see also JP 3-27 *Homeland Defense* 12 July 2007 and its glossarial appendices.

[12] http://www.rdr.com/jobs/13-54.pdf; USSOCOM = United States Special Operations Command, AFB = Air Force base.

[13] "The University-Industrial Complex," *The New York Times* 18 September 1994; http://www.nytimes.com/1994/09/18/business/l-the-university-industrial-complex-281158.html.

Heremite": "That loving lord, shall take vs by the Hand, / And with Him lead vs, to the Home Land."[14] The second attestation is economic, "Neither need I nominate the homeland commerce of this kingdome to Scotland and Ireland," from the *Merchants Mappe of Commerce* (1638) of Lewes Roberts (1596–1641), in the simple sense of 'A person's home country or native land; the land of one's ancestors.' Phrasal *the homeland* dates to the 19th century and later, while there is also the South African sense of *homelands* or *Bantustans* (Afrikaans *Bantoestan*, 'Bantu-stan'; *-stan* in the sense 'state/region' is from Persian, though ultimately of Sanskrit origin). The collocation *homeland security* first occurs in Hiroshi Saito 1935 book *Japan's Policies and Purposes: Selections from Recent Addresses and Writings* ("it would not be essential to any Western nation's proper homeland security to go to war"; s.v. *homeland*, compounds). And the next occurrence does not come until after (September 11) in a *Time* magazine article on President Bush's establishment of an OHS, by which we have the sense still in use: 'national security, now esp. with regard to the threat of terrorism within a country's borders.' One might say that continued use of the term in conjunction, or even interchangeably, with *War on Terror* has led to semantic broadening: that 'foreign soil' operations are not just an extension of but actual matters concerning *homeland security*. The semantic displacement has only been partial, and not necessarily interchangeable, as the semantic ranges of *national security* (a term evocative of the Cold War and *nuclear deterrence*) and *homeland security* (terrorism by non-state actors or agents) do not fully overlap. To an extent, *national security* may retain its older, broader sense of conflict between or threat from nation-states (OED: 'the safety of a nation and its people, institutions, etc., esp. from military threat or from espionage, terrorism, etc.,' s.v. *national security*), while *homeland security* seems to bear implications of unconventional threats from non-state groups – namely, from *terrorism*. While the original connection between *terrorism* and 'The Terror' is from the French Revolution, the OED's succinct second sense of the term is telling: 'the unofficial or unauthorized use of violence and intimidation in the pursuit of political aims' (s.v. *terrorism*). The emphasis upon 'unofficial' and 'unauthorized' makes the distinction best summed up in the rather negative adage that a government is an entity that has a monopoly on the resources of violence. The attestations in the OED entry dating 1796–1989 range from ancient Greece to Northern Ireland, and encompass references to insurrection, rebellion, and guerilla warfare. Later 20th-century use of the term *terrorism* had its antecedents in press coverage of IRA bombing campaigns in BrE in particular.

The impact of the GWOT on 21st-century English is most immediately seen in the lexical realm: *Homeland Security, global terrorism, counterterrorism, al Qaeda, ISIS/ISIL, the surge* (campaign in Baghdad and al-Anbar provinces of Iraq 2007), *social media monitoring tools, sleeper cells, data-mining, Threat Mitigation Units, Urban Areas*

[14] The line from Craig (ca. 1567–1627) may be a ghost reference in the OED; the Hunterian edition of Craig's poetry prints "And with Him lead vs, to the HOLIE LAND," which scans, while 'home land' does not meet the metrical requirements. The poem was published posthumously in 1631 in Aberdeen by Edward Raban, only one copy of which survives (now in the Huntington Library, San Marino, California). See *the Poetical Works of Alexander Craig, of Rose-Craig, 1604-1631, Now First Collected* (Glasgow: The Hunterian Club, 1873).

Security Initiatives; *Truthers*: originally skeptics of the official version of the events of September 11, and the form has produced in turn *Birthers* (those skeptical of the official birth certificate of President Barack Obama, a skepticism extended to *globalists*, *banksters*, *Bilderbergers*, the *Davos crowd*, members of the *NWO* [New World Order]). The *Occupy Wall Street* protest that began in September of 2011 spread globally, producing not only a ready-made template for other 'Occupy X' formations but a language of the 1% versus the 99% ("We are the 99%"). Social media sped the growth of such movements, and some existed largely in cyberspace (Anonymous). The use of Guy Fawkes masks by Occupy street protesters and those delivering Anonymous communiques on *YouTube* pointed to a curious mixture of popular and traditional culture: the Fawkes mask was employed by the titular protagonist in 2005's *V for Vendetta* (based on David Lloyd's *graphic novel*, a term that has understandably displaced *comic book*), and there seemed to be as well varying awareness of the original 1605 Gunpowder Plot against the Houses of Parliament. The *tale of the tape*, the role of video technology, has gone digital. The protests and petitions, surveillance and spying, have increasingly been reduplicated in *cyberspace*, that is, to use a term that originally referred to that great defining transport of the 19th century, the railroads: *online*.

The much-vaunted *24-hours news cycle* is now outpaced by the *Twitterverse* (or *X-verse* or *-sphere*) and *alternative media* platforms such that *disinformation* has, especially since the highly contentious 2016 and 2020 US Presidential elections, become one of the highest-frequency forms in search analytics of media coverage. The word seemingly has its origins in the Cold War, the earliest attestations in the OED dating to 1955–1967 and perhaps deriving from Russian Дезинформация (*dezinformatsija*). The word now seems so highly partisan in application that its use seems akin to that of *sin* in earlier Christian texts and preaching or *wickedness* in Puritan New England. Of course, as can be seen in the semantic history of any human language, the semantic content of words is shaped by the intentions of users and their sense (often impressionistic, even at times erroneous) of what a word means.

But crises in particular drive vocabulary expansion and awareness of new vocabulary tokens and even registers – all speakers of contemporary English have some knowledge of the computer/digital register, and now, in the *COVID-19/COVID/covid* era (frequency of use has often reduced the acronym to the simplex *covid*), a renewed or expanded knowledge of medical and epidemiological registers. When linguists look back over the development of the lexicon of English in the first quarter of the 21st century the events of 9/11 and the *War on Terror* will likely be seen as the signal events that began to mark a new age of 'postmodern' English lexis. But it is likely the SARS-CoV-2 epidemic 2019-present that will be seen as the more prolific. A first grouping of terms includes some that are fairly to highly technical, part of medical or epidemiological registers, but which entered reportage, public announcements (billboards, PSAs [*public service announcements*], etc.), and general discourse as massive media campaigns sought to sound the alarm over the crisis.

SARS (Sudden Acute Respiratory Syndrome)
SARS-1 (2002–2004; origin: Southern China)
SARS-2 (2020–; origin: Southern China)
MERS (Middle East Respiratory Syndrome; 2012–; origin: Saudi Arabia)

ARDS (Acute Respiratory Distress Syndrome (also called 'wet lung')
RSV (Respiratory Syncytial Virus; also called 'human orthopneumovirus')
CDC (Centers for Disease Control and Prevention; the United States)
WHO (World Health Organization)
PHE (Public Health England)
Coronaviridae (family of coronaviruses)
zoonotic (spread of an infectious disease from animals to humans, especially if previously limited to animals; in popular usage, it "jumps" from one species to another)
Wuhan virus (the original name for SARS-CoV-2; still used for the original 'strain,' as by Dr. Anthony Fauci at a press briefing 12 April 2021)
2019nCoV (designation in January 2020 of a 'novel' coronavirus in Wuhan, China)
SARS-CoV-2 (Sudden Acute Respiratory Syndrome Coronavirus 2; official designation for the virus causing COVID-19 to distinguish it from SARS-CoV-1 that originated in China in 2002)
novel coronavirus (designation that a new member of the family Coronaviridae had been identified but not yet officially named, thus it is new or 'novel') COVID-19 (also 'covid-19,' now commonly just 'covid': official designation as of 2 November 2020 for 'coronavirus disease 2019')
VBM, VOI, VOC, VOHC (AmE): Centers for Disease Control and Prevention (CDC) classifications of SARS-CoV-2 variants: Variants Being Monitored, Variant of Interest, Variant of Concern, Variant of High Consequence
VUS, VOC, VUI, VIM (BrE): Public Health England (PHE) classifications of Variants Under Surveillance (the cover term), Variants of Concern, Variants Under Investigation, Variants in Monitoring
alpha (B.1.1.7) variant: detected in the United Kingdom in December 2020
beta (B.1.351) variant: detected in South Africa in December 2020
gamma (P.1) variant: detected in Brazil in December 2020
epsilon (B.1.427, B.1.429) variant: detected in California in March 2021
zeta (P.2): detected in Brazil in February 2021
eta (B.1.525) variant: detected in Nigeria and the United Kingdom in December 2020
theta (P.3) variant: detected in the Philippines in February 2021
iota (B.1.526) variant: detected in NYC in February 2021
kappa (B.1617.1) variant: detected in India in May 2021
lambda (C.37) variant: detected in Peru in August 2020
mu (B.1.621, B.1.621.1) variant: detected in Colombia in January 2021
*nu (B.1.1.529): this was first applied to the variant detected in Botswana and South Africa in November 2021
omicron (B.1.1.529) variant: this is now the official name applied to what had briefly been known as the 'nu' variant
escape variant (variants that 'escape' the 'vaccines')
Messenger RNA (ribonucleic acid): hence mRNA vaccine/shot
spike protein
ACE-2 receptor (angiotensin-converting enzyme)
booster

vaccine mandate
lockdown (hard lockdown, soft lockdown)
bend the curve, flatten the curve; zero covid
"we're all in this together" (this dates back to 2012 as a campaign slogan of the United Kingdom's Conservative Prime Minister David Cameron)
social distancing, physical distancing
PPE (personal protective equipment)
N95, P100 masks
face covering
rapid testing
positivity rate
surveillance testing
vaccine exemption
CARES (Coronavirus Aid, Relief, and Economic Security) US Congress, Act, HR 748, 20 March 2020
PPP (Paycheck Protection Program) loans, established by US Congress, CARES Act, ended 31 May 2021
contact tracing
contact investigators (2020)
contact tracers (2021)

Another set of vocabulary, of generally mid to high frequency, might be classed as part of a secondary or second-phase register: the vocabulary generated once the crisis was identified and publicized.

Zoom
Zoom fatigue
Zoom-bombing
fully remote
shelter-in-place
self-isolate
quarantine
community spread
community transmission
person-to-person transmission
surface transmission
hand hygiene
"not a big ask, wear a mask"
R0 (R naught) number: basic reproduction rate of an infectious agent
depletion of susceptibles
long covid
vax hesitancy
vax(x)ed, vax, unvax(x)ed
IM (intramuscular) injection
VAERS (Vaccine Adverse Event Reporting System [of the CDC])
EudraVigiliance (EU equivalent to VAERS)
adverse reaction
ADE (antibody-dependent enhancement)
cytokine storm
double-vaxxed, triple-vaxxed
undervaxxed
fully vaccinated
vaccine card
vaccine passport
covid passport
vaccine regimen
vaccine schedule
asymptomatic carrier
super-spreader
super-spreader event
self-monitoring
temperature screening
hybrid (model, learning)
drive-thru testing
hydroxychloroquine
Ivermectin
Remdesivir
Paxlovid (new Pfizer covid pill)
Molnupiravir (new Merck covid pill)
gain-of-function (research)
BSL-4 lab (biosafety level)
herd immunity
natural immunity
patient zero
congregate settings
low-density (model)
presumptive positive case
immunocompromised

outdoor dining
remote quarantine (Australia)
isolation camp (Australia; Howard Springs isolation camp)
close contact
(covid) exposure
exposure notice
covid notice
antibody test (serology test)
antibody shedding
antigen test
cluster
convalescent plasma therapy
swab test
nasopharyngeal swab (test, specimen)
EUA (Emergency Use Authorization)
viral load
viral shedding
breakthrough infection
vaccine effectiveness
anti-vaxxer (this has semantically broadened to refer also to those who only refuse the experimental mRNA shots rather than all vaccines)
covid protocols
(contact) tracing protocols
contactless delivery
contactless pickup
contact-free (vs. contactless or no-touch)
no-touch trash can (pedal trash can)
gloving
fully gowned, gown up
physical (distance) guides (pieces of tape or decals on floor, etc.)
negative pressure room (air pressure in room in hospital covid ward is lower than that outside the room – to prevent virus escape)
covid billionaire
mask up (as verb, especially in imperative mood)
mask down (as in 'with mask down')
cordon sanitaire (a recycled term from earlier crises: attempt to stop spread of virus/disease by preventing people from leaving an area; more common outside AmE)
essential workers
essential activities
presymptomatic
epidemic, pandemic, endemic
outbreak, cluster
positivity rate
travel ban
travel restrictions (AmE; travel curbs BrE)
WFH (working from home)
remote learning
remote work(place)
ACH (air changes per hour – guidelines for indoor air circulation)
HEPA (high-efficiency particulate-absorbing filter; industry standard for air/HVAC
monoclonal antibody treatment
remote patient monitoring
surge (in case numbers)
wave (of pandemic)
public health expert
droplet range
GAVI (Global Alliance for Vaccines and Immunology; now known as 'Gavi, The Vaccine Alliance')
COVAX (Covid-19 Vaccines Global Access; a program of donation of vaccine doses by wealthier nations to lower-income nations headed by Gavi)
The New Normal
The Great Reset; reset (in collocations such as *reset X*, *the reset*, *economic reset*)
Build Back Better

This is of course nowhere near a complete "Vocabulary of covid" – left out are many brand-name vaccines, therapies, and tests and protocols, but the sheer mass of new lexical items in so relatively short a period of accession (Spring 2020–Summer 2022) raises interesting questions about the role of mass media – and even more so social media – in not just informing people about events but perhaps also driving and shaping perceptions of them. It is difficult to think of any other medical or epidemiological crisis that has so altered the lexicon in recent times, and even the broader register of public discourse (this was at first the result of panic, but the after-effects look to be long-lasting). But there is some precedent within recent memory, the HIV-AIDS crisis of 1981 to present; in fact, a considerable number of terms are recycled from that crisis, as was the register of pronouncements by *public health officials*.

Inevitably, any crisis or event that so deeply marks public discourse and lexis affects popular discourse and vocabulary as well. The "slang lexicon" of covid encompasses several hundred items, many of them revivals or adaptations of existing formations or expressions already in the informal register. A form such as *Zoom fatigue* ('fatigue' or simply irritation at having to use the remote meeting technology) likely began its lexical course as slang, modeled on other X-*fatigue* formations (-*fatigue* has become not just a frequent second element in compounds but a productive suffix); frequent use in workplace and academic settings seems to have allowed it to 'leap up' in level within the *covid*-register from informal to more formal use. Only a small sample can be given, and even that, naturally, gives a sense of how a public health crisis, like a war, can be an eminently divisive matter.

face diaper
maskhole
Branch Covidian
covidiot
Lockdownista
medical tyranny
maskne (mask + acne)
clot shot
China Originated Virus
commie flu, commie cold
CCP Virus
Red Death
WuFlu
deputized nobodies
Plandemic
scamdemic
scariant
hamstering (panic buying/hoarding, as of toilet paper; 2020)
quarantinis (blend: quarantine + martini)
Miley Cyrus (= 'corona virus' in Cockney rhyming slang; BrE)
BT ([the] 'before time," i.e., before corona virus); also BV, PV (before/post-virus)
waist-up dressing (for Zoom meetings, i.e., pajamas down below)
Blursday (notion that days blur together with lockdowns/remote work or learning)
Hot Girl Summer (that the vaccines would allow freedom to resume the old normal and *'gram*, etc. Turned into 'vax girl summer')
'Rona
coronacation (lockdown staycation)
quarantine 15 (modeled on 'freshman 15')
'pandemic pounds' (weight gain during lockdowns)
The Corona 19s (variant of above)
coronaspeak
morona
pureblood (unvaccinated)
Boomer Remover

WYH (wash your hands)
Quarantunes (quarantine playlist)
bacbac (antibacterial gel, hand sanitizer)
panno (pandemic; Australian English)
vaxhole[15]
death shot, kill shot
stimmy (stimulus payments)
Covid Karen, Lockdown Karen
JOMO (joy of missing out)
anti-masker
Coronapocalypse
Fauci ouchie (mRNA shot)
vaxxie (vaccination selfie, especially by politicians)
halfvaxxed, halfcination (partially vaccinated)
the jab, double-jabbed
doomscrolling, gleefreshing

This "cycling back" in lexical patterns may have a parallel in coverage of the Ukraine crisis from February 2022 to present, which seems to have reawakened layers of the Cold War vocabulary to be repurposed for a *hot war*.

Donbas(s): the Donbas Basin, the coal and industrial heartland of Eastern Ukraine
DPR = Donetsk People's Republic
LPR = Luhansk People's Republic
special operation (Спецоперация) = Russia's official term for the invasion of Ukraine
AFU = Armed Forces of Ukraine
UA = Ukrainian Army; also, ZSU збройні сили україни (*zbroyni syly ukrayiny*) in Ukrainian, or VSU вооруженные силы украины (*vooruzhennyie sily ukrainy*) in Russian; in English coverage the ZSU and VSU acronyms are seen in use, and these seem to be generally understood not just by analysts but by those following the news coverage fairly closely
terobonist: Ukrainian territorial defense forces
hohol/khokhol (хохол): Russian pejorative term for Ukrainians deriving from *khokhol*, a topknot or top tuft hairstyle with rest of head shaved characteristic of medieval Ukrainian Cossacks
Spetsnaz (спецназ): Russian Special Forces
Shahed drone: Iranian *kamikaze* drone (drone sent on one-way destructive mission) employed (and now manufactured) by the Russian Federation; because of its blunt triangular shape it has been given the slang name *Dorito* (after the American brand of corn chips) and now called *geran* 'geranium' in Russian use
Kalibr (Калибр): Russian cruise missile that can travel up to 2200 mph; launched in present crisis mainly from Russian navy ships in Black Sea

[15] Like *maskhole*, the mocking blend *vaxhole* can be semantically ambivalent or bivalent; the former seems to have become auto-antonymous, applied at first to those resisting mandatory masking, then to those persisting in their use in situations that did not seem to warrant *masking* (itself a covid-era repurposing); for example, alone in an automobile in the countryside. The case of *vaxhole* may be more complex, as its antonymous use may have been simultaneous, applied equally to those seen as resisting *vaccine mandates* and those insisting on increasingly draconian means of *encouraging* what officialdom termed *vaccine distribution/uptake*.

Kinzhal (Кинжал, 'dagger'): Russian hypersonic cruise missile used for the first time in striking Ukraine in March 2022; capable of traveling in excess of 8000–9000 mph

Z: Z-group of Russian Federation Armed Forces in Ukraine 2/2022–present; there is speculation that it stands for запад (*zapad*) 'west,' but the following group designations would seem to contradict that; "Z" is in wider use in Russia as a symbol for the war, its display a sign of support for the war effort; thus *V* (V-group Russian Armed Forces) and *O* (O-group)

Wagner Group: a Russian PMC used by that nation in various conflicts around the world, including Syria and Ukraine most recently

Ghost of Kiev (Привид Києва): alleged MIG-29 pilot of Ukrainian Air Forces said to have downed an unusually high number of Russian planes (10 alone on 27 February 2022), a story since debunked (but one of many propaganda efforts employed by both sides in the conflict)

Kyiv (Київ): a disambiguation only given attention with the war in Ukraine, with western media adopting the Ukrainian spelling as opposed to the traditional Russian *Kiev* (Киев); the Romanization *Kyiv* is now conventional, but confusing (it produces *kih-eev* or *KEE-yuv* or *kee-yuf*; one even hears *keeve* in the media). The form Kyiv is part of the program of **derussification** adopted in the Ukraine following the fall of the Soviet Union

Snake Island (зміїний острів, zmiinnyi ostriv): tiny Ukrainian island in the Black Sea west of Odessa near the Ukrainian-Romanian border, from February 2022 site of small-scale fighting that has loomed large in propaganda warfare

peremogy/peremohy (Russian and Ukrainian перемоги): 'victory'; both Russia and Ukraine have introduced the term in their press releases about alleged territorial gains/pushbacks

SBU: Служба безпеки України/Sluzhba bezpeky Ukrayiny 'Security Service of Ukraine'; the 'secret police' of Ukraine [as this is at times used as a pejorative and as an allusion to the Communist era rather than a contemporary gloss on 'SBU']

denazification (денацификация, denatsifikatsiya): Russia has claimed its invasion of the Ukraine is to 'denazify' the strongholds of neo-Nazi parties and militias in the Ukraine, particularly for their role in the Euromaidan protests (and 'Odessa Trade Unions House massacre' of ethnic Russians) and attacks on the Donbas 2014 to present.

Pravy Sektor (Ukrainian правий сектор): 'Right Sector,' one of a number of ultranationalist Ukrainian organizations (some are also militias with links to, or integration within, the AFU); it is, with its logo and flag, a 'Banderite' group

Banderite, Banderist: a term loosely referring to movements in Ukraine identifying as inspired by Ukrainian nationalist Stepan Bandera (1909–1959), a controversial figure in modern Ukraine

As with the covid crisis, the Ukraine crisis is subject to partisan claims and recriminations by supporters of one side or the other; no military crisis goes without such fault lines being discovered. It may be precisely this heated partisanship that drives lexical innovation, as sides develop alternative language to describe the same things (and the crisis in Ukraine has its linguistic side, as recent elections in the nation have often seen the vote fall along ethnolinguistic lines). The language of press release and protest, by innovation or repurposing, of the Gaza crisis 2023-present once again expands the popular vocabulary, with forms of high, mid-, and low frequency. Partisanship seems particularly acute, as it has been with regard to Israel and the Palestinians since 1948. The vocabulary can have a declarative power to the speaker's identity, sympathy, or allegiance: reference to the *Hamas massacre* (BrE *7/10*, AmE *10/7*) will rankle those who chant "From the river to the sea," or who replace IDF (Israeli Defense Force) with IOF ('Israeli Occupation Force'). There is a general pattern in 'revolutionary' conflicts for vocabulary to proliferate on the rebel rather than state-actor side; with regard to the renewed Gaza crisis the Arabic terms used in English-language coverage likely outnumber those from Israeli Hebrew: *nakba* ('disaster') and *intifada* ('uprising') beside Hebrew *aliyah* (literally 'ascent,' but used to refer to immigration to Israel) and *kiryat* ('town,' or, a more politically charged term, 'settlement'). The protests against Israel's response to the events of October 7/7 October have been particularly vociferous in Anglophone countries, enough so that measures have been proposed to consider "From the river to the sea" a form of hate speech or even a call for genocide (the US House of Representatives passed a measure, H.R. 883, on 16 April 2024, condemning the slogan as *antisemitic*). Others have in turn pointed out the slogan's use by conservative Israelis to refer to a return of Judaea and Samaria to *Eretz Yisrael* (the 'land of Israel'). The term *genocide* has been liberally used by all parties to the conflict, with especial frequency among pro-Palestinian voices (along with references to Gaza as an *open-air prison*). The term is particularly emblematic of the conflict; it was coined by lawyer Rafael Lemkin, a Polish Jew who fled to Sweden during the Second World War but lost much of his family in the Holocaust. It formed the linguistic basis for the *Genocide Convention* passed by the United Nations General Assembly on 9 December 1948, to which appeal has been made numerous times since – and currently, on behalf of the Palestinians of Gaza. The force of the appeal and term pitches at the memory of the Holocaust, and may likely be meant to undermine the force of its original application to the Holocaust and other systematic massacres of World War II. As the toll of the conflict mounts, the voices of protesters catch mainstream media attention – the protests and signage largely in English, with some Arabic loans (most not new): as global reach of protests and media can influence both governmental policy (the United States being the largest supplier of weapons to Israel), the use of English has increased: the Qatari Al Jazeera (from Arabic *al-jazīra*, 'island, peninsula') network has a dedicated English service; Lebanese Al-Mayadeen (Arabic *al-mayādīn*, 'the fields,' or 'squares'), launched in Beirut in 2012, also has an English-language service. The battle to *control the narrative* is often waged on X (formerly Twitter) in English. The Chief of the General Staff of the IDF (Israel Defense Forces) Herzi Halevi gives briefings in Hebrew and English; Prime Minister Benjamin Netanyahu (the original patronym Mileikowsky) spent his later formative years in the Philadelphia area while his father taught at Dropsie College (a fellow Hebraist on the faculty there was William Chomsky, father of the linguist Noam Chomsky) – Netanyahu speaks impeccable American English. In post-Cold War America few issues have so dominated policy and media coverage as "the Middle East," and where there is focus, and fervor, there is linguistic innovation. *De-escalation*, or *deconfliction* (a more recent political science *buzz-word*), when possible, often involves toning down the language, and the postconflict settlements and rhetoric can shape what words will survive the conflict to become permanent parts of the vocabulary (whether of low, mid-, or high frequency), and which will be more or less forgotten – until the next crisis that is.

12.5 A DIGITAL AGE: THE INTERNET AND ENGLISH

A salient development in the language of 'Homeland Security' is the expansion of 'defense' into cyberspace – indeed since 2009 the US military has had a 'cybercommand' (United States Cyber Command; USCYBERCOM) based in Fort Meade, Maryland. Like the United States Space Command (USSPACECOM; and now *Space Force*), established in 1985, USCYBERCOM is a break from the traditional Unified Combatant Command (UCC) of the U.S. Department of Defense, which has always had before a geographical *area of responsibility* (e.g., USCENTCOM, which views its responsibility as extending from Egypt through the Middle East to West Asia, forces of which have been deployed to the wars in Afghanistan and Iraq). Now the leap has been made from the terrestrial sphere to space, and from there to *cyberspace*. The prefix *cyber-* is among the most prolific of affixes in 21st-century English, even tediously so. It is freely found in collocative use and in compound formations: *cyberattack*, *cyber-bullying*, *cyberpunk*, *cyberwarfare*. As with *e-* ('electronic-') and *i-* ('intelligent-') formations, active generation of new collocations and compounds will continue apace with technological innovation, consumer trends, and what might be called a sort of techno-savvy pretension (a need to sound "in the know" about new technologies, even if one is not). *Cyber-* as a morpheme actually antedates the PC (personal computer) and Internet – *cyberspace* is first attested in science fiction writer William Gibson's short story "Burning Chrome" from 1982 (though the OED seems guarded here: "Apparently coined by William Gibson"; s.v. *cyberspace*). While *web/the web* is still in common use, if secondary to *I/internet*, *WorldWideWeb/the World Wide Web* is now rarer, though *www* is in many web addresses (or URLs, *uniform resource locators*) even if not noticed by many users of the *web/Internet*, and *cyberspace* seems more semantically abstract in some locutions, such as *lost in cyberspace*. Indeed, the economist and *New York Times* columnist Paul Krugman entitled a blog entry "Lost in Cyberspace"[16] after access was lost to blog entries on the *Times* website, then spread to the rest of the site on 14 August 2013. The *Times* denied that their site had been *hacked* or subject to a *malicious external attack*[17]; nonetheless, precisely that happened two weeks later as the *Times* website (the self-described *paper of record* in the United States employs *web site* by in-house style guidelines rather than the more common *website*) was *taken down* by a *cyberattack* claimed by the 'Syrian Electronic Army,'[18] allegedly a group of Syrian hackers supportive of the embattled regime of former Syrian President Bashar al-Assad. As Western powers (the

[16] *New York Times* (online), 14 August 2013; http://krugman.blogs.nytimes.com/2013/08/14/lost-in-cyberspace/#postComment.

[17] Noam Cohen, "Times Says Web Site Failure Is Not a Result of Cyberattack," *New York Times* (online) 14 August 2013; http://www.nytimes.com/2013/08/15/business/media/new-york-times-web-site-returns-after-hours-offline.html.

[18] Julianne Pepitone, "New York Times hit with 'malicious attack,'" *CNNMoney.com* 28 August 2013; http://money.cnn.com/2013/08/27/technology/security/new-york-times-hacked/index.html.

United States, Britain, and France) have supported opposition fighters in the Syrian civil war since March 2011, the 'real-world' fight has been shadowed by a parallel struggle in cyberspace. As is the pattern with 21st-century conflicts, an 'online' propaganda and 'information war' component often drives news coverage nearly as much as the events on the ground. Videos are posted on YouTube and Vimeo and other video-hosting platforms (and now *streaming platforms* and *video feeds*), 'tweets' from rival organizations or even combatants appear on Twitter/X, and online news sites have their comment boards flooded with thousands of postings (many allegedly by *sock puppets* or *bots*). This has reached a level of peak propaganda with the Ukraine and Gaza conflicts since 2022–2023 (as with the *NAFO* 'meme wars').

With so much going on or being lost in 'cyberspace,' it is interesting to note that *cyber(-)* is a clipping of *cybernetic*, the adjective form of *cybernetics*, a field of study outlined by MIT mathematician Norbert Wiener in his 1948 book *Cybernetics, or Control and Communication in the Animal and the Machine*; OED simply follows Wiener's formulation of the discipline as it is a term that has since varied widely in application in mathematics, philosophy, social sciences, engineering, and artificial intelligence among other disciplines: "The field of study concerned with communication and control systems in living organisms and machines" (s.v. *cybernetics*). Wiener derived *cybernetics* from Greek κυβερνήτης (*kubernētēs*), 'helmsman,' the form behind *govern, government*, and the 'kappa' in the honors society Phi Beta Kappa, the oldest in the United States, founded on 5 December 1776, whose motto is Φιλοσοφία βίου Κυβερνήτης (*philosophīa bīou kubernētēs*) 'Philosophy the helmsman of life.'[19] The steering or helmsman metaphor is apt, part of a nautical metaphoric scheme, found also with *aeronautical* and *cosmonaut*, and by extension in the nebulous formations *cloud-computing, the cloud, cloud storage*; what is interesting is the jump to Gibson's *cyberspace* neology. Such an awkward form of truncation is not unusual in the history of English – one that detaches a seeming affix or compound element from the original form and attempts to transport the full sense by means of the detached part (*church* is a clipping of the Greek phrase *kuriakòn dõma*, 'the house of the Lord,' or more literally, 'the lordly home,' whereby the English noun preserves only the Greek adjective 'lordly'). Interesting too is the pressing of *cyber-* into service as a sort of 'electronic' or 'computerized' descriptor or *metatag*. Strictly speaking, *cyberspace* is semantically empty, and somewhat ambiguous and tenuous anyway as a synonym for *the Internet* (unless one allows that *cyberspace* may be that *virtual reality* in which the Internet exists). The OED suggests as much in its definition of *cyberspace*: 'The space of virtual reality; the notional environment within which electronic communication (esp. via the Internet) occurs.' *Cyberspace* is cross-referenced with *Cyberia*, an evident play on, and not just homophone of, Siberia; the OED glosses: 'The notional environment within which electronic communication occurs; the space of virtual reality, esp. viewed as a global village or sphere of human interaction; cyberspace.' Or a global gulag? Does *Cyberia* fully escape semantically the clutches of Siberia's popular associations?

[19] The organization itself uses the slightly less literal version: "Love of learning is the guide of life"; http://www.pbk.org/infoview/PBK_InfoView.aspx?t=&id=8.

One of the OED's attestations for *Cyberia* is Douglas Rushkoff's *Cyberia: Life in the Trenches of Cyberspace* (Rushkoff 1994), in which the writer – who specializes in what might now be called 'digital studies' – explores the emergence of an *online culture* with a view toward promises of the democratization of culture, though subsequent work has also warned of the 'dark side' of this *cyber-culture and cyber-world*, especially its commercialization and consumerism, and there is no dearth of literature about the perils of *cyber-bullying* and *-stalking*, of *identity theft*. Before turning to more of this new world of terms, the use of 'notional' by the OED in its definitions of *cyberspace* and *Cyberia* seems vital – that the entire 'virtual' enterprise of the web involves an act of imagination, that the data, the texts, e-mails, links, images, audio, and video are anything more than just electrical signals. It is this imagining that is vital, but also unstable; how often is an e-mail not 'real' until it is printed out or saved or forwarded? Are there really *e-books*, or is 'digital' or 'electronic facsimile' the better term? Will a 'book' published only in 'electronic format' really be considered as durable and prestigious as the printed item? (The *hack* of the Internet Archive and related sites in October-November 2024 cautions against relying on digital archives to the exclusion of print and other hard-copy formats.) An interplay between the 'real' and 'virtual' worlds has produced interesting lexical fruit: *digital currencies* such as *eCoin*, *Bitcoin*, their *e-wallets*, and proposed variants of a *CBDC* (Central Bank Digital Currency) all maintain their link to the tangible progenitor. And the notional world of 'virtual reality' has probably been far less jarring to the average web user than may have been thought: one clicks items into virtual shopping carts to be clicked through to virtual checkouts, takes virtual tours of locations across the globe or just outside one's window, or, quite frankly, and unremarkably, just watches television and movies on a computer.

At the chapter's outset among the major concerns raised with describing 21st-century English only two decades into its history was the matter of lexical innovation. As seen earlier, no major linguistic component of contemporary English seems static – there are significant phonological and syntactic developments in the world's English varieties and English-based pidgins and Creoles. And these may be the most significant players in the vexed matter of 'global English' versus 'World Englishes.' Within the 'home country' and major Anglophone national varieties (American, Canadian, Australian, Indian, etc.) dialectal development and innovation still occur – a good deal of it as we have seen driven by matters of linguistic affectation, especially among younger speakers. In terms of standard global varieties of English, as would be expected, the greatest innovation is to be found in morphology and lexis. And while English is still the most common language of the Internet in terms of users (with Mandarin not far behind) and content (English-language content still dwarfs any near competitors), the gap is narrowing somewhat. Advances in displaying non-Roman scripts in the 1990s have allowed for a certain typographic parity – no longer is there a need to Romanize devanāgarī (for Hindi and a number of other South Asian languages), nor to depend upon pinyin renderings for Chinese varieties. The web has become friendlier to the scripts of the world's languages. The rise of discussion and message boards (LISTSERVs were an early form), texts, tweets, and other messaging systems in their immediacy and informality naturally inclines the user to the language he/she/they is/are most comfortable with. But it is not just the great abundance of web content in English that bolsters the global online reach of English. The late 20th and early 21st centuries have seen not only the continued dominance politically, economically, and culturally by the United States and the Anglo-American alliance that has driven Western foreign policy in the Middle East, Central Asia, and now Africa, but also the rapid worldwide spread of American popular culture and adaptation of it in virtually every corner of the world (seen earlier was the example of American hip-hop, arguably the most influential musical style globally). Looking to the future, it is inevitable to ask which areas of innovation will persist – does the 'Global War on Terror,' which has likely generated already a broader vocabulary than the entire Cold war era, indeed become the 'Long War' marking English for decades to come? Or technological innovation continue its rapid pace and mark English lexis more so than any other vocabulary field? For the moment, it may be useful to briefly survey the contours of the 'Digital Age' vocabulary of English.

A variety of processes of word coinage and derivational morphology are at work in the technological registers of the Internet, computerization/digital technology:

clipping:
bit < *binary digit*
blog < *web-log* (an interesting case of 'false-cutting')
techno- < *technological*

***de novo* and 'arbitrary' formations:**
byte: 8-bit unit of information [expandable by affixation to extraordinary multiples of units of digital information: *kilobytes* (KB), *megabytes* (MB), *gigabytes* (GB), *terabytes* (TB), *petabytes* (PB), *exabytes* (EB), *zettabytes* (ZB), *yottabytes* (YB)][20]

acronyms:
FTP: file transfer protocol
IP: Internet protocol (address)
IRC: Internet Relay Chat
ISP: Internet Service Provider
RSS: Rich Site Summary (often in collocation *RSS feed*)
TCP: Transmission Control Protocol (more commonly in the combination TCP/IP)
URL: uniform resource locator
VOIP: Voice over Internet Protocol (by which phone calls are made over the Internet)

affixation:
net-: *netizen* (here a detached suffix *-net* < *Internet* is converted to a prefix, and a blend formed of *Internet* + *citizen*)
-net: *ARPANET* (= Advanced Research Projects Agency Network, a U.S. Department of Defense forerunner of the Internet; here the prefix *net-* < *network* has been converted to a suffix)
wiki-: *Wikipedia*, *Wikileaks*

---

[20] The U.S. National Security Agency's vast Utah Data Center, is said to have capacity in the zettabytes: units of 10^{21} bytes.

One of the more morphologically rich areas of computer jargon is compounding: *data transfer*; *data storage*, *data encryption*; *file transfer*; *file protocol*; *uploads*, *downloads*, *downloaded music*, *downloaded movies*, *uploaded videos*; *hypertext*, *hyperlink*, *hotlink*. Acronyms and alphanumeric acronyms, such as of file formats and extensions, are enormously common: *MP3/MP4*, *CD-ROM*, *DVD-ROM*, *streaming services* (as opposed to cable subscriber services), *2GL/3GL*/etc. (*second-*, *third-generation programming language*). Alphanumeric combinations also come into play with the selection of passwords and PINs ('personal identifications numbers') or the generation of device technology (such as *4G* and *5G* broadband cellular technology: *fourth* and *fifth generation*); the average user of an *ATM* (in the Delaware Valley region of PA-NJ-DE the vestigial term *MAC* is still heard, for *Money Access Center*), *online bill-pay*, *online banking*, and *online shopping* (or *-retail*), and a host of other cyber-activities that require a username and password or *two-factor authentication* scrambles to come up with something both memorable and secure. It might be said that *digital* as a productive compounding element has undergone some semantic bleaching: a formation such as *digital humanities* broadly encompasses any electronic form of scholarship, performance, commentary, or pedagogy. A *digital library* might include hard-copy storage formats or *cloud storage* (or just, *the cloud* or *cloud server*). One can speak of wanting a *digital version*, *digital format*, *digital option*, and so forth, the first element being used rather loosely; similarly, *streaming* seems to be broadening into a catch-all term.

The vocabulary itself belongs to a number of registers, from that of programmers, coders, and hackers to everyday users of computers and the Internet, with a tendency for terms to 'leak down' from the specialist registers to 'end-users' (as in those who may or may not read EULAs, *End-User License Agreements* for software). Acronyms abound in any technical jargon, and they positively fill "techie talk": CSS (*Cascading Style Sheets*), HTML (*hypertext markup language*), XML (*extensible markup language*); BT (*BitTorrent*), DES (*data encryption standard*), OS (*operating system* or *open source*). *Software* and *hardware* generate their own subfields of tech vocabulary, though the latter has undergone significant changes to the once-dominant model of stand-alone or networked PCs (*personal computers*) with their CPUs (*central processing units*), monitors, printers, and other 'peripherals.' Every element of computing has its terminological subfields, from hardware matters such as ports and connections: for example, USB, *Universal Serial Bus*, in which the *bus*, the means of communication between computer components, such as between CPU and printer or *external storage device*, is said to derive from the Latin dative plural form *omnibus* 'for/with all,' and is thus connected to the history of this Latin loan earlier applied to publishing (*omnibus edition*) and politics (an *omnibus bill*). File extensions morphologically are usually acronyms or clippings: *.doc* (*plain-text document file*), *.exe* (*executable file*), *.jpeg* (a common image file format created by the *Joint Photographic Experts Group*, a collaboration of the ISO [International Organization for Standardization] and IEC [International Electrotechnical Commission]). So too with web domains (*domain names*): *.com*/*.co.uk* ('commercial'), *.edu* (colleges and universities – 'higher education'), *.org* (organizations, originally limited to nonprofit organizations); country domain names are normally clippings: *.ca* (Canada), *.in* (India), *.se* (Sweden). ICANN (the Internet Corporation for Assigned Names and Numbers, a nonprofit private corporation based in Los Angeles) coordinates the assignment of domain names through registering entities it accredits; the latterly mentioned country codes themselves are formally known as *ccTLDs*, a nearly inscrutable acronym for *country code Top-Level Domain.*

As with nearly every other aspect of life in the 21st century, computer and Internet security is a major concern. It is also an enormously profitable business for *virus-protection* providers. So pervasive is the need for computer prophylaxis that the compound adjective *anti-virus* has undergone conversion to the nominal form *antivirus* and is marketed as such by the major software providers in the field (as with so much else in tech jargon, many of the terms are proprietary). And while *hackers* and *hacktivists* will break into systems or code for the 'fun of it' or 'laughs' (or *lulz*, a pluralized play on *LOL* 'laugh out loud,' one of many acronyms that populate texting discourse and the 'Twitterverse'), more mysterious and malevolent hackers (*black hats*) launch the *malware* (a blend < *malicious software*) and *spyware* and *viruses* and *Trojans* (malware with a *malicious payload* – the term a literary allusion to the Trojan Horse). As do the cyberwarfare and espionage commands of many nations, Israel, the United States, and China foremost among them. The Stuxnet virus is a famous example of a 'computer worm' (a form of malware that unlike a virus does not need to infiltrate a program on the computer or network of computers it *infects*) likely developed by *nation-state actors* (as opposed to an individual hacker or 'collective' of hackers) that wound up infecting the computer system at Iran's Natanz nuclear facility causing centrifuges to spin out of control until damaged. Press reports credited the United States and Israel with the *cyberattack*; what was interesting in the coverage was that *cyber-command* defensive capabilities turned out to be offensive as well, and that a headline such as "Israeli Test on Worm Called Crucial in Iran Nuclear Delay"[21] presumed readers would suffer no semantic ambiguity over the use of *worm* – as with *mouse* (for what was originally called *computer-aided display control*) and *virus*, semantic differentiation has occurred.

Obfuscation both deliberate and inadvertent can be found in the emerging style of e-mail and text messaging language use. Clippings abound: *newbie* > *newb* – as do phonetic spellings – *noob* varying with *newb*. The style is most often associated with younger users, especially teenagers, and older users may resort nonetheless to such forms, abbreviations, acronyms, and spellings with strained irony. Much decried as yet another example of the "decline of English," *LOL*-speak is in part a result of constraints in the technology: character limits to texts and tweets, attempts to avoid overcharges in a cell phone/mobile industry that is highly monopolistic. But, as seen before, century after century, lamentations over alleged declines in literacy are commonplace. And the vast spread of at least functional literacy needs to be taken into account. Which is not to say that the many phonetic spellings, confusions, and malapropisms teachers note in student writing are not worrying. Something is happening with the new media and electronic devices; while the 'Millennials' are not exceptional

[21] William J. Broad, John Markoff and David E. Sanger, "Israeli Test on Worm Called Crucial in Iran Nuclear Delay," *New York Times* (online), 15 January 2011; http://www.nytimes.com/2011/01/16/world/middleeast/16stuxnet.html?pagewanted=all.

in their informal uses and orthographical errors, neither are they the multitasking generation of geniuses touted by self-esteem-raising workshops and best-selling parenting handbooks. Have electronic devices produced a certain laziness in recording English? Or has a generation of text-messagers simply committed spontaneous thoughts too quickly into 170- or 140-character-limited transmissions? While adults may find many of the abbreviations, acronyms, and alphanumeric combinations teens text and tweet irritating, there does not seem to be anything terribly new about the truncation – one thinks of the conventions of telegrams (in which one was charged per word) or secretarial shorthand. It may be more a matter of content and tone that adults are exposed more than ever to 'teen culture': one need only look to the recent major Hollywood feature-length film releases, nearly every one of which slated for summer release is based upon comic book figures: superheroes with superpowers enacting crude revenge fantasies in dystopic landscapes. Or one can turn to television, with so much teen-centric programming – a landscape of 'BFF' ('best-friends-forever') serio-comedies, dramedies, and sitcoms (not to mention the heavily scripted and market forces-cast and -driven *reality programs* attractive to networks largely in that they are cheaper to produce). But there is nonetheless a utility, economy, and inventiveness to this text-/tweetspeak that one finds in comment boards and Twitter/X replies:

BTW: by the way
IDK: I don't know
IMHO: in my humble opinion
LOL: laugh out loud
ROTFL: rolling on the floor laughing
TLDR: too long, didn't read
FIFY: fixed it for you
AFAIK: as far as I know
FWIW: for what it's worth
IRL: in real life
LMAO: laughing my ass off
OTOH: on the other hand
ICYMI: in case you missed it

Left out of this very brief sample of a 'textspeak' lexicon are emphatic variations that almost invariably add the 'F-word' (or *F-bomb*): LMAO 'laughing my ass off' > LMFAO; ROTFL 'rolling on the floor laughing > ROTFLMFAO, GTFO, and so forth. Emoticons too have been glossed over – the scores of typographic icons, many of them facial expressions such as the 'wink';) – as they transcend just English and belong to a nearly universal electronic iconographic notation system.

The new gadgets, devices, software, and smart phones that are now ubiquitous enough that they are taken for granted – no news event seems complete without cell camera video, and the tourist with camera or cell phone or *selfie-stick* has been joined by the awkward sight of people holding up tablets to take pictures – are vital to the *information economy*. No doubt part of the appeal of such devices and *apps* is their novelty and severely short half-lives. News coverage of devotees lining up overnight for the debut of the latest Apple offering is not really anything new – fans have lined up for game consoles, sneakers/trainers, or concert tickets. And for all the convenience and entertainment provided by these electronic devices and media, there are the perils of *over-sharing* and surveillance. But how much of all this is really new or lasting? This matters to its ultimate impact on the history of the English language. Which is all rather underwhelming, and makes one think of the curious postmodern consumerist paradox of a digital subscriber television package with 900 channels (many in HD) with nothing worth watching.[22] Inasmuch as e-mail, video-conferencing, CCTV, and satellite surveillance have made for a *global village* in closer contact, one wonders whether the alleged *future shock* has worn off with oversaturation. The question might be ventured: for all the lexical enrichment the Digital Age has provided, will the Internet, for instance, have as great and lasting an impact on the history of English as, say, William Caxton's introduction of the printing press to England or the King James Bible? At the risk of promulgating heresy, a tentative 'no' might be ventured.[23] David Crystal has seen in the Internet a profound source of future change for the language:

> Because the Internet is uncontrolled by the hierarchy of grammarians, lexicographers, publishers, printers, copy editors, and proof-readers who have traditionally established, disseminated, and controlled standard English, it seems likely that we will see a much greater presence of informal written interaction than at any previous stage in the history of the language, and thus the rapid emergence and consolidation of local group norms of usage – several of which will privilege non-standard forms. These new varieties are bound to achieve a more developed written representation than would ever have been possible before, and through the global reach of the Internet they may well extend their influence beyond their locality or country of origin. A whole new range of Internet-mediated regional written standards is the likely outcome. And as the amount of written language on the Internet will eventually far exceed that available in traditional print form, a new type of relationship between non-standard varieties and standard English will one day emerge (Crystal 2006, 404–405).

As seen above in "The Business of English," there are likely constraints to a "whole new range of Internet-mediated regional written standards" – the nature of social media networks that link people who are family or friends or acquaintances but located in different regions; the need for clarity to an immediate, known audience and a presumed, broader audience; orthographical constraints to all online activity: the need for spelling and form to be at least approximate for searches and indexing to be productive. There is also the matter of what much Internet "writing" consists of: actual written English or just graphically recorded speech. Advances in video- and tele-conferencing programs (Skype, now defunct; or Zoom) are allowing for what appeared before as written versions of discussions, or live, scrolling

[22] An admittedly weak adaptation of Bruce Springsteen's 1992 song "57 Channels (And Nothin' On)."
[23] Crystal 2006, especially at "The Long-Term Consequences of the Internet" (401–408).

transcripts or conversations to occur in real time and in person. Both activities may produce interesting archives for linguists: the off-the-cuff informal texting and tweeting of conversational English and the more natural and no less informal voice archive of actual Internet-broadcast conversations. What is likely happening is the recording, or transcribing, for now, of informal conversational English on the Internet, often with *ad hoc* rules of orthography and grammar as participants try to put into electronic text what had been free-flowing conversation before. But the examples above from Giriama text messaging in Kenya likely do bear out Crystal's prediction in a fairly radical way: ***usiku*** *I coud no sleep,* ***nakuwaza wewe*** *my lve,* ***tangu juzi naku*** *mis*: 'I couldn't sleep **at night, I think of you**, my love, **I've** missed **you since the other day**,' a mixture of Kigiriama, Sheng, and textspeak English (McIntosh 2010, 344). But, as seen earlier, the printing press generated, eventually, an orthographic fixity that was revolutionary, and no amount of informal or semi-literate tweets, however much the more curmudgeonly may fear their corrosive influence, can undo its legacy.

12.6 THE MEDIUM IS THE MESSAGE: 21ST-CENTURY MEDIA

While Canadian philosopher Marshall McLuhan's dictum "the medium is the message" (McLuhan 1964) has been endlessly repeated, it has not escaped the fate of many other dicta turned into *sound-bites* – modern mass media have indeed at times actually "become the message," growing beyond the embedding and symbiosis McLuhan envisioned. As seen earlier, McLuhan contributed toward the founding of a number of modern disciplines that examine human and mass media communication, as well as contributing the 'meta-language' used to describe these postmodern phenomena (we may owe *surfing the web* at least in part to McLuhan, in addition to *global village*). The increasing drive to extract profit from the *news business*, paralleled in the United States at least by the capitalization of *health care*, has yielded a much lamented coalescence with the entertainment industry – *infotaintment*, a blend similar to *infomercial* though the *info-* prefix performs differing semantic work: in the compound *infotainment* there is a sense of debasement or dilution of the *information* element of the blend by *entertainment*, while the *infomercial* purports to elevate the *commercial* (*advertisement*) with actual information beyond the sales pitch, though still primarily in the service of pushing and selling a product. Blends themselves seem subject to a kind of semantic alterity in this media age, which may be a function of an increasing sense of irony, even 'snarkiness' in media coverage and public reception of such coverage, and a sense of the semantic space of blends formed out of the native stock of English morphemes feeling some crowding – a salient example may be the AmE innovation *craptastic*, which has a general sense of something so 'crappy' it has ironic redemptive value, though it can be 'unpacked' semantically somewhat differently by various users.

The commodification of 'news' has spanned the range from the early days of television when news programs were *money losers* but recouped some expenses from incessant breaks for "some words from our sponsors," to a present age in which *content* is there to drive the advertisements, often with the products and services being hawked spilling over into the news covered.[24] The desire for more or more accurate 'content' has driven the rise of *alternative media* and *independent media* ('indymedia'); in addition to independent journalists are so-called *citizen journalists*, such as those who submit the photographs and videos that networks so often cite as news organizations close bureaus and cut staff. But as 'citizen journalists' increasingly provide for the network's photojournalism needs, the news divisions of major networks seem determined to merge their product with the dramatic, comedic, and other fare from their entertainment divisions. *Jump-cut* editing (an influence of MTV when it actually showed *music videos*), bold, flashing graphics (nearly everything bursts or explodes onto the screen – no more graceful *wipes* or *fade-outs*), loud, dramatic sound-effects and punctuation – the news program as crime drama or *homeland security* thriller. The ubiquitous *tickers* and *crawls* (and *chyrons*) suggest drama and immediacy, and they have multiplied to the point that nearly the bottom third of the screen has three and four tickers blotting out the main frame. Even the delivery of the news has changed – in terms of the tone, volume, and velocity of verbal delivery. Most reporters and *on-air personalities* seem chosen on the basis of their looks – the profit-motive's need for *eye candy* to keep viewers – but even the 'serious reporters' have resorted to gimmickry and salesmanship. The CNN late afternoon/early evening prime news program "The Situation Room" is a prime example of the drive for *immediacy* in news reporting. The bar for what constitutes *breaking news* has been lowered relentlessly and the 'Breaking News' or 'Breaking Now' banners can remain on at CNN or BBC for hours at a time. And the breathlessness of a 'breaking news' pace seems to have had an effect also on syntax: newscasters now can break up normal English syntax into a faux-telegraphic, ticker-tape delivery, and no better example can be found than CNN's Wolf Blitzer:

> 1 October 2013, 5 pm Eastern Standard Time (US).
>
> Wolf Blitzer: Happening now, push finally comes to shove as the government shutdown idles close to a million federal employees across the country. On day one, the effects are already being felt across the United States. President Obama vows his health care law is here to stay. It's also day one for the insurance exchanges, where so many Americans can now get coverage. Dr. Sanjay Gupta will tell you what you need to know.
>
> WB: And are Republicans starting to look for a way out of the shutdown stalemate? Will Democrats be willing to make any concessions? I'll ask Senator Dick Durbin, one of the top Democratic leaders on Capitol Hill.
>
> I'm Wolf Blitzer. You're in THE SITUATION ROOM.

---

[24] See, for instance, "CNBC Drops 'World Business'," *Politico.com* 3 August 2011; http://www.politico.com/blogs/onmedia/0811/CNBC_drops_World_Business.html; Howard Kurtz, "CNBC's Baritoromo Flies into Citigroup Controversy," *The Washington Post* (online) 26 January 2007; http://www.washingtonpost.com/wp-dyn/content/article/2007/01/25/AR2007012502049.html.

WB: It's also day one of the health insurance exchanges, a key part of Obamacare, which is at the heart of all the political shoving match – match that's going on up on Capitol Hill.

The president now digging in his heels, blaming Republicans for the shutdown.

Let's go to the White House.

Our senior White House correspondent, Jim Acosta, is standing by.

With the latest – Jim.

WB: But up next, fireworks at the United Nations today as Israel's prime minister speaks out about Iran.

[video clip of Prime Minister Binyamin Netanyahu speaking at the U.N. General Assembly.]

WB: ...Let's bring in our chief national security correspondent Jim Sciutto.

Very tough words from Bibi Netanyahu.

CNN.com transcript:

http://transcripts.cnn.com/TRANSCRIPTS/1310/01/sitroom.01.html

Aside from the dearth of actual content, and the immediate move to commentary over reporting of facts, the jagged syntax of host Blitzer gives the sense of a just-received telegram being read. The presumed excitement of being in "The Situation Room" gives a sense of being less in an actual newsroom than in a live-action drama. And this breathless, jagged telegraphic syntax has spread to other newscasters and reporters, just as have tickers and crawls and *breaking news flashes*. As with the narrative and lexical culture of the 'homeland security' era, the contemporary media landscape is predicated upon constant alarm and vigilance to breaking news alerts. Such pins-and-needles wall-to-wall 24-hour coverage has led to what has been called *news fatigue,* and the collocative pattern "X-fatigue" has been productive in 21st-century English: the appeals for financial donations that follow almost immediately upon those for food and medical supplies in the wake of attacks or natural disasters but go on for longer duration have produced *donor fatigue* and *compassion fatigue* (or STS: *secondary traumatic stress*). The nearly nonstop cycle of elections in democratic nations – the kick-off of the next *campaign season* now within days of an election's settling as political experts nominate frontrunners and *dark horse* candidates – has given rise to *election fatigue*, as has a sense in general that one's vote does not matter, that "things will not change" – now called *voter fatigue.*[25] This productiveness of the formation of *X-fatigue* has extended to another form of *donor fatigue*, such that, by the

[25] The anonymous adage that "no matter who you vote for, the government always wins" is well-worn enough that it is subject to productive inversion; see Gary Younge, "US elections: no matter who you vote for, money always wins," *The Guardian* (online), 29 January 2012; http://www.theguardian.com/commentisfree/cifamerica/2012/jan/29/us-politics-vote-money-wins.

time the much-anticipated counteroffensive of the Armed Forces of Ukraine began in June 2023, one could see mention of *Ukraine fatigue*.

The snark and confidence of news reporters, guest experts, and commentators belie the low regard with which modern journalists are held by the general public – a Gallup poll in December 2024 entitled "Honesty/Ethics in Professions" saw a majority of respondents hold journalists in 'low' to 'very low' regard, and in a professional ranking saw them placed only above "lobbyists"[26] As seen before, mistrust of media reports and official pronouncements can lead to alternative views of events as presented by the *establishment*, the search for alternative, *unredacted* information, or, with increasing frequency in the 21st century, the heavy censorship on *national security* grounds and dearth of verifiable information can feed *conspiracy theories*. Existing at first on partisan message and discussion boards, alternative websites and blogs and social media platforms (i.e., on Telegram instead of Twitter/X), occasionally on comment boards of online news sites, these 'conspiracy theories' occasionally break through to the MSM (*mainstream media*), an acronym usually derisory in application. That a number of speculations are fairly quickly debunked does not seem to deter adherents or those whose level of suspicion is such that they trust nothing from the mainstream media; nor does the fact that at other times the theories or alternative information of dismissively termed *conspiracy theorists* prove to be true enter much into the mainstream 'narrative' (there is the adage: What is a 'conspiracy theory'? Six months early). Anger over the *TARP* (Troubled Asset Relief Program) in response to the fiscal crisis in October 2008 and following (triggered by the financial meltdown of *sub-prime mortgages* and other *derivatives* and risky *financial instruments*), over similar *housing bubble* bursts in Ireland, Britain, and other nations, or *austerity* measures in the EU, led to a climate of recriminations against the *globalist bankers*, the IMF, World Bank, and U.S. Federal Reserve, targets already under the aim of academic and regulatory economists. More extended, or to their detractors, paranoid, theories posit the malefaction of the Bilderbergers, Illuminati, 'One-Worlders,' and others. The term *conspiracy theory* has clearly undergone semantic extension, a broadening from that core notion of at least two persons engaged in a concerted effort to anything organized, secretive, 'elitist,' and nefariously anti-populist. Few events in the 21st century have engendered as much suspicion as 9/11. A vocabulary of 9/11 can be said to exist at two levels, the official, with its *first responders*, *Let's roll*, *9/11 widows*, *Falling Man*, and the alternative *WTC 7*, *controlled demolition*, *9/11 Truth Movement*, pre-9/11 *put options*, *nanothermite*, *New Pearl Harbor*, *Operation Northwoods*, *false-flag attacks*. Similarly, covid era (December 2019–2023) slang formations such as *covidiot* and *maskhole* could be semantically bivalent, applied to one's opponents on either "side" of the issue.

If a general malaise has settled into 21st-century culture, suspicion was no doubt already primed by an advertising culture whose claims simply never could be believed. And 21st-century citizens are bombarded with advertising: on cable television, in papers and magazines, and nowhere more so than on the Internet with popup, scrolling, and other types of invasive ads that seem to occupy much of a net surfer's bandwidth or CPU power. Ads are plastered across city buses, sports stadia, and through

[26] https://news.gallup.com/poll/1654/honesty-ethics-professions.aspx

product placement in popular entertainment. And while some advertising firms have sought to recapture an ad-weary viewership with new campaigns that are 'cool,' 'edgy,' 'socially conscious,' 'environmentally friendly,' they are nonetheless tasked with being 'visible': in this overall *ad* (AmE) or *advert* (BrE) culture *corporate visibility* and *name/brand recognition* are paramount (even universities seek to market their *brand* and launch *branding* campaigns). One difficulty in discussing the phenomenon is that nearly every example is proprietary; the recent fad of the *cronut* (a blend of 'croissant' and 'donut'), said to have been created by French chef Dominique Ansel and first available at his eponymous New York City bakery in May 2013, has witnessed the parallel blend formations *dosant* and *crodough* as the confection crossed from New York to London, allegedly over matters of copyright in an age of 'intellectual property.'[27]

The *intellectual property* of the proprietary trademark is for *Madison Avenue* (the AmE metonym has no exact BrE equivalent) no small investment. Fortunes are spent on advertising campaigns, and success often depends upon a memorable tagline or sound bite and an evocative product name. Even in the 21st century the Latin language has its appeal, even if it is no longer one of the languages of British literature nor even taught widely in English-language schools. As with medical and other sciences, Latin still has *gravitas*. But neither Varro nor Cicero could anticipate their tongue being pressed into service to sell luxury automobiles or pharmaceuticals. With regard to automobile manufacturers, the resort to Latinate and pseudo-Latin formations was economically necessary. As Japanese cars were through the 1980s and early 1990s associated with reliability and affordability – which sounds like an ad/advert for them – the *luxury car* market was dominated by the topline of American automakers and European imports. To break the psychological barriers, Honda became also Acura, Nissan became Infiniti, and Toyota became Lexus. Names that preserve that sense of reliability but also seemingly justify a higher 'sticker price.' No one has taken to pseudo-Latin in English as have the pharmaceutical corporations, whose advertising campaigns for prescription medications dominate not just news program ad/advert-breaks but nearly all prime-time and evening breaks with brand names such as Allegra, AndroGel, Fosamax, Lipitor, Lunesta, Lyrica, Nasonex, Nexium, Restasis, Ventolin, Viagra. Medical jargon has deep historical ties that necessitate its continued use of Greek and Latin. Advertisers hope to appeal to that authority, but also have an ear toward the sounds involved and the pithiness of one-word Latinate forms over a lengthy chemical compound formula.

While 'technical' vocabulary items make for a great many of the additions to modern lexica such as the AHD and OED – the latter has noted that some 500,000 technical terms remain uncatalogued – their inclusion is hardly controversial: one could hold only relative low frequency or obscurity against their favor. With popular media coverage of the *WOTY* ('Word of the Year'), even lexicographers have caught the

---

[27] "London jumps on Cronut craze with the Dosant and the Crodough," *New York Daily News* 10 October 2013, http://www.nydailynews.com/life-style/eats/london-jumps-cronut-craze-dosant-crodough-article-1.1481799; and on the 'Duffin' (donut + muffin) controversy, see "Starbucks and UK baker in 'Duffin' kerfuffle," *CNN.com* 10 October 2013, http://eatocracy.cnn.com/2013/10/10/starbucks-and-uk-baker-in-duffin-kerfuffle/?hpt=hp_t3.

publicity bug, and 'buzz' about 'buzzwords' sells dictionaries. Twenty-first-century English abounds in clumsy blend formations – *cronut* may be appetizing, but hardly sounds so – and a relatively recent announcement noted the addition of *twerking*, *derp*, and *selfie* to the OED.[28] A posting from Oxford University Press's blog by noted etymologist Anatoly Liberman on *twerk* sees it as most likely a blend of *twist* + *jerk* with reference to dancing[29]; though this misses the vector of transmission of *twerk* into broader popular use (and incessant use after Miley Cyrus's performance at the MTV VMAs show on 25 August 2013): from hip-hop, the AAVE form 'to work [it]' syncopating to *twerk* (the particulars of which are to be found all over the Internet and no further glossing is necessary). But the tone of *twerk* and *selfie* (as a colloquial form of *selfshot*), the sexual suggestiveness and maximal informality, highlight the apparent incongruity pointed up in media coverage of OED's announcement – that the stuffy old lexicon has entered the 21st century. Tone of course does matter to the lexicographer, whose duty is to apply usage labels as necessary and record as complete a picture of the lexis of a language as possible.

And the tone has mattered, as the partisan divide allegedly increases, vitriol is the usual response in online discussions, with *trolls* and *flamewars*, or on streets with demonstrations and counter-demonstrations. The *loss of civility* – a phrase often applied in AmE to the election campaigns of 2016–2024 – has likely been in-process for quite some time, and debate whether on 'talk shows' or 'Question Time' has resembled more a shouting match or *brannigan*. Which returns us to McLuhan's notion of language as a communicative tool separate from a moral scheme, and the perennial question of the extent to which language is shaped by the events and experiences of its users, or that to which language shapes or predisposes or drives the reactions of its users to observed phenomena. In some regards – at least those covered in the last few sections – the 21st century is off to an acrimonious start.

12.7 EN CONTACTO

A major study of Spanish in Los Angeles, CA (Silva-Corvalán 1994), looked to wide-ranging matters of internal change in the Spanish spoken by, at the time of the study, some three million residents of Los Angeles County of varying levels of Spanish and English proficiency, from primarily Spanish monolinguals (often recent immigrants to the United States) to proficient bilinguals to partials bilinguals more comfortable expressing themselves in English (to give a broad range of subjects interviewed; there are many more striations to the English-Spanish contact situation). Los Angeles has the largest urban population of Spanish speakers in the United States (as a percentage of the population, El Paso, TX, has a higher figure of Spanish use). Despite the influx of new Spanish speakers to the region, language attrition of Spanish as a heritage language is still being observed (often among third-, but also

[28] "'Twerking' and 'selfie' added to Oxford dictionary," *BBC* (online), 28 August 2013.

[29] "Twerk, twerp, and other tw-words," *OUPblog*, 13 March 2013 (http://blog.oup.com/2013/03/twerk-twerp-tw-etymology-word-origin/).

second-generation speakers). Silva-Corvalán's study is interesting in looking at the contact situation in terms of its effect on the Spanish spoken in LA rather than just the English produced by bilingual speakers of Spanish and English. One of the marked patterns of Spanish use in an urban environment in which it is often the second language is a reduction in verbal inflection in Los Angeles Spanish (in which, in contact terms, English is the superordinate language). The distinction in use, in the indicative mood, of the Spanish copular verbs *ser* and *estar*, seems to have been weakening in favor of extension of *estar* to uses normally reserved for *ser* (both are Latin-derived verbs, *estar* < *stāre* 'to stand,' while *ser* is a suppletive verb < *essere* 'to be' [in an existential sense] and *sēdere*, 'sit, reside in place'). In general, *ser* is preferred to express things that are "inherent or essential," stative, permanent as to a person, *Mis padres son mexicanos* 'My parents are Mexican'; *estar* can express what is "accidental or circumstantial" and thus "temporary, subject to change" (Silva-Corvalán 1994, 92–95): *Hoy el tianguis está cerrado* 'Today the bazaar/farmer's market is closed." The gradual simplification of verbal inflection, which can occur across other verb paradigms, may be to an extent an autonomous change, from "the need to simplify and generalize rules, perhaps to make oral production quicker and more automatic" (Silva-Corvalán 1994, 92). The influence of English as the "superordinate" language might reinforce or encourage such changes already in-progress; another significant factor is the variety and level of Spanish of the bilingual user (a term that encompasses varying levels of proficiency[30]); and there are external factors at work: "highly infrequent or steadily decreasing use of Spanish; its restriction to the domain of the family and close friends; and neutral or negative subjective attitudes towards the maintenance of Spanish" (Silva-Corvalán 1994, 14). In an educational setting, language attrition can be seen even in regions with large Hispanic/Latino/a populations within which there are high numbers of Spanish speakers; thus, even in the American Southwest, for example, one finds high schools and universities offering "heritage Spanish" classes (in what now resembles a three-track system: more advanced classes for native or near-native speakers with active use in the household; 'from-scratch' learners of Spanish with no background or heritage use of the language in the family; and students of Hispanic background who have not had as much exposure to the language at home or in the neighborhood as native speakers).

As seen earlier, such contact situations, and educational situations (e.g., the bilingual classroom, or "Spanish immersion" schools in Los Angeles, San Diego, and other cities) can provide a vector for loan formation in both directions. Tijuana *norteño* Spanish is rife with English loans, some partially to fully Hispanicized: the *-ería* suffix is highly productive (*lonchería*, 'lunch counter/place,' *mofletería*, 'muffler [repair] shop,' *washetería*, 'laundromat' [in place of Spanish *lavandería*]). Such hybrid forms can be found on both sides of the border, on signage and in speech, but are generally

[30] In general terms bilingualism can be: *native*, with enough exposure to comprehensible input at a young age to both language systems such that speaker is equally proficient in both; *additive*, in that the learner maintains the heritage or native L1 (generally an acquired system) while learning the L2 (in this example, Spanish plus English); or *subtractive*, that there can be language attrition of the heritage or native L1 as the L2 is learned (i.e., some loss of Spanish to gain proficiency in English).

seen as part of an informal register. Phonological 'interference' is a highly productive form of contact; seen earlier are the forms code-switching and code-mixing can take in the various contact varieties of English and in American English-Spanish historical contact situations. One small example from San Diego, CA, may give an idea of the phenomenon of being "caught between two languages," or of incomplete phonological and orthographical inventories of the developing bilingual. The following is a sample from a 6th-grade essay response from "Javier," a first-generation Mexican American student – born in the United States, parents born in Mexico – in a bilingual education program in Southeast San Diego (Barrio Logan) from 1994 (cited in a student-teacher project for the teacher-credentialing course "Development of the English Language" at the University of San Diego). The essay assignment involved a written response to a class viewing of the video "Victor" about a young Mexican American growing up in East Central Los Angeles with the general rubric "how is this video like your life"?

> How's thisvideolikmy life?
> this video re mainds mea wen im introuble and icant
> sey wat i haf tosay and i get in troble and awer famili
> is gust like theres at houm we talk inglish and spanish
> mixt together and me and may Brother wen we get howm
> its gust like victor and teresa But we onli doiton
> fraidays we order a extra larg pitzza its alwis fun in
> awer famili. some taims its voring or sad.

One can see in the sample that the student is struggling with the graphic representation of a language not his own (English) that he speaks with strong phonological interference from the home language (Spanish). The essay was clearly not to grade level, but it shows someone thinking in phonological terms.

thisvideolikmy: here the difficulty is phonological, *lik* without the *-e* to mark preceding vowel length, an innovation of late Middle English to Early Modern English, but also morphological. A challenge to a learner of a new language is at first to simply discern word boundaries as opposed to syllable or affix-and-root boundaries. Intonation patterns can cause confusion when stress is shifted onto, for example, a prefix (as in the emphatic pronunciation of *prepare*, v.). The learner often looks to frequently repeated elements, which are usually function (closed class) words such as articles, pronouns, prepositions, and conjunctions. The running together of *thisvideolikmy* seems an unusual example, but the following *introuble* (the prepositional phrase taken as a single unit) and *re mainds* (prefix detached from root, for [aɪ] rendered phonetically – and correctly – as the diphthong) show, inversely, the effect intonation pattern may be having on his writing of English (as with *doiton* in line 5).

icant similarly exhibits difficulty with word boundaries in the target language, and the absence of the apostrophe is almost unremarkable among younger learners regardless of language background.

sey wat i haf tosay: *Sey* for *say* once again is a phonetic rendering of an English diphthong (here [eɪ]), but likely also with interference from Spanish forms such as *ley* 'law' [leɪ] *rey* 'king' [reɪ]. Irregular capitalization is both a function of inexperience with English orthographical norms and the differences in practice between Spanish and English (e.g., *I* versus *yo*, or the following *we talk inglish and spanish*, with *talk* for *speak* but with the influence of Spanish on the rendering of the language names (*inglés*, *español*). *Wat* may be a case of the student spelling English *what* as he says and hears it, that is, unaspirated (compare *wen* in line 4). The verb form *haf* shows devoicing and is highly common with native Spanish speakers of English as a second language.

awer famili (lines 2 and 7): once again, the spellings render English pronunciation phonetically (['aʊ(ə)r] or [ar] in American English, but one does hear an intrusive /w/ at the syllable break in many American dialects); the student's pronunciation is closer to [ɑwər] or [owər]. *Famili* spells it likely as the student pronounces it [fɑmili], that is, with a "Spanish accent" (compare *onli* for *only* in line 5).

gust like theres at houm: Confusion over earlier lessons about English "hard g" and "soft g" seem behind *gust* for *just* (also in line 5), *theres* is a common confusion over homophonous *there/their* and *houm* may have the same vowel as in the rendering of *our* as *awer* (compare in line 4 *howm* for *home*, likely transferred from such English forms as *own* or *show*).

mixt together: *mixt* with <t> for <d> and without *-e-* reflects contemporary pronunciation, the unstressed suffix having undergone devoicing.

me and may Brother wen we get howm: Inconsistent use of capitalization can lead to hypercorrection (or possibly a sense of *Brother* being of enough importance to be capitalized); *may* for *my* shows the influence of Spanish forms such as *hay* [aɪ] (similar phonetic rendering with Spanish influence as with *fraidays* in line 6) while *mea* borrows the digraph from English forms such as *read* (v.) and *lead* (v.) for /i/.

extra larg pitzza: The *-e* is otiose and commonly left off with the writing of young learners; *pitzza* inserts a letter for a sound that is present but not recorded in standard orthography (/t/); the student's Spanish-influenced pronunciation is actually closer to the Italian, as some American English speakers voice /t/ to /d/: [pi:dzə].

alwis: This form shows even more strongly the influence of L1 Spanish with a common Southwest Spanish-influenced pronunciation [ɔlwis], with monophthongization of /eɪ/ to /i/ or /ɪ/ and devoicing of final /z/.

some taims its voring or sad: separation of compound *sometimes* likely a matter of how the student hears English intonation patterns, *taims* once again a phonetic rendering of the diphthong /aɪ/; *voring* for *boring* is commonplace in

> Chicano English, with what amounts to, at times, an interchange of the voiced bilabial stop /b/ and voiced labiodental fricative /v/ (/ß/), and pronunciation of sounds intermediate between the two common in American Spanish dialects (a local Southern California supermarket chains *Vons* is often pronounced *Bons* by native Mexican Spanish speakers).

The original assignment, of course, had one goal: to write a response in English, based on the experiences of students whose home language is Spanish. Attitudes to Spanish use by first- and second-generation Chicano/a speakers of Spanish were shown to be variable and subject to a wide variety of factors in Silva-Corvalán's 1994 study of Spanish in Los Angeles (her Appendix 4 consisted of "Attitude Questionnaires"); despite the Chicano Pride movements of the 1970s onward, and the renewed emphasis upon language as custodian of culture, language attrition has taken its toll, but so have attitudes. There may be a similar cycle of language attitudes seen in the attempts at maintenance of Irish and Welsh; as it is younger learners who are especially the target of such programs, their attitudes toward the language affect language learning and maintenance – something so intangible yet omnipresent as what is 'cool' can influence heritage language trends. The situation with Spanish in the United States is aided by new waves of immigration from Mexico and other Spanish-speaking countries, though immigration patterns have broadened in the United States in the past few decades to see a larger share of new immigrants from the rest of the world, Asia in particular. Intra-community attitudes toward what it means to be "Mexican" are vitally important, and knowledge of Spanish has long been one such indicator of 'authenticity.' Every language has its terms of derogation for the outsider or foreigner; Anglo-Americans bristle at *gringo/a*, though regionally there are many more: *bolillo*, 'white bread (roll)' and *güero* are racially marked terms; the latter can also be applied to a Mexican seen as uncharacteristically pale, 'de pelo amarillo o claro' (i.e., someone with blonde or fair hair; DdM, s.v.); *gabacho* in Peninsular Spanish was first applied to the French, but in Mexican Spanish it is similar to *güero* in referring to fair-haired and -skinned Americans 'extranjera y rubia' ('foreign and blonde,' and so by extension their customs: 'En Ciudad Juárez hay gente de costumbres muy gabachas,' i.e., that the people of the border city Juárez, Chihuahua, have ways that are *gabacha*, too Americanized; DdM, s.v.). But there can be a particular punchiness to *pocho*, as applied by Mexicans to Chicanos, with the sense of having become less Mexican, more American, or 'white': *Mis primos pochos festejan el 4 de Julio* ('My pocho cousins celebrate the 4th of July'; DdM, s.v.). José Antonio Villareal's 1959 novel *Pocho*, published in English, has been seen as one of the first to capture the cultural and linguistic dilemmas of identity and language among first-generation Mexican Americans in an era in which Chicano/a shifted from a derogatory term for working-class Mexican Americans to a term for 'persons born and resident in the United States of America, of Mexican ancestry, and who incorporate elements emblematic' *de ambas culturas* ('of both cultures'; DdM, s.v.).

12.8 THE QUEEN'S ENGLISH/THE KING'S ENGLISH

Dating to 1382, the *Liber regalis* ('Royal Book') is today MS 38 in the collection at Westminster Abbey and it provided through to the coronation of Elizabeth I the 'Order of Service' for the ceremony, in Latin, until 'Englished' with the Reformation.

The tradition of royal coronation services at Westminster Abbey dates back to William I the Conqueror, who in 1066, as a usurping and foreign monarch, sought legitimation in the abbey Edward the Confessor (reigned 1041-January 1066) had built as his 'burial church' beside his Palace at Westminster. On Saturday 6 May 2023 this medieval ritual was witnessed by 2200 officially invited guests and, by the modern media of cable television and the Internet, by some 20 million viewers in the United Kingdom and perhaps 400 million viewers globally with the Coronation of King Charles III and Queen Camilla. The Order of Service proceeded in many ways as it has for centuries, the *ordo consecrandi regem solum* ('order for consecrating the king alone'), and *ordo consecrandi reginam solam* ('order for consecrating the queen alone'), but with greater linguistic representation of the languages of the United Kingdom: the *kyrie eleison* 'Lord, have mercy' from the Introduction was sung in Welsh (*Arglwydd trugarhâ*. 'Lord have mercy'), while at the Anointing Hrabanus Maurus's Latin hymn *Veni, Creator Spritus* ('Come, Creator Spirit'), in a four-stanza version of the original seven, was sung in English, Welsh, Scots Gaelic, and Irish. There is a long-ago connection between the German monk Hrabanus Maurus (ca. 784–856, abbot of the Benedictine abbey at Fulda, later archbishop of Mainz) and England. Irish and English monks in their missions to the Continent in the 7th–9th centuries brought manuscripts from the British Isles to build the libraries of these new foundations, and Hrabanus had been a student of English monk Alcuin of York (ca. 735–804), often described as the "architect of the Carolingian Renaissance" (Levison 1946, 136–138).

A decade earlier it was still the run of *Cool Britannia*, a bad pun on "Rule, Britannia!" and awkward media campaign to "update" the image of Britain. Two events of 2011–2012 marked the "Cool Britannia" era: one was meant to showcase the new image, the other, a year earlier, gave off rumblings of discontent. One year apart, the London riots of 6–10 August 2011 (which spread also to Birmingham, Bristol, Liverpool, Manchester, and broader areas in the West Midlands and Merseyside) and London 2012 Olympics of 25 July–12 August offered on display two sides of the 'Cool Britannia' of New Labour and the aggressive marketing of London as a 'cool' or 'hip' metropolis. Film director Danny Boyle's Britpop-saturated opening and closing ceremonies to the London Olympics were self-congratulatory extravaganzas (as were the handing-off and -on pageants put on by China and Brazil; less ceremonious were those between Paris and Los Angeles in August 2024). Reference to 'Cool Britannia' had grown increasingly ironic even snide during the decade of Tony Blair's leadership of New Labour; lurking somewhere uncomfortably in the background was the knowledge that 'Cool Britannia' was a 'riff' on 'Rule, Britannia!,' an un-ironic imperial anthem. The 'London Riots' were deeply embarrassing as Britain was caught in a 'cant-happen here' moment (despite relevant historical links to the Brixton riots). And while the BBC, Sky, and other British news outlets covered intensively the voice from the 'Arab street' during the 'Arab Spring,' notably missing from coverage of the riots was the voice from the 'London street.' Media reported the view of the police and *security forces* and focused particularly on property damage in Tottenham, Peckham, Croydon, Enfield (where a Sony distribution center went up in flames), and a score of other neighborhoods. Twitter, Facebook, BlackBerry Messenger (BBM – now facing obsolescence), and other *social media* were widely reported in *rolling news coverage* as facilitating the spread of rioting in London and thence to other cities in England, as was the 'rolling coverage' itself. And while there is no doubt some truth to the role of handheld electronic devices and social media in the *pace* of the spread of rioting, worse rioting had occurred in Britain before the electronic age. And the role of social media in the *Arab Spring* from late 2010 to present – a phrase with antecedents in the *Prague Spring* of 1968 and earlier upheavals – was singled out for effusive praise in Western media. Instead, one read again and again of the BBM text messages inviting young people to Oxford Circus for "pure terror and havoc & free stuff," with the "free stuff" segment rising in British popular journalism to the level of AmE 'F.S.A.' – the *Free Stuff/Shit Army*, a derogatory term for public assistance recipients who allegedly sport designer goods (the *benefits cheats* of BrE), an acronym now overlapping in frequency with the *Free Syrian Army*.

In retrospect, a high watermark in how the riots would be received in 'sober analysis' and the role of language in 21st-century Britain was the live interview on the BBC on 9 August 2011 of late writer and activist Darcus Howe (Leighton Rhett Radford Howe) by presenter Fiona Armstrong. The contrast in personalities, backgrounds, and accents was stark. Armstrong, who, since her marriage to Sir Malcolm Gregor Charles MacGregor, 7th baronet and chief of Clan Gregor, is Lady MacGregor of MacGregor, had spent a decade in Nigeria in her youth as her father had been in the colonial service, and in her career in broadcast journalism has worked for ITV and the BBC, covering Africa and, within Britain, focusing on the North. Howe, a Trinidad native who came to England at 18 years of age, was a noted broadcaster himself, writer (and nephew of celebrated Trinidadian essayist C.L.R. James), and activist (he has been part of the 'Mangrove Nine' protests and trial of 1970–1971). At this point in the riots, after extensive property damage in more than a score of London neighborhoods with violence and looting having spread to other English cities, it was a media encounter meant to 'generate sparks,' that is, a media-contrived provocation. And the lines had been drawn in advance: media coverage had focused nearly exclusively on what could be done to stop the 'rioters,' deploring the 'senselessness' of the looting and violence. Linkage to previous outbreaks of riots in Britain was kept to a minimum, often to shorthand forms such as 'Brixton.' It is an understatement to say Howe was being put on the spot; indeed, the entire tone of the interview seemed to be one of expecting some sort of apology from Howe – standing in Croydon in front of a burned-out business – for the rioting, or at least the extraction of his condemnation of the young rioters.

> FA: Marcus Dow, are you shocked by what you've seen there last night. [After announcing the next interview segment was to be with 'Darcus Howe,' Armstrong twice uses the form 'Marcus Dow.']
>
> DH: No, not a t'all. I have been living in London for fifty years, there are so many different mood and moments. But what I was certain about, listening to my grandson, and my son, is that something very, very serious was going to take place in this country. Our political leaders had no idea, the police had no idea, but if you looked at, at young blacks, and young whites, with a discerning eye, and a careful hearing, they have been telling us, and we would not listen, that what is happening in this country to them...

FA: Mr. Howe, if I could just...if I could just stop you Mr. Howe for a moment. You're not, you say you're not shocked, does this mean that you condone what happened in your community last night?

DH: I condone, if I...Of course not, what I'm gonna condone it for? What I am not, What I'm concerned about more than anything else, there is a young man called Mark Duggan, he has parents, he has brothers, he has sisters, and a few yards away from where he lives a police office blew his head off, blew his face off with

FA: Well Mr. Howe...

DH: Let me finish...

FA: Mr. Howe, we have to...Mr. Howe we have to let, we have to wait for the official inquiry before we can say things like that, we don't know what happened to Mr. Duggan, we are going to wait for the police report on it. If I can take you on a little bit...

DH: ...but Mr. Duggan is dead...

FA: ...you were talking about young people...you were talking about your grandson, you were talking about...

DH: They, they have been stopping and searching young blacks for no reason a t'all. I have a grandson he's an angel, and he began to think, he was coming of age, when the police slapped him up against a wall and searched him.... I say, how many times have the police searched you, he said, papa, I can't count, there are so many times.

FA: Mr. Howe, that may well have happened, and if you say it did, I'm, I'm not to gainsay you, but that isn't, that is not, that is not an excuse to go out rioting and cause the sort of damage that we have been seeing over the last few days.

DH: Where were you in 1981 in Brixton?

FA: Mr. Howe...

DH: They had, I don't call it rioting, I call it an insurrection of the masses of the people. It is happening in Syria, it is happening in, uh, Clapham, it's happening in Liverpool, it's happening in Port-of-Spain, Trinidad, and that is the nature of the historical moment...

FA: ...Mr. Howe, if I can just ask you, you are not a stranger to riots yourself, I understand [checking notes], are you? You have taken part in them yourself.

DH: I'm not a.... I have never taken part in a single riot, I've been on demonstrations that ended up in a conflict, and, have some respect for an old West Indian Negro and stop accusing me of being a rioter, because I, you wanted me to get abusive, you just sound idiotic. Have some respect.

FA: Darcus Howe, thank you very much for joining us from Croydon, Darcus Howe the writer and broadcaster.

Armstrong's more 'establishment' accent was not the only disparity to the interview format, linguistically speaking; Howe tried to hear the studio-based presenter from the street in Croydon, the sound of helicopters passing overhead at times. And as is so many times the case too, an adversarial interview format has interviewer and interviewee talk over one another. Howe's Trinidadian accent is still marked – *our* [aʊ'wə], *discerning* [di:zɛrniŋ], *for* [fɔ:] – so too the intonation pattern, with just trace elements of Caribbean Creole syntax (*what I'm gonna condone it for?*). The plaintiveness of Howe's personal recollection of his grandson being stopped by police – immediately undercut by Armstrong's "and if you say it did, I'm not going to gainsay you" – no doubt struck some viewers as the BBC using its 'bully pulpit;' sufficient viewers took offense at the interview and lodged complaints with the BBC review board that the network issue a muted apology:

> We forwarded concerns on this issue ["viewers who felt that Fiona Armstrong was rude towards Darcus Howe and accused him of taking part in riots during her interview on the BBC News Channel that was broadcast on 9 August 2011"] to BBC News Channel Editors and while they accept that this interview was not ideal, they stressed that the presenter did not intend to show Mr Howe any disrespect and the questions were simply intended to gauge his reaction to the events in Croydon the night before.
>
> In particular they acknowledge that the interview included a poorly phrased question about rioting. This can and does happen on occasions during live interviews and was compounded by a number of technical issues during the interview which led to the presenter and Mr Howe talking over each other.
>
> Therefore while Fiona Armstrong was trying to make a general point about protests, we'd like to apologise for any offence that this interview has caused.[31]

A 21st-century speaker of English is so used to the turns of phrase and rhetorical strategies of officialdom-speak that parsing the network apology is hardly necessary. The 'London Riots' of summer 2011 and the 'rolling' media coverage of looting, street-fighting, burning buildings, police crackdowns, and official pronouncements of ending the riots "by any means necessary" (always a chilling statement, if meant in any way literally) pointed out that many people simply "didn't get it" about any number of things. Lurking in the coverage of the riots was the fear of the pall they would cast over London's hosting of the 2012 Summer Games. But the Games themselves, despite an unprecedented military buildup in 'civilian' areas of the capital (surface-to-air missile batteries near tower blocks no less), were a reassuring success. The same youthful, frenzied energy on display destructively in the summer of 2011 was there in 2012, in the frenetic pop-infused – in music and sensibility – opening and closing ceremonies. Though not by any means an exact counterpart to the London riots, the demonstrations (and rioting) of the summer of 2020 (with subsequent police

[31] http://www.bbc.co.uk/complaints/complaint/res_bbcnewsriotscoverage.

shootings and deaths in custody; protest and unrest continued during 2020–2023) in the United States similarly fed a media frenzy that broadened the reach of a vocabulary limited previously to activists and college campuses: Antifa (given a vaguely Continental pronunciation [anti:fə]), BLM (Black Lives Matter), ACAB ("All Cops Are Bastards"), Proud Boys, the CHAZ ('Capitol Hill Autonomous Zone' in Seattle, June–July 2020), and scores of other new vocabulary items entered or re-entered the general lexicon with an urgency and partisan fervor that can make study of them difficult (though it is quite clear that acronyms, in the smart phone-and-texting age, will remain a major source of neologies). And if to the trained ear there had been a shift in the late Queen's vowels over the years (Harrington et al. 2000), there was steadiness nonetheless in the voice of her son and grandson and other members of the Royal Family: tradition as expressed in language. The surprise success of 'imperial-nostalgic' television series such as *Downton Abbey* and *The Crown* (which indulge as well an RP-nostalgia, in a TOWIE age) in the United States closes the economic-military gap between Britain and the United States with a cultural-prestige loop.

Londinium. A prize too great to go unclaimed for long by the Germanic-speaking invaders of the 5th century, though London disappears for more than a century from the records. By the time Chaucer, a Londoner, helps fix English as the national literary language once again, and permanently so, the city too occupies a central role it has not since lost. The Caribbean rhythms and pronunciations brought from Trinidad to London with the Windrush Generation are part of the city's contemporary linguistic picture, as are the vowels and clippings and profanities of "baseball-capped, tracksuited, trainered" Lionel Asbo (Amis 2012, 172). The story of English across those 15 centuries is as interesting as it was once unlikely, and so remarkable a story in this scripted, managed media age – because it is true. In his acerbic travel account *Remote People* (1931) London-born (West Hampstead) Evelyn Waugh had traveled across great stretches of Africa, from Abyssinia (Ethiopia) to Aden, Zanzibar, Kenya, Tanganyika (united in 1964 with Zanzibar as modern Tanzania), Uganda, Belgian Congo, Rhodesia (Zimbabwe), the Union of South Africa (now the Republic), and, outward bound, St. Helena (with its local dialect of English simply called 'Saint'). Along thousands of miles colonial Englishes were spoken, which are now emerging world varieties of English. The return to London is disorienting; all the formerly "latest places" are long gone. A new trendy restaurant is suggested: "I was back in the centre of the Empire, and in the spot where, at the moment, 'everyone' was going. Next day the gossip-writers would chronicle the young M.P.s, peers, and financial magnates who were assembled in that rowdy cellar, hotter than Zanzibar, noisier than the market at Harar, more reckless of the decencies of hospitality than the taverns of Kabalo or Tabora" (Waugh 1931, 240). Waugh hears English spoken so very widely while abroad – and though his observations and style (including his prose style) are now firmly out of fashion, he is never truly oblivious to how English got there. Back in the heart of the empire, where Modern English took root, Waugh is nonetheless beset by an ironically discomfiting sense of being in an alien and unfamiliar place, despite the familiarity of language and people:

> Why go abroad?
> See England first.

REFERENCES

Abdulaziz, Mohamed H. and Ken Osinde, "Sheng and Engsh: development of mixed codes among the urban youth in Kenya," *International Journal of the Sociology of Language* 125 (1997), 125–143

Altendorf, Ulrike. *Estuary English: Levelling at the Interface of RP and South-Eastern British English.* Tübingen: Gunter Narr, 2003

Amis, Martin. *Lionel Asbo: State of England.* London: Jonathan Cape, 2012

Baron, Dennis. "Royal Rhetoric: Yo, Prince! Quit Dissing Us With Your Verbal Venom," *Chicago Tribune* 7 April 1995

Baron, Naomi S. "The Impact of Electronically-Mediated Communication on Language Standards And Style," in Nevalainen, Terttu and Elizabeth Closs Traugott, eds. *The Oxford Handbook of The History of English.* Oxford: Oxford University Press, 2012, pp. 329–340.

Bayley, Robert. "Latino Varieties of English," in Momma, Haruko and Michael Matto *A Companion to the History of the English Language.* Oxford: Wiley-Blackwell, 2008, pp. 521–530

Bolton, Kingsley. *Hong Kong English: Autonomy and Creativity.* Hong Kong: Hong Kong University Press, 2002

Bolton, Kingsley. *Chinese Englishes: A Sociolinguistic History.* Cambridge: Cambridge University Press, 2006a

Bolton, Kingsley. "World Englishes today," in Kachru Braj B., Yamuna Kachru, Cecil L. Nelson, eds. *The Handbook of World Englishes.* Oxford: Blackwell, 2006b, pp. 240–270.

Bryson, Bill. *Notes from a Small Island.* New York: Morrow, 1995

Cameron, Deborah. "The Commodification of Language: English as a Global Commodity," in Nevalainen, Terttu and Elizabeth Closs Traugott, eds. *The Oxford Handbook of The History of English.* Oxford: Oxford University Press, 2012, pp. 352–361.

Clayton, Thomas. *Language Choice in a Nation Under Transition: English Language Spread in Cambodia.* Lexington, KY: Springer, 2006

Crystal, David. "Into the Twenty-First Century," in *The Oxford History of English*, ed. Lynda Mugglestone. Oxford: Oxford University Press, 2006, 394–413

DdM. *Diccionario de mexicanismos: Propios y compartidos.* Mexico City: Academia Mexicana de la Lengua/ESPASA, 2022

Fukuyama, Francis. *The End of History and the Last Man.* New York: Free Press, 1992

Githiora, Chege. "Sheng: peer language, Swahili dialect or emerging Creole?" *Journal of African Cultural Studies* 15.2 (2002): 159–181

Gonzalez, Br. Andrew, FSC. "The Transplantation of American English in Philippine Soil," in Momma, Haruko and Michael Matto, *A Companion to the History of the English Language.* Oxford: Wiley-Blackwell, 2008, pp. 313–322.

Graddol, David. *The Future of English?* London: British Council, 1997. http://www.britishcouncil.org/learning-elt-future.pdf

Graddol, David. *English Next.* London: British Council, 2006 http://www.britishcouncil.org/learning-research-english-next.pdf

Harrington, Jonathan, Sallyanne Palethorpe, and Catherine I. Watson, "Does the Queen Speak the Queen's English?" *Nature* 408 (2000), 927–928

Kachru, Braj B. *The Indianization of English: The English Language in India*. Delhi: Oxford University Press, 1983

Kachru, Braj B. "The Sacred Cows of English," *English Today* 4 (1988): 3–8

Kachru, Braj B. "World Englishes in World Contexts," in Momma, Haruko and Michael Matto, *A Companion to the History of the English Language*. Oxford: Wiley-Blackwell, 2008, pp. 567–580

Kachru Braj B., Yamuna Kachru, Cecil L. Nelson, eds. *The Handbook of World Englishes*. Oxford: Blackwell, 2006

Kiessling, Roland, and Maarten Mous. "Urban Youth Languages in Africa," *Anthropological Linguistics* 46.3 (2004): 303–341

Kortmann, Bernd, Clive Upton, et al., eds. *Varieties of English*. 4 vols. Berlin: Mouton de Gruyter, 2008. 1. *The British Isles*, ed. Bernd Kortmann and Clive Upton; 2. *The Americas and the Caribbean*, ed. Edgar W. Schneider; 3. *The Pacific and Australasia*, ed. Kate Burridge and Bernd Kortmann; 4. *Africa, South and Southeast Asia*, ed. Rajend Mesthrie

Leech, Geoffrey, Marianne Hundt, Christian Mair, and Nicholas Smith. *Change in Contemporary English: A Grammatical Study*. Cambridge: Cambridge University Press, 2012

Levison, Wilhelm. *England and the Continent in the Eighth Century*. Oxford: Clarendon Press, 1946

Lozano, Rosina. *An American Language: The History of Spanish in the United States*. Berkeley, CA: University of California Press, 2018

Mazrui, Alamin M. "English in Africa," in Momma, Haruko and Michael Matto, *A Companion to the History of the English Language*. Oxford: Wiley-Blackwell, 2008, pp. 423–430

McIntosh, Janet. "Mobile phones and Mipoho's prophecy: the powers and dangers of flying language," *American Ethnologist* 37.2 (2010): 337–353

McLuhan, Marshall. *Understanding Media: The Extensions of Man*. New York: McGraw-Hill, 1964

Meierkord, Christiane. *Interactions across Englishes: Linguistic Choices in Local and International Contact Situations*. Cambridge: Cambridge University Press, 2012

Mesthrie, Rajend. "English circling the globe," *English Today* 93, 24.1 (March 2008): 28–32

Michaelis, Susanne Maria, Philippe Maurer, Martin Haspelmath, and Magnus Huber, eds. *The Atlas and Survey of Pidgin and Creole Languages*. 4 vols. Oxford: Oxford University Press, 2013. I. *English-based and Dutch-based Languages*; II. *Portuguese-based, Spanish-based, and French-based Languages*; III. *Contact Languages Based on Languages from Africa, Asia, Australia, and the Americas*; [IV.] *The Atlas of Pidgin & Creole Languages Structures*

Momma, Haruko and Michael Matto, eds. *A Companion to the History of the English Language*. Oxford: Wiley-Blackwell, 2008

Mufwene, Salikoko S. "Creoles and Pidgins," in Momma, Haruko and Michael Matto, *A Companion to the History of the English Language*. Oxford: Wiley-Blackwell, 2008, pp. 553–566

Nevalainen, Terttu and Elizabeth Closs Traugott, eds. *The Oxford Handbook of The History of English*. Oxford: Oxford University Press, 2012

Nunberg, Geoffrey. *Ascent of the A-Word: Assholism, the First Sixty Years*. New York: PublicAffairs, 2012

O'Leary, John. "Prince says Americans are ruining the language," *The Times* 24 March 1995

Price, Jenny. "Old News: Rethinking Language Change Through Australian Broadcast Speech," in Nevalainen, Terttu and Elizabeth Closs Traugott, eds. *The Oxford Handbook of The History of English.* Oxford: Oxford University Press, 2012, pp. 341–351

Rosewarne, David. "Estuary English," *The Times Educational Supplement* 19 (October 1984)

Rosewarne, David. "Estuary English: Tomorrow's RP?" *English Today* 37, 10.1 (January 1994): 3–8

Rushkoff, Dougals. *Cyberia: Life in the Trenches of Hyperspace.* New York: HarperCollins, 1994

Schiller, Robert J. *Irrational Exuberance.* 2nd ed. Princeton, NJ: Princeton University Press, 2005

Schneider, Edgar W. *Postcolonial English: Varieties around the World.* Cambridge: Cambridge University Press, 2007

Schneider, Edgar W., Kate Burridge, Bernd Kortmann, Rajend Mesthrie, and Clive Upton, eds. *A Handbook of Varieties of English: A Multimedia Reference Tool.* 2 vols. Berlin: Mouton de Gruyter, 2004

Schreier, Daniel, Peter Trudgill, Edgar W. Schneider, and Jeffrey P. Williams, eds. *The Lesser-Known Varieties of English: An Introduction.* Cambridge: Cambridge University Press, 2010

Schreier, Daniel, and Marianne Hundt, eds. *English as a Contact Language.* Cambridge: Cambridge University Press, 2013

Silva-Corvalán. *Language Contact and Change: Spanish in Los Angeles.* Oxford Studies in Language Contact. Oxford: Clarendon Press, 1994

Sridhar, Kamal K. "South Asian English," in Momma, Haruko and Michael Matto, *A Companion to the History of the English Language.* Oxford: Wiley-Blackwell, 2008, pp. 404–412

Uchitelle, Louis. "Irrational exuberance," *The New York Times* 21 April 1997

Upton, Clive, David Parry, J.D.A. Widdowson. *Survey of English Dialects: The Dictionary and Grammar.* London: Routledge, 1994

Upton, Clive, Bethan Davies, eds. *Analysing 21st Century British English: Conceptual and Methodological Aspects of the 'Voices' Project.* London: Routledge, 2013

Wa-Mungai, Mbugua and David A. Samper. "'No Mercy, No Remorse': Personal Experience Narratives About Public Passenger Transportation in Nairobi, Kenya," *Africa Today* 52.3 (2006), 51–81

Waugh, Evelyn. *Remote People.* London: Duckworth, 1931

Wiener, Norbert. *Cybernetics, or Control and Communication in the Animal and the Machine.* New York: Chapman & Hall, 1948

Williams, Alex. "Americans are Barmy over Britishisms," *The New York Times* 10 October 2012.

Winford, Donald. "English in the Caribbean," in Momma, Haruko and Michael Matto, *A Companion to the History of the English Language.* Oxford: Wiley-Blackwell, 2008, pp. 413–422

Zentella, Ana Cecilia. *Growing up Bilingual: Puerto Rican Children in New York.* Oxford: Blackwell, 1997

Abbreviations

AAVE	African American Vernacular English
abl.	ablative
acc.	accusative
act.	active
adv.	adverb, adverbial
AIPE	American Indian Pidgin English
AmE	American English
AN	Anglo-Norman
aor.	aorist
BrE	British English
Celt.	Celtic
comp.	comparative
dat.	dative
eMdE	Early Modern English
eME	early Middle English
gen.	genitive
Gmc	Germanic
Grk	Greek
GVS	Great Vowel Shift
imper.	imperative
instr.	instrumental
IPA	International Phonetic Alphabet
Lat	Latin
MdE	Modern English
ME	Middle English
NWGmc	Northwest Germanic
OBrit	Old British
OE	Old English
OFr	Old French
OFris	Old Frisian
OHG	Old High German
OIr	Old Irish
ON	Old Norse
opt.	optative

OS	Old Saxon
pass.	passive
PDE	Present Day English (=MdE)
pers.	person
PGmc	Proto-Germanic
PIE	Proto-Indo-European
pl.	plural
PNWGmc	Proto-Northwest Germanic
pret.	preterite
ptc.	participle
PWGmc	Proto-West Germanic
RP	Received Pronunciation
sing.	singular
Skt.	Sanskrit
subj.	subjunctive
superl.	superlative
s.v.	sub verbo ('under the word')
s.vv.	sub verbis ('under the words')
Ved.	Vedic (Sanskrit)
WAPE	West African Pidgin English
WS	West Saxon

ADS	American Dialect Society
AHD5	*The American Heritage Dictionary of the English Language*. Fifth Edition. Boston: Houghton Mifflin Harcourt, 2011
ANAE	*The Atlas of North American English: Phonetics, Phonology and Sound Change*. William Labov, Sharon Ash, Charles Boberg. Berlin: Mouton de Gruyter, 2006
APCLS	*The Atlas of Pidgin and Creole Language Structures*. Ed. Susanne Maria Michaelis, Philippe Maurer, Martin Haspelmath, and Magnus Huber. Oxford: Oxford University Press, 2013. Online: https://apics-online.info/
BT	*An Anglo-Saxon Dictionary*. Joseph Bosworth, edited and enlarged by T. Northcote Toller. Oxford: Clarendon Press, 1898/rpt. 1989
BTS	*An Anglo-Saxon Dictionary. Supplement*. T. Northcote Toller, revised and enlarged by Alistair Campbell. Oxford: Oxford University Press, 1921/rpt. 1980
Campbell OEG	Campbell, Alistair. *Old English Grammar*. Oxford: Clarendon Press, 1959
CDEPN	*The Cambridge Dictionary of English Place-Names: Based on the Collections of the English Place- Name Society*. Ed. Victor Watts, John Insley, and Margaret Gelling. Cambridge: Cambridge University Press, 2004

CHEL *The Cambridge History of the English Language*. 6 vols. Cambridge: Cambridge University Press, 1992–2001

CHEL1 *The Cambridge History of the English Language*. Volume I: *The Beginnings to 1066*. Ed. Richard M. Hogg. Cambridge: Cambridge University Press, 1992

CHEL2 *The Cambridge History of the English Language*. Volume II: *1066–1476*. Ed. Norman Blake. Cambridge: Cambridge University Press, 1992

CHEL3 *The Cambridge History of the English Language*. Volume III: *1476–1776*. Ed. Roger Lass. Cambridge: Cambridge University Press, 2000

CHEL4 *The Cambridge History of the English Language*. Volume IV: *1776–1997*. Ed. Suzanne Romaine. Cambridge: Cambridge University Press, 1998

CHEL5 *The Cambridge History of the English Language*. Volume V: *English in Britain and Overseas: Origins and Development*. Ed. Robert Burchfield. Cambridge: Cambridge University Press, 1994

CHEL6 *The Cambridge History of the English Language*. Volume VI: *English in North America*. Ed. John Algeo. Cambridge: Cambridge University Press, 2001

CHM *A Concise Anglo-Saxon Dictionary*. J.R. Clark Hall, with a supplement by Herbert D. Meritt. 4th ed. Medieval Academy Reprints for Teaching 14. Toronto: University of Toronto Press/Medieval Academy of America, 1960/rpt. 2004

CIIC *Corpus Inscriptionum Insularum Celticarum*, 2 vols. Ed. R.A.S. Macalister. Dublin: Stationery Office, 1945–1949

CIL *Corpus Inscriptionum Latinarum*. Berlin: Georg Reimer, 1862–. Online: http://www.attalus.org/docs/cil/

CSASE Cambridge Studies in Anglo-Saxon England

DARE *Dictionary of American Regional English*, 6 vols. Cambridge, MA: The Belknap Press of Harvard University Press, 1985–2013. Volume I: A-C. Ed. Frederic G. Cassidy (1985); Volume II: D-H. Ed. Frederic G. Cassidy and Joan Houston Hall (1991); Volume III: I-O. Ed. Frederic G. Cassidy and Joan Houston Hall (1996); Volume IV: P-Sk. Ed. Joan Houston Hall (2002); Volume V: Sl-Z. Ed. Joan Houston Hall (2012); Volume VI: Contrastive Maps, Index to Entry Labels, Questionnaire, and Fieldwork Data. Ed. Joan Houston Hall with Luanne von Schneidemesser (2013)

DdM *Diccionario de mexicanismos: Propios y compartidos*. Mexico City: Academia Mexicana de la Lengua/ESPASA, 2022

DOE *The Dictionary of Old English*. Toronto: University of Toronto Press, 1986–
Fascicles A-Le, 1986–present. Online: https://doe.artsci.utoronto.ca/

DSAE	*Dictionary of South African English*. Dictionary Unit of South African English. Rhodes University, Makhanda/Grahamstown. Online: https://dsae.co.za/
EDD	*The English Dialect Dictionary*. Ed. Joseph (and Elizabeth) Wright. 6 vols. London: Henry Frowde, 1898–1905
EETS	The Early English Text Society (O.S. = Original Series)
EPNS	English Place-Name Society
LAEME	Laing, Margaret. *A Linguistic Atlas of Early Middle English, 1150–1325*. Version 3.2. Edinburgh: The University of Edinburgh, 2013. Online: http://www.lel.ed.ac.uk/ihd/laeme2/laeme2.html
LALME	McIntosh, Angus, M.L. Samuels, and Michael Benskin. *A Linguistic Atlas of Late Middle English*. 4 vols. Aberdeen: Aberdeen University Press, 1986
LAMSAS	*Linguistic Atlas of the Middle and South Atlantic States*. Ed. Raven McDavid, Jr. and Raymond K. O'Cain. Fascicles 1–2. Chicago: University of Chicago Press, 1980
LANE	*Linguistic Atlas of New England*. Ed. Hans Kurath et al. 3 vols. Providence: Brown University, 1939–1943
LAP	Linguistic Atlas Project (LAMSAS, LANE, etc.; cf. ch. 9). Online: https://www.lap.uga.edu/ https://linguisticatlasproject.org/
LHEB	*Language and History in Early Britain: A Chronological Survey of the Brittonic Languages, 1st to 12th c. AD*. Kenneth Hurlstone Jackson, Edinburgh: Edinburgh University Press, 1953 rpt. Dublin: Four Courts Press, 2000
MED	*Middle English Dictionary*. Ann Arbor, MI: University of Michigan Press, 1954–2001. Online: https://quod.lib.umich.edu/m/middle-english-dictionary/dictionary
OCT	Oxford Classical Texts
ODBPN	*A Dictionary of British Place Names*. A.D. Mills. Oxford: Oxford University Press, 2011
ODEG	*The Oxford Dictionary of English Grammar*. Sylvia Chalker and Edmund Weiner. New York: Oxford University Press, 1994
ODEPN	*The Concise Oxford Dictionary of English Place-Names*. Eilert Ekwall. 4th ed. Oxford: Clarendon Press, 1960
ODES	*A Dictionary of English Surnames*. Ed. P.H. Reaney and R.M. Wilson. Oxford: Oxford University Press, 2005
ODFN	*The Oxford Dictionary of Family Names in Britain and Ireland*. Ed. Patrick Hanks, Richard Coates, and Peter McClure. 4 vols. Oxford: Oxford University Press, 2016
OED	*The Oxford English Dictionary*. 2nd ed. 20 vols. Oxford: Oxford University Press, 1989. 3rd ed. [in-progress]. Online: https://www.oed.com/
OEG	*The Oxford English Grammar*. Sidney Greenbaum. Oxford: Oxford University Press, 1996
OS	Ordnance Survey. Online: https://www.ordnancesurvey.co.uk/

PADS	Publications of the American Dialect Society
RIB	*The Roman Inscriptions of Britain*. 3 vols. Oxford: Clarendon Press. Volume I: *Inscriptions on Stone*. Ed. R.G. Collingwood and R.P. Wright (1965); Volume II: *Instrumentum Domesticum*. Ed. S.S. Frere and R.S.O. Tomlin (1990–1995); Volume III: *Inscriptions on Stone*. Ed. R.S.O. Tomlin, R.P. Wright, and M.W.C. Hassall (2009)
RIC	*The Roman Imperial Coinage*. Ed. Harold Mattingly and Edward A. Sydenham. London: Spink, 1923–; rev. ed. C.H.V. Sutherland and R.A.G. Carson. London: Spink, 1984–
SND/eSND	*Scottish National Dictionary* (10 volumes, 1931–1976), in the *Dictionaries of the Scots Language* (DSL) project; included also is the *Dictionary of the Older Scottish Tongue* (12 volumes, 1931–2002). Online: https://dsl.ac.uk/
SPCL1	*The Survey of Pidgin and Creole Languages*, volume I: *English-based and Dutch-based languages*. Ed. Susanne Michaelis, Philippe Maurer, Martin Haspelmath, and Magnus Huber. Oxford: Oxford University Press, 2013
SPCL2	*The Survey of Pidgin and Creole Languages*, vol. II: *Portuguese-based, Spanish-based, and French-based Languages*. Ed. Susanne Michaelis, Philippe Maurer, Martin Haspelmath, and Magnus Huber. Oxford: Oxford University Press, 2013
SPLC3	*The Survey of Pidgin and Creole Languages*, vol. III: *Contact Languages Based on Languages from Africa, Asia, Australia, and the Americas*. Ed. Susanne Michaelis, Philippe Maurer, Martin Haspelmath, and Magnus Huber. Oxford: Oxford University Press, 2013
TOE	*A Thesaurus of Old English*. Ed. Jane Roberts and Christian Kay, with Lynne Grundy. 2 vols. Costerus New Series 131–132. Amsterdam: Rodopi, 2000
TPS	*Transactions of the Philological Society*
WALS	*The World Atlas of Language Structures*. Ed. Martin Haspelmath, Matthew S. Dryer, David Gil, and Bernard Comrie. Oxford: Oxford University Press, 2005. Online: https://wals.info/

Glossary

allophone The OED glosses, 'Each of the different phonetic realizations of a phoneme' (s.v.), and one might add that an *allophone* (literally 'other-sound') is a variant of a sound but not one so distinct as to constitute a separate phoneme. Such judgments about what is a sound, a **phoneme**, and what is a variant of that sound, an *allophone*, can be language-dependent. For example, the aspirated stops in English are considered *allophones* of those sounds: thus the *t* in *stop* is /t/ while the *t* in *top* is also a variant of /t/, but an aspirated ('breathy,' with a trailing puff of air in its articulation) variant of /t/ that is transcribed /t^h/. As with a number of phonological phenomena, environment seems important, the particular environment of the sound in a word, or "types of realizations of phonemes that are systematically related to particular contexts, or...to particular phonological environments" (Catford 2001, 192).

alternant The OED very precisely glosses, 'Any of the possible variants of a particular feature of speech or language' (s.v.). This can apply especially to phonological and morphological features, such as a 'Verner's Law alternant,' that is, those seeming exceptions to **Grimm's Law** when Germanic languages exhibited a voiced fricative instead of an expected voiceless fricative if between voiced sounds in a word in PIE (and Sanskrit) where the preceding syllable is unaccented: PIE **b^{h}ráh$_2$tēr* 'brother' and Sanskrit *bhrātṛ* but PGmc **brōþēr*, Gothic *broþar*, and Old English *brōðor*; where PIE and Sanskrit have /t/ between voiced sounds, the Germanic languages have /ð/, the voiced *alternant* (compare also PIE **d^{h}éh$_2$ti-* 'act of putting' but PGmc **dēdiz* 'deed,' Old English *dǣd*). Any sound change rule may produce such alternants, and these variants can also be leveled or analogically restored (i.e., 'go back to' the original form through other processes).

apocope The loss of a sound or sounds at a word's end; also called *clipping* or *truncation*; the g-dropping common in Modern English might involve the substitution of one nasal /n/ for another /ŋ/, but there are many examples of historical *apocope* (of short high vowels in early Germanic: Proto-West Germanic **ahslu* 'shoulder' > Old English *eaxl*; Ringe in Ringe and Taylor 2014, 285) and contemporary *apocope* (*want* > *wan'*, *don't* > *don'* [do:n]).

aspect As a category of the verb, verbal or grammatical aspect is not fully separate or inflectionally marked in English, though it may be argued that auxiliary verbs in non-preterite (simple past) forms mark such aspects as *habitual*, *durative*, and *inceptive* (or *inchoative* or *ingressive*), indicating action through time (what is usually classified as *tense*), that is, respectively, repeated, enduring (or enduringly repeated), and being just undertaken. For example, *I'm about to go* and *I'm fixin' to go* can be taken as inceptive or inchoative, or *I'm used to getting there early* as habitual; or, *I have been reading that* *paper for two weeks now* is present perfect progressive in terms of tense and durative in aspect. That said, many grammarians consider the *perfective* (completed action) and *progressive* (continuing action) to involve aspectual marking and not simply compound tense forms. To which some linguists would add the *imperfective*, marking durative or continuing action without marking its inception or termination. Modern German and the earlier Germanic languages by and large did not mark for aspect (at least not inflectionally; but see Lloyd 1979 for an alternative view with Gothic). Indeed, Bruce Mitchell in his magisterial *Old English Syntax* (Mitchell 1985) did not think "aspect a valid category for OE" (§676, and §§865–868). More recently, Taylor in Ringe and Taylor 2014 discusses *HAVE* and *BE* perfects in Old English (*habban*, *bēon-wesan*) as well as 'aspectualizer' verbs such as *beginnan* and *onginnan* (both with the sense 'begin, attempt, try, undertake'), the latter indicating a type of inceptive/inchoative aspect expressed in early modal auxiliaries (428–439, 488–494). See also Section 4.3.

assimilation The phonological process by which a sound or sound segment becomes partially to fully like a neighboring sound; as with **metathesis**, certain classes of sounds and environments seem conducive to the change (that is, some sounds seem likelier to assimilate while others resist assimilative processes). The term *assimilation* itself underwent the process: Latin *ad-* 'to, toward' + *similāre* 'to make like, resemble' > *assimilāre*. Similarly *assure* < Latin *ad-* + *sēcūrus* > *assēcūāre,* or English *cupboard* > [kʌbəd] (BrE) [kʌbɚd]/[kʌbərd] (AmE).

conjugation From Latin *coniungere* 'to join together,' the pattern of inflections added to a verb to mark its various grammatical distinctions: person (1st/2nd/3rd), number (singular, plural), tense (present, past/**preterite**, future), voice (active/middle-mediopassive/passive), mood (indicative, subjunctive, imperative), **aspect**, etc.

contact variety When language contact situations arise, as they always have, speakers in the encounter who do not share the same language face a number of choices (some contact situations of course can involve compulsion): learn something of the language of the others, or attempt to communicate through a form of *interlanguage*, a sometimes radically simplified composite variety with a limited vocabulary, reduced inflections and grammatical rules, in what may seem like a learner's or child's variety. Normally, but not absolutely (as in the case of *mixed languages*; see the example of Michif in Section 10.3, and Bakker 1997), the simplified composite 'mixed' variety has one of the languages in contact as the 'base,' the 'donor' of most of the vocabulary (the **lexifier**), and many of the grammatical forms and rules; the other languages of the contact variety can influence quite significantly pronunciation and vocabulary (though there are many variables at work in such systems). This initial contact variety may only be used in the contact situation, with speakers of the various languages returning to use of their native languages outside the contact situation (such a contact variety is called a **pidgin**). If the contact situation persists, there may develop a need for a more complex mixed system, one that increases in complexity and may even become the L1 of a speech community in the contact situation (which is called a **Creole**). A speech community employing a Creole may, such as in many colonial contact situations, shift to the language at the base of the contact variety, and the original contact variety may undergo **decreolization** (this is one theory behind **AAVE**). The contact varieties themselves (pidgins, Creoles) may be scalar in terms of degree of reliance upon the 'base' lexifier language and degree of input from the 'donor' languages, from **basilectal** varieties that may be the least intelligible to speakers of a standard variety of the base language, to **mesolectal** varieties (closer to the base language than the *basilectal*), to **acrolectal** varieties closest to the base language; for example, varieties of French-based Creole *Ayisyen* (*Kreyòl ayisyen* < *Haïtien*): Port-au-Prince varieties can include those acrolectal, closer to standard Haitian French, while those in the upland interior can be more basilectal.

Creole See **contact variety**.

declension From Latin *dēclīnātiō* < *dēclīnāre* 'to change direction, turn, put out of alignment; deviate from, diverge,' with the sense, like *inflection*, of altering: here, changing the word endings to indicate grammatical information. Similar to *conjugations* for verbs, declensions are the paradigms for nominals indicating such grammatical markings as number (singular, **dual**, plural), **case**, gender. Section 4.3 looks at the strong and weak declensions of nouns and adjectives in Old English, which would undergo inflectional decay/**deflexion** in Middle through Early Modern English.

deflexion *Deflexion*, or *inflectional decay*, is the historical process by which a *synthetic* language becomes less so by loss of inflections, often by *leveling* in its paradigms (verbal conjugations, nominal declensions). This leveling, or generalization, sees fewer distinctions in the paradigms of word classes, as by the spread of remaining affixes to more instances in the paradigm; for example, English nouns ceased to be clearly marked for case (nominative, accusative, genitive, dative) by late Middle English, though this was a process of 'decay' in the paradigms beginning in late Old English. The demonstratives saw a reduced paradigm in Middle English (though we preserve the marking for number: *this/these*, *that/those*), while the definite article (originally from an Old English demonstrative) became indeclinable (not changing form) such that only *the* survives in Modern English (compare the Old English forms *se þone þæs* etc. in Section 4.3, which were once marked for case, number, and gender).

deixis From the Greek for 'reference, indication,' this term covers the various forms of content-dependency in language as a *pragmatic* function of human language; *deictic* expressions are those whose meaning depends upon context, such as who is speaking and the referents involved. For example, in the sentence *Please place your order two weeks before the holiday* the sense depends upon which 'holiday' is being referred to (this may be obvious if one sees a date on the notice, but will be ambiguous if there is no such contextual information). In *She gave her her book back* the sentence may be clear to the speaker, who knows the referents of *her* (1) and *her* (2) and whether *her* (1–2) refer to the same person or, if not, who is the lender and who the recipient. Or, if given a verbal instruction *Turn left when you get downtown* adverbial *left* is deictic ('left' is dependent upon what direction one approaches *downtown* from).

grammaticalization In general, *grammaticalization* is the process by which lexical (semantic content) morphemes are 'reduced' to function (grammatical) morphemes, undergoing semantic weakening (or 'bleaching'). What is now the indeclinable (invariant, not marked for case, number, or gender) definite article *the* was once a demonstrative in Old English with the sense 'this, this one'; what is now the indefinite article *a(n)* was in Old English the cardinal number *ān* 'one,' which when used adjectivally followed the strong declension (see Section 4.3). In the Middle English period a weakened pronunciation developed, *an*, and it came to function also as an indefinite article (OE *ān* > Middle English *on* whence Modern English *one*). Partial to full grammaticalization occurred with a number of Old English verbs that came to be used as auxiliaries (*willan* 'wish' > modal auxiliary expressing futurity and, somewhat more weakly, desire; *habban* 'possess, have,' maintained its primary sense as a main verb but grammaticalized into the modal in verb forms such as *will have gone*).

inflection From Latin *inflectere*, 'to bend, turn,' inflections are those affixes (word-endings, but also infixes; see **infix**) that convey grammatical distinctions: e.g., *-es/-s* genitive singular marker in Old English (*cyning* 'king,' nominative singular, *cyninges* 'of [the] king,' gen. sing.). Old English was more **synthetic** in its **morphological typology**, with nouns, pronouns and other nominals, adjectives, adverbs, articles and demonstratives, and verbs all inflected. Many of these **inflectional morphemes** were lost in the history of English in a process of **inflectional decay** or **deflexion** (such that since Early Modern English the language might be better classified as an **analytic** language). The noun *inflection* derives from the addition of the **derivational morpheme** *-tio* to the 1st-person singular present active indicative form *inflectō*, which by an assimilative process in Latin became *inflexiō* (hence British English uses the spelling *inflexion*, a vestige of the tradition of classical education in England).

inflectional decay See **deflexion**.

lexeme An 'item of vocabulary' (OED, s.v.) as an abstract unit distinct from **morpheme**; basically, a headword in the dictionary is a *lexeme*, subsumed under which are its inflectional forms and, in some definitions, its derivatives. To an extent, *lexeme* may be said to have displaced *root* in the philological sense: that is, a root form, such as a verbal root, that includes all of its inflected and derivative forms. So, for example, following OED's example of *run*, under the lexeme **run** are included its conjugated forms *run runs running ran*, the deverbal noun *run*, and gerund *running*, and derived forms such as *outrun* and *overrun*.

lexifier The language that is the 'donor' of most of the vocabulary in a **contact variety** is called the *lexifier*; linguists often then speak of the contact variety (pidgin, at first) as being 'based' on that language, though the classification is usually also based on morphological and other features. Thus Tok Pisin is classified as an English-based Creole as most of its vocabulary does derive from English (if in pronunciations heavily influenced by native Papuan languages).

lexis The words of a language in terms of their role in the overall vocabulary, i.e., as part of the lexicon rather than just the language's morphology. As with **register**, there is variable usage of the term in linguistics and philology, in particular the distinction between an overall *lexis* (Lexis) as the total set of words of a language's vocabulary, and a *lexis* (lexis) peculiar to a profession, discipline, pursuit, etc. From Greek λέξις (*léksis*) 'diction,' there is often some overlap with *semantics*, the study of meaning (as with the subdiscipline *lexicosemantics*). Lexicography is literally the 'writing of the lexicon,' or dictionary-making, and as such it does seek to record word class and other grammatical information (morphology) but is primarily geared toward meaning. In referring to, for example, Old English lexis, the overall vocabulary of that stage of English is indicated (as are considerations such as word origin, native or loan formation).

metathesis The reordering or transposition of neighboring sounds or sound segments. In the historical view, metathesis has been an important sound change in the history of English: Old English *āscian* 'ask' occurred commonly also in the forms *ācsian*, *āhsian*, *āxian* (thus Modern English vernacular form *aks/axe* is not an unusual development); Old English *bridd* 'young bird': the MED notes that *bird* "is not attested until 1419 and occurs before 1450 chiefly in Northern MSS [manuscripts], but it must be old" (s.v. *brid*). If the manuscript evidence is not simply chance occurrence of what written evidence survived, this may indicate that the metathesis began in Northern dialects of Middle English and spread southward. Metatheses in English seem to involve specific types of sounds and environments for change: liquids, nasals, and labials in particular seem subject to the change (*animal* > *aminal*; *cavalry* > *calvary*). It is also a feature of child language and certain types of language processing errors and learning disabilities. Metatheses of entire syllables across words are sometimes called *Spoonerisms*, after Rev. William Archibald Spooner, sometime dean at New College, Oxford, who was said, perhaps exaggeratedly, to have been subject to making them (*coin toss* > *toin coss*, *no doubt about it* > *no bout adoubt it*).

morpheme A discrete unit of grammatical meaning, that is, in contrast to a **lexeme**, which is primarily a discrete unit of meaning (with its related forms derived from the same root), the smallest grammatical unit in a language that cannot be further subdivided (see **morphology** below). Every word is a *morpheme*, but words may consist of two or more morphemes; for example, the word *deconstruction* consists of four morphemes, **de-** + **con-** + **-struct-** + **-(t)ion**, all of which are *bound morphemes* (i.e., they do not stand on their own but are affixes that form words). The affixes *de-*, *con-*, and *-tion* are *derivational morphemes* added to the root morpheme *- struct(-)*, which carries the primary meaning or 'semantic content.' The root *-struct(-)* is highly productive: **in**struct, **in**struct**ion**, **con**struct**ion**, **con**struct**ive**, **re**struct**ure**, etc. *Inflectional morphemes* are those whose primary function is grammatical rather than semantic; for example, the *-s* plural marker for nouns, the *'s* possessive marker (genitive case), or the *-s* 3rd person singular present tense marker for verbs.

morphological typology This involves the classification of a language by the 'type' of its morphological system. Old English was more a **synthetic** language, 'creating' word endings (inflections) to carry grammatical information. Over the course of the history of English the language saw a sharp reduction in use and maintenance of inflectional morphemes and became more **analytic**; for example, the four forms in the present system of verbs, marking for 1st, 2nd, 3rd singular and plural (all numbers), were reduced to just two in Modern English: 3rd singular (*she goes*) and the rest in what was once the 1st singular form (*I go*, from Old English *iċ gā*), which spread, by **levelling**, to the remaining forms (*you go*, *we go*, *you* [pl.] *go*, *they go*). An *isolating* language such as Vietnamese has essentially all of the grammatical information borne by inflections in *synthetic* languages conveyed instead by free **morphemes** (that is, a nearly 1:1 ratio of words and morphemes – thus grammatical distinctions such as pluralization would be indicated by separate (not 'bound') morphemes: *một ca sĩ* = 'a singer' or 'one singer,' *hai ca sĩ* = 'two singers' (literally, 'two singer'), *một trăm ca sĩ* '100 singers' (literally. 'one hundred singer'). In some instances, contact varieties of English and 'learner English' involving native (source) languages that are isolating can involve a sort of morphological transfer (e.g., 'Vietnamese English' may drop the *-s* plural marker for nouns as it has no equivalent in Vietnamese). An *agglutinative* language such as Hungarian adds affixes to a base morpheme (e.g., adding prefixes and suffixes bearing grammatical information to a base nominal morpheme). A *polysynthetic* language such as Akwesasne Mohawk (St. Regis Reserve/Reservation on the St. Lawrence in New York State and the provinces of Ontario and Québec) can use multiple prefixes and other affixes attaching to a base morpheme (verbal, nominal): *wakekstv́:ha* 'I am old' (*wa-* an objective marker applied to *-ke-* 1st person singular pronoun 'I' both added to *kstv́:ha* 'be old'), *ukekst′v:hahne?* 'I became old' (*u-* a declarative modal prefix and objective marker + *-ke-* + *kst′v:hahne?* 'become old'; Bonvillain 1973, 118).

morphology Morphology is the study of 'forms,' here linguistic or, more specifically, grammatical or grammatically meaningful forms. The *morpheme* is therefore the discrete unit of morphological meaning or function: *inflectional morphemes* encode grammatical distinctions through affixes (prefixes, infixes, suffixes), such as number for nouns (singular, plural) or gender (in Old English for all nominals, in Modern English 3rd-person singular personal pronoun forms *he/she/it* and nouns with natural [*mare, stallion*] or attributive gender [such as traditional association of ships as feminine: *Christen her; her maiden voyage*]); *derivational morphemes* are the 'building blocks' of new forms often, but not always, by affixation: the denominal suffix *-ise/-ize* allows for the creation of a verb from a noun; the deverbal suffixes *-er/-or, -ing,* or *-(a)tion* allow for the creation of nouns from verbs (*act > actor, read > reading, animate > animation*). *Conversion* refers to the derivation of a new form without affixation (or by 'zero-formation'); e.g., *a walk* (< *to walk*), or *throw a pitch* (< *to pitch*). Morphemes can be further classified as *free* or *bound*; all words are free morphemes, though they may be used to form more complex morphemes (as by compounding: *free-form*); bound morphemes cannot 'stand alone,' but must be joined to a free morpheme (*freedom* < *free* + *-dom*, the latter a bound morpheme). Occasionally free morphemes can become bound, as by becoming otherwise obsolete (the *luke-* in *lukewarm*) or **grammaticalization**. Morphemes may additionally be specified as belonging to either an *open* (lexical or content) class (nouns, verbs, adjectives, adverbs) or *closed* (function) class (pronouns, articles, prepositions, conjunctions). With this last categorization, interjections and pronouns complicate things: the interjection word class does admit new members, especially in informal usage; pronouns as function words generally do not, though English has long struggled with the gender-bearing 3rd-person singular personal pronouns (*he/she/it*) and a search for a gender-neutral singular form; more recent debate over pronouns involve matters of gender itself (e.g., how to represent 'nonbinary' and other identification linguistically).

philology Literally 'love of language' (or 'the word,' *logos*), philology refers most broadly to the study of language, often in a pre-Modern (or pre–postmodern) sense (i.e., before the rise of modern linguistics or Chomskyan linguistic theory). Philologists of the 18th and especially 19th centuries produced many still valuable resources for the study of older languages: critical editions of texts, manuscript studies, comprehensive grammars, and early comparative grammars. At present the term can refer to more 'traditional' approaches to language study that reserve their focus upon 'natural' languages, especially earlier stages of recorded languages. The *comparative method* and advances such as a number of *sound laws* (Grimm's Law, Verner's Law, etc.) were the product of the philological approach.

phoneme A discrete unit of sound, such as a unit that cannot be further reduced – i.e., a basic, constituent sound of a language, part of a language's *phonemic inventory*. The classical philological approach classified this inventory of sounds into consonants (obstruents) and vowels, with further refinements of each class; consonants: obstruents such as stops, fricatives, and affricates with partial to full blockage of the airflow in their articulation, and sonorants (with continuous unobstructed airflow in articulation) such as nasals, liquids, and semi-vowels; vowels: simple vowels and diphthongs (two-part vowel sounds, consisting of a nuclear and glide vowels that 'count' as one syllable). The classical scheme is useful in analyzing and teaching languages, if unavoidably a bit oversimplified (vowels are also sonorants; 'semi-vowels,' the /j/ and /w/ phonemes in English are the least 'consonant-y' of consonants, or most vowel-like in their articulation. It is customary in phonemic analysis to place sound symbols between angled brackets, e.g., the voiceless stops /p/ /t/ /k/, and phonetic transcriptions in square brackets (e.g., [haʊs]).

phonology The study of the sounds of a language, of its inventory of phonemes. More broadly, any consideration of oral language falls under this heading, such as articulatory and acoustic phonetics (how phonemes are actually produced and heard), diachronic ('through time,' historical), and synchronic (the study of a language at a moment or in time or stage in its development, though often this indicates 'contemporary') sound change. See also **phoneme** and **allophone**.

pidgin See **contact variety**.

pragmatics As a sort of 'fifth' area of inquiry about human languages (after *phonology*, *morphology*, *syntax*, *semantics*) *pragmatics* looks to applied or 'pragmatic' matters of language; pragmatic concerns include semiotics (the study of signs, and their use and nature and means of signification), context, speech acts (language that is not merely 'signs' or 'signifies' or 'means something' but *does* things: promises, oaths, oblique commands, etc.), implicature, deixis ('pointing out' functions, such as context-dependency).

rhotacism Broadly, *rhotacism* refers to pronunciation of medial and final /r/; one of the salient dividing features between BrE varieties and AmE varieties is the pronunciation of /r/: standard BrE is non-rhotic, standard AmE now rhotic in a majority of dialects. But many BrE dialects are rhotic (or R+), in the West and Southwest, and North; a majority of AmE dialects were non-rhotic (or R-) in the later colonial and early independence periods, and non-rhotic varieties persist in New England (east of the Connecticut River), the New York metropolitan region, coastal regions of Southern states such as South Carolina and Georgia, and to a lesser extent in New Orleans. *Rhotacism* can also refer to a historical process of alveolar consonants shifting ro /r/, as with the language of early Runic inscriptions (see Section 4.6), or in the verb forms *was* and *were* < Proto-Germanic **wesaną* (the preterite forms were all non-rhotic originally: **was *wāzī *was* (sing.) / **wāzum *wāzud *wāzun* (pl.; Ringe in Ringe and Taylor 2014, 113).

RP 'Received Pronunciation,' a somewhat more neutral term for standard British English (BrE) than 'the Queen's/King's English,' but one which still has the entailment that the standard variety is 'traditional' and 'acceptable' or 'preferred.' For American English (AmE) the term *Standard English* is the most common. A critical difference between the sets of varieties is a scalar class distinction between them, with British English standard varieties felt to be higher on the class scale (closer to upper class, 'public school,' or 'BBC-speak' varieties) than the American (which are more solidly middle-middle class, college-educated, suburban, or gentrified urban). The differences, which are not entirely perceptual (though the labeling of BrE RP as 'posh' is in part a matter of perception), reflect as well social differences, with the observation (perceptual, again, to some extent) that with Americans class is determined rather more by money than breeding or connections or other inherited privilege. As such, RP may create a sense of belonging more closely to the 'right' class while Standard AmE somewhat more simply suggests one 'got educated.' Insofar as one adheres to the norms in pronunciation, grammar, and use in a standard variety, the matter is linguistic; the perceptual observations about standard varieties, which do indeed have real-world consequences, are more the province of **sociolinguistics**.

semantics *Semantic* has to do with a word's meaning, and *semantics*, as a linguistic subdiscipline, looks to word meaning and *semantic change*. Just as languages in the diachronic perspective can undergo phonological, morphological, and syntactic change, so too the semantic. Words can undergo various types of semantic change: metaphorical extension (as from literal to figurative sense, physical to metaphysical, concrete to abstract); metonymy, in which an attribute or characteristic, stands in for the form, 'the action of substituting for a word or phrase denoting an object, action, institution, etc., a word or phrase denoting a property or something associated with it' (OED, s.v.); synecdoche, a subspecies of metonymy, by which a part stands in for the whole (*pars pro toto*); intensification or loss of intensity: certain 'curse words' seem to have lost some of their intensity in 21st-century informal speech), while racial and ethnic epithets have intensified and pejorized (pejoration or pejorization refers to a word taking on a more negative sense; meliorization/amelioration refers to a word taking on a more positive sense, or losing more negative associations); tabooization indicates a word whose sense enters the lowest stratum of the lexicon, when it no longer has any socially accepted occasion of use (and if used may incur disapprobation or worse). For example, the 'f-word' seems to have lost some of its taboo status; conversely, the 'n-word' has pejorized further, from 'offensive' to 'taboo.' Various other shifts in meaning can occur over the 'lifetime' of a word. Perhaps the most dramatic is autoantonymy, when a word can have two contrary meanings or shift to a reversal in original meaning; a number of informal forms have undergone the shift in popular usage: *bad* or *wicked* indicating 'good,' 'admirable,' 'cool,' or *cool* itself indicating what is 'hot' (in a metaphorical sense). Words can narrow or specialize in their meaning or generalize or broaden.

sociolinguistics In the broadest definition *sociolinguistics* is the branch of linguistics that studies 'language in society'; the work of linguist Uriel Weinreich and his student William Labov is often pointed to as the starting point of (at least American) sociolinguistics, in particular Labov's 1966 study of *The Social Stratification of English in New York City* (Labov 2006). Labov's study is most famous for its urban fieldwork example of social and workplace-conditioned rhotic ~ non-rhotic NYC English among sales staff, floorwalkers, and other employees of a set of class-marked department stores in the city (Klein's, Macy's, Saks Fifth Avenue, in ascending social-class order), which found that workers adjusted their pronunciation of medial and final /r/ according to the climate of the establishment, instructions from management, and the clientele being served; the staff were in the main working class and would be expected to be non-rhotic in their variety of NYC English (which varies by borough, e.g., Bronx English and Brooklyn English), but more rhotic pronunciations were found the higher one went in the scale up to Saks Fifth Avenue. But the study covered much more than the "department store study" and broke new ground in the examination of 'language in society,' in particular the role of the **speech community** and class and social stratification – as by neighborhood, social networks, race, ethnicity, and religion (see especially Labov 2001, 1–145). Many other studies have followed in the wake of the NYC study, of BrE varieties (from Northern BrE dialects to 'Estuary English' [Section 12]) to World English varieties, and has been applied to many others of the world's languages. In a way, sociolinguistics returns to earlier philological studies of language that focused on 'language and people,' of language as an expression of a people's culture and identity. The matter of 'identity' has seen a tremendous broadening in the scope of sociolinguistics as the study of the social aspects of language and the role language can play in shaping and projecting identity (see Sections 9 and 12 on *linguistic affectation* of how speakers can modify their variety or *register* based on audience, peer groups, or social expectations, desire to 'fit in,' etc.).

speech community A group of people who have a dialect, variety (here used as a unit within a dialect), or way of speaking or using a dialect/variety in common. In the narrowest sense, a group of people who may not have anything else in common (religion, race, ethnicity, national origin) but who share a speech variety can form a *speech community*. This may be geographically bounded and constitute a *regional dialect*: for instance, people from the same inner-city neighborhood, as bounded by particular streets or arterial roads (expressway, motorway, etc.), or river or shoreline, or by zoning or social constraints or wishes (forms of voluntary and involuntary association: 'ghettoization,' gentrification). It may also be constituted socially and extend beyond original geographical bounds: varieties of AAVE/AAE (African American Vernacular English/African American English or 'Language'; on the latter term see Lanehart 2015) are often classified as *social dialects* in that characteristics of the varieties (pronunciations, grammatical features) deriving from the American South can be found in African American speech communities throughout the United States (Seattle, Chicago, Boston, Philadelphia, Baltimore, etc.). In general, *speech community* seems to be used in sociolinguistic work in a positive sense in that linguistic ties create a sense of belonging to a *community* with at least one set of ties.

suppletive verb Verbs whose paradigm is supplemented by forms from originally separate verbs. This may be due, historically, to displacement by semantic overlap (having two or more verbs whose semantic range was similar), by leveling of forms in one verb and suppletion of missing forms from a verb of similar meaning, or some other early processes not fully understood. It can seem unusual at first that high-frequency verbs should supplement their paradigm with forms borrowed from other verbs, but it is not an uncommon phenomenon (see Section 4.3 on Old English suppletive verbs). So, for example, English *to be* derives from Old English *bēon-wesan*, a "multiply suppletive" verb (Ringe in Ringe and Taylor 2014, 372–374). Both verbs had original sense 'to be, exist, happen,' and a modern observer can readily note that the *am* and *are* and *is*, *was* and *were*, and *been being been* forms cannot all derive from the same verb etymologically. It may be that the very high frequency of the 'to be' verbal form, and vestigial senses of 'be' and 'exist' (that is, more temporary and more lasting states of being, or the stative and existential) led to coalescence of multiple verbs that express existence and being (and function also in a temporal sense as auxiliary forms: *am going*, *have been reading*, *was amused*). Modern English 'to go' is also suppletive: present forms and the past participle derive from Old English *gān* (*go*, *goes*, *going*, *gone*), while the past forms derive from Old English *wendan* (*went*), which survives only in the phrasal form *wend one's way*.

syntactic typology English is in its *syntactic typology* an SVO language, that is, its normative syntactic arrangement of a sentence in the indicative mood is Subject-Verb-Object (*She* [S] *read* [V] *the book* [DO]). This designation English has in common with Romance languages such as Spanish and French, also members of the Indo-European family of languages. But this similarity exists at the level of normative syntax, and other languages related to English in Indo-European have other normative patterning; for example, the Celtic languages are VSO in their syntactic typology, or 'verb-first' languages.

uniformitarian principle Fundamental to the enterprise of historical linguistics is the idea, or principle, that essentially the same processes observable in contemporary human languages can be expected to have been operant in the past (at least so far back as 'complex' human language is known or can be inferred to have existed; Weinreich et al. 1968, 103). That is, that languages change and are subject to change several millennia ago in much the same manner as they do today. The uniformitarian principle has been particularly useful, or necessary even, to the study of phonology; Labov (1994) observed that, "To the extent that this principle depends on uniformities in the physiological basis of language, it must be correct, since there is no indication of differences between the linguistic past and the present in this respect" (23). If human articulators for the production of speech were the same at the time of Proto-Indo-European (perhaps ca. 4000–3500 BC), then *ceteris paribus* ('other things being equal'), we can expect sound change to have proceeded in much the same manner in the daughter languages. Labov (1994) does offer caveats about the applicability of the principle to all elements of language, especially the role of social factors (21–25).

REFERENCES

Bakker, Peter. *A Language of Our Own: The Genesis of Michif, The Mixed Cree-French Language of the Canadian Métis*. Oxford Studies in Anthropological Linguistics volume 10. New York: Oxford University Press, 1997

Bonvillain, Nancy. *A Grammar of Akwesasne Mohawk*. Ethnology Division Paper No. 8. Ottawa: National Museum of Man, 1973

Catford, J.C. *A Practical Introduction to Phonetics.* Oxford Textbooks in Linguistics. 2nd ed. Oxford: Oxford University Press, 2001

Labov, William. *Principles of Linguistic Change.* Volume 2: *Social Factors.* Language in Society 20. Malden, MA: Blackwell, 2001

Labov, William. *The Social Stratification of English in New York City.* 2nd ed. Cambridge: Cambridge University Press, 2006

Lanehart, Sonja, ed. *The Oxford Handbook of African American Language.* Oxford: Oxford University Press, 2015

Lloyd, Albert. *Anatomy of the Verb: The Gothic Verb as a Model for a Unified Theory of Aspect, Actional Types, and Verbal Velocity.* Studies in Language Companion Series, Volume 4. Amsterdam: John Benjamins, 1979

Mitchell, Bruce. *Old English Syntax.* 2 vols. Oxford: Clarendon Press, 1985

Ringe, Don and Ann Taylor. *The Development of Old English.* A Linguistic History of English, Volume II. Oxford Linguistics. Oxford: Oxford University Press, 2014

Weinreich, Uriel, William Labov, and Marvin I. Herzog. *Empirical Foundations for a Theory of Language Change.* Austin, TX: University of Texas Press, 1968

Index

Q